WATERFOWL

OF NORTH AMERICA, EUROPE, AND ASIA

WATERFOWL

OF NORTH AMERICA, EUROPE, AND ASIA

An Identification Guide

Sébastien Reeber

PRINCETON UNIVERSITY PRESS

PRINCETON AND OXFORD

First published 2015

© Delachaux et Niestlé, Paris, 2015
Title of the original edition: *Canards, cygnes et oies d'Europe, d'Asie et d'Amérique du Nord.*

Sébastien Reeber asserts his moral right to be identified as Author of this work.

Published in North America by
Princeton University Press
41 William Street
Princeton, NJ 08540

press.princeton.edu

ISBN: 978-0-691-16266-9

Library of Congress Control Number: 2015944232

Printed on acid-free paper. ∞
Printed in Hong Kong

1 3 5 7 9 10 8 6 4 2

CONTENTS

*This book is dedicated to my wife, Gwenn, and my two sons,
Quentin and Valentin, for their help, support and good humour
throughout the completion of this book.*

ACKNOWLEDGEMENTS

First, I want to thank all of the photographers who have contributed images: Anand Arya, Ron Bielefeld (whistlingwingsphotography.com/blog/home), Anders Blomdahl, Mark Curley, Mike Danzenbaker, Philippe J. Dubois, Joe Fischer, Eva Foss Henriksen, Ian Fulton, Julien Gonin, Tom Grey, Manuel Grosselet, Stefano Guiducci, Nidal Issa, Mikaël Jaffré, Ayuwat Jearwattanakanok, Zbigniew Kajzer, Jainy Kuriakose, Vincent Legrand, Peiqi Liu, Nis Lundmark Jensen, Niall Moores, Dennis Morrison, Silas Olofson, Otto Plantema, Christopher J. G. Plummer, Stuart Price, William Price, Sébastien Provost, Johannes Rydström, Bob Steele, Harold Stiver, Kannan Achi Sundararajan, Singhal Sunil, Amit Thakurta, Seraf Van der Putten, Rick & José Van der Weijde, Matthieu Vaslin, Alain Verneau, Ingo Waschkies, Michelle & Peter Wong and Thomas Zgirsky.

Special thanks and sincere gratitude go to my main contributors: Tormod Amundsen (Tormod runs Biotope, an architectural company specialising in bird hides, photographic hides and other equipment designed for birding: www.biotope.no), Aurélien Audevard (www.ouessant-digiscoping.fr), Yann Kolbeinsson, Greg Lavaty (Greg guides nature observation and photographic trips in Texas and elsewhere: www.texastargetbirds.com), Steven Mlodinow, Jean-Baptiste Mouronval, Vincent Palomares and Alan D. Wilson.

All of the people with whom I exchanged and discussed information contained in this book are too numerous to be mentioned here, but I would like to thank the following for their special assistance: Pierre Brousseau, Colin Bowen, Peter Campainolo, Robert C. Faucett, Michel Gosselin, Christoph Randler and, especially, Peter Pyle for information on moult in Anseriformes, Frédéric Jiguet for his advice and proof-reading, Steven Mlodinow for his expertise on several issues, Philippe Rambaud for welcoming me to his huge wildfowl collection, Ker Anas, in Brière (France), and Alain Verneau for his patience during trips that were not originally planned only to photograph ducks!

I am very grateful to the team at Editions Delachaux & Niestlé (Michel Larrieu, Philippe J. Dubois, Chloé Cosnefroy and Sophie Postollec) and Bloomsbury Publishing (Nigel Redman, Guy Kirwan, Julie Dando) for their confidence in me, patience and availability. Finally, I cannot conclude without offering my deep gratitude to the Société Nationale de Protection de la Nature (www.snpn.com), the oldest NGO for nature conservation in France, which manages two national nature reserves – both major sites for European wildfowl – the Camargue and the Lac de Grand-Lieu. The SNPN, by providing me the opportunity to work at the second of these, also helped make this book possible.

HOW TO USE THIS BOOK

This guide's main aim is to summarise current knowledge concerning the specific and subspecific identification, ageing and sexing of the 83 breeding species of geese, swans and ducks found in Europe, Asia and North America, in plates, texts, photographs and maps. The index indicates for each species the pages of text (and photographs) and the relevant plate of illustrations. A second index is specifically dedicated to hybrids of 100 different crosses that are more or less regular in the wild. Each hybrid is cross-referenced to each of its parent species (e.g., American Wigeon × Eurasian Wigeon, and Eurasian Wigeon × American Wigeon), with references to the texts where they are described (chapter on Hybridisation), or photographs, and to the plate on which they are illustrated.

PLATES

To facilitate their use, the plates and facing-page texts are organised to act as a quick identification guide. Each plate is numbered and every image is labelled, and their captions indicate the species, subspecies, sex, age and plumage concerned. The texts present a summary of identification (including to subspecies), and sexing and ageing features.

TEXTS

The species texts present more comprehensive information following the same sequence of sections. Within each account, at first mention both the vernacular and scientific names are given, but thereafter only the English name. Alternative English names are occasionally given, mainly where they differ in European and American usage.

TAXONOMY This section provides reference to the type used in the description of the species, its date and author, followed by information on the species' phylogenetic placement and any geographic variation. In many cases these topics have been the subject of much discussion, which is then summarised. For others, the debate is ongoing, which is reflected in the lack of consensus among recent authors and different taxonomic committees. This book does not claim to provide new information concerning the taxonomy of Anseriformes, and its aim is not to propose new treatments. A discussion of current treatments is presented, and the most widely accepted view is adopted here, although further work will of course either confirm or refute these decisions.

IDENTIFICATION Firstly, this section describes the risks of misidentification, either with other species or with hybrids. Distinguishing characters compared to other species are discussed in detail. Lists of distinguishing features are ranked in order of importance, from diagnostic to informative. The abbreviations used for some tracts of feathers are the same as used in the following section.

PLUMAGE This section describes each of the species' plumages (usually referring to the nominate subspecies for polytypic species) for each sex and age group. The terminology adopted to describe these plumages is that of Humphrey-Parkes, modified as described below under 'Moult'. However, for convenience, the different subheadings also indicate the age of the bird (e.g. first-winter male, adult female, etc.), which also corresponds with the most frequently used terminology, which is less accurate but in more widespread use. The texts in parentheses indicate the time of year when the plumage is usually observed. For example, Oct–Dec/Mar–Apr means that the plumage can be acquired as early as October, but sometimes only from December and is kept until March or April, when it is replaced by the next plumage. However, this information is not well established for all of the tropical species whose ranges just reach the Holarctic, and which mostly show no obvious seasonal change in plumage. For these species, when information is available, the timing mentioned concerns Holarctic populations. Where a plumage is similar to another (e.g.

formative and definitive basic plumages), the description indicates the similarity and, instead of providing a full description, emphasises the features that distinguish it. Unless otherwise stated, references to the wing-coverts relate to the upperwing. Note that colours used here do not refer to the standardised colour charts sometimes used in the ornithological literature. Although the latter undeniably have the advantage of greater precision, they do not permit much discussion of individual variation in coloration, which depends on diet, substrate, age, bleaching, wear and, most of all, on the observer and viewing conditions. Moreover, the basic colours used herein are frequently used and easily understood.

GEOGRAPHIC VARIATION This section describes geographic variation compared to the main description (above), whether clinal or not. Differences vary from those populations whose individuals are only marginally distinguishable (though average differences still exist), to subspecies for which, on the contrary, the majority of the individuals are distinctive. Each subspecies is treated separately, emphasising the important features that distinguish it from the other(s).

MEASUREMENTS and MASS These are indicated for each subspecies treated in the book, as well as by sex, and sometimes by age group, in millimetres (mm) and grams (g), respectively. The information presented here generally includes the length of the folded wing, tail, bill or culmen, tarsus and mass. Biometrics may have been taken using different methods, depending on the author, and where known this is stated (e.g. culmen length from tip of forehead feathering, bill length from gape or from proximal or distal edge of the nostril, etc.). Where available, the range, mean, the sample size and, optionally, standard deviation are given. Depending on their relevance to identification, other measurements are occasionally indicated, especially when data for different taxa or populations are comparable. Note that some datasets can differ significantly depending on the techniques of the authors. Note also that mass varies considerably even within a day, but also during the year, especially in females.

VOICE This section outlines the main vocalisations of both sexes, during and outside the breeding season. However, the subject is treated in detail only if voice is a useful feature for identification, which is rarely the case among wildfowl. Note that other sounds produced by the birds, such as the rustling of wings, if characteristic, is also described here.

MOULT Understanding moult is essential, especially for ageing, and is therefore described here for every species, by first describing the strategy (number and type of moults during the first and subsequent annual cycles). The list of different moults is detailed, with for each of them information on their timing and extent (i.e. the plumage tracts usually replaced). Note, however, while such information is generally well described in the literature for North American and European species, this is not yet the case in East and South Asia, especially in subtropical and tropical regions, where moult schedule varies regionally depending on rainfall. The nomenclature used for moults, plumages and moult strategies is Humphrey-Parkes terminology.

HYBRIDISATION This section details the frequency of hybridisation in nature. For each species, the list of other species with which it has hybridised, in the wild and captivity, is indicated. There follows descriptions of the hybrids more or less regularly seen in the wild. Descriptions are more detailed if the hybrid concerned is likely to be confused with either species, and thus pose identification problems. However, most crosses result in hybrids of rather variable appearance, including in relation to the sex of each parent, so it is important not to consider the descriptions as exhaustive. In most cases, the description applies to definitive basic male plumage, and gives an idea of the known variability of the hybrid.

HABITAT and LIFE CYCLE This section provides an overview of habitats, migration, breeding season and various biological traits of interest, especially in an identification context. Gregariousness during breeding, migration or wintering periods, movements associated with moult and/or other information possibly useful for finding and identifying the species are addressed here. This section is obviously not a comprehensive synthesis of a species' biology, for which there is often extensive literature.

RANGE and POPULATIONS Information is presented concerning distribution during the annual cycle, population size, demographic trends, conservation status and threats, using the most recent global data available, including those available online.

CAPTIVITY Because Anseriformes are among the most popular and widely kept birds for ornamental purposes, the question of origin often arises for a bird seen outside its normal range. This short section indicates the frequency of each species in captivity, the prices at which the species is usually offered for sale, and the difficulty of maintaining and breeding them in captivity. The likelihood of a bird seen in the wild having escaped from captivity is obviously much stronger if that species is frequently kept in captivity, easy to breed or inexpensive.

PHOTOGRAPHS

Photographs are presented at the end of each account to illustrate the main plumages of each species, as well as a number of more or less regularly encountered natural hybrids. With very few exceptions (where the term 'captivity' is clearly indicated), all photographs are of birds taken in the wild, thereby avoiding the many captive individuals that show atypical characters (linked to inbreeding, more or less ancient hybridisation, impact of diet on colour, altered moult strategy, etc.). Like the plates, taxon, sex, age and plumage are indicated when known with sufficient certainty. The month and country in which the photo was taken are also given, as well as the photographer's name.

MAPS

These provide a graphic representation of range during the breeding and wintering periods. Three colours are used: breeding season (orange), winter (blue) and present year-round (violet).

TAXONOMY AND SYSTEMATICS

The Order Anseriformes broadly includes ducks, geese and swans, which total, according to previous authors, between 147 and 173 species[217]. The majority of these are long known to science, with only three species described since the end of the 19th century. Within this order there are the Anhimidae (screamers; three species) and Anseranatidae (Magpie Goose *Anseranas semipalmata*; one species), with all other species grouped in the family Anatidae[775]. Some previous authors considered the Dendrocygninae to be a distinct family[1192], whereas others placed the Anseranatidae within Anatidae[646]. Whatever the treatment, the Anatidae includes the vast majority of species of Anseriformes. In the region covered by this book, only the Anatidae are represented, by four families and eight tribes: Dendrocygninae (Dendrocygnini), Anserinae (Anserini and Cygnini), Tadorninae (Tadornini) and Anatinae (Anatini, Aythyini, Mergini and Oxyurini). Depending on the treatment adopted, Eurasia and North America host about half of the Anseriformes in the world.

Several classifications have been proposed since that of Delacour & Mayr[297], based on interspecific comparisons of varying external morphological, anatomical, behavioural, ecological and genetic characters, as well as frequency of hybridisation and fertility of the resultant offspring. The organisation of the Anseriformes as described above is almost unanimously recognised today, as well as their proximity to Galliformes, it being considered that no other orders of birds are as close to each other than the Anseriformes and Galliformes[217]. These two orders, grouped under the Galloanseres, are now placed together at the beginning of avian sequences proposed by most authors.

Despite the fact that the Anseriformes are clearly one of the most widely studied orders, including their taxonomy and systematics, many differing views exist between various current authorities. Regarding the sequence of species, it is worth mentioning the position of the swans (before or after the geese) and of the stifftails. Generic nomenclature is also not unanimously agreed. For example, the 'white' and 'blue' geese in North America are sometimes included in genus *Anser*, and sometimes in their own genus, *Chen*.

Nevertheless, those topics of most interest to field ornithologists relate to the taxonomic rank afforded to taxa within several superspecies, with some supporting their 'splitting' (treating these groupings as two or more species) and others their 'lumping' (i.e. as a single species). Until recently, the Biological Species Concept[814] was generally applied, determining a species to be a group of individuals or populations that breed freely with each other, but almost never so with others, because of reproductive isolation or the sterility of hybrids[1021]. Not only is this concept difficult to apply in the case of two similar allopatric populations (which therefore cannot naturally breed with one another, irrespective of their potential ability to do so), but it is not very suitably applied to Anseriformes. The huge diversity of crosses between species and the frequency of hybrids, even in the wild, suggests that reproductive barriers are not very effective compared to the rule in many other orders. Moreover, with the exception of some intergeneric hybrids, most hybrids are obviously fertile.

The rise of the Phylogenetic Species Concept recently has overturned the previous approach. This concept refers to a species as a group of individuals sharing a set of characters not shown by neighbouring groups[263,1372,1392]. Logically, this treatment results in a significantly larger number of species, and can even identify genetically distinct clades almost devoid of noticeable phenotypic differences. Furthermore, the results of phylogenetic analyses can be biased by homoplasy, that is to say, any evolutionary phenomenon leading two species to resemble one another (convergent or reverse evolution). A phylogenetic analysis therefore can consider two species to be very closely related (i.e. having diverged recently), despite that their last common ancestor may be very ancient. The even more recent arrival of DNA analysis, when based on sufficiently dense sampling, has yielded much interesting information concerning the relationships between taxa, including within superspecies. Nevertheless, there is still no comprehensive treatment of all taxa of Anseriformes, sufficient to produce a comprehensive cladistic classification.

Among recent taxonomic and systematic changes, some are now more or less widely accepted, such as the specific treatment of Green-winged Teal *Anas carolinensis* and Black Scoter *Melanitta americana*. These two Nearctic taxa were long considered subspecies respectively of the Eurasian Teal *Anas crecca*, and the

Common Scoter *Melanitta nigra* of Europe and western Asia. However, many other superspecies remain the subject of sometimes heated discussions.

- Bean Goose *Anser fabalis* (1–4 species depending on authority).
- Brent Goose *Branta bernicla* (the three main subspecies are sometimes considered full species).
- Canada Goose *Branta canadensis* and Cackling Goose *B. hutchinsii* (once conspecific, currently considered two distinct species, and taken together including 11 subspecies; the organisation of this superspecies is undoubtedly the most complex taxonomic topic among Anseriformes).
- Tundra Swan *Cygnus c. columbianus* and Bewick's Swan *C. c. bewickii* (one or two species).
- Old World Comb Duck *Sarkidiornis melanotos* and South American Comb Duck *S. sylvicola* (one or two species).
- Mallard *Anas p. platyrhynchos* and Mexican Duck *A. (p.) diazi* (one or two species, *diazi* having also been considered a subspecies of American Black Duck *A. rubripes* and, more recently, of Mottled Duck *A. fulvigula*).
- Eastern Spot-billed Duck *Anas zonorhyncha* and Indian Spot-billed Duck *A. poecilorhyncha* (one or two species, with the position of an intermediate taxon, *haringtoni*, also being debated).
- Common Eider *Somateria mollissima* (six subspecies, including at least one, *S. m. v-nigrum*, which could be considered a full species).
- Velvet Scoter *Melanitta fusca*, White-winged Scoter *M. deglandi* and Siberian Scoter *M. stejnegeri* (considered as 1–3 species depending on authority).

No doubt genetics will soon provide additional answers, but currently both the rapidity with which knowledge improves and affects the interpretations we make has promulgated diverse views. This is amply reflected in the many differences between species lists proposed by different taxonomic committees and the main works on Anseriformes. Study of the lists proposed by the AERC-TAC[272] and BOURC-TSC in Europe, the AOU in North America, BirdLife International[142], the Clements Checklist[236] or the IOC[437], for example, swiftly reveals this fact. The positions adopted here, which do not claim to be based on new information, are based on current references and online resources, and, where necessary, are explained in the 'Taxonomy' sections. Note that, for more information on this topic, the synthesis proposed by Callaghan & Harshman[217] is helpful.

AVIAN TOPOGRAPHY

The nomenclature used herein is the same as that typically used in identification guides, as shown in Figs. 1–3 and the photos thereafter. However, a few terms frequently used when describing Anseriformes merit explanation.

'Grinning patch' In several species of geese, the cutting edges of the two mandibles are disjunct, revealing, in profile, a gap whose length and depth varies with species. Up close, it permits the 'teeth' inside the bill to be seen.

Lamellae Some ducks have developed a unique water-filtration system, with the tongue (in the upper mandible) acting as a piston to fill and empty the 'mouth'. This creates a movement of the water in both directions via a filter composed of parallel lamellae, equivalent to the baleen plates in some whales. In species adapted to grazing or catching fish underwater, the sides of the bill possess more or less sharp teeth.

Several species of geese possess grooves on the neck-sides, which are typically more obvious on adults than young birds.

Nail Small curved growth at the tip of the bill, used primarily to grasp or hold food items.

Speculum Refers broadly to the upperside of the secondaries, especially the iridescent area of them that shows a metallic gloss, usually green or blue.

Tertials and **tertial coverts** These feathers are sometimes referred to as the inner secondaries and coverts.

In Snow Goose *Chen caerulescens*, the 'grinning patch' is tinged black. Its size and shape are useful in distinguishing several species and subspecies of geese.

The lamellae, here in a Northern Shoveler *Anas clypeata*, act like a filter to trap phytoplankton and zooplankton on which the species feeds.

Neck grooves Feathers arranged in rows and separated by grooves, generally obvious, on the sides of the neck of several species of *Anser* and *Chen* geese.

Tomium Refers to the cutting edge of the mandibles.

Bill protuberance A bulge present at the base of the culmen in males of several species of swans (e.g. Mute Swan) and ducks (e.g., Knob-billed Duck *Sarkidiornis melanotos*, Common Scoter *Melanitta nigra*, White-winged Scoter *Melanitta deglandi*, King Eider *Somateria spectabilis*).

Femoral coverts or area Feathers covering the base of the legs (thighs), which are distinguished, for example in some ducks, by a white patch between the flanks and the undertail.

MOULT AND PLUMAGES

It is impossible to deal precisely with species identification, ageing or sexing without addressing the topic of moult and how to name the various plumages. But often, simply to address these issues causes at best some reluctance among field ornithologists. While moult undoubtedly remains a complex issue, it is not necessarily difficult to acquire the rudiments useful to interpret what we observe.

Above all, two basic concepts must be addressed: what is a moult and what is a plumage? A moult is defined by the partial or complete replacement of feathers necessary to keep plumage in good condition. A feather is considered to be moulted when the follicle is activated, generating the growth of a new feather. The plumage is simply the set of feathers that results from a given moult, irrespective of its appearance.

MOULT IN ANSERIFORMES

In the Holarctic, moult of Anseriformes is rather simple, with many similarities between the moulting patterns of different species, influenced especially by the strongly seasonal climate. Indeed, cold winters not only force birds to migrate south, but also to concentrate the high-energy activities (breeding, migration and moult) into a relatively short period, especially for birds that breed at high latitudes. The main moult period, involving the wings, is critical. Over a two-month period, not only must a female take care of her offspring, recover the mass lost during incubation and lay down the reserves needed for autumn migration,

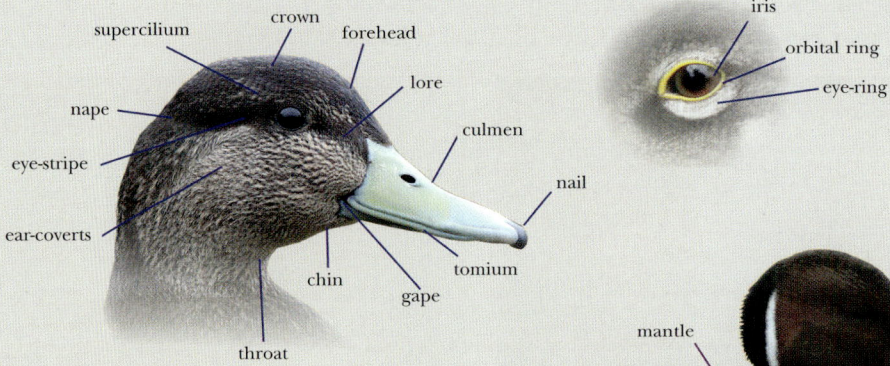

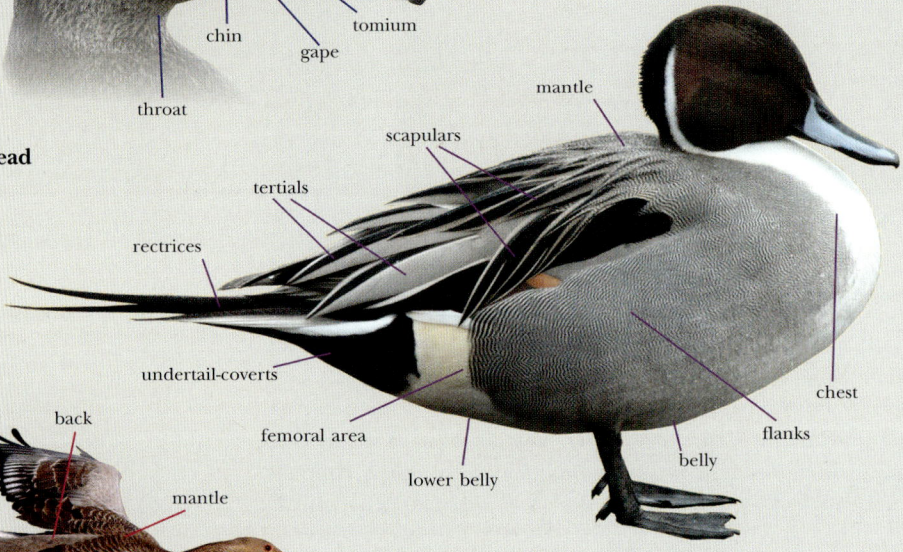

Fig. 1. Head

Fig. 2. Body

Fig. 3. Wing

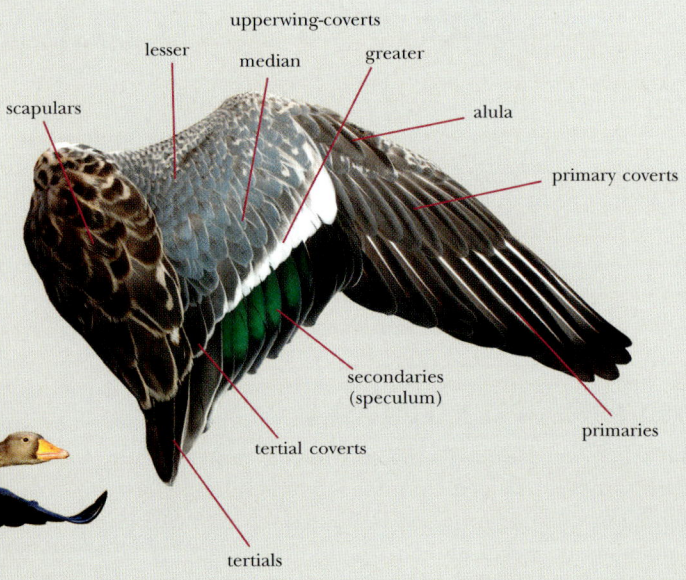

but also replace the flight feathers, which too requires energy expenditure. It is therefore unsurprising that in temperate latitudes and further north, such accumulation of energy is best conducted in summer. Climatic aspects not only determine the timing of breeding and migration, but also, directly and indirectly, the moult timing of all species.

Among adults, the majority of ducks moult their flight feathers simultaneously in summer, rendering them unable to fly (for 20–50 days, depending on species). This is the first singularity of the Anseriformes, because the vast majority of other birds moult their flight feathers gradually, in order to maintain their ability to fly. Perhaps this reflects an adaptation demanded by morphology, they being heavy compared to the size of their wings[590]. Given that the loss of 2–3 remiges is sufficient to severely affect their ability to fly, perhaps it is better to become flightless for a month, rather than to fly weakly for 4–5 months, which would be the result of gradually moulting the flight feathers? Once the wings are effective again, and following any migration, a complete moult of the rest of the body commences, resulting in the 'beautiful' plumage of males, mostly between autumn and spring. It is in this plumage that mating occurs, usually on the wintering grounds, which again is unusual, as the vast majority of Holarctic birds acquire breeding plumage at the end of winter or in spring.

Between February and July, another partial moult occurs, including some body feathers (the flight feathers, most wing-coverts and sometimes the rectrices are replaced just once per year). This moult occurs before breeding, leading to the female's more cryptic plumage, which is on average browner and more barred. This permits the female to become better concealed during incubation, brood-rearing and the flightless period. Adult males do not moult at quite the same time, but instead replace the 'beautiful' plumage with a much duller plumage in May–July, also aiding the bird's concealment during the flightless period. This partial moult constitutes a third peculiarity of the Anseriformes, in that timing differs according to gender. It has been suggested that their ancestors had two annual partial body moults, just before and after breeding in both sexes, but that the former was gradually lost in males (or almost so) and the latter disappeared in females[590,1013,1015].

To sum up, the majority of ducks have two moults of the head and body per year, plus a single wing moult in summer. Geese, swans and whistling-ducks perform a single wing moult followed by a complete body moult. During the first year of life, there is an additional moult in almost all species, in between that producing the juvenile plumage and the one similar to that of adults in spring.

Note that these generalities reflect the situation for Anseriformes only in the Holarctic. The situation is different in tropical and equatorial regions, where breeding, migration and, therefore, moult follow different timings. The biological cycle can be heavily influenced by the seasonality and intensity of rainfall, and may not be regular between years.

A NAME FOR EACH MOULT AND EACH PLUMAGE

To address these topics, it is first necessary to define the terminology, which is not ubiquitous. In Europe and Asia, terminology includes a 'post-juvenile' moult, and a 'pre-' or a 'post-nuptial' moult. The resultant plumages are termed 'juvenile', 'first-winter', 'first-summer', 'breeding', 'non-breeding' or 'eclipse' (adult male), with a tendency for many users to mingle ages and plumages. So the 'first-winter' plumage of a young goose is worn between November and June! Also, what many ornithologists agree to term 'first-summer' is, for the vast majority of Anseriformes, the summer of the second calendar year, i.e. their second summer. We should also mention the example of young female ducks, for which 'first-winter plumage' is actually a sequence of three successive generations of feathers.

Similarly, within the genera *Anas*, *Aythya* and *Somateria*, for example, 'breeding plumage', which is bright and colourful in males, is acquired following 'pre-breeding moult', in autumn. This plumage is worn by males to mate in winter and until their contribution to breeding is complete. But, in females, the same plumage, the result of the same pre-nuptial moult is succeeded by a partial body moult in February–May, which is included in the 'post-nuptial moult'. This moult results in a more cryptic plumage for concealment during nesting and brood-rearing. In other words, they undertake a 'post-nuptial' moult and lose their 'breeding' plumage just before breeding! In fact, names are rarely applied to the two annual plumages worn by female ducks, probably because of their great similarity. Such terminology includes some inaccuracies, which can lead to misinterpretation and greatly complicates understanding of moult!

DISTINGUISHING PLUMAGE AND ASPECT

More than half a century ago, Humphrey & Parkes[610] proposed an alternative classification, simultaneously more precise and clearer. This terminology completely ignores the coloration of the feathers, which is not directly linked to seasons, to biological periods (nesting, wintering), or to the age or sex of the bird. Indeed, the physiological processes controlling the colour and shape of feathers are independent of those controlling moult timing[590,1012,1323]. A feather's shape and colour is actually controlled by hormonal activity, which itself varies with the age of the bird and during the annual cycle. Advanced, delayed or protracted moult timing, and level of hormonal activity at a given time, can therefore result in different coloration between individual feathers, even if they are part of the same moult. Likewise, the juxtaposition of differently coloured feathers on usually uniform parts of a definitive plumage does not necessarily indicate their formation during different moults. Such differences may also reflect follicles activated at different times, under the influence of different levels of hormonal activity.

To give a more concrete example, the cheeks of a young male Common Eider *Somateria mollissima* at the end of its first winter exhibit variable brown, black and white feathers. Retained juvenile feathers are brown. The other juvenile feathers were replaced by black feathers in November, then more or less quickly with grey or white feathers. So, the presence of feathers of different coloration, in place of all-white feathers in the adult, do not necessarily require more than one moult (or activation of follicles) after juvenile plumage.

Taking coloration into account when determining the moult status or plumage of a given bird can be misleading. In the example of the young male Common Eider, in early spring, many observers would think that a bird with a largely white head is 'advanced' and one with black head is 'less advanced' in its moult. In this case, given equal levels of hormonal activity, the opposite is true: the bird that has moulted more feathers in autumn will have almost blackish cheeks, whereas the bird that has moulted these feathers 1–2 months later, as a result of increased hormonal activity, will have whiter feathers. One can also mention the case of senescent females, in which female hormonal activity declines with age, leaving male hormones to take over and resulting in an intermediate appearance between the two sexes, visible in the colour and shape of the feathers and in the colour of the bare parts.

THE REVISED HUMPHREY-PARKES TERMINOLOGY

Once the dissociation between the different notions of plumage, appearance (feather colour and shape), season, age and sex is accepted, it is much easier to distinguish moulting patterns common to individuals and between species, and to establish a nomenclature. This was the basis on which Humphrey & Parkes laid the groundwork for a new terminology, which was subsequently adapted and modified by two other pioneers in the study of moult, Pyle and Howell[593,594,590,1012,1013,1015]. To avoid needless complexity, only the last version of this terminology is detailed below, leaving aside the various intermediate proposals.

Firstly, it should be remembered that the prefix 'pre-' is added to the name of a given plumage to designate the moult from which it results (e.g. 'pre-basic moult' leads to 'basic plumage'). The term 'pre-basic' refers to the single annual complete moult (in Holarctic Anseriformes), while 'pre-alternate' applies to the complementary partial moult. Furthermore, a moult is referred to as definitive when it is repeated identically from year to year, i.e. in adults. Conversely, moults and plumages are numbered when they differ from the following analogous moults and plumages (e.g. first pre-basic moult, second pre-basic moult, etc.).

The revised Humphrey-Parkes terminology leads, in Holarctic Anseriformes, to the sequence of moults hereafter. Much information on the extent of various moults among different genera was presented in the groundbreaking work by Pyle[1012]. Names used in traditional European nomenclature are given in italics.

FIRST PRE-BASIC MOULT (*pre-juvenile moult*) results in the first genuine plumage, which replaces the down of ducklings, starting at the age of a few weeks (cf. Howell *et al.*[593,594] for more details on the name of this moult). First basic plumage is generally duller and plainer, characterised by narrower, more pointed feathers than the equivalent adult ones. Their texture is typically looser than the same feathers produced during subsequent moults, which makes them more prone to wear and bleaching, especially at their tips. Indeed, heavy wear to feathers such as the rectrices, remiges, upperwing secondary- and tertial-coverts are often a sign of retained juvenile feathers.

AUXILIARY PRE-FORMATIVE MOULT (*post-juvenile moult*) is partial and poorly understood, but is apparently present at least in young males of some ducks, especially in July–August, involving a small number of feathers on the head, neck, mantle, breast and flanks. This moult occurred in fewer than half of the birds considered by Pyle, with an extent ranging from 8% to 19% of these feathers in males of the genus *Anas*[1012]. This moult could have developed in populations that undertake long-distance migrations, which also typically undertake pre-formative moult more slowly and later. An additional plumage would have been inserted after juvenile plumage, which is too weak to last until spring. For example, young males (at least) of Northern Shoveler *Anas clypeata* show a largely adult-type plumage as early as their first winter in the north of the wintering range, whereas they frequently show an intermediate, variegated plumage in the south. This appears true on both the European–African and American flyways. However, many questions remain concerning this moult: is its extent more related to species or to individuals that migrate long distances? Could it simply be a delayed part of the first pre-basic moult, with the activation of additional follicles being linked to the increasing skin surface due to body growth?[1012]

PRE-FORMATIVE MOULT (*first pre-breeding moult*) is partial and only undertaken during the first cycle, between September–November and December–April in most Anseriformes. It can be protracted, suspended or undertaken more slowly during the coldest part of the winter. It leads to an appearance closer to that of the adult, even though many formative feathers are duller and show a shape intermediate between those of the juvenile and the adult (e.g., scapulars in geese). In many cases, this moult involves most feathers of the head, neck, much of the breast, flanks, mantle and scapulars, and a smaller proportion of the back, rump, belly and undertail feathers. It also includes a variable number of tertials and tertial-coverts, rectrices and inner secondary upperwing-coverts. This moult is on average more extended in dabbling ducks (*Anas*) and scaups (*Aythya*) than in geese, swans (Anserinae) and sea ducks (Mergini), which corresponds to the fact that the former two often breed as early as their second calendar year (hence the need for adult-type plumage), unlike the latter groups. This moult is also more extended on average in young males than in young females, contrary to the subsequent first pre-alternate moult[1012]. Finally, as mentioned above, pre-formative moult frequently appears slower and more protracted in some species of dabbling ducks that undertake long migrations (e.g. Northern Shoveler, Garganey *Anas querquedula* and Blue-winged Teal *A. discors*). It is also often the case in vagrants that have wandered far from their normal range, in which moult is often suspended, in many other species, including geese.

DEFINITIVE PRE-ALTERNATE MOULT (*adult post-breeding moult*) is partial, varies in timing and extent by gender, but generally relates to some feathers of the head, neck, breast, mantle, scapulars and flanks, a smaller number on the rest the body, sometimes the inner secondary-coverts, and often some tertials and rectrices. It is on average more extended in females than males of the genus *Anas*[1012], and more prolonged in paired females than unpaired birds[590,785]. In females of most sea ducks, dabbling and diving ducks (except scoters in which it is absent or very limited), this moult is performed on the wintering and staging grounds, just prior to breeding. It often results in a cryptic plumage (with strong barring even on the tertials) that permits females to more easily conceal themselves during nesting, brood-rearing and wing moult, when females are most prone to predation. In males of the same species, pre-alternate moult results in a plumage also termed 'eclipse' and often starts shortly after egg laying. Most males desert the females during breeding, and gather to complete this moult (sometimes at dedicated sites), which also produces a much duller plumage for the flightless period that follows. The first pre-alternate moult is often reduced in the second calendar year among individuals and species that do not breed at this age, and/or may be characterised by a slightly earlier timing. Similarly, young birds of these species that over-summer on the wintering grounds tend to perform a first pre-alternate moult that is more limited than conspecifics that accompanied the adults to the breeding grounds.

DEFINITIVE PRE-BASIC MOULT (*adult pre-breeding moult*) is complete or almost complete, and like the previous one, occurs once per annum. The wings are moulted first and then, in general, the head, neck and body backwards, often culminating with the tertials and undertail-coverts. It is usually performed in two stages: the wings on the moulting grounds (males of most Anatinae and non-breeders in all species) or nesting areas (most Anserinae and breeding females of many Anatinae), and the body feathers during or after the autumn migration. This moult seems to terminate on average slightly later in those Anatinae wintering in East Asia than elsewhere, and many in representatives of the genus *Anas* that do not achieve full basic plumage before early winter. The same is true of pre-formative moult, at least on average. Pre-basic moult also starts earlier in non-breeders, including individuals in their second calendar year in many species.

NB: Whether under Humphrey-Parkes terminology or in European nomenclature, it has often been considered that the autumn moult of the head and body represented a partial pre-alternate moult (pre-breeding in Europe), unrelated to the wing moult. The latter is in fact the second part of the complete annual moult, the first part (head and body) being undertaken in spring, as described above. Pyle[1012] subsequently proposed to group the wing and autumn body moults into a single complete moult (so called pre-basic), and considered the partial spring moult as pre-alternate. Geese, swans, whistling-ducks and scoters perform only one annual moult, which begins with the wings and rectrices, and continues through autumn with a complete head and body moult. Given the homologies between the Anatinae and Anserinae (insofar as they descend from the same ancestor), this makes sense. Indeed, under the original system, not only was the body moult associated with complete moult actually only partial, but in addition this moult preceded wing moult. It is, however, not easy to interpret this situation to understand its evolution, i.e. to conclude whether the pre-alternate moult (and any pre-supplemental moults) existed in the ancestor of the Anseriformes and whether it disappeared in some species, or rather progressively appeared in others.

DEFINITIVE PRE-SUPPLEMENTAL MOULT Among the issues deserving further study are reports of a limited moult (mostly the head and neck) in males (at least) of certain species of *Anas*. Such a moult has been reported in February–March[96,242,591,1014] during the pre-alternate moult of females described above, perhaps to refresh those parts of the plumage most critical for courtship, although by this time many pairs have already formed in these species. It has also been suggested that it could represent a delayed part of pre-basic moult from the previous autumn[1012] and that this moult could have a counterpart in females in June–July, when males undertake their definitive pre-alternate moult.

Another moult has been reported, especially among the same species that undertake an auxiliary pre-formative moult in their first year (Northern Shoveler, Garganey, Blue-winged Teal, Cinnamon Teal *Anas cyanoptera*, Northern Pintail *Anas acuta*), and also involves a small proportion of the feathers of the head and possibly the neck, upperparts, breast and flanks. In Northern Shoveler, this supplemental plumage is visible in the presence of a vertical white crescent between the eye and the bill base in September–November, which is absent in July (head all brown) and in basic plumage (head black with green sheen). As indicated for the auxiliary pre-formative moult, it is also possible that this moult explains the more variegated brown plumage of adult males that winter furthest south, while those wintering in the north are in full basic plumage from November/December. This moult remains to be studied more precisely, including the relationships between its extent and migratory movements/wintering latitudes, as well as the extent of the previous pre-basic moult. Given that this moult is inserted between the first part of pre-basic moult (wings) and what is generally understood as its end (bright plumage of the head and body), it might be necessary to redefine the various moults and plumages of such birds.

The revised Humphrey-Parkes nomenclature thus designates the various moults and plumages worn by the Anseriformes, as referred to in this book. However, it should be kept in mind that our understanding of the subject will surely evolve. Similarly, as well noted by Howell[590], such efforts reflect our desire to place complex natural phenomena in small boxes. Like any nomenclature, it nevertheless permits us to name moults and plumages, which is an essential first step in the study and understanding of these topics.

VARIOUS MOULT STRATEGIES

One of the major benefits of a single nomenclature for moults and plumages is to permit comparisons between species, and thus to establish shared 'strategies'[591,593]. There are four fundamental moulting strategies, differentiated by the number of moults (one or more) per cycle (or year for the Holarctic Anseriformes) and the existence of inserted moult(s) during the first cycle. Both strategies termed 'basic' display only one plumage per definitive (= adult) cycle and the two strategies termed 'alternate' result, additionally, in an alternate plumage once per year. Furthermore, the two strategies termed 'complex' possess an additional moult (and plumage) during the first cycle, whereas the two 'simple' strategies do not.

COMPLEX BASIC STRATEGY includes a single plumage (and just one moult) per year in adults and an additional moult (pre-formative) during the first cycle. This strategy is displayed by whistling-ducks, swans and geese. In the latter, a possible additional moult of the head and neck feathers in spring has often been mentioned. If this moult really exists in a significant proportion of birds, and does not constitute a delayed part of pre-basic moult, the strategy would be simple alternate (same number of moults per cycle). The basic plumage being the only one in adults, this obviously implies that appearance remains the same throughout the year, with a juvenile plumage (duller) and an intermediate formative plumage appearing different.

COMPLEX ALTERNATE STRATEGY includes at least two plumages during an adult cycle (basic and alternate plumage) and at least three in the first cycle (first basic, formative and first alternate plumage). This strategy is adopted by the genera *Tadorna, Aix, Anas, Netta, Aythya, Polysticta, Somateria, Histrionicus, Clangula, Bucephala, Lophodytes, Mergellus* and *Mergus*. Nevertheless, there are variations. *Aix* and *Anas* exhibit a rather extensive pre-alternate moult that is sexually differentiated (in extent and timing) in the first cycle as well as possible additional plumages (cf. remarks concerning 'auxiliary pre-formative' and 'definitive pre-supplemental' moults). The genus *Aythya* shows a sexually differentiated pre-alternate moult too, but less extended, especially in males. The genus *Somateria* has a pre-alternate moult less extended in the first cycle than thereafter (approaching the scoters and their simple alternate moult strategy), and sexually differentiated (timing) in adults. Other genera also show a limited first pre-alternate moult, but the latter is not or very little sexually differentiated in adults.

SIMPLE ALTERNATE STRATEGY includes a pre-basic moult and one inserted moult in both the first and subsequent cycles. This is the case among scoters (*Melanitta*) in which the single moult inserted in the first cycle is closer to a pre-formative moult than to a pre-alternate moult in terms of homologies[1014]. This strategy has perhaps evolved from a complex alternate strategy, with two moults inserted in the first cycle having eventually merged into one. Indeed, what is understood as the pre-formative moult in scoters is remarkably protracted, often ending only in April or May. The extent of the definitive pre-alternate moult is also probably reduced or even absent in some birds, especially females[1012]. This strategy is perhaps that adopted by Ruddy Duck *Oxyura jamaicensis*, but numerous questions remain for this species.

For other genera covered here, knowledge (in the wild) is insufficient to assign a moult strategy, namely the genera *Sarkidiornis, Alopochen, Cairina, Asarcornis, Nettapus* and *Marmaronetta*, all of which are represented by a single species in the Holarctic. All of these (except *Nettapus*) show a constant appearance year-round and the extent of pre-alternate moult is poorly known, as well as that of the first cycle. These species share a primarily inter-tropical or Mediterranean (*Marmaronetta*) distribution, living in tropical or equatorial climatic conditions, very different from those prevailing over most of the Holarctic. Species at tropical latitudes (plus White-headed Duck *Oxyura leucocephala* and Masked Duck *Nomonyx dominicus*) have their

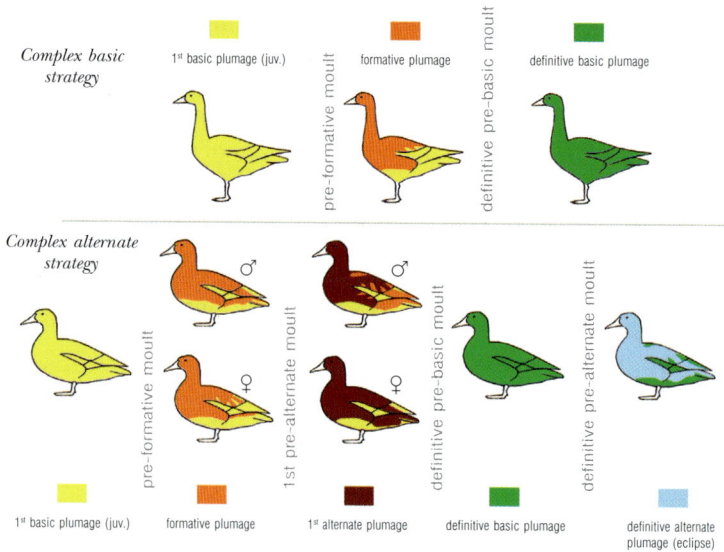

Fig. 4. Schematic representation of the two main moulting strategies in Anseriformes. In the complex alternate strategy, the extent and timing of the pre-formative and pre-alternate moults vary between sexes in certain species (male represented above, female below).

lifecycle strongly influenced by rainfall conditions, which produce temporary wetlands in otherwise dry or arid regions. These rains can be variable (in season and/or intensity) from one region to another and/or between years. This may result in timing differences between populations of the same species, or force the birds to be opportunistic, breeding where and when conditions permit. It is therefore unsurprising that the information available for these species, which is in any case limited, suggests that general moult patterns are not as well defined as elsewhere in the Holarctic. One must also bear in mind that moult strategy is not necessarily as rigid as one might guess and many cases exist of radical changes at individual level due to changes in conditions. This fact also explains why using captive individuals (or feral populations) to study moult is not recommended, as strategies adapt very well to radically different environments (affecting overall fitness) compared to those in a species' native range.

AGEING AND SEXING

In many species, sex can be determined using plumage and/or colour of the bare parts (iris, bill, legs) at least from the first winter onwards. The same is true for ageing, as for the majority of species it is possible, even easy, to distinguish young birds (until their second pre-basic moult, i.e. a little after the age of one year). Birds in their second year of life can occasionally be aged, even (rarely) up to their third year of life (some eiders *Somateria* for example). Ageing and sexing features are detailed for each species, but it is worth recalling some general characters useful for several, sometimes all, species.

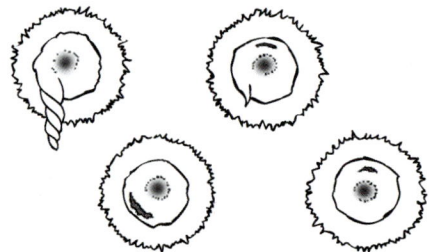

Fig. 5. Cloacae for age and sex determination, left to right: ad male, ad female, juv male and juv female (in birds viewed upside-down).

SEXING

The rare cases of gynandromorphs, defined as the juxtaposition of two genetically distinct sets of cells, one male and the other female, must be discussed. In birds, this is phenotypically manifest by the individual showing characters of both sexes, or sometimes intermediate characters. This rarely happens in Anseriformes, but is more frequent in hybrids, in which gynandromorphy can sometimes be relatively common in some crosses. Note that older or senescent females can acquire characters like adult males, which process is attributed to a decrease in oestrogen levels, with male hormones taking over[943,1247,1323].

SIZE AND WEIGHT Body size usually varies between individuals of the same age and sex within the same population. This may reflect normal variability, sometimes induced by food availability during the first months of life. For example, goslings of Arctic geese, especially the colonial species which may be more exposed to shortages, are prone to a highly variable growth rate, which can be reflected subsequently in adult size. These variations partly obscure mean differences in size and weight between males and females, but for the majority of species, observing a pair will reveal that the male is larger and heavier. Also in direct comparison, the head often appears stronger and more angular in the male, and the neck thicker.

POSTURES AND BEHAVIOUR In family groups of geese and swans, the adult male assumes the responsibility to remain alert, often standing a little apart from the rest of the family (the young staying closer to the adult female, often following her) and adopting a typically more upright posture. It is also often the male that first gives the alert calls. Similarly, brief conflicts sometimes break out between two birds within a flock, with males often being the most aggressive.

BROOD PATCH In order to optimise incubation, females (of many bird species) lose some feathers on the belly, so that the skin comes into direct contact with the eggs thereby improving the transmission of body heat. Just before and during incubation, the presence of a brood patch indicates a female. However, its absence does not point to a male. Similarly, in the female, the naked skin of the belly is typically slightly wrinkled and distended immediately after laying, whereas in the male at the same time, the diaphragm is usually more prominent under the abdominal skin.

CLOACAE In the hand, an examination of the cloaca permits sexing in many cases[352,562,732] and can also enable ageing (see below). The male's penis is right in front of the cloacal opening. Small (c.1cm) and translucent pink in juveniles, it quickly becomes much more visible in the adult by its size and its more coloured sheath. It is also much better developed before and during the nesting period. At this time, the cloaca forms a characteristic bump in the male, noticeable even without detailed examination. In

Fig. 6. Bill shape in geese by age. Adult on the left, juvenile on the right.

contrast, the adult female's opening to the oviduct (to the left of the cloacal opening) is a little more difficult to discern. During breeding, the female's cloaca also appears distended, longer and wider (more open) than that of the male. This feature is generally associated with a net brood patch (Fig. 5).

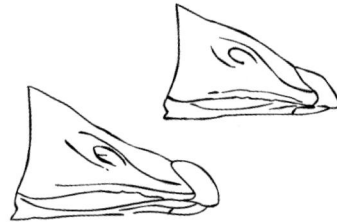

AGEING

BILL SHAPE Generally, the bill of juveniles thickens more quickly at the base than it lengthens. Therefore, it appears typically quite thick and rather short in juveniles, often with the culmen bulging in its central part, which feature is often well visible, e.g. in geese (Fig. 6) until the end of the first autumn.

SIZE, MASS AND WING LENGTH In all Anseriformes, young birds until their first winter are on average smaller and lighter than adults by sex, but with much overlap in many species. The most interesting feature is probably wing length (wing chord), which differs significantly between age groups in many species, and is even discriminatory if sex can be determined. Unlike many other measurements in young birds, wing length remains the same until the first summer, whereas other measurements have progressively increased to match those of adults during the first year of life.

OUTER PRIMARIES Besides wear being more pronounced on average at the tips in juveniles, the outer primaries have a weaker texture and are also narrower at the tips (Fig. 7). This feature can be assessed in the hand or under very favourable viewing conditions.

SECONDARIES Typically, many species show adult secondaries that are broader at the tips and more truncated (often with a small protruding arrow at the tip of the shaft), while juveniles have on average more rounded feathers, or 'teat-shaped' tips. In many species, the tips to the greater coverts are reminiscent of those of the secondaries, and vary in the same way according to age. However, this is a general trend, more or less pronounced depending

Fig. 7. Shape of the tips to the outer primaries: adult on the left (worn and fresh), juvenile on the right.

on the species and individuals, and should be used with caution and prior experience of the species. In many ducks of the genus *Anas*, the gloss of the speculum is more pronounced in the adult male, slightly less in the juvenile male and adult female, and duller in the juvenile female.

RECTRICES Juvenile rectrices show a unique wear pattern. These feathers are initially tipped with fluffy filaments that disappear very quickly due to wear, leaving a bare segment (Fig. 8). During the first autumn and winter, the presence of rectrices (sometimes just two) with this pattern is diagnostic of this age. In spring, some rectrices are replaced as part of pre-formative moult and/or pre-alternate moult, leading to the juxtaposition of two or three generations of rectrices, typical of second-calendar-year birds. Note that all rectrices are often replaced during pre-formative moult (depending on the individual and species) and individuals showing all new rectrices at this time are not necessarily adult. Moreover, adults can have one or more damaged rectrices, with tips that appear forked. In such cases, however, the bare shaft is always broken. Finally, some large Anseriformes sometimes do not replace all of their rectrices annually, also leading to the presence of two feather generations, without being indicative of immaturity.

SCAPULARS These feathers, especially the longest, also vary in shape with age, averaging shorter and more rounded in young than in adults. However, huge variation in the shape of these feathers by species and different definitive plumages of both sexes make it difficult to define a pattern shared by all species. In *Anser* geese, however, scapulars (and secondary-coverts) are very useful to distinguish juvenile plumage from subsequent ones. Juvenile scapulars are narrow and round-tipped, while adult scapulars are distinctly truncated, with an almost square shape. The fringes are pale brown and fuzzy in juveniles, creating a scaly appearance. The fringes (tips alone) of the adult scapulars are white and clear-cut, creating a regularly streaked overall appearance. The formative scapulars, usually acquired by the middle of the first autumn onwards, are like those of the adult but remain intermediate, narrower at the base and slightly rounded at the tip (Fig. 9).

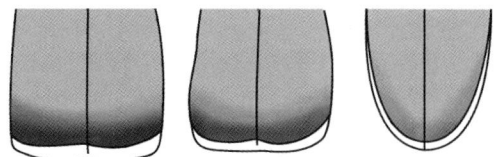

Fig. 8. Shape of the rectrices: adult on the left, juvenile on the right.

Fig. 9. Shape of the scapulars in grey geese *Anser* spp., from left to right: adult, formative and juvenile.

TEXTURE AND FEATHER WEAR As a general rule, juvenile feathers are less dense, with a looser texture than in adults. This results in them being more prone to wear, whether due to sun exposure (bleaching) or to abrasion. Typically, by the first autumn, it should be noted in juveniles that the tips of the rectrices, outer primaries, upperwing-coverts (especially secondary- and tertial-coverts) and tertials are significantly worn, appearing frayed at the tips. Wear to the feathers is more pronounced in pale parts of the plumage, which do not benefit from the strengthening effects of melanin. Thus, pale fringes to feathers exposed to sunlight (scapulars, rectrices) tend to wear prematurely compared with dark parts of the same feathers, and also compared with the pale fringes of concealed feathers (on the underwing for example).

UPPERWING-COVERTS Another feature that cannot be generalised across all species, even if the differences between age groups are similar to those in other feathers. Juvenile coverts are narrower-tipped than in the adult. In species where adult coverts are rounded, juveniles usually have rather pointed or trapezoidal coverts (with straight convergent sides), whereas in species with truncated or square-tipped adult coverts, the juvenile coverts are more rounded.

NB: The five features detailed above relating to the size and shape of the feathers are generally valid for many other feathers. As a rule, they are narrower, shorter and weaker in juveniles. It is, however of particular relevance to the rectrices and the majority of wing feathers insofar as they are retained until the second pre-basic moult, i.e. throughout the first year of life.

MOULT CONTRAST Irrespective of the shape and colour of the feathers, the simplest way to determine age is generally to look for moult contrast (in the hand). This contrast is caused by the juxtaposition of two generations of feathers. Because Anseriformes undertake a complete pre-basic moult between summer and autumn their plumage normally consists of a single generation of feathers from the end of the moult (between November and January for the majority of species). Until the subsequent summer, young birds sometimes retain part to all of their tail and especially many of their juvenile wing feathers. The pre-formative and pre-alternate moults may involve the tertial-coverts and a variable number of inner coverts. This results in a moult limit between the new formative feathers (adult-like) and the juvenile outer feathers. Close scrutiny will thus reveal a moult contrast in the wing typical of young birds. However, young birds whose pre-formative moult was reduced can show a completely juvenile wing (including tertials). If there is moult contrast, check the outermost feathers and determine if these are definitive basic feathers (possibly contrasting with newer inner feathers) or juvenile feathers. This general character is useful for many species, but in some it is of little use or much less pronounced (see species texts).

FLANK FEATHERS In juveniles (especially of dabbling ducks), the flank feathers (upper row) are more pointed and narrower, and form an alignment typical of this age, a series of '7-shaped' feathers. The same definitive alternate feathers in adults, present until autumn, are usually more rounded. This feature is particularly useful as these feathers are among the last body feathers (together with the lower scapulars and tertials) to be replaced during pre-formative moult.

HEAD FEATHERS This feature is even more useful in species with a crest or long feathers on the crown or nape. These feathers are always shorter in juveniles, producing a dishevelled appearance, with a lack of a crest and often a thinner, more angular and smaller head. Among the species concerned, this feature is often visible, at least until the first autumn, in direct comparison with adults.

CLOACAE Diagnostic and generally easy to use with a little practice in the hand, even if it is not very useful for distinguishing age groups between early spring and the end of the breeding period, at least in species that nest during their first spring. Until early winter at least the cloacae of young birds show the openings to the bursa of Fabricius (see below), which are virtually absent in all breeders. The young male has an embryonic penis and, in the young female, the opening to the oviduct is covered by a membrane. These sexual characters (cloacal protuberance and penis in the male, oviduct opening in females) are usually obvious in adults at the same time, especially during the nesting period (cf. sexing features above; Fig. 5). The colour of the cloaca is usually pale pink and translucent in juveniles, but becomes more or less dark red in adults.

Upperwing of Northern Shoveler *Anas clypeata*: note the age and sex characters, common to many species of ducks, in the shape of the secondary and tertial coverts, the shape of the tertials and gloss of the speculum (Jean-Baptiste Mouronval).

Shape of the greater coverts in Eurasian Teal *Anas crecca* and Red-crested Pochard *Netta rufina*; adults on left, juveniles on right (Jean-Baptiste Mouronval).

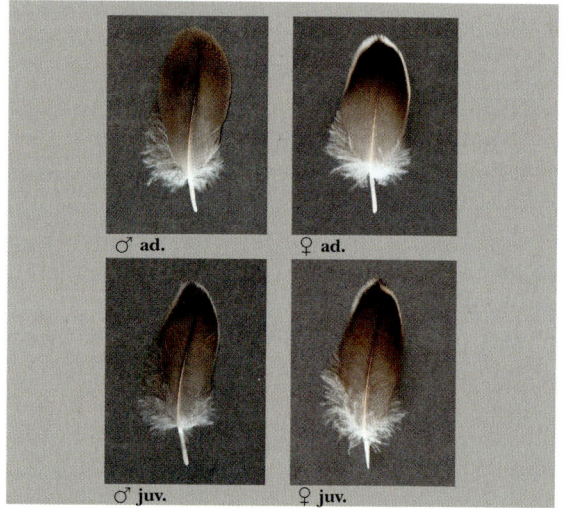

Shape and fringes of the greater tertial coverts, here in Northern Pintail *Anas acuta*. The pale fringe is absent in the adult male, faint and often interrupted at the tip in juvenile male, more marked (often brownish) in the juvenile female, and white and clear-cut in the adult female (Jean-Baptiste Mouronval).

Note the shape of the upper flank feathers in dabbling ducks (here Eurasian Teal *Anas crecca*). In juveniles (right), these feathers are pointed and form a characteristic pattern.

BURSA OF FABRICIUS An epithelial lymphoid organ that contributes to the immune system in the early stages of life, it is adjacent to the cloaca, and its opening is just behind the cloacal opening. The bursa is present in juveniles, but disappears quite quickly during the first two years of life, being virtually absent in adults. In live birds it is possible to measure (with care and experience) the depth of the bursa using a probe. The lengths at different ages for different species of Anseriformes are unknown, but usually it will be possible to distinguish two or three age groups, depending on species. The length of the bursa reaches 8–10 mm to 30–50 mm in juveniles, depending on the size of the species, and 0–5 mm in adults[1014]. Externally, the presence and development of the bursa of Fabricius is characterised by the presence of a usually clearly visible hole in juveniles, which disappears gradually until the age of the first breeding.

HYBRIDISATION

WHAT IS A HYBRID?

Hybridisation is the breeding of two individuals of two different species, leading to offspring with mixed physical and genetic characters. When the term designates a bird (rather than a population), it will usually be considered as a first-generation individual (or First Filial Generation = F1). After backcrossing (i.e. breeding between a hybrid and one of its parent species), the visible hybrid characters can greatly diminish, to the point where, under normal viewing conditions, it can be difficult to differentiate the hybrid from the species with which the backcross occurred. Further generations of backcrosses will produce individuals visually indistinguishable from the species in question. Here, backcrossing and second-generation hybrids (F2) will be distinguished, the latter actually being the offspring of two hybrid parents. Finally, multiple-hybrid designates a hybrid resulting from breeding between an F1 hybrid and an individual of a third species (this is probably very rare in the wild).

STERILITY AND VIABILITY

Hybrid sterility has long been considered the rule, and helped define the Biological Species Concept (species being assumed to be reproductively isolated from one another), with 'hybrids' between subspecies being fertile. However, the reality is more complex. Many hybrids, especially intra-generic ones (between closely related species) are fertile, but their ability to produce offspring varies depending on the parent species and their genetic closeness. The degree of fertility also varies within a given cross and between individuals, depending on the age of the bird, and the sex of each parent species[817]. This also leads to a rule proposed by Handale[497] indicating that within a given cross, the sex that is numerically less numerous (or even non-existent), sterile (no egg production or eggs infertile) or non-viable is the heterogametic sex, i.e. the female in birds. This explains why, for many crosses, male hybrids are more numerous (even the only sex known). However, note that, especially among waterfowl, the discreet female plumages make the detection and identification of hybrids much more difficult, which partly explains their rarity.

HYBRIDS, INTERMEDIATES AND INTROGRESSION

A hybrid can result from inter-generic crosses (between species of different genera) or intra-generic crosses (species of the same genus). When dealing with individuals of different subspecies, ornithologists prefer to speak of intermediates or intergrades. The same is true of populations at the junction of their ranges, where they interbreed freely, termed hybrid zones in reference to species and intergradation zone for subspecies, although intergradation implies that one taxon merges gradually into another. But a hybrid zone can be relatively narrow, and therefore the transition from one taxon to another is not genuinely clinal. Such hybrid zones are often stable in time.

Extensive hybridisation can also occur through introgression, which implies a more dynamic phenomenon, ancient or ongoing, based on the transfer (or flow) of genes from one species to another. This happens, for example, when a species rapidly expands its range into that of another species, making cases of hybridisation increasingly numerous as the zone of sympatry widens. Introgression also implies the generality of backcrossing and, of course, the fertility of at least the majority of hybrids.

Note that a clinal transition between two taxa is not necessarily linked to intergradation (i.e. the flow of current or former unilateral or bilateral genes), but for example can also be due to environmental factors that have led to a differentiated evolution of successive populations. Many species are naturally phenotypically variable, and not always due to hybridisation. One can recognise the variability due to hybridisation especially when the variability within a species is not homogeneous throughout its range and/or if the variability increases at the edges of its range. Furthermore, if these variable characters tend toward those shown by a neighbouring species with which interbreeding is possible, hybridisation will often be the explanation for the variability in character states. This is probably the case in the green iridescence in the dark eye patch of male Eurasian Wigeon *Anas penelope*. The percentage of individuals showing a clear green gloss behind the eye is stronger in parts of its range where American Wigeon *Anas americana* is likely to occur, e.g. in East Asia and, to a lesser extent, in north-west Europe. It is therefore possible that this represents the expression of hybrid characters, rather than 'normal' variability in Eurasian Wigeon.

CONSERVATION PROBLEMS

Hybridisation is often cited as a source of serious conservation concern for the genetic integrity of certain animal and plant populations, and the Anseriformes are no exception. In some cases, the ease with which some ducks hybridise naturally has even been said to potentially constitute a further threat to the precarious situation of a species, whose representatives, instead of searching a partner of their own kind, hybridise. This has, for example, been suggested for the Ferruginous Duck *Aythya nyroca* in western Europe[1032]. However, the most serious threats are due to extensive introgression caused by the introduction of one species into the range of another. There are many examples among Anseriformes, but the most notorious concerns Mallard *Anas platyrhynchos*, which was introduced extensively as an ornamental species and for hunting in many places throughout the world. It now hybridises regularly and widely with American Black Duck *A. rubripes*, Mottled Duck *A. fulvigula*, Mexican Duck *A. (platyrhynchos) diazi*, Pacific Black Duck *A. superciliosa rogersi* from Australia, Hawaiian Duck *A. wyvilliana*, Laysan Duck *A. laysanensis* and Meller's Duck *A. melleri*. These species are now threatened to various degrees by hybridisation with introduced Mallards. The example of the Ruddy Duck *Oxyura jamaicensis*, which was introduced in England, spread across Western Europe and came into contact with the Iberian population of White-headed Duck *O. leucocephala*, which was already threatened by habitat loss, should also be mentioned. Brought into contact partly due to man's agency, these two species frequently hybridised, especially as male Ruddy Ducks out-compete the native species and mate with their females. Starting with the culling in Spain of dozens of hybrids, considerable efforts are now being made to eradicate European populations of Ruddy Ducks.

WHY DO BIRDS HYBRIDISE?

Hybridisation occurs in the wild for several reasons. Among the prerequisites is genetic closeness, since if the parent species' genomes are too distant the resultant hybrids are sterile or unviable. Several reproductive barriers may also make breeding more difficult or prevent hybridisation: these barriers can be of an ethological or ecological nature, such as the type of courtship, choice of habitats, nesting periods, etc. However, in Anseriformes, geographic barriers appear to be most effective. Indeed, it appears that the majority of the species can be crossed if they are brought into contact and the choice of partners is reduced, as is often the case in captivity. This results in totally unexpected crosses such as Wood Duck *Aix sponsa*

× Common Shelduck *Tadorna tadorna*, Greylag Goose *Anser anser* × Mallard, Brent Goose *Branta bernicla* × Mute Swan *Cygnus olor* or Northern Pintail *Anas acuta* × Common Eider *Somateria mollissima*. In captivity, where reproductive barriers are reduced or removed, many combinations are possible.

In nature, however, these reproductive barriers are effective and, as indicated above, large-scale hybridisation only occurs when a species has been introduced by man into the range of another phylogenetically and ecologically close species, thereby surmounting the geographical barrier. However, hybridisation is a spontaneous phenomenon even among naturally sympatric species. Sometimes, it may be due to interspecific parasitism, which leads some species of ducks to lay some of their eggs in the nests of other species, and is rather frequent for example among the genus *Aythya*. This can produce an imprinting phenomenon on the female of the host species, which may affect the choice of sexual partners in adulthood. The same may happen in the case of very early adoptions of ducklings into the brood of another species. Other commonly reported causes for hybridisation are the lack of a partner of their own species, especially when a bird strays far from its original range or the species becomes rarer. In such cases, a bird will prefer to mate with a partner from another species, rather than not breed at all. Finally, transformation of natural environments is mentioned as a cause of hybridisation. This is, for example, the case in the American Black Duck and Mallard in coastal wintering areas of the former. The creation of many freshwater ponds, including within urban recreation areas, close to saltwater coastal habitats, has contributed to weaken their segregation by habitat. In addition, hybridisation can be facilitated by the fact that males often force females to mate, and female plumages of many species are quite similar.

DETECTING HYBRIDS

Our notions of frequency of natural hybridisation are obviously related to our ability to detect them. This frequency is undeniably greater in Anseriformes, firstly because they can often be studied in large numbers and in good conditions, and their plumages are varied and easily separable, at least in males. Needless to say, an equivalent frequency of hybrids among tyrant-flycatchers *Empidonax* or reed warblers *Acrocephalus*, many of which are similar-looking, dull-coloured and secretive, would be much harder to detect.

Compared to other orders, the species of Anseriformes are phylogenetically rather close to each other, making them more likely to hybridise. Moreover, Anseriformes being among the most popular species for ornament and hunting, are certainly (among birds) the most prone to escape within other species' ranges, which is a major cause of hybridisation. Finally, also because these species are commonly kept in captivity, hybridisation has been well known for a long time and knowledge of different hybrids is consequently much more accurate than for other orders, e.g. the remarkable syntheses prepared by Sibley, in 1938[1190], and Gray, in 1958[465]. Later, Gillham & Gillham (1996–2002)[439, 440, 441, 442, 443] compiled an outstanding inventory of hybrids among the Anatinae based on descriptions and photographs of nearly 220 combinations. There are also countless online resources. Other significant syntheses are those by McCarthy in 2006[817], Randler[1040] and the continuously updated website of Serge Dumont (http://www.bird-hybrids.com/) for all species of birds. Information in the 'Hybridisation' section of each species are based on these resources, among others.

IDENTIFICATION PROBLEMS

The frequency of natural hybrids is difficult to quantify, and highly variable depending on species group and region of the world. But, they are sufficiently numerous to be a regularly discussed topic among ornithologists, and to constitute real identification pitfalls. Without detailing the genetic mechanisms underlying hybridisation, it leads to the existence of individuals with mixed phenotypic characters (i.e. a combination of characters identical to those of both parents) or intermediate characters uncommon to either (typically coloration of the bare parts). Note that other traits useful for identification (vocalisations, behaviour, ecological preferences) can also be either mixed or intermediate.

In the case of combined characters, those corresponding to the dominant genes of one parent or the other are usually expressed in the hybrid. In other cases, the hybrid shows features not shown by either parent. For example, adult male hybrid Northern Shoveler *Anas clypeata* × Gadwall *Anas strepera* frequently has whitish cheeks, unlike either parent. Many hybrids between *Anas* dabbling ducks possess what is known as a 'bimaculated' pattern on the head-sides, with two bright patches, one at the base of the bill and below the lores, and the other on the rear cheeks. This pattern recalls that of the Baikal Teal *Anas formosa*, even when neither hybrid's parent shows this pattern. It has been suggested, for this case and others, that hybridisation could cause ancestral characters to reappear. Other similarly odd features include the striped upper- and undertail-coverts of some geese *Branta* spp. × *Anser* spp. hybrids, or a size greater or smaller than either parent.

In some cases, a hybrid can strongly resemble one parent more than the other, or even a different species, causing identification problems. One example is the case of Lesser Scaup *Aythya affinis*, which in Eurasia, where it is rare, can be mistaken for hybrids involving this species, but also Tufted Duck *A. fuligula* × Common Pochard *A. ferina* and Tufted Duck × Greater Scaup *A. marila*. In North America, Eurasian Wigeon *Anas penelope* and Tufted Ducks *Aythya fuligula* are rare, but hybrids involving these species are relatively common and very likely to constitute pitfalls.

The field ornithologist can also be faced by obvious hybrids without knowing either or one of the parent species involved. Establishing the parentage of a hybrid is obviously interesting and useful, but it must be remembered that identifying such birds, especially if they have probably escaped from captivity, requires much caution. Not only a bird's characters may have been affected by captivity (due to the type of feeding and care, and possible inbreeding among its ancestry) but the possibilities for each of its parents are much more numerous than in the wild. Moreover, there is no certainty as to the 'genetic quality' of each parent, which might also be hybrids. In this book, the legends to the photographs and artwork urge caution in this respect, often using the terms 'probable' or 'putative' if the parentage of a hybrid is not established with sufficient certainty.

Mute Swan *Cygnus olor* × Whooper Swan *C. cygnus*. Russia, Jun (Matthieu Vaslin).

Mute Swan *Cygnus olor* × Black Swan *C. atratus*. France, Feb (Sébastien Reeber).

Snow Goose *Chen caerulescens* × Cackling Goose *Branta hutchinsii*. Colorado, USA, Feb (Steve Mlodinow).

Ross's Goose *Chen rossii* × Cackling Goose *Branta hutchinsii*. Colorado, USA, Nov (Steve Mlodinow).

Greylag Goose *Anser anser* × Canada Goose *Branta canadensis*. Netherlands, Feb (Sébastien Reeber).

Putative American Wigeon *Anas americana* × Green-winged Teal *A. carolinensis*. Colorado, USA, Mar (Steve Mlodinow).

Eurasian Wigeon *Anas penelope* × Mallard *A. platyrhynchos*. Denmark, Dec (Nis Lundmark Jensen).

Gadwall *Anas strepera* × Mallard *A. platyrhynchos*. Poland, Mar (Zbigniew Kayzer).

Mallard *Anas platyrhynchos* × Northern Pintail *A. acuta*. France, Feb (Aurélien Audevard).

Mallard *Anas platyrhynchos* × Eastern Spot-billed Duck *A. zonorhyncha*. Japan, Oct (Stuart Price).

Green-winged Teal *Anas carolinensis* × Blue-winged Teal *A. discors*. Texas, USA, Mar (Greg Lavaty).

Blue-winged Teal *Anas discors* × Northern Shoveler *A. clypeata*. France, Apr (Matthieu Vaslin).

Blue-winged Teal *Anas discors* × Cinnamon Teal *A. cyanoptera*. Captivity, Dec (Steve Mlodinow).

Northern Pintail *Anas acuta* × Red-crested Pochard *Netta rufina*. Switzerland, Nov (Christopher J. G. Plummer).

Northern Pintail *Anas acuta* × Red-crested Pochard *Netta rufina*. England, Feb (Sébastien Reeber).

Mallard *Anas platyrhynchos* × Red-crested Pochard *Netta rufina*. Switzerland, Jan (Vincent Palomares).

Mallard *Anas platyrhynchos* × Red-crested Pochard *Netta rufina*. France, Mar (Sébastien Reeber).

Mallard *Anas platyrhynchos* × Red-crested Pochard *Netta rufina*. Captivity, Feb (Sébastien Reeber).

Common Pochard *Aythya ferina* × Ferruginous Duck *A. nyroca*. Switzerland, Nov (Christopher J. G. Plummer).

Common Pochard *Aythya ferina* × Ferruginous Duck *A. nyroca*. France, Nov (Sébastien Reeber).

Common Pochard *Aythya ferina* × Ferruginous Duck *A. nyroca*. Switzerland, Nov (Christopher J. G. Plummer).

Common Pochard *Aythya ferina* × Canvasback *A. valisineria*. Captivity, May (Sébastien Reeber).

Common Pochard *Aythya ferina* × Tufted Duck *A. fuligula*. Switzerland, Nov (Christopher J. G. Plummer).

Putative Tufted Duck *Aythya fuligula* × Lesser Scaup *A. affinis*. British Columbia, Canada, Feb (Alan D. Wilson).

31

PLATE 1

Black-bellied Whistling-duck *Dendrocygna autumnalis* Text p. 177

Usually unmistakable. Two subspecies, but *fulgens* is the only one in the Holarctic. Complex basic moult strategy (one plumage per adult cycle). Sexes very similar.

D. a. autumnalis

a **Adult definitive basic** (year-round). Note broad greyish band across lower breast, the slightly smaller size, shorter legs and, on average, paler bill.

D. a. fulgens

b **Adult definitive basic** (year-round).

c **Juvenile first basic** (until Nov–Dec). Overall dull grey-brown, rather uniform. From juvenile dull greenish-grey colour, legs become pinkish through first winter, as does the bill. Pre-formative moult occurs during first winter, and most birds are easy to age at least until Jan.

d **First-winter/first-summer, formative** (Dec–Feb/Aug). Much like adult after pre-formative moult but most birds show some juvenile feathers mixed with new formative ones, giving a rather mottled aspect especially to the belly. Some birds with limited pre-formative moult may appear very 'messy' during their first spring.

e **Adult definitive basic** (year-round). In flight, unmistakable with its broad white wingbars. Clear-cut white base to primaries typical of adults. Almost black from below.

Lesser Whistling-duck *Dendrocygna javanica* Text p. 183

Easy to identify, although superficially resembles Fulvous Whistling-duck *D. bicolor*. Complex basic moult strategy (one plumage per adult cycle). Sexes very similar.

f **Adult definitive basic** (year-round).

g **Juvenile first basic** (until Jan–Feb). Duller and plainer than adult, but ageing may require good views.

h **Adult definitive basic** (year-round). In flight, note rather stocky shape and tricoloured upperwing with blackish remiges, slate-grey greater and median coverts, and reddish lesser coverts.

Black-bellied Whistling-duck

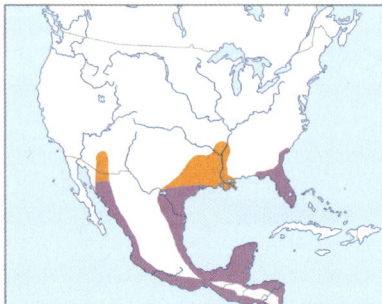

Lesser Whistling-duck

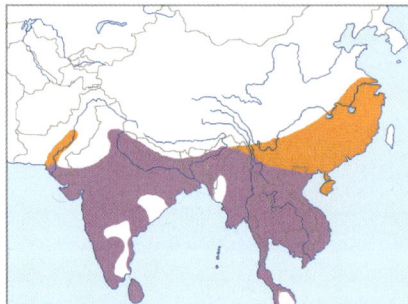

PLATE 2

Fulvous Whistling-duck *Dendrocygna bicolor* Text p. 180

Easily identified. Complex basic moult strategy (one plumage per adult cycle). Sexes similar but slight differences in size and shape often visible within pairs.

a **Adult definitive basic** (year-round).

b **Adult definitive basic** (year-round).

c **Adult ♀ definitive basic** (year-round). Note dark vertical stripe on nape, reaching dark crown.

d **Adult ♂ definitive basic** (year-round). This stripe is usually clearly interrupted in ♂.

e **Adult definitive basic** (year-round). In flight from above, appears uniformly dark, with a white crescent on the uppertail.

f **Adult definitive basic** (year-round). In flight from below, underwing is black contrasting with reddish belly. Note typical posture when landing, with the neck stretched downwards.

g **Juvenile first basic** (until Oct–Dec). Recalls adult, but less brightly coloured. Pale fringes to upperparts feathers much narrower, crown darker and contrasts with paler cheeks, and flanks lack white shafts of adult.

Hybrid Fulvous Whistling-duck *D. bicolor* × White-faced Whistling-duck *D. viduata*

Hybridisation occurs very rarely within this genus.

h **Juvenile first basic** (until Oct). Shows features of both parents, with finely barred belly, overall dull cinnamon colour, including cheeks, and inconspicuous crescent on uppertail-coverts.

Fulvous Whistling-duck

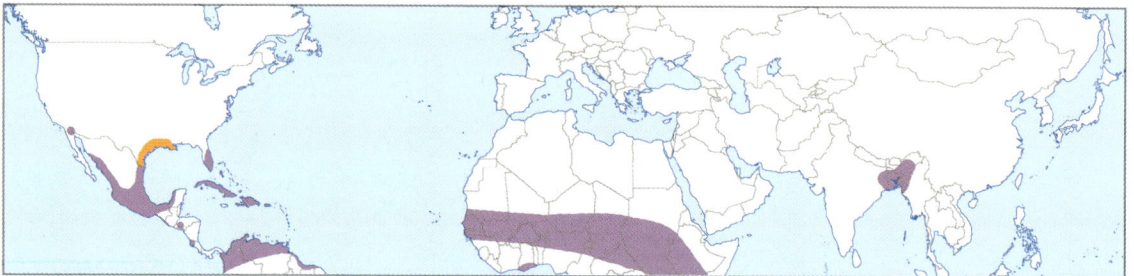

PLATE 3

Swan Goose *Anser cygnoides* (see also Plate 8) Text p. 186

Distinctive grey goose, easy to identify in any plumage, but care should be given to hybrids with the various domestic forms escaped from captivity. Complex basic moult strategy (one plumage per adult cycle). Sexes similar but slight differences in size and shape often visible within pairs.

a   **Adult definitive basic** (year-round). Note very long bill (longer in ♂ as shown here) and white line at its base.

b   **Juvenile first basic** (until Oct–Dec). Resembles adult, but has finely scalloped upperparts, plainer flanks, no white line at base of bill and bill is shorter.

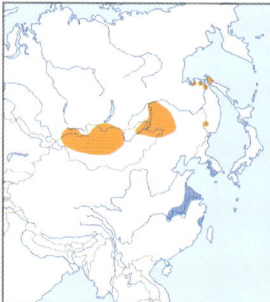

Greylag Goose *Anser anser* (see also Plate 8) Text p. 203

The largest 'grey goose', with stocky shape, thick neck and head, rather pale plumage, pale pink legs and orange or pinkish bill. Two subspecies, distinguishable when comparing birds from western and eastern ends of range, but many intermediates in C Europe. Complex basic moult strategy (one plumage per adult cycle). Sexes similar but slight differences in size and shape often visible within pairs.

A. a. anser

c   **Adult definitive basic** (year-round).

d   **Juvenile first basic** (until Oct–Nov). Compared to adult, slightly smaller with plainer plumage (flanks uniform, scapulars rounded and faintly fringed pale, forming a clean scaly appearance). Could be mistaken for juvenile Greater White-fronted Goose *A. albifrons*, but latter is smaller, slenderer and distinctly darker overall.

e   **First-winter, formative** (Nov–Apr/Aug). This bird is in pre-formative moult, with mix of juvenile and adult-type feathers (flanks and scapulars). The bill's nail is often not completely whitish until the beginning of the first spring.

A. a. rubrirostris

f   **Adult definitive basic** (year-round). A little larger, paler and greyer overall. Bill slightly longer and its pale pink colour is typically similar to that of the legs and orbital ring.

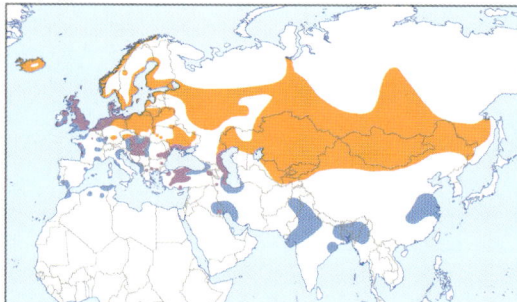

Bar-headed Goose *Anser indicus* (see also Plate 8) Text p. 226

Unmistakable at all ages. Complex basic moult strategy (one plumage per adult cycle). Sexes similar.

g   **Adult definitive basic** (year-round).

h   **Juvenile first basic** (until Oct–Nov). Recalls adult, but note plainer flanks and upperparts, with scapulars lacking adult white fringes, and blackish hindneck and nape.

Swan Goose   Greylag Goose   Bar-headed Goose

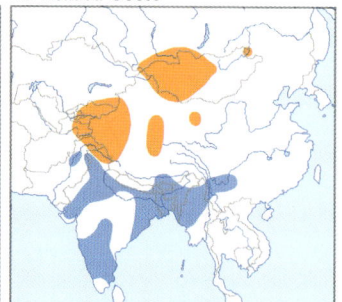

b

a

f

c

d

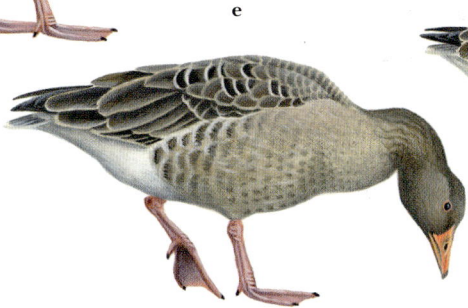
e

g

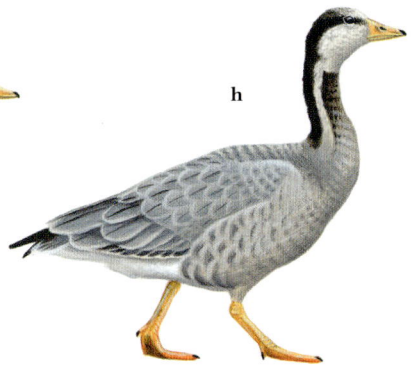
h

PLATE 4

Pink-footed Goose *Anser brachyrhynchus* (see also Plates 5 & 8) Text p. 199

Medium-sized goose, with pinkish legs and small dark bill with a rosy patch. Appears stocky and relatively short-necked. Complex basic moult strategy (one plumage per adult cycle). Sexes similar.

a **Adult definitive basic** (year-round). Typical, with rear flanks the darkest part of body, darker than greyish upperparts. Dark head and upper neck contrasting with pale breast. Note also grey tail-band.

b **Adult definitive basic** (year-round). Can show browner upperparts, and thus more easily be mistaken for Russian Bean Goose *A. fabalis rossicus*.

c **Juvenile first basic** (until Oct–Nov). Often arrives on wintering grounds in full juvenile plumage, with overall plain coloration, no dark markings on flanks, typical 'U-shaped' scapulars with only faintly paler fringes and an ill-defined bill pattern.

Bean Goose *Anser fabalis* (see also Plates 5 & 8) Text p. 189

Very variable, with bright orange legs and yellow-orange patch of variable extent on bill. From east to west, *serrirostris* and *rossicus* breed in the Eurasian tundra, whereas *middendorffii* and *fabalis* occur within the taiga belt. See Plate 5 for details of the bills of the different subspecies. Complex basic moult strategy (one plumage per adult cycle). Sexes similar.

A. f. serrirostris (**Thick-billed Bean Goose**)

d **Adult definitive basic** (year-round). A large subspecies, as heavy as *fabalis*, but neck typically shorter, colder toned overall with a very thick bill. When alert, the bill often appears snub.

A. f. rossicus (**Tundra Bean Goose**)

e **Adult definitive basic** (year-round). The smallest subspecies. Compared to *fabalis*, has a shorter neck and a distinctive head and bill shape.

f **Juvenile first basic** (until Oct–Nov). At this age, note plain plumage, lack of bars on flanks, 'U-shaped' scapulars (more distinctly fringed than in juvenile Pink-footed Goose), darker crown and forehead, and dull-coloured bill and legs until at least mid-autumn.

A. f. middendorffii (**Middendorff's Bean Goose**)

g **Adult definitive basic** (year-round). The largest subspecies, with overall pale plumage, especially head and neck. The latter seems very long when stretched. Long thick bill, flattened forehead and often gently curved neck may recall shape of Whooper Swan *Cygnus cygnus*.

A. f. fabalis (**Taiga Bean Goose**)

h **Adult definitive basic** (year-round). Close to Greylag Goose *A. anser* in size, with a long neck, longer and relatively thinner bill, and paler head and neck (vs. *rossicus*).

i **First-winter, formative** (Nov–Apr/Aug). During pre-formative moult, note two generations of scapulars, with adult-type feathers appearing on flanks. Bare parts much like adult.

Pink-footed Goose   Bean Goose

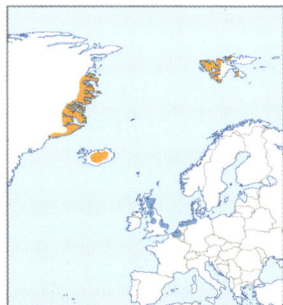

a
b
c
d
e
f
g
h
i

PLATE 5

All birds shown here are adult (definitive basic).

Pink-footed Goose *Anser brachyrhynchus* (see also Plates 4 & 8)   Text p. 199

a   Typical smallish, rounded head, with a short bill. Bill blackish with rosy patch, usually extending along the tomium towards the gape. Some birds show a thin white band around the base of the bill.

b   In many birds, the rosy colour is restricted to a narrow band behind the nail.

Bean Goose *Anser fabalis* (see also Plates 4 & 8)   Text p. 189

As in Pink-footed Goose, some show a thin white band around the bill's base.

A. f. rossicus (Tundra Bean Goose)

c   Bill thicker and longer than in Pink-footed Goose, with an orange patch. Head square-shaped with a steep forehead, forming an angle with culmen. Lower mandible slightly concave at its base, and the culmen is straight. 'Grinning patch' deeper and shorter than in *fabalis*. The bill pattern here is that most commonly shown in W Europe.

d   A slightly thicker bill as here, with a larger orange patch, is shown by *c*.30% of birds wintering in W Europe.

e   *A. f. rossicus* and *fabalis* overlap in bill length, coloration and structure. This extent of orange on the bill is shown by *c*.5% of birds wintering in W Europe.

A. f. fabalis (Taiga Bean Goose)

f   Compared to *rossicus*, head appears flatter and more elongated, with a flattened forehead and paler cheeks. The bill is the same depth at its base, but *c*.10% longer. Note the straight or concave culmen, the tomium almost straight compared to other taxa, and thin 'grinning patch'. Bill coloration is variable, but this is the common type.

g   A rather dark bill, as shown by *c*.15% of birds wintering in the Netherlands. A few show an orange patch restricted to a narrow band behind the nail, as in *c*.5% of *rossicus*.

h   Almost all-orange bill, as shown by *c*.20% of birds wintering in the Netherlands.

A. f. serrirostris (Thick-billed Bean Goose)

i   The thickest-billed subspecies, and averages slightly longer than in *fabalis*. Note deep, oval-shaped 'grinning patch' and restricted yellow-orange patch. The head is stocky.

A. f. middendorffii (Middendorff's Bean Goose)

j.   The longest-billed subspecies, and bill as thick as *serrirostris* at its base. Head elongated with flattened forehead and no angle with culmen, giving a Whooper Swan-like shape. Yellow patch on bill restricted. Head and neck paler, and washed gingery, compared to *serrirostris*.

PLATE 6

Lesser White-fronted Goose *Anser erythropus* (see also Plates 7 & 8)   Text p. 221

The smallest grey goose. Closely resembles Greater White-fronted Goose *A. albifrons* and, especially, hybrids between these species. Lesser White-fronted Goose is small, chunky and has long wings. Complex basic moult strategy (one plumage per adult cycle). Sexes similar. [Map on Plate 7]

a   **Adult definitive basic** (year-round). Compared to *albifrons*, note dark head contrasting with ochre-yellow upper breast. Black barring on belly reduced (often less than shown here).

b   **Juvenile first basic** (until Oct–Nov). Dark brown, lacking the white 'front', white streaks on upperparts and black bars on rear flanks and belly.

Greater White-fronted Goose *Anser albifrons* (see also Plates 7 & 8)   Text p. 208

Highly variable, with five subspecies currently recognised. Within each, individual variation occurs in size, bill shape and colour, extent of white 'front' and black barring on the belly. 'Average' birds are shown here. Complex basic moult strategy (one plumage per adult cycle). Sexes similar.

A. a. albifrons (Eurasian White-fronted Goose)

c   **Adult definitive basic** (year-round). The smallest and palest subspecies, but closest to *sponsa* in E Asia. Black sometimes covers up to 75% of the belly.

d   **Juvenile first basic** (until Oct–Nov). Bill pale pink, sometimes yellow-orange (much more frequently than adult).

A. a. sponsa (Pacific White-fronted Goose)

e   **Adult definitive basic** (year-round). Like *albifrons* but slightly larger and darker, with a longer and paler bill. Overall greyish (less brown) compared to other North American subspecies, especially *elgasi*, with which it occurs sympatrically on Pacific coasts.

A. a. gambelli (Gambell's White-fronted Goose)

f   **Adult definitive basic** (year-round). Under current definitions, *gambelli* comprises birds from the tundra (closer to *sponsa*) and the taiga, as shown here (closer to *elgasi* and *flavirostris*).

A. a. flavirostris (Greenland White-fronted Goose)

g   **Adult definitive basic** (year-round). Large and very dark, with a thick neck and an orange bill.

h   **Juvenile first basic** (until Oct–Nov). Compared to *albifrons*, darker brown plumage, with barely paler belly and poorly defined pale buff edges to tertials, median coverts and scapulars.

A. a. elgasi (Tule White-fronted Goose)

i   **Adult definitive basic** (year-round). The largest subspecies, with a long, thick neck and head.

j   **First-winter, formative** (Nov–Apr/Aug). Closer to adult than in other subspecies.

Greater White-fronted Goose

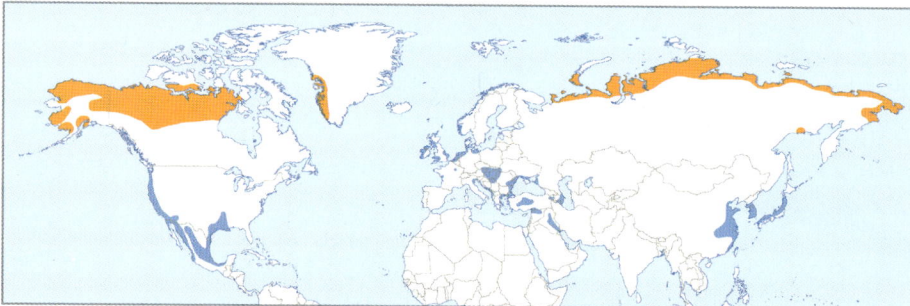

PLATE 7

Lesser White-fronted Goose *Anser erythropus* (see also Plates 6 & 8) Text p. 221

a **Adult definitive basic** (year-round). Note small pink bill and striking yellow orbital ring. The white forehead extends far onto the crown.

b **Adult definitive basic** (year-round). From the front, the white facial patch is usually sharply pointed.

c **First-winter, formative** (Nov–Apr/Aug). Dark head with a contrasting yellow orbital ring.

Hybrid Greater White-fronted Goose *A. albifrons* × Lesser White-fronted Goose *A. erythropus*

Text p. 223

d **Adult definitive basic** (year-round). Variable. Intermediate in size, but may look much like Lesser White-fronted Goose, with less extensive white 'front' and less obvious orbital ring, often thicker above the eye and thinner below.

Greater White-fronted Goose *Anser albifrons* (see also Plates 6 & 8) Text p. 208

Variation occurs within each subspecies in overall darkness of the head, extent of the white 'front', colour of the orbital ring, and colour, size and shape of the bill. [Map on Plate 6]

A. a. albifrons (Eurasian White-fronted Goose)

e **Adult definitive basic** (year-round). This race has palest head, accentuating blackish area around rather reduced white facial patch. Bill short, triangular with an almost straight culmen, bright pink (occasionally yellowish). Orbital ring usually inconspicuous, but sometimes yellowish.

f **Adult definitive basic** (year-round). White mask often more rounded (vs. Lesser White-fronted Goose).

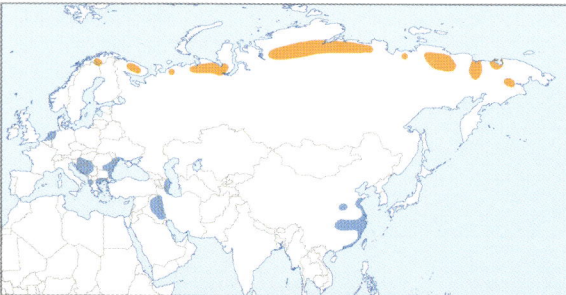

g **First-winter, formative** (Nov–Apr/Aug). Note dark nail, less well-marked neck grooves and reduced white 'front'. Bill more often yellow or orangey than in adult.

A. a. sponsa (Pacific White-fronted Goose)

h **Adult definitive basic** (year-round). Compared to W Eurasian birds, head slightly darker, bill longer and more peach-coloured, with a more concave culmen (teat-shaped tip); *albifrons* of E Asia very similar.

A. a. gambelli (Gambell's White-fronted Goose)

i **Adult definitive basic** (year-round). Rather dark head with a longish bill, but variable.

j **Adult definitive basic** (year-round). Bill colour can vary from pale pink to bright orange.

k **First-winter, formative** (Nov–Apr/Aug). White facial patch often extensive and bill often peachy yellow.

A. a. flavirostris (Greenland White-fronted Goose)

l **Adult definitive basic** (year-round). Head very dark, with a bright orange bill.

m **First-winter, formative** (Nov–Apr/Aug.).

A. a. elgasi (Tule White-fronted Goose)

n **Adult definitive basic** (year-round). Head very dark, frequently with a yellow orbital ring. White facial patch can be very large (as shown here), and the bill is thick-based and long.

Lesser White-fronted Goose

PLATE 8

All birds shown here are adult (definitive basic).

Bean Goose *Anser fabalis* (see also Plates 4 & 5)   Text p. 189

Note dark upperwing, blackish underwing, rump and tail-band. Variable in size and body coloration.

a   *A. f. middendorffii.* Very large, with long neck, head and bill.

b   *A. f. rossicus.* This species typically appears very dark in flight.

c   *A. f. fabalis.* Larger and paler than *rossicus*, often with a longer neck.

d   *A. f. rossicus.* Underwing dark, sharply contrasting with the underparts in this species.

Pink-footed Goose *Anser brachyrhynchus* (see also Plates 4 & 5)   Text p. 199

e   Note the typically bluish-grey and uniform aspect from above (no contrast between the upperwing and scapulars), with a grey rump and pale grey tail-band.

f   Note slight contrast on underwing (more marked than in Bean Goose but less than in Greylag Goose).

Bar-headed Goose *Anser indicus* (see also Plate 3)   Text p. 226

g   Unmistakable.

Greylag Goose *Anser anser* (see also Plate 3)   Text p. 203

h   The only species with a strong contrast between the pale upperwing and darker scapulars. Rump pale grey-brown.

i   Note strong contrast on the underwing.

Swan Goose *Anser cygnoides* (see also Plate 3)   Text p. 186

j   Unmistakable.

Lesser White-fronted Goose *Anser erythropus* (see also Plates 6 & 7)   Text p. 221

Appears compact in flight with long pointed wings.

k   Very dark and uniform from above.

l   Note the ventral patches are often much reduced.

Greater White-fronted Goose *Anser albifrons* (see also Plates 6 & 7)   Text p. 208

Variable in size, shape and overall coloration, but always has dark upper- and underwing, with blackish rump and tail-band.

m   *A. a. albifrons.* Appears a little larger, paler and greyer than Lesser White-fronted Goose.

n   *A. a. flavirostris.* Larger, darker and browner than *albifrons*

PLATE 9

These species possess two colour morphs. White morphs are shown on this plate(see Plates 10–11 for blue morphs and intermediates).

Snow Goose *Chen caerulescens* (see also Plates 10 & 11)   Text p. 233

Can be mistaken only with Ross's Goose. Complex basic moult strategy (one plumage per adult cycle). Sexes similar. [Map on Plate 11]

C. c. atlanticus (Greater Snow Goose)

a   **Adult definitive basic** (year-round). The largest subspecies (with overlap), with a very strong bill, a deep 'grinning patch' and flat forehead.

C. c. caerulescens (Lesser Snow Goose)

b   **Adult definitive basic** (year-round). Note the strong bill with deep black 'grinning patch', flat crown, rounded feathering at base of bill and 'almond-shaped' eye.

c   **Adult definitive basic** (year-round). A small-billed individual shown here.

d   **Adult definitive basic** (year-round). All white except primaries, with head often washed rusty or ochre-yellow.

e   **First-winter, formative** (Nov–Mar/Aug). Typically shows mix of brownish or dusky and white feathers. Appears much more variegated than Ross's Goose at same age.

f   **Juvenile first basic** (until Oct–Nov). Much browner and darker than Ross's Goose at same age.

Hybrid Snow Goose *C. caerulescens* × Ross's Goose *C. rossii*   Text p. 243

Variable in size and shape, these hybrids can resemble Ross's Goose.

g   **Adult definitive basic** (year-round). Here a bird with a long thin bill, intermediate feathering at base of bill and 'grinning patch'.

h   **Adult definitive basic** (year-round). Some show a bill much like Ross's Goose, but slightly stronger and with an obvious black 'grinning patch'. Also note that the bill is dark basally.

i   **Adult definitive basic** (year-round). Some hybrids show several features not matching pure Ross's Goose (thick bill, thin 'grinning patch', feathering at base of bill, head shape, etc.), but are much closer to the latter than to Snow Goose.

Ross's Goose *Chen rossii* (see also Plates 10 & 11)   Text p. 240

Complex basic moult strategy (one plumage per adult cycle). Sexes similar. [Map on Plate 11]

j   **Adult definitive basic** (year-round). Note tall, rounded head, round eye located close to the bill base, small triangular bill with dark bluish base and straight feathering at base of bill.

k   **Adult definitive basic** (year-round). A small-billed individual shown here.

l   **Adult definitive basic** (year-round). Appears stockier than Snow Goose, with thinner legs.

m   **Juvenile first basic** (until Oct–Dec). Much whiter and more adult-like than Snow Goose at same age.

d

a

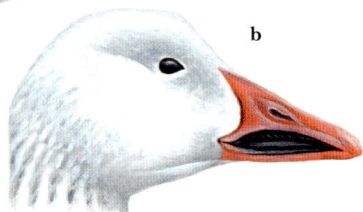
b

e

c

f

g

l

h

i

m

j

k

PLATE 10

Snow Goose *Chen caerulescens* (see also Plates 9 & 11)

Text p. 233

The blue morph is rare among birds wintering along the Pacific coast, and occasional in *atlanticus*. Many intermediates with white morph occur as well. [Map on Plate 11]

a   **Adult definitive basic** (year-round). A typical blue morph, with dark belly.

b   **First-winter, formative** (Oct–Dec/Aug). Pre-formative moult appears to be shorter and less extensive than in white morph, young birds typically showing many juvenile brown feathers until first summer.

c   **Juvenile first basic** (until Oct–Dec). Usually very dusky, with blackish bare parts.

d   **Adult definitive basic** (year-round). An intermediate bird close to dark morph, but has a pale belly.

e   **Adult definitive basic** (year-round). A typical intermediate bird.

f   **Adult definitive basic** (year-round). In some intermediates, white of neck joins white underparts on breast.

Ross's Goose *Chen rossii* (see also Plates 9 & 11)

Text p. 240

Dark morph very rare. [Map on Plate 11]

g   **Adult definitive basic** (year-round). From blue Snow Goose (other than size and shape differences), by blacker dark areas, belly, tertials and upperwing-coverts whiter, and presence of black on nape and crown.

h   **First-winter, formative** (Oct–Dec/Aug). Note the paler upperwing in this species.

Emperor Goose *Chen canagica* (see also Plate 11)

Text p. 230

Readily identified, but shows superficial similarity with blue Snow Goose. Complex basic moult strategy (one plumage per adult cycle). Sexes similar.

i   **Adult definitive basic** (year-round).

j   **First-winter, formative** (Nov–Mar/Aug). Note rounded scapulars, and browner juvenile feathers retained on head, neck, breast and/or flanks.

Emperor Goose

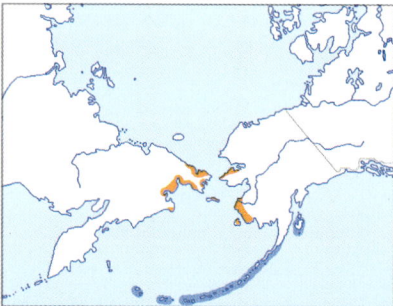

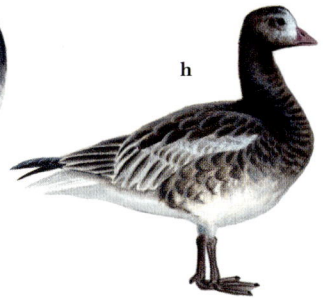

PLATE 11

Snow Goose *Chen caerulescens* (see also Plates 9 & 10) Text p. 233

a **Adult definitive basic** (year-round), white morph. Extent of black on remiges (and grey on primary coverts) varies individually, many showing black over all ten primaries.

b **Adult definitive basic** (year-round), white morph. This bird has only seven black primaries.

c **Adult definitive basic** (year-round), white morph. Here, black extends over three outermost secondaries.

d **Juvenile first basic** (until Oct–Dec), white morph.

e **Adult definitive basic** (year-round), blue morph. Underwing lesser and median coverts are whitish in many birds, but can also be pale grey.

f **Juvenile first basic** (until Oct–Dec), blue morph.

Ross's Goose *Chen rossii* (see also Plates 9 & 10) Text p. 240

g **Adult definitive basic** (year-round), white morph. Distinguished from Snow Goose only by size and shape in flight.

h **Adult definitive basic** (year-round), blue morph. Upperwing, underwing and rump are almost white.

i **Juvenile first basic** (until Oct–Dec), white morph.

Emperor Goose *Chen canagica* (see also Plate 10) Text p. 230

[Map on Plate 10]

j **Adult definitive basic** (year-round). Note, among other features, the typical dark underwing.

k **Juvenile first basic** (until Oct–Dec).

Snow Goose

Ross's Goose

PLATE 12

Several hybrids among the genera *Anser, Chen* and *Branta* which are reported in the wild more or less regularly (adult in definitive basic plumage shown). It should be kept in mind that all of these hybrids are variable, and may resemble more one parent or the other (see text). See also Plate 7 (Greater White-fronted Goose *A. albifrons* × Lesser White-fronted Goose *A. erythropus*), Plate 9 (Snow Goose *C. caerulescens* × Ross's Goose *C. rossii*) and Plate 15 (Brent Goose *B. bernicla* × Barnacle Goose *B. leucopsis*, Canada Goose *B. canadensis* × Barnacle Goose *B. leucopsis*, and Barnacle Goose *B. leucopsis* × Red-breasted Goose *B. ruficollis*).

a	**Hybrid Greater White-fronted Goose** *A. albifrons* × **Greylag Goose** *A. anser*	Text p. 213
b	**Hybrid Greater White-fronted Goose** *A. albifrons* × **Canada Goose** *B. canadensis*	Text p. 214
c	**Hybrid Greater White-fronted Goose** *A. albifrons* × **Canada Goose** *B. canadensis* Head variant.	Text p. 214
d	**Hybrid Greylag Goose** *A. anser* × **Barnacle Goose** *B. leucopsis*	Text p. 205
e	**Hybrid Greylag Goose** *A. anser* × **Canada Goose** *B. canadensis*	Text p. 205
f	**Hybrid Barnacle Goose** *B. leucopsis* × **Snow Goose** *C. caerulescens*	Text p. 260
g	**Hybrid Barnacle Goose** *B. leucopsis* × **Bar-headed Goose** *A. indicus*	Text p. 228
h	**Hybrid Greater White-fronted Goose** *A. albifrons* × **Snow Goose** *C. caerulescens*	Text p. 213
i	**Hybrid Greater White-fronted Goose** *A. albifrons* × **Snow Goose** *C. caerulescens* (blue morph)	Text p. 213
j	**Hybrid Canada Goose** *B. canadensis* × **Snow Goose** *C. caerulescens* (blue morph)	Text p. 236
k	**Hybrid Canada Goose** *B. canadensis* × **Snow Goose** *C. caerulescens*	Text p. 236
l	**Hybrid Greater White-fronted Goose** *A. albifrons* × **Barnacle Goose** *B. leucopsis*	Text p. 213
m	**Hybrid Greater White-fronted Goose** *A. albifrons* × **Red-breasted Goose** *B. ruficollis*	Text p. 257

PLATE 13

Brent Goose (Brant) *Branta bernicla* (see also Plate 14)   Text p. 246

Plates 13–14 employ a nomenclature wherein Pacific breeders (Black Brant) are called *B. b. orientalis*, with *B. b. nigricans* being used for breeding populations on Queen Elizabeth Is, Arctic Canada (Grey-bellied Brant). Complex basic moult strategy (one plumage per adult cycle). Sexes similar.

B. b. bernicla (**Dark-bellied Brent Goose**) The greyer and most uniform subspecies, with a faint but visible contrast between breast and flanks (variable between a and b), and rear flanks appear variably whitish, depending on the light.

a   **Adult definitive basic** (year-round).

b   **Adult definitive basic** (year-round).

c   **Juvenile first basic** (until Oct–Dec). Note plain grey-brown flanks, scaly upperparts and lack of white collar at this age.

d   **First-winter, formative** (Nov–Dec/Jul–Aug.). First formative feathers appear on head and neck, making the collar visible during the first autumn.

e   **First-summer, formative** (Nov–Dec/Jul–Aug). In first summer, the retained juvenile feathers become very bleached and worn, especially for birds that summer at southern wintering sites.

B. b. hrota (**Pale-bellied Brent Goose**) The palest subspecies, with strong contrast between the breast and flanks, and belly and brown upperparts.

f   **Adult definitive basic** (year-round).

g   **Juvenile first basic** (until Oct–Dec). The upperparts show a strongly scaly pattern, and the flanks are initially pale grey-brown.

h   **First-winter/first-summer, formative** (Nov–Dec/Jul–Aug). After pre-formative moult, much like adult with fringes to upperwing-coverts forming obvious white lines.

B. b. orientalis (**Black Brant**) The darkest subspecies, with very faint contrast between the breast and fore flanks (variable, between i and j, in most North American birds), and contrasting white patch on flanks.

i   **Adult definitive basic** (year-round).

j   **Adult definitive basic** (year-round).

k   **Juvenile first basic** (until Oct–Dec).

l   **First-winter/first-summer, formative** (Nov–Dec/Jul–Aug). During first autumn, juvenile and formative scapulars are both visible, the formative ones often being slightly better fringed than adult scapulars.

Brent Goose

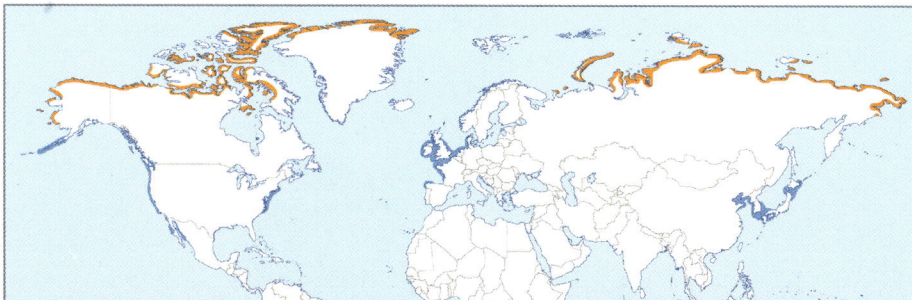

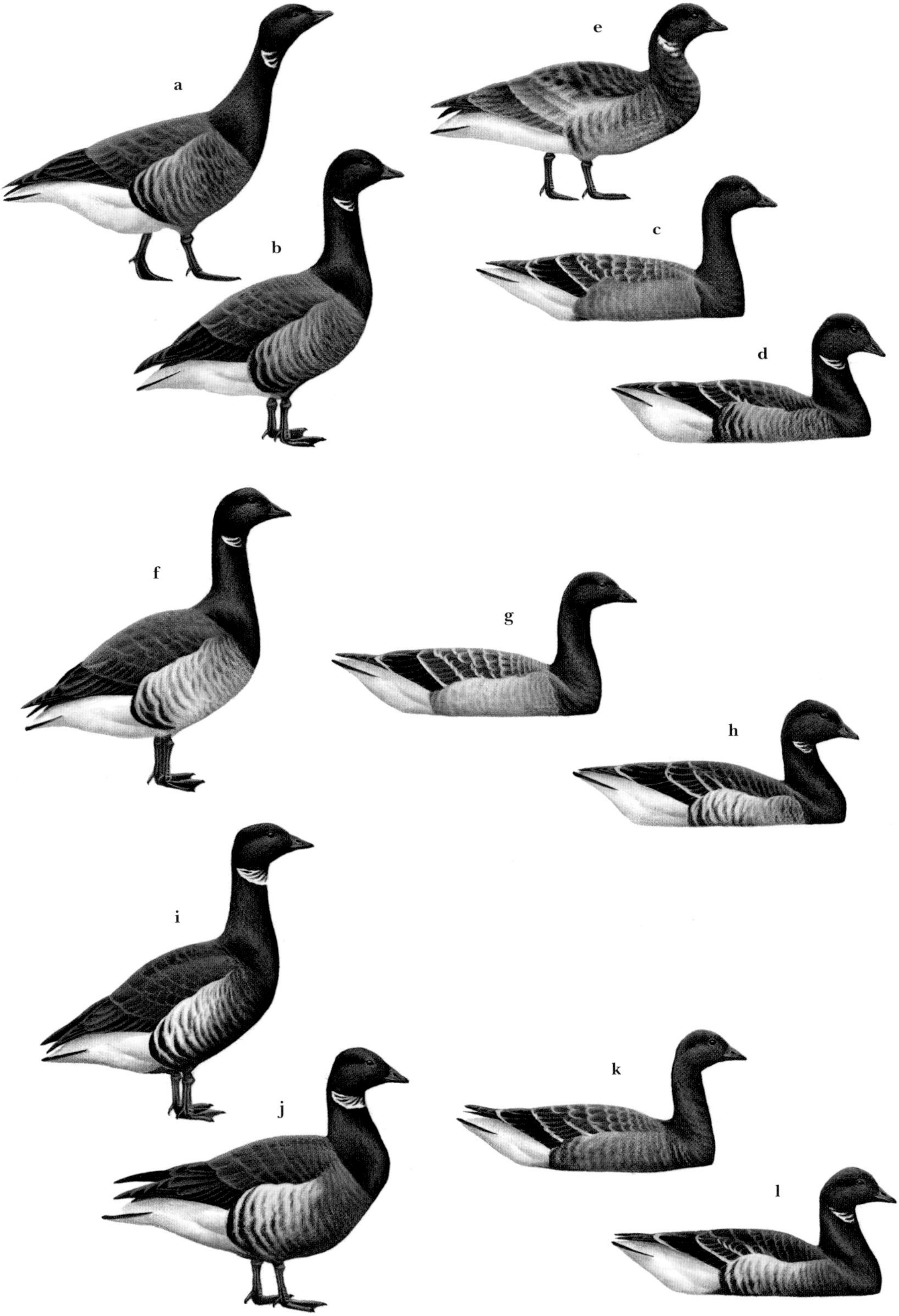
a
e
b
c
d
f
g
h
i
k
j
l

PLATE 14

Brent Goose (Brant) *Branta bernicla* (see also Plate 13) Text p. 246

Plates 13–14 employ a nomenclature wherein Pacific breeders (Black Brant) are called *B. b. orientalis*, with *B. b. nigricans* being used for breeding populations on Queen Elizabeth Is, Arctic Canada (Grey-bellied Brant). See text. [map on Plate 13]

***B. b. nigricans* (Grey-bellied Brant)** This subspecies is rather variable and intermediate between *orientalis* and *hrota*, with a belly browner than grey.

a   **Adult definitive basic** (year-round). Such birds still have an extensive collar, but are otherwise indistinguishable from *hrota*.

b   **Adult definitive basic** (year-round). A typical bird with brown fore flanks and belly, and an extensive white collar.

c   **Adult definitive basic** (year-round). Birds at the darker end resemble *orientalis*, but are often browner on the flanks and upperparts.

Intermediates

d   **Adult definitive basic** (year-round). Such birds are regularly seen in W Europe, and are considered to be intermediates between *bernicla* and *orientalis*.

e   **Adult definitive basic** (year-round). Rarely reported, this intermediate usually shows flanks washed pale grey.

***B. b. orientalis* (Black Brant)**

f   **Adult definitive basic** (year-round).

***B. b. hrota* (Pale-bellied Brent Goose)**

g   **Adult definitive basic** (year-round).

The extent of the white collar varies between subspecies and among them. The birds depicted here show the variation from in front (**h–k**) and behind (**l–n**).

***B. b. bernicla* (Dark-bellied Brent Goose)**. Typical pattern is j and m.

***B. b. hrota* (Pale-bellied Brent Goose)**. Most like k and n, but sometimes j (rarely i) and m.

***B. b. nigricans* (Grey-bellied Brant)**. In front, many birds are close to i or j (rarely h or k).

***B. b. orientalis* (Black Brant)**. Most birds show a pattern close to h (sometimes i) and l.

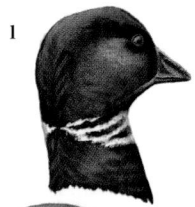

PLATE 15

Barnacle Goose *Branta leucopsis*

Text p. 259

No risk of confusion. Complex basic moult strategy (one plumage per adult cycle). Sexes similar.

a **Adult definitive basic** (year-round).

b **Adult definitive basic** (year-round). Note variability in wash to face (white to pale buff or yellowish) and thickness of loral stripe.

c **First-winter/first-summer, formative** (Nov–Dec/Jul–Aug). During first autumn, many show a mix of juvenile and formative (adult-type) scapulars, as depicted here. Juvenile belly feathers distinctive at close range, as well as juvenile median and greater coverts (more round-tipped, less clearly patterned).

d **Adult definitive basic** (year-round).

Red-breasted Goose *Branta ruficollis*

Text p. 256

No risk of confusion. Complex basic moult strategy (one plumage per adult cycle). Sexes similar.

e **Adult definitive basic** (year-round). Median and greater coverts form two broad, clear-cut white wingbars, with a faint third one often visible.

f **First-winter/first-summer, formative** (Nov–Dec/Jul–Aug). Following pre-formative moult, age can be determined by the wing pattern. The median and greater coverts are more rounded, dark grey-brown (vs. black) with pale diffuse fringes (vs. white and clear-cut). These form a succession of several thin, dull wingbars. Also note contrast between black scapulars and dark grey-brown upperwing.

g **Adult definitive basic** (year-round).

Hybrid Red-breasted Goose *B. ruficollis* × Barnacle Goose *B. leucopsis*

Text p. 257

h **Adult definitive basic** (year-round).

Hybrid Canada Goose *B. canadensis* × Barnacle Goose *B. leucopsis*

Text p. 277

i **Adult definitive basic** (year-round). Hybrid Barnacle Goose × Cackling Goose is similar, but distinctly smaller (even smaller than *B. leucopsis*).

Hybrid Brent Goose *B. bernicla* × Barnacle Goose *B. leucopsis*

Text p. 260

j **Adult definitive basic** (year-round).

Barnacle Goose

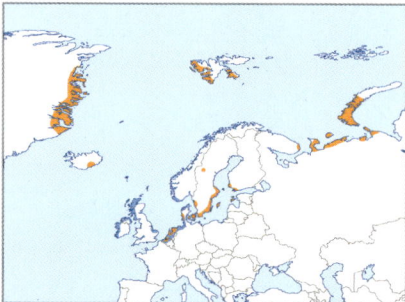

Red-breasted Goose

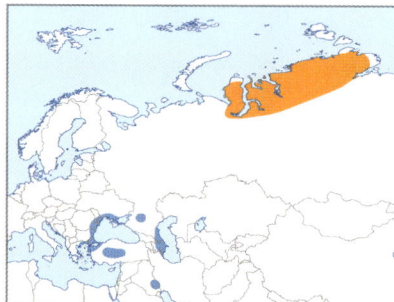

PLATE 16

The different subspecies of Canada and Cackling Geese are all variable, with many intermediates between typical birds of both species. Subspecific identification of Canada Geese is usually difficult, and often impossible for lone out-of-range birds. On the other hand, many Cackling Geese can be identified to subspecies in good views. Both species can be hard to distinguish when it comes to medium-sized birds (see text and Plate 17 for details of head and bill structure). All plumages depicted here adult definitive basic (year-round).

Canada Goose *Branta canadensis* (see also Plate 17) Text p. 272

Complex basic moult strategy (one plumage per adult cycle). Sexes similar. [Map on Plate 17]

a   ***B. c. maxima***. The largest and palest subspecies.

b   ***B. c. maxima***. Variant with white speckles on foreneck, which can occur in all taxa.

c   ***B. c. maxima***. Another variant with a white patch on the forehead, which can also occur in other subspecies, but appears more frequent in *maxima*. Other birds can show all-dark cheeks.

d   ***B. c. moffitti***. Also pale (some populations darker) and large, but averages smaller than *maxima*. These two widely interbreed and are not safely distinguished in most populations.

e   ***B. c. canadensis***. Smaller and slimmer than *maxima/ moffitti*.

f   ***B. c. canadensis***. Some are distinctly darker with a hint of pale collar sometimes visible.

g   ***B. c. interior***. Averages slightly smaller, longer-necked, shorter-legged and darker than *canadensis* (variable).

h   ***B. c. fulva***. Smaller and distinctly darker than *canadensis*.

i   ***B. c. occidentalis***. The darkest subspecies.

j   ***B. c. parvipes***. The smallest subspecies, with some birds being very dark like this one.

k   ***B. c. parvipes***. Most *parvipes* are pale and even larger than the largest Cackling Geese.

Cackling Goose *Branta hutchinsii* (see also Plate 17) Text p. 263

Complex basic moult strategy (one plumage per adult cycle). Sexes similar. [Map on Plate 17]

l   ***B. h. taverneri***. The largest Cackling Goose subspecies, with long thin neck when stretched.

m   ***B. h. taverneri***. Feeds with neck held oblique, compared to *leucopareia* (o) and *minima* (q).

n   ***B. h. leucopareia***. A variably dark subspecies, usually with a distinct white collar.

o   ***B. h. leucopareia***. A dark-breasted bird, most having a black gular stripe.

p   ***B. h. minima***. The smallest subspecies, usually very dark with distinctly patterned upperparts.

q   ***B. h. minima***. Some birds show a white collar and can then resemble *leucopareia*.

r   ***B. h. hutchinsii***. A small subspecies, usually pale with well-patterned upperparts.

s   ***B. h. hutchinsii***. Some variation exists in size and overall darkness.

PLATE 17

Canada Goose *Branta canadensis* (see also Plate 16) Text p. 272

Compared to Cackling Goose, the bill is usually much longer and thinner, especially at the tip, with a concave culmen.

a   ***B. c. maxima/B. c. moffitti***. The largest subspecies, with a heavy bill and sloping forehead.

b   ***B. c. canadensis***. Bill thinner, with a concave forehead/culmen line in profile.

c   ***B. c. canadensis***. Adult definitive basic (year-round).

d   ***B. c. canadensis***. Adult definitive basic (year-round).

e   ***B. c. canadensis***. Juvenile first basic (until Oct–Dec). Duller blackish neck, slightly swollen culmen, and flanks and upperparts appear scaly, rather than clearly streaked pale.

f   ***B. c. parvipes***. Adult definitive basic (year-round). Head often appears square, with a thin bill.

g   ***B. c. parvipes***. Adult definitive basic (year-round).

Cackling Goose *Branta hutchinsii* (see also Plate 16) Text p. 263

Usually shows a rather short, stubby bill, with a straighter culmen.

h   ***B. h. taverneri***. Often shows a pear-shaped head, with a deep-based, rather triangular bill.

i   ***B. h. hutchinsii***. Head typically square, with a marked forehead and flat crown peaking well behind the eye. The white cheeks usually show an indentation behind the eye.

j   ***B. h. hutchinsii***. Adult definitive basic (year-round).

k   ***B. h. hutchinsii***. Adult definitive basic (year-round).

l   ***B. h. hutchinsii***. Juvenile first basic (until Oct–Dec). Ageing as in Canada Goose.

m   ***B. h. minima***. Small square head with very short triangular bill. A black gular stripe is sometimes present.

Canada Goose

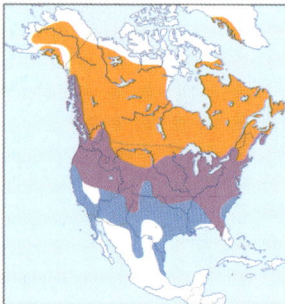

Canada Goose (introduced)

Cackling Goose

a

e

b

c

d

f

g

k

h

j

i

l

m

PLATE 18

Mute Swan *Cygnus olor*   Text p. 283

Usually readily identified by shape, including long pointed tail, and bill coloration. Complex basic moult strategy (one plumage per adult cycle). Slight sexual dimorphism.

a   **Adult ♂ definitive basic** (year-round). Wings often held 'puffed out' by ♂ in breeding period. Head and neck often tinged yellowish or rusty depending on the environment.

b   **Adult definitive basic** (year-round). Long tail and reddish-orange and black bill distinctive.

c–d   **Juvenile first basic** (until Jan–Feb). Two colour morphs exist in juvenile.

e   **First-winter/first-summer, formative** (Feb–Mar/Oct–Dec). Brownish parts of plumage darker than in other species, making this plumage more variegated.

f   **First-winter/first-summer, formative** (Feb–Mar/Oct–Dec). Typically variegated in flight as well.

g   **Adult ♂ definitive basic** (year-round). For much of the year, sex can be assessed by the size of the bill knob, being more developed in ♂.

h   **Adult ♀ definitive basic** (year-round). Smaller bill knob.

Hybrid Mute Swan *C. olor* × Whooper Swan *C. cygnus*   Text p. 285

i   **Adult definitive basic** (year-round). Rarely reported, in Eurasia, this hybrid has the bill typically with yellow, whitish, pinkish and black.

Hybrid Mute Swan *C. olor* × Black Swan *C. atratus*   Text p. 284

j   **Adult definitive basic** (year-round). This hybrid has been reported several times in Europe as a consequence of the introduction of Black Swan.

Mute Swan

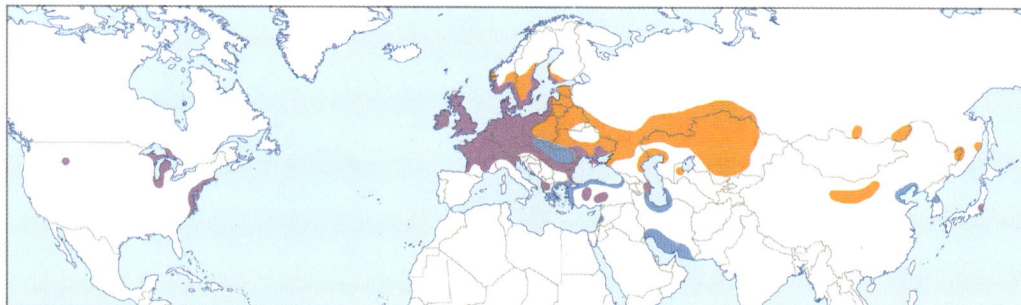

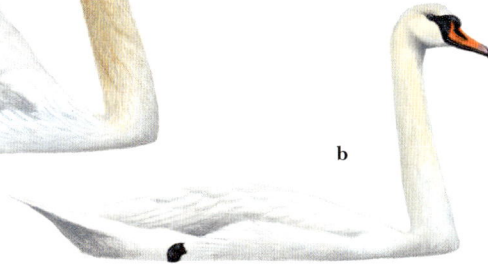

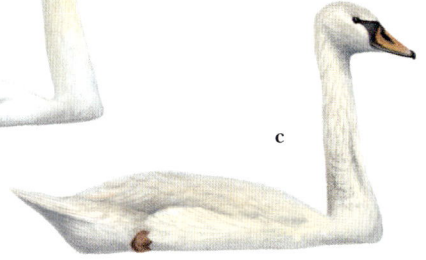

PLATE 19

Separating these three swans is mostly based on size, shape and bill coloration. For the latter, see Plate 20. Trumpeter Swan can be mistaken for Tundra Swan in North America (both are occasional in Eurasia), and Whooper Swan with Bewick's Swan in Eurasia (both are occasional in North America).

Trumpeter Swan *Cygnus buccinator* (see also Plate 20)   Text p. 287

Large, with a very long neck and long all-black bill. Complex basic moult strategy (one plumage per adult cycle). Sexes similar.

a   **Adult definitive basic** (year-round). Note very long neck, usually held gently curved.

b   **First-winter/first-summer, formative** (Feb–Mar/Oct–Dec). Juvenile plumage rather dark grey-brown, which is kept well into first winter compared to Tundra Swan at same age.

c   **Juvenile first basic** (until Jan–Feb.). Two colour morphs, with the white morph depicted here.

d   **Adult definitive basic** (year-round). In flight, neck appears very long, with a notch between the lower neck and belly.

Whooper Swan *Cygnus cygnus* (see also Plate 20)   Text p. 298

Large, with a very long neck and long straight bill, which is predominantly yellow. Complex basic moult strategy (one plumage per adult cycle). Sexes similar.

e   **Adult definitive basic** (year-round). Neck long and often held curved when feeding on water, with the bill pointing down.

f   **Adult definitive basic** (year-round). Often shows a rusty tinge to the head and neck (rare in Bewick's Swan).

g   **First-winter/first-summer, formative** (Jan–Mar/Nov–Jan). In alert posture, neck often surprisingly long and straight, with a clear angle at its base.

h   **Adult definitive basic** (year-round).

Tundra Swan *Cygnus columbianus* (see also Plate 20)   Text p. 292

Structure appears less disproportionate than those of the two larger swans, with a shorter neck and smoother head and bill shape. Complex basic moult strategy (one plumage per adult cycle). Sexes similar.

C. c. columbianus **(Tundra Swan)** [Map on Plate 20]

i   **Adult definitive basic** (year-round). When swimming, back peaks closer to neck (vs. back regularly rounded in Trumpeter and Whooper Swans).

j   **Adult definitive basic** (year-round). When stretched, the neck appears very thin in this species.

k   **First-winter/first-summer, formative** (Jan–Mar/Nov–Jan). By early winter, appears whiter (especially the upperparts) than Trumpeter Swan.

l   **Adult definitive basic** (year-round).

C. c. bewickii **(Bewick's Swan)**. Averages smaller than Tundra Swan. [Map on Plate 20]

m   **Adult definitive basic** (year-round).

n   **First-winter/first-summer, formative** (Jan–Mar/Nov–Jan).

Trumpeter Swan

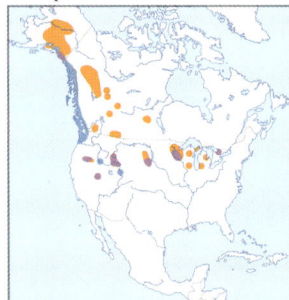

Whooper Swan

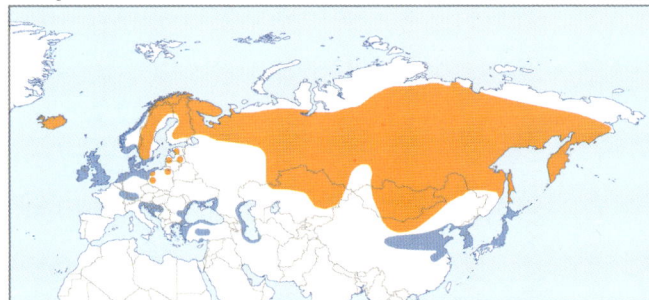

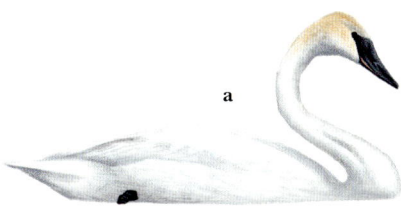

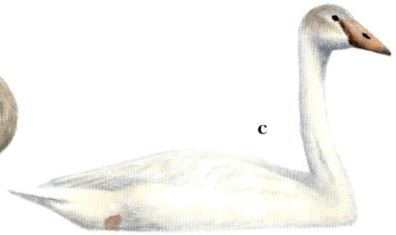

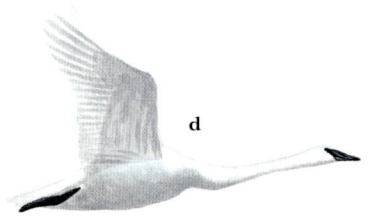

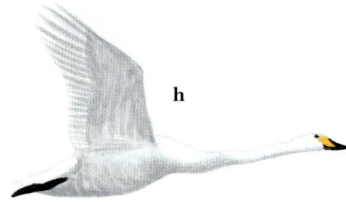

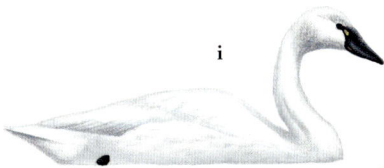

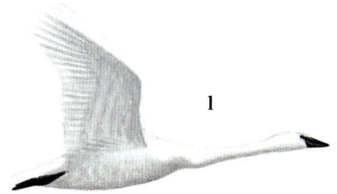

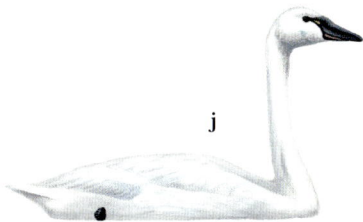

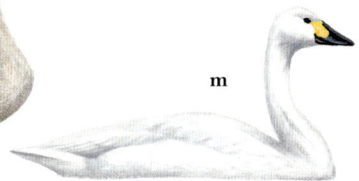

PLATE 20

Trumpeter Swan *Cygnus buccinator* (see also Plate 19)   Text p. 287

Black skin at the bill base is not narrower than the eye just in front of it, and its delineation between the gape and eye is almost straight.

a   **Adult definitive basic** (year-round). Bill entirely black with a pink shaft often visible at base of the tomium.

b   **Juvenile first basic** (until Jan–Feb.). The base of the bill is black (vs. Tundra Swan).

c   **Adult definitive basic** (year-round). From front, the forehead feathers often form a 'V'.

Whooper Swan *Cygnus cygnus* (see also Plate 19)   Text p. 298

Large yellow pointed patch on bill-sides is typical, the yellow often extending on the lower mandible and around the eye.

d   **Adult definitive basic** (year-round). The yellow patch usually tapers to a point under the nostril.

e   **Juvenile first basic** (until Jan–Feb). Initially, the black parts of the bill are pink, and the yellow parts pale grey or whitish, but adult pattern quickly becomes obvious.

f   **Adult definitive basic** (year-round). The black-and-yellow pattern varies individually, but less so than in Bewick's Swan. This is the commonest type, with a yellow upper culmen.

g   **Adult definitive basic** (year-round). All-black culmen rare in Europe and even rarer in E Asia.

Tundra Swan *Cygnus columbianus* (see also Plate 19)   Text p. 292

Bill coloration highly variable between and among subspecies.

C. c. columbianus (**Tundra Swan**). Note that the black skin is much narrower just in front of the eye, and that the feathering between the eye and gape is well rounded.

h   **Adult definitive basic** (year-round). Frequent pattern, with a reduced yellow patch.

i   **Juvenile first basic** (until Jan–Feb). Bill largely pink (even at base), with yellow patch initially whitish becoming increasingly visible until first summer.

j   **Adult definitive basic** (year-round). Here a bird with a reduced yellow patch, which is sometimes completely lacking.

k   **Adult definitive basic** (year-round). Here a bird with a large yellow patch, but does not usually match that shown by Bewick's Swan.

C. c. bewickii (**Bewick's Swan**). Yellow-and-black bill pattern very variable individually.

l   **Adult definitive basic** (year-round). Compared to Whooper Swan, note rounded yellow patch, which usually does not reach the nostril.

m   **Juvenile first basic** (until Jan–Feb).

n   **Adult definitive basic** (year-round). All-black culmen, which type is termed 'darky'.

o   **Adult definitive basic** (year-round). Culmen entirely yellow in this type, called 'yellowneb'.

p   **Adult definitive basic** (year-round). A yellow patch is visible on the otherwise black culmen, which type is termed 'pennyface' or 'diamond-shape'.

Tundra Swan

Bewick's Swan

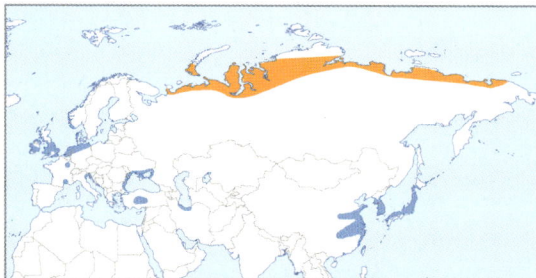

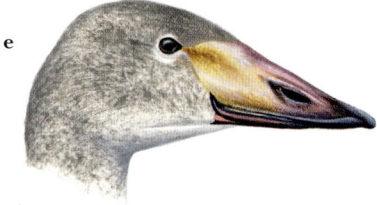

PLATE 21

Egyptian Goose *Alopochen aegyptiacus*   Text p. 305

Highly variable in coloration. Complex alternate moult strategy (two plumages per adult cycle, three in first cycle), but no seasonal change in appearance. Sexual dimorphism in size and weight. Unmistakable.

a   **Adult ♂ definitive basic/definitive alternate** (year-round). ♂ is distinctly larger than ♀, with a thicker head and often more alert posture.

b   **Adult ♀ definitive basic/definitive alternate** (year-round).

c   **Adult ♂ definitive basic/definitive alternate** (year-round). A greyer and paler plumage variant.

d   **Adult definitive basic/definitive alternate** (year-round).

e   **Juvenile first basic** (until Oct–Nov).

Common Shelduck *Tadorna tadorna*   Text p. 312

Complex alternate moult strategy (two plumages per adult cycle, three in first cycle). Slight sexual dimorphism. Unmistakable.

f   **Adult ♂ definitive basic** (Oct–Dec/May–Jun). Sexing possible by presence of bulge on upper culmen, deep red bill, all-black head with green gloss and larger size.

g   **Adult ♀ definitive basic** (Oct–Dec/May–Jun).

h   **Adult ♂ definitive basic** (Oct–Dec/May–Jun).

i   **Juvenile first basic** (until Oct–Nov). May resemble alternate plumage ♀, but lacks breast-band.

j   **Juvenile first basic** (until Oct–Nov). In flight, young birds (until first summer) distinguished from adult by white trailing edge to the wing.

Egyptian Goose   Common Shelduck

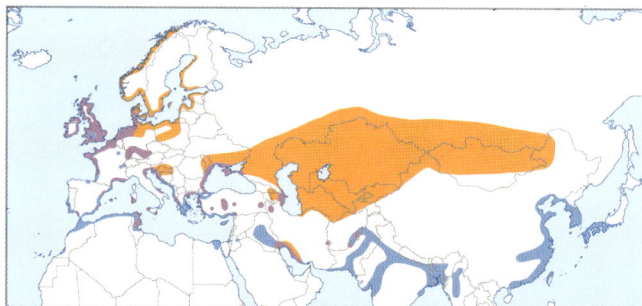

a

b

d

c

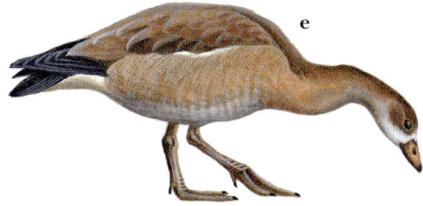

e

f

h

g

j

i

PLATE 22

Crested Shelduck *Tadorna cristata*

Text p. 316

Almost certainly extinct. A rather small and compact shelduck, with unique coloration. Clear sexual dimorphism. Moult strategy unknown. Illustration here based on photographs of mounted specimens in Tokyo Natural History Museum and descriptions in the literature.

a **Adult ♂ definitive basic**. Note unique long black crest.

b **Adult ♀ definitive basic**.

c **Adult ♂ definitive basic**. In flight, upper- and underwing similar to other *Tadorna* species.

Ruddy Shelduck *Tadorna ferruginea*

Text p. 308

Easily distinguished from all other species within its range, but beware escaped Cape Shelduck *T. cana* of South Africa which is frequent in captivity. Complex alternate moult strategy (two plumages per adult cycle, three in first cycle), but only slight seasonal changes. Slight sexual dimorphism.

d **Adult ♂ definitive basic** (Nov–Mar/May–Jun). Sexed by the larger and longer, almost whitish head, black collar, and brighter orange breast.

e **Adult ♀ definitive basic** (Nov–Mar/May–Jun). Sexed by whitish patch at base of bill and forehead, encircling the eye (variably visible according to plumage condition).

f **Juvenile first basic** (until Oct–Dec). Full juvenile plumage depicted here has dark-centred scapulars and mantle feathers, and dark smudges on flanks and breast. Quickly resembles adult.

g **Adult ♀ definitive basic** (Nov–Mar/May–Jun). Upperwing like other *Tadorna*. In flight, young birds (until first summer) distinguished by dark grey centres to greater coverts.

Hybrid Ruddy Shelduck *T. ferruginea* × Egyptian Goose *Alopochen aegyptiacus*

Text p. 309

h **Adult definitive basic**.

Hybrid Ruddy Shelduck *T. ferruginea* × Common Shelduck *T. tadorna*

Text p. 313

Bill variable in coloration: some have pinkish areas near base, around nostril and behind nail, others are all blackish. Legs and feet vary too, from dull pink to pale fleshy-grey.

i **Adult ♂ definitive basic**.

j **Adult ♀ definitive basic**.

Ruddy Shelduck

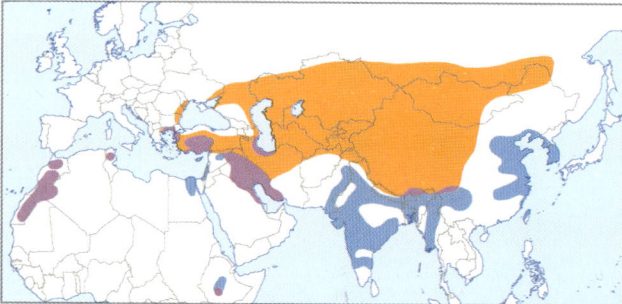

PLATE 23

Muscovy Duck *Cairina moschata*   Text p. 317

All black with white under- and upperwing-coverts, this duck should not be mistaken for any other species. Strong sexual dimorphism in size and mass (no overlap). Moulting strategy not well known in the wild.

a   **Adult ♂ definitive basic**. ♂ shows bare and variably swollen black skin at bill base, across cheeks and around eye, and long feathers on crown and nape are often held erect, giving head its typical shape. Upperparts and secondaries show beautiful green and bronze sheen.

b   **Adult ♀ definitive basic**. Clearly smaller. No bulge at bill base and no bare facial skin.

c   **Adult ♂ definitive basic**. In flight, extensive white on forewing.

d   **Juvenile first basic**. Plumage blackish overall with variable brown mottling on flanks, breast, neck and head.

e   **Juvenile first basic**. In flight, appears all dull blackish.

White-winged Duck *Asarcornis scutulata*   Text p. 320

A large, heavy duck with dark plumage and a pale head. Huge variation in the extent of white on the head, neck and breast (see text). Slight sexual dimorphism. Moult strategy not well described in the wild, but no significant seasonal change in appearance.

f   **Adult ♂ definitive basic**.

g   **Adult ♂ definitive basic**. Variant with a white head and neck.

h   **Adult ♀ definitive basic**. Smaller, culmen more concave (no swelling at base) and head more heavily spotted.

i   **Juvenile first basic**. Mostly distinguished by its duller plumage and plain brownish head at this age.

j   **Adult ♂ definitive basic**. In flight, extensive white on forewing, and white head.

Comb Duck *Sarkidiornis melanotos*   Text p. 302

Unmistakable. Clear sexual dimorphism. Moult strategy not well known in wild, but no significant seasonal change in appearance.

***S. m. sylvicola* (South American Comb Duck)** [not mapped]

k   **Adult ♂ definitive basic**. Distinguished by its blackish flanks.

***S. m. melanotos* (Old World Comb Duck)**

l   **Adult ♂ definitive basic**.

m   **Adult ♂ definitive basic**. In non-breeding season, the knob on bill shrinks significantly.

n   **Adult ♀ definitive basic**. Much smaller, without knob on bill and duller, less glossy, overall.

o   **Juvenile first basic**.

p   **Adult ♂ definitive basic**. In flight, wings all-dark.

Muscovy Duck

White-winged Duck

Comb Duck

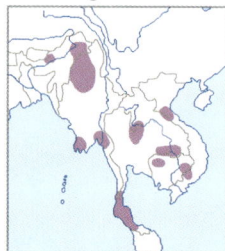
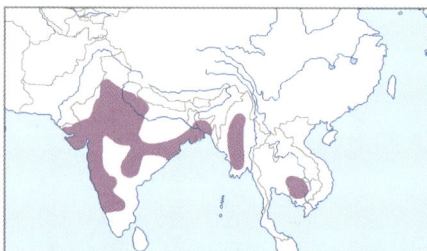

a

b

c

d

e

f

h

i

g

j

k

m

p

l

n

o

PLATE 24

Mandarin Duck *Aix galericulata*

Text p. 332

Juvenile and ♀ can be mistaken for those of Wood Duck *A. sponsa*. Clear sexual dimorphism, especially in definitive basic plumage. Complex alternate moult strategy (two plumages per adult cycle, three in first cycle).

a   **Adult ♂ definitive basic** (Sep–Nov/May–Jun). Unmistakable.

b   **Adult ♂ definitive alternate** (Jun–Jul/Sep–Oct). Much more like ♀, but retains pinkish bill.

c   **Adult ♀ definitive basic** (Oct–Nov/Jan–Apr). Compared to Wood Duck (k), note flanks pattern and duller brown upperparts.

d   **Adult ♀ definitive basic** (Oct–Nov/Jan–Apr). Compared to Wood Duck (l), note whitish nail to bill, greyer head and narrower eye-ring prolonged by a white bridle.

e   **Adult ♀ definitive alternate** (Feb–Apr/Oct–Nov). Head pattern less clearly defined when breeding.

f   **Adult ♀ definitive basic** (Oct–Nov/Jan–Apr). A senescent ♀ depicted here, showing mix of ♂ and ♀ characters.

g   **Adult ♀ definitive basic** (Oct–Nov/Jan–Apr). In flight, best identified by plainer and darker underwing.

h   **Juvenile first basic** (until Oct–Nov). Like ♀ in definitive alternate plumage, but has regularly and neatly streaked breast, no crest, white eye-ring interrupted behind eye, and dark grey bill with a pinkish hue and darker nail.

Wood Duck *Aix sponsa*

Text p. 326

Juvenile and ♀ can be mistaken for those of Mandarin Duck. Clear sexual dimorphism, especially in definitive basic plumage. Complex alternate moult strategy (two plumages per adult cycle, three in first cycle).

i   **Adult ♂ definitive basic** (Oct–Nov/May–Jun). Unmistakable.

j   **Adult ♂ definitive alternate** (Jun–Jul/Oct–Nov). This bird in pre-alternate moult still has some basic head feathers, which disappear in full alternate plumage. Iris and bill still bright (useful for sexing).

k   **Adult ♀ definitive basic** (Oct–Nov/Jan–Apr). Note glossy upperparts (vs. Mandarin Duck).

l   **Adult ♀ definitive basic** (Oct–Nov/Jan–Apr). Note dark nail to bill, large white almond-shaped eye-patch without bridle, contrasting white throat, white line encircling bill base and yellow orbital ring, all of which identify the species.

m   **Adult ♀ definitive alternate** (Feb–Apr/Oct–Nov). Duller than basic plumage.

n   **Adult ♀ definitive basic** (Oct–Nov/Jan–Apr). In flight, note strongly spotted or streaked underwing.

o   **Juvenile first basic** (until Oct–Nov). Some head feathers are replaced in Jul–Aug (either in an auxiliary pre-formative moult or early pre-formative moult). These feathers generally allow birds to be sexed, as young ♂ has white stripes on ear-coverts and towards nape well before it can be sexed using iris and bill coloration.

p   **First-winter ♂ formative** (Nov–Dec/May–Jun). Easily aged in autumn by retained juvenile feathers (e.g. tertials, upperwing-coverts) and duller bare parts, but ageing much harder once pre-formative moult completed.

Mandarin Duck

Wood Duck

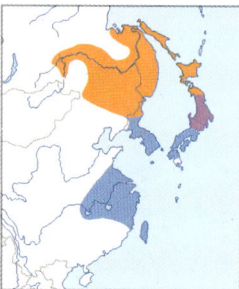
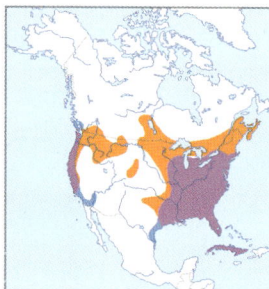

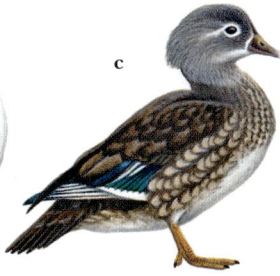

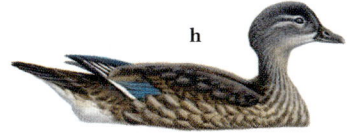

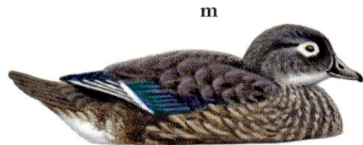

PLATE 25

Cotton Pygmy-goose *Nettapus coromandelianus* Text p. 323

A very small duck, unmistakable. Complex alternate moult strategy (two plumages per adult cycle, three in first cycle). Clear sexual dimorphism.

a   **Adult ♂ definitive basic** (Jan–Mar/Jun–Aug).

b   **Adult ♂ definitive alternate** (Jul–Sep/Dec–Feb). Whiter and greyer than adult ♀, with faint dark eyestripe.

c   **Adult ♀ definitive basic/definitive alternate** (year-round).

d   **Juvenile first basic** (until Jan–Apr.). Similar to adult ♀, but browner flanks, and duller, browner upperparts.

e   **Adult ♂ definitive basic** (Jan–Mar/Jun–Aug). Wing pattern typical.

f   **Adult ♀ definitive basic/definitive alternate** (year-round).

g   **First-winter ♂ formative** (Jan–Apr/Jun–Aug). Often shows hint of adult ♂ pattern on upperwing, with pale tips to underwing feathers.

Hybrid Wood Duck *Aix sponsa* × Mallard *Anas platyrhynchos* Text p. 329

Sometimes reported in Europe and North America. Both sexes well known but quite variable in appearance.

h   **Adult ♂ definitive basic.**

i   **Adult ♀ definitive basic.**

Hybrid Wood Duck *Aix sponsa* × Hooded Merganser *Lophodytes cucullatus* Text p. 329

j   **Adult ♂ definitive basic.**

Hybrid Wood Duck *Aix sponsa* × Ring-necked Duck *Aythya collaris* Text p. 473

k   **Adult ♂ definitive basic.**

Cotton Pygmy-goose

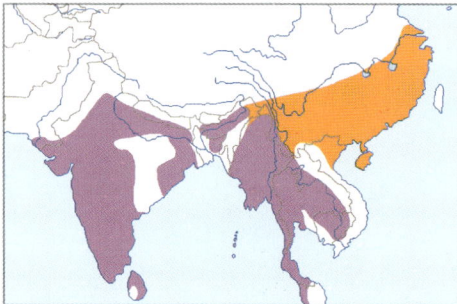

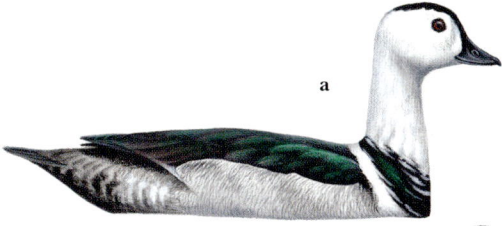

a

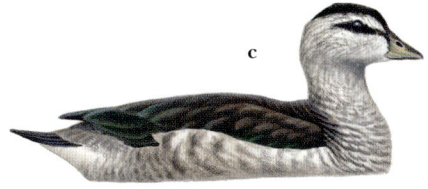

c

b

d

e

f

g

i

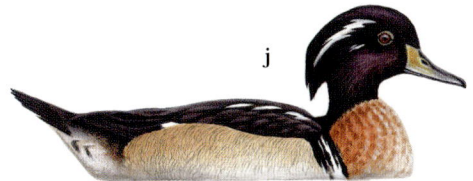

j

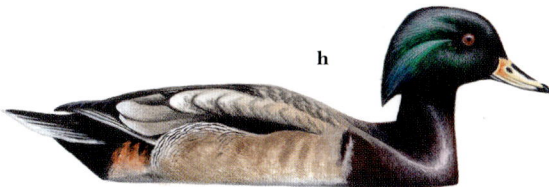

h

k

PLATE 26

Falcated Duck *Anas falcata*

Text p. 340

Juvenile and ♀ superficially resemble those of Gadwall *A. strepera* and Eurasian Wigeon *A. penelope*, but should be readily identified in good views. Complex alternate moult strategy (two plumages per adult cycle, three in first cycle). Clear sexual dimorphism, especially in definitive basic plumage.

a   **Adult ♂ definitive basic** (Oct–Nov/May–Jun).

b   **First-winter ♂ formative** (Oct–Jan/May–Jun). Much like adult ♂ by early in first winter. After pre-formative moult, best aged by partly juvenile grey-brown upperwing-coverts and shorter tertials.

c   **Adult ♂ definitive alternate** (May–Jul/Sep–Oct). Basic feathers often retained on head, mantle and anterior scapulars. Basic tertials are also often retained.

d   **Adult ♀ definitive basic** (Oct–Nov/Jan–Mar). Distinctive, with a rather plain head.

e   **Juvenile first basic** (until Sep–Nov). Closely resembles adult ♀, but differs in that scapulars are more uniformly dark (almost lacking pale inner marks), flank feathers darker with broader, less well-defined black chevrons, browner forehead and shorter, greyer tertials.

f   **Adult ♂ definitive basic** (Oct–Nov/May–Jun).

g   **Adult ♀ definitive basic** (Oct–Nov/Jan–Mar).

Gadwall *Anas strepera*

Text p. 335

Juvenile and ♀ superficially resemble those of Falcated Duck *A. falcata* and Mallard *A. platyrhynchos*. Complex alternate moult strategy (two plumages per adult cycle, three in first cycle). Clear sexual dimorphism, especially in definitive basic plumage.

h   **Adult ♂ definitive basic** (Oct–Nov/May–Jun).

i   **Adult ♂ definitive basic** (Oct–Nov/May–Jun). This variant is relatively frequent in North America and E Asia, but also occurs elsewhere. It perhaps reflects ancient hybridisation with another *Anas* species.

j   **Adult ♂ definitive alternate** (May–Jul/Sep–Oct). Basic tertials often retained.

k   **Adult ♀ definitive basic** (Oct–Nov/Jan–Mar).

l   **Juvenile first basic** (until Sep–Nov). Note darker and more reddish plumage, often contrasting with grey head. Tertials shorter and plainer grey. Bill initially darker, the orange tinge becoming increasingly visible (vs. often heavily marked with black spots in adult ♀ in summer).

m   **Adult ♂ definitive basic** (Oct–Nov/May–Jun).

n   **Adult ♀ definitive basic** (Oct–Nov/Jan–Mar).

Falcated Duck

Gadwall

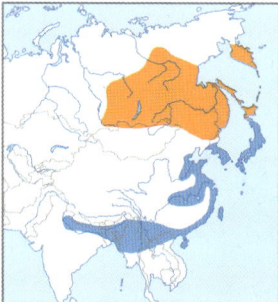
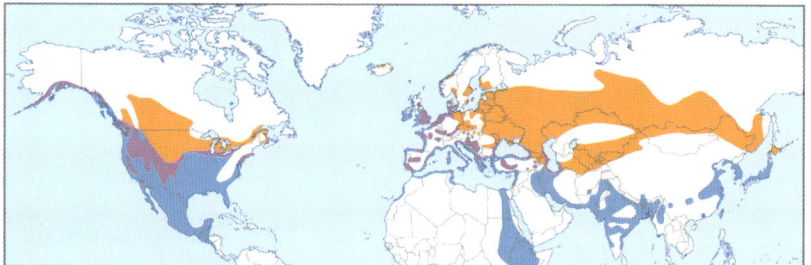

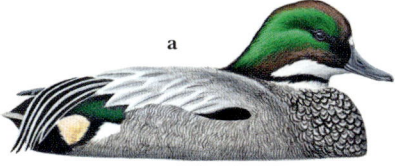

a

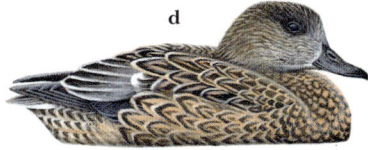

d

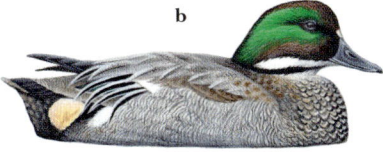

b

e

c

f

g

i

m

h

n

j

k

l

PLATE 27

Eurasian Wigeon *Anas penelope* (see also Plate 28)   Text p. 344

♂ resembles that of American Wigeon *A. americana*, but they are easily separated. Hybrids between these two species represent the only serious identification pitfalls. Complex alternate moult strategy (two plumages per adult cycle, three in first cycle). Clear sexual dimorphism, especially in definitive basic plumage.

a   **Adult** ♂ **definitive basic** (Oct–Dec/May–Jun).

b   **Adult** ♂ **definitive basic** (Oct–Dec/May–Jun). Forehead can be golden-yellow, tinged buff or paler yellow, sometimes extending into reddish fore cheeks, revealing faint dark vermiculations. Some also show a black patch with a green gloss behind the eyes.

c   **First-winter** ♂ **formative** (Nov–Jan/May–Jul). Some undergo an extensive pre-formative moult and resemble adult ♂. Age then can be assessed by upperwing pattern, and the presence of brownish spots in the white upperwing patch.

d   **Adult** ♂ **definitive alternate** (May–Jun/Sep–Nov).

e   **Adult** ♂ **definitive basic** (Oct–Dec/May–Jun.). Note plain greyish underwing compared to American Wigeon.

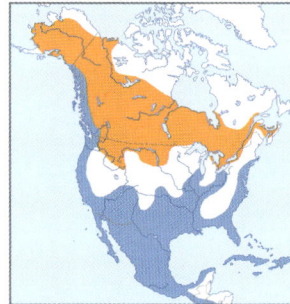

American Wigeon *Anas americana* (see also Plate 28)   Text p. 351

Hybrids with Eurasian Wigeon can be very misleading. Complex alternate moult strategy (two plumages per adult cycle, three in first cycle). Clear sexual dimorphism, especially in definitive basic plumage.

f   **Adult** ♂ **definitive basic** (Oct–Nov/May–Jun).

g   **Adult** ♂ **definitive basic** (Oct–Nov/May–Jun). Rare variant with very pale to creamy-white cheeks, lores and forehead.

h   **Adult** ♂ **definitive basic** (Oct–Nov/May–Jun). More colourful than adult ♀, with white upperwing patch often visible even when the wing is folded.

i   **First-winter** ♂ **formative** (Oct–Jan/May–Jun). This bird has retained some juvenile feathers (head, lower scapulars, tertials).

j   **Adult** ♂ **definitive alternate** (May–Jul/Sep–Oct). White axillaries and underwing median coverts contrast strongly with the orangey flanks.

Hybrid American Wigeon *A. americana* × **Eurasian Wigeon** *A. penelope*   Text p. 354

k–p   **Adult** ♂ **definitive basic** The huge variability in hybrids from this cross is illustrated here. Most show attenuated contrast between the breast and flanks, and a head pattern that more closely evokes that of the ♂ involved in the cross. A bird matching a backcross to American Wigeon is depicted (m) and one to Eurasian Wigeon (p).

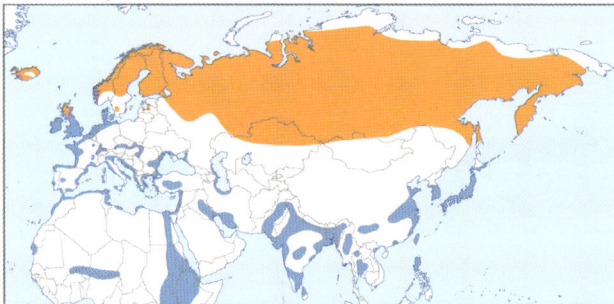

Eurasian Wigeon

American Wigeon

PLATE 28

Eurasian Wigeon *Anas penelope* (see also Plate 27) Text p. 344

♀ closely resembles that of American Wigeon *A. americana*, and juvenile is hard to distinguish. Adult ♀ quite variable, with some being deeper reddish, others paler and buff. Complex alternate moult strategy (two plumages per adult cycle, three in first cycle). Clear sexual dimorphism, especially in definitive basic plumage. [Map on Plate 27]

a   **Adult ♀ definitive basic** (Oct–Dec/Feb–Mar). A rather dark, reddish-brown bird.

b   **Adult ♀ definitive alternate** (Feb–Mar/Oct–Dec). This ♀ is paler, rather buff-brown, but irrespective of overall coloration, contrast between the head and flanks is usually faint.

c   **Adult ♀ definitive alternate** (Feb–Mar/Oct–Dec). Note the alternate tertials.

d   **First-winter ♀ formative** (Nov–Jan/Feb–Mar). Note the plainer scapulars, darker head, culmen often marked dusky and upperwing secondary coverts often visible.

e   **Adult ♀ definitive basic** (Oct–Dec/Feb–Mar). Note typical pattern to greater coverts (tipped black) and lesser and median coverts (broadly fringed white).

f   **First-winter ♀ formative** (Nov–Jan/Feb–Mar). Note pattern of lesser and median coverts, faintly fringed pale brownish.

American Wigeon *Anas americana* (see also Plate 27) Text p. 351

Complex alternate moult strategy (two plumages per adult cycle, three in first cycle). Clear sexual dimorphism, especially in definitive basic plumage. [Map on Plate 27]

g   **Adult ♀ definitive basic** (Oct–Dec/Feb–Mar).

h   **Adult ♀ definitive alternate** (Feb–Mar/Oct–Dec). Contrast between head, breast and flanks is somewhat reduced, with alternate tertials depicted here.

i   **First-winter ♀ formative** (Nov–Jan/Feb–Mar). Note plain scapulars, dark culmen (autumn) and faintly fringed upperwing-coverts.

j   **Juvenile first basic** (until Oct–Nov). Duller overall, with darker crown, and juvenile tertials, shorter and rounded.

k   **Adult ♀ definitive basic** (Oct–Dec/Feb–Mar). Greater coverts tipped black, sometimes with a faint white fringe (in both species). The median and posterior lesser coverts are whiter than in Eurasian Wigeon.

l   **First-winter ♀ formative** (Nov–Jan/Feb–Mar.). Note pattern of secondary coverts.

Hybrid American Wigeon *A. americana* × Eurasian Wigeon *A. penelope* Text p. 354

m   **Adult ♀ definitive basic**.

Hybrid Chiloe Wigeon *A. sibilatrix* × Eurasian Wigeon *A. penelope* Text p. 347

n   **Adult ♀ definitive basic**.

PLATE 29

Mallard *Anas platyrhynchos*

Text p. 358

♀ resembles those of Mexican Duck *A. (p.) diazi*, American Black Duck *A. rubripes* and Mottled Duck *A. fulvigula*. Complex alternate moult strategy (two plumages per adult cycle, three in first cycle). Strong sexual dimorphism, especially in definitive basic plumage.

A. p. platyrhynchos

a   **Adult ♂ definitive basic** (Sep–Nov/May–Jun).

b   **Adult ♂ definitive alternate** (May–Jul/Sep–Oct). Closer to ♀, but some keep their basic tertials, and the bill remains yellow.

c   **Adult ♀ definitive basic** (Oct–Dec/Feb–Apr).

d   **Juvenile ♂ first basic** (until Sep–Nov). Note juvenile tertials, flanks (creating bold longitudinal streaks), scapulars (plainer) and breast (finely streaked). Young ♂ quickly develops a yellowish bill and often a soft green sheen on the sides of the crown.

e   **Juvenile ♀ first basic** (until Sep–Nov).

f   **Adult ♂ definitive basic** (Sep–Nov/May–Jun).

A. p. conboschas (Greenland Mallard)

g   **Adult ♂ definitive basic** (Sep–Nov/May–Jun). Barely distinguishable from nominate subspecies, but paler, larger, with proportionately longer wings and shorter bill.

Hybrid Mexican Duck *A. (p.) diazi* × Mallard *A. platyrhynchos*

Text p. 360

These hybrids are rather common, even if first-generation (F1) hybrids are not the most common.

h–i   **Adult ♂ definitive basic**. Two types of hybrids depicted here, some F1 hybrids being closer to Mallard, with for example much more green on the head.

j   **Adult ♂ definitive basic**. Typical wing pattern of F1 hybrid.

Mexican Duck *Anas (platyrhynchos) diazi*

Text p. 360

Both sexes resemble a ♀ Mallard, without strong seasonal changes. The most reliable distinguishing features are the grey-brown tail, belly mottled dark, dark grey-brown tertials (pale shafts) and upperwing pattern. The precise variability of 'pure' *diazi* remains unclear. Complex alternate moult strategy (two plumages per adult cycle, three in first cycle). Slight sexual dimorphism.

k   **Adult ♂ definitive basic** (Sep–Nov/May–Jun). Note yellow bill compared to female.

l   **Adult ♀ definitive basic** (Oct–Dec/Feb–Apr). Compared to ♀ Mallard (c), note the dark tertials and tail, and mottled belly.

m   **Adult ♀ definitive basic** (Oct–Dec/Feb–Apr). The bill is quite variable in coloration, sometimes all olive-grey with more or less orange, and sometimes orange with well-defined slate-grey spots/patches on the culmen.

n   **Adult ♂ definitive basic** (Sep–Nov/May–Jun). Wing pattern typical of birds from north of range (white of greater coverts extends along outer fringes of each feather). In the south, many birds show less or no white in the wing.

Mallard

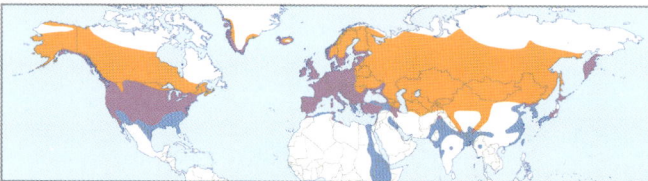

Mexican Duck

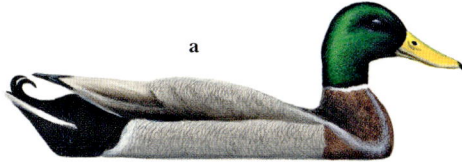

a

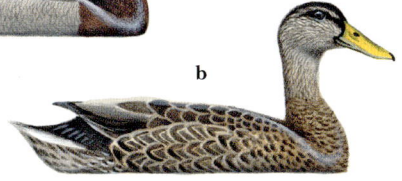

b

c

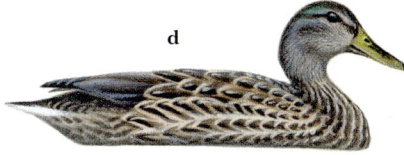

d

f

e

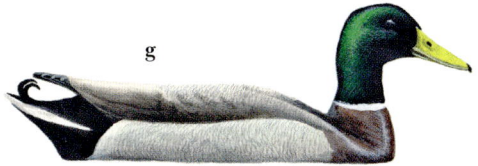

g

j

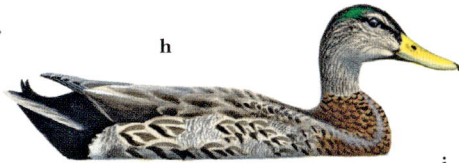

h

n

i

m

l

k

PLATE 30

American Black Duck *Anas rubripes* Text p. 367

Both sexes resemble ♀ Mallard, but are plainer and darker overall, without strong seasonal changes in appearance. The more reliable distinguishing features are the dark belly, tail and tertials, and upperwing without white wingbars. Hybrids between the species can be very misleading. Complex alternate moult strategy (two plumages per adult cycle, three in first cycle). Slight sexual dimorphism.

a–b Adult ♂ **definitive basic** (Oct–Dec/May–Jun). Bill appears yellow more or less washed olive.

c Adult ♀ **definitive basic** (Oct–Dec/Feb–Mar).

d **Juvenile first basic**. Note shorter tertials, and narrower flank feathers and scapulars.

e Adult ♂ **definitive basic** (Oct–Dec/May–Jun). Normally, does not show white wingbars, and at most a narrow trailing edge.

f **Adult definitive basic/definitive alternate**. A very thin pale line is sometimes visible in birds that do not show any other hybrid features.

g Adult ♂ **definitive basic** (Oct–Dec/May–Jun). Note dark patches near the 'wrist'. The number of dark feathers is a diagnostic feature for distinguishing pure birds from hybrids.

h **Adult definitive basic/definitive alternate**. Some hybrids may show up to ten dark patches near the 'wrist', but this pattern matches pure American Black Ducks as well.

Hybrid American Black Duck *A. rubripes* × Mallard *A. platyrhynchos* Text p. 371

Quite numerous in the wild, this hybrid backcrosses freely with both parent species, leading to a huge variety of appearances.

i–j Adult ♂ **definitive basic**. Typical F1 hybrids depicted here.

k Adult ♂ **definitive basic**. Such a bird far more closely resembles American Black Duck, and could be a backcross with the latter.

l Adult ♀ **definitive basic**. Difficult to separate from both parent species, even at close range, but does not match the normal appearance of either.

m–n **Adult definitive basic/definitive alternate**. Typical hybrid upperwing patterns (n is a ♀, the white wingbar extending to the tertial coverts).

o–p **Adult definitive basic/definitive alternate**. Typical hybrid underwing patterns.

American Black Duck

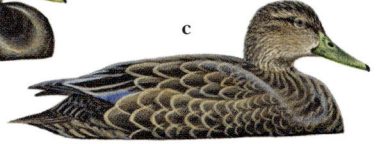

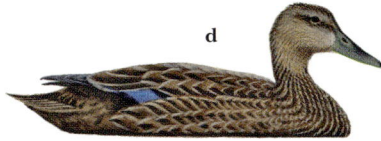

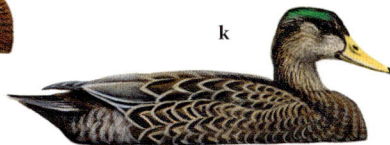

PLATE 31

Mottled Duck *Anas fulvigula*
Text p. 375

Both sexes resemble ♀ Mallard, without strong seasonal changes in appearance. The most reliable distinguishing features are the belly mottled dark, dark tail and tertials, and upperwing almost devoid of white wingbars. Hybrids between them can be very confusing. Complex alternate moult strategy (two plumages per adult cycle, three in first cycle). Slight sexual dimorphism.

a   **Adult ♂ definitive basic** (Oct–Dec/May–Jun). Note yellow bill and black gape running along base of bill.

b   **Adult ♂ definitive basic** (Oct–Dec/May–Jun). *A. f. maculosa* appears a little stockier, with a thicker bill and shorter neck on average.

c   **Adult ♂ definitive alternate** (Oct–Dec/May–Jun). Alternate tertials shorter with faint inner marks, and alternate scapulars and flank feathers shorter and rounded. Bill is yellow-tinged year-round.

d   **Adult ♀ definitive basic** (Oct–Dec/Feb–Mar). Bill is orange, not yellow, and shows a very variable slate-grey patch on culmen, sometimes absent and sometimes covering most of bill.

e   **Juvenile first basic**. Plumage duller, with flank feathers and scapulars shorter and almost devoid of pale inner marks.

f   **Adult ♂ definitive basic/definitive alternate**. Note lack of white wingbar and very thin trailing edge. The speculum often appears more green-glossed than in Mallard and Mexican Duck.

g   **Adult definitive basic/definitive alternate**. Some that apparently do not show other hybrid features have a thin whitish or pale wingbar and trailing edge to the inner wing.

Hybrid Mottled Duck *A. fulvigula* × Mallard *A. platyrhynchos*
Text p. 378

Quite frequent in the wild, especially in Florida, this hybrid backcrosses freely with both parent species, leading to a huge variety of appearances.

h–i   **Adult ♂ definitive basic**. Typical F1 hybrids depicted here.

j   **Adult ♂ definitive basic**. Such birds are very close to Mottled Duck, but show clearly curved central rectrices, which could reflect ancient hybridisation.

k   **Adult definitive basic**. This wing pattern is shown by many F1 hybrids, and can even be shown by birds that more closely resemble Mottled Duck.

Mottled Duck

e

d

a

b

c

f

g

j

k

h

i

PLATE 32

Indian Spot-billed Duck *Anas poecilorhyncha*

Text p. 386

Not difficult to identify, but some eastern birds (*haringtoni*) appear more or less intermediate with the formerly conspecific Eastern Spot-billed Duck *A. zonorhyncha*. Complex alternate moult strategy (two plumages per adult cycle, three in first cycle), but moult schedule not well described in the wild. Slight sexual dimorphism.

A. p. poecilorhyncha

a   **Adult ♂ definitive basic.**

b   **Adult ♀ definitive basic.** Slightly less contrasting, browner, with smaller red patches at base of culmen and less clear-cut tertials.

c   **Juvenile first basic.** Overall plainer and browner. Yellow patch at tip of bill often runs along tomium.

d   **Adult definitive basic/definitive alternate.** Note clear white wingbars and glossy green speculum.

A. p. haringtoni

e   **Adult ♂ definitive basic** (Oct–Dec/May–Jun). Much like *poecilorhyncha* but red patches at base of culmen much reduced or lacking, slightly smaller and browner ground colour.

Eastern Spot-billed Duck *Anas zonorhyncha*

Text p. 382

Complex alternate moult strategy (two plumages per adult cycle, three in first cycle), without clear seasonal change in appearance. Moult schedule not well described in the wild. Slight sexual dimorphism.

f   **Adult ♂ definitive basic.**

g   **Adult ♀ definitive basic.** A little browner and less contrasting, with narrower and less clear-cut white fringes to tertials, and paler iris.

h   **Juvenile first basic.** Duller scaly pattern overall, with tertials shorter and washed brownish.

i–j   **Adult definitive basic/definitive alternate.** White wingbars appear very variable individually.

Hybrid Eastern Spot-billed Duck *A. zonorhyncha* × Mallard *A. platyrhynchos*

Text p. 384

Regularly reported in the wild.

k   **Adult ♂ definitive basic.** Some variation occurs, especially in head pattern.

Hybrid Indian Spot-billed Duck *A. poecilorhyncha* × Mallard *A. platyrhynchos*

Text p. 388

Rarely described in the natural range, but fairly common in captivity.

l   **Adult ♂ definitive basic.**

Indian Spot-billed Duck

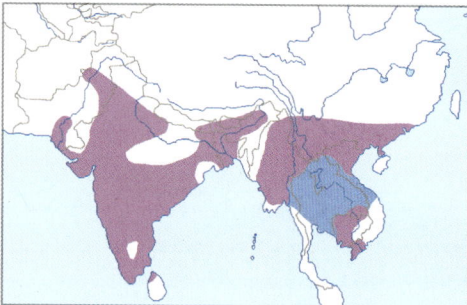

Eastern Spot-billed Duck

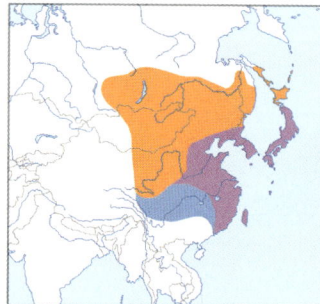

a

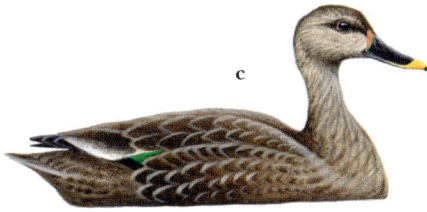

c

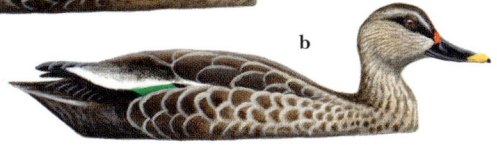

b

e

d

f

i

j

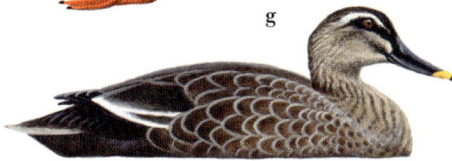

g

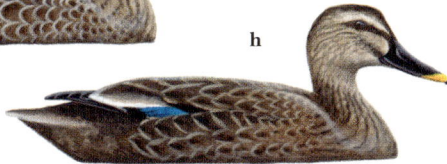

h

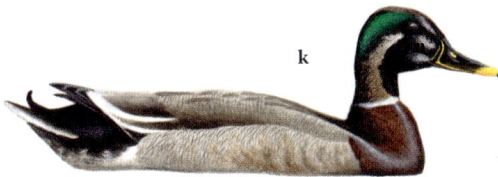

k

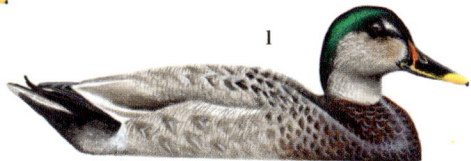

l

PLATE 33

Blue-winged Teal *Anas discors* (see also Plate 34) Text p. 391

♂ resembles that of Cinnamon Teal *A. cyanoptera* in alternate plumage. Complex alternate moult strategy (two plumages per adult cycle, three in first cycle). Strong sexual dimorphism, especially in definitive basic plumage. [Map on Plate 34]

a   **Adult ♂ definitive basic** (Jan–Mar/Jun–Jul).

b   **Adult ♂ definitive alternate** (Jul–Aug/Dec–Feb). Note adult tertials and sharp inner marks to flank feathers. Upperwing pattern (e) is very useful too.

c   **First-winter ♂ formative** (Jan–Mar/Jun–Jul). Shows formative feathers on head and upper flanks, but still has juvenile tertials.

d   **First-winter ♂ formative** (Jan–Mar/Jun–Jul). In spring, much like adult ♂, but age can be determined by upperwing pattern (dusky traces in blue patch, black spots on greater coverts and reduced green gloss on speculum) and the barred or pale-mottled belly.

e   **Adult ♂ definitive basic** (Jan–Mar/Jun–Jul).

Hybrid Blue-winged Teal *A. discors* × Northern Shoveler *A. clypeata* Text p. 394

Regularly reported in Europe and North America.

f   **Adult ♂ definitive basic.**

Hybrid Blue-winged Teal *A. discors* × Cinnamon Teal *A. cyanoptera* Text p. 394

Sometimes observed in North America.

g   **Adult ♂ definitive basic.** Quite variable in head pattern and flanks coloration.

Hybrid Cinnamon Teal *A. cyanoptera* × Northern Shoveler *A. clypeata* Text p. 400

Rare in North America.

h   **Adult ♂ definitive basic.**

Cinnamon Teal *Anas cyanoptera* (see also Plate 34) Text p. 398

♂ resembles those of Blue-winged Teal *A. discors* and Northern Shoveler *A. clypeata* in alternate plumage. Complex alternate moult strategy (two plumages per adult cycle, three in first cycle). Strong sexual dimorphism, especially in definitive basic plumage. [Map on Plate 34]

i   **Adult ♂ definitive basic** (Oct–Dec/May–Jun).

j   **Adult ♂ definitive basic** (Oct–Dec/May–Jun). Typical alert posture.

k   **Adult ♂ definitive basic** (Oct–Dec/May–Jun).

l   **Adult ♂ definitive alternate** (May–Jul/Sep–Nov). Distinguished from Blue-winged Teal and ♀ by red, orange or yellow iris and by overall reddish wash.

m   **First-winter ♂ formative** (Nov–Jan/May–Jul). Note juvenile tertials, tertial coverts and upper flank feathers.

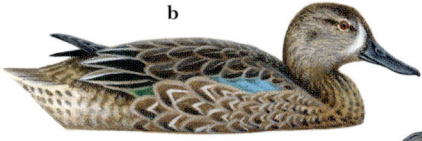

PLATE 34

Blue-winged Teal *Anas discors* (see also Plate 33)   Text p. 391

♀ resembles that of Cinnamon Teal *A. cyanoptera*.

a   **Adult ♀ definitive basic** (Jan–Mar/Mar–May).

b   **Adult ♀ definitive basic** (Jan–Mar/Mar–May).

c   **Adult ♀ definitive basic** (Jan–Mar/Mar–May). Note cold coloration, striking white eye-ring and pale supercilium that is interrupted over the eye.

d   **Juvenile first basic** (until Oct–Feb.). Note duller and browner appearance, juvenile tertials and flank feathers (narrower, more pointed without inner marks).

e   **First-winter ♀ formative** (Jan–Mar/Mar–May). Note dusky traces in blue wing patch, dark traces on greater coverts (often with two thin white wingbars) and speculum almost devoid of gloss.

Hybrid Blue-winged Teal *A. discors* × Northern Shoveler *A. clypeata*   Text p. 394

Reported occasionally in Europe and North America.

f   **Adult ♀ definitive basic**. Slightly variable, may constitute a serious pitfall with Blue-winged Teal and, especially, Cinnamon Teal.

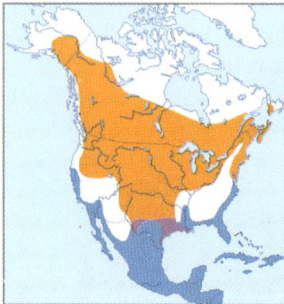

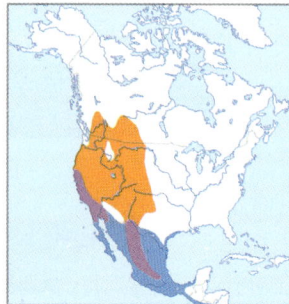

Cinnamon Teal *Anas cyanoptera* (see also Plate 33)   Text p. 398

♀ resembles those of Blue-winged Teal *A. discors* and Northern Shoveler *A. clypeata*, being somewhat intermediate in size and shape.

g   **Adult ♀ definitive basic** (Jan–Mar/Jun–Jul).

h   **Adult ♀ definitive basic** (Jan–Mar/Jun–Jul). Note warmer tones, broad pale supercilium reaching pale cheeks behind dark eyestripe, as well as pale eye-ring and patch at base of bill less obvious.

i   **Adult ♀ definitive basic** (Jan–Mar/Jun–Jul).

j   **Juvenile first basic** (Jan–Mar/Jun–Jul). This appearance is shown by many birds in early autumn, just before start of pre-formative moult.

k   **Juvenile first basic** (Jan–Mar/Jun–Jul).

Blue-winged Teal   Cinnamon Teal

a

d

b

c

e

f

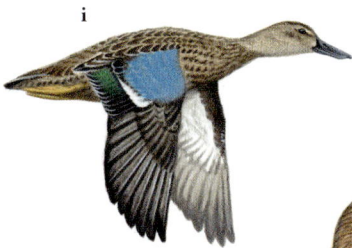

i

h

g

j

k

PLATE 35

Northern Shoveler *Anas clypeata*

Text p. 402

Bill shape alone should be sufficient to prevent any identification mistake. The ♀ of this species resembles that of the Cinnamon Teal *A. cyanoptera*. Complex alternate moult strategy (two plumages per adult cycle, three in the first cycle). Strong sexual dimorphism, especially in definitive basic plumage.

a   **Adult ♂ definitive basic** (Nov–Mar/May–Jun).

b   **Adult ♂ definitive alternate** (May–Jun/Jul–Sep). Follows basic plumage and is acquired in late spring.

c   **Adult ♂ definitive alternate/definitive supplemental** (Aug–Sep/Nov–Feb). In late summer and early autumn, many ♂♂ show an appearance different from basic and alternate plumages, which may be at least partially due to pre-supplemental moult (see text).

d   **First-winter ♂ formative** (Oct–Mar/May–Jun). Resembles previous plumage, but reliably aged by darker iris, bill tinged dull orange, and juvenile tertials, tertial coverts, rectrices and upperwing.

e   **Adult ♀ definitive basic** (Jan–Mar/Mar–May).

f   **Adult ♀ definitive basic** (Jan–Mar/Mar–May). Bill highly variable, from pale orange to slate-grey, spotted dusky.

g   **Juvenile first basic** (until Oct–Feb.). Note duller appearance with ill-defined inner marks on scapulars and flank feathers, as well as juvenile tertials.

h   **Adult ♂ definitive basic** (Nov–Mar/May–Jun).

i   **Juvenile/first-winter ♂ first basic/formative** (until May–Jun). Note dusky traces within bluish wing patch, dark bases to greater coverts and reduced green gloss to speculum.

j   **Adult ♀ definitive basic** (Jan–Mar/Mar–May).

k   **Juvenile/first-winter ♀ first basic/formative** (until May–Jun). Note greyer-brown upperwing, without gloss on speculum, and darker greater coverts.

Hybrid Garganey *A. querquedula* × Northern Shoveler *A. clypeata*

Text p. 405

Reported occasionally in Europe.

l   **Adult ♂ definitive basic.**

Garganey *Anas querquedula*

Text p. 413

Distinctive in all plumages, but ♀ resembles those of several other small species of dabbling ducks. Complex alternate moult strategy (two plumages per adult cycle, three in first cycle). Strong sexual dimorphism, especially in definitive basic plumage.

m   **Adult ♂ definitive basic** (Feb–Mar/Jun–Jul).

n   **Adult ♂ definitive basic** (Feb–Mar/Jun–Jul).

o   **Adult ♂ definitive alternate** (Jun–Jul/Jan–Feb).

p   **First-winter ♂ formative** (Jan–Mar/Jun–Jul). Some juvenile feathers often retained until Feb at least.

q   **Juvenile first basic** (until Oct–Feb).

r   **Adult ♀ definitive basic** (Jan–Mar/Mar–May).

s   **Adult ♀ definitive basic** (Jan–Mar/Mar–May).

Northern Shoveler

Garganey

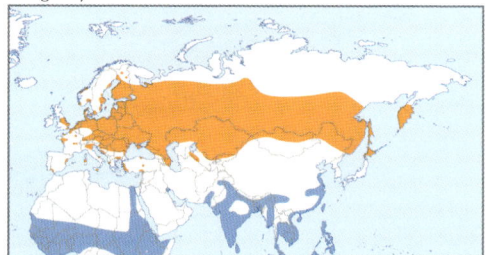

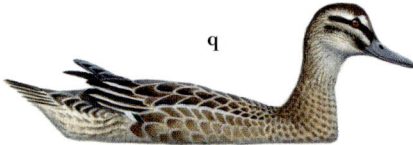

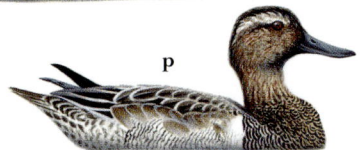

PLATE 36

Northern Pintail *Anas acuta*

Text p. 408

No confusion risk. Complex alternate moult strategy (two plumages per adult cycle, three in first cycle). Strong sexual dimorphism, especially in definitive basic plumage.

a   **Adult ♂ definitive basic** (Oct–Nov/May–Jul). Underparts often tinged ochre-yellow or rusty, depending on the environment.

b.   **First-winter ♂ formative** (Nov–Dec/May–Jul). A bird in pre-formative moult depicted here, with growing tertials, rectrices and scapulars. This stage is attained in Oct–Nov, when adult ♂ is more advanced in its pre-basic moult.

c   **Adult ♂ definitive alternate** (Jun–Jul/Sep–Oct.). Note basic tertials retained here, as well as sharply defined inner marks on many body feathers, and adult bill coloration.

d   **Adult ♂ definitive basic** (Oct–Nov/May–Jul).

e   **Adult ♀ definitive alternate** (Mar–Apr/Oct–Nov). Basic plumage is similar, but note alternate tertials.

f   **Adult ♀ definitive basic** (Nov–Dec/Feb–Apr).

g   **Juvenile first basic** (until Nov–Jan). Best aged by upperwing pattern (shape, fringes and inner marks of secondary and tertial coverts), but note juvenile tertials, scapulars and flank feathers narrower with inner marks less well-defined, blurred bill coloration and head often more patterned.

Marbled Duck *Marmaronetta angustirostris*

Text p. 437

No confusion risk. Complex alternate moult strategy (two plumages per adult cycle, three in first cycle), without strong seasonal changes. Moult schedule not well known in the wild. Slight sexual dimorphism.

h   **Adult ♂ definitive basic.**

i   **Adult ♀ definitive basic.** Basically similar to ♂, but has shorter crest. Bill has a triangular greenish patch at its base and lacks pale subterminal band.

j   **Adult ♀ definitive alternate.** Breeding plumage quickly becomes worn and looks 'messy'.

k   **Juvenile first basic.** Similar to ♀, but less distinct pale spotting on flanks and upperparts.

l   **Adult ♂ definitive basic.**

Northern Pintail

Marbled Duck

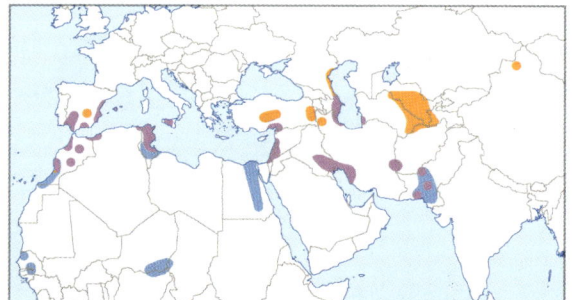

a

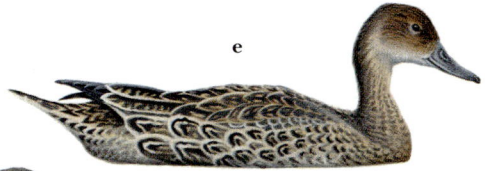

e

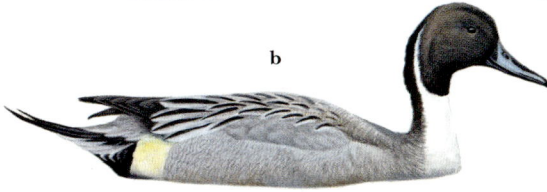

b

d

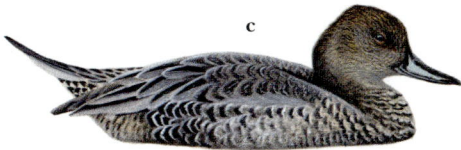

c

f

g

h

l

i

k

j

PLATE 37

Eurasian Teal *Anas crecca* (see also Plate 38)   Text p. 423

♂ can be mistaken for that of Green-winged Teal, and especially with hybrids between them. Complex alternate moult strategy (two plumages per adult cycle, three in first cycle). Strong sexual dimorphism, especially in definitive basic plumage.

a   **Adult ♂ definitive basic** (Oct–Nov/May–Jul). Note white bar on lower scapulars and pale line surrounding the eye-band.

b   **Adult ♂ definitive alternate** (Jun–Jul/Oct–Nov). Here a bird in pre-alternate moult.

c   **First-winter ♂ formative** (Nov–Jan/May–Jul). At end of pre-formative moult, the lower scapulars and upper flank feathers are among the last feathers replaced (note remaining pointed juvenile feathers). At this stage, the white horizontal line is invisible.

d   **Adult ♂ definitive basic** (Oct–Nov/May–Jul). Note mostly white wingbar, broadening externally.

Green-winged Teal *Anas carolinensis* (see also Plate 38)   Text p. 430

Complex alternate moult strategy (two plumages per adult cycle, three in first cycle). Strong sexual dimorphism, especially in definitive basic plumage. [Map on Plate 38]

e   **Adult ♂ definitive basic** (Oct–Nov/May–Jul). Note white vertical line on fore flanks, and breast often strongly washed salmon-pinkish.

f   **Adult ♂ definitive alternate** (Jun–Jul/Oct–Nov).

g   **First-winter ♂ formative** (Nov–Jan/May–Jul). After pre-formative moult, can be difficult to distinguish from adult under field conditions. Note differences in pattern of scapulars and upper flank feathers. Note that pre-formative moult in young ♂ ends *c.*1–2 months after the pre-basic moult of adult ♂.

h   **Adult ♂ definitive basic** (Oct–Nov/May–Jul). Note reddish wingbar, more even in width.

Hybrid Green-winged Teal *A. carolinensis* × Eurasian Teal *A. crecca*   Text p. 433

Reported occasionally in Europe and North America, these hybrids can be very confusing.

i   **Adult ♂ definitive basic**. Here a bird more like *crecca*, with a strong white horizontal bar.

j   **Adult ♂ definitive basic**. Here a bird that resembles *carolinensis*, but with a pale grey horizontal bar.

Baikal Teal *Anas formosa* (see also Plate 38)   Text p. 417

Unmistakable. Complex alternate moult strategy (two plumages per adult cycle, three in first cycle). Strong sexual dimorphism, especially in definitive basic plumage. [Map on Plate 38]

k   **Adult ♂ definitive basic** (Nov–Dec/Jun–Jul).

l   **Adult ♂ definitive basic** (Nov–Dec/Jun–Jul). In fresh plumage, black pattern often concealed.

m   **First-winter ♂ formative** (Dec-Jan/Jun-Jul). Note shorter ornamental scapulars than adult.

n   **Adult ♂ definitive alternate** (Jun–Jul/Oct–Nov).

o   **Adult ♂ definitive basic** (Nov–Dec/Jun–Jul). Wing pattern unique.

Eurasian Teal

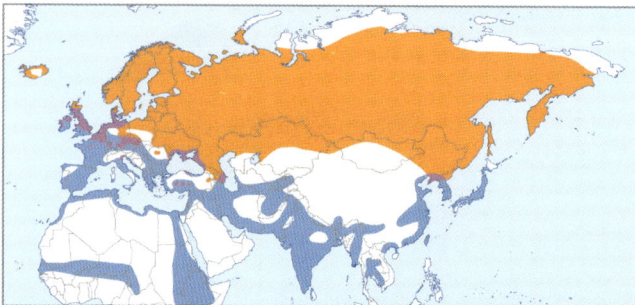

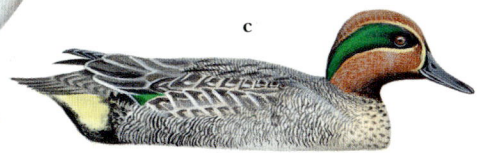

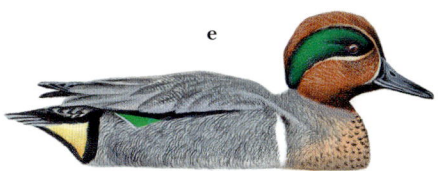

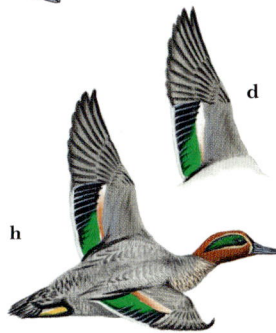

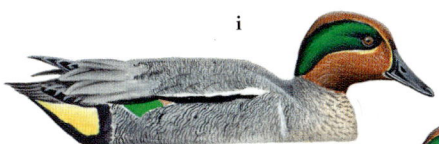

PLATE 38

Eurasian Teal *Anas crecca* (see also Plate 37)   Text p. 423

♀ very similar to that of Green-winged Teal, but some at least can be safely identified in the hand or very good views. Useful features are upperwing pattern (colour and width of wingbar on greater coverts, width of trailing edge to secondaries), colour of the undertail and head pattern (see text).

a   **Adult ♀ definitive basic** (Nov–Dec/Feb–Apr). Note the overall rather warm tones.

b   **Adult ♀ definitive basic** (Nov–Dec/Feb–Apr). Bill often heavily spotted dusky in adult ♀.

c   **Adult ♀ definitive basic** (Nov–Dec/Feb–Apr). Rather plain warm-toned head, with a frequent pinkish or orangey wash at the bill base.

d–e   **Adult ♀** (year-round). The wingbar on the greater coverts is usually clearly broader than the white trailing edge to the secondaries. It varies between all white (d) and washed reddish (e)

f   **Juvenile first basic** (until Oct–Feb). Note plainer flank feathers and scapulars, and juvenile tertials. The pale wash at the base of the bill is usually more pronounced.

Green-winged Teal *Anas carolinensis* (see also Plate 37)   Text p. 430

See above.

g   **Adult ♀ definitive basic** (Nov–Dec/Feb–Apr). Usually greyer and colder than *crecca*.

h   **Adult ♀ definitive basic** (Nov–Dec/Feb–Apr). Head pattern more contrasting and also colder than *crecca*, with often a clear white rounded patch at the bill base and a diffuse dark bar running from the gape. Many have an entirely dark bill.

i   **Adult ♀ definitive basic** (Nov–Dec/Feb–Apr). A somewhat intermediate pattern, which can be shown by both species.

j–k   **Adult ♀** (year-round). The wingbar is often as broad as or scarcely broader than the trailing edge, and averages more reddish (by age and sex) than in *crecca*.

Baikal Teal *Anas formosa* (see also Plate 37)   Text p. 417

♀ resembles Eurasian Teal and especially Green-winged Teal by its head pattern. Usually rather easy to separate, especially using head and upperwing patterns.

l   **Adult ♀ definitive basic** (Nov–Dec/Feb–Apr). Note the plain, often elongated scapulars.

m   **Adult ♀ definitive basic** (Nov–Dec/Feb–Apr). Head shape and pattern are usually distinctive.

n   **Adult ♀ definitive basic** (Nov–Dec/Feb–Apr). The secondaries and greater coverts form a succession of four lines, white, black, glossy green and reddish, typical of the species.

o   **Juvenile first basic** (until Oct–Feb). Juvenile tertials and scapulars typically shorter, but after pre-formative moult age is determined mainly using upperwing pattern.

Green-winged Teal

Baikal Teal

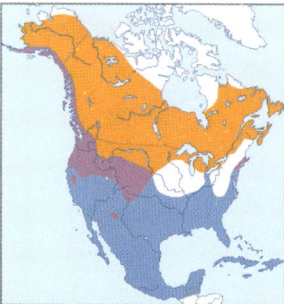

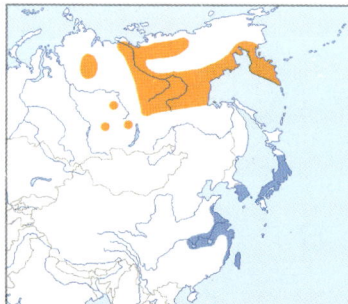

PLATE 39

This plate and the next one present several hybrids, mostly in the genus *Anas*, which are reported in the wild more or less regularly (adult in definitive basic plumage shown here). It should be kept in mind that all of these hybrids are variable, and can resemble one parent more than the other (see text). The head pattern is especially variable in all crosses. For other hybrids within the genus *Anas*, see also Plates 27–35 and 37.

a	**Hybrid Wood Duck** *Aix sponsa* × **Tufted Duck** *Aythya fuligula*	Text p. 329
b	**Hybrid American Wigeon** *Anas americana* × **Green-winged Teal** *A. carolinensis*	Text p. 432
c	**Hybrid American Wigeon** *Anas americana* × **Northern Shoveler** *A. clypeata*	Text p. 354
d	**Hybrid American Wigeon** *Anas americana* × **Mallard** *A. platyrhynchos*	Text p. 355
e	**Hybrid Northern Pintail** *Anas acuta* × **American Wigeon** *A. americana*	Text p. 410
f	**Hybrid Eurasian Wigeon** *Anas penelope* × **Mallard** *A. platyrhynchos*	Text p. 347
g	**Hybrid Eurasian Wigeon** *Anas penelope* × **Chiloe Wigeon** *A. sibilatrix*	Text p. 347
h	**Hybrid Northern Pintail** *Anas acuta* × **Eurasian Wigeon** *A. penelope*	Text p. 410
i	**Hybrid Eurasian Wigeon** *Anas penelope* × **Gadwall** *A. strepera*	Text p. 347
j	**Hybrid Eurasian Teal** *Anas crecca* × **Eurasian Wigeon** *A. penelope*	Text p. 426
k	**Hybrid Falcated Duck** *Anas falcata* × **Eurasian Wigeon** *A. penelope*	Text p. 347
l	**Hybrid Falcated Duck** *Anas falcata* × **Gadwall** *A. strepera*	Text p. 342

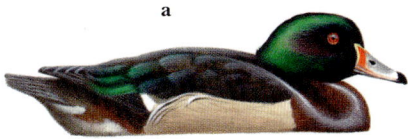

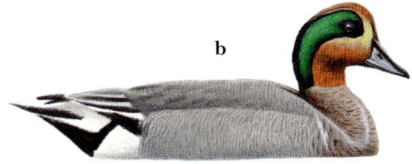

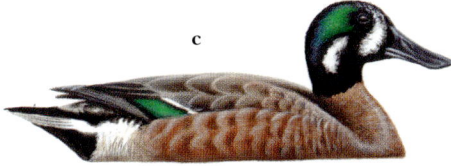

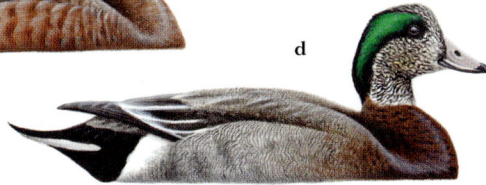

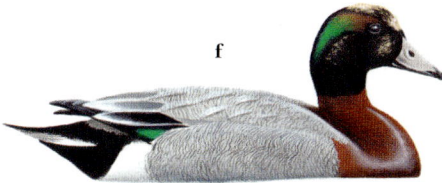

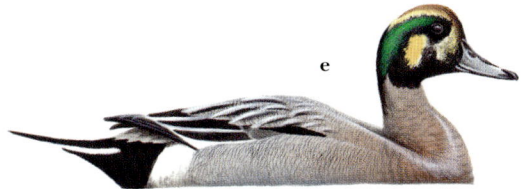

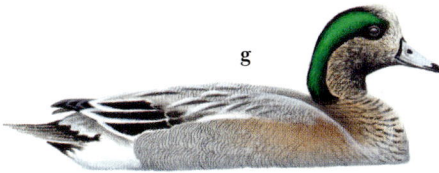

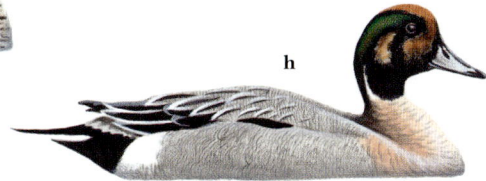

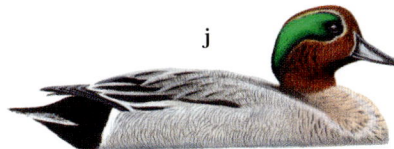

PLATE 40

Hybrid dabbling ducks (continued)

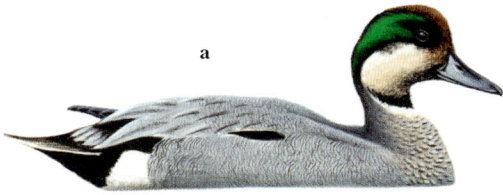

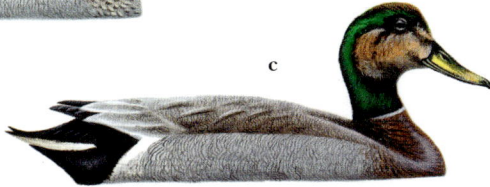

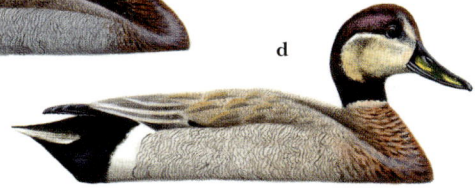

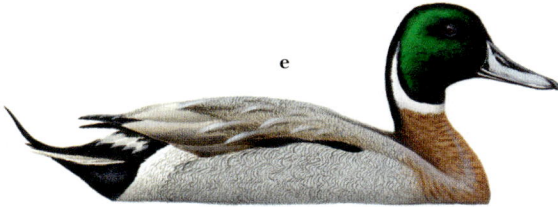

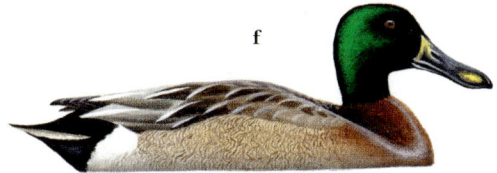

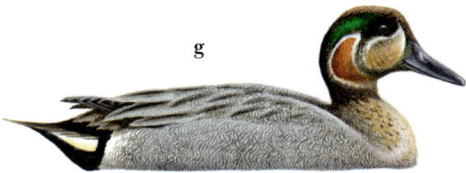

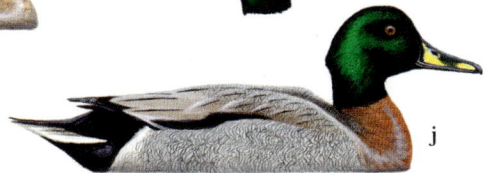

PLATE 41

Red-crested Pochard *Netta rufina* Text p. 440

Usually unmistakable. Complex alternate moult strategy (two plumages per adult cycle, three in first cycle). Strong sexual dimorphism, especially in definitive basic plumage.

a **Adult ♂ definitive basic** (Oct–Nov/May–Jun).

b **Adult ♂ definitive basic** (Oct–Nov/May–Jun). The ♀ also shows a broad white wingbar.

c **First-winter ♂ formative** (Dec–Feb/Aug). Almost identical to adult ♂ once pre-formative moult completed, but age can be determined by presence of juvenile feathers especially on belly, among tertials and on upperwing.

d **Adult ♂ definitive alternate** (Jun–Jul/Sep–Oct). Resembles ♀ but has red eye and bill.

e **Juvenile ♂ first basic** (until Sep–Nov). Eye and bill begin to acquire adult colours before first adult-type feathers appear.

f **Adult ♀ definitive basic** (Oct–Dec/Dec–Apr).

g **Juvenile ♀ first basic** (until Sep–Jan). Note duller and greyer coloration, and juvenile tertials.

Hybrid Red-crested Pochard *N. rufina* × Ferruginous Duck *Aythya nyroca* Text p. 464

Rarely encountered in the wild, and does not resemble any species.

h **Adult ♂ definitive basic.** At least sometimes, this hybrid shows obvious vermiculations on the flanks and anterior scapulars, a feature not shown by either parent species.

Hybrid Red-crested Pochard *N. rufina* × Common Pochard *Aythya ferina* Text p. 442

Regularly encountered in the wild in Europe. Both sexes may recall Redhead *Aythya americana*, even the wingbar which most often seems off-white on secondaries and greyer on primaries.

i **Adult ♂ definitive basic.**

j **Adult ♀ definitive basic.**

Red-crested Pochard

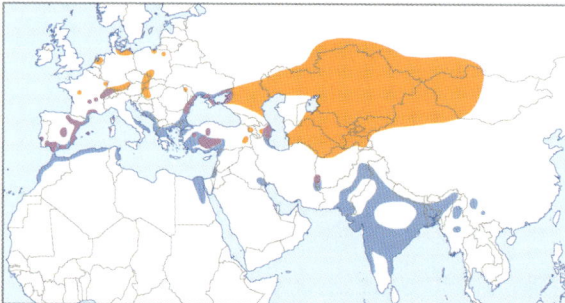

c

b

a

d

e

f

g

h

i

j

PLATE 42

Common Pochard *Aythya ferina* (see also Plates 43 & 44) Text p. 455

Usually easily identified in Eurasia, but the existence of hybrids should be taken into account in a North American context. Complex alternate moult strategy (two plumages per adult cycle, three in first cycle). Strong sexual dimorphism, especially in definitive basic plumage.

a–b **Adult ♂ definitive basic** (Nov–Dec/May–Jun).

c **Adult ♂ definitive basic** (Nov–Dec/May–Jun).

d **First-winter ♂ formative** (Oct–Mar/May–Jun). Pre-formative moult usually ends with tertials, lower scapulars and upper flank feathers.

e **First-winter ♂ formative** (Oct–Mar/May–Jun). In flight, note contrast between formative scapulars and browner and darker juvenile upperwing.

f **Adult ♂ definitive alternate** (May–Jun/Oct–Nov).

Redhead *Aythya americana* (see also Plates 43 & 44) Text p. 450

♂ easily identified in all plumages. Complex alternate moult strategy (two plumages per adult cycle, three in first cycle). Strong sexual dimorphism. [Map on Plate 43]

g **Adult ♂ definitive basic** (Oct–Nov/Jun–Jul).

h **Adult ♂ definitive basic** (Oct–Nov/Jun–Jul). In flight, note broad wingbar, paler on secondaries.

i **First-winter ♂ formative** (Nov–Feb/May–Jun). Many birds retain some juvenile feathers on belly, femoral area, rump, undertail-coverts and tertials. Age also determined based on contrast between formative scapulars and juvenile upperwing (e).

j **Adult ♂ definitive alternate** (Jun–Jul/Oct–Nov). In many birds, alternate plumage is even closer to definitive basic plumage than here.

Canvasback *Aythya valisineria* (see also Plates 43 & 44) Text p. 445

Shape and size usually distinctive. Complex alternate moult strategy (two plumages per adult cycle, three in first cycle). Strong sexual dimorphism. [Map on Plate 43]

k **Adult ♂ definitive basic** (Nov–Dec/May–Jun).

l **Adult ♂ definitive basic** (Nov–Dec/May–Jun).

m **First-winter ♂ formative** (Oct–Mar/May–Jun). In flight, age can be determined by contrast between formative scapulars and juvenile upperwing (e).

n **Adult ♂ definitive alternate** (May–Jun/Oct–Nov). Most birds retain an all-black bill, but some have a very faint pale subterminal area as shown here.

Common Pochard

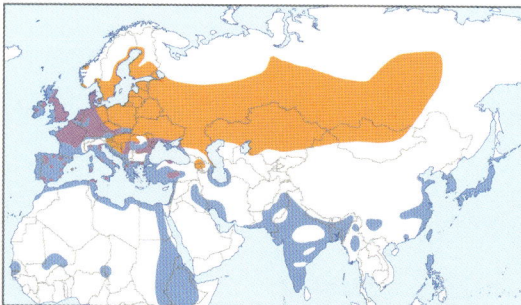

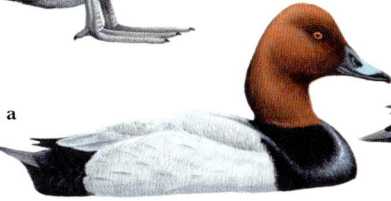

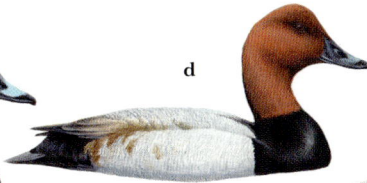

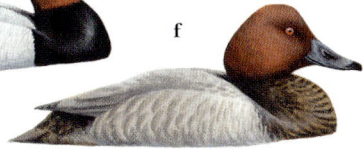

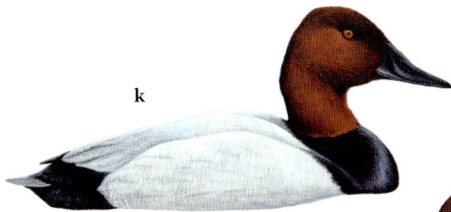

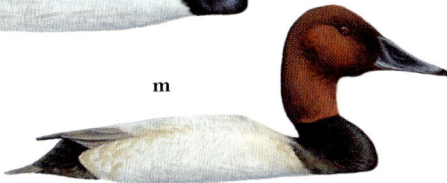

PLATE 43

Redhead *Aythya americana* (see also Plates 42 & 44)   Text p. 450

a   **Adult ♂ definitive basic** (Oct–Nov/Jun–Jul). Brighter orange and rounded head, with yellow-orange eyes and steep forehead. Bill has clear-cut whitish subterminal band and black tip.

Canvasback *Aythya valisineria* (see also Plates 42 & 44)   Text p. 445

b   **Adult ♂ definitive basic** (Nov–Dec/May–Jun). The head and bill shape is long and pointed, a usually obvious feature. Head deep reddish (darker than Redhead), blackish in front of eye. Iris red. Culmen slightly swollen at base, and bill very long and thin at tip, usually all black.

Common Pochard *Aythya ferina* (see also Plates 42 & 44)   Text p. 455

c   **Adult ♂ definitive basic** (Nov–Dec/May–Jun). Oval- or pear-shaped head, with a gently curved forehead and culmen, more concave than in Canvasback and without any clear break as in Redhead. The pale area on the bill appears more contrasting with age. [Map on Plate 42]

Apart from the three 'red-headed' *Aythya*, this plate shows the hybrids (♂♂ in definitive basic plumage) that resemble those species, and which could cause confusion, especially when trying to identify an out-of-range bird. All these hybrids can show some variation in many respects, apparently mainly due to the sex of each parent species.

d–e   **Hybrid Redhead** *A. americana* × **Canvasback** *A. valisineria*   Text p. 452

f–g   **Hybrid Common Pochard** *Aythya ferina* × **Canvasback** *A. valisineria*   Text p. 457

h–i   **Hybrid Common Pochard** *Aythya ferina* × **Ferruginous Duck** *A. nyroca*   Text p. 463

j   **Hybrid Redhead** *Aythya americana* × **Ring-necked Duck** *A. collaris*   Text p. 473

k   **Hybrid Ring-necked Duck** *Aythya collaris* × **Canvasback** *A. valisineria*   Text p. 473

l   **Hybrid Common Pochard** *Aythya ferina* × **Tufted Duck** *A. fuligula*   Text p. 480

Redhead

Canvasback

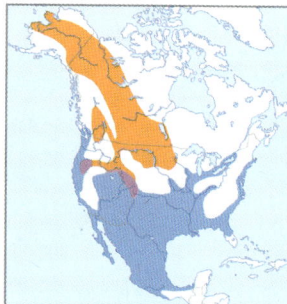

a

b

c

d

f

h

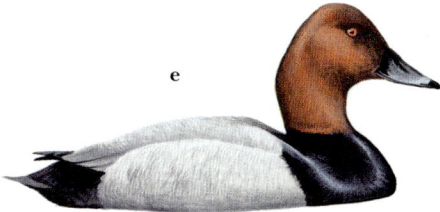

e

j

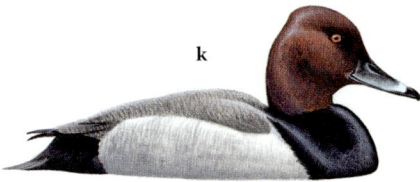

k

i

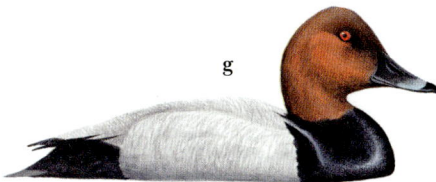

g

l

PLATE 44

Canvasback *Aythya valisineria* (see also Plates 42 & 43) Text p. 445

♀ usually not difficult to identify in North America, but an out-of-range vagrant should be checked carefully due to the existence of hybrids, especially with Common Pochard *A. ferina*. Both definitive plumages often appear very pale.

a   **Adult ♀ definitive basic** (Nov–Dec/Mar–Apr).

b   **Adult ♀ definitive basic** (Nov–Dec/Mar–Apr). Note distinctive head profile, with an all-black bill.

c   **Adult ♀ definitive alternate** (Apr.-May/Oct–Nov).

d   **Adult ♀ definitive basic** (Nov–Dec/Mar–Apr).

Redhead *Aythya americana* (see also Plates 42 & 43) Text p. 450

In North America, can be confused with ♀ Ring-necked Duck, which is much smaller but whose plumage shows some similarities.

e   **Adult ♀ definitive basic** (Nov–Dec/Apr–May).

f   **Adult ♀ definitive basic** (Nov–Dec/Apr–May). Note head and bill pattern recalling Ring-necked Duck.

g   **Adult ♀ definitive alternate** (Apr–May/Oct–Nov). This plumage appears more streaked, with an ill-defined bill pattern.

h   **Adult ♀ definitive basic** (Nov–Dec/Apr–May).

i   **Juvenile first basic** (until Sep–Nov).

Common Pochard *Aythya ferina* (see also Plates 42 & 43) Text p. 455

Rarely misidentified in Eurasia, but in North America, where it is a very rare vagrant, should be identified with great care due to its resemblance to some hybrids involving Canvasback *A. valisineria*.

j   **Adult ♀ definitive basic** (Nov–Dec/Mar–Apr).

k   **Adult ♀ definitive basic** (Nov–Dec/Mar–Apr). Note distinctive bill pattern, which appears more contrasting with age.

l   **Adult ♀ definitive alternate** (Apr–May/Oct–Nov). Distinctly warmer brown than basic plumage, with much-reduced contrast between the head, breast, flanks and upperparts.

m   **Adult ♀ definitive basic** (Nov–Dec/Mar–Apr).

n   **Juvenile first basic** (until Oct–Nov). Plainer and browner than adult ♀. The bill pattern gradually appears during the first winter.

Hybrid Redhead *A. americana* × Canvasback *A. valisineria* Text p. 452

Reported occasionally in North America.

o   **Adult ♀ definitive basic.** This hybrid can recall both parent species, but also ♀ Common Pochard by its intermediate overall coloration and bill pattern.

Hybrid Common Pochard *A. ferina* × Canvasback *A. valisineria* Text p. 457

Reported occasionally in Eurasia.

p   **Adult ♀ definitive basic.** This hybrid can resemble both parent species in the same plumage and constitutes a real identification pitfall.

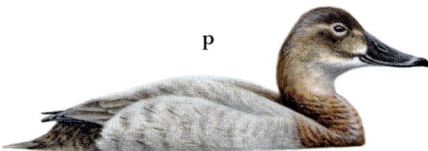

PLATE 45

Ferruginous Duck *Aythya nyroca*

Text p. 460

A small to medium-sized diving duck, overall dark brown with white undertail-coverts. Rounded head without any hint of crest. Can be mistaken for some ♀ Tufted Ducks *A. fuligula* and especially several hybrids (see Plate 46). Complex alternate moult strategy (two plumages per adult cycle, three in first cycle). Slight sexual dimorphism.

a–b   **Adult ♂ definitive basic** (Oct–Nov/May–Jun). Dark collar visible when neck is stretched.

c–d   **Adult ♂ definitive basic** (Oct–Nov/May–Jun). Typical bill pattern (c) with black tip reduced to the nail, but in some birds (d) the black can extend slightly on its sides.

e   **Adult ♂ definitive basic** (Oct–Nov/May–Jun). In flight, broad white wingbar somewhat recalls Red-crested Pochard *Netta rufina*.

f   **Adult ♂ definitive alternate** (Jun/Oct). Much duller but iris still white and, usually, some bright reddish feathers retained on the head.

g   **First-winter ♂ formative** (Oct–Mar/Jun). Strongly resembles adult ♂ by Jan–Mar (once pre-formative moult completed). Some browner juvenile feathers often retained among undertail-coverts (though often entirely white) and on belly, which appears streaked. Iris is not usually clean white until early spring, and the bill pattern is somewhat diffuse. Wingbar slightly less white than in adult.

h   **Adult ♀ definitive basic** (Nov/Mar–May). Appears browner and darker than ♂, with dark iris.

i   **Adult ♀ definitive alternate** (Apr–May/Oct). Plumage somewhat colder and darker, with more obvious patches on the head-sides, roughly barred flanks and darker 'cap'. Bill almost blackish.

j   **Adult ♀ definitive basic** (Nov/Mar–May). Usually shows clear pale bluish subterminal band on bill.

k   **Adult ♀ definitive basic** (Nov/Mar–May).

l   **First-winter ♀ formative** (Oct–Mar/Mar–May). Like adult ♀, but some juvenile feathers usually retained on belly, which appears faintly streaked pale grey-brown with less well-defined contours. Bill pattern ill-defined.

m   **Juvenile first basic** (until Sep–Oct). Note very dark bill with faint subterminal pale band, darker crown and obvious pale reddish patches on the head-sides. Iris initially greyer than adult ♀, quickly varying according to sex.

n   **Juvenile first basic** (until Sep–Oct). Belly and undertail-coverts washed pale buff and neatly spotted brown.

Ferruginous Duck

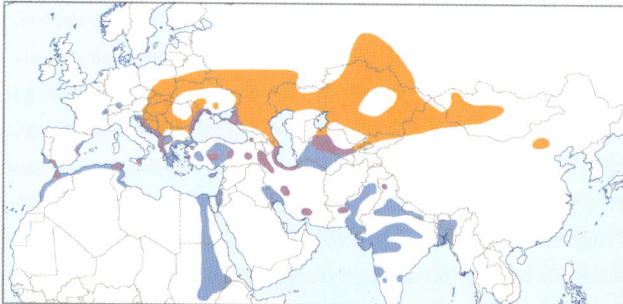

PLATE 46

This plate presents several hybrids (in definitive basic plumage) resembling Ferruginous Duck *Aythya nyroca* and involving this species in their parentage. These hybrids are rather numerous in the wild, and even more frequent than Ferruginous Duck itself in W Europe. Moreover, some (especially ♀♀) are very confusing. Many of these hybrids are rather variable, depending among other things on the sex of either parent species. See Plates 43, 47 and 49 for other hybrids involving Ferruginous Duck.

Hybrid Ferruginous Duck *A. nyroca* × Common Pochard *A. ferina* Text p. 463

The second most frequently encountered hybrid duck in Europe.

a–c   **Adult ♂ definitive basic**. Note variability in several features, including coloration of the head (more or less reddish-mahogany), breast (from reddish to near blackish) and body (more or less brownish or grey). The iris can be pale, circled reddish (a), whitish (b) or dull orange (c). The bill pattern varies between those of the parents, but usually shows more black than in Ferruginous Duck. The undertail-coverts show more or less white. See also Plate 43.

d   **Adult ♀ definitive basic**. This hybrid is very misleading but is usually distinguished by the contrast between the breast and flanks, the coarsely streaked pale grey-brown belly and greyer wingbar.

e   **Adult ♀ definitive basic**. Some show a more patterned bill (reminiscent of Common Pochard) and a faint pale bridle.

f   **Adult ♀ definitive basic**. A typical hybrid, with darker reddish-brown head and breast, strong contrast with the flanks and no blackish bar on the femoral coverts.

g   **Adult ♀ definitive basic**.

h   **Adult ♀ definitive basic**. Most hybrids show this type of wingbar, pale greyish on primaries.

Hybrid Ferruginous Duck *A. nyroca* × Tufted Duck *A. fuligula* Text p. 464

Rarer than the previous hybrid, but regularly reported in Eurasia. The ♀ of this cross is shown on Plate 49.

i   **Adult ♂ definitive basic**. This type can superficially resemble a Ferruginous Duck.

j   **Adult ♂ definitive basic**. This type appears more common and should not be difficult to identify (see also Plate 47).

k   **Adult ♀ definitive alternate**. Very dark plumage, usually identified by pale yellow iris, not matching either parent.

a

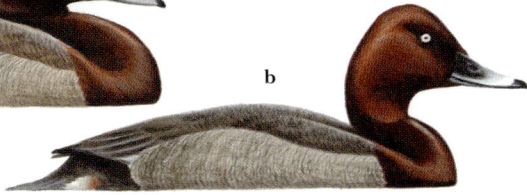

b

c

e

d

f

g

h

i

j

k

PLATE 47

Baer's Pochard *Aythya baeri* Text p. 467

A medium-sized diving duck, overall dark brown with a glossy green head and white undertail-coverts. Identification should be made with great care, this species being now very rare, and because of the existence of hybrids. Complex alternate moult strategy (two plumages per adult cycle, three in first cycle). Moult schedule not well known in the wild. Slight sexual dimorphism.

a–b **Adult ♂ definitive basic** (Oct–Dec/Jun–Aug?).

c **Adult ♂ definitive alternate** (Jul–Aug/Oct–Dec?). Duller, with less white on fore flanks and browner head.

d **First-winter ♂ formative** (Nov–Mar/Jun–Jul?). After pre-formative moult, almost identical to adult ♂, but iris not completely white usually until at least midwinter and belly appears faintly streaked or mottled brownish.

e **Adult ♀ definitive basic** (Nov–Dec/Mar–May?).

f **Juvenile first basic** (until Oct–Nov?). Much duller than adult, with a brownish head (blackish after pre-formative moult).

g **Adult ♀ definitive basic** (Oct–Dec/Jun–Aug?).

Hybrid Baer's Pochard *A. baeri* × Common Pochard *A. ferina* Text p. 468

This hybrid has been reported occasionally in E Asia.

h **Adult ♂ definitive basic.**

Hybrid Ferruginous Duck *A. nyroca* × Tufted Duck *A. fuligula* Text p. 464

i **Adult ♂ definitive basic.** This hybrid bears a superficial resemblance to Baer's Pochard. See also Plate 46.

Hybrid Baer's Pochard *A. baeri* × Ferruginous Duck *A. nyroca* Text p. 464

The most misleading hybrid, whose frequency seems to have increased recently, perhaps due to the decline of Baer's Pochard (and the local increase of Ferruginous Duck?).

j **Adult ♂ definitive basic.** Note presence of both green and reddish sheens on the head and white on fore flanks lacking or reduced.

Baer's Pochard

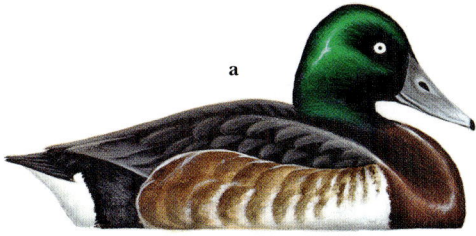

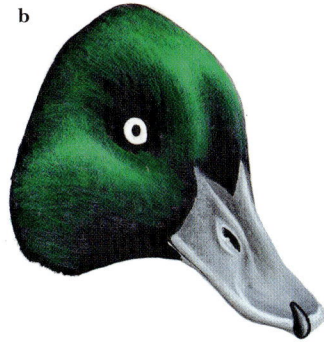

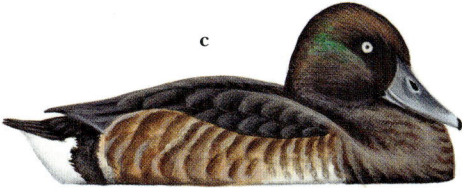

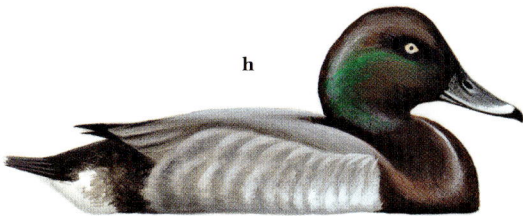

PLATE 48

Ring-necked Duck *Aythya collaris* (see also Plate 49)   Text p. 471

A medium-sized diving duck, which bears a superficial resemblance to Tufted Duck *A. fuligula*, the only other species whose adult ♂ (definitive basic) has blackish head and upperparts. Hybrids between these two species can constitute serious pitfalls. Complex alternate moult strategy (two plumages per adult cycle, three in first cycle). Strong sexual dimorphism, especially in definitive basic plumage.

a–b   **Adult** ♂ **definitive basic** (Oct–Dec/Jun).

c   **Adult** ♂ **definitive alternate** (Jul–Jul/Oct–Nov). Note presence of white at the bill base and on the fore flanks.

d   **First-winter** ♂ **formative** (Sep–Mar/Jun). After pre-formative moult, much like adult, but often some juvenile feathers are retained on the belly and lower flanks, rump and/or undertail-coverts. The bill is less strikingly patterned.

Tufted Duck *Aythya fuligula* (see also Plate 49)   Text p. 477

Much like previous species, but usually has a distinctive crest. Some hybrids can be confusing. Complex alternate moult strategy (two plumages per adult cycle, three in first cycle). Strong sexual dimorphism, especially in definitive basic plumage. [Map on Plate 49]

e–f   **Adult** ♂ **definitive basic** (Nov/May–Jun).

g   **Adult** ♂ **definitive alternate** (Jun–Jul/Oct–Nov). Usually no white patch at the bill base.

h   **First-winter** ♂ **formative** (Oct–Mar/Jun). Flanks usually not pure white at this age and has shorter crest.

Hybrid Tufted Duck *A. fuligula* × Ferruginous Duck *A. nyroca*   Text p. 464

i   **Adult** ♂ **definitive basic.** The bird depicted here is a backcross with Tufted Duck, obviously resembling the latter, but has a shorter crest, whiter iris and reduced black tip to the bill.

Hybrid Lesser Scaup *A. affinis* × Tufted Duck *A. fuligula*   Text p. 494

j   **Adult** ♂ **definitive basic.** This hybrid can recall Tufted Duck, with its dark upperparts and almost white flanks, but the crest is usually truncated. See also Plate 51.

Hybrid Ring-necked Duck *A. collaris* × Tufted Duck *A. fuligula*   Text p. 480

k   **Adult** ♂ **definitive basic.**

Hybrid Common Pochard *A. ferina* × Tufted Duck *A. fuligula*   Text p. 480

l   **Adult** ♂ **definitive basic.** Such birds could be backcrosses with Tufted Duck.

Ring-necked Duck

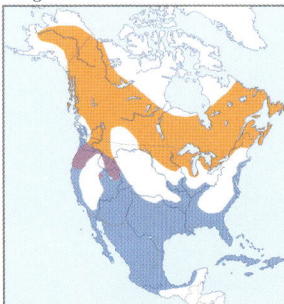

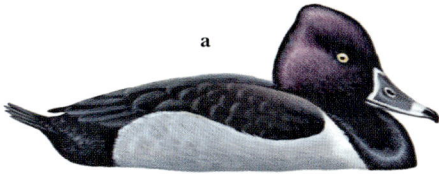

PLATE 49

Ring-necked Duck *Aythya collaris* (see also Plate 48)   Text p. 471

Can recall ♀ Redhead *A. americana* in general coloration and bill pattern, but distinctly smaller. Several hybrids within the genus *Aythya* can also resemble this species.

a   **Adult ♀ definitive basic** (Oct–Dec/Apr).

b   **Adult ♀ definitive alternate** (May–Jun/Oct–Nov). Similar to basic plumage, but on average duller, with less contrasting head pattern and pale band on bill reduced or near-absent.

c   **Juvenile ♂ first basic** (until Sep–Oct). This ♂ has begun its pre-formative moult (Sep/Oct) and already shows formative feathers on head, breast and fore flanks.

d   **Juvenile first basic** (until Sep–Oct). Note overall dull brownish tinge, poorly marked eye-ring and bridle, and faint contrast between breast and flanks. Iris is dark dull brown and bill shows a very faint or no pale subterminal band.

e   **Adult ♀ definitive basic** (Oct–Dec/Apr). Note greyish wingbar and underwing.

Tufted Duck *Aythya fuligula* (see also Plate 48)   Text p. 477

An overall dark diving duck in these plumages, which can be mistaken for ♀ Ferruginous Duck and ♀♀ of several hybrids.

f   **Adult ♀ definitive alternate** (May–Jun/Oct–Nov). Similar to definitive basic plumage, but on average darker, browner on flanks (often with a clear reddish hue), bill darker and patch at bill base ill-defined or washed reddish-brown.

g   **Adult ♀ definitive alternate** (May–Jun/Oct–Nov). A variant showing much white at the bill base.

h   **Adult ♀ definitive basic** (Nov/Apr). Rather variable, with flanks from pale grey-brown to deep brown, breast more or less reddish, undertail variably stained white and sometimes approaching Ferruginous Duck *A. nyroca*.

i   **Adult ♀ definitive basic/definitive alternate** (year-round). Note clear-cut white wingbar.

j   **Juvenile ♂ first basic** (until Sep–Oct.). Overall darker and colder, lacking contrast between upperparts, breast and flanks. Iris dark dull brown. Bill dark grey with blackish culmen and often ill-defined black tip.

Hybrid Tufted Duck *A. fuligula* × Ferruginous Duck *A. nyroca*   Text p. 464

Rarely reported and probably overlooked.

k   **Adult ♀ definitive basic** Can be difficult to separate from either parent species in the wild.

Hybrid Common Pochard *A. ferina* × Tufted Duck *A. fuligula*   Text p. 480

Quite frequently reported and rather variable in appearance.

l   **Adult ♀ definitive basic** The bird shown here is typical (see also Plate 53).

Hybrid Redhead *A. americana* × Ring-necked Duck *A. collaris*   Text p. 473

Occasional in the wild and poorly known.

m   **Adult ♀ definitive basic** Resembles both parents and often difficult to identify unless direct comparison with both species is possible.

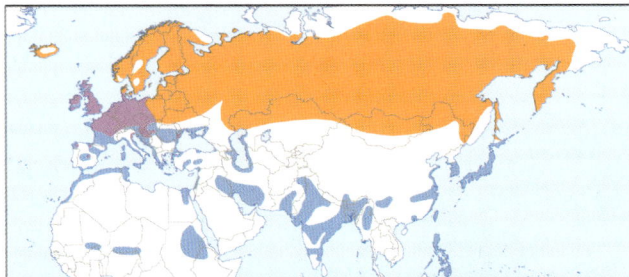

Tufted Duck

PLATE 50

Greater Scaup *Aythya marila* (see also Plates 51 & 52)   Text p. 484

A medium to large-sized diving duck, whose ♂ closely resembles that of Lesser Scaup, the only other species whose adult ♂ (definitive basic) has a blackish head and vermiculated upperparts. Distinction relies on size, shape and a few plumage details. Complex alternate moult strategy (two plumages per adult cycle, three in first cycle). Strong sexual dimorphism, especially in definitive basic plumage.

A. m. marila

a   **Adult ♂ definitive basic** (Nov/Jun). Compared with Lesser Scaup, note large rounded head, strong bill and back peaking near its mid-point.

b   **Adult ♂ definitive alternate** (Jun–Jul/Oct–Nov). Like basic plumage, but duller and stained brown.

c   **Juvenile ♂ first basic/first-winter ♂ formative** (until Jun). Here, in early pre-formative moult, with some adult-type feathers appearing on head and among scapulars.

d   **First-winter ♂ formative** (Oct–Mar/Jun). After the pre-formative moult, many show obvious traces of juvenile plumage. Formative scapulars show coarser vermiculations and head is less shiny. Age can also be determined using contrast between upperwing and scapulars like in Lesser Scaup (l).

e   **Adult ♂ definitive basic** (Nov/Jun).

A. m. nearctica

f   **Adult ♂ definitive basic** (Nov/Jun). Note differences in head shape (see also Plate 51) and coarser vermiculations on upperparts.

Lesser Scaup *Aythya affinis* (see also Plates 51 & 52)   Text p. 492

A medium-sized diving duck which closely resembles Greater Scaup. Complex alternate moult strategy (two plumages per adult cycle, three in first cycle). Strong sexual dimorphism, especially in definitive basic plumage. [Map on Plate 51]

g   **Adult ♂ definitive basic** (Nov/Jun). Note smaller and taller head with a notch on nape, smaller bill, coarser vermiculations on body and back usually peaking close to the neck.

h   **Adult ♂ definitive basic** (Nov/Jun). Contrast in wingbar (white on secondaries and pale grey-brown on primaries) is typical of this species.

i   **Adult ♂ definitive alternate** (Jun–Jul/Oct–Nov).

j   **First-winter ♂ formative** (Oct–Mar/Jun). A bird in late pre-formative moult (Dec–Feb) shown here. Note the tail held slightly upward, which is frequently the case in Lesser Scaup and Tufted Duck *A. fuligula*, but rarer in Greater Scaup.

k   **First-winter ♂ formative** (Oct–Mar/Jun). An early stage of pre-formative moult.

l   **First-winter ♂ formative** (Oct–Mar/Jun). In flight, note browner back and rump, as well as contrast between formative (adult-like) scapulars and mostly juvenile (blackish-brown) upperwing.

Greater Scaup

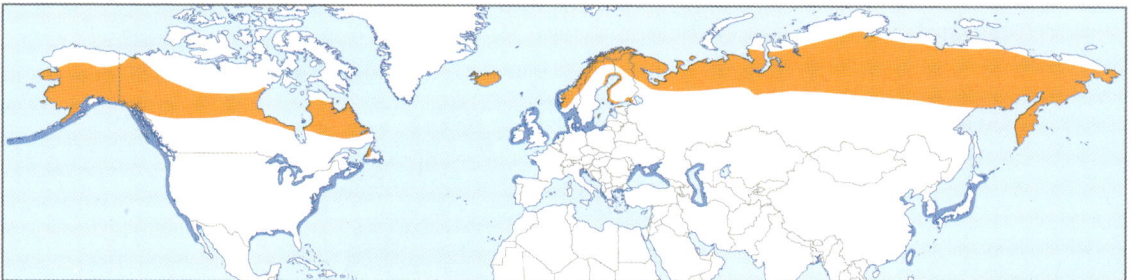

PLATE 51

The head and bill shape, and pattern of the latter, are important features for distinguishing Greater and Lesser Scaups from each other and from hybrids. It is worth noting that head shape changes with the crown feathers' position. These are held tight against the head when feeding, giving a more flattened shape in both species. [Map on Plate 50]

Greater Scaup *Aythya marila* (see also Plates 50 & 52) Text p. 484

A. m. marila

a **Adult ♂ definitive basic.** Note rounded head peaking above eye, green gloss and strong spatulate bill with an almost straight culmen. The black tip is usually reduced to the nail.

b **Adult ♂ definitive basic.** When head-on, note 'chubby' cheeks, spatulate bill and oval-shaped nail.

c **Adult ♂ definitive basic.** In some birds, the black extends on both sides of the nail, apparently more commonly in *nearctica* than *marila*. Young also show more black near the nail and on the culmen, as here.

A. m. nearctica

d **Adult ♂ definitive basic.** Both head and bill features (b–c) are valid for *nearctica* too. In profile, the forehead often shows a bump and the nape a slight angle. The crown peaks slightly in front of the eye.

Lesser Scaup *Aythya affinis* (see also Plates 50 & 52) Text p. 492

e **Adult ♂ definitive basic.** Typical head shape of a relaxed bird, taller than long, peaking well behind the eye. Note the thinner bill and black tip reduced to the nail, which can be hard to see in profile.

f **Adult ♂ definitive basic.** From the front, note the thinner head, parallel-sided bill and thinner nail.

Hybrid Tufted Duck *A. fuligula* × Greater Scaup *A. marila* Text p. 487

g **Adult ♂ definitive basic.** This hybrid most frequently shows a short pointed crest peaking above the rear crown.

h **Adult ♂ definitive basic.** At a distance, the upperparts appear plain grey, strongly contrasting with the white flanks.

Hybrid Common Pochard *A. ferina* × Tufted Duck *A. fuligula* Text p. 480

i **Adult ♂ definitive basic.** The most frequent bill pattern, with a broad black tip and black at the base.

j **Adult ♂ definitive basic.** Some variants resemble Lesser Scaup, the iris varying from yellow to reddish.

k **Adult ♂ definitive basic.** A different variant, closer to Common Pochard, possibly a backcross with the latter.

l **Adult ♂ definitive basic.** The wingbar is variable, but many show a pattern close to Lesser Scaup.

Hybrid Redhead *A. americana* × Greater Scaup *A. marila* Text p. 488

m **Adult ♂ definitive basic.** Very rare in the wild.

Hybrid Common Pochard *A. ferina* × Greater Scaup *A. marila* Text p. 488

n **Adult ♂ definitive basic.** Exceptional in the wild, this hybrid resembles that depicted in k.

Lesser Scaup

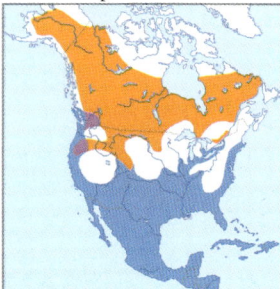

Hybrid Ring-necked Duck *A. collaris* × Lesser Scaup *A. affinis*
Text p. 494

o **Adult ♂ definitive basic.** Relatively rare, this hybrid shows obvious features of both parents.

Hybrid Tufted Duck *A. fuligula* × Lesser Scaup *A. affinis*
Text p. 494

p **Adult ♂ definitive basic.** Sometimes reported in North America and W Europe.

PLATE 52

♀ Greater and Lesser Scaups can be difficult to distinguish, and several hybrids with other species of *Aythya* can cause additional confusion. This plate shows the different plumages of ♀ of these species, while Plate 53 shows the relevant hybrids.

Greater Scaup *Aythya marila* (see also Plates 50 & 51)   Text p. 484

Appears distinctly larger and stockier, with a stronger head and bill shape, very useful in direct comparison, but lone birds can be difficult to identify. [Map on Plate 50]

A. m. marila

a–b **Adult ♀ definitive basic** (Nov/Apr). Note large white round patch at bill base, heavy bill with an almost straight culmen and a usually distinct pale patch on the ear-coverts.

c **Adult ♀ definitive alternate** (May–Jun/Oct–Nov). The upperparts and flanks feathers are browner, instead of pale grey with vermiculations, making the whole bird plainer, with obvious pale patches around the bill, on the ear-coverts and often the throat and foreneck.

d **Juvenile first basic** (until Sep–Oct). Note the darker upperparts, ochre-brown flanks, dark iris and ill-defined bill pattern, with a dark culmen and barely distinguishable dark nail.

A. m. nearctica

e–f **Adult ♀ definitive basic** (Nov/Apr). Note differences from *marila* in head shape.

g **Adult ♀ definitive basic** (Nov/Apr). Underwing whiter than in Lesser Scaup (both races).

h **Adult ♀ definitive basic** (Nov/Apr). The white wingbar extends onto the inner primaries (even more in *marila* than in *nearctica*).

i **First-winter ♀ formative** (Oct–Mar/Apr). By early winter, young ♀♀ can still retain many juvenile feathers, a less extensive white facial patch stained brownish, blackish culmen, diffuse blackish tip to the bill and brownish eyes, often browner around the pupil, which appears larger.

Lesser Scaup *Aythya affinis* (see also Plates 50 & 51)   Text p. 492

Smaller than Greater Scaup, with a typically thinner and more delicate shape. [Map on Plate 50]

j–k **Adult ♀ definitive basic** (Nov/May–Jun). Note typical head and bill shape. Iris usually yellow, but can be amber and browner, even in adult birds.

l **Adult ♀ definitive basic** (Nov/May–Jun). Note greyer greater underwing-coverts.

m **Adult ♀ definitive basic** (Nov/May–Jun). Like ♂, white on wingbar usually restricted to secondaries.

n **Adult ♀ definitive alternate** (Jun–Jul/Oct–Nov). Browner and darker overall in this plumage, with a duskier bill.

o **Juvenile first basic** (until Sep–Oct.). Often shows a blackish 'cap', with darker upperparts and plain ochre-brown flanks. Lone juvenile can be very difficult to separate from same-age Greater Scaup.

PLATE 53

This plate shows ♀♀ resulting from several crosses that resemble the scaups. Note that hybrids between Greater Scaup and Lesser Scaup are not well described in the literature, probably because they are very difficult to detect in the field, and probably almost impossible in ♀♀.

Hybrid Common Pochard *A. ferina* × Tufted Duck *A. fuligula* Text p. 480

a–c **Adult ♀ definitive basic**. This cross produces very variable hybrids, although ♀♀ are less well known than ♂♂. Some can recall Greater Scaup, Lesser Scaup, Tufted Duck or even Ring-necked Duck. Note the variation in size and shape, in head coloration (with or without a pale bridle behind the eye) and in overall darkness of the upperparts and flanks. On the other hand, the white facial patch, the colour of the iris and bill pattern seem more constant.

Hybrid Tufted Duck *A. fuligula* × Greater Scaup *A. marila* Text p. 487

d–f **Adult ♀ definitive basic**. Another variable hybrid, whose size can match that of both parent species. Variation occurs in the presence of a crest, in the bill shape, presence of pale patches on the ear-coverts and in the darkness of the upperparts. Some may constitute real pitfalls, especially with both scaups.

Hybrid Ring-necked Duck *A. collaris* × Lesser Scaup *A. affinis* Text p. 494

g **Adult ♀ definitive basic**. This hybrid shows obvious characters of both parent species.

Hybrid Lesser Scaup *A. affinis* × Tufted Duck *A. fuligula* Text p. 494

h **Adult ♀ definitive basic**. The ♀ resulting from this cross is not well described, but could occur anywhere in the Holarctic. It closely resembles hybrid Tufted Duck × Greater Scaup, but can be distinguished by smaller size, a crest more like a bump, smaller bill, darker head and possibly less white on primaries.

Hybrid Ring-necked Duck *A. collaris* × Tufted Duck *A. fuligula* Text p. 480

i **Adult ♀ definitive basic**. In good views, this hybrid generally presents characters of both parents.

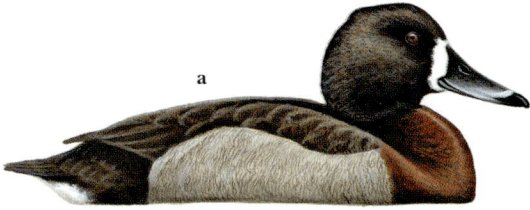

a

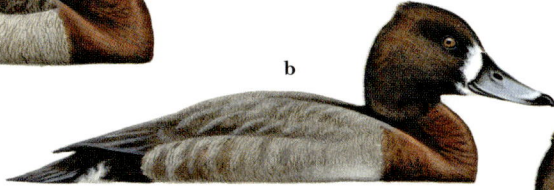

b

c

d

e

f

g

h

i

PLATE 54

This plate presents several hybrids between dabbling and diving duck species, and between diving ducks. None resembles another species in this plumage (all are adult ♂ definitive basic, except c), but they are encountered in the wild on a more or less regular basis.

a	**Hybrid Northern Pintail** *Anas acuta* × **Red-crested Pochard** *Netta rufina*	Text p. 442
b	**Hybrid Mallard** *Anas platyrhynchos* × **Red-crested Pochard** *Netta rufina*	Text p. 441
c	**Hybrid Mallard** *Anas platyrhynchos* × **Red-crested Pochard** *Netta rufina*	Text p. 441
	Adult ♀ definitive basic.	
d	**Hybrid Tufted Duck** *Aythya fuligula* × **Red-crested Pochard** *Netta rufina*	Text p. 479
e	**Hybrid Mallard** *Anas platyrhynchos* × **Tufted Duck** *Aythya fuligula*	Text p. 363
f	**Hybrid Mallard** *Anas platyrhynchos* × **Common Pochard** *Aythya ferina*	Text p. 363
g	**Hybrid Common Goldeneye** *Bucephala clangula* × **Smew** *Mergellus albellus*	Text p. 578
h	**Hybrid Bufflehead** *Bucephala albeola* × **Common Goldeneye** *B. clangula*	Text p. 562
i	**Hybrid Bufflehead** *Bucephala albeola* × **Hooded Merganser** *Lophodytes cucullatus*	Text p. 562

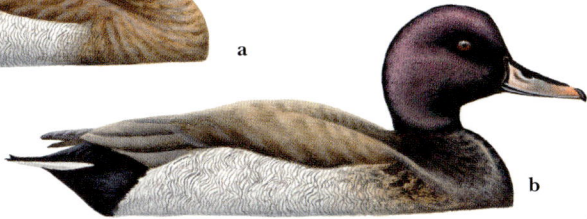

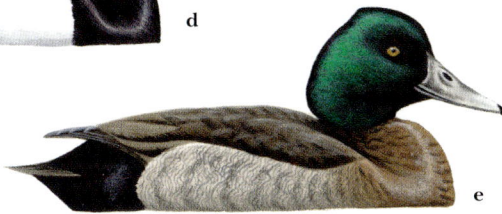

PLATE 55

Steller's Eider *Polysticta stelleri* (see also Plate 56)   Text p. 497

An Arctic sea duck, usually easily identified. Bill shape unique, with two flaps visible from below, and a rather truncated appearance in profile. Complex alternate moult strategy (two plumages per adult cycle, three in first cycle). Strong sexual dimorphism, especially in definitive basic plumage. [Map on Plate 56]

a   **Adult ♂ definitive basic** (Oct–Dec/May–Jul).

b   **Adult ♂ definitive alternate** (May–Jul/Sep–Nov). From adult ♀ and imm ♂ by clean white upperwing-coverts.

c   **First-winter ♂ formative** (Nov–Mar/May–Jul). Note grey and rounded tertials. From juvenile ♀ by whitish spots on breast and plain dark tertials (see Plate 56b).

d   **First-summer ♂ first alternate** (Jun–Jul/Sep–Dec). At start of first alternate moult, typically shows a ghost-like pattern of definitive basic coloration, with heavily worn brown tertials.

Spectacled Eider *Somateria fischeri* (see also Plate 56)   Text p. 502

Complex alternate moult strategy (two plumages per adult cycle, three in first cycle). Strong sexual dimorphism, especially in definitive basic plumage. [Map on Plate 56]

e   **Adult ♂ definitive basic** (Nov–Dec/Jun–Jul).

f   **Adult ♂ definitive alternate** (Jun–Jul/Oct–Nov). This plumage is mostly seen at sea.

g   **First-winter/first-summer ♂ formative** (Nov–Mar/May–Jun). A variable number of adult-type feathers appear by first summer, especially on head, breast, mantle, scapulars and flanks.

h   **Second-winter ♂ second basic** (Oct–Nov/Jun–Jul). Note shorter and greyer tertials at this age.

King Eider *Somateria spectabilis* (see also Plate 56)   Text p. 506

Complex alternate moult strategy (two plumages per adult cycle, three in first cycle). Strong sexual dimorphism, especially in definitive basic plumage. [Map on Plate 56]

i   **Adult ♂ definitive basic** (Dec/Jul).

j   **Adult ♂ definitive alternate** (Jul/Nov). Note typical bill, tertials and white upperwing.

k   **First-winter ♂ formative** (Nov–Mar/May–Jul). Appearance by early to midwinter.

l   **First-summer ♂ formative/first alternate** (Jun–Jul/Sep–Oct). Variable in appearance after pre-formative moult, but juvenile tertials and upperwing retained.

m   **Second-winter ♂ second basic** (Oct–Nov/May–Jul). Like adult ♂, except upperwing, the reduced swelling on the bill, shorter tertials and 'sails' on the back.

Hybrid Common Eider *Somateria mollissima* × King Eider *S. spectabilis*   Text p. 509

n   **Adult ♂ definitive basic** The hybrid depicted here corresponds to birds seen in N Atlantic, having for example the subspecies *borealis* of Common Eider in its parentage. This hybrid differs slightly when involving another North American subspecies of Common Eider (see text).

Steller's Eider

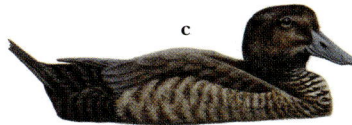

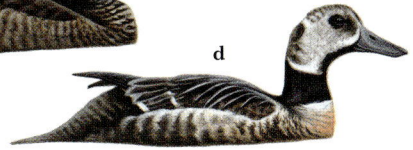

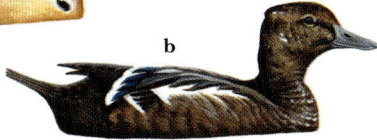

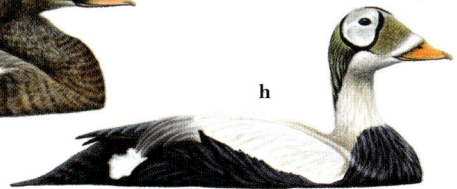

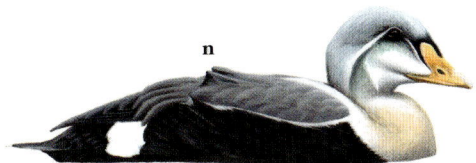

PLATE 56

Steller's Eider *Polysticta stelleri* (see also Plate 55)   Text p. 497

[Map on Plate 55]

a **Adult ♀ definitive basic** (Oct–Dec/Feb–Mar).

b **Juvenile ♀ first basic** (until Sep–Jan). Duller brown than adult ♀, best aged by juvenile tertials and narrower white tips to greater coverts and secondaries. At this age, the tertials fringed pale reddish-brown and all-dark breast indicate a ♀.

c **Adult ♂ definitive basic** (Oct–Dec/May–Jul).

d **Second-winter ♂ second basic** (Nov–Dec/Jul). Note brown leading edge to wing at this age.

e **Adult ♀ definitive basic** (Oct–Dec/Feb–Mar).

Spectacled Eider *Somateria fischeri* (see also Plate 55)   Text p. 502

f **Adult ♀ definitive basic** (Nov–Dec/Apr). A plumage rarely seen near shore.

g **Adult ♀ definitive alternate** (May–Jun/Oct–Nov). This plumage is paler, which makes the black barring appear coarser, especially on upperparts. A blackish band is often visible in front of the eye.

h **First-summer ♀ formative/first alternate** (Jun–Jul/Sep–Oct). Less coarsely streaked, with duller head pattern and juvenile tertials retained.

i **Adult ♂ definitive basic** (Nov–Dec/Jun–Jul). Birds with full adult plumage except some blackish anterior lesser coverts are perhaps in their third winter/third spring.

j **Adult ♀ definitive basic** (Nov–Dec/Apr). In flight, best distinguished from other eiders by head pattern and grey axillaries and underwing (use with caution).

King Eider *Somateria spectabilis* (see also Plate 55)   Text p. 506

k **Adult ♀ definitive basic** (Dec/Apr–May). Overall rufous to cinnamon-brown, with distinct black crescents on flanks. Dark grey bill with blackish nail and pale subterminal band.

l **Adult ♀ definitive alternate** (May–Jun/Nov). Like all *Somateria*, this plumage is much paler, grey-beige, more or less washed with a caramel tone, and more strongly barred. Tertials ochre-yellow to copper, centred black. Breast often shows a neat scaly pattern. Bill blackish, lacking pale subterminal band.

m **First-winter ♀ formative** (Nov–Mar/May–Jul). Overall duller brown, with breast more buff and head greyer. Dark markings on flanks coarser and less well defined. Tertials shorter, straighter and more round-tipped.

n **Adult ♂ definitive basic** (Dec/Jul). Birds in full adult plumage except some blackish anterior lesser coverts are perhaps in their third winter/third spring.

o **Adult ♀ definitive basic** (Dec/Apr–May). Note whitish axillaries and underwing median coverts, unlike Spectacled Eider.

Spectacled Eider

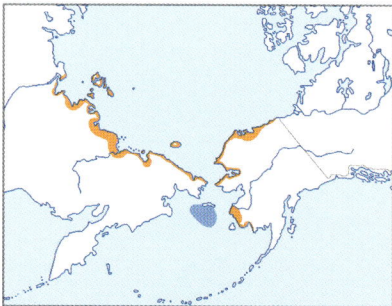

King Eider

142

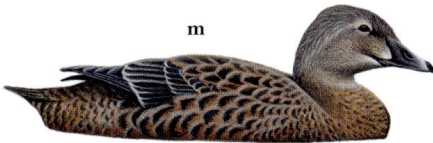

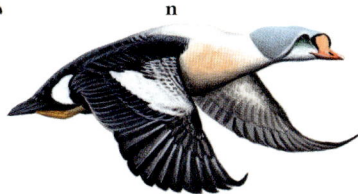

PLATE 57

Common Eider *Somateria mollissima* (see also Plate 58)   Text p. 513

A highly polymorphic species; ♂ should prove unmistakable. Complex alternate moult strategy (two plumages per adult cycle, three in first cycle). Strong sexual dimorphism, especially in definitive basic plumage.

S. m. mollissima

a   **Second-winter ♂ second basic** (Oct–Nov/Jun–Jul). Like adult ♂ but tertials visibly tipped grey or blackish, and lesser coverts variably stained brownish (see Plate 58d).

b   **Adult ♂ definitive alternate** (Jun–Jul/Oct–Nov). Dark with basic white upperwing and tertials retained.

c–e   **First-winter ♂ formative** (Nov–Mar/May–Jun). Different variants depicted here, illustrating the huge variability during the protracted pre-formative moult.

f   **Adult ♂ definitive basic** (Nov–Dec/Jun–Jul).

S. m. v-nigrum

g   **Adult ♂ definitive basic**. Note 'sails' on back and typical posture, with bill held down when neck is stretched.

h   **Adult ♂ definitive basic**. Note rounded feathering at base of bright orange bill, short and pointed bill processes and the extent of green wash below eye.

i   **First-winter ♂ formative**. The shape of the bill and feathering are the same, the bill usually quickly becoming bright yellow.

S. m. dresseri

j   **Adult ♂ definitive basic**. The head shape is typical.

k   **Adult ♂ definitive basic**. Note the long and pointed feathering at the bill base, the broad, long and rounded bill lobes and extent of green wash below the eye.

l   **First-winter ♂ formative**. The shape of bill and feathering are less marked but quickly become diagnostic during first autumn.

S. m. borealis

m–n   **Adult ♂ definitive basic**. Rather variable, with feathering at bill base slightly shorter and more rounded than *mollissima* and *dresseri*, bill processes rather short and thin and sometimes a green wash under black eye-band. The first bird (m) has typical head shape, with a tall crown and slight angle between forehead and culmen. Southern populations tend towards *sedentaria* (N Hudson Bay), *dresseri* (E Arctic Canada) and *mollissima* (N Atlantic).

S. m. mollissima

o   **Adult ♂ definitive basic**. Usually shows no green under black eye-band and long, pointed feathering at the base of the bill.

S. m. sedentaria

p   **Adult ♂ definitive basic**. Somewhat intermediate between *dresseri* and *borealis*, but typical birds (S Hudson Bay) are closer to *dresseri*.

S. m. faeroeensis

q   **Adult ♂ definitive basic**. Barely distinguishable from *mollissima*, but averages smaller with shorter and thinner bill processes.

Common Eider

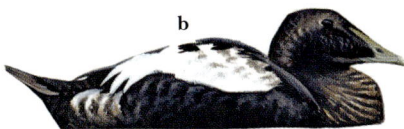

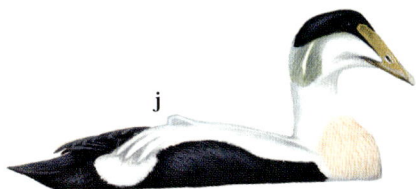

PLATE 58

Common Eider *Somateria mollissima* (see also Plate 57)

Text p. 513

♀♀ of the different subspecies are depicted here in definitive alternate plumage. Like other *Somateria*, this plumage has a paler, more grey-beige ground colour, making the dark barring appear stronger. Features described for ageing (a–f) are valid for all subspecies. [Map on Plate 57]

S. m. mollissima

a   **Adult ♀ definitive alternate** (May/Oct–Nov).

b   **Juvenile first basic** (until Oct–Nov). At the start of pre-formative moult, plainer and greyer, with plain scapulars and tertials, and flanks less distinctly barred.

c   **First-winter ♀ formative** (Nov–Mar/May–Jun). After pre-formative moult, some parts of the body are similar to those of adult ♀, but tertials and upperwing are still juvenile.

d   **Second-winter ♂ second basic** (Oct–Nov/Jun–Jul). Note dark leading edge to the wing.

e   **Adult ♂ definitive basic** (Nov–Dec/Jun–Jul).

f   **First-winter ♀ formative** (Nov–Mar/May–Jun). During first year, note lack of white wingbars.

g   **Adult ♀ definitive alternate** (May–Jun/Nov).

h   **Adult ♀ definitive alternate** (May–Jun/Nov). Note the long, pointed feathering at the base of the bill in this subspecies.

S. m. borealis

i   **Adult ♀ definitive alternate** (May/Oct–Nov). Note shorter and more rounded feathering at the base of the bill and shorter bill processes (variable).

j   **Adult ♀ definitive alternate** (May/Oct–Nov). Often shows a beautiful caramel or coppery wash.

S. m. sedentaria

k   **Adult ♀ definitive alternate** (May/Oct–Nov).

l   **Adult ♀ definitive alternate** (May/Oct–Nov). The palest subspecies, some ♀♀ showing an almost whitish ground colour in this plumage.

S. m. dresseri

m   **Adult ♀ definitive alternate** (May/Oct–Nov). Note long pointed feathering at the bill base and broad rounded lobes.

n   **Adult ♀ definitive alternate** (May/Oct–Nov). Clear reddish tones overall, with browner bars.

S. m. v-nigrum

o   **Adult ♀ definitive alternate** (May/Oct–Nov). Note short and broadly rounded feathering at the base of the bill and short bill processes.

p   **Adult ♀ definitive alternate** (May/Oct–Nov).

King Eider *Somateria spectabilis* (see also Plates 55 & 56)

Text p. 506

q   **Adult ♀ definitive alternate** (May–Jun/Nov). Head and bill pattern, for comparison.

PLATE 59

Harlequin Duck *Histrionicus histrionicus*

Text p. 526

Should prove unmistakable, given to its distinctive plumages and specific habitats (fast-flowing rivers in breeding season, rocky coasts in winter). Complex alternate moult strategy (two plumages per adult cycle, three in first cycle). Strong sexual dimorphism, especially in definitive basic plumage.

a **Adult** ♂ **definitive basic** (Sep–Oct/Jun–Jul.).

b **First-winter** ♂ **formative** (Oct–Jan/Jun–Jul). Early in the first winter, many ♂♂ have plumage much like that of adult ♂, being distinguished only by the whitish-barred belly and retained juvenile upperwing (plus at least some tertials and rectrices).

c **First-winter** ♂ **formative** (Oct–Jan/Jun–Jul). The timing and extent of pre-formative moult is variable, thus some ♂♂ still resemble juvenile in early winter. The bird here is typical of moult state in autumn (Oct/Dec), with some formative (adult-type) feathers on head, upper neck, upper flanks and back. At the same time, many show one or more moulted black-and-white tertials.

d **Adult** ♂ **definitive alternate** (Jun–Jul/Sep–Oct). Like ♀, but darker overall, with glossier and blacker upperparts, head and wings, and warmer brown flanks. The white marks on the head are more clearly defined.

e **Adult** ♀ **definitive basic** (Oct–Nov/May–Jul).

f **First-winter** ♀ **formative** (Oct–Jan/Jun–Jul). Belly more extensively whitish. Also note juvenile rectrices and tertials, quickly becoming browner and worn.

g **Adult** ♂ **definitive basic** (Sep–Oct/Jun–Jul).

h **Adult** ♀ **definitive basic** (Oct–Nov/May–Jul). In flight, the upperwing appears uniformly dark (paler brown in first basic and formative plumages).

i **Adult** ♀ **definitive basic** (Oct–Nov/May–Jul).

Harlequin Duck

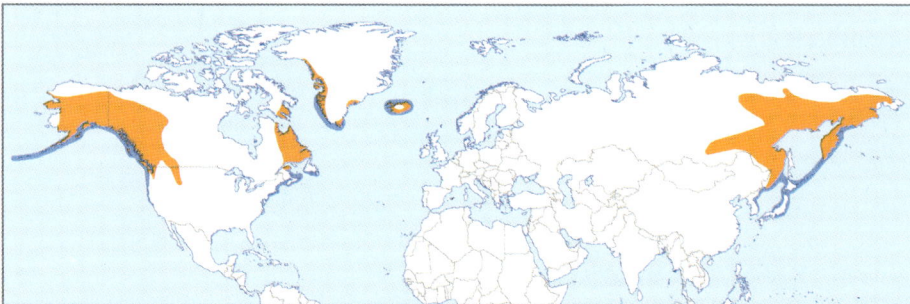

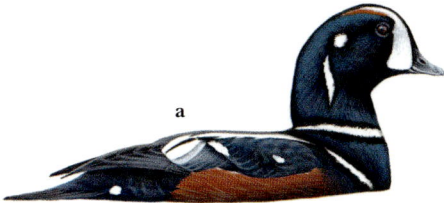

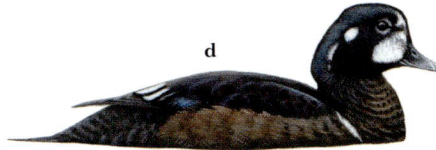

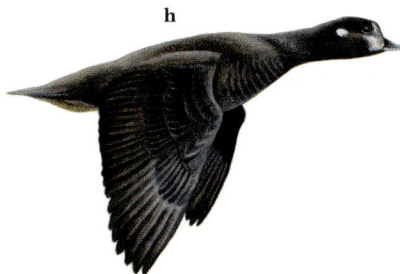

PLATE 60

Surf Scoter *Melanitta perspicillata*   Text p. 531

Usually not difficult to identify, being the only black-winged scoter except Black *M. americana* and Common Scoters *M. nigra*. Surf Scoter clearly differs from these two species in head and bill shape and coloration (all sexes and ages). Diving movement also differs, both Black and Common Scoters performing a slight jump above the surface, with wings held tight against the body. Surf Scoter does not jump before diving, and holds its wing slightly open. Simple alternate moult strategy (two plumages per cycle?). Clear sexual dimorphism.

a **Adult ♂ definitive basic** (Nov/Apr). No obvious seasonal change during the year.

b **Second-winter ♂ second basic** (Oct/Apr). Differs from adult by browner belly and some slight differences in head and bill pattern: bill less swollen at base of culmen, white forehead reduced or even lacking, and white patch on nape stained dusky.

c **First-winter/first-spring ♂ formative** (Oct/Jun). In early stage of pre-formative moult (mid-autumn), with some adult-type feathers visible on head. Note bill coloration appears at same time, permitting sex determination.

d **First-winter/first-spring ♂ formative** (Oct/Jun). This stage is often reached by midwinter.

e **First-winter/first-spring ♂ formative** (Oct/Jun). After pre-formative moult, juvenile feathers are retained on belly, rear body, wing and tertials. The contrast between the formative and juvenile parts is accentuated by wear during the first spring and subsequent summer.

f **First-winter/first-spring ♂ formative** (Oct/Jun). In flight, note whitish belly.

g **Adult ♀ definitive basic** (Nov/Apr).

h **First-winter/first-spring ♂ formative** (Oct/Jun). From first winter to subsequent summer, note lack of white nape, stronger pale patches on face, and wing and tertials becoming paler brown with wear.

i **First-winter/first-spring ♀ formative** (Oct/Jun). Like ♂, the white belly is diagnostic at this age.

j **Juvenile first basic** (until Nov). Initially, plain dark brown, with a dark iris, short pointed tertials, no white patch on nape, and bill less swollen at base of culmen.

Surf Scoter

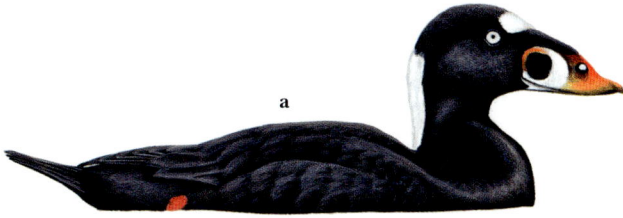

PLATE 61

These three species, the 'white-winged' scoters, were and sometimes still are considered conspecific. All have a large white patch on the secondaries, striking in flight, but also often visible on the water, especially as these species slightly spread their wings when diving. These three scoters are easy to distinguish from other scoters, and rather easy to separate from each other in adult ♂ plumages, but more difficult in adult ♀ plumages (see Plate 62).

Velvet Scoter *Melanitta fusca* (see also Plate 62) Text p. 535

Simple alternate moult strategy (two plumages per cycle?). Clear sexual dimorphism.

a **Adult ♂ definitive basic** (Nov/Apr). Note reduced white eye-patch, slight bulge at the bill base and its yellow sides.

b **Adult ♂ definitive basic** (Nov/Apr). The white patch on the inner wing includes the tips of the greater coverts in adult, but not in young birds in their first year.

c **Adult ♂ definitive basic** (Nov/Apr).

d **First-winter ♂ formative** (Oct/Jun). By late autumn, some formative adult-type feathers have appeared, here on the head, flanks and among scapulars. The bill shows a hint of adult coloration by mid-autumn (see Plate 62).

e **First-spring ♂ formative** (Oct/Jun). After pre-formative moult, in spring many body feathers have been replaced, the retained juvenile feathers appearing worn and bleached (tertials, outer or all rectrices, rump, upperwing). The belly is whitish. The bill is not fully coloured, the iris pale greyish and eye-patch less obvious or incomplete.

White-winged Scoter *Melanitta deglandi* (see also Plate 62) Text p. 540

Simple alternate moult strategy (two plumages per cycle?). Clear sexual dimorphism. [Map on Plate 62]

f **Adult ♂ definitive basic** (Nov/Apr). Note forehead bump, square bulge on upper culmen, black tomium and pinkish and yellow sides to the bill.

g **Adult ♂ definitive basic** (Nov/Apr). Compared to the other two species, note the reddish-washed flanks (between dives, the wing often covers the flanks when half-opened, as in k).

h **First-winter/first-spring ♂ formative** (Oct/Jun). During first winter, the bill coloration and head pattern are less marked, but already diagnostic in good views (see Plate 62).

Siberian Scoter *Melanitta stejnegeri* (see also Plate 62) Text p. 544

Simple alternate moult strategy (two plumages per cycle?). Clear sexual dimorphism. [Map on Plate 62]

i **Adult ♂ definitive basic** (Nov/Apr). Note more pear-shaped head, with a small protuberance on the bulge of the upper culmen, the rounded nostrils in profile, and red bill-sides with yellow along the tomium.

j **Adult ♂ definitive basic** (Nov/Apr).

k **First-winter/first-spring ♂ formative** (Oct/Jun).

Velvet Scoter

PLATE 62

♀♀ and immature ♂♂ are more difficult to separate, but still possible in good views, especially using head and bill shape, and the feathering at the base of the bill.

Velvet Scoter *Melanitta fusca* (see also Plate 61) Text p. 535
[Map on Plate 61]

a   **Second-winter** ♂ **second basic** (Oct/Apr). Early in second winter, almost like adult ♂, except reduced white eye-patch, dusky lower culmen and nail, and iris slightly darker greyish.

b   **First-winter** ♂ **formative** (Oct/Jun). Young birds can be sexed as early as mid-autumn by the new formative adult-type feathers and bill coloration.

c   **Adult** ♀ **definitive basic** (Nov/Apr). Compared to *deglandi* and *stejnegeri*, note gently concave forehead and bill profile. Furthermore, note the bill base feathering (like ♂). Iris brown to medium grey (vs. dark brown in young ♀). Bill blackish, sometimes with vague paler orange or pinkish hue to sides of tip (absent in young ♀ and its extent may be age-related).

d   **Ad** ♀ **definitive basic** (Nov/Apr). At a distance, the slightly 'snub' bill is typical.

White-winged Scoter *Melanitta deglandi* (see also Plate 61) Text p. 540

e   **Second-winter** ♂ **second basic** (Oct/Apr). The best ageing features are the smaller eye-patch, slightly smaller bulge at the bill base, lower culmen and nail often showing diffuse dark marks and the slightly darker grey iris. However, some second basic ♂♂ are almost identical to adult ♂♂, and each of these features can be shown by adult.

f   **First-winter** ♂ **formative** (Oct/Jun). This bird has completed its pre-formative moult, with bill colour clearly recalling adult, but has a duller blackish head with a hint of an eye-patch.

g   **Adult** ♀ **definitive basic** (Nov/Apr). Typical head profile, with slight but clear, partially feathered, swelling at the bill base. The shape of the feathering at the bill base is diagnostic, forming a right-angle. The pale patches on the face tend to be more clearly marked in this species compared to the others.

h   **Adult** ♀ **definitive basic** (Nov/Apr).

i   **First-winter** ♀ **formative** (Oct/Jun). Between first spring and the start of second pre-basic moult (Jul–Aug), most birds show bleached plumage, with pale grey-brown body feathers, a whitish belly and very contrasting facial patches.

Siberian Scoter *Melanitta stejnegeri* (see also Plate 61) Text p. 544

j   **Second-winter** ♂ **second basic** (Oct/Apr). Differs from adult in same way as the other species.

k   **First-winter** ♂ **formative** (Oct/Jun). Even during first spring, bill colour should permit separation from the other two white-winged scoters when seen at close range.

l   **Adult** ♀ **definitive basic** (Nov/Apr). Distinctive head shape, with an almost straight line between the forehead and the bill tip. Often shows an extensive orange-reddish patch on the bill-sides. The feathering at the bill base forms a slightly acute angle.

m   **First-winter** ♀ **formative** (Oct/Jun).

n   **Adult** ♀ **definitive basic** (Nov/Apr).

White-winged Scoter

Siberian Scoter

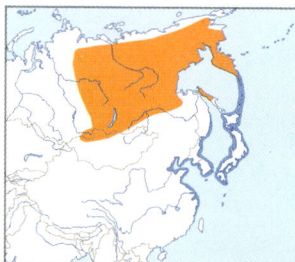

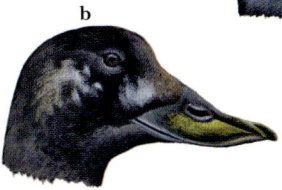

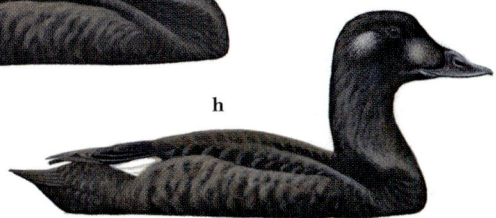

PLATE 63

These two species were long considered conspecific. Adult ♂♂ are rather easy to distinguish in good views, but identification of ♀♀ is harder, or at least, requires close scrutiny. They are usually readily distinguished from other scoters by the absence of white on the wing and/or the head and bill shape.

Black Scoter *Melanitta americana*   Text p. 551

Simple alternate moult strategy (two plumages per cycle?). Clear sexual dimorphism.

a   **Adult ♂ definitive basic** (Nov/Apr).

b   **First-winter ♂ formative** (Nov/Jun). This bird has almost completed pre-formative moult, with some juvenile feathers on the breast, lower flanks, upperwing, tertials and rear body. The bill already has near-adult coloration, but its swollen part is not fully developed yet.

c   **First-winter ♂ formative** (Nov/Jun). A less-advanced bird, with somewhat bleached juvenile feathers.

d   **Adult ♀ definitive basic** (Nov/Apr).

e   **First-winter ♀ formative** (Nov/Jun). When close, the body shows a faint scaly pattern, the bill less yellow and initially without swollen part, and paler cheeks. However, the best ageing feature is the pale belly (o).

f   **Adult ♀ definitive basic** (Nov/Apr). Distinguished by steeper forehead, broader black nape, straight or concave feathering at the bill base (gape salient), bill with swollen upper culmen and more yellow on average, and a slightly more hooked nail.

g–h   **Adult ♂ definitive basic** (Nov/Apr). Head and bill diagnostic, with a rounded head, grey orbital ring and strong yellow-orange bump on the bill base.

Common Scoter *Melanitta nigra*   Text p. 546

Simple alternate moult strategy (two plumages per cycle?). Clear sexual dimorphism.

i–k   **Adult ♂ definitive basic** (Nov/Apr). Note more angular head shape, yellow orbital ring, black band of feathers near the bill, black bulge on upper culmen, more oval nostrils, and yellow patch, variable in extent.

l   **Adult ♀ definitive basic** (Nov/Apr). Note straighter culmen, flatter nail and convex feathering at the bill base. The cheeks are often more stained dusky.

m   **Adult ♂ definitive basic** (Nov/Apr). In equivalent postures, the head and neck are thinner, and the tail is less often held raised.

n   **First-winter ♂ formative** (Nov/Jun). A typical early-winter moult state.

o   **First-winter ♀ formative** (Nov/Jun). For both sexes and all scoters, the best ageing feature is the pale to whitish belly.

Black Scoter

Common Scoter

PLATE 64

Long-tailed Duck *Clangula hyemalis*

Text p. 554

A medium-sized sea duck, usually not difficult to identify. Complex alternate moult strategy (two plumages per adult cycle, three in first cycle). Strong sexual dimorphism in all plumages after first winter. Note that, as in scoters, the wings often hide the flanks between two dives (j–l).

a Adult ♂ definitive basic (Sep–Oct/Mar–May).

b **Adult ♂ definitive basic** (Sep–Oct/Mar–May). This facial appearance is shown in autumn, prior to the previous one (a).

c **Adult ♂ definitive alternate** (Mar–Jul/Sep–Nov).

d **Adult ♂ definitive alternate** (Mar–Jul/Sep–Nov). Appearance in spring on breeding grounds, while other ♂♂ look like the bird in c. The scapulars vary in length, shape and coloration (reddish, buff or whitish at tip).

e **Adult ♂ definitive basic** (Sep–Oct/Mar–May).

f **First-winter ♂ formative** (Oct–Mar/May–Aug). This bird is in almost full juvenile plumage.

g **First-winter ♂ formative** (Oct–Mar/May–Aug). Typical appearance in early to midwinter, already whiter than ♀♀, often with a pale patch on the bill.

h **First-winter ♂ formative** (Oct–Mar/May–Aug). By end of first winter, resembles adult ♂, often with central rectrices moulted (thus shorter than adult ♂). Formative scapulars usually show dark centres and are shorter.

i **First-winter ♀ formative** (Oct–Mar/May–Aug). Scapulars forming a grey patch are typical of this age. Tertials bluntly pointed, shorter and fringed brown (reddish in adult).

j **Adult ♀ definitive alternate** (Mar–Jul/Oct–Dec).

k–m **Adult ♀ definitive basic** (Oct–Dec/Mar–May). Rather variable, with more or less marked blackish patch on cheeks, overall hue grey, brown or reddish, as are scapulars. The bill can be dark grey, bluish or greenish.

Long-tailed Duck

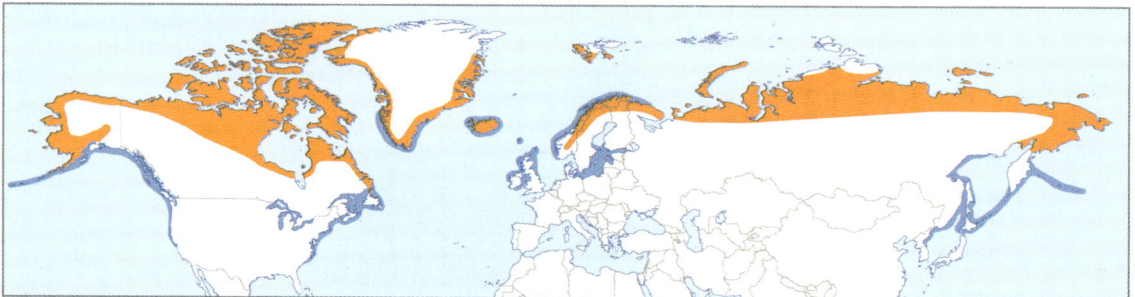

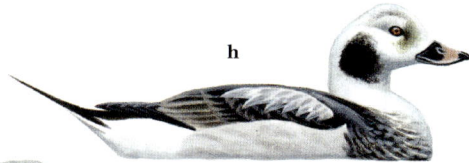

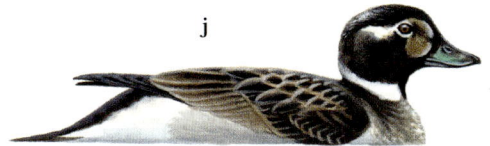

PLATE 65

These two species are relatively similar to one another, but ♂♂ are usually not difficult to separate. The existence of hybrids should be kept in mind though.

Common Goldeneye *Bucephala clangula* (see also Plate 66) Text p. 564

Complex alternate moult strategy (two plumages per adult cycle, three in first cycle) with first pre-alternate moult limited or absent. Strong sexual dimorphism, especially in definitive basic plumage.

B. c. clangula

a **Adult** ♂ **definitive basic** (Oct–Nov/Jun).

b **Adult** ♂ **definitive basic** (Oct–Nov/Jun).

c **First-winter** ♂ **formative** (Nov–Jan/Jun–Aug). Initially resembles ♀, but by late autumn usually shows hint of white facial patch in the otherwise blackish head, iris becoming yellowish-brown and whitish patches on anterior scapulars.

d **First-winter** ♂ **formative** (Nov–Jan/Jun–Aug). After pre-formative moult, resembles dull definitive basic plumage. Iris often pale yellowish outwardly and brownish around pupil.

e **Adult** ♂ **definitive basic** (Oct–Nov/Jun). Note upperwing pattern compared to Barrow's Goldeneye.

f **Adult** ♂ **definitive alternate** (Jun/Oct–Nov). Like adult ♀, but greyer with darker head and basic upperwing retained.

B. c. americana

g **Adult** ♂ **definitive basic** (Oct–Nov/Jun). Note stronger bill. On average, the bill is as deep-based as in Barrow's Goldeneye but distinctly longer. In *B. c. clangula*, the bill averages the same length as Barrow's Goldeneye, but is distinctly thinner at the base.

Hybrid Common Goldeneye *B. clangula* × Barrow's Goldeneye *B. islandica* Text p. 568

Reported regularly in North America, much rarer elsewhere.

h **Adult** ♂ **definitive basic.** Head shape and facial patch closer to Common Goldeneye, but coppery sheen on head and scapulars closer to Barrow's Goldeneye.

i **Adult** ♂ **definitive basic**. Head shape and pattern closer to Barrow's Goldeneye here but, among other features, scapulars too white for that species.

Barrow's Goldeneye *Bucephala islandica* (see also Plate 66) Text p. 572

Complex alternate moult strategy (two plumages per adult cycle, three in first cycle) with first pre-alternate moult limited or absent. Strong sexual dimorphism, especially in definitive basic plumage. [Map on Plate 66]

j–k **Adult** ♂ **definitive basic** (Oct–Nov/Jun).

l **Adult** ♂ **definitive basic** (Oct–Nov/Jun).

m **Adult** ♂ **definitive alternate** (Jun/Oct–Nov).

n **First-winter** ♂ **formative** (Nov–Jan/Jun–Aug). Like Common Goldeneye, shows a succession of plumages intermediate between that of juvenile and adult ♂ until second pre-basic moult.

Common Goldeneye

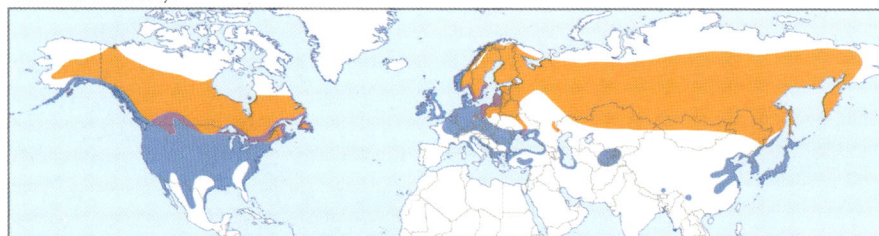

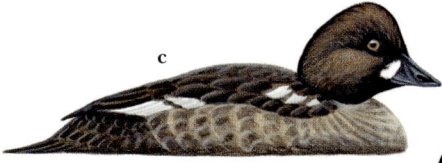

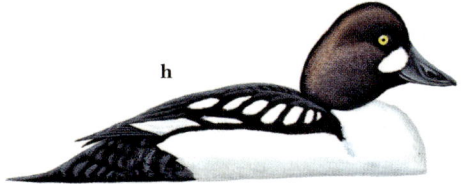

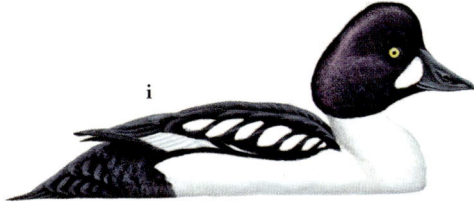

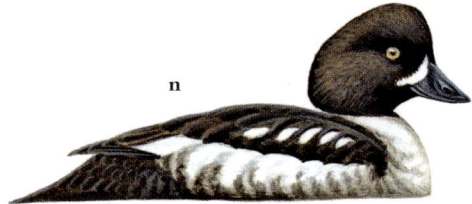

PLATE 66

♀♀ of these species are more difficult to distinguish than ♂♂, but is possible, mainly using head and bill shape, bill coloration and upperwing pattern. Note that head shape is drastically influenced by the position of the feathers. Figures b–d (Common Goldeneye) and h–j (Barrow's Goldeneye) illustrate variations in head shape for both species, with feathers held flat (b & h), e.g. between dives or when alarmed, normally erect (c & i) or strongly erect (d & j). Bill size in Common Goldeneye varies between subspecies as in ♂♂ (nominate subspecies illustrated here). Variation in iris coloration (from golden-yellow to whitish) occurs in both species.

Common Goldeneye *Bucephala clangula* (see also Plate 65)   Text p. 564

a   **Adult ♀ definitive basic** (Nov–Dec/May–Jun).

b–d   **Adult ♀ definitive basic** (Nov–Dec/May–Jun). Note variation in bill pattern, with b and c being the common types. All-yellowish bills are exceptional, and possibly linked to age. When yellow reaches nostrils, it is often more extensive above them than below (compare h).

e   **Adult ♀ definitive basic** (Nov–Dec/May–Jun). Note presence on wing of three white patches separated by black lines, which distinguishes adult ♀ from young ♀ and from both ages of Barrow's Goldeneye.

f   **Juvenile ♀ first basic/first-winter ♀ formative**. Usually no black line formed by tips to greater coverts. A pale greyish patch is formed by the median and posterior lesser coverts (unlike Barrow's Goldeneye).

Barrow's Goldeneye *Bucephala islandica* (see also Plate 65)   Text p. 572

g   **Adult ♀ definitive basic** (Nov–Jan/Jun–Aug). Note darker and warmer head colour, which extends further down upper neck, and greyer breast (vs. Common Goldeneye).

h–j   **Adult ♀ definitive basic** (Nov–Jan/Jun–Aug). Bill brighter yellow-orange, thicker at base and proportionately more triangular, as well as concave lower mandible. Birds in Iceland show a pattern close to h, whereas the other two patterns are typical in North America.

k   **Adult ♀ definitive basic** (Nov–Jan/Jun–Aug). Note upperwing pattern, which distinguishes it both from young ♀ and from Common Goldeneye.

l   **Juvenile ♀ first basic/first-winter ♀ formative**. Underwing-coverts darker than Common Goldeneye (compare f).

Barrow's Goldeneye

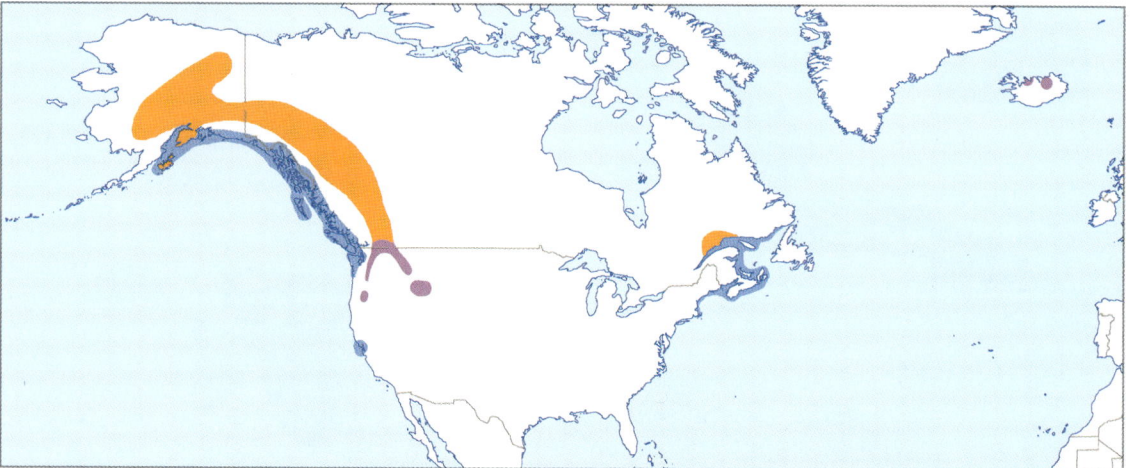

PLATE 67

Smew *Mergellus albellus*

Text p. 576

Unmistakable. Complex alternate moult strategy (two plumages per adult cycle, three in first cycle) with first pre-alternate moult limited or absent. Strong sexual dimorphism, especially in definitive basic plumage.

a–b   **Adult ♂ definitive basic** (Nov–Dec/Jun–Jul).

c   **Second-winter ♂ second basic** (Nov–Dec/Jun–Jul). From adult by greyish tips to longest scapulars and sometimes ill-defined face pattern.

d   **Adult ♂ definitive alternate** (Jun–Jul/Oct–Nov). Closer to ♀ but darker head (often with retained white feathers), darker upperparts, and basic upperwing and often some anterior scapulars retained.

e   **First-winter ♂ formative** (Nov–Jan/Jun–Aug). Juvenile can be sexed as soon as some adult ♂-type feathers appear, generally in the crown (white spots) and around the eye (black). Birds in this plumage often seen in Dec–Feb.

f–g   **Adult ♀ definitive basic** (Nov–Dec/Jun–Jul).

h   **Juvenile first basic/first-winter formative.** Until second pre-basic moult (first summer), age can be determined using the upperwing, which shows a broader white wingbar and trailing edge, and brownish stains within the white wing patch.

i   **First-winter ♀ formative** (Nov–Jan/Jun–Aug). Note smaller and squarer head, lores of same colour as crown, and shorter, brownish, juvenile tertials.

Bufflehead *Bucephala albeola*

Text p. 560

A small diving duck, easily identified. Complex alternate moult strategy (two plumages per adult cycle, three in first cycle) with first pre-alternate moult limited or absent. Strong sexual dimorphism, especially in definitive basic plumage.

j–k   **Adult ♂ definitive basic** (Oct/Jun–Jul).

l   **Adult ♂ definitive alternate** (Jun–Jul/Nov). Closer to ♀ but blacker and whiter overall, without brownish hue, and often some basic feathers retained, on breast, fore flanks and/or anterior scapulars.

m   **First-winter ♂ formative** (Nov–Jan/Jun–Aug). This plumage is typical of early to midwinter, with formative adult-type feathers on head, anterior scapulars, breast and fore flanks.

n–o   **Adult ♀ definitive basic** (Nov/Jun–Aug).

p   **Juvenile first basic** (until Oct–Dec). Much like adult ♀, with a paler throat, smaller whitish patch on head-sides, and pointed, brownish and shorter tertials.

q   **First-winter ♀ formative** (Nov–Jan/Jun–Aug). Young ♀ usually shows no white on greater coverts (vs. young ♂ and adult ♀).

Smew
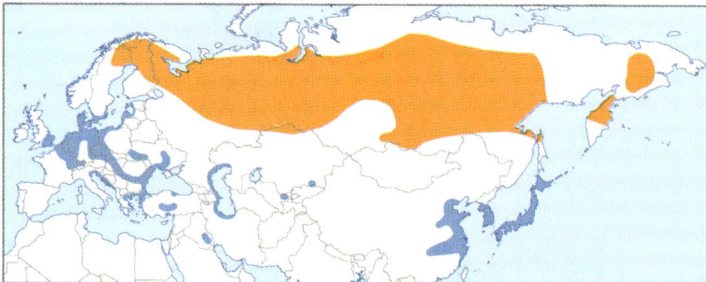

Bufflehead
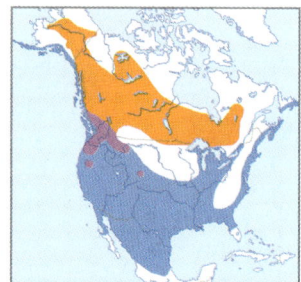

PLATE 68

Hooded Merganser *Lophodytes cucullatus* Text p. 580

Unmistakable. Complex alternate moult strategy (two plumages per adult cycle, three in first cycle) with first pre-alternate moult limited or absent. Strong sexual dimorphism, especially in definitive basic plumage.

a   **Adult ♂ definitive basic** (Oct/May–Jun). The head feathers held flattened here.

b   **Adult ♂ definitive basic** (Oct/May–Jun). When erect, the crest creates a unique head shape.

c   **Adult ♂ definitive alternate** (Jun–Jul/Sep–Oct). Shown here in pre-alternate moult.

d   **Adult ♂ definitive alternate** (Jun–Jul/Sep–Oct). Much like ♀ in full alternate plumage, but sex determined by yellow iris.

e–g   **Adult ♀ definitive basic** (Oct/May–Jun). Note differences in head shape depending on position of feathers.

h   **First-winter ♂ formative** (Oct–Jan/Sep–Oct). Like ♀, but shows ♂-type feathers by mid-autumn (around eye, upper flanks, etc.).

i   **First-winter ♀ formative** (Oct–Jan/Sep–Oct). Like adult ♀, but crest shorter, flank feathers and scapulars narrower and browner, and tertials shorter and without whitish rachis stripe.

j   **Adult ♂ definitive basic** (Oct/May–Jun).

k   **Adult ♀ definitive basic** (Oct/May–Jun). Compared to young birds (l), has more white on greater coverts.

l   **Juvenile first basic/first-winter formative.**

Hybrid Common Goldeneye *Bucephala clangula* × Hooded Merganser *L. cucullatus*

Text p. 582

m   **Adult ♂ definitive basic.**

Hybrid Barrow's Goldeneye *Bucephala islandica* × Hooded Merganser *L. cucullatus*

Text p. 582

n   **Adult ♂ definitive basic.**

Hooded Merganser

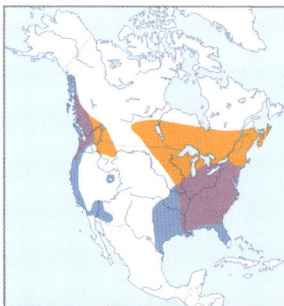

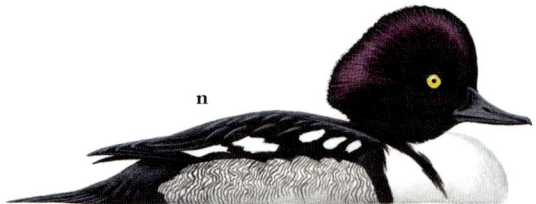

PLATE 69

Scaly-sided Merganser *Mergus squamatus*

Text p. 591

Unmistakable. Complex alternate moult strategy (two plumages per adult cycle, three in first cycle) with first pre-alternate moult limited or absent. Strong sexual dimorphism, especially in definitive basic plumage.

a   **Adult ♂ definitive basic** (Oct–Nov/Apr–May).

b   **Adult ♂ definitive basic** (Oct–Nov/Apr–May). With head feathers erected.

c   **Adult ♂ definitive basic** (Oct–Nov/Apr–May).

d   **Adult ♂ definitive alternate** (May–Jun/Sep–Oct.). Like ♀ but head and upperparts darker, and white upperwing and tertials clearly visible.

e   **Adult ♀ definitive basic** (Oct–Nov/Apr–May?). Easily distinguished from other mergansers by scaly pattern on flanks and long crest.

f   **Adult ♀ definitive basic** (Oct–Nov/Apr–May?). Note pale grey area in front of white greater coverts. Ageing based on upperwing pattern like in Red-breasted Merganser (h, k, m & o).

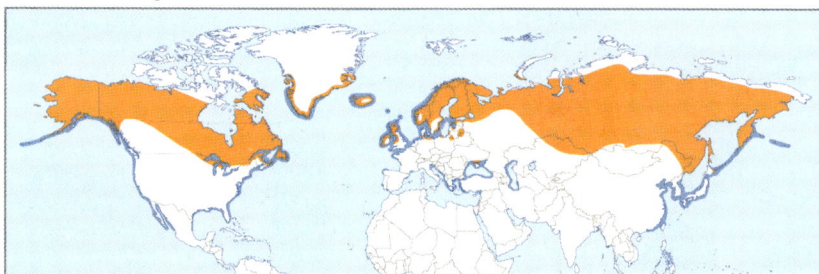

Red-breasted Merganser *Mergus serrator*

Text p. 595

♀♀ and juvenile can be mistaken for those of Scaly-sided Merganser and Goosander, but distinguished by size, head shape, bill shape and by lack of contrast between neck and breast. Complex alternate moult strategy (two plumages per adult cycle, three in first cycle) with first pre-alternate moult limited or absent. Strong sexual dimorphism, especially in definitive basic plumage.

g   **Adult ♂ definitive basic** (Nov–Dec/Apr–May).

h   **Adult ♂ definitive basic** (Nov–Dec/Apr–May).

i   **Adult ♂ definitive alternate** (May–Jun/Oct–Nov). Resembles ♀ but, as in other mergansers, head and upperparts darker, and white upperwing and tertials retained.

j   **Adult ♀ definitive basic** (Nov–Dec/Apr–May). Crest often forms two separate tufts.

k   **Adult ♀ definitive basic** (Nov–Dec/Apr–May). Note dark bar on tips of greater coverts.

l   **First-winter ♂ formative** (Aug–Sep/Jul–Aug). By late autumn or early winter, adult-type formative feathers appear on head.

m   **First-winter ♂ formative** (Aug–Sep/Jul–Aug). Bar on greater coverts is almost absent.

n   **First-winter ♀ formative** (Aug–Sep/Jul–Aug). Note shorter crest, lores more striped and juvenile brownish tertials.

o   **First-winter ♀ formative** (Aug–Sep/Jul–Aug). Dark bar on greater coverts often faint or partial as shown here.

Scaly-sided Merganser

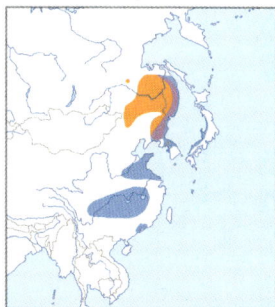

Red-breasted Merganser

PLATE 70

Goosander (Common Merganser) *Merganser merganser* Text p. 584

♀♀ and juvenile can be mistaken for those of Scaly-sided and Red-breasted Mergansers, and are distinguished by larger size, head shape, stronger bill and clear-cut contrast between neck and breast. Three subspecies recognised, identified using head and bill shape, feathering at the base of the bill and upperwing pattern. Complex alternate moult strategy (two plumages per adult cycle, three in first cycle) with first pre-alternate moult limited or absent. Strong sexual dimorphism, especially in definitive basic plumage.

M. m. merganser

a　**Adult ♂ definitive basic** (Nov–Dec/Apr–May).

b　**Adult ♂ definitive basic** (Nov–Dec/Apr–May). Compared to *americanus*, note greater coverts appear all white.

c　**Adult ♂ definitive basic** (Nov–Dec/Apr–May). Note feathering at base of bill is acutely pointed, reaching almost halfway between gape and proximal end of nostril. Also, strongly hooked nail, concave culmen and steep, 'bumped' forehead.

d　**Adult ♂ definitive alternate** (May–Jun/Oct–Nov). Resembles ♀ but, as in other mergansers, head and upperparts darker, with white inner upperwing and tertials.

e　**Adult ♀ definitive basic** (Nov–Dec/Apr–May). Note clear-cut throat and contrast between neck and breast (good species characteristic). Tertials are rounded at tips, pale grey with black outer fringes at this age.

f　**Adult ♀ definitive basic** (Nov–Dec/Apr–May). The only plumage with a clear black bar formed by the tips to the greater coverts.

g　**First-winter ♂ formative** (Aug–Sep/Jul–Aug). Resembles adult ♀, but note formative adult-type feathers appearing around eye, on lores, among scapulars (pale-centred grey feathers) and on flanks (whitish vermiculated grey).

h　**First-winter ♂ formative** (Aug–Sep/Jul–Aug). Usually no dark bar at tips of greater coverts but a diffuse pale area in front of them.

i　**First-winter ♀ formative** (Aug–Sep/Jul–Aug). Note pale iris in autumn and browner juvenile tertials.

j　**First-winter ♀ formative** (Aug–Sep/Jul–Aug). Often shows trace of dark bar on greater coverts and no pale grey area on median and lesser coverts.

M. m. comatus

k–l　**Adult ♂ definitive basic** (Nov–Dec/Apr–May). Thin bill with concave culmen, reduced red on lower mandible, feathering at bill base almost vertical and crest appears longer and flatter.

M. m. americanus

m–n　**Adult ♂ definitive basic** (Nov–Dec/Apr–May). Note slimmer head and thicker bill with a short nail, feathering at the bill base is almost vertical making the pinkish-red base more striking, even on the lower mandible.

o　**Adult ♂ definitive basic** (Nov–Dec/Apr–May). Note blackish bar at base of greater coverts.

p　**Adult ♀ definitive basic** (Nov–Dec/Apr–May). Like ♂, identified by bill shape and feathering at base of bill.

q　**Adult ♀ definitive basic** (Nov–Dec/Apr–May). Upperwing as in *merganser*.

Goosander

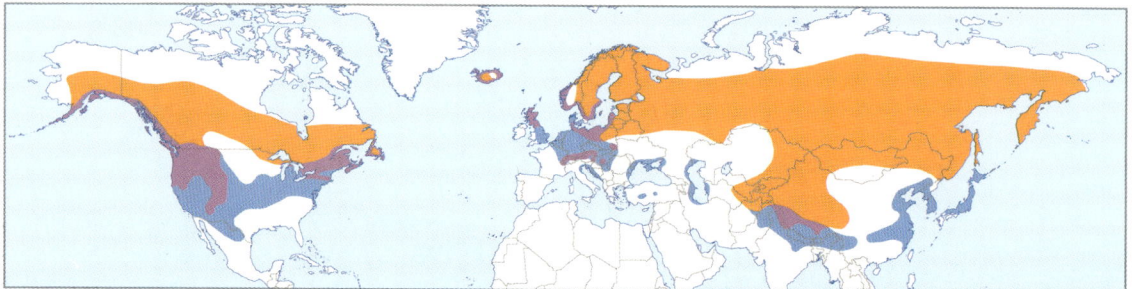

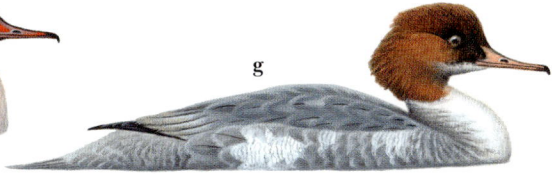

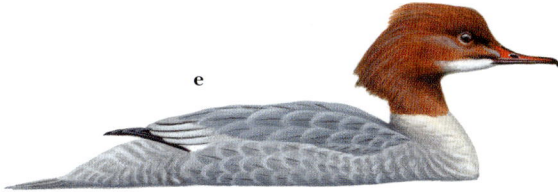

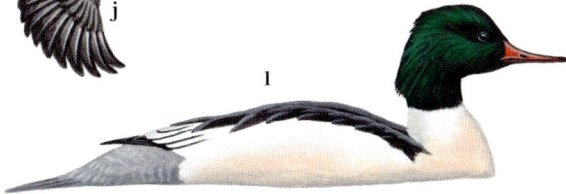

PLATE 71

White-headed Duck *Oxyura leucocephala* (see also Plate 72)   Text p. 610

In Europe, can be mistaken for the introduced Ruddy Duck (♀ and juvenile), and their hybrids. Complex alternate moult strategy (two plumages per adult cycle, two or three in first cycle). Unlike other Anseriformes treated here, alternate plumage is worn during breeding even by ♂ in all stifftails (see text). Strong sexual dimorphism, especially in definitive alternate plumage.

a   **Adult ♂ definitive alternate** (Apr–May/Aug–Sep). Such birds correspond to dark morph described in Spain.

b   **Adult ♂ definitive alternate** (Apr–May/Aug–Sep).

c   **Adult ♂ definitive basic** (Aug–Dec/Apr). Similar to alternate plumage, but head darker and bill blackish.

d   **First-winter/first-summer ♂ formative** (Nov–Mar/Apr–Jun.). Like alternate adult, but head more spotted dusky, often has all-blackish nape and bill less swollen at base.

e   **First-winter/first-summer ♂ formative** (Nov–Mar/Apr–Jun). In first spring and subsequent summer, head can be almost entirely black.

Ruddy Duck *Oxyura jamaicensis* (see also Plate 72)   Text p. 604

Complex alternate moult strategy (two plumages per adult cycle, two or three in first cycle), and alternate plumage is worn during breeding even by ♂ (see text). Strong sexual dimorphism, especially in definitive alternate plumage. [Map on Plate 72]

f   **Adult ♂ definitive alternate** (Mar–Apr/Aug–Sep).

g   **Adult ♂ definitive alternate** (Mar–Apr/Aug–Sep). Note tufts shown by ♂ in courtship.

h   **Adult ♂ definitive alternate** (Mar–Apr/Aug–Sep). All-black head variant, occurs both in North America and among introduced birds in Europe.

i   **First-winter/first summer ♂ formative** (Nov–Feb/Apr–Jun).

j   **Adult ♂ definitive basic** (Sep–Nov/Mar–Apr). More like ♀ but cheeks entirely white.

k   **Adult ♂ definitive basic** (Sep–Nov/Mar–Apr). Note whitish or silvery belly in this species.

l   **First-winter ♂ formative** (Nov–Feb/Apr–Jun). Like ♀, but often has some reddish feathers on upperparts, and cheeks whiter.

Hybrid Ruddy Duck *O. jamaicensis* × White-headed Duck *O. leucocephala*   Text p. 613

Six different types of hybrids shown, including some described and photographed by Urdiales & Pereira[1299].

m   **Adult ♂ definitive alternate**. A backcross with Ruddy Duck.

n–o   **Adult ♂ definitive alternate**. Two different types of first-generation hybrids.

p–q   **Adult ♂ definitive basic**. Two different types of first-generation hybrids.

r   **Adult ♂ definitive alternate**. A backcross with White-headed Duck.

White-headed Duck

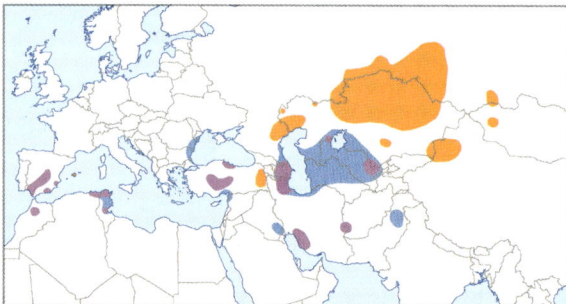

PLATE 72

White-headed Duck *Oxyura leucocephala* (see also Plate 71)   Text p. 610

Much closer to Ruddy Duck in ♀ and juvenile plumages. Distinguished by larger size, more contrasting head pattern, swollen bill, feathering at base of bill straight or concave (convex in Ruddy Duck), longer tail and no or only faint contrast between flanks and upperparts. [Map on Plate 71]

a   **Adult ♀ definitive basic** (Aug–Dec/Apr).

b   **Adult ♀ definitive basic** (Aug–Dec/Apr). A dark morph as reported from Spain.

c   **Adult ♀ definitive alternate** (Apr–May/Aug–Dec). In summer, the head can be very dark.

d   **Juvenile/first-winter/first-spring ♀ first basic/formative** (Nov–Mar/Apr–Jun). Initially, bill is much less swollen at base, and head pattern is paler and greyer than in alternate ♀. During first winter, age much harder to determine, and preferably requires close scrutiny of rectrices.

Ruddy Duck *Oxyura jamaicensis* (see also Plate 71)   Text p. 604

e   **Adult ♀ definitive alternate** (Mar–Apr/Aug–Sep). This plumage appears browner, plainer and has a warmer hue.

f   **Adult ♀ definitive basic** (Sep–Nov/Mar–Apr).

Hybrid Ruddy Duck *O. jamaicensis* × White-headed Duck *O. leucocephala*   Text p. 613

g–h   **Adult ♀ definitive basic.** These hybrids constitute real pitfalls, but close scrutiny should reveal that they do not properly match either parent species.

Masked Duck *Nomonyx dominicus*   Text p. 600

♀ and juvenile plumages can be mistaken for those of Ruddy Duck. Complex alternate moult strategy (two plumages per adult cycle, two or three in first cycle), and alternate plumage is worn during breeding even by ♂ (see text). Strong sexual dimorphism, especially in definitive alternate plumage. Depending on the (variable) breeding season, the different plumages may be encountered year-round.

i–j   **Juvenile ♀ first basic** . Note pale yellowish-buff overall plumage, appearing more streaked than spotted. The broad pale tips to the scapulars are diagnostic of this age.

k   **Adult ♀ definitive alternate**. A darker and warmer plumage.

l   **Adult ♀ definitive basic**. This 'non-breeding' plumage appears darker and duller, with the upperparts finely spotted pale yellowish.

m   **Adult ♂ definitive basic**.

n   **Adult ♂ definitive alternate**. The neck is swollen during courtship.

o   **Adult ♂ definitive alternate**. The extent of white on the upperwing distinguishes adult from first-year bird.

Ruddy Duck (native)

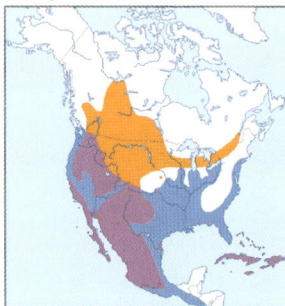

Masked Duck

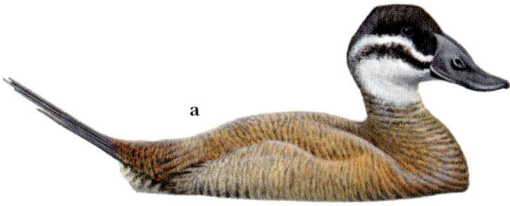

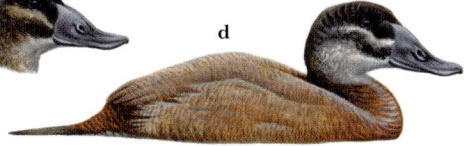

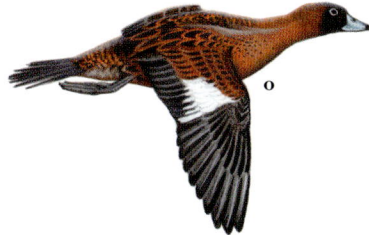

BLACK-BELLIED WHISTLING-DUCK
Dendrocygna autumnalis   **Plate 1**

TAXONOMY *Anas autumnalis* Linnaeus, 1758, *Syst. Nat.*, edn. 10, p. 127. Long considered the morphologically close relative of White-faced Whistling-duck *D. viduata*[769] but recent molecular studies reveal it to be closer to West Indian Whistling-duck *D. arborea*[534]. Until recently, birds in South America were considered to represent subspecies *D. a. discolor*, with the nominate subspecies north of the Isthmus of Panama. Friedmann[405] proposed to split northern populations into two subspecies: *D. a. fulgens* in Texas and NE Mexico and *D. a. lucida* further west and south to Panama. James & Thompson[626] pointed out that the type specimen of the species originated from South America, and that this population should therefore be named *autumnalis*, *fulgens* being used by the same authors for North and Central American populations. Differences between *fulgens* and '*lucida*' seem too weak to merit subspecific differentiation (see Geographic Variation).

IDENTIFICATION Unique colour pattern among whistling-ducks makes this species unlikely to be misidentified: the only species with pink legs, a reddish bill, black belly and, in flight, two broad white wingbars. Only two congenerics encountered within its range, White-faced Whistling-duck *D. viduata* and Fulvous Whistling-duck *D. bicolor*, both very different.

PLUMAGES *D. a. fulgens*. Sexes similar. Complex basic moult strategy (no seasonal change).

Adult male

Definitive basic plumage (year-round). Crown dark rufous extending as a vertical blackish line down the hindneck. Sides of head, throat and upper neck grey, variably tinged brown or yellowish. Dark brown iris, appearing black, with a large white eye-ring. Bill pale pink to reddish with a yellow area on the culmen and a pale grey nail. Breast, lower neck and upperparts (mantle and back) cinnamon-red. Scapulars same colour, centred dull brown to slate-grey. Tertials dark brown. Rump dark reddish-brown merging into the black lower rump and tail. Underparts (flanks and belly) entirely black, clearly delineated from breast. Lower belly and undertail black with strong white markings. Upperwing: tertial coverts grey, leading edge blackish brown, lesser coverts yellowish-brown fringed pale, median coverts pale grey to whitish, greater coverts and primary coverts white,

alula black fringed grey on the outer web. Primaries and secondaries black with a white stripe on the inner web, extending further on each feather towards the outer wing (*c.* half of length on outer primaries). Underwing all black, including axillaries. Legs bright pink.

Adult female

Definitive basic plumage (year-round). Sexing difficult but possible if both members of pair seen side by side. ♀ is slightly duller, with underparts duller black, browner ear-coverts and darker pink legs[1014].

Juvenile

First basic plumage (until Nov–Dec). Like very dull adult. Head pale greyish-brown, with a blackish line from the forehead and crown own the nape to the mantle. Clear-cut white eye-ring. Dark brown iris. Lead-grey bill with a darker nail, quickly becoming paler. Pale brown to beige breast, warmer on neck-sides. Pale belly looks neatly streaked and flank feathers centred dark, giving a well-marked overall appearance. Lower belly and undertail-coverts whitish stained blackish. Upperparts (including tertials) warmer cinnamon-brown. Upperwing as adult, but whitish basal parts of remiges smaller and less clear-cut, and greater coverts speckled grey, producing a slightly narrower and less contrasting wingbar. Lesser coverts more uniform, without pale fringes. Greyish legs, becoming pink during early winter.

First-winter/first-summer

Formative plumage (Dec–Feb/Aug). Pre-formative moult occurs between Aug–Oct and Jan–Mar, many birds showing two generations of feathers simultaneously. At the same time, the bare parts acquire their definitive colours. Following pre-formative moult (variable in extent), similar to adult, but most birds still have at least scattered juvenile feathers on the upperparts, breast, rump and especially the belly, which typically appears mottled. Except a few inner primary coverts and median coverts, the wing is fully juvenile until the second pre-basic moult (first-summer). Outer primaries are narrower, more pointed and frayed, and often browner, at the tips.

Second-winter

Second basic plumage (year-round). Following second

pre-basic moult, some birds may be aged by a few juvenile feathers retained on the belly until Dec[1014].

GEOGRAPHIC VARIATION Two subspecies widely accepted, with probable intergrades in Central America. Nominate *autumnalis* from South America best distinguished from *fulgens* by its slightly greyer upperparts and broad pale grey breast-band between the reddish upper breast and black belly. Moreover, *autumnalis* is slightly smaller, with shorter legs. Another subspecies described, '*lucida*', is very close to *fulgens*, with underparts said to be more uniform black. Individual variation within *autumnalis* and *fulgens*, including age- or sex-related, make these differences of little use.

MEASUREMENTS and MASS *D. a. autumnalis*. Bolen *in* Kear[160]: wing chord 227–259 (242) and tarsus 47–59 (52) (*n*=160). Bourne[165]: mass 530–890, with a mean 741 for ♂♂ and 725 for ♀♀.

D. a. fulgens. North America. ♂ adult (*n*=80): wing chord 243–260 (adult) and 235–252 (juvenile), culmen 48–56, bill depth at distal end of forehead feathering 21.6–24.2, tarsus 56–65; adult ♀ (n=80): wing chord 237–256 (adult) and 231–248 (juvenile), culmen 46–55, bill depth at distal end of forehead feathering 21.2–23.7, tarsus 55–63[1014]. Adult tail: 65–76, mass: 680–907 (816)[159].

VOICE Flocks often noisy and chattering, in flight as well as on the ground. The typical call comprises 4–6 squeaky whistled syllables: *tut-tweeet-tut-twee-twee-doo*, the second being longest and loudest. The distress call is a repeated *pieew*.

MOULT (North America). Complex basic strategy. Young birds begin their pre-formative moult between Aug and Oct, mainly on the wintering grounds. The extent of this moult is variable, sometimes limited to a few body feathers, especially in late broods. Usually, it includes most body feathers, 0–3 tertials, some inner primary coverts and median coverts, and all rectrices, replaced before Jan–Mar[1014]. The formative feathers are retained until the next pre-basic moult, which is similar in timing to the adult (definitive) pre-basic moult, between Aug and Oct–Dec. No pre-alternate moult, or alternate (eclipse) plumage.

HYBRIDISATION Hybrids reported with West Indian Whistling-duck, Fulvous Whistling-duck and White-faced Whistling-duck[817]. Natural hybrids with the latter

occur very occasionally in South America[238,817]. Outside its native range, escaped birds may hybridise with other whistling-duck species, e.g. Plumed Whistling-duck *D. eytoni*[802]. Hybrids involving Black-bellied Whistling-duck should not be difficult to identify, as the parents look very different.

HABITAT and LIFE-CYCLE Arrives at their breeding sites in Mar (S Texas), and in Apr in northernmost parts of its range[626]. Breeding habitats include shallow freshwater marshes, lakes and ponds, especially those surrounded by riparian woods with dead trees. Unlike Fulvous Whistling-duck, often perches on dead branches, rooftops, powerlines, and favours tree holes to nest, or nestboxes if available. Migrants depart breeding areas between Aug and Oct. Like other whistling-ducks, very gregarious in non-breeding season, gathering in noisy flocks at wetlands, often near meadows, lawns and golf courses. Faced with a predator or other danger, the whole group simultaneously adopts an upright and alert posture.

RANGE and POPULATION Nominate subspecies occurs over much of South America. Further north, *fulgens* is found along the Pacific coast to Sonora, Mexico. The first breeding record in Baja California, Mexico, was in 2005[1136]. In the Gulf of Mexico, the species reached S Texas during 20th century, and subsequently Louisiana and Florida (where first bred 1990), while recent breeding records in South Carolina (2003), Arkansas and SE Arizona reflect ongoing range expansion[516,647,626]. Some of these populations may have benefited from escapees or introduction schemes (Louisiana). Rare or vagrant further west and north in the USA, including California, Minnesota, New York and even Ontario, Canada. Mainly sedentary within its breeding range, but northernmost populations move south in winter, gathering in huge flocks, mainly using coastal marshes such as in S Texas. Population (*fulgens*) estimated at 100,000–1,000,000 individuals.

CAPTIVITY Both subspecies are kept in captivity, but in Europe much less frequently than Fulvous and White-faced Whistling-ducks. The nominate subspecies is sometimes present in captivity in North America, and does escape there.

REFERENCES Bolen (1964)[159]; Bolen *in* Kear (2005)[160]; Bourne (1979)[165]; Coimbra-Filho (1965)[238]; Dale & Thompson (2001)[276]; Friedmann (1947)[405]; Harrigal & Cely (2004)[516]; Harshman (1996)[534]; James & Thompson (2001)[626]; Johnsgard (1979)[647]; Johnsgard (2010)[648];

Livezey (1995)[769]; Marchant & Higgins (1990)[802]; McCarthy (2006)[817]; Pyle (2008)[1014]; Sauma *et al.* (2005)[1136]; Wetlands International (2014)[1348].

1. *D. a. fulgens*, adult (definitive basic). Texas, USA, Feb (Tom Grey).

2. *D. a. fulgens*, adult (definitive basic). Texas, USA, Feb (Sébastien Reeber).

3. *D. a. fulgens*, adult (definitive basic); note typically downward-stretched neck on landing (common to all *Dendrocygna*). Florida, USA, Aug (Ron Bielefeld).

4. *D. a. fulgens*, adult (definitive basic); note long well-defined white tongues on primaries at this age. Texas, Jan (Alan D. Wilson).

5. *D. a. fulgens*, juvenile (first basic); note grey bill and legs, and pale brownish underparts at this age. Mexico, Aug (Steve Mlodinow).

6. *D. a. fulgens*, first-winter (formative); ill-defined white tongues on outer primaries (worn at tips) and bill flecked dusky at this age. Florida, USA, Mar (Ron Bielefeld).

FULVOUS WHISTLING-DUCK
Dendrocygna bicolor

Plate 2

TAXONOMY *Anas bicolor* Vieillot, 1816, *Nouv. Dict. Hist. Nat.*, Nouv. Édn. 5, p. 136. Only slight geographic variation despite huge range on four continents. No subspecies.

IDENTIFICATION There is little risk of confusion with other whistling-ducks, and even less with other wildfowl. Only Lesser Whistling-duck *D. javanica* could be confused, especially juveniles, as their ranges overlap in SE Asia. Adult Lesser Whistling-duck is easily separated by the lack of long, white, arrow-shaped feathers on the flanks, by the plain neck and much duller head and neck. In addition, at any age, the wing is slate-grey with dark red lesser coverts, as are the uppertail-coverts (white in Fulvous Whistling-duck). In Oceania, shows a very superficial resemblance to Wandering Whistling-duck *D. arcuata*, especially in juvenile plumage. Note that adult-type plumage is acquired very quickly in whistling-ducks, often before independence. Thus, juveniles are most likely to be seen in direct company of adults.

PLUMAGES Sexes similar. Complex basic strategy (one plumage per definitive cycle, two in the first cycle). A typical whistling-duck, with a proportionately long neck, short body and long legs. In flight, shape very different from other ducks, with broad and rounded wings, and feet extending well beyond the tail. On landing, spreads legs and stretches neck towards the water.

Adult male

Definitive basic plumage (year-round). Orangey head, with whitish chin and throat. Crown and lores darker brown, extending as a brown line down the neck. Dark brown iris. Bluish-grey bill with blackish nail. Rows of white feathers on sides of neck recall the grooves shown by most grey geese *Anser* spp. The lower neck, chest and underparts are orangey, except the white lower belly and undertail. The upper row of flank feathers are elongated and pointed, with a broad white line in their centres. At a distance, these form large, oblique, more or less neatly-arranged stripes. The upperparts are blackish, with broad reddish fringes to the feathers of the mantle and scapulars, giving a roughly barred appearance. Rump and tail black, separated by the whitish to pale buff uppertail-coverts. The underwing, including axillaries, is blackish. Upperwing blackish,

with thin reddish fringes to the primary coverts and median coverts. Long, dark grey legs, projecting far beyond the short tail in flight.

Adult female

Definitive basic plumage (year-round). Similar to ♂, but has slightly duller plumage and by a broad dark stripe down hindneck from the crown (broken on the nape in ♂). Furthermore, ♀ usually appears somewhat less pot-bellied[84]. These differences are subtle and most useful in direct comparison. No difference in measurements.

Juvenile

First basic plumage (until Oct–Dec). Duller, with fringes to scapulars and mantle feathers thinner, paler and ill-defined, sometimes barely visible. Juvenile upperparts and flank feathers are narrower and more rounded at the tips, with a looser texture. Also note dirty pale brownish uppertail-coverts, which is a useful feature in flight.

First-winter/first-summer

Formative plumage (Nov–Mar/Jun–Jul). Once the pre-formative moult is completed (end of first winter), barely distinguishable from adult. Look for moult contrast among the tertials, secondary coverts and rectrices. Retained juvenile feathers appear worn, pointed and bleached compared to blacker and broader formative feathers. Moreover, second-year birds keep their juvenile primaries, which in spring and summer typically appear narrow, usually noticeably worn and bleached. The fringes of the scapulars usually appear slightly darker and browner than in adult.

GEOGRAPHIC VARIATION No recognised subspecies. Slight, poorly understood geographic variation despite a huge range on four continents. Birds in North and Central America have sometimes been treated as a separate subspecies, *D. b. helva*, mainly because said to be a little paler, with a shorter and thinner bill than South American populations. These differences seem too subtle and inconsistent to deserve subspecific rank[577,1014]. Genetic studies of the different populations may provide further information.

MEASUREMENTS and MASS ♂♂ on average very slightly larger and heavier than ♀♀. More significant differences in wing length by age.

North America. ♂: wing chord 209–220 (217, *n*=8), culmen 44–50 (46, *n*=8), tarsus 54–60 (57.5, *n*=8); ♀: wing chord 212–220 (216, *n*=4), culmen 45–49 (47, *n*=4)[945]. ♂ (*n*=100): wing chord 204–224 (adult) and 198–219 (juvenile), culmen 43–49, bill depth at distal end of forehead feathering 19.3–21.9, tail 45–59, tarsus 53–61; ♀ (*n*=100): wing chord 200–222 (adult) and 194–216 (juvenile), culmen 42–48, bill depth at distal end of forehead feathering 18.9–21.5, tail 42–56, tarsus 52–60[1014]. ♂: mass 545–958 (770.5, *n*=138); ♀: 595–964 (743.3, *n*=148)[577]. *Africa.* ♂ (*n*=12): wing chord 202–242 (216), culmen 43.1–48.1 (46.2), tarsus 52.1–57.2 (54.2); ♀ (*n*=15): wing chord 203–235 (217), culmen 41.5–50 (46.1), tarsus 50.1–58.9 (54)[197]. *Trinidad.* ♂: wing chord 209–238 (228, *n*=10), tarsus 54.6–59.9 (57.7, *n*=11), mass 790–1,050 (921.4, *n*=11); ♀: wing chord 212–238 (224.3, *n*=10), tarsus: 52.1–59.4 (56.5, *n*=11), mass 770–1,000 (905, *n*=11)[629].

VOICE Flocks often noisy, like all whistling-ducks. Most frequent calls have 2–3 syllables, *pit-weeoo, pit-pit-weew* or *pit-weee*. The last syllable is slightly louder, longer and less resonant in ♀[197]. Other calls less conspicuous, e.g. a repeated *kup kup kup*. In flight at night, easily recognised by its voice and whistling sound produced by the wingbeats.

MOULT (*North America*). Complex basic strategy. Pre-formative moult starts upon arrival on non-breeding grounds in Aug–Oct, and lasts until the end of the first winter. It includes most of the body feathers, none to a few inner lesser coverts and median coverts, 0–3 tertials and usually all rectrices[1014]. In some birds (especially those hatched in summer or which did not undertake normal southward migration), more juvenile feathers are retained. Pre-basic moult is complete, also starting upon arrival on wintering grounds in Jul–Oct, and completed by Jan. Some juvenile feathers (body and secondary upperwing-coverts) may be retained through the second pre-basic moult, meaning that some birds can by aged (in hand) until the beginning of the third calendar year. Moult timing varies regionally, depending on the breeding and wet seasons. In E & S Africa, the pre-formative and definitive pre-basic moults occur in Apr–Jul[197,234].

HYBRIDISATION Natural hybridisation exceptional, the few reported cases often involving escaped birds, outside the ranges of the parent species, but reported in the wild with White-faced Whistling-duck *D. viduata*[235,439,817], including a mixed pair in W France that produced three fledglings. In captivity, hybridisation mentioned more frequently, with White-faced Whistling-duck, West Indian Whistling-duck *D. arborea*, Wandering Whistling-duck *D. arcuata*, Black-bellied Whistling-duck *D. autumnalis*, Plumed Whistling-duck *D. eytoni* and Lesser Whistling-duck[97,817].

HABITAT and LIFE-CYCLE North American migrants arrive on the breeding grounds between mid-Feb and mid-Apr. Frequents both fresh and brackish wetlands, preferring shallow marshes with much emergent vegetation. Favours the proximity of tall grass or wet meadows, as well as rice fields, where locally said to cause damage[629]. Nests on floating or emergent aquatic vegetation. Eggs laid mainly early Apr to early Jul, sometimes until late Aug[577]. Outside the breeding season moves in loose groups, unlike most ducks and geese. Noisy day and night, often mixes with other whistling-ducks where two or more species co-exist. In India, often seen in the company of Lesser Whistling-duck, the latter being by far more abundant. Unlike Black-bellied Whistling-duck, does not frequently perch on dead branches, rooftops, boardwalks, etc.

RANGE and POPULATION The only whistling-duck with such an extensive distribution but disjunct populations. The Asian population extends from S & E India to Myanmar, and comprises *c*.50,000 birds[1348]. In Africa, found south of the Sahel, outside forested regions, with *c*.1.1 million birds[1095], but more recent estimates are of 170,000–390,000[1348]. Vagrants reported Morocco and Spain, but probably not a natural visitor so far north, due to regular escapees from captivity, including occasional breeding records. In South America, present in the eastern and northern lowlands, south to N Argentina. Absent from Central America. Further north, from C Mexico to Texas and Louisiana, the Greater Antilles and more recently in Florida, where it is now abundant. Small numbers or rare in S California and S Arizona. Casual visitor over much of the USA (especially in the south-west and the Atlantic coast), north to British Columbia, Alberta, Quebec and Nova Scotia, Canada[648]. The North American population on the W Gulf coasts winters mainly in S Mexico[629]. Overall, the Neotropical population is estimated at one million birds[1095], and is declining due to hunting in rice-growing regions [629].

CAPTIVITY Common and frequently encountered in collections. Easy to maintain and breed, and usually offered at low prices (often the cheapest whistling-duck). Very likely to escape from captivity. Observations far outside normal range should therefore be treated with caution.

REFERENCES Bell (1997)[84]; Bird Hybrids Database (2014)[97]; Bottjer (1983)[163]; Brown *et al.* (1982)[197]; Clancey (1967)[234]; Clark (1974)[235]; Delacour (1954–64)[295]; Gillham & Gillham (1996)[439]; Harshman (1996)[534]; Hohman & Lee (2001)[577]; Jarrett *in* Kear (2005)[629]; Johnsgard (1961)[640]; Johnsgard (2010)[648]; Livezey (1995)[769]; Livezey (1996)[774]; McCarthy (2006)[817]; Palmer (1976)[945]; Perennou (1992)[964]; Pyle (2008)[1014]; Rose & Scott (1997)[1095]; Wetlands International (2014)[1348].

7. Adult (definitive basic); broad blackish bar on nape typical of ♀. France (escaped), Jun (Sébastien Reeber).

8. Adult (definitive basic). France (escaped), Jun (Sébastien Reeber).

9. Adult (definitive basic); note black underwing pattern shared by all whistling-ducks. Texas, USA, May (Greg Lavaty).

10. Adult (definitive basic); in flight, white uppertail-coverts distinctive (vs. Lesser Whistling-duck *D. javanica*). Texas, USA, May (Greg Lavaty).

11. Adult (definitive basic). Florida, USA, Apr (Ingo Waschkies).

LESSER WHISTLING-DUCK
Dendrocygna javanica

Plate 3

TAXONOMY *Anas javanica*, Horsfield 1821, *Trans. Linn. Soc. Lond.* 13, p. 199, pl. 1. Considered the sister species of Wandering Whistling-duck *D. arcuata*, based on morphological[769] and genetic[534] characters. No geographic variation or subspecies.

IDENTIFICATION Only two other whistling-ducks occur in the range of this species: Fulvous Whistling-duck in S India and Myanmar, and Wandering Whistling-duck in Indonesia (Borneo and Java). Easily distinguished in good conditions. Compared to Fulvous Whistling-duck, stockier and smaller, head and underparts duller (beige) and has less pronounced vertical stripe on neck. Lesser Whistling-duck has slate-grey upperparts without orangey crescents, but large deep red areas on the leading edge of the wings (lesser coverts). In flight, reddish uppertail-coverts often visible. Wandering Whistling-duck is closer in size and shape, but distinguished by its brighter orange underparts, obvious white arrows on the upper flanks (like Fulvous Whistling-duck), the scaly upperparts (pale fringes to the scapulars), breast finely spotted black, contrast between the dark crown and cheeks, and black bill. In flight, note the browner uppertail-coverts. From below, Wandering Whistling-duck has an orangey-brown belly, separated from the blackish underwing by a broad white line (the upper flanks), whereas Lesser Whistling-duck has a grey-beige and paler belly, reaching the blackish underwing.

PLUMAGES Sexes identical. No alternate (eclipse) plumage. The smallest whistling-duck, with a stubby shape and a short neck. In flight, typically stockier than congenerics, with broad rounded wings.

Adult

Definitive basic plumage (year-round). Grey-beige at a distance. Forehead, crown and nape dark grey-brown, contrasting slightly with the beige cheeks, neck and breast. Chin and throat marginally paler. Dark brown iris with a diagnostic yellow orbital ring. Blue-grey bill, somewhat paler near forehead, rest of culmen blackish. Belly and flanks washed pale orange, the upper flanks showing small white shafts (much shorter and less conspicuous than in Fulvous Whistling-duck). Lower abdomen and undertail-coverts white. Mantle and scapulars brownish-grey to slate-grey, with buff fringes, becoming paler and thinner towards the rear. Tertials uniform slate-grey. Back and rump grey-brown, uppertail-coverts deep reddish. Tail blackish. Upperwing rather pale slate-grey, except reddish lesser coverts and darker trailing edge. Underwing black. Legs and feet blue-grey.

Juvenile

First basic plumage (until Nov–Jan?). Plainer and slightly duller than adult, especially the underparts (tinged yellowish or greyish, less orangey) and uppertail-coverts and lesser coverts (more brownish). Scapulars more rounded with thinner, browner and more ill-defined pale fringes. These differences are most obvious in direct comparison, which is often possible, as most young birds do not achieve independence before the first winter.

First-winter/first-summer

Formative plumage (Nov–Feb/Aug?). The extent of the pre-formative moult in the wild is still unclear and probably varies in timing depending on region. In India, the moult seems very similar to that of Fulvous Whistling-duck. Like the latter, the distinction between young birds that have undertaken an extensive pre-formative moult from the adult can be difficult. Ageing possible by the presence of juvenile feathers especially among the tertials, secondary coverts and rectrices.

GEOGRAPHIC VARIATION None described.

MEASUREMENTS and MASS ♂ marginally larger. ♂: total length 325–340, head 83–87, tail 53–60; ♀: total length 325–330, head 80–84, tail 50–55[1350]. Both sexes: wing chord 170–204 (187), tail 53–55 (54), culmen 38–42 (40), tarsus 40–50 (45), mass 450–600 (525)[11]. Sample size not specified in either work.

VOICE Recalls Fulvous Whistling-duck. Several different high-pitched whistles, including a somewhat dissonant *teeeh*, *wee-wee-oo* or a softer, chattering *dee-dee-dee*, especially in flight or when taking off. Produces a lower *kwak* too. The wings produce a soft rustle, especially on take-off.

MOULT Few specific data on the extent of pre-formative moult in the wild, even its timing, or on that of definitive pre-basic moult. Timing is obviously influenced by that of breeding, which is variable, for example between India and Sri Lanka (depending on the monsoon). Pre-formative moult probably follows fledging, which in India occurs between Sep and Dec.

HYBRIDISATION The only hybridisation event documented in the literature was with Fulvous Whistling-duck, and occurred in captivity[1190].

HABITAT and LIFE-CYCLE Inhabits brackish to freshwater wetlands, but prefers ponds, marshes and shallow oxbows, with substantial aquatic vegetation and often fringed by trees. Also seen in flooded fields, rice fields, mangroves, and artificial tanks near villages, but avoids open lakes and streams, especially if reedbeds, aquatic or riparian vegetation is absent. Often rests in small groups on islands or dead branches. In India, eggs are laid Jun–Sep, sometimes as late as Nov[150], depending mainly on the monsoon. Nests can be sited on the ground or just above it, in dense vegetation or reedbeds, but usually several metres high in a tree, in old nests of crows or raptors, or in a cavity[1350]. Mass movements may occur after fledging, especially depending on rainfall and regional flooding, and the resultant water levels. In non-breeding season, often seen with Fulvous Whistling-ducks where their ranges overlap, but Lesser Whistling-duck is usually far more numerous.

RANGE and POPULATION Widespread in S Asia and W Indonesia. The commonest species of sedentary Anseriformes in SE Asia and still abundant over much of its range[228,1223]. However, it is declining due to excessive hunting and habitat destruction in many parts of its range. The global population was estimated at 233,000 individuals in 2003–07 [757], with other estimates of 100,000–1,000,000 birds for both S & SE Asia[1095,1348].

CAPTIVITY Common in captivity or as a pet within its range, but more rarely kept elsewhere in Asia, Europe and North America, particularly because of its sensitivity to cold and the fact that it rarely breeds. Not frequently offered for sale, and usually much more expensive than other whistling-ducks.

REFERENCES Ali & Ripley (1987)[11]; Blanford (1898)[150]; Choudhury *in* Kear (2005)[228]; Harshman (1996)[534]; Hillgarth & Kear (1982)[558]; Li *et al.* (2009)[757]; Livezey (1995)[769]; Rose & Scott (1997)[1095]; Sibley (1938)[1190]; Sonobe & Usui (1993)[1223]; Wetlands International (2014)[1348]; Whistler (1949)[1350].

12. Adult (definitive basic). India, May (Anand Arya).

13. Adult (definitive basic); in flight, deep red uppertail-coverts distinctive (vs. Fulvous Whistling-duck *D. bicolor*). India, Mar (Sunil Singhal).

14. Adult (definitive basic). India, Feb (Julien Gonin).

15. Adult (definitive basic). India, Feb (Sunil Singhal).

SWAN GOOSE
Anser cygnoid

TAXONOMY *Anas Cygnoid* Linnaeus, 1758, *Syst. Nat.*, edn. 10, p. 122. Usually placed in the genus *Anser*, but in many respects differs from the other species therein. Has sometimes been placed in its own genus, *Cygnopsis*, sister to *Anser* and *Chen*[772]. Along with Greylag Goose *A. anser* and their hybrids, this goose is the ancestor of *c.*20 domestic races, including the most widespread, Chinese Goose. No geographical variation or subspecies.

IDENTIFICATION A large brownish goose similar in size to Greylag Goose, but more slender with a unique two-tone head and neck, and a thick, long and straight bill grading into the rather flat forehead. In flight, the neck seems long and is often held slightly upwards. Unlikely to be confused, but be mindful of the many, more or less domestic, hybrids resembling this species.

PLUMAGES Sexes similar, ♂♂ being slightly larger and heavier than ♀♀, which is often visible within pairs. Note also that ♀ has shorter neck and bill and a thinner head. Complex basic moult strategy (one plumage per definitive cycle).

Adult

Definitive basic plumage (year-round). Plumage dark brown, tan-beige and white. Head and neck bicoloured with a clear-cut delineation. Lores and crown chestnut-brown extending as a dark brown stripe down the hindneck. Cheeks pale ochre to beige. A narrow white band encircles the bill base (including forehead), on average more pronounced in ♂. Iris warm chestnut-brown. Bill notably long with a straight culmen, and slightly spatulate and elongated nail, entirely charcoal-black. Foreneck whitish merging into pale ochre breast. Flanks and belly creamy, with white fringes to the upper/rear flank feathers forming regular vertical streaking and a broad white line encircling the flanks, like all 'grey geese'. Mantle pale brown to beige. Broad square-tipped scapulars, dark brown with a faint blackish subterminal band and sharp white fringe, the latter forming neat barring on the upperparts. Tertial coverts and tertials broad, rounded at tips, dark brown fringed white. Lower belly, undertail- and uppertail-coverts white. Tail has a brown bar at base, rump and back dark brown. Upperwing grey (including primary coverts) with darker brown inner median coverts and remiges. Primaries blackish towards tips with clear white rachis. Greater underwing-coverts and remiges dark grey to blackish, rest of coverts and axillaries paler grey. Legs and feet bright orange.

Juvenile

First basic plumage (until Oct–Dec). Like definitive basic plumage, but note smaller size and more slender shape, often obvious in direct comparison with adult. Also note significantly shorter bill (but quite thick, or even has slightly swollen culmen) until early first winter. The delineation between the dark brown and beige tones of the head and neck is less sharp and the white band encircling the bill base is lacking. As in other grey geese, juvenile scapulars are narrower, round-tipped, and duller brown with yellowish to pale brown fringes, affording the upperparts a scaly appearance. The flanks are more uniform, without the dark and white barring at the rear. The legs are pale brownish or yellowish-orange.

First-winter/first-summer

Formative plumage (Nov–Jan/Aug). Until early winter, juvenile feathers are usually visible at close range, especially on the rear flanks and/or scapulars. Once pre-formative moult is completed, close inspection should reveal juvenile feathers on the belly, contrasting with the surrounding formative (adult-like) breast and flank feathers. Until first summer, note narrower juvenile primaries and rectrices becoming frayed at tips and worn, often paler and browner than in adult. At same time, at least most secondary coverts are still juvenile, more rounded and worn at the tips, without subterminal dark bars and browner, more diffuse pale fringes.

GEOGRAPHIC VARIATION None.

MEASUREMENTS and MASS Few data published from the wild. ♂ (*n*=4): wing chord 460–473, culmen 89.0–98.5, tarsus 80–82; ♀: wing chord 437–445 (*n*=4), culmen 87.0 (*n*=1), tarsus 80–82[308,794]. ♂: mass *c.*3,500; ♀: 2,850–3,450 (samples not specified)[646].

VOICE The commonest call is a prolonged *an-ang*, very nasal and close to that given by the various forms of Chinese Goose. Also utters a *gaa* or *gang* similar to Bean Goose *A. fabalis*, mainly in flight, on take-off or when alert.

MOULT Complex basic strategy. Few data on the moult of this species in the wild, but the available information and that obtained from captive birds suggests that the moult strategy is identical to those of other strictly migratory grey geese. It is not well known if pre-formative moult is suspended or delayed during the coldest months and completed in late winter. Definitive pre-basic moult starts with the flight feathers, mainly in Jul–Aug (earlier for non-breeders[918,1271]). Moulting birds gather in large flocks near open water or on large tidal mudflats[456,1327].

HYBRIDISATION Reported with Greylag Goose within its Asian range, but hybrids are probably mostly escapees (sometimes of a domestic form) or the product of feral populations. Furthermore, a free-flying population is established in Germany, including many hybrids[1036]. Backcrosses frequently reported too, but only 50–60% of eggs hatch[817]. First-generation hybrids are usually easy to separate from their parents, having obviously mixed characters. The bill often looks quite long with variable orange and black colouring. Hybridises with other species in the wild very occasionally, e.g. Bean Goose[496,717] and Snow Goose *Chen caerulescens*[465,496,817]. Hybridisation has sometimes been mentioned (involving escapees, most of them domestic forms) with Bar-headed Goose *A. indicus* in Germany (see that species), Canada Goose *Branta canadensis*[817] and perhaps Barnacle Goose *B. leucopsis*[128,585]. In captivity, hybridisation described with Mute Swan *Cygnus olor*, Spur-winged Goose *Plectropterus gambensis*, Greater White-fronted Goose *Anser albifrons*, Hawaiian Goose *Branta sandvicensis*, Egyptian Goose *Alopochen aegyptiacus*, Muscovy Duck *Cairina moschata* and Mallard *Anas platyrhynchos* (only one of 38 fertile eggs hatched[1378])[817]. This list is obviously not comprehensive, and it should be kept in mind that the vast majority of domestic individuals show more or less marked hybrid features. Many reported cases of hybridisation are unlikely to have involved 'pure' Swan Geese.

HABITAT and LIFE-CYCLE Arrives on breeding grounds between late March and early May, slightly earlier than other geese[902,918], eggs being laid between early May and early Jun[1271]. Inhabits a wide variety of habitats, whether lowlands, high plateaux or mountains, steppe or forested areas, near fresh or brackish marshes and ponds, even steep-sided, fast- or slow-flowing rivers. Adults moult their flight feathers on the breeding grounds, and are able to fly again at the same time that their offspring fledge. Before fledging, young may gather in crèches in areas of high breeding density[210,1002]. Departure from the breeding areas occurs when both adult and young birds are able to fly, in Aug–Sep. A study using GPS tags on 25 birds in NE Mongolia found that the birds moved in Aug towards the mouth of the Yalu River, in the N Yellow Sea and stayed there several weeks before heading to wintering sites in the Yangtze Valley in Dec[74]. Other birds may, however, arrive much earlier, by mid-Oct. During migration, uses a wide variety of habitats, even dry steppes far from water. In winter, prefers shallow lowland wetlands, marshes, floodplains, lakes, rice fields, mudflats in estuaries and coastal bays[138,772]. Most leave the wintering grounds between early Feb and late Mar[74,210,902,918,1002,1271].

RANGE and POPULATION Four distinct breeding populations. The first breeds in NE & C Mongolia, the second in extreme NE Mongolia and neighbouring China, the third at Lake Khanka on the Sino-Russian border in Manchuria, and the last in the lower Amur Valley and N Sakhalin. Formerly mentioned in E Kazakhstan, but probably extirpated there[455,772]. Possibly breeds in NE North Korea too[138]. The bulk usually winters near Lake Poyang, Jiangxi, and in Anqingyanjiang and Shengjinhu reserves, Anhui[757]. A few dozen winter in South Korea. Scarce visitor to Japan and Taiwan. Current population estimated at 60,000–80,000 individuals[138], and has markedly declined during recent decades, being considered Endangered by BirdLife International[138]. Recent counts in the 2000s yielded 70,000 at Lake Poyang, which would raise the global population to 100,000–120,000 birds[757]. However, major changes (wrought by droughts caused by the construction of the Three Gorges Dam) have occurred there in recent years and may threaten this major wintering site for many wildfowl species in E Asia, including Swan Goose[74]. In addition, there has been heavy hunting pressure at migration stop-over, breeding and wintering sites, eggs and goslings are harvested, and there is massive habitat loss throughout the range, mainly for agriculture and development. A Russian/Japanese joint conservation programme was initiated in 2000 with the participation of China, Japan, South Korea and Mongolia[452,1004]. Feral populations exist in Europe (Netherlands, England, Ireland, Sweden and Germany, where 140 free-flying birds were counted near Heidelberg[1037]).

CAPTIVITY Birds belonging to one or other of the many domestic races, more or less hybridised with Greylag Goose, are abundant in captivity and sometimes establish small semi-domestic or feral populations. 'Pure' Swan Geese are much rarer, because they tend to hybridise readily in captivity, and they also seem susceptible to gizzard worm infections. Observations of this species outside its normal range require much caution to eliminate the possibility of a hybrid.

REFERENCES Batbayar *et al.* (2011)[74]; Bird Hybrids Flickr Forum (2010)[128]; BirdLife International (2001)[138]; Callaghan *in* Kear (2005)[210]; Dementiev & Gladkov (1952)[308]; Gombobaatar *et al.* (2003)[452]; Goroshko (2001)[455]; Goroshko (2003)[456]; Gray (1958)[465]; Hachisuka (1928)[496]; Hopkinson (1933)[585]; Johnsgard (1978)[646]; Kuroda (1924)[717]; Li *et al.* (2009)[757]; Livezey (1996)[772]; McCarthy (2006)[817]; Madge & Burn (1988)[794]; Nechaev (1992)[902]; Nowak (1970)[918]; Poyarkov (1984)[1002]; Poyarkov (2006)[1004]; Randler (2003)[1036]; Randler (2004)[1037]; Tkachenko (1995)[1271]; Voronov & Pronkevich (1991)[1327]; Yamashina (1953)[1378]; Zhang *et al.* (2011)[1385].

16. Adult (definitive basic); note unique bill size and shape among geese, as well as bicoloured head and neck. Captivity (Sébastien Reeber).

17. Adult (definitive basic). Mongolia, Jun (Matthieu Vaslin).

18. Adult (definitive basic). Mongolia, Jun (Matthieu Vaslin).

19. Adult (definitive basic). Mongolia, Jun (Matthieu Vaslin).

BEAN GOOSE
Anser fabalis

Plates 4, 5, 8

TAXONOMY *Anas Fabalis* Latham, 1787, *Gen. Synopsis Birds*, Suppl. p. 297. A polytypic species, genetically closely related to the other six species of *Anser*[1103]. Forms a superspecies with *A. brachyrhynchus*. The taxonomic organisation of this complex has long been discussed, and further research seems needed to fully understand it. Evolution of the taxonomic units within this group has been fully addressed recently[1102]. The number of species recognised in this group has varied between one and six, with up to eight different subspecies. Pink-footed Goose *A. brachyrhynchus* has sometimes been placed in *A. fabalis*[1232], but is now widely accepted as a separate monotypic species.

Many taxa were described based on abnormal birds, such as those with white chin patches (*mentalis* Oates, 1899), flesh- or rose-coloured (rather than the normal orange) bare parts[636] (*neglectus* Sushkin 1897) or a rosy bill and orange legs (*carneirostris* Buturlin, 1901). These birds are now considered rare variants that can occur in all subspecies[294,1102]. *A. f. curtus* Lönnberg, 1923 was separated from *serrirostris* by its darker crown, neck and forehead. Ruokonen & Aarvak[1102] studied seven specimens from China and Mongolia; these were genetically similar to *serrirostris/rossicus*, with an intermediate-length nail, and it is possible that *curtus* represents an intergrade population between the two tundra subspecies.

Until recently, Bean Geese were generally split into two groups across the Palearctic: the taiga group, including three taxa from west to east (*fabalis*, *johanseni* Delacour, 1951, and *middendorffii* Severtzov, 1872), and the tundra group including *rossicus* Buturlin, 1933, and *serrirostris* Swinhoe, 1871. This view was first promulgated by Johansen[637] and adopted by numerous authors thereafter. Several studies conducted recently in Europe, especially in the Netherlands, have confirmed the morphological and ecological differences between the two groups[207,1307,1309], e.g. Burgers *et al.*[207], who studied 12,176 birds caught in the Netherlands between 1954 and 1986, concluded that there are clearly two distinct groups, despite the existence of strong variation within both. However, Liebherr & Rutschke[759], having analysed 1,114 birds in the hand in Germany between 1987 and 1991, were more cautious, and deemed the distinctions very difficult, particularly because of frequent overlap in the different features. Van Impe[1309] studied the ecology of the two groups on the Dutch wintering grounds and found obvious differences between them. Burgers *et al.*[207] also showed, via the distribution of 154 summer sightings and recoveries of banded geese from the Dutch wintering grounds, that the two forms nest in different geographical regions, indicating strong reproductive isolation. In E Palearctic, Ogilvie & Young[928] consider intergradations between the two groups to be unlikely, but Yokota *et al.*[1380] estimated that 10–20% of Bean Geese wintering in Japan are intermediates between *serrirostris* and *middendorffii*, at least under field conditions.

Sangster & Oreel[1130] proposed to split *fabalis* and *rossicus* into two species, the first including *fabalis*, *johanseni* and *middendorffii*, and the second *rossicus* and *serrirostris*. They also assumed that clinal variation in both species from west to east (see Geographical Variation) is not linked to subspecific differentiation, and therefore considered both species to be monotypic: *A. fabalis* and *A. serrirostris*. This split was accepted in North America by the AOU[67]. On the other hand, Mooij & Zöckler[868] considered *A. fabalis* as a single species with four subspecies, which treatment has been adopted in Europe by the AERC-TAC.

More recently, further genetic studies have been conducted on the *fabalis/brachyrhynchus* complex[1108], sampling 199 birds from 14 geographical areas within the breeding range. The authors of this molecular phylogeny recognised three species: *A. brachyrhynchus*, *A. middendorffii* and *A. fabalis*, the first two being monotypic with small degrees of genetic and morphological variation. Here, *A. fabalis* is considered a polytypic species including *rossicus*, *serrirostris* and the nominate subspecies, the latter appearing to constitute an almost monophyletic group within the species. The same study highlighted the distinctiveness of *middendorffii*, based on both genetics and morphology, although stating the need for bi-parentally inherited nuclear markers to corroborate their interpretation.

Simultaneously, the status of *A. f. johanseni* has been questioned[207,544,868,1130]: *johanseni* has been described as resembling *fabalis* but larger and longer-billed with yellow-orange restricted to a band just behind the nail, or thought to be intermediate between *fabalis* and *middendorffii*, and to interbreed with *rossicus* northward[294]. Based on extensive work, Emel'yanov[361] included '*johanseni*' within *fabalis*. Heinicke[544] studied a small population, numbering 2,000–5,000 individuals, wintering in C Asia and clearly belonging to subspecies *fabalis*. This is supported by two recoveries of Taiga Bean Geese ringed in the Netherlands, and shot in the Sayan Mts, just south-west of Lake Baikal. However, Ruokonen & Aarvak[1102] found two individuals from C Russia that both genetically and morphologically matched *middendorffii*. Ruokonen *et al.*[1108] did not recognise this taxon because they did not find any *middendorffii* haplotypes in 150 birds studied from Europe, whereas this should have been the case if interbreeding between *fabalis* and *middendorffii* was extensive. Intermediates could be the result of interbreeding between *fabalis* and *middendorffii*, where their breeding range meet or overlap, but this is rather unlikely (see below). Equally, *johanseni* could also be a stable 'hybrid' population, or represent the western end of clinal variation in *middendorffii* or could be explained both by interbreeding and by convergent evolution towards *fabalis*.

There are undoubtedly four valid taxa into the Bean Goose complex: *rossicus* (Tundra Bean Goose), *serrirostris* (Thick-billed Bean Goose), *fabalis* (Taiga Bean Goose) and *middendorffii* (Middendorff's Bean Goose). The tundra (*rossicus*/*serrirostris*) and taiga groups (*fabalis*/*middendorffii*) appear to be well segregated, by breeding and wintering habitat, genetically and by morphology. However, the number of species within this group is still discussed. The extent of interbreeding between the four taxa is still unclear. Furthermore, it would be useful to know if genetically intermediate birds occur. Pending further research, the treatment adopted here is a single polytypic species.

IDENTIFICATION Bean Goose is a rather variable species, especially in size and shape, bill size, shape and colour, and head and neck coloration. Both eastern taxa *serrirostris* and *middendorffii* have a dark and heavy bill, usually with a small yellow-orange patch that distinguishes them from the other large species in E Asia, Greylag Goose *A. anser* and Greater White-fronted Goose *A. albifrons*, and the latter in North America.

In Europe and W Asia, Taiga Bean Goose *A. f. fabalis* should be easily separated from other species too. Compared to Greylag Goose, which can be similar in size, it is more slender, with a thinner neck when stretched. Also note the overall darker and more brownish colour, bill generally black (at least the nail), and usually orange (not pink) legs, even if the light and distance may be misleading, especially with young birds whose bare parts are duller. Compared to juvenile Greater White-fronted Goose *A. albifrons*, which can also

show a black nail on a pale bill, note the larger size, the more elongated shape and the longer bill. Some adult Bean Geese can have a variable amount of white at the bill's base, although never as much as an adult Greater White-fronted Goose. Some first-winter Greater White-fronted Geese show limited white at the bill's base, especially above it. These can be separated from Bean Goose by their overall uniform juvenile plumage, an age at which Bean Goose does not show any white around the bill base.

Identification is trickier when distinguishing Tundra Bean Goose *A. f. rossicus* from Pink-footed Goose *A. brachyrhynchus*. At close range, they are easily told apart, especially if the orange legs and bill patch of the Bean Goose are visible. Nevertheless, it should be kept in mind that bare-parts colour can be safely checked only in good light, and that very rarely some Bean Geese can have rosy rather than orange parts, and conversely some Pink-footed Geese can show orange legs[196]. Size is not very useful, but shape differs, although is only easily used with experience. Tundra Bean Goose has a more slender body, with a longer neck, longer legs and more angular head shape, with a heavier bill. It is browner and darker overall, further differing from Pink-footed Goose by the lack of contrast between the flanks and upperparts, and an ill-defined contrast between the head and lower neck. In flight, Bean Goose shows a unique pattern that makes its identification relatively easy. Both under- and upperwings are darker than in Greylag and Pink-footed Geese, with only poor contrast between the coverts and remiges, especially in Tundra Bean Goose. All subspecies show a broad blackish tail bar that distinguishes them from both other species.

The juvenile, as seen on the wintering ground from autumn, has an overall less patterned plumage, with more scaly upperparts, and dullish bare parts. Juvenile Bean Goose can be distinguished from Pink-footed Goose at the same age by the darker plumage, especially the head and rear flanks, and by head and bill shape. The bare-parts colours are quickly acquired during the first winter.

PLUMAGES Sexes similar, but slight differences in size, stance and behaviour are useful for sexing within pairs. The male is slightly larger, has a thicker neck and a more upright posture when alert, and is frequently aggressive towards other geese. Complex basic moult strategy (one plumage per definitive cycle, two in the first cycle). Ageing easy until the end of first autumn, and with more careful examination until the end of the following spring.

Adult

Definitive basic plumage (year-round). The head and upper neck are medium chocolate-brown, being very dark in poor light. A faint ring of white feathers sometimes encircles the bill (with occasionally a few small patches above it, and sometimes a continuous line surrounding the entire bill base). This was once thought to be a reliable feature to separate *rossicus* from *fabalis*[73], but even if it is more frequent in *fabalis*, all four taxa can show it. Iris brown, encircled by an inconspicuous pale orbital ring. The bill is long, not swollen at the base, with a typically concave upper mandible and an almost flat lower mandible in profile. The nail is on average shorter than in all other taxa. The 'grinning patch' is also distinctive, as it is half as wide and as long as in *rossicus*. At a distance, the 'grinning patch' is often invisible on *fabalis*, whereas it is often visible in *rossicus*. The bill colour is more variable in this subspecies than all others, ranging from almost entirely yellow-orange (almost always paler than the legs) to blackish with a small pale subterminal band encircling the mandibles (exceptionally, only the upper mandible). In the Netherlands, *c.*20% of wintering birds have an orange bill with black restricted to the nail and part of the culmen[207]. The most frequent pattern consists of a black proximal half to the culmen, up to the nostrils, with yellow along the cutting edges and a black nail. The dark head continues over the neck and nape, but the foreneck is paler, approaching the beige colour of the breast. Dark streaks (formed by the feathers being arranged in grooves) are visible on the sides of the neck, as in all other grey geese. The belly is pale, highlighting the darker flanks in flight. The rear flanks appear almost black. Lower belly, under- and uppertail-coverts white. The tail has a broad blackish bar, contrasting with the white rump and narrow white terminal band. Mantle, scapulars, tertials and upperwing-coverts brown with white fringes forming a succession of thin broken lines on the upperparts. Back dark brown. Upperwing dark grey-brown with lesser coverts and primary coverts slightly paler grey. Tips of median coverts and greater coverts white forming thin wingbars. Remiges dark grey with blackish tips. Underwing grey-brown, lacking clear contrast. The legs and feet are a deep orange. Rarely, the orange colour of the bill and/or legs is replaced by a rosy colour.

Juvenile

First basic plumage (until Oct–Nov). Slightly smaller and more slender than adult. Resembles adult in plumage, but more uniform overall, with a paler and slightly more yellowish-brown ground colour. Head pattern slightly more contrasting, with paler cheeks and darker nape and rear crown. The upperparts feathers are narrower, rounded at the tips, and show duller pale fringes that are not restricted to the tips, creating a typically reduced scaly appearance, rather than the white-streaked adult upperparts. The flanks are poorly marked, lacking the broad blackish and thin pale crescents of the adult. Also note that young birds do not show any white at the base of the bill. Legs paler and duller than in adult, often tinged brownish-yellow until first winter. Bill shorter than in adult, gradually growing during first year of life. The yellow-orange and blackish pattern of the adult is initially completely obscured but is gained progressively during the first winter.

First-winter/first-summer

Formative plumage (Nov–Apr/Aug). The young bird undertakes its first southward migration in juvenile plumage, and starts moulting on migration or even soon after arrival on the wintering grounds. Pre-formative moult can be protracted into late winter. By Nov–Dec, young birds are generally still easy to age by the juvenile features of late autumn. The mix of juvenile and formative feathers affords an untidy aspect to the upperparts and flanks. Look especially for the 'U-shaped' scapulars with buff fringes between the formative ones, which are more adult-like (square-tipped with a clear-cut white fringe at the tip). Bare-parts coloration is almost like that of adult by Mar–Apr. Thereafter, ageing can require very close inspection to spot some juvenile scapulars or mantle feathers between the formative ones. Also look for the abraded, faded and more pointed primaries, secondary upperwing-coverts and rectrices, the latter strongly abraded and typically notched at the tip.

Second-winter

Second basic plumage (Sep–Aug). Generally indistinguishable from adult after second pre-basic moult, but some birds may retain a few greater coverts. More study needed.

GEOGRAPHIC VARIATION There is significant variation across this species' range, with four taxa being safely identifiable. The following sections describe the typical appearance of each subspecies. However, it is essential to bear in mind that there is some variation within each taxon, and that intermediates occur. It is always easier to identify small parties or family groups (families often remain intact until the subsequent spring), which permit a better assessment of the different features, based on the average appearance. If two different subspecies are seen in the same group, this will allow interesting comparisons. It is more difficult to identify lone birds or vagrants, and sometimes impossible when faced with atypical birds.

A. f. rossicus. Differs from *fabalis* by size, shape, head and bill pattern, and slightly different coloration. In Europe, most birds should be distinguishable in good conditions. It is nonetheless useful to bear in mind that size, shape and bill are the most useful clues, and that these also vary with age and sex. Therefore, individual differences within a group do not generally signify the presence of different subspecies. In W Europe for example, *rossicus* and *fabalis* present different ecological traits, and most flocks of both subspecies are monospecific. A. f. *rossicus* is c.20% smaller than *fabalis*, with some overlap. The shape is typically stockier, with a shorter neck and relatively longer legs. Head shape differs in being more squared or rounded than oval, with a more angular nape, higher crown and steeper forehead, clearly forming a break with the culmen line. The neck is often held straight when stretched, compared to the gentle bend shown by *fabalis* and *middendorffii* in most postures. The bill appears thick and triangular, accounting for c.40–43% of total head length[196]. Very similar to *fabalis* in plumage, but slightly darker overall, especially the head and cheeks, making the eyes often less conspicuous at a distance than in *fabalis*. Overall coloration colder brown, lacking any gingery or cinnamon tones to the breast, neck and head, which are sometimes visible in *fabalis* and usual in *middendorffii*. The tail-band is reportedly blacker and reaches closer to the tail tip, leaving a very thin white terminal band. The bill is, on average, very slightly deeper-based and shorter, but there is overlap. The lower mandible generally looks concave and the culmen straight or convex. The yellow-orange patch is generally restricted to a band between the nail and the nostrils, often running up along the cutting edges, but as Burgers et al.[207] stated, c.5% of Tundra Bean Geese show some yellow on at least half of the bill, matching typical *fabalis*. The same authors did not find any *rossicus* with an almost or entirely yellow-orange bill, whereas this occurred in 20% of *fabalis*. Another useful clue is the 'grinning patch' between the mandibles, if seen closely. It is thicker and shorter in *rossicus*, and far more obvious than in typical *fabalis*. Although it requires close inspection, the bill is a key element, and in the majority of birds is usually sufficient to distinguish the two

western subspecies. Also note that the patch on the bill often looks orange in *rossicus*, but slightly paler yellow in eastern subspecies. Legs as *fabalis*, but on average very slightly shorter.

A. f. serrirostris. In differentiating it from *rossicus*, consider size as well as bill shape and colour. The differences between *serrirostris* and *middendorffii* are similar to those separating *fabalis* from *rossicus* in Europe, although bill coloration is not very useful. Size close to *fabalis*, but with a *rossicus*-type shape: proportionately short thick neck and high, angular or squared head. Forehead less steep than in *rossicus* due to the bill's depth at its base, but still more clearly marked than in *middendorffii*. In alert posture, usually not too difficult to separate from *middendorffii* by the shorter neck, higher and larger head, and conical bill, often held slightly upward. The bill is on average very slightly longer than in *fabalis*, and as deep as *middendorffii*, affording the head a hefty appearance, and represents c.33–37% of the head's total length (vs. c.50% in *middendorffii*). Other very useful clues are the deep, oval-shaped 'grinning patch', the markedly concave lower mandible base and straight or convex culmen that can sometimes appear rather swollen, especially in juveniles whose bill is not fully developed. Also note that at close range, the line formed by the edges of the upper mandible is rounded. The yellow patch is restricted to a band just behind the nail, sometimes reaching the nostrils, but is generally less extensive than in *rossicus*. Very rarely, some birds show a slightly larger yellow patch, and almost entirely yellow bills are reported very exceptionally. Plumage as *rossicus* or slightly paler overall. Subtly darker and colder than *middendorffii* but this is only useful in direct comparison. Head usually distinctly darker brown, more strongly contrasting with the breast, the eyes being inconspicuous at mid-range.

A. f. middendorffii. Typical birds have a very distinctive size, shape and head/bill pattern. It is nevertheless worth noting that some birds in E Asia do not clearly match any taxon, appearing intermediate between *middendorffii* and *serrirostris*, closer to the latter in their size and short neck, but resembling *middendorffii* in rather pale plumage and gentle head shape. The bill is intermediate in length, depth and culmen outline. Such birds have been regarded as westernmost populations of *middendorffii* or as '*johanseni*'[423], but this seems questionable as the influence of *fabalis* does not appear convincing. By far the largest Bean Goose subspecies, 30–50% heavier than Greylag Goose, but some overlap in size with *serrirostris*. Typical birds show a distinctly elongated and handsome shape, with the long neck often held gently curved. As in *fabalis* vs. *rossicus*, the head is typically slimmer, oval-shaped and longer, with a flatter crown, forming a smooth curve without obvious angles. The flattened forehead line continues without a break into the long bill. Head and neck shape may be astonishingly reminiscent of Whooper Swan *Cygnus cygnus*. When quiet, the bill is often held downwards, and horizontally when alert (tilted upwards in *serrirostris*). Bill structure is also useful for identification: *middendorffii* has a very long and thick bill, which represents about half of total head and bill length. The culmen is usually straight, or slightly convex over its proximal half, and when seen in profile the lower mandible's basal two-thirds bulge below the chin and the tip. The lower mandible accounts for c.30% of bill depth at its midpoint, vs. 20–25% in *fabalis*[196]. The 'grinning patch' is similar in height to *serrirostris*, but appears much longer, with the edges of both mandibles more parallel. The yellow patch is usually restricted to a small band behind the nail, not reaching the nostrils. As this patch is on average smaller than in *serrirostris*, and the bill is longer in *middendorffii*, the yellow patch usually appears closer to the bill's tip, well beyond its midpoint. Plumage paler overall than *serrirostris*, with a slightly warmer tinge on breast, neck and head (gingery), and paler head (eyes often clearly visible, even at long range). Underwing very slightly less uniform, due to dark axillaries contrasting slightly with the paler median coverts.

MEASUREMENTS and MASS ♂♂ larger and c.10% heavier on average than ♀. Young differ from adults in being smaller, lighter and having a slightly shorter bill. There is relatively strong variation in mass during the annual cycle, both adults and young being lighter in Jan and heavier in Mar–Apr, before their departure northward. Ruokonen *et al.*[1108] found significant differences between Pink-footed Goose and all four taxa of Bean Goose in bill length and height, nail length and 'grinning patch' depth; *middendorffii* differed from all others in bill length, and from *fabalis* in all measurements; *fabalis* and *rossicus* only differed significantly in 'grinning patch' depth and *rossicus* and *serrirostris* differed in both bill length and height.

A. f. fabalis. ♂: wing chord 452–520 (adult, 481, n=87) and 436–487 (juvenile, 461, n=87), culmen 57–70 (63.6, n=93), 'grinning patch' depth 5.5–7.3 (6.4, n=13), tarsus 76–90 (82.2, n=21), mass 2,690–4,060 (3,198,

n=68). ♀: wing chord 434–488 (adult, 460, n=73) and 418–476 (juvenile, 442, n=48), culmen 55–66 (60, n=75), 'grinning patch' depth 5.3–7.0 (6.2, n=6), tarsus 73–80 (76.7, n=11), mass 2,220–3,470 (2,843, n=58)[267]. All sex and age groups: bill 61.5 (σ =4.24, n=20), bill depth at tip of forehead feathering 30.5 (σ =1.89, n=20), 'grinning patch' depth 5.8 (σ =1.18, n=17), nail 15.3 (σ =1.11, n=20); compare measurements for other taxa by same author[1108].

A. f. rossicus. ♂: wing chord 430–478 (adult, 454, n=144) and 390–451 (juvenile, 429, n=31), culmen 52–63 (57.7, n=142), 'grinning patch' depth 7.0–10.0 (7.9, n=13), tarsus 70–81 (75.2, n=13), mass 1,970–3,390 (2,668, n=126); ♀: wing chord 405–458 (adult, 433, n=133) and 378–443 (juvenile, 417, n=36), culmen 49–60 (54.6, n=134), 'grinning patch' depth 6.9–8.6 (7.5, n=10), tarsus 69–79 (73.9, n=13), mass 2,000–2,800 (2,374, n=117)[267]. All sex and age groups: bill 57.8 (σ =2.42, n=10), 'grinning patch' depth 7.29 (σ =1.01, n=10), nail 16.5 (σ =0.84, n=9); compare measurements for other taxa by same author[1108].

A. f. serrirostris. ♂: wing chord 440–524 (474, n=28), culmen 59–72 (65.9, n=30), 'grinning patch' depth 8.0–12.5 (10.4, n=26); ♀: wing chord 420–491 (449, n=20), culmen 58–69 (63.3, n=17), 'grinning patch' depth 8.1–11.3 (9.3, n=10)[267]. Mass 3,200[180]. All sex and age groups: bill 62.9 (σ =3.00, n=14), bill depth at tip of forehead feathering 33.8 (σ =1.52, n=14), 'grinning patch' depth 7.7 (σ =1.12, n=14), nail 18.2 (σ =1.84, n=14); compare measurements for other taxa by same author[1108].

A. f. middendorffii. ♂: wing chord 440–558 (492, n=16), culmen 64–81 (73.3, n=15), 'grinning patch' depth 7.0–10.5 (8.6, n=15); ♀: wing chord 465–524 (488, n=9), culmen 63–80 (72.7, n=9), 'grinning patch' depth 7.0–9.8 (8.6, n=8)[267]. Mass 4,600[180]. All sex and age groups: bill 69.7 (σ =4.98, n=14), bill depth at tip of forehead feathering 34.1 (σ =2.80, n=14), 'grinning patch' depth: 8.4 (σ =1.04, n=10), nail: 17.5 (σ =1.46, n=14); compare measurements for other taxa by same author[1108].

VOICE Usually less vocal and noisy than other grey geese, except when groups take off or land, for example near resting places during migration and in winter. Frequently heard on migration at night. Usual calls quite close to those of other grey geese, but produces a doubled *hang-hung*, like Pink-footed Goose, but deeper.

Voice less harsh and more nasal than Greylag Goose. Identification by voice at night possible but requires practice. The different subspecies differ slightly[267,859,1380]. In Asia, the call of *serrirostris* is lower than Greater White-fronted Goose, whereas *middendorffii* calls are much deeper and more honking. Similar differences are noticeable between *rossicus* and *fabalis* in Europe.

MOULT Complex basic strategy. Juvenile undergoes pre-formative moult during their first autumn on migration and on arrival at the wintering sites. This moult may be protracted, until early spring, or suspended during the coldest part of the winter. Involved are many to most head, neck and body feathers (fewer on rump and rear body, almost none on belly), occasionally 1–2 tertials and a variable number of rectrices. Second pre-basic moult by Jun–Sep, slightly earlier than breeding adult. Definitive pre-basic moult starts Jul–Aug with a *c.*3-week flightless period, in large flocks near open water. Once able to fly again, moves to moulting grounds on Arctic Ocean coasts[390]. Replacement of body feathers and rectrices in Aug–Nov, on moulting grounds and during autumn migration. Timing may vary slightly depending on population and latitude of breeding sites.

HYBRIDISATION Natural hybridisation involving Bean Goose seems very rare. In the wild, reported several times with Greater White-fronted Goose *A. albifrons*, Swan Goose *A. cygnoid*, Canada Goose *Branta canadensis* and Barnacle Goose *B. leucopsis*. In captivity, hybrids also reported with Greylag Goose *A. anser*, Pink-footed Goose *A. brachyrhynchus*[899,995,1158] and Snow Goose *Chen caerulescens*[817]. About 4–5 hybrids with Canada Goose have been reported in Sweden[668], where a local reintroduction scheme using Canada Goose as parents has been established.

HABITAT and LIFE-CYCLE Long-distance migrant, but some southernmost (taiga) populations undertake only short migrations. Leaves wintering grounds between mid-Feb and mid-Apr, with traditional long stop-overs en route. There are differences in both breeding and wintering habitats between the different subspecies: *fabalis* and *middendorffii* form the 'taiga' group, which preferentially inhabits wet taiga with more or less wooded swamps and bogs; *rossicus* and *serrirostris* (tundra group) inhabit Arctic tundra regions. Eggs laid by early May in the taiga and *c.*1 month later in the tundra. Breeds in solitary pairs, rarely in small loose colonies. More gregarious on the moulting grounds, but in winter typically less gregarious than other geese,

often feeding in more scattered small flocks. Several ecological and behavioural differences have been described, e.g. by Van Impe[1309] in the Netherlands. For example, *fabalis* is less diurnal in winter, arriving earlier at its foraging grounds and leaving later in the evening. This subspecies also seems to bathe and drink more frequently. It seems that grazing while on ground is not a characteristic of *fabalis*, but is more related to ambient temperatures[327]. Such differences have also been identified between *middendorffii* and *serrirostris*, the former feeding by night, far from its roost sites, and the latter usually feeds by day close to the roost[402]. In winter, the tundra group generally prefers cultivated areas such as crops or rice fields in Japan. The taiga group prefers grasslands, marshes and vegetated lakeshores, where it often feeds while swimming[859,1309]. Both use large waterbodies or small islands to roost.

RANGE and POPULATION Strongly migratory, breeding in N Eurasia, north to the high Arctic, and wintering in temperate to subtropical regions. The precise distribution of each subspecies is not well known, and obscured by the uncertain taxonomic status of '*johanseni*'.

A. f. fabalis. Breeds in the taiga (W Siberia to C Scandinavia). Immature non-breeders move further north to moult, probably N Lapland and the White Sea coast[993]. The winter range extends from S Scandinavia to the Netherlands (where now less numerous) and Germany, with small numbers in England. The wintering population in W Europe was estimated at 100,000 birds and thought to be stable[797] in the 1990s, but during the following decade at just 40,000–45,000 individuals, and declining[400]. The subspecies is much rarer further south (e.g. Belgium, France), where it appears to have declined in recent decades.

'*A. f. johanseni*' (included here in *fabalis*). This name has been applied to populations east of *fabalis*, from the Urals to the Krasnoyarsk Krai, and south to Lake Baikal, Russia. These migrate along the Ob and Yenisei Rivers, and winter in C Asia (SE Kazakhstan, E Kyrgyzstan and NW China)[544]. The taxonomic status of birds wintering in C China is unknown, but at least one collected on the Yellow Sea, at Qingdao, E China pertained to *fabalis*[544]. Some birds banded in winter in the Netherlands show features and measurements of '*johanseni*', and have been recovered east of the Urals[207], and other individuals seen elsewhere in Europe have been assigned to this taxon[1308]. Population size poorly known.

A. f. middendorffii. Breeds across the Siberian taiga between Lake Baikal and the Sea of Okhotsk, N Mongolia and south to the Altai. Winters mainly in E China (*c.*50,000 birds), South Korea and Japan (*c.*6,000 birds each), and overall in decline[858]. More recently (2010), only 13,000–35,000 individuals estimated, due to a decline in China[1348] linked to habitat loss (drainage for agriculture) and over-hunting. Moulting sites known from some river mouths on E Siberian Arctic coasts (the Yana, Indigirka and Lena[290]) and two sites in W Kamchatka[433]. Very rare vagrant in W North America, from Alaska to California.

A. f. rossicus. Breeds in the Russian tundra east to the Taimyr Peninsula, which forms the approximate dividing line between population migrating westwards and those moving east[1091]. Winters in Europe with several populations on North Sea coasts (mainly Belgium, the Netherlands and Germany), in NE France, N Italy, Hungary, Moravia and W Black Sea coasts. Moulting sites are distributed along Arctic Ocean coasts, north of its breeding range. One record from Quebec, E Canada. The commonest subspecies with a wintering population numbering 600,000 in the 1990s[797] and 550,000 in the 2000s [400], and considered stable. Introduction attempts in Germany in the 1950s and 1960s failed[710].

A. f. serrirostris. Breeds in the tundra zone from the Taimyr Peninsula east to the Bering Sea and Kamchatka. Wintering population in the 1990s numbered 45,000–65,000 individuals and was declining, with most in China (20,000), South Korea (30,000) and Japan

(6,000)[858]. At the end of the first decade of the present century, the population was estimated at 81,000–157,000 individuals[1348], but was still thought to be declining. Very rarely recorded in W North America.

CAPTIVITY Generally infrequent in captivity, especially the eastern subspecies. Almost absent from North American collections. Occasional breeding by escapees reported in the UK, Netherlands and Belgium. Only the latter has a feral population, which numbered up to 400 birds in the late 1990s[62].

REFERENCES Banks *et al.* (2008)[62]; Barthel & Frede (1989)[73]; Bloomfield (2004)[153]; Brazil (1991)[180]; Brown (2010)[196]; Burgers *et al.* (1991)[207]; Cramp & Simmons (1977)[267]; Degtyarev (1995)[290]; Delacour (1951)[294]; Dronneau (2006)[327]; Emelyanov (2000)[361]; Fox *in* Kear (2005)[390]; Fox *et al.* (2010)[400]; Fox *et al.* (2013)[402]; Garner (2010)[423]; Gerasimov & Gerasimov (1995)[433]; Heinicke (2009)[544]; Johansen (1945)[636]; Johansen (1959)[637]; Kampe-Persson & Lerner (2007)[668]; Kreutzkamp (2003)[710]; Liebherr & Rutschke (1993)[759]; Madsen *et al.* (1999)[797]; McCarthy (2006)[817]; Miyabayashi *et al.* (1994)[859]; Miyabayashi & Mundkur (1999)[858]; Mooij & Zöckler (1999)[868]; Nagy (1950)[899]; Ogilvie & Young (1998)[928]; Pirkola & Kalinainen (1984)[993]; Pitt (1944)[995]; Rogacheva (1992)[1091]; Ruokonen & Aarvak (2011)[1102]; Ruokonen *et al.* (2000)[1103]; Ruokonen *et al.* (2008)[1108]; Sangster & Oreel (1996)[1130]; Scott (1947)[1158]; Stepanyan (1990)[1232]; van den Bergh (1985)[1307]; van den Bergh (2003)[1308]; Van Impe (1980)[1309]; Wetlands International (2014)[1348]; Yokota *et al.* (1982)[1380].

20. *A. f. fabalis*, adult (definitive basic); note large size, compared to Greylag Goose *A. anser*. Denmark, May (Nis Lundmark Jensen).

21. *A. f. fabalis*, adult (definitive basic); a trickier individual, but still has longish, thin bill. Sweden, Feb (Nis Lundmark Jensen).

22. *A. f. fabalis*, adult (definitive basic); contrast between whitish belly and dark underwing typical of this species. Sweden, Feb (Johannes Rydström).

23. *A. f. fabalis*. Adult (definitive basic); typical bill pattern of this subspecies. Sweden, Feb (Nis Lundmark Jensen).

24. *A. f. middendorffii*, adult (definitive basic); a very large subspecies, with a long, gently curved neck, and long head and bill, without any salient angle. Japan, Oct (Stuart Price).

25. *A. f. middendorffii*, first-winter (juvenile/formative); aged by presence of some new scapulars and flank feathers, but rest are juvenile (narrow and rounded), while bill has almost adult colours, but is still not fully grown. Japan, Nov (Ayuwat Jearwattanakanok).

26. *A. f. middendorffii* and *A. f. serrirostris* (left), adult (definitive basic); note oval head shape, longer bill and neck, and paler head (eye easily discerned). Hong Kong, China, Nov (Michelle & Peter Wong).

27. *A. f. middendorffii*, adult (definitive basic); bill colour is rather constant in both eastern subspecies – *middendorffii* has a long bill with a swollen lower mandible and a longish 'grinning patch'. Japan, Sep (Stuart Price).

28. *A. f. middendorffii* and *A. f. serrirostris* (left), first-winter (juvenile/ formative); both birds in formative plumage (scattered juvenile scapulars, rounded at tip, and retained rectrices), and separated subspecifically by longer bill of right-hand bird, longer 'grinning patch' and lower mandible bulge, as well as more yellow bare parts (vs. more orange). Japan, Jan (Ayuwat Jearwattanakanok).

29. *A. f. rossicus*, adult (definitive basic); compared to other subspecies, appears stocky with a short neck and rather short bill. Scotland, Jan (Ian Fulton).

30. *A. f. rossicus*, adult (definitive basic); in flight from below, dark underwing contrasting with pale uniform belly are typical of the species. Netherlands, Feb (Sébastien Reeber).

31. *A. f. rossicus*, adult (definitive basic); like Pink-footed Goose, but note orange hue to bare parts. Iceland, Feb (Yann Kolbeinsson).

32. *A. f. rossicus*, adult (definitive basic); most birds of this subspecies have a broad orange subterminal bill-band like this. Scotland, Jan (Ian Fulton).

33. *A. f. serrirostris*, adult (definitive basic); typically thick bill and dark head of this subspecies, while the right-hand bird is juvenile. South Korea, Dec (Philippe J. Dubois).

34. *A. f. serrirostris*, adult (definitive basic); like other taxa, some birds show white at the base of the bill. South Korea, Dec (Philippe J. Dubois).

35. *A. f. serrirostris*, adult (definitive basic). South Korea, Dec (Philippe J. Dubois).

36. *A. f. serrirostris*, adult (definitive basic); square or rounded head (vs. elongated in *middendorffii*) and thick bill with a deep, down-sloping, 'grinning patch'. Hong Kong, China, Nov (Michelle & Peter Wong).

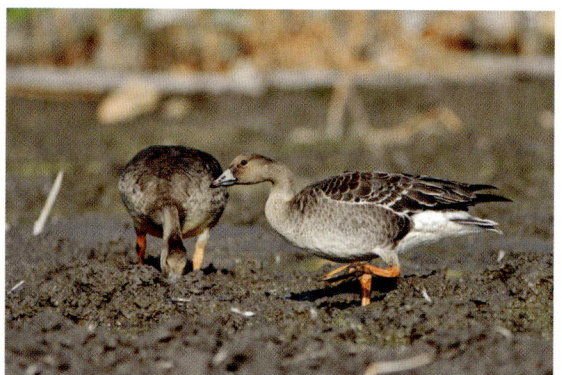

37. *A. f. serrirostris*, first-winter (juvenile/formative); still in mostly juvenile plumage, with flank feathers and scapulars with rounded tips and fringed pale brownish. Japan, Nov (Ayuwat Jearwattanakanok).

PINK-FOOTED GOOSE
Anser brachyrhynchus

TAXONOMY *Anser Brachyrhynchus* Baillon, 1834, *Mém. Soc. Roy. Emulation Abbeville*, sér. 2(1) (1833), p. 74. Phylogenetically very close to Bean Goose *A. fabalis*[772]. Although described as a species, long considered by many authors a subspecies of Bean Goose[1233], as the westernmost representative of the tundra group. However, recent studies confirm that it is better treated as a distinct species, the morphological similarities with Tundra Bean Goose *A. f. rossicus* being partly due to convergence, and adaptation to similar environments. A study of mitochondrial DNA of 142 individuals from the species' entire range has recently revealed significant differentiation between western breeders in Greenland and Iceland, and the eastern population on Svalbard[1106].

IDENTIFICATION Usually easily distinguished from Greylag Goose *A. anser*, which is much larger, with paler head and underwing-coverts, and a much bulkier all-pink or orange bill. Greater White-fronted Goose *A. albifrons* is similar in size, but the adult has a distinctive white mask and heavily marked black underparts. Moreover, at any age, this species has an all-pink or orange bill, significantly darker brown upperparts and a strong blackish tail bar.

Confusion is easier with Tundra Bean Goose, which is of equivalent size, has a black bill with an orange spot often limited to a subterminal band and an all-dark head (a white line encircling the bill base is rare to reasonably common in both species). Note, however, that the bill is thicker and longer, with an orange (vs. pink) patch, the legs are bright orange and the upperparts darker brown. In flight, the upperparts (including wings) of Bean Goose are much darker with a broad blackish tail-band (see this species for more details). At a distance, best distinguished from all other geese by its paler upperparts (often appearing silvery), with rear flanks darker than the upperparts and dark head contrasting with upper chest, which is often tinged ochre.

The identification of the grey geese is more difficult in juvenile plumage in autumn, as the bare parts are much duller and often confusing. The upperparts and flanks are different from those of the adult, and are of less use for identification purposes. In this plumage, specific distinction should be based on size, general shape and bill shape. Juvenile Bean Goose has darker upperparts and more obvious fringes to the scapulars, tertial coverts and tertials, contrasting more clearly with the flanks. In contrast, juvenile Pink-footed Goose is more uniform, with barely visible pale fringes to the upperparts and hardly any contrast between the latter and the underparts.

PLUMAGES Sexes similar, except for a few differences in size and behaviour. Complex basic moult strategy (a single plumage by definitive cycle, two in the first cycle). Ageing rather easy until the beginning of winter and still possible under good conditions, or in hand, until the end of the first summer.

Adult

Definitive basic plumage (year-round). Medium-sized goose, with rather long wings and a stocky body, short legs, a rather short, thick neck, a rounded head and tiny bill. Head chocolate-brown, darker around and in front of eye, with a narrow band at the base of the bill in some individuals. Dark brown iris. Short triangular bill, mostly black with a bright pink subterminal band. This patch can be restricted to a small pink spot on the upper mandible, or extend over much of the sides of the bill and along the tomium towards the gape. Exceptionally, it is orange. Upper neck chocolate-brown, contrasting sharply with the pale breast and lower neck, often tinged ochre or ginger. Underparts beige with rear flanks dark brown, where fine white fringes form vertical streaks like in all grey geese. Feathers of the mantle and scapulars square-shaped, pale brown to grey-blue, with a vaguely darker subterminal area and clear white fringes. From a distance, these fringes appear like pale streaking, as in other geese, but are wider than in Bean, Greater and Lesser White-fronted Geese *A. erythropus*. Greater coverts and tertials of similar coloration, and do not contrast with the scapulars (vs. formative). Lower belly and undertail-coverts white. Back and rump grey like the scapulars, being much darker in Bean and Greater White-fronted Geese, and paler in Greylag Goose. Uppertail-coverts form a white crescent and tail white with a medium-grey band at base, which is shared only by Greylag Goose. Typical upperwing with the lesser coverts, primary coverts and bases of the remiges pale blue-grey, median coverts and greater coverts (especially proximal feathers) darker with pale fringes forming narrow wingbars. The relatively pale upperwing offers little contrast with the scapulars, back and rump, but the whole contrasts with the blackish remiges. Underwing median coverts, primary coverts and axillaries uniform grey, darker than in Greylag Goose, but paler than in other grey geese, and no contrast with the flanks visible in flight from below (vs. often strong contrast in Bean Goose). Legs pale to bright pink, with rare individuals rather dull orange and, even more rarely, as bright as in Bean Goose[137,196].

Juvenile

First basic plumage (Jun/Oct–Nov). Many arrive on the wintering sites in juvenile plumage, which differs from adult in being much plainer, with little contrast between the upper- and underparts. Scapulars have rounded tips with narrow light brown fringes, forming a very faint scaly pattern, very different from the adult. The rear flanks are also more uniform, without the bold dark and fine white streaks of the adult. The greater coverts and tertials have broader and more diffuse grey fringes. The breast typically has a mottled appearance. Bill coloration is duller and ill-defined, initially olive-brown. Its shape is also distinctive, very short, with the culmen being slightly swollen. The legs are brownish or greyish-pink, duller than the adult.

First-winter/first-summer

Formative plumage (Nov–Apr/Aug). Following pre-formative moult, completed between Dec and Mar, appearance is closer to that of adult, with head, neck, flanks and upperparts almost identical, at least for those birds that undertake extensive moult. Others can often show a mixture of formative feathers (like adult, but less square-tipped) and juvenile feathers (round-tipped with poorly defined brownish fringes). Legs and bill gain adult coloration at the beginning of the first winter. Ageing can be difficult after pre-formative moult. However, close observation should detect the presence of juvenile feathers on the belly (moult contrast sometimes obvious) and/or the mantle and scapulars. The secondary upperwing-coverts are typically narrower, round-tipped, with diffuse pale fringes and no dark subterminal bars. In profile, juvenile pattern contrasts with adult-patterned scapulars. Tertials differ in the same way, being narrower, slightly shorter, with browner and less well-marked fringes. During the first spring and until the second pre-basic moult (first summer), primaries, rectrices and median coverts often seem obviously worn, brown and faded.

Second-winter

Second basic plumage (Sep–Aug). The second pre-basic moult ends at the start of the second winter, with a few remaining juvenile feathers sometimes visible in the secondary upperwing-coverts, belly, mantle or back, but are usually only discernible in the hand.

GEOGRAPHIC VARIATION No geographic variation described despite the existence of two widely allopatric populations, differing significantly genetically (mitochondrial DNA)[1106].

MEASUREMENTS and MASS ♂ slightly larger and 10–20% heavier than ♀, with differences often visible within pairs. ♂: wing chord 430–540 (adult, 450, n=139) and 400–450 (juvenile, 430, n=34), culmen 40–54 (adult, 46.4, n=108) and 40–51 (juvenile/first-winter, 45.9, n=41), tarsus 65–86 (adult, 74.9, n=84) and 71–82 (juvenile/first-winter, 73.7, n=23); ♀: wing chord 410–530 (adult, 435, n=114) and 390–450 (juvenile, 415, n=41), culmen 40–55 (adult, 44.8, n=71) and 40–59 (juvenile/first-winter, 43.8, n=41), tarsus 64.5–81.5 (adult, 71.0, n=62) and 68–76 (juvenile/first-winter, 71.8, n=31). ♂: mass in winter 1,900–3,860 (adult, 2,800, n=1,249) and 1,410–3,080 (juvenile/first-winter, 2,431, n=1088), in Jul (wing moult) 1,990–3,120 (2,610, n=180); ♀: mass in winter 1,790–3,150 (adult, 2409, n=1,307) and 1,450–2,800 (juvenile/first-winter, 2,207, n=984), in Jul (wing moult) 1,650–2,810 (2,332, n=125)[169].

Ruokonen *et al.*[1108] compared measurements for Pink-footed Goose and the different subspecies of Bean Goose. Bill: 45.8 (σ=2.92, n=26), bill depth: 25.5 (σ=1.77, n=26), nail length: 12.8 (σ=1.17, n=25) and 'grinning patch' depth: 4.7 (σ=0.99, n=26). Measurements of *A. f. rossicus* as follows: bill 57.8 (σ=2.42, n=10), bill depth 30.7 (σ=1.52, n=10), nail length 16.5 (σ=0.84, n=9) and 'grinning patch' depth 7.3 (σ=1.01, n=10).

VOICE Calls similar to Bean Goose, with nasal and somewhat rasping tones, but higher in pitch. In particular, the loudest call, *ang* or a doubled *ang-ang*, is squeaky and well audible from afar, albeit less high pitched and less melodious than Greater White-fronted Goose. Another frequent, softer call *gik-week* recalls the latter. With some experience, easily distinguished from other geese. Young utter higher-pitched and more rasping calls than ad[169].

MOULT Identical to that of other grey geese. Juvenile undertakes pre-formative moult between Oct and Jan–Mar, often briefly paused or slowed during coldest months of winter. Starts with the head and neck, often in Oct–Nov, then the chest, mantle, scapulars and flanks until Dec–Jan[56]. The appearance of many birds is then already very close to that of adult. The moult ends between Jan and Mar with a variable number of back and rear body feathers, and a variable number of rectrices. Some of these feathers and most of those on the belly may be retained until the end of the second pre-basic moult, i.e. until the end of the second calendar year. Adult begins definitive pre-basic moult with the wings, on the breeding grounds (with their young), and moults the body feathers on the moulting grounds, completing at staging sites or on arrival at the wintering grounds.

HYBRIDISATION Very rare natural hybridisation cases have been reported with Canada Goose *Branta canadensis*[740,1190], Greylag Goose[465,668] and Bean Goose[153,668,817,995]. Hybrids with the latter may be more regular than reported. Indeed, photographs and reports on the internet show birds with intermediate characters in coloration of bare parts, in shape of head and bill, tail-band and in the colour of the centres to the scapulars, greater coverts and tertials. Hybridisation often seems the best explanation, but variability in the bare parts (mainly legs) of Pink-footed Goose is 'normal'. Similarly, the centres to the upperparts feathers can be very dark brown (tertials included) in birds that are otherwise similar in every respect to Pink-footed Goose. So such variations do not necessarily stem from hybridisation. In captivity, hybrids have been described with Snow Goose *Chen caerulescens*[295,465], Emperor Goose *Chen canagica*[295] and Greater White-fronted Goose. Finally, a hybrid not formally identified but which accompanied Pink-footed Geese for several consecutive winters in England was perhaps the result of a cross with Ross's Goose *Chen rossii*, but this remains hypothetical[126].

HABITAT and LIFE-CYCLE Arrives at nesting sites between mid-May and late June. On Svalbard, mostly uses rugged and inaccessible habitats, such as cliffs, and different hilly landscapes and rocky outcrops, often in spots with more lush vegetation and where the snow melts early. Nests alone or in loose colonies[1213]. Pair-bond often lifelong, with the ♂ remaining with the ♀ throughout the nesting season, defending the territory, nest and ♀ from other ♂♂. Post-breeding,

moves to moulting sites, usually in quiet areas of open water (e.g. islands with dense vegetation). Some Icelandic birds (mainly non-breeders) moult their flight feathers in Greenland from mid-Jun and return to Iceland in late Aug[169]. The first migrants are reported in Denmark soon after mid-Sep, with birds shortly after reaching Belgium. The bulk of the population concentrates in Denmark in Oct and then Belgium in Nov. Return movements depend on weather conditions, and may occur as early as mid-Dec, with birds appearing again in Denmark. In mild winters, most leave Belgium in Jan, the bulk of the population staging in Jutland, Denmark, between Feb and early May[797]. In winter and during migration, now primarily uses fertilised grassland and secondary stubbles[169], where the birds feed by day, forming large roosts on open water at night.

RANGE and POPULATION Two allopatric populations. The first breeds on Svalbard and winters mainly in Belgium and to a lesser extent in the Netherlands and NW Germany. Cold winters force Belgian birds to move south, but hunting pressure and absence of protected wetlands in N France are not conductive to long stays. Migration is mostly noticeable on the W & N coasts of Norway and Denmark, and in smaller numbers along Baltic Sea coasts, including W Finland. Breeding was reported in the 1990s on Novaya Zemlya[666], where several hundred to 1,000 birds over-summer (see Van Impe[1311] for a recent review of status in W Siberia). Rare or occasional visitor south of its wintering range, south to the Mediterranean. This population was estimated at 10,000 birds in the 1930s and 1940s, then increased to 25,000–30,000 birds in 1980[169] and 63,000 in the early 2000s[400]. The second population breeds in E Greenland and C Iceland, and winters mainly in Scotland and N & NE England, with many fewer in Ireland and occasionally W France, and exceptionally in NE North America[1179]. The total population was estimated at 20,000–30,000 birds in the 1930s, 260,000 in 1994 and 350,000 birds in the early 2000s[169,400].

CAPTIVITY Rarely kept in captivity, either in Eurasia or North America, and much more expensive than other grey geese, but said to breed fairly easily.

REFERENCES Baker (1993)[56]; Bird Hybrids Flickr Forum (2011)[126]; Bird Hybrids Flickr Forum (2013)[137]; Bloomfield (2004)[153]; Boyd *in* Kear (2005)[169]; Brown (2010)[196]; Delacour (1954)[295]; Fox *et al.* (2010)[400]; Gray (1958)[465]; Kalyakin (2001)[666]; Kampe-Persson & Lerner

(2007)[668]; Leck (1967)[740]; Livezey (1996)[772]; Madsen *et al.* (1999)[797]; McCarthy (2006)[817]; Nagy (1950)[899]; Pitt (1944)[995]; Ruokonen *et al.* (2005)[1106]; Ruokonen *et al.* (2008)[1108]; Sherony (2008)[1179]; Sibley (1938)[1190]; Snow & Perrins (1998)[1213]; Stepanyan (2003)[1233]; Van Impe (2008)[1311].

38. Adult (definitive basic); combination of black-and-pink bill and pink legs unique among geese. Scotland, Jan (Ian Fulton).

39. Adult (definitive basic); among typical features of the species, note smallish bill, dark chocolate head, gingery breast and blue-grey upperparts paler than flanks. Netherlands, Dec (Rick Van der Weijde).

40. Adult (definitive basic); this bird has rather more pink on bill than most. Iceland, May (Yann Kolbeinsson).

41. In flight, note pale upperwing-coverts and darker back. Denmark, Apr (Nis Lundmark Jensen).

42. First-winter (juvenile/formative); at this age has narrow, rounded flank feathers, and much plainer overall appearance (juvenile *A. fabalis rossicus* behind). Poland, Oct (Zbigniew Kayzer).

43. First-winter (juvenile/formative), with plain flanks, rounded scapulars, and a faintly scaly appearance. Sweden, Feb (Nis Lundmark Jensen).

GREYLAG GOOSE
Anser anser

TAXONOMY *Anas Anser* Linnaeus, 1758, *Syst. Nat.*, edn. 10, p. 123. Phylogenetically closer to the Bean Goose *A. fabalis*/Pink-footed Goose *A. brachyrhynchus* complex than to Swan Goose *A. cygnoid*, Greater White-fronted Goose *A. albifrons* and Lesser White-fronted Goose *A. erythropus*[772]. Two subspecies described, nominate in Iceland and W Europe and *A. a. rubrirostris* Swinhoe, 1871, in the rest of Eurasia. The many domestic forms are grouped under the name of *A. a.* var. *domesticus*.

IDENTIFICATION The largest and heaviest grey goose, except the largest subspecies of Bean (*A. f. middendorffii*) and Greater White-fronted Geese (*A. a. elgasi*), which are more slender and easily distinguished by plumage and bare-parts coloration. Greylag Goose is distinguished from all other species by its combination of fairly heavy and stocky shape, large head, massive pink or orange bill, rather pale grey plumage and pale pink legs. In flight, the upperwing has a pale grey leading edge (lesser coverts) and 'hand', contrasting with the rest of the wing. Strong contrast on the underwing, between the lesser and median coverts on one hand and the greater coverts and remiges on the other, is unique among grey geese. The main confusion risk is probably with juvenile Greater White-fronted Goose, which also has a plain orangey bill, but structural differences, the dark brown plumage (especially in flight), broad black tail-band and orange legs should easily distinguish it from Greylag Goose.

PLUMAGES Nominate subspecies. Sexes identical except for some differences in size and behaviour (visible especially in paired birds). Complex basic moult strategy (one plumage by definitive cycle, two in the first cycle). Ageing relatively easy until autumn and possible until the end of the first summer under good conditions or in the hand.

Adult

Definitive basic plumage (year-round). Plumage rather uniform, mostly grey-brown and white. Head and upper neck rather pale grey-brown (eye easily discerned at distance) with clear grooves on the sides of the neck, more obvious from afar than in other grey geese. Iris dark brown with a pink to orange orbital ring. Bill thick, triangular, orange but paler pink on the distal third, with an ivory nail. Breast, belly and flanks pale grey-beige with rear flanks having long dark crescents and fine vertical white stripes (fringes to the feathers), like other grey geese. Clear white line demarcating flanks and upperparts. A variable number of black spots are visible on the centre of the lower breast and belly. Feathers of the mantle and scapulars dark grey-brown fringed beige or pale grey (appearing neatly streaked). Greater coverts and tertials darker blackish-brown, also fringed with conspicuous white line. Lower belly, undertail- and uppertail-coverts white. Back and upper rump pale grey-brown and look scaly, slightly darker than the surrounding scapulars in flight. White tail with bases to rectrices forming a dark grey bar. In flight, upperwing has lesser coverts, primary coverts and alula pale grey, contrasting with the median and greater coverts, which are dark brown fringed white, and the dark grey remiges. Outer primaries with paler bases and white rachis clearly visible. Underwing has axillaries, lesser coverts and median coverts pale grey contrasting with the darker rest of wing. Pale pink to fleshy legs, rarely orangey, often assuming brighter colours during breeding.

Juvenile

First basic plumage (June/Oct–Nov). Similar to adult, best distinguished (like other grey geese) by poorly marked grooves on sides of the neck, shorter bill with blackish nail, more uniform flanks (grey-beige with yellowish hue, vaguely mottled dark) and by juvenile scapulars. The latter are rounded at the tips, grey-brown with diffuse pale brownish fringes forming a faint scaly (rather than obviously streaked) pattern. This scaly pattern is often more clearly visible than in other grey geese in the same plumage. Pale greyish orbital ring. Legs dull flesh to yellowish-brown, sometimes darker.

First-winter/first-summer

Formative plumage (Nov–Apr/Aug). Like other grey geese, very similar to adult at end of pre-formative moult, which occurs earlier in winter (cf. Moult), many birds being in fully formative plumage in Nov. Differs from adult by the lack of black markings on the belly, which is still mostly juvenile. At close range, note the contrast between the formative (adult-like) scapulars and the juvenile wing-coverts. The latter are more rounded with duller pale fringes and no dark subterminal bars. Also note that the orbital ring does not gain its full colours until spring. Some birds also retain juvenile scapulars and/or rectrices, but many can be aged only on close inspection of the wing-coverts. Formative scapulars are generally narrower at the base than their tip, and less square-ended, but this is useful only in the hand.

Second-winter

Second basic plumage (Sep–Aug). Like other grey geese, a few juvenile feathers are sometimes retained among the wing-coverts (especially the median coverts[56]), mantle and belly, but require close examination to see. An adult-type plumage in autumn without any black markings on the belly could be indicative of this age, but requires confirmation.

GEOGRAPHIC VARIATION The eastern subspecies *rubrirostris* is distinguished by its paler and greyer plumage, especially the head, the paler and slightly coarser fringes to the upperparts, bright pink orbital ring and more intense pink legs. In addition, the bill is marginally longer, slightly thinner at the tip (faintly concave culmen) and pink, not orange (but juvenile can show a flesh or dull orange base). Typical birds are fairly easy to distinguish from the nominate subspecies. Difficulties arise given the broad clinal transition zone, where many birds have variable and intermediate characters. This zone covers Finland and much of C Europe to the Balkans, with a wintering range west to Algeria. W European sightings of *rubrirostris*-type birds usually relate to intermediates. On the other hand, some records of groups with all these characters are more likely to represent an influx of continental birds. Note that birds from Scotland, Iceland and Norway have sometimes been regarded as a third subspecies, *A. a. sylvestris* C. L. Brehm, 1830, primarily based on the shorter bill[794], but this taxon is no longer accepted.

MEASUREMENTS and MASS ♂♂ slightly larger and 10–20% heavier than ♀♀, with the difference often visible in paired birds. Adult larger and heavier than young until first spring at least.

A. a. anser. ♂: wing chord 448–480 (adult, 465, *n*=7) and 418–482 (juvenile, 450, *n*=122), bill 59–74 (66.6, *n*=32), tarsus: 78–93 (84.7, *n*=32); ♀: wing chord 412–465 (adult, 442, *n*=16) and 390–466 (juvenile, 433, *n*=119), bill 58–65 (61.5, *n*=24), tarsus 71–87 (78.8, *n*=24). Iceland. ♂: wing chord 436–480 (467, *n*=191), bill 54–66 (60.0, *n*=125), mass in Oct (arrival

in Scotland) 3,030–3,790 (adult, 3,454, *n*=42) and 2,730–3,170 (juvenile/first-winter, 2,900, *n*=9), in winter (Scotland) 2,740–4,250 (adult, 3793, *n*=52) and 2,450–4,250 (juvenile/first-winter, 3,297, *n*=21); ♀: wing chord 417–480 (adult, 447, *n*=157), bill 47–62 (56.2, *n*=117), mass in Oct (arrival in Scotland) 2,540–3,470 (adult, 3,039, *n*=45) and 2,430–2,990 (juvenile/first-winter, 2,722, *n*=8), in winter (Scotland) 2,070–3,960 (adult, 3170, *n*=25) and 2,810–3,540 (juvenile/first-winter, 3,174, *n*=22)[267,813,922].

A. a. rubrirostris. ♂: wing chord 435–513 (adult, 468, *n*=16), bill 59–78 (68.8, *n*=19), mass in spring, Kazakhstan 2,800–4,100 (3,455, *n*=10); ♀: wing chord 395–470 (adult, 448, *n*=7), bill 47–73 (63.8, *n*=7), mass in spring, Kazakhstan 2,450–3,600 (2,921, *n*=7)[267].

VOICE Utters a variety of loud, hoarse and guttural calls, the commonest in flight being tri-syllabic, with the first syllable longer and louder *ge-ang ang ang.* Also an *ang ang ang*, more nasal and with equal syllables, sometimes two or four as well.

MOULT Complex basic strategy, identical to other grey geese, but timing more variable depending on breeding latitude. Pre-formative moult occurs primarily between Aug and Nov, with some birds still moulting in Feb. Starts with the head, neck, flanks, scapulars and a variable number of rectrices and proximal upperwing-coverts. Definitive pre-basic moult begins in May–Aug, depending on latitude, with the simultaneous loss of the flight feathers. Replacement of the body feathers starts once able to fly again, starting with the underparts, back, head and neck and ending with the rectrices in Sep–Nov.

HYBRIDISATION Natural hybridisation quite rare, very occasionally mentioned with Pink-footed Goose, Bean Goose[668,1142] and Greater White-fronted Goose (see latter species). The frequency of natural hybridisation seems to have considerably increased with the many introductions of several goose species in NW Europe. For several years, hybrids have been reported with Canada Goose *Branta canadensis*, Cackling Goose *B. hutchinsii*, Barnacle Goose *B. leucopsis* (which see), as well as Swan Goose and Bar-headed Goose *A. indicus*[668,1033] (which see), and more occasionally with Emperor Goose *Chen canagica*[668] and Egyptian Goose *Alopochen aegyptiacus*[35,582,668]. In captivity, hybrids involving Greylag Goose (or one of its domestic races) have been described with Black Swan *Cygnus atratus*, Whistling Swan *C.*

columbianus, Whooper Swan *C. cygnus*, Mute Swan *C. olor*, Lesser White-fronted Goose[668,1107], Snow Goose *Chen caerulescens*, Ross's Goose *C. rossii*, Brent Goose *Branta bernicla*, Muscovy Duck *Cairina moschata* and Mallard *Anas platyrhynchos*[97,817].

Greylag Goose × Canada Goose. Appears intermediate with variable characteristics, including white at the base of the bill, and can then resemble hybrid Greater White-fronted Goose × Canada Goose (see Greater White-fronted Goose). Feathers of the flanks, mantle, scapulars, greater coverts and tertials are centred brown with pale brown to beige fringes, forming faint streaking on the upperparts and flanks. Beige-brown belly and chest, which may appear darker than in either species. Neck and head black without sharp transition to the chest. Cheeks (same pattern as in Canada Goose) coloured beige or grey, sometimes darker. Pale eye-ring often prominent, accentuated by a variable small white patches around eyes and the bill base (sometimes very extensive, and merging into pale cheeks). Bill variegated and dull, dark grey (often culmen and base to nostrils) and pale pink or pale orange. Black nail. Tail mainly blackish. Last rows of undertail-coverts frequently barred dark, a feature shown by many hybrids between *Anser* and *Branta* spp., even if neither parent does. Legs usually dull pale pink. Such hybrids have yet to be seen in NW Europe, where Canada Goose has established feral populations. In North America, this cross is likely to involve one the domestic races of Greylag Goose, which will probably lead to different-looking hybrids.

Greylag Goose × Cackling Goose. Hybrid rarely described in the literature, but images published on the internet[109] show birds similar to those involving Canada Goose, but substantially smaller than Greylag Goose, with a shorter bill and a more square-shaped head, which corresponds to what might be expected from this cross.

Greylag Goose × Barnacle Goose. Much rarer than hybrids with Canada Goose. Quite close to the previous two in appearance and general coloration, which is intermediate between the two parents. Scapulars centred paler grey with dark subterminal bars and diffuse pale brown fringes. Similar in size and shape to hybrids involving Cackling Goose, including square head and short, triangular bill. Best distinguished by the brown chest, darker than the underparts, and the pale face including the eye and forehead, thus recalling Barnacle Goose. Also shows small white spots

in the black neck, an essentially dark grey bill with a black nail and a variable pink patch on the sides of the mandible. Tail completely blackish, with uppertail- and undertail-coverts showing (always?) dark stripes. Legs pinkish or fleshy.

HABITAT and LIFE-CYCLE Inhabits a wide variety of wetlands, from Mediterranean brackish or fresh coastal marshes and islands to above the Arctic Circle in places. Favours large quiet wetlands, with some safety from predators (islets, flooded reedbeds[711]) and meadows or grasslands, flooded or not, used for grazing. Breeds in single pairs or in colonies. Depending on latitude, eggs are laid between late Mar (SW Europe) and mid-Jun on the Arctic tundra. Many populations lay between mid-Apr and late May. Both parents take care of the goslings, and begin pre-basic moult (wings) well before they fledge. Other families form large flocks and migrate, often only short distances, to moulting grounds used by thousands of birds[922]. Very gregarious outside the breeding season, often performing massive migrations, sometimes linked to weather conditions. Severe cold fronts may cause movements, especially with heavy snow cover. In winter, usually frequents large, sparsely hunted or protected wetlands, and often prefers to feed on flooded areas, rather than on stubble and crops.

RANGE and POPULATION Distributed across temperate zones of Eurasia with a total population estimated at 1,000,000–1,100,000 individuals[305]. Occasional visitor as far as the Azores and Canary Is, Greenland, and several Arctic archipelagos east to Japan. One observed on a boat off Newfoundland was considered wild, but other North American records are considered to be escapees[1007].

A. a. anser. Many disjunct populations from Iceland to coasts of Norway and the Baltic Sea, south-west to W & S France. Breeding populations in W Russia and C Europe show intermediate characters between this subspecies and *rubrirostris*. Population estimated at 98,000 individuals in Iceland, wintering in the British Isles[393,797]; 35,000 in N Scotland, which are mostly sedentary[682]; 610,000 elsewhere in NW Europe, which are sedentary or winter in SW Europe; and 56,000 in C Europe and south and east of Baltic Sea, wintering in W Balkans, Italy and N Africa[682,1348]. These populations all show stable or increasing trends, although the presence of introduced and rapidly growing population, particularly in England and the Netherlands, can 'muddy' censuses of 'natural' populations. Recent censuses of feral geese populations[667] suggest that almost half of W European population derive from the many introduction attempts conducted mainly in the 20th century, including individuals of the subspecies *rubrirostris*.

A. a. rubrirostris. Nests and winters further east. The Black Sea and Turkish population is estimated at 85,000 individuals and is mostly sedentary. That in W Russia, the Caspian Sea to Red Sea is estimated at 100,000 individuals[400]. The C Asian population winters south of the Himalayas (mainly India) and is estimated at 25,000 birds[1348] while the population breeding in E Asia and wintering in SE Asia numbers 50,000–100,000 individuals[222,1007].

CAPTIVITY Abundant in captivity, even if most birds belong to one or other of the domestic forms or derive from crosses with Swan Goose. Less numerous in North America, where the observation of a potential vagrant requires careful examination, to detect any domestic characters.

REFERENCES Antonius (1933)[35]; Baker (1993)[56]; Bird Hybrids Database (2014)[97]; Bird Hybrids Flickr Forum (2009)[109]; BirdLife International (2014)[145]; Cao *et al.* (2010)[222]; Cramp & Simmons (1977)[267]; Delany & Scott (2006)[305]; Fox *et al.* (2010)[400]; Gray (1958)[465]; Gustavsson (2010)[494]; Hopkinson (1926)[582]; Kampe-Persson (2010)[667]; Kampe-Persson & Lerner (2007)[668]; Kershaw & Cranswick (2003)[682]; Kristiansen (1998)[711]; Li *et al.* (2009)[757]; Livezey (1996)[772]; Madsen *et al.* (1999)[797]; Madge & Burn (1987)[794]; Matthews & Campbell (1969)[813]; Mitchell *et al.* (2000)[854]; McCarthy (2006)[817]; Nyeland *in* Kear (2005)[922]; Pranty *et al.* (2008)[1007]; Randler (2001)[1033]; Ruokonen *et al.* (2007)[1107]; Scherrer & Hilsberg (1982)[1142]; Wetlands International (2014)[1348].

44. *A. a. anser*, adult (definitive basic); easily separated from other grey geese by rather pale head and neck, and massive pale bill, while some birds have small white feathers at base of bill. England, Feb (Sébastien Reeber).

45. *A. a. anser*, adult (definitive basic); nominate subspecies is browner with an orange bill, which like the legs are bright orange here, as is often the case pre-breeding. France, Feb (Aurélien Audevard).

46. *A. a. anser*, adult (definitive basic); note relatively massive bulk. Netherlands, Feb (Sébastien Reeber).

47. *A. a. anser*, juvenile (first basic); typically rounded scapulars (fringed pale brownish), plain flanks, faint grooves on neck-sides and slimmer head at this age. France, Jul (Sébastien Reeber).

48. *A. a. anser*, adult (definitive basic); in flight, the only grey goose with a pale forewing contrasting with clear-cut darker scapulars. England, Feb (Sébastien Reeber).

49. *A. a. anser*, adult (definitive basic); characteristic underwing of this species, with lesser coverts, median coverts and axillaries pale grey. England, Feb (Sébastien Reeber).

50. *A. a. rubrirostris*, adult (definitive basic); this subspecies has a pink bill, matching the leg colour. Mongolia, Jul (Matthieu Vaslin).

51. *A. a. rubrirostris*, adult (definitive basic); aside of bill colour, in this subspecies the bill is also rather long and thin, and overall coloration is greyer. India, Jan (Sunil Singhal).

GREATER WHITE-FRONTED GOOSE
Anser albifrons   Plates 6, 7, 8

TAXONOMY *Branta albifrons* Scopoli, 1769, *Annus I Hist.-Nat.*, p. 69. Phylogenetically close to Lesser White-fronted Goose *A. erythropus*. Taxonomy of Greater White-fronted Goose is debated, with up to six subspecies recognised, primarily based on winter-collected specimens. The species was described from a bird probably taken in N Italy. In 1852, Hartlaub considered Nearctic birds to be distinct, *A. gambelli*[535]. This name was then applied to all Nearctic birds except those of Greenland, as well as some large European birds[1275]. Note that the correct spelling is *gambelli* and not *gambeli*, despite the latter still being in widespread use[65]. During the first half of the 20th century, Swarth & Bryant[1246] reported the existence of two different wintering populations in California, with large birds referred to *A. a. gambelli* and smaller ones to the nominate subspecies. *A. a. flavirostris* which breeds in Greenland and winters mainly in Ireland was described by Dalgety & Scott in 1948[277]. During the second half of the 20th century, other changes occurred; first Todd[1275] gave the name *frontalis* to smaller North American birds, thus separating them from the nominate subspecies. Then Delacour[295] ; proposed to place E Asian birds in *frontalis* too, but admitted that the limit between the two taxa was not clearly defined. A third North American subspecies was described in 1975 by Delacour & Ripley[298]: *A. a. elgasi*, for the largest birds wintering in C California, then considered different from *A. a. gambelli* wintering east of the Rocky Mts. This treatment, with five subspecies, was commonly accepted until the early 21st century.

Recent changes have been proposed by Mooij & Zöckler[868] and Mooij[866], who emphasised the need to separate Eurasian birds. They applied the name *A. a. albicans* to Asian populations west of the Khatanga River, Russia, and *frontalis* to North American birds, a view supported by the apparent lack of exchange between these populations, as evidenced by the absence of ringing recoveries[356]. However, large-scale study into mensural variation throughout the species' breeding range[359] has revealed no significant differences between E Asian birds and *frontalis* from Alaska and Arctic Canada, and also found that the increase in size from west to east in Siberia is clinal. Finally, a recent study of phylogenetic relationships among Palearctic populations[344] showed that East Asian birds are clearly differentiated from those east of the Rocky Mts.

The nomenclature of the species was reassessed recently[65], highlighting the invalidity of two widely used subspecies names. First, the name *albicans* was rejected as it was previously used to designate the nominate subspecies[65], but without addressing the question of subspecific status for E Asian birds. Secondly, this study reconsidered the issue of the name *frontalis*, initially assigned by Baird (1858) to birds belonging to *gambelli*, making *frontalis* a junior synonym of the latter. Banks[65] therefore proposed a new subspecies, *A. a. sponsa*, for populations breeding in W Alaska. Two distinct populations (see Range and Populations) with different migration phenology and minor plumage differences, however, do not seem sufficient to justify subspecific distinction[358,935,1202].

According to this treatment, there are three Nearctic subspecies, in addition to *A. a. flavirostris*: *A. a. sponsa* and *A. a. elgasi*, nesting in W & S Alaska and wintering west of the Rocky Mts, and *A. a. gambelli*, which includes all other breeding populations over the interior of Alaska and Canada, wintering east of the Rocky Mts. However, this view does not seem entirely satisfactory, insofar as *gambelli*, under its new definition, includes both taiga (larger and darker) and tundra breeders, these birds being further distinguished by migration timing and winter habitat preferences. In fact, *gambelli* now includes birds whose appearance can be close to the three other North American taxa including *flavirostris*. The new treatment is based primarily on the fact that the range of *gambelli* does not overlap with those of the other taxa[356,359].

Finally, it is interesting to note the similarities between this species and Bean Goose, both being polymorphic with clinal variation in size, coloration and habitat preferences (tundra vs. taiga breeders). This is true for Greater White-fronted Geese in North America, but probably also in E Asia, with the birds in the vicinity of the Kava River in S Magadan Oblast, SE Siberia, being geographically distinct from northern breeders, described as larger, and have even been afforded subspecific status[708]. Therefore, some questions remain, especially the status of birds in E Asia and the definition of *gambelli*, which may lead to further subspecific differentiation. Pending future research, the treatment proposed by Banks[65] is adopted here, with five subspecies: *albifrons* (Eurasian Greater White-fronted Goose), *gambelli* (Gambell's Greater White-fronted Goose), *flavirostris* (Greenland Greater White-fronted Goose), *elgasi* (Tule Greater White-fronted Goose) and *sponsa* (Pacific Greater White-fronted Goose).

IDENTIFICATION In North America, Greater White-fronted Goose is the only 'grey goose', and easily distinguished from other species. In Eurasia, adult Greater White-fronted Goose is usually easily separated from Greylag Goose *A. anser*, Pink-footed Goose *A. brachyrhynchus* and Bean Goose by its smaller size, stocky shape, relatively long narrow wings, bright orange legs, uniformly pink or orange bill, strong black ventral markings and white facial mask. The juvenile and first-winter (formative) are more uniform with a slightly paler face and distinctly smaller facial patch. At this age, the rather short bill is entirely pink, orange or pale flesh, with an initially blackish nail, which is usually sufficient to distinguish the species from Pink-footed Goose and Bean Goose. Can recall Greylag Goose, but in addition to the shorter bill, darker brown plumage and orange legs, it has a rather uniform dark upperwing. The only really similar species is Lesser White-fronted Goose, which is usually much rarer. Separating the two species and identifying hybrids is detailed in the latter species' texts. Identification of the different subspecies of Greater White-fronted Goose is detailed under Geographic Variation.

PLUMAGES Nominate subspecies. Sexes identical, but sexing often possible within pairs by differences in size, posture and behaviour. Complex basic moult strategy (one plumage par definitive cycle, two in the first cycle). Ageing easy until the beginning of the first winter and possible until the end of the first summer, and sometimes (in the hand) after the second pre-basic moult.

Adult

Definitive basic plumage (year-round). Uniform brown head, neck, upperparts, pale brown-beige chest and underparts, and white lower belly and undertail. Lacks sharp contrast between head/upper neck and lower neck/breast, typical of Pink-footed and Bean Geese. Medium-brown head, more blackish towards white facial mask, which extends from the gape, the sides of the bill base and forehead. Brown iris with a usually inconspicuous orbital ring, which is sometimes yellow

(most frequently in breeding ♂♂). Bill pinkish, more heavily tinged at base, whitish nail; can show a fleshier or pale orange tinge, often depending on the light, season and probably individual physical condition[395]. Lower neck and breast pale brown to beige. Belly same colour, often whiter in centre. Upper belly and lower breast variably marked with black bars, usually much more obvious than other grey geese. The black can even extend across much of the belly, according to age and also sex (stronger in ♂♂), albeit with much overlap between age and sex groups[1014], but varies at subspecific and individual levels too[1014]. The rear flank feathers are dark brown with pale grey-brown fringes giving a finely streaked appearance, and a clear-cut white line separates the flanks from the upperparts. Feathers of the mantle and scapulars are square-tipped, medium brown with white fringes and black subterminal bars, the upperparts being finely streaked pale like other grey geese, though less obviously in this species and Lesser White-fronted Goose. Dark brown to blackish tertials, finely but distinctly fringed beige. Lower belly and undertail-coverts white. Dark grey back and rump. Uppertail forms a white crescent. Dark grey tail with white fringes to outer rectrices and broad white tip conspicuous in flight. Upperwing has rather dusky greater, lesser and outer median coverts, alula and primary coverts blue-grey contrasting with blackish remiges. Underwing uniform dark grey. Bright orange legs and feet.

Juvenile

First basic plumage (until Oct–Nov). Differs from adult as in other grey geese: slightly smaller size, often more slender shape, scapulars rounded at tips with pale fringes browner and less clearly defined (upperparts faintly scaly), underparts without black spots, and even-coloured flanks. Greater coverts are more pointed with broader, less well-defined greyish fringes. The white tip to the tail is less contrasting than in adult, and the head lacks the white face patch and grooves on the neck-sides. The bill is dull yellow-brown with a dark nail. Legs also significantly duller.

First-winter/first-summer

Formative plumage (Nov–Apr/Aug). Like most grey geese, young birds begin their first autumn migration in juvenile plumage, and start their pre-formative moult on the staging or wintering grounds. White feathers on the face are usually absent until Oct, but often very visible by early winter. The underparts are uniformly pale, except the rear flanks, gradually becoming adult-like (large dark crescents finely fringed whitish). The upperparts show a mixture of juvenile and formative (adult-like, but narrower based and less square-tipped) feathers. Once pre-formative moult is completed, flanks and upperparts similar to adult. This moult is suspended during the coldest months in some birds, but is completed as early as Jan in others. In winter, one should expect both adult-type birds and others with an obvious mixture of two generations of feathers among young birds. However, the white face patch is often incomplete and the black ventral bars are absent or reduced to a few spots until second pre-basic moult. The legs and the bill gain adult colours between midwinter and spring. Thereafter, and until the second pre-basic moult (first summer), the wing feathers, including primaries, are juvenile, often obviously worn, as well as the rectrices.

Second-winter

Second basic plumage (Oct/Jun). Identical to adult, but adult-type birds in autumn/winter lacking black ventral bars (black over <10%) could be in their second winter, but this feature also depends on sex and subspecies. In the hand, second-winter birds may retain some juvenile secondary upperwing-coverts[1014].

GEOGRAPHIC VARIATION Huge, partly clinal and imperfectly assessed over entire Holarctic range. Variation relates to size, head and neck structure, general coloration and thickness, length and colour of the bill. One should bear in mind that these features also vary individually and depend on age, sex and physical condition. It is therefore much easier to assess each feature in small flocks. Identifying the subspecies of a group of geese is relatively simple where two subspecies regularly winter together, e.g. *elgasi* and *sponsa* in C California, or *albifrons* and *flavirostris* in NW Europe. Vagrants that have joined a flock of another subspecies require perfect viewing conditions and a good knowledge of normal variation in the local geese to identify, and in many cases it will be difficult to subspecifically identify a lone vagrant.

Along the Pacific coast of North America, groups of *elgasi* and *sponsa* will usually be fairly easy to distinguish using size, shape, coloration and behaviour: *elgasi* is distinctly larger with a thicker and longer neck, is very dark (especially on the neck and head in direct comparison with *sponsa*), with a large white forehead, and thicker-based and longer bill. In addition, *elgasi* usually forages in small parties, swimming in shallow marshes with much aquatic vegetation, whereas *sponsa* prefers to graze by walking in rice fields, crops and meadows. In the American Pacific context, it would be much harder to detect another subspecies, especially *gambelli* which is intermediate between *elgasi* and *sponsa* in many ways (size, structure, colour), especially as, according to the new definition proposed by Banks[65], it now includes birds from the tundra of N Alaska, very close to *sponsa*, and some birds from the northern taiga, closer to *elgasi*. East of the Rocky Mts, where *gambelli* is the only regularly occurring subspecies, *sponsa* and *elgasi* are occasional visitors. Nevertheless, their distinction from *gambelli* is more than challenging, given the same problems in the variability of 'modern' *gambelli*, although *elgasi* would probably be identifiable under perfect viewing conditions.

Greater White-fronted Goose is a rare visitor to the Atlantic coast of North America, where *gambelli* is the subspecies most likely to occur, but where *flavirostris* is also reported occasionally. These two taxa can be surprisingly alike[669,1202] because of the existence within *gambelli* of large dark birds with a fleshy-orange bill. This difficulty has often been under-estimated. The nominate subspecies may also occur in E North America. In direct comparison with *gambelli*, distinction may be possible, given its smaller, more stocky shape, paler plumage (especially head), white forehead rather reduced at all ages and fairly short bill, with a bright pink base. Within a group of *gambelli*, the differences could be fairly obvious, but much more difficult to evaluate in a lone bird.

In W Europe only two subspecies are regular, *flavirostris* being almost restricted to Ireland and Scotland. These subspecies are usually fairly easy to distinguish, while *gambelli* has never been reported there, although it could occur, the breeding range of *gambelli* being similar to that of Cackling Goose *Branta hutchinsii* and Ross's Goose *Chen rossii*, both occasional visitors to Europe. Identifying *gambelli* would remain problematic because of the similarity to *flavirostris*. Any *flavirostris* with a pale pink or flesh bill (rather than orange) should be carefully checked. Birds of E Asia could also be found in Europe, and several have been reported, including in the Middle East. Larger size, slender shape, long, pale pink bill, largely blacker tail (thin white tip) and large white face patch are all clues that could reliably distinguish an Asian bird in Europe.

In E Asia, detection of another taxon would be very difficult, as *sponsa*, from the Pacific coast of America, is virtually identical. On the other hand, some taiga breeders[708] apparently differ significantly from usual tundra breeders by their larger size and darker plumage, as also the case in North America.

It is important to emphasise that criteria vary within each taxon and that structural differences between the sexes are far from negligible. A large ♂ of the smallest subspecies can therefore exceed a small ♀ of any of the other taxa (except *elgasi*) in mass, head length, bill length, wing chord and tarsus. Bill coloration is also variable; some *albifrons* have an orangey bill, while *flavirostris* occasionally has a rather pink bill. The yellow orbital ring is often considered a good distinguishing feature for *elgasi*, which subspecies certainly shows this feature most frequently, but it can occur in all taxa. The black ventral markings are variable too, but more marked on average in *flavirostris* than *albifrons* and *sponsa*, or to be more precise, individuals with largely black bellies are commoner in *flavirostris*. On the other hand, *elgasi* rarely shows black bars over >50% of the upper abdomen.

A. a. albifrons (W Asia/Europe), see Plumages. The smallest and palest subspecies, with a relatively short neck and short, triangular, pink bill. The pale fringes to the flank feathers, scapulars and greater coverts are broad and obvious, and plumage is more clearly streaked than in other subspecies. The tail-band is paler grey-brown than in other taxa and the white tip broader. In formative plumage, the white face patch is often small, rarely reaching the gape.

A. a. albifrons (E Asia). Larger than W Eurasian birds, but overlap. Neck distinctly longer, as well as the bill (*c.*10% on average), which is also deeper-based, with a slightly concave culmen and the distal third has parallel edges in profile, producing a typical 'teat-shaped' appearance. Pale pink bill, paler and with a more fleshy or peachy hue than in western birds, sometimes pale orange. Head and upperparts are darker on average, with a slightly darker underparts, while the back is blackish-brown (dark grey in Europe). The tail-band is usually blacker with a narrower white tip. Note that southernmost birds nesting in taiga (e.g. along the Kava River[708]) may be larger, with longer neck and tarsi, and a longer and more orange bill.

A. a. sponsa. Almost identical to tundra breeders from E Siberia. In North America, the smallest subspecies, rather grey and pale plumaged (but slightly browner than *albifrons* from W Eurasia). Bill generally pinkish with a variable orange shade, fairly uniform (paler at base in *elgasi*). Orbital ring usually dark and hard to see. Ventral markings on average more pronounced than in other Nearctic taxa. Two populations differ slightly in colour and size (that from Bristol Bay lowlands slightly larger and darker).

A. a. gambelli. Under its new definition[65], this subspecies includes breeders from the tundra and taiga, whereas the name was formerly applied only to the latter. Tundra breeders tend towards *sponsa* while being slightly larger, longer-necked and overall browner (including underparts), while taiga breeders, by far less numerous and less well known, tend more towards *elgasi*. Ely et al.[359] stated that structure and colour differences are moderate, and correlated with temperature on nesting grounds and habitat. Taiga breeders are smaller than *elgasi*, and paler than *flavirostris*. The bill is rather long, usually pale peach with a pinkish or orange hue (often more orange towards the tip and pinkish at the base). Many first-winter birds have a yellow-orange bill, dark flanks, an extensive white face patch and dark greater coverts.

A. a. flavirostris. Probably the most distinct subspecies both morphologically and ecologically[1338], considered as to have first diverged from the common ancestor[397]. The second-largest subspecies, although barely bigger than *gambelli*, with much overlap. Shape typically more massive, neck almost as thick as the head, which is a useful feature compared to other taxa whose neck is thinner, especially *gambelli*). Dark brown with very dark head, appearing plain compared to *albifrons* and *sponsa*, in which the cheeks contrast with a black area bordering the white face patch. The bill is bright orange (occasionally pink), slightly paler and more yellow at the base, with a pale nail (although more dusky than other taxa).

The difference vs. other birds wintering in Europe is obvious, but is slighter vs. *gambelli*, in which the bill may be peach-coloured or pale orange. It can be useful to compare the colour of the bill with the legs, which are often similar in *flavirostris*. Compared to other North American taxa, the bill is proportionately thicker and seems shorter, without the 'teat-shaped tip' of many Nearctic birds. Scapulars, median and greater coverts, tertials and flank feathers have pale brown rather than white fringes, very narrow and scarcely visible at a distance (overall appearance is uniformly dark). Furthermore, the white line separating the sides from the upperparts (which is formed by the fringes to the flank feathers is thinner, shorter and less visible than in other taxa, especially *albifrons*. Black ventral marks are significantly larger than in *albifrons* and *gambelli*, and the central abdomen is often entirely blackish, extending well beyond the legs in profile. The ground colour of the belly and breast is often pale brown, distinctly darker than in other taxa. The tail-band is darker than in *albifrons*, with a considerably thinner white tip.

A. a. elgasi. The largest subspecies, *c.*25% larger than *sponsa*[359], visible even in flight, with its long neck and slower wingbeats[334]. Compared to *sponsa* or *gambelli*, note the proportionately longer legs and strong, visibly thicker and longer neck, sometimes even recalling a swan. When stretched, the neck is typically very long, with the nape, crown and bill forming a gently curved shape, often without any obvious angle. Head is usually very dark chocolate-brown with little contrast between the blackish bar adjoining the white face patch. The dark head emphasises the white face patch, which is typically very contrasting and large, generally covering the whole forehead (looking like a white bump), around the gape and sometimes even almost reaching the eye. The very pale pink base to the mandible, often whitish and shiny, contributes to the impression of a large white face patch. Note that the patch is also larger in formative plumage (more than *sponsa*). A black streak descends from the crown over the hindneck. The bill is deep-based and very long, with a slightly concave culmen and 'teat-shaped' tip. Some birds (40–50% of those wintering in California[334]) have a prominent yellow orbital ring. Overall plumage is dark chocolate-brown with small black ventral bars.

MEASUREMENTS and MASS ♂ slightly larger and heavier than ♀, except in *flavirostris* where differences are smaller. Ely *et al.*[359] indicate differences of 4.6–5.7% in different measurements (head, tarsus, culmen and bill depth at the base), with ♂♂ being 10% heavier. Adult larger and heavier than young birds during the first winter.

A. a. albifrons. W Eurasia. ♂: wing chord 377–464 (adult, 423, n=73) and 375–419 (juvenile, 399, n=15), bill 43–53 (adult, 47.1, n=74), tarsus 68–80 (72.8, n=49), mass in winter 2,450 (adult, ± 29.1, n=87) and 2,130 (first-winter, ± 11.9, n=238); ♀: wing chord 379–438 (400, n=60) and 359–410 (juvenile, 388,

n=18), bill 40–51 (adult, 44.9, n=64), tarsus 64–76 (69.3, n=34), mass in winter: 2,180 (adult, ± 27.1, n=92) and 1,905 (first-winter, ± 8.4, n=287)[267].

A. a. gambelli. Northwest Territories. ♂: tail 125.3 (± 1.0, n=30), culmen 53.5 (± 0.47, n=32), tarsus 88.9 (± 0.58, n=31), mass in Jul 2,400 (± 70, n=32); ♀ (n=30): tail 125.3 (± 1.0), culmen 50.5 (± 0.08), tarsus 82.8 (± 0.63), mass in Jul 2,100 (± 80)[356]. Saskatchewan. ♂: culmen 53.2 (± 0.37, n=66), tarsus 91.1 (± 0.32, n=64), mass in Sep 2,725 (± 24, n=66); ♀: culmen 49.6 (± 0.25, n=67), tarsus 86.3 (± 0.39, n=65), mass in Sep 2,454 (± 22, n=67)[356].

A. a. elgasi. ♂: culmen 58.3 (± 0.54, n=26), tail 135 (± 1.6, n=20), mass in winter 3,000 (± 30, n=53); ♀: culmen 54.4 (± 0.58, n=12), tail 132 (± 1.8, n=13), mass in winter 2,700 (± 30, n=54)[356]. ♂ (n=70): wing chord 426–468 (adult) and 415–452 (juvenile), culmen 54–64, depth of bill at tip of forehead feathering 25.2–32.2, tail 124–147, tarsus 76–88; ♀ (n=50): wing chord 400–441 (adult) and 387–425 (juvenile), culmen 51–61, depth of bill at tip of forehead feathering 23.5–30.2, tail 121–144, tarsus 73–85[1014]; compared measurements by same author for *flavirostris*.

A. a. sponsa. California. ♂: wing chord 440.9 (± 1.1, n=124), tail 126.8 (± 1.0, n=40), culmen 50.7 (± 0.12, n=371), tarsus 89.8 (± 0.21, n=250), mass in winter 2,348 (± 11, n=407); ♀: wing chord 420.5 (± 1.0, n=126), tail 122.8 (± 1.0, n=42), culmen 48.4 (± 0.12, n=344), tarsus 84.8 (± 0.19, n=256), mass in winter 2,075 (± 11, n=384)[356]. Mexico. ♂: wing chord 432 (± 3.2, n=7), tail 129.5 (± 6.4, n=6), culmen 55.0 (± 0.56, n=17), tarsus 90.3 (± 0.8, n=15), mass in winter 2,637 (± 36, n=17); ♀: wing chord 410 (± 7.4, n=4), tail 120.1 (± 1.2, n=3), culmen 50.9 (± 0.55, n=10), tarsus 83.1 (± 1.1, n=10), mass in winter 2,335 (± 37, n=10)[356].

A. a. flavirostris. ♂: wing chord: 389–463 (adult, 426, n=232) and 370–441 (juvenile, 410, n=94), bill 46–60 (adult, 52.7, n=326), tarsus 65–84 (74.9, n=326), mass in winter 2,050–3,600 (adult, 2714, n=229) and 1,900–3,510 (first-winter, 2497, n=277); ♀: wing chord 389–461 (423, n=261) and 361–439 (juvenile, 405, n=149), tail 90–98 (94.7, n=21), bill 44–60 (adult, 52.0, n=410), tarsus 63–83 (74.4, n=410), mass in winter 1,800–2,900 (adult, 2409, n=223) and 1,700–2,875 (first-winter, 2 262, n=245)[267,395]. ♂ (n=100): wing chord 396–453 (adult) and 383–437 (juvenile), culmen 46–59, depth of bill at tip of forehead feathering: 21.0–27.9, tail

105–135, tarsus 67–83; ♀ (*n*=100): wing chord 393–450 (adult) and 379–433 (juvenile), culmen 44–58, depth of bill at tip of forehead feathering 19.8–26.6, tail 101–132, tarsus 66–82[1014]; compare measurements by same author for *elgasi*.

VOICE Very loquacious. Utters various calls close to those of Greylag Goose but more melodious and high-pitched, less raucous and nasal. The most typical call is a whistled *kyew-lyew* or *kyeew-gluk* with a longer first syllable, or *kyew-lyew-lyew* (tri-syllabic). Voice higher pitched in ♂[7395]. That voice of *elgasi* is described as lower and harsher than that of *sponsa*[861].

MOULT Complex basic strategy. Pre-formative moult during migration and on wintering grounds, starting in Sep–Nov, lasting until first winter, ending as early as Jan in some, but often suspended in early winter and completed in Mar–Apr in others. Winter moult suspension could be the source of the claim of a pre-alternate moult in spring[267], but this moult has not been recorded in adults[1014]. Pre-formative moult includes most to all head and neck feathers, a variable number of scapulars and flanks, fewer mantle, back and rear body feathers and very few to no belly feathers, occasionally 1–2 tertials and a variable number of rectrices[1014]. Definitive pre-basic moult begins Jul–Aug (*c.*1 month earlier for non-breeding second-years) with simultaneous loss of flight feathers. The body feathers and rectrices are moulted Aug–Nov, at different sites along the Arctic coast, during migration and on arrival at the wintering sites. Moult timing varies slightly depending on population and latitude of nesting grounds.

HYBRIDISATION In the wild, hybridisation has been reported regularly with Snow Goose *Chen caerulescens*, Canada Goose *Branta canadensis* and Cackling Goose *B. hutchinsii*. In Europe, hybridisation has also been reported with introduced Canada Geese and Barnacle Goose *B. leucopsis*, which now nests in the winter range of Greater White-fronted Goose. Natural hybrids with Greylag Goose are rare. Although they do not produce particular identification problems with one or another species, these hybrids are described below. Hybrids with Bar-headed Goose *A. indicus* have been reported a few times in N Europe (see that species). Other natural hybridisation events are very rare, with Bean Goose, Red-breasted Goose *B. ruficollis* (a few recent reports in Europe) and possibly Brent Goose *B. bernicla*[668,817]. The only really misleading hybrid is with Lesser White-fronted Goose, which is sometimes reported in the wild as well as in captivity (see that species). Finally, in captivity, Greater White-fronted Goose has hybridised with Swan Goose *A. cygnoid*, Pink-footed Goose *A. brachyrhynchus*, Emperor Goose *Chen canagica*, Red-breasted Goose, Egyptian Goose *Alopochen aegyptiacus* and Ashy-headed Goose *Chloephaga poliocephala*[97,817].

Greater White-fronted Goose × Greylag Goose is rarely reported and may be difficult to detect, given its resemblance to some domestic variants of the latter, especially those with much white at the base of the bill. Moreover, Greylag Goose can show black ventral spots and a pink bill that matches that usually shown by the adult hybrid. The latter can be identified by its intermediate size, rather dark upperparts (vs. Greylag Goose), dark area adjacent to white face patch, yellow-orange orbital ring, clear orange hue to the legs and less contrasting underwing pattern (vs. Greylag Goose). At least some hybrids have more obvious pale fringes to the median and greater coverts than in Greater White-fronted Goose. Finally, the white fringes to the flank feathers are slightly broader than in Greylag Goose and form a more visible white line on the upper flanks (at least when *A. a. albifrons* is involved in the cross).

Greater White-fronted Goose × Snow Goose is regularly reported in North America, where no other natural hybrid has the same appearance, as Greater White-fronted Goose is the only Nearctic grey goose. Note, however, that hybrid Greater White-fronted Goose × Ross's Goose has apparently not been described to date. In Europe, this hybrid is much rarer and can be mistaken for hybrids involving another grey goose, but also any of the domestic forms of Greylag. Most hybrids from this cross have entirely white underparts below the breast or even the lower neck, except a few grey-brown feathers on the upper flanks. The head, neck, upper breast (sometimes flecked with white) and upperparts are irregularly grey-brown, often with some white scapulars and usually a large white face patch. The blackish tertials, secondaries and greater coverts have clear white fringes. Thick, long bill, pinkish or peach-coloured. Legs pink to pale orange.

Greater White-fronted Goose × Barnacle Goose hybrids have been reported on several occasions, mainly in Europe, where in many cases at least one parent pertains to a feral population or an escape from captivity. It is often difficult to distinguish this hybrid from others involving Greater White-fronted Goose and another *Branta* species (see below). This hybrid is generally dark and uniformly-plumaged, with the chest, neck, nape and crown blackish, and a beige-coloured circular area on the cheeks and chin. An ill-defined white face patch is inherited from Greater White-fronted Goose, with a variable white spot often visible on the forehead as well. The bill is variable, with both blackish and dull pinkish areas, sometimes almost entirely blackish. The culmen and nail are often blackish, the sides of the bill variably stained orange or pink. Scapulars are like those of Barnacle Goose, grey-brown with blackish subterminal bars and faint pale fringes. Upperwing dusky with faint pale fringes. Flanks grey-brown, slightly paler than the breast, lightly streaked pale. Belly flecked whitish. Tail blackish. Bright yellow-orange legs.

Greater White-fronted Goose × Canada Goose: typical birds from this cross look like a browner, faded version of Canada Goose, with pale brownish or beige cheeks, a white face patch often completely surrounding the base of the bill, variable white eye-ring and bright yellow-orange legs. The bill is longish, different from hybrids involving Barnacle or Cackling Geese. The bill can be almost entirely blackish, dull grey-orange or pale orange, sometimes with just a few dark spots. The foreneck is sometimes blackish to the breast (as in Canada Geese), but can also be browner, without any sharp contrast. Compared to Greylag Goose × Canada Goose hybrids, the European version of this cross (including *A. a. albifrons*) is smaller and more slender, darker and browner overall, with a white face patch and thinner bill. Note, this is a general description, as the variability of each of the parents will inevitably lead to hybrids, depending on the subspecies involved.

Greater White-fronted Goose × Cackling Goose is also potentially highly variable in appearance (mainly size and general paleness), as are the two parents. Also note, at least in some birds (perhaps those involving *B. h. minima*), the smaller size than Greater White-fronted Goose and significantly stockier bill. These will probably be the only individuals safely distinguishable from a hybrid involving a Canada Goose.

HABITAT and LIFE-CYCLE Different populations differ in their nesting and wintering habitat preferences, as well as in their migration and time of breeding. All subspecies are strictly migratory, wintering populations south of the Gulf of Mexico (*gambelli*) undertaking the longest migration among geese. Nesting season and habitat are directly related to latitude. In SW Alaska, *sponsa* inhabits marshes in coastal lowlands, the ponds formed by snowmelt, sloughs and slow rivers, up to the dry tundra and 30 km from the Bering Sea coast[356]. Eggs are laid during the first half of May in Bristol Bay, Alaska, and at the end of the month in Yukon-Kuskokwim Delta. Race *elgasi* lays mainly in the last three weeks of May and inhabits fresh and brackish coastal marshes, as well as bushy fringes to ponds and bogs in spruce taiga[1265]. In Greenland, *flavirostris* mainly lays during the second half of May[1238] and inhabits coastal marshes, as well as fresh ponds at higher altitudes than other taxa[395]. Under its new definition, *gambelli* inhabits a wide variety of habitats from coastal floodplains and large Arctic delta tundra to grassy or bushy fringes of rivers, ponds, bogs and taiga marshes dominated by conifers, birches and willows. Taiga populations (C Alaska, Yukon) lay in May, while breeders on the Arctic fringe and Nunavut lay during the first half of Jun. Eurasian birds are tundra breeders, laying mainly during the first three weeks of Jun[359]. Sometimes joins other species of geese to moult[356]. Non-breeders and adults that have failed to breed moult earlier.

In winter, gathers in large flocks, especially if hunting activity and other disturbances force birds to congregate in protected areas. Tundra-nesting populations mainly use grasslands, meadows, wet or flooded crops and rice fields to feed, mainly by grazing in large flocks. Taiga populations prefer to feed in marshes with abundant vegetation, swimming and even up-ending to search for food at the bottom. They often feed in family groups or relatively small flocks. The same differences in habitat choice and feeding behaviour exist among different subspecies of Bean Goose (tundra vs. taiga groups).

RANGE and POPULATION With Brent Goose (Brant), Greater White-fronted Goose is the only goose with an almost continuous circumpolar distribution. The available information on the populations of the different subspecies is complicated by changed nomenclature. The world population is estimated at just over three million individuals.

A. a. albifrons. Breeds in the tundra and northern taiga, with an isolated population around the Kava River, Magadan Oblast, E Russia[708]. Western breeders winter in Europe, east to around the Caspian Sea, while eastern birds winter in E Asia, the species being a scarce visitor to the Indian Subcontinent and SE Asia. The dividing line between the two populations has been placed around the Kolyma River by several authors[295,395], but Mooij[866] and Mooij & Zöckler[868] suggested it to be the Khatanga River, NC Siberia. The same authors stated that westernmost breeders winter in NW Europe, based on recoveries and controls of banded birds. However, the measurements of birds on the Kanin and Taimyr Peninsulas[359] correspond to those of European wintering birds and are significantly smaller than birds measured from the mouth of the Lena River and further east, suggesting that the dividing line might further east, between the Khatanga and Lena Rivers. The western population is c.1.2 million birds (mainly in the Netherlands and, to a lesser extent, the UK, N Germany and Belgium), with 100,000–110,000 birds in C Europe, 200,000 in Turkey and the Black Sea[400,1347] and c.15,000 in the Caspian Sea and Iraq[1154]. Numbers have recently increased in NW Europe, whereas they are stable or declining elsewhere.

The Asian wintering population was estimated at 100,000–150,000 birds[395], but the most recent censuses seem higher, with a gradual shift of Chinese birds towards Japan and South Korea. A total of 175,000–210,000 was given for Japan and 70,000–100,000 in South Korea during 2008–11[833], while in China, 110,000 birds were reported in 2007 at Lake Poyang, Jiangxi, alone[757]. The same authors indicate the total E Asian population as 218,000–311,000 birds in 2005–07.

In the Netherlands, a feral population was first reported in 1980 and now numbers 745 pairs[633,1328,1329]. Elsewhere in Europe, a few pairs nest or have nested recently in England, Belgium and Germany, but none of these populations is self-sustaining[62]. Some older introduction attempts (both *albifrons* and *flavirostris*) took place in SE Sweden in the 1930s, but failed[667].

A. a. sponsa. Two main populations. The first breeds in W Alaska (mainly the Yukon-Kuskokwim Delta area) and winters on the Pacific coast from Oregon to Mexico. The second breeds in the Bristol Bay lowlands and winters on the Chihuahuan Plateau, in NC Mexico. The total population was estimated at 605,000 individuals in 2009–11[1292], 664,200 in 2012 and 579,900 in 2013, with a mean annual growth rate of 5% during the last decade[1292]. Very few birds stray east of the Rocky Mts (into the range of *gambelli*), since

only 1.3% of controls of banded birds occurred there (with 0.5% elsewhere outside the Pacific Flyway)[395].

A. a. gambelli. Following Banks[65], this subspecies breeds in the tundra from NW Alaska to W Hudson Bay, Canada, and in the taiga of the Alaskan interior (south to 60°N). Tundra populations winter in the lower Mississippi Valley to Louisiana and Texas, with small numbers on Gulf of Mexico coasts (Tamaulipas and Veracruz, Mexico). Taiga populations preferentially winter on the plateaux of Zacatecas and Durango, Mexico, migrating earlier than tundra breeders[360]. It is a rare but regular visitor elsewhere in North America, particularly along the Atlantic coast of the USA. Total population estimated at 710,000 individuals in 2010, 681,700 in 2011 and 777,900 in 2012[1292]. No clear trend between 2004 and 2013, but the population peaked near 1.1 million birds during the 1990s.

A. a. flavirostris. Breeds in W Greenland between 64°N and 76°N, and migrates across Iceland to wintering grounds in Ireland and W Scotland, less frequently south to W Wales. Small numbers reach further south and east in the UK. A rare to occasional visitor elsewhere in W Europe and on the North American Atlantic coast. The population increased steadily to 35,500 birds in the late 1990s, but has declined since then, to a mean of 24,000 birds between 2006 and 2011[401].

A. a. elgasi. The most range-restricted and rarest subspecies. Breeds in a small area of coastal marshes and taiga around the Cook Inlet, S Alaska. Winters mainly in the Sacramento Valley and at Suisun Marsh, east of San Francisco Bay, California. Its population numbers 5,000–10,000 birds[1187]. Banded birds have occasionally been reported east of the Rocky Mts, while several sightings of large, dark Greater White-fronted Geese among the local tundra *gambelli* east of the Rockies might also have involved this subspecies.

CAPTIVITY Generally rare in captivity, except in some specialised collections, and often much more expensive than most other grey geese, including Lesser White-fronted Goose.

REFERENCES Alisauskas (1998)[13]; Banks (2011)[65]; Banks *et al.* (2008)[62]; Bird Hybrids Database (2014)[97]; Cramp & Simmons (1977)[267]; Dalgety *et al.* (1948)[277]; Delacour (1954)[295]; Delacour & Ripley (1975)[298]; Dunn (2005)[334]; Dzubin *et al.* (1992)[339]; Eda *et al.* (2013)[344]; Ely & Dzubin (1994)[356]; Ely & Takekawa

(1996)[358]; Ely *et al.* (2005)[359]; Ely *et al.* (2013)[360]; Fox & Owen *in* Kear (2005)[395]; Fox & Stroud (2002)[397]; Fox *et al.* (2010)[400]; Fox *et al.* (2011)[401]; Hartlaub (1852)[535]; van der Jeugd *et al.* (2006)[633]; Kampe-Persson (2010)[667]; Kampe-Persson & Lerner (2007)[668]; Kaufman (1994)[669]; Krechmar (1996)[708]; Li *et al.* (2009)[757]; McCarthy (2006)[817]; Meijuan *et al.* (2012)[833]; Moffitt (1926)[861]; Mooij (2000)[866]; Mooij & Zöckler (2000)[868]; Orthmeyer *et al.* (1995)[935]; Pyle (2008)[1014]; Rutt (2006)[1112]; Scott & Rose (1996)[1154]; Shuford & Gardali (2008)[1187]; Sibley (2011)[1202]; Stroud (1982)[1238]; Swarth & Bryant (1917)[1246]; Timm & Sellers (1981)[1265]; Todd (1950)[1275]; USFWS (2011)[1292]; USFWS (2013)[1294]; Voslamber (2002)[1328]; Voslamber *et al.* (2010)[1329]; Warren *et al.* (1993)[1338]; Wetlands International (2012)[1347].

52. *A. a. albifrons*, adult (definitive basic); the smallest subspecies, with a smallish, stubby bill, and compared to the orange legs, the bill appears clearly pink. Netherlands, Feb (Sébastien Reeber).

53. *A. a. albifrons*, adult (definitive basic); species is unmistakable in adult plumage, although this shows few black ventral patches (frequent in second-winter birds). Netherlands, Feb (Sébastien Reeber).

54. *A. a. albifrons*, adult (definitive basic); a moulting bird (perhaps in its second year); in E Asia, the bill is often longer and more orange. Japan, Oct (Stuart Price).

55. *A. a. albifrons*, juvenile (first basic); like other geese, note rounded scapulars, plain flanks and near-lack of grooves on neck-sides at this age, although bare-parts coloration should still make identification easy. France, Dec (Vincent Palomares).

56. *A. a. albifrons*, first-winter (formative); similar to adult after pre-formative moult, and best distinguished by smaller face patch, dark nail to bill and lack of black ventral patches. Netherlands, Feb (Sébastien Reeber).

57. *A. a. albifrons*, adult (definitive basic); in flight, note ventral patches, dark underwing and long pointed wings of this species. Netherlands, Feb (Sébastien Reeber).

58. *A. a. albifrons* (left) and *A. a. flavirostris* (right), adult (definitive basic): *flavirostris* has darker head (eye barely noticeable), larger white face patch, narrower fringes to upperparts (including greater coverts), more extensive black ventral patches and broader and blacker tail bar; however, this bird lacks the typical orange bill, thereby matching some *gambelli*. Netherlands, Feb (Sébastien Reeber).

59. *A. a. albifrons*, adult (definitive basic); compared to European wintering birds, the bill looks longer, thinner, with a more 'teat-shaped' tip, and tinged flesh to orangey. South Korea, Dec (Philippe J. Dubois).

60. *A. a. elgasi*, adult (definitive basic); typical shape of this subspecies; while fringes to upperparts are rather narrow, the underparts have a pale ground colour with less black than *sponsa*. California, USA, Nov (Sébastien Reeber).

61. *A. a. elgasi*, adult (definitive basic); the largest subspecies, typically dark brown, bill pale pink (almost whitish at base), deep-based and very long, large white face patch, and often a yellow orbital ring. California, USA, Nov (Sébastien Reeber).

62. *A. a. elgasi*, family group; note typical shape of adult (right), with long, thick neck and large head. California, USA, Nov (Sébastien Reeber).

63. *A. a. elgasi*, juvenile (first basic); ageing **as** in other subspecies. California, USA, Nov (Sébastien Reeber).

64. *A. a. elgasi*, adult (definitive basic); tail pattern with rather thin white tip. California, USA, Nov (Sébastien Reeber).

65. *A. a. sponsa*, adult (definitive basic); compared to European wintering *albifrons*, note browner, darker plumage (tinged rusty here), and the longer, paler bill, very similar to E Asian *albifrons*. California, USA, Nov (Sébastien Reeber).

66. *A. a. sponsa*, first-winter (formative); the foreground bird is a first-winter (black nail, reduced white face patch, some juvenile body feathers). California, USA, Nov (Sébastien Reeber).

67. *A. a. sponsa*, adult (definitive basic); note variability of ventral coloration. California, USA, Nov (Sébastien Reeber).

68. *A. a. gambelli*, adult (definitive basic); birds wintering E of Rockies are this subspecies, which groups birds sharing characters of *sponsa*, *flavirostris* and *elgasi*; apart from the rather pale belly and thinner neck, this bird recalls *flavirostris* in its orange bill, large white face patch and dark head, while the complete yellow orbital ring can be present in all subspecies. Colorado, USA, Feb (Steve Mlodinow).

69. *A. a. flavirostris*, adult (definitive basic); a large, dark brown subspecies, with a clearly orange bill (becoming redder pre-breeding). Iceland, Apr (Yann Kolbeinsson).

70. *A. a. gambelli*, juvenile (first basic); aged by rounded scapulars, plain flanks, no face patch and dark nail, while many young birds have a clear orangey hue to bill. Colorado, USA, Jan (Steve Mlodinow).

71. *A. a. gambelli*, adult (definitive basic); such birds can be very difficult to separate from *sponsa* – rather pale head (eye easily visible), pale pinkish bill, small face patch, obvious pale fringes to upperparts, and pale underparts with well-marked black ventral patches. Texas, USA, Jan (Joe Fischer).

72. *A. a. flavirostris*, adult (definitive basic); most birds of this subspecies have large black ventral patches, and also note narrower pale brown fringes to upperparts and thick neck when stretched. Iceland, Apr (Yann Kolbeinsson).

73. *A. a. flavirostris*, juvenile (first basic); plain dark plumage, with slightly bulging culmen, typical of this age. France, Oct (Aurélien Audevard).

74. *A. a. flavirostris*, first-winter (formative); like adult, but note reduced white face patch and dark nail, while broad blackish tail bar and thin white tip identify the subspecies. Scotland, Mar (Ian Fulton).

75. *A. a. flavirostris*, adult (definitive basic); typical head pattern of this subspecies, with long orange bill and large white face patch. Scotland, Mar (Ian Fulton).

LESSER WHITE-FRONTED GOOSE
Anser erythropus   **Plates 6, 7, 8**

TAXONOMY *Anas erythropus* Linnaeus, 1758, *Syst. Nat.*, edn. 10, p. 123. Within the genus *Anser*, very close to Greater White-fronted Goose *Anser albifrons*, which it closely resembles also with which it hybridises relatively frequently. No geographic variation or subspecies.

IDENTIFICATION The smallest grey goose, usually distinguished fairly easily by its small size, rather stocky look, long wings, short neck, relatively large oval head and tiny triangular bill. The only real confusion species is Greater White-fronted Goose, which is the second smallest grey goose in Eurasia and shares several similar characters (pale pink bill surrounded by white mask, rather dark brown plumage with black markings on underparts). When flocks of the two species are seen side by side, identification is usually pretty easy, using the following features.

- *Size*: Slightly smaller than Greater White-fronted Goose, with overlap. An adult ♂ Lesser White-fronted Goose in a flock of Greater White-fronted Geese may not stand out by size, whereas a young female may seem surprisingly small within a flock of other grey geese.

- *Shape*: Often more striking and useful than size. Lesser White-fronted Goose is generally stubby, compact, elongated and rather small, due to its short, thick neck, oval head (whose thickness often equals that of the neck) with a rather steep forehead and small bill. Legs are approximately 25% shorter than in Greater White-fronted Goose. In Lesser White-fronted Goose in profile, the wings extend well beyond the tip of the tail, while in Greater White-fronted Goose, they reach the tip of the tail or project just beyond it. In flight, the wings of Lesser White-fronted Goose seem quite long and narrow, with rapid wingbeats.

- *Head and neck coloration*: In Greater White-fronted Goose (in Eurasia), the head-sides are a paler brown with greyish tones, contrasting with a vertical black area next to the white face patch. In Lesser White-fronted Goose, the cheeks are more uniform and darker brown, providing little contrast with black border to the face patch. The lower neck and sides of the chest often show a clear ochre or gingery tinge in Lesser White-fronted Goose.

- *Size and shape of bill*: In Lesser White-fronted Goose, the bill is very small, short and triangular (culmen straight in profile). Compared to the head, its size is more reminiscent of Barnacle Goose *Branta leucopsis* than of any of the grey geese.

- *White face patch* (adult): In Lesser White-fronted Goose, the white face patch extends further over the forehead, often up to the mid-crown. In profile, the white extends just above the eye or even slightly to the rear of it, forming a concave delineation with the dark brown head. In Greater White-fronted Goose, the white usually does not reach above the eye and forms a straighter delineation. Viewed from the front, the white often tapers on the crown, while in Greater White-fronted Goose the border to the white face patch is often rounded or truncated. However, the white very rarely can extend further onto the crown in Greater White-fronted Goose (hybrids?). Between the first winter and early summer, young of both species show a partially marked white facial patch, making this feature less useful for identification purposes).

- *Orbital ring*: The orbital ring of Lesser White-fronted Goose is bright yellow, usually large and obvious, especially as the surrounding head is dark brown. It is wider in front and above the eye. Greater White-fronted Goose of the nominate subspecies usually has a dark grey orbital ring, invisible at any distance. However, in some birds (especially breeding ♂♂), the orbital ring is pale or yellow, but usually still rather narrow.

- *Body coloration*: Lesser White-fronted Goose is slightly darker brown and more uniform overall, with pale streaks barely visible on the upperparts and a brownish-ochre tinge to the belly. The white line on the upper flanks (adult) is slightly thinner than in Greater White-fronted Goose, but of constant width and clear-cut.

- *Ventral patches* (adult): On average less developed, smaller and fewer in Lesser White-fronted Goose. For identification purposes, this feature should be used with caution and this criterion is only indicative, varying with age and sex in both species.

- *Tail*: The white tip to the tail is slightly broader in Lesser White-fronted Goose and the rectrices are blacker (dark grey in Greater White-fronted Goose), making the tip appear more contrasting.

- *Foraging action*: When feeding, the movements of Lesser White-fronted Goose are slightly faster and more nervous, which can be useful, especially in direct comparison.

A lone bird, especially outside the usual range of Lesser White-fronted Goose, may prove harder to identify, especially given the risk of a hybrid between the two species. Such birds show intermediate characters and are sometimes hard to distinguish from Lesser White-fronted Goose without perfect viewing conditions (see Hybridisation).

PLUMAGES Sexes identical, but can be determined within pairs, based on differences in size, posture and behaviour. Complex basic moult strategy (one plumage per definitive cycle, two in the first cycle). Ageing is easy until the beginning of the first winter, requires closer views until the end of the first summer and is possible in the hand after the second pre-basic moult.

Adult

Definitive basic plumage (year-round). Darkish brown head, neck and upperparts, pale ochre-yellow or ginger chest, and white lower belly and undertail. Head, upper neck and nape brown, darker brown towards white face patch, which surrounds the base of the bill and extends from the forehead onto the forecrown. Iris brown with a bright yellow orbital ring, wider (slightly distended) in front of and above the eye. Bill pink with a pale nail. Lower neck, foreneck, breast, belly and flanks rather uniform pale brown with yellow-ochre or ginger tones. The upper belly is has variable black patches, heavier than in other grey geese except Greater White-fronted Goose. Like other grey geese, feathers of the flanks are dark brown with pale brownish fringes forming a faint streaked pattern and a white line separating the sides from the upperparts. Feathers of the mantle and scapulars are square-tipped, medium brown (subterminal bars barely darker) with pale brown to whitish fringes that form pale streaks, less visible than in all other grey geese. Dark brown to blackish tertials with fine white fringes, often reduced at the tips. Lower belly and undertail-coverts white. Back and rump dark grey-brown. Uppertail-coverts form a white crescent. Tail black with white fringes, including broad trailing edge. Upperwing has dark grey-brown secondary coverts and narrow bars formed by the paler grey tips to the greater coverts. Lesser coverts (the palest area of the wing) contrast with blackish flight feathers (clear white shafts to primaries). Underwing uniform grey with blackish flight feathers. Bright orange legs and feet.

Juvenile

First basic plumage (until Oct–Dec). Differs from adult by slightly smaller size (in direct comparison), marginally thinner head, lack of white face patch, absence of grooves on sides of the neck, scapulars with rounded tips and barely visible yellowish-brown fringes, and underparts rather uniform pale ochre-brown. The white tips to the greater coverts are less clear-cut. The bill is dull pinkish with a pale brown nail, quickly becoming whitish. Legs much duller orange-yellow, with darker brownish stains.

First-winter/first-summer

Formative plumage (Nov–Apr/Jul–Aug). Young birds begin their first autumn migration in juvenile plumage, and start their pre-formative at migration stop-over sites or on arrival at the wintering grounds. White feathers around the bill begin to appear in Nov, quickly followed by the scapulars and rear flank feathers, which are marginally narrower at the base and slightly more rounded on the tips. As in Greater White-fronted Goose, pre-formative moult is completed by Jan–Feb in some, suspended or slowed during the coldest month(s) in others, in which moult finishes in Mar–Apr. During the winter, some will be almost adult-like, but others show two feather generations. Following pre-formative moult, most birds have a white face patch, albeit visibly smaller than in adult. Belly still almost entirely juvenile (small round feathers centred brown and fringed whitish) initially neatly and faintly barred, without black markings of adult. During following spring, contrast between the new scapulars and flank feathers, and the worn, dull juvenile upperwing coverts without fringes, is often obvious. The bill coloration is similar to the adult during the first winter, but the legs remain more yellow and duller until the following spring.

Second-winter

Second basic plumage (Jul/Aug). Usually undistinguishable from adult after second pre-basic moult. In the hand, some second-winter birds may retain a few upperwing-coverts, especially outer median coverts.

GEOGRAPHIC VARIATION None described, although three genetically distinct populations exist[1105].

MEASUREMENTS and MASS ♂♂ and adult slightly

larger than ♀♀ and young, respectively. ♂: wing chord 370–407 (adult, 387, n=17) and 350–376 (juvenile, 367, n=6), bill 29–35 (33.1, n=12); ♀: wing chord 342–392 (adult, 363, n=16) and 331–359 (juvenile, 344, n=4), bill 28–35 (31.2, n=10)[1122]. ♂: wing chord 370–388 (adult, 378, n=8) and 360–369 (juvenile, 364, n=5), bill 31–37 (33.6, n=13), tarsus 59–68 (63.7, n=13), mass in winter 1,950–2,300 (n=4); ♀: wing chord 361–387 (adult, 373, n=7) and 329–356 (juvenile, 345, n=10), bill 29–34 (31.3, n=17), tarsus 57–65 (61.0, n=15), mass in winter 2,100 and 2,150 (n=2)[267]. Adult ♂ (n=24): wing chord 380.5 (±14.7), culmen from forehead feathers 33.8 (±3.5), bill depth 19.3 (±1.7), tail 105.6 (±5.1), tarsus 63.5 (±3.1), middle toe 62.1 (±3.7)[911].

VOICE Close to that of Greater White-fronted Goose, but a little faster, sharper and squeaky, not very loud but generally acute. Can be transcribed, depending on its frequency (perhaps linked to sex), *kya-rya-rya* or *rew-lii-lip*, with the first syllable slightly longer and lower. Usually fairly easy to pick out among Greater White-fronted Geese. Also utters a *kak*, sharper when worried.

MOULT Complex basic strategy. Extent and timing very similar or identical to Greater White-fronted Goose (which see), except pre-basic moult starts a week or two earlier[56].

HYBRIDISATION In the wild, the only hybrids reported involved Greater White-fronted Goose (which see). Hybridisation has also been reported very occasionally with Snow Goose *Chen caerulescens*[300,465], Barnacle Goose[582,585,817], especially in the Scandinavian reintroduction programme[668], and Red-breasted Goose *Branta ruficollis*[465,899]. Hybrids also reported in NW Europe, where there are important natural populations of several species of geese, and feral populations of many others. Apart from Lesser White-fronted Goose, these hybrids involved Bar-headed Goose *A. indicus*[121,619] (which see), probably Cackling Goose *Branta hutchinsii*[104] and Canada Goose *B. canadensis*[668], and possibly Ross's Goose *Chen rossii*[132] and Emperor Goose *C. canagica*[107]. In captivity, hybridisation also documented with Greylag Goose *Anser anser*[668,1107] and Brent Goose *Branta bernicla*[619,817].

Lesser White-fronted Goose × Greater White-fronted Goose: hybridisation between the two species is reported occasionally, especially in captivity, and has even caused problems for the reintroduction efforts in Europe. Indeed, the genetic analysis of both captive and wild birds has demonstrated the presence of haplotypes of Greater White-fronted Geese in 15 captives, while no such haplotypes were found among the 81 wild birds sampled[1105]. Hybridisation has occurred during the formation of the captive stock for the reintroduction scheme in Scandinavia[962,1104,1105,1107,1258].

Hybridisation is probably rare in nature, even if the difficulties in detecting such hybrids makes estimating its frequency difficult. These hybrids pose real identification issues, especially when faced by a lone Lesser White-fronted Goose (which is the rarest species). Suspected hybrids were first described long ago[300,746,911,947,1177,1310,1326].

Measurements of two hybrids in museums (Amsterdam and Tring) were intermediate between those taken of samples of 26 Lesser White-fronted Geese and 24 Greater White-fronted Geese[911] for wing chord, tarsus, middle toe, and culmen length and depth. One of the two was closer to Greater White-fronted Goose and other to Lesser White-fronted Goose. Many hybrids show a clear yellow orbital ring, which may not seem complete, or as obvious as in Lesser White-fronted Goose. The white face patch appears intermediate in extent between those of the two parents, and often is irregularly defined on the forecrown. Other features (contrast in the pale fringes on the upperparts, coloration of the head, neck and underparts, extent of black ventral markings) also appear intermediate, but because they are also variable in both parent species, they may be less useful. Such hybrids are likely to be misidentified, especially when an individual recalling Lesser White-fronted Goose in several respects is seen in company of Greater White-fronted Geese.

HABITAT and LIFE-CYCLE Highly migratory, leaving the wintering grounds from Feb, arriving on the breeding grounds between early May and late Jun, with eggs being laid between 5 Jun and 10 Jul, most frequently in mid-Jun[391,1248]. Breeding habitat often the transition zone between tundra and taiga, in bushy fringes to wetlands (bogs, waterbodies resulting from melting snow, slow-flowing rivers, etc.), up to 700 m above sea level[391]. Mostly in lone pairs[145]. Adults begin moulting their flight feathers on or near nesting sites, in tall grass near wetlands where both flightless adults and young can hide[391]. Once able to fly again, usually by late Aug or Sep[145], moults the contour feathers at both dedicated sites away from the nesting areas or at migratory stop-over sites. Non-breeders and those that fail usually gather to moult at higher latitudes and/or altitudes than nesting sites[794]. Scandinavian non-breeders may moult along the Arctic coast of C Siberia[1]. Gregarious in the non-breeding season. Inhabits open steppe with short grass (often on brackish substrates[391]), swampy or agricultural areas (pastures and grasslands). Lesser White-fronted Geese may be forced to use pastures with less nutritional value because of locally heavy human disturbance[1334]. Similarly, the species may switch sites during winter depending on food resources[244].

RANGE and POPULATION Globally threatened and listed as Vulnerable[145]. Nest sites distributed discontinuously or sparsely through S Palearctic tundra belt, from N Scandinavia to E Siberia (Anadyr Valley, River Kanchalan[545]). Formerly more widespread in montane Scandinavia, but population collapsed (30–50 pairs in 1990s vs. *c.*10,000 in early 20th century[913]). Reintroduction schemes were implemented in Finland in 1989–97 (143 birds released, unsuccessfully)[1104] and Sweden in 1981–2000 (348 birds released[30]), using semi-captive Barnacle Geese as adoptive parents[23,911]. These geese winter in NW Europe (especially the Netherlands), where hunting pressure is less and survival rates greater. The project was suspended due to the discovery of haplotypes of Greater White-fronted Geese in some birds[911,1104,1105], as a result of past hybridisation in the captive stock. The Scandinavian breeding population is currently estimated at 60–80 individuals[400], wintering in the E Mediterranean and Hungary to W Black Sea.

Fragmentation of the population has occurred also in Russia[391]. Some of those birds breeding in W Siberia winter around the Black and Caspian Seas, to SW Asia, and this population is estimated at 10,000–21,000 individuals[400,1348] or perhaps 8,000–13,000 individuals[305,662]. Breeding populations of E & C Siberia winter in E China, and were estimated at 25,000–28,000 in the 2000s[1333,1348], but perhaps just 20,000[305,662]. East Dongting Lake Nature Reserve, Hunan, in China, hosts the majority of wintering birds (up to 20,000 in 1997[757]). Increases noted locally, e.g. 500–600 pairs in spring 2010 in the Rauchua Basin, Chukotka, whereas it was absent there in 1983[1220]. The species is rare to occasional in the Bering Sea, Japan, South Korea, Hong Kong, Taiwan, India, Bangladesh, Pakistan, and the Middle East south to Oman, as well as in most European countries, where the origin of birds is often unclear. Escapees have bred occasionally in the UK and more recently in the Netherlands (three pairs in 2008[1329]).

The world population is currently estimated at 28,000–33,000 birds[145], vs. 250,000–300,000 individuals during the second half of the 19th century[867]. This sharp decline seems to be ongoing. The causes seem mainly related to hunting pressure, probably more in Russia and SW Asia than elsewhere, which does not permit a sufficient survival rate. Both hunting tourism and harvesting by natives, legal or illegal, is to blame, but also unintentional shots while hunting other geese[145]. The second major cause of the decline is extensive habitat destruction, mainly on the staging and wintering grounds (especially for agriculture), due to the construction of dams in Scandinavia and China (including the Five Gorges Dam, threatening the world's major wintering sites), oil pollution or peat extraction[145,391,662,795,810,867].

Disturbance caused by tourism, agriculture and hunting is also cited as an aggravating factor over the entire range. Actions needed to conserve this species include improving knowledge of the key sites in Russia, Azerbaijan and Kazakhstan, and better control of hunting and other disturbance at both newly discovered and already known sites. Restarting the Scandinavian reintroduction programme, using genetically pure individuals, should also be discussed[911,937].

CAPTIVITY Easy to keep in captivity and deemed fairly easy to breed. In fact, offered for sale more frequently (and at lower prices) than all other grey geese except Greylag Goose. Regularly escapes from captivity (at least in W Europe), and at least some observations involve breeding birds with rings of captive breeders. Observations outside regular wintering sites should therefore be checked, especially for the presence of such rings, behaviour and context (season, movements of other geese, etc.).

REFERENCES Aarvak & Øien (2003)[1]; Anderson (2003)[23]; Andersson & Larsson (2006)[30]; Baker (1993)[56]; Bird Hybrids Flickr Forum (2008)[104]; Bird Hybrids Flickr Forum (2009)[107]; Bird Hybrids Flickr Forum (2010)[121]; Bird Hybrids Flickr Forum (2011)[132]; BirdLife International (2014)[145]; Cong *et al.* (2012)[244]; Cramp & Simmons (1977)[267]; Delany (1993)[300]; Delany & Scott (2006)[305]; Fox *in* Kear (2005)[391]; Fox *et al.* (2010)[400]; Fox *et al.* (2013)[402]; Gray (1958)[465]; Heinicke *et al.* (2009)[545]; Hopkinson (1926)[582]; Hopkinson (1933)[585]; IZY (1971; 1974)[619]; Jones *et al.* (2008)[662]; Kampe-Persson & Lerner (2007)[668]; Lerner (2005)[746]; Li *et al.* (2009)[757]; Madge & Burn (1988)[794]; Madsen (1996)[795]; Marchant & Musgrove (2011)[803]; Martin (2005)[810]; McCarthy (2006)[817]; Mooij (2010)[867]; Morozov (2006)[878]; Nagy (1950)[899]; Nijman *et al.* (2010)[911]; Norderhaug & Norderhaug (1984)[913]; Ottvall (2008)[937]; Panov

(1989)[947]; Pedall *et al.* (2007)[962]; Ruokonen (2001)[1101]; Ruokonen *et al.* (2000)[1104]; Ruokonen *et al.* (2004)[1105]; Ruokonen *et al.* (2007)[1107]; Ruokonen *et al.* (2010)[1109]; Salminen (1983)[1122]; Shackelton (1956)[1177]; Snow & Perrins (1998)[1213]; Solovieva & Vartanyan (2013)[1220]; Syroechkovski (1996)[1248]; Tegelström *et al.* (2001)[1258]; Van Impe (1982)[1310]; Voous & Wattel (1967)[1326]; Voslamber (2010)[1329]; Wang *et al.* (2013)[1333]; Wang *et al.* (2014)[1334]; Wetlands International (2014)[1348].

76. Adult (definitive basic); note stubby shape, with short neck, large rounded head, small bill and long wings, while this species usually has only a few black ventral patches. Netherlands, Feb (Sébastien Reeber).

77. Adult (definitive basic); with Greater White-fronted Goose *A. albifrons*, the only other species showing a large white face mask, distinguished by smaller bill with steeper forehead, white patch extending onto crown above eye and broad yellow orbital ring. India, Dec (Kannan Sundararajan).

78. Adult (definitive basic); rather uniform dark upperwing pattern. Netherlands, Feb (Sébastien Reeber)

79. Adult (definitive basic); pale fringes to upperparts faintly marked (especially on median and greater coverts), head and upper neck dark brown and broad white tip to tail clearly contrasts with blackish bar. Netherlands, Feb (Sébastien Reeber).

80. Juvenile (first basic); birds in pre-formative moult, but still largely juvenile (rounded scapulars, plain flanks, no or small face patch), while at same age Greater White-fronted Goose *A. albifrons* has dark nail to bill. Hong Kong, China, Nov (Michelle & Peter Wong).

BAR-HEADED GOOSE
Anser indicus   **Plates 3,8**

TAXONOMY *Anas indica* Latham, 1790, *Index Orn.*, p. 839. Quite distinct from other geese in the genus *Anser*, by many aspects including skull[625]. Phylogenetically close to Snow Goose *Chen caerulescens*, Ross's Goose *C. rossii* and Emperor Goose *C. canagica*. These species form a clade, which is sister to the grey geese (*Anser*) and the genus *Branta*[772]. This finding could justify placing Bar-headed Goose in the genus *Chen*, whereas it is treated by all taxonomic lists within *Anser*. Very slight geographical variation.

IDENTIFICATION Very distinctive in all plumages, and should not be confused with any other species. Some hybrids may show a very superficial resemblance.

PLUMAGES Sexes identical, but can often be sexed based on differences in size, posture and behaviour among pairs. Complex basic moult strategy (one plumage per definitive cycle, two in the first cycle). Ageing easy until the beginning of the first winter.

Adult

Definitive basic plumage (year-round). Medium-sized goose with distinctive plumage. Head and sides of neck mostly white (often tinged yellow-ochre depending on substrate) with a dark brown vertical black line on the hindneck from the nape to upper back. Two short bars on the rear head, one towards the cheeks and the other towards the eye. Dark brown iris. Bill bright orange-yellow with black nail. Pale grey breast, with a sharply defined band extending up the foreneck and darkening. Pale grey flanks and belly, with feathers on flanks darker brown. The pale fringes to these feathers form neat vertical stripes. Lower belly, undertail- and uppertail-coverts white. Tail grey with broad white tip and lateral edges. Feathers of mantle and scapulars grey-brown, more bluish rearwards, with pale fringes forming regularly spaced pale streaks. Pale blue-grey greater coverts, fringed white. Dark grey back. Upperwing has all coverts pale grey, the fringes of the greater and median coverts forming fine paler lines. Secondaries and inner primaries blackish. Outer primaries greyer, tipped black with clear white rachis. Underwing has pale grey coverts, greater coverts medium grey with pale tips and remiges darker, rather like Greylag Goose *A. anser*. Bright yellow-orange legs.

Juvenile

First basic plumage (until Oct–Nov). Like adult, but black band on the hindneck is less clear-cut, broader and extends to the middle crown and up to the eye, without the two crossbars. Hint of dark loral line. Foreneck, breast, belly and flanks appear pale grey mottled dusky, slightly darker on the rear flanks, without the vertical streaks. Scapulars round-tipped, not forming parallel pale streaks. Bill and legs a trifle duller.

First-winter/first-summer

Formative plumage (Nov–Apr/Aug). Very similar to adult basic plumage from first winter, after pre-formative moult. Formative plumage is distinguished by limited number of juvenile feathers, especially on the belly, rear body and wings. Good views should reveal contrast between the new, adult-like, formative scapulars and the worn juvenile secondary upperwing-coverts. However, as juvenile and formative feathers are very much alike, their distinction will often require close examination (or in the hand).

GEOGRAPHIC VARIATION Slight morphological differences recently described between wintering populations in China and Mongolia. Culmen length similar for ♂♂ in both populations, but a difference between ♀♀ of *c.*3.5 mm. Moreover, tarsus length of Chinese birds (both sexes) 8–10 mm shorter than in Mongolia[1254].

MEASUREMENTS and MASS ♂ slightly larger and heavier than ♀. Few datasets available, especially with sufficient sample size. ♂ (*n*=4): wing chord 450, culmen 47, tarsus 82, mass 2,600; ♀ (*n*=6): wing chord 419, culmen 45, tarsus 72, mass 2,014[789]. Würdinger[1376] and Takekawa[1254] indicate other sources.

VOICE Rather loquacious, and even noisy in flight, when landing or taking off. Utters a *hin* or *han*, typically sounding rather tinny. In flocks on ground, also various types of whistles and chattering sounds.

MOULT Complex basic strategy. Pre-formative moult rarely described in the wild, but seems close to that of other geese in extent. Occurs in autumn, during migration and on wintering grounds, extending into first winter, with some young moulting until end of winter. Definitive pre-basic moult begins in Jun–Jul [1254], typically 24–28 days after hatching, with birds able to fly again c.1 month later, at the same time that young birds fledge. Body feathers are moulted in Aug–Oct. Non-breeding adult and immature moult later than breeding ad[308].

HYBRIDISATION In nature, hybridisation has been reported very occasionally with Greylag Goose *A. anser*[149,465]; the resulting hybrids are described below. Very few reported cases with Brent Goose *Branta bernicla*[639] and possibly Common Shelduck *Tadorna tadorna*[1303]. Recently, hybrids have been reported with growing frequency as a result of Bar-headed Goose being introduced in Europe, with Canada Goose *Branta canadensis*[300,817], Barnacle Goose *B. leucopsis*[465,582,817], Swan Goose *A. cygnoid*, Lesser White-fronted Goose *A. erythropus*, Greater White-fronted Goose *A. albifrons*[817] and Snow Goose *Chen caerulescens*. See descriptions below. All these hybrids are very scarcely reported and none should actually be misidentified as the present species. In captivity, at least, it can probably hybridise with virtually any other goose. Hybrids have been mentioned in the literature with all of the above species, and with Emperor Goose *C. canagica*. Fertility of eggs and viability of chicks appear high[1231].

Bar-headed Goose × Swan Goose: very few descriptions of this hybrid exist in the literature, but some reports published on the internet with photographs probably relate to it. A feral population in Kiel, Germany, includes birds of this cross and/or crossed with Snow Goose. First-generation (or presumed) specimens of this cross have an elongated head profile, a broad dark band covering the crown, nape and hindneck, and a yellow bill with variable dark patches all seem inherited from Swan Goose. The modest size, presence of yellow on the bill and pale grey-blue tones to the flanks and upperparts indicate Bar-headed Goose as the other parent. A rather narrow white face patch occurs in the two species.

Bar-headed Goose × Greater White-fronted Goose: very occasional in the wild, this hybrid has a long, rather thin bill, which is pale yellow-orange with a pale nail (always?). The upperparts (including tertials) are rather plain grey-brown with narrow pale fringes, and the greyish underparts are pale with dark blackish-brown flanks and faint white vertical stripes. The head and neck are brown, the crown darker than the cheeks, more or less flecked white, with a clear-cut pale eye-ring.

Another bird photographed in Germany could also represent this cross and had the head and neck-sides stained white and pale grey-brown, with a 'ghost'-like pattern of that shown by Bar-headed Goose. The tail had a broad pale grey bar. The legs were brighter orange than the bill.

Bar-headed Goose × Lesser White-fronted Goose: a hybrid probably from this cross was photographed in England, and was similar to the previous one but smaller, with a more rounded head and shorter bill, clear yellow orbital ring, and larger white patches on the forecrown and chin. The influence of Lesser White-fronted Goose is quite obvious in this type of bird.

Bar-headed Goose × Greylag Goose: this hybrid seems surprisingly rare even in Europe, where feral populations co-exist. Intermediate general coloration, and easily distinguished from each of its parents. The head resembles that of Bar-headed Goose but with a less well-defined pattern on a grey-brown dirtier background. The bill, intermediate in thickness, is bright orange-yellow with a black nail (always?). The legs are darker orange[134,203,300].

Bar-headed Goose × Snow Goose: very few reports in N Europe, with multiple-generation hybrids derived from a feral population in Germany. This hybrid is rather variable, usually a largely white head, the black pattern of Bar-headed Goose is variably marked, the neck-sides are white and the hind- and foreneck brown or blackish, more or less flecked white. The bill is (often at least) pale yellow on its proximal half and pinker towards the tip and on the tomium. The upperparts are like those of Pink-footed Goose, except the blackish-centred tertials fringed with white. At least some birds have white scapulars scattered among those of Bar-headed Goose type. The underparts are variably white, sometimes almost entirely so, with grey-brown or black-centred feathers confined to the upper flanks and breast. Tail with a broad pale grey band. Legs pale orange with a more or less pink hue.

Bar-headed Goose × Canada Goose: very rarely reported, but recorded in England and Germany at least. An illustration on the internet[124] shows a bird intermediate in size and coloration, including the pale grey-brown upperparts and flanks. The neck is almost blackish and its sides flecked white. The head is largely white except the nape, rear crown and a black bar abutting the eye. The bill is dull yellowish-grey and the legs dull grey-pinkish. The author reported a rusty tinge to the breast that is present in neither parent.

Bar-headed Goose × Barnacle Goose: a few sightings in N Europe. Quite close to the previous hybrid, with a grey-brown body, with a darker breast, the latter often streaked blackish. Head and neck pattern varies individually, possibly suggestive of both parents. Upper neck, nape and crown often black flecked white, the rest of the head being white. Usually a large black bar runs from the nape towards the eye. Dull olive bill with a black nail (sometimes more grey-pinkish). Olive-grey or yellowish-olive legs. Tail grey.

HABITAT and LIFE-CYCLE Arrives on the breeding grounds in Apr–May depending on latitude and weather, eggs being laid mainly from the first half of May[1376]. At this season, inhabits permanent or temporary wetlands often in mountainous regions or plateaux, lakes and marshes as well as flooded steppe areas. Breeds in lone pairs, or in small or large colonies of up to a thousand pairs[308,789,1376]. After moulting their flight feathers, mainly in Jun–Jul, the birds begin southbound migration in Jul–Aug, with a significant proportion of the population crossing the Himalayas. Sightings have been made near the summit of Mount Everest, but are not unanimously accepted. It is now recognised that migrants preferentially follow valleys and mountain passes, at maximum altitudes of 6,400–7,300 m[539,538]. This ability to fly at high altitudes has been the subject of many studies, including the physiological adaptations needed for such performance. Arrives on the wintering grounds in Oct–Nov. In winter, frequents various types of wetlands with surrounding grasslands and pastures, either alone, in family groups or flocks formed of several such groups. More gregarious at roosts. Returning from the Indian plains to the nesting areas on the Tibetan Plateau, many birds cross the Himalayas again, in a single flight of seven hours with a maximum altitude reported of 6,540 m[538].

RANGE and POPULATION Breeds in C Asia, wintering in S Asia. Rare visitor to Indochina and E China. Two populations totalling 32,300–36,400 individuals winter south of the Himalayas and in China[1376]. Other estimates are more optimistic, 52,000–60,000 individuals[758] and 63,110 individuals counted in 2007[757]. Apparently declined during much of the 20th century, due to excessive hunting, egg harvesting and heavy loss of habitat[223], but appears to be stable or slightly increasing now.

A feral population seems well established in N Europe. The species was first deliberately introduced into Sweden in the 1930s, but this attempt failed[667]. It then bred regularly in Norway in the 1950s and 1960s, and sporadically thereafter. In Finland, there several recent breeding records[149] and a few pairs have nested in France and the UK. Larger populations are in Germany (15–18 pairs in 2005), Belgium (30–40 pairs at present) and the Netherlands (100 pairs in 2008)[667]. The European population was estimated at 140–190 pairs in the early 2000s[62].

CAPTIVITY Common in captivity, being offered for sale at affordable prices, usually just twice the price of domestic geese. Easy to keep and breed. Frequently escapes in North America, Europe and Asia, where breeding attempts are often reported in the wild.

REFERENCES Banks *et al.* (2008)[62]; Bird Hybrids database (2014)[97]; Bird Hybrids Flickr forum (2011)[124]; Bird Hybrids Flickr forum (2012)[134]; Blair *et al.* (2000)[149]; Bruns (1985)[203]; Carboneras (1992)[223]; Delany (1993)[300]; Dementiev & Gladkov (1952)[308]; Graham *et al.* (2011)[464]; Gray (1958)[465]; Hawkes *et al.* (2011)[538]; Hawkes *et al.* (2012)[539]; Hopkinson (1926)[582]; Jacob & Glaser (1975)[625]; Johnsgard (1960)[639]; Kampe-Persson (2010)[667]; Lee *et al.* (2008)[741]; Li *et al.* (2009)[757]; Li Laixing (2001)[758]; Livezey (1996)[772]; Ma & Cai (2002)[789]; McCarthy (2006)[817]; Steklenev (1993)[1231]; Takekawa *et al.* (2009)[1254]; Vale (1900)[1303]; Würdinger *in* Kear (2005)[1376]; Zhang *et al.* (2011)[1384].

81. Adult (definitive basic). Mongolia, Jun (Aurélien Audevard).

82. Adult (definitive basic). India, Nov (Anand Arya).

83. Adult (definitive basic). India, Feb (Julien Gonin)

84. Adult (definitive basic). India, Feb (Julien Gonin).

85. First-winter (first basic/formative); the first-winter bird (right) has a stained head and neck, and mix of juvenile and formative feathers on flanks. India, Dec (Amit Thakurta).

229

EMPEROR GOOSE
Chen canagica

TAXONOMY *Anas Canagica* Sewastianoff, 1802, *Nova Acta Acad. Sci. Imp. Petropolitanae*, 13, p. 349, pl. 10. Placed in the genus *Chen* along with Snow Goose *C. caerulescens* and Ross's Goose *C. rossii*, but the latter two species are much closer morphologically to one another than to Emperor Goose[772]. Its generic placement, however, has long been debated[1089], the species having also been placed in a monotypic genus, *Philacte* Bannister, 1870, or in *Anser* (along with all *Chen*). It was also assumed that the species derived from the blue form of Snow Goose[1249], with which it shares many plumage traits.

IDENTIFICATION Should prove unmistakable despite that its white head and dark blue-grey body could provoke thoughts of the blue form of Snow Goose. The adult is easy to distinguish by the white extending not only across the head but also the entire hindneck, as well as by the black foreneck extending onto the chin, and by its much smaller bill. Also note the white tail framed by dark under- and uppertail-coverts, bright yellow-orange legs and, in flight from below, the plain grey underwings. The juvenile is more similar to the blue form of Snow Goose given its wholly dark grey appearance, but the size of the bill, tail colour and underwings are diagnostic. At all ages, note the rather heavy silhouette, with a stocky body, short neck and strong head.

PLUMAGES Sexes identical, but ♂ slightly larger and stockier, which may be useful for sexing within pairs. Complex basic moult strategy (one plumage in definitive cycle, two in the first cycle). Ageing easy until the first winter and requires a little more attention until the following summer.

Adult

Definitive basic plumage (year-round). Two-toned overall. Head, nape and hindneck down to mantle white, and clearly delineated. White sometimes stained yellow-orange or rusty in spring, due to ferrous substrate. Foreneck, neck-sides, throat and chin up to bill black. In profile, the black area extends along the tomium to the nail. The rest of the bill has a complex pastel coloration: pale blue covers the sides of the base and around the black nostrils, the culmen is greyish-pink, with a broad pink subterminal band and the top of the nail is yellowish to ivory. Iris dark brown, sometimes

hazel if seen close. Feathers of the breast, flanks, mantle and scapulars pale blue-grey with blackish subterminal bands and clear-cut whitish or beige fringes, producing a neatly streaked effect, and more strongly barred on the underparts. Tertials dark grey to blackish with sharp white fringes. Belly slightly paler, lower belly and undertail-coverts more coarsely mottled dark. Rectrices mostly white with grey bases (usually invisible). Back, rump and uppertail-coverts grey with pale fringes. Upperwing grey, secondary coverts similar to scapulars, pale grey with blackish subterminal areas and whitish fringes. Remiges grey basally, darkening towards the tips, with sharp white fringes to the outer webs of secondaries, and white shafts to primaries. Underwing including axillaries uniform grey, slightly darker on the tips of the remiges. Bright yellow-orange legs. Adult ♀ has on average a stronger rust coloration to the head and paler fringes to the body feathers, and especially the greater coverts[1150].

Juvenile

First basic plumage (until Oct–Nov). Quite similar to adult, but the head and neck are dark grey to blackish. Feathers of the breast, flanks, mantle, scapulars and secondary upperwing-coverts are narrower and more round-tipped than adult, but similar in coloration, except that the black subterminal area is diffuse and browner. Overall, appears more mottled or scaly than regularly streaked. Back and rump as adult. Feathers of rear flanks rather plain grey. Belly and lower breast whitish mottled dusky. Dark blue-grey to blackish bill. Duller orange-brown legs.

First-winter/first-summer

Formative plumage (Nov–Mar/Jul). Plumage acquired during first winter, similar to that of adult. Best distinguished by variable dark flecks on the white head and hindneck (e.g. on upper cheeks and in front of the eye), but most birds are largely white-headed by Dec[1151]. Formative feathers of the upperparts, breast and flanks are similar to those of adult, but slightly narrower at the base and less square-tipped. These adult-type feathers contrast with the juvenile secondary upperwing-coverts, which have diffuse and browner bars. The black area of the chin and the foreneck is interspersed by short brownish or whitish streaks (fringes to the feathers).

The upperwing is plainer than in the adult, the black subterminal bars and whitish fringes being less marked and/or abraded. Rectrices may be partly or wholly juvenile, narrow and increasingly worn by summer. The bill achieves adult coloration in Apr[1151]. The legs become more orange at the beginning of the first winter, but bright orange only in the first spring.

GEOGRAPHIC VARIATION. None.

MEASUREMENTS and MASS ♂: culmen 39.0 (*n*=13), tarsus 83.8 (*n*=13), mass during wing moult 2,316 (*n*=75); ♀: culmen 35.5 (*n*=18), tarsus 80.0 (*n*=18), mass during wing moult 1,945 (*n*=206)[1150]. ♀ (Yukon-Kuskokwim): culmen 35.7 (SE=0.2, *n*=82), mass 1,757.8 (SE=14.0, *n*=82); (Manokinak River): wing chord 377.3 (SE=0.9, *n*=121), culmen 36.0 (SE=0.3, *n*=32), tarsus 80.2 (SE=0.2, *n*=127), mass 1,638.3 (SE=10.4, *n*=126)[945,1151]. ♂ (*n*=20): wing chord 375–403 (adult) and 362–389 (juvenile), culmen 34–43, bill depth at tip of forehead feathering 22.9–25.1, tail 106–131, tarsus 63–72; ♀ (*n*=20): wing chord 364–390 (adult) and 349–376 (juvenile), culmen 31–40, bill depth at tip of forehead feathering 22.0–24.5, tail 97–122, tarsus 61–70[1014].

VOICE The commonest call, often heard in flight, is a *ga-anh*, or a tinny nasal trumpeting call sometimes ended with an acute note *ta-di-lik*. Also utters an acute *gik* or low grunts when disturbed. Voice usually diagnostic.

MOULT Pre-formative moult occurs between Oct–Nov and Jan–Mar and is variable in extent, including many of the feathers of the head and neck, a variable number of feathers in the upperparts and flanks (sometimes many), few or no belly feathers, lesser coverts or inner median coverts, no tertials and none to all rectrices[1014]. Definitive pre-basic moult is complete, starts in Jul with the wing feathers, and continues at stop-over sites or wintering grounds until Oct (sometimes Dec). Pre-basic moult of second calendar-year birds, non-breeding adult and those that failed at the egg stage occurs on average one month earlier.

HYBRIDISATION Apparently unknown in the species' native range. However, there are some reports from W Europe involving escaped Emperor Geese or birds from feral populations, with Lesser White-fronted Goose *Anser erythropus* and Greylag Goose *A. anser*[107,668]. In captivity, hybridisation has been reported with Swan Goose *A. cygnoid*[97], Pink-footed Goose *A. brachyrhynchus*[465,817], Greater White-fronted Goose *A. albifrons*[1190], Bar-headed Goose *A. indicus*[817], Snow Goose[465,586,817], including the blue form[114], Ross's Goose[465,586,1184,1190], Brent Goose *Branta bernicla*[1190], Barnacle Goose *B. leucopsis*[115,817] and Upland Goose *Chloephaga picta*[97,817].

HABITAT and LIFE-CYCLE Short- to medium-range migrant (generally <1,800 km between breeding and wintering grounds). Leaves wintering sites between mid-Mar and mid-May, depending on weather along coasts and in breeding areas (especially timing of ice and snow melt) and distance to the latter[616,1151]. Arrives at nest sites between mid-May and early Jun, depending on latitude, and eggs laid soon after. Breeding habitat consists of marshy coastal lowlands in the Arctic tundra (large deltas such as Yukon-Kuskokwim) with many inlets, brackish tidal ponds and freshwater snowmelt ponds, generally within 15 km of the coast[709,1150]. Nests are usually sited on banks, often exposed, even if the nest is usually in an area where the vegetation is slightly taller than in the surroundings. Predation by Arctic Foxes *Vulpes lagopus* and skuas *Stercorarius* spp. can cause extensive losses (0–95% of nests[977]). Adult begins pre-basic moult with the wing feathers soon after young hatch, and then lead their clutch to coastal areas. Once young and adults able to fly, families head to moulting sites where adults replace head and body feathers. Leaves moulting grounds between mid-Aug and mid-Sep, for wintering grounds in the Aleutians, mostly in Nov[616,1151]. On migration, uses shallow coastal lagoons with large tidal mudflats, resting on beaches, islands and rocky outcrops. Can occur along more exposed, rocky shores in winter[1150], at which season the species often gathers in flocks of a few dozen up to 500 birds[1150]. Takes invertebrates in the intertidal zone (especially molluscs) in winter, but is herbivorous just before and during the nesting season, when the rusty tint to head and neck is acquired.

RANGE and POPULATION Entirely restricted to the Bering Sea, south-east to Kodiak I, and west to Chukchi Sea. Most of the Alaskan population breeds in the Yukon-Kuskokwim Delta and the main moulting areas are on St. Lawrence I, Alaska, and along Arctic coasts of the Chukchi Peninsula[695,1150]. In winter, present from Kodiak I and S Alaska Peninsula (Izembek Lagoon being a major staging site), through the Aleutian chain west to the coast of Kamchatka. May winter even further north, if winter weather permits Much rarer further east along the US Pacific coast (British Columbia and Washington) and regular vagrant south to California, but less frequent south along the Asian coast, the species being rare in S Kamchatka and accidental in Japan and South Korea[182]. Also accidental in Hawaii[1151]. A few dozen escapees occur in England, the Netherlands and even Switzerland. Up to five pairs breed annually in the first two countries[62,1329].

Global population estimated at 139,000 individuals in spring 1964[690]. Numbers then declined until the mid-1980s[691], then increased slowly, at a mean annual rate of 2% between 2003 and 2012. The current population has fluctuated between 50,000 and 90,000 birds since 2000, reaching 74,200 individuals in spring 2011 and 68,800 in spring 2012[1293]. Considered Near Threatened[145], especially due to harvesting by indigenous peoples (2,000–3,000 birds annually[648]) and, to lesser extent, risk of oil pollution.

CAPTIVITY Relatively easy to keep and breed in captivity, but usually sold at fairly high prices. It nevertheless escapes occasionally, as evidenced by its presence in NW Europe. Given its restricted distribution and preference for strictly coastal habitats, sightings far inland and well outside its normal range should be treated with caution.

REFERENCES Banks *et al.* (2008)[62]; Bird Hybrids Database (2014)[97]; Bird Hybrids Flickr Forum (2009)[107]; Bird Hybrids Flickr Forum (2009)[114]; Bird Hybrids Flickr Forum (2009)[115]; BirdLife International (2014)[145]; Blurton Jones (1972)[155]; Brazil (2009)[182]; Dau *et al.* (2006)[281]; Eisenhauer & Kirkpatrick (1977)[350]; Gibson (2002)[434]; Gray (1958)[465]; Hopkinson (1934)[586]; Hupp *et al.* (2007)[615]; Hupp *et al.* (2008)[616]; Johnsgard (1960)[639]; Johnsgard (2010)[648]; Kampe-Persson & Lerner (2007)[668]; King (1965)[690]; King & Dau (1992)[691]; Kistchinski (1971)[695]; Krechmar & Kondratiev (1982)[709]; Livezey (1996)[772]; McCarthy (2006)[817]; Palmer (1976)[945]; Petersen (1992)[977]; Petersen & Gill (1982)[981]; Pyle (2008)[1014]; Rockwell *et al.* (1996)[1089]; Schmutz (2001)[1149]; Schmutz *in* Kear (2005)[1150]; Schmutz *et al.* (2011)[1151]; Shoffner *et al.* (1979)[1184]; Sibley (1938)[1190]; Syroechkovski (2000)[1249]; USFWS (2012)[1293]; Voslamber (2010)[1329]; Watkins (2006)[1339].

86. Adult (definitive basic); typical dark blue-grey and white coloration, and stocky shape. Chukotka, Russia, Jul (Anders Blomdahl).

87. First-winter (formative); note numerous retained juvenile feathers (lower scapulars, belly, breast, rump, tail and wing). California, USA, Apr (Mike Danzenbaker).

88. Adult (definitive basic); the dusky underwing distinguishes this species from many blue Snow Geese. Chukotka, Russia, Jul (Anders Blomdahl).

89. Adult (definitive basic). Netherlands, Feb (Otto Plantema).

SNOW GOOSE
Chen caerulescens

Plates 9, 10, 11

TAXONOMY *Anas caerulescens* Linnaeus, 1758, *Syst. Nat.*, edn. 10, p. 124 (the scientific name relates to the type specimen, a blue morph, the white morph having initially been described as a separate species, *Anser hyperboreus* Pallas, 1769). Snow Goose is phylogenetically very close to Ross's Goose *C. rossii*, these two species being sister to Emperor Goose *C. canagica*[772], and all three species form the genus *Chen*[142,437], but in Europe the AERC-TAC includes them in *Anser*. There are two colour morphs ('white' and 'blue') and many intermediates, as well as two subspecies differing mainly in measurements and the relative frequency of the blue morph (see Geographic Variation).

IDENTIFICATION In all plumages, usually confused only with Ross's Goose or, especially, the various hybrids between these two species. These issues are discussed under Identification and Hybridisation in the account for Ross's Goose. Moreover, many hybrids involving Snow Goose and any other species of *Anser* and *Branta* can be variegated grey-brown and white, and can resemble the blue and intermediate morphs of Snow Goose. Misidentification easily avoided by checking bill and leg colours, the coloration of the under- and upperwings, and the precise hue of the dark parts of the plumage. Among other usual pitfalls, there are also white or variegated domestic geese, which, however, should be distinguished easily.

PLUMAGES Sexes identical, but birds can be sexed within pairs based on the larger size and alert posture (more erect and aggressive) of the ♂. Complex basic complex moult strategy (one plumage per definitive cycle, two in the first cycle). Ageing easy until the first summer. Two colour morphs, controlled by a single locus, the white morph being partially recessive. Individuals of the blue or white morph are generally homozygote, intermediates being heterozygote[247,250,1048]. Of all the birds hunted in North America, about one-third are of the blue morph.

Adult (white morph)
Definitive basic plumage (year-round). All-white plumage except black primaries, with white shafts and grey primary coverts. Very rare birds (leucistic?) have silvergrey primaries. Dark brown iris. Reddish-pink bill with nail often slightly paler and 'grinning patch' blackish.

Pink legs and feet, sometimes appearing more orange or brownish.

Adult (blue and intermediate morphs)
Definitive basic plumage (year-round). Iris, bill and legs like white morph. Head white, often tinged rusty or yellowish, heavier towards bill base and forehead. This iron staining is more pronounced in birds feeding in coastal saltmarshes[247], and therefore visible especially in late winter and the next spring. Upper neck white, with blackish hind- and foreneck. Lower neck, breast, flanks, mantle and scapulars dark grey with violet hues. Belly slightly paler. White undertail-coverts. Rectrices pale grey fringed white. Back and rump grey, paler towards uppertail (whitish fringes). Tertials black-centred with large white fringes and tips. Upperwing has alula, primary, lesser coverts and median coverts pale grey. Outer greater coverts identical, but increasingly black-centred and fringed white on inner feathers. Remiges black with white shafts on primaries. Underwing (variable) pale grey, with whitish axillaries and median coverts, darker grey greater coverts and remiges blackish. Iris, bill and legs like white morph.

There is a complete range of intermediates between the white and blue morphs, which have sometimes been placed in 5–7 different types[250,254]. White types only vary in the shade of grey on the upperwing primary coverts and the extent of black on the remiges (seven black outer primaries in all, but black can extend across four outer secondaries in some). The true intermediate type has dark wings, upperparts and flanks, but white belly and chest. Variation among dark types occurs mainly on the underparts, with the dark coloration ranging from a simple indistinct collar, the rest being white, to all dark.

Juvenile (white morph)
First basic plumage (until Oct–Feb). Whitish and pale grey-brown, somewhat variable, obviously smaller and more slender than adult in direct comparison. Pale grey forehead and cheeks, crown and nape slightly darker grey-brown with clear dark bar on lores, tapering behind eye. Iris dark brown to blackish. Dark grey bill with nail ivory to pale buff. Back of head, hindneck, breast-sides, mantle and scapulars grey-brown with pale fringes. Rear scapulars and tertials dark grey-brown with

broad white fringes. Lower neck and breast mottled grey. Flanks and belly to undertail-coverts white, with vague brown patches on rear flanks. Back, rump and uppertail-coverts white with subtle grey speckles. Rectrices pale grey fringed white. Upperwing like that of adult but less contrasting: primaries blackish with white shafts, secondaries and lesser coverts pale grey, greater coverts (except innermost) and outer secondary coverts whitish. Young often show variable dark flecks around the shafts (more common than in ad[1014]). Other secondary coverts grey with clean white fringes. Tertial coverts white. Underwing has black primaries, pale grey secondaries and whitish coverts and axillaries. Dull olive-brown legs.

Juvenile (blue morph)

First basic plumage (until Oct–Dec). Uniformly dark, but rather variable. Head and neck dark brown to blackish, scapulars and flanks duller brown than adult of same morph. Often shows blurred pale patch at base of bill and on chin. Belly neatly and faintly barred pale, slightly paler than flanks. Lower belly and uppertail-coverts whitish. Tertials and inner secondary upperwing-coverts centred dark grey to blackish, variably fringed white. Bill much like that of white morph at same age, but legs darker, sometimes even blackish. Upper- and underwing close to adult of the same morph. Intermediate characters already visible at this age, especially on the belly, and the upper- and underwing.

First-winter/first-summer (white morph)

Formative plumage (Oct–Apr/Aug). Variable with rather variegated appearance due to slow acquisition of formative plumage. A variable number of white feathers gradually appears between autumn and early spring, on the head, neck and whole body, sometimes inner secondary upperwing-coverts and a few tertials. Following pre-formative moult, quite similar to the adult, essentially white but generally shows clear signs of immaturity with grey marks on the head, upperparts and upperwing at least. The bill's pink colour appears in Oct–Nov, becoming gradually dull pink with dusky marks in spring.

First-winter/first-summer (blue and intermediate morphs)

Formative plumage (Oct–Dec/Aug). Pre-formative moult seems less extensive and less protracted than in the white morph (see Moult). Similar to juvenile plumage, and thus easily distinguished from adult, with a variable

number of white flecks on the head and upper neck during autumn. Following pre-formative moult, a limited but variable number of scapulars, breast and flank feathers have been moulted and are similar to those of the adult, as well as those of the head, which can appear mostly white or spotted dark.

GEOGRAPHIC VARIATION Two subspecies separated primarily based on measurements (see below). Breeders in NE Nunavut and Greenland winter along the North American Atlantic coast, *C. c. atlantica* Kennard, 1927, and are larger, with a longer bill, slightly thicker at the base and with a wider 'grinning patch' (9–14 mm[1014]). The nominate subspecies nests south and west of the previous subspecies, and winters in C, S & W USA. It is slightly smaller, with a smaller and less prominent bill, and a 'grinning patch' of maximum width 7–12 mm[1014]. Head rounder and seems 'gentler' (vs. nape slightly more prominent and forehead marginally flatter in *atlantica*). Typical individuals can be identified to subspecies, but there is much overlap in the measurements. Thus, ♀ *atlantica* approaches ♂ of the nominate subspecies in size. Identifying an individual to subspecies within a flock of the other race will partly depend on the sex of the bird. There are also variations between populations in general size and bill size, such as between birds on the coasts of the Gulf of Mexico and those wintering in the Mississippi Valley, the latter being smaller[13]. This makes subspecific identification outside the normal range difficult, and even weakens the justification for two subspecies[254].

The relative frequency of the colour morphs is highly variable between the different breeding populations. The blue morph and intermediates are exceptional in *atlantica*, and are rare among the western breeding and wintering populations, although their frequency has recently increased[338,659,886]. On the other hand, the blue morph forms the majority among the colony at Koukdjuak, south-west of Baffin I (85–90% of birds). Within the nominate subspecies, which reaches its eastern limit there close to the range of *atlantica*, the proportion of dark birds decreases north and west[254,1024]. Because migration routes are mainly orientated north–south, the proportions of the two forms on the wintering grounds matches that on the breeding grounds further north: the blue form is rare in winter along the coasts of both oceans, but dominant in the lower Mississippi Valley and on the Gulf of Mexico [254,886].

Analysis of mitochondrial DNA has revealed the existence of two major clades, which do not correlate with subspecies distribution, or the colour morphs.

This seems to be the result of allopatric distribution of two populations confined to distinct biological refugia during Pleistocene glaciations, which have largely become mixed since[46,1024]. Many phenotypic differences between populations are essentially maintained via assortative mating, birds preferably choosing the colour form of its parents[252], their choice also being influenced by age and size[254]. The strong philopatry of ♀♀ and lifelong pair-bond[247] also limit gene flow between populations. Like other geese, gene flow is mainly conditioned by the degree of sympatry in winter, when pairing occurs. Thus, two breeding populations of Snow Geese occur on Wrangel I, are genetically distinct and winter in the Puget Sound (British Columbia and Washington) and S California, respectively. Despite the fact that they now frequently nest in the same colonies, they are still segregated in winter[720]. Similarly, it has been highlighted that the white and blue morphs have long been allopatric, and remained so until the third decade of the 20th century[253,1341]. It was also assumed that the two morphs represented two distinct taxa, whose merging was facilitated by them both using the newly established rice fields in Louisiana and Texas in winter.

MEASUREMENTS and MASS Like other geese, feeding conditions experienced by youngsters during their first few months can influence their size, even when fully grown[248,744]. In addition, a decrease in the species' general size, linked to a decline in the quality of the environment, has been reported over the last several decades[249,1053]. ♂♂ and adult slightly larger than ♀♀ and young, respectively.

C. c. caerulescens. Queen Maud Gulf, Canada. ♂: wing chord 423.9 (± 14.5, n=60), culmen 55.6 (± 3.7, n=78), tarsus 82.9 (± 3.6, n=70), mass 2,557.8 (± 273.2, n=81); ♀: wing chord 415.7 (± 17.9, n=233), culmen 55.1 (± 2.8, n=389), tarsus 79.7 (± 3.8, n=70), mass 2,538.8 (± 376.1, n=289) Alisauskas in Mowbray *et al.*[886]. Banks I, Canada. ♂: culmen 53.9 (± 2.7, n=376), tarsus 96.3 (± 3.7, n=376), mass 2123.7 (± 175.4, n=376); ♀: culmen 51.1 (± 2.6, n=384), tarsus 92.5 (± 3.6, n=384), mass 1,906.8 (± 159.6, n=384) Samuel in Mowbray *et al.*[886]. Wrangel I, Russia. ♂: culmen 58.4 (± 2.4, n=339), tarsus 95.4 (± 3.4, n=343), mass 2,041.9 (± 153.8, n=343); ♀: culmen 55.8 (± 2.3, n=356), tarsus 91.9 (± 3.1, n=355), mass 1,867.5 (± 132.6, n=359)[886]. ♂ (n=100): wing chord 413–461 (adult) and 403–440 (juvenile), culmen 52–63, bill depth at tip of forehead feathering 29.3–37.4, tail 112–148, tarsus 78–91; ♀ (n=100): wing chord 398–449 (adult) and 377–426 (juvenile), culmen 49–60, bill depth at tip of forehead feathering 27.8–36.0, tail 105–140, tarsus 75–87[1014]; compared with measurements given by Pyle[1014] for *atlantica* and Ross's Goose.

C. c. atlantica. Bylot I, Canada. ♂: culmen 66.3 (± 3.2, n=92), tarsus 88.5 (± 3.0, n=92), mass 2,847.3 (± 230.8, n=92); ♀: culmen 62.5 (± 2.7, n=100), tarsus 83.6 (± 3.0, n=100), mass in Aug 2,455.7 (± 148.7, n=100)[886]. ♂ (n=100): wing chord 429–479 (adult) and 412–456 (juvenile), culmen 61–73, bill depth at tip of forehead feathering 31.0–38.7, tail 125–150, tarsus 85–98; ♀ (n=100): wing chord 421–471 (adult) and 397–437 (juvenile), culmen 58–70, bill depth at tip of forehead feathering 29.1–37.2, tail 118–142, tarsus 80–93[1014]; compared with measurements given by Pyle[1014] for *caerulescens*.

VOICE Very loquacious, even noisy, especially in flight, when taking off or landing. Produces loud, raucous, barking calls *gwok* or *ga-ik*, as well as other sounds more like those of grey geese, lower and hoarser: *gung, wa-iir* or *hun-hrr*. Large flocks utter these calls continuously and at different pitches, linked to the birds' size.

MOULT Complex basic strategy. Pre-formative moult takes place between Sep–Oct and Mar–Apr, during migration and on wintering grounds, often suspended or slowed during coldest part of the winter. In the white morph of the nominate subspecies, pre-formative moult is rather variable and includes the same feathers as other geese: many of the feathers of the head, neck and body, a small proportion of the inner upperwing-coverts, 0–2 tertials and rectrices. This moult seems less extensive and protracted in the blue morph of the nominate subspecies and in *atlantica*[886,945,1014], occurs in Sep–Jan and includes many feathers of the head and neck, only some (<50%) of the breast and upperparts feathers and few or no inner coverts[1014]. Definitive pre-basic moult starts from mid-Jul with the simultaneous loss of the remiges, then continues on the moulting and/or staging grounds and ends on wintering sites. Second pre-basic moult (and pre-basic moult by non-breeding adult) takes place on average one month earlier.

HYBRIDISATION Hybrids are sometimes reported with Ross's Goose, but are difficult to distinguish among large flocks of 'white' geese, making it difficult to estimate their real frequency. These hybrids can be misidentified, mainly as Ross's Goose (see that species). Hybridisation is also relatively frequently reported with

Canada Goose *Branta canadensis* and Cackling Goose *B. hutchinsii* (see below), and much more rarely with Bar-headed Goose *Anser indicus*, Greater White-fronted Goose *A. albifrons* and Barnacle Goose *Branta leucopsis* (see those species). Exceptional reports exist with Swan Goose *Anser cygnoid*[465,817], Lesser White-fronted Goose *Anser erythropus*[465] and Brent Goose *Branta bernicla*[117,188]. In captivity, hybridisation is mentioned fairly frequently with Greylag Goose *Anser anser* and its different domestic forms, including those involving Swan Goose *A. cygnoid* in their parentage[817]. Other captive mixed pairs have been reported occasionally with Bean Goose *A. fabalis*[582,817], Pink-footed Goose *A. brachyrhynchus*, Emperor Goose[112,465,586,817], Mute Swan *Cygnus olor*[1190], Egyptian Goose *Alopochen aegyptiacus*[1190] and Muscovy Duck *Cairina moschata*[1190].

Snow Goose × Canada Goose: quite variable in size, shape, and bill shape, especially depending on the subspecies involved. The coloration also varies probably much depending on the morph of Snow Goose involved. Mantle, scapulars and upperwing grey-brown with regular, narrow pale streaks, more reminiscent of Canada Goose pattern. Inner greater coverts and tertials variably fringed white. Flanks often paler but usually neatly streaked. Head and neck white, with a variable number of black flecks on crown, nape, back, neck-sides and hindneck. Belly often whitish. Bill pale pink to greyish, with tomium and nail mostly black. Legs dull greyish-pink.

Snow Goose × Cackling Goose: difficult to separate from the previous hybrid, and those involving one of these two *Branta* geese and Ross's Goose (see also Cackling Goose). Size and structure are key elements, as well as the size of the bill compared to the head. The shape of the 'grinning patch' is also important. In general, it is probable that such a hybrid will accompany a flock of one of the species involved its parentage. Thus, if the hybrid follows a group of Cackling Geese, for example, a stronger size and longer bill would better designate a Snow Goose as a parent. However, if the size is barely larger or equivalent, and the bill shorter, triangular and appears very small compared to the head, the other species involved is probably a Ross's Goose. Similarly, if such a hybrid is seen with Snow Geese, smaller size may point towards Cackling Goose as the second parent, and a similar or greater size towards Canada Goose.

HABITAT and LIFE-CYCLE Highly migratory, travelling to its breeding grounds between Mar and May (leaving southernmost wintering sites in mid-Feb). Inhabits the Arctic tundra, usually close to shores, lakes or estuaries, preferably using islands and islets away from terrestrial predators. Favours areas with swift succession in vegetation from the shore, the different types of vegetation being used for food (for both adult and young birds) depending on the progressive thaw[247,254]. In the north of its range, inhabits hillier landscapes up to 10 km from shore[886]. Often establishes dense colonies (up to 1,700 nests per km²)[247]. These huge densities have been cited as the cause of local damage, both to natural grassland habitats (colonies) and crops on migration routes[247,631]. Eggs are mostly laid in Jun, shortly after arriving on the breeding sites. Adult loses its remiges while their offspring are still small, and are able to fly again at about the same time that young fledge[247]. Autumn migration occurs between mid-Sep and mid-Nov. Movements occur in noisy flocks of thousands, even tens of thousands of birds, in which families often remain together. At this season, inhabits mostly coastal marshes (fresh or brackish), tidal mudflats, shallow lagoons, using short-vegetation habitats to feed, as well as crops, especially rice fields[886].

RANGE and POPULATION Essentially Nearctic, breeding in large colonies in Arctic tundra from NW Greenland east to NE Siberia. The two subspecies have adjoining breeding areas and have both been reported in NW Europe (Iceland, British Isles, Norway, the Netherlands, etc.), where escapes from captivity also occur.

C. c. caerulescens. Breeds from S Baffin Island and the coast of Hudson Bay to the New Siberian Is. Populations from Nunavut and Hudson Bay winter between C USA and coasts of the Gulf of Mexico. Those breeding further west winter in Central Valley and S California (north to British Columbia) and on the coasts of Sonora, Mexico, as well as locally inland in SW USA and on the Chihuahuan plateau, Mexico. Birds breeding in the Queen Maud Gulf winter either in California, in Mexico or along the coast of the Gulf of Mexico. Rare further south to Honduras, in the Greater Antilles, Hawaii and on coasts of E Asia (mostly N Japan but also South Korea and China). Significantly more common in the past in E Siberia (now breeds mostly on Wrangel I), and was formerly a common winter visitor to Japan in the 19th century[182]. Breeding populations as follows: 3,170,000–3,180,000 individuals around Hudson Bay, 1,230,000 birds in Nunavut, 653,800 birds estimated for the W Canadian Arctic and 210,000 on Wrangel I[1348], totalling 5.2 million birds, perhaps even 6–8 million birds[247]. All populations have increased sharply in recent decades (estimated at 600,000 individuals in the 1950s) and continue to do so[1294].

C. c. atlantica. Breeds in NW Greenland, N Nunavut to SE Baffin I. Winters along the Atlantic coast between Massachusetts and South Carolina, mostly in New Jersey and on the Delaware Peninsula. One report of this subspecies in Japan[182]. This population's numbers fluctuate on average below one million birds (1,005,000 in 2012, 921,000 in 2013[1294]), having steadily increased during the 20th century (population estimated at 10,000 individuals in the early 1900s).

In Europe, pairs or small populations have bred following introductions in Norway, Sweden, Finland[667], Germany, the Netherlands and England (fewer than ten pairs established in each country in 2004–07[62]).

CAPTIVITY Said to easy to keep and breed, although pairs may be relatively aggressive towards other geese when breeding. Generally more expensive than domestic geese, but significantly cheaper than most goose species. Quite common in collections and likely to escape from captivity outside its range.

REFERENCES Alisauskas (1998)[13]; Avise *et al.* (1992)[46]; Banks *et al.* (2008)[62]; Bird Hybrids Flickr Forum (2009)[112]; Bird Hybrids Flickr Forum (2009)[117]; Avise *et al.* (1992)[46]; BirdLife International (2012)[142]; Brazil (2009)[182]; Brimley (1927)[188]; Clements *et al.* (2013)[236]; Cooch & Cooch *in* Kear (2005)[247]; Cooch *et al.* (1991)[248]; Cooch *et al.* (1991)[249]; Cooke & Cooch (1968)[250]; Cooke *et al.* (1976)[252]; Cooke *et al.* (1988)[253]; Cooke *et al.* (1995)[254]; Dzubin (1979)[338]; Gill & Donsker (2014)[437]; Gray (1958)[465]; Hopkinson (1926)[582]; Hopkinson (1934)[586]; Jefferies & Rockwell (2002)[631]; Johnson & Troy (1987)[659]; Kampe-Persson (2010)[667]; Kutnezsov *et al.* (1998)[720]; Lepage *et al.* (1998)[744]; Livezey (1996)[772]; McCarthy (2006)[817]; Mowbray *et al.* (2000)[886]; Ogilvie (1978)[925]; Palmer (1976)[945]; Pittaway (1992)[997]; Pyle (2008)[1014]; Quinn (1992)[1024]; Quinn *et al.* (1987)[1025]; Rattray & Cooke (1984)[1048]; Reed & Plante (1997)[1053]; Reed *et al.* (1998)[1054]; Sibley (1938)[1190]; USFWS (2013)[1294]; Weckstein *et al.* (2002)[1341]; Wetlands International (2014)[1348].

90. *C. c. atlanticus*, adult (definitive basic), white morph; note thicker and longer bill, with straighter culmen and deeper 'grinning patch'. Quebec, Canada, Sep (Mikaël Jaffré).

91. *C. c. atlanticus*, adult (definitive basic), white morph. Quebec, Canada, Sep (Mikaël Jaffré).

92. *C. c. caerulescens*, adult (definitive basic), white morph; distinguished from Ross's Goose *C. rossii* by flatter crown, bigger bill with broad black 'grinning patch' and upward-tilted rear body. California, USA, Nov (Sébastien Reeber).

93. *C. c. caerulescens*, juvenile/first-winter (first basic/formative), white morph; during pre-formative moult, typically shows mix of greyish/dusky and white feathers. California, USA, Nov (Sébastien Reeber).

94. *C. c. caerulescens*, group, with adult (below) and juvenile (above), white morph. California, USA, Nov (Sébastien Reeber).

95. *C. c. caerulescens*, adult (definitive basic), white morph. California, USA, Nov (Sébastien Reeber).

96. *C. c. caerulescens*, adult (definitive basic), blue morph; a typical blue morph, with dark underparts. Texas, USA, Jan (Joe Fischer).

97. Possible hybrid Snow Goose *C. caerulescens* × Ross's Goose *C. rossii*, adult (definitive basic), white morph; length and thin shape to bill not typical of Ross's Goose, although other features could match that species. New Jersey, USA, Nov (Sébastien Reeber).

98. Possible hybrid Snow Goose *C. caerulescens* × Ross's Goose *C. rossii*, adult (definitive basic), white morph; a strange-looking bird, with rather thick bill and 'grinning patch' looks deep but bill is apparently not completely shut. California, USA, Nov (Sébastien Reeber).

99. Possible hybrid Snow Goose *C. caerulescens* × Ross's Goose *C. rossii*, adult (definitive basic), white morph; probably a hybrid, with a long bill, thin towards tip with concave culmen, head looks rather long and crown flat, with feathering at base of bill obviously convex. California, USA, Nov (Sébastien Reeber).

100. *C. c. caerulescens*, adult (definitive basic), blue/intermediate morph; flanks and breast with white patches make this a blue/intermediate morph, and note rather black upperparts. California, USA, Nov (Sébastien Reeber).

101. *C. c. caerulescens*, adult (definitive basic), blue morph; note pale grey upperwing, contrasting with scapulars and remiges. Texas, USA, Dec (Greg Lavaty).

102. *C. c. caerulescens*, adult (definitive basic), blue/intermediate morph; note differences in coloration of underparts. Texas, USA, Jan (Joe Fischer).

103. *C. c. caerulescens*, adult (definitive basic) blue/intermediate morph (below), first-winter (first basic/formative) blue morph (above) and first-winter (first basic/formative) white morph (middle); note contrasting underwing pattern in both ages of blue morph. California, USA, Nov (Sébastien Reeber).

104. Putative hybrid Snow Goose *C. caerulescens* × Ross's Goose *C. rossii*, adult (definitive basic), blue/intermediate morph; note bill pattern (intermediate 'grinning patch' and feathering at base of bill) which does not match either parent species. California, USA, Jan (Bob Steele).

105. *C. c. caerulescens*, adult (definitive basic), white morph; a bird with only eight black primaries. California, USA, Nov (Sébastien Reeber).

ROSS'S GOOSE
Chen rossii

Plates 9, 10, 11

TAXONOMY *Anser Rossii* Cassin, 1861, *Proc. Acad. Nat. Sci., Philadelphia*, 13: 73. Phylogenetically very close to Snow Goose *C. caerulescens*[772], both species being placed in the genus *Anser* in Europe (AERC-TAC) and by some authors[454]. There are two colour morphs, but the blue one is very rare. No geographic variation or subspecies.

IDENTIFICATION Its white plumage (in vast majority of adults) with black primaries make it unlikely to be mistaken for any other species except Snow Goose. Distinction will be easier in direct comparison, based on size, shape and bill shape.

- *Size*: Ross's Goose is significantly smaller than the nominate subspecies of Snow Goose, with a mass on average 40% lighter, and the difference is even greater compared to *atlantica*, which Ross's Goose often joins on the Atlantic coast of North America.

- *Structure*: In Ross's Goose, the neck is noticeably shorter and thicker, with a higher and more rounded head, which does not appear thicker than the upper neck. In Snow Goose, the neck is thinner than the head (a useful clue in flight as well).

- *Shape*: On water (slow swimming or resting), the back in Snow Goose typically appears stronger and points upwards, with the tip of the wings and the tail held well above the level of the back. In Ross's Goose, the rear body is less prominent, the tip of the wings and tail often being held a little below the level of the back, which is slightly curved.

- *Head*: Higher and more rounded in Ross's Goose, more elongated in Snow Goose, with a flatter crown. The forehead is steeper in Ross's Goose than in the nominate subspecies of Snow Goose, and much more than in *atlantica*. These impressions are emphasised by the respective bill sizes of the three taxa. Also note that from early winter Snow Geese acquire a yellowish or rusty tinge to the head (birds feeding in brackish or saltwater habitats), while it usually remains all white in Ross's Goose.

- *Shape and position of the eye*: In Ross's Goose, the eye is typically round (more almond-shaped in Snow Goose), which makes it appear 'surprised' and 'cute'. The eye's position is also different, being centred vertically in Ross's Goose but closer to the crown in Snow Goose. Similarly, the eye is closer to the base of the culmen in Ross's Goose (this distance nearly equals the diameter of the eye in Ross's Goose, and nearly twice its diameter in Snow Goose).

- *Bill shape*: In Ross's Goose, the bill is much shorter and smaller, especially compared to the size of the head. It almost forms an equilateral triangle with straight edges in profile. This is accentuated by the vertical feathering at the base of the bill, which is virtually straight. In the nominate subspecies of Snow Goose, the culmen is somewhat concave just before the nail, and the lower mandible slightly convex (even more bulging in *atlantica*). The feathering at the base of the bill is clearly convex in profile.

- *Bill coloration*: In Ross's Goose, it is pink over the central portion and tip, and blue-grey (sometimes greenish) at the sides of the base. The base also shows small caruncles which are more marked in the ♂ and increase with age. They also perhaps indicate social status and constitute a reproductive barrier with Snow Goose[829]. In the latter, the bill is completely pink to the base without caruncles.

- *Spacing between mandibles* ('grinning patch'): Seen in profile, the cutting edges of the mandibles are contiguous or nearly so in Ross's Goose. In Snow Goose, they form a flattened oval opening in the black lamellae, which is even more visible in *atlantica*.

- *Legs*: In direct comparison, the legs of Ross's Goose are visibly thinner than in Snow Goose. They are generally more reddish-pink in Snow Goose, and pale purple in Ross's Goose.

Plumage (adult dark morph): The blue morph of Ross's Goose (very rare) is completely dark over the neck, nape and crown, encircling the large white face, and together with the mantle and scapulars is also darker (almost black) than the blue morph of Snow Goose. Among other noticeable differences, the upperwing-coverts are white (vs. grey in Snow Goose), forming a broad white bar between the upperparts and flanks, merging in a large pale area on the secondaries and tertials, which are pale grey to whitish with dark areas reduced to the shaft (vs. blackish feathers with white fringes in Snow Goose).

Plumage (juvenile): Juvenile plumage of the white morph (until first winter) is much whiter than that of Snow Goose. Particularly, the neck, scapulars, upperwing-coverts and tertials are whitish (grey in Snow Goose). In flight, the median coverts and outer secondaries are also whiter in young Ross's. Overall, young Ross's Goose more closely resembles the adult.

Distinguishing these two species is usually not that difficult, but is greatly complicated by the existence of hybrids between them, which are relatively frequent in the wild and some individuals with mixed characters can be very misleading. A hybrid in a flock of Snow Geese in a region where Ross's Goose is rare can easily be mistaken for the latter, due to its smaller size and significantly different head shape from the surrounding geese, making it necessary to eliminate the possibility of a hybrid when faced by a possible vagrant Ross's Goose, especially as hybrids may well adopt the migration routes of Snow Goose. The proportion of hybrids among 'Ross's-like' geese outside of the species' regular range may be higher than it is in the overall population (see Hybridisation). Also note that, even after detailed observation, it is sometimes impossible to determine whether some birds very similar to typical Ross's are actually multiple-generation hybrids or simply atypical Ross's Geese. Moreover, intra-specific variability and the effects of extensive hybridisation can be linked, especially as two episodes of extensive gene exchange occurred in the past[1341].

PLUMAGES Sexes identical, but can be sexed based on the larger size, more alert and upright posture, and the more aggressive behaviour of the ♂. Complex basic moult strategy (one plumage per definitive cycle, two in the first cycle). Ageing easy until the first summer. See also Identification. The dark morph is very rare (fewer than one bird per 10,000)[830].

Adult (white morph)

Definitive basic plumage (year-round). All white except blackish primaries (greyer at base with white shafts, especially on outer primaries) and alula, with grey primary coverts. Many show some white on the inner primaries or black markings on the outer secondaries. Iris dark brown. Reddish-purple to pale pink bill with hardly paler, ivory nail. Base of bill covered in caruncles, on average more developed in older birds, before and during the nesting season and in ♂♂[664,829]. From a distance, the bill base appears bluish-grey to olive-grey. Legs and feet pale pink or pale purple.

Adult (blue morph)

Definitive basic plumage (year-round). Appears black and white, more contrasting than the blue morph of Snow Goose. Broad white patch over cheeks, face, forehead, chin, throat and around the eyes, contrasting with blackish neck, nape and crown. Breast, mantle and inner scapulars blackish too, but flanks greyer or have narrow white fringes to feathers. Belly, rear body and rump white. Rectrices dark grey at base, broadly fringed white. Longest scapulars and tertials centred black and fringed white. Secondary upperwing-coverts white or very pale grey, with dark grey shafts tapering to a point on the greater coverts and inner median coverts. Secondaries centred black and fringed white. Alula and primary coverts grey. Underwing whitish, with greater coverts darker grey and blackish remiges. Iris, bill and legs as in the white form.

This morph has often been considered the result of occasional hybridisation with the blue morph of Snow Goose, or backcross hybrids with Ross's Goose[251,830]. To date, no 'blue allele' specific to Ross's Goose has been found in its genome[664]. There are hybrid individuals, clearly showing intermediate general structure, bill shape and dark parts to the plumage, but most of these show at least one of the following features, intermediate between blue morphs of the two species: partially dark belly, more extensive white on the upper neck, crown, nape or hindneck irregularly flecked white, dark blue mantle and grey scapulars, light grey secondary upperwing-coverts and black centres to greater coverts and inner median coverts significantly larger than in blue morph of Ross's Goose. Besides the obvious hybrids, there are also birds such as those described above for the blue morph, which do not show obvious structural differences (or measurements[794]) compared to typical Ross's. Their coloration differs significantly from the homozygous morph of blue Snow Goose, including features difficult to explain as hybridisation with a white Ross's Goose (extensively dark head and blacker upperparts than in blue Snow Goose). Genetic analysis of such individuals would therefore be very interesting.

Juvenile (white morph)

First basic plumage (until Oct–Feb). Overall white with indistinct grey marks on the head and upperparts. Cheeks and forehead white, crown and nape pale grey, and a dark grey loral stripe. Iris dark grey-brown. Bill dark olive-grey (with paler nail), pinkish being initially restricted to the lower culmen but spreading over the rest of the bill from Oct. Mantle grey. Hindneck and scapulars whitish with pale grey markings. Tertials whitish centred grey. Rest of neck, chest and flanks white slightly mottled pale grey. Belly to undertail-coverts white. Back, rump and uppertail whitish, with subtle grey speckles. Rectrices pale grey fringed white. Upperwing has blackish primaries (white shafts), outer secondaries pale grey fringed white, becoming all white inwards. Secondary coverts whitish and primary coverts pale grey. Underwing has blackish primaries, pale grey secondaries (darker outwards) and axillaries and coverts whitish. Legs dull greyish-pink, brighter in ♂ and more olive-tinged in ♀[664].

Juvenile (blue morph)

First basic plumage (until Oct–Dec). Poorly described in the literature. Head, neck, chest, mantle and scapulars dull dark grey-brown. Flank feathers identical, with irregular whitish fringes. Belly and rear body pale grey-brown to whitish. Upperwing and tertials close to those of adult but grey centres appears more pronounced on the latter and inner greater coverts. Bare parts as white form (?).

First-winter/first-summer *(white morph)*

Formative plumage (Nov–Mar/Aug). Acquisition of formative plumage usually extends over the first winter. The overall appearance is whiter than in juvenile plumage, including the head, mantle and scapulars, which still show some pale grey traces. From Mar–Apr, the formative neck feathers show similar grooves to those of adult. The pink on the bill is close to that of adult (but caruncles absent) which, combined with the white plumage, can make distinction from adult challenging. The most obvious ageing feature is often the outer secondaries, largely centred grey, and less strongly contrasting with the black primaries. The iris is dark grey becoming dark brown during the first winter (not very useful in field conditions).

First-winter/first-summer (blue morph)

Formative plumage (Oct–Dec?/Aug). Poorly documented, including potential differences with the white morph in extent and timing of pre-formative moult (such differences exist between the two morphs of Snow Goose[1014]). Many of the feathers of the head and neck are moulted, however, and the plumage appears quite close to that of adult with variable brown smudges on upperparts and flanks.

GEOGRAPHIC VARIATION None described.

MEASUREMENTS and MASS ♂♂ and adult slightly larger and heavier than ♀♀ and young, respectively. Saskatchewan. ♂ (n=31): wing chord 360–403 (386), tail 114–131 (121.8), culmen 36–46 (41.2), tarsus 81–89 (84.8); ♀ (n=32): wing chord 355–382 (368.5), tail 108–124 (116.2), culmen 35–43 (39.1), tarsus 75–86 (80.5)[664]. Nunavut. ♂ (n=52): culmen 39.0–49.3 (43.4), tarsus 79.2–91.5 (85.2); ♀ (n=47): culmen 35.0–45.0 (40.1), tarsus 75.5–88.2 (81.0)[664]. ♂ (n=70): wing chord 356–396 (adult) and 346–385 (juvenile), culmen 37–47, bill depth at tip of forehead feathering 21.1–26.6, tail 110–131, tarsus 65–76; ♀ (n=70): wing chord 344–380 (adult) and 330–370 (juvenile), culmen 35–44, bill depth at tip of forehead feathering 20.6–25.9, tail 105–124, tarsus 62–72[1014]; compare with measurements given by Pyle[1014] for both subspecies of Snow Goose. ♂: mass in winter 1,239–1,570 (1,426.0, n=10), mass in Jun 1,350–1,955 (1,632.2, n=25)[247], mass in Sep 1,320–1,880 (1,679, n=31)[945]; ♀: mass in winter 1,099–1,407 (1,269.0, n=12), mass in Jun 1,155–2,040 (1,640.2, n=20)[247], mass in Sep 1,270–1,660 (1,500, n=32)[945].

VOICE Less vocal and noisy than Snow Goose, with higher pitched and less powerful calls. Commonly produces a nasal and high-pitched *geek* or *ong* (slightly lower in ♂). Also utters a lower and more raucous *kowk*, including in migratory flight[825].

MOULT Complex basic strategy. Pre-formative moult occurs between Sep–Nov and Feb–Mar, includes many feathers of the head, neck and body, often a small proportion of the inner upperwing-coverts, 0–4 tertials and most to all rectrices. Definitive pre-basic moult begins in mid-Jul with the simultaneous loss of the remiges, then continues on the moulting and/or staging grounds, ending on the wintering grounds in Nov. The second pre-basic moult and definitive pre-basic moult of non- or failed breeders occurs on average one month earlier[664,1014].

HYBRIDISATION In the wild probably occurs on a regular basis with Snow Goose (see below), is reported occasionally with Barnacle Goose *Branta leucopsis* (see below), and is very occasional with other species: Cackling Goose *B. hutchinsii*[1190] (see that species), Red-breasted Goose *B. ruficollis*[465,1158] and possibly Lesser White-fronted Goose *Anser erythropus*[132], partly related to feral populations and/or escapees in NW Europe. Note, however, that the list of potential hybrids is probably longer, but doubts remain in many cases whether either Ross's or Snow Goose is involved in the cross. In captivity, hybridisation has been mentioned with Greylag Goose *A. anser*[1190], Emperor Goose *C. canagica*[295,465,586,817] and Blue-winged Goose *Cyanochen cyanopterus*[1282].

Ross's Goose × Snow Goose: thought to be rather common in the wild. Studies found 32 hybrids among 6,489 white-morph Snow Geese, 1,666 blue-morph Snow Geese and 5,471 Ross's Geese captured[1282], i.e. 0.23% of 13,626 geese of both species combined were hybrids. These same figures led to estimates that, among wintering birds in C & S USA, the number of hybrids represented 0.5% of Snow Geese and 4.7% of Ross's Geese[1282]. The hybrid element was estimated at 1.9% in the Queen Maud Gulf in 1989–92[680]. Like many crosses, hybridisation seems more frequent where one of the two species involved is rare, pairing occurring in winter. It is therefore likely that the frequency of hybrids is higher in E North America than in California, for example.

The description of these hybrids has been detailed[1282], including precise data on useful measurements. The culmen length of hybrids – adult ♂: 45.1 (40–48, n=7), adult ♀: 46.6 (45–50, n=5) – is a little closer to that of Ross's Goose – adult ♂: 41.9 (39–47, n=47), adult ♀: 39.0 (37–44, n=32) – than that of Snow Goose – adult ♂: 56.2 (53–61, n=32), adult ♀: 53.5 (50–59, n=36). It is the same with tarsus length and wing chord. Mass data detailed in the same work give an idea of overall size: ♂: 1,955 (1,680–2,160, n=7) in hybrids, 1,780 (1,580–2,010, n=47) for Ross's Goose and 2,403 (2,030–2,860, n=32) for Snow Goose. For ♀♀, mass: 1,778 (1,334–2,240, n=4) in hybrids, 1,583 (1,390–1,840, n=32) for Ross's Goose and 2,274 (1,890–2,590, n=36) for Snow Goose[1282]. These figures suggest that a ♀ hybrid can have a body size similar to ♂ Ross's Goose, and that a hybrid ♂ is more intermediate in general size.

The most obvious distinguishing features of a hybrid reside in bill structure, the form of the feathering at the base of the bill and the spacing between the mandibles. The bill is slightly longer and appears thinner towards the tip than in Ross's Goose, with usually a slightly concave culmen in profile. According to the data indicated above[1282], there is no overlap in culmen length between hybrids and Snow Goose, giving a significantly different appearance. Furthermore, the shape of the head is typically intermediate, rather elongated (not as high as Ross's Goose), but less wedge-shaped than Snow Goose. The feathering at the bill base forms a slightly convex line, intermediate between the two parent species. The 'grinning patch' is more visible in hybrids, averaging 6–8 mm, i.e. the minimum shown by Snow

Goose of the nominate subspecies (7–12 mm)[1014,1282]. The spacing is tinged black in hybrids. Note that the sides of the bill base in hybrids are mostly blue-grey or greyish-green, but the colour is less pronounced and less extensive than in Ross's Goose on average. There are no small caruncles. The delicate legs recall those of Ross's Goose and are distinctly shorter than in Snow Goose on average, with much longer feet than in Ross's Goose[1282].

There are also hybrids of the blue morph, which show intermediate coloration between the blue morphs of both species (see above). Finally, note that the plumage of a juvenile hybrid seems to vary in coloration between juvenile Ross's Goose and Snow Goose[1282].

Ross's Goose × Barnacle Goose: reported occasionally in North America[817,830,1282], Russia[702] and the UK[110]. Quite variable in appearance but, fairly typically, size and structure similar to those of the two parent species, with scapulars, upper breast, mantle and flanks dark brown to blackish, fringed pale. Greater coverts and tertials blackish with clear white fringes. White belly and rear body, except rectrices, black fringed white. Some show a largely white head and neck with some blackish flecks, while others show a black head and neck with variable and ill-defined white cheeks and around the eye[110]. Some birds at least have well-marked white secondaries. The bill is typically very small and short, pink to grey-pink with a black nail. Greyish-pink legs. Distinction may be difficult vs. any other hybrid involving a Barnacle, Canada or Cackling Goose on the one hand and a Ross's or Snow Goose on the other.

HABITAT and LIFE-CYCLE Highly migratory, leaving the wintering grounds between late Feb and late Mar, and arriving on the Arctic breeding grounds in early Jun. Inhabits Arctic tundra, preferring coastal lowlands, where colonies are established preferably on islands covered with boulders, grass and lichens, or scattered short shrubs[664,825]. Breeds in dense colonies (tens to several hundreds of nests per ha[664,1114], often mixed with Snow Geese[664,680,819]. Eggs are laid soon after arriving at breeding sites, at least when the weather permits, between early Jun and mid Jul. Pre-basic moult begins with non-breeders or failed breeders, from Jun, on moulting grounds. Adult with goslings moult on breeding sites or gather in dense flocks[664]. The drop in temperatures and increasing scarcity of food triggers autumn migration from Sep, with arrivals on the wintering grounds occurring until early Dec. In winter, feeds mainly in crops, slightly flooded fields and shallow grassy wetlands. Roosts in huge numbers on deeper waterbodies, preferably in quiet or protected areas. May join Snow Geese, but prefers to form monospecific flocks where the two species are numerous.

RANGE and POPULATION Breeds in the Canadian Arctic, where the species has undergone a spectacular geographical expansion and numerical increase since the mid-20th century. It then bred almost only in the Queen Maud Gulf, Nunavut, this region still hosting the main colony of the species today, at Lake Karrak with 726,000 birds in 2008[648]. Besides the current range (see map), rarer west to Alaska and north on the islands of Nunavut[664], and present in small numbers at most of Snow Geese colonies in E Canadian Arctic[825]. Previously, the species wintered almost exclusively in C California, but it is much more widespread today (see map). Less numerous far inland (S Great Plains and lower Mississippi Valley) and smaller numbers in east (New Jersey to North Carolina). Uncommon migrant in the interior of E USA. Casual visitor in Russian Far East, and Europe (Iceland, Faroe Is, Ireland, UK, the Netherlands, Norway and Germany). The presence of escapees makes judging natural vagrancy difficult, with occasional breeding records in the Netherlands and England[62,834,1329]. Total population estimated at <6,000 individuals in 1930[664], just 2,000 birds in 1949, 188,000 in 1988, 500,000 in 1997[4], 1,050,000 individuals in 2002[1348] and more than two million at the end of the first decade of the present century[14], and is still increasing rapidly.

CAPTIVITY Rather uncommon in captivity, at least in Eurasia, but deemed fairly easy to keep and breed. Still quite expensive (typically more so than Snow Goose). Escapees are regularly reported in W Europe, including some with ornamental rings. The context of a sighting is important when considering the origin of a potential vagrant (date, location, species of geese alongside which the individual has arrived, etc.).

REFERENCES Abraham & Jefferies (1997)[4]; Alisauskas *et al.* (2012)[14]; Banks *et al.* (2008)[62]; Bird Hybrids Flickr Forum (2009)[110]; Bird Hybrids Flickr Forum (2011)[132]; Cooke & Ryder (1971)[251]; Delacour (1954)[295]; González *et al.* (2009)[454]; Gray (1958)[465]; Hopkinson (1934)[586]; Johnsgard (2010)[648]; Jónsson & Afton (2008)[663]; Jónsson *et al.* (2013)[664]; Kaufman *et al.* (1979)[671]; Kerbes (1994)[680]; Kondratyev & Zöckler (2009)[702]; Livezey (1996)[772]; Madge & Burn (1988)[794]; McCarthy (2006)[817]; McCracken *et al.* (1997)[819]; McGill *in* Kear (2005)[825]; McLandress (1983)[829]; McLandress & McLandress (1979)[830]; Meininger (2004)[834]; Palmer (1976)[945]; Ploeger (1968)[998]; Prevett & Johnson (1977)[1009]; Pyle (2008)[1014]; Ryder (1969)[1114]; Ryder (1972)[1115]; Scott (1947)[1158]; Sibley (1938)[1190]; Trauger *et al.* (1971)[1282]; van den Berg (2004)[1306]; Voslamber (2010)[1329]; Weckstein *et al.* (2002)[1341]; Wetlands International (2014)[1348]; Williamson (1957)[1359].

106. Adult (definitive basic), white morph; two adults with Snow Goose *C. caerulescens* (right), note differences in size and shape, especially on water, where Snow Goose often has larger rear body, held upwards. California, USA, Nov (Sébastien Reeber).

107. Adult (definitive basic), blue morph; compared to Snow Goose *C. caerulescens* (beside size and shape), dark parts are blacker, upperwing and tertials whiter, belly always white, and nape and crown most frequently marked with black. California, USA, Dec (Bob Steele).

108. Adult (definitive basic), white morph; head features, including straight limit between base of bill and feathers, are also useful in flight. California, USA, Nov (Sébastien Reeber).

109. Juvenile/first-winter (first basic/formative), white morph; compared to Snow Goose *C. caerulescens*, much whiter and closer to adult at this age, and aged by dusky traces on upper head (especially lores and rear crown) and mantle, as well as by darker and duller bare parts. California, USA, Nov (Sébastien Reeber).

110. Adult (definitive basic), white morph; round head with small bill characteristic, but also note round eye, olive-grey tinge at base of bill and 'grinning patch' almost lacking. California, USA, Nov (Sébastien Reeber).

245

BRENT GOOSE (BRANT)
Branta bernicla

TAXONOMY *Anas Bernicla* Linnaeus, 1758, *Syst. Nat.*, edn. 10, p. 124. Within the genus *Branta*, the Brent Goose forms a clade with Red-breasted Goose *B. ruficollis* and Barnacle Goose *B. leucopsis,* which is the close sister group of the three other species[772]. Three subspecies are generally accepted: Dark-bellied Goose *B. b. bernicla* on Arctic coasts of C Siberia and wintering in Europe, Pale-bellied Goose *B. b. hrota* O. F. Müller, 1776, breeding in E Canadian Arctic and on Svalbard, wintering in E North America, Ireland and Denmark, and Black Brant *B. b. nigricans* Lawrence, 1846, breeding on Arctic coasts of W North America and E Siberia, wintering on N Pacific coasts. It has been proposed to treat them as three species[182,427,847,1096,1180], given their distinctive plumages and the apparent rarity of hybrids, despite that two of the three taxa winter in sympatry. In this respect, it is worth mentioning that where the wintering grounds of *bernicla* and *hrota* overlap (Netherlands, Denmark[724], France, British Isles), flocks do not usually mix, their activity rhythms are often different and interactions between them do not seem higher than those between other species of geese. Despite this, European and North American taxonomic committees, as well as the majority of authors, currently consider these taxa as conspecific[142,170,299,437,794,928].

This treatment, if it has the advantage of recognising three easily discernible taxa, does not reflect the greater genetic diversity and the fact that fully parapatric populations occur in two of the three taxa[173,753,1055,1170]. Moreover, it ignores a distinct population, the Grey-bellied Brant, breeding on the W Queen Elizabeth Is, in Arctic Canada and wintering in Puget Sound, on the North American Pacific coast. It has an intermediate appearance between *nigricans* and *hrota* and is geographically proximate to two taxa. These birds are nevertheless quite variable in appearance (see Geographic Variation). Mitochondrial DNA analysis indicates that their origin is not necessarily reflective of ancient or ongoing hybridisation. This population is phylogenetically closer to *nigricans* than *hrota*, but it has been reproductively isolated for *c.*400,000 years[1180]. It was also reported that some DNA fragments could not derive from *hrota* or *nigricans*[1181]. Although larger samples are needed to confirm these findings, it could therefore be a genetically isolated population, ancient and stable[1256,999], rather than a clinal variation or the

result of ancient hybridisation. No scientific name for it is unanimously accepted yet.

Another issue lies in the name *nigricans*, applied to Pacific birds, although the type specimen was collected in 1846 in New Jersey, where Black Brant is only an occasional visitor. Moreover, the description of this specimen suggests Grey-bellied Brant[204,299], including a plate by Peter Scott in 1957[1159] of this bird, which is also known as Lawrence's Goose, for the author of its description. It is therefore questionable to name the Pacific population on the basis of an individual with atypical characters of *nigricans*, and taken far from the usual range. If it is confirmed that Grey-bellied Brant is genetically stable and reproductively isolated, it should be named and, in this case, the name *nigricans* should be assigned to it[753] (see below).

Another subspecies has also been described, breeding in EC Siberia and wintering on the Pacific coast of Asia, *B. b. orientalis* Tugarinov, 1941. Geographically, it is located between *bernicla* of C Siberia and *nigricans* in far E Siberia and W North America. Differences compared to *nigricans* are slight, but some individuals clearly look intermediate between *bernicla* and *nigricans* (see Geographic Variation). However, genetic exchange with *bernicla* is probably not extensive, nor is there clinal variation between them. Indeed, pair formation occurs in winter, when the two populations are very distant from one another. In addition, intermediates would probably be sufficiently frequent to be detected on the wintering grounds. Most authors include *orientalis* in *nigricans*.

A recent overview has proposed to address these issues[753,999], based on the work of Delacour & Zimmer[299], who considered that the name *nigricans* cannot be applied to Pacific birds and therefore applied the next oldest available name to them, i.e. *orientalis*. This treatment, however, ignores the differences in coloration between birds breeding in the west of the range (Siberia) and those in the east (far E Siberia, Alaska and NW Canada). Delacour & Zimmer[299] attributed the name *nigricans* to Grey-bellied Brant, assuming that the bird described by Lawrence originated from this population. If the first conclusion seems robust, it would be useful to confirm the second. Further genetic analysis confirming the results of Shields[1180] would be welcome, i.e. that Gray-bellied Brant is stable and sufficiently isolated genetically (gene flow from *hrota* or *nigricans* low or non-existent). This population is intermediate in appearance between *hrota* and *nigricans*, and variable, despite its small population. Moreover, known first-generation hybrids between Black Brant and Pale-bellied Goose (including young observed in the company of both parents) are similar to typical Grey-bellied Brant, and it is possible that the initial description of *nigricans* was actually based on such a hybrid, rather than a pure Grey-bellied Brant. Similarly, it has been suggested that this bird, two of the same type from the US Atlantic coast (at the Smithsonian Institution, Washington DC) and two others taken on the Labrador coast (Canadian Museum of Nature, Ottawa), emanate from a dark-bellied population that probably bred formerly in E Canada[170]. The same source indicates that this morph was familiar to hunters on the North American Atlantic coast until the early 20th century. In this case, *nigricans* would designate an extinct intermediate population.

Taking the above into account and following the recommendations of Lewis *et al.*[753], the following treatment is adopted here:

- Dark-bellied Brent Goose *B. b. bernicla* (Arctic coasts of C Siberia, wintering in Europe)

- Pale-bellied Brent Goose *B. b. hrota* (E Canadian Arctic to Svalbard, wintering on both coasts of N Atlantic).

- Black Brant *B. b. orientalis* (Arctic coasts of W North America and E Siberia, wintering on both coasts of N Pacific)

- Grey-bellied Brant *B. b. nigricans* (Queen Elizabeth Is, wintering in Puget Sound).

In the following sections, *orientalis* therefore designates Black Brant and *nigricans* Grey-bellied Brant.

IDENTIFICATION Should not be mistaken for other geese, although Pale-bellied Brent Goose superficially resembles Barnacle Goose. Easily distinguished by its smaller size, darker overall plumage and all-black head in all plumages. Note also that Brent Goose inhabits some different habitats to those used by other geese, preferentially feeding in shallow coastal waters, whereas other species prefer grassy areas to graze. See Geographic Variation for separation of the subspecies.

PLUMAGES *B. b. bernicla*. Sexes identical, but ♂ slightly larger and 10% heavier, with a slightly larger head and body structure and often more aggressive behaviour

towards intruders. These differences may be useful for sexing pairs. Complex basic moult strategy (one plumage per definitive cycle, two during the first cycle). Ageing relatively easy until the first summer.

Adult

Definitive basic plumage (year-round). Dark, with rear body white. Head, neck and chest matt blackish, with two white marks, on average slightly larger in ♂, on the neck-sides (white tips to the feathers) which usually do not merge on the front. Iris dark brown. Bill dark and rather small. Belly and flanks grey-brown slightly contrasting with the breast, the broad whitish fringes to the rear flanks forming a series of long pale crescents. The paleness of the rear flanks strongly depends on the light. Lower belly, under- and uppertail white, concealing much of the black tail. When foraging in water by upending, seen from behind, the dark belly appears slightly above the surface of the water (see other taxa). On a standing bird in profile, the dark coloration extends between the legs. Upperparts uniform grey-brown (like the fore flanks), except the blackish remiges (and tertials). Upperwing has all coverts grey-brown like the mantle and scapulars. Underwing dark grey-brown, with pale spots on outer webs of median coverts and inner greater coverts. Back black extends as fine line across the rump. Legs blackish.

Juvenile

First basic plumage (until Oct–Dec). Similar to adult but duller and paler. Head, neck and chest dull dark grey-brown, rather than blackish, without white marks on the neck-sides (or at most a few pale flecks). Flanks and belly paler grey-brown, much plainer than in adult. Mantle feathers, scapulars and upperwing-coverts slightly narrower, less square-tipped, grey-brown with whitish fringes towards the tips. The entire upperparts appear regularly streaked at a distance. Tertials also fringed white at the tips. Sexes identical.

First-winter/first-summer

Formative plumage (Nov–Dec/Jul–Aug). Like adult after pre-formative moult, but differs in clear whitish fringes to the upperwing-coverts, forming obvious bars on the wing (visible in flight and at rest). Belly feathers usually still juvenile, forming a uniform grey-brown patch, easily visible at short range. The white marks on the neck are slightly smaller than in the adult and, on average among young birds, smaller in ♀ than ♂[1014]. By the following spring, the juvenile feathers have become very worn, especially the upperwing-coverts (in particular the median coverts[56]) and the belly feathers become increasingly pale brown or even whitish in first summer. Similarly, the juvenile primaries and rectrices are also narrow, worn and faded. Wear also makes the white fringes to the upperwing-coverts inconspicuous or absent, and thus less useful for ageing. However, variegated appearance is typical of this age; adult also worn at this time, but the wear is much more uniform overall.

Second-winter/second-summer

Second basic plumage (Nov–Jan/May–Jul). Identical to adult, but some birds (especially those that summer on the wintering grounds[56]) retain one or more juvenile outer lesser coverts and/or median coverts, which are very worn and faded, at least until Dec. Birds showing these characters, visible as clear contrast between juvenile feathers and the rest between Oct and winter, are certainly second-winter birds.

GEOGRAPHIC VARIATION See Taxonomy for the names of subspecies used here. There is huge geographical variation, generally corresponding to the three commonly accepted subspecies. This variation is visible in belly coloration (and contrast with the flanks and breast), the extent of dark coloration from the belly rearwards (up to or behind the legs), the size of the patches on the neck-sides and the pattern of the upperparts. Secondarily, some subtle differences in size and structure are also known.

The following features may be useful once age known. Especially in Sep–Nov, juvenile feathers must be distinguished from formative ones (which are adult-like) to correctly assess the coloration of the upperparts and flanks. In juvenile plumage, the upperparts are streaked pale, and the flanks uniform, but both are more or less dark depending on subspecies. In formative plumage (from Nov–Dec), the flanks and upperparts (but not wings) are close to those of adult, but the belly remains mostly juvenile, paler than the adult (whitish in *hrota*, grey-brown in *bernicla* and dark brown in *orientalis*). Similarly, the white marks on the neck-sides are on average smaller in formative plumage (first-winter) than in adult, but vary between subspecies in the same way in both plumages. Also note that the pale/white fringes to the flank feathers decrease in width with wear, making the flanks appear increasingly barred dark until the following summer. Similarly, the contrast between the breast and fore flanks tends to increase with wear. Finally, light conditions must be considered when assessing subtle contrasts (breast/body) and colour

tones (grey or brown) of the upper- and underparts, as well as the precise colour of the flanks (pure white or washed pale grey-brown).

B. b. bernicla (Dark-bellied Brent Goose). See Plumages. The most uniform and grey-toned subspecies, with the belly and fore flanks grey slightly washed brownish, contrasting faintly with the blackish chest, but not with the upperparts. Upper flanks marked with barely contrasting pale crescents. The white spots on the neck-sides do not usually merge on the foreneck.

B. b. hrota (Pale-bellied Brent Goose). Distinctive, having four colours overall. Head, neck and breast like *bernicla* with white marks on the neck-sides slightly smaller, sometimes reduced to two short lines or, more rarely, scarcely visible. This feature varies: in USA, birds wintering in New Jersey more frequently show a complete collar on the foreneck, while it is rare in New York or Virginia[1314]. Upperparts slightly paler, visibly browner, the pale fringes to the scapulars forming subtle streaks. The sides and belly are entirely whitish, with pale brown markings concentrated on the upper flanks (meeting the blackish breast) and better-marked long dark crescents on the rear flanks. There is slight variation in both the coloration of the fore flanks and the intensity of the white patch on the rear flanks. When a swimming bird feeds by upending, seen from behind, no dark is usually visible between the legs, unlike in *bernicla*, *orientalis* and some *nigricans*. Beware, however, that young birds, with juvenile belly feathers until the first summer, may appear pale brown between or behind the legs. In direct comparison with *bernicla*, *hrota* is sometimes noted as being slightly larger.

B. b. orientalis (Black Brant). The most contrasting taxon, mostly blackish and white. Neck, head and chest as *bernicla* but white marks on the neck-sides much larger, usually meeting on the foreneck, and sometimes even almost on the hindneck, thereby forming a near-complete necklace. The majority of birds in which the collar is interrupted on the foreneck are ♀♀. Upperparts plain and very dark brown (darker and without the pale fringes of *hrota*, darker and less grey than *bernicla*). The fore flanks and belly only slightly contrast with the blackish breast, on average slightly more in ♀. Rear flanks form a large white patch, contrasting strongly with the very dark body. Long grey-brown crescents (feather bases) are visible on the white flanks, but from a distance they do not reach the upper flanks. Note that *orientalis* looks slightly more hefty, with a fairly thick neck[427], which is sometimes visible in direct comparison with the other taxa.

Western populations are sometimes recognised as subspecifically distinct from those breeding in North America and in far E Siberia. They are described as having the upperparts, fore flanks and belly slightly more contrasting with the blackish breast and neck. This contrast appears rather obvious in many birds wintering in Japan, for example, intermediate between *bernicla* and birds wintering on Pacific North American coasts. Compared to *bernicla*, the upperparts and fore flanks are browner (less ashy) and the white neck markings are extensive and meet on the foreneck, at least in the large majority.

B. b. nigricans (Grey-bellied Brant). The most variable subspecies, often described as intermediate between *hrota* and *orientalis*[173,175,204]. This variation is sometimes reported as being clinal, the plumage being darker on Prince Patrick I in the west of the range and virtually identical to *hrota* in the east, on Melville I[999]. Huge variability exists, particularly in the colour of the fore flanks and belly at the junction with the black breast. Some are difficult to distinguish from *hrota* in this respect while others are similar to *orientalis*[427,801]. Many are still more like *hrota* though, with most frequently a brown patch next to the chest, contrasting with both the latter and the white rear flanks. The belly may also appear barred dark. However, unlike the English name, the belly is usually more brown than grey, this colour often also extending beyond the legs when seen in profile[427]. The rear flanks are whitish as in *hrota* and *orientalis*, with variable dusky crescents. The mantle and scapulars are generally similar to those of *hrota*, brown with fine pale streaks or slightly darker and plainer brown. The white marks on the neck-sides are also variable, but many show marks larger than in *hrota*, often almost meeting on the foreneck. However, it has been reported that paler individuals have incomplete necklaces, and the darkest, complete necklaces[566].

Distinguishing the subspecies usually poses no problem in relation to *bernicla*, *hrota* and *orientalis*. In E Asia, only *orientalis* is present. In W Europe, *bernicla* and *hrota* are the two common taxa, albeit in different regions. Races *orientalis* and *nigricans* are occasional visitors, but their identification is complicated by the existence of hybrids between the taxa. In North America, *hrota* winters on the Atlantic coast and *orientalis* along the Pacific coast. Both are casual on the opposite coasts and in the interior, and are easily distinguished.

Identification problems therefore concern mainly Grey-bellied Brant.

Outside its normal range, *orientalis* is usually easily detected in flocks of *hrota* or *bernicla* but, obviously, the identification features often do not take into account the existence of birds in which breast/body contrast is stronger, e.g. Siberian breeders. These birds are often suspected of being hybrids between *orientalis* and *bernicla* (the commonest intra-specific hybrid in many countries in W Europe[154,427,1377]), but this is not necessarily the case. True hybrids are characterised by stronger contrast between chest and body, white patch on the rear flanks less prominent (more obscured by dusky crescents, even in fresh plumage, when washed pale buff-grey) and/or white collar often interrupted at the front (not always the case[816]). The distinction between such a hybrid and pale *orientalis* will often be tricky, if not impossible. Although, it is worth noting that true *orientalis* usually has a generally complete and extensive necklace, browner upperparts (vs. greyer in the hybrid) and a more striking white rear flanks patch.

Race *nigricans* is a casual visitor in the interior and E North America, and in NW Europe (reported in Ireland[425,427]), where it may be overlooked. Indeed, populations of *hrota* from the northernmost Canadian breeding grounds, in contact with *nigricans*, winter in the British Isles. Birds wintering in E North America nest further south and east. Two intermediates may be mistaken for this subspecies: that (in Europe) between *bernicla* and *hrota*[627] has the rear flanks largely white (more than *bernicla*) and the fore flanks and belly shows moderate contrast with the breast (less than *hrota*). Pending further information on such hybrids, the belly, fore flanks and upperparts, however, appear more grey than brown, upper flanks have stronger smoke-grey crescents and the white marks on the neck-sides are reduced compared to *nigricans*. The other hybrid recalling this taxon is between *orientalis* and *hrota*, and is probably not safely distinguishable from *nigricans* other than genetically, e.g. because of the phenotypic variability of the latter. Faced with a vagrant *nigricans*, concentrate on the other members of the family group. If the other birds also show *nigricans* features, it is unlikely that they are hybrids.

MEASUREMENTS and MASS See Taxonomy for the subspecies names used here. ♂♂ and adult slightly larger than ♀♀ and young, respectively. Data are given for the four subspecies, but no significant differences between them have been recorded in measurements[170,1014].

B. b. bernicla. ♂: wing chord 330–353 (adult, 340, *n*=18), bill 32–38 (34.9, *n*=17), tarsus 60–67 (63.7, *n*=17); ♀: wing chord 317–335 (adult, 324, *n*=13), bill 29–33 (31.7, *n*=14), tarsus 56–61 (58.1, *n*=13)[1122]. ♂: wing chord 323–355 (adult, 337, *n*=43) and 308–342 (juvenile, 323, *n*=24), bill 30–38 (34.4, *n*=42); ♀: wing chord 313–337 (adult, 324, *n*=22) and 291–326 (juvenile, 307, *n*=16), bill 30–36 (32.7, *n*=23)[267].

B. b. hrota. ♂: wing chord 338–348 (adult, 344, *n*=3) and 321–332 (juvenile, 326, *n*=7); ♀: wing chord 323–333 (adult, 329, *n*=7) and 308–325 (juvenile, 316, *n*=4)[267]. ♂: culmen 34.3 (± 0.3, *n*=33), mass in Jul 1,346 (± 19, *n*=33), mass in Jan 1,446 (± 24, *n*=54); ♀: culmen 31.5 (± 0.3, *n*=38), mass in Jul 1,199 (± 13, *n*=38), mass in Dec 1,236 (± 30, *n*=40)[31,753].

B. b. nigricans. ♂: culmen 34.6 (± 0.3, *n*=42), mass in Jul 1,362 (± 15, *n*=25), mass in Dec 1,630 (± 27, *n*=43); ♀: culmen 32.5 (± 0.2, *n*=56), mass in Jul 1,217 (± 15, *n*=25), mass in Dec 1,480 (± 21, *n*=57)[753].

B. b. orientalis. ♂: culmen 32.4 (± 0.3, *n*=106), mass in Jul 1,215 (± 14, *n*=82), mass in Jan 1,519 (± 14, *n*=69); ♀: culmen 31.0 (± 0.2, *n*=142), mass in Jul 1,071 (± 14, *n*=62), mass in Jan 1,396 (± 15, *n*=84)[753].

VOICE The loudest call, a rising *crank*, slightly nasal and gargling, produces the characteristic chorus of flying flocks, familiar to observers where the species winters. Many variations (*rrr-wek*, *kronk*, *kok*, etc.), usually less loud or chattering in foraging or resting flocks for example. No differences between subspecies known, but precise comparison seems to be lacking.

MOULT Complex basic strategy. Pre-formative moult begins between Sep and Nov and ends in Jan–May, during migration and on wintering sites, and is often suspended or slowed down during the coldest part of the winter. It begins with the head, neck and upper flanks, then chest, most scapulars, mantle and the rest of flanks, sometimes 1–3 tertials, some of the inner upperwing-coverts (sometimes most[56]) and a variable number of rectrices[1014]. The juvenile feathers of the belly are usually retained. Note that timing may slightly vary depending on breeding period, itself influenced by latitude and weather. Until early winter, there may be slight differences between populations in the advancement of pre-formative moult. For example, in North America, *orientalis* may be more advanced by mid-Nov than *hrota* and even more than *nigricans*. Definitive pre-basic moult begins in Jul–Aug

(sometimes earlier in second-year birds) with the simultaneous loss of remiges at breeding or moulting sites (immature, non-breeders), continues with the body feathers and rectrices until Oct–Dec, and arrival on the wintering grounds.

HYBRIDISATION Natural hybridisation involving this species occurs very casually, and has been reported with Barnacle Goose and Red-breasted Goose (see the latter two species), and on even fewer occasions with Snow Goose *Chen caerulescens*[188] and/or Ross's Goose *C. rossii*[117], Canada Goose *B. canadensis* or Cackling Goose *B. hutchinsii*. Hybrids have also been reported with Greater White-fronted Goose *Anser albifrons*[817,1190] and Bar-headed Goose *A. indicus*[639,1317], but these may be escapees or linked to feral populations. In captivity, hybridisation has been mentioned in the literature with Greylag Goose *A. anser*, Lesser White-fronted Goose *A. erythropus*[817], Emperor Goose *Chen canagica*[97,1190], Mute Swan *Cygnus olor*[639] and possibly Swan Goose *Anser cygnoid*[639].

HABITAT and LIFE-CYCLE Strictly migratory, and ecologically rather specialised. Spring migration occurs between mid-Feb and mid-May, the birds concentrating near the nesting areas until snowmelt. Egg laying peaks between late May and 20 Jun[170], with more than three weeks separating different populations depending on latitude (earliest in Alaska, later in Nunavut and Arctic Siberia[753]). Breeds in loose colonies or isolated pairs (especially depending on habitat quality[145,753]), using coastal lowlands and marshes in Arctic tundra. Nests on small grassy islands or near gull colonies and raptor nests for protection from predators[145]. Breeding adults start moulting their wings on average ten days after the chicks hatch[170,1154]. Other birds, as well as groups of southern nesting birds[386], form large gatherings usually on open water. Autumn migration occurs between early Sep and early Dec, the first birds arriving near the wintering grounds by mid-Sep. Gregarious in the non-breeding period, but uses large areas, with scattered flocks of tens to a few hundred individuals, rather than very large flocks. In winter, exclusively coastal, using large sandy or muddy bays, estuaries, tidal mudflats, brackish or saltmarshes and lagoons. Primarily herbivorous, feeding especially on eelgrass beds *Zostera* spp. The species has also recently developed a tendency to use coastal cultivation (meadows, grasslands, crops). Generally rare inland, where migrating flocks usually occur only at high altitudes, although adverse weather can force birds to land at otherwise unoccupied sites.

RANGE and POPULATION See Taxonomy for subspecies names used here. Polytypic species within circum-Arctic breeding range, wintering in temperate coastal regions of the Holarctic.

B. b. bernicla. Breeds along W & C Arctic coasts of Siberia, east to the Lena River Delta, where it meets the range of *orientalis*, with which it is even said to form mixed colonies[170]. Highest densities occur in the east, on the Taimyr Peninsula. Migrates via the White Sea and Baltic Sea to the W European winter quarters. Rare in C Europe and the Mediterranean, and reported as accidental on the North American Atlantic coast[205]. Movements occur during winter following depletion of local food resources. Estimated population 200,000–280,000 birds, with a slight decline noted over the last two decades[400,1348].

B. b. hrota. Three major populations, largely allopatric especially in winter. The first breeds on Svalbard (few on Franz Josef Land), winters in Denmark and to a lesser extent elsewhere on North Sea coasts. This population numbers 7,600 birds and is increasing[400,1348]. The second breeds in N Nunavut and Greenland, migrates via Iceland and winters mainly in Ireland (with a few hundred birds in NW France) and is estimated at 40,000 birds, with a slight increase recently[400,1348]. The third breeds in C & E Nunavut, migrates via Hudson Bay, NE USA and Quebec, and winters on coasts of USA, mainly between Massachusetts and North Carolina. It has fluctuated between 100,000 and 180,000 birds over the last 30 years (149,200 in 2012 and 111,800 in 2013)[1294]. Rare inland and south to Gulf of Mexico.

B. b. nigricans. Breeds on W Queen Elizabeth Is (Melville, Prince Patrick and Borden Is) and migrates offshore, firstly heading west, bypassing Alaska, to its wintering area in Puget Sound, British Columbia (Canada) and Washington (USA), with some further south on the Pacific coast (to Baja California[1055]), regularly on the Atlantic coast of the USA and recently reported in Iceland (ringed)[204] and Ireland[427]. Population fluctuates between 7,000 and 15,000 individuals[170], up to 16,200 birds in 2009[1291], but only 8,500 individuals in 2011[1292].

B. b. orientalis. Two or three distinct populations. The first breeds in North America from the Beaufort Sea west to the Yukon-Kuskokwim Delta, SW Alaska, and on the Arctic coast of Chukotka. This population winters on the North American Pacific coast, mainly

between Washington and Baja California, and in Gulf of California, Mexico. Scarce in winter further north, in S Alaska and the coast of Queen Charlotte I. Population recently estimated at 147,000–148,000 individuals[1292,1348], and is increasing. The second breeds on the Arctic coast of Siberia between the deltas of the Rivers Olenyok and Lena (where in contact with *bernicla*) and Chukotka, in contact with the previous population. These birds winter in China (Bohai Sea and Yellow Sea) and North Korea (2,500–5,700 birds[1251]) on the one hand, and Japan and South Korea on the other (2,500–3,000 individuals[1251,1348]), perhaps forming two distinct populations. This subspecies occasionally wanders to the interior and the Atlantic coast of North America, and Europe, where they arrive either from the west, among Pale-bellied Brent Geese, or from the east, in company of Dark-bellied Brent Geese. Also note that many of these vagrants are known to return to the same wintering grounds year after year.

CAPTIVITY Fairly easy to maintain in small flocks, but difficult to breed. Thus, only rarely encountered in collections and generally traded for significantly higher prices than Red-breasted Goose, and much higher than for Barnacle, Canada and Cackling Geese. Therefore, it is generally unlikely that out-of-range individuals have escaped from captivity.

REFERENCES Ankney (1984)[31]; Baker (1993)[56]; Bird Hybrids Database (2014)[97]; Bird Hybrids Flickr Forum (2009)[117]; BirdLife International (2012)[142]; BirdLife International (2014)[145]; Bloomfield & McCallum (2001)[154]; Boyd *in* Kear (2005)[170]; Boyd & Maltby (1979)[173]; Boyd & Maltby (1980)[174]; Boyd *et al.* (1988)[175]; Boyd *et al.* (2013)[176]; Brazil (2009)[182]; Brimley (1927)[188]; Buckley & Mitra (2002)[204]; Buckley *et al.* (2004)[205]; Cramp & Simmons (1977)[267]; Delacour & Zimmer (1952)[299]; Flint *et al.* (1984)[386]; Fox *et al.* (2010)[400]; Garner (1998)[419]; Garner & Millington (2001)[425]; Garner *et al.* (2008)[427]; Gavin (1947)[430]; Gill & Donsker (2014)[437]; González *et al.* (2009)[454]; Handley (1950)[500]; Harrison *et al.* (2010)[527]; Hoffman & Elliott (1974)[566]; Jansen & Ebels (2004)[627]; Johnsgard (1960)[639]; Lambeck (1981)[724]; Lewis *et al.* (2013)[753]; Livezey (1996)[772]; Madge & Burn (1987)[794]; Madsen *et al.* (1989)[796]; Manfred & Ebels (2006)[799]; Manning *et al.* (1956)[801]; Martin (2002)[807]; McCallum (2014)[816]; McCarthy (2006)[817]; Millington (1997)[847]; Novak *et al.* (1989)[917]; Ogilvie & Young (1998)[928]; Poole *et al.* (2014)[999]; Pyle (2008)[1014]; Reed *et al.* (1989)[1052]; Reed *et al.* (1998)[1055]; Roselaar & Sluys (1999)[1096]; Salminen (1983)[1122]; Schamber *et* *al.* (2007)[1141]; Scott & Rose (1996)[1154]; Scott (1957)[1159]; Sedinger *et al.* (1993)[1170]; Sedinger *et al.* (1995)[1171]; Sedinger *et al.* (1998)[1172]; Shields (1990)[1180]; Shields & Cotter (1998)[1181]; Sibley (1938)[1190]; Sibley (2011)[1201]; Summers *et al.* (1994)[1243]; Syroechkovski (2006)[1251]; Syroechkovski & Litvin (1998)[1252]; Talbot (2013)[1256]; USFWS (2009)[1291]; USFWS (2011)[1292]; USFWS (2013)[1294]; Vangilder & Smith (1985)[1314]; Vesterinen (1998)[1317]; Wetlands International (2014)[1348]; Wilson & Guthrie (1999)[1363]; Wynn (2002)[1377].

111. *B. b. bernicla*, adult (definitive basic); the most uniform subspecies, overall greyish rather than brown, although contrast between breast and flanks is easily visible. Netherlands, Feb (Sébastien Reeber).

112. *B. b. hrota*, first-winter (formative); wing-coverts still juvenile with clear white fringes, and note large patch with small dusky spots on belly, another juvenile feature. Netherlands, Feb (Sébastien Reeber).

113. *B. b. hrota*, adult (definitive basic); clear contrast between flanks and breast in this subspecies, with reduced white neck-side patches and browner upperparts with obvious paler fringes. New Jersey, USA, Nov (Sébastien Reeber).

114. *B. b. hrota*, juvenile (first basic); still in almost full juvenile plumage (note broadly fringed upperparts feathers and reduced or absent neck-side patches). New Jersey, USA, Nov (Sébastien Reeber).

115. *B. b. hrota*, adult (definitive basic); note white underparts and much-reduced white neck-side patches in this subspecies. New Jersey, USA, Nov (Sébastien Reeber).

116. *B. b. bernicla*, adult (definitive basic); in flight from below, appears very dark. France, Mar (Matthieu Vaslin).

117. *B. b. bernicla*, juvenile (first basic); only part of head and upper neck have been moulted, the rest of the plumage being juvenile. France, Oct (Sébastien Reeber).

118. *B. b. bernicla*, adult (definitive basic); following pre-formative moult, ageing remains easy given obvious white fringes to median and greater coverts on young bird (right), which are absent in adult (left). France, Jan (Matthieu Vaslin).

119. *B. b. bernicla*, adult (definitive basic); according to the light, the flanks coloration can vary strongly; note incomplete white collar. Netherlands, Feb (Sébastien Reeber).

120. *B. b. bernicla*, adult (definitive basic). France, Oct (Matthieu Vaslin).

121. *B. b. bernicla*, adult (definitive basic); when feeding, extent of dark belly beyond and between legs is a good feature, vs. *hrota*, in which dusky colour is less extensive. France, Mar (Matthieu Vaslin).

122. *B. b. orientalis*, adult (definitive basic); a paler bird like some wintering in E Asia – contrast between belly and breast is almost like *bernicla*, but the flanks, upperparts and neck-ring match typical *orientalis*. Japan, Mar (Stuart Price).

123. *B. b. orientalis*, family group; two adult (right) with a juvenile (left), which has already moulted part of its head, upper neck and rear flanks. California, USA, Nov (Sébastien Reeber).

124. *B. b. orientalis*, adult (definitive basic); white upper flanks often barely visible in flight. Japan, Mar (Stuart Price).

125. *B. b. orientalis*, first-winter (formative); as in other subspecies, juvenile wing-coverts show typical white bars, and also note large ventral patch (still juvenile), slightly paler and browner. Japan, Mar (Stuart Price).

126. *B. b. orientalis*, adult (definitive basic); this subspecies is the darkest and most contrasting, with striking white flanks patch, surrounded by fore flanks, belly and upperparts barely contrasting with blackish breast, brown hue to upperparts and complete white neck-ring. Japan, Feb (Stuart Price).

127. *B. b. nigricans*, adult (definitive basic); palest birds are not safely distinguishable from *hrota*, but note extensive (near-complete) white collar in this bird. Captivity (injured wild bird), Dec (Steve Mlodinow).

128. *B. b. nigricans*, adult (definitive basic); note variability in underparts coloration and extent of white neck-side patches, while belly and fore flanks are more brown than grey. Captivity (injured wild birds), Dec (Steve Mlodinow).

RED-BREASTED GOOSE
Branta ruficollis

Plate 15

TAXONOMY *Anas ruficollis* Pallas, 1769, *Spicilegia Zool.*, fasc. 6, p. 21, pl. 4. Within the genus *Branta*, Red-breasted Goose is phylogenetically closer to Barnacle Goose *B. leucopsis*[772] (which see). Monotypic.

IDENTIFICATION Distinctive appearance in all plumages, preventing any confusion with other species or potential hybrids. However, where it is rare, this species mixes readily with other *Branta*, and can be surprisingly difficult to detect in such flocks, especially in flight or while grazing.

PLUMAGES Sexes identical, but ♂ slightly larger and heavier (see Measurements and Mass) and often easily distinguished within pairs by more demonstrative behaviour. Complex basic moult strategy (one plumage per definitive annual cycle, two during the first cycle). Ageing relatively easy until the beginning of the first summer.

Adult

Definitive basic plumage (year-round). Somewhat variegated dark plumage, black, white and dark reddish. Head and neck coloration complex: forehead, crown, nape and hindneck black, with white oval spot at base of bill, large red patch surrounded by white on cheeks, the white extending in a line separating the black hindneck from the reddish foreneck and breast. Dark brown iris. Bill very small and short. All-black upperparts, with the exception of clearly defined white tips to the median and greater coverts, forming two very distinctive lines. Back, rump and tail black, with uppertail forming a broad white crescent. Flanks black with broad white border at top and large white and black crescents at rear. Belly mostly black, white on lower belly and undertail-coverts. Upperwing entirely blackish with two white lines formed by tips of greater and median coverts, broader on the outer feathers. Upperwing-coverts typically large and square-tipped. Underwing black with variable whitish spots on the tips of greater coverts. Legs black.

Juvenile

First basic plumage (until Oct–Dec). Resembles adult, but black and reddish parts duller and lack gloss. The rusty cheek patch is smaller (larger white borders) and duller. Rear flanks have scattered dusky blotches instead of evenly spaced crescents in adult. White mark at base

of the bill and white lines on head and neck less clearly defined, and/or mottled brown. The upperwing pattern is also different, and often constitutes the clearest ageing feature. The tips of the secondary coverts are pale brown to whitish, somewhat ill-defined, forming pale and rather diffuse lines, visible both in flight and on ground (two broader white bars in adult). Rectrices white at tips[56].

First-winter/first-summer

Formative plumage (Nov–Dec/Jul–Aug). During pre-formative moult, the contrast between dull dark grey upperparts (including primary coverts and median coverts) and blacker remiges and hindneck is usually obvious. Much closer to adult once moult completed, and may be difficult to age. Usually retains juvenile wing and tail feathers, but can moult many secondary coverts (except median coverts)[56], and thus closer to adult in appearance. The white bar formed by the tips of the median coverts usually still thin and ill-defined. Other wing features, like juvenile coverts being narrower, more worn and round-tipped, are only easily checked in the hand.

Second-winter/second-summer

Second basic plumage (Jul–Aug/Jul–Aug). Some birds retain at least some juvenile median coverts, which appear bleached, very worn and lack white fringes, contrast obviously with new feathers. However, this requires a close inspection (in the hand or good photographs).

GEOGRAPHIC VARIATION None.

MEASUREMENTS and MASS Few data available. ♂ and adult larger and heavier than ♀ and young, respectively. ♂: wing chord 355–379 (367, *n*=8), culmen 23–27 (24.9, *n*=9), tarsus 58–65 (61.3, *n*=8); ♀: wing chord 332–352 (343, *n*=7), culmen 22–26 (24.2, *n*=8), tarsus 54–61 (57.1, *n*=8)[267]. ♂: mass 1,200–1,625 (1,375, *n*=5); ♀: mass 1,058–1,130 (1,094, *n*=2)[79].

VOICE Typical disyllabic call, high-pitched and slightly hoarse, *kik-kwik* quite slow and with a short break between the two notes. ♂ and ♀ have similar calls[612].

MOULT Pre-formative moult occurs between Oct and

Mar, starting with the head, neck, mantle and chest[56]. It includes many of body feathers, sometimes one or two tertials, and sometimes a significant number of secondary upperwing-coverts and rectrices[56]. Definitive pre-basic moult begins between mid-Jul and late Aug with the simultaneous loss of the remiges, on or near the nesting grounds, and continues with the body feathers and rectrices until Oct–Nov. Non-breeders commence their moult two weeks earlier[1300].

HYBRIDISATION Very rare in the wild, but reported especially with Greater White-fronted Goose *Anser albifrons*, Barnacle Goose, Brent Goose (Brant) *B. bernicla* (see below). Even more occasionally, hybridisation has been mentioned with Lesser White-fronted Goose *Anser erythropus*[465] and Ross's Goose *Chen rossii*[465,1158]. In captivity, other crosses include with Canada Goose *B. canadensis*[639,817,1190] and Cackling Goose *B. hutchinsii*[465,1142].

Red-breasted Goose × Greater White-fronted Goose: exceptional in the wild[639], but recent reports in Europe. Hybrids from this cross are stocky, with a thick neck, round head and small bill. Very dark overall, with almost black sides, the foreneck, chest and upperparts are dark grey-brown (thin pale fringes on latter), hindneck, crown and head blackish with a large round pale reddish patch on the cheeks, and a poorly defined white line around the base of the bill. Legs dull pink.

Red-breasted Goose × Barnacle Goose: a very dark hybrid, appearing almost blackish or sooty from afar, with flanks and underparts slightly browner than the black chest and neck. Black crown and nape, but broad whitish patch on head-sides, similar to Barnacle Goose, with reddish tinge towards rear cheeks. Small and very short bill with slightly duskier loral stripe. At least one bird photographed in Norfolk, England[133] had a hint of a pale half-collar on the foreneck.

Red-breasted Goose × Brent Goose: like the previous hybrid, very dark overall, with brown crescents on upper flanks and faint pale fringes to upperparts. Rear body and uppertail-coverts white with a very short black tail, inherited from Brent Goose. Head and neck black with a large comma-shaped white patch on the neck-sides, much more contrasting than the collar of Brent Goose[135].

HABITAT and LIFE-CYCLE Strictly migratory, spring migration between Mar and early Jun, with several rather long stop-overs. Breeds in the Arctic tundra south to the transition zone with the taiga, usually near steep-sided rivers, rocky outcrops or cliffs. Often in loose colonies of usually 5–15 pairs[145], with a reported maximum of 37 pairs[705]. Eggs are laid in the month of Jun, depending on snowmelt. Nest concealed under tall grass, dwarf birches and willows, often near a raptor nest, as protection against predators[1011]. Like with other Arctic geese, breeding success is probably also indirectly linked to lemming density. Indeed, when the latter's numbers are reduced, predators switch to the eggs and chicks of wildfowl and waders. Pre-basic moult begins with the loss of the remiges shortly after the chicks hatch. Autumn migration occurs from Sep, birds arriving on their wintering grounds in Oct–Nov[145]. In winter and on migration, very gregarious and often seen with Greater White-fronted or Lesser White-fronted Geese[612]. Inhabits open landscapes of grassy steppes, meadows, pastures and fields for foraging, and coastal lakes and lagoons to drink and rest.

RANGE and POPULATION Restricted range. Breeds mainly on the Taimyr (70% of the world population), and Gydan and Yamal Peninsulas, NC Siberia[145,613]. Migrates via a relatively narrow route, along the lower Ob Valley, heading to N Kazakhstan and the N Caspian Sea. Four traditional staging areas are known in Russia and Kazakhstan[145]. Prior to the 1950s, the main wintering area was on the W coast of the Caspian Sea, but now 80–90% of the population winters on the coasts of Ukraine, Romania and Bulgaria[271,1110]. According to weather conditions, small numbers reach Greece, Turkey and Azerbaijan. Some wintering areas are perhaps still unknown along the migration routes, especially in mild winters[145]. Regular visitor to Hungary, W & C Turkey, SE Iraq and, very small numbers, in Netherlands and Belgium. Occasional or accidental in most other European countries, although some birds are considered escapes from captivity.

Estimates of the global population fluctuate, from 25,900 (1976–90) to 88,425 (1996)[1,145], but it is unclear if these variations are real or due to methodological bias (especially during mild winters, when part of the population may winter further north). Winter population estimated at 44,000 birds in 1996–2006[400,1348], and more recently, 40,800 in spring 2008 and 44,300 in spring 2009[271].

The species is considered Endangered by Birdlife International[145]. Breeding areas suffer disturbance related to oil and gas exploitation, and are at major risk due to global warming. On migration stop-over and wintering sites, hunting pressure (especially hunting tourism) is heavy in Ukraine, Russia and Kazakhstan, and undertaken illegally in Romania and Bulgaria[1100]. Hunting also produces indirect disturbance when other species of geese are targeted, with which Red-breasted Geese mix. In winter, increasing tourism pressure, lack of effective non-hunting areas (especially important in geese), changes in agricultural uses and construction of windfarms (e.g. in Romania[986]) are all considered as threats[145,612]. An international action plan to conserve the species has been produced[271] in an attempt to assess and counteract these threats.

CAPTIVITY Frequently encountered in captivity, where it is appreciated for its ornamental qualities and easy maintenance. However, breeding is quite difficult (apparently easier if kept in small groups). Therefore, the species is usually one of the most expensive geese, with prices often three or four times higher than for Barnacle Goose. Birds outside their normal range should therefore not necessarily be considered escapees, especially when sightings are made during migration periods and alongside *Anser* or other *Branta* geese.

REFERENCES Aarvak *et al.* (1996)[1]; Baker (1993)[56]; Bauer & Glutz von Blotzheim (1968)[79]; Bird Hybrids Flickr Forum (2011)[133]; Bird Hybrids Flickr Forum (2012)[135]; BirdLife International (2014)[145]; Cramp & Simmons (1977)[267]; Cranswick *et al.* (2010)[271]; Delany & Scott (2006)[305]; Dereliev (2000)[312]; Fox *et al.* (2010)[400]; Gray (1958)[465]; Hunter *in* Kear (2005)[612]; Hunter & Black (1996)[613]; Hunter *et al.* (1999)[614]; Johnsgard (1960)[639]; Kostin & Mooij (1995)[705]; Livezey (1996)[772]; Madge & Burn (1988)[794]; McCarthy (2006)[817]; Ogilvie & Young (1998)[928]; Petkov *et al.* (2012)[986]; Prop & Quinn (2003)[1011]; Quinn *et al.* (1996)[1023]; Rozenfeld (2011)[1100]; Rusev *et al.* (2008)[1110]; Scherer & Hilsberg (1982)[1142]; Scott (1947)[1158]; Sibley (1938)[1190]; Uspenski (1965)[1300]; Wetlands International (2014)[1348].

129. Adult (definitive basic); note plain black upperparts except the two white wingbars at this age. Netherlands, Mar (Seraf van der Putten).

130. First-winter (formative) on left and adult (definitive basic) on right; young birds have several wingbars, which are less well defined, and the folded wing is slightly greyer than scapulars. Netherlands, Apr (Rick Van der Weijde).

131. First-winter (formative). Netherlands, Nov (Otto Plantema).

BARNACLE GOOSE
Branta leucopsis

Plate 15

TAXONOMY *Anas leucopsis* Bechstein, 1803, *Orn. Taschenbuch Deutschland*, 2, p. 424. The tribe *Anserini* includes three genera, *Anser, Chen* and *Branta*, with the second sometimes included in the former. In the Holarctic, the genus *Branta* comprises five species: Canada Goose *B. canadensis*, Cackling Goose *B. hutchinsii*, Brent Goose *B. bernicla*, Red-breasted Goose *B. ruficollis* and Barnacle Goose. The first three show much geographical variation over their respective ranges, which is not the case for the latter two, which are monotypic. A sixth species, Hawaiian Goose (Nene) *B. sandvicensis*, is restricted to Hawaii and derived from an ancestor close to Cackling Goose[953]. Within *Branta*, Barnacle Goose is phylogenetically closer to Red-breasted Goose[772].

IDENTIFICATION Should not be mistaken for any other goose, although superficially resembles other *Branta*. Easily distinguished from Brent Goose by the white cheeks, from Canada Goose by its black chest, and from both species by its upperparts streaked pale blue-grey and black, whitish belly and overall paler and greyer coloration.

PLUMAGES Sexes identical, but ♂ slightly larger and 10% heavier (see Measurements and Mass) and paired ♂ often differs by being more demonstrative or aggressive toward intruders. Complex basic moult strategy (one plumage per definitive cycle, two during the first cycle). Ageing relatively easy until the beginning of the first winter and possible until the end of the following summer, under good viewing conditions or in the hand.

Adult

Definitive basic plumage (year-round). Rather stocky with long wings and very small bill. Head, neck and breast black, with large whitish, pale yellowish or pale buff area covering forehead, forecrown, supercilium, cheeks and throat, with a variable black stripe across the lores to the eye. Iris dark brown. Bill dark slate-grey, darker towards the tip. Feathers of mantle black with white fringes. Scapulars broad, square-tipped, pale blue-grey with large diffuse black subterminal bands and clear-cut white fringes. Secondary coverts and tertials the same colour, the whole forming a regular succession of pale blue-grey, black and white stripes

on upperparts. Remiges (including tertials) pale grey with diffuse blackish areas on tips and shafts. Pale grey lesser coverts. Underwing has dark grey remiges, greater coverts hardly paler grey (lighter tips) and rest pale grey. Flanks pale grey with bases to feathers forming large dark stripes. Pale grey to whitish belly more or less spotted dusky. Lower belly, under- and uppertail white. Back, rump and uppertail blackish. Legs dark grey.

Juvenile

First basic plumage (until Oct–Dec). Similar to adult but duller. White cheeks as well as black parts of the head, neck and breast dull blackish mottled grey. These dusky smudges are particularly visible on the forehead and around the eye, often making the latter seem connected to the dark crown. The mantle, scapulars and secondary upperwing-coverts are narrower, more round-tipped, slightly darker grey basally, with barely visible dark subterminal bands and blurred pale grey-brown fringes. The pale flanks are irregularly mottled grey. Finally, note that juvenile is often visibly smaller than adult in direct comparison.

First-winter/first-summer

Formative plumage (Nov–Dec/Jul–Aug). Like adult from early winter. Following pre-formative moult, at least when it is extensive, ageing requires close examination. First look for the presence of juvenile feathers among the scapulars and upper flanks and, in the hand, moult contrast between the juvenile outer secondary coverts (faded, dull, rounded and worn at tip) and formative inner ones (with black subterminal bands and sharp white fringes, often square-tipped). These formative coverts are also typically narrower basally than at the tip, which is not the case in adult feathers or in juvenile ones[56]. Birds which have undertaken a limited pre-formative moult are even easier to age, by the scattered juvenile feathers, especially on the mantle and scapulars.

Second-winter/second-summer

Second basic plumage (Jul–Aug/Jul–Aug). Identical to definitive basic plumage, with the exception of a few outer secondary upperwing-coverts (faded or bleached, very worn), preferably checked in the hand.

GEOGRAPHIC VARIATION. None, despite the existence of several almost or wholly allopatric populations[938], with clear differences between populations in breeding and moult timings[939], and habitat selection.

MEASUREMENTS and MASS ♂ and adult larger and heavier than ♀ and young, respectively. ♂: wing chord 388–429 (adult, 410, n=23) and 374–399 (juvenile, 389, n=9), culmen 28–33 (29.6, n=32); ♀: wing chord 376–410 (adult, 392, n=19) and 362–393 (juvenile, 372, n=9), culmen 27–32 (28.6, n=28)[267]. ♂: wing chord 370–444 (412, n=300), tarsus 60–81 (72.1, n=560); ♀: wing chord 353–414 (389, n=281), tarsus 58–81 (68.2, n=541)[938,941]. Mass: 1,700–2,400, ♂ being on average 180 g heavier than ♀[939].

VOICE Loquacious, and even noisier in flocks, especially in flight. The call is a repeated nasal *gaa*, recalling a small dog barking when heard from afar. Within a flock, it is easy to notice that this sound is uttered at very different pitches, depending on the individual. The pitch is linked to how wide the bill is opened when calling, which is constant in any individual bird[939].

MOULT Complex basic strategy. Pre-formative moult occurs between Oct and Mar, during migration and at wintering sites, often suspended or slowed down in midwinter. It includes many to almost all of the head, neck and body, including a variable number of scapulars, mantle and flank feathers, sometimes 1–2 tertials, some inner upperwing-coverts and a variable number of rectrices[56]. Definitive pre-basic moult begins between mid-Jul and mid-Aug with the simultaneous loss of remiges on or near the nesting grounds, continues with the body feathers and rectrices until Oct–Nov, and arrival on the wintering grounds, at least in Arctic breeders. Populations established in N Europe breed and moult one month earlier on average[939].

HYBRIDISATION Relatively frequently reported in the wild, but often involving feral populations in N Europe. These reports concern Greylag Goose *Anser anser*, Greater White-fronted Goose *A. albifrons*, Bar-headed Goose *A. indicus*, Ross's Goose *Chen rossii*, Canada Goose, Cackling Goose, Red-breasted Goose (see these species), Brent Goose, Snow Goose *Chen caerulescens*[300,465,817] (see below), and more rarely, Lesser White-fronted Goose *Anser erythropus*[582,584,817],

Bean Goose *A. fabalis*[275], Pink-footed Goose *A. brachyrhynchus*[97,668] and Mallard *Anas platyrhynchos*[817]. In captivity, has also hybridised with Swan Goose *Anser cygnoid*[584], Emperor Goose *Chen canagica*[817], Magellanic Goose *Chloephaga picta*, Ashy-headed Goose *C. poliocephala* and Egyptian Goose *Alopochen aegyptiacus*[97].

Barnacle Goose × Brent Goose: a very rare hybrid in the wild, and identification can be difficult due to its resemblance to some crosses between Barnacle and Red-breasted Geese. A hybrid observed in W France was dark overall with a large white face patch and a hint of white collar on the upper neck. Unlike the hybrid involving Red-breasted Goose, it had a broad black loral stripe, a slightly longer bill, clear contrast between the black chest and flanks (the latter pale grey-brown streaked dusky) and clear pale streaks on the upperparts. The lower scapulars and wing-coverts visible on the folded wing were reminiscent of Barnacle Goose. On the other hand, a typical feature of Brent Goose was the very short black tail.

Barnacle Goose × Snow Goose: much like hybrid Canada Goose × Snow Goose (see the latter). The body is grey-brown with a white head and neck variably flecked black (sometimes almost all white, others like Barnacle Goose, with black of head and neck mixed with white spots). Bill has tomium and nail blackish, and variable dark patches in the pink or pale grey sides. The shape and length of the bill, and size of the bird are essential features to distinguish hybrid Canada Goose × Snow Goose from Barnacle Goose × Ross's Goose. The influence of Barnacle Goose is usually visible in the upperparts (grey-blue bases), by chest blackish or dusky brown reaching to belly, and head and neck often obviously inherited from Barnacle Goose, including black loral stripe. The influence of Snow Goose is visible in the presence of white where *Anser* and *Branta* geese lack it, especially the head, neck and belly. Grey legs, with more or less strong pink hue.

HABITAT and LIFE-CYCLE Several natural populations in the Arctic, but also naturally established populations and others, feral and introduced in N Europe, with habitats, migratory behaviour and breeding season varying as result. Arctic populations nest and winter in relatively restricted areas, and migrate via narrow routes. Migrants arrive in May–Jun and lay eggs soon after arrival, if snowmelt permits. Nests on cliffs, rocky ridges and boulders along coasts up to mountainous areas (Greenland, Russia) as well as on islands in coastal marshes or at sea (Svalbard, Sweden) in small colonies (5–50 pairs, sometimes up to 150)[1213]. Pre-basic moult of adult starts on the nesting sites, shortly after hatching. Families leave the breeding grounds when the young fledge and adults are able to fly again, in Aug–Sep. After several halts at traditional stop-over sites, arrives on wintering grounds from late Sep, mostly between Oct and Dec. In winter, inhabits tidal mudflats, saltmarshes, meadows, marshes and improved pastures, the latter having become predominant lately, at least locally where agriculture has replaced natural habitats[961]. Roosts at night on open water, or on islets of sand or gravel, preferably within 5–7 km of feeding areas[1318]. Birds leave the wintering grounds between mid-Mar and mid-May, with some traditional long stop-overs en route, up to 20–30 days[939].

RANGE and POPULATION Three Arctic breeding populations and others at temperate latitudes. The first nests on coast of E Greenland and winters mainly in Scotland and Ireland. Estimates in the early 2000s reached 70,500 birds[400], including a small number of breeders in Iceland. The second breeds on Svalbard, migrates along coasts of N & W Norway and winters mainly in Scotland. It has been estimated at c.30,000 individuals[400]. The last population nests on the Arctic coast of W Siberia, north to Novaya Zemlya, migrates across the Baltic to its wintering range from Denmark to Belgium. It was estimated at 770,000 individuals in the early 2000s[400], including populations established in recent decades along the migration route and on the wintering grounds: 1,300 pairs in Denmark, >300 in Norway, 1,800 in Sweden, >2,000 in Finland, 8,300 in the Netherlands, 30 in Germany and 200 in Belgium[667,1329]. Other feral and sedentary populations have been established especially in the British Isles (120 pairs[667]) and at scattered places elsewhere in NW Europe. The impact of captive, escaped and introduced

populations in N Europe on the recent increase in the global population is not well known. However, it is possible that the temperate populations would never have established without introductions[667]. Currently, populations are still increasing rapidly, compensation for farmers accepting the presence of geese on their pastures being one essential action benefiting the species[258].

Barnacle Goose is a rare or occasional visitor in S & C Europe, and a rare but annual vagrant to North America[1179], mainly on the Atlantic coast, but also reported west to Alberta, Canada, and south to Texas. Many birds there are suspected to be escapees or to emanate from introduced populations, as even escapees are known to be prone to long-distance movements[93].

CAPTIVITY Generally available for sale at cheap prices, this goose is very frequently kept in captivity, including in mixed collections, and is easy to breed. Its ubiquity in captivity makes the species very likely to escape and captive individuals survive very well in the wild at temperate latitudes, and breed easily, even in urban habitats.

REFERENCES Baker (1993)[56]; Bengtsson (2007)[93]; Bird Hybrids Database (2014)[97]; Bird Hybrids Flickr Forum (2008)[105]; Cope et al. (2003)[258]; Cramp & Simmons (1977)[267]; Csörgey (1926)[275]; Delany (1993)[300]; Delany & Scott (2006)[305]; Fox et al. (2010)[400]; Gray (1958)[465]; Hopkinson (1926)[582]; Hopkinson (1933)[584]; Kampe-Persson (2010)[667]; Kampe-Persson & Lerner (2007)[668]; Larrson (1993)[729]; Larrson & Forslund (1991)[730]; Livezey (1996)[772]; McCarthy (2006)[817]; McLandress & McLandress (1979)[830]; Owen (1980)[938]; Owen & Black in Kear (2005)[939]; Owen & Ogilvie (1979)[941]; Paxinos et al. (2002)[953]; Peberdy (1991)[961]; Sherony (2008)[1179]; Snow & Perrins (1998)[1213]; Trauger et al. (1971)[1282]; Vickery & Gill (1999)[1318]; Voslamber (2010)[1329]; Wetlands International (2014)[1348].

132. Adult (definitive basic). Netherlands, Feb (Sébastien Reeber).

133. Adult (definitive basic); note individual variation in width of black loral stripe and tinge to face (from whitish to pale yellow). Netherlands, Feb (Sébastien Reeber).

134. First-winter (first basic/formative) birds easy to age until pre-formative moult is completed; this bird has only replaced some scapulars, head and flank feathers. Netherlands, Feb (Sébastien Reeber).

135. Family groups; these adults have shed their remiges and juveniles are unable to fly yet; despite being duller, juvenile resemble adult as soon as they acquire their first plumage. Iceland, Jul (Julien Gonin).

136. Adult (definitive basic); in flight, easy to identify by pale blue-grey areas on upperwing. Netherlands, Feb (Sébastien Reeber).

CACKLING GOOSE
Branta hutchinsii

Plates 16, 17

TAXONOMY *Anser Hutchinsii* Richardson, 1832. *Richardson's Fauna Bor. Amer.*, vol. 2, p. 470. This species contains the four smallest types of small 'white-cheeked' geese, all once considered conspecific with Canada Goose *B. canadensis* (see that species). Several genetic studies have revealed the presence of two paraphyletic groups within this superspecies, which diverged *c.*1 million years ago. One of the two clades comprises the small taxa breeding in the Arctic tundra and has recently been split from Canada Goose. Thus Cackling Goose involves four subspecies: *hutchinsii* Richardson, 1832, *leucopareia* Brandt, 1836, *minima* Ridgeway, 1885, and *taverneri* Delacour, 1951. A fifth subspecies has been described, *asiatica* Aldrich, 1946, which formerly bred on the Kuril and Commander Is off the Russian coast in the Bering Sea, and wintered in Japan. It has disappeared since, but is now considered a population of *leucopareia*[887,1111,1162]. Another distinct population, numbering *c.*350 individuals was described in 1979 on Kiliktagik, Semidi Is, Alaska. These birds show intermediate morphometric characters between *taverneri* and *leucopareia* and have been said to potentially deserve subspecific status[537].

IDENTIFICATION Should not be mistaken for any other species than Canada Goose, which is on average larger and paler. However, the largest subspecies of Cackling Goose, *taverneri*, is also rather pale and can be difficult to distinguish from subspecies *parvipes* of Canada Goose. The distinguishing features are detailed under the latter species. See also Geographic Variation below. Separation from Barnacle Goose is easier, but one should be aware of the resemblance of Cackling Goose to hybrid Barnacle Goose × Canada Goose (see the latter).

PLUMAGES Nominate subspecies. Sexes identical, but ♂ slightly larger and heavier, with usually more demonstrative attitude within pairs. Complex basic moult strategy (one plumage per definitive cycle, two during the first cycle). Ageing relatively easy until the beginning of the first winter and possible until the end of the first summer under good viewing conditions or in the hand. See also Geographic Variation.

Adult

Definitive basic plumage (year-round). Head and neck black with white oblong spot from the throat across the cheeks to behind the eyes. Dark gular stripe sometimes present. Iris brown. Bill blackish, relatively short and thick-based. Feathers of the mantle, scapulars and secondary upperwing-coverts grey brown with visible duskier subterminal bars and thin pale fringes producing a regularly streaked appearance. Chest usually whitish or beige (rarely light brown), contrasting sharply with black lower neck. White half-collar infrequent and, when visible, often limited to a few white flecks on the foreneck. Belly and fore flanks grey-beige more clearly streaked dusky. Flanks strongly marked with long dark brown crescents. Rump blackish. Upper- and undertail-coverts and lower belly white. Tail black. Upperwing has secondary and primary coverts grey-brown, with subterminal darker bars and pale fringes, sharper in fresh plumage. Dark remiges, blackish around shafts and towards tips. Underwing has dark brown lesser coverts, median and greater coverts paler silver-grey, pale grey axillaries and dark grey-brown remiges (primaries more silvery-grey at base). Legs blackish.

Juvenile

First basic plumage (until Oct–Jan). Similar to adult but duller, plainer and less contrasting. Easy to age under good viewing conditions. Head and neck duller and browner, somewhat merging into pale breast, with whitish cheeks speckled brown. Usually no white collar or, at most, poorly defined pale flecks forming a short, irregular band (all taxa). Iris initially dull grey and pale. Juvenile body feathers narrower, shorter and rounded at tip, differing obviously from adult pattern on upperparts (larger and squarer feathers) and flanks (very broad feathers). Pale fringes to these feathers are more yellowish-brown and extend along their sides (restricted to tip in adult). The whole body appears typically scaly and mottled whereas it looks streaked in adult. Breast, belly and flanks appear mottled dark. White uppertail-coverts. Rectrices substantially narrower, with a bare shaft at tip and more brown and fade more rapidly than adult. Primaries narrower.

First-winter/first-summer

Formative plumage (Nov–Feb/Jul–Aug). Pre-formative moult sometimes starts late in autumn and ends in Mar–

Apr. During their first winter, many young have a mix of juvenile and formative (adult-like) feathers, evident on the scapulars and flanks, but will generally require close scrutiny once moult is well advanced. Once formative plumage is completely acquired, looks very like adult. The majority of lesser, median and outer greater coverts are still juvenile, narrower and round-tipped, browner at base, blackish subterminal bar barely visible and very faint or no pale fringes. At close range, contrast between juvenile upperwing (folded) and formative scapulars is usually the best ageing feature. Outer primaries and at least some rectrices narrow and quickly fade or bleach towards tips. Dark gular stripe may be on average more pronounced in young bird than in ad[1014].

Second-winter/second-summer

Second basic plumage (Jul–Aug/Jul–Aug). Identical to definitive basic plumage, except that 1–4 juvenile rectrices (very worn) are sometimes retained[1014].

GEOGRAPHIC VARIATION Four subspecies of Cackling Goose breed in the Arctic tundra from N Hudson Bay to the Aleutian Is. The nominate subspecies is the easternmost and occurs virtually throughout the species' Canadian range. The next subspecies, *taverneri*, breeds in W Alaska, the extent of sympatry and/or intergradation with *hutchinsii* being poorly defined, as well as the precise subspecific identity of birds nesting on coasts of N Alaska[860]. The regular presence of *B. c. parvipes* in contact with *taverneri* and *hutchinsii* is not proven by analyses of birds from the tundra[559,860] or appears at most marginal[958]. Further south-west in Alaska, subspecies *minima* occurs in the Yukon-Kuskokwim delta, with apparently no clinal transition to *taverneri*[860]. Finally, subspecies *leucopareia* breeds in the Aleutians and Semidi Is.

Each subspecies shows variation, between individuals and populations, in colour (of the breast, presence of a white collar) and shape (also varying by sex and age), but also show useful trends in each of these characters. Subspecific identification of many individuals is possible, especially when faced with small flocks that can be compared to well-known local geese. Note also that flocks of different subspecies tend to separate on any shared wintering grounds[860]. Based on huge field experience, Mlodinow *et al.*[860] stated that, in good viewing conditions, 90–95% of Cackling Geese can be identified to subspecies. The same authors estimate that identification based on photographs is much trickier, and that only 10–20% of lone individuals on single photographs would be positively identifiable.

These authors produced a remarkable overview of the identification of the different subspecies.

B. h. hutchinsii. Pale and rather small. Slightly larger than *minima* and smaller than the other two subspecies, but variable: eastern breeders are slightly larger than those in the west[860], which contradicts the theory of a cline towards *taverneri*. Neck typically quite short and thick. Head square and angular in profile, with steep but short forehead (often vertical). At rest, the head peaks well behind the eye, and the crown appears typically flat and slightly forward-inclined. Bill generally quite thin and rather long, the culmen being straight in profile. The white cheeks typically show a notch behind the eye, which is more frequent and pronounced in *hutchinsii* than all other taxa. Gular stripe present in about one-quarter of birds[860]. White collar in small proportion of birds, never underlined by a band darker than rest of breast. However, the white collar can be difficult to discern due to the chest being usually whitish itself. Underparts rather plain. Scapulars and adult upperwing pattern less marked than *minima*, with feathers browner basally, dark subterminal bar quite marked and faint pale brown fringes.

B. h. taverneri. Large and medium dark (western birds on average slightly darker than in N Alaska). The largest subspecies, with a rather massive shape and prominent breast, but much overlap with *leucopareia* and some with *hutchinsii*. Usually visibly smaller than *B. c. parvipes* in direct comparison. Neck typically longer than other subspecies, appearing distinctly oblique or slightly curved when feeding. The alert posture often gives it a typical shape with massive breast, long neck ending in drop-shaped head and thick bill. Proportionately longer tail, projecting further beyond wingtips compared to other taxa[860]. Head like *minima*, somewhat angular in appearance, but thicker, oval or pear-shaped. The angle between the forehead and culmen is often very flat. In comparison, *B. c. parvipes* has a slightly steeper forehead extending into a concave (and longer) culmen in profile, with a thinner bill tip. Bill stronger than other subspecies, thick-based and appearing quite triangular. The base of the lower mandible sometimes shows a slight downwards bulge. Gular stripe present in 40–75% of individuals wintering in Washington, varying between flocks[860]. In *B. c. parvipes*, gular stripe is usually absent, except in the dark population of the Anchorage area (25–50% of birds[860]). White collar rare (present in 2–5% of ad[860]), which is also the case in *B. c. parvipes*, although in the latter the whitish breast may obscure the white collar, as in *hutchinsii*. In most birds, the breast is medium grey-brown, much paler than the majority of *minima* and darker than most *hutchinsii* and *B. c. parvipes*. Some rare birds may show the classic pattern of either taxa. The breast is also typically paler than the flanks, including in birds with pale breast[860], which resemble *B. c. parvipes*. Little contrast among the scapulars and secondary upperwing-coverts (bases vs. subterminal bars), as in *hutchinsii* and *B. c. parvipes*, but <5% of adult show a pattern similar to 'standard' *minima*, with grey bases and crisp white fringes.

B. h. minima. The darkest and smallest subspecies, with size of a large Mallard *Anas platyrhynchos*. Somewhat 'dwarf' shape, with short thick bill, rounded head, short thick neck, but wings and legs proportionately long. Wings usually project well beyond the tail. When feeding, the short neck is held almost straight and vertically towards the ground. Rather rounded head with high crown, less angular than *leucopareia* and *hutchinsii*. Bill really small, short with straight or slightly convex culmen. Gular stripe present in many, but variable: Mlodinow et al.[860] mentioned its presence in 40–95% of birds, depending on the flock. Sometimes shows hint of a white collar, rarely a clear, complete one. Very rarely, it is underlined by a black collar and/or extends around hindneck. On average, breast and a belly almost as dark as upperparts, with a purple or bronze hue often visible on the sides. Little contrast between breast and lower neck. Races *leucopareia* and *taverneri* may have breast as dark, but the former also often shows a clear white half-collar. On the other hand, *minima* almost never has a pale breast, which distinguishes it from most *hutchinsii*, the closest subspecies in size and shape. The breast of *minima* is usually darker than the flanks, while the opposite is true in *taverneri* and *hutchinsii*[860]. Most adult have scapulars and secondary upperwing-coverts typically more bluish-grey basally, more contrasting with a blackish subterminal bar and clear white fringe, the upperparts pattern being reminiscent of Barnacle Goose.

B. h. leucopareia. Taller and more slender than *minima* and most *hutchinsii*, but smaller on average than *taverneri*. Neck slightly longer and thinner than *minima*, with proportionately long legs. When feeding, neck is often slightly bent or curved towards the ground[860]. Has a more angular head than *minima*, with a steep forehead and flat crown, but head slightly more elongated than in *hutchinsii*, appearing more rectangular than square.

Bill on average longer and thicker based than *minima*, slightly thicker than *hutchinsii* but usually thinner and shorter than *taverneri*, with a more elongated, flatter nail. Gular stripe present in almost all birds. White collar (broad crescent on foreneck) in almost all adult. Collar sometimes complete (exceptional in other subspecies) and frequently underlined by a dark collar (rare in *minima*, exceptional in *hutchinsii* and *taverneri*). Collar present only in definitive and formative plumages, i.e. only often from the end of first winter (so ageing is necessary before concluding that the collar is absent). Breast varies in coloration, ranging from beige to dark grey-brown, sometimes with bronze sheen, on average slightly paler than *minima* but darker than the other taxa. Birds with pale breasts usually have flanks and belly slightly darker[860]. Secondary upperwing-coverts pattern intermediate between *minima* and *hutchinsii* with pale brown bases, darker blurred subterminal bar and rather large pale fringes, cream to pale brown (rarely white). Semidi Is birds are intermediate between *leucopareia* and *taverneri*, with white collar less strongly marked, mass reportedly lower than *leucopareia* and tarsus length approaching *B. c. parvipes*[537].

MEASUREMENTS and MASS ♂ and adult larger and heavier than ♀ and young birds respectively during first year of life.

B. h. hutchinsii. Adult ♂ (*n*=129): culmen 39.0 (±0.2), head and bill 96.7 (±0.4), tarsus 90.1 (±0.5), mass 2,180 (±3). Adult ♀ (*n*=125): culmen 37.7 (±0.5), head and bill 92.5 (±0.5), tarsus 84.5 (±0.5), mass 1,920 (±20)[887]. Adult ♀: wing chord 349–392 (371, *n*=24), tail 117 (*n*=7), culmen 32–39 (35, *n*=142), mass 1,610–2,330 (1950, *n*=25)[172]. ♂ (*n*=100): wing chord 383–436 (adult) and 370–422 (juvenile), culmen 34–43, bill depth at tip of forehead feathering 18.4–22.9, tail 110–139, tarsus 69–83; ♀ (*n*=100): wing chord 369–420 (adult) and 357–407 (juvenile), culmen 31–41, bill depth at tip of forehead feathering 17.3–21.9, tail 103–131, tarsus 64–78; compare measurements from Pyle[1014] for other taxa.

B. h. taverneri. Adult ♂ (*n*=60): culmen 37.8 (±2.3), tarsus 92.8 (±3.9), middle toe 62.3 (±3.5), mass 2,606 (±267.4). Adult ♀ (*n*=61): culmen 36.1 (±2.2), tarsus 87.1 (±3.4), middle toe 59.4 (±3.3), mass 2,421 (±238.2)[651]. ♂ (*n*=100): wing chord 401–436 (adult) and 381–413 (juvenile), culmen 34–42, bill depth at tip of forehead feathering 18.9–21.8, tail 116–133, tarsus 72–81; ♀ (*n*=100): wing chord 380–429 (adult) and 365–389 (juvenile), culmen 32–40, bill depth at tip of forehead feathering 17.7–20.4, tail 112–128, tarsus 65–75; compare measurements from Pyle[1014] for other taxa.

B. h. leucopareia. Adult ♂ (*n*=36): culmen 36.6 (±2.1), tarsus 92.4 (±3.4), middle toe 63.3 (±4.7), mass 1,946 (±136.6). Adult ♀ (*n*=46): culmen 35.1 (±1.4), tarsus 86.7 (±3.7), middle toe 59.5 (±3.5), mass 1,704 (±156.6)[887]. Adult ♀: wing chord 369 (*n*=20), tail 120 (*n*=9), culmen 32 (*n*=21)[172]. ♂ (*n*=100): wing chord 373–416 (adult) and 362–405 (juvenile), culmen 32–41, bill depth at tip of forehead feathering 18.0–22.8, tail 107–131, tarsus 72–81; ♀ (*n*=100): wing chord 362–405 (adult) and 351–394 (juvenile), culmen 30–38, bill depth at tip of forehead feathering 16.5–21.4, tail 101–125, tarsus 68–77; compare measurements from Pyle[1014] for other taxa.

B. h. minima. Adult ♂ (*n*=152): culmen 29.7 (±2.1), tarsus 83.2 (±3.1), middle toe 56.2 (±5.2), mass 1,546 (±199.5). Adult ♀ (*n*=152): culmen 28.1 (±1.7), tarsus 77.9 (±1.7), middle toe 53.9 (±5.4), mass 1,311 (±199.6)[651]. Adult ♀ (*n*=11): wing chord 354, tail 104, culmen 28, mass 1,310 (*n*=24)[172]. ♂ (*n*=100): wing chord 359–400 (adult) and 351–389 (juvenile), culmen 25–34, bill depth at tip of forehead feathering 16.3–20.6, tail 99–127, tarsus 64–76; ♀ (*n*=100): wing chord 345–384 (adult) and 335–373 (juvenile), culmen 23–32, bill depth at tip of forehead feathering 14.8–19.0, tail 93–121, tarsus 60–72; compare measurements from Pyle[1014] for other taxa.

VOICE From afar, flocks produce a chorus of high-pitched squeaking and barking calls, like *yap* or *yeek*. Among other calls, also short and acute sounds like *rok*, *rook* or *urr-lik*, produced in rhythm by pairs taking off, for example. The call's pitch is linked to the size of the bird, *minima* and *hutchinsii* producing more acute calls, *leucopareia* uttering a lower, more harmonious call, while *taverneri* gives a hoarser *ga-rok* (first syllable low and barely audible from far), closer to that of Canada Goose, but sharper and less resonant, often uttered on take-off. Precise studies of the vocalisations and sonograms of the different populations are still lacking.

MOULT Complex basic strategy. Apparently identical to that of Canada Goose (which see), but both breeding and moult timing depend on latitude. Adult moults wings in Jul–Aug and complete pre-basic moult soon after arriving on wintering grounds, if not before. This is not the case for young birds, however, many of which are still in full juvenile plumage until Nov–Dec and even

sometimes Feb. In many birds, pre-formative moult is slow or protracted during winter, and not completed until early spring. Pre-formative moult is more extensive on average than in Canada Goose with, for example, rectrices often completely replaced[1014].

HYBRIDISATION Mixed pairings with Canada Goose at the junction of the two species' range is often said to be widespread. Even clinal evolution between these two species, as well as the existence of numerous intermediates between more 'typical' populations of each taxon, is widely accepted. However, evidence of hybridisation is infrequent, e.g. between *B. c. parvipes* and *B. hutchinsii*, even though that is the most expected pairing[860]. Moreover, genetic studies that led to the split of the two species[1182,1183] suggest that gene flow between them is at most limited. Reports of natural hybridisation with other species seem casual, many references not always making clear whether Canada Goose or Cackling Goose is involved. Recent reports have been documented with Greater White-fronted Goose *Anser albifrons*, Greylag Goose *A. anser*, Snow Goose *Chen caerulescens*, Ross's Goose *C. rossii* and Barnacle Goose (see the first three species, respectively, and below). Natural hybridisation has also been mentioned very occasionally with Bean Goose *Anser fabalis*[931], Pink-footed Goose *A. brachyrhynchus*[465,947] and Brent Goose *B. bernicla*[97]. In captivity, other references mention hybridisation with Red-breasted Goose *B. ruficollis*[1142] and Mallard *Anas platyrhynchos*[465].

Cackling Goose × Ross's Goose: like hybrid Canada Goose × Snow Goose as its plumage is variegated grey-brown and white. Most birds have the head, neck and most of the belly white (more or less mottled grey), the white extending variably on the flanks. The upperparts are (always?) rather grey, with barely visible dark subterminal bars and very faint pale fringes. Bill pale pink to greyish, with dark tomium and nail. Dull greyish-pink legs. Hybrid Canada Goose × Ross's Goose and Cackling Goose × Snow Goose are also reported occasionally and are, depending on the subspecies involved, only marginally distinguishable from each other and the present hybrid. One should base identification on head shape (usually rectangular), shape and size of bill (small and rectangular) and 'grinning patch' (absent). The company it keeps is also likely to be one of the parent species, which may help.

Cackling Goose × Barnacle Goose: rarely reported, including in Europe, where both parents are escapes from captivity or from feral populations[668]. Like hybrid Barnacle Goose × Canada Goose (see the latter), and mainly distinguished by overall size, and shape of the head and bill. The hybrid involving Cackling Goose is usually close in size to Barnacle Goose, while that involving Canada Goose is usually visibly larger. Hybrid Cackling Goose × Barnacle Goose can closely recall subspecies *minima*, including the dark breast, paler than the neck and darker than the flanks. The head is small and square, with a remarkably small bill. Finally, this hybrid has upperparts coloration close to that of *minima*, with bluish-grey bases to scapulars and secondary coverts, blackish subterminal bars and conspicuous whitish fringes. Separated from *minima* by frequent presence of white mark on forehead or even above eyes and by wider white cheeks (especially towards the throat, usually or always without a gular stripe). Also note the very dark breast (almost blackish variably marked with pale, vs. brown with purple sheen in *minima*) and contrast between breast and flanks is noticeably stronger. Finally, at least some hybrids have an upperwing pattern similar to Barnacle Goose (lesser and median coverts pale grey).

HABITAT and LIFE-CYCLE Highly migratory, inhabiting Arctic and subarctic regions of North America, migrating in large flocks and sometimes making long stop-overs at traditional sites, especially between mid-Apr and mid-May. Arrival on the breeding grounds occurs, depending on latitude and snowmelt, from early May to mid-Jun. Breeding habitats vary depending on subspecies: *hutchinsii* occurs in the tundra, mainly coastal lowlands with many small ponds, slow-flowing rivers and sloughs. Also nests on cliffs[915], and irrespective of habitat, often in quite dense colonies of several hundred pairs. Race *minima* inhabits the coastal fringe, from the margins of the tidal zone to floodable tundra lowlands, up to 24 km from Bering Sea coasts[976]. Race *leucopareia* selects slopes overlooking coastal cliffs. In wet tundra lowlands, most pairs nest on small islands or hummocks. Eggs are laid between mid-May and mid-Jul depending on population. Adult begins pre-basic moult with the remiges during the first weeks after hatching, while non-breeders and adults that fail gather on moulting grounds. Pre-basic moult of breeding adult is completed on same moulting sites once young able to fly. Autumn migration peaks in Oct. In winter, uses a small number of traditional coastal lowlands, floodplains and huge agricultural areas, plateaux or valleys.

RANGE and POPULATION Restricted breeding range along American Arctic coasts from Baffin I to the Aleutian chain, with four subspecies.

B. h. hutchinsii. Breeds on Arctic coasts of Canada, between S Baffin I and NW Quebec, west to near the mouth of the Mackenzie River, Northwest Territories. Breeds or used to breed rarely in Greenland[398,458]. The western boundary of its range is not well known, nor the extent of sympatry and/or hybridisation with *taverneri*, thus may extend along N coast of Alaska. Migrates over the centre of the continent to winter in two main regions, along W coasts of the Gulf of Mexico (eastern breeders, west to Queen Maud Gulf) and over S Colorado, W Texas, E Arizona and N Mexico (western breeders). The winter range may vary depending on temperatures. Eastern populations estimated at 300,000 individuals in the 1990s, more recently at 405,800 in 2012 and 263,300 in 2013, without any clear trend[1294]. The western population's trend is more difficult to assess, as censuses in winter of the 'short-grass population' produced 292,800 birds in 2012 and 256,300 in 2013[1294], including an unknown proportion of *B. c. parvipes* and even perhaps *taverneri*[860]. This population has increased over the past ten years and is probably the subspecies found in E North America, where it is seen regularly in small numbers. Reported annually in NW Europe (British Isles, the Low Countries, Scandinavia), where birds are sometimes (perhaps wrongly) considered escapees.

B. h. taverneri. Restricted breeding range on coasts of N & W Alaska, including the Yukon-Kuskokwim Delta, where *minima* also breeds, and the Seward Peninsula to the south. Eastern boundary unclear (see *hutchinsii*). Winters mainly in valleys of the Willamette and Columbia Rivers, Oregon and Washington, with smaller numbers further south to Central Valley of California and north to Puget Sound, where numbers unknown. Reported occasionally (status unclear) within the winter range of subspecies *hutchinsii* and *B. c. parvipes* east of the Rockies (Colorado, New Mexico, Texas, N Mexico). USFWS[1294] lists this subspecies as part of 'Lesser and Taverner's Canada Geese' thus including western *B. c. parvipes*. This population was estimated at 40,300 (22,500–58,100) birds in 2013[1294], mostly *taverneri*, and is decreasing.

B. h. minima. Very local, breeding on a small stretch of coast in SW Alaska (Yukon-Kuskokwim Delta). Wintered mainly in the Central Valley of California (south to Mexico), with traditional stop-overs in the

Klamath Basin, but winter range has gradually shifted north since the 1990s. Primary winter sites now include the Willamette and Columbia Valleys, of Oregon and Washington, with much smaller numbers now using California's Central Valley. Its population, initially estimated at *c*.400,000 birds, collapsed due to excessive hunting pressure throughout the annual cycle, to just 20,000 birds in the 1980s. Appropriate regulations permitted an impressive recovery thereafter, with an estimated 202,300 birds in 2012 and 312,200 in 2013[1294]. Rare outside its normal range, with two records in Japan[180], and others in E Siberia, Hawaii and the Yukon, as well as scattered observations (including banded birds) east of the Rocky Mts, in Nevada, Idaho, North Dakota, Minnesota, Colorado, Arizona, Alabama, Illinois, North Carolina and Connecticut[860]. European records are generally considered to relate to escapes from captivity.

B. h. leucopareia. Breeds on several Aleutian Is (especially Buldir I, Attu, Agattu, Alaid-Nizki and Chagulak) and Semidi Is (Kiliktagik and Anowik). The latter winter mainly in Oregon, near Pacific City[706], while the Aleutian population winters primarily in California, in the San Joaquin Valley and the delta of the Sacramento and San Joaquin Rivers. Like *minima*, migrates over the Pacific Ocean to and from their breeding range, but frequents several traditional stop-over sites (briefly in autumn, for longer periods in late winter) on the coast of N California and Oregon. Formerly more widespread (east to Kodiak and west to the Kuril Is; see '*asiatica*' below), this goose was close to extinction due to the introduction of foxes on many islands and by the 1960s only 200–300 individuals remained on Buldir[706]. Conservation actions designed to save it (removal of foxes on some islands, introduction of breeders, protection of wintering areas, hunting restrictions in winter, etc.) permitted a rapid increase, with the total population reaching 1,630 birds in 1977, 7,000 in 1991, 37,000 in 2000 and 166,300 in 2013, with a mean rate of increase of 4% per year over the last decade[1294]. Reported very occasionally away from its normal range, including in S California, Mexico and British Columbia.

'B. h. asiatica'. Extinct. Usually treated as a western population of *leucopareia*[887]. Formerly bred on Commander and Kuril Is, NE Russia, and wintered in Japan, on Hokkaido and Honshu[718], where the last record was obtained in 1929, although Brazil[180] mentioned its existence until the 1980s. Extinction appears to have been caused by hunting, as well as introduction of rats and foxes to the nesting grounds. Since then, *leucopareia* has been reintroduced in the former range of '*asiatica*' and this subspecies is now found more frequently in Japan.

CAPTIVITY Quite frequently kept in captivity, but many individuals possess a more or less hybrid ancestry, making them difficult to assign to taxon. Furthermore, only *minima* is widely kept, both in North America and Europe. This subspecies is regularly reported in the wild in several countries in W Europe (British Isles, Low Countries, France, Scandinavia, etc.) and is even more frequently reported than *hutchinsii*, suggesting a captive origin for at least the majority. Nominate *hutchinsii* is reported in Europe occasionally, but is rare in captivity. Race *leucopareia* is very rarely held in captivity in Europe or North America, and *taverneri* is very rarely kept in North America and almost never in Europe.

REFERENCES Bird Hybrids Database (2014)[97]; Brazil (1991)[180]; Fox *et al.* (1996)[398]; Gotfredson (2002)[458]; Gray (1958)[465]; Hatch & Hatch (1983)[537]; Hines *et al.* (2000)[559]; Johnsgard (2010)[648]; Kampe-Persson & Lerner (2007)[668]; Kraege (2005)[706]; Krueger (2004)[713]; Kuroda (1939)[718]; Martin *et al.* (1982)[806]; McCarthy (2006)[817]; Mlodinow *et al.* (2008)[860]; Mowbray *et al.* (2002)[887]; Norment *et al.* (1999)[915]; Oreshnikova (1985)[931]; Panov (1989)[947]; Pearce *et al.* (2006)[958]; Peterson (1990)[976]; Price (2008)[1010]; Pyle (2008)[1014]; Rush *et al.* (1994)[1111]; Scherer & Hilsberg (1982)[1142]; Scribner *et al.* (2003)[1162]; Shields & Wilson (1987)[1182]; Shields & Wilson (1987)[1183]; USFWS (2013)[1294].

137. *B. h. hutchinsii*, adult (definitive basic); a typical bird, with a flat crown peaking well behind eye and pale breast, while upperparts are also typical (bases tinged greyish with dusky subterminal area), but the bill is rather small. Colorado, USA, Mar (Steve Mlodinow).

138. *B. h. hutchinsii*, adult (definitive basic); a rather dark-breasted individual, with a small bill reminiscent of *minima*. Colorado, USA, Mar (Steve Mlodinow).

139. *B. h. hutchinsii*, adult (definitive basic); two birds with white neck-rings that could match *leucopareia*, but breast pale and no dark neck-band below neck-ring. Colorado, USA, Mar (Steve Mlodinow).

140. *B. h. hutchinsii*, adult (definitive basic); this bird shows white marks on forehead, but is otherwise typical of the subspecies (the most likely in E North America). New Jersey, USA, Nov (Sébastien Reeber).

141. Adult (definitive basic); intermediate between *minima* (dark breast, upperparts feathers with blue-grey bases, clear subterminal bars and whitish fringes) and *taverneri* (appears large, with 'drop-shaped' head and long neck). Washington, USA, Jan (Steve Mlodinow).

142. *B. h. taverneri*, adult (definitive basic); oval-shaped head, rather large bill and plain upperparts (almost no subterminal bands) typical of this subspecies. Washington, USA, Dec (Steve Mlodinow).

143. *B. h. taverneri*, first-winter (formative); note two generations of feathers among scapulars and juvenile upperwing-coverts (rounded with faint pale brownish fringes), while the long neck is often distinctive of this subspecies. Washington, USA, Mar (Steve Mlodinow).

144. *B. h. taverneri*, adult (definitive basic) at front, and first-winter (formative) behind; note medium-dark breast and plain upperparts of this subspecies. Washington, USA, Dec (Steve Mlodinow).

145. *B. h. minima*, adult (definitive basic); the smallest and darkest Cackling Goose subspecies; the middle bird has undergone its preformative moult and is best distinguished from nearby adult by unpatterned median and greater coverts. Washington, USA, Jan (Steve Mlodinow).

146. *B. h. minima*, first-winter (first basic/formative); note differences in size and shape compared to *taverneri* (front left). Washington, USA, Jan (Steve Mlodinow).

147. *B. h. minima*. Adult (definitive basic); note pointed wings and short neck of this subspecies. Vancouver, Canada, Oct (Steve Mlodinow).

148. *B. h. minima*, adult (definitive basic); note rounded head with very small bill and neck only slightly contrasting with dark breast. California, USA, Nov (Bob Steele).

149. *B. h. leucopareia*, adult (definitive basic); rectangular head, long bill, black gular stripe and distinct white collar underlined by darker 'subcollar' are typical of this subspecies. California, USA, Nov (Sébastien Reeber).

150. *B. h. leucopareia*, adult (definitive basic); breast coloration varies and can match both *taverneri* and *minima*; this is a rather dark-breasted bird, matching the usual appearance of *minima*. California, USA, Nov (Sébastien Reeber).

151. *B. h. leucopareia*, first-winter (first basic/formative); from adult by moulting scapulars (the lower row typically lacking as here), less well-defined white collar and juvenile flanks and belly feathers, producing typically mottled appearance (vs. adult which is streaked). California, USA, Nov (Sébastien Reeber).

152. *B. h. leucopareia*, adult (definitive basic); note variation in breast colour and extent of white collar. California, USA, Nov (Sébastien Reeber).

153. *B. h. leucopareia*, juvenile (first basic); pre-formative moult seems to have not yet started, the typical juvenile scaly upperparts and neatly spotted belly being clearly visible. California, USA, Nov (Sébastien Reeber).

154. *B. h. leucopareia*, adult (definitive basic); the black gular stripe (which is variably present in all four subspecies) is usually visible in flight. California, USA, Nov (Sébastien Reeber).

CANADA GOOSE
Branta canadensis

Plates 16, 17

TAXONOMY *Anas canadensis* Linnaeus, 1758, *Syst. Nat.*, edn. 10, p. 123. Canada Goose *sensu lato* (including Cackling Goose *B. hutchinsii*) is the closest relative of Hawaiian Goose (Nene) *B. sandvicensis*, endemic to Hawaii. However, it has been highlighted that small subspecies are also close to Barnacle Goose *B. leucopsis*[51,953,1026,1227].

Among the Anseriformes, this complex of 'white-cheeked' geese is certainly the most discussed taxonomically. Many forms occur across the North American continent with clinal transitions between some of them, sometimes related to environmental factors[738]. Basically, there is variation in size (on average, increasing from north to south) and overall darkness (the darkest birds occur in the west). Authors like Hellmayr & Conover[549], recognised nine taxa and Delacour[295] 12, his treatment having been widely accepted thereafter[87,503,645], even though Palmer[945] accepted just eight. 12 subspecies are generally accepted nowadays and placed in two distinct species: the Canada Goose with the largest subspecies (*canadensis, parvipes* Cassin, 1852, *occidentalis* Baird, 1858, *interior* Todd, 1938, *moffitti* Aldrich, 1946, *maxima* Delacour, 1951, *fulva* Delacour, 1951) and the Cackling Goose *B. hutchinsii* with the smallest subspecies (*minima* Ridgway, 1885, *hutchinsii* Richardson, 1832, *leucopareia* Brandt, 1836, *asiatica* Aldrich, 1946 and *taverneri* Delacour, 1951).

The overall situation is even more complex due to the existence of many populations, some of which intergrade and others not, despite their geographic proximity. Furthermore, unlike other geese, pair formation seems to occur later in Canada Geese, even on the breeding grounds[860,887,942], which, combined with a strong fidelity to nest site, strong philopatry[887] and long-lasting pair-bonds, has been described as potentially favouring genetic structure and divergence between colonies/populations[357]. In contrast, the massive introduction of individuals of various origins (mainly *maxima* and *moffitti*) to many southern areas has certainly counteracted this diversification. Finally, the expansion and recent and rapid increase in numbers of many populations could contribute to these difficulties, and also go against possible ongoing genetic structuring. It is possible that part of the difficulty in assessing the phylogeography of this superspecies is due to a more dynamic evolution than expected.

It is generally accepted that intergradation occurs between many subspecies at the boundaries of their respective ranges, but frequency of this is poorly known. Several genetic analyses revealed small differences (<1% in mitochondrial DNA sequences) between populations of small geese (*hutchinsii, leucopareia, minima, taverneri*) and those of large Canada Geese (all other taxa cited above)[1026,1182,1313]. Nevertheless, up to ten populations appear identifiable using mitochondrial DNA[50,1312], even if gene flow between 11 populations of western taxa are continuous, albeit at varying degrees[1162].

Morphologically, a large proportion of individual birds of the small subspecies are subspecifically identifiable, but it is more complicated for the largest subspecies. Within each of them, there is clear variation, with a significant proportion of individuals unidentifiable, at least when alone. However, this variability is not fully understood. For example, within a given subspecies, it could reflect differences between subpopulations, themselves being relatively homogeneous. Or perhaps the variability within each subpopulation is similar to that of the subspecies as a whole? Geographically, at least, the authorities responsible for wildfowl management in North America have identified 18 populations, distinguished by their migratory routes, and breeding and wintering grounds[172,1294]. Apart from the three most range-restricted taxa (*occidentalis, leucopareia* and *minima*), these different populations, primarily designated for management purposes, do not correspond to usually recognised subspecies.

In the early 2000s, other authors[24,508,509] proposed a very different approach to the taxonomy of this species, based on a detailed description of morphological characters. Anderson[24] assigned scores for 16 plumage characters and nine measurements using a huge sample of various origins, resulting in a decision to recognise nine species of large geese (and 98 subspecies) and six species of small geese (83 subspecies). Earlier, Hanson[508,509] had recognised 217 subspecies in six species. Although impressive in their scale, these studies have been widely discussed and justifiably criticised for their methodology and resulting decisions, and are not currently accepted by the major taxonomic committees. Indeed, they leave little room for intra-population variability, many taxa being proposed on the basis of weak morphological differences or minute small samples (one or a few individuals). Finally, they result in a taxonomy so plethoric that it becomes virtually unusable. The basis of the currently accepted taxonomy, i.e. a huge range with large-scale clinal variation, is, however, far from faultless. The authors mentioned above demonstrated that among diagnosable populations, the nearest geographically are not necessarily the closest phenotypically. The different 'official' subspecies thus include geographically and morphologically separate populations together, despite limited or no gene flux between them, at times resulting in highly variable subspecies, and difficulties in distinguishing them.

Nevertheless, 12 subspecies are currently accepted by the AOU[66] and AERC-TAC[273] as well as by most other authors[172,236,887]. However, it is likely that the species' dynamic phylogeography, improved knowledge of the range of several subspecies, extensive banding and use of genetic tools (including nuclear DNA[989]) will result in some changes to this treatment.

If the designation of the different taxa remains a fairly open topic, the recent decision to split 'Canada Goose' into two species seems less questionable. During the 20th century, between one and 15 species have been recognised, until several genetic studies (mitochondrial DNA) demonstrated the existence of two paraphyletic clades within the complex[50,953,956,1026,1162,1182,1227,1313], which diverged c.1 million years ago[1183], suggesting very little gene exchange and the existence of effective reproductive barriers[956].

The first clade comprises seven taxa, breeding over most of North America, except the tundra: *canadensis*, *interior*, *maxima*, *moffitti*, *occidentalis*, *fulva* and *parvipes*. These are also the largest subspecies, although *parvipes*, the northernmost and whose breeding range almost penetrates the tundra, is also the smallest.

The second clade includes four taxa, *hutchinsii*, *leucopareia*, *minima*, *taverneri*, plus *asiatica*, which is extinct and usually considered a synonym of *leucopareia*[887]. These subspecies are smaller and occupy the Arctic tundra of N Canada west to the Aleutian Is.

The two groups not only differ genetically, but are generally distinguishable in the field (see Identification), differ in size, coloration, structure and their skeletons[1313], as well as vocally, and inhabit different breeding habitats. They were therefore split into two species: Canada Goose B. *canadensis* (the seven larger

subspecies) and Cackling Goose B. *hutchinsii* (the four small subspecies). This treatment is now widely accepted nowadays and has been adopted here.

IDENTIFICATION The only other goose with a black neck and head, and white cheeks is Barnacle Goose, which differs in size, stockier structure, overall greyer (less brown) coloration, the black of the neck extends to the breast, the white cheeks extend behind and above the eye and on forehead, pale grey to whitish underparts, and upperparts appear streaked pale blue-grey, black and white.

Separating Canada Goose and Cackling Goose is much more difficult, but depends on the taxa involved. A *minima* Cackling Goose among large Canada Geese is easily picked out, due to the huge difference in size. Difficulties occur with medium-sized individuals, especially single individuals with no relevant species for comparison. In particular, the problem culminates with the subspecies *taverneri*, the largest Cackling Goose, and *parvipes*, the smallest Canada Goose, which two taxa are rather pale on average and have even been considered synonymous. Their sizes are close, with some overlap in measurements. The distinguishing features are listed below (see also *taverneri* under Geographic Variation of Cackling Goose).

The identification of these two species (and their subspecies) is based on many subtle differences in size, neck length, head shape and especially bill. It will be easier to judge these features only once a good knowledge of 'local' geese has been acquired, and preferably by checking family groups, which will permit an 'average' impression of several individuals presumably of the same subspecies, and to compare them directly with birds of known identity. Conversely, a 'white-cheeked goose' observed alone can cause many problems. Finally, take into account the variation in size depending on age, sex and feeding conditions during the first months of life, especially in northernmost populations. It is also known that captive-bred birds of clear parentage are 5–8% larger than wild birds from the same region[738], emphasising the impact of food resources, themselves variable between years and different areas. Finally, outside North America, much caution is needed owing to the existence of birds whose parentage may involve one or even two escapes from captivity. Such birds may not match any typical subspecies, as several populations or even subspecies may be involved in their parentage.

Canada Goose is significantly larger than Cackling Goose, but the differences are more tenuous between *parvipes* and *taverneri*, which together represent the interface between the two species in terms of size and shape. *B. c. parvipes* usually is on average slightly but distinctly larger than *taverneri*.

The breast is paler on average in *parvipes* than in *taverneri*, but there is some overlap (for example the darker *parvipes* from the Anchorage area).

On average, the head profile is more angular and square in Cackling Goose, accentuated by the shorter bill. However, in the subspecies *taverneri*, the head profile is more elongated and rounded, and the forehead is not salient. The head is quite typically pear- or drop-shaped, with the bill rather short and thick-based compared to *parvipes*. The latter often has a more angular head profile than *taverneri*.

The bill is longer in *B. canadensis*, with a culmen slightly concave in profile. In *B. hutchinsii*, the bill is shorter, proportionately thicker and triangular, with a straight culmen.

The chin and throat show a large longitudinal dark gular stripe, dividing the white cheeks, common in *B. hutchinsii* (depending on taxon), while it is usually absent in *B. canadensis*, except in certain populations from the Rockies and Pacific coast. This stripe is on average more pronounced in young birds than adults[1014], but another study found this not to be true in *B. hutchinsii*[860].

From the side, the white cheeks show a slight notch at the rear of the eye. This is commoner in *B. h. hutchinsii* than any other subspecies, but is also common in *parvipes* (especially those overwintering in Colorado[860]).

The width and colour of the pale fringes to the upperparts vary slightly. They are darker and thinner in Canada Goose, giving Cackling Goose a more clearly streaked appearance.

On average and in the same posture, the tail is slightly longer and projects further in Cackling Goose.

The legs can seem short compared to the body in *parvipes* compared to all taxa of Cackling Goose.

PLUMAGES Nominate subspecies. Sexes identical, but ♂ slightly larger and heavier, with usually more demonstrative and 'proud' attitude visible in pairs. Complex basic moult strategy (one plumage per definitive cycle, two during the first cycle). Ageing relatively easy until the beginning of the first winter and possible until the end of the first summer under good viewing conditions or in the hand. See also Identification and Geographic Variation for more details. NB: In all subspecies, there are more or less frequent abnormalities like white on the forehead (more frequent in *maxima* and *moffitti*) and/or above the lores,

the cheeks may be largely or wholly black, and the neck can show variable white speckles.

Adult

Definitive basic plumage (year-round). Head and neck all black with large white oblong patch starting on throat and extending to rear of cheeks. Iris brown. Bill blackish. Feathers of mantle, scapulars and secondary upperwing-coverts grey-brown with a slightly duskier subterminal band and sharp whitish fringe at the tip, producing a quite regularly streaked appearance. Breast beige with whitish half-collar usually barely visible, contrasting sharply with black lower neck. The fringes of feathers, paler than their centres, afford a faintly barred appearance, and also change slightly with wear. Belly and flanks grey-beige, barely darker than breast. Flanks clearly marked with large dark streaks and pale narrow streaks. Rump blackish. Lower belly, upper- and undertail-coverts white. Tail black. Upperwing has secondary and primary coverts grey-brown with darker subterminal bands and sharper pale fringes when fresh. Grey-brown remiges, darker or blackish around shafts and towards tips. Underwing has lesser coverts brown, median and greater coverts greyer with pale tips, axillaries pale grey centred dark, dark grey-brown remiges (primaries basally paler grey). Legs blackish.

Juvenile

First basic plumage (until Oct–Dec). Similar to adult but duller and less contrasting. Head and neck more faded, brownish and merging into pale breast, with whitish cheeks speckled brown. Iris paler and duller grey. Juvenile body feathers narrower, shorter and round-tipped, distinctly different from adult pattern on upperparts (large and square feathers) and flanks (very broad feathers). The fringes of the same feathers, tinged pale brown (vs. whitish) and less distinct than in adult, form a typical scaly appearance, vs. streaked in adult. For the same reasons, the breast, belly and flanks are mottled dark rather than finely streaked, slightly paler than adult. Uppertail-coverts white with brown on centres and tips[887]. Rectrices notched at tips (bare shafts), browner and duller. Primaries narrower.

First-winter/first-summer

Formative plumage (Nov–Dec/Jul–Aug). Pre-formative moult occupies the autumn and ends between early and late winter. During this period, young birds typically show a mixture of juvenile and formative feathers (adult-type), which is most visible among the scapulars and flanks, but can require closer scrutiny from the beginning of the first winter. Following pre-formative moult, very similar to adult. Most primary coverts, median coverts and outer greater coverts are still juvenile, narrow, round-tipped, virtually no subterminal bar and very faint or on pale fringes (especially outer greater coverts[1014]). This juvenile pattern usually contrasts with the formative scapulars, but may require close examination. Outer primaries and at least some rectrices narrow quickly become visibly worn and bleached. The dark gular stripe may be more pronounced on average vs. adult[1014].

Second-winter/second-summer

Second basic plumage (Jul–Aug/Jul–Aug). Identical to definitive basic plumage, except of 1–4 juvenile rectrices, which if retained are very worn[1014].

GEOGRAPHIC VARIATION Complex and at least partially clinal (see Taxonomy and Identification). Seven recognised subspecies, most of them variable and whose sub-populations differ slightly. The identification of an unusual individual is much simpler if seen with birds from a local population whose identity is known, but potentially very difficult if alone.

Of the seven subspecies, *canadensis*, the easternmost, is large and pale. Further west is *interior* which is the same size but darker, and further south, *maxima*, the largest and palest subspecies. In the western half of North America, *moffitti* is the equivalent of *maxima*, which it resembles strongly. Both subspecies have been the source of countless introduction programmes, contributing to blur the differences between them. Further north, *parvipes* is close in colour to *moffitti* but is the smallest subspecies, hardly larger on average than the largest Cackling Geese. Finally, on the Pacific coast of North America there are two subspecies with rather restricted ranges: *occidentalis*, which is medium-sized and very dark, and *fulva* a little further south, which is slightly larger and paler on average. These taxa are sometimes considered synonymous[945,1014]. Note that many features – gular stripe, cheek colour (white, mottled brown or yellowish), breast colour (pale to dark brown, contrasting with the black or not lower neck) and feathering on the upper legs (white, various shades of brown or black), upperparts streaked or not, etc. – are linked to overall dark or pale plumage.

B. c. canadensis (see Plumages). Rather tall and slender, with a long neck, long bill whose culmen is markedly concave, and long legs. The neck in relaxed position is 155–200 mm long[1014]. Plumage quite pale, without clear whitish collar at base of black neck. Dark gular stripe usually lacking. Cheeks white, frequently finely speckled brown. Very pale grey-brown to beige breast. Rather pale upperparts with pale fringes and duskier subterminal bars barely contrasting (upperparts faintly streaked). Neck and upper mantle pale, contrasting sharply with black neck. Many birds cannot be distinguished from *interior* (see below).

B. c. interior. On average slightly smaller and paler than *canadensis*, but many overlap. Nevertheless, differs genetically[1163]. Shape slightly different due to wings being somewhat longer, and often has visibly longer neck too (in relaxed position 170–220 mm[1014]), but marginally shorter tarsi on average and shorter and slightly less deep-based (proportionately thinner) bill. Differs in having slightly darker and browner upperparts with pale fringes slightly better marked. Neck and mantle usually fairly dark too, reducing the contrast with black neck. Breast slightly darker grey-brown (but variable), often with a trace of whitish half-collar. When the collar is absent, the breast/neck contrast may subdued. Unless dealing with typical individuals in respect of these features, it will often be difficult to certainly identify a lone individual. However, identification will be facilitated by comparing small flocks of either subspecies.

B. c. maxima. The largest of the Canada Geese, with bill and tarsi longer than in the previous two subspecies, with overlap. Very pale, especially the underparts. White cheeks tend to reach further above and behind the eye than in *canadensis* and the gular stripe is usually completely absent. Often has a small patch or white line on the upper forehead. Distinction from *moffitti* tricky, especially as the widespread introduction of birds of either subspecies in the range of the other has further complicated the problem.

B. c. moffitti. Close to the previous subspecies in size and coloration, and the two intergrade widely. Slightly smaller on average. Length of neck in relaxed position 175–230 mm[1014]. Frequently has some white markings on forehead and, in some populations (especially between the Rockies and the Cascade), a dark gular stripe. On average marginally darker than *maxima*, often with a broad whitish collar (upper breast paler than lower).

B. c. parvipes. Probably the subspecies that causes the most significant identification problems. Not only does it seem to consist of geographically distinct populations, but many of them intergrade (at an unknown frequency) with neighbouring taxa, especially *maxima/moffitti*, *interior* and perhaps *B. h. taverneri* (?). Its size and structure are also at the 'crossroads' between Canada and Cackling Goose, thereby constituting the 'crux' of the problem. Distinguished by its relatively small size (the smallest Canada Goose), albeit with structure typical of the species, different from Cackling Goose. More precisely, the bill is quite long and thin-tipped with a slightly concave culmen. A subtle break is visible in profile between the culmen and forehead. The legs can seem short compared to the body, especially compared to Cackling Goose. Length of neck in relaxed position 115–150 mm[1014]. Overall, rather pale, similar to *moffitti* with beige chest and usually lacks a gular stripe. Some individuals are darker, with a more grey-brown breast, a broad whitish area on the upper breast and sometimes a narrow, sharper white collar. An isolated breeding population in the vicinity of Anchorage, Alaska, for example, has the breast substantially darker and gular stripe more frequent (25–50% of birds[860]), approaching *occidentalis*, and may constitute a different subspecies.

B. c. occidentalis. Medium-sized, the second smallest subspecies after *parvipes* and dark (the darkest race) with chocolate-brown underparts contrasting sharply with white lower belly. The breast is also chocolate-brown becoming paler and often greyish at the border with the black neck, and, rarely, has a clear whitish half-collar. The fringes to the upperparts feathers are narrow and quite dark (reddish-brown), lacking clear contrast with the black neck. The white cheeks are rather small and narrow compared to other subspecies, with a clear dark gular stripe. Neck length in relaxed position 120–170 mm[1014].

B. c. fulva. On average slightly larger and paler than *occidentalis*, with bill 10% longer on average. Distinct from *occidentalis* by range and mitochondrial DNA[1181,1255].

MEASUREMENTS and MASS ♂ and adult larger and heavier than ♀ and young, respectively.

B. c. canadensis. Adult ♂ (*n*=10): culmen 57.4 (±2.7), head and bill 128.4 (±4.4), mass 4,931 (± 456.2). Adult ♀ (*n*=10): culmen 53.4 (±3.2), head and bill 119.4 (±2.7), mass 4,280 (±237.0)[887]. Adult ♀ (*n*=7): wing chord 435–488 (465), tail 134–158 (147), culmen 51–56 (54), mass 3,450[172]. ♂ (*n*=100): wing chord 448–506 (adult) and 430–488 (juvenile), culmen 51–60, bill depth at tip

of forehead feathering 25.9–32.1, tail 136–172, tarsus 87–98; ♀ (*n*=100): wing chord 435–483 (adult) and 418–467 (juvenile), culmen 49–56, bill depth at tip of forehead feathering 23.4–29.7, tail 130–166, tarsus 82–93[1014]; compare measurements from Pyle[1014] for other taxa.

B. c. interior. Adult ♂ (*n*=22): culmen 52.9 (±3.3), head and bill 120.1 (±5.1), mass 4,472 (± 30). Adult ♀ (*n*=18): culmen 49.1 (±2.6), head and bill 113.1 (±3.7), mass 4,188 (±109.0)[882,887]. Adult ♀ (*n*=90): wing chord 438–509 (466), tail 132–162 (142), culmen 43–56 (50), mass 2,590–3,990 (3,330, *n*=36)[172]. ♂ (*n*=100): wing chord 469–524 (adult) and 452–509 (juvenile), culmen 48–60, bill depth at tip of forehead feathering 23.9–31.1, tail 119–165, tarsus 74–87; ♀ (*n*=100): wing chord 444–501 (adult) and 427–484 (juvenile), culmen 44–55, bill depth at tip of forehead feathering 21.7–28.5, tail 108–157, tarsus 69–83[1014]; compare measurements from Pyle[1014] for other taxa.

B. c. maxima. Adult ♂ (*n*=6): culmen 57.3 (±1.7), head and bill 129.5 (±3.9), tarsus 115.1 (±5.5), middle toe 84.6 (± 4.4), mass 4,858 (± 280.3). Adult ♀ (*n*=10): culmen 52.6 (±2.1), head and bill 122.0 (±2.4), tarsus 104.8 (±2.7), middle toe 78.5 (± 2.5), mass 4,825 (± 425.1)[241,887]. Adult ♀ (*n*=26): wing chord 472–513 (496), tail 136–166 (154), culmen 55–63 (57), mass 5,030 (*n*=25)[172]. Hanson[507] described individuals weighing up to 10 kg.

B. c. moffitti. Adult ♂ (*n*=18): culmen 49.6 (±4.0), head and bill 120.3 (±5.4), tarsus 118.8 (±7.6), mass 4,017 (± 431.7). Adult ♀ (*n*=3): culmen 45.7 (±0.9), head and bill 111.4 (±1.4), tarsus 106.9 (±4.2), middle toe 78.5 (± 2.5), mass 3,450 (± 300.0)[887]. Adult ♀ (*n*=20): wing chord 472–513 (478), tail 136–159 (147), culmen 51–56 (52), mass 3,720 (*n*=9)[172]. ♂ (*n*=100): wing chord 492–548 (adult) and 478–533 (juvenile), culmen 50–66, bill depth at tip of forehead feathering 24.9–34.0, tail 141–188, tarsus 85–103; ♀ (*n*=100): wing chord 466–525 (adult) and 451–510 (juvenile), culmen 46–62, bill depth at tip of forehead feathering 23.1–31.9, tail 130–177, tarsus 80–99[1014]; compare measurements from Pyle[1014] for other taxa (*maxima* included in *moffitti* by this author).

B. c. parvipes. Adult ♂ (*n*=70): culmen 42.4 (±2.1), head and bill 108.6 (±3.1), tarsus 85.3 (±2.8), middle toe 68.2 (± 2.5), mass 3,266 (± 319.6). Adult ♀ (*n*=59): culmen 40.6 (±2.1), head and bill 107.8 (±3.6), tarsus 84.0 (±2.4), middle toe 62.6 (± 2.8), mass 2,854 (± 334.7)[887]. Adult ♀ (*n*=194): wing chord 422, culmen 42 (54), mass 2,450[172]. ♂ (*n*=100): wing chord 445–476 (adult) and 424–453 (juvenile), culmen 39–47, bill depth at tip of forehead feathering 21.4–24.8, tail 130–148, tarsus 76–85; ♀ (*n*=100): wing chord 424–449 (adult) and 408–429 (juvenile), culmen 37–44, bill depth at tip of forehead feathering 20.2–23.4, tail 125–143, tarsus 71–81[1014]; compare measurements from Pyle[1014] for other taxa.

B. c. occidentalis. Adult ♂ (*n*=130): culmen 46.3 (±2.6), tarsus 106.2 (±3.9), middle toe 80.8 (±7.4), mass 3,232 (± 260.7). Adult ♀ (*n*=131): culmen 43.5 (±2.4), tarsus 97.3 (±3.4), middle toe 74.6 (±6.5), mass 2,640 (±201.5)[651]. Adult ♀: wing chord 408–492 (450, *n*=61), tail 137 (*n*=60), culmen 40–50 (44, *n*=199), mass 2,580–4,000 (3,450, *n*=98)[172]. ♂ (*n*=100): wing chord 440–497 (adult) and 422–482 (juvenile), culmen 41–57, bill depth at tip of forehead feathering 24.0–29.5, tail 125–164, tarsus 84–100; ♀ (*n*=100): wing chord 413–479 (adult) and 400–459 (juvenile), culmen 39–54, bill depth at tip of forehead feathering 21.4–27.8, tail 118–156, tarsus 77–93[1014]; compare measurements from Pyle[1014] for other taxa (*fulva* included in *occidentalis* by this author).

B. c. fulva. Adult ♂ (*n*=175): culmen 51.2 (±0.5), tarsus 93.8 (±0.5), middle toe 80.3 (±2.8), mass 3,689 (± 405.0). Adult ♀ (*n*=134): culmen 47.6 (±0.4), tarsus 87.1 (±0.7), middle toe 77.3 (±3.7), mass 3,043 (±463.0)[1047].

VOICE Seems to vary slightly according to general size of subspecies, but a precise comparative study of the vocalisations of different populations of this species and Cackling Goose is still lacking[887]. The most typical call is a *war-wonk*, the first syllable being low and rising and the second louder and explosive (only the latter heard from afar). This call is honking, strong and rather musical when heard in chorus. Different variations can be written *wak* or *wok* shorter and barked, or *ha-ang* trumpeting and longer. Thirteen types of vocalisations described, with different social functions[1352].

MOULT Complex basic strategy. Pre-formative moult occurs between Sep–Oct and Feb–Apr, and includes many to all feathers of the head, neck and body, sometimes 1–2 tertials, some inner lesser and median coverts (up to 50%[1014]) and a variable number of rectrices, with most birds retaining some juvenile rectrices. Definitive pre-basic moult begins between Jul and Aug with the simultaneous loss of the remiges on or near the breeding sites, continues on moulting sites with the body feathers and rectrices until Oct–Nov and arrival on the wintering grounds. Second pre-basic moult is similar, but *c*.1 month earlier on average. Both moults are delayed in northern populations.

HYBRIDISATION Natural hybridisation is rare, except with Cackling Goose, but their frequency is poorly known. Hybrids from this cross are probably barely identifiable. Other natural reports are mentioned occasionally with Snow Goose *Chen caerulescens* or Ross's Goose *C. rossii*, but hybrids resulting from hybridisation between Canada or Cackling Goose on the one hand and Snow Goose or Ross's Goose on the other are very difficult to distinguish, and variable according to the subspecies involved (see Snow Goose and Cackling Goose). Natural hybridisation is also rarely reported with Greater White-fronted Goose *Anser albifrons*, and, involving feral populations in Europe, with Greylag Goose *A. anser*, Bar-headed Goose *A. indicus* (see these three species), Swan Goose *A. cygnoid*[465,817] of more or less domestic forms, Barnacle Goose *B. leucopsis* (see below) and Mute Swan *Cygnus olor*. Other reports in the wild are obtained very occasionally with Pink-footed Goose *Anser brachyrhynchus*[740,817,1190], Brent Goose *B. bernicla*[817] and Mallard *Anas platyrhynchos*[1190]. In captivity, hybridisation also mentioned with Red-breasted Goose *B. ruficollis*, Black Swan *Cygnus atratus*, Trumpeter Swan *C. buccinator*, Whistling Swan *C. columbianus*, Whooper Swan *C. cygnus*, Egyptian Goose *Alopochen aegyptiacus* and Muscovy Duck *Cairina moschata*[97,639,1190,1194].

Canada Goose × Barnacle Goose: reported fairly regularly in NW Europe, where feral populations of both species are established. Such birds can be mistaken for Cackling Goose, being smaller with a darker breast than Canada Goose. Depending on the subspecies of Canada Goose, appearance probably varies, but most birds seen in Europe are larger than Barnacle Goose with an obviously longer bill, which would match *parvipes*. The head pattern is intermediate, with large white cheeks and two white spots varying in extent above the lores, which may extend to above the eye and merge on the forehead, or be quite reduced. The breast is usually dark and contrasts quite sharply with the flanks and belly, but often has a distinctly browner hue than the black neck. Most hybrids have feathers with pale blue-grey bases close to Barnacle Goose, with clear dusky subterminal bars. See also hybrid Cackling Goose × Barnacle Goose, under Cackling Goose.

HABITAT and LIFE-CYCLE Breeding season, migratory behaviour and habitat choice vary among populations and subspecies. Northernmost populations highly migratory, whereas coastal or southern ones are short-distance migrants, while others, including introduced ones, are sedentary or nearly so. In the southern tundra, mainly inhabits the edges and islands of small waterbodies, e.g. *occidentalis*, which breeds on the coastal plains of the Copper River, Alaska, in a vast area covered with ponds of varying size. These northern populations (including *parvipes*) also favour the banks of rather fast-flowing rivers[489]. In the taiga, uses all kinds of lakes, ponds, marshes and bogs, where nests are sited especially on islands, using lodges of Muskrat *Ondatra zibethicus* and Beaver *Castor canadensis*. The subspecies *fulva* breeds in tall pine and hemlock forests, often nesting in trees[739]. On rocky coasts, it often forms colonies on cliffs[945]. Further south, very eclectic in choice of breeding habitat, using wetlands, ponds, natural lakes and slow-flowing streams, as well as artificial environments including agricultural (reservoirs, tanks) urban or suburban areas. Favours short grass, urban parks, roadsides, lawns and golf courses to feed. Breeds in lone pairs, loose colonies or more compact aggregations, especially in the north. Egg laying occurs between mid-Mar to mid-May in the south and where it has been introduced, and mid-May to mid-Jul in the north. Breeding adults begin to shed their remiges when their chicks are a few weeks old. When both adults and offspring are able to fly, families travel to moulting sites, often located further north. Autumn migration peaks in Oct in the majority of migratory populations. In winter, prefers wetlands near vast agricultural lands, which have been favoured foraging areas in recent decades (especially corn). Also uses all types of lawns and short-grass meadows.

RANGE and POPULATION In North America, seven subspecies occur over most of the continent. Range limits and degree of intergradation with neighbours not established precisely for all taxa. Overall North American population at least six million birds, mainly *moffitti* and *maxima*, and increasing rapidly. Some northern and migratory populations are more threatened.

B. c. canadensis. Breeds in E Canada (extreme SE Baffin I, E Quebec, Labrador and Newfoundland) and winters on coasts from S Newfoundland to NE USA, south to New Jersey, and occasionally even North Carolina (casual to Georgia). Population fluctuated between 45,000 and 70,000 breeding pairs in 2000–13[1294], or 79,500–233,000 individuals in 2011[1292], and is declining.

B. c. interior. Occurs west of *canadensis*, from S Baffin I and around Hudson Bay, south-west to near the border of Manitoba and Nunavut. In the north-east, breeds in S Ungava Bay, N Quebec and has recently expanded to SW Greenland[1163]. Winters mainly in E USA, the northern limit varying according to winter temperatures, south to C Texas and N Florida. Four populations are distinguished by USWFS[172,1294]. The 'Atlantic population' breeds in N Quebec, winters in EC USA (Pennsylvania to South Carolina), and is estimated at 150,000–240,000 breeding pairs in the last decade[1294], or 780,000–1,060,000 individuals in 2011[1292], and is stable. The second, 'southern James Bay population', breeds in S James Bay and winters from W Pennsylvania to S Michigan, south to N Florida and Mississippi. It is estimated to number 40,000–130,000 breeding birds during the last decade[1294] (60,900 in 2013) or 69,400–105,000 birds in 2011[1292], and is increasing. The third, 'Mississippi Valley population,' breeds to the south, in S Hudson Bay lowlands and winters mainly in S Wisconsin, Indiana and Illinois. It comprises 240,000–400,000 individuals (319,700 in 2013[1294]) and is stable. The fourth is the 'Eastern Prairie population', which breeds in SE Hudson Bay and winters from SE Nebraska to Illinois, and south to Louisiana. It has 120,000–170,000 birds (136,600 in 2013[1294]), and is decreasing. The total population for this subspecies is 1,450,000 individuals.

B. c. maxima. Virtually extinct due to hunting in the early 20th century, but reintroduced and now very common throughout its range. Breeds in SE Canada and E USA, south to N Florida and Kansas, and is essentially sedentary or a short-distance migrant. Several isolated introduced populations south of this range. Numerous introduction schemes have facilitated intergradation with *moffitti*, its western counterpart at temperate latitudes. Four populations are distinguished: the 'Atlantic Flyway resident population' numbered 845,000–1,190,000 in 2011[1292] and 797,700–1,107,000 in 2013[1294], and is present in the east coast states. The second, 'Mississippi Flyway resident population' extends further west from S Manitoba, Canada, to Louisiana, and had 1.6 million individuals at the start of the present decade[1292,1294]. The other two populations of the Great Plains, known as the 'Great Plains population' and 'Western Prairie population' breed further west and are migratory. If they belong to *maxima* or *moffitti* is not well known. These two numbered 768,800 birds in 2013[1294].

B. c. moffitti. Breeds in W USA and widely intergrades with *maxima* (see above) especially between the Appalachians and Rockies. Besides the two 'mixed' populations mentioned for *maxima*, two other populations are typically assigned to the present taxon. The first is the 'Hi Line population', east of the Rocky Mts that winters south to C New Mexico. It numbered 338,900 birds in 2013[1294], and is increasing. The other is called 'Rocky Mountains population' and breeds further west (S Alberta, Montana, Wyoming and NW Colorado to N California) and winters in the south of this range and along the N Gulf of California, Mexico. It had 112,000 birds in 2011[1292] and 158,400 in 2013[1294].

B. c. parvipes. Breeds in W Canada, W Nunavut (where in contact with *B. h. hutchinsii*) and NW Manitoba (where in contact with *interior*) west to C British Columbia (in contact with *moffitti* in south and *fulva* in west) and C Alaska (where in contact with *B. h. taverneri* and *B. h. minima*). Two populations distinguished, mainly on their wintering range, birds of the eastern range (NW Canada) wintering in the Great Plains, E Colorado and Kansas south to NE New Mexico and C Texas. Known as the 'Short Grass Prairie population', it was estimated at 292,800 birds in 2012 and 256,300 in 2013[1294], having increased over the last ten years. The second population breeds in the west, from extreme W Canada to C Alaska, wintering in Washington, Oregon and also in California (Central Valley). Estimates given for this population also include some *B. h. taverneri*, with 27,400–67,600 individuals in 2011[1292] and 22,500–58,100 in 2013[1294]. A breeding population in the vicinity of Anchorage, Alaska, which is phenotypically distinct, winters in Oregon[860].

B. c. fulva. Breeds on Pacific coast of Canada, in Vancouver and north to extreme S Alaska. Mainly sedentary but reported south to Oregon. Numbers difficult to assess. *B. c. fulva* is probably only the coastal part of the 'Pacific population'[172,1294]. The latter breeds from SE Alberta and British Columbia to N California and Nevada, wintering in the south of this range and south to S California. The 'Pacific population' is probably composed of several taxa or intermediate populations, with *parvipes* further north. It had 221,600 birds in 2012[1294].

B. c. occidentalis. Restricted range on S coast of Alaska (mainly Copper River Delta, near Cordova). Winters on S coast of British Columbia, in Washington and Oregon. Following an earthquake in 1964 which affected the entire breeding area, the population grew to 25,500 birds in 1979. Thereafter, habitat change and the arrival of new predators limited breeding success, and the population was estimated at 10,000–18,000 individuals in 1980 and just 6,700 in 2009[648], but on average 13,700 between 2010 and 2012[1294].

In Europe, introduced and feral populations are often considered as being of the nominate subspecies, but many birds also show features of *maxima/moffitti*. Many captive birds at the start of this introduction are likely to have ancestors from two subspecies or more. On the other hand, most of the Swedish population, of nearly 10,000 breeding pairs, originated from just five birds[1257], and therefore a low genetic diversity. The species is now widely established in Europe, breeding mainly in the British Isles and from Scandinavia to France. Overall numbers were 48,500–73,750 breeding pairs in 2004–07, and are still increasing rapidly. The species is locally considered a problem, mainly because of its aggression towards other geese, ducks, loons (divers) and other waterbirds, competing for food and habitat with these species, and because of the damage it causes to agriculture[62,1062]. Some birds showing features of *interior* in Europe and the Azores are regarded as true vagrants, like *B. hutchinsii*[77,78]. Also introduced to New Zealand before 1876 and now well established and sedentary there.

CAPTIVITY Very common in captivity and could escape anywhere in the Holarctic. Semi-captive and introduced populations are established in many urban areas of the world. The identification of accidental subspecies, especially in W Europe, is complicated not only by difficulties in differentiating 'pure' individuals, but also by the existence in Europe of birds of mixed ancestry.

REFERENCES Anderson (2010)[24]; Baker (1998)[50]; Baker & Marshall (1997)[51]; Banks *et al.* (2008)[62]; Banks *et al.* (2004)[66]; Batty & Lowe (2001)[77]; Batty *et al.* (2001)[78]; Bellrose (1980)[87]; Bird Hybrids Database (2014)[97]; Boyd & Dickson *in* Kear (2005)[172]; Clements *et al.* (2013)[237]; Coluccy (2001)[241]; Crochet *et al.* (2010)[273]; Delacour (1954)[295]; Ely & Scribner (1994)[357]; Fox *et al.* (1996)[398]; Gray (1958)[465]; Grieb (1970)[489]; Hansen & Nelson (1964)[503]; Hanson (1951)[506]; Hanson (1997)[507]; Hanson (2006)[508]; Hanson (2007)[509]; Hatch & Hatch (1983)[537];

Hellmayr & Conover (1948)[549]; Johnsgard (1960)[639]; Johnsgard (1975)[645]; Johnsgard (2010)[648]; Johnson *et al.* (1979)[651]; Kristiansen *et al.* (1999)[712]; Krueger (2004)[713]; Kuroda (1939)[718]; Leaflor *et al.* (1998)[738]; Lebeda & Ratti (1983)[739]; Leck (1967)[740]; MacInnes (1966)[791]; Marquardt (1961)[805]; Martin *et al.* (1982)[806]; McCarthy (2006)[817]; Millington & Gantlett (1999)[850]; Mlodinow *et al.* (2008)[860]; Morgan (2001)[876]; Moser & Rolley (1990)[882]; Mowbray *et al.* (2002)[887]; Ogilvie & Young (1998)[928]; Oreshnikova (1985)[931]; Owen *et al.* (1988)[942]; Paxinos *et al.* (2002)[953]; Palmer (1976)[945]; Pearce *et al.* (2000)[956]; Pierson *et al.* (2000)[989]; Pyle (2008)[1014]; Quinn *et al.* (1991)[1026]; Ratti & Timm (1979)[1046]; Ratti *et al.* (1977)[1047]; Rehfisch *et al.* (2006)[1062]; Richards (1999)[1069]; Rush *et al.* (1994)[1111]; Scribner *et al.* (2003)[1162]; Scribner *et al.* (2003)[1163]; Sheaffer *et al.* (2007)[1178]; Shields & Cotter (1998)[1181]; Shields & Wilson (1987)[1182]; Shields & Wilson (1987)[1183]; Sibley (1938)[1190]; Sibley (1994)[1194]; Sibley (2010)[1197]; Sorenson *et al.* (1999)[1227]; Talbot *et al.* (2003)[1255]; Tegelström & Sjöberg (1995)[1257]; USFWS (2011)[1292]; USFWS (2013)[1294]; US Geological Survey (2001)[1295]; Van Wagner & Baker (1986)[1312]; Van Wagner & Baker (1990)[1313]; Whitford (1987)[1352]; Whitford (1998)[1353]; Wilson (2005)[1362].

155. *B. c. canadensis*, adult (definitive basic). New Jersey, USA, Nov (Sébastien Reeber).

156. *B. c. canadensis*, adult (definitive basic); note head and bill shape compared to Cackling Goose *B. hutchinsii*. New York, USA, Nov (Sébastien Reeber).

157. *B. c. canadensis*, adult (definitive basic). New York, USA, Nov (Sébastien Reeber).

158. *B. c. interior*, adult (definitive basic). Hudson Bay, Canada, Jul (Philippe J. Dubois).

159. *B. c. interior*, adult (definitive basic). Hudson Bay, Canada, Jul (Philippe J. Dubois).

160. Adult (definitive basic); a rather dark bird recalling *fulva*, but head and bill shape could match *parvipes*. Idaho, USA, Dec (Bob Steele).

161. *B. c. moffitti/B. c. maxima*. California, USA, Nov (Sébastien Reeber).

162. *B. c. moffitti/B. c. maxima*, adult (definitive basic). California, USA, Apr (Sébastien Reeber).

163. *B. c. parvipes* (two left-hand birds), *B. c. moffitti/B. c. maxima* (two at rear) and *B. h. hutchinsii* (right). Colorado, USA, Dec (Steve Mlodinow).

164. *B. c. parvipes*, first-winter (formative); contrast between scapulars and wing-coverts indicates a first-winter bird. Colorado, USA, Jan (Steve Mlodinow).

165. *B. c. parvipes*, adult (definitive basic). Colorado, USA, Feb (Steve Mlodinow)

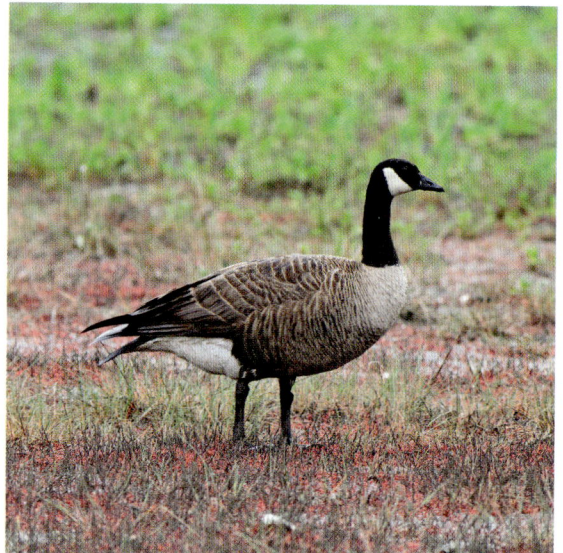

166. *B. c. occidentalis*, adult (definitive basic). Alaska, USA, Jun (Anders Blomdahl).

MUTE SWAN
Cygnus olor

Plate 18

TAXONOMY *Anas Olor* J. F. Gmelin, 1789, *Syst. Nat.*, 1, p. 502. The swans constitute the tribe Cygnini, in which Livezey[772] recognised two genera, *Coscoroba* and *Cygnus*, and three subgenera, of which two of the latter occur in the Holarctic: *Cygnus* (Mute Swan) and *Olor* (Trumpeter Swan *C. buccinator*, Tundra Swan *C. columbianus* and Whooper Swan *C. cygnus*). Relationships within this tribe are still debated[218].

No subspecies are recognised, but one colour morph known as the 'Polish morph', originally named *Cygnus immutabilis* Yarrell, 1838, and which is based on a form imported from coastal Poland to England. It is distinguished by the colour of immature plumages and the bare parts at all ages (see Plumages). This is an inherited mutation corresponding to leucism, encountered in all swans. It is very frequent in some populations of Mute Swan, especially where the species has been introduced, recently or not. Such populations descend from captive birds in which these characteristics were selected until the 19th century, in order to breed a domestic variant whose whiteness from an early age was more attractive. Currently, this form is common in all populations, but especially in Europe and North America[47,147,232,1360]. For example, in W France, the frequency of both morphs is almost equal: in a sample of 142 broods (1998–2013), 33 had only 'Polish' cygnets, 37 had cygnets only of the normal morph and 72 broods were mixed. A total of 391 chicks were of the 'Polish' morph and 377 normal.

IDENTIFICATION Easy to identify by its shape and colour of the bill. In Eurasia, its silhouette distinguishes the species from the other two by the much longer tail, pointed and upturned, more 'inflated' looking body and thick neck often held in a 'S' (straight and somewhat broken in Whooper Swan, slightly curved in Bewick's Swan). In flight, the tail projects well beyond the legs, while the reverse is true in other swans. The head profile differs significantly, with a knob on the bill in adult Mute Swan, whereas Whooper Swan has a flat forehead aligned with the culmen and Bewick's Swan a forehead/culmen that appear gently concave. The bill of Mute Swan is reddish-orange with a black base. In the other swans, the bill is bright yellow up to the eye, with a broad black tip. The coloration of the bill base also differs in the juvenile and immature, being black in Mute Swan, and pink-grey in the other two species. Also note that at these ages, Mute Swan is either white (Polish form) or variegated grey-brown and whitish. The young 'yellow-billed' swans are paler grey-brown, with less contrast. In North America, Mute Swan differs from the other two swans present by the same shape characters, including head profile. The coloration of the bill is also very useful, as Trumpeter and Whistling Swans have a largely to all-black bill. Also note that other Holarctic swans produce various trumpeting calls, which is not the case in Mute Swan. However, the latter produces a strong wing rustling in flight.

PLUMAGES Slight sexual dimorphism from second winter, especially in the breeding period. Complex basic strategy (one plumage by definitive cycle, two in the first cycle). Ageing possible (Polish morph) or easy (normal morph) until the first summer, and possible until the second summer for the normal form.

Adult

Definitive basic plumage (year-round). Plumage all white with head and neck often slightly tinged yellow or pale rusty ochre, depending on habitat. Top of head often little more strongly coloured. Iris pale brown. Bright orange to reddish bill with nail, nostrils, tomium and base black, the latter merging into bare black skin reaching the eye. The base of the culmen has a black knob, larger in ♂ and when breeding. Legs blackish in normal morph, greyish-pink in 'Polish' morph. Also note that during breeding, adult ♂ often holds his wings slightly raised, producing a typically 'inflated' shape, different from ♀ (and from both sexes in other species of swans).

Juvenile

First basic plumage (until Jan–Feb). Normal morph: grey-brown overall, with foreneck, breast and belly paler. Initially blackish bill, quickly becoming like adult, but without the black knob and olive-grey instead of orange. Legs dark grey. 'Polish' morph: all white (often dirtied pale brown) with legs and orange part of bill a dull, pale flesh-pink.

First-winter/first-summer

Formative plumage (Feb–Mar/Oct–Dec). Normal morph: variegated white and grey-brown, the latter especially on top of head, cheeks, neck, sides of breast, belly, rump, some scapulars, median coverts and tips of remiges. Nevertheless, there is considerable individual variation, especially depending on the extent of pre-formative moult. Feathering more extensive on top of bill (>50 mm) after second pre-basic moult[56]. Bill like adult but knob initially absent, and not fully developed until first summer. The orange tinge is replaced by grey-pink during first winter. Legs blackish. 'Polish' morph: all white, although the presence of two generations of feathers (juvenile ones can look dirtier) often easily distinguishes it from adult. Bill like adult but small or barely developed knob and orange replaced by dull pink. Legs pinkish.

Second-winter

Second basic plumage (Oct–Dec/Jun–Dec). Often a few juvenile feathers retained on head, neck and especially the rump, as well as among the upperwing-coverts. These differences may be visible in the normal morph, but much more difficult to detect in the 'Polish' morph. Possibly up to six juvenile rectrices retained, pale brown and very worn[56]. Bill often duller orange, knob less developed than in adult during at least second winter. See also Moult for distinguishing birds in second basic plumage from adult.

GEOGRAPHIC VARIATION None. The 'Polish' morph occurs spontaneously in all populations, albeit with a higher frequency among introduced birds in W & C Europe and North America.

MEASUREMENTS and MASS ♂ and adult slightly larger than ♀ and young, respectively. ♂: wing chord 580–623 (adult, 606, n=12) and 552–598 (juvenile, 582, n=4), bill 74–88 (adult, 80.6, n=12), tarsus 107–118 (114, n=12); ♀: wing chord 533–589 (adult, 562, n=10) and 540–572 (juvenile, 556, n=7), bill 69–79 (adult, 74.2, n=13), tarsus 99–114 (104, n=10)[267]. ♂ (n=52): bill 94–113 (103.5), knob depth 6–25 (13.7), knob length 16–34 (23.3), knob width 10–26 (14.8); ♀ (n=42): bill 92–118 (97.7), knob depth 4–20 (10.5), knob length 12–28 (19.7), knob width 7–22 (12.3)[232]. Bill depth at base (top of knob–gape) 44–49 (juvenile/first-winter/first-summer), 47–55 (second-winter, second-summer) and 53–63 (adult)[1014]. Adult ♂: mass 9,200–14,300 (winter, 11,800, n=59) and 10,600–13,500 (summer, 11,900, n=21); first-winter ♂/first-summer: mass 8,100–12,100 (winter, 9,700, n=159) and 9,300–13,500 (summer, 10,900, n=42); adult ♀: mass 7,600–10,600 (winter, 9,700, n=35) and 8,300–10,800 (summer, 9,600, n=6); 1st

winter ♀/first-summer: mass 5,500–9,500 (winter, 7800, n=221) and 6,400–9,700 (summer, 8,300, n=36)[1065].

VOICE The most frequent call is a *wee-rrrr* or *wiingrr-iew* with a high-pitched second syllable. Also an *in-rrr* and strong hissing in aggression (towards congeners, predators or humans). In flight, the wings produce a strong rustling sound, typical of the species.

MOULT Complex basic strategy. Pre-formative moult begins in Aug–Sep, is relatively slow and usually ends between Jan and Mar. It includes many feathers of the head, neck, breast, sides, mantle, back and scapulars. Number of feathers moulted elsewhere on the body lower. No rectrices and tertials replaced. Second and third pre-basic moults from May–Jun to Oct–Dec, complete or nearly so, starting with the wings at moulting sites (usually large waterbodies). A small number of body feathers, lesser coverts and up to six rectrices may be retained. Definitive pre-basic moult complete and slightly later, between Jun–Jul. and Nov–Jan. Within pairs with cygnets, ♀ often loses its flight feathers first, usually shortly after chicks hatch. ♂ loses its remiges later, while those of ♀ are already partially grown[301,1014]. However, this sequence can be reversed[56], permitting at least one adult to be able to fly at any time. Remiges shed simultaneously, leading to a 6–8-week flightless period.

HYBRIDISATION Rare in the wild, though cases occasionally reported with Whooper Swan. Cases involving Black Swan *Cygnus atratus* are mentioned more frequently in W Europe and where this species escapes from captivity or establishes feral populations. Such hybrids have also been reported in Australia and New Zealand, within the natural range of Black Swan[817] (see below). In nature, hybridisation also reported very rarely with Greylag Goose *Anser anser*, Canada Goose *Branta canadensis*[97,817] and recently with Trumpeter Swan. In captivity, it has been described with the following species: Swan Goose *Anser cygnoides*[817], Snow Goose *Chen caerulescens*[1190], Brent Goose *Branta bernicla*[639], Bewick's Swan[817], Tundra Swan[1190] and Black-necked Swan *C. melanocorypha*[817,1190].

Mute Swan × Black Swan. Unmistakable by its inter-mediate shape, often closer to Black Swan, however, with bill often held downwards, a straight neck and upperwing feathers (tertials included) slightly wrinkled. Bill usually dark pink to reddish with sometimes a slight bump on the culmen. The nail is pale or dusky. Overall coloration variegated and mottled grey, black and white, unlike any other swan.

Mute Swan × Whooper Swan. Plumage all white in adult, of course, but head profile and bill are intermediate. There is sometimes a flattened bump at the base of culmen. The colour of the bill is mostly variegated yellow, whitish, pink and black, and very recognisable. Yellow is mainly distributed towards the base, recalling Whooper Swan. The middle sides of the bill often show a whitish patch, variable in extent, and a pink patch is usually visible towards the tip, also variable in extent (sometimes just a faint band around the nail). Black lines often separate these areas. Tomium and nail black, as are the centre of the culmen and a thin line at the base of the bill.

HABITAT and LIFE-CYCLE Wild populations mainly use large lakes and wetlands in steppe regions or southern taiga and are largely migratory. Introduced populations are sedentary or short-distance migrants, and occur in various types of wetlands, lakes, ponds, marshes and slow-moving streams, often lined with reeds where the swans nest. Favours waters with much floating or submerged aquatic vegetation. Very territorial, and often very aggressive towards intruders, human or otherwise. Laying dates depend on latitude, mainly from Mar to May in Europe and early Apr to mid-May in North America[232,301]. Non-breeders form huge gatherings at moulting sites – usually large shallow lakes of fresh or brackish water, on which they often remain far from shore. In autumn and winter, inhabits a variety of wetlands, favouring lakes, shallow ponds and marshes, grasslands and flooded fields, estuaries and urban waterbodies, where they benefit from feeding. Also frequently uses vast farmlands and grasslands feeding in the manner of other swans. Also occurs frequently on eutrophic or dystrophic waters, such as wastewater treatment plant lagoons. In winter, often forms small flocks, but also larger gatherings.

RANGE and POPULATION Patchy distribution (see map). Introduced across much of Europe (frequently since the 16th century, but since as long ago as 1186 in UK), South Korea, Japan, Australia, New Zealand (19th century) and North America (coasts of NE USA and Great Lakes region during second half of the 19th century). Present in many cities elsewhere, especially urban parks, where can establish small populations, at least temporarily. Global population *c.*630,000 individuals: 290,000 in CN & W Europe, 45,000 around the Black Sea, 260,000–275,000 birds in C Asia, 1,000–3,000 in E Asia and *c.*23,000 in North America[648,757,1348]. The majority of these populations are increasing[301,1348].

CAPTIVITY Often held captive or left free, being easier to breed on small ponds than in mixed collections, where it can be very aggressive towards other large species. Therefore, very likely to be seen outside its normal range and even to breed locally.

REFERENCES Bacon (1980)[47]; Baker (1992)[56]; Bird Hybrids Database (2014)[97]; Birkhead & Perrins (1986)[147]; Callaghan *et al. in* Kear (2005)[218]; Ciaranca *et al.* (1997)[232]; Cramp & Simmons (1977)[268]; Delany *in* Kear (2005)[301]; Johnsgard (1960)[639]; Johnsgard (2010)[648]; Lever (1987)[751]; Li *et al.* (2009)[757]; Livezey (1996)[772]; McCarthy (2006)[817]; Pyle (2008)[1014]; Reynolds (1972)[1065]; Sibley (1938)[1190]; Wetlands International (2014)[1348]; Wilmore (1979)[1360].

167. Juveniles (first basic); note two coloration forms. France, Sep (Sébastien Reeber).

168. Adult (definitive basic); compared to other swans, note orange bill, with black knob at its base, and long tail. England, Feb (Sébastien Reeber).

169. First-winter (formative); typical mix of white and brownish feathers at this age. England, Feb (Sébastien Reeber).

170. Adult (definitive basic); note defence posture, with wings held 'inflated'. France, Apr (Sébastien Reeber).

171. First-winter (formative); more contrasting than other swans in same plumage. England, Feb (Sébastien Reeber).

TRUMPETER SWAN
Cygnus buccinator   **Plates 19, 20**

TAXONOMY *Cygnus buccinator* Richardson, 1832, *Fauna Boreali-Americana*, 2 (1831), p. 464. Belongs to the tribe Cygnini (see Mute Swan), within which it is closer to Whooper *C. cygnus* and Tundra Swans *C. columbianus*. Sometimes considered a subspecies of Whooper Swan[61], and it can be considered the Nearctic equivalent, as Tundra Swan is to Bewick's Swan, but whereas clinal variation shown by Tundra Swan in North America represents a continuation from that in Bewick's Swan in Eurasia, suggesting significant gene flow between them near the Bering Strait, this is not the case in Whooper and Trumpeter Swans. Monotypic (see Geographic Variation). There is a stable leucistic morph (see Plumages), equivalent to the 'Polish' morph of Mute Swan *C. olor*, of varying frequency, reaching 13% of cygnets in Yellowstone National Park[59], <2% in Minnesota and virtually zero elsewhere[824,857].

IDENTIFICATION North American species, easily distinguished from Mute Swan (which see) but much more difficult to separate from Tundra Swan. The recent expansion of Trumpeter Swan makes it now possible to occur where Tundra Swan regularly winters. Differences in shape and size, very important for distinguishing the two species, can be difficult to assess especially given little previous experience or with lone birds. Furthermore, there is overlap in all of the following features, and it is therefore better to base identification on application of several of them.

- *Head profile*: That of Trumpeter Swan is typically very long and prominent. From the side, the head forms an almost straight line from the tip of the bill to the rear crown, the nape being often distinctly angular. The whole is reminiscent of the profile of ♂ Canvasback *Aythya valisineria*[826]. Conversely, Tundra Swan has a usually slightly concave forehead/culmen profile (although some, probably ♂♂, have a massive bill with straight culmen[1214]) and a round head. Before the first winter, the bill shape is different, as it reaches adult thickness before achieving adult length. This gives it a shorter, thicker appearance with the culmen even appearing slightly bumped, affecting the overall head profile.

- *Bill length*: Longer in Trumpeter Swan than Tundra Swan, the distance between the distal edge of the nostril and the tip of the bill being generally >48 mm in the former and below this in the latter[1014]. Slight overlap was found for this feature by Limpert *et al.*[761], but still confirmed its usefulness. Note the relative position of the nostril on the bill: almost centred in Tundra Swan (between the gape and tip) but closer to the gape in Trumpeter Swan.

- *Bill base feathering*: Important, but sometimes difficult to assess. The black skin at the base of the bill forms a broad triangle pointing towards the eye in Trumpeter Swan, while this skin is narrower, often reduced to a thin line just before the eye in Tundra Swan. Whereas the eye seems encompassed by a black mask in Trumpeter Swan, it is more distinct in Tundra Swan[826]. Similarly, from the side, the delineation of the feathers between the eye and gape is almost straight in Trumpeter Swan yet visibly curved in Tundra Swan.

- *Bill coloration*: In most Tundra Swans (from 80–85%[1214] to 90%[1196]), a small yellow spot is visible in the dark of the bill near the eye. This spot is usually absent in Trumpeter Swan, except very occasionally. The bill of immature Trumpeter Swan (until first winter) is greyish-pink with a blackish base (the white morph has a much more pink or fleshy bill), while young Tundra Swan has an almost entirely pink bill, pale grey at the base.

- *Pink line at base of tomium*: Trumpeter Swan has a clear pinkish or orangey line along the tomium (more obvious at the base), due to the space between the two mandibles when the bill is closed. In Tundra Swan, this line is less marked or absent.

- *Forehead feathering*: Indicative but often difficult to assess. Front-on (when bird feeding on surface of the water or grazing), the feathering over the bill forms a rather sharp 'V' in Trumpeter Swan and more rounded 'U' in Tundra Swan. Feathers extend slightly more onto the bill in young birds, but the differences between the species is the same.

- *Bill nail*: From the front, the nail is more triangular in Trumpeter Swan (length 15–22 mm, width 16–20 mm), rounded in Tundra Swan (length 11–16 mm, width 12–17 mm)[1014]. This is especially useful in the hand, or under very good viewing conditions.

- **Size**: Trumpeter Swan is slightly larger than Mute Swan, whereas Tundra Swan is significantly smaller. In direct comparison, the two species should be relatively easy to distinguish, but this is not the case with lone birds. In direct comparison, the stretched neck appears distinctly longer in Trumpeter Swan, which is also slower when it walks or moves its neck when feeding on water.

- **Posture**: Usually very little difference[1196] but, like Whooper Swan, Trumpeter Swan generally has a more obvious 'break' on the lower neck, its top often being held straight, both on water or land. Tundra Swan often shows a more regularly curved neck. When feeding on land, Trumpeter Swan often lowers it[1196]. On the water and when relaxed, the base of the hindneck (i.e. its lowest point) is held at the surface of the water or even below the surface in Trumpeter Swan, while it is clearly held above the surface in Tundra Swan.

- **Plumage**: Adult white and can show a yellowish to pale rusty tinge, mostly on the neck and head, but more useful to separate birds in their first year of life. Juvenile Trumpeter Swan is slightly darker and more contrasting, the feathers of upperparts, head and neck being a stronger grey than Tundra Swan. Furthermore, first-winter Trumpeter Swan has grey upperparts, whereas they are noticeably whiter in Tundra Swan between Nov and Jan at least (the neck and head often still grey at this time). In Trumpeter Swan, the formative feathers grown between Oct and Jan are grey, while those acquired between Jan and Mar are white[857,1014]. Most young Tundra Swans have moulted their scapulars by mid-Jan, and appear largely white at this time[1196].

- **Legs**: In direct comparison, the tarsi appear thicker and more robust in Trumpeter Swan. The legs are slightly darker in young Tundra Swans in first autumn/winter but become black in both species soon after.

- **Flight**: Trumpeter Swan is large with a longer neck in direct comparison, and shows an angle between the breast and belly, while the breast/belly line is flatter in Tundra Swan. The 'bump' formed at the base of the neck in certain positions in Trumpeter Swan is also visible in flight. Also note the thicker neck of rather constant thickness. Tundra Swan generally shows a straighter and thinner neck, especially just below the head.

- **Voice**: Calls of the two species differ markedly.

Trumpeter Swan utters, as its name suggests, nasal low-pitched calls recalling a honk or a toy-trumpet: *hunk* or *hoo-onk*. Tundra Swan emits higher pitched, rather barked, more musical calls, e.g., *kiew* more reminiscent of Sandhill Cranes *Grus canadensis* heard from afar.

PLUMAGES Sexes identical, ♀ nevertheless slightly smaller and lighter than ♂, albeit with much overlap. These differences are often noticeable within pairs, but useless on lone birds. Head of ♀ seems on average slightly finer. Complex basic moult strategy (one plumage per definitive cycle, two in the first cycle). Ageing relatively easy until the middle of the first winter and possible until second winter.

Adult

Definitive basic plumage (year-round). All white with head and neck often slightly tinged yellow or pale rusty, depending on concentration of iron in the water. Rarely, scapulars and humeral coverts and/or secondaries have grey shaft-streaks[1014], perhaps also linked to immaturity. Iris dark brown. Bill and area towards black eye sometimes with a small diffuse pale or whitish spot, just in front of the eye. The inside of the lower mandible is pink and usually visible in the form of a pink streak between the mandibles. Legs blackish or black, but pale yellowish to olive in the leucistic morph.

Juvenile

First basic plumage (until Jan–Mar). Plumage pale greyish, darker on head and neck, upperparts, tail, tertials and inner median coverts , whitish or very pale grey on breast, underparts, back and rest of the upperwing, white on remiges (except grey-brown tips). Bill pale flesh-pink with black nail and around the nostrils. Skin at base of bill variably stained dark grey. Legs dull pink. Cygnets of leucistic form are white, with yellowish legs and a completely pale pink bill[906].

First-winter/first-summer

Formative plumage (Jan–Mar/Nov–Jan). Similar to juvenile, but some formative feathers whitish or white especially on upperparts, head and neck. Most of the juvenile feathers of the wing, rump and rectrices retained. The bill gains its adult colour at 12–16 months[59]. The legs usually acquire their adult colour during the second calendar year, many birds in formative plumage having a clear olive or yellowish hue. The leucistic form is largely white, with bill more clearly marked pink in winter, and pale dull yellowish legs.

Second-winter

Second basic plumage (Nov–Jan/Nov–Jan). Second pre-basic moult can be near-complete, individuals then being identical to adult. When moult is partial, juvenile or formative feathers remain visible mainly on the rump, among the upperwing-coverts and/or rectrices. These feathers are by now very worn and bleached, and easily overlooked even in the hand. The bill is like that of adult but pale pinkish spots or patches are visible on the sides until Dec[1014]. Similarly, the legs can be tinged yellowish or olive until the second winter.

GEOGRAPHIC VARIATION Small differences in measurements (tarsus length and middle toe) reported among populations, those in Alaska being largest. However, it appears that these differences are insufficient to justify subspecific status, and may even reflect methodological bias[323]. At a genetic level, comparisons between three populations (Alaska, Canada and Montana) revealed only weak differences[70]. A more recent study found slight differences between the Pacific population and those in the Rockies (including Montana and Canada), but found that intraspecific differences in mitochondrial DNA were much lower than in most Anseriformes, probably due to past bottlenecks in both populations[70,944].

MEASUREMENTS and MASS ♂ and adult slightly larger than ♀ and young, respectively. ♂: wing chord 545–680 (adult, 618.6, n=5)[1056], bill 108.9–131 (adult, 120.4, n=13) and 109.8–132.8 (adult, 117.6, n=8)[501], tarsus 105–160 (119, n=13)[501], mass in winter 9,100–14,500 (adult, 11,900, n=152)[323]; ♀: wing chord 604–636 (adult, 623.3, n=3)[1056], bill 108–127 (adult, 116, n=12) and 99.9–116.9 (adult, 109.7, n=7)[501], tarsus 107–152.5 (119.6, n=12)[501], mass in winter 7,000–12,500 (adult, 10,300, n=120)[323].

VOICE Various typical calls reflected in both the species' scientific and English names, *hoo-onk* or *hoo-wor*, trumpeting or honking, rather soft and low-pitched, or *oh-oh*, which is less audible. Young until first winter give higher *hunk*, recalling a toy-trumpet. All calls are harsher and lower than those of Tundra Swan, which is more loquacious.

MOULT Complex basic strategy. Pre-formative moult begins in Aug–Oct and ends Jan–Mar[1014]. It includes a variable number of body feathers, at most a few lesser coverts, but neither rectrices nor remiges. Formative feathers are either grey or white[1014]. Second pre-basic

moult occurs from May to Nov–Jan, and is complete with the exception of sometimes a few body feathers, upperwing-coverts and/or rectrices. This moult is nevertheless usually more complete during the second calendar year than thereafter (after definitive pre-basic moult, c.75% of the adults retain some body feathers and up to six rectrices of the previous generation). Definitive pre-basic moult is thus complete or almost so, and takes place slightly later, from Jun to Nov–Jan in ♀♀ and a month later in ♂♂[1014] in the Rockies, but the reverse in Alaska[857].

HYBRIDISATION Has rarely occurred in captivity with Tundra Swan[856,1190], and it is probable that such birds would be difficult to detect in the wild, although some well-documented individuals[98] appear clearly intermediate. In captivity, hybridisation also reported with Canada Goose *Branta canadensis*[1190], Whooper and Mute Swans[97,817,1190]. Recently, natural hybrids involving the latter have been reported in NW USA.

HABITAT and LIFE-CYCLE Migratory behaviour and egg-laying schedules vary by population, latitude and thaw of favoured wetlands. Most eggs are laid between mid-May and late Jun[857], but up to one month earlier in south of range[1056]. Inhabits various types of permanent freshwater wetlands for breeding, preferring lakes and shallow ponds, large enough to permit take-off, with ample submerged vegetation (waters neither too acidic nor too eutrophic) and nest sites (islands, vegetation mounds, Beaver *Castor canadensis* or Muskrat *Ondatra zibethicus* lodges)[412,857,1056]. Usually breeds for the first time at age of 4–7 years[412]. Can be sensitive to human disturbance. Both parents remain with cygnets and undertake asynchronous moult, the first adult losing its remiges soon after hatching (see Moult). Pacific populations migrate mostly to the coast, where they use various types of wetlands including estuaries and brackish lagoons. Inland populations breeding in regions where waterbodies freeze in winter migrate short distances (up to 700–1,000 km[857]) to regions with similar habitats (streams, hot springs, etc.) that remain ice-free. Post-breeding migration occurs between early Oct and mid-Nov[857].

RANGE and POPULATION Once widespread in North America, its numbers were greatly reduced by harvesting for its skin and feathers. By 1935 just 69 individuals were known, but the major populations of Alaska and W Canada remained to be discovered[881]. Numbers have greatly increased since, due to several conservation programmes, habitat restoration schemes and hunting regulations. In 2005, the global population was estimated at 34,803 birds[881] or 46,225 individuals, of which 11,976 were first-year birds, in 2010[1260]. Nowadays, its range includes *c.*30 distinct breeding populations, some of them restored or introduced. The bulk of the world population breeds between Alaska and W Canada (26,790 birds including 6,011 first-years in 2010[1260]), wintering on the coasts from S Alaska to NE Washington. The Rockies population extends from W Canada to Yellowstone Park (Wyoming, Montana, Idaho) and numbered 9,626 birds, 3,310 of them first-years, in 2010[1260]. Further east to the Great Lakes, inland populations from reintroduction programmes totalled *c.*9,809 birds, including 2,655 first-years, in 2010[1260]. Accidental in Japan and Chukotka (Russia).

CAPTIVITY Rarely held in captivity, especially in Eurasia (a few hundreds in Europe). North American observations outside the breeding range are generally regarded as concerning genuine vagrants, especially as the species is currently expanding its range.

REFERENCES Banko (1960)[59]; Banko & Schorger (1976)[61]; Barrett & Vyse (1982)[70]; Bird Hybrids Database (2014)[97]; Bird Hybrids Flickr forum (2014)[98]; Drewien & Bouffard (1994)[323]; Gale *et al.* (1987)[412]; Hansen *et al.* (1971)[501]; Johnsgard (2010)[648]; Kraft (1991)[707]; Limpert *et al.* (1987)[761]; McCarthy (2006)[817]; McEneaney (2005)[824]; McGowan (2001)[826]; Mitchell (1994)[856]; Mitchell & Eichholz (2010)[857]; Moser (2006)[881]; Nelson (1993)[906]; Oyler-McCance *et al.* (2007)[944]; Pyle (2008)[1014]; Rees *in* Kear (2005)[1056]; Sibley (1938)[1190]; Sibley (2010)[1196]; Snowden (1987)[1214]; Trumpeter Swan Society (2014)[1260].

172. Adult (definitive basic); note the long neck, often held gently curved. Wyoming, USA, Jul (Joe Fischer).

173. Adult (definitive basic); the black base to the bill is typically the same width as the eye just behind it (narrower than eye in Tundra Swan *C. c. columbianus*). Minnesota, USA, Nov (Yann Kolbeinsson).

174. Juvenile (first basic); note blackish base to bill and yellowish legs. British Columbia, Canada, Nov (Alan D. Wilson).

175. Adult (definitive basic); bill usually all black with pinkish stripe on tomium, and also note straight delineation of feathering between eye and gape. Minnesota, USA, Nov (Yann Kolbeinsson).

176. Adult (definitive basic); forehead feathering is usually V-shaped (U-shaped in Tundra Swan *C. c. columbianus*), but this is variable. Wyoming, USA, Jul (Joe Fischer).

177. Adult (definitive basic); in flight (upper left) with a Tundra Swan *C. c. columbianus* (middle) and an unidentified swan, perhaps a hybrid (right). Colorado, USA, Apr (Steve Mlodinow).

TUNDRA SWAN
Cygnus columbianus

TAXONOMY *Anas Columbianus* Ord, 1815, *in* Guthrie's Geography, Amer. Ed. 2, p. 319. See Taxonomy under Mute Swan *C. olor* for information on the tribe Cygnini. Tundra Swan is the North American equivalent of Bewick's Swan *C. bewickii* Yarrell, 1830. These two were initially considered separate species, then as conspecifics during the 20th century. More recently, some authors have split them again[417,688,1131,1134,1232]. Nevertheless, there appear to be no genetic data demonstrating two distinct monophyletic groups or how much they differ. In addition, E Asian birds, sometimes considered a separate subspecies *C. c. jankowskyi* Alphéraky, 1904, appear intermediate between Tundra and Bewick's Swan, albeit closer to the latter. This suggests the existence of clinal variation across the Holarctic[696,949], although there is a clear gap at the Bering Sea. Finally, it should be mentioned that the two taxa are now sympatric in E Siberia, with reported hybridisation, at an unspecified frequency[182,844,1250]. All this suggests that unless further genetic studies show the opposite, it is best to consider the two taxa conspecific, which position is adopted by most taxonomic committees for now[20,1134]. The nominate form of Tundra Swan *C. c. columbianus* was formerly known as Whistling Swan.

IDENTIFICATION Separating Tundra and Bewick Swans is discussed in Geographic Variation. In North America, Tundra Swan can be difficult to distinguish from Trumpeter Swan *C. buccinator*, which is larger, with a longer and generally all-black bill (see that species). In Eurasia, Bewick's Swan can be mistaken for Whooper Swan *C. cygnus*, which is also larger, with a longer bill and more yellow on it (see Whooper Swan).

PLUMAGES Nominate subspecies. Sexes similar except slight differences in size (see Measurements and Mass) and posture, which can often be noticed within pairs. Complex basic moult strategy (one plumage per definitive cycle, two in the first cycle). Ageing easy until the beginning of the first winter, but requires more attention to the first summer and is still possible in some cases until second winter.

Adult

Definitive basic plumage (year-round). White plumage, sometimes tinged yellow or pale rusty (particularly on the head and neck), in relation to iron concentration in the water. Some birds show grey shaft-streaks on the scapulars, upperwing-coverts and/or secondaries[1014], perhaps related to immaturity. Iris dark brown. Bill and skin before eye black, with a yellow spot just in front of the eye, whose length is 0–16% of total bill length[1014]. This spot varies in extent, reduced to a small whitish or yellowish oval patch in 80% of adults, absent in 10% of them and more extensive in the remaining 10%[1196]. In the latter, the patch extends as yellow stains, more or less clearly defined, mainly at the base of the bill. The distance between the tip of the yellow spot and the proximal edge of the nostril is nearly always >25 mm[1014]. Birds in the east of the continent seem to show a smaller yellow spot on average than in the west[1155]. The pale or pinkish streak at the base of the bill, between the mandibles, is less marked than in Trumpeter Swan and often absent. When visible, it is often due to the fact that the bird opens its bill slightly. Legs blackish to black, or dull yellow to orangey in leucistic individuals of both subspecies[375,499,841], which are much rarer than in Mute Swan or Trumpeter Swan.

Juvenile

First basic plumage (until Jan–Mar). Pale grey-brown overall, darker on head and neck, upperparts, tail, tertials and inner median coverts, and pale grey to white on the breast, underparts, back and rest of the upperwing. Bill and skin at its base almost entirely pink to pale grey-pink, with nail and area around the nostrils blackish. Legs initially dull grey-pink, becoming dark grey and black during first winter.

First-winter/first-summer

Formative plumage (Jan–Mar/Nov–Jan). Most juvenile feathers grey, gradually replaced between Oct and Mar by white or whitish feathers. The remaining juvenile feathers (most wing and rump feathers as well as rectrices) are bleached by early spring. The bill becomes grey and black during the first winter, and achieves adult colours during first summer; the yellow spot in front of the eye is initially whitish and poorly defined, and is the last part to gain its adult colour. The feathers of the forehead extend further onto the culmen (distance between eye and tip of feathering >35 mm, vs. <35 mm in ad[1014]). The legs darken during the first winter and are like those of adult by end of first summer.

Second-winter

Second basic plumage (Nov–Jan/Nov–Jan). Before the end of the second pre-basic moult, some grey-brown juvenile feathers (very worn) are usually still visible (under good conditions), mainly on the rump, among the upperwing-coverts and rectrices. Until the second winter, the largely black bill can nevertheless show some diffuse pinkish-grey stains. By the end of the second pre-basic moult, the majority of birds cannot be distinguished from adult.

GEOGRAPHIC VARIATION There is significant variation in bill colour, partly inherited[75] and noticeable variation in measurements. European wintering birds (*C. c. bewickii*) are smallest, have the smallest and thinnest bills, with more yellow. In contrast, North American birds (*C. c. columbianus*) are largest, with a strong, almost all-black bill. On average, the yellow spot in front of the eye is smaller or more frequently absent in the east than in W North America, with the exception of the Aleutians, where this spot is also reduced[1155]. In Asia, wintering birds (sometimes attributed to *C. c. jankowskyi*) are on average smaller than *columbianus* but larger than 'European' *bewickii*, with more black on the bill (including culmen) than the latter. These birds could suggest clinal variation from Siberia to E North America, or indicate increasing intergradation between the two taxa in far E Russia[1196]. The existence of intermediates makes identification in W North America and E Asia trickier, but these individuals are much rarer elsewhere. In fact, there is actually very little overlap in bill coloration between populations wintering in C & E North America and those wintering in Europe.

C. c. bewickii. Differs from Tundra Swan mainly in bill coloration. In adult, its base and the skin that reaches the eye is largely bright yellow, with a highly variable pattern between individuals, which locally may even permit individual identification[373]. The yellow extends 22–42% of the bill length (0–16% in Tundra Swan). The distance between the tip of the yellow patch and the proximal edge of the nostril is at most 25 mm[1014], but the yellow can also include most of the nostril. Variability of the yellow and black pattern has resulted in a classification into three types: those with yellow covering the entire culmen ('yellowneb'), those with black covering the entire culmen ('darky') and those with a black pattern more or less continuous on the culmen

or an isolated yellow spot in the culmen ('pennyface' or 'diamond-type')[373,1155,1160]. Based on this typology, the type with most yellow ('yellowneb') is represented by 63% of individuals at Slimbridge, UK (*n*=2,400) and 51% in Japan (*n*=312), the medium type ('pennyface') comprises 19.1% of individuals at Slimbridge and 13.1% in Japan, while the type with a black culmen ('darky') constitutes 17.9% of individuals at Slimbridge and 35.9% in Japan[376,1155]. Similarly, Knapton[696] indicated that individuals with the culmen largely or partially black are dominant among Bewick's Swans reported occasionally in North America (from E Russia). Note also that yellow may extend over all or part of the orbital ring. Bewick's Swan also has a variably extensive area of yellow under the lower mandible, not shown by Tundra Swan. Juvenile of both subspecies have fairly identical bills, but their coloration reveals what will be the extent of the yellow patch by the early first winter.

Other differences between *columbianus* and *bewickii* mainly lie in measurements (see below), the former being larger on average (all biometrics), albeit with much overlap. In particular, the bill is longer and thicker at the base in Tundra Swan, with a straighter culmen (often clearly concave in Bewick's). Mixed breeding pairs have been reported for several decades in E Asia[376,701,844] and the range of sympatry has recently expanded[895,1250]. Resultant bill colorations have been described as intermediate[896].

MEASUREMENTS and MASS ♂ and adult slightly larger than ♀ and young, respectively.

C. c. columbianus (in winter, Maryland and North Carolina[761]). ♂: bill 103.7 ± 5.2 (adult, *n*=305) and 88.4 ± 7.1 (juvenile/first-winter, *n*=34), distance distal edge of nostril–tip 44.6 ± 2.8 (adult, *n*=305) and 43.3 ± 2.5 (juvenile/first-winter, *n*=34), tarsus 115.7 ± 6.6 (adult, *n*=290) and 113.7 ± 4.0 (juvenile/first-winter, *n*=33), mass 7,200 ± 800 (adult, *n*=1447) and 6,100 ± 900 (juvenile/first-winter, *n*=299); ♀: bill 101.1 ± 5.1 (adult, *n*=164) and 89.1 ± 7.5 (juvenile/first-winter, *n*=38), distance distal edge of nostril–tip 43.4 ± 2.7 (adult, *n*=164) and 43.0 ± 2.3 (juvenile/first-winter, *n*=38), tarsus 110.3 ± 5.9 (adult, *n*=160) and 111.3 ± 6.4 (juvenile/first-winter, *n*=37), mass 6,300 ± 700 (adult, *n*=1,290) and 5,600 ± 800 (juvenile/first-winter, *n*=403). ♂: wing chord 501–569 (538.0, *n*=8), tail 162–181 (170.8, *n*=8); ♀: wing chord 505–561 (531.6, *n*=15), tail 146–186 (165.3, *n*=15)[945]. ♂ (*n*=100): wing chord 511–574 (adult) and 493–556 (juvenile), culmen 92–120, bill depth at distal edge of nostril 41.9–51.7, tail 155–190, tarsus 101–124; ♂ (*n*=100): wing chord 483–556 (adult) and 467–539 (juvenile), culmen 87–116, bill depth at distal edge of nostril 39.6–49.6, tail 149–183, tarsus 96–119[1014]; compared with data given by Pyle[1014] for *C. c. bewickii*.

C. c. bewickii (winter, UK). ♂: wing chord 480–570 (adult, 529.0, *n*=152) and 468–538 (juvenile, 500, *n*=69), tarsus 93–119 (106.6, *n*=111), mass 4,536–8,391 (6,380, *n*=211); ♀: wing chord 474–542 (509.0, *n*=133) and 445–525 (juvenile, 482, *n*=65), tarsus 87–113 (102.4, *n*=110), mass 4,300–7,825 (5,642, *n*=189)[374]. ♂ (*n*=100): wing chord 489–561 (adult) and 469–538 (juvenile), culmen 82–105, bill depth at distal edge of nostril 36.0–45.1, tail 132–166, tarsus 90–117; ♀ (*n*=100): wing chord 468–544 (adult) and 444–521 (juvenile), culmen 78–101, bill depth at distal edge of nostril: 33.8–42.8, tail 126–160, tarsus 86–113[1014].

VOICE Tundra Swan emits high-pitched, barked and resonant calls, e.g. *kyoo*, *oo-wooo* and sometimes a tri-syllabic *hoo-woo-woo*, like distant Sandhill Cranes *Grus canadensis* in chorus. Many variations of these sounds, including softer social calls or low chattering *ouh* or *trrou*. Juvenile and immature (until first winter at least) calls are higher-pitched, more hissing or wheezy. Few differences described in the literature between the two subspecies, but, in captivity, it has been stated that they can sound different to an expert ear[166]. See Identification of Whooper and Trumpeter Swans for differences from those species.

MOULT Complex basic strategy. Pre-formative moult between Aug–Oct and Jan–Mar, begins with the head and neck, then mantle and scapulars, breast and flanks until Jan, possibly some inner upperwing-coverts. Replacement of some tertials and rectrices reported in Bewick's Swan[56,267] but not in Tundra Swan[1014]. Second pre-basic moult occurs from May–Jul to Nov–Jan[945], is complete, with the exception of at most a few body feathers, upperwing-coverts and /or rectrices. Definitive pre-basic moult occurs from Jun–Jul to Dec[56,1014], but seems to continue at a slower pace until Mar at least[265]. It is reported that the two adults moult simultaneously[56], or *c.*1 month later in ♂ like other swans[60,1014,1360]. Other sources indicate that ♂♂ start their pre-basic moult just three days after ♀♀[342].

HYBRIDISATION Natural mixed pairs or hybrids reported very occasionally between Tundra Swan and Whooper Swan[817,1190] and it is probable that hybridisation sometimes occurs with Trumpeter Swan. Hybrids resulting from the latter cross would be very difficult to detect under field conditions. In captivity, Bewick's Swan has bred with Whooper and Mute Swans[817], while Tundra Swan has bred with Black Swan *C. atratus*, Greylag Goose *Anser anser* and Canada Goose *Branta canadensis*[1190].

HABITAT and LIFE-CYCLE Arctic and subarctic breeder, exclusively migratory, which spends *c.*6 months per year at stop-over sites[265,760]. In spring, return migration occurs from mid-Feb to late May, most arriving near their breeding grounds during the latter month. Eggs are laid soon after arrival, between mid-May and early Jul[166,760] depending on snow and ice melt. Uses riverbanks, lakes, large ponds and waterbodies in the Arctic tundra, mainly in low-lying coastal plains and large deltas. Rarer further south near wooded tundra. Occurs in lone, territorial pairs, constructing their nest on hummocks, islets or mounds of vegetation (often visible from afar). Both parents remain with cygnets and begin wing moult soon after chicks hatch. Non-breeders (estimated at 67–72% of European population[166]) gather at large shallow waterbodies and wetlands. Post-breeding migration starts soon after fledging, with a succession of long stop-overs. On southernmost wintering grounds, numbers peak between early Dec and mid-Feb. During migration and winter, uses large wetlands (estuaries, deltas, lakes, etc.), with abundant submerged aquatic vegetation or near agricultural land for feeding. Usually forms large flocks, with for example 90% of European winterers concentrated at fewer than 15 sites[83]. Young remain with their parents throughout the winter and leave them during the spring migration. However, they may join their parents regularly each winter up to their fifth [166].

RANGE and POPULATION Breeds in the Arctic tundra from the White Sea, Russia, east to NW Quebec and S Baffin I, Canada. In winter, concentrated in four relatively small areas: NW Europe, E Asia, and on west and east coasts of the USA.

C. c. columbianus. Breeds in the Canadian Arctic tundra west to the Chukchi Peninsula, where it seems to have expanded west during recent decades[701]. Winters mainly on both American coasts, the breeding populations of W Alaska wintering on the Pacific coast and those breeding in N Alaska and Canada on the Atlantic coast. Rare or occasional visitor elsewhere in the USA and N Mexico. Rare but regular in Japan. Accidental in Greater Antilles, Hawaii and UK. The Pacific population fluctuates, being stable or slightly increasing, and was estimated at 117,200 birds in 2012 and 75,300 in 2013. The Atlantic population numbered 107,100 in 2013 and 111,700 in 2012, and was stable over the previous decade[1294].

C. c. bewickii. Breeds in Russian Arctic tundra from the Kanin Peninsula to Kolyuchinskaya Bay, near the Chukchi Peninsula[701]. Birds breeding east of the mouth of the Lena winter in E Asia, where numbers in 2007 were estimated at 92,000–110,000 birds[221] with 100,000 (80,000 in China)[757]. Western breeders winter in W Europe. This population was estimated at 21,500 birds[1348], in slight decline from a peak of 29,000 birds in mid-1990[82]. A third population winters around the Black Sea, Caspian Sea and Aral Sea, numbers 1,000 birds[1250] and is declining, at least locally[166]. Rare or occasional visitor over much of Palearctic and to the Aleutians, with some records (including intermediates with *bewickii*) in the USA, from Alaska to California and Alberta, Canada[760], as well as Hawaii[648].

CAPTIVITY Rarely kept in captivity outside a few specialised collections, and said to be quite difficult to breed. Thus rather unlikely to escape, although it is often considered that birds seen in North America east to the Rockies are escapes from captivity[760].

REFERENCES AOU (1983)[20]; Baker (1992)[56]; Banko & Mackay (1964)[60]; Bateson *et al.* (1980)[75]; Beekman (1997)[82]; Beekman *et al.* (1994)[83]; Bowler *in* Kear (2005)[166]; Brazil (2009)[182]; Cao *et al.* (2008)[221]; Craigie & Petrie (2003)[265]; Cramp & Simmons (1977)[268]; Earnst (1992)[342]; Evans (1977)[373]; Evans & Kear (1978)[374]; Evans & LeBret (1973)[375]; Evans & Sladen (1980)[376]; Gantlett *et al.* (1996)[417]; Hanby (1986)[499]; Hayashi (1982)[541]; Johnsgard (2010)[648]; King (1997)[688]; Knapton (2000)[696]; Kondratiev (1991)[701]; Li *et al.* (2009)[757]; Limpert & Earnst (1994)[760]; Limpert *et al.* (1987)[761]; Livezey (1996)[772]; McCarthy (2006)[817]; Merne & Walsh (1991)[841]; Mikami (1989)[844]; Murase (1992)[895]; Murase (1994)[896]; Palmer (1976)[945]; Patten & Heindel (1994)[949]; Pyle (2008)[1014]; Rees (2010)[1058]; Sangster *et al.* (1997)[1131]; Sangster *et al.* (2004)[1134]; Scott (1981)[1155]; Sibley (1938)[1190]; Sibley (2010)[1196]; Stepanyan (1990)[1232]; Syroechkovski (2002)[1250]; USFWS (2013)[1294]; Wetlands International (2014)[1348]; Wilmore (1979)[1361].

178. *C. c. bewickii*, adult (definitive basic); in flight, neck appears distinctly thin when stretched. England, Feb (Sébastien Reeber).

179. *C. c. bewickii*, adult (definitive basic); from Whooper Swan *C. cygnus* by more 'gentle' shape, neck gently curved and bill pattern. England, Feb (Sébastien Reeber).

180. *C. c. bewickii*, adult (definitive basic) and Whooper Swan *C. cygnus* (left); note differences in size and shape between them; both Bewick's and Tundra Swans *C. c. columbianus* often hold the bill slightly upwards in alert posture. England, Feb (Sébastien Reeber).

181. *C. c. bewickii*, first-winter (formative). England, Feb (Sébastien Reeber).

182. *C. c. bewickii*, first-winter (formative); bill shows 'ghost' of adult coloration, whereas at same age, Whooper Swan *C. cygnus* usually has a more adult-like bill. England, Feb (Sébastien Reeber).

183. *C. c. bewickii*, adult (definitive basic); compared to Whooper Swan *C. cygnus*, yellow patch usually does not reach nostrils. England, Feb (Sébastien Reeber).

184. *C. c. bewickii*, adult (definitive basic); upper culmen mostly yellow, known as the 'yellowneb' variant. England, Feb (Sébastien Reeber).

185. *C. c. bewickii*, adult (definitive basic); upper culmen with yellow patch, known as the 'pennyface' or 'diamond-shape' variant. England, Feb (Sébastien Reeber).

186. *C. c. bewickii*, adult (definitive basic); upper culmen mostly black, known as the 'darky' variant. England, Feb (Sébastien Reeber)

188. *C. c. columbianus*, first-summer (formative); note brown traces on upperwing at this age. Alaska, USA, Jun (William Price).

187. *C. c. columbianus*, adult (definitive basic). Alaska, USA, Jun (William Price).

189. *C. c. columbianus*, adult (definitive basic), with comparatively extensive yellow on bill; note rounded limit of feathers at base of bill. California, USA, Jan (Tom Grey).

190. *C. c. columbianus*, adult (definitive basic), with typical bill pattern; the black base typically narrows just in front of the eye (vs. Trumpeter Swan). Texas, USA, Feb (Greg Lavaty).

191. *C. c. columbianus*, adult (definitive basic); note variation in extent of yellow patch on bill. Alaska, USA, Jun (Tom Grey).

192. *C. c. columbianus*, adult (definitive basic). Alaska, USA, Jun (Tom Grey)

WHOOPER SWAN
Cygnus cygnus

Plates 19, 20

TAXONOMY *Anas Cygnus* Linnaeus, 1758, *Syst. Nat.*, edn. 10, p. 122. See Mute Swan *C. olor* for organisation of the tribe Cygnini. In the past, sometimes considered conspecific with Trumpeter Swan *C. buccinator*[61,257,644], and even with Tundra Swan *C. columbianus*[794]. Nowadays considered a monotypic species, although there is clinal variation in size and bill colour (see Geographic Variation), which led to Icelandic birds being described subspecifically, *C. c. islandicus* C. L. Brehm, 1831, but overlap with birds of Fennoscandia makes its validity questionable[1059].

IDENTIFICATION Superficially similar to all other Holarctic Swans by its white (adult) or pale grey-brown (juvenile) plumage, easily distinguished from Mute Swan (which see). Among the other Holarctic swans, Whooper shows most yellow on the bill, which is sufficient to distinguish it from Trumpeter Swan and nominate Tundra Swan, both of which do not overlap with the present species, and they are rarely seen together. Identification issues mostly concern Bewick's Swan *C. columbianus bewickii*, which is widely sympatric with Whooper Swan in Eurasia. The features distinguishing the two species are in many respects similar to those separating Trumpeter Swan and nominate Tundra Swan (see Identification under Trumpeter Swan).

- *Size*: Much larger than Bewick's Swan with little overlap in most biometrics (see Measurements and Mass). Differences are often obvious in direct comparison, but size can be difficult to assess on lone birds. However, both species are often seen with Mute Swan, which is useful for comparison: Whooper is similar in overall size, with a noticeably longer neck, while Bewick's seems significantly smaller, with a shorter neck and head/bill.

- *Shape and posture*: Whooper Swan always seems larger, with a longer thicker neck, held upright with a prominent breast. When held vertical, the neck marks a clear break at its junction with the body. Bewick's Swan seems smaller, with more gentle proportions, suggesting a goose. Its neck is often held gently curved. When swimming or resting on water, the bill of Whooper is often held somewhat downwards, while it is usually held horizontally by Bewick's.

- *Head shape*: Whooper Swan has the head and bill very long, with the line formed by the crown, forehead and culmen being almost straight, without a break. The nape often forms an angle from the side. The nape of Bewick's Swan is more rounded, the head can appear proportionately larger, the bill shorter with a slightly concave culmen/forehead profile.

- *Bill coloration*: Bill and facial skin bright yellow and black in adult of both species. Overall, the yellow is more extensive in Whooper Swan, so that, at a distance, it shows more yellow than black, while the reverse is true in Bewick's Swan. In Whooper, the yellow extends from the periphery of the eye (often), on the culmen (not always) and base of the lower mandible, and tapers to a point under the nostril or just beyond its distal edge. The bill of Bewick's is more variable, but the yellow patch is almost always rounded at the distal tip, and rarely reaches the proximal edge of the nostril or exceptionally its centre. In young, the bill is initially pinkish, more or less tinged pale greyish, the adult pattern gradually becoming apparent during first winter. However, the black and yellow are on average acquired faster by young Whooper, in which they are often close to the adult (albeit pale yellow) from the middle of the first winter. At the same time, most Bewick's still show a pale greyish, pink and dark grey bill.

- *Plumage coloration*: Adult of both species has white plumage, often tinged yellowish or rusty on head and neck, which is more common in Whooper Swan. Juvenile of both species variegated pale grey-brown and whitish, but less than Mute Swan, which is darker. Young Whooper is usually slightly darker and more contrasting than Bewick's. From midwinter, the replacement of certain juvenile feathers and the fading or bleaching of the rest give young birds a very pale appearance.

- *Flight*: Whooper Swan has a very long neck accentuated by the rather thin head and bill, and a more prominent breast. Its wingbeats are slightly heavier and slower than Bewick's Swan.

- *Voice*: Both species are very loquacious, in flight and on the ground, and calls are useful for identification. Whooper Swan typically emits a soft *woop* or *oh-oop* mono- or disyllabic, often repeated, as well as several honking or hoarse sounds, reminiscent of those of large domestic geese or a toy trumpet. The calls of Bewick's Swan are clearly softer, higher pitched, more hooting, and more musical. They are easily distinguished in flight by call with a little experience.

PLUMAGES Sexes similar, with some slight differences in size (see Measurements and Mass) and posture, often obvious within pairs. Complex basic moult strategy (one plumage per definitive cycle, two in the first cycle). Ageing fairly easy until the beginning of the first winter, but requires more care until the first summer, and is sometimes possible to the second winter. No leucistic morph known (vs. Mute and Trumpeter Swans).

Adult

Definitive basic plumage (year-round). White plumage, sometimes tinged yellowish or pale rusty (especially head and neck), depending on iron concentration in water. Iris dark brown, occasionally blue-grey[1057]. Bill and facial skin bright yellow (often including orbital ring), the patch extending below the nostril and sometimes beyond it. Base of lower mandible often marked yellow too and a pink line is sometimes visible towards the base between the mandibles. Rest of bill black. There is variation in bill pattern across the range (see below), but also individually, albeit less than in Bewick's Swan. Most birds have yellow on the upper third of the culmen. A common variant has a black forked pattern near the forehead, with a thin, transversal, more or less regular, black band on the feathers of the forehead (rarely extending to the sides of the bill). Others, much more rarely, have an all-black culmen, or an isolated yellow spot in the middle of the black culmen. Legs and feet black.

Juvenile

First basic plumage (until Jan–Mar). Like other swans, overall pale grey-brown plumage, darker on the head and neck, upperparts, tail, tertials and inner median coverts, and paler on the breast, underparts, back and rest of upperwing. Bill and facial skin greyish-pink, paler at the base, with tomium, nail and nostrils dusky-grey, becoming blackish rather quickly. Legs initially dull grey-pink, becoming dark grey and then black during first winter.

First-winter/first-summer

Formative plumage (Jan–Mar/Nov–Jan). Some body feathers are replaced with grey or white ones, giving the bird a slightly variegated appearance during first winter. The grey-brown feathers, however, tend to fade or bleach rapidly. By the end of the first winter, mainly white, grey often being visible only on the head and upper neck. The remaining juvenile feathers (rectrices, tertials and scattered feathers elsewhere), even if they appear whitish, are heavily worn if seen close. The adult-like black bill develops early in the first winter. The yellow appears later, usually in early spring, though it often remains duller or pale greyish until the beginning of the first summer.

Second-winter

Second basic plumage (Nov–Jan/Nov–Jan). Before the end of the second pre-basic moult, juvenile feathers (grey-brown and very worn) are sometimes visible under perfect viewing conditions or in the hand, mainly on the head, neck, rump, upperwing-coverts and rectrices, at least in a small proportion of birds[56]. Definitive pre-basic moult is not always absolutely complete. Adult can therefore also show two generations of feathers between pre-basic moults.

GEOGRAPHIC VARIATION There are differences in the frequency of different bill colour patterns between populations wintering in the British Isles (and breeding in Iceland) and those of Japan. One analysis[181] was made on the basis of four coloration types: top of culmen yellow ('yellowneb'), culmen with black forked pattern or spots ('black-based yellowneb'), black culmen with isolated yellow spot or patch ('pennyface ') and black culmen ('darky'). Of 264 individuals in Europe, these four types represented 22%, 74%, 3% and 1%, respectively. In Japan, 634 individuals were distributed as follows: 95%, 4%, 1% and 0%[181]. Another study, based on 552 birds in Finland (breeding in Scandinavia and W Russia, wintering in N Europe), produced the following results: 60%, 38%, 2% and 0%[929]. This population is intermediate between Icelandic breeders and those of E Siberia, while differing statistically from both. Geographic variation has also been reported in biometrics, breeding birds in Iceland being smaller than continental birds. Recent measurements[1059] and genetic analyses[536], however, tend to minimise these differences.

MEASUREMENTS and MASS ♂ and adult slightly larger than ♀ and young, respectively. Adult ♂: wing chord 553–674 (612, $n=534$), head-bill 138.0–192.0 (174.6, $n=630$), tarsus 106.8–142.2 (123.5, $n=411$), mass in winter 7,200–13,500 (10,200, *n*=655); adult ♀: wing chord 521–674 (596, *n*=589), head–bill 140.0–189.0 (170.4, *n*=678), tarsus 102.4–132.8 (118.9, *n*=453), mass in winter 5,600–13,100 (9,200, *n*=718); juvenile/first-winter ♂: wing chord 504–647 (591.0, *n*=156), head–bill 144.0–191.0 (175.6, *n*=177), tarsus 111.6–129.1 (122.6, *n*=95), mass in winter 5,200–12,100 (9,000, *n*=177) ; juvenile/first-winter ♀: wing chord 452–628 (577.0, *n*=197), head–bill 140.0–187.6 (171.5, *n*=217), tarsus 113.0–130.0 (118.9, *n*=136), mass in winter 5,600–11,300 (8,400, *n*=220)[1059]. Measurements from UK at site where food is provided, which may lead to artificially high mass data[1059]. ♂: bill 98–116 (adult, 106, *n*=19); ♀: 92–111 (adult, 102, *n*=15)[1161]. Extinct population on Greenland was possibly slightly smaller (wing chord 562, tarsus 114, *n*=7 adult)[1144].

VOICE The most frequent calls, a *whoop* or *wo-hoop* with higher pitched second syllable, as well as other trumpeting or honking sounds, like domestic geese or a toy trumpet. Sings with acute clarion tones, alternating long and shorter, rapidly repeated syllables: *wooooh-oo-oo-oo-wououh….*

MOULT Complex basic strategy. Pre-formative moult occurs between Oct and Jan–Mar, starting with the head and neck, then mantle and scapulars, breast and flanks, sometimes some tertials, rectrices and inner upperwing-coverts. Second pre-basic moult occurs from Jun to Dec, is complete, except in some birds[56], which keep a few feathers on the head, neck, rump and some upperwing-coverts (and rectrices?). Definitive pre-basic moult begins with the remiges in ♀, when cygnets are small, and almost one month later in ♂. It ends in Dec[56]. Definitive pre-basic moult therefore takes place on the nesting grounds for adults that raise young, and in gatherings on open water for others[349].

HYBRIDISATION Natural hybridisation reported very occasionally with Tundra Swan[817,1190], but only in captivity with Bewick's Swan[817]. Other natural hybrids have occasionally been mentioned with Mute Swan (which see). In captivity, hybridisation described very occasionally with Trumpeter Swan[817,1190], Black Swan *C. atratus*[802], Greylag Goose *Anser anser* and Canada Goose *Branta canadensis*[639].

HABITAT and LIFE-CYCLE Whooper Swans leave the wintering grounds in Mar–Apr, sometimes even early May[1057]. Offspring from the previous year often migrate with their parents, then leave them to gather at moulting sites, where adults that fail to breed also gradually congregate. Depending on progress of thaw, eggs are laid between late Apr and May in Iceland and Scandinavia, and from the second half of May in Russia[1059]. Inhabits various types of wetlands, mainly in steppe (C Asia), taiga and the southern tundra. Particularly favours lakes and shallow ponds bordered by forest or reeds, slow-flowing rivers, bogs, marshes, especially in plains but sometimes in low hills, preferentially with abundant aquatic vegetation and islets where the impressive heap of vegetation that constitutes the nest is often well visible. Pairs nest alone, although density may be relatively high, with a minimum distance of 50 m between nests[349]. Begins migrating to wintering sites in late Sep or Oct, departures often being determined by the weather[1057]. Arrives in Oct–Nov on its wintering grounds, spending less time at stop-over sites than Bewick's Swan. Form groups of a few hundred birds in winter, at large lakes, estuaries and coastal bays, with large bodies of water necessary for resting or preening. For foraging, uses marshes, but now mainly flooded or dry croplands and grasslands.

RANGE and POPULATION Outside of mapped range in Palearctic, a local breeder in Belarus and Poland, and occasionally further south, in Scotland, Ireland or France. In winter, occasional rare visitor to SW Europe, N Africa, the Middle East, India, SE Asia and even the Aleutians. Accidental in mainland Alaska and on the Pacific coast of Canada and USA. The Icelandic population is relatively distinct from continental birds and winters almost exclusively in N Scotland, Ireland and Norfolk (E England). Several banding recoveries have nevertheless been reported elsewhere on coasts of the North Sea, mainly in Denmark[909]. The Icelandic breeding population numbered 29,232 individuals in Jan 2010[498]. Between 52,000 and 80,000 individuals winter over the rest of Europe to the Black Sea[139], and *c*.20,000 around the Caspian Sea[1154]. Approximately 60,000 winter in E Asia[757,858]. Trend increasing in west of range, declining for the C Siberian population wintering in the Caspian Sea, and unknown in E Asia[1348]. Windfarms are potentially problematic at wintering sites[731].

CAPTIVITY Usually rare in captivity outside a few specialised collections, its aggressive behaviour often requiring that it be kept in isolated pairs in their own pen. Generally sold at rather high prices, despite that the species is fairly easily bred in good conditions. It should, however, escape from captivity only infrequently.

REFERENCES Baker (1992)[56]; Banko & Schorger (1976)[61]; BirdLife International (2004)[139]; BirdLife International (2014)[145]; Brazil (1981)[178]; Brazil (2003)[181]; Cooper (1979)[257]; Cramp & Simmons (1977)[268]; Delany & Scott (2006)[305]; Einarsson (1996)[349]; Hall *et al.* (2012)[498]; Harvey (1999)[536]; Johnsgard (1960)[639]; Johnsgard (1974)[644]; Larsen & Clausen (2002)[731]; Li *et al.* (2009)[757]; Ma & Cai (2002)[790]; Madge & Burn (1988)[794]; Marchant & Higgins (1990)[802]; McCarthy (2006)[817]; Miyabayashi & Mundkur (1999)[858]; Newth *et al.* (2013)[909]; Ohtonen (1988)[929]; Rees *in* Kear (2005)[1057]; Rees *et al.* (1997)[1059]; Schiøler (1925)[1144]; Scott & Rose (1996)[1154]; Scott & The Wildfowl Trust (1972)[1161]; Sibley (1938)[1190]; Wetlands International (2014)[1348].

193. Adult (definitive basic); note typical long neck, head and bill, the latter appearing more yellow than black (vs. Bewick's Swan *C. c. bewickii*). England, Feb (Sébastien Reeber).

194. Adult (definitive basic); a rare bird with an all-black culmen (called 'darky'). England, Feb (Sébastien Reeber).

195. Adult (definitive basic); yellow bill patch typically wedge-shaped at the front, ending below the nostrils. France, Feb (Vincent Palomares).

196. Adult (definitive basic). Japan, Feb (Aurélien Audevard).

197. First-winter (formative); note scattered pale brownish areas, but by Feb, the bill is almost coloured like that of adult (vs. Bewick's Swan *C. c. bewickii*). England, Feb (Sébastien Reeber).

198. Adult (definitive basic) and cygnets. Iceland, Jul (Julien Gonin).

COMB DUCK (KNOB-BILLED DUCK)
Sarkidiornis melanotos

Plate 23

TAXONOMY *Anser melanotos* Pennant, 1769, *Ind. Zool.*, p. 12, pl. 11. Placed among the Tadorninae[765], the genus *Sarkidiornis* belongs to the tribe Plectropterini, with Spur-winged Goose *Plectropterus gambensis*. South American populations were previously called *S. regius* Eyton, 1838, and African birds *S. africanus* Eyton, 1838. Both taxa were lumped with *S. melanotos* by Gray[466]. Subsequently, two taxa were again generally recognised: *melanotos* in the Old World and *sylvicola* H. & R. Ihering, 1907, in the New World. They are sometimes considered conspecific[142,1063,1192] and by others as separate species[239,437,1381]. The first option is followed here, but only *melanotos* is present in the Holarctic (see Geographic Variation).

IDENTIFICATION Little risk of confusion in the Holarctic, although bear in mind that juvenile and ♀ Cotton Pygmy Goose *Nettapus coromandelianus* have similar overall coloration. Nevertheless, there are very strong differences in size, bill shape and head coloration.

PLUMAGES Nominate subspecies. Strong sexual dimorphism in size and structure starting from first winter. Ageing ♂♂ possible until the first summer. ♀♀ more difficult to age from beginning of second calendar year. Moult timing and strategy poorly described in the wild and vary geographically.

Adult ♂

Definitive basic plumage. Top of head and upper neck white with buff, yellowish or creamy tones and many irregular black dots, concentrated on the crown and nape. Bill dark grey with a large knob, as tall as the top of the head and as long as the tip of the bill, but narrow. Base of lower mandible tinged pink. Iris brown. Breast and lower neck white. All-whitish underparts, with pale grey-toned flanks, a thin black vertical bar between flanks and chest and a broader black bar on rear flanks. Undertail-coverts more or less strongly tinged yellowish-buff. Mantle, scapulars, uppertail-coverts and tail black with strong blue, purple, green or bronze gloss, depending on light. Back more variable pale grey (blackish in some, white in others). Upperwing uniform black with bronze sheen on coverts, greener on speculum. Underwing entirely blackish, including axillaries, except white fringes to lesser coverts. Legs dark grey.

Definitive alternate plumage. Poorly studied and only marginally different from basic plumage, mainly in ground colour of the head and undertail-coverts, which is white. Knob on culmen much less prominent outside breeding season, but remains more obvious than in ♀.

Adult ♀

Definitive basic plumage. Mainly distinguished from ♂ by biometrics and mass, with almost no overlap. Head on average slightly more heavily spotted (less contrasting black crown). Mantle, scapulars and upperwing have softer gloss than in adult ♂, often restricted to the speculum. Grey of back extends onto rump in ♀. The flanks are less uniform pale grey, more strongly marked with brownish crescents, with black vertical line absent or faint. The white fringes to the lesser underwing-coverts are absent. The bill shows no knob or swelling at the base of the culmen.

Definitive alternate plumage. No seasonal changes described.

Juvenile

First basic plumage. Structure initially similar to that of adult ♀ but head and upper neck pale brownish and not spotted black, with a dark eyestripe and pale eyebrow. Black-brown iris darker than in adult. Upperparts brown, not black, without metallic gloss. Underparts more brownish (with yellowish or pale rust hue), and diffuse, uneven spotting.

First-winter

Formative plumage. Timing and accurate descriptions of post-juvenile plumages poorly documented in the wild. Following pre-formative moult, the head and neck are similar to those of adult but the gloss on the upperparts is slightly less pronounced. Young ♂ has blackish-grey upperparts, while ♀ is browner. Dirty white underparts.

GEOGRAPHIC VARIATION The South American subspecies *S. m. sylvicola* is slightly smaller (see Measurements and Mass) and has black flanks in the adult ♂ (dark grey in ♀). However, individuals with black flanks have been reported occasionally both in Africa (e. g. in N Kenya[1381]) and in India[380].

MEASUREMENTS and MASS *S. m. melanotos*. ♂

distinctly larger and heavier than ♀. In South Africa: ♂ (*n*=10): wing chord 347–380 (360), tail 117–150 (136), culmen 57–66 (62), tarsus 56–67.5 (63.9); ♀ (*n*=6): wing chord 279–300 (286.6), tail 100–120 (109), culmen 42.5–52 (46.6), tarsus 42–50 (48.2)[793]. In India (sample unknown): ♂: wing chord 339–406, tail 139–153, culmen 63–70, tarsus 64–75; ♀: wing chord 280–309, culmen 59–66 [11]. ♂ (sample unknown): mass 2,250; ♀ (sample unknown): mass 1,750[794].

S. m. sylvicola. ♂: wing chord (*n*=7) 336, culmen (*n*=7) 55–57, mass (*n*=5) 1,863; ♀: wing chord (*n*=8): 283, mass (*n*=5) 1,069[211].

VOICE Usually quiet. Utters fairly discreet croaks when disturbed. During breeding season, emits various wheezing whistles and some more raspy calls, like *kerk*, sometimes repeated.

MOULT Very few data on timing and moult strategy[1381]. These are probably variable within the range, which is very large and extends across both N & S Hemispheres. Difficulties in defining moult strategy also result from the lack of seasonal changes in appearance during the annual cycle. Finally, life-cycle (including breeding and probably subsequent pre-basic moult) is influenced by weather conditions (including seasonality of rains). ♂ in basic plumage has a yellowish-buff hue to the head and undertail, which is lost after breeding. This is probably manifestation of pre-alternate moult, but perhaps only a colour related to diet[1381]. More research is clearly needed.

HYBRIDISATION In the wild, reported in Oman, between a vagrant Comb Duck and a Mallard *Anas platyrhynchos*[831]. Other reports are from captivity, with Muscovy Duck *Cairina moschata* (domestic form) and Rosy-billed Pochard *Netta peposaca*[817].

HABITAT and LIFE-CYCLE Mostly sedentary, but movements regularly undertaken depending on weather and water conditions, especially for breeding, which occurs during the monsoon in continental Asia. Inhabits various types of freshwater, temporary or permanent wetlands, often lined with wooded areas. Often perches high above water, for example on dead branches. In India, eggs are laid mainly in Jul–Sep, usually in cavities, hollow trees or under dense cover of tall grassy or brushy vegetation, never far from water. In Sri Lanka, seems to mostly breed in Feb–Mar[150]. Nests in isolated and territorial pairs, but can also be polygamous, although this behaviour is described as

rare in Asia and Africa[994]. Outside the nesting season, usually found in small parties of fewer than ten birds, but occasionally in flocks of up to 100 individuals. May also use rice fields at this season.

RANGE and POPULATION Broad distribution on three continents like that of Fulvous Whistling-duck *Dendrocygna bicolor*, including South America (race *sylvicola*), sub-Saharan Africa to E Africa and Madagascar, as well as S & SE Asia. The latter population has a fragmented range through India and Bangladesh, with much smaller numbers from Myanmar into N Cambodia, and is a rare or irregular visitor, primarily in winter, elsewhere in Indochina. Rare visitor to Pakistan (probably extinct as a breeder[490,1044]), more accidental west to Oman. Asian population estimated at 10,000–25,000 individuals[1348], with a global population probably of 150,000–700,000 birds.

CAPTIVITY Generally rare in captivity outside a few specialised collections, as reportedly sensitive to temperatures in temperate regions, rather aggressive (often must be kept apart from other species) and rather difficult to breed. Moreover, relatively expensive, and thus unlikely to escape from captivity.

REFERENCES Ali & Ripley (1987)[11]; BirdLife International (2012)[142]; Blanford (1898)[150]; Brown *et al.* (1982)[197]; Callaghan *in* Kear (2005)[211]; Collar & Andrew (1988)[239]; Finn (1915)[380]; Gill & Donsker (2014)[437]; Gray (1841)[466]; Grimmett *et al.* (1999)[490]; Livezey (1986)[765]; Maclean (1993)[793]; Madge & Burn (1988)[794]; McCarthy (2006)[817]; McLeish (1993)[831]; Pitman (1965)[994]; Rasmussen & Anderton (2005)[1044]; Remsen *et al.* (2014)[1063]; Robson (2005)[1088]; Sibley & Monroe (1990)[1192]; Wetlands International (2014)[1348]; Young *in* Kear (2005)[1381].

199. *S. m. melanotos*, adult ♂. Outside breeding season, knob on bill is much reduced. India, Dec (Christopher J. G. Plummer).

200. *S. m. melanotos*, adult ♂. India, Feb (Sunil Singhal).

201. *S. m. melanotos*, adult ♂. India, Feb (Sunil Singhal).

202. *S. m. melanotos*, adult ♀. Tanzania, Oct (Rick Van der Weijde).

EGYPTIAN GOOSE
Alopochen aegyptiacus   **Plate 21**

TAXONOMY *Anas aegyptiaca* Linnaeus, 1766, *Syst. Nat.*, edn. 12, 1, p. 197. The sole representative of the genus *Alopochen*, which, within the subfamily Tadorninae, is placed near the genera *Neochen* and *Chloephaga*[765].

IDENTIFICATION Its structure like that of a large shelduck, unique coloration and large white patches on the upperwing should prevent any risk of confusion. In flight and under poor viewing conditions, compare Ruddy Shelduck *Tadorna ferruginea*.

PLUMAGES Weak sexual dimorphism from first winter onwards. Complex alternate moult strategy (two plumages per annual cycle, three during the first cycle). Ageing relatively easy until the beginning of the first winter and possible until the end of the first summer under good viewing conditions or in the hand. Moult timing and strategy varies geographically in Africa, but is poorly known in introduced European population.

Adult

Definitive basic plumage. Overall coloration brownish, beige and russet. Head variegated, with crown, forehead, fore cheeks, throat and foreneck whitish. Large oval patch around eye and line encircling bill base dark reddish-brown, and the two often linked by a dark line. Rear cheeks, hindneck and nape vermiculated dark brown to reddish-brown. Bill pale pink with base, tomium, nail and nostrils dark brown to blackish. Iris pale brown to orange. Breast paler and brighter, tinged yellowish to peach, with a slightly darker collar above and a dark patch in centre of lower breast. Note that breast does not really contrast with underparts. Flanks and belly pale grey-brown. Mantle and scapulars plain, quite variable from dark brown to reddish-brown or greyish-beige. Tertials longish, tinged cinnamon to reddish. Back, rump and tail black. Lower belly pale grey. Undertail-coverts tinged pale orange. Upperwing has remiges, alula and primary coverts black, with green or purple reflections on speculum. All secondary coverts white, with fine black bar on greater coverts, forming a line parallel to base of secondaries. Underwing has lesser coverts and remiges black, and axillaries and secondary coverts white. Legs bright pink. ♀ similar to ♂ but has legs and bill less bright pink in breeding season. Easier to assign sex based on its more slender shape, thinner neck and head, and slightly smaller size, especially when in pairs. Note that there are many variations in colour, accentuated in Europe by the influence of selected ornamental variants. Dark birds are dull grey-brown overall, others more mixed with much redder shades, and finally paler individuals are overall tinged greyish or beige.

Definitive alternate plumage. Same as basic plumage, marginally duller and less contrasting[284].

Juvenile

First basic plumage . Close to adult, but lacks dark patches around eyes, at base of bill and on centre of lower breast, and without dark neck-ring. The head and neck are more uniform and lack contrast. The bill is pale pink, with black areas of the adult browner and poorly defined. Underparts less vermiculated but appear mottled. Upperwing has secondary coverts washed light grey, and darker diffuse grey fringes. Median coverts slightly darker, as are the bases to the greater coverts, which contrast with the white tips, the bases and tips being separated by a distinct black band. Legs pale pink.

First-winter

Formative plumage. Following pre-formative moult, resembles the adult, and easily distinguished only by upperwing pattern, which is identical to that of juvenile described above.

GEOGRAPHIC VARIATION None.

MEASUREMENTS and MASS ♂ and adult significantly larger than ♀ and young, respectively. ♂: wing chord 378–407 (396.1, *n*=11), tail 116–150 (131.6, *n*=11), culmen: 45–55 (49.1, *n*=12), tarsus 74.5–95 (82.4, *n*=12), mass 2,348 (*n*=41); ♀: wing chord 340–390 (369.8, *n*=12), tail 111–145 (127.4, *n*=11), culmen: 43–54 (49.0, *n*=15), tarsus 67–85 (76.7, *n*=15), mass 1,872 (*n*=98)[267,284,793].

VOICE ♀ utters some loud, nasal, raspy, coarse *hu-rr* calls, sometimes repeated in rapid series. ♂ emits a coarse, guttural hiss, recalling the intimidation call of a male domestic goose. Both sexes emit a repeated *hong* when alarmed, disturbed or on take-off. The tone, loudness and duration of sounds vary with their function[284].

MOULT Complex alternate strategy (?). In Africa, the timing of remiges moult varies: it takes place post-breeding, which in turn is determined by the wet season and/or local water conditions[287,851,900,901,1287], and can therefore be at any time of year[197,284], possibly with two annual peaks in numbers of moulting birds[431]. However, this schedule cannot be applied to the introduced European population, whose moult does not seem to have been studied. Young undertake a pre-formative moult with most (exact proportion unknown) of the feathers of the head, neck and body, but retain at least the majority of the wing feathers and some rectrices. The possible pre-alternate moult is undescribed and, if it occurs, does not lead to seasonal change in plumage. However, it appears that at least the feathers of the head and neck are more brightly coloured during breeding and seem fresh, but it remains unclear if this is the result of a partial moult. Pre-basic moult occurs after breeding.

HYBRIDISATION In the Holarctic, hybrids in the wild are very rare, and exclusively linked to the European feral population. A few cases of hybridisation have been reported with Ruddy Shelduck (see this species) and Common Shelduck *Tadorna tadorna*. Rare cases have been reported with Greylag Goose *Anser anser*[465,668] and Mallard *Anas platyrhynchos*[817]. In Africa, in the native range, hybrids have been reported with Spur-winged Goose *Plectropterus gambensis*[403], South African Shelduck *Tadorna cana*[139,817] and the introduced Muscovy Duck *Cairina moschata*[817], but these are very unlikely to occur in Eurasia. In captivity, hybridisation has been mentioned in the literature with the following species: Greater White-fronted Goose *Anser albifrons*[1190], Snow Goose *Chen caerulescens*[1190], Swan Goose *Anser cygnoides*, Canada Goose *Branta canadensis*[439,465,817], Andean Goose *Chloephaga melanoptera*, Upland Goose *C. picta*, Blue-winged Goose *Cyanochen cyanoptera*[465,817], Orinoco Goose *Neochen jubata*, Maned Duck *Chenonetta jubata*[439,582,817] and Australian Shelduck *Tadorna tadornoides*[619].

HABITAT and LIFE-CYCLE In Europe, uses a variety of wetlands, from small wooded ponds to rivers, and from canals in cultivated areas to lakes, reservoirs and estuaries. Usually breeds early, with eggs laid between Mar and May, usually on the ground under dense brushy vegetation or high up, like the shelducks. Particularly aggressive towards perceived threats to nest or chicks. Does not migrate in Europe, but small parties undertake erratic movements and may sometimes appear where the species is not established.

RANGE and POPULATION This species occurs across the southern two-thirds of Africa, south of a line from S Mauritania to S Egypt, except the rainforest areas, especially over broad band on equatorial Atlantic coasts. The total population has been estimated at 200,000–500,000 individuals[1154]. Absent from the extreme Horn of Africa and Madagascar. Scarce visitor to the Maghreb. Previously reported in the Middle East and even along the Danube[267,1154]. Its introduction into mainland Europe began with some breeding cases in the wild in the Netherlands in 1967, and two decades later, the birds began to disperse to Germany, Denmark, Belgium and France. Local breeding in all these countries has also been enhanced by escapees. In 2010, the breeding population was estimated at 10,000 pairs (45,000 individuals) in the Netherlands, and 16,000 pairs in Belgium and Germany[495]. During 2004–07, the long-established English population was estimated at 2,520–3,160 individuals, with a few dozen pairs in France, Denmark and Switzerland. In the same period, 30–50 pairs were also reported in Israel, and 100–200 pairs in United Arab Emirates[62]. These populations seem likely to increase rapidly where they are not subject to control measures.

CAPTIVITY Very common in captivity, where it breeds readily. Usually sold at very low prices, at least in Europe. Highly likely to escape from captivity, the majority of birds seen outside the usual range being considered escapes. However, note that like Ruddy Shelduck, historical records exist far beyond the usual range, at a time when they were rare in captivity, suggesting that the species may also occur naturally in the Middle East and Europe[851].

REFERENCES Baker (1993)[56]; Banks *et al.* (2008)[62]; Brown *et al.* (1982)[197]; Cramp & Simmons (1977)[268]; Davies *in* Kear (2005)[284]; Dean (1978)[287]; Frade & Pinho (1971)[403]; Geldenhuys (1975)[431]; Gillham & Gillham (1996)[439]; Gray (1958)[465]; Gyimesi & Lensink (2012)[495]; Harrop (1998)[531]; Hopkinson (1926)[582]; IZY (1968)[619]; Johnson & Sorenson (1999)[654]; Kampe-Persson & Lerner (2007)[668]; Livezey (1986)[765]; Maclean (1993)[793]; McCarthy (2006)[817]; Milstein (1993)[851]; Ndlovu *et al.* (2010)[901]; Ndlovu *et al.* (2013)[900]; Scott & Rose (1996)[1154]; Sibley (1938)[1190]; Underhill *et al.* (2000)[1287].

203. Juvenile (first basic/formative). France, Jul (Vincent Palomares).

204. Adult (definitive basic); sexing is much easier if comparing two birds within a pair than when faced by a lone bird. France, Feb (Vincent Palomares).

205. Adult ♂ (definitive basic); the thick neck indicates a ♂. Netherlands, Feb (Sébastien Reeber).

206. Pair (definitive basic); note large white forewing patch typical of the species; the ♂ (on left) is larger and has more glossy secondaries. Netherlands, Feb (Sébastien Reeber).

RUDDY SHELDUCK
Tadorna ferruginea

Plate 22

TAXONOMY *Anas ferruginea* Pallas, 1764, *in* Vroeg, *Cat. Raisonné Coll. Oiseaux, Adumbr.*, p. 5. Close to South African Shelduck *T. cana*. In captivity, known to hybridise readily with all other shelducks and to produce fertile hybrids [295].

IDENTIFICATION In the Holarctic, no other species resembles Ruddy Shelduck. However, bear in mind the possibility of rare hybrids with Common Shelduck *Tadorna tadorna* (see that species), and possibly South African Shelduck. The latter is actually very similar to Ruddy Shelduck, the adult ♂ being distinguished by its pale grey head and upper neck, the ♀ by its contrasting dark grey and white head.

PLUMAGES Slight sexual dimorphism from first winter onwards. Complex alternate moult strategy (two plumages by definitive cycle, three in first cycle). Ageing easy until the first autumn and possible until the following summer based on the upperwing, in good viewing conditions or in the hand.

Adult ♂

Definitive basic plumage (Nov–Mar/May–Jun). Entire plumage a beautiful rufous-orange, slightly brighter on the breast and marginally paler and more yellowish on the upperparts and head. Upper head paler, often whitish, without clear demarcation and extending towards nape. Thin whitish band surrounding bill base. Iris dark brown. Frequently, a small dark mark on the central crown. Thin, clear-cut black collar. Rump, lower belly, rear flanks, uppertail-coverts and tail black. Upperwing has secondary coverts white slightly to strongly tinged buff or pale orange, becoming whitish with wear (spring/summer). Alula, lesser coverts and remiges black with metallic green sheen on speculum. Underwing white (all coverts except black tips to outer lesser coverts) and black (remiges). Legs dark grey to blackish.

Definitive alternate plumage (Jun/Nov–Mar). Identical to basic plumage, only differing in the black neck-ring being absent or much reduced.

Adult ♀

Definitive basic plumage (Nov–Mar/Jun–Jul). As ♂ except small differences in size and structure, often visible in direct comparison. ♂ shows a bulge on hindneck, reminiscent of a long drooping crest, not shown by ♀. The ♂'s head profile thereby seems longer, while the head of ♀ is typically thinner, squarer, with steeper forehead and bill looks slightly up-curved. Among plumage differences, note the complete lack of black collar, and well-demarcated whitish area covering entire bill base, with an extension around eye in ♀. The white area around the eye of ♂ is more vague, extends to the crown but does not usually reach the bill base (unless most of the head is white, as in worn plumage).

Definitive alternate plumage (Jun–Jul/Nov–Mar). Identical to definitive basic plumage.

Juvenile

First basic plumage (until Oct–Dec). Similar to ♀ but upperparts darker and duller, with blackish centres to scapulars. A dark grey-brown patch is visible on the central crown. Underparts duller rufous-brown. Feathers of the back, rump and outer rectrices black fringed pale. Pale buff head, fairly plain. Upperwing distinctive with lesser and median coverts white, lacking the buff or orange hue of adult but have grey tips. Greater coverts centred dark grey and fringed pale.

First-winter

Formative plumage (Oct–Dec/Jun–Jul). Similar to adult basic plumage of each sex respectively, except a variable quantity, often few, of retained juvenile feathers on underparts and scapulars, which are nevertheless difficult to detect not only because many birds moult almost all the head and body feathers, but also because adult pre-basic moult is protracted well into winter, and can also show two generations of feathers simultaneously. The best ageing feature is the upperwing being juvenile (until the beginning of the second pre-basic moult), except sometimes a few inner coverts. The pale greyish tips to the lesser and median coverts are often bleached or faded, making all secondary coverts often seem entirely white (usually tinged pale buff or pale orange in adult). The broad dark grey centres to the greater coverts are usually visible under good conditions. Some birds at least retain up to several juvenile tertials until first pre-alternate or second pre-basic moult.

GEOGRAPHIC VARIATION Monotypic. Variation has been reported in the colour of the head of ♀, its pale mask being absent in birds in the east of the range[532]. It appears that this is a rather variable feature in all populations and that the appearance of this mask changes during the annual cycle. This merits further study.

MEASUREMENTS and MASS ♂ and adult larger than ♀ and young, respectively. ♂: wing chord 333–402 (adult, 368, n=30) and 325–352 (juvenile, 340, n=4), tail 116–135 (125, n=8), bill 40–49 (44.1, n=31), tarsus 59–64 (61.5, n=11), mass 1,200–1,600 (n=29); ♀: wing chord 321–371 (adult, 340, n=36) and 313–346 (juvenile, 326, n=3), tail 112–122 (118, n=6), bill 35–44 (40.1, n=36), tarsus 52–57 (54.6, n=10), mass 925–1,500 (1,100, n=9)[267,1122].

VOICE Loquacious, even noisy, and often heard before being seen. Emits a trumpeting *hung* or *ang* with nasal tone and loud, often preceded and/or followed by a shorter, less audible note. Sometimes also gives a cooed *hooh* or falling *hang*, included within a quick cackling 'chat'. Also frequently an *arrrr* lasting one to a few seconds. Calls of ♀ slightly deeper and more raucous than those of ♂[606].

MOULT Complex alternate moult strategy. Pre-formative moult usually starts early, from Jul, and ends in Dec[56]. It includes the head and body feathers and a variable number of inner upperwing-coverts and none to all tertials. Definitive pre-alternate moult starts in both sexes when the chicks hatch, mostly in Jun, slightly later in ♀, and includes the head and body feathers starting with scapulars and flanks, then the head and rest of the body[56]. It is unknown if first pre-alternate moult differs from definitive in the wild. The final pre-basic moult begins thereafter, with the loss of the remiges and a flightless period, especially in Aug, then the rest of the body between Sep and Mar–Apr, with a suspension or slowdown in Dec–Feb[56]. This moult ends with the tertials, which are often heavily worn by early winter.

HYBRIDISATION Reported very occasionally in wild with Falcated Duck *Anas falcata*[465] and occasionally with Common Shelduck *Tadorna tadorna* (see that species) and Egyptian Goose *Alopochen aegyptiacus*[817] (see below), especially in Europe where Ruddy Shelduck frequently escapes. In captivity, hybrids have been described in the literature with Spur-winged Goose *Plectropterus gambensis*, Orinoco Goose *Neochen jubata*[1142], Barnacle Goose *Branta leucopsis*, South African Shelduck[439,817], Radjah Shelduck *Tadorna radjah*, Paradise Shelduck *T. variegata*, Australian Shelduck *T. tadornoides*, Wood Duck *Aix sponsa*[97], Mallard *Anas platyrhynchos*[817] and Rosy-billed Pochard *Netta peposaca*[817].

Ruddy Shelduck × Egyptian Goose. A few cases of hybridisation reported in Europe (see, e.g. Harrop[531]), where both species have escaped, been introduced or established feral populations. Recalls Ruddy Shelduck in overall reddish coloration, especially the upperparts (including tertials), breast and head. The latter is often darker than the breast, and, sometimes at least, a large dark collar is visible. The head can also look quite pale, especially around the eye (only ♀?), which can be surrounded by pure white. The bill is blackish, with a variable pink hue in the centre of the mandible. The flanks are mostly grey, especially at the rear. Undertail-coverts pale orange to yellowish. Legs pale pinkish-grey.

HABITAT and LIFE-CYCLE In N Africa, eggs generally laid between mid-Mar and late Apr, and from late Apr to early Jun in Asia[606]. In N Africa, inhabits temporary or permanent marshes, and undertakes erratic movements linked to local hydrology[197]. In Asia, inhabits banks of rivers and freshwater, salt or brackish lakes, especially in the interior, in steppe zone or on plateaux up to 5,000 m in the Himalayas[145,267]. Like Common Shelduck, nests in cavities, on the ground or above it, on different types of substrates, sometimes far from water. African populations sedentary or erratic, depending on rainfall and available wetlands. Populations of the Black Sea and Middle East are partially migratory. Those in Asia are mainly migratory and winter in different lowland habitats, often in small flocks along slow-moving rivers, ponds, marshes and flooded areas with fresh or brackish water. Prefers open inland habitats and avoids coastal areas or heavily vegetated marshes[794].

RANGE and POPULATION Several distinct populations. The first is fragmented, between Tunisia, Algeria, Morocco and Mauritania, numbers *c*.3,000 individuals, and is declining[484]. The second is confined to Bale Mountains National Park, Ethiopia, and is in very critical situation: flocks of 200–500 birds were still reported in the 1990s[1154,1298] but more recently the population was estimated at just 30–80 birds[371]. Other populations are mostly or strictly migratory. Those of Greece, the Black Sea, W and C Turkey overwinter partly on the breeding grounds (where unfrozen), and in E

Mediterranean and along the Nile Valley, with *c*.20,000 birds[606,864], and is also declining[1348]. A population has also been re-introduced in S Ukraine[1395]. Further east, *c*.35,000 birds recorded from E Turkey to C Asia (mainly in Iran and Iraq[445,606]), and again probably declining[1395]. Most birds breeding further east winter from Pakistan to E China, with *c*.50,000–100,000 birds in S & SE Asia and perhaps as many in E Asia, and this population is stable or slightly increasing[222,757]. In Europe, a population introduced in Switzerland has spread to S Germany and numbered nearly 600 birds in the first decade of the 21st century, and is currently subject to control. There are also some scattered pairs elsewhere in W Europe[62], usually considered to be escapes from captivity or from feral populations, although some influxes could represent natural vagrants[532]. In North America, all records are regarded as concerning escapes, including a recent record of six in Jul 2000 on the island of Southampton, Nunavut, Canada[1073].

CAPTIVITY Very common in captivity, where it is easily bred, even if rather aggressive towards other species or conspecifics during nesting. Sold at low prices.

REFERENCES Baker (1993)[56]; Banks *et al.* (2008)[62]; Bird Hybrids Database (2014)[97]; BirdLife International (2014)[145]; Brown *et al.* (1982)[197]; Cao *et al.* (2010)[222]; Cramp & Simmons (1977)[268]; Delacour (1954–64)[295]; Ethiopian Wildlife & Natural History Society (2001)[371]; Gillham & Gillham (1996)[439]; Gillissen *et al.* (2002)[445]; Gray (1958)[465]; Green *et al.* (2002)[484]; Harrop (1998)[531]; Harrop (2002)[532]; Hughes & Green *in* Kear (2005)[606]; Li *et al.* (2009)[757]; Madge & Burn (1988)[794]; McCarthy (2006)[817]; Monval & Pirot (1989)[864]; Popovkina (2006)[1000]; Quan *et al.* (2001)[1020]; Robbins *et al.* (2004)[1073]; Salminen (1983)[1122]; Scherer & Hilsberg (1982)[1142]; Scott & Rose (1996)[1154]; Urban (1993)[1298]; Wetlands International (2014)[1348]; Zubko *et al.* (2001)[1395].

207. First-winter (formative/first alternate), with grey-centred greater coverts typical of this age, the two birds on left having seemingly replaced some inner coverts. India, Apr (Ingo Waschkies).

208. Adult ♂ (definitive basic), with pre-basic moult just completed, showing the typical orangey hue to the wing-coverts of an adult. India, Feb (Amit Thakurta).

209. Adult ♂ (definitive basic), with thin black collar visible. Mongolia, May (Sébastien Provost).

210. Pair (definitive basic/definitive alternate); these birds moult their body feathers as part of pre-basic moult; the best feature for sexing is head coloration (♂ above, ♀ below). India, Feb (Julien Gonin).

211. Adult ♀ (definitive basic/definitive alternate); white facial patch more clearly delineated in ♀; this bird has not yet finished its pre-basic moult (tertials are replaced last). India, Jan (Amit Thakurta).

212. Juvenile (first basic); many body feathers, especially scapulars and tertials, have dusky centres, a feature unique to this plumage. Captivity, Jul (Sébastien Reeber).

COMMON SHELDUCK
Tadorna tadorna   **Plate 21**

TAXONOMY *Anas Tadorna* Linnaeus, 1758, *Syst. Nat.*, edn. 10, p. 122. The six species of shelducks form one of 11 genera within the subfamily Tadorninae, the majority of which are represented primarily or exclusively in the S Hemisphere. Of the 24 species in this subfamily, only four reach north of the Tropic of Cancer, Common Shelduck having the northernmost range. No subspecies or geographic variation.

IDENTIFICATION Distinctive in all plumages.

PLUMAGES Slight sexual dimorphism from first winter onwards. Complex alternate moult strategy (two plumages per definitive cycle, three in first cycle). Ageing fairly easy until the beginning of the first summer. Shelducks are characterised by size and shape intermediate between those of a duck and goose.

Adult ♂

Definitive basic plumage (Oct–Dec/May–Jun). Variegated and contrasting coloration. Head and upper neck black with green sheen. Iris black. Bill with strong knob at base of culmen, bright pinkish-red to red, except the nail and around the nostrils, which are black. Flanks, lower neck and nape pure white, contrasting sharply with the upper neck, black lower scapulars and broad orange-chestnut full collar. This collar is blackish in the centre of the breast, extending as a diffuse band between the legs to the lower belly. Centre of undertail-coverts ochre-orange up to the tail. The sides of the rear body, uppertail-coverts, rump and back are white. Tail white with black terminal band. Upperwing-coverts all white, but outer webs and tips to the alula, primary coverts and remiges black. Strong metallic green gloss to secondaries. Outer tertials form a dark rufous area on folded wing. Underwing has black remiges and rest of wing white. Legs bright pink.

Definitive alternate plumage (May–Jun/Oct–Nov). Similar to definitive basic plumage, but duller and less clear-cut coloration. The head is black without any gloss and white spots around the bill base. The bill is pink with a less bulky knob. The reddish breast-band is less clearly demarcated and has small black and white stripes. Scapulars dull blackish-brown with faint pale fringes. Finally, the white parts of definitive basic plumage appear slightly grey-tinged or irregularly marked with pale grey-brown dots or short streaks.

Adult ♀

Definitive basic plumage (Oct–Dec/May–Jun). Like definitive basic plumage of ♂, but distinguished by substantially smaller size (obvious in direct comparison), by its bill lacking bulge at base of culmen, which is distinctly concave, and bill duller and marked with black towards tip and on culmen. The head is black with white flecks concentrated at the base of the bill (white increases with wear), incomplete white eye-ring, slightly less clearly-defined reddish breast-band and undertail less strongly tinged yellowish.

Definitive alternate plumage (May–Jun/Oct–Nov). Differs from definitive basic plumage as in ♂, by its duller coloration and less contrast. Upperparts often stained with grey, and scapulars browner, fringed pale. The whitish facial patch is larger, and can include the forehead, throat and part of the cheeks. Can then resemble juvenile, from which it is distinguished by red bill, reddish breast-band and the lack of clean broad white trailing edge to secondaries.

Juvenile

First basic plumage (until Aug–Sep). Recalls adult ♀ in alternate plumage, but has dull grey-rosy bill, dark brown to blackish head less sharply contrasting with the white breast, foreneck often white, no reddish breast-band (at most a few vague brown traces on the breast-sides) and all grey-brown upperparts. Tail blackish. In flight, note conspicuous white tips to secondaries and 3–4 inner primaries forming a sharp white trailing edge, as well as the greater coverts and tips of the median coverts tinged grey-brown. Legs dull flesh-pink.

First-winter

Formative plumage (Sep–Oct/Dec–Feb). Resembles definitive basic plumage of either sex respectively. Young ♂ may seem intermediate between adult ♀ and ♂ by having bill less swollen at the base and less pronounced gloss to the head. Seen closely or in the hand, look for retained juvenile feathers, especially on the lower belly, undertail, mantle or among the scapulars. The best ageing feature is the broad white trailing edge to the inner wing and grey greater coverts and tips to the median coverts, identical to the juvenile, as the wing is not moulted until the second pre-basic moult.

Second-winter

Second basic plumage (Oct–Dec/May–Jun). Identical to definitive basic plumage, except, in some birds, grey marks to the tips of the greater and median coverts (visible in the hand)[56].

GEOGRAPHIC VARIATION None, despite the existence of distinct populations with different ecological preferences.

MEASUREMENTS and MASS ♂ and adult larger than ♀ and young, respectively. ♂: wing chord 312–350 (adult, 334, n=33) and 291–334 (juvenile, 315, n=13), tail 108 (n=27), bill 50–58 (53.0, n=37), tarsus 52–60 (55.8, n=34), mass in Feb, SW Caspian Sea 830–1,500 (1,180, n=?), mass in Apr–May 1,100–1,450 (1,261, n=11), mass in summer 1,000–1,350 (1,167, n=7) ; ♀: wing chord 284–316 (adult, 303, n=28) and 277–307 (juvenile, 290, n=13), tail 96.9 (n=27), bill 44–50 (47.3, n=36), tarsus 46–54 (50.1, n=36), mass in Feb, SW Caspian Sea 562–1,085 (813, n=?), mass in Apr–May 926–1,250 (1,043, n=5), mass in summer 850–1,075 (952, n=5)[267].

VOICE Quite loquacious, especially before and during breeding. The ♂ emits sharp whistling sounds and a series of harsh wheezing *sew siew sew siew*, mainly during courtship, chasing the ♀ or when nervous. The ♀ utters different types of low and loud calls: nasal cackles often in crescendo, a repeated rattling *grrr* or *ga ga ga ga* (up to 12 notes per second[302]), in long series, first increasing in pitch, then lowering and speeding up.

MOULT Complex alternate moult strategy close to that of *Anas*, but few or no differences in timing between the sexes. Pre-formative moult usually starts in Aug–Sep and ends between Dec and Feb, with possibly a slowdown or suspension during the coldest part of winter[447]. It includes head and body feathers with a variable number of feathers on the breast, flanks, scapulars and mantle[56]. Definitive pre-alternate moult starts in both sexes when the chicks hatch, first the head and underparts, then the upperparts[56]. Definitive pre-basic moult occurs just after, at moulting sites or on nesting grounds for those adults protecting crèches. It begins with the wings and tail, and ends in Oct–Dec on wintering grounds.

HYBRIDISATION Natural hybridisation involving Common Shelduck has been reported a few times with Falcated Duck *Anas falcata*[947] and Common Eider *Somateria mollissima*[439]. Mixed pairs have occurred recently in W Europe with escapees or feral Egyptian Goose *Alopochen aegyptiacus* and Ruddy Shelduck *Tadorna ferruginea*. Hybrids with the latter are described below. In captivity, hybridisation reported in the literature with Spur-winged Goose *Plectropterus gambensis*[465], Orinoco Goose *Neochen jubata*, South African Shelduck *Tadorna cana*, Radjah Shelduck *T. radjah*, Paradise Shelduck *T. variegata*[442], Australian Shelduck *T. tadornoides*, Muscovy Duck *Cairina moschata*, Wood Duck *Aix sponsa*[439,817], Mallard *Anas platyrhynchos*[439,442], Gadwall *Anas strepera*[817], Red-crested Pochard *Netta rufina*, Common Pochard *Aythya ferina*[439], Goosander *Mergus merganser* and possibly Bar-headed Goose *Anser indicus*, but crosses between *Tadorna* and *Anser* cited previously are now considered dubious[817].

Common Shelduck × Ruddy Shelduck. Reported occasionally in the wild, this hybrid can appear superficially like Ruddy Shelduck in its reddish plumage, but is readily separated by the darker head and, frequently, a white collar. The available descriptions concur in the existence of plumage differences according to sex[108,439,442,443]. The ♂ has breast, scapulars and fore flanks dark reddish-brown, often becoming paler rufous on the rear flanks and mantle. Dark reddish-brown head sometimes with paler patches in front of the eyes and on cheeks. Belly dark brown with pale rump. A large white collar is usually present. Tertials forming a large white patch. Legs pale grey-pink and bill blackish (though some have a partially red bill). The ♀ has a paler brown head with a large white area at the base of the bill and large white eye-patch, the white collar can be more subdued or absent, overall colour is paler and has vermiculated paler grey flanks. The bill is essentially black with a dark pink area on the culmen or around nostrils.

HABITAT and LIFE-CYCLE Inhabits bays, estuaries and coastal marshes with large mudflats or sandy/muddy intertidal areas, and islands and sand dunes to nest, often in rabbit burrows, but also in all kinds of holes, including tree cavities up to 8 m above ground[302]. Locally in W Europe, the deterioration of many coastal habitats has resulted in the species colonising freshwater inland wetlands. Asian populations are coastal and inhabit semi-permanent or temporary, salt, brackish or fresh waterbodies, in steppe and semi-desert regions, as well as on banks of rivers and streams[302,794]. Eggs are mainly laid between early Apr and mid-Jun (depending on latitude, among other factors). Both parents take care of the nest and chicks, but many of them leave their offspring when 15–20 days old under the supervision of a few remaining adults, forming crèches of up to 100 young[302]. The adults then regroup at moulting sites on huge coastal mudflats, where they are protected from predators. The main W European moulting site, Helgoland Bight, NW Germany, hosts >100,000 moulting Shelducks[302,223]. Asian populations may moult near their breeding areas[302]. After moulting, groups move towards the wintering grounds and/or return to their breeding sites via several long stop-overs.

RANGE and POPULATION W European populations sedentary or perform short-distance migrations, and Asian populations migratory. In addition to main Eurasian range, nests along N African coast, in lower Nile Valley, Egypt, along the Tigris and Euphrates, Iraq, and coasts of the Caspian Sea. More local in Iran, Pakistan, Bangladesh, the S coast of China and South Korea. Global population estimated at 580,000–710,000 individuals[305].

CAPTIVITY Commonly kept, and said to breed readily even if it is often aggressive during courtship and the nesting period. Scarcer in North America than in Eurasia, where it is among the cheapest species sold. In W Europe, some small populations inland may be derived from and/or enhanced by individuals escaped from captivity.

REFERENCES Baker (1993)[56]; Bird Hybrids Flickr forum (2009)[108]; BirdLife International (2014)[145]; Carboneras (1992)[223], Cramp & Simmons (1977)[268]; Delany *in* Kear (2005)[302]; Delany & Scott (2006)[305]; Gillham & Gillham (1996)[439]; Gillham & Gillham (2000)[442]; Gillham & Gillham (2002)[443]; Ginn & Melville (1983)[447]; Gray (1958)[465]; Madge & Burn (1988)[794]; McCarthy (2006)[817]; Panov (1989)[947].

213. Adult ♂ (definitive basic). England, Feb (Sébastien Reeber).

214. Pair (definitive basic); note differences in bill shape and coloration (♂ left and ♀ right). France, Mar (Aurélien Audevard).

215. Adult ♀ (definitive basic), often has whitish marks on head, especially around eyes and at base of bill. England, Feb (Sébastien Reeber).

216. Adult ♂ (definitive basic). France, Apr (Matthieu Vaslin).

217. Juvenile (first basic) has no pectoral band, with brown scapulars and dull pinkish bare parts. France, Jun (Sébastien Reeber).

218. Adult ♀ (definitive basic). France, May (Sébastien Reeber).

CRESTED SHELDUCK
Tadorna cristata

Plate 22

TAXONOMY *Pseudotadorna cristata* Nagamichi Kuroda, 1917, *Tori*, I, pp. 1–2, fig. 1. Very probably extinct[80,411], known from three specimens taken in Korea (a ♂ during winter 1913 or 1914, and ♀ in Dec 1916) and Vladivostok, Russia (♀ in Apr 1877). The first two are held in Tokyo and the third in Copenhagen. The species was first described only in 1890 as a hybrid between Ruddy Shelduck *T. ferruginea* and Gadwall *Anas strepera*[1053]. Later, Kuroda contradicted this identification and thereafter described the Crested Shelduck, assigning it to a separate genus[44,411].

IDENTIFICATION Plumage distinctive, but should be identified with great care given its rarity.

PLUMAGES Strong sexual dimorphism. The three specimens appear adult, and were collected in winter. No information available on juvenile, formative and alternate plumages. Moult strategy unknown.

Adult ♂

Definitive basic plumage. Forehead, cap down to eye, nape and hindneck black with green gloss, forming long drooping crest. Rest of head pale grey with narrow dark vermiculations. Bill pinkish-red. Black patch on chin. Lower neck, breast and upper mantle black with green sheen. Underparts and scapulars grey vermiculated white, with reddish tones on posterior scapulars and tertials. Rump and tail black. Undertail-coverts ochre-yellow. Upper- and underwing close to those of Ruddy Shelduck, mostly black and white with green gloss on speculum. Legs bright pink.

Adult ♀

Definitive basic plumage. ♀ only superficially similar to ♂, but has facial patch, forehead, cheeks, upper neck and broad eye-ring continuing as a thin bridle rearwards, whitish. Rest of head black. Rest of body grey-brown clearly streaked dark, with posterior scapulars and tertials tinged reddish. Bill and legs a slightly paler pink.

GEOGRAPHIC VARIATION None described.

MEASUREMENTS and MASS The data presented here were published by Delacour[295] and involve the two specimens in Tokyo. ♂ (*n*=1): wing chord 320, tail 117,

culmen 45, tarsus 49.5; ♀ (*n*=1): wing chord 310, tail 115, culmen: 41.5, tarsus 47.

VOICE No information.

MOULT No information.

HYBRIDISATION No hybrid involving this species in its parentage is known.

HABITAT and LIFE-CYCLE The presumed breeding habitat consists of banks of rivers and lakes in forested montane regions. In winter, probably moved to lower valleys and coasts, and even the sea[919,920]. Other behavioural traits supposedly close to those of other shelducks, but few certain details exist.

RANGE and POPULATION The former range probably extended over extreme SE Russia to coastal regions of NE China, North Korea, South Korea, and N & S Japan[212,920]. The species might possibly still persist in the Chang-bai Shan, a mountain range on the border between China and North Korea. In addition to the three individuals mentioned above, only two sightings are generally accepted since 1950: one ♂ and two ♀♀ in May 1964 with Harlequin Ducks *Histrionicus histrionicus* at sea off the Rimsky-Korsakov Is, south-west of Vladivostok, Russia[721] and two ♂♂ and four ♀♀ reported in Mar 1971 at the mouth of the Pochon-gang River, on the N coast of North Korea[898]. This record, however, has been recently debated[145]. Unconfirmed observations have been reported more recently in E China (Heilongjiang, Jilin, Liaoning and Hebei provinces) and around the North Korean border[1042,1043,1288,1386]. The complete lack of proven sightings for many decades and the degradation of potential habitats leave little hope for the species' survival.

CAPTIVITY No captive individual reported.

REFERENCES Austin & Kuroda (1953)[44]; Beacham (1997)[80]; BirdLife International (2014)[145]; Callaghan *in* Kear (2005)[212]; Delacour (1954–64)[295]; Fuller (2001)[411]; Labzyuk & Nazarov (1967)[721]; Myong Sok (1984)[898]; Nowak (1983)[919]; Nowak (1984)[920]; Rank (1991)[1042]; Rank (1992)[1043]; Sclater (1890)[1153]; UNEP (2008)[1288]; Zhao (1993)[1386].

MUSCOVY DUCK
Cairina moschata

Plate 23

TAXONOMY *Anas moschata* Linnaeus, 1758, *Syst. Nat.*, edn. 10, p. 124. The phylogenetic position of this species and several other atypical ducks is not unanimously accepted. Long considered a member of the tribe Cairini (8–9 genera and 13 species[297,646]), it is now more frequently placed in the Anatini, usually near White-winged Duck *Asarcornis scutulata* (although not by Johnson & Sorenson[654]), the genus *Aix* and Hartlaub's Duck *Pteronetta hartlaubi*[767,776]. Monotypic. The domestic form is very common in captivity and readily establishes feral populations.

IDENTIFICATION Its mainly black plumage with a large white patch on the wing should prevent confusion with any other species. In Texas and N Mexico, special care is necessary to eliminate the possibility of birds resulting from reproduction between wild and domestic individuals.

PLUMAGES Strong sexual dimorphism in size and structure from first winter onwards. Moult timing and strategy not well known, but lack of obvious seasonal change during annual cycle in adult (see Moult). Ageing rather easy during first year of life, and possible in second year at least for some birds. Large, with broad wings and tail. Perches frequently. Possesses both claws and webs, as well as caruncles above the bill and around eyes.

Adult ♂

Definitive basic plumage (?). Black, with brown tones on head and flanks, purple to green gloss on mantle, scapulars, back, rump and tail, and metallic green on tertials. Elongated erectile feathers with green gloss often form a characteristic bump on the top of the head and a swollen nape. The head has a naked area of blackish skin extending from the bill base to around the eye, with a variable number of small red caruncles around the mask and eye, their quantity increasing with age[567]. The bill is pale pink to whitish with the nail, oblique median band and base black, and a small knob above the base of the culmen. Iris yellow to amber. Secondary upperwing-coverts and area around the alula white, remiges black with metallic green gloss on the secondaries. Underwing has all secondary and primary coverts white, and remiges black. Legs and feet dark grey. Domestic forms are heavier and plumper, with a variable number of white feathers (usually on the head and breast, sometimes the whole body, but rarely the remiges), more extensive facial skin, with many more caruncles and mainly or entirely bright red, and often has yellow to orange legs.

Adult ♀

Definitive basic plumage. Similar to ♂ but two to three times lighter. Bumps less marked on crown and nape (thinner head profile). Bill lacks knob at base and face almost without bare skin, devoid of red caruncles, apart from a line between the top of the bill to above the eye, or at most around it. Iris brown to yellowish-brown, often darker than ♂.

Juvenile

First basic plumage. Similar to definitive basic plumage being completely dark, but lacks the green and purple sheen of adult. No bare skin between the bill base and eye. The bill is coloured like the adult, but with less contrast. Iris pale brown to amber. The head, breast and underparts are usually dull brown and are variably mottled light brown. Upperwing initially completely or almost wholly dark.

First-winter

Formative plumage. The timing, duration and extent of pre-formative moult have not been described in the wild, and are probably variable, the species breeding year-round. Young are close to adult, but duller black, with a variable number of inner lesser and median coverts white. The subsequent plumages show more white on the upperwing, but it seems that after the second pre-basic moult, at least some birds still show some dark outer secondary coverts.

GEOGRAPHIC VARIATION None.

MEASUREMENTS and MASS ♂ much larger than ♀. Differences in size obvious from as early as a few months old. ♂ (*n*=9): wing chord 345–408 (383), tail 164–184 (176), bill 60.9–76.2 (67.9), tarsus 62.1–69.1 (64.7), mass 1,990–4,000; ♀ (*n*=4): wing chord 294–318 (307), tail 139–156 (148), bill 47.2–54.3 (51.4), tarsus 48.3–54.2 (51.9), mass 1,100–1,470[743,945].

VOICE Mostly silent. The ♂ emits an asthmatic

wheezing, often repeated in rapid series. The ♀ produces a *quack* like those of many ♀ dabbling ducks.

MOULT Not fully described in the wild. The moulting strategy observed in captivity cannot be applied to natural populations, which can breed year-round. Like many species with an inter-tropical distribution, the breeding season is more related to rainfall conditions and the availability of habitat that results. Pre-basic moult usually occurs after breeding, and also requires suitable habitats (resources, shelter). It is thus probable that weather conditions also affect the timing (and perhaps extent) of moults. The extent (and even occurrence) of pre-formative and pre-alternate moults have not been defined in the wild. In captivity, the moult strategy may differ in relation to climate, lack of movements, food quality and availability. Moreover, some captives may have domestic birds in their ancestry; the latter are also likely to have a different moult strategy.

HYBRIDISATION Very few cases of hybridisation documented in the wild, but many reports involving this species involving domestic feral birds. For example, this is the case for Common Shelduck *Tadorna tadorna* (very rare) and Mallard *Anas platyrhynchos*. The latter hybrid is very likely to be observed in the wild, since it is widespread in poultry being obtained by artificial insemination and deemed to have very low fertility[817]. In Africa, crosses involving domestic birds have been reported with Egyptian Goose *Alopochen aegyptiacus* and Meller's Duck *Anas melleri*, the fragile conservation status of the latter even being threatened by hybridisation. In captivity, crosses involving Muscovy Duck (again often domestic forms) have been reported with Spur-winged Goose *Plectropterus gambensis*, Swan Goose *Anser cygnoides*, Greylag Goose *A. anser*, Snow Goose *Chen caerulescens*, Canada Goose *Branta canadensis*, White-winged Duck *Asarcornis scutulata*, Comb Duck *Sarkidiornis melanotos*, American Wigeon *Anas americana*, American Black Duck *A. rubripes*, Pacific Black Duck *A. superciliosa* and Northern Shoveler *A. clypeata*[465,817,1190].

HABITAT and LIFE-CYCLE Little known. Frequents various habitats, especially rivers, backwaters, marshes and ponds with wooded shores, as well as mangroves. In S Texas, found in parts of the Rio Grande where riverine habitat is protected and where it is most easily seen flying along the river. Usually breeds in holes in trees near water, but often away from the riverbed. Often undertakes movements in response to heavy rainfall, to use habitats that have become temporarily suitable. The ♂ leaves the ♀ quickly after the eggs are laid. In non-breeding season, often in parties of <20 individuals. Feeds mostly in morning and evening, spending much time perching on branches in the shade.

RANGE and POPULATION Distributed mainly in Central and South America, on the coast of the Gulf of Mexico to extreme S Texas. In the USA, individuals showing characteristics of wild birds are regularly reported along the lower Rio Grande, Texas. Natural populations numbered 50,000–500,000 birds at the end of the last decade[145], but were estimated at twice as large a few years earlier[567]. Declining due to habitat destruction and excessive hunting. Locally in Mexico, its populations have been reinforced by nestbox programmes.

Domestic feral populations are present in many places in the N Hemisphere, mainly in the vicinity of urban or suburban wetlands and parks. Currently present around many large cities, in Florida (introduced in 1967), Texas and California[657]. In Europe, just a few viable populations, often reinforced by escapees. Populations of fewer than several dozen pairs are known in Britain, the Netherlands, Germany, Austria and Israel[62], and even more locally in France and Spain at least.

CAPTIVITY Very common in captivity in its domestic form, but birds with natural characters are much harder to find.

REFERENCES Banks *et al.* (2008)[62]; BirdLife International (2014)[145]; Delacour & Mayr (1945)[297]; Gray (1958)[465]; Hoffmann in Kear (2005)[567]; Johnsgard (1978)[646]; Johnson & Sorenson (1999)[654]; Johnson & Hawk (2012)[657]; Leopold (1959)[743]; Livezey (1991)[767]; Livezey (1997)[776]; McCarthy (2006)[817]; Palmer (1976)[945]; Sibley (1938)[1190].

219. Adult ♂. Texas, USA, Oct (Mike Danzenbaker).

220. Adult ♂. Brazil, Aug (William Price).

221. Adult ♂. Brazil, Feb (Otto Plantema).

222. Adult ♂. Texas, USA, Dec (Greg Lavaty).

WHITE-WINGED DUCK
Asarcornis scutulata

Plate 23

TAXONOMY *Anas scutulata*, S. Müller, 1842, *Verh. Nat. Ges. Ned. Over. Bez., Land-Volkenk.*, p. 159. Long considered close to and even congeneric with Muscovy Duck *Cairina moschata*, but now placed in a monotypic genus[654]. Traditionally considered a member of the Tadornini but more recently placed within the Aythyini[1079]. Two subspecies are often recognised, but this treatment is debated (see Geographic Variation) and merits further investigation[485]. The subspecies in mainland Asia is named *A. s. leucoptera* Blyth, 1849.

IDENTIFICATION Size, structure, dark coloration with pale head and large white wing patches, and its ecological preference for densely forested habitats, make confusion difficult. Attention should be paid, though, to feral domestic Muscovy Ducks, which can be vaguely similar.

PLUMAGES Birds described here are from mainland SE Asia, including Bangladesh and extreme E India (sometimes attributed to *A. s. leucoptera*). Slight sexual dimorphism from first winter onwards. Moult strategy unclear, but no seasonal change during year. Ageing possible until first summer, but more difficult than for Muscovy Duck, for example, the upperwing showing a large white patch from juvenile plumage.

Adult ♂

Definitive basic plumage. Head and upper neck white with highly variable number of small grey and black spots, mainly concentrated on the nape and rear crown. From afar, the head may look dark grey in some birds and mostly white in others. Bill yellow-orange variably mottled brown or black, often more densely towards the base, with a pale nail. A slight bulge is visible at the base of the culmen during the nesting period. Iris yellow to orange-hazel, and quite variable. Mantle, back, scapulars, rump and uppertail-coverts black with metallic green sheen. Lower neck and breast have dark green gloss, grading into dark brown with a variable reddish hue on flanks. Belly black with variable grey flecks. Outer tertials white with black inner webs, forming two long white and black lines beside the speculum. White secondary coverts and a black band formed by the tips of the greater coverts, and glossy blue-grey secondaries. Primaries and primary coverts black. Underwing black (remiges) and white (coverts). Tail

dark brown. Legs yellow-orange. Significant variation in the extent of white on the head, breast and even body, some birds having a white head and others, in the extreme, the head, neck, breast and mantle all white.

Adult ♀

Definitive basic plumage. Similar to ♂ but smaller and lacks swelling at the base of the culmen. On average, iris darker brown with denser dark speckles on the head and upper neck.

Juvenile

First basic plumage. Browner and duller overall, without gloss of adult. The flanks are duller brown (less reddish), with less contrast vs. the breast. The head and upper neck are brownish-grey initially, more uniform than adult. Breast, mantle and lower neck always brownish, even in birds that become white there when adult. Upperwing has large white patches like adult. Iris dark brown.

First-winter

Formative plumage. Poorly described in the literature but close to that of adult, including head becoming white with variable dark flecking.

GEOGRAPHIC VARIATION The nominate subspecies occurs in Indonesia and has the plumage more marked with white on average. Birds on Sumatra, especially ♂♂, can be entirely white, except the remiges, tertials and rectrices[208,324]. Only 20% of birds show a pattern similar to that of continental birds (head and upper neck white speckled grey and black)[469,485,792], and just one of 19 birds observed in SE Sumatra did so[208]. Moreover, these birds were also described as more variable in overall appearance and smaller[208,485,792], with a smaller and rounder head, shorter and slightly up-curved bill and a relatively long neck and shorter body, thus their posture is typically more upright, like that of a shelduck[485]. Finally, the bare parts are possibly redder on average[485]. Other differences in habitat selection and diet have also been reported[485].

MEASUREMENTS and MASS ♂ larger than ♀. Continental birds, sample unknown[53]: ♂: wing chord 363–401, tail 127–178, bill 58–66, tarsus 54–61, mass 3,800–4,300; ♀: wing chord 305–355, tail 127–178, bill 56–61, tarsus 53–61, mass 2,100–3,600 g. Captive birds at Slimbridge, England, originating from Assam, India[485]. ♂ (n=20): wing chord 351–380 (367.2), bill 57.3–67.2 (60.7), tarsus 54.4–65.8 (60.3), mass 2,200–3,225 (2,666); ♀ (n=7): wing chord 327–358 (340.7), bill 54.0–61.2 (57.4), tarsus 55.0–57.6 (56.6). Mass 1,700–2,250 (1,914). The mass of 'numerous' ♂♂ collected in S Sumatra said to fluctuate between 2,500 and 2,800 g[485,581].

VOICE Unique, rather mournful honking that gave rise to the name 'Spirit Duck' in Assam[485]. Different honking and nasal calls *ang* or *hong*, singly or repeated, or a higher pitched *wii*. In flight, the wings produce a slight hiss.

MOULT Occurrence and extent of pre-formative and pre-alternate moult very poorly studied in the wild, but the former is probably completed quickly and results in the loss of the plain greyish feathers on the head and upper neck, and at least some dull brownish body feathers. In captivity, pre-basic moult occurs quite late and starts with the remiges in Sep. The few data available from the wild confirm this schedule, especially on Sumatra[485], as well as the rather late breeding period for continental populations.

HYBRIDISATION Very few reports in captivity with Mallard *Anas platyrhynchos* and Muscovy Duck *Cairina moschata* (or one of its domestic forms)[582,817]. No cases reported in the wild, but hybridisation with domestic ducks has been mooted to explain the leucistic and highly variable appearance of populations on Sumatra[579,792], although this requires confirmation through genetic studies.

HABITAT and LIFE-CYCLE Mostly sedentary, usually not gregarious and difficult to see because of its rarity, largely crepuscular habits and densely forested habitats. Most frequently seen or heard in flight[472]. Inhabits mature natural forests and wetlands, with many ponds, oxbows or slow-flowing streams, usually in remote areas. Its favoured habitats are usually in the lowlands, but the species does occur up to 1,400 m[145,473,485], especially in areas where lowland habitats have been extensively impacted. Eggs laid mainly in Mar–Jul (laying dates probably influenced regionally by the monsoon), usually in tree cavities up to 23 m above the ground[485]. ♂ remains with ♀ during incubation and the first weeks of life of the chicks. In non-breeding season, mostly alone or in small groups, usually on or near the breeding sites.

RANGE and POPULATION Listed as Endangered and is locally close to extinction in some areas. Highly fragmented distribution from E India (Assam, Arunachal Pradesh) and Bangladesh to W & S Sumatra, with a few small and isolated populations in Myanmar, Thailand, Laos (possibly extinct[313]), Cambodia and S Vietnam. Once widespread over this range, with an initial population estimate of 50,000–500,000 birds[470,472]. Rare or extinct in Malaysia and Java, but recently reported in Bhutan[229]. More recently, population estimated at just 336 individuals in the early 1990s[473] and 450 (130 in SE Asia, 170 in India and 150 in Sumatra) subsequently[1095]. Several estimates have been published since, based on more optimistic guesses, but its ongoing decline is unanimously accepted. Population most recently estimated at 1,000 birds: c.200 in SE Asia, c.450 in India and Bangladesh, c.150 on Sumatra and c.200 in Myanmar[145]. Its decline is primarily related to large-scale destruction of its natural habitats, hunting pressure and disturbance. Protection measures have been implemented in SE Asia to preserve suitable sites, but these appear insufficient to assure the future of the species, especially as the increasingly fragmented populations are also threatened by inbreeding.

CAPTIVITY Requires good maintenance conditions, preferably with the possibility to fly, and may be aggressive toward conspecifics and other species when breeding. Deemed to be particularly subject to avian tuberculosis. Once considered difficult to breed in captivity, but possible if suitable conditions are achieved. For all these reasons, generally very rare in captivity, difficult to find and expensive, and consequently very unlikely to escape.

REFERENCES Baker (1908)[53]; BirdLife International (2014)[145]; BirdLife International Cambodia Programme (2012)[146]; Burn & Brickle (1992)[208]; Choudhury (2007)[229]; Dersu *et al.* (2008)[313]; Drilling (2000)[324]; Drilling (2001)[325]; Evans *et al.* (1996)[377]; Green (1992)[468]; Green (1992)[469]; Green (1992)[470]; Green (1993)[471]; Green (1993)[472]; Green (1993)[473]; Green *et al. in* Kear (2005)[485]; Holmes (1977)[579]; Hoogerwerf (1950)[581]; Hopkinson (1926)[582]; Johnson & Sorenson (1999)[654]; Mackenzie (1990)[792]; McCarthy (2006)[817]; Robertson & Goldstein (2012)[1079]; Rose & Scott (1997)[1095].

223. Adult (definitive basic?); head shape and heavy speckling indicate a ♀. India, Dec (Jainy Kuriakose).

224. Adult (definitive basic?). Captivity, Apr (Harold Stiver).

COTTON PYGMY-GOOSE
Nettapus coromandelianus

Plate 25

TAXONOMY *Anas coromandeliana* Gmelin, 1789, *Syst. Nat.*, 1, p. 522. Complex and controversial systematic position[1228], although the genus *Nettapus* is now considered part of the tribe Anatini. Within the genus, closer to *N. pulchellus* (Oceania) than to *N. auritus* (sub-Saharan Africa)[767]. Two recognised subspecies, the nominate over most of the range, except Australia, where replaced by *N. c. albipennis* Gould, 1842, which was sometimes regarded as a separate species in the past.

IDENTIFICATION No risk of confusion with any other species in the Holarctic. ♀♀ and juvenile show a superficial resemblance to Green Pygmy-Goose *N. pulchellus*, from Australia and New Guinea.

PLUMAGES Nominate subspecies. Strong sexual dimorphism from first winter onwards. Complex alternate moult strategy (two plumages per definitive cycle, three in first cycle). The immature moult sequences and plumage are poorly understood in the wild. Ageing young ♂ easy until the beginning of second pre-basic moult, but more difficult for ♀. One of the smallest Anseriformes, lighter than Eurasian Teal *Anas crecca* or Green-winged Teal *A. carolinensis*, with shape characterised by thick neck, often held vertical, rather rectangular head and short and triangular bill. Fast flight. The neck of ♂ is slightly longer than that of ♀, which is thought might permit them to exploit different depths when feeding[1297].

Adult ♂

Definitive basic plumage (Jan–Mar/Jun–Aug?). Mainly black and white. Head and breast white with forehead, crown and breast-band black. Eye surrounded by thin black line. Iris red. Bill black. Underparts white with narrow grey vermiculations on the flanks. Lower belly, under- and uppertail-coverts more strongly marked with blackish flecks and patches. Tail blackish. Mantle, scapulars, tertials and upperwing-coverts black with metallic green sheen. Secondaries black (green gloss to outer webs) with broad white tips and central primaries also white, forming unique wing pattern with broad trailing edge extending as a large wingbar. Underwing has the same pattern. Legs grey to greyish-green.

Definitive alternate plumage (Jul–Sep/Dec–Feb?). Plumage somewhat intermediate between basic adult

♂ and ♀. Head whiter than ♀, with dark eyebrow often confined to behind the eye. Breast finely streaked dark without the black band of basic plumage, flanks tinged slightly browner and upperparts duller. The red iris and basic wing pattern also distinguish it from ♀.

Adult ♀

Definitive basic plumage. More grey and brown than ♂. Head and breast grey-beige with narrow darker grey vermiculations and cap, loral stripe and short eyestripe blackish. Iris dark brown. Bill lead-grey, with a yellowish patch at the base and on lower mandible. Flanks, rump and uppertail-coverts beige-brown, the latter variably flecked white. Belly and undertail-coverts (and centre of breast) white in older birds, with more pronounced brownish streaks in young ♀♀. Tail and upperparts uniform dark brown with bronze or green sheen on scapulars. Upperwing dark grey-brown, except tips of secondaries which form a broad white trailing edge that extends onto the inner primaries. The white is usually wider on the inner web than the outer web, unlike the ♂. Underwing mostly blackish, including axillaries, but greater coverts often paler. Legs and feet grey with variable yellow-brown hue.

Definitive alternate plumage. Very close to basic plumage, but often seems browner, especially on the upperparts, flanks and rump. Bill appears (on average) more yellow-green at the base.

Juvenile

First basic plumage (until Jan–Apr?). Plumage similar to adult ♀ but duller. The head, neck, breast and flanks are browner, more coarsely flecked and streaked, and darker than adult. The upperparts are browner and paler, reducing the contrast between scapulars and flanks. The upperwing is similar to that of adult ♀ but browner and duller, without any metallic sheen on the coverts, and a variable pale bar (related to age or sex?) formed by the tips to the greater coverts. Underwing has the tips of the axillaries and coverts forming a succession of pale lines, unlike the uniform blackish adult underwing. Young ♂ shows a hint of pale wingbar, more obvious than young ♀, and a blacker bill.

First-winter ♂

Formative plumage (Jan–Apr/Jun–Aug). Body coloration

323

close to that of adult ♂ but duller, except the wing, which remains juvenile. Only slight green reflections on the secondary coverts and at best a vague pale area replacing the white band across the primaries.

First-winter ♀

Formative plumage (Jan–Apr/?). Few data available, but both wing surfaces mostly juvenile. Moreover, the eyestripe is slightly broader, flanks more washed pale brownish and belly more clearly barred dark.

Further investigation is needed into the different plumages. For example, some birds that are obviously ♂ (black bill) have a white wingbar intermediate in size, with white mainly restricted to the inner webs of the primaries, and underwing-coverts like adult (second-cycle birds?).

GEOGRAPHIC VARIATION Two subspecies recognised, including the nominate described above, present in S & SE Asia, and *N. c. albipennis* on the coast of NE Australia. The latter is slightly larger but otherwise similar in appearance, with a different moulting schedule linked to its distribution in S Hemisphere, and a definitive alternate plumage said to be much shorter-lived[928].

MEASUREMENTS and MASS Biometrics of ♂ and ♀ very close. ♀ heavier than ♂ during monsoon[1297]. ♂ (*n*=27): wing chord 168–171 (169.3), tail 63.4–65.9 (64.6), bill length 26.2–26.9 (26.6), bill depth 15.1–15.6 (15.4), bill width 12.0–12.7 (12.3), tarsus 29.0–29.2 (29.1), middle toe 34.0–34.5 (34.3), mass 180–260 (221.2); ♀ (*n*=15): wing chord 168–171 (169.1), tail 63.2–65.3 (64.5), bill length 26.2–26.8 (26.5), bill depth 15.1–15.4 (15.3), bill width 11.5–12.0 (11.8), tarsus 29.0–29.2 (29.1), middle toe 34.1–34.5 (34.3), mass 215–236 (227.0)[1297].

VOICE The male utters, among other sounds, a multi-syllabic rhythmic *kar kwaack ka-ka-ka*, rather nasal and low-pitched. The ♀ gives a *kwik* or *kwak*, which is weaker and squeakier. Descriptions of various other calls and sonograms are given in Fullagar[409] and Rasmussen & Anderton[1044].

MOULT Very few data available concerning moult of the nominate subspecies in the wild. Given its broad inter-tropical distribution, moult timing and strategy are probably linked to latitude and wet season. In India, there is clearly a pre-formative moult in young ♂ in spring, which includes some to most head and body

feathers and an unknown number of upperwing-coverts. After this, it look like adult ♂, except for lacking or having only faint white wingbar on the primaries. Pre-alternate moult essentially includes the body feathers, and starts in the ♂ shortly after breeding (between Jun and Sep in India). It may occur before nesting in ♀, but this remains to be established. Definitive pre-basic moult occurs shortly after pre-alternate moult and seems to end between Jan and Mar, at least in adult ♂.

HYBRIDISATION None reported in the literature, either in captivity or in the wild[97,817]. The only report in captivity, relating to the genus *Nettapus* concerns an African Pygmy-goose *N. auritus* and a Chiloe Wigeon *A. sibilatrix*[465].

HABITAT and LIFE-CYCLE Inhabits shallow freshwater wetlands with abundant emergent or submergent vegetation. In India, eggs are laid mainly during the wet season, especially between Jun and Sep, depending on the locality, often in cavities or hollow trees near water. The ♂ often remains with ♀ during incubation or to rear the chicks, but may also gather in small flocks nearby. Tame or shy, it may use small waterbodies even near or within villages. Usually encountered in pairs or small flocks, but more gregarious in non-breeding season, especially in drought periods, when birds are forced to concentrate at the remaining wetlands.

RANGE and POPULATION Outside the main range, several smaller or isolated populations in Oceania (in Australia, *N. c. albipennis*). Migratory in north of range, but mostly sedentary elsewhere. Long movements may be promoted by heavy rainfall. Regular visitor to Oman and the Persian Gulf, rarer in Iran and Iraq[409], accidental west to Socotra, Yemen. Population in S Asia estimated at 100,000 individuals[757] and fewer than 100 breeding pairs in China[182]. Total population 130,000–1,100,000 individuals, with most uncertainty in SE Asia[757,1348]. Stable or trend unknown[1296,1348].

CAPTIVITY Rarely kept in captivity, at least outside its range. Reportedly quite difficult to breed, and preferably kept in flocks, in large aviaries with water that does not freeze in winter. Generally uncommonly offered for sale and unlikely to escape from captivity.

REFERENCES Baker (1929)[54]; Bird Hybrids Database (2014)[97]; Brazil (2009)[182]; Fullagar *in* Kear (2005)[409]; Gray (1958)[465]; Li *et al.* (2009)[757]; Livezey (1991)[767]; McCarthy (2006)[817]; Ogilvie & Young (1998)[928];

Rasmussen & Anderton (2005)[1044]; Sraml *et al.* (1996)[1228]; Upadhyaya & Saikia (2010)[1296]; Upadhyaya & Saikia (2011)[1297]; Wetlands International (2014)[1348].

225. *N. c. coromandelianus*, ♂ (formative/definitive basic), still showing some traces of alternate plumage. India, Feb (Sunil Singhal).

226. *N. c. coromandelianus*, first-winter ♂ (first basic/formative); this ♂ is in pre-formative moult and closely resembles adult ♂ in pre-basic moult at same time, but still has different-coloured bare parts, while only some rectrices have been replaced and note narrow upper flanks feathers. India, Dec (Christopher Plummer).

227. *N. c. coromandelianus*, ♀ (formative/definitive basic). India, Mar (Sunil Singhal).

228. *N. c. coromandelianus*, adult ♂ (definitive alternate). This plumage is duller, and lacks black breast-band, but wing pattern remains the same and is typical of adult ♂. India, Dec (Sunil Singhal).

229. *N. c. coromandelianus*, group; upperwing patterns correspond to adult ♂ in definitive alternate (left), ♀ (centre) and first-winter ♂ (first basic/formative). Oman, Nov (Anders Blomdahl).

230. *N. c. coromandelianus*, ♂ (first alternate/definitive alternate); resembles ♀ in this plumage, even if eyestripe is often reduced or absent, but sexed by its dark red iris. India, Oct (Anand Arya).

WOOD DUCK
Aix sponsa
Plate 24

TAXONOMY *Anas sponsa* Linnaeus, 1758, *Syst. Nat.*, edn. 10, p. 128. The genus *Aix* includes two monotypic species, of which ♂♂ are very distinctive, and is usually placed at the root of the subfamily Anatinae, near the genera *Cairina* and *Pteronetta*, with which it forms the subtribe Cairineae.

IDENTIFICATION ♂ in definitive basic and formative plumage cannot be mistaken for any other species. All other plumages (alternate ♂, juvenile and ♀) are similar and are close to the equivalent plumages of Mandarin Duck *A. galericulata*. Both species have completely allopatric ranges, but are very likely to escape from captivity and have established many feral populations, especially near urban areas. The identification features are as follows.

- The head of Mandarin Duck is grey with thin whitish stripes on the cheeks, whose longest feathers reach the upper neck. In Wood Duck, the head is darker grey, almost blackish with a green or purple sheen on the crown. The head of juvenile Mandarin Duck is quite similar to the adult, while that of juvenile Wood Duck shows clear contrast between pale lores and dark cap.

- The white peri-ocular patch amounts to a rather narrow clean eye-ring, with a white stripe from the back of the eye that fades on the rear cheeks in Mandarin Duck. In Wood Duck, the eye is surrounded by a large white drop-shaped patch, often irregularly outlined, pointed backward but without a bridle.

- The orbital ring is dull yellow (juvenile), bright yellow (♀) or reddish (♂) in Wood Duck, while it is very narrow, dull greyish or pale yellowish, and barely visible in Mandarin Duck.

- The white throat of Mandarin Duck extends as a fine white line up the base of the bill (which is straight or almost so), and fades in front of the lores. In Wood Duck, this white line is generally more marked, well rounded (as is the feathering at the bill base), and completely encircles the bill, including on the forehead. Juvenile of the two species do not show the same pattern, rather they often have two diffuse horizontal, parallel lines behind the eye. The white eye-ring is narrow or absent (the orbital ring is visible). ♂♂ in juvenile

and definitive alternate plumage of Wood Duck also have two short whitish bands starting at the white throat, one towards the back of the eye and the other below the cheeks. Some adult ♀♀ (senescent?) possess a similar pattern.

- Adult ♀ Mandarin Duck has a brownish-grey bill more or less strongly tinged pink or pale purple with a white nail and usually a yellow patch at the base of the culmen. Adult ♀ Wood Duck has a grey bill with a blackish nail. ♂♂ in definitive alternate plumage of both species show a pink to reddish bill with a white nail in Mandarin Duck and blackish nail (and culmen) in Wood Duck.

- The pale spots on the flanks (to a lesser extent the breast) are larger, round and whitish in Mandarin Duck, but reduced to vague pale buff streaks along the feather shafts in Wood Duck. The underparts of the former are marked with broad lines of round whitish patches, but are darker in the latter.

- The scapulars of Mandarin Duck are uniform brown whereas they frequently show an obvious bronze, purple or blue sheen in ♀ Wood Duck.

- The legs are on average brighter yellow in Mandarin Duck than Wood Duck.

- The inner secondaries have a white stripe at the base of the inner web in Mandarin Duck, visible at a distance on perched birds, as well as in flight from above. Furthermore, the speculum of ♀ Mandarin Duck shows only very limited gloss, whereas these are strong in ♀ Wood Duck, and extend over a large part of the inner wing.

- The underwing is distinctive at all ages. The coverts of Wood Duck show strong dark streaks on a pale background, whereas they are uniformly dark in Mandarin Duck.

PLUMAGES Strong sexual dimorphism from first basic (juvenile) plumage onward. Complex alternate moult strategy (two plumages by definitive cycle, three in first cycle). Ageing ♂♂ relatively easy until the beginning of the first winter and possible until the end of the subsequent summer under good viewing conditions or in the hand. ♀♀ harder to age from the beginning of the second calendar year. Rather small dabbling duck with characteristic shape. Spends much time perched on branches.

Adult ♂

Definitive basic plumage (Oct–Nov/May–Jun.). Very colourful. Head pattern complex, black with a white throat from which emanate two short stripes, one over the cheeks to behind the eye and the other under the cheeks, around the neck. Two thin white lines frame the broad eyestripe which extends into a drooping pointed crest. A strong green gloss is visible on the forehead, lores and eye-patch, where a patch of purple gloss is usually also visible. Iris red surrounded by a yellow-orange to reddish orbital ring. Bill red on sides and at base, pink on top except a black line on the centre of culmen, with bright yellow lines at the upper base of the mandible, and black nail. Breast purplish-brown with delicate longitudinal lines of white dots. Hindneck and mantle black. Pale tan to yellowish-grey flanks finely vermiculated dark, with strong black and white vertical bars at border with breast. The fringes of the upper rear flank feathers form a sharp black and white border. Belly white. Femoral area dark purple. Under- and uppertail-coverts, tail, rump, back and scapulars black with metallic blue or green sheen. Inner greater coverts and median coverts have dark blue sheen and black tips, rest of the secondary and primary coverts duller grey-brown. Speculum strongly glossed blue (extending along tips of primaries) and a white trailing edge. Outer webs of primaries white (more marked on outer half), also visible on folded wing. Underwing dark grey except axillaries, lesser and median coverts whitish with bold dark grey stripes, tips of greater coverts broadly white and streaked dark, and tips of secondaries white. Legs and feet brownish-yellow.

Definitive alternate plumage (Jun–Jul/Oct–Nov). Similar to ♀ but upperparts slightly darker with more pronounced gloss. More contrasting head, with two bands starting from white throat to central cheeks and around the neck, and white eye-patch almost lacking, making the yellow orbital ring more obvious. The bill's coloration is close to that in basic plumage, but paler and duller. Distinctive red iris.

Adult ♀

Definitive basic plumage (Oct–Nov/Jan–Apr). Slightly flecked greyish-brown overall. Structure and shape identical to ♂, but crest shorter. Head grey to slate-coloured, with a contrasting clear-cut white throat extending as a line surrounding the bill base. White peri-ocular, drop-shaped patch, pointed at its rear. Forehead, lores and crown black with subtle green to violet sheen. Some ♀♀ (perhaps age-related) have short white stripes across and below cheeks. Bill dark grey with nail black and tomium often tinged pink. Iris brown with prominent yellow orbital ring. Breast and flanks brown with pale yellowish to pale buff patches along the shafts forming fine longitudinal lines on the breast and diffuse streaks on the flanks. Whitish belly. Undertail-coverts mottled brown. Tail, rump, back, mantle, scapulars and tertials fairly uniform brown with purple to bronze sheen. Upperwing similar to ♂, distinguished mainly by secondaries having rounded white tips on the outer webs, forming a much broader white trailing edge than in ♂, which is obvious in flight or on folded wing. Also note innermost secondary (s10) without white tip and plain black, different from that in ♂. Underwing like ♂ except larger white trailing edge to secondaries. Legs dull brownish-yellow.

Definitive alternate plumage (Feb–Apr/Oct–Nov). Very like basic plumage, but crest shorter or almost absent, and overall colour marginally darker and duller, usually without gloss on upperparts. Head shows no sheen on the crown, and white pattern somewhat less clearly demarcated.

Juvenile

First basic plumage (until Oct–Nov). Close to ♀ but duller and less contrasting. In particular, head pattern less clearly defined, with matt blackish crown. Pale eye-ring extends as two parallel lines bordering dark eyestripe behind eye. Also note pale loral patch, and a brown-beige to grey throat. Breast and flanks have yellowish-buff streaks, which are longer but slightly more diffuse than in adult ♀. Tertials paler brown, narrower and pointed. Upperwing greater and median coverts least square-tipped, the blue glossy speculum extending over the first two rows of secondary coverts (three rows or more in adult)[224] and often not exceeding the inner half of the speculum in length. Belly mottled brown. In juvenile plumage, ♂ distinguished from ♀ by two pale bars extending from the throat, one towards the back of the eye and the other below the cheeks. Moreover, adult coloration at the bill base and iris appear early in autumn, and may be useful for sexing young birds, although at this time, formative feathers usually also appear, which should make sexing easy. Finally, note the much broader tips to the secondaries in ♀, already distinctive at this age.

First-winter ♂

Formative plumage (Nov–Dec/May–Jun). Very similar to adult ♂, and generally best separated in the hand, via a close examination of upperwing pattern until the beginning of second pre-basic moult. When pre-formative moult is limited on the wing, the juvenile pattern (described above) is distinctive, with a particularly small glossy blue area and narrow, worn and round-tipped coverts. Formative coverts are much closer to definitive basic plumage, but are slightly paler and the greater coverts, in particular, less square-tipped. The formative wing is thus distinguished by its inner formative coverts slightly paler than the tertial coverts[224], as well as by contrast between the juvenile and formative coverts. Note that when pre-formative moult is extensive, the wing cannot be distinguished from that of adult from the first autumn[224,1014]. The juvenile rectrices are partly or all retained.

First-winter ♀

Formative plumage (Nov–Dec/Jan–Apr). Very similar to adult ♀ from end of pre-formative moult, and distinguished mostly by retained juvenile rectrices and upperwing pattern until the beginning of second pre-basic moult as described for ♀ above. However, pre-formative moult is often less extensive in the wing of young ♀.

GEOGRAPHIC VARIATION None.

MEASUREMENTS and MASS ♂ and adult very slightly larger than ♀ and young, respectively. ♂ (*n*=12): wing chord 218–240 (228), tail 100–118 (115), bill 32–36 (35), tarsus 34–39 (36); ♀ (*n*=12): wing chord 211–231 (221), tail 91–106 (98), bill 31–35 (34), tarsus 33–36 (35)[945]. ♂ (*n*=30): wing chord 217–239 (adult) and 208–233 (juvenile), tail 94–119, culmen 32–38, bill depth at end of forehead feathering 14.3–18.3, tarsus 34–38; ♀ (*n*=30): wing chord 195–232 (adult) and 188–226 (juvenile), tail 87–113, culmen 31–36, bill depth at end of forehead feathering 13.5–17.5, tarsus 32–36[1014]. ♂: mass 544–862 (adult, 680, *n*=84) and 499–817 (juvenile/first-winter, 667, *n*=45); ♀: mass 499–862 (adult, 671, *n*=60) and 454–817 (juvenile/first-winter, 612, *n*=47)[85]. ♂: mass 694 (adult, σ=61, *n*=150) and 662 (juvenile/first-winter, σ=63, *n*=49); ♀: mass 647 (adult, σ=52, *n*=76) and 627 (juvenile/first-winter, σ=51, *n*=40)[307].

VOICE Usually quiet outside courtship period. The ♂ utters a high-pitched, shrill whistle, a prolonged and rising *dweezz* and *dee-dee-djizz* recalling a whistling-duck. The wings of the ♂ also produce a typical whistling. The ♀ emits different calls, the most typical being loud, slightly squealing or trumpeting: a prolonged, rising *gang* or a *hee-yik*, acute and with a louder second syllable.

MOULT Complex alternate moult strategy close to that of *Anas*. An auxiliary pre-formative moult is reported in Jul–Aug in the young and concerns some feathers of the head[89], even if this moult has been described as more extensive, at least in ♂[945] (see above). Pre-formative moult occurs between Aug and Nov, starting at age 100 days[692]. It includes many to all head and body contour feathers, 1–4 tertials (most birds replace all[224]) and tertial coverts, none to a few rectrices and a variable number of secondary upperwing-coverts. It is reported that some birds (♂♂?), especially those in the south of the range, moult all their secondary coverts[224]. Primaries and primary coverts are retained. Definitive pre-alternate moult occurs in Jan–Apr in ♀ and May–Jul in ♂, starting sometimes while ♀ is still on eggs[560]. It includes the feathers of the upperparts and a variable number (up to 60%) of inner secondary coverts, none to all tertials, but few or no rectrices[555,1014]. Definitive pre-basic moult is complete, between Jun and Nov, and begins with the remiges. It is slightly delayed in ♀♀ that successfully raise young[555].

HYBRIDISATION Natural hybridisation is rare, reported occasionally with Mallard *Anas platyrhynchos* (see below), involving escapees in Eurasia. Other much rarer cases have been reported with Ring-necked Duck *Aythya collaris* (see that species), Common Goldeneye *Bucephala clangula*, Hooded Merganser *Lophodytes cucullatus* (see below) and possibly Redhead *Aythya americana*[817] in North America. Hybrids involving many other species have been described in the wild, but their origin may be captive, so they are listed below.

In captivity, Wood Duck has a deserved reputation as a 'seducer', whatever the species. Cases of hybridisation are known with *c*.50 different species, but, strangely, hybridisation with Mandarin Duck, the only congeneric, is very rare as are any crosses involving this species. The list of species mentioned in the literature[97,439,442,582,639,817,1190] as having hybridised with Wood Duck is as follows (references are listed only for rare cases): Common Shelduck *Tadorna tadorna*, Ruddy Shelduck *T. ferruginea*[97], Maned Duck *Chenonetta jubata*[802], Mandarin Duck, Brazilian Teal *Amazonetta brasiliensis*[639], Yellow-billed Duck *Anas undulata*, American Wigeon

A. americana[439], Eurasian Wigeon *A. penelope*, Chiloe Wigeon *A. sibilatrix*, Gadwall *A. strepera*, Northern Pintail *A. acuta*[1190], Yellow-billed Pintail *A. georgica*, Kerguelen Pintail *A. eatoni*[97], White-cheeked Pintail *A. bahamensis*, Red-billed Duck *A. erythrorhyncha* (?)[103], Philippine Duck *A. luzonica*[439], Spot-billed Duck *A. poecilorhyncha*, Pacific Black Duck *A. superciliosa*, Chestnut Teal *A. castanea*[817], Hottentot Teal *Anas hottentota*, Puna Teal *A. puna*[442], Garganey *A. querquedula*, Northern Shoveler *A. clypeata*, Eurasian Teal *A. crecca*, Green-winged Teal *A. carolinensis*, Speckled Teal *A. flavirostris*, Baikal Teal *A. formosa*[442], Cinnamon Teal *A. cyanoptera*[439], Blue-winged Teal *A. discors*[439], Ringed Teal *Callonetta leucophrys*[439], Marbled Duck *Marmaronetta angustirostris*[101], Rosy-billed Pochard *Netta peposaca*, Red-crested Pochard *N. rufina*, Canvasback *Aythya valisineria*[439], Common Pochard *A. ferina*, Baer's Pochard *A. baeri*, Ferruginous Duck *A. nyroca*, New Zealand Scaup *A. novaeseelandiae*[97], Tufted Duck *A. fuligula*, Greater Scaup *A. marila* (?)[127], Lesser Scaup *A. affinis*[1190] and Red-breasted Merganser *Mergus serrator*[439].

Wood Duck × Mallard[439,443]. The basic plumage of adult ♀ is usually quite easy to detect the influence of both parents. The head is dark with a strong metallic green gloss and thick crest on the nape (of variable length). The rather short bill has whitish, greyish or yellowish sides, with a pink or reddish base, and black culmen and nail. A white collar is sometimes visible, and the foreneck can be pale too. Breast purplish-brown and flanks grey, sometimes tinged buff, with a hint of black bar between them. Rear flanks reddish to mahogany-brown. Undertail-, uppertail-coverts and tail mostly black, with a varying amount of white on the outer rectrices. Tertials usually broad and pale grey. Scapulars more variable, from dark to pale grey, more or less tinged brown. Belly white. Legs yellow-orange. The ♀ is variable in colour too, but looks more like a ♀ Mallard with a shape more typical of Wood Duck. Of particular note is the short bill, blackish crown with a hint of a crest, black lores and clear eyestripe. A second black line, parallel to the latter, often runs across the upper cheeks (more obvious in juvenile plumage). The eye is variably surrounded by white. Breast, flanks and upperparts variably streaked, and generally barely useful for identification. Rather long square tail, pale at its sides, more typical of Wood Duck.

Wood Duck × Hooded Merganser: very rarely reported in the wild, this hybrid shows readily detectable features of both parents. Head blackish with purple sheen and variable white flecks behind the eye. Long bill mainly grey or blackish with a variably marked pinkish base. Breast reddish-buff. Broad black band split by thin white vertical stripe on fore flanks. The latter are yellowish-grey, darker reddish towards the rear. Pale undertail-coverts. Tail and upperparts dark brown. See also Gillham & Gillham[439].

HABITAT and LIFE-CYCLE Inhabits marshes, ponds, lakes and slow-flowing streams in deciduous or mixed forests. Favours more enclosed habitats than other waterfowl, with many branches in the water, on which the birds spend much time perched. Pairs form between Feb and Apr. depending on latitude. Nests are established in cavities and holes in trees, often old Pileated Woodpecker *Dryocopus pileatus* holes, as well as nestboxes. Eggs are laid mainly between mid-Apr and late Jun[555]. ♂ leaves ♀ later than most waterfowl and many remain close to the nest site, which seems to be an advantage in case of failure and may even permit two annual broods in the south of the range[672]. Autumn migration occurs mainly from mid-Sep to mid-Nov[555] over short to medium distances, depending on latitude and habitat[553,672]. In winter, inhabits a wider variety of habitats, including more open wetlands, and more rarely brackish water. At this season, keeps mostly alone or in small groups, forming larger flocks only at roosts (up to 200–1,000 individuals[672]).

RANGE and POPULATION A strictly Nearctic species, rarely wintering south to C Mexico. Regular in the Azores and possibly in W Europe, where the presence of accidental visitors may be obscured by frequent escapes. The overall population was considered very low in the early 20th century, mainly because of overhunting[89]. Its numbers have recovered since protection in 1918, and also in response to the massive installation of nestboxes[672]. Population difficult to estimate because of its habitat, and discreet and relatively solitary habits. Current estimates are based on old figures of 2.8 million birds in E North America, 665,000 in the centre-north of its range and 66,000 in the west[1348]. The trend is stable or increasing. In Eurasia, the species frequently escapes from captivity but seems generally unable to establish viable feral populations. A total of 50–100 pairs is given for Europe, mainly in Belgium and Germany. These populations appear to subsist only through the regular arrival of new escapes[62].

CAPTIVITY Very common in captivity throughout the Holarctic, easy to breed and usually very cheap. Very likely to escape into or near urban areas, although the fact that the species is a rather regular visitor to the Azores suggests that at least some birds in W Europe are genuine vagrants.

REFERENCES Banks *et al.* (2008)[62]; Bellrose (1976)[85]; Bellrose (1976)[86]; Bellrose (1990)[88]; Bellrose & Holm (1994)[89]; Bird Hybrids Data Base (2014)[97]; Bird Hybrids Flickr Forum (2008)[101]; Bird Hybrids Flickr forum (2014)[102]; Bird Hybrids Flickr forum (2014)[103]; Bird Hybrids Flickr forum (2014)[127]; Brown (2010)[195]; Carney (1992)[224]; Delnicki & Reinecke (1986)[307]; Gillham & Gillham (1996)[439]; Gillham & Gillham (2000)[442]; Gillham & Gillham (2002)[443]; Hepp & Hines (1991)[553]; Hepp & Bellrose (2013)[555]; Hipes & Hepp (1995)[560]; Hopkinson (1926)[582]; Johnsgard (1960)[639]; Kear *in* Kear (2005)[672]; Kirby & Fredrickson (1990)[692]; Marchant & Higgins (1990)[802]; McCarthy (2006)[817]; Nichols & Johnson (1990)[910]; Palmer (1976)[945]; Pylc (2008)[1014]; Sibley (1938)[1190]; Wetlands International (2014)[1348].

231. Adult ♀ (definitive basic); note glossy primaries, upperparts and crown, as well as adult-type tertials, and broad, dark blue greater coverts with black terminal bar. New York, USA, Nov (Sébastien Reeber).

232. Adult ♂ (definitive alternate); easily distinguished from ♀ by bare-parts coloration, and from juvenile ♂ by adult upperwing pattern (including tertials) visible here. Azores, Sep (Vincent Legrand).

233. First-winter ♂ (formative), resembles adult ♂, but note bare-parts coloration, and at this time of year, adult ♂ is usually more advanced in its pre-basic moult than young ♂ in pre-formative moult. New York, USA, Nov (Sébastien Reeber).

234. Adult ♂ (definitive basic); in all ages and sexes, from Mandarin Duck *A. galericulata* in flight by streaked/spotted underwing pattern (vs. uniformly dark). Texas, USA, Nov (Greg Lavaty).

235. Adult ♂ (definitive basic). California, USA, Jan (Tom Grey).

236. Juvenile (first basic), with dull bare parts, and plain brownish upperparts and flanks; the front bird is a ♂ (white stripes on cheeks, pinkish hue to the bill, thin white trailing edge to secondaries) and the other apparently a ♀ (grey bill, plainer face, broad rounded tips to secondaries). Texas, USA, Aug (Greg Lavaty).

MANDARIN DUCK
Aix galericulata
Plate 24

TAXONOMY *Anas galericulata* Linnaeus, 1758, *Syst. Nat.*, edn. 10, p. 128. Close to Wood Duck *A. sponsa*, the only congeneric, and its equivalent in the New World. Monotypic.

IDENTIFICATION Easily identified by its distinctive plumage and unusual habits. ♂♂ and ♀♀ in their alternate and juvenile plumages, however, are very similar to those of Wood Duck (see that species).

PLUMAGES Strong sexual dimorphism from the first autumn onward. Complex alternate moult strategy (two plumages per definitive cycle, three in first cycle). Ageing ♂♂ relatively easy until the first spring. Ageing ♀♀ harder from the beginning of the second calendar year. Small dabbling duck with a characteristic shape, in particular in basic ♂ plumage, with very prominent tertials. In all other plumages, note the short bill and the long tail. Spends a lot of time perched on branches.

Adult ♂

Definitive basic plumage (Sep–Nov/May–Jun). Very colourful. Forehead, crown and nape blackish, coloured green and rufous. Large white eye-patch tapers rearward down neck. Feathers of nape and cheeks very long and thin, producing a long drooping crest, and an orange striated white ruff. Iris dark brown. Bill short and triangular, reddish-pink with white nail. Upper breast black with purple sheen. Sides of breast with alternately two white and two black vertical bars. Flanks yellowish to orange with fine dark vermiculations, the latter broadening on upper and rear flanks. Femoral coverts dusky purplish-red (shared by Wood Duck). Central and lower breast, belly and undertail white, the underparts being often visible because of the frequently erect posture. Mantle and scapulars olive-brown with blue gloss on latter. The longest outer scapulars are white centred black. Central tertials form large square 'sails', orange, fringed white. Upperwing uniform grey-brown with turquoise to blue gloss on inner half of speculum. Trailing edge of speculum white, as are shafts to primaries, especially the outers. Underwing uniform dark brown. Legs yellow with brownish tone.

Definitive alternate plumage (Jun–Jul/Sep–Oct). Like alternate plumage of ♀, though eye-ring and bridle often reduced to thin line. The white streaks on the cheeks are more pronounced and the flanks show vague pale yellow-brown streaks instead of the white round and well-defined patches of ♀. Femoral patch and undertail generally whiter. Bill raspberry-coloured, often with dark marks on culmen.

Adult ♀

Definitive basic plumage (Oct–Nov/Jan–Apr?). Head grey with a strong white eye-ring extending as a line above the cheeks, which are marked with thin whitish streaks. White throat extends into a fine white line at the sides of the bill. Iris dark brown. Bill grey with a variable pinkish hue (probably accentuated with age), pale nail and often a yellow patch at the base of culmen. Brown breast with white spots forming strong, irregular longitudinal streaks. Flanks also brown with large neat round white patches (the feather centres), often arranged in rows. Femoral area washed brownish. Underparts to undertail-coverts whitish. Upperparts, including tertials (except innermost) black with blue sheen, uppertail-coverts and tail brown with hazelnut tone and subtle green sheen visible in sunlight. Upper- and underwing like those of ♂ but blue or green gloss limited to inner speculum and softer. Legs brownish-yellow.

Definitive alternate plumage (Feb–Apr/Oct–Nov?). Similar to basic plumage, with slight differences: top of head a little paler, hindneck less swollen (head squarer) and white line at base of bill less pronounced or lacking.

Juvenile

First basic plumage (until Oct–Nov). Like ♀ but crest less swollen (head thinner and more angular) and overall coloration of head duller and less contrasting. Eye-ring often interrupted behind eye and prolonged in a faint pale eyebrow, parallel to the whitish bridle. No white line at the bill base and poorly demarcated white throat. Breast often has thin well-defined streaks and belly faintly streaked, dotted or mottled pale brown. The bill, at first orange-brown darker on the culmen, quickly becomes pink in ♂ and grey-brown in ♀, the best feature for sexing before formative plumage acquired.

First-winter ♂

Formative plumage (Oct–Nov/May–Jul). Very close

to adult ♂, often characterised by less to much less-developed tertial 'sails'. Also, scapulars are duller brown with green or blue gloss less or absent. Similarly, the sheen is often less pronounced on primaries. No difference in pattern of white tips to secondaries[202], nor significant differences between ♂ and ♀ by age group, although ♀ has white tip a little broader on shaft on average (much overlap).

First-winter ♀

Formative plumage (Oct–Nov/Jan–Apr). Almost identical to adult ♀ and difficult to separate. On average, bill may become pink with age, and an all-pink bill could indicate an older ♀. The white tips to the secondaries are on average more mottled dark on the inner web in adult, but this feature is not diagnostic[202]. The white fringe is complete on both webs in 22% of young ♀ (until second pre-basic moult), but in 75% of adult ♀[202]. Wing length is also a good feature, but there is overlap between age groups[202].

GEOGRAPHIC VARIATION None.

MEASUREMENTS and MASS ♂ slightly larger and heavier than ♀ on average. ♂: wing chord 226–242 (235, n=11), tail 94–111 (101, n=13), bill 27–31 (28.6, n=15), tarsus 36–40 (38.1, n=14); ♀ (n=8): wing chord 215–234 (226), tail 94–104 (99.3), bill 27–30 (28.2), tarsus 35–38 (36.7)[267]. ♂: P9: 170–179 (adult, 174.4, n=10) and 160–173 (juvenile, 167.8, n=20); ♀: P9: 165–178 (adult, 170.6, n=12) and 155–169 (juvenile, 162.9, n=26). Mass (sample unknown): ♂: 571–693 (628); ♀: 428–608 (512)[267].

VOICE Rather quiet. The ♂ gives a *weeeb*, very sharp and rising, and the ♀ a high-pitched, rising and rather rough *heerb*, reminiscent of a stilt *Himantopus* sp.

MOULT Complex alternate moult strategy. Little has been published on the extent of the different moults in the wild, but information obtained in captivity and from several of feral populations suggest that moult strategy is very similar to that of Wood Duck (see that species). An auxiliary pre-formative moult is reported in Aug–Sep in young birds[447].

HYBRIDISATION Unlike Wood Duck, which is known to hybridise with numerous species in captivity, Mandarin Duck rarely hybridises, even with Wood Duck. The following hybrids are mentioned from captivity or are probably of captive origin: Wood Duck, Laysan Duck *Anas laysanensis*, Mallard *A. platyrhynchos*, Gadwall *A.*

strepera, Redhead *Aythya americana* and Long-tailed Duck *Clangula hyemalis*[97,439,465,582,643,817,1190]. No hybridisation described in the wild.

HABITAT and LIFE-CYCLE Very like those of its North American counterpart, the Wood Duck. In breeding season, frequents slow-flowing streams, ponds and other wetlands lined with tall deciduous forest and many trees above the water. Nests in high tree holes, including old nests of Black Woodpecker *Dryocopus martius* but also in other cavities and nestboxes. Pairs arrive near the nesting grounds between Feb and Jun, depending on latitude. ♀♀ can begin definitive pre-basic moult (with the remiges) while still tending their broods[673]. In winter, usually in small groups, either near nesting sites or in slightly more open habitats.

RANGE and POPULATION Outside E Asia in breeding range, rare visitor to Mongolia, Bangladesh and extreme NE India. Global winter population estimated at 65,000–66,000 birds[1346]: 20,000 in China[858], 350–500 in Taiwan[439], 3,000–4,000 in South Korea[874] and 40,000 in Japan[858]. Trend decreasing mainly due to loss of its forested habitats[673]. European feral populations have been introduced, intentionally or not, with breeding reports in the wild in several countries during the second half of the 20th century. Currently, the European population is estimated at c.3,000 breeding pairs[62], including c.2,500 in the UK (mainly S England and a few localities in Scotland)[195]. Several tens to hundreds of pairs reported in Germany, the Netherlands, Belgium, Austria, France, Poland and Switzerland. Rare elsewhere. Can potentially out-compete other species using tree cavities (e. g. Common Goldeneye *Bucephala clangula*[259]), by monopolising the sites, even destroying eggs it finds in potential nests. In North America, many escaped from captivity locally (mostly in Florida), but apparently no viable population established[233].

CAPTIVITY Considered by many the ultimate ornamental species, and very widespread in captivity. Available at very affordable prices and easily bred if nestboxes made available. Very likely to escape from captivity.

REFERENCES Banks *et al.* (2008)[62]; Bird Hybrids database (2014)[97]; Brown (2010)[195]; Bruggers (1978)[202]; CISEH (2014)[233]; Cosgrove (2003)[259]; Cramp & Simmons (1977)[268]; Gillham & Gillham (1996)[439]; Ginn & Melville (1983)[447]; Gray (1958)[465]; Hopkinson

(1926)[582]; Johnsgard (1968)[643]; Kear *in* Kear (2005)[673]; McCarthy (2006)[817]; Miyabayashi & Mundkur (1999)[858]; Moores *et al.* (2010)[874]; Shurtleff (1996)[1188]; Sibley (1938)[1190]; Wetlands International (2006)[1346]; Wetlands International (2014)[1348].

237. Adult pair (definitive basic). England, Feb (Sébastien Reeber).

238. Adult ♂ (definitive basic). Scotland, Mar (Ian Fulton).

239. Adult ♂ (definitive alternate), growing its remiges; from ♀ by bill coloration. Scotland, Sep (Dennis Morrison).

240. Adult pair (definitive basic). France, Feb (Julien Gonin)

GADWALL
Anas strepera

Plate 26

TAXONOMY *Anas strepera* Linnaeus, 1758, *Syst. Nat.*, edn. 10, p. 125. A member of the tribe Anatini. Livezey[767] placed the species within a clade comprising Cape Teal *A. capensis*, Falcated Duck *A. falcata*, Chiloe Wigeon *A. sibilatrix*, Eurasian Wigeon *A. penelope* and American Wigeon *A. americana*, and assigned all of them to the genus *Mareca*. However, Johnson & Sorenson[654] excluded Cape Teal from this group, regarding the clade as comprising Gadwall and Falcated Duck on the one hand, and the three wigeon on the other. The fact that the first two species form a paraphyletic group has been explained by introgression of Falcated Duck into Gadwall, rather than still incomplete lineage sorting[970]. An extinct subspecies is sometimes recognised (see Geographic Variation).

IDENTIFICATION Medium-sized dabbling duck; the adult ♂ in basic plumage differs from those of other species by its colourless uniform plumage. Other plumages are more like those of Mallard *A. platyrhynchos*. The white inner secondaries are visible in flight (a white square surrounded by black and deep reddish) and even on the water. The adult ♀ in basic plumage resembles that of Mallard by its pale brown plumage mottled black, sides of the bill orange, yellow legs and pale facial pattern marked by dark eyestripe. However, distinction is not difficult given the slimmer shape, more angular head and steeper forehead, head-sides paler and greyer with a shorter dark eyestripe and narrower dark crown (broader supercilium), more strongly marked orange bill, dark grey tertials (pale grey in Mallard), belly with a white oval patch (pale buff in Mallard) and finally the different upperwing. Adult ♂ in alternate plumage and juvenile differ from those of Mallard by their body strongly marked with warm tones (hazel or rufous) contrasting with the grey head, bill orange at sides and dark grey on culmen, whitish belly (less sharply demarcated in juvenile) and upperwing pattern.

PLUMAGES Clear sexual dimorphism from first winter onward. Complex alternate moult strategy (two plumages per definitive cycle, three in first cycle). Ageing ♂♂ relatively easy until beginning of the first winter and possible until end of the subsequent summer under good viewing conditions or in the hand. ♀♀ harder to age from the beginning of the second calendar year.

Adult ♂

Definitive basic plumage (Oct–Nov/May–Jun). Head pale grey to pale grey-brown (whitish-beige finely speckled dark grey), darker on the centre of the crown with a faint eyestripe. Some show a trace of wide eye-band, darker and contrasting with the cheeks (see Geographic Variation). Iris brown. Bill lead-grey to glossy black. Breast darker grey with fine scaly pattern (centre and fringes of individual feathers whitish, separated by broad black subterminal band). Mantle and upper scapulars grey (whitish with dark grey vermiculations). Central and lower scapulars elongated, pointed, with dark rachis stripe, plain grey variably tinged buff and white inner web towards the tip. Tertials broad, long, pointed and curved at tips, pale grey (the palest part of the plumage from afar). Rump, upper- and undertail-coverts black. Flanks grey (dark grey with fine white vermiculations). Belly whitish. Lower belly more strongly streaked dark. Upperwing basically has four colours, mostly grey-brown, with white square formed by outer webs to three inner secondaries, black area formed by outer webs to next four, by about one-third of inner secondary- and tertial coverts (outer webs). Finally, a reddish area is formed by the distal parts of the central and outer median coverts (and some lesser coverts) as well as the outer fringes of the greater coverts. Underwing whitish, with greater coverts pale grey and remiges darker. Legs bright yellow-orange with dark grey webs.

Definitive alternate plumage (May–Jul/Sep–Oct). Rather like basic plumage of adult ♀. Head is grey with a dusky grey-brown crown and a short diffuse eyestripe. Chin, throat and foreneck slightly paler. Bill with yellow-orange sides and dark grey culmen. Scapulars short and rounded, blackish in centre with clean buff to creamy fringes. Tertials grey-brown to olive-brown, rounded and shorter than in basic plumage. Breast with a reddish hue and sharp dark grey-brown spots. Flanks dark yellowish-buff with internal marks. Belly whitish sometimes with a variable number of dark patches. Undertail-coverts whitish mottled dark. Basic upperwing retained.

Adult ♀

Definitive basic plumage (Oct–Nov/Jan–Mar). Light brown mottled blackish, like other ♀♀ of genus *Anas*. Sides of head and neck pale yellowish-buff finely streaked dark grey-brown, with crown, nape and eyestripe darker, and chin and throat creamy. Iris brown. Bill yellow-orange (variable) with culmen lead-grey and variably numerous dark spots on the sides of the upper mandible. Feathers of mantle and scapulars blackish-brown with crisp, broad pale buff fringes, and internal marks the same colour. Tertials short, straight and slightly blunt-tipped, grey-brown fringed pale. Tertial coverts dark brown or blackish on outer webs, grey on inner webs and fringed white at tips. Feathers of back and rump centred blackish-brown, fringed buff. Breast pale buff strongly marked with blackish spots loosely aligned. Flank feathers dark brown with internal pale buff marks and fringes paler beige. Belly and undertail-coverts whitish, the latter with strong round, blackish spots. Tail grey-brown with pale brown fringes, whitish on outer rectrices. Upperwing mostly grey-brown with lesser and median coverts rather square, edged pale (possibly some internal pale marks). Blackish restricted to 30–50% of inner feathers on lower 2–4 rows of secondary coverts. Cinnamon or reddish hue restricted to fringes of a few greater coverts. The two innermost secondaries have white outer webs (pale grey on the next), the whole forming a smaller white square than in adult ♂. Central and outer secondaries darker grey with pale tips. Underwing similar to ♂. Legs similar to those of ♂, but duller yellow.

Definitive alternate plumage (Feb–Apr/Oct–Nov). This plumage looks more irregularly streaked, spotted or even messy. The crown and eyestripe are blackish and often more obvious, with a broad contrasting pale supercilium. Sides of head and neck more strongly and irregularly mottled grey-brown. Tertials shorter, dark grey-brown to blackish with pale fringes and sometimes internal pale bars. Belly pale, more or less strongly mottled or spotted dusky. The marks on the undertail-coverts are arrow-shaped, instead of round like basic plumage.

Juvenile

First basic plumage (until Sep–Nov). Resembles basic plumage of adult ♀, but somewhat darker brown, with hazel or reddish tones. Sides of head more regularly and 'cleanly' speckled blackish. Crown and eyestripe dark brown. Iris dark brown. Bill initially washed olive-brown, but quickly becomes similar to adult ♀. Chin and throat greyish. Breast buff to reddish finely spotted dark. Scapulars, mantle and flank feathers dark dull grey-brown with pale brown fringes, and pale internal marks inconspicuous or absent. Tertials short, but pointed, of

constant width, dark grey with paler tips and sometimes diffuse internal pale crossbars. Tertial coverts pointed with whitish tips. Belly whitish finely streaked dusky, more heavily in young ♀[1014]. Juvenile. rectrices typical (bare rachis at tip), grey-brown (♂) or brown (♀). Upperwing with red-cinnamon present on 1–2 rows of lower secondary coverts (♂), or restricted to fringes of at most a few coverts, or absent (♀). The black extends over three rows of inner secondary coverts (♂) or two rows alone (♀)[224], the black coverts being obviously fringed pale in ♀ and almost not at all in young ♀. White is restricted to 1–2 innermost secondaries (outer fringes), often pale grey in ♀, the following secondary (s9) showing white on outer web (♂) or only the tip (♀)[1014]. Lesser and median coverts rather narrow, round-tipped, quickly frayed, frequently with whitish inner marks (♀) or thin straight or 'V'-shaped streaks (♂)[56,224]. Legs washed grey-brown, quickly becoming yellower.

First-winter ♂

Formative plumage (Oct–Dec/May–Jun). The appearance of adult-type body feathers occurs in Nov–Dec, the young ♂ strongly resembling the adult from early winter. The bill, however, frequently retains traces of orange on its sides until Jan–Feb. The whitish belly is often more cream-coloured, diffusely demarcated, and is more or less obviously blotched dusky. The lower belly is less clearly streaked. Some juvenile feathers are sometimes visible on the body (including one or a few lower scapulars). The black undertail-coverts often retain two or a few juvenile feathers, brown with whitish tips Similarly, one or more juvenile tertials (short, dark grey and frayed at the tips) are sometimes retained, the formative tertials being the same colour as the adult, but often shorter and less curved. Also distinguished by juvenile upperwing pattern (see above), with reddish and black restricted, and secondary coverts narrow and round-tipped.

First-winter ♀

Formative plumage (Oct–Dec/Feb–Mar). Very similar to definitive basic ♀. Ageing is based on upperwing pattern retained until the beginning of the second pre-basic moult (see above), with cinnamon and black very limited or almost absent, and narrower, round-tipped secondary coverts. Other features are the ill-defined whitish belly with a variable number of dusky blotches, as well as the sometimes retained juvenile tertials, faded and visibly frayed at the tips.

GEOGRAPHIC VARIATION An extinct subspecies,

A. s. couesi Streets, 1876, was described on the basis of two immature specimens from Washington I, Republic of Kiribati, in the Pacific Ocean and now at the Smithsonian Institution, Washington DC. It is mainly distinguished by its smaller size, close to that of a teal *A. crecca/carolinensis*, and is often recognised as a separate subspecies, but sometimes also as a short-lived and very small population, descending from vagrant Gadwalls on the island[487,787,1349]. No differences found between Palearctic and Nearctic populations, either in phenotypic characters[945], or genetically[638]. Nevertheless, there is variation in face and neck coloration, which is not necessarily geographic. Some birds show a white neck-ring, especially marked on the foreneck. Others show a whitish-beige area around the bill base, including forehead. Finally, other birds have the upper head and hindneck visibly darker than the cheeks, often with a copper or purplish gloss. Cheeks are sometimes pale buff and can even appear as if surrounded by a pale line. This form occurs very rarely in Europe, but is more regularly encountered in North America, and, at least sometimes, in Asia. It has been suggested that some or all of these characters could be related to recent or ancient hybridisation, and could also reflect the introgression of Falcated Duck into Nearctic populations of Gadwall[970,969]. In North America, analysis of mitochondrial DNA from 348 Gadwalls revealed two clades (A and B), the first corresponding to the vast majority of Nearctic birds and also present in Eurasia, and the second (5.5% of birds) with haplotypes nearer to those of Falcated Duck than from clade A[969]. However, it should also be borne in mind that several hybrids involving Gadwall show clear contrast between the cheeks and upper head and nape, including with species that do not show such contrast at all (Northern Shoveler *A. clypeata*, Mallard, Falcated Duck, Eurasian Wigeon). It is therefore possible that these features are indicative of ancient hybridisation with other species as well.

MEASUREMENTS and MASS ♂ and adult slightly larger than ♀ and young, respectively. ♂: wing chord 261–282 (adult, 269, n=24) and 251–274 (juvenile, 264, n=37), bill 39–46 (42.4, n=60), tarsus 38–42 (40.3, n=42); ♀: wing chord 243–261 (adult, 252, n=14) and 233–262 (juvenile, 246, n=32), bill 37–43 (39.8, n=48), tarsus 36–42 (38.8, n=34)[267]. ♂ (n=12): wing chord 262–281 (271.7), tail 80–92 (86.3), culmen 41–50 (45.6), tarsus 40–43 (41.5), mass 908 (n=68); ♀ (n=10): wing chord 246–268 (255), tail 81–91 (85.8), culmen 40–43 (41.8), tarsus 37–43 (40.0), mass 808 (n=66)[945]. ♂: mass in winter 782.5 (adult, n=150) and

765.9 (juvenile/first-winter, n=317); ♀: mass in winter 706.3 (adult, n=127) and 678.2 (juvenile/first-winter, n=290)[392]. ♂: mass 726–1,043 (adult, 966, n=37) and 590–1,043 (juvenile/first-winter, 857, n=204); ♀: mass 635–1,043 (adult, 835, n=45) and 499–953 (juvenile/first-winter, 776, n=200)[87].

VOICE The ♂ produces a distinctive, nasal, low *heeb*, often mixed with much higher pitched whistled sounds, uttered especially during courtship and when several ♂♂ pursue a ♀. The ♀ emits 'quacks' much closer to that of a ♀ Mallard, but more nasal.

MOULT Complex alternate strategy. Pre-formative moult occurs between Jul and Dec, and includes most of the head and body feathers (smaller numbers on the lower breast, belly, undertail-coverts, back and upper rump), sometimes a few inner upperwing-coverts, with some rectrices and tertials (none to all). It is on average less extensive in ♀[56,1014]. Definitive pre-alternate moult occurs in May–Jul in ♂ and in Jan–Apr in ♀, and includes some of the upperparts (occasionally all), none to all tertials (up to two inner secondaries in ♀), up to 60% of the inner upperwing-coverts[1014] and none to all rectrices. Definitive pre-basic moult is complete, begins with the wings between late Jun and late Sep, ♀♀ that bred successfully being latest. This moult ends between mid-Sep and Nov.

HYBRIDISATION In the wild this is reported from time to time with Mallard (see below), Eurasian Wigeon, Falcated Duck, Northern Pintail *A. acuta* and Northern Shoveler (see these species). Much less frequent cases have been reported in the wild with American Black Duck *A. rubripes*[639], Eurasian Teal *A. crecca*[947], Green-winged Teal *A. carolinensis*[435], Garganey *A. querquedula*[442] and possibly American Wigeon[439,947] and Hooded Merganser *Lophodytes cucullatus*[1194]. In captivity, hybrids or mixed pairs have been reported with Common Shelduck *Tadorna tadorna*[439], Mandarin Duck *Aix galericulata*[817,1190], Wood Duck *Aix sponsa*[439,582,817,1190], Chiloe Wigeon[439,1266], Pacific Black Duck *A. superciliosa*[639,1190], Yellow-billed Duck *A. undulata*[1190], Chestnut Teal *A. castanea*[1190] and Yellow-billed Pintail *A. georgica*[439,465,582,817].

Gadwall × Mallard: a rare hybrid, first reported almost two centuries ago, when it was described as a species, Brewer's Duck *A. breweri* Audubon, 1838. Adult ♂ in basic plumage has coloration that falls into two types similar to the two parent species, with a highly variable head pattern. The 'Mallard' type (or 'Brewer's Duck') has upperparts, breast-sides and flanks grey (whitish vermiculated blackish), lower scapulars darker, breast purplish-brown in centre, broad pale grey-beige tertials, femoral coverts white, undertail-coverts black, tail-sides white with two central rectrices dark, slightly elongated and often up-curved. The whole is more reminiscent of a Mallard, often with a trace of white collar and upper neck blackish with green sheen. Lores and cheeks can be dark, pale grey, light buff, pale orange-brown or darker reddish-brown. A broad eye-band extends behind the eye, with strong green gloss, and the crown often has a hazelnut, reddish or purplish hue. A bimaculated pattern (vertical dusky line under eye splitting the cheeks into two distinct pale patches) is sometimes visible. The bill is usually bicoloured, blackish with long pale patches on the sides, but can also be mainly blackish or yellow. The upperwing pattern is mixed, with greater coverts grey or white and broad black tips, and green speculum framed black, except two innermost secondaries partly white (large black oval patch on outer webs). Legs dull yellow-orange. The 'Gadwall' type has a more vermiculated grey-brown body, with a black rear body, tail-sides white, tertials longer, pointed and very pale at the tips, pinkish-brown breast barely darker than the flanks with small dusky crescents, all closer to Gadwall. The rear flanks are sometimes marked by a thin pale vertical bar. A white collar is often visible, topped by a large black collar sometimes with a green sheen. The cheeks are pale grey-beige more or less tinged buff or yellowish (rear cheeks, throat), and frequently surrounded by a paler line. The upper head and nape are darker, usually with strong copper or purplish reflections behind the eye and crown tinged chestnut. Bill, legs and upperwing similar to the 'Mallard' type. In a total of 17 hybrids, Gillham & Gillham placed eight in 'Mallard' type 443. However, there are also clearly intermediates between the two types. The adult ♀ from this cross is obviously more difficult to distinguish, and is described as closer to Gadwall[443], with at least one inner secondary white or very pale grey, bill variably mottled blackish and orange, and head intermediate in appearance (width of pale supercilium, overall tone, etc.).

HABITAT and LIFE-CYCLE Species of temperate latitudes whose northern and continental populations are generally migratory, the others being short-distance migrants or more or less sedentary. Spring migration occurs mainly in Mar–May, but the species is a rather late breeder. Eggs are mostly laid between early May and early Jul, even in the south of its range. Usually nests in isolated pairs, at fresh eutrophic wetlands, with much floating and helophytic vegetation, and banks covered with *Carex* spp., *Phragmites*, *Typha* spp. etc.). Favours natural shores of lowland lakes, ponds (including fish farms), deltas and slow-flowing streams. Less common in oligotrophic, acidic (peat) or moderately alkaline waters, in montane regions and in the taiga. The ♂ leaves the ♀ during incubation and gathers in small groups at sites dedicated to moult. ♀♀ start their pre-basic moult often shortly before their offspring fledge. Autumn migration occurs mainly in Oct–Nov. More gregarious on migration and in winter, but tends to form smaller flocks than other dabbling ducks, even where it is numerous. Usually inhabits the same habitats year-round, but the main wintering sites often comprise large lagoons and shallow wetlands, with much helophytic vegetation, often in coastal regions.

RANGE and POPULATION Holarctic distribution mapped here (local in Iceland, S Scandinavia, N Africa or N Japan, for example). Rare winter visitor to the Caribbean, Central America, SW Asia and elsewhere north of its breeding range. The bulk of the world population breeds in North America, where populations were estimated at 3,586,000 individuals in 2012 and 3,351,000 in 2013, having increased since the early 1990s, when there were around 1.5 million[1294]. In S Asia, the population has been estimated at 400,000 birds[757] (previously 300,000[1348]). The population in E Asia was estimated at 500,000–1,000,000 birds[858], but is probably <500,000[757] and has even been estimated at 50,000[928]. Numbers wintering in SW Asia and NE Africa have been estimated at 130,000, in the Mediterranean at 75,000–130,000 birds and W Europe at 60,000[1348]. American, European and S Asian populations show positive trends, which is not the case in E Asia. Does not seem threatened at present, despite locally significant harvesting (e.g. 1.46 million birds taken annually in 2004–08 in the USA[648], corresponding to half the breeding population).

CAPTIVITY Reportedly fairly easy to keep and breed, and usually sold at prices among the lowest for ornamental ducks. Despite this, relatively uncommon in captivity, perhaps because of its rather dull plumage.

REFERENCES Baker (1992)[56]; Bellrose (1980)[87]; Carney (1993)[224]; Cramp & Simmons (1977)[268]; Fox *in* Kear (2005)[392]; Gibson & Byrd (1973)[435]; Gillham & Gillham (1996)[439]; Gillham & Gillham (2000)[442];

Gillham & Gillham (2002)[443]; Gray (1958)[465]; Greenway (1967)[487]; Hopkinson (1926)[582]; Johnsen *et al.* (2010)[638]; Johnsgard (1960)[639]; Johnsgard (2010)[648]; Johnson & Sorenson (1999)[654]; Leschack *et al.* (1997)[747]; Li *et al.* (2009)[757]; Livezey (1991)[767]; Luther (1996)[787]; McCarthy (2006)[817]; Merrifield (1998)[842]; Miyabayashi & Mundkur (1999)[858]; Ogilvie & Young (1998)[928]; Oring (1968)[933]; Paulus (1984)[952]; Palmer (1976)[945]; Panov (1989)[947]; Peters & Omland (2007)[969]; Peters *et al.* (2007)[970]; Peters *et al.* (2008)[971]; Pyle (2008)[1014]; Sibley (1938)[1190]; Sibley (1994)[1194]; Tipling (1989)[1266]; USFWS (2013)[1294]; Wetlands International (2014)[1348]; Wetmore (1925))[1349].

241. ♀ (first alternate/definitive alternate) is distinguished from all other ♀ dabbling ducks by white patch visible at rear flanks; this ♀ is in pre-alternate moult (two generations of scapulars visible, tertials growing), with adult-type tertial coverts. England, Feb (Sébastien Reeber).

242. Adult ♂ (definitive basic); first-winter ♂ (formative) can be almost identical, even if tertials are often shorter and straighter-tipped; reliably aged by wing pattern and some juvenile feathers (undertail-coverts, scapulars, back). France, Feb (Sébastien Reeber).

243. Juvenile (first basic) has scapulars plainer (no internal markings) and duller, and also note short dark tertials. New Jersey, USA, Sep (Sébastien Reeber).

244. Adult ♂ (definitive alternate/definitive basic), completing its pre-basic moult. New Jersey, USA, Nov (Sébastien Reeber).

245. ♀ (first alternate/definitive alternate); note alternate tertials. France, Mar (Sébastien Reeber).

246. In flight, white patch on inner speculum is typical of the species (♀ left, ♂♂ right). France, Nov (Sébastien Reeber).

FALCATED DUCK
Anas falcata

Plate 26

TAXONOMY *Anas falcata* Georgi, 1775, *Bemerkungen Reise Russischen Reich*, p. 167. Close to the Gadwall *A. strepera* (see Taxonomy of latter). No subspecies or geographical variation.

IDENTIFICATION Medium-sized dabbling duck distinguished by strong, rather angular head, often held hunched when resting on the water. The bill is mid-length but rather thin, and the tail short. ♂♂ in formative and definitive basic plumages are sufficiently distinctive to avoid confusion with other species. Juvenile and ♀♀ may require more care and their brown plumage mottled dark can resemble Eurasian *A. penelope* and American Wigeon *A. americana* in the plain head (no eyestripe or supercilium), though easily distinguished by longer all-blackish bill. Shape also recalls Gadwall, but latter's face is more patterned and bill marked orange. In flight, black speculum with green gloss framed white can be close to that of a wigeon, but differs from Gadwall. It is worth mentioning that while identification of Falcated Duck is usually quite easy, a lone ♀ within a flock of wigeon or Gadwalls (in whose company the species is most frequently recorded outside its range) can be very hard to pick out.

PLUMAGES Strong sexual dimorphism from first winter onwards. Complex alternate moult strategy (two plumages by definitive cycle, three in first cycle). Ageing ♂♂ relatively easy until the beginning of the winter and possible until the end of the subsequent summer under good viewing conditions or in the hand. ♀♀ are harder to age from the beginning of the second calendar year.

Adult ♂

Definitive basic plumage (Oct–Nov/May–Jun). Lovely plumage, grey (body), black (rear body) and black with green and red sheen (head). Long crest falling on hindneck, tricoloured head, with strong green gloss around and behind eye (and coppery shades towards nape), centre of crown and nape with purple tones, lores black and chin, throat, sides and top of neck clearly delineated white. A round white spot is visible on the forehead meeting the bill. A blackish-green collar across the white upper neck. Iris dark brown. Bill blackish. Breast finely scaled with round feathers, black in their centre, with a white inner crescent, black subterminal crescent and white fringe. Flanks dark

grey finely vermiculated white, with white vertical bar at side of undertail. Mantle, back, rump and inner scapulars strongly vermiculated black and white. The two outer rows of scapulars are long and pointed, with fine black vermiculations and white fringes. Tertials very long, falling over the tail and rear flanks, dark grey to blackish, with white fringes and contrasting rachis line. Upper- and undertail-coverts black, with well-delineated triangular patch on sides, coloured yellow to pale buff, like Eurasian *A. crecca* and Green-winged Teals *A. carolinensis* in same plumage. Rectrices short, dark grey-brown fringed whitish. Belly white with pale grey streaks, more marked on lower part. Upperwing grey, similar to upperparts, with trailing edge of the primaries darker, and broad black speculum with green gloss, with a sharp white trailing edge on the tips of the secondaries and a white bar formed by the greater coverts, pale grey to off-white at tips. Underwing has axillaries, lesser and median coverts white, greater coverts and bases to primaries pale grey, and leading and trailing edges darker grey. Grey legs with yellow tone more or less marked, dark webs.

Definitive alternate plumage (May–Jul/Sep–Oct). Like ♀ in definitive basic plumage. Head a little darker and browner, sometimes with a few remaining basic feathers, especially with green gloss on rear cheeks. The breast and flanks show blackish feathers with large internal 'U'-shaped marks and pale buff fringes. Scapulars darker, blackish variably speckled pale at the base, often with narrow internal 'V'-shaped marks and thin whitish to cold buff fringes. Frequent basic feathers are visible on the mantle and back of neck. Rear flanks and undertail white to pale buff with blackish arrow-shaped patches. The alternate tertials are shorter (longer than ♀) centred black and fringed white. Note that the basic tertials are retained until wing moult is completed, i.e. when the body has already acquired its dominant brown coloration. Basic upperwing retained.

Adult ♀

Definitive basic plumage (Oct–Nov/Jan–Mar). Overall coloration buff-brown mottled blackish. Head whitish to pale buff, heavily speckled and vermiculated dark grey, darker from forehead to around the eyes, which is thus surrounded by a dark patch reminiscent of ♀♀ of both wigeon. The feathers of the nape are elongated and form a short thick but obvious crest. Iris dark brown. Bill lead-grey, with culmen often mottled blackish. Breast, flanks, mantle and scapulars pale reddish-buff mottled blackish. These feathers are dark grey-brown with a pale internal arrow-shaped mark (scapulars, flanks) or a crescent (breast) and whitish fringe. Tertials long, slightly drooping, slightly rounded-tipped, grey, paler towards the base of the inner web with pale buff to whitish fringes. Femoral and undertail-coverts whitish with blackish streaks or arrows. Back, rump and uppertail-coverts dark brown with pale buff fringes. Rectrices short, dark grey-brown fringed white. Belly pale brown mottled dusky. Upperwing like that of ♂ but secondary coverts darker, with crisp white fringes and softer, less extensive green gloss. Underwing like ♂ but leading edge browner, appearing more spotted blackish (feathers fringed pale). Legs grey.

Definitive alternate plumage (Feb–Apr/Oct–Nov). Very like basic plumage, but slightly less contrasting as the ground colour of the head is a little darker brown. The breast is marked by coarse, ill-defined longitudinal streaks. Alternate tertials differ significantly from basic tertials being centred dark grey-brown with broad buff to grey fringes, and often diffuse pale internal marks. Belly more strongly mottled dark brown.

Juvenile

First basic plumage (until Sep–Nov). Like adult ♀, but slightly more yellowish (less buff) and duller. Distinguished by thinner, more square-shaped, slightly darker top of head (with blackish speckles less visible), contrasting with the cheeks, and a shorter crest. The bill is grey with a more contrasting culmen, breast with neat longitudinal streaks and feathers of the mantle and scapulars blackish-brown with no internal marks (or at most barely visible). Tertials short, dark brown (♀) to grey-brown (♂), browner than adult ♀, and whitish fringes which quickly become worn and frayed. The upperwing has narrower coverts with oval tips (broader and rounded or almost blunt-tipped in adult ♀). Lesser and median coverts grey to brownish-grey with dusky rachis and slight pale fringes (♂) or brown with clear pale fringes (♀). Greater coverts narrower at tip, and broadly pointed whitish. Secondaries dull dark grey, with little or no green sheen (♀) or stronger green gloss (♂). Femoral coverts have blurred brown streaks, and dark spots under tail less well-defined. Belly neatly streaked grey-brown.

First-winter ♂

Formative plumage (Oct–Dec/May–Jun). Pre-formative moult is usually rapid, with the first adult basic-type feathers appearing in early autumn on the head and neck. Often closely resembles adult ♂ by early winter. The crest is often virtually absent, producing a square head typical of this age. The formative tertials resemble the definitive basic tertials but are shorter, more round-tipped. The juvenile upperwing is retained (narrow coverts, pale fringes to lesser, median and tertial coverts narrower, pointed and at least partially fringed pale, greater coverts with narrow pale grey tips). Sometimes, some juvenile brownish feathers are visible on the breast, scapulars (especially the lower ones) and upper flanks. The belly and back are still largely juvenile as well, the former being finely streaked dusky, and the latter dull brown. Also look for juvenile tertials or rectrices, which are brown, faded and worn. Note that if the mix of adult basic-type and brownish feathers suggests both an adult ♂ in pre-basic moult or a young ♂ in pre-formative moult, the former will have completed its body moult by Nov, ending with the longest tertials in Dec. At same time and often until Jan at least, the young ♂ still has obvious brown feathers. Finally, a bird in autumn showing two generations of rectrices or tertials is probably a young bird, the adult usually moulting all rectrices and tertials simultaneously.

First-winter ♀

Formative plumage (Oct–Dec/Feb–Mar). Difficult to separate from adult ♀ following pre-formative moult, but note head shape, which is thinner, more square-shaped with crest barely marked, and juvenile upperwing retained until the second pre-basic moult (useful in the hand or under very good viewing conditions). Ageing can also be based on the presence of juvenile tertials and rectrices until midwinter (often first shed during first pre-alternate moult). Finally, the belly often has a typical juvenile appearance, finely streaked pale grey-brown.

GEOGRAPHIC VARIATION None described.

MEASUREMENTS and MASS ♂ and adult slightly larger than ♀ and young, respectively. ♂ ($n=12$): wing chord 244–268 (253), tail 70–80 (73.5), bill 39–48 (42.8, $n=41$), tarsus 37–44 (39.8), mass 590–770 (713, $n=4$); ♀ ($n=9$): wing chord 226–236 (231), tail 68–76 (71.3), bill 36–40 (38.8), tarsus 36–40 (37.7), mass 422–700 (585, $n=4$)[184,945].

VOICE Generally silent except during courtship, when ♂ produces a short series of whistled sounds *tyu-tyu-witt*, di- or trisyllabic[308] or a low whistle followed by a short rattling sound, *hoo-wiik-brrr*. The ♀ utters rather low-pitched *quack*, typical of ♀♀ of the genus *Anas*.

MOULT Little known concerning the timing and extent of different moults, but information available from the wild and the observation of captive birds suggests that they are very similar to those of Gadwall (which see). Nevertheless, it is possible that at least pre-formative moult may occur earlier and be more extensive in captive birds. Pre-formative moult occurs between Sep–Oct and Dec–Feb. Definitive pre-alternate moult occurs in Jan–Apr in ♀ and in mid-May to Jul in ♂. Definitive pre-basic moult then occurs in Jul–Nov, starting with the wings in Jul–Aug (♂♂ and non-breeding ♀♀ first).

HYBRIDISATION Seems rare but is reported occasionally in the wild with Gadwall (see below) and Eurasian Wigeon (which see). Exceptionally, natural hybridisation has also been mentioned with Common Shelduck *Tadorna tadorna*[947], Ruddy Shelduck *T. ferruginea*[465,817,1241], Mallard *A. platyrhynchos*[719,947,1244] and Garganey *A. querquedula*[439]. In captivity, hybridisation has been described with American Wigeon[439,465], Chiloe Wigeon *A. sibilatrix*[442,582], Laysan Duck *A. laysanensis*[439], White-cheeked Pintail *A. bahamensis*[442], Chestnut Teal *A. castanea*[584,817], Northern Shoveler *A. clypeata*[584,865], Australasian Shoveler *A. rhynchotis*[442] and Eurasian Teal *A. crecca*[439].

Falcated Duck × Gadwall: hybrid whose adult ♂ in basic plumage is occasionally reported in the wild. Has a large round head (flattened crest on neck) that is dark, with red tones in front and around eye, and green (sometimes purple[439]) gloss towards the rear. A clearly delineated pale area (often whitish vermiculated reddish-brown) includes the lower cheeks, chin, bill base and usually the forehead. This area is sometimes divided into two by a dark vertical bar. A broad black neck-ring is underlined by a thin white collar. Body mainly vermiculated pale grey-brown with tertials generally (but variably) elongated, pointed and drooping, which can be either pale grey (Gadwall-type) or centred black and fringed white (Falcated Duck-type). A white bar separates the grey flanks and black undertail, the latter sometimes showing a hint of the pale yellow lateral triangle of Falcated Duck or being all black. The upperwing pattern is described as similar to that of an adult ♀ Falcated Duck.

HABITAT and LIFE-CYCLE Migratory and inhabits freshwater wetlands (lakes, ponds, swamps, slow-flowing streams) including wooded habitats[945], with banks and shores with dense cover. Breeds in isolated pairs. Eggs are laid between late May and early Jun in Russia, especially Jun in China[945]. The ♂ leaves the ♀ during incubation. Outside the breeding season, usually occurs alone or in small flocks with other dabbling ducks, in lowland shallow wetlands such as lakes, marshes, flooded meadows, rice fields and even brackish coastal lagoons with nearby vegetation (tall grass, reeds, etc.), as well as grasslands and meadows, where the species grazes in the manner of wigeon.

RANGE and POPULATION Breeds in E Siberia and winters in E Asia, with a few south to Bangladesh, N India, Nepal, Taiwan and N Indochina. Accidental visitors reported to the US Pacific coast (especially Aleutians, rarer south to British Columbia and even California), in several countries of SW Asia and the Middle East, and even west to Europe, where most are nevertheless considered to be escapes from captivity (see below). Population initially estimated at 35,000 individuals, but recent evidence tends to suggest that it is 78,000–89,000 individuals[145,221,304,1348]. The species is still thought to be declining, especially in China[145,222,1348], primarily due to harvesting for food and feathers[223], and, more recently, large-scale destruction of its habitats, mainly to make way for agriculture.

CAPTIVITY Deemed fairly easy to keep and breed in captivity, but usually still quite expensive. Among Holarctic species of *Anas*, it is usually the most expensive with Baikal Teal *A. formosa*. Reports in Europe or North America are often considered to be escapees, but some reports in late autumn within large flocks of Eurasian Wigeon or Gadwalls merit fuller investigation.

REFERENCES BirdLife International (2014)[145]; Brewer *in* Kear (2005)[184]; Cao *et al.* (2008)[221]; Cao *et al.* (2010)[222]; Carboneras (1992)[223], Delany & Scott (2002)[304]; Dementiev & Gladkov (1952)[308]; Gillham & Gillham (1996)[439]; Gillham & Gillham (2000)[442]; Gray (1958)[465]; Hopkinson (1926)[582]; Hopkinson (1933)[584]; Kuroda (1960)[719]; Livezey (1991)[767]; Martin & Garner (2012)[808]; McCarthy (2006)[817]; Moody (1932)[865]; Palmer (1976)[945]; Panov (1989)[947]; Poyarkov (2006)[1003]; Sibley (1938)[1190]; Suchetet (1897)[1241]; Suter (1953)[1244]; Wetlands International (2014)[1348].

247. Adult ♂ (definitive basic). California (Tom Grey).

248. ♀ (formative/definitive basic); overall, plumage rather plain, especially the head. Japan, Dec (Ayuwat Jearwattanakanok).

249. Adult ♂ (definitive basic). India, Dec (Amit Thakurta).

250. Adult ♂ (definitive basic). Japan, May (Stuart Price).

251. ♀ (formative/definitive basic); aged by upperwing pattern, with the tertials (longish, tapering to a point) suggesting an adult ♀. Japan, Mar (Ayuwat Jearwattanakanok).

252. ♀ (formative/definitive basic). Japan, Feb (Aurélien Audevard).

343

EURASIAN WIGEON
Anas penelope

TAXONOMY *Anas Penelope* Linnaeus, 1758, *Syst. Nat.*, edn. 10, p. 126. Closely related to its South American and Nearctic counterparts, Chiloe Wigeon *A. sibilatrix* and American Wigeon *A. americana*, respectively (which see)[654,767].

IDENTIFICATION ♀, juvenile and alternate plumages of ♂ are fairly easy to distinguish from other ducks by the typical shape (rather strong head, short triangular bill) and rather plain reddish-brown head. Only American Wigeon poses real identification issues (which see). Note that the difficulties in distinguishing the two species will depend partly on the coloration of the bird in question, some ♀ Eurasian Wigeon being an overall reddish colour and fairly easy to distinguish. In North America, where Eurasian Wigeon is infrequent but regular on both coasts, the existence of frequent hybrids with American Wigeon must be remembered, some adult ♂♂ in basic plumage being reminiscent of Eurasian Wigeon. Be wary, especially of first-generation hybrids with a pale grey body, reddish eye-patch and/or golden-yellow forehead. The latter often extends well onto the crown, whereas the eye-band frequently shows clear contrast with the paler (often vermiculated) cheeks. Finally, the breast, flanks and scapulars often show at least a slight pinkish hue. Backcrosses with Eurasian Wigeon are much more problematic. Some Eurasian Wigeon clearly have a whitish forehead reaching the crown and/or merging into the cheeks, a green gloss behind the eye and axillaries/underwing median coverts largely white. It is unknown if these characters are indeed linked to past hybridisation with American Wigeon (see also Geographic Variation). Nonetheless, such individuals, which are most frequent in E Asia, strongly resemble 'pure' Eurasian Wigeon.

PLUMAGES Strong sexual dimorphism from first winter onwards. Complex alternate moult strategy (two plumages per definitive cycle, three in first cycle). Ageing ♂♂ is relatively easy until first summer. Ageing ♀♀ is possible up to first summer as well, but will require detailed examination of upperwing and/or rectrices.

Adult ♂

Definitive basic plumage (Oct–Dec/May–Jun). Head reddish-brown, darker to blackish around eye and rearwards, and on chin, with golden-yellow forehead extending to centre of crown. Iris dark brown. Bill rather short and triangular (barely curved culmen), pale blue-grey with broad black tip reaching along the tomium. Breast flesh-pink, paler in centre, a little more purplish at sides. Mantle, flanks and scapulars appear grey (actually whitish finely vermiculated blackish). Belly white, extending on femoral coverts. Tertials have black inner webs, grey-brown outer webs, fringes and rachis white. Black undertail-coverts, base of tail and lower row of uppertail-coverts (except central pair, which are pale grey). Tail grey at sides with the central pair of rectrices longer and black. Upperwing dark grey-brown with large contrasting white patch on some lesser coverts, median coverts and bases of greater coverts, their square tips being black. Secondaries blackish with green gloss covering almost the entire length of the speculum. The innermost secondaries have their outer webs largely white and black fringes on the distal half. Underwing dark grey, with tips of secondaries, greater coverts, median coverts and axillaries paler grey (the latter streaked or speckled grey-brown) and appearing slightly paler than the flanks in flight. Legs blue-grey.

Definitive alternate plumage (May–Jul/Sep–Nov). Closer to basic plumage of adult ♀ but with brighter colours. Head and upper neck dark reddish-brown, almost black on fore cheeks, around and behind eye. Breast and flanks brighter red-orange that adult ♀. Scapulars rather short and rounded, centred blackish with broad orange fringes. Alternate upper- and undertail-coverts centred blackish and pale-fringed, more patterned than in ♀. Some pale grey basic feathers are usually retained, especially on the mantle and rump. These feathers are more scattered among scapulars and on flanks.

Adult ♀

Definitive basic plumage (Oct–Dec/Feb–Mar). Variable in general coloration (grey-beige to reddish-brown) and to lesser extent in the intensity of streaks and dark marks. There is a tendency towards two main forms, but all intermediates are possible. Head tinged reddish-brown, buff or grey-beige, with blackish vermiculations that vary in intensity, but more visible if the ground colour is paler. The eye-surround and nape are darker than the rest of the head. Iris dark brown. Bill like that of ♂ but darker blue-grey, less sharply contrasting. Breast buff to grey-beige in centre, darker at sides, with dark stripes (centres) variably marked. Flanks buff-orange to reddish-brown, with fine pale fringes to feathers visible only when close. Well-demarcated white belly. Undertail-coverts also whitish with black spots more concentrated on undertail. Mantle grey-brown. Scapulars buff-brown more or less bright, with diffuse blackish centres and fine pale yellowish fringes. Tertials elongated, pointed, grey-brown on outer webs, blackish on inner webs with a white rachis line on the proximal half, and fine white fringes. Back and rump feathers dark grey fringed pale grey. Rectrices blackish, the outer ones fringed white. Lesser and median coverts broad, rounded, dark grey and broadly fringed white. Greater coverts rather variable, usually pale grey with broad black tips and white fringes poorly marked, restricted to tips or lacking (Fig. 10). Subtle green gloss to inner secondaries (except innermost, which is essentially white). Underwing like that of ♂ but axillaries on average somewhat more strongly streaked or flecked dusky. Legs grey.

Definitive alternate plumage (Feb–Mar/Oct–Dec). Close to definitive basic plumage but slightly more cryptic, with more obvious dark crescents on flanks and pale internal marks better marked on alternate scapulars and tertials.

Juvenile

First basic plumage (until Oct–Nov). Like ♀, but more brownish and duller, with crown (down to eye) more strongly streaked or mottled blackish (affording capped appearance). Bill dark blue-grey, with diffuse dusky marks on the culmen. Differs from adult ♀ by the upperwing pattern as in formative plumage (see below). Tertials short and frayed at tips, without white rachis line. Scapulars dull grey-brown without pale inner marks, and rather diffuse pale brownish fringes. In hand, note juvenile rectrices. Sexing possible based on pattern of greater coverts, speculum and tertial coverts (see below).

First-winter ♂

Formative plumage (Nov–Jan/May–Jul). Following pre-formative moult, similar to definitive basic plumage, except in some birds in which moult was less extensive, and which still have juvenile feathers on the breast, flanks, undertail, among scapulars and/or tertials. Easily separated by upperwing pattern until the beginning of the second pre-basic moult, the broad, clean white patch of the adult being less extensive, poorly demarcated and mottled dusky. Greater coverts quite different from those of adult ♂ . Narrower and

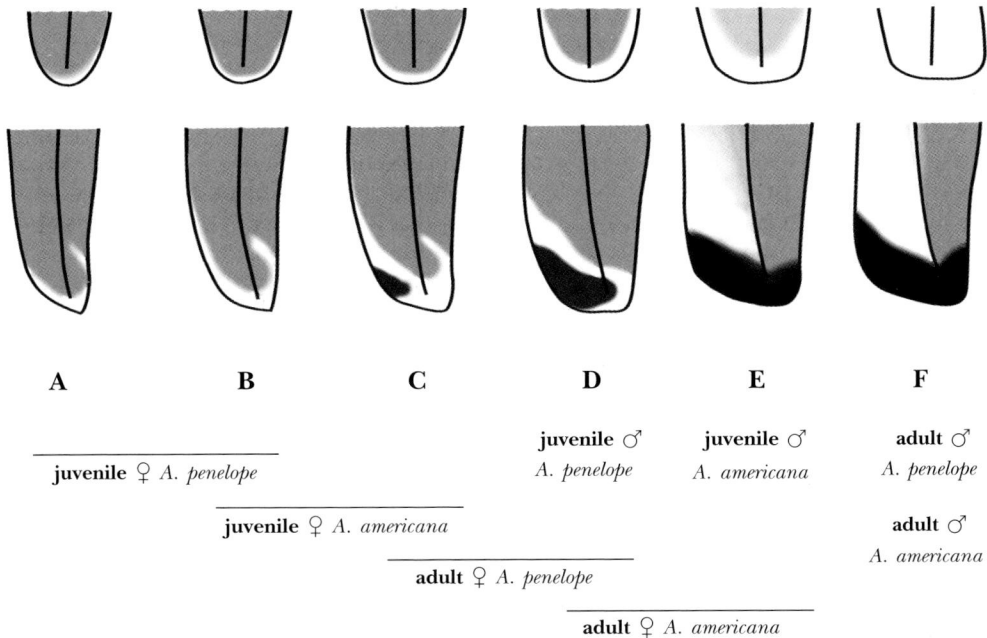

A	B	C	D	E	F

| | | | **juvenile** ♂ *A. penelope* | **juvenile** ♂ *A. americana* | **adult** ♂ *A. penelope* |

juvenile ♀ *A. penelope*

juvenile ♀ *A. americana*

    adult ♂ *A. americana*

adult ♀ *A. penelope*

adult ♀ *A. americana*

Fig. 10. Shape and pattern of upperwing median and greater coverts in American Wigeon *Anas americana* and Eurasian Wigeon *A. penelope.*

rather pointed, with outer webs often all or partly greyish, an off-white fringe or some black spots at tip and thin white fringe (Fig. 10). Black speculum with green sheen usually limited to ss7–9 (innermost secondaries being pale grey or whitish on outer webs). Tertial coverts pointed with narrow pale fringes often interrupted at tips.

First-winter ♀

Formative plumage (Nov-Jan/Feb-Mar). Very similar to adult ♀, but easily distinguished by upperwing pattern until the beginning of second pre-basic moult. Pre-formative moult is less extensive in young ♀ than in young ♂, and signs of juvenile plumage (especially tertials) often remain. The whitish belly is often finely streaked pale brown and diffusely demarcated. Lesser and median coverts narrower, frayed at tips, plainer with pale brown fringes. Greater coverts narrow, rather pointed, mostly grey with large white fringes on outer webs. Sometimes also has black patch towards the tip and a white inner bar (Fig. 10). Speculum grey (not black) with usually very faint or no gloss. Tertial coverts have pale fringes narrower than in adult ♀, but usually unbroken at tip (vs. young ♂).

GEOGRAPHIC VARIATION None. However, in ♂♂ in definitive basic or formative plumage, the presence of a green glossy patch behind the eye is apparently more common in NW Europe and even more in E Asia, where *c.*10% of birds show this[872]. Many also show a slightly broader creamy forehead, merging into the fore cheeks. One can see in this geographical prevalence the genetic influence of American Wigeon, a casual visitor more expected at the eastern and western extremes of the Palearctic. It would be interesting to have genetic analysis of such birds.

MEASUREMENTS and MASS ♂ and adult slightly larger than ♀ and young, respectively. ♂ : wing chord 252–281 (adult, 267, *n*=45) and 246–266 (juvenile, 257, *n*=42), tail 102–119 (106, *n*=19), bill 32–38 (34.7, *n*=84), tarsus 37–44 (39.5, *n*=49); ♀: wing chord 242–262 (adult, 250, *n*=19) and 228–261 (juvenile, 244, *n*=32), tail 86–95 (90.7, *n*=13), bill 31–37 (33.8, *n*=51), tarsus 35–41 (38.6, *n*=40)[267] ; ♂ : 267 (adult, *n*=781) and 260 (juvenile, *n*=400), tarsus 40.1 (adult, *n*=18) and 40.3 (juvenile, *n*=24), mass 790 (adult, *n*=800) and 712 (juvenile, *n*=384); ♀: 250 (adult, *n*=473) and 248 (juvenile, *n*=449), tarsus 38.9 (adult, *n*=14) and 38.7 (juvenile, *n*=30), mass 719 (adult, *n*=481) and 645 (juvenile, *n*=438) from WWT ringing stations[852].

♂ (*n*=40): wing chord 245–271 (adult) and 238–262 (juvenile), tail 82–112, culmen 32–38, bill depth at tip of forehead feathering 15.2–17.8, tarsus 37–42; ♀ (*n*=40): wing chord 229–254 (adult) and 220–245 (juvenile), tail 73–100, culmen 30–37, bill depth at tip of forehead feathering 14.4–17.0, tarsus 35–40; compare data for American Wigeon in Pyle[1014].

VOICE Loquacious, especially in flocks, whatever the circumstances. ♂ produces a typical whistling sound: *weee-oor* or *rew-wee-oorr*, with the *wee* louder and higher pitched. ♀ produces a harsh *kerr*.

MOULT Complex alternate strategy. Pre-formative moult occurs in Sep–Dec, mainly on staging and wintering grounds, and involves a large number (variable) of head and body feathers, none to all tertials and rectrices, most birds retaining at least some of the latter until second pre-basic moult (first summer). A small number of inner upperwing-coverts may be replaced too. Definitive pre-alternate moult occurs between Jan and May in ♀ and May–Aug in ♂. It includes some body feathers, none to all tertials and rectrices and possibly inner upperwing-coverts. Definitive pre-basic moult takes place in Jul–Dec and begins with the flight feathers. It is delayed for 1–2 months in ♀♀ that breed successfully. Most of the head and body feathers are replaced once southbound migration starts, and it ends mostly at wintering sites. The earliest ♂♂ show an almost complete basic plumage from late Oct but the majority complete their moult in Dec. However, Baker[56] indicated that *c.*15% of adult ♂♂ retain some tertials, central rectrices and other scattered feathers until Mar–Apr.

HYBRIDISATION In the wild, this species hybridises rarely, the majority of the reports involving American Wigeon (see that species). Other natural hybridisation events have been described with Falcated Duck *A. falcata*, Gadwall *A. strepera*, Mallard *A. platyrhynchos*, Northern Pintail *A. acuta* and Eurasian Teal *A. crecca*. The first three hybrids are described below and the latter two under the other two species respectively. Much more infrequent reports have been published concerning Northern Shoveler *A. clypeata*, Baikal Teal *A. formosa*[465,582] and Garganey *A. querquedula*[465,947]. In captivity, hybridisation has been mentioned with Wood Duck *Aix sponsa*[97,817], Chestnut Teal *A. castanea*[582], White-cheeked Pintail *A. bahamensis*[443], Yellow-billed Pintail *A. georgica*[465,587], Red-crested Pochard *Netta rufina*, Common Pochard *Aythya ferina*[442], Tufted Duck *Aythya fuligula*[442,817], Ring-necked Duck *Aythya collaris*[443] and possibly Common Scoter *Melanitta nigra*[752]. Finally, this species also regularly hybridises in captivity with Chiloe Wigeon *A. sibilatrix*, and these may escape. As this hybrid's resemblance to American Wigeon can be misleading, it is described below.

Eurasian Wigeon × Chiloe Wigeon. Such hybrids (♂♂ and ♀♀) are often reported as American Wigeons in Europe[439,523,1330]. Their shape is often more reminiscent of Chiloe Wigeon with the tail held upward more often than in Eurasian and American Wigeons, revealing the more massive rear body of Chiloe Wigeon. In definitive basic plumage, the ♂ has a head close to that of American Wigeon, with white to buff cheeks clearly vermiculated blackish, bill base and lores more yellowish extending into a buff-yellow forehead, which is short (ending above the eye), of even width and squared-off. Neck has reddish hue (always?) inherited from Eurasian Wigeon. Rear crown, nape and broad eye-band blackish with green gloss. Breast purplish-pink. Fore flanks pale orange merging into grey-toned rear flanks. Large white spot between the flanks and undertail, the latter variably stained dark grey and white, but always paler than Eurasian and American Wigeons. Scapulars and mantle grey to grey-brown, the former being distinctly elongated and dark-centred, especially the longest ones. Rump pale grey. ♀ is very similar to ♀ American Wigeon or a ♂ in alternate plumage. The blackish eye-patch extends more upwards (to the centre of the cap), reducing the pale forehead as in ♂ and often shows subtle green hues. Moreover, further distinguished by the blackish-centred scapulars, which are also more elongated and pointed, with more contrasting pale fringes. Rear flanks and undertail whitish with fewer dusky patches than American Wigeon.

Eurasian Wigeon × Falcated Duck. Sometimes encountered in the wild, mostly in E Asia[385,524,817,947] and well known in captivity[100,439], at least ♂ in definitive basic plumage. It has a reddish head reminiscent of Eurasian Wigeon, with the strongly green eye-patches meeting on the lower hindneck. The bill is black with two long blue-grey triangles at the sides. Chin and throat white, more or less clearly demarcated[100,439], underlined by a large black neck-ring and sometimes a thin white one. The breast is dull peachy pink with small dusky crescents. Rest of the body as both parents (upperparts and flanks pale grey, white patches on femoral area, black undertail-coverts and black horizontal line on the scapulars), with long, curved tertials intermediate between those of the parents.

Eurasian Wigeon × Gadwall. Adult ♂ in basic plumage is variable, with up to four types described[439]. The head can be close to that of Gadwall albeit with a trace of eye-band darker than yellowish cheeks. The latter may be more variegated, with a blackish eye-band with a reddish hue and possibly a green gloss. Paler yellow vermiculated grey-brown surrounds the dark eye-band on the cheeks and lores, and spreads toward the forehead and black chin. This type can easily be mistaken for hybrid Eurasian Wigeon × American Wigeon. Bill rather long, black with pale blue-grey or dull pink triangles at the sides. Breast usually pink to pale brownish-grey with dusky crescents forming regular streaks. Body intermediate between the parents, vermiculated dark grey with a more or less brownish hue. Femoral area has a variable white patch. Tertials elongated, pointed and, in many birds, more or less uniform grey. Upperwing variable, but some white often present on innermost secondaries. ♀ more reminiscent of Eurasian Wigeon or Falcated Duck, but with a rather long bill, pinkish at the sides (always?).

Eurasian Wigeon × Mallard. Reported occasionally in the wild, and difficult to distinguish from hybrid American Wigeon × Mallard (see American Wigeon). Adult ♂ in basic plumage is quite variable, particularly the head colour, which can have a broad black eye-patch with green sheen, cheeks pale yellowish or reddish with dark vermiculations merging on lores and forehead, and a blackish chin, but can also be mainly dark with green gloss, closer to Mallard. Bill intermediate in structure and length, grey to pale pink, with black tip. Breast flesh-pink to purplish-brown, with small black spots, well demarcated from the rest of the body, which is mostly pale grey vermiculated blackish. Femoral white patch variable. Under- and uppertail-coverts black, with central rectrices black elongated and slightly up-curved. Like many hybrids, the pattern of the head and bill is often closer to one parent, and the body closer to that of the other. The upperwing pattern often recalls that of Eurasian Wigeon with white nevertheless restricted to the base of the greater coverts. Tertials essentially uniform grey with variable black on the inner webs. Legs dull yellow-orange. ♀ quite close to that of Eurasian Wigeon, but often has a longer bill, variably tinged pink or yellowish.

HABITAT and LIFE-CYCLE Migrant that reaches its nesting grounds between early Apr and mid-Jun, depending on latitude, and eggs laid soon after. Usually breeds in isolated pairs or loose colonies, using various types of freshwater lowland wetlands, preferably lined with low vegetation (marshes, slow-flowing rivers, shallow lakes with abundant aquatic vegetation)[145,852]. Favours vast open bogs in taiga or wetlands fringed by cultivation. Rarer in Arctic tundra, in montane or in brackish habitats[267]. ♂ leaves ♀ during incubation and forms large gatherings at sites dedicated to wing moult. Successful ♀♀ moult their flight feathers near or on nesting grounds. Begins migration southward as soon as able to fly again. Very gregarious on migration and in winter, at large shallow wetlands near grassy areas (flooded or not), eelgrass beds, etc. The majority of the main wintering areas are on coasts (bays, estuaries). Usually feeds by day, but may do so by night if the tidal rhythm and/or hunting pressure dictate.

RANGE and POPULATION Huge Palearctic range. Total estimated population 2,800,000–3,300,000 birds[305], of which 1,500,000 birds winter in N & E Europe, 300,000 in Mediterranean and Black Seas, 250,000 in E Africa and Middle East, 250,000 in S Asia and 500,000–1,000,000 in E Asia[1348]. Stable in west of its range, with slight increase in S Asia[757] and declining in E Asia[1348]. Rare visitor that has become more regular since the 1970s in North America, primarily on the Pacific coast and to lesser extent in the north-east, with local concentrations exceeding 100 birds. Over 2,000 birds killed annually in USA[648]. Potentially found throughout North and Central America where American Wigeon occurs, although breeding does not appear to have been proven in North America yet.

CAPTIVITY Quite frequently held in captivity, usually cheap and deemed fairly easy to keep and breed. Considered of natural origin in inland North America, although birds seen alone, away from flocks of American Wigeon should be considered with caution.

REFERENCES Baker (1992)[56]; Bird Hybrids Database (2014)[97]; Bird Hybrids Flickr forum (2008)[100]; Bird Hybrids Flickr forum (2010)[123]; Bird Hybrids Flickr Forum (2011)[136]; BirdLife International (2014)[145]; Cramp & Simmons (1977)[268]; Delany & Scott (2006)[305]; Flint & Anzigitova (1993)[385]; Gillham & Gillham (1996)[439]; Gillham & Gillham (2000)[442]; Gillham & Gillham (2002)[443]; Gray (1958)[465]; Harrison & Harrison (1968)[523]; Harrison & Harrison (1968)[524]; Hopkinson (1926)[582]; Hopkinson (1933)[584]; Hopkinson (1935)[587]; Johnsgard (2010)[648]; Johnson & Sorenson (1999)[654]; Leverkühn (1890)[752]; Li *et al.* (2009)[757]; Livezey (1991)[767]; McCarthy (2006)[817]; Mitchell *in* Kear (2005)[852]; Moores & Moores (2003)[872]; Panov (1989)[947]; Pyle (2008)[1014]; Votier *et al.* (2003)[1330]; Wetlands International (2014)[1348].

253. Adult ♂ (definitive basic). England, Feb. Sébastien Reeber.

254. Adult ♂ (definitive alternate); sexing easy due to reddish-brown plumage and many basic-type feathers on mantle and scapulars. Denmark, Oct (Nis Lundmark Jensen).

255. Adult ♂ (definitive alternate). Scotland, Sep (Ian Fulton).

256. Adult ♂ (definitive basic); aged using upperwing pattern, with adult having large clear-cut white oval patch in winter and spring. Denmark, Mar (Nis Lundmark Jensen).

257. First-winter ♂ (formative); note the many juvenile feathers, especially on undertail, as well as shorter and more rounded formative tertials. Netherlands, Feb (Sébastien Reeber).

258. Adult ♂ (definitive basic); such birds, which are regularly reported on both Asian and North American Pacific coasts and in W Europe, show odd features like extensive green sheen behind eye, white forehead extending far onto crown and/or merging into fore cheeks, slight pinkish hue to scapulars and/or fore flanks, all probably signs of a mixed ancestry. Japan, Jan (Ayuwat Jearwattanakanok).

259. Adult ♀ (definitive basic-definitive alternate), with paler axillaries, but still has distinct creamy ground colour and brownish speckles. UK, Feb (Sébastien Reeber).

260. Juvenile (first basic); among several juvenile characters, note tertial coverts (narrow with faint brownish fringes), tertials (short, frayed at tips), dusky culmen and 'capped' appearance to head, while uninterrupted pale fringe to the tertial coverts indicates a ♀. France, Oct (Aurélien Audevard).

261. First-winter ♀ (formative); aged by brownish spots forming a neat line around belly, and by juvenile tail, upper- and undertail-coverts (compare to adult ♀ above). UK, Feb (Sébastien Reeber)

262. Adult ♀ (definitive basic/definitive alternate); note grey, speckled axillaries and underwing pattern, here at darkest end of individual variation. UK, Feb (Sébastien Reeber).

263. Adult ♀ (definitive basic); among adult features, note broad and rounded, black and white-edged tertial coverts, and broadly white-fringed upperwing-coverts. England, Feb (Sébastien Reeber).

264. Adult ♀ (definitive alternate), well advanced in pre-formative moult (including tertials); a rather variably coloured plumage, here a pale, greyish ♀. Netherlands, Feb (Sébastien Reeber).

AMERICAN WIGEON
Anas americana

Plates 27, 28

TAXONOMY *Anas americana* J. F. Gmelin, 1789. *Syst. Nat.*, 1, p. 526. Very close to its Eurasian and South American counterparts, Eurasian Wigeon *A. penelope* and Chiloe Wigeon *A. sibilatrix*, respectively. These three species form a clade with Gadwall *A. strepera* and Falcated Duck *A. falcata*[654], and all five species have even been placed together with Cape Teal *Anas capensis* in the genus *Mareca*[767]. No geographic variation or subspecies.

IDENTIFICATION In Eurasia, American Wigeon is a rare visitor (mainly to W Europe and E Asia), usually in the company of Eurasian Wigeon. ♂♂ are usually not difficult to identify in definitive basic and formative plumages, but even then they can be surprisingly difficult to detect in Eurasian Wigeon flocks, either on the water or grazing on land, because of similar shape and size. In bad light, the head can appear quite dark and plain pinkish hues to the body inconspicuous. In such conditions, the large white forehead is often the most obvious feature. The potential for misidentification is increased by the regular presence of hybrids in the wild, even if first-generation hybrids are rarely very similar to American Wigeon. Hybrids backcrossed with American Wigeon are less likely to occur in Europe, but much trickier. See also Eurasian Wigeon.

♂ in definitive alternate plumage distinguished from ♀ by large oval patch on the upperwing, which is pure white and clearly demarcated. In this plumage, ♂ American Wigeon differs from its Eurasian counterpart in being paler with bright orange flanks (vs. deep red in Eurasian Wigeon) and pale grey contrasting head (brown in Eurasian Wigeon, usually slightly darker than the breast and flanks, but without sharp contrast). American Wigeon generally has a large dark patch around the eye, tapering at the rear, which can recall the eye-band of basic plumage. Also useful when seen close, a thin black line often runs from the gape upward along the bill base in American Wigeon.

♀♀ of the two species are very similar, with that of Eurasian Wigeon being more variable in overall coloration, the reddish-brown form generally being easy to identify. Their sizes are similar but their shapes slightly different: ♀ American Wigeon often has a less square head and appears stronger, with a slightly steeper forehead and less angular nape when relaxed. The bill and neck appear slightly longer and often stretched

when feeding on water. Note also that American Wigeon feeds more frequently on water than Eurasian Wigeon, which prefers to graze. The tail of American Wigeon is longer, the tips of the wings often barely exceeding the longest uppertail-coverts, while the wings reach the tip of the tail in Eurasian Wigeon. Overall colour usually differs, with contrast between the grey and pale head, and the orange tint of the breast and flanks. Some ♀ Eurasian Wigeon also show a rather greyish head, but they then usually have rather dull buff-coloured flanks. Conversely, some ♀♀ have deep orange-brown flanks (rarely as bright orange as in American Wigeon though), but in such cases the head is usually dark reddish-brown. If a bird is suspected to be different due to this general contrast, consider the following features.

- The head of American Wigeon is greyish with the cheeks, lores and forehead pale grey vermiculated dark grey. ♀ Eurasian Wigeon has a similar pattern, especially in alternate plumage, but the dark brown ground colour conceals the vermiculations. In American Wigeon, a large dark oval patch surrounds the eye, and offers sharp contrast, visible even at long range.

- The axillaries and underwing median coverts form a pure white area in American Wigeon. The axillaries are sometimes speckled grey-beige, which does not alter the white impression. In Eurasian Wigeon, this area is tinged or stained/streaked grey-brown. However, direct sunlight may 'over-expose' the underwing.

- A black line is sometimes visible at the base of the bill, which is not usually the case in Eurasian Wigeon. It is more visible in adult ♂♂, often present in adult ♀♀, but rare in juveniles.

- Upperwing pattern is useful in adult ♀♀: that of American Wigeon has paler secondary coverts. The greater coverts are usually pale grey to whitish basally (paler on the outer webs) with broad black tips, giving the impression of a clear white wingbar, while Eurasian Wigeon is plainer grey, often greater coverts have grey bases and black tips, but many intermediate patterns occur in both species. In American Wigeon, the median coverts have broad sharp white fringes, with grey centres, which may be pale grey or even whitish, affording an upperwing close to the ♂ (Fig. 10 on p. 345). This rarely occurs in Eurasian Wigeon.

- The scapulars have paler, broader and sharper fringes in adult ♀ American Wigeon in basic plumage, giving the upperparts a less uniform and more scaly appearance. The same is true of the rump, which has a finely streaked appearance, whereas it is plainer in Eurasian Wigeon.

- The tertials are slightly more contrasting in adult ♀ American Wigeon, the outer web being blacker, and the fringes whiter and broader.

- The breast of adult ♀ American Wigeon is usually more heavily spotted with black.

- The innermost secondary has a largely white outer web in adult ♂ Eurasian Wigeon (with a black fringe on the distal half), the same feather being pale grey in American Wigeon. In all plumages, this feather shows more white in Eurasian Wigeon.

- The eyelid of American Wigeon is whitish, whereas that of Eurasian Wigeon is pale buff[726].

The identification problems linked to hybridisation are poorly known in ♀♀, because of the similarity of the two species in this plumage, and the difficulty to detect hybrids.

DESCRIPTION. Strong sexual dimorphism from first winter onward. Complex alternate moult strategy (two plumages per definitive cycle, three in first cycle). Ageing ♂♂ relatively easy until first summer. Ageing ♀♀ possible until first summer too, but requires detailed examination of the upperwing and/or rectrices.

Adult ♂

Definitive basic plumage (Oct–Nov/May–Jun). Creamy forehead (whitish to yellowish) extending onto crown and tapering towards the nape. Cheeks and neck pale greyish to pale buff, vermiculated and flecked dark grey. Broad eye-band blackish with green gloss (often bronze near eye), meeting on the hindneck. In some birds, this band is restricted to a dark patch around and behind the eye, merging into fine streaks and flecks on a beige ground colour towards the rear. The cheeks are variably vermiculated, sometimes sufficient to make the eye-band barely contrast. Sometimes, however, vermiculations are absent on lores and fore cheeks. Fewer than 1% of adult ♂♂ show entirely creamy cheeks without vermiculations. Iris dark brown. Bill pale blue-grey with base, tomium, nail and around nostrils black. The black base typically appears as a black vertical line

in contact with the feathers (concealed by feathers in Eurasian Wigeon). Mantle, breast and flanks pinkish-brown, slightly more purplish on fore flanks and more orange on rear flanks. Belly and femoral patch white and sharply defined. Undertail-coverts and final row of uppertail-coverts black (except central pair, which are pale grey). Outer rectrices have large white fringes, central rectrices longer, pointed and black. Rump grey. Scapulars pinkish-brown, the longest feathers greyish with a black line on the shaft. Tertials long and pointed, black on inner webs, grey on outer webs with a white fringe and rachis line. Tertial coverts have lateral whitish fringes. Upperwing dark grey with broad white patch over much of lesser and median coverts and bases of greater coverts. This patch is frequently visible even if the bird does not fly, as a horizontal line between the flanks and scapulars. Tips of greater coverts black (Fig. 10). Secondaries with black outer webs and green gloss more marked basally, except on the innermost secondary, which is pale grey with a black fringe on the outer web at the tip. Underwing grey, axillaries and median coverts white. Legs pale grey.

Definitive alternate plumage (Jun–Jul/Sep–Oct). Like adult ♀, but distinguished by upperwing pattern and large well-defined white patch, by stronger contrast between orange flanks and pale grey head, more pronounced black eye-patch and paler blue-grey bill, with the black parts more clear-cut.

Adult ♀

Definitive basic plumage (Oct–Nov/Feb–Mar). Mainly orange-brown with a greyer and paler head and whitish rear body. Head and neck pale grey to pale buff vermiculated dark grey, with dark oval patch often well marked around eye. Iris dark brown. Bill as ♂ but slightly darker and less sharply marked black. The vertical bar at the bill base is often visible, but can be hidden by feathers. Breast brown-orange with small dark spots (feather centres). Flanks a brighter and paler orange, especially rearwards. Mantle and scapulars orange-brown with darker centres and well-defined buff fringes. Back and rump grey-brown with disorderly pale stripes formed by pale fringes to the feathers. Belly and undertail whitish to cream-coloured, the latter being marked with brown spots. Tertials like definitive ♂ in basic plumage but shorter, less pointed and lacking white shaft. Tertial coverts round-tipped and clearly fringed whitish. Upperwing similar to ♂, but lower lesser coverts and median coverts centred grey to whitish with broad white fringes. When centres are pale, the upperwing shows a large whitish patch similar to that of ♂, but less well demarcated and speckled pale grey. The white bases to the greater coverts form a broad wingbar (Fig. 10). The whiteness of lesser and median coverts might increase with age, at least in some birds, but this requires further study. Secondaries blackish with moderate green sheen at the base. Underwing like ♂ but most lesser coverts mottled brown and fringed pale. The axillaries may show very slight pale grey speckling at the tips. Legs grey.

Definitive alternate plumage (Feb–Mar/Sep–Oct). Very like definitive basic plumage, but slightly duller and more cryptic, especially scapulars (longest elongate and pointed) and tertials, which have pale brown inner markings. Dark crescents well marked on flanks. Lateral uppertail-coverts striped white.

Juvenile

First basic plumage (until Oct–Nov). Resembles adult ♀, with duller plumage, less vermiculated head and often has a diffuse dark eye-patch that merges into a dusky crown (capped effect). Young ♀ mainly differs from adult by upperwing pattern: median coverts with diffuse pale brownish fringes, greater coverts narrower and more pointed, with fine pale fringes at sides widening towards the tips. A pale crossbar is often also present, the whole then forming two narrow parallel wingbars (Fig. 10). The secondaries are dull grey-brown, paler and duller than in adult ♀ and young ♂. The latter has greater coverts with outer webs whiter, a dusky patch towards the tip and an inconspicuous pale fringe (Fig. 10)[224]. The speculum has no green sheen (♀) or gloss is limited to 1–3 inner secondaries (♂). Tips of secondaries clearly show more white (especially on outer webs) in young ♀ than young ♂, forming a more visible white trailing edge[1014]. Other significant age features include the short rounded tertials with frayed tips, and the tertial coverts with continuous pale fringes in ♀ and thin pale fringes interrupted at tips in ♂. Scapulars largely dull grey-brown, with pale fringes rather diffuse and no pale internal marks. The undertail has elongated dark patches in ♂, more rounded in ♀. Bill dark blue-grey and dull, with poorly defined blackish nail, tomium and blackish traces on culmen. In the hand, note the juvenile rectrices.

First-winter ♂

Formative plumage (Nov–Dec/May–Jun). Following pre-formative moult, similar to definitive basic plumage ♂. The broad white patches on the upperwing of adult ♂

are replaced by a more or less pale but ill-defined area, with juvenile coverts centred brown (a small number of replaced inner coverts are white). This feature, as well as the pattern of juvenile greater coverts and tertial coverts, is retained until the second pre-basic moult. Other features can be useful: one to several juvenile tertials (shorter, more round-tipped and without white rachis), some scapulars or upper flanks are juvenile and the belly feathers are largely juvenile, forming neat brownish streaking.

First-winter ♀

Formative plumage (Nov–Jan/Feb–Mar). Very similar to adult ♀, but easily separated using upperwing pattern until the second pre-basic moult. The juvenile tertial coverts are narrower with a pale diffuse brownish fringe (white and sharp in adult ♀). As pre-formative moult is less extensive in ♀ than ♂, more juvenile feathers will occur with formative feathers, even if the formative plumage is worn briefly. Until the next pre-alternate moult, the plumage usually shows clear juvenile traces, with scapulars, breast and flanks browner and duller, and reduced contrast between head and breast. Tertials often entirely juvenile, short, rounded, frayed at the tips and without white rachis.

Second-winter

Definitive basic plumage (Oct–Nov/May–Jun). Cannot usually be distinguished from definitive basic plumage, but sometimes one or a few juvenile greater and median coverts are retained (visible in the hand).

GEOGRAPHIC VARIATION None.

MEASUREMENTS and MASS ♂ and adult slightly larger than ♀ and young, respectively. Mass varies noticeably throughout the year, especially in ♀. ♂ (*n*=12): wing chord 256–275 (264), tail 98–123 (111), culmen 35–39 (37), tarsus 37–43 (40), mass 590–1,089 (adult, 821) and 318–1134 (juvenile/first-winter, 794), during wing moult 567–794 (674); ♀ (*n*=12): wing chord 236–256 (246), tail 81–92 (88), culmen 35–40 (36), tarsus 37–40 (37), mass 544–1,043 (adult, 767) and 408–952 (juvenile/first-winter, 708)[171]. ♂ (*n*=100): wing chord 247–277 (adult) and 240–266 (juvenile), tail 96–127, culmen 33–41, bill depth at end of forehead feathering 15.3–18.0, tarsus 37–43; ♀ (*n*=80): wing chord 228–258 (adult) and 224–247 (juvenile), tail 86–113, culmen 31–39, bill depth at end of forehead feathering 14.4–17.1, tarsus 35–41; compare data by Pyle[1014] for Eurasian Wigeon.

VOICE Flocks often noisy, mainly in flight, but also when resting or feeding. ♂ utters a whistling sound, usually of three notes, the second louder and higher pitched (more often mono- or di-syllabic, slightly louder in Eurasian Wigeon). ♀ gives a harsh *kerrr* or *rrreg*, more reminiscent of a female *Aythya*.

MOULT Complex alternate strategy. Pre-formative moult occurs in Aug–Dec, mainly in staging and wintering areas, and includes many to almost all head and body feathers, none to all tertials and rectrices (20% of ♂♂ replace all, but very few ♀♀ do so[1014]), and possibly a small proportion of inner upperwing-coverts. Definitive pre-alternate moult occurs between Feb and May in ♀ and Jun–Aug in ♂. It includes roughly the same feathers as pre-formative moult, but is more extensive on average in ♀. Definitive pre-basic moult occurs in Jul–Dec and begins with the flight feathers. Southbound migration begins as soon as the birds can fly, when body plumage still largely alternate. ♂♂ at least may perform a pre-supplemental moult including some feathers of the head and neck in spring[1372] (see Introduction, perhaps vestigial).

HYBRIDISATION Natural hybridisation involving this species is relatively common with Eurasian Wigeon. These hybrids are described below, as well as those involving Mallard *A. platyrhynchos*, which are much rarer in the wild. Two other hybrids reported very occasionally, with Northern Pintail *A. acuta* and Green-winged Teal *A. carolinensis* (see those two species). Hybridisation in nature with Northern Shoveler *A. clypeata* and Blue-winged Teal *A. discors* seems exceptional[1190], while that with Gadwall *A. strepera*[125] remains to be confirmed. In captivity, cases of hybridisation documented with the following species: Muscovy Duck *Cairina moschata*[1190], Wood Duck *Aix sponsa*[439], Chiloe Wigeon[1190], White-cheeked Pintail *A. bahamensis*[582,817], American Black Duck *A. rubripes*[1190], Falcated Duck *A. falcata*[439,465], Baikal Teal *A. formosa*[1190], Red-crested Pochard *Netta rufina*[817], Redhead *Aythya americana*[1190], Lesser Scaup *A. affinis*[465,817], Tufted Duck *A. fuligula*[1190] and possibly Canvasback *A. valisineria*[817]. Also note that hybrid Chiloe Wigeon *Anas sibilatrix* × Eurasian Wigeon is sometimes reported in captivity and might escape. It can resemble American Wigeon (see Eurasian Wigeon).

American Wigeon × Eurasian Wigeon: quite regular in nature, even as frequent or more so than American Wigeon in W Europe and E Asia, or than Eurasian Wigeon on North American Pacific coast. These hybrids are fertile and many backcrosses with each of the two parent species have been reported. These backcrosses are usually very close to the parent with which backcrossing occurred. Adult ♂ in definitive basic plumage quite variable, each of the following features may be close to either parent or intermediate: width, length and colour of forehead patch, colour and gloss (red or green) of eye-band, ground colour of cheeks and upper neck, and coloration of breast, flanks and scapulars. Axillaries and median underwing-coverts usually average white or off-white. The most common type of hybrid has a whitish, yellowish or cream-coloured forehead, dark eye-patch with green sheen reddish or both, cheeks and upper neck pale reddish-beige with vermiculations, and mixed colours on flanks (often pale pinkish-orange with pale grey patches or vice versa). Overall, the appearance of this hybrid is closer to that of the male of the parent species[443], and many hybrids show a head closer to American Wigeon with a body closer to Eurasian Wigeon, or vice versa.

It is not easy to distinguish the features related to recent or ancient hybridisation, and normal phenotypic variability within both species (extensive hybridisation often being a source of variability). In W Europe, it is easy to observe Eurasian Wigeon with a broad forehead, reaching far onto the crown. These birds often show the pale forehead merging into the lores and even the fore cheeks up to below the eye. This highlights the dark vermiculations, which are present in most Eurasian Wigeon but obscured by the dark red ground colour. Such birds often show a glossy green patch behind the eye, off-white or whitish axillaries and median underwing-coverts, and/or a more purplish hue to the pinkish breast. Conversely, other birds have an overall appearance very similar to American Wigeon, but with a much less contrasting eye-band, the cheeks being tinged more reddish-brown. The eye-band frequently has a red or coppery sheen behind the eye, instead of the green gloss, and the chin is often black or reddish-brown[439,443]. Birds closely resembling American Wigeon are probably second-generation hybrids (or late) if several unusual features tend toward Eurasian Wigeon, and vice versa.

♀♀ from the same cross have been described on several occasions in captivity[439,443], including multiple-generation hybrids[634]. They are just as variable as hybrid ♂♂, with characters that can vary between each parent species: coloration of the head, flanks, and axillaries or pattern of greater coverts. Identification should be based on as many features as possible to prevent confusion with the two parent species in the same plumage. It is certain that the vast majority of hybrid ♀♀ go unnoticed.

American Wigeon × Mallard. ♂ in definitive basic plumage has the head quite close to that of American Wigeon (lores and cheeks whitish vermiculated blackish, black eye-patch with green sheen), except the forehead and crown are dark or pale streaked dark. Some birds show a bimaculated pattern (vertical black bar below the eye)[439]. Bill like that of American Wigeon, but a little longer, with pale blue replaced by pinkish or dull yellowish (always?). Breast and mantle blackish-brown with copper and red tones, sometimes pinkish or paler. Flanks and scapulars mainly grey with brownish traces. Tertials pale grey, rather narrow with diffuse black patches on inner webs. Belly whitish, becoming grey-streaked lower down. Femoral coverts show a white vertical patch. Under- and uppertail-coverts black. Tail whitish at sides, with central rectrices black, elongate and curved slightly upward. Upperwing pattern also intermediate, with large pale grey or grey-brown patch on lesser and median coverts[439], greater coverts as American Wigeon, but blue or violet gloss on speculum (variable?). Legs orange-yellow to dull yellow-brown.

HABITAT and LIFE-CYCLE Pair formation occurs both on wintering grounds and on arrival at breeding grounds, which takes place mainly between Mar and mid-May, depending especially on the latitude and thaw Inhabits great variety of open wetland habitats from Arctic tundra to different marshes and lakes, from lowlands to plateaux. Being largely herbivorous, American Wigeon is less tied to seeds than other dabblers[171], and prefers shallow wetlands lined with grasslands and meadows[884]. Eggs are laid May–Jun[884]. Most ♂♂ abandon the ♀♀ during incubation and gather at sometimes very distant moulting sites, while ♀♀ moult their remiges on or near the nest sites, often with their offspring[884,1372]. On migration and winter, uses different types of shallow, fresh or brackish wetlands, but favours large estuarine systems, lagoons or coastal bays, where it especially feeds on eelgrass beds *Zostera* sp. In the interior, found at waterbodies bordered by grassy

areas, rice fields, pastures and flooded crops. Its short bill is adapted to grazing, even if it is less specialised than Eurasian Wigeon. Frequently forms numerous small flocks to feed, and large compact gatherings for preening or resting.

RANGE and POPULATION Occurs in the New World, with a small population in the Anadyr Valley of extreme E Siberia[182]. In winter, outside the mapped range, small numbers occur further south to Central and South America, and rare but regular visitor in E Asia (Russia, Japan, South Korea, etc.) and W Europe, south to Morocco, where it is the second commonest Nearctic dabbling duck after Green-winged Teal *A. carolinensis*, with a few (in Europe) to several tens (Asia) of birds per year. Estimated global population of 2,700,000 birds in 1995–97, 2,470,000 in 2009 and 2,644,000 in 2013[1294]. After a slight decline between the 1950s and 1980s, the population now seems stable.

CAPTIVITY Fairly frequently kept for ornamental purposes, without being one of the commonest species, at least outside specialised collections. More frequent in North America, but in Eurasia usually sold at a price slightly higher than most dabbling ducks, and often more expensive than the other two wigeon with which it is said to hybridise readily. Could escape from captivity, although the geographical pattern and timing of appearance in W Europe and E Asia leave little doubt as to the natural origin of most birds. However, birds seen alone, away from the company of Eurasian Wigeon, may not be genuine vagrants.

REFERENCES Bird Hybrids Database (2014)[97]; Bird Hybrids Flickr forum (2011)[125]; Boyd *in* Kear (2005)[171]; Brazil (2009)[182]; Carney (1992)[224]; Cox & Barry (2005)[262]; Gillham & Gillham (1996)[439]; Gillham & Gillham (2002)[443]; Gray (1958)[465]; Harrop (1994)[529]; Harrop (1994)[530]; Hopkinson (1926)[582]; Howell (2010)[590]; Jiguet (1999)[634]; Johnsgard (2010)[648]; Johnson & Sorenson (1999)[654]; Larkin (2000)[726]; Livezey (1991)[767]; McCarthy (2006)[817]; Mowbray (1999)[884]; Panov (1989)[947]; Pyle (2008)[1014]; Sibley (1938)[1190]; Sibley (1957)[1191]; USFWS (2013)[1294]; Votier *et al.* (2003)[1330]; Wishart (1985)[1372].

265. Adult ♂ (definitive basic). New Jersey, USA, Nov (Sébastien Reeber)

266. Adult ♂ (definitive basic); this rare but regular variant has a wide whitish forehead and cheeks, almost without dark speckling, making its head very contrasting. Florida, USA, Dec (Ron Bielefeld).

267. Adult ♂ (definitive alternate), resembles ♀, but is brighter and more contrasting; note green sheen on eyestripe and white upperwing patch. New Jersey, USA, Sep (Sébastien Reeber).

268. Adult ♂ (definitive pre-alternate); note diagnostic underwing pattern, with white axillaries and median coverts contrasting with dark orange-brown flanks. New Jersey, USA, Sep (Sébastien Reeber).

269. Adult ♀ (definitive basic); whitish upperwing patch and greater coverts typical of adult, but former is individually variable, this bird having an extensive white patch. British Columbia, Canada, Jan (Alan D. Wilson).

270. First-winter ♀ (pre-formative/first alternate), still showing juvenile rectrices and tertials. Texas, USA, Feb (Sébastien Reeber)

271. Adult ♂ (right) and adult ♀ (left) (definitive basic); note upperwing pattern, typical of adults; the ♂ has a clear-cut white oval patch, whereas in the ♀, this is much whiter in adults than immatures; in both sexes, the greater coverts have white bases and black tips. California, USA, Nov (Sébastien Reeber).

272. Adult ♀ (definitive basic), compared to Eurasian Wigeon *A. penelope*, note orangey flanks, greyish and distinctly speckled head, and contrasting dark eye-patch; the long pointed tertials, neatly white-fringed tertial coverts and upperwing-coverts are typical of this age. New Jersey, USA, Nov (Sébastien Reeber)

273. First-winter ♂ (formative) in pre-formative moult, when resembles dull adult ♂, but note juvenile feathers (tertials, all rectrices except two central ones) and dusky trace on upper culmen. Texas, USA, Nov (Greg Lavaty).

274. American Wigeon *A. americana* × Eurasian Wigeon *A. penelope*, adult ♂ (definitive basic); the influence of Eurasian Wigeon is obvious, while the broad green eye-band, pale forehead extending far onto crown and long tail are known to be inherited from American Wigeon. Japan, Feb (Aurélien Audevard).

275. American Wigeon *A. americana* × Eurasian Wigeon *A. penelope*, adult ♂ (definitive basic); a typical hybrid of this cross. Washington, USA, Jan (Steve Mlodinow).

276. American Wigeon *A. americana* × Eurasian Wigeon *A. penelope*, adult ♂ (definitive basic), with a more reddish eye-band and paler cheeks. Washington, USA, Dec (Steve Mlodinow)

MALLARD
Anas platyrhynchos Plate 29

TAXONOMY *Anas platyrhynchos* Linnaeus, 1758, *Syst. Nat.*, edn. 10, p. 125. The Mallard forms part of a clade of relatively similar species grouped under the subgenus *Anas* by Livezey[767] (see Taxonomy of American Black Duck *Anas rubripes* for further details). The taxonomic position and status of many of these taxa have long been discussed and are still debated today. Mottled Duck *A. fulvigula*, American Black Duck, Indian Spot-billed Duck *A. poecilorhyncha* and Eastern Spot-billed Duck *A. zonorhyncha* also form part of this group and are regarded as full species, although the first two and last two were considered conspecific, respectively, in the past. In the Pacific Is, three related taxa have been described: Hawaiian Duck *A. wyvilliana*, Laysan Duck *A. laysanensis* and Mariana Duck *A. (p.) oustaleti*. The first two are currently recognised as species[21,236,437]. The latter, described by Salvadori in 1894, endemic to some of the Mariana Is but not seen since the 1980s, is now considered to represent an unstable hybrid population between Mallard and Pacific Black Duck *A. superciliosa*[410,767].

Another close relative is Mexican Duck *A. (p.) diazi* Ridgway, 1886, which is distinguished from Mallard by the adult ♂ plumage being like that of ♀ throughout the year. Its status and placement are still discussed, some authors considering it to be a separate species[437,1382] and others as a subspecies of Mallard[21,236,326,597]. Livezey[767] considered *platyrhynchos* part of a clade that also includes *oustaleti*, *wyvilliana* and *laysanensis*, and neighbour to another clade including *diazi* and *fulvigula*. These results are consistent with the analyses conducted by Avise *et al.*[45] and Kulikova *et al.*[715,716], who established the existence of two genetically distinct clades (differing in mitochondrial DNA by 0.6–0.8%) in the nominate subspecies of Mallard. The first clade is widespread throughout the Holarctic and genetically close to Indian Spot-billed Duck and Eastern Spot-billed Duck. The second occurs in North America, the Aleutians and Primorye in the Russian Far East. It is very close genetically to American Black Duck, Mottled Duck, Mexican Duck and Hawaiian Duck[822,1067]. Finally, note the same analysis[45] showed that Mallards on the Aleutians are sedentary and differ significantly from Mallards in both Eurasia and North America.

Johnson & Sorenson[654] also recovered two clades within Mallard, and placed them in monophyletic

groups similar to those above, except that they added Philippine Duck *A. luzonica* and Laysan Duck to the first group, although subsequently it has been suggested that Laysan Duck is actually more distant[1067]. More recently, Kulikova *et al.*[715] detected haplotypes specific to each group in Eastern Spot-billed Duck of E Asia, also suggesting that this species is actually closer to American Black Duck, Mottled Duck and Mexican Duck than Mallard even though the latter is sympatric. Other authors have placed Mexican Duck near Mottled Duck, either as full species[64,749,822], or as subspecies[293]. The possibility of treating Mottled and Mexican Ducks as subspecies of American Black Duck has also been discussed[64], given that *diazi*, *fulvigula* and *rubripes* are closer to each other than *platyrhynchos*[454].

For *diazi*, up-to-date information is lacking on historical and current hybridisation, which may be overestimated[1340]. There is also a need for genetic analyses based on sufficient samples for all taxa within the 'Mallard' group, to arrive at a more global view of the complex. Mexican Duck *A. (p.) diazi* is treated within Mallard here, following the current view of the AOU[21], despite a recent proposal to treat it specifically[64]. There is, however, little doubt that further information will lead to changes in this status, and to a more consensual treatment. Another taxon, *A. p. conboschas* C. L. Brehm, 1831, endemic to S Greenland, is also considered a subspecies of Mallard.

IDENTIFICATION The identification of adult ♂ in basic plumage is straightforward. All other plumages can, however, be mistaken for those of other *Anas*, especially American Black Duck (including in Europe, where it is accidental) and Mottled Duck. Identification issues are emphasised by the fact that these species readily hybridise with Mallard in the wild. The identification features to distinguish these three species and their hybrids are detailed under American Black Duck and Mottled Duck. The only other species that may pose (less significant) identification problems is Gadwall *A. strepera* (which see). The features for separating Mexican Duck from the nominate subspecies of Mallard are discussed under Geographic Variation (see also Mottled Duck).

PLUMAGES Nominate subspecies. Strong sexual dimorphism from first winter onwards. Complex alternate moult strategy (two plumages per definitive cycle, three in first cycle). Ageing relatively easy until mid-autumn and possible until the subsequent summer under good viewing conditions or in the hand. See also American Black Duck, including a detailed description of upperwing and underwing patterns compared to those of American Black Duck and hybrids between the two species. Finally, see Kirby et al. [693] for the frequency of atypical upperwing patterns in North America, England and E Palearctic.

NB: The description hereafter deals with wild birds, and does not apply to the countless domestic forms (see, e.g., Delacour[295] and Kear[674]) and vast numbers of intermediates. Such birds escape frequently from captivity, and breed with wild congeners. Finally, the genetic 'quality' of birds bred and released for hunting is, even today, not always controlled, and many descendants of more or less domestic forms breed well in the wild.

Adult ♂

Definitive basic plumage (Oct–Nov/May–Jun). Head and upper neck dark with strong green metallic gloss (can appear blue or purple depending on light). Iris dark brown. Bill yellow, slightly greenish, with black nail. Narrow, sharply defined white collar, more or less interrupted on hindneck. Breast dark purplish-brown. Mantle grey-brown, vermiculated slightly reddish. Scapulars and flanks whitish, finely vermiculated grey (appearing pale grey-beige). A broad diffuse horizontal bar is formed by dark reddish-brown tint to the lower scapulars, and inner webs of the tertials, which are broad, long, lanceolate and centred pale grey. Back, rump and uppertail-coverts black, with blue sheen to latter. Belly pale grey and undertail black. Two pairs of central rectrices are almost completely curled. Other rectrices grey becoming white at the sides. Upperwing grey-brown with outer webs and tips of primaries blackish. Speculum has strong blue gloss (can appear turquoise or purple) except 1–3 outermost secondaries. The glossy area is framed by black stripes (subterminal bands on secondaries and tips to greater coverts) and white lines (tips to secondaries and subterminal bands on greater coverts), see Fig. 11 on p. 369. Underwing whitish with cream-coloured tones and greyer greater coverts, and dark grey flight feathers. Legs and feet orange with variably greyer webs.

Definitive alternate plumage (May–Jul/Oct–Nov). More discreet plumage, overall brownish, but easily distinguished from ♀. Head grey-beige vermiculated blackish-brown with a blackish area from forehead,

across crown and down nape, and a broad dusky eyestripe. Bill yellowish, with stronger olive tone. Mantle dark grey-brown with narrow buff to reddish fringes. Scapulars similar with paler grey bases on inner webs, often with a buff inner mark on outer web. Back to uppertail-coverts blackish more or less streaked brown (fringes to feathers). Alternate tertials (some to all basic tertials often retained) shorter, broad and pointed, grey-brown like basic tertials of adult ♀. Breast reddish-brown mottled dark. Flanks feathers variable, usually pale ochre-brown with broad subterminal 'U'-shaped marks or essentially dark brown with buff to reddish fringes and inner marks. Femoral area pale brown irregularly mottled dark. Belly also variable, pale buff variably stained dark, or basic feathers more widely retained. Lower belly and undertail-coverts whitish strongly stained blackish. Tail as basic plumage, except central rectrices, which are slightly up-curved or flat.

Adult ♀

Definitive basic plumage (Oct–Dec/Feb–Apr). Mainly buff-brown mottled dark brown. Head and upper neck pale buff finely streaked blackish-grey (except bill base, chin and throat, sometimes pale buff or cream-coloured), with crown more distinctly streaked blackish and dusky eyestripe. Iris warm brown to hazelnut-brown. Bill variable, yellow-orange, yellow-brown or even olive-grey, with a variable number of blackish spots, usually more concentrated on the central culmen. The orange often covers the distal culmen, just above the black nail. Mantle and scapulars dark brown broadly fringed pale buff, more or less tinged ochre-yellow. Strong 'J'-shaped marks visible on outer webs of scapulars. The pale fringes and marks, however, vary in width between individuals, making ♀♀ look more or less dark and variegated. Tertials broad and pointed, grey-brown, paler towards centre, finely fringed pale. Tertial coverts broad, round and sharply fringed whitish or pale brown. Back and rump dark brown to blackish with frequent pale centres and fine pale buff fringes, often interrupted at tip. Uppertail-coverts blackish-brown with pale buff centres. Rectrices have dark grey-brown centres and broad pale brownish to whitish fringes. Breast bright buff, with blackish subterminal bands. Breast-sides and flanks blackish-brown with broad 'U'-shaped marks and pale buff fringes. Belly slightly paler than flanks, tinged buff with diffuse, broad dusky streaks. Undertail-coverts centred dark with broad whitish fringes (appear whitish, irregularly stained brown and dark grey). Upperwing grey-brown with dark trailing edge. Lesser and median coverts broad and rounded, with pale fringe variably marked, sometimes absent. Speculum has strong blue gloss (less pronounced on ss2–3 than in adult ♂) framed with black and white as ♂, but greater coverts have slightly narrower white subterminal bands (width at the shaft 9–12 mm in adult ♀, 11–13 mm in adult ♂[1014], Fig. 11). Sometimes has small white spots at tips of greater coverts, mostly the outermost. Underwing as ♂. Legs and feet like ♂ but less bright.

Definitive alternate plumage (Mar–May/Oct–Dec). Very similar to basic plumage, the differences in plumage being slight and obscured by individual variation. Plumage slightly stronger buff and darker overall. Crown marginally darker and head somewhat more contrasting. Head-sides, particularly bill base, chin and throat more clearly buff. Bill on average less bright, sometimes largely lead-grey. Flanks and scapulars have broader inner marks and fringes more contrasting and buff. Alternate tertials (usually the third innermost) have a short buff-brown inner band on inner web.

Juvenile

First basic plumage (until Sep–Dec). Similar to adult ♀ in basic plumage but duller overall, slightly darker and appearance more striated. Crown and eyestripe blackish (slight green gloss often present in young ♂), cheeks and upper neck strongly vermiculated dark grey-brown and buff (overall darker in young ♂). Iris dark brown. Bill dark olive-brown with orange initially limited to the gape and tomium. Scapulars like adult ♀ but pale inner marks and fringes restricted or very faint. Overall, scapulars duller brown, darker and plainer. Back and rump blackish with green tips in young ♂, dark brown with pale brown fringes in ♀. Rectrices fringed dark tan or light brown, without white of adult. Tertials shorter and narrower, quickly fray at tips, fairly uniform brown (without grey and deep reddish tones of adult), and slightly darker in ♀. Tertial coverts have narrow diffuse whitish fringes (♀), or fringe very faint, incomplete or lacking in ♂, constituting a useful tip for sexing at any age: the white wingbar extends above the tertials in ♀, but not in ♂, in which it stops at the inner edge of the speculum. Breast reddish-brown with irregular dark spots. Flanks pale yellowish with long blackish longitudinal stripes, formed by alignment of broad dark rachis streaks. Rear flanks pale brown vaguely mottled dark. Undertail-coverts whiter spotted dark. Upperwing similar to that of adult but greater coverts more pointed,

with black terminal bars narrower, less well-defined and often small whitish bars at tips. Lesser and median coverts narrower, frayed at tips with variable edges (absent or faint in ♂, absent to strong in ♀[224]). The blue speculum generally extends to the second outermost secondary in the ♂ and fourth outermost in ♀.

First-winter ♂

Formative plumage (Nov–Dec/May–Jul). Pre-formative moult is completed relatively quickly, so from mid- to late autumn is close to adult ♂. The bill and legs reach their definitive colours at this time. Juvenile tertials are often moulted before Dec. Once moult completed, often retains some juvenile feathers on the back and upper rump, which appear browner and more untidy. Formative central rectrices often poorly or incompletely curled. Formative tertials slightly shorter and less clearly lanceolate. However, ageing is easier based on the upperwing (see Juvenile) until the second pre-basic moult.

First-winter ♀

Formative plumage (Nov–Jan/Feb–Apr). Very like basic plumage of adult ♀. Cannot usually be aged except using upperwing (until the second pre-basic moult). As in ♂ at same age, look for contrast between inner coverts (often moulted) and outer ones, which are still juvenile. The features described for juvenile are often still useful, e.g. the tertial coverts, greater coverts and other secondary coverts narrower and frayed at the tips. Note also the inner webs to the four outer primary coverts have pale fringes strongly marked to absent (never strong in adult ♀)[224]. The intensity of the pale edges to the secondary coverts and tertial coverts is not a reliable ageing feature in ♀♀ (variable at any age).

GEOGRAPHIC VARIATION In the treatment adopted here (see Taxonomy), Mallard has three subspecies, the nominate being by far the most widespread, and described above. The other two subspecies are described below.

A. (p.) diazi (Mexican Duck). Like Mottled and American Black Ducks, all plumages resemble each other and that of nominate ♀ Mallard. There is clinal variation within the range of this subspecies in general coloration, including the upperwing. Birds in the south are slightly darker, with warmer brown tones[9] and show little or no white on the greater coverts. Such variation is at least partly due to introgression with nominate Mallard in the northern range of *diazi*[326]. However, such variation is not recent, the northernmost populations of *diazi* having been described subspecifically as *A. (p.) novimexicana* Huber, 1920. In the 1980s, Scott & Reynolds[1157] indicated that introgression was probably historical, as reports of Mallards in Mexico were less frequent than before. More recently, hybridisation has been considered rare in Arizona[1340], whereas other authors consider that hybridisation could cause the extinction of *diazi*[215,1382]. Similarly, if populations with characters potentially inherited from hybridisation occur widely, birds showing characters of a first-generation hybrid are rare[749], which may indicate a rather ancient introgression that is not currently ongoing. There is a high variability of phenotypes, and even some difficulties in defining that of a 'pure' Mexican Duck. For example, Hubbard[597] ranked seven phenotypes with 'pure' *platyrhynchos* at one extreme and 'pure' *diazi* at the other, while Scott & Reynolds[1157] assigned a score based on 18 characters to 92 individuals from six localities of Mexico, from the US border to Jalisco. Under current knowledge, it is difficult to set a precise limit between normal variability within Mexican Duck and that due to a more or less ancient hybridisation. In the north of the range, virtually no bird has the full set of features shown by indisputably 'pure' Mexican Ducks, including no white on the leading edge of the speculum. The following features describe birds that can be considered 'typical', specifying the variability found in nature (see Leukering & Mlodinow[749] for a complete overview).

General appearance: ♂♂ in definitive basic or formative plumages are easily distinguished, as those of *diazi* resemble the ♀ but have a fairly bright yellow bill. Misidentification therefore concerns all other plumages, including definitive alternate plumage of ♂. First-generation hybrid ♂♂ can appear like those between *platyrhynchos* on one hand, and American Black Duck or Mottled Duck on the other. Others show more subtle hybrid characters (sides of upper head with green sheen, some pale grey vermiculated feathers at sides, tertials centred grey but paler than fringes, central rectrices slightly up-curved).

- *Size*: Race *diazi* is on average 10% smaller (cf. Measurements and Mass).
- *Coloration*: Darker and warmer brown, thus the inner marks on the scapulars and flanks are less clear than in *platyrhynchos*. Light velvety (not metallic) green sheen to the crown-sides is normal in adult

♂.

- *Tail*: Grey-brown with little or no white on outer rectrices. In ♀♀, the outer rectrices of *platyrhynchos* show a clear inverted 'U', while in *diazi*, this mark is narrower and more pointed ('V'-shaped)[598].
- *Undertail-coverts*: Brownish with small (♀) or strong (♂) black spots, and pale fringes in *diazi* (vs. white or cream-coloured with narrow dark arrow along the shaft)[598].
- *Uppertail-coverts*: In adult ♀ (alternate plumage) dusky with white fringes in *diazi* (vs. dusky with broad white rachis and fringes).
- *Tertials*: Browner, with soft green sheen[598] and pale grey-brown fringes in *diazi* (vs. greyer, especially in centre, with pale grey or whitish fringes in ♀ and largely pale grey in adult ♂ *platyrhynchos*).
- *Speculum*: Glossed turquoise, sometimes green (♂♂?[749]), rarely (?) bluish-purple, but many (intermediates?) have a blue speculum exactly like that of *platyrhynchos*.
- *Central greater coverts*: In adult, black tip is larger than in *platyrhynchos*. Along the rachis, the white subterminal band is narrower than or as broad as the black tip, while in *platyrhynchos* the white band is broader than the black tip. On the greater coverts corresponding to s5, the white on the shaft is 5–7 mm wide in young ♀ (vs. 8–10 mm in *platyrhynchos*), 7–9 mm in adult ♀ (vs. 9–12 mm), 6–8 mm in young ♂ (vs. 9–11 mm) and 8–10 mm in adult ♂ (vs. 11–13 mm)[1014]. Other authors consider this white band to be usually absent[1157] or reduced/interrupted[598] in 'pure' individuals. The white subterminal band frequently extends along the outer web, especially on the outer coverts.
- *White trailing edge to secondaries*: The white is more likely to reach along the outer web of each feather (especially the outer ones). On the shaft of s5, the white is 4–9 mm wide in *diazi* and 8–13 mm in *platyrhynchos*[1014].
- *Inner lesser underwing-coverts*: Distinctly barred (vs. entirely white)[598].
- *Bill*: A beautiful yellow with slight olive hue in ♂. The bill of ♀ averages darker and more uniform than in ♀ *platyrhynchos*, frequently largely slate grey to yellow-olive, with brighter yellow-orange tones often limited to the base and tomium. In some, a dark spot is visible at the gape, which is usually shown by Mottled Duck, but normally hardly ever

by *platyrhynchos*.

- **Breast**: In ♀, darker and more strongly spotted in *diazi* (individual feathers have three spots, sometimes merging into a single mark).

- **Head**: The cheeks and throat are usually more strongly coloured and vermiculated dark in *diazi*.

Identification of a ♀ must be based on as many as possible of the above-mentioned features, but keeping in mind that some birds will be very difficult to identify, given the existence of a complete and uninterrupted spectrum of intermediates. Finally, studies linking phenotypic variability to genetics are still lacking, but is needed to define more precisely the current nature of *diazi*.

A. p. conboschas. Endemic to S & W Greenland; like the nominate subspecies, and the only other dimorphic taxon in this group. Described as slightly larger on average, with marginally different proportions (bill significantly shorter and wing chord longer, see Measurements and Mass), in adaptation to cold climate conditions, and to coastal saltwater habitats in winter. Adult ♂ in basic plumage also has upperparts on average greyer, and scapulars less strongly vermiculated, but more heavily on flanks. Lower belly darker. Breast purplish-brown and more strongly streaked blackish. Adult ♀ slightly paler, greyer and has more strongly mottled dark underparts.

MEASUREMENTS and MASS ♂ and adult slightly larger than ♀ and young, respectively.

A. p. platyrhynchos. UK. ♂: wing chord 250–298 (274.8, n=665), bill 45.6–63.1 (54.6, n=500), tarsus 40.8–51.0 (45.7, n=500); ♀: wing chord 235–280 (258.6, n=880), bill 45.5–58.9 (51.3, n=500), tarsus 39.9–48.0 (43.4, n=500)[940]. Europe. ♂: wing chord 272–285 (adult, 279, n=13) and 258–287 (juvenile, 272, n=27) ; bill 51–61 (55.4, n=58), tarsus 42–48 (45.3, n=45); ♀: wing chord 257–273 (adult, 265, n=13) and 245–272 (juvenile, 257, n=23); bill 47–56 (51.8, n=48), tarsus 41–46 (43.4, n=37)[267]. North America. ♂ (n=100): wing chord 271–303 (adult) and 265–295 (juvenile), tail 84–103, culmen 52–59, bill depth at tip of forehead feathering 19.4–23.6, tarsus 43–50; ♀ (n=100): wing chord 255–287 (adult) and 249–279 (juvenile), tail 80–98, culmen 48–55, bill depth at tip of forehead feathering 18.6–22.6, tarsus 41–47; compare with measurements given by Pyle[1014] for *A. (p.) diazi*, *A. fulvigula* and *A. rubripes*. Mass in Dec (Europe) ♂: 1,017–1,442 (1,216, n=15); ♀: 921–1,320

(1,084, n=14)[267,1382]. Mass in winter (Mississippi) ♂: 1,246 (adult, n=1,308, SE=3) and 1,181 (first-winter, n=169, SE=8); ♀: 1,095 (adult, n=453, SE=5) and 1,040 (first-winter, n=188, SE=8)[307].

A. p. conboschas. ♂ (n=69): wing chord 275–306 (292), bill 44–51 (46.6); ♀ (n=41): wing chord 261–285 (272); bill 45–52 (48.1)[267].

A. (p.) diazi. Six sites across Mexico. ♂ (n=52): wing chord 257–297 (281), culmen 35.6–46.1 (42.0), bill width 18.7–22.2 (21.0), mass 1,028 (849–1,243); ♀ (n=46): wing chord 248–277 (261), culmen 34.1–42.2 (38.8), bill width 18.0–21.0 (19.2), mass 908 (647–1,267)[1157]. Northern part of range. ♂: (n=18) wing chord 260–289 (273.9), bill 50.4–56.4 (53.0), tarsus 40.1–47.4 (44.2); ♀: (n=27) wing chord 237–271 (254.7), bill 47.1–55.1 (51.0), tarsus 38.3–49.3 (42.6)[9]. Southern part of range. ♂: (n=13) wing chord 260–282 (269.9), bill 51.1–55.6 (53.3), tarsus 43.1–48.4 (46.3); ♀: (n=13) wing chord 232–268 (253.4), bill 45.5–52.7 (50.3), tarsus 40.2–43.6 (42.0)[9]. ♂ (n=100): wing chord 264–297 (adult) and 257–289 (juvenile), tail 78–93, culmen 48–57, bill depth at tip of forehead feathering 19.1–22.6, tarsus 42–48; ♀ (n=45): wing chord 247–279 (adult) and 239–270 (juvenile), tail 75–91, culmen 46–54, bill depth at tip of forehead feathering 18.2–21.8, tarsus 40–46; compare with the measurements given by Pyle[1014] for *A. p. platyrhynchos*, *A. fulvigula* and *A. rubripes*.

VOICE The ♂ gives a repeated, low and rasping *rreb*, and several whistled calls during courtship. The ♀ produces a familiar series of *quack* notes in decrescendo, the syllables being shorter and lower in terminating. Also various other quacking and whistled calls. The voice of *A. (p.) diazi* has rarely been described in the literature, but is at least partly similar to that of Mallard.

MOULT Complex alternate moult strategy. The timing of the various moults is strongly influenced by latitude and timing of breeding, with much variation in the introduced populations in S Hemisphere. Pre-formative moult occurs from Aug to Nov–Dec, perhaps preceded by an auxiliary pre-formative moult[1014]. It includes a large number of head and body feathers (usually few on the back, rump and belly), 0–4 tertials (all in most ♂♂ and 1–2 in most ♀♀) and corresponding tertial coverts (often none in ♀♀[326]) and none to all rectrices (all in 40% of ♂♂, generally fewer if any in ♀♀)[1014]. Few or no inner secondary coverts replaced. Definitive pre-alternate moult occurs between Jan and May in ♀ and May–Jul in ♂ and includes approximately the same feathers as pre-formative moult, but is more extensive in ♀ than ♂. Definitive pre-basic moult is complete and occurs in Jun–Nov with a flightless period of *c.* 3 weeks starting late Jul to mid-Aug[783], and slightly later in ♀♀ that breed successfully than ♂♂ and non-breeders.

HYBRIDISATION As the species most frequently raised in captivity, with an extremely large natural range and many introduced feral populations, it might be expected that Mallard would be the species to have hybridised with the largest number of other species (62 known here). Note that hybrids descending from Mallard show some variability due to the frequent involvement of domestic individuals, at least in those that escape from captivity or derived from feral populations.

In the wild, hybridisation has been reported fairly regularly with Wood Duck *Aix sponsa*, American Wigeon *Anas americana*, Eurasian Wigeon *A. penelope*, Indian Spot-billed Duck, Eastern Spot-billed Duck, Gadwall, Northern Pintail *A. acuta*, Northern Shoveler *A. clypeata*, Eurasian Teal *A. crecca*, Green-winged Teal *A. carolinensis* and Red-crested Pochard *Netta rufina*. Hybrids from these crosses are described under those species. In the wild, individuals of introduced feral populations hybridise regularly or widely with the following species: American Black Duck, Mottled Duck (see these species), Meller's Duck, Pacific Black Duck (including *A. s. rogersi*), Yellow-billed Duck *A. undulata*, Laysan Duck[883] and Hawaiian Duck. For these species, as well as for Mexican Duck, the introduction of the Mallard and hybridisation that results constitutes a serious threat, of 'genetic pollution'.

Much rarer natural cases of hybridisation reported with Canada Goose *Branta canadensis*[1190], Muscovy Duck *Cairina moschata*, Falcated Duck *Anas falcata*[719,1190], Blue-winged Teal *A. discors*[1190], Common Pochard *Aythya ferina*, Tufted Duck *A. fuligula*, Steller's Eider *Polysticta stelleri*[817], Common Eider *Somateria mollissima*, Common Goldeneye *Bucephala clangula*[817], and possibly (origin uncertain) Mandarin Duck *Aix galericulata*, Ferruginous Duck *Aythya nyroca*, Canvasback *A. valisineria*, Goosander *Mergus merganser* and Red-breasted Merganser *M. serrator*[407]. Other infrequent or occasional natural cases, probably involving escapes or birds from introduced feral populations, are mentioned with Barnacle Goose *Branta leucopsis*[817], Comb Duck *Sarkidiornis melanotos*[831], Australian Shelduck *Tadorna tadornoides*[802], Egyptian Goose *Alopochen aegyptiacus*, Philippine Duck *Anas luzonica*, Chestnut Teal *A. castanea*[802], Grey Teal *A. gibberifrons*[465], Australian Grey Teal *A. gracilis*[914], New Zealand Brown Teal *A. chlorotis*, Silver Teal *A. versicolor*, Rosy-billed Pochard *Netta peposaca* and Hardhead *Aythya australis*[802]. In captivity, hybridisation has been reported with Greylag Goose *Anser anser*, Swan Goose *A. cygnoides*, Cackling Goose *Branta hutchinsii*[465], White-winged Duck *Asarcornis scutulata*[582,988], Common Shelduck *Tadorna tadorna*, Ruddy Shelduck *T. ferruginea*, Paradise Shelduck *T. variegata*, Chiloe Wigeon *Anas sibilatrix*, African Black Duck *A. sparsa*[187], Bronze-winged Duck *A. specularis*[439], White-cheeked Pintail *A. bahamensis*, Yellow-billed Pintail *A. georgica*, Brown Teal *A. aucklandica*[639], Speckled Teal *A. flavirostris*, Garganey *A. querquedula*[439,988], Redhead *Aythya americana*[1190] and Ring-necked Duck *A. collaris*.

HABITAT and LIFE-CYCLE Southern populations including *A. (p.) diazi)*, and coastal populations (including *A. p. conboschas*) are generally sedentary or perform at most short movements, while northern and continental populations are migratory or move in response to prolonged freezes. Timing of migration and breeding depend on latitude and population. It is, however, an early migrant, and many birds leave wintering grounds at temperate latitudes in Feb–Mar. Wild populations generally lay between Mar and Jul, but in urban areas and the south of its range, semi-domesticated individuals are able to breed almost year-round. Uses almost all types of wetlands, including very small waterbodies (ditches, small ponds.) and in urban areas. However, shuns flowing oligotrophic waters, the deep parts of large waterbodies, rocky shores or saltwater (which it may nevertheless use if fresh waters freeze, or as daytime roost, when local hunting pressure forces them to do so). ♂♂ abandons ♀♀ during incubation, gather in small flocks and then proceed to moulting sites, wetlands with abundant vegetation, where flightless birds find food and shelter. ♀♀ usually moult near breeding sites. Autumn migration occurs between Sep and Dec. In winter, mostly in small scattered parties in rather enclosed habitats, like Eurasian and Green-winged Teals. More rarely forms large compact flocks on open water.

RANGE and POPULATION The most abundant species of Holarctic wildfowl, widespread across the entire region, with the exception of high mountains, deserts and most Arctic coastal areas, usually reaching its southern limit at 32–35°N. Many populations have been introduced into the natural winter range of the species, especially for hunting or ornamental purposes, and have mingled with wild populations. Outside the normal breeding range, the species especially inhabits urban parks. Better-established feral populations are present in SW & SE Australia, New Zealand, South Africa, Madagascar, the United Arab Emirates and Mauritius[62,1382]. Rare or occasional outside its usual range, being recorded on Spitsbergen, several Pacific islands, in sub-Saharan Africa and SE Asia.

A. p. platyrhynchos. Inhabits most of the range. Abundant (nearly 20 million birds) with estimates of 5,500,000 birds in N & W Europe, 2,000,000 in E Europe, Black Sea and E Mediterranean, 800,000 wintering birds in SW Asia, 75,000 in S Asia, 1,500,000 in E Asia and 9,180,000 estimated in North America[1348,1391].

A. p. conboschas. Present in SW & SE Greenland, with a population estimated at 15,000–30,000 birds[1154], and more recently at 10,000–100,000 birds[1348].

A. (p.) diazi. Distributed in SE Arizona and W Texas, south across C Mexico (to Jalisco and around Mexico City, uncommon further east to Oaxaca). Population estimated at 55,000 birds[304,1348], mainly concentrated in a small area between the states of Guanajuato, Jalisco and Michoacán. The available censuses show strong annual fluctuations (5,188–49,510 individuals in 1960–2000) with a tendency to be slightly increasing[966]. Rare visitor or erratic outside its breeding range (California, Central USA, Lesser and Greater Antilles, Central America)[326].

CAPTIVITY By far the most abundant species in captivity, most domestic ducks descending from Mallard. Its huge range and abundance mean the species could be seen almost anywhere in the Holarctic, and the question of the origin of vagrants rarely arises.

REFERENCES Aldrich & Baer (1970)[9]; AOU (1998)[21]; Avise *et al.* (1990)[45]; Baker (1992)[56]; Banks *et al.* (2008)[62]; Banks (2010)[64]; Bird Hybrids database (2014)[97]; Brickell (1988)[187]; Callaghan & Green (1993)[215]; Carboneras (1992)[223], Carney (1992)[224]; Clements *et al.* (2013)[237]; Cooper *et al.* (1996)[256]; Cramp & Simmons (1977)[268]; Delacour (1964)[295]; Delany & Scott (2002)[304]; Delnicki & Reinecke (1986)[307]; Drillin *et al.* (2002)[326]; Fritsch (1905)[407]; Fullagar *in* Kear (2005)[410]; Gill & Donsker (2014)[437]; Gillham & Gillham (1996)[439]; Gillham & Gillham (2000)[442]; Gillham & Gillham (2002)[443]; González *et al.* (2009)[454]; Gray (1958)[465]; Heitmeyer (1987)[547]; Hopkinson (1926)[582]; Hubbard (1977)[597]; Huey (1961)[598]; Johnsgard (1960)[639]; Johnsgard (1961)[641]; Johnson & Sorenson (1999)[654]; Kear (2005)[674]; Kulikova *et al.* (2004)[715]; Kulikova *et al.* (2005)[716]; Kuroda (1960)[719]; Leukering & Mlodinow (2012)[749]; Livezey (1991)[767]; Livezey (1993)[768]; Marchant & Higgins (1990)[802]; McCarthy (2006)[817]; McCracken *et al.* (2001)[822]; McLeish (1993)[831]; Moulton & Marshall (1996)[883]; Norman (1990)[914]; Owen & Montgomery (1978)[940]; Palmer (1976)[945]; Pérez-Arteaga *et al.* (2002)[966]; Phillips (1922–26)[988]; Pyle (2008)[1014]; Remsen *et al.* (2014)[1063]; Rhymer (2001)[1067]; Scott & Rose (1997)[1154]; Scott & Reynolds (1984)[1157]; Sibley (1938)[1190]; Webster (2006)[1340]; Wetlands International (2014)[1348]; Williams (1980)[1358]; Young *in* Kear (2005)[1382]; Zimpfer *et al.* (2011)[1391].

277. *A. p. platyrhynchos*, adult ♂ (definitive basic). France, Apr (Sébastien Reeber).

278. *A. p. platyrhynchos*, adult ♂ (definitive alternate); note adult tertials (long, acutely pointed and pale grey in centre) and tertial coverts (broad, rounded, pale grey without paler fringe). France, Jul (Sébastien Reeber).

279. *A. p. platyrhynchos*, adult ♂ (definitive basic). California, USA, Nov (Sébastien Reeber).

280. *A. p. platyrhynchos*, adult ♀ (definitive basic/definitive alternate); compared to Mottled Duck *A. fulvigula*, Mexican Duck *A. (p.) diazi* and American Black Duck *A. rubripes*, note extent of white in tail and two broad white wingbars. Netherlands, Feb (Sébastien Reeber).

281. *A. p. platyrhynchos*, juvenile ♀ (first basic), with narrow pointed flank feathers and juvenile tertials. France, Jul (Sébastien Reeber).

282. *A. p. platyrhynchos*, juvenile ♀ (first basic); narrow scapulars and flank feathers, with at most ill-defined markings, typical of this age, as are rather pointed tertial coverts, while the white wingbar extending to the inner tertial covert, the longest having a visible pale fringe, indicates sex. France, Jul (Aurélien Audevard).

283. *A.* (*p.*) *diazi*, ♀ (formative/definitive basic); rather extensive white in tail, but still has narrow wingbar and trailing edge to secondaries. Arizona, USA, Feb (Steve Mlodinow).

284. *A. p. platyrhynchos*, adult ♀ (definitive basic/definitive alternate); note broad rounded lesser and median coverts, gloss extending onto s2, the lack of light edging to the outermost primary covert (with rounded tip), and black tip to second greater covert. France, Feb (Vincent Palomares).

285. *A.* (*p.*) *diazi*, ♂ (formative/definitive basic). Colorado, USA, Jan (Steve Mlodinow).

286. *A.* (*p.*) *diazi*, adult ♂ (definitive basic); note thinner wingbars than in Mallard, and all-grey tail. Arizona, USA, Feb (Steve Mlodinow).

287. *A. p. platyrhynchos* × *A.* (*p.*) *diazi*, adult ♂ (definitive basic) with obvious mixed characters. Arizona, USA, Dec (Steve Mlodinow).

288. *A. p. platyrhynchos* × *A.* (*p.*) *diazi*, adult ♂ (definitive basic), closer to latter taxon, but still shows green reflections on head, pale tertials and tail, and up-curved central tertials. Arizona, USA, Feb (Steve Mlodinow).

AMERICAN BLACK DUCK
Anas rubripes

Plate 30

TAXONOMY *Anas obscura rubripes* Brewster, 1902, *Auk* 19, p. 184. Within the genus *Anas*, apart from the six species that he placed in the genus *Mareca*, Livezey[767] distinguished two major clades, each constituting a subgenus. The first (subgenus *Anas*) includes the species of the 'Mallard' group and the second (subgenus *Spatula*) the 'blue-winged' ducks. Within the subgenus *Anas*, African Black Duck *A. sparsa* diverged early, and two lineages appeared thereafter, the first including the species from Africa, Madagascar, Oceania and Asia, with the only Holarctic representatives being Indian Spot-billed Duck *A. poecilorhyncha* and Eastern Spot-billed Duck *A. zonorhyncha*. The second clade includes Mallard *Anas platyrhynchos* and several local taxa often considered close to it (*wyvilliana, laysanensis, oustaleti* and *diazi* – see Taxonomy of Mallard), Mottled Duck *A. fulvigula* and American Black Duck, the latter having diverged first. Avise *et al.*[45] revealed the existence of two paraphyletic groups within Mallard, and found that American Black Duck recently diverged from a common ancestor with Mallard. Johnson & Sorenson[654] confirmed the existence of two groups among Nearctic Mallards, the first one belonging to a clade also comprising Mottled Duck, Mexican Duck and American Black Duck, the latter the closest relative of Mallard. Initially considered conspecific with Mottled Duck, the two species being grouped under the name *Anas obscura*. No recognised subspecies.

IDENTIFICATION Large dabbling duck with shape similar to Mallard and Mottled Duck (marginally in contact with American Black Duck), these three species often being mistaken for each other. American Black Duck is wholly dark blackish, which provides strong contrast in flight with the largely white underwing. Distinction from Mallard (♀ and juvenile) is based on the following features:

- *General coloration*: Much darker in American Black Duck, in which the paler part of the body is formed by the head-sides, chin, throat and neck, which are pale buff vermiculated or flecked dark grey-brown. The rest of the body appears dark brown, quite devoid of warm colours.

- *White wingbars around speculum*: Absent or very limited in American Black Duck, irrespective of age or sex, but strongly marked in Mallard (see

also Hybridisation below). More precisely, the white trailing edge may be present in American Black Duck, but is usually absent or at most very narrow. In contrast, the greater coverts normally show, at most, a very thin and inconspicuous pale greyish or brownish bar (see below).

- *Underwing*: Typically silvery-white and highly contrasting with rest of dark body in American Black Duck. The median and lesser primary coverts are marked dark brown, creating a blackish comma or crescent near the 'wrist'. The lesser coverts are often marked dusky near the leading edge. Mallard has the underwing more creamy white, with at most a few small brown spots in these areas (especially ♀ or juvenile). Kirby *et al.*[693] mentioned that Mallard can show up to seven dark spots, but these were not noted on birds collected before 1935, suggesting that introgression with American Black Duck has occurred since then.

- *Scapulars and flank feathers*: Entirely dark brown except clearly defined pale fringes, but lacking the pale inner marks of Mallard.

- *Tail*: In all plumages, American Black Duck shows no white in the tail, the rectrices being dark brown, fringed pale grey-brown. In Mallard, the rectrices are clearly marked white to largely white.

- *Legs and feet*: Slightly more reddish-orange in adult ♀ American Black Duck than in Mallard (dull orange).

- *Belly*: Plain dark brown in American Black Duck (vs. beige to pale brown in Mallard).

- *Speculum*: The secondaries (except 1–3 outermost) have a strong metallic blue gloss, more violet or purplish, usually less bright and darker in American Black Duck. In Mallard, the gloss is usually azure (variable and sometimes difficult to assess).

- *Bill*: Tinged dull yellow-green, more or less olive or grey, with blackish spots more marked on culmen.

Among domestic variants of Mallard, some show largely black or dark plumage, recalling American Black Duck (see, e.g., Delacour[295]). However, such birds usually have the wings, tail and legs typical of Mallard. When this is not the case, e.g. when even the wing is all black, the plumage is often strongly glossy and/or the underwing is often marked dark.

Distinction from Mottled Duck is slightly more complicated for this species, which in all plumages shares many characters among those mentioned above with American Black Duck: rather overall dark plumage (including belly) and white bars around speculum poorly marked or absent. However, both sexes have more brightly coloured bills, face and a neck pale buff slightly vermiculated dark (or not at all), shorter dark eyestripe not reaching dark nape, broad pale supercilium (narrow dark cap) and warmer brown body, with clear pale inner marks on flanks and scapulars, forming elongated blackish chevrons, more pronounced in adult ♀ than ♂. At same sex and age, American Black Duck has legs slightly more red. Finally, Mottled Duck typically has a black spot at the gape and small dark patches on the 'wrist' of the underwing. Juvenile distinguished from one another by general plumage coloration, the paleness of face and neck, length of eyestripe and width of supercilium.

The distinction will be more difficult with hybrid American Black Duck × Mallard, except first-generation adult ♂♂. All other plumages and birds originating from backcrosses with American Black Duck will pose tougher problems. It is useful to look for one or preferably several of the features listed above showing intermediate characteristics, especially on the upperwing (width/presence of white wingbars around the speculum) and underwing (number of dark primary coverts; see Hybridisation).

PLUMAGES Weak sexual dimorphism from first winter. Complex alternate moult strategy (two plumages per definitive cycle, three in first cycle). Ageing possible until end of the first summer under good viewing conditions or in the hand. The different plumages (sex and age) are similar to one another. See wing chord for differences between ages and sexes.

Adult ♂

Definitive basic plumage (Oct–Nov/May–Jun). Dark brown to blackish with face and upper neck slightly paler, with remarkably-coloured bare parts. The sides of the head and neck, the chin and throat are pale buff vermiculated dark grey-brown. Faint pale supercilium visible (mostly behind eye) between the blackish eyestripe and dark crown (feathers finely fringed pale grey-brown). A slight green sheen is sometimes visible on the crown-sides[783,1014]. Iris dark brown. Bill rather dull yellow, more or less tinged greenish, with black

nail and black at base, visible especially at the gape. Possibly has some diffuse dark patches on the culmen. Breast dark clearly contrasting with paler area on the sides of the head and neck. Breast, mantle, flanks and scapulars dark brown with narrow grey-beige to pale brown fringes, and sometimes diffuse faint 'U'-shaped inner markings, forming a neat scaly appearance when close. The belly, back, rump and upper- and undertail-coverts are blackish-brown with pale fringes less clearly defined, these parts appearing more uniformly dark. Dark brown rectrices finely fringed paler brown (outer webs) or uniform, and tail does not contrast sharply with the body. Tertials broad, elongated and pointed, pale grey-brown at centre with whitish rachis, purple sheen on inner web and narrow or no pale buff fringes. Tertial coverts rounded, with faint cinnamon fringes marked or absent. Upperwing dark brown with secondaries forming a purple-blue speculum (except outer secondaries, mostly ss1–3). The tips of the secondaries form a broad black bar, sometimes a faint white trailing edge. Pyle[1014] indicated that the length of white at the tip of the shaft of s5 measures 0–2 mm in American Black Duck, 1–4 mm in Mottled Duck, 4–9 mm in Mexican Duck and 8–13 mm in Mallard. Kirby *et al.*[693], however, stated that the width of the white trailing edge can equal that of Mallard. Lesser and median coverts broad and round-tipped. Greater coverts broad, almost square, with broad black tips, sometimes topped with a narrow pale brown to whitish line (Fig. 11). The extent of pale subterminal bands on greater coverts and white tips to secondaries are not mentioned historically and appear to have been acquired by the species during the 20th century[693]. Underwing has secondary coverts and axillaries silvery-white (often pale grey on bases of lesser and greater coverts). A variable number (at least ten[693]) lesser and median primary coverts are marked dark brown, forming a crescent or comma near the 'wrist', with some lesser coverts also marked dusky near leading edge. Blackish-brown marginal coverts. Darker grey remiges. Legs bright red with black webs. Some birds have the webs mottled reddish and black. Their frequency reaches 12.4% (*n*=916) in ♀♀ and 10.3% (*n*=968) of ♂♂ in Maryland, and 7% (*n*=358) of ♀♀ and 4.5% (*n*=694) of ♂♂. This pattern has been mentioned only in adults in Labrador[783].

Definitive alternate plumage (Jun–Jul/Sep–Oct). Like basic plumage, and essentially characterised by pale parts of the head more speckled dark and less contrasting, and lack of pale inner marks on feathers of breast and flanks. Alternate tertials shorter and rounded. Tertial coverts may be slightly fringed pale. The bill is duller, tinged grey or olive, and legs slightly paler red.

Adult ♀

Definitive basic plumage (Oct–Nov/Jan–Apr). Close to ♂. Distinguished by less contrasting appearance with body more visibly scaly or streaked pale brown. The pale areas of the head are more heavily speckled/vermiculated dark and the ground colour is warmer, often buff-brown. The pale parts thus contrast less with the body. The crown is also paler, duller, more streaked and lacks green sheen, while the black eyestripe is slightly more pronounced. Iris paler brown than ♂. Bill dull yellowish-green with variable dark patches on the upper mandible (denser on culmen). The buff or pale cinnamon fringes to the feathers of the upperparts, breast and flanks are broader, creating stronger scaling, sometimes with pale internal 'V'-shaped marks (more rounded, 'U'-shaped in ♂) on the breast-sides. Note that basic feathers are more elongated than in ♂ and alternate plumage of ♀, where they are rounded[783]. Tertials shorter than in ♂ (in longest tertials, distance from tip to that of

corresponding tertial covert <90 mm in ♀, >90 mm in ♂[224]), more round-tipped and less tinged grey around shaft. Tertial coverts broad and rounded, like adult ♂ (vs. juvenile), but usually has clear pale fringe, often narrower at the tip. The purple gloss of the speculum is usually absent on 3–4 outer secondaries. Greater coverts show less clearly defined blackish tips, usually without pale subterminal band[1014] (Fig. 11). Legs dark orange to dull red with black webbing (see adult ♂).

Definitive alternate plumage (Feb–May/Sep–Oct). Similar to basic plumage, but slightly darker and duller. Background coloration of pale parts of head and neck more whitish than buff, and appears more speckled than vermiculated dark. The fringes of the upperparts, breast and flanks often appear slightly greyer and colder, than buff or cinnamon, mostly without pale inner marks. Alternate tertials sometimes show one or two pale inner bars. The bill and legs are duller.

Juvenile

First basic plumage (until Sep–Oct). Close to basic plumage of ♀ with pale parts of head and neck, duller, paler and more diffuse. ♂ differs from ♀ at this age by

Anas platyrhynchos platyrhynchos

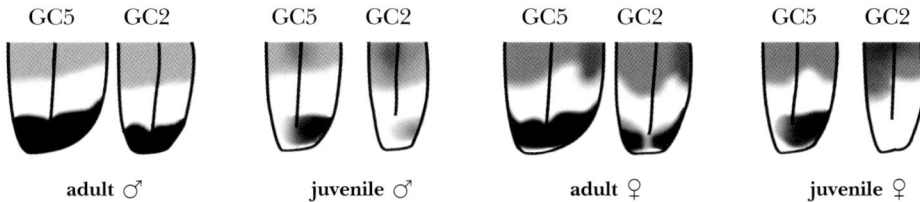

GC5 GC2 GC5 GC2 GC5 GC2 GC5 GC2

adult ♂   juvenile ♂   adult ♀   juvenile ♀

Anas (platyrhynchos) diazi

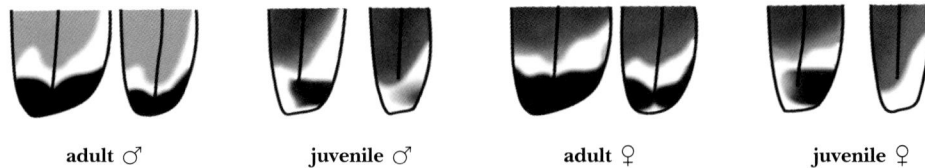

adult ♂   juvenile ♂   adult ♀   juvenile ♀

Anas rubripes and *Anas fulvigula*

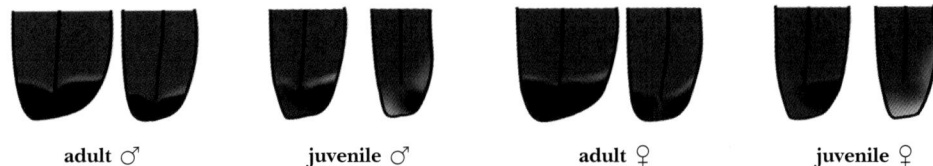

adult ♂   juvenile ♂   adult ♀   juvenile ♀

Fig. 11. Shape and pattern of outer greater upperwing-coverts in Mallard *Anas platyrhynchos*, Mexican Duck *Anas (p.) diazi*, Mottled Duck *Anas fulvigula* and American Black Duck *Anas rubripes*.

differences similar to those separating adults, including darker, more contrasting crown (pale supercilium barely visible in front of eye), and scapulars have narrower, less obvious fringes. Bill olive grey-brown. Scapulars and flank feathers narrower and round-tipped, with less clearly defined pale olive-brown fringes. Underparts have paler central longitudinal bars giving a more streaked appearance[1014]. Tertials shorter and narrower, quickly fraying at tips, all brown, without dark area and purple sheen on outer web. Rachis stripe and pale buff fringes thin or almost lacking. Tertial coverts narrow with continuous pale fringes (often interrupted in ♂♂). Rectrices juvenile with rachis bare at tip. Otherwise, essentially differs from adult by upperwing pattern. Greater coverts narrower, rounded with ill-defined (♂) or diffuse, barely marked (♀) blackish tips (Fig. 11). Lesser and median coverts narrower, quite pointed rather than rounded at tips, quickly frayed, fringed pale or not in both sexes[224]. Iridescence of speculum like that of adult, sometimes permitting sexing. Primary coverts dark brown with pale fringes on inner webs. If this edging is present on four outermost primary coverts, age is juvenile (edging absent in adult)[994]. Legs dull brown-grey, quickly becoming flesh-coloured (♀) or orange (♂), with dusky webs.

First-winter ♂

Formative plumage (Oct–Nov/May–Jun). Pre-formative moult completed relatively quickly, producing a plumage very close to definitive basic plumage. It is usually necessary to examine the tertials, tertial coverts and upperwing (see Juvenile), useful until the second pre-basic moult. Tertials are usually replaced as part of pre-formative moult[37], which is not the case in ♀. Formative tertials slightly shorter and less lanceolate than definitive basic tertials. Tertial coverts, whether juvenile or formative[1014], generally show subtle pale fringes interrupted at tips. Feathers of flanks and scapulars slightly narrower[783], and belly often appears pale-streaked. Crown-sides have green sheen very slight or absent.

First-winter ♀

Formative plumage (Oct–Nov/Jan–Apr). Sexing as adult from first winter onward. Age determined largely through juvenile tertials until pre-alternate moult (Feb–Apr), or beginning of second pre-basic moult in Jun. These are short, rounded and frayed at tips, brown and fringed pale. Age and sex also established (in hand or very good conditions) base on tertial coverts

and upperwing as in juvenile. Bill duller greyish than adult ♀. Legs dull brownish-orange and dusky at first, gradually acquiring adult colour during first winter. Also note the duller and colder fringes (less buff) to the flank feathers and scapulars, and belly appears more streaked pale.

GEOGRAPHIC VARIATION Suspected in size[945]. Western and northern populations have been described as slightly larger, marginally paler and showing some other differences probably related to age and sex. These populations have been named *A. r. tristis*[186]. However, these differences, if present, are clinal and do not appear to warrant subspecific differentiation[693]. Moreover, any past geographic variation may have been confused by extensive hybridisation with Mallard, and it is worth mentioning that no genetic differentiation has been found between different populations[32,45].

MEASUREMENTS and MASS ♂ and adult slightly larger than ♀ and young, respectively. Morphometrically similar to Mallard[505]. Adult ♂: wing chord 285.0 ± 7.6 (*n*=377), culmen 54.3 ± 2.4 (*n*=377), tarsus 46.2 ± 2.1 (*n*=377); adult ♀: wing chord 268.7 ± 6.9 (*n*=335), culmen 51.1 ± 2.0 (*n*=355), tarsus 43.1 ± 2.3 (*n*=335)[783,1072]. Juvenile/first-winter ♂: wing chord 244–300 (280.8 ± 7.5, *n*=858)[783], culmen 54.5 ± 2.2 (*n*=195), tarsus 45.5 ± 1.7 (*n*=195)[505]; juvenile/first-winter ♀: wing chord 225–288 (265.5 ± 7.0, *n*=659)[783], culmen 51.3 ± 2.1 (*n*=240), tarsus 43.3 ± 1.6 (*n*=240)[1072]. ♂ (*n*=100): wing chord 271–300 (adult) and 265–294 (juvenile), culmen 50–59, bill depth at tip of forehead feathering 19.4–23.6, tail 85–103, tarsus 42–50; ♀ (*n*=100): wing chord 255–283 (adult) and 249–277 (juvenile), culmen 47–55, bill depth at tip of forehead feathering 18.6–22.6, tail 81–98, tarsus 40–47[1014]. Wing chord diagnostic of sex once age assessed: 94% of adult ♂♂ >281, 94% of adult ♀♀ <281, 93% of juvenile ♂♂ >273 and 94% of juvenile ♀♀ <273[224]. Mass in autumn: adult ♂ 960–1,640 (± 130, 1,317, *n*=222); adult ♀: 810–1,380 (± 102, 1,090, *n*=227); ♂ juvenile/first-winter 825–1,755 (± 113, 1158, *n*=857); ♀ juvenile/first-winter 720–1,285 (± 96, 1,016, *n*=664)[783].

VOICE Similar to Mallard. The ♂ gives a low, quiet and rasping *rreeb*, as well as whistled calls, some of them more reminiscent of those of ♂ Gadwall *A. strepera*. The ♀ utters various quacks, the commonest being described as slightly lower pitched than Mallard[630], but also gives classic series of nasal *quack* notes in decrescendo, with a mean of six syllables, the second being loudest and prolonged.

MOULT Complex alternate strategy. Pre-formative moult occurs from Aug to Nov–Dec (perhaps preceded by auxiliary pre-formative moult[783,1014]) and includes many to the majority of head and body feathers, 0–4 tertials (all in most ♂♂, and 1–2 in majority of ♀♀), none to some tertial coverts (not all[37]) and none to all rectrices (all in 40% of ♂♂, fewer in ♀♀)[37,1014]. Moult of a variable number of inner secondary coverts is probable, like many congenerics, but Ashley *et al.*[37] did not find any wing-coverts being replaced during this moult. In captive birds, the same authors reported that 92% of tertials were replaced in ♂♂ by Dec, while this was the case for only 43.3% of tertials in ♀♀. Definitive pre-alternate moult occurs between Jan and May in ♀ and May–Jul in ♂, and overall includes the same feather tracts as pre-formative moult. It is more extensive in ♀♀ than ♂♂ in their second calendar year. Definitive pre-basic moult is complete and occurs in Jul–Nov, with a flightless period of *c.*3 weeks starting late Jul to mid-Aug[783]. It is slightly delayed in ♀♀ that breed successfully compared to ♂♂ and non-breeders.

HYBRIDISATION Frequent in nature with Mallard in North America, and is considered a major threat to the future of American Black Duck (see below). In the wild, ancient and very occasional cases have been reported with Mottled Duck[1190,1234] and Northern Pintail *A. acuta*[16,817], even if hybrids of the former are liable to go undetected. In captivity, hybridisation reported with Muscovy Duck *Cairina moschata*[354], Meller's Duck *A. melleri*[465], Indian Spot-billed Duck[465], Pacific Black Duck *A. superciliosa*[465], American Wigeon *A. americana*[1190], Gadwall *A. strepera*[639], Yellow-billed Duck *A. undulata*[465,817,1190] and Common Pochard *Aythya ferina*[752,988].

American Black Duck × Mallard. The introduction of Mallard to E North America and its expansion within the natural range of American Black Duck has led to a massive introgression. Mallard populations have also benefited from urbanisation[556,694] and massive releases for hunting[32,694,783]. American Black Duck and Mallard, initially allopatric, have very similar morphological and behavioural characters[191,192], and there is conflicting evidence of the effectiveness of reproductive barriers[32]. Experiments have demonstrated that, even in mixed flocks, intra-specific pairing remains the rule[191] and that ♂ Mallards attempt to mate with ♀ American Black Ducks only once all ♀♀ of their own species have paired[554]. This recent sympatry has led to frequent hybridisation, especially where Mallards are bred in

captivity and released into the wild. Indeed, domestic strains of Mallard are more capable of hybridising with American Black Duck than wild birds, especially by monopolising those ♀♀ that failed in their first nesting attempt[694].

The proportion of hybrids within 4,608 wings of American Black Duck and hybrids collected in 1977 was 13.2% and did not include at least some backcrossed hybrids indistinguishable from 'pure' American Black Ducks. These estimates are confirmed by examination of hunting bags, with (detected) hybrid samples estimated at 14,300 per year in 2004–08, representing *c.*10% of American Black Duck and American Black Duck-type hybrids[648]. Some analyses have found a significant reduction in genetic distance between American Black Duck and Mallard, suggesting even that the distinction between them is only subspecific[32,45], but that the introgression is not necessarily the only cause[800]. A comprehensive study, however, revealed that genetic distance decreased during the 20th century, by comparing samples of both species collected pre-1940 (genetic differentiation measure, Gst = 0.146), and others taken in 1998 (Gst = 0.008)[800]. The same study also concluded that this strong reduction also affects northern populations of American Black Duck, which previously were believed to have been relatively spared. The impact of this introgression is not unanimously accepted, sometimes being considered as the main threat to American Black Duck, and sometimes only as a contributory factor[33,245,694,783,1068].

Adult ♂ in basic plumage (first generation) generally has obvious characters of both species, although be aware of the strong resemblance of some of these hybrids to gynandromorph Mallards. The upperwing pattern (width of white bars around the speculum) and intermediate bill coloration are helpful. Hybrids are usually overall brown, being almost as dark and plain as American Black Duck, or reflect the colours of Mallard (flanks and scapulars strongly marked pale grey and vermiculated dark). The face, cheeks and neck are beige-grey to pale buff vermiculated dark, but the head-sides can be largely blackish. The broad eye-patch with strong green gloss includes the eyestripe, supercilium and sometimes the whole crown. The bill is similar to that of both parents, but sometimes shows black traces on the culmen. The breast is often slightly reddish. The flank feathers show clear pale fringes and a variable number of pale grey vermiculated dark patches, usually with a strongly barred appearance. Tertials more strongly tinged pale grey in the centre and uppertail-coverts slightly to strongly up-curved. Even if variable, this hybrid is not usually difficult to distinguish from either parent, at least in this plumage. Distinction is much harder in alternate plumage, when it is usually preferable to rely on upperwing pattern (see below).

Adult ♀ (first generation) is intermediate in colour, with inner marks quite visible on scapulars and flanks, resembling a dark ♀ Mallard. Distinction of a hybrid is, however, much more difficult than for ♂♂ and it will usually be necessary to check the upperwing pattern (again, see below).

A very useful identification key to hybrids has been published[693], permitting the distinction of all first-generation hybrids, and an unknown proportion of backcrossed hybrids based on examination of the wing. When the wing is Mallard-type (broad white bars around the speculum) and, in ♂♂, at least one dark patch is visible on the lesser and median underwing-coverts (especially near the 'wrist' and leading edge), it is a hybrid. In ♀♀, if there are more than ten feathers marked brown-black on the same tract, it is a hybrid. If the wing is different from that of Mallard (white bars incomplete, missing and/or narrow), and if two or more greater coverts show a white subterminal bar, it is a hybrid. If no greater coverts has a white subterminal bar, but <10 underwing-coverts near the 'wrist' and leading edge are marked brown or blackish, without white tips to the secondaries, it is a hybrid.

Backcrossed hybrids (second generation or more) can be indistinguishable from either species if the wing features do not permit distinction. Regarding American Black Duck, it is well established that the presence of green sheen on the crown-sides, and the extent of faint pale subterminal bands on greater coverts and thin white tips to the secondaries do not necessarily indicate hybridisation, although at least the last two features were not mentioned historically and appear to have been acquired by the species during the 20th century[693].

HABITAT and LIFE-CYCLE Mainly migratory, although southern breeding populations are sedentary or perform only short-range movements. Spring migration starts early, from early Feb, the birds arriving on nesting grounds between Feb and May depending on latitude. Pair formation occurs mainly in late autumn. In North Carolina between 1978 and 1980, 95% of ♀♀ were mated by Nov[552]. Eggs are laid between mid-Mar and mid-Aug (mainly late Mar to mid-Jun)[783]. When nesting, the species is very eclectic, using various types of wetlands, including saltwater or brackish marshes on coasts, estuaries, bogs, ponds and lakes in the boreal taiga as well as slow-moving streams and various temporary wetlands. Most ♂♂ abandon ♀♀ during incubation, and gather to moult. They can perform quite significant movements towards northern coasts, or moult closer to breeding sites[783,945]. ♀♀ moult on breeding grounds or nearby. Autumn migration occurs mainly between mid-Oct and mid-Dec. In winter, primarily uses saltmarshes in the tidal zone, where concentrations are even larger if nearby freshwater wetlands freeze. Also inhabits fresh waterbodies near coasts, including urban andsuburban ponds, especially in response to hunting pressure. In the interior, present in various types of shallow wetlands with abundant aquatic vegetation and sometimes even woody edges.

RANGE and POPULATION Outside mapped area (NE North America), occasional breeding records have occurred in the south and west[630,783]. Scarce winter visitor to coastal states on Gulf of Mexico. Its northern limit generally depends on winter conditions. On coasts, winters north to Newfoundland. The species is accidental in W USA to Alaska and California, as well as the Bahamas, Puerto Rico[1027], British Isles and several other countries in N & W Europe (including the recovery in France of a bird banded in New Brunswick, Canada), and South Korea. Population estimated at a mean of 621,000 birds between 1990 and 2012, and 622,000 in 2013[1294], and is decreasing[1391], mainly due to competition for nesting sites with introduced Mallards[630] but also because of local habitat destruction including forested sites. The hunting harvest also seems very high compared to the species' estimated numbers: 153,000–243,000 per year in Canada in 1990–98, and 125,000 on average in USA in 2004–08. Finally, hybridisation with Mallard is a major concern (see Hybridisation).

CAPTIVITY Reportedly easy to keep and fairly easy to breed (less than Mallard), but generally uncommon in collections and rare in Eurasia, probably due to its rather dull plumage. European sightings of the species (including the Azores) match a pattern expected of natural vagrancy. However, in the American West it has been suggested that some records could involve escaped individuals[1074].

REFERENCES Alison & Prevett (1976)[16]; Ankney *et al.* (1986)[32]; Ankney *et al.* (1987)[33]; Ashley *et al.* (2007)[37]; Avise *et al.* (1990)[45]; Brewster (1902)[186]; Brodsky & Weatherhead (1984)[191]; Brodsky *et al.* (1988)[192]; Carney (1992)[224]; Conroy *et al.* (1989)[245]; Delacour (1964)[295]; Elliot (1892)[354]; Godfrey & Crosby (1986)[451]; Gray

(1958)[465]; Hanson & Ankney (1994)[505]; Hepp & Hair (1983)[552]; Hepp *et al.* (1988)[554]; Heusmann (1974)[556]; Jarrett *in* Kear (2005)[630]; Johnsgard (1960)[639]; Johnsgard (2010)[648]; Johnson & Sorenson (1999)[654]; Kirby *et al.* (2000)[693]; Kirby *et al.* (2004)[694]; Leverkühn (1890)[752]; Livezey (1991)[767]; Longcore *et al.* (2000)[783]; Mank *et al.* (2004)[800]; McCarthy (2006)[817]; Palmer (1976)[945]; Patton & Avise (1986)[950]; Phillips (1922–26)[988]; Pyle (2008)[1014]; Raffaele *et al.* (1998)[1027]; Rhymer & Simberloff (1996)[1068]; Robb (1997)[1072]; Roberson (1980)[1074]; Shortt (1943)[1186]; Sibley (1938)[1190]; Stevenson & Anderson (1994)[1234]; USFWS (2013)[1294]; Zimpfer *et al.* (2011)[1391].

289. Adult ♂ (definitive basic); note long, lanceolate adult tertials. New York, USA, Nov (Sébastien Reeber).

290. Adult pair (definitive basic); bill coloration is often the easiest way to distinguish ♂ (left) and ♀ (right). New York, USA, Nov (Sébastien Reeber).

291. Adult ♂ (definitive basic). New York, USA, Nov (Sébastien Reeber).

292. First-winter (definitive basic), showing dark iris and upper head, more typical of ♂; tertial coverts pointed and their pale fringes are interrupted at tips; still has some juvenile rectrices. New York, USA, Nov (Sébastien Reeber).

293. Adult ♀ (definitive basic), with adult-type tertials, tertial coverts and rectrices, which are rare in first-winter (formative) ♀. New York, USA, Nov (Sébastien Reeber)

294. Adult ♀ (first alternate/definitive alternate). Quebec, Canada, Jul (Mikaël Jaffré).

295. Adult ♂ (definitive basic); blue or purple speculum has, at most, very faint whitish lines in front (greater coverts) and behind (tips to secondaries). New York, USA, Nov (Sébastien Reeber).

296. Adult ♂ (definitive basic); the extent of the black patch on the primary coverts can be used to detect hybrids with Mallard *A. platyrhynchos*. New York, USA, Nov (Sébastien Reeber).

297. Mallard *A. platyrhynchos* × American Black Duck *A. rubripes*. New York, USA, Nov (Sébastien Reeber).

298. Mallard *A. platyrhynchos* × American Black Duck *A. rubripes*; adult ♂ hybrids frequently show heavy green glossed crown-sides and up-curved central rectrices. New York, USA, Nov (Sébastien Reeber).

MOTTLED DUCK
Anas fulvigula **Plate 31**

TAXONOMY *Anas obscura* var. *fulvigula* Ridgway, 1874, *Amer. Natur.*, 8, p. 111. Member of a group of closely related species including Mallard *A. platyrhynchos* (see Taxonomy of that species). In North America, very close genetically[681] to American Black Duck *A. rubripes* (with which it was considered conspecific), one of the two clades of Mallard[45,654] and Mexican Duck *A. (p.) diazi*. The latter has recently been considered a subspecies of Mottled Duck[293,822], but at present this position is not widely accepted (see Taxonomy of Mallard).

Two subspecies, *A. f. fulvigula* Florida, and *A. f. maculosa* Sennett, 1889, between Louisiana and NE Mexico. There are significant genetic differences between the two populations, with >50% of 219 Mottled Ducks sampled falling into two reciprocally monophyletic haplotype groups of Mottled Ducks, each of them endemic to a region. The nearest neighbour of these two clades together is another monophyletic group comprising Mexican Duck (based on four individuals). The same study showed that the two populations of Mottled Duck diverged a long time ago and without detectable ongoing gene flow between them[822,1357]. Analyses of Florida birds found no differences between four regional subpopulations[1355] and a genetic variability somewhat stronger among populations from Texas[1357]. The two populations differ marginally, at best, in plumage and measurements (see Geographic Variation). Many authors recognise two taxa[64,213,236,437], but the species is sometimes considered monotypic[95,1014].

IDENTIFICATION In the range of this species, which is rather unlikely to wander far, confusion can occur with ♀ and juvenile Mallard and Mexican Duck (see below) and marginally with American Black Duck (see that species). Note that Mottled Duck hybridises regularly with Mallard, possibly with Mexican Duck and very rarely with American Black Duck. The latter hybrid is rarely mentioned in the literature, but some characters of southern populations of American Black Duck (plainer face with dark vermiculations less marked) could be linked to possible hybridisation with Mottled Duck[783]. Hybrids with these three taxa, especially Mallard because of their frequency, are the main risks of confusion with Mottled Duck (see Hybridisation).

Distinction of Mexican Duck and ♀ Mallard is based on the following features (see Leukering & Mlodinow[749] for a complete overview).

- Overall coloration hazelnut-brown, warmer and darker than ♀ Mallard, but slightly less reddish-brown than Mexican Duck.
- Size somewhat smaller than those of the three related taxa, with a very slightly longer and stronger bill on average, which affects overall shape.
- Head paler and less patterned in Mottled Duck, with dark (crown, eyestripe) less extensive. The crown is paler and finely streaked dark, and the pale supercilium is broader. The eyestripe is thinner and shorter, not reaching the dark nape, making the eye more easily discerned.
- The pale areas of the face show a pale buff tinge, usually visible even from afar. The bill base, fore cheeks, throat and foreneck are devoid of flecks or dark vermiculations, the latter being only slightly marked over the rest of the head.
- Bill yellow (usually bright) in ♂. More variable in ♀ (yellowish-olive, dull or bright orange), with variable dark marks towards the culmen, but often less contrasting than in ♀ Mallard.
- The bill base has a clear black spot at the gape (at most, reduced or diffuse in Mexican Duck and American Black Duck). In adult ♂, this black mark extends as a vertical line along the edge of the feathers.
- Tail grey-brown, with fringes of outer rectrices slightly paler, as in Mexican Duck, but very different from Mallard at all ages. The central rectrices are straight (not curled or up-curved as in ♂ Mallard and hybrids).
- Upperwing pattern similar to American Black Duck, but usually has a thin white trailing edge and more obvious pale brownish subterminal line on greater coverts. The width of the white tip on the shaft of s5 varies 0–2 mm in American Black Duck, 1–4 mm in Mottled Duck, 4–9 mm in Mexican Duck and 8–13 mm in Mallard[1014]. The speculum has a green to blue gloss, averaging greener than in other taxa.
- Underwing pattern: the coverts near the 'wrist' often show a few dark patches, on average fewer

than American Black Duck, but more than the two other taxa

- Longest flank feathers are typically elongated and pointed, centred blackish with broad fringes and long, pointed arrow-shaped inner marks, buff-coloured. The rear flanks pattern is typical.

- Belly is not usually paler than adjacent flanks and breast. In the other two taxa, the belly is slightly (Mexican Duck) to significantly (Mallard) paler.

- Undertail-coverts brown mottled dusky, close to American Black Duck, but different from Mallard.

PLUMAGES Nominate subspecies, the other, *A. f. maculosa*, being very similar. Weak sexual dimorphism from first winter onward. Complex alternate moult strategy (two plumages by definitive cycle, three in first cycle). Ageing possible until end of the first summer under good viewing conditions or in the hand. The species' different plumages (sex and age) are close to one another. See also wing chord measurements for differences by ages and sex classes.

Adult ♂

Definitive basic plumage (Sep–Oct/May–Jun). Warm brown with sides of head and foreneck pale buff. Head and upper neck pale buff with fine dusky streaking on crown and short dark eyestripe. The rear cheeks and neck-sides are usually faintly flecked and vermiculated grey (barely visible in some). Bill base, chin, throat and foreneck pale buff. Iris dark brown. Bill bright yellow with black nail and black contrasting spot at gape, which extends along feathering to forehead. Breast yellowish-buff coarsely streaked blackish, darker on average than in ♀. Scapulars and flank feathers elongated, oval or pointed at tip, dark grey-brown with broad fringes, and clear-cut arrow-shaped inner marks, brightly coloured yellowish to reddish-buff. Belly, back, rump, under- and uppertail-coverts the same colour with pale 'U' or 'V'-shaped marks. These parts are as dark as the rest of the body, but appear typically speckled dusky. With wear, the pale fringes are reduced and the birds visibly darker. Tertials pointed at tip, usually dark grey-brown without pale inner marks, but clear bright buff fringes. The 2–3 outer tertials show a wide blackish area with green or bluish sheen on inner webs. Rectrices centred dark grey-brown with crisp greyish to buff fringes, sometimes with very thin fringes on outer webs. A significant proportion of ♂♂ have the two central rectrices slightly up-curved, probably a sign of ancient hybridisation despite the absence of other signs of it. Tertial coverts rounded

with variable light brown fringes (fine to rather broad). Upperwing dark brown with secondaries forming a turquoise to green speculum (except 1–2 outer secondaries). White trailing edge to secondaries thin or virtually absent (see Identification). The greater coverts have large black tips and thin buff subterminal lines, which are rarely paler and more greyish. Underwing has secondary coverts and axillaries silvery-white, greater coverts slightly greyer and remiges dark grey. Some coverts near the 'wrist' often tinged dark grey-brown. Marginal coverts (leading edge) blackish-brown. Legs and feet bright orange often with grey webs.

Definitive alternate plumage (Jun–Jul/Sep–Oct). Very similar to basic plumage. The feathers of the flanks, tertials and scapulars are slightly shorter and rounded or truncated at the tips. The crown and eyestripe are a little sharper and more contrasting. The breast is more regularly and heavily streaked dark. The rectrices may show slight pale inner marks. The bill is duller yellow in some birds, tinged orange or olive. However, *c*.60% of ♂♂ (at least) in Florida have a bright yellow bill all year[467]. The legs are less bright orange.

Adult ♀

Definitive basic plumage (Sep–Oct/Jan–Apr). Very like ♂ but pale fringes to most feathers, especially the breast, flanks and belly, broader and often paler (more yellowish than reddish or with greyer tones). The plumage thus appears slightly paler overall, and more distinctly striped dark. The speckles and vermiculations on the cheeks and neck-sides are more inconspicuous than in ♂. The rectrices have inner marks slightly paler buff and more contrasting. Tertials shorter and less pointed, dark brown with broader pale fringes and frequently a diffuse buff inner mark. The 2–3 outermost tertials are blackish with a soft sheen on the inner webs. On average, the pale fringes to the tertial coverts are more clearly marked. Upperwing similar to ♂ but metallic gloss on speculum reduced in length and width. Absence of gloss on the three (or more) outermost secondaries indicates a ♀: 75% of ♀♀ have at least three outer secondaries without gloss, the other 25% have 1–2[224]. Bill orange and rather dull, with variable dark spots (olive, slate or blackish) concentrated towards the centre of the culmen, but often extending around the nostrils. The black patch of the gape is easily visible, but does not extend along the feathering like the ♂. Iris dark brown. Legs duller orange than ♂.

Definitive alternate plumage (Feb–May/Sep–Oct). Very like basic plumage, but slightly darker and duller. The pale fringes to the feathers, especially the upperparts, wear quickly, leading to a particularly dark plumage in summer. Alternate tertials generally show clear pale buff inner marks. The bill is generally plainer and drabber in this plumage.

Juvenile

First basic plumage (until Oct–Nov). Resembles adult basic plumage but duller and more greyish-brown. The pale parts of the head are more irregularly marked with diffuse grey-brown traces (vs. neatly vermiculated). Bill tinged olive. Scapulars and feathers of flanks narrower, more round-tipped, with fringes and inner marks thinner, more diffuse and duller. Breast feathers narrower and centred dark, creating a narrowly streaked aspect. Belly feathers appear more disordered and mottled dark. Tertials shorter and narrower, quickly fray at tips, all brown without any dark area and purple sheen on inner webs. Tertial coverts narrower and more pointed, with pale fringes continuous (♀) or interrupted at tips (♂). Rectrices juvenile with tips of rachis bare. The upperwing pattern of young birds is distinguished by narrower, almost triangular secondary coverts. The speculum has similar sheen to adult and thus often permits sexing (1–2 secondaries without gloss in young ♂, c.80% of ♀♀ with at least three non-glossy secondaries[224]). Bill and legs initially dusky, acquiring coloration closer to that of adult from first winter.

First-winter ♂

Formative plumage (Oct–Dec/May–Jun). Pre-formative moult is completed swiftly and early, leading to plumage very like definitive basic ♂. From first winter, it may be necessary to examine the upperwing to determine age. Note shape and wear of juvenile secondary coverts, the outer primaries (sharper and frayed at tip) and juvenile tertials and tertial coverts (at least one of each), pointed, brown and worn. These features can be used until the beginning of the first summer (start of second pre-basic moult).

First-winter ♀

Formative plumage (Oct–Dec/Jan–Apr). Sexes distinguished like adult from first winter. Age determined largely via juvenile tertials and tertial coverts, which are often retained until pre-alternate moult (Feb–Apr), or until second pre-basic moult in Jun. These feathers are short, rounded and worn, brown and fringed pale. Age also determined by examining upperwing like juvenile. Bill and legs dull brownish-orange, dark at

first, gradually acquiring adult coloration during winter. These features can be used until the beginning of the first summer (second pre-basic moult).

GEOGRAPHIC VARIATION Subtle differences described between Florida populations (nominate) and those of Louisiana, Texas and NE Mexico (*A. f. maculosa*). The latter have been described as darker[641,822], with stronger dark marks, a stronger bill[1014] and a neck appearing shorter on average[928]. These differences appear insufficient to warrant recognition of two subspecies, and would certainly be unreliable to identify an individual outside its range. In contrast, both subspecies are quite distinct genetically, probably because of the prolonged lack of gene flow[822,1357]. Note that Mottled Duck has been introduced in South Carolina, but it at least partly involved birds of the subspecies *maculosa*, which are now established and have spread to Georgia. Some of these birds have come into contact with those of Florida, creating new gene flow[1345] (see also Hybridisation).

MEASUREMENTS and MASS ♂ and adult slightly larger than ♀ and young, respectively. Subspecies and localities not specified. ♂ (*n*=60): wing chord 242–267 (adult) and 235–260 (juvenile), culmen 51–61, bill depth at tip of forehead feathering 19.4–22.5, tail 81–93, tarsus 43–49; ♀ (*n*=50): wing chord 230–253 (adult) and 223–248 (juvenile), culmen 48–57, depth at tip of forehead feathering 18.1–21.2, tail 78–90, tarsus 40–47[1014].

A. f. fulvigula (Florida). ♂: wing chord 259 (*n*=82), culmen 54 (n=21), tarsus 46 (*n*=90), middle toe 69 (*n*=21); ♀: wing chord 243 (*n*=61), culmen 51 (*n*=21), tarsus 44 (*n*=65), middle toe 66 (*n*=21)[95]. Adult ♂: mass 876–1,241 (1,043, SE=9.3, *n*=86); adult ♀: mass 699–1,151 (934, SE=10.6, *n*=71)[467]

A. f. maculosa (Texas). ♂: wing chord 262 (244, *n*=26), bill from gape 65 (*n*=219), tarsus 56 (*n*=106), middle toe 60 (*n*=106), mass 810–1,330 (1,081, *n*=116); ♀: wing chord 249 (*n*=27), bill from gape 60 (*n*=221), tarsus 53 (*n*=110), middle toe 57 (*n*=110), mass 590–1,380 (967, *n*=136)[1239].

VOICE Seems very similar to that of Mallard (which see).

MOULT Complex alternate strategy. Pre-formative moult occurs between Aug and Nov–Dec, perhaps following an auxiliary pre-formative moult (existence unconfirmed)[95,1014]. Early-hatched birds may have completed their moult by Nov. Pre-formative moult includes part to most head and body feathers, possibly some inner secondary coverts, 0–4 tertials and tertial coverts[224,1014] and none to all rectrices (all in *c*.50% of ♂♂ but a small proportion of ♀♀[1014]). Definitive pre-alternate moult occurs between Jan and May in ♀ and May–Jul in ♂, and overall includes the same feathers as pre-formative moult, but is more extensive in ♂ than ♀ in their second calendar year. Definitive pre-basic moult is complete and undertaken between late Jun and Oct–Nov, starting with the wings between late Jun and early Aug in ♂, *c*.3 weeks later in ♀♀ that raised young (flightless period 27 days[95]). Note that Bielefeld *et al.*[95] described a third moult in the definitive cycle, in Dec–Mar, producing an additional plumage identical to the basic one.

HYBRIDISATION In the wild regularly hybridises with Mallard (see below), which poses conservation issues. Natural cases are more occasionally reported with American Black Duck[465,1190,1234], although detecting these hybrids in the wild would be tricky. An old record exists with Northern Shoveler *A. clypeata*[465,1190]. In captivity, very few records with Chiloe Wigeon *A. sibilatrix*[619], Pacific Black Duck *A. superciliosa*[465,817] and Yellow-billed Duck *A. undulata*[465,1190].

Mottled Duck × Mallard. Hybrids between these two species recorded in Florida, where Mallard is an introduced ornamental species (mostly of domestic origin)[467], and is considered the main threat to Mottled Duck, the nominate subspecies being restricted to this state. Genetic studies[1356] have shown that 10.9% of Mottled Ducks sampled were hybrids. However, this proportion varied from virtually 0% in S Florida to 24% in the east. Note that this hybridisation is asymmetric (lower introgression level), as only 3.4% of Mallards sampled in Florida were hybrids[1356]. The same analyses have not, however, found any genetic differences between Mottled Duck populations introduced in South Carolina and Mallard[1356]. Within the range of *A. f. maculosa*, hybridisation appears less problematic, although the introduction of Mallards should be strictly controlled to avoid a similar situation to that in Florida[95].

Unsurprisingly, this hybrid resembles that between Mallard on the one hand and American Black Duck or Mexican Duck on the other. The first-generation ♂ in definitive basic or formative plumage usually recalls Mottled Duck more by its rather brown and uniform overall coloration, while showing clear signs

of both species. Typically, the head has the crown, bill base and eyestripe strongly marked blackish (pale supercilium slightly marked), and cheeks, throat and neck pale beige-buff slightly vermiculated dark (often has duskier patch on upper and rear cheeks). Breast reddish mottled black. Feathers of the flanks, mantle and scapulars usually brownish with blackish similar to Mottled Duck, but with a variable number of Mallard-type feathers (pale grey finely vermiculated dark) often visible. Tertials often have diffuse pale grey centres. The rear body and back vary between those of the two species, with outer rectrices strongly marked white and central rectrices distinctly up-curved. The upperwing pattern is intermediate, with two conspicuous white or whitish lines bordering the blue glossy speculum. Other plumages and hybrid ♂♂ backcrossed with Mottled Duck are much more difficult to detect, but many hybrids very close in appearance to Mottled Duck can be identified using the following features.

- Bill base shows a black spot, but only in adult ♂ (age and sex should be checked first), and the black line at the bill base is often lacking or incomplete.

- Upperwing pattern consists of two white or whitish lines bordering the speculum in hybrids. That on greater coverts is usually virtually absent or clearly tinged buff in Mottled Duck. The trailing edge of the secondaries is usually more visible than in American Black Duck, but a strong white bar indicates a hybrid. The speculum colour is of little value, as it is too variable and difficult to assess.

- Central rectrices normally straight in Mottled Duck (adult ♂ in basic plumage). In hybrids, they are usually slightly up-curved. Note this character appears to be retained after two or more generations, as ♂♂ apparently identical to 'pure' Mottled Ducks, including the upperwing, have such rectrices.

- Outer rectrices frequently show clear white, whitish or pale grey outer fringes in hybrids. These fringes can be visible in Mottled Duck as well, but are usually thinner and tinged buff or brown.

- Belly and undertail-coverts of adult ♀ are brown-buff in Mottled Duck, more often paler (beige or cream-coloured) in hybrids.

- In a bird otherwise identical to Mottled Duck, the presence of one or more of these characters should arouse suspicion of hybridisation in its lineage. Conversely, the 'purity' of a Mottled Duck may be affirmed by examining all of these features, especially in Florida where introgression is extensive.

HABITAT and LIFE-CYCLE Largely sedentary, performing only short seasonal movements, especially depending on local water conditions. Subtropical conditions in its range permit a very long breeding period, eggs being laid between late Jan and mid-Jul, even Aug[95,213], albeit peaking in late Mar to mid-May. Inhabits a variety of fresh and brackish wetlands, usually shallow and with abundant aquatic vegetation, including marshes, ponds, rice fields, etc., at low densities (up to three nests per ha in good conditions[213]). May also use man-made habitats[1315], including suburban waterbodies, especially in Florida where a significant portion of its coastal habitats has been destroyed. May rapidly switch sites in response to rainfall conditions, which affect both the depth and salinity of favoured coastal wetlands. The ♂ abandons ♀ during incubation to form small flocks (sometimes up to a few thousand birds), and then head to moulting grounds, e.g. large swampy or agricultural areas[95]. ♀♀ that raised young usually moult alone and close to breeding sites, along with their offspring or not. After moulting, usually overwinters in small flocks of up to several dozen birds. Events affecting food supplies (hurricanes, droughts, etc.) may provoke larger gatherings.

RANGE and POPULATION Two distinct populations: the first (nominate subspecies) over a large part of the Florida peninsula and is estimated at 40,000 birds in the early 2000s, being probably stable[652]. The second (*A. f. maculosa*) nests in coastal areas of NW Gulf of Mexico, from Louisiana to NE Mexico. Extends slightly further south along coast of Mexico in the non-breeding season, especially depending on local water conditions. The population is estimated at *c*.600,000 birds, with trend unknown[652]. May extend its usual range temporarily following tropical storms, which may cause the flooding of coastal marshes with sea water, and thus alter their salinity[95]. Some records have occurred further north, as far as Nebraska, Colorado, Kansas and Arkansas, including birds banded in Florida (in Georgia, Virginia and New Jersey[95]). Introduced in 1975 and 1982 to South Carolina, and now established locally in the south-east of the state, near Savannah, and SE Georgia[1345].

Hunting harvests are estimated at 70,000 birds annually (2004–08)[648]. The risks represented by introgression of Mallard (see Hybridisation) are serious, and should lead to better control of the species' feral populations, mainly in Florida where the introgression appears deeper. Unfortunately, many Mallards and hybrids occur in urban and suburban wetlands, where removing the birds and controlling releases are not easy. The future of this species' (especially the nominate subspecies) genetic integrity therefore probably relies on strong measures (ban of free-flying Mallards, control of feral populations), which is politically difficult[95]. Note that extensive hybridisation also produces greater genetic diversity in Mottled Duck, which potentially favours its adaptability[974].

CAPTIVITY Uncommon in collections, probably due to its unattractive plumage compared to Mallard in particular. Rarely offered for sale, despite it being reportedly easy to keep and breed. North American records outside the species' natural range are generally considered to be genuine vagrants.

REFERENCES Avise *et al.* (1990)[45]; Bielefeld *et al.* (2010)[95]; Bird Hybrids Database (2014)[97]; Callaghan in Kear (2005)[213]; Carney (1992)[224]; Clements *et al.* (2013)[237]; Gill & Donsker (2014)[437]; Gray (1958)[465]; Gray (1993)[467]; del Hoyo & Collar (2014)[293]; IZY (1989)[619]; Johnsgard (1961)[641]; Johnsgard (2010)[648]; Johnson (2009)[652]; Johnson & Sorenson (1999)[654]; Kerr *et al.* (2007)[681]; Leukering & Mlodinow (2012)[749]; Livezey (1991)[767]; Longcore *et al.* (2000)[783]; Mazourek & Gray (1994)[815]; McCarthy (2006)[817]; McCracken *et al.* (2001)[822]; Ogilvie & Young (1998)[928]; Peters *et al.* (2014)[974]; Pyle (2008)[1014]; Sibley (1938)[1190]; Stevenson & Anderson (1994)[1234]; Stutzenbaker (1988)[1239]; Varner *et al.* (2013)[1315]; Weng (2006)[1345]; Williams *et al.* (2002)[1355]; Williams *et al.* (2005)[1356]; Williams *et al.* (2005)[1357].

MOTTLED DUCK (continued)

299. *A. f. fulvigula,* ♂ (formative/definitive basic), sexed by black of gape extending along base of bill. Florida, USA, Jan (Joe Fischer).

300. *A. f. maculosa,* pair; note differences in extent of gloss on speculum between ♀ (behind) and ♂. Texas, USA, Mar (Greg Lavaty).

301. *A. f. fulvigula,* ♂ (formative/definitive basic); central rectrices slightly up-curved, which may indicate past hybridisation. Florida, USA, Dec (Tom Grey).

302. *A. f. maculosa,* first-winter ♂ (formative?); the rounded flank feathers and scapulars, with attenuated inner markings, and short brown tertials might indicate a first-winter ♂. Texas, USA, Feb (Joe Fischer).

304. *A. f. fulvigula*, adult ♂ (definitive alternate); a thin white trailing edge is normal in this species (wider than American Black Duck *A. rubripes* but narrower than Mallard *A. platyrhynchos*). Florida, USA, Aug (Ron Bielefeld).

303. *A. f. fulvigula*, ♂ (first alternate/definitive alternate). Florida, USA, Aug (Ron Bielefeld).

305. *A. f. maculosa*, pair (formative/definitive basic). Texas, USA, Apr (Greg Lavaty).

306. *A. f. fulvigula*, pair (formative/definitive basic); ♀ distinguished by its orange bill with black normally reduced to the gape, paler iris, and tertials with clearly defined inner markings. Florida, USA, Dec (Tom Grey).

EASTERN SPOT-BILLED DUCK
Anas zonorhyncha

Plate 32

TAXONOMY *Anas zonorhyncha* Swinhoe, 1866, *Ibis* (2)2, p. 394. See Taxonomy of Indian Spot-billed Duck *A. poecilorhyncha*. Eastern Spot-billed Duck was considered conspecific with the latter, but local sympatry of the two species during breeding does not seem to result in frequent hybridisation[736]. Both species appear to be more closely related to American Black Duck *A. rubripes*, Mottled Duck *A. fulvigula* and Mexican Duck *A. (platyrhynchos) diazi* than to Mallard *A. platyrhynchos*. Its phylogenetic relationships to Pacific Black Duck *A. superciliosa* remain to be studied further, but the two taxa have many similarities.

IDENTIFICATION Within its range, should not pose identification problems, due to the rather cold coloration (pale grey-brown and blackish-brown), the bill pattern (black with a broad yellow patch at the tip) and heavily striped head-sides. However, where the species is rare, beware hybrids with Mallard (see Hybridisation). At the southern end of the range, separation from Indian Spot-billed Duck and Pacific Black Duck, which are relatively close in many respects, should be made with care. In all plumages, Eastern Spot-billed Duck differs from Indian Spot-billed Duck by its overall browner hue, plainer and darker plumage, the centres to the feathers of the flanks and scapulars being blacker and the fringes narrower. The breast is tinged pale buff-brown, irregularly spotted/striped dark, gradually merging into the blackish rear body. The head is more contrasting, with crown and stripe on the hindneck wider and more uniformly dark, broad whitish supercilium typically with flat inverted 'V'-shape and broad dark line from gape across the upper cheeks. The yellow patch at the tip of the bill is on average slightly reduced compared to Indian Spot-billed Duck, particularly on the tomium. The longest tertials show clear white outer fringes, but inner webs are not completely white (or almost white) as in Indian Spot-billed Duck. The speculum has a strong blue gloss, not green, bounded by two white lines that are narrow (trailing edge) or virtually absent (greater coverts). Finally, compared to nominate Indian Spot-billed Duck, Eastern Spot-billed Duck never shows red spots on the top of the culmen.

PLUMAGES Weak sexual dimorphism from first winter onward. Complex alternate moult strategy (two

plumages per definitive cycle, three in first cycle). Ageing possible until end of first summer under good viewing conditions or in the hand. The species' different plumages (sex and age) are close to each other.

Adult ♂

Definitive basic plumage. Head contrasting with crown, stripe on hindneck and eyestripe blackish-brown and a dark area from the gape across the cheeks fading on ear-coverts. Large white supercilium, chin and throat whitish (or washed pale buff) and contrasting. Rest of cheeks and neck pale vermiculated greyish-brown. Iris dark warm brown. Bill blackish-slate with bright yellow patch towards tip and black nail. Breast pale grey-brown to whitish with brown spots (feather centres) often loosely aligned. Feathers of mantle, flanks and scapulars broad, rounded and centred dark brown, finely fringed pale grey to white, giving an overall finely scaled appearance. Belly dark brown finely striped pale, gradually becoming blackish on undertail-coverts. Back, rump and uppertail-coverts blackish, slightly fringed pale. Tertials broad, rather pointed, with white fringes quite variable in width, which can extend over up to half of inner web of longest tertials. Tertial coverts round-tipped, with pale fringes barely visible. Tail has central rectrices black and outer rectrices more greyish-brown with whitish outer fringes. Upperwing dark grey-brown with strong blue gloss on speculum (sometimes green or purple depending on light), bordered by two black bars (greater covert tips and subterminal bars on secondaries). Very narrow white trailing edge. The subterminal white bar on the greater coverts varies in width, being often virtually absent or barely discernible under field conditions. Others, however, show a wingbar almost as large as in Mallard or Indian Spot-billed Duck. The causes of this variability are not fully understood, but do not appear (always) to be associated with hybridisation, even ancient, insofar as birds with such bars do not appear to possess other hybrid characters. Further study is needed. Lesser and median coverts have pale fringes faint or lacking. Underwing has axillaries, lesser and median coverts white with cream or pale yellowish hue, pale grey greater coverts, marginal coverts centred grey with whitish fringes, and dark grey remiges. Legs and feet bright orange, with slightly darker webs (variable).

Definitive alternate plumage. Very similar in appearance to basic plumage (extent of the pre-alternate moult not well known in the wild).

Adult ♀

Definitive basic plumage. Very similar to ♂, but somewhat browner overall. Crown more distinctly streaked pale and slightly less contrasting with the rest of the head (often a distinct feature within pairs). Essentially distinguished by upper- and undertail-coverts black with velvety sheen in ♂, but browner and duller in ♀, with fringes and possibly inner marks pale brown. Belly of adult ♂ is dark reddish-brown, contrasting with breast, whereas that of adult ♀ is more distinctly mottled dark brown contrasting less with breast, but more with lower belly and undertail-coverts[617]. However, similar characters can be shown by young ♂♂ that have not moulted the same feathers, thereby retaining juvenile brown and worn plumage, instead of having black feathers of adult ♂. Tertial coverts round-tipped, with clear white fringes, slightly thinner in the centre. Tertials narrower, with less extensive white fringes.

Definitive alternate plumage. The extent of pre-alternate moult and its timing are poorly known in the wild. However, the appearance during breeding is largely similar to that during the rest of the year, although the breast is often less distinctly spotted/striped dark.

Juvenile

First basic plumage. Like adult ♀. Best distinguished by darker and duller coloration. Cheeks and neck appear more uniform pale brown than adult. Breast and belly appear more irregularly marked with vague dark brown streaks. Bill like adult but yellow tip often extends as a thin line along the tomium. Tertial coverts narrower, somewhat pointed and fringed pale (better marked in ♀). Tertials centred brown (blackish-brown on inner web in adult), short and rather round-tipped. The upperwing pattern has secondary coverts slightly more trapezoidal, with inconspicuous pale fringes (varies, probably by sex?), often interrupted or frayed at tips. Greater coverts narrower with rounded tips (vs. square in adult), with black marks from tips smaller than in adult (obvious on outer greater coverts). The white subterminal bars on the greater coverts are typically narrow in their centres, and frequently extend towards the base on the outer webs. The extent of white may be age-related, but deserves further study. The blue, purple or turquoise gloss to the secondaries of young ♂ is close to that of adult ♀ (1–2 outer secondaries without gloss) while that of young ♀ is reduced in length (3–4 outer feathers without gloss) and width (black subterminal band almost as broad as glossy area on outer half of speculum).

Immature ♂

Formative/first alternate plumage. The extent of pre-formative moult and its timing are not well known in the wild but appear similar to those of congenerics in the Holarctic. Appearance is similar to that of adult from first winter. Apart from upperwing pattern still juvenile (see above), ageing must be based on juvenile feathers (brown fringed pale) of upper- and undertail coverts, rump and/or back. Among other remaining juvenile feathers, also check the rectrices (faded, brown and worn) and tertials (browner, narrower and frayed at the tips, lanceolate, with white fringes smaller and less clearly demarcated).

Immature ♀

Formative/first alternate plumage. Age established as for ♂ by presence of juvenile feathers (wings, rectrices, tertials, belly and rear body, best assessed in hand), but as for latter, the extent and timing of pre-formative moult are not well known. Differences in pattern between juvenile, formative, alternate and definitive basic tertials in the ♀ are poorly described.

GEOGRAPHIC VARIATION None described.

MEASUREMENTS and MASS Very few published data, generally without information on sample sizes and localities. ♂ and adult slightly larger than ♀ and young, respectively. ♂: wing chord 263–293, bill 50–55, tarsus 43–49, mass 1,000–1,340 (1,156, $n=13$); ♀: wing chord 255–262, bill 45–49, tarsus 42–44, mass 750 and 980 ($n=2$)[408,646,988].

VOICE Very similar to that of Mallard, but some calls at least are described as being louder[182].

MOULT Very few data seem to have been published on the timing and extent of different moults in the wild, their study being complicated by the similarity of different plumages. The information available, however, suggests that the moult strategy is similar to that of Mallard.

HYBRIDISATION This species hybridises readily with Mallard in the wild, leading to hybrids that are distinctive in the first generation (see below). Also many backcrossed hybrids with Eastern Spot-billed Duck, which are far less easy to detect. The range of Eastern Spot-billed Duck also appears to extend north-west and into that of Mallard, which is likely to increase the frequency of hybridisation at least locally. It was assumed that the two species hybridised extensively in the Russian Far East in the past[715]. Hybridisation or intergradation with Indian Spot-billed Duck, especially the subspecies *haringtoni* of the latter, is more enigmatic. Hybrids and mixed pairs have been reported in Hong Kong[736], with the same source reporting that the two species' ranges overlap only very locally, and that such natural hybrids had not been mentioned in the literature previously. Regarding reports of hybridisation in captivity, many references do not specify if Eastern or Indian Spot-billed Duck was involved, as the two taxa were long considered conspecific.

Eastern Spot-billed Duck × Mallard. Adult ♂ in basic plumage is quite variable. Among ten individuals, Gillham & Gillham[443] did not define any particular type. These hybrids generally have a dark head, irregularly marked with black, brown and metallic green gloss, traces of pale areas at the bill base, on the supercilium in front and/or behind the eye, and on the rear cheeks. The bill often resembles that of Eastern Spot-billed Duck being dark with a broad yellow patch at the tip, but can also be more broadly yellow with blackish spots limited to the culmen. A white collar generally separates the neck from the breast, which is usually tinged purplish-brown like Mallard. The rest of the body is often like Mallard in coloration, but duller and variably mottled/stained brown. The tertials can resemble Mallard, but are often darker and browner, or Eastern Spot-billed Duck, i.e. blackish-brown with broad white fringes. The central rectrices are often (in six of ten birds studied by Gillham & Gillham[443]) up-curved or more strongly curled. Adult ♀ of this cross is more difficult to distinguish, but many have a bill like that of Eastern Spot-billed Duck, with body coloration closest to Mallard (pale inner marks and broad fringes to the feathers of the flanks and, often, scapulars). The head is usually intermediate with a prominent white supercilium and a hint of a line starting from the gape.

HABITAT and LIFE-CYCLE Largely migratory, wintering in the south of its breeding range. The breeding season lasts from Apr to Jul[180,408], but does not start before May in the north[182]. Favoured habitats are diverse during the breeding season, but preferentially inhabits lowland wetlands, mainly shallow freshwater areas with dense emergent and riparian vegetation. Common also in rice fields, but less numerous on fast-flowing streams, large open waterbodies and brackish water. Few data available on movements and timing of pre-basic moult, which occurs post-breeding. In the non-breeding season, occurs in freshwater wetlands (marshes, flooded crops, rice fields), brackish (estuaries, coastal lagoons, aquaculture ponds) and marine habitats (intertidal mudflats). Its liking for saltwater habitats recall Mottled Duck and American Black Duck, but distinguish the species from Indian Spot-billed Duck and Mallard, which prefer fresh water. Also appears to form larger gatherings than Indian Spot-billed Duck.

RANGE and POPULATION E Asia. The species appears to have expanded north and north-west since the mid-20th century at least[715]. The southern limit is not clearly established, but is located along a line between Hong Kong and C Yunnan, China (perhaps including N Laos and NE Vietnam?). It winters along the coastal and southern parts of the range, mainly in South Korea, Japan, in Jiangxi (Poyang Lake) and on coasts of E China, only rarely wandering further south. It appears occasionally in NE Russia and on the Aleutians and Kodiak I, Alaska[1280], as well as in NE India and the Philippines[1044]. Population estimated at 800,000–1,600,000 birds, and is declining[756,858,1348], but this estimate was subsequently considered to be too optimistic[757].

CAPTIVITY Rather rarely kept in captivity outside its native range, although fairly easy to breed and offered at low prices.

REFERENCES Brazil (1991)[180]; Brazil (2009)[182]; Fullagar *in* Kear (2005)[408]; Gillham & Gillham (2002)[443]; Imamura & Sugimori (1989)[617]; Johnsgard (1978)[646]; Kulikova *et al.* (2004)[715]; Leader (2006)[736]; Li & Mundkur (2007)[756]; Li *et al.* (2009)[757]; Miyabayashi & Mundkur (1999)[858]; Phillips (1922–26)[988]; Trapp & Macintosh (1978)[1280]; Wetlands International (2014)[1348]; Zhuravlev *et al.* (2002)[1389].

307. Adult ♂ (definitive basic), with dark and contrasting plumage; note broad tertials and broad, rounded, hardly fringed pale tertial coverts. Japan, Mar (Aurélien Audevard).

308. Adult (definitive basic); the broad white wingbar extending onto the rounded tertial coverts, paler brown plumage, faintly warmer and paler iris, and less white on tertials suggest a ♀. Japan, Nov (Ayuwat Jearwattanakanok).

309. ♀ (formative/definitive basic). South Korea, Dec (Philippe J. Dubois).

310. Adult ♀ (first alternate/definitive alternate). Japan, May (Stuart Price).

311. Adult ♀ (definitive basic). Note variation in white on greater coverts, which is still poorly understood. Japan, Nov (Ayuwat Jearwattanakanok).

312. First-winter (formative). Hebei, China, Oct (Sébastien Reeber).

INDIAN SPOT-BILLED DUCK
Anas poecilorhyncha

Plate 32

TAXONOMY *Anas poecilorhyncha* J. R. Forster, 1781, *Ind. Zool.*, p. 23, pl. 13, fig. 1. Phylogenetically related to Mallard *A. platyrhynchos* and placed in the subgenus *Anas* by Livezey[767]. Its taxonomic status and position within this group have long been discussed (see Taxonomy of Mallard). Livezey[767] recovered two major clades, the first including species from Africa, Madagascar, Oceania and Asia, in which the only Holarctic representatives are Indian Spot-billed Duck and Eastern Spot-billed Duck *A. zonorhyncha*. The phylogeny in relation to Mallard then evolved, especially after the discovery of two paraphyletic groups within the latter species[45,654], one of them being sister to Eastern and Indian Spot-billed Ducks. More recently, Kulikova *et al.*[715] detected specific haplotypes from both groups within Eastern Spot-billed Duck, also suggesting that this species is closer to the Nearctic taxa (*rubripes*, *fulvigula* and *diazi*) than to sympatric nominate Mallard. This study did not include Indian Spot-billed Duck, which highlights the lack of a comprehensive analysis based on sufficient samples of all taxa in the 'Mallard' group.

The Spot-billed Duck *sensu lato* has long been regarded as including three subspecies. The nominate subspecies is widespread across the Indian subcontinent, then merges into *haringtoni* Oates, 1907, in SE Asia, which is in contact with *zonorhyncha* Swinhoe, 1866, of E Asia. This treatment was maintained[408,928] until Leader[736] reported sympatric breeding of *haringtoni* and *zonorhyncha* in Hong Kong, with only two mixed pairs of 23 studied, and one of the two mixed pairs involving a hybrid ♀. According to this author, the fact that 91% of pairs observed mated intra-specifically suggests a high level of homogamy and supports their specific distinction. This treatment has been widely adopted since, *haringtoni* being considered a subspecies of *poecilorhyncha*[68,142,236,437,794].

IDENTIFICATION Within its usual range, should not be mistaken for any other species, the nearest in size and shape being Mallard. Indian Spot-billed Duck, in all plumages, is distinguished by its mainly black-and-white appearance, scaly and spotted, with a large white patch on the outer tertials, speculum with green gloss and blackish bill with a sharp yellow patch on tip and red spots at base of culmen. The distinction between the two subspecies is described under Geographic Variation,

while the separation of Indian and Eastern Spot-billed Ducks is treated under the latter species.

PLUMAGES Weak sexual dimorphism from first winter onward. Complex alternate moult strategy (two plumages by definitive cycle, three in first cycle). Ageing possible until end of first summer, under good viewing conditions or in the hand. The different plumages of the species (sex and age) are much alike. Moult strategy and timing not well described and vary geographically (see Moult).

Adult ♂

Definitive basic plumage. Sides of head and neck whitish with a buff or brown hue and fine dark vermiculations. Throat and foreneck paler. Crown neatly streaked blackish-brown, extending as a faint stripe on the hindneck. Broad dark loral stripe encircling eye and extending as a short eyestripe tapering quickly behind the eye. Iris warm brown. Bill blackish-slate with waxy red spots (swollen during nesting) on the upper mandible near the forehead. Large bright yellow patch covering tip of bill (extending further along the tomium than the culmen) and black nail. Breast, mantle and fore flanks beige with dark centres to feathers. The pale fringes, broad on the breast and mantle, become thinner and browner towards the rear flanks and on longest scapulars. The fine pale grey-brown fringes on a dark brown to blackish ground form a neat scaly appearance. The belly appears paler with smaller dark spots forming irregular longitudinal streaks. The black spots become denser towards the rear body, lower belly (black finely streaked pale) and undertail-coverts (entirely blackish). Back, rump and uppertail-coverts blackish with velvety sheen in ♂. Inner tertials blackish and longest tertials elongated, pointed, with white inner webs, forming a large contrasting patch. Corresponding tertial coverts broadly tipped white. Tail has central rectrices black, slightly longer and pointed, and outer rectrices more grey-brown with whitish outer fringes. Dark grey-brown upperwing with large speculum with strong green gloss (can appear blue or purple depending on light), bordered by two black bars (greater covert tips and subterminal bars on secondaries) and two white bars (broad subterminal bars to greater coverts and thin white tips to secondaries). Lesser and median coverts fringed pale or almost uniform. Underwing has axillaries, lesser and median coverts white to cream-coloured, greater coverts pale grey, marginal coverts centred grey fringed white, and remiges dark grey. Legs and feet bright orange, with slightly darker webs (variable).

Definitive alternate plumage. Very similar to basic plumage, the extent of pre-alternate moult being poorly understood in the wild. The red spots on the culmen are less swollen and duller (orange or yellow).

Adult ♀

Definitive basic plumage. Similar to ♂ but blackish parts often a little paler and browner, making the overall plumage look slightly less contrasting. In particular, the dark centres to the breast and above all the flanks form smaller spots, making the flanks appear paler, which is useful mostly in direct comparison. The main feature for sexing is the smaller and less swollen red spots on the bill, even if this is variable and also especially useful within pairs. In profile, in ♂ the red often extends halfway down the base of the bill. Also note plumage details, such as the paler crown with more distinct dark streaks and rump and undertail-coverts more brownish, without velvety sheen but with fine brown streaks. The tertials are shorter and less pointed, but variably washed pale grey-brown, especially at the base of the inner web of the longest feathers. Tertials very similar to adult ♂ in some ♀♀, but largely pale grey-brown in others (alternate tertials?). Upperwing pattern identical to ♂, but frequently two secondaries without metallic gloss and/or glossy area narrower over the outer speculum, with black subterminal bar on average wider than in ♂. Pale fringes to the lesser and median coverts are more clearly marked (they can be rather well marked in some ♂♂). Iris paler on average.

Definitive alternate plumage. The extent and timing of pre-alternate moult, presumably linked to the breeding period, which varies across the range of the species, are poorly described in the wild. Observations of captive birds suggest that moult is quite similar to that in other Holarctic ducks. Furthermore, there is little change in general appearance during the annual cycle, except that ♀♀ with ducklings often show very worn and 'messy' plumage. Similarly, the tertials are usually largely pale grey-brown, often with irregular patterns, inner marks, pale or dark bars and stripes. These tertials are generally short, round-tipped and almost devoid of white, except for fringes to the inner webs. The longest flank feathers and scapulars also often show pale inner marks.

Juvenile

First basic plumage. Very close to ♀, but a little duller. The ground colour of the cheeks, neck, breast and flanks is tinged pale grey-brown instead of whitish in adult. The streaks and vermiculations of the face are much thinner, making the whole appear plainer. The centres to the feathers of the breast and flanks are smaller, and form stripes rather than spots (especially visible on the breast). Similarly, these spots are less black (browner) than adult. The bill quickly resembles the adult but the limit between the yellow and black (which is stained brownish, olive or orangey) is rather diffuse. Furthermore, the spots at the base of culmen are dull yellow-orange initially, and the yellow patch extends along the tomium towards its base. The upperwing pattern has narrower and more triangular secondary coverts, with variably marked fringes (probably by sex?). Greater coverts narrower with rounded tips (vs. squarer in adult), black terminal bars narrower as well (absent on outermost 3–4 greater coverts) and often show white patches at the tips. The white bars on the greater coverts are thinner, often very narrow in their centres, and frequently extend to the outer webs (♂ only?). The green gloss to the secondaries of young ♂ is like that of adult ♀ (1–2 outer secondaries without gloss) while that of young ♀ is reduced in length (2–3 outer secondaries without gloss) and width (black subterminal bars almost as wide as glossy parts). Sexing based on wing pattern poorly studied.

Immature ♂

Formative/first alternate plumage. It appears that like Mallard and other species in this group, young birds become very like adult a few months after fledging. More research is needed, but many birds at least can be aged by the presence of juvenile-type feathers (fringed pale) on the undertail, rump and/or back. Age can also be determined by the presence of juvenile rectrices and upperwing pattern.

Immature ♀

Formative/first alternate plumage. Aged like ♂ by presence of juvenile feathers (upperwing, rectrices, tertials, belly and rear body). Differences in pattern between juvenile, formative, alternate and definitive basic tertials of ♀ are poorly described.

GEOGRAPHIC VARIATION The only other subspecies, *A. p. haringtoni*, occurs in the north-east of the species' range, in contact with Eastern Spot-billed

Duck, and, in many respects, is intermediate between Indian and Eastern Spot-billed Ducks, but is still much closer to the former (tertials white, speculum green, no dark bar from gape across cheeks). *A. p. haringtoni* is somewhat smaller than the nominate (with overlap), the red spots on the culmen are absent or reduced, and its overall colour is slightly paler, more uniform and less distinctly spotted. Especially the sides of the head, neck, breast, belly and flanks are tinged more buff to brownish, with fewer dark spots, reducing the overall contrast. Other features are more variable: *haringtoni* usually shows a clear white wingbar on the greater coverts, which can seem on average thinner (and perhaps more variable) than in *poecilorhyncha*, but the wingbar can be much less marked, suggesting hybridisation with *zonorhyncha*. An overview of variation within *haringtoni* is currently lacking, especially in the contact zones with *poecilorhyncha* and *zonorhyncha*.

MEASUREMENTS and MASS Few data available, and sample sizes not indicated. ♂ and adult slightly larger than ♀ and young, respectively.

A. p. poecilorhyncha. ♂: wing chord 260–280, tail 105–113, bill 52–55, tarsus 46–48, mass 1,230–1,500; ♀: wing chord 250–268, tail 90–102, bill 31–37, tarsus 40–48, mass 790–1,360[408,794,988,1044].

A. p. haringtoni. ♂: wing chord 245–267; ♀: wing chord 237–258; sex unknown: bill 49–57[54].

VOICE Vocalisations similar to those of Mallard (see sonograms in Rasmussen & Anderton[1044]). The typical call of ♀ consists of a loud *quack* followed by several others in decrescendo, but with a more constant tempo than Mallard.

MOULT Very little information available on the extent and timing of different moults in the wild. In captivity, the moult strategy seems similar to Mallard. Study of moult is complicated by the great similarity between all plumages throughout the year. It has been reported that the species undertakes pre-basic moult in Aug–Sep in India, and that it moults its remiges shortly after breeding [54]. However, it seems that eggs can be laid between Mar and Dec, depending on region and the intensity of the monsoon. It is therefore possible that the moult strategy varies geographically.

HYBRIDISATION Many references (especially historical ones) do not specify whether *poecilorhyncha* or *zonorhyncha* is involved in hybrid events. The bibliography is particularly confusing concerning crosses with Mallard, which frequently hybridises with *zonorhyncha*. However, natural hybridisation occurs regularly, and mixed breeding is frequent in captivity, where many birds possess hybrid characters. Similarly, hybrids including both Mallard and Indian Spot-billed Duck in their lineage but of unknown precise parentage, are reported regularly in C Europe (Switzerland, E France). Natural hybridisation with Eastern Spot-billed Duck may be regular, but seems to have been reported just once in the wild, in Hong Kong[736], making available descriptions very rare. In captivity, Indian and/or Eastern Spot-billed Ducks have bred with Mandarin Duck *Aix sponsa*[465,587], Northern Pintail *Anas acuta*[465], Yellow-billed Pintail *A. georgica*[443], Grey Teal *A. gibberifrons*[639], Meller's Duck *A. melleri*[465,817], Philippine Duck *A. luzonica*[97,642], American Black Duck *A. rubripes*[465], Pacific Black Duck *A. superciliosa*[465,817], Yellow-billed Duck *A. undulata*[465,587,988] and Red-crested Pochard *Netta rufina*[97,439,465,817].

Indian Spot-billed Duck × Mallard. First-generation adult ♂ in basic plumage resembles a faded Mallard, overall washed pale grey. The head is black with green gloss behind the eyes and on the nape, with cheeks variably pale (sometimes entirely so, sometimes two small patches form a bimaculated pattern), tinged grey and/or pale buff, and finely vermiculated. The pale supercilium can be strongly marked even behind the eyes (in pale-cheeked birds) or reduced to a small patch above the lores. The bill is orange-yellow, often with a well-defined black patch on central culmen. The breast is pale reddish-brown with a variable quantity of blackish crescent-shaped streaks, and sometimes a white collar. Flanks quite variable, mixing feathers with broad subterminal blackish marks and others whitish vermiculated dark grey. Mantle and scapulars may also be closer to those of one or the other species. Tertials broad, lanceolate, centred grey, darker on inner webs with broad ill-defined whitish fringes. Back to uppertail-coverts black, undertail-coverts variably marked black. Outer rectrices fringed white. Central rectrices usually visibly up-curved or curled. Backcrosses with Indian Spot-billed Duck obviously much more closely resemble this species, but differ in being paler and more faded (centres to flank feathers and scapulars paler), with bill variably stained black and yellow-orange (including the tomium) and slightly up-curved central rectrices. First-generation ♀ hybrid poorly described in the literature.

HABITAT and LIFE-CYCLE Sedentary or short-distance migrant, especially depending on regional rainfall and available habitat. These same weather conditions also affect timing of breeding. Breeds mainly Jul–Oct in N India and Nov–Dec in S India, but may do so from Mar to Dec[54,1350]. Nests also mentioned in spring, Feb–Jun, for *A. p. haringtoni*. Inhabits lowland wetlands, fresh, standing and shallow water, with much emergent vegetation, and has a preference for small wooded waterbodies. Rarely on rivers, large open waterbodies and brackish water, whereas the latter is one of the principal habitats of Eastern Spot-billed Duck. Usually nests on the ground under dense cover, near water or not, and sometimes high in trees[54]. Like many species of equatorial regions and S Hemisphere, pair-bond is likely to be long-lasting, the ♂ staying with ♀ and its brood[54,408,988]. Few data on moult, but usually follows breeding. Outside the breeding season, less gregarious than most ducks, usually remaining in pairs or small parties, and not generally associating with congenerics.

RANGE and POPULATION Restricted to S & SE Asia. The limits between the ranges of the two subspecies are located somewhere between E Assam and W Myanmar, but are not known precisely, nor are those between *haringtoni* and *zonorhyncha* further north. Similarly, the possible overlap between the different taxa (and the degree of intergradation) is poorly documented.

A. p. poecilorhyncha. Widespread from S & E Pakistan over much of India, except mountainous regions of the north, and Bangladesh, east to the borders of Myanmar. Also in N & W Sri Lanka. Population estimated at 50,000–100,000 birds[858], perhaps closer to 100,000[1348], but in moderate decline[757].

A. p. haringtoni. Present from Myanmar to extreme S China (Yunnan), Laos, Vietnam (rare in east), Cambodia (rare) and Thailand (rare in south). Population estimated at 10,000–100,000 birds in the late 1990s[1348] but other estimates suggest 100,000–1,000,000 birds[408,858], probably due to the inclusion of some *zonorhyncha* populations in S China. Trend unknown.

CAPTIVITY Rather rare in captivity outside its natural range. Reportedly fairly easy to keep and breed, and generally offered for sale at very affordable prices. Occasionally escapes from captivity and may then breed with local Mallards, even establishing small, hybrid populations. In captivity, many birds presented as this species clearly have Mallard in their ancestry.

REFERENCES Ali *et al.* (1987)[11]; Avise *et al.* (1990)[45]; Baker (1929)[54]; Banks *et al.* (2008)[68]; Bird Hybrids database (2014)[97]; BirdLife International (2012)[142]; Clements *et al.* (2013)[236]; Fullagar *in* Kear (2005)[408]; Gill & Donsker (2014)[437]; Gillham & Gillham (1996)[439]; Gillham & Gillham (2002)[443]; Gray (1958)[465]; Hopkinson (1935)[587]; Johnsgard (1960)[639]; Johnsgard (1965)[642]; Johnson & Sorenson (1999)[654]; Kulikova *et al.* (2004)[715]; Leader (2006)[736]; Li *et al.* (2009)[757]; Livezey (1991)[767]; Madge & Burn (1988)[794]; McCarthy (2006)[817]; Miyabayashi & Mundkur (1999)[858]; Ogilvie & Young (1998)[928]; Phillips (1922–26)[988]; Rasmussen & Anderton (2005)[1044]; Wetlands International (2014)[1348]; Whistler (1949)[1350].

313. *A. p. poecilorhyncha*, pair (definitive basic); note reduced red patch on top of culmen, the clearly scaled appearance, brown tertials and rear body of ♀ (right). India, Feb (Julien Gonin).

314. *A. p. poecilorhyncha*, pair, ♀ on right, with browner plumage (including rear body), smaller red patch on bill and slightly paler iris. India, Dec (Kannan Sundararajan).

315. *A. p. haringtoni*; pointed and faintly fringed tertial coverts, very worn rectrices, pointed and fringed primary coverts, and mix of juvenile (pointed, fringed whitish) and formative (rounded, fringed pale buff) scapulars and flank feathers indicate this bird is in pre-formative moult. Hong Kong, China, Jan (Michelle & Peter Wong).

316. *A. p. poecilorhyncha*, adult ♂ (definitive basic). India, Dec (Sunil Singhal).

317. *A. p. poecilorhyncha*. India, Feb (Julien Gonin).

BLUE-WINGED TEAL
Anas discors

TAXONOMY *Anas discors* Linnaeus, 1766, *Syst. Nat.*, edn. 12(1), p. 205. Phylogenetically, morphologically and behaviourally very close to Cinnamon Teal *A. cyanoptera*[654,767,1094]. Analysis of mitochondrial DNA (cytochrome *b* and ND2)[654] showed very low divergence (0.19%) with North American populations of Cinnamon Teal *A. c. septentrionalium*. Blue-winged Teal, Cinnamon Teal and the four species of shovelers constitute the subgenus *Spatula*, and have bluish secondary upperwing-coverts in common. Birds of the North American Atlantic coast were considered a distinct subspecies (*A. d. orphna*, Stewart & Aldrich 1956), but its validity is rarely accepted (see Geographic Variation).

IDENTIFICATION Definitive basic and formative plumages of ♂ are distinctive and should not pose identification problems. Juvenile, ♀ and ♂ in alternate plumage (eclipse) are more difficult to identify, firstly because of their strong resemblance to similar plumages of Cinnamon Teal and, secondly, because of the existence of hybrids in the wild. In Eurasia, where Blue-winged Teal is a rare visitor, one must first eliminate ♀♀ and juvenile of other teals. Blue-winged Teal is slightly larger with a long somewhat spatulate bill, an oblong pale patch at the bill base and a large blue patch on the upperwing, highlighted by a white/pale wingbar, but no white trailing edge (vs. all other Eurasian teals).

Separation from Northern Shoveler *A. clypeata* is normally easy, this species being larger, stockier, has a much stronger and spatulate bill that is orange at least towards the base. Note also the warmer head and body, underwing without characteristic blackish leading edge, greyish upperwing-coverts (♀) and bright orange legs in Northern Shoveler (vs. yellow). Hybrid Blue-winged Teal × Northern Shoveler is much more problematic in its ♀ plumage (see Hybridisation), as is ♀ hybrid Cinnamon Teal × Northern Shoveler (see Hybridisation under Cinnamon Teal).

The main identification pitfall in female/juvenile plumage is undoubtedly posed by Cinnamon Teal, which is subtly larger and slightly stockier, especially the head/bill. The latter is thicker, longer and more spatulate in Cinnamon Teal, thus recalling slightly more the bill of Northern Shoveler. The head pattern is very important, and appears plainer and devoid of contrast in Cinnamon Teal, with a warmer reddish hue (especially to the cheeks). In Blue-winged Teal, the overall colour is grey. A broad, diffuse, round or oval patch is visible at the bill base and merges into the pale chin and throat, while in Cinnamon Teal this patch is often reduced to a rather thin crescent at the base of the bill. Blue-winged Teal has a clear dark eyestripe extending almost to the nape, whereas it is less marked in Cinnamon Teal, especially behind the eye. In Cinnamon Teal, the dusky patch on the ear-coverts is generally more pronounced than the eyestripe, the dark eyes being typically more obvious in the plain face. Blue-winged Teal has a near-complete obvious white eye-ring and a prominent pale supercilium, the latter interrupted above the eye, where the dark crown meets the white eye-ring. In Cinnamon Teal, the supercilium is part of the relatively plain face and the eye-ring is much less contrasting. The flanks are slightly different too, warmer and with scaly appearance less marked in Cinnamon Teal. Up close, the bill has pale orange at the base of the tomium in Cinnamon Teal, which is very inconspicuous or absent in Blue-winged Teal. The colour of the iris is paler brown (hazel) in Cinnamon Teal. Note that the juvenile ♂ of this species has a distinctive reddish iris from age two months, while plumage is still juvenile. These differences are subtle, but quite easy to judge with experience. ♂ Blue-winged Teal in full alternate plumage often has a plainer and slightly warmer coloured head[427]. For identification purposes, it is helpful to age the bird first.

Hybrid ♀ Cinnamon Teal × Blue-winged Teal appears not to have been described in the literature, while ♂♂ of this cross are regularly reported in North America. This is undoubtedly due to these two species strong similarity in ♀ and juvenile plumages, which obviously suggests that such hybrids go undetected.

PLUMAGES Strong sexual dimorphism from first winter onwards. Complex alternate moult strategy (see Moult). Ageing ♂♂ relatively easy until beginning of first winter and possible until end of subsequent summer under good viewing conditions or in the hand. ♀♀ harder to age from beginning of second calendar year.

Adult ♂

Definitive basic plumage (Jan–Mar/Jun–Jul). Small to medium-sized dabbling duck with proportionately long bill. Head dark violet-grey with chin, base of bill and cap blacker (thin yellow streaks on latter), and a contrasting white vertical crescent on the fore cheeks reaching above the lores, and sometimes extending as a thin white line along the crown towards the nape (see Geographic Variation). Iris warm brown, but may appear dark in low light and mahogany-red in direct sunlight. Bill slate-grey to blackish. Breast, flanks and belly yellowish to ochre-brown heavily spotted dusky and striped on upper flanks. Lower belly more whitish, also mottled, with two large round white patches on the femoral areas, visible when swimming. Under- and uppertail-coverts black. Rectrices fringed pale brown. Upperparts yellowish-buff with lower scapulars elongated, pointed, black and centred pale yellow. Back and rump yellowish-buff striped blackish. Tertials long, pointed, black on inner webs, dark grey on outer webs with a pale yellow line on the rachis and soft green sheen. Lesser and median coverts blue, greater coverts largely white-tipped (especially outer webs) forming a wingbar that broadens externally. Small number of adult ♂♂ show dark spots on greater coverts, including outer ones. Speculum black with clear green gloss on outer webs of innermost 6–7 secondaries. Rest of wing dark to blackish (except white rachis stripes on primaries). Underwing has axillaries and median coverts white, greater coverts pale grey, remiges medium grey and leading edge dark grey. Legs bright yellow with dull brown webs.

Definitive alternate plumage (Jul–Aug/Dec–Feb). Similar to basic plumage of adult ♀ but hint of white facial crescent is visible at many stages between Jul and following winter. The dark crown is generally more marked, and the rest of the head plainer, stained brownish and the supercilium barely visible. The breast often has a clear reddish-cinnamon hue. Also distinguished from ♀ by upperwing pattern (basic feathers retained except a variable number of inner coverts) and slightly more brightly coloured legs.

Adult ♀

Definitive basic plumage (Jan–Mar/Mar–May). Plumage cold and mottled grey-brown. Dark crown, dark eyestripe variably defined on lores, through eye and reaches dark nape. Striking white eye-ring. Supercilium and cheeks appear pale grey (beige with blackish vermiculations, white patch at base of bill, with chin and throat the same colour). Iris dark grey-brown. Bill dark grey with reduced pale orange near gape and broad blackish spots (variable), denser towards culmen. Breast

beige with strong blackish streaks. Scapulars blackish-brown with broad well-defined beige to whitish fringes, giving upperparts a scaly appearance. Flank feathers quite dull dark brown with pale brownish fringes and 'U'-shaped inner marks. Femoral coverts and undertail-coverts beige with clear dusky spots. Belly paler and less strongly mottled than surrounding parts. Back and uppertail-coverts dark brown fringed beige. Tail dark, vaguely barred, with white fringes to rectrices. Upperwing similar to ♂ but tertial coverts fringed whitish to pale brown, lesser and median coverts slightly duller blue (scattered dusky traces), tips of greater coverts with white fringes, to largely white with dark subterminal spots (Fig. 12), producing a variably visible white wingbar, sometimes like that of ♂ and often split in two on distal half. Soft green sheen to inner half of speculum (secondaries are fringed pale). Underwing as ♂ with leading edge appearing slightly paler, less black and speckled whitish. Legs marginally duller yellow.

Definitive alternate plumage (Apr–May/Dec–Feb). Very similar to basic plumage, but head and neck more buff-coloured, with more irregular dusky speckles/vermiculations. Bill darker with less visible dusky spots. Scapulars slightly larger, with fringes thinner and more buff or pale brown, and inner markings on both sides of rachis more obvious. Belly pale, coarsely stained brown. Femoral area paler. Undertail-coverts and rectrices more clearly barred.

Juvenile

First basic plumage (Jun/Oct–Feb). Like adult ♀, but more yellowish-brown throughout and less contrasting. Head vermiculated and patch at base of bill less clearly defined. Breast has reddish-buff hue, finely striped dark. Iris dull brown. Bill like ♀ in basic plumage but dark spots generally <1 mm in diameter. Flank feathers have inner marks and fringes less clear-cut and tinged pale yellowish-brown. Belly whitish with narrow lines of pale brown dots. Scapulars grey-brown finely fringed whitish and no inner markings (upperparts darker than adult ♀). Tertials short, slightly round-tipped, with pale brown fringes but no bronze or green sheen. Humeral area and undertail-coverts whitish with elongated, 'messy' brown markings. Legs greyish becoming yellowish-brown during first winter. Upperwing less contrasting than adult, lesser and median coverts dull greyish-blue with numerous dusky traces, and greater coverts largely white at tips (♂♂) or have little or no white (♀). Underwing lesser coverts darker than ad[1094]. Young ♀ distinguished from ♂ by pale patch at bill base marginally clearer (often slightly buff in young ♂), especially following auxiliary pre-formative moult in Jul–Aug. Sexing juveniles also possible based on inner half of speculum (ss5–10) having clear green gloss (♂) or very faint gloss (♀), and pattern of the greater coverts (beware of adult ♀ with pattern intermediate between those of young ♂ and young ♀). Note also pale fringes to tertial coverts, rather well defined in ♀ and interrupted at tips to almost absent in ♂.

First-winter ♂

Formative plumage (Jan–Mar/Jun–Jul). Pre-formative moult lasts several months and is often suspended temporarily. If ♂ characters are usually visible from early autumn, the plumage is similar to that of adult only during the first winter. At that time, moult ends with some inner wing-coverts and tertials. Those that are not replaced are shorter, rounded, and non-glossy but have clear and broad pale fringes. Juvenile tertial coverts are clearly fringed pale. After pre-formative moult, difficult to distinguish from adult ♂, except a few birds whose pre-formative moult is less extensive. The head generally has a duller hue, often without the purple sheen of adult ♂ and a variable number of undertail-coverts are pale brown. The upperwing is essentially juvenile until the second pre-basic moult, the lesser and median coverts being duller blue (note contrast between new and old feathers), the tips of the greater coverts slightly less white with black patches, and the green gloss to the inner secondaries softer and less extensive. Also note that inner secondaries tend to show clear whitish fringes towards the tips of outer webs, which are absent in adults. Finally, the belly is still partially juvenile at least, paler, and irregularly mottled or striped dusky. All these features, however, can require exceptional viewing conditions or an in-hand inspection.

First-winter ♀

Formative plumage (Jan–Mar/Mar–May). Pre-formative moult can be long-lasting, delayed and overlap with the beginning of pre-alternate moult. From midwinter, very like basic plumage of adult ♀. Distinguished mainly by the whitish belly, smaller dark spots on the bill (diameter <1 mm) and juvenile tertials shorter, frayed at the tips and washed brownish. Rectrices blackish, uniform (not vaguely barred) and fringed pale. Distinction is easier using wing pattern (until the second pre-basic moult), since, except for some inner secondary coverts, the wing feathers are still fully juvenile. The juvenile greater coverts are typically darker (Fig. 12) and those with broad white tips are usually adult, but both age classes can show a limited amount of white at the tips. Young ♀ usually shows no (or little) green gloss on inner half of speculum. In hand, look for contrast (colour and shape) between inner secondary coverts that have been replaced (formative) and the outer ones that are still juvenile.

GEOGRAPHIC VARIATION Birds in Texas and Louisiana were described as *A. d. albinucha*, Kennard 1919, on the basis of more pronounced white lines extending from white facial crescent along sides of the cap in basic plumage of adult ♂. Similarly, birds on North American Atlantic coasts were named *A. d. orphna*, Stewart & Aldrich, 1956, based on greyer and darker plumage, with black spots more marked on the underparts in definitive basic plumage of ♂[1235]. In both cases, these variations seem weak, prone to much overlap between populations and insufficient to merit subspecific distinction.

MEASUREMENTS and MASS ♂ and adult slightly larger and heavier than ♀ and young, respectively. ♂ (n=33): wing chord 182.9, tail 65.0, culmen 40.2, tarsus 32.2; ♀ (n=18): wing chord 174.3 (n=18), tail 63.9, culmen 39.1, tarsus 31.4[1235]. ♂ (n=34): wing chord 180–199 (187.6), tail 62.9–84.6 (73.5), culmen 37.7–44.7 (41.3), bill depth at distal edge of nostril 12.1–15.9 (13.7), bill width at distal edge of nostril 13.7–17.2 (15.7), tarsus 29.1–32.5 (30.5); ♀ (n=13): wing chord 171–186 (177.2), tail 66.9–81.4 (72.9), culmen 37.1–44.3 (39.6), bill depth at distal edge of nostril 12.1–14.5 (12.9), bill width at distal edge of nostril 14.1–15.7 (14.9), tarsus 29.1–31.2 (30.0)[1368]. Adult ♂: mass 427 (n=10) in autumn, 376 (n=9) in spring; juvenile ♂: mass 409 (n=14) in autumn, 388 (n=13) in spring; juvenile ♀: mass 388 (n=15) in autumn, 382 (n=6) in spring[1351]; ♂: mass 380 (± 35.7, n=110) in winter; ♀: mass 340 (± 28.1, n=82) in winter[1262]. Mass of ♀ fluctuates: from 329 (± 19.7, n=64) at end of incubation[784] to 422 (± 24.8, n=19) at start of incubation[1093].

VOICE Usually quiet, voice being unhelpful for identification. ♂ utters weak whistles, sometimes singly, sometimes in series or decrescendo, different from voice of ♂ Cinnamon Teal during courtship. ♀ gives a *quack*, higher-pitched than that of Northern Shoveler.

MOULT Complex alternate moult strategy very similar to Northern Shoveler (which see). An auxiliary pre-formative moult may occur between Jul and Sep in young birds. Pre-formative moult takes place between Sep and Mar–Apr, mainly on the wintering grounds, being temporarily suspended or slowed during migration. It mainly includes the body feathers (except a variable number of belly feathers), a variable number of inner secondary upperwing-coverts, 1–4 tertials and tertial coverts, and none to all rectrices (on average more in ♂[1014]). Definitive pre-alternate moult occurs between Mar and May in ♀, and Jun–Sep in ♂. It includes a variable number of body feathers (most upperparts), sometimes up to four tertials, but no upperwing-coverts or rectrices. A definitive pre-supplemental moult seems to occur in autumn, but further study is needed[1014]. Definitive pre-basic moult occurs from Sep to Jan–Mar in both sexes, starting with the wing feathers at moulting sites, then the rest of the body mainly on the wintering grounds. The longest scapulars are among the last to be replaced[1094].

HYBRIDISATION Natural hybridisation is relatively frequent with Cinnamon Teal and Northern Shoveler in North America and W Europe for the latter. Hybridisation involving Green-winged Teal *A. carolinensis* is rare in North America. These three hybrids are described below. A natural case has also been reported with American Wigeon *A. americana*[1190]. Hybridisation in captivity has been reported with Wood Duck *Aix sponsa*, Northern Pintail *Anas acuta*, Chestnut Teal *A. castanea*, Mallard *A. platyrhynchos* and Garganey *A. querquedula*[439,1190].

Blue-winged Teal × Northern Shoveler. The basic plumage of the adult ♂ of this hybrid strongly resembles Australasian Shoveler *A. rhynchotis*, which could escape from captivity in our region. Intermediate between the two parents in biometrics[227] and shape. Head and upper neck have dark green to purplish gloss, forehead and crown blackish, with a clear narrow vertical white crescent between the bill base and eye. Iris red-brown. Bill black, intermediate in size and shape, but still significantly spatulate. A white collar delimits the base of the dark head. Breast and upper flanks white to pale grey heavily spotted or vermiculated dark. Flanks and belly washed reddish (paler than Northern Shoveler) with dusky spots and/or streaks. Femoral coverts show as a clear round white patch. The longest scapulars are often closer to those of Northern Shoveler, black with broad white lines on the rachis. Legs yellow-orange. Slight variations occur in facial pattern, and that of the flanks and the anterior scapulars[439]. The ♀ of this hybrid is less well known, but generally has a bill with

a very straight culmen, visibly too thick basally, long in profile and to spatulate for Blue-winged Teal, but can resemble a Cinnamon Teal. Moreover, the base of the bill shows (always?) orange, easily visible. Note also the intermediate head pattern between the two species, slightly faded with warm colours for Blue-winged Teal. The upperwing pattern is distinctly bluish and could suggest Blue-winged Teal, especially in a Eurasian context. The legs are more orange (always?) than Blue-winged Teal. Faced by such an odd bird, it would be interesting to record the leading edge (lesser /marginal coverts) of the underwing, as they differ markedly between the two parents.

Blue-winged Teal × Cinnamon Teal. ♂ well known in North America and overall looks like Cinnamon Teal with its reddish, brown and black plumage. Distinguished by broader and darker eye-patch (with frequent blue tones) and hint of pale crescent between eye and bill (often white in front of eye and pale reddish near bill base, but variable, sometimes all white or completely light tan). Cheeks, neck, breast, flanks and belly pale reddish with dark spots and coarse vermiculations (sometimes absent) on lower flanks. Femoral area has large round whitish patches, sometimes pale reddish. Like many hybrids, variability may be linked with the male and female parent, respectively, the head pattern often resembling one and the body being closer to the other. Indeed, some birds have a pronounced white facial crescent and chest and flanks largely reddish, while others, with the head more reddish and only a faint crescent have the flanks more ochre-yellow and more heavily spotted. Gillham & Gillham[443] presented photographs of two hybrids (♂ and ♀) from backcrosses with Blue-winged Teal. ♂ best distinguished from Blue-winged Teal by chestnut hue to sides and top of head, white facial crescent partially washed pale reddish and somewhat stronger bill. The ♀ hybrid does not appear to have been described in the literature and would undoubtedly be a challenge to identify.

Blue-winged Teal × Green-winged Teal: distinctive hybrid well known in North America. Head pattern unique, with chin, bill base and forehead black, crown brown streaked black (like Blue-winged Teal), large dark eye-patch with green gloss extending towards nape and bounded by a whitish line (recalling Green-winged Teal), and a pale orange-brown area covering cheeks, upper neck and lores. The latter is often surrounded by white too, and sometimes divided into two by a white vertical line below the eye (bimaculated pattern). Iris dark brown. Bill dark slate, intermediate in size and shape. The underparts are grey-beige with well-defined marks on the central breast and narrow stripes on its sides. The flanks show a mix of feathers of both parents: whitish background with fine blackish vermiculations like Green-winged Teal and light tan background with dark strong stripes recalling Blue-winged Teal. Belly whitish and variably spotted, becoming thinly striped lower with a vertical white patch on the femoral region. Upper- and undertail-coverts black with a thin white line (variable) underlining the base of the tail at its sides. Feathers of mantle with fine ochre-yellow fringes and inner marks. Scapulars grey-brown. Upperwing has glossy green speculum and whitish wingbar formed by tips to greater coverts. Legs dull yellow with dark webs. Variation occurs, with some birds showing more contrast between breast (browner) and flanks (greyer), and longest scapular having a pale line on its centre. The ♀ of this cross does not seem to have been described in the literature, at least with a certified kinship.

HABITAT and LIFE-CYCLE Highly migratory, and among the last ducks to reach their breeding grounds. In North America, spring migration peaks in Apr and eggs are laid mainly between mid-May and mid-Jul. For breeding, prefers semi-permanent marshes with shallow-water areas and tall herbaceous vegetation. In dry years, uses largest wetlands, but usually shuns shrubby or wooded banks. ♂♂ and non-breeding ♀♀ move towards moulting grounds mainly in Jun, sometimes gathering in thousands. Others moult their flight feathers near the nest sites, including the vast majority of ♀♀ that breed successfully[827]. Autumn migration occurs mainly in Sep–Oct, i.e. earlier than the majority of Nearctic Anatidae. More eclectic habitat use during migration and winter, when found at a large variety of wetlands, from flooded rice fields and forested ponds to mangroves, brackish marshes and lake shores. However, tends to avoid areas devoid of vegetation, and deep or turbid waters[1094].

RANGE and POPULATION North American distribution centred on taiga belt with a few isolated populations further north, along coasts of S Hudson Bay and Newfoundland[1094], and in SE USA. Winters from S USA to N South America, with southern boundary between Peru and N Brazil, but a rare but regular visitor south of the Tropic of Capricorn. The bulk of the population is concentrated at a few large wetlands along the coast of the Gulf of Mexico. Regular vagrant to W Europe, south to NW Africa. Much rarer in the Pacific, with exceptional records in the Aleutians, Japan and Hawaii.

Estimates of the breeding population averaged 4,839,000 birds between 1955 and 2012, with an irregular increase, primarily since the early 1990s, and recent maxima of 9,242,000 individuals in 2012 and 7,732,000 in 2013[1294].

CAPTIVITY Fairly frequently kept and bred in captivity, even if the species is said to favour a more natural environment than many other species to breed. Usually among the least expensive duck species. The presence of this species in captivity can raise doubts concerning the origin of lone birds outside the usual range, although in W Europe most are considered genuine vagrants, which is supported by the pattern of occurrence (geographic and temporal), their ability to migrate (many birds that arrived in autumn head to Africa and return north in the subsequent spring with Northern Shovelers) and the fact that the species is rather frequent in the Azores.

REFERENCES Carney (1992)[224]; Childs (1952)[227]; Garner *et al.* (2008)[427]; Gillham & Gillham (1996)[439]; Gillham & Gillham (2002)[443]; Johnson & Sorenson (1999)[654]; Kennard (1919)[679]; Livezey (1991)[767]; Loos (1999)[784]; McHenry (1971)[827]; Pyle (2005)[1012]; Pyle (2008)[1014]; Rohwer (1986)[1093]; Rohwer *et al.* (2002)[1094]; Sibley (1938)[1190]; Stewart & Aldrich (1956)[1235]; Thompson & Baldassarre (1990)[1262]; USFWS (2013)[1294]; White *et al.* (1981)[1351]; Wilson *et al.* (2011)[1367]; Wilson *et al.* (2012)[1368].

318. Adult ♂ (definitive basic). Texas, USA, Feb (Sébastien Reeber).

319. Adult ♂ (definitive basic). Texas, USA, Feb (Sébastien Reeber).

320. Adult ♂ (definitive alternate) is very like ♀ or juvenile, but note black bill, glossy speculum and rusty tinge to face and breast (♂), as well as pointed tertials, new rectrices, and broad well-fringed scapulars and flank feathers (adult); some tertial coverts visible, black without fringes, also typical of adult ♂. New Jersey, USA, Sep (Sébastien Reeber).

321. ♂ (first basic/definitive alternate); note pale blue lesser and median coverts, and broad white wingbar on greater coverts, typical of adult ♂ but can also be shown by juvenile ♂. New Jersey, USA, Sep (Sébastien Reeber).

322. Adult ♀ (definitive basic/definitive alternate); in flight, the only other species with blue wing patches is Cinnamon Teal *A. cyanoptera*. Texas, USA, Mar (Greg Lavaty).

323. First-winter ♂ (formative); note still juvenile wing (faintly pale-edged tertial coverts, black spots on greater coverts) and scattered juvenile feathers (including on head). Texas, USA, Feb (Greg Lavaty).

324. Adult ♀ (definitive alternate); dark leading edge to underwing distinguishes this species from Northern Shoveler *A. clypeata*. New Jersey, USA, Sep (Sébastien Reeber).

325. Adult ♀ (definitive alternate/definitive basic); note adult tertials, two generations of body feathers and coarse speckling on face. New Jersey, USA, Sep (Sébastien Reeber).

326. ♀ (formative); note overall cold tones and contrasting head pattern, with pale patch at base of bill and almost complete white eye-ring. Texas, USA, Feb (Sébastien Reeber).

327. First-winter ♂ (first basic/formative), with narrow and faintly edged tertial coverts, glossy speculum, and almost white greater coverts (♂), and many juvenile rectrices. Florida, USA, Oct (Ron Bielefeld).

328. Adult ♀ (definitive alternate), with adult-type tertials, greater coverts, clean blue patch on wing, soft gloss to speculum and all rectrices moulted; bill shows large dusky spots. Florida, USA, Oct (Ron Bielefeld).

CINNAMON TEAL
Anas cyanoptera

TAXONOMY *Anas cyanoptera* Vieillot, 1816, *Nouv. Dict. Hist. Nat.*, Nouv. édn., 5, p. 104. Very close to Blue-winged Teal *A. discors* phylogenetically, morphologically and behaviourally[654,767,1094]. Five subspecies currently recognised, although just one occurs in the Holarctic, in North America (*A. c. septentrionalium*; see Geographic Variation).

IDENTIFICATION Basic plumage of adult ♂ cannot be confused, being the only largely reddish Holarctic species. ♂♂ in juvenile plumage aged more than 2–3 months and those in alternate plumage (eclipse) are more like ♀♀ and could be confused with same plumages of Blue-winged Teal. However, they all show a distinctive yellow-orange to bright red iris. ♀♀ are harder to distinguish from those of Blue-winged Teal (see latter species). ♀ and juvenile Northern Shoveler show some resemblance to Cinnamon Teal, but are easily distinguished by the much longer, stronger and more spatulate bill, often largely tinged orange at the base at least, face pattern slightly more contrasting and lesser and median coverts significantly greyer. The smaller size and yellow legs (not orange) of Cinnamon Teal are also useful. Hybrid ♂ Cinnamon Teal × Northern Shoveler is distinctive in definitive basic plumage, by dark head, frequently with green sheen and vertical whitish crescent in front of eye (shown by neither parent in same plumage; see Hybridisation below). Other plumages produced by this cross are less well described and would probably be much harder to distinguish from similar plumages of hybrid Blue-winged Teal × Northern Shoveler (see Hybridisation under Blue-winged Teal). The ♀-type plumage of this hybrid also constitutes a pitfall vs. Cinnamon Teal. Indeed, Cinnamon Teal and its hybrids are both intermediate between Blue-winged Teal and Northern Shoveler by size, bill shape and overall coloration.

PLUMAGES *A. c. septentrionalium.* Strong sexual dimorphism from first winter onwards. Complex alternate moult strategy (see Moult). Ageing ♂♂ relatively easy until early winter and possible until end of first summer under good viewing conditions or in the hand. ♀♀ harder to age from beginning of second calendar year.

Adult ♂

Definitive basic plumage (Oct–Dec/May–Jun).

Unmistakable. Medium-sized dabbling duck with a relatively long, strong bill. Head, neck, breast and underparts ochre-red to reddish-orange. Belly often freckled blackish. Forehead and crown darker, striped yellow and dark brown. Bill rather long and visibly spatulate, glossy black. Iris orange to red, sometimes yellow-orange. Feathers of mantle, back and rump dark brown with fringes and internal marks pale yellowish. Tertials long, pointed, dark with green to bronze sheen and white rachis line. Under- and uppertail-coverts black. Rectrices dark grey-brown fringed pale grey (tail appearing pale). Scapulars long and pointed, blackish with large pale yellow line along shaft. Upperwing similar to Blue-winged Teal, with lesser and median coverts bright blue, greater coverts broadly pointed, white, forming a wingbar that broadens outwardly, and black speculum with strong green gloss. Underwing like Blue-winged Teal, with a dark leading edge to secondary coverts. Legs yellow with dark brown webs.

Definitive alternate plumage (May–Jul/Sep–Nov). Similar to ♀, but appearance more 'disordered' and warmer, with crisp orange or reddish shades, especially on flanks, breast and sides of head. Also differs from ♀ (in all plumages) by its red-orange iris and largely white greater coverts.

Adult ♀

Definitive basic plumage (Oct–Dec/Feb–Mar). Head uniform, with slight reddish hue red absent in Blue-winged Teal, and eyestripe, loral stripe and pale supercilium barely contrasting. Brown vermiculations on face coarser. Crown dark, whereas bill base, throat and area around eye are paler. Bill dark grey with sides pale orange at the base. Iris brown. Breast and flanks tinged beige to pale reddish with base and subterminal marks dark brown, forming streaks on breast and 'V'- and 'U'-shaped marks on flanks. Fringes more coloured and centres to feathers less dark than Blue-winged Teal, thus flanks look more uniform. Belly whitish variably mottled brown. Feathers of mantle, scapulars and tertials dark, with longest feathers fringed beige-reddish with faint green to bronze sheen. Note that there is substantial variation between ♀♀ in overall coloration (more or less dark and/or reddish). Upperwing like ♂ but blue duller and marked with dusky, and less white on tips of greater coverts (Fig. 12 on p. 403), thus wingbar less striking. Inner secondaries with white fringes on outer webs and speculum has non-iridescent green sheen. Underwing like Blue-winged Teal. Legs yellow, duller than ♂, with dark webs.

Definitive alternate plumage (Feb–Mar/Oct–Dec). Similar to definitive basic plumage. Head and neck have dark vermiculations wider and crisper, tertials more brownish-red with broader buff fringes[113] and whitish belly usually heavily mottled or streaked brown.

Juvenile

First basic plumage (Jun/Sep–Jan). Similar to ♀ but overall coloration duller and somewhat washed out. Rear flanks and undertail less distinctly spotted dark, with diffuse 'messy' brown streaks. Close examination of wing useful for ageing, by duller speculum with soft (♂) or no green gloss (♀), narrower and rounded secondary coverts, lesser and median coverts duller blue with dusky traces (often noticeably barred), and greater coverts with more (♂) or less (♀) white at tips than adult ♀ (Fig. 12). Note general features related to age (width and colour of outer primaries, rectrices, etc.). Sexing juvenile is relatively easy as the orange-red colour of the iris of ♂ is usually visible from age of two months. The fore cheeks and feathers at the bill base are also often a visibly redder coloration in juvenile ♂. The lower scapulars are usually elongated and pointed, and the tertial coverts much more clearly pale-fringed in ♀. Finally, the dark markings on the rear body are diffuse and rounded in ♀ and rather arrow-shaped in ♂. Note that in Oct, juvenile often appears pale and uniform. It remains to be established whether this appearance is related to gradual wear of the feathers, to a delayed element of the first pre-basic moult or to head and body feathers being replaced as a part of an auxiliary pre-formative moult.

First-winter ♂

Formative plumage (Nov–Jan/May–Jul). Similar to definitive basic plumage, but overall duller reddish-brown with breast and flanks having variable mix of orange-reddish and pale brown feathers. Traces of juvenile plumage sometimes more obvious on belly, with clear pale freckles. Upperwing features still very useful as for juvenile, the wing feathers being retained except for a few inner secondary coverts (until second pre-basic moult).

First-winter ♀

Formative plumage (Nov–Jan/Feb–Mar). Identical to ♀ in definitive basic plumage, but slightly duller, often appearing 'messier' in autumn and early winter. The femoral area and undertail often show diffuse and ill-defined dark marks, whereas adult ♀ has crisper blackish spotting. Certain ageing often possible only based on upperwing pattern: shape and contrast in colour between inner (formative) and outer (juvenile) secondary-coverts, little or no white at tips of outer greater coverts, dull dark grey speculum without green gloss. Most juvenile ♀♀ retain some juvenile rectrices until first spring at least.

GEOGRAPHIC VARIATION Five subspecies currently recognised, including *A. c. septentrionalium* which is the only race in the Holarctic, and is described above, the other four occurring in South America. Subspecific differences are expressed mainly in size, sexual dimorphism in size and coloration of the speculum and, in adult ♂ (definitive basic plumage), the coloration of the head (crown and cheeks), breast and underparts, the extent of dark spotting on these parts and, in ♀, coloration of the upperwing (blue patch and speculum)[1366]. Based on colorimetric pairwise comparisons between subspecies, the same study[1366] demonstrated that the differences between *septentrionalium* and the other subspecies were five times greater than those among the South American subspecies.

A. c. septentrionalium is distinguished from the South American taxa by its more ochre coloration, the lack of dark spotting on underparts of ♂ and strong sexual dimorphism in size. The ♀ has the lesser and median coverts more blue, less purple. *A. c. tropica* (lower altitudes locally in Colombia) is the smallest subspecies with no sexual dimorphism in size. ♂ has underparts strongly spotted with black and blackish belly. ♀ dark. *A. c. borreroi* (high altitudes in Colombian Andes, possibly extinct). Medium-sized with fairly strong sexual dimorphism in size. ♂ less red, browner and darker with strong spotting on underparts. *A. c. orinomus* (Peruvian Andes in Chile and Bolivia). The largest subspecies, with a long bill. ♂ same colour as *septentrionalium* (rather pale). ♀ quite heavily mottled dark. *A. c. cyanoptera* (S South America). Medium-sized. ♂ has browner belly, rather darker and more chestnut or brown, sides and centre of breast mottled dark. ♀ quite pale.

MEASUREMENTS and MASS ♂ and adult slightly larger than ♀ and young, respectively. ♂ (*n*=50): wing chord 168–201 (189), tail 66.0–87.0 (80.5), culmen

42.5–47.9 (45.6), bill depth at distal end of nostril 12.3–15.1 (13.4), bill width at distal end of nostril 15.7–17.8 (16.8), tarsus 28.1–33.4 (31.0), mass 310–420 (361.8); ♀ (*n*=10): wing chord 171–187 (181), tail 67.0–86.0 (76.3), culmen 40.1–46.0 (43.1), bill depth at distal end of nostril 11.1–13.8 (12.6), bill width at distal end of nostril 15.0–17.4 (16.1), tarsus 29.2–34.9 (30.7), mass 315–430 (363.5)[1368]; compare data for Blue-winged Teal by same authors. See also Pyle[1014] for other measurements and Gammonley[413] for measurements of South American subspecies.

VOICE Quieter than many other waterfowl including Blue-winged Teal. ♂ gives different, short, rattling, repeated or single calls: *drrer*, soft, low, sometimes included in a phrase recalling rhythm of ♂ Northern Shoveler in courtship. Call of ♀ similar, but often louder and more nasal, often when taking off or when nervous or disturbed.

MOULT Complex alternate moult strategy very similar to Blue-winged Teal (which see), but timing earlier by 1–2 months on average (North American populations). An auxiliary pre-formative moult probably occurs in Jun–Sep, pre-formative moult in Sep–Feb, mainly on wintering grounds, pre-alternate definitive moult Jan–Mar in ♀, and May–Aug in ♂. Definitive pre-basic moult in Jul–Jan[1014].

HYBRIDISATION In the wild hybridises regularly with Blue-winged Teal (see Hybridisation under latter), and rarely but regularly with Northern Shoveler in North America (see below). Natural cases involving Green-winged Teal *A. carolinensis* seem much rarer in North America, and others involving Speckled Teal *A. flavirostris* and Red Shoveler *A. platalea* reported in South America. Hybrids resulting from latter crosses are obviously not expected in the Holarctic. Finally, in captivity cases have been reported with Wood Duck *Aix sponsa*, White-cheeked Pintail *A. bahamensis*, Eurasian Teal *A. crecca*, Baikal Teal *A. formosa* and Garganey *A. querquedula*[442,782,817].

Cinnamon Teal × Northern Shoveler. ♂ in definitive basic plumage usually has a dark green head with a well-defined white crescent between the eye (which is yellow-orange) and the black bill base, sometimes almost as broad as in ♂ Blue-winged Teal, and can extend above the eye and on chin. The breast is ochre-brown with small dark marks, flanks bright red (often with some dark stripes on their upper part), belly dark reddish-brown, fringes to upperparts more ochre-yellow. Beige to pale red patch on femoral area. Appearance is very close to Australasian Shoveler *A. rhynchotis*, albeit with a less spatulate bill, breast and flanks less spotted black and fringes to upperparts reddish. The ♀ of this cross is less frequently described and would be difficult to detect. Under good viewing conditions, the bill should nevertheless be different from those of both parents in size and shape, and its coloration unusual for Cinnamon Teal. See also Lockwood & Cooper[782].

HABITAT and LIFE-CYCLE Migrant (usually short-distance) or sedentary in some southernmost populations. Before many other species, breeding birds arrive as early as Feb in south of range, but until mid-May in the north. Eggs are laid between Apr and Jul (mainly May–Jun). Eclectic habitat choice, using all kinds of fresh wetlands, sometimes highly alkaline, with a preference for temporary or semi-permanent marshes with abundant floating vegetation and dense herbaceous cover on banks[413]. ♂ abandons ♀ early during incubation and usually moults in vicinity or sometimes migrates to specific moulting grounds. ♀♀ that raise young moult at the nest sites. Having moulted, ♂♂ move to wintering sites between mid-Sept and early Nov. In winter, inhabits same habitats as during breeding where species is sedentary, but also flooded crops, rice fields, coastal marshes, estuaries and tidal flats.

RANGE and POPULATION Subspecies *septentrionalium* breeds in North America and has its main wintering sites at large lagoons along coast of W Mexico[413]. Rare visitor to much of the rest of North America (regular along coast of Gulf of Mexico) and south to N South America. Records in W Europe and some from E North America are considered to represent escapes. Overall population of *A. c. septentrionalium* estimated at 260,000 individuals[1285], and is stable or slightly decreasing[209]. South American populations total <200,000 birds[378], including *A. c. borreroi* which does not seem to have been definitely recorded since the 1950s[144] and is possibly extinct.

CAPTIVITY Inexpensive and frequently kept in captivity, where it breeds readily and is said to frequently hybridise with Blue-winged Teal, to the point that it is recommended to keep them separately. It would be interesting to ascertain the subspecies involved in records outside known range. Only *A. c. septentrionalium* is likely to occur as a vagrant outside its range in the Holarctic.

REFERENCES BirdLife International (2013)[144]; Butcher & Niven (2007)[209]; Evarts *in* Kear (2005)[378]; Gammonley (2012)[413]; Gillham & Gillham (2000)[442]; Harrison & Harrison (1965)[522]; Johnson & Sorenson (1999)[654]; Livezey (1991)[767]; Lockwood & Cooper (1999)[782]; McCarthy (2006)[817]; Pyle (2008)[1014]; Rohwer *et al.* (2002)[1094]; Trost & Drut (2001)[1285]; Wilson & McCracken (2008)[1365]; Wilson *et al.* (2008)[1366]; Wilson *et al.* (2012)[1368].

329. *A. c. septentrionalium*, pair (definitive basic). California, USA, Nov (Tom Grey).

330. *A. c. septentrionalium*, adult ♀ (definitive basic); compared to Blue-winged Teal *A. discors*, note warmer plumage tones, plainer head and larger, more spatulate bill. California, USA, Dec (Sébastien Reeber).

331. *A. c. septentrionalium*, adult ♂ (definitive basic). California, USA, Dec (Sébastien Reeber).

332. *A. c. septentrionalium*, ♀. California, USA, Dec (Mike Danzenbaker).

333. *A. c. septentrionalium*, adult ♂ (definitive basic); note upperwing pattern, shared only with Blue-winged Teal *A. discors*. Texas, USA, Apr (Greg Lavaty).

334. *A. c. septentrionalium*, first-winter ♂ (formative), replacing its tertials, the old ones being juvenile; at same time, adult ♂ is usually in near-complete basic plumage. California, USA, Dec (Tom Grey).

NORTHERN SHOVELER
Anas clypeata   **Plate 35**

TAXONOMY Anas clypeata Linnaeus, 1758, *Syst. Nat.*, edn. 10, p. 124. Forms a clade with its three S Hemisphere counterparts: Red Shoveler *A. platalea* in South America, Cape Shoveler *A. smithii* in S Africa and Australasian Shoveler *A. rhynchotis* in Australia and New Zealand. These four species comprise the subgenus *Spatula* with Blue-winged *A. discors* and Cinnamon Teals *A. cyanoptera*[767]. Monotypic.

IDENTIFICATION Medium-sized dabbling duck, with stocky shape, the head often held hunched down at rest or when swimming. This typical shape combined with its massive and strongly spatulate bill make the species difficult to confuse with any other Holarctic species. Note also the strong wing rustling produced by adult ♂ when taking off. Blue-winged and Cinnamon Teals superficially resemble ♀♀ / juveniles by their slightly spatulate bill and blue wing-patches, but careful scrutiny should avoid any mistakes. Various hybrids involving Northern Shoveler in their ancestry have been reported in the wild, some of which could be misleading in plumages other than definitive basic and formative ♂.

PLUMAGES Strong sexual dimorphism from first winter. Complex alternate moult strategy (see Moult). Ageing ♂♂ is relatively easy until middle of the first winter and at least possible until end of subsequent summer under good viewing conditions or in the hand. Ageing ♀♀ harder from beginning of the second calendar year.

Adult ♂

Definitive basic plumage (Nov–Mar/May–Jun). Head and upper neck black with green gloss on rear cheeks. Iris golden-yellow. Bill very long, thick-based, with straight culmen in profile and strongly spatulate tip. Breast, lower neck and upper flanks white (except centre of hindneck, streaked black). Flanks red darkening towards belly. White spot on femoral area. Lower belly, undertail- and uppertail-coverts, rump and back black. Tertials long, pointed, black with clean white line on rachis (often extending onto outer web). Lesser and median coverts pale blue-grey, and broad white-tipped greater coverts (black bases usually hidden by median coverts). Clear green gloss to speculum (usually 7–9 glossy secondaries at least six). Rest of wing dark grey with white rachis lines on primaries. Underwing has

axillaries, lesser and median coverts white with pale brown spots on leading edge, greater coverts and remiges greyer, darkening towards trailing edge. Legs and feet bright orange.

Definitive alternate plumage (May–Jun/Dec–Mar). Quite different from plumages of adult ♀, with grey head finely vermiculated dark, eyestripe, crown and nape blackish. Iris often amber-yellow. Bill plain olive-brown to slate-brown, with sides (tomium) dull ill-defined orange-brown. Breast and flanks have feathers centred dark brown, broadly fringed beige to reddish-orange on flanks. Femoral and undertail-coverts brown, fringed whitish. Upperparts blackish-brown, often with soft green or bronze sheen, and sharp beige fringes. Basic wing feathers, part of back, rear body and belly retained. Legs orange.

Definitive supplemental plumage (Aug–Sep/Oct–Nov). The extent of this pre-supplemental moult seems to vary between individuals and needs further study. Compared to definitive alternate plumage, cheeks more mottled pale, around eye and base of bill blackish, with white crescent between eye and bill, sometimes sharply defined and sometimes reduced to a trace. Feathers of breast mainly white with blackish subterminal bands, flanks brown with broad rounded pale crossbars, femoral coverts white with blackish bars. Bill mainly black.

Adult ♀

Definitive basic plumage (Dec–Apr/Mar–May). Fairly uniform pale brown overall. Dark brown crown and dark eyestripe quickly fading behind eye. Iris dull yellow-brown, with olive or hazel hue. Bill orange with variable part of culmen dull slate-grey, but not clearly demarcated, and variable small dark spots. Rest of head and underparts beige with more or less buff tones and fine dusky vermiculations becoming streaks on breast. Flank feathers dark brown with beige, pale buff or pale brown fringes, belly hardly paler than flanks (unlike many other ♀ dabbling ducks). Feathers of mantle, back and scapulars dark brown fringed pale buff, affording scaly appearance. Tertials dark grey, blunt-tipped with clear pale fringe on inner web. Tertial coverts rounded and broadly fringed pale. Rectrices brown fringed pale (tail appears whitish at sides). Lesser and median coverts bluish-grey, variably fringed beige (broad to almost absent). Secondaries blackish with broad pale fringes at tips and soft green gloss on some feathers (SS2–10[224]). Legs orange.

Definitive alternate plumage (Apr–May/Dec–Apr). Very like definitive basic plumage, but slightly browner overall, especially upperparts, with broader pale fringes to body feathers, making this plumage appear a little more streaked. Belly more clearly mottled dark brown. Lesser and median coverts often appear greyer with wear. Definitive supplemental plumage, equivalent to ♂, if any, is undescribed.

Juvenile

First basic plumage (Jun/Jul–Aug). Similar to definitive basic plumage of ♀ but fringes to upperparts and flanks less crisp, their centres being duller brown without pale inner marks, thus appearing plainer overall. Dark centres to flank feathers often form diffuse longitudinal lines. Crown and nape uniform dark. Bill olive-brown with orange sides. Iris yellow-brown (♂) to grey-brown (♀). Femoral and undertail-coverts vaguely punctuated (♀) or barred (♂). Legs dull yellow or pale orange with dark webs. Tertials shorter, browner towards tips (which are rounded and quickly fray), fine pale fringes and rachis stripe barely visible. Tertial coverts narrow, often frayed and slightly pale-fringed. Lesser and median coverts bluish in young ♂ with dull brown bases, grey-brownish in young ♀. Sexing also possible based on green sheen to secondaries (at least five innermost in ♂

and 0–5 in ♀) and on greater coverts with white tips in ♂ (black bases not entirely concealed by median coverts) often with dark spot near tips on inner webs. In ♀, the white is reduced or restricted to the fringes (Fig. 12).

First-autumn ♂

Auxiliary formative plumage (Jul–Aug/Sep–Nov). Between juvenile and formative plumages, there is seemingly a plumage resulting from a limited to partial moult, equivalent to additional plumage of adult (♂ at least). However, it is unclear whether the feathers involved should be considered within a delayed part of first pre-basic moult, an advanced part of pre-formative moult, or its own auxiliary pre-formative moult. The plumage is characterised by the sides of the head and neck beige and finely vermiculated, with forehead, crown and eyestripe blackish. Scapulars round-tipped, dark brownish slightly fringed brown, making upperparts rather dark and uniform. Flanks and belly tinged reddish to warm hazelnut-brown, without scaly pattern of ♀. Back partly black with green sheen. Upper rump barred black and white, seemingly unique to this plumage. Two inner tertials round-tipped and uniformly dark, the next two with white on the shafts[330]. Iris yellow-brown, usually still distinct from adult.

First-autumn ♀

Auxiliary formative plumage (Jul–Aug/Sep–Nov?). Extent of auxiliary pre-formative moult poorly known

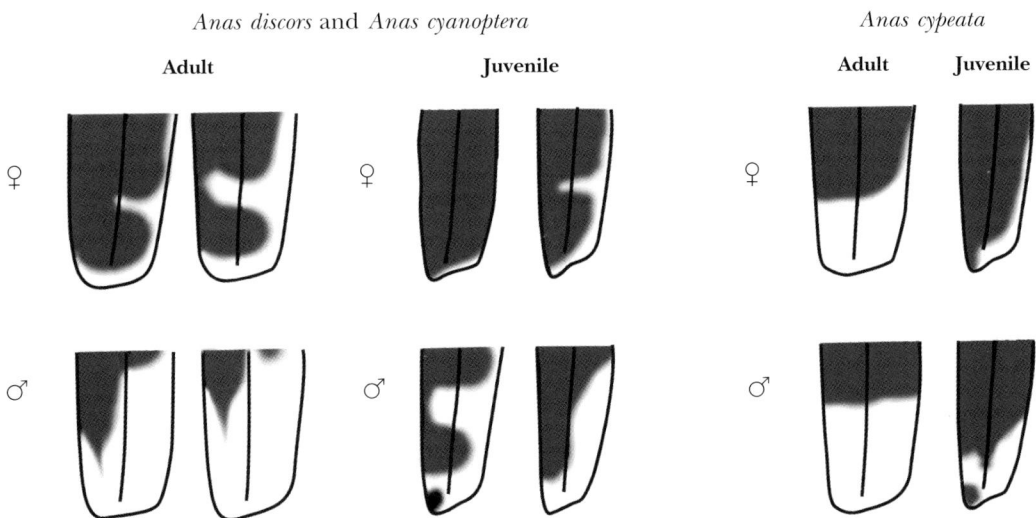

Fig. 12: Shape and coloration of outer greater upperwing-coverts by age and sex in Northern Shoveler *Anas clypeata*, Blue-winged Teal *A. discors* and Cinnamon Teal *A. cyanoptera*.

in ♀, but leads, in any case, to a plumage much like formative and definitive basic. Note paler fringes on upperparts[330], belly and undertail-coverts regularly spotted brown (forming longitudinal streaks) and two innermost tertials with fine white fringes[945].

First-winter ♂

Formative plumage (Oct–Mar/May–Jun). Pre-formative moult is protracted until early spring, with some intermediate stages resembling definitive additional plumage of ♂, often with a pale crescent in front of eye. Ageing possible as upperwing pattern still juvenile (until second pre-basic moult), feathers of rump often fringed pale, small white patch in front of folded wing (unique to this plumage?), and inner secondaries well-fringed white towards tips of outer webs (no fringe in adult). Iris often amber-yellow at six months, and yellow by end of first winter. The bill, initially orange with olive-brown tones, becomes black at age *c.*10 months[330]. Note that acquisition of formative plumage (in young) occurs later than acquisition of definitive basic plumage (adult). From early winter, formative plumage differs by some pale grey and barred undertail-coverts, often a pale crescent in front of eye, a few dark feathers mixed with white feathers of breast, lower belly blackish speckled white and shorter tertials, less pointed and duller (often without green sheen).

First-winter ♀

Formative plumage (Oct–Apr/Feb–May). Ageing difficult from middle of first winter, as formative plumage is very similar to definitive basic plumage. The best features are on upperwing (until second pre-basic moult), including lesser and median coverts being worn and grey-brown, greater coverts with little or no white at tips (Fig. 12), and secondaries with green gloss lacking or reduced (at most to s6).

GEOGRAPHIC VARIATION None described, despite huge range and largely allopatric populations. Apparently, no significant differences between North American and European birds in measurements.

MEASUREMENTS and MASS North America. ♂ and young larger than ♀ and young, respectively. ♂ (n=72): wing chord 235–255 (adult) and 229–248 (juvenile), tail 76–90, culmen 60–71, bill depth at tip of forehead feathering 18.9–23.9, tarsus 35–42; ♀ (n=67): wing chord 223–242 (adult) and 216–235 (juvenile), tail 68–84, culmen 57–66, bill depth at tip of forehead feathering 17.8–22.7, tarsus 33–40[1014]. Adult. ♂ (n=40):

culmen 65.2, max. bill width 29.8, nail width 5.68; adult ♀ (n=12): culmen 60.5, max. bill width 28.4, nail width 5.70[329]. Europe. ♂: wing chord 247 (adult, n=38) and 238 (juvenile, n=66), tarsus 37.5 (n=30), mass in winter 636 (adult, n=36) and 598 (juvenile/first-winter, n=66); ♀: wing chord 230 (adult, n=24) and 228 (juvenile, n=46), tarsus 36.2 (n=14), mass in winter 577 (adult, n=23) and 555 (juvenile/first-winter, n=46). Data from WWT[853]; ♂: wing chord 239–249 (adult, 244, n=27) and 227–251 (juvenile), 235, n=66), bill length from tip of forehead feathering 62–72 (66.1, n=61), tarsus 35–40 (37.2, n=48); ♀: wing chord 222–237 (adult, 230, n=18) and 213–229 (juvenile, 222, n=29), bill length from tip of forehead feathering 56–64 (60.7, n=47), tarsus 35–38 (36.0, n=39)[267].

VOICE During courtship, ♂ utters dry *khuk* or *tshuk*, given alternately (*tshuk-huk*) in fast rhythm, e.g. during pursuit of ♀, while stretching and lowering the neck. ♀ gives different types of *quack* notes, often descending.

MOULT Complex alternate moult strategy. An auxiliary pre-formative moult is reported in Jul–Oct in young birds and involves some head and body feathers, inner upperwing-coverts and some rectrices. This moult seems more extensive in this species, Blue-winged and Cinnamon Teals (perhaps especially ♂♂) than in all other Holarctic ducks, but its extent remains to be ascertained[1012,1014]. Pre-formative moult occurs between Sep and Jan (sometimes until Mar) in ♂ and until Mar–Apr in ♀, and is often paused or slowed during migration. It involves a large proportion of the head and body feathers (except part of the belly and back), some inner secondary coverts, 1–4 tertials and tertial coverts, and none to all rectrices (on average more in ♂). Rarely, in some ♂♂, this pre-formative moult is so reduced (or even almost absent) that the plumage is like auxiliary, but extremely pale and worn until next pre-basic moult. Definitive pre-alternate moult occurs from mid-Feb to mid-May in ♀ and Jun–Aug in ♂. It includes some head and body feathers, and a variable number of rectrices and tertials. Definitive pre-basic moult starts with the remiges between mid-Jun and Aug in ♂ and on average *c.*1 month later in ♀. It ends later than in many ducks, between Dec and Mar in ♂, although many birds have largely basic plumage by mid-Nov, and *c.*1 month later in ♀. A definitive pre-supplemental moult occurs in adults (at least ♂) in autumn, but more research is required to define its extent, especially in ♀.

HYBRIDISATION Natural hybridisation is reported

frequently with Blue-winged Teal and Cinnamon Teal in North America, and sometimes in Europe for the former (see these two species respectively). Reports involving Mallard A. *platyrhynchos*, Gadwall A. *strepera* and Garganey A. *querquedula* are rarer in the wild (see below). Hybrids including Northern Pintail A. *acuta*[465], Baikal Teal A. *formosa*[947], Eurasian Teal A. *crecca*[439], Green-winged Teal A. *carolinensis*, American Wigeon A. *americana* and Eurasian Wigeon A. *penelope*[439,517,518] are much rarer in nature, but are reported occasionally. Adult ♂♂ in basic plumage generally have a dark head with two clear pale patches on fore and rear cheeks (bimaculated pattern). Also reported in the wild, hybrids with Red Shoveler[817] are very unlikely in the Holarctic. Mixed breeding has been reported in captivity with Muscovy Duck *Cairina moschata*, Wood Duck *Aix sponsa*, Falcated Duck *Anas falcata*, Mottled Duck A. *fulvigula*, Ringed Teal *Callonetta leucophrys*, Redhead *Aythya americana* and Ferruginous Duck A. *nyroca*[97,817].

Northern Shoveler × Gadwall. A hybrid whose ♂ in definitive basic plumage is distinctive and unlike any other species. Head and upper neck blackish often with reddish-brown tones on crown, and green gloss on rear cheeks, contrasting sharply with whitish-beige area over much of rest of cheeks (except black bill base), lores and throat. A vertical dark line is often visible under the eye (bimaculated pattern). Black bill obviously spatulate at tip. Breast, flanks, mantle and scapulars pale grey-brown finely streaked (breast) or vermiculated dark, with scattered reddish patches (variable). Longest scapulars elongated, pointed and pale (recalling Gadwall) or white-centred (like Northern Shoveler). Tertials intermediate, often slightly curved, sometimes white-centred. Ill-defined white area on femoral coverts. Back, rump and uppertail-coverts black. Rectrices fringed white. Belly has an often well demarcated whitish oval patch. Lesser and median coverts grey to grey-brown, tips to outer median and greater coverts pale, sometimes tinged reddish. Speculum black with green reflections on inner half (always?). Legs orange. The ♀ does not appear to have been described in the literature to date.

Northern Shoveler × Mallard. Rarely reported hybrid, but distinctive. Adult ♂ in basic plumage distinguished by head and upper neck black with strong green gloss, long spatulate bill, black with diffuse yellow patches near tip and at base of culmen (which is sometimes extensively yellow), breast pale reddish, flanks ochre with greyish tones on upper part, belly slightly paler,

scapulars dark grey-brown fringed pale grey, crisp white spots on femoral area, and tertials broad and pale grey. Rear body black with white-fringed rectrices. Some birds show a white collar[439]. Few data available on ♀ of this hybrid.

Northern Shoveler × Garganey. A few reports in the wild in W Europe. Intermediate in size, adult ♂ in basic plumage has a dark head (black with pale green sheen), pale reddish-brown breast gradually merging into flanks, which are greyer and vermiculated at rear and upper part. Bill clearly spatulate. Upperparts closer to those of Garganey, with long, pointed, white-centred grey scapulars. Rear body dark mottled pale, undertail-coverts vermiculated white and black. This type of bird clearly has a head closer to Northern Shoveler and a body closer to Garganey, but the reverse is probably possible as well.

HABITAT and LIFE-CYCLE Very broad range and inhabits a wide variety of wetlands, from Mediterranean marshes to Arctic tundra. Timing of migration and breeding depends on latitude, but in most regions the species is a late spring and early autumn migrant. Eggs are laid mainly between mid-May and mid-Jun in N Russia[853] and North America[330], but by late Mar in S Europe. Wetlands used for breeding include flooded meadows, and shallow freshwater temporary or permanent marshes, usually lined with tall, dense herbaceous vegetation (grasses, sedges, cattail, reeds). The species requires a sufficient area of open water, shuns heavily wooded banks and prefers waters with abundant aquatic invertebrates. Also frequents rice fields, artificial lakes and fish ponds[330,853]. ♂♂ do gather to moult at favoured sites, but this is generally less frequent than in many other dabbling ducks[330]. Indeed, many ♂♂ moult their remiges near the nesting grounds or with ♀♀ and their broods. Moves south to the wintering grounds once able to fly again. On migration and in winter, uses same habitats, preferring flooded meadows and shallow marshes, but also found in coastal lagoons, brackish marshes and tidal flats. Also feeds in deep water, on surface plankton, the birds swimming with their bill ajar below the surface of the water. In shallow water, up to two dozen birds form a tight group that turns on itself. The birds then filter the water whose turbidity was increased by the circular movement.

RANGE and POPULATION Holarctic range, with a few isolated breeding populations south of mapped area.

World population estimated at 5,500,000–6,000,000 birds[305], but probably currently closer to 6,500,000 of which *c*.40,000 birds winter in W Europe, 450,000 in Black Sea, Mediterranean and W Africa, and 400,000 in SW Asia and E Africa, these populations appearing to be stable or slightly declining since the 1980s[305]. In S Asia, population estimated at 500,000–1,000,000[755] but reliability of counts needs to be improved, and *c*.500,000 in E Asia[757]. North American population close to 2,000,000 birds between the 1950s and early 1990s, but closer to 4,000,000 birds during current decade, peaking at 5,018,000 birds in 2012 and 4,751,000 in 2013[1294].

CAPTIVITY Fairly frequently encountered in captivity, and quite affordable, but may require grassy areas to breed. The question of escapes rarely arises, as it is a common species over much of the Holarctic.

REFERENCES Bird Hybrids database (2014)[97]; Carney (1992)[224]; Cramp & Simmons (1977)[268]; Delany & Scott (2006)[305]; Dubowy (1987)[329]; Dubowy (1996)[330]; Gillham & Gillham (1996)[439]; Gray (1958)[465]; Harrison (1959)[517]; Harrison (1964)[518]; Li & Mundkur (2004)[755]; Li *et al.* (2009)[757]; Livezey (1991)[767]; McCarthy (2006)[817]; Mitchell *in* Kear (2005)[853]; Palmer (1976)[945]; Panov (1989)[947]; Payn (1941)[954]; Pyle (2005)[1012]; Pyle (2008)[1014]; USFWS (2013)[1294].

335. Adult ♂ (definitive basic). France, Feb (Sébastien Reeber).

336. Adult ♂ (definitive basic); note adult wing pattern, with bluish forewing patch and greater coverts almost all white. California, USA, Nov (Sébastien Reeber).

337. Adult ♀ (definitive basic); this sex has variable spotting on bill; best aged by upperwing pattern, here by clear bluish hue to coverts. France, Feb (Sébastien Reeber).

338. Adult ♂ (definitive supplemental/definitive basic); at least some feathers (e.g., head and flanks) are not part of basic or alternate plumage, and could represent part of pre-supplemental moult. California, USA, Nov (Sébastien Reeber).

339. Juvenile ♂ (first basic); note overall dull juvenile plumage including scapulars, tertials, tertial coverts and greater coverts typical of this age, as well as dull bare parts and dark iris; sexed by glossy green speculum, yellowish iris, ill-defined pale fringes to tertial coverts and white-tipped greater coverts. France, Aug (Sébastien Reeber).

340. First-winter ♂ (auxiliary formative/formative); many young ♂♂ have not finished their pre-formative moult by Feb; note dusky base to blue-grey median coverts, narrow, pale-fringed tertial coverts and dark iris. France, Feb (Sébastien Reeber).

NORTHERN PINTAIL
Anas acuta   **Plate 36**

TAXONOMY *Anas acuta* Linnaeus, 1758, *Syst. Nat.*, edn. 10, p. 126. Forms a clade with Eaton's Pintail *A. eatoni*, of the Kerguelen Is and formerly considered a subspecies of Northern Pintail, Yellow-billed Pintail *A. georgica* from South America, White-cheeked Pintail *A. bahamensis* of Central and South America, and Red-billed Duck *A. erythrorhyncha* in Africa[654]. These species form the subgenus *Dafila* Stephens, 1824, which also comprises Speckled Teal *A. flavirostris* and Andean Teal *A. andium*[767]. Monotypic.

IDENTIFICATION Large dabbling duck, with bill, neck, body and tail typically long and thin, affording it a unique elegant look, including in flight. Basic plumage of adult ♂ cannot be mistaken. Other plumages recall those of other ♀ *Anas* in their brown and spotted coloration, but are usually easily distinguished by size and shape, as well as by the dark grey bill, grey legs, white belly and dark grey speculum bordered by two large pale wingbars. Moreover, note the remarkably uniform head coloration, in which the dark eye is frequently obvious.

PLUMAGES Strong sexual dimorphism from first winter onward. Complex alternate moult strategy (two plumages per definitive cycle, three in first cycle). Ageing ♂♂ easy until beginning of first winter and possible in good viewing conditions or in the hand until second pre-basic moult (subsequent summer). Ageing ♀♀ harder from first winter onwards, requiring close scrutiny of the upperwing.

Adult ♂

Definitive basic plumage (Oct–Nov/May–Jul). Head and upper neck uniform dark brown, with purple sheen on rear cheeks and fine dark streaks on crown and nape. Iris dark brown, rarely hazelnut. Bill long, pale blue with clear-cut black base, culmen, tomium and nail. Underparts, breast and lower neck white, extending as a fine vertical line colour the neck-sides. Flanks, mantle and anterior scapulars whitish finely vermiculated black. Belly white, but often tinged ochre-yellow or even red, depending on the mineral substrate on wintering grounds. Femoral area pale yellowish. Posterior scapulars long, pointed and drooping, pale grey and centred black. Tertials of same coloration, rather long, pointed and even-coloured. Feathers of back and rump pale grey, centred blackish in latter. Undertail-coverts

black. Uppertail-coverts form beige and black bands at base of tail. Tail has central rectrices very long and black, the others forming white areas at the sides. Entire upperwing grey (same as flanks and mantle), except broad pale reddish band formed by tips to greater coverts, black speculum with clear green gloss (can seem bronze or purple) and broad white trailing edge (often somewhat reddish distally). Underwing has large dark grey-brown area on leading edge, with a white central area (posterior median coverts and axillaries, the latter with grey-brown vermiculations on shafts), and lesser and greater coverts grey with broad white crescents on tips. Legs pale grey with darker webs.

Definitive alternate plumage (Jun–Jul/Sep–Oct). Closer to ♀ but nevertheless easily separated by paler breast (white and spotted) and flank feathers grey-beige with dark brown crescents affording a barred effect (rather than scaly). Upperparts often show a mix of alternate scapulars (black barred white) and basic scapulars (pale grey vermiculated). Also distinguished from ♀ by bill having more clear-cut coloration, tertials pale grey, long and pointed (centred black) and central rectrices longer. The centre of the tail (central rectrices and corresponding uppertail-coverts) is darker than the sides.

Adult ♀

Definitive basic plumage (Nov–Dec/Feb–Apr). Head, neck, breast and flanks pale yellowish-brown, almost whitish on throat, foreneck, centre of breast and belly. Sides and top of head are rather plain (no eyestripe or supercilium, the eye being the only contrasting character) and warmer brown. Head and breast finely vermiculated or streaked brown. Bill lead-grey with variable blackish on culmen and pale blue pattern like that of ♂ more or less well defined (age-related?). Iris dark brown. Feathers of flanks have dark inner arrow marks and subterminal 'U'-shaped marks. Scapulars dark brown with pale buff to reddish-beige fringes and inner marks. Tertials dark grey fringed white, with diffuse pale yellowish-brown inner marks (variable, sometimes lacking). Rear flanks, lower belly and undertail-coverts whitish with dark spots forming streaks. Feathers of back and rump dark brown fringed white. Rectrices dark brown, barred pale and fringed white. Upperwing like that of ♂ but lesser and median coverts browner with crisp pale fringes, greater coverts have whitish tips, outer secondaries with outer webs brown and soft bronze sheen (rarely green) to speculum and broad white trailing edge. Underwing like adult ♂ but more heavily spotted dark and median coverts and axillaries whitish clearly barred brownish. Legs grey with dark webs.

Definitive alternate plumage (Mar–Apr/Oct–Nov). Similar to definitive basic plumage, but more strongly streaked and less uniform, slightly more brown or reddish overall, with belly on average more mottled dark. Pale fringes and inner marks to flank feathers and upperparts, especially the scapulars, more pronounced. Breast darker and heavily streaked. The central alternate tertials are straighter, pointed, with often heavily marked whitish to buff indentations. Rectrices distinctly barred and have reddish-buff fringes. The two central rectrices are broader and shorter than in definitive basic plumage[43].

Juvenile

First basic plumage (Jun/Nov-Jan). As adult ♀ but scapulars and flank feathers more pointed with less contrasting dark centres, darker (tan to pale brown) and narrower fringes. Belly beige with narrow regular streaking formed by dark centres to feathers (especially in young ♀). Tertials grey-brown fringed buff at tip. Outermost tertial has inner web blackish in ♂. Lesser and median coverts narrow and rather pointed, fringed grey-beige (at least over central part[333]), greater coverts have narrow reddish tips, speculum has pale green or bronze sheen, black subterminal band and trailing edge white to pale buff, narrower than adult. Upperwing pattern of juvenile ♀ differs in buff tips to greater coverts are reduced and gloss on speculum is faint or lacking. Axillaries whitish and vermiculated in young ♂, well spotted or barred in young ♀ (and some ♂♂[224]). An auxiliary pre-formative moult occurs in Jul–Sep, leading to a plumage very close to juvenile, but head, neck and breast more heavily streaked dark, giving head a less uniform appearance (dark crown and eyestripe visible). Central rectrices distinctly darker than outer ones.

First-winter ♂

Formative plumage (Nov–Dec/May–Jul). Similar to basic plumage of adult ♂, but acquired on average *c.*1 month later[43], and not until midwinter in latest individuals (whose frequency seems higher in southern wintering populations). It seems that birds with tertials still growing after Nov are almost always young[224]. Once

pre-formative moult completed, differs from adult ♂ by variable number of worn and brown juvenile feathers on belly and especially among black undertail-coverts. Also note that iridescence on head-sides, speculum and tertials is usually less bright than in adult, and that central rectrices and longest scapulars are distinctly shorter. Further distinguished from adult ♂ by upperwing pattern (until second pre-basic moult), especially the juvenile lesser and median coverts being narrower, pointed, frayed at tips and fringed pale (broad, rounded or square tips, and plain grey in adult). Also look for tertial coverts that might not have been replaced, being pointed, brownish and fringed beige.

First-winter ♀

Formative plumage (Dec–Jan/Feb–Apr). Very like adult ♀ after pre-formative moult, which ends in early winter. Traces of juvenile plumage often obvious on belly (appears finely streaked pale brown), even if some juvenile scapulars and flank feathers are sometimes also retained until first pre-alternate moult in subsequent spring. However, the most reliable ageing features are on the upperwing (until second pre-basic moult), which requires detailed inspection (in the hand or very good viewing conditions). Note juvenile lesser and median coverts, trapezoidal and pointed, and, on some feathers, pale lateral indentations joining the pale fringes. In adult ♀ the pale inner marks can be present, but never connect with the fringe. The retained tertial coverts are narrower, worn at the tips, duller with pale fringes slightly marked.

GEOGRAPHIC VARIATION None.

MEASUREMENTS and MASS ♂ slightly larger than ♀, but adult and young very close in size. No significant differences found in measurements between Nearctic and Palearctic. North America. ♂: wing chord 261–294 (adult, 274.5, n=189) and 260–279 (juvenile, 266, n=25)[43], culmen 44.3–59.8 (51.2, n=191)[43], tail 162–223 (187, n=12)[945], tarsus 49.8–57.3 (53.7, n=191)[43], mass in autumn/winter 605–1,245 (adult, 1,006, n=188) and 640–1,110 (juvenile/first-winter, 961, n=26)[43]; ♀: wing chord 225–275 (adult, 255.3, n=150) and 244–265 (juvenile, 252, n=40)[43], culmen 40.4–50.8 (46.8, n=152)[43], tail 98–112 (101, n=12)[945], tarsus 46.8–53.2 (50.1, n=152)[43], mass in autumn/winter 615–1,100 (adult, 887, n=151) and 515–920 (juvenile/first-winter, 715, n=114)[43]. Europe. ♂: wing chord 268–281 (adult, 275, n=20) and 252–286 (juvenile, 269, n=101)[1122], culmen 47–56 (50.9, n=55)[267], tarsus 40–45 (42.6,

$n=40)^{267}$; ♀: wing chord 247–265 (adult, 258, $n=12$) and 238–273 (juvenile, 254, $n=126)^{1122}$, culmen 44–51 (46.7, $n=31)^{267}$, tarsus 39–43 (41.0, $n=30)^{267}$.

VOICE The ♂ gives a soft but loud *drroob* and also a more discreet *Dendrocygna*-like *sweee-wuu*. The ♀ utters several quacking notes like that of Mallard, but usually lower pitched and softer.

MOULT Complex alternate moult strategy. An auxiliary pre-formative moult is reported between Jul and Sep in young birds, involving an unknown proportion of head, body, inner wing and some tail feathers, but questions remain as to the definition of this moult (see Introduction). Pre-formative moult occurs between Aug and Nov–Dec (slightly later in ♀). It includes many body feathers (lower proportion on belly, back, rump and uppertail-coverts), a small number of inner secondary coverts, 0–4 tertials and tertial coverts, and none to all rectrices (more extensive in ♂ than in ♀)[56,1014]. Definitive pre-alternate moult occurs Jan–Apr in ♀ and May–Jul in ♂. It includes some upperparts feathers and a variable number of inner upperwing-coverts, rectrices and tertials. Definitive pre-basic moult starts with the remiges in Jun in ♂ at sites dedicated to moult and on average *c*.1 month later in ♀. It is completed in Oct–Nov with the body feathers, ending with tertials, ornamental scapulars and central rectrices, mostly on wintering grounds. Note that in North America, it has been shown that wet autumns permit earlier acquisition of definitive basic plumage[846,1212].

HYBRIDISATION Crosses reported occasionally with Eurasian Wigeon *A. penelope*, American Wigeon *A. americana*, Mallard *A. platyrhynchos*, Gadwall *A. strepera*, Eurasian Teal *A. crecca* and Green-winged Teal *A. carolinensis* (see below). Hybrids with Baikal Teal *A. formosa*[226,817] and Red-crested Pochard *Netta rufina* are even rarer (see these species respectively). Natural hybridisation has been reported much more infrequently with American Black Duck *A. rubripes*[16], Pacific Black Duck *A. superciliosa*[817,1190], Yellow-billed Duck *A. undulata*[465], Northern Shoveler *A. clypeata*[817], Garganey *A. querquedula*[465,947], Common Pochard *Aythya ferina*[465] and Common Eider *Somateria mollissima*[996]. In captivity, hybridises readily, hybrids or mixed pairs reported with Paradise Shelduck *Tadorna variegata*[1231], Wood Duck *Aix sponsa*, Chiloe Wigeon *Anas sibilatrix*[439], Meller's Duck *A. melleri*, Indian Spot-billed Duck *A. poecilorhyncha*[465], White-cheeked Pintail[439,1190], Cape Teal *A. capensis*[439], Yellow-billed Pintail[465,1190], Chestnut Teal *A.*

castanea [465], Blue-winged Teal *A. discors*[465,639], Speckled Teal[1190], Rosy-billed Pochard *Netta peposaca*[465,817], Redhead *Aythya americana*[439,817], Tufted Duck *A. fuligula*[588] and Ferruginous Duck *A. nyroca*[588,817].

Northern Pintail × Eurasian Wigeon. Very rarely reported, mostly in N Europe. Adult ♂ in basic plumage has an intermediate shape with a variegated head, black base of bill, throat, upper neck, nape and wide eye-band (green sheen on latter), wide yellowish to beige patches on cheeks extending in front of eye, separated by a vertical line across the cheeks just behind eye. This is typically a cross where an obvious bimaculated pattern is shown despite being absent in both parents. However, it seems obvious especially in young birds[443]. The centre of the crown is often red-ochre (variable). Bill similar to Northern Pintail, but shorter. Breast pale peach, flanks and upperparts similar to Northern Pintail, pale grey vermiculated black, longest scapulars centred black and broad white patches on femoral areas. A pale vertical bar can be visible on the fore flanks[441]. Rear body as in both parents. Tail intermediate but two central rectrices rarely elongate. Plumage of ♀ unknown, but some published photographs show gyandromorphic plumages and ♂♂ in definitive alternate plumage[443].

Northern Pintail × American Wigeon[415]. Very rarely reported. Adult ♂ in basic plumage resembles previous hybrid, with a shape closer to Northern Pintail and, especially, central rectrices very long, which seems unique among hybrids involving Northern Pintail[441]. Rear body as both parents, flanks and upperparts grey vermiculated but with brownish tone, breast pinkish merging into flanks and upperparts, with (always?) a pale pinkish line across fore flanks. Head mainly black with green sheen on eye-band and two pale diffuse patches on cheeks, separated by a black vertical bar. Reddish-brown crown at least sometimes framed by two thin buff lines[441]. Axillaries white with some light grey speckling, whereas they are more coarsely vermiculated grey-brown in hybrid with Eurasian Wigeon[441]. Bill similar to Northern Pintail, but shorter and black often interrupted on culmen. In flight, upperwing has tips of greater coverts reddish as in Northern Pintail, but broad pale grey patch on lesser and median coverts, recalling white pattern of adult ♂ American Wigeon. Note that ♀♀ from cross between Northern Pintail and one of the wigeons seem to show a number of ♂-type feathers. Gillham & Gillham[441] stated that the ♂ of this hybrid has a call similar to American Wigeon, while ♀ calls like Northern Pintail.

Northern Pintail × Mallard. Regularly reported in wild, in Europe as well as in Asia and North America. Adult ♂ in basic plumage has shape similar to Northern Pintail, but typically has the two central rectrices elongated and curved upwards. Head all dark with brown tones visible on cheeks and green or purple sheen behind eye and sometimes over entire face. Bill like that of Northern Pintail, but with black culmen, nail and tomium less clear-cut. Breast pinkish-brown bordered by broad white half-collar extending back as vertical lines onto rear cheeks (variable), indicating Northern Pintail as one parent. The flanks are grey-vermiculated and the upperparts slightly browner. Broad grey-brown tertials indicating Mallard. Green speculum bordered by two white lines, possibly with a reddish hue to the tips of the outer greater coverts. Legs dull yellow-brown. ♀ is intermediate between the two species, with an elegant shape reminiscent of Northern Pintail, but a short neck. Rather reddish overall, with legs pale dull pink and bill blue-grey with a large black patch on culmen and possibly yellow patches at the tip[439].

Northern Pintail × Gadwall. Uncommon hybrid, adult ♂ in basic plumage being distinctive. Slender shape recalling Northern Pintail with breast, flanks and upperparts whitish vermiculated grey (like Northern Pintail) and scapulars and tertials elongated (the latter broad and curved down like Gadwall), grey with dark centres hardly marked. The breast may be tinged reddish or marked with dark semicircle-shaped spots (as Gadwall). Head characteristic with forehead and crown hazelnut-brown merging into large black eye-band with green, copper or purple gloss. The eye-bands extend to the nape and merge into a broad black collar, which runs up over the throat to the bill base. Cheeks pale ochre-yellow to beige, sometimes split into two by a clear-cut or diffuse vertical dark line. A broad white half-collar is visible below the black collar. Bill similar to Northern Pintail but black pattern ill-defined, sometimes almost all blackish. Inner speculum white with black trailing edge. Legs dull yellow with dark webs.

Northern Pintail × Eurasian Teal. Rare in the wild. Adult ♂ in basic plumage described as being closer in appearance to one or other parent[439]. Throat, chin, base of bill, forehead, crown and nape have reddish hue, dark eye-band with green or bronze sheen and completely buff-reddish cheeks, sometimes divided by a dark vertical line joining the throat. Sometimes each buff patch is surrounded by a paler line. Bill blackish with variable blue areas at sides. Has a whitish to pale grey-brown body vermiculated dark grey, dark scapulars with dusky centres and central rectrices sufficiently long to identify Northern Pintail as one parent. Centre of breast pale peach. Undertail black except small white area at base of outer rectrices (always?). Green speculum with broad white trailing edge and tips to greater coverts reddish. Legs grey. See also Sage[1117] and Harrison & Harrison[525,526].

Northern Pintail × Green-winged Teal. First reported several decades ago[16,595], although this hybrid is very rare in the wild. Adult ♂ in basic plumage is very similar to previous hybrid, but differs in having breast (always?) more tinged salmon-pink and presence of a vertical line of same colour between the flanks and breast. Often seems to have a less contrasting head pattern, largely reddish without bimaculated pattern on cheeks and a bill whose pale blue sides are clearly outlined in black.

HABITAT. Usually among the earliest spring migrants, as departs southern wintering areas from mid-Jan, peaking Feb–Mar. Arrives on breeding grounds in Apr–May. They settle in the Arctic tundra as soon as snow and ice melt, and lay eggs a few days after arriving. Uses open landscapes in lowland tundra, large marshy areas in taiga or flooded meadows further south. Requires shallow wetlands, usually temporary, favouring shores with low herbaceous vegetation. ♂ abandons ♀ early during incubation and starts pre-basic moult on average 12 days later[932]. Most ♂♂ undertake a moulting migration among the longest in dabbling ducks[1126]. ♀♀ that raise ducklings start their pre-basic moult on the nest sites or nearby. During summer, one of the first migrant ducks to appear south of its breeding range, often from late Jul or early Aug, but southernmost wintering sites often only host significant numbers between early Dec and mid-Jan. On migration and in winter, uses all types of fresh and brackish waters, preferably large, open and shallow wetlands. Feeds in water by up-ending and using its long neck to reach deeper bottoms than other dabbling ducks.

RANGE and POPULATION Has the largest breeding range among Anseriformes. Isolated pairs or small populations breed in Greenland and locally south of mapped range. In winter, uncommon or scarce visitor south to the Lesser Antilles, N South America, South Africa and S Philippines. Total population estimated at 5,300,000–5,400,000 individuals[144]. In North America, recent estimates of 3,473,000 in 2012 and 3,335,000 in 2013[1294], a slight increase since the early 1990s, but below the level of 1950s (*c.*10,000,000 birds). European population estimated at 320,000–360,000 breeding pairs[139]. Wintering Eurasian populations estimated at 60,000 birds in NW Europe, 750,000 in S & E Europe and W Africa[1154], 700,000 in SW Asia and E Africa[445], >1,000,000 birds in South Asia and 200,000–300,000 in E & SE Asia [757].

CAPTIVITY Frequently kept in captivity being much appreciated for its ornamental character and easy to maintain and breed. Generally offered for sale at very affordable prices. Nevertheless, the species is present over much of the Holarctic and the question of natural or captive origin rarely arises.

REFERENCES Alison & Prevett (1976)[16]; Austin & Miller (1995)[43]; Baker (1993)[56]; BirdLife International (2004)[139]; BirdLife International (2013)[144]; Carney (1992)[224]; Chiba *et al.* (2007)[226]; Cramp & Simmons (1977)[268]; Duncan (1985)[333]; Gantlett (1989)[415]; Gillham & Gillham (1996)[439]; Gillham & Gillham (1999)[441]; Gillham & Gillham (2002)[443]; Gillissen *et al.* (2002)[445]; Gray (1958)[465]; Harrison & Harrison (1969)[525]; Harrison & Harrison (1971)[526]; Hopkinson (1935)[588]; Howell (1959)[595]; Johnsgard (1960)[639]; Johnson & Sorenson (1999)[654]; Li *et al.* (2009)[757]; Livezey (1991)[767]; McCarthy (2006)[817]; Miller (1986)[846]; Oring (1964)[932]; Palmer (1976)[945]; Panov (1989)[947]; Pitt (1944)[996]; Pyle (2008)[1014]; Sage (1960)[1117]; Salminen (1983)[1122]; Salomonsen (1968)[1126]; Scott & Rose (1996)[1154]; Sibley (1938)[1190]; Smith & Sheeley (1993)[1212]; Steklenev (1993)[1231]; USFWS (2013)[1294].

341. Adult ♀ (definitive basic/definitive alternate); note adult median and tertial coverts, broad with clear whitish fringes. England, Feb (Sébastien Reeber).

342. Adult ♂ (definitive basic); in flight, note blackish speculum, framed by white trailing edge and deep buff wingbar. England, Feb (Sébastien Reeber).

343. First-winter ♂ (first basic/formative); note tertial coverts and median coverts, which are narrow and clearly pale-fringed. France, Oct (Aurélien Audevard).

344. Adult ♂ (definitive basic). England, Feb (Sébastien Reeber).

345. First-winter ♀ (formative); longest tertials and corresponding tertial coverts apparently juvenile. France, Feb (Sébastien Reeber).

346. First-winter ♀ (first basic/formative); aged by tertials and tertial coverts pattern, the latter narrow and faintly edged whitish. California, USA, Nov (Sébastien Reeber).

GARGANEY
Anas querquedula

Plate 35

TAXONOMY *Anas Querquedula* Linnaeus, 1758, *Syst. Nat.*, edn. 10, p. 126. Phylogenetically rather close to Silver Teal *A. versicolor* and Puna Teal *A. puna*, from South America, and Hottentot Teal *A. hottentota*, of Africa. These four species together form a clade, which is sister to the subgenus *Spatula* (the 'blue-winged' ducks)[654]. Other works include the first three-named species and Garganey in the subgenus *Querquedula* Stephens 1824, along with Eurasian Teal *A. crecca*, Green-winged Teal *A. carolinensis* and Baikal Teal *A. formosa*[767].

IDENTIFICATION Definitive basic and formative plumages of ♂ unmistakable. Other plumages are similar to each other and distinguished from other small dabblers by the dark grey bill, head pattern appearing typically strongly striped, with clear white spot at the base of the bill and a dark bar from the gape across the cheeks. Also note the absence of a white patch on the basal tail-sides. In flight, note especially the upperwing with base of primaries, primary coverts and alula uniform pale grey, as well as the broad trailing edge to the secondaries, which is thicker than the wingbar formed by the tips to the greater coverts. Finally, the leading edge of the underwing is much darker, recalling Cinnamon and Blue-winged Teals.

In North America, the species is occasional and can be mistaken for Green-winged Teal and Blue-winged Teal *A. discors*. Garganey differs from the former by its slightly greater size, longer bill, more contrasting facial pattern, whitish fringes to scapulars and tertials, grey legs and broad double white wingbars bordering the narrow speculum. Blue-winged Teal, closer to Garganey in size, has a more spatulate bill, lacks the dark bar running from the gape across the cheeks, has lesser and median coverts blue, always paler than primary coverts (all secondary- and primary coverts are grey-brown in Garganey), broad white trailing edge to the secondaries and yellow legs.

PLUMAGES Strong sexual dimorphism from first winter onward. Complex alternate moult strategy (two plumages per definitive cycle, three in first cycle). Ageing ♂♂ relatively easy until early winter and possible until end of subsequent summer under good viewing conditions or in the hand. Ageing ♀♀ harder from first winter, but possible based on a thorough scrutiny of upperwing.

Adult ♂

Definitive basic plumage (Feb–Mar/Jun–Jul). Forehead, base of bill, chin, crown and nape blackish-brown, with clear-cut white eye-bands from in front of eye, above lores, towards the nape where the bands merge. Cheeks and neck purplish-brown with well-defined whitish vermiculations. Dark eyestripe. Iris hazel to reddish-brown. Bill blackish to slate-grey. Breast feathers centred black with broad yellow-ochre fringes, forming a scaly appearance that appears streaked at border with fore flanks. Flanks whitish with strong blackish vermiculations, except vertical white stripe at border with breast and white line around flanks at top and rear. Belly whitish. Mantle grey-brown with diffuse blackish centres. Scapulars elongated and pointed, pale grey with diffuse black centres and broad white rachis lines. Tertials long, pointed, dark grey with white sharp fringes (interrupted at tips). Femoral coverts, lower belly and undertail beige-yellowish with crisp dark brown spots. Uppertail, rump and back barred black and white. Rectrices dark grey finely fringed pale brown. Upperwing unique, with lesser and median coverts, alula, primary coverts and base of primaries pale bluish-grey. Greater coverts have broad white tips forming wingbar. Secondaries black with green gloss, and white tips form broad trailing edge. The speculum is distinctly narrow, due to the broad white trailing edge and reduced length of exposed secondaries, the greater coverts extending further rearwards. Underwing has dark grey remiges, greater coverts pale grey, axillaries and median coverts white, lesser coverts blackish-grey. Legs grey.

Definitive alternate plumage (Jun–Jul/Jan–Feb). Similar to ♀, but somewhat brighter (particularly on breast), with head pattern slightly more contrasting, due to dark bars (from gape across cheeks and eyestripe) being more heavily marked and supercilium and throat white. Belly is also whiter. The most useful feature for sexing remains the upperwing, which is not replaced and thus still basic (see above). During the definitive cycle, an additional plumage may be present after alternate plumage, as in Northern Shoveler, but the precise nature of this plumage and the extent of moult leading to it remain unknown (see Moult under Northern Shoveler).

Adult ♀

Definitive basic plumage (Jan–Mar/Mar–May). Brown and spotted overall, like all ♀ *Anas*, but rather pale, with head-sides coarsely barred and contrasting. Crown and strong eyestripe dark. The eyestripe is framed by a pale supercilium (almost interrupted above eye) and whitish upper cheeks. Dark brown vermiculations on nape, neck-sides and central cheeks, becoming denser in a dark band that runs from the gape across the cheeks. A round whitish patch is usually obvious at the bill base, well separated from the whitish throat. Iris hazel. Bill grey, slightly darker at the tip. Flank feathers centred brown and fringed beige, scapulars with darker brown centres, with pale inner marks barely visible or lacking in both. Tertials blackish with contrasting white fringes. The broad trailing edge to the secondaries is often visible on the folded wing. Rear body beige with brown spots but no pale horizontal patch under tail-sides.

Definitive alternate plumage (Apr–May/Dec–Feb). Very similar to basic plumage, with head more tinged hazel-brown, thus appearing plainer, whitish patches at base of bill, throat and supercilium often being the only striking characters. Flanks appear roughly barred rather than scaly.

Juvenile

First basic plumage (until Oct–Feb). Similar to basic plumage of adult ♀ with a more 'tidy' and scaly appearance in direct comparison. Breast more ochre-yellow and belly neatly streaked or marked pale brown. The most obvious feature for ageing, however, is the wing, with the trailing edge to the secondaries much narrower. Young ♂ has the lesser and median coverts slightly bluish-grey, often stained brown (feather bases) and greater coverts have broad white tips, often with a small dark spot at tip of each inner web (the whole forming a broad white wingbar). The secondaries show a slight to moderate pale green sheen to the inner speculum. Young ♀ has lesser and median coverts dull grey-brown, often fringed pale brown, greater coverts with white tips often limited to fringes, sometimes slightly wider (usually <5 mm of white along shafts of outer feathers) with or without a small dark spot at tip. Dark grey speculum usually lacks green gloss.

First-winter ♂

Formative plumage (Jan–Mar/Jun–Jul). Very like adult ♂ at end of pre-formative moult, and separated (with difficulty) by presence of juvenile feathers, for example on back, rump or belly, and possibly one or more tertials.

This distinction is usually possible only in the hand or perfect viewing conditions. Best aged by upperwing pattern, which is quite different from adult ♂ (see juvenile), until second pre-basic moult.

First-winter ♀

Formative plumage (Feb–Apr/Mar–May). Virtually identical to basic plumage adult ♀, and differs only by retaining one or more juvenile tertials and upperwing pattern, especially the width of two white stripes framing speculum and sheen to latter: dull brown-grey in ♀ in formative plumage and black with green gloss in adult.

GEOGRAPHIC VARIATION None.

MEASUREMENTS and MASS ♂: wing chord 190–211 (adult, 198, n=34) and 187–201 (juvenile, 194, n=35), bill from tip of feathers 38–43 (39.6, n–70), tarsus 29–33 (31.3, n=38), tail 57–73 (n=69); ♀: wing chord 184–196 (adult, 189, n=16) and 182–194 (juvenile, 186, n=17), bill from tip of feathers 36–40 (38.0, n=34), tarsus 28–32 (30.1, n=20), tail 54–69 (n=33)[267]. ♂: mass 260–520 (adult, 368, n=110) and 230–480 (juvenile/first-winter, 359, n=126); ♀: mass 240–585 (adult, 335, n=122) and 200–660 (juvenile/first-winter, 348, n=115)[448].

VOICE The ♂ gives a typical dry rattle or clicking call, mainly during courtship and nesting period, and frequently heard at night. The ♀ utters (rather rarely) a short, low *quack*.

MOULT Complex alternate moulting strategy, much like that of Northern Shoveler *A. clypeata* (which see). An auxiliary pre-formative moult (extent unclear) occurs between Aug and Oct–Nov in young birds, followed by protracted pre-formative moult until Feb–Apr. Some head and body feathers, rectrices, one to all tertials and some inner secondary upperwing-coverts are replaced from Sep[56]. A variable number of feathers on the mantle, back, rump and possibly up to several juvenile tertials are retained until second pre-basic moult[56]. Definitive pre-alternate moult occurs Mar–May in ♀ and mid-May to Jul in ♂. It includes a variable number of head and body feathers, up to all tertials, but few inner upperwing-coverts. Definitive pre-basic moult begins between late Jun and mid-Aug in ♂ with the simultaneous loss of the remiges (*c*.1 month later in ♀♀). Some feathers of the head, breast, flanks and scapulars are replaced during late summer at moulting sites or migration stop-overs, but birds arrive on their wintering grounds in mostly alternate-type plumage. Pre-basic moult, leading to definitive basic plumage ends between mid-Feb and mid-Mar, typically with the longest scapulars. This very progressive moult, with some feathers possibly grown twice since the previous summer, could suggest the existence of a definitive pre-supplemental moult, but this remains to be assessed.

HYBRIDISATION Natural hybridisation involving Garganey is very rare. The most frequently reported cross is probably that with Northern Shoveler (which see). Other cases have been reported even more occasionally with Eurasian Wigeon *A. penelope*[465,947], Falcated Duck *A. falcata*[439], Northern Pintail *A. acuta*[465], Eurasian Teal *A. crecca*, Tufted Duck *Aythya fuligula*[439] and Common Pochard *A. ferina*[817]. In captivity, hybridisation has been described with Wood Duck *Aix sponsa*, Mallard *A. platyrhynchos*[439], Gadwall *A. strepera*[442], Cinnamon Teal[439], Blue-winged Teal[439] and Hottentot Teal[439].

HABITAT and LIFE-CYCLE Strictly migratory and the only species of Anatidae breeding exclusively in the Holarctic that is virtually absent from this region in winter. Migrants arrive at nesting sites mainly in Mar–Apr, sometimes up to mid-May in north. Usually breeds in habitats similar to those of Northern Shoveler, with a preference for grassy marshes, flooded grasslands and steppes, ponds and shallow wetlands with herbaceous riparian vegetation[144,1152]. Prefers wetlands with abundant submerged vegetation, rich in invertebrates, which are main food resource in spring. ♂ abandons ♀ during incubation, and some then gather to moult, whereas others moult their primaries near nest sites. ♀♀ that raise young start wing moult when the young fledge. Migration to wintering grounds starts early, usually as soon as the birds can fly again, before moulting at least most body feathers. Arrives in Africa by early Sep, with a peak in Oct. During winter, uses all types of large, permanent or temporary, shallow wetlands, fresh or brackish, with a preference for those with abundant submerged and floating vegetation[448]. At this season, the species is much more gregarious. Often undertakes erratic movements in response to local conditions[144].

RANGE and POPULATION Eurasian breeder with scattered breeding locations south of mapped range, e.g.

in Spain, Turkey, on W Caspian Sea and Turkmenistan. In winter, present south of Sahara, in E Africa from Nile Valley to Tanzania and Zambia. In Asia, winters south of Himalayas (Pakistan, India, Bangladesh), south to Myanmar, S & SE China. Scarcer in Indonesia, the Philippines and to Papua New Guinea. Migrant anywhere between these two areas and to Japan in the east. Uncommon visitor to Aleutian Is, and occasionally along both coasts of North America.

Wintering population estimated at 1,500,000 birds in W Africa[1284] in early 2000s, with only older estimates available for E Africa, where 500,000 in 1980s[864], 100,000–200,000 in SW Asia[1154], 350,000 in India and Sri Lanka, and 100,000–200,000 in SE Asia. This corresponds to a total of 2,600,000–2,800,000 individuals[144]. Estimated to be decreasing, especially in E Asia[757], although some populations appear stable. The reasons given are the destruction of both breeding and wintering habitats, mainly through drainage for agriculture, the construction of dams or use of water for domestic or agricultural purposes. Hunting pressure also seems excessive, with annual harvests estimated at >500,000 birds, mainly in Russia, Ukraine, Poland and France[448]. Weather conditions during spring migration have also been listed as a major concern in the dynamics of the population[1006].

CAPTIVITY Regular in captivity and usually sold at quite low prices, but rather difficult to breed. Some North American records are attributed to escapees. Vagrant individuals may tend to join migratory flocks of Blue-winged Teals or Northern Shovelers, species with which the Garganey is often associated in Eurasia, at least due to similar ecological preferences and migration timing.

REFERENCES Baker (1993)[56]; Bird Hybrids database (2014)[97]; BirdLife International (2013)[144]; Cramp & Simmons (1977)[268]; Gillham & Gillham (1996)[439]; Gillham & Gillham (2000)[442]; Girard *in* Kear (2005)[448]; Gray (1958)[465]; Johnson & Sorenson (1999)[654]; Li *et al.* (2009)[757]; Livezey (1991)[767]; McCarthy (2006)[817]; Monval & Pirot (1989)[864]; Panov (1989)[947]; Pöysä & Väänänen (2014)[1006]; Schricke (2002)[1152]; Scott & Rose (1996)[1154]; Trolliet *et al.* (2003)[1284].

347. Adult ♂ (definitive basic). Denmark, Apr (Nis Lundmark Jensen).

348. Adult ♂ (definitive basic). France, Apr (Aurélien Audevard).

349. Adult ♂ (definitive basic); in flight, note unique wing pattern, also shown in definitive alternate plumage. Denmark, Apr (Nis Lundmark Jensen).

350. Adult ♀ (definitive alternate); aged and sexed by heavy dusky patches on bill, typical of this age and sex, and rather pale, long tertials, well fringed whitish (as well as tertial coverts). France, Aug (Aurélien Audevard).

351. First-winter ♀ (formative/first alternate), still with many juvenile feathers (some upper flanks and scapulars), short pale brown tertials and narrow trailing edge to secondaries, typical of young birds. Switzerland, Mar (Christopher J. G. Plummer).

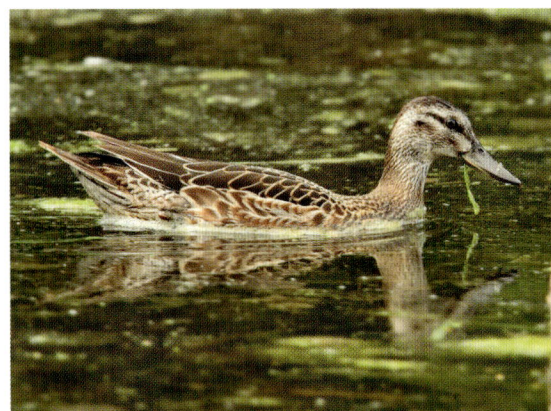

352. Juvenile (first basic); aged by narrow tertial coverts incompletely edged pale, duller and browner body feathers, dull pale brown iris and pale greenish base to bill. Switzerland, Aug (Christopher J. G. Plummer).

BAIKAL TEAL
Anas formosa

Plates 37, 38

TAXONOMY *Anas formosa* Georgi, 1775, *Bemerkungen Reise Russ. Reich*, p. 168. The phylogenetic position of this species is not unanimously accepted, sometimes being placed within a clade including Eurasian Teal *A. crecca* and Green-winged Teal *A. carolinensis*[767], but Johnson & Sorenson[654] placed it alongside the clade of 'blue-winged' ducks. The same authors, however, indicated that the phylogenetic relationships with this group are loose and that Baikal Teal should not be considered close to any other species of Anatidae. This was also the position expressed in several earlier works[158,295,297].

IDENTIFICATION Adult ♂ in basic plumage is so strikingly patterned to make confusion with any other species virtually impossible, although many hybrids, not involving Baikal Teal, show a 'bimaculated' facial pattern recalling this species, while hybrids that do include Baikal Teal in their lineage can be even more confusing. Therefore, even adult ♂ of the Baikal Teal should be identified with care. Other plumages are more difficult to identify, primarily due to risk of confusion with ♀ Eurasian and especially Green-winged Teals, which are slightly smaller, as well as with definitive alternate (eclipse) ♂♂ of these species. For juvenile and ♀♀, the following features are most useful.

- **Facial pattern**: Distinctive and characterised by a white round spot at the base of the bill, usually surrounded by dark. The characteristic pale reddish supercilium is often interrupted above the eye and more pronounced behind it. The throat is white and extends as a whitish vertical line, variably marked and fading on the central cheeks. A pale area usually intersects the dark loral stripe just in front of the eye. This facial pattern is unique among ♀♀ Anatidae, but Green-winged Teal can also have a rather contrasting head pattern, with a sharp round whitish spot at the bill base. Eurasian Teal, on the other hand, has a plainer face. The juvenile has a slightly less contrasting face pattern, more greyish, with a variable whitish vertical line on the cheeks. The whitish spot is visible at the bill base and often highlighted by a dark line starting at the gape and extending over the cheeks. Garganey *A. querquedula* and some Green-winged Teals also have a dark line across the cheeks.

- **Structure**: Baikal Teal is slightly different from the other two teals, being slightly larger (useful in a direct comparison). The top of the head is typically a little higher and more angular, peaking just behind the eye, with a slightly more rounded nape. The rear body is remarkable for its longer wings and tail. In flight, appears more elongated.

- **Scapulars**: ♀ in definitive basic and formative (from beginning of first winter) plumages are more uniform than Eurasian and Green-winged Teals, with browner feather centres and more reddish-buff fringes, quite dark, greatly reducing the scaly appearance. The scapulars also have pale inner marks very faint or lacking, and are often distinctly longer and more pointed, sometimes even approaching shape in ♂♂ (oldest ♀♀?). However, in juvenile plumage, the scapulars of all three species are much more similar.

- **Upperwing pattern**: Characteristic in adult, with tips to greater coverts forming rust-coloured wingbar (narrower in ♀ than ♂). White tips to the secondaries form a very broad white trailing edge. These white tips often have a straight or convex boundary with the dark centre of each feather, whereas in the other teals the white tip is much more extensive along the outer edge and its border is concave (Fig. 13 on p.418). In flight, the reddish wingbar is narrow compared to other species, of even width, usually inconspicuous and offers very little contrast, unlike the white trailing edge, which is often two to three times wider[427]. It is the reverse in Eurasian Teal, in which the wingbar is large and white, with a narrower white trailing edge. Green-winged Teal has an intermediate pattern, but the impression of two pale bars bordering the speculum is obvious. However, in young Baikal Teal (until first summer), the tips to greater coverts are paler and duller, more like those of other two teals.

- **Dark speculum**: Narrower in Baikal Teal, because of the broad white trailing edge, but also because greater coverts cover a larger part of the wing (as in Garganey), which is often visible even on the folded wing. Unlike other teals, the colour of the speculum is split, the fore half (at the greater coverts) glossed green and the rear (at the white trailing edge) black. However, the green gloss is slightly wider on the inner secondaries, and almost absent on the outermost 1–4, depending on the bird's age. Finally, the green is less shiny, more bronze than iridescent[427]. In Eurasian and Green-winged Teals, the inner secondaries form a green square with narrow black subterminal bar.

- *Rump and back*: In Baikal Teal plainer, brown-grey with feathers only slightly pale-fringed (slightly more in juvenile), whereas they are typically scaly (dark brown with sharp pale fringes) in the other teals. In flight, this feature, combined with the more uniform scapulars, is distinctive.

- *Basal tail-sides*: The pale patch of Eurasian Teal, often slightly yellowish or pale orange in Green-winged Teal, is also present in Baikal Teal, but is much narrower.

- *Belly*: Whitish to cream-coloured in adult ♀ Baikal Teal, beige or pale brown in the two other teals.

- *Bill*: Grey with a paler blue tone at the base of the tomium, but lead-grey in the other teals, usually with a yellow or pale orange area at the base and along the tomium, especially in Eurasian Teal.

- *Legs*: ♀ Baikal Teal's are greyish with a yellowish or flesh tone, whereas those of Eurasian Teal are dull grey with a brown-green tone and in Green-winged Teal they are on average slightly paler and more brightly coloured.

- *Underwing pattern*: Leading edge to secondary coverts blacker and better marked in Baikal Teal[427].

PLUMAGES Strong sexual dimorphism from first winter onwards. Complex alternate moult strategy (two plumages per definitive annual cycle, three in first cycle). Ageing ♂♂ relatively easy until end of autumn and usually not difficult on basis of upperwing pattern until first summer. Ageing ♀♀ harder from first winter onwards.

Adult ♂

Definitive basic plumage (Nov–Dec/Jun–Jul). Head colourful. Cap black with fine pale spotting, underlined by a complete white coronal line around the head. Lores, base of bill, fore cheeks and throat pale yellow, crossed by a vertical black line from eye to chin. Large glossy green eye-band, covering back of eye, rear cheeks and upper nape, ending in neat crescent below the cheeks. White line forming half-collar and extending behind green eye-band. Nape black. In fresh basic plumage, the pale fringes to the feathers of the head make it appear somewhat faded or 'frosted', often concealing the black vertical line below the eye. Bill lead- to blackish-grey. Iris dark brown. Breast purplish-pink in centre, finely and regularly spotted black. Sides of breast and flanks

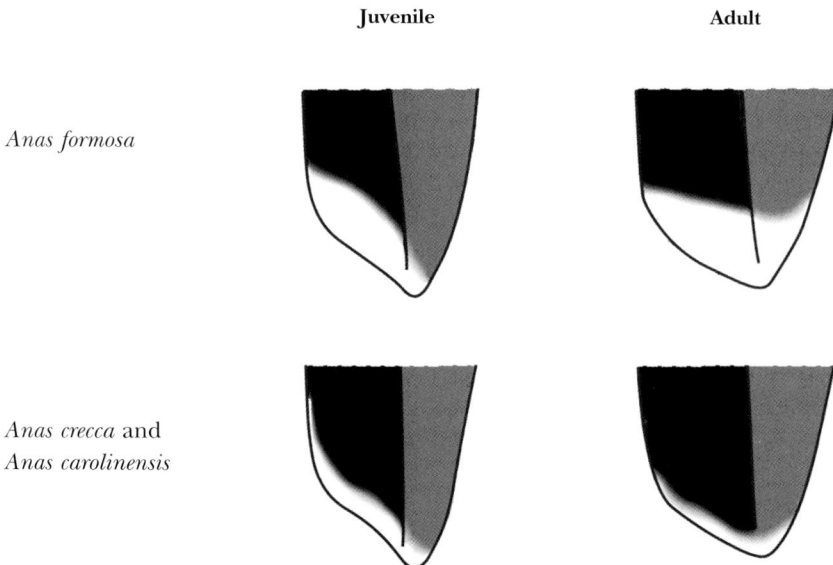

	Juvenile	Adult
Anas formosa		
Anas crecca and *Anas carolinensis*		

Fig. 13. Pattern of white tips to outer secondary remiges in Baikal Teal *Anas formosa*, Eurasian Teal *Anas crecca* and Green-winged Teal *Anas carolinensis*. The pattern is identical in the two latter species, but the white trailing edge is broader on average in Green-winged Teal.

pale grey with fine dark grey vermiculations. A white vertical bar is visible on the fore flanks, from the front of the folded wing to the waterline. Mantle and anterior scapulars grey-brown with more or less pronounced hazelnut tone. Longest scapulars very long, pointed and show three longitudinal stripes of equal width: white on outer webs, black along shafts and reddish on inner webs. Tertials dark grey-brown, slightly paler around shafts, and on two outermost a thick black band on inner webs. Tertial coverts dark grey. Femoral area pale brown with a clear-cut white vertical line next to black undertail. A reddish-orange horizontal bar is visible at the basal tail-sides. Uppertail-coverts dark grey with inner webs fringed white. Feathers of rump and back paler grey with blackish shafts. Rectrices grey-brown finely fringed pale. Upperwing grey with narrow reddish wingbar on tips of greater coverts, with three bands of equal width on secondaries, the first green in contact with greater coverts (except on 1–2 outermost secondaries), then black and white on trailing edge. The white tips to the secondaries are broader than in other ages and sexes, and extend over inner webs (Fig. 13). Underwing dark grey without pale fringes on lesser coverts, whitish on median coverts and axillaries (the latter often vermiculated greyish) and pale grey on greater coverts and remiges. Legs dull yellow with dark grey-brown webs.

Definitive alternate plumage (Jun–Jul/Oct–Nov). Similar to ♀ except basic feathers often kept until early Aug (including scapulars) or begin to grow as early as Sep–Oct. Thus generally warmer than ♀, with often diffuse face pattern, generally without vertical white line below eye, but round spot at bill base remains generally obvious. Forehead and crown usually blackish, reaching eye. Throat, neck and breast often paler than ♀. Alternate tertials rather long. Bill often tinged black at base and on tomium.

Adult ♀

Definitive basic plumage (Nov–Jan/Feb–Apr?). See Identification for additional information. Brown overall, but slightly less clearly mottled or streaked than many other ♀ dabbling ducks. Head with forehead, crown and eyestripe (behind the eye) dark brown. Round white spot at base of bill, surrounded by dark, and throat white extending as a vertical line to behind eye. Pale breast, finely mottled. Centre of breast and lower belly whitish. Flanks and upperparts centred dark brown to blackish with reddish to pale brown fringes. Scapulars fairly narrow and elongated, sometimes remarkably

long. Upperwing like ♂ but all coverts browner and green iridescence is reduced in extent.

Definitive alternate plumage (Mar–Apr?/Nov–Jan). Very like definitive basic plumage, but browner, duller and darker overall. Belly more mottled brown, inner marks on flank feathers and scapulars at best faint, and face pattern significantly reduced, often only the pale patch at the bill base contrasting at any distance[353].

Juvenile

First basic plumage (until Nov–Dec). Like adult ♀ but slightly less contrasting and duller, usually without reddish tones. Face pattern generally reduced, the crown being rather pale brown, and the spot (washed pale yellowish-brown) at the bill base is usually the only contrasting feature. The bill has a pale grey-blue patch at base. Breast often washed coppery or ochre-yellow, and its centre is noticeably paler, often with very few dark spots. Flank feathers elongated, narrow, pointed, dull cold brown, with fairly neat sandy-whitish fringes, and diffuse pale central marks. Scapulars dark brown with dull brown fringes, shorter and more round-tipped, unlike those of many adult ♀♀. Body as a whole rather plain, close in this plumage to juvenile Eurasian or Green-winged Teals. The whitish belly is ill-defined, and usually faintly streaked with small dusky spots in rows. The wingbar formed by tips to the greater coverts is paler than in adult. Upperwing-coverts show diffuse pale fringes, often not obvious in field conditions, but easily so in the hand. Tertial coverts fringed pale, more continuously in young ♀ than young ♂.

First-winter ♂

Formative plumage (Dec–Jan/Jun–Jul). Similar to basic plumage of adult ♂. Adult ♂♂ are generally in basic plumage from early Nov and most have finished pre-basic moult by mid-Dec. Young ♂♂ finish their pre-formative moult in Jan–Feb. In Dec–Jan, some juvenile feathers should therefore be obvious, e.g. on upper flanks. If some feathers there are juvenile-type (cold brown, narrow, pointed, with crisp beige fringes and diffuse inner mark), age can be safely assessed. However, the presence of rounded feathers does not always indicate an adult, as it appears that such feathers, redder-toned with hazelnut fringes, can be present along with juvenile-type feathers, perhaps as part of an auxiliary pre-formative moult (see below). Adult alternate flank feathers are broad and rounded, warm, but also have a reddish inner bar. Finally, adult ♂♂ have the head profile taller and more pointed, while young ♂♂ show a flatter head, closer to that of ♀.

Once formative plumage acquired, ageing should be based on the following features. Adult has a sharper white line above the eye, which usually reaches the top of the bill, a clear green iridescence on the rear head-sides and a wider and longer white vertical line on the fore flanks. The bill of first-winter ♂ often has a pale blue-grey patch near the base. The longest scapulars are shorter (usually one elongated feather, vs. 2–3 in adult), with a more diffuse black centre and less sharply defined inner web[424]. Tertials slightly thinner and round-tipped. Tertial coverts usually show a slight pale fringe, interrupted at tip. On the upperwing, the tips of the secondaries are white almost only on outer web[424] (Fig. 13) and the green sheen to the speculum is reduced (2–4 outer secondaries without gloss in young ♂, vs. generally one in adult). Also look for signs of juvenile plumage on rump and back (feathers brownish with pale fringes), belly (rows of small pale brown spots) and undertail (pale or brown patch in black area).

First-winter ♀

Formative plumage (Nov–Jan/Feb–Apr). Differs from adult ♀ in retained juvenile feathers on wing, rear body and belly, but more reliably assessed in hand. The wingbar appears slightly paler than in adult ♀. Precise knowledge is lacking on the distinguishing characters between first basic (juvenile) and definitive basic plumages, apart from the shape of the primaries and primary coverts, narrower and more pointed, with diffuse pale brown fringes on the latter.

GEOGRAPHIC VARIATION None.

MEASUREMENTS and MASS Few data available. ♂ (*n*=12): wing chord 203–225 (211), tail 74–87 (77.6), bill from tip of feathers 38–40 (38,7), tarsus 36–39 (37), mass 360–520 (437); ♀ (*n*=12): wing chord 201–214 (206.5), tail 74–83 (78), bill from tip of feathers 36–38 (37), tarsus 33–38 (35.7), mass 402-505 (431, *n*=8)[871,945].

VOICE ♂ gives a chuckled *wog-wog-wog* and a soft *prup*. The ♀ gives low quacks and more rarely, a decrescendo recalling that of Eurasian and Green-winged Teals[182,871].

MOULT Complex alternate moult strategy. Few data published on moult in the wild. An auxiliary pre-formative moult including some feathers of the head, the body and tail is possible, but, if present, its extent remains undefined (see Introduction). Pre-formative moult occurs between Oct and Jan–Feb. It includes many body feathers (smaller numbers on the belly, back and rear body, varying individually), and an unknown number of inner secondary upperwing-coverts, tertials and tertial coverts, and probably often all rectrices in young ♂ at least. Definitive pre-alternate moult occurs in Feb–Apr in ♀ (in captivity at least) and Jun–Aug in ♂. It includes some upperparts feathers and a variable number of inner lesser coverts, rectrices and tertials. Definitive pre-basic moult starts with the wings in Jul–Aug in ♂ and *c*.1 month later in ♀ with young. It ends between Oct and Dec on wintering grounds.

HYBRIDISATION Many hybrids between species of *Anas*, even those not involving Baikal Teal, show a face pattern recalling this species. Natural hybridisation involving Baikal Teal is rare, but has been reported a few times with Eurasian Teal (see that species) and Northern Pintail *A. acuta* (see below). Even more occasional cases have been reported in the wild with Northern Shoveler *A. clypeata*[439], Eurasian Wigeon *A. penelope*[465,817] and perhaps Red-crested Pochard *Netta rufina*[817]. In captivity, hybridisation described with Wood Duck *Aix sponsa*[442], American Wigeon *Anas americana*[1190], Cinnamon Teal *A. cyanoptera*[639], Speckled Teal *A. flavirostris*[439], Chiloe Wigeon *A. sibilatrix*[442] and Silver Teal *A. versicolor*[817].

Baikal Teal × Northern Pintail. Rarely reported, but nonetheless the most frequently observed hybrid involving Baikal Teal, mainly in E Asia (especially Japan[226]), but very occasionally in Europe. Recalls a large Baikal Teal with a long tail, intermediate size and rather high, peaked head. The crown is brown with black stripes, underlined by a long white line, of variable width. Rest of head black, often glossed green on rear cheeks, with two clear whitish patches, one on fore cheeks and the other crescent-shaped on rear cheeks. Bill blackish-grey. Breast white and finely spotted with dark centres, tinged pale pinkish above and at sides. Belly whitish. Sides of breast and flanks whitish finely vermiculated dark grey (the whole appearing bluish-grey), with a thin or broken white vertical bar in front of flanks. Scapulars centred with a broad black line, edged pale grey or yellowish, vermiculated, but can be closer to Baikal Teal, especially in shape and length. Rear flanks yellowish with vertical white bar against black undertail-coverts. Outer rectrices broadly fringed white and central rectrices markedly elongated. Legs grey. ♀ has seemingly not been described.

HABITAT and LIFE-CYCLE Most birds leave the

wintering grounds by mid-Mar and arrive on the nesting grounds between late May and early Jun, laying mainly between late May and mid-Jun. Rather few data available on breeding and ecological preferences[871]. Inhabits mainly grassy marshes in taiga and wetlands along major rivers or estuaries in tundra. ♂♂ seem to moult their remiges either near breeding sites or at moulting grounds where they gather. ♀♀ raise the young and moult their wings at the breeding sites. In autumn, first arrivals at Korean wintering areas reported in Sep, and numbers increase rapidly between Oct and Jan[291]. On migration, uses a wide variety of wetlands, including coastal estuaries and capable of roosting at sea. In winter frequents huge wetlands, e.g. large lakes or wide rivers, where it rests in monospecific flocks by day. In South Korea, a large part of the global population can gather in a single flock. In evening, the birds leave in small parties and congregate progressively in the air, until the whole flock heads to a feeding site (which changes from day to day), where they disperse in smaller parties. Mainly uses rice fields. Said to undertake erratic movements depending on food resources, especially linked with freezing weather conditions.

RANGE and POPULATION Restricted to E Asia, and nests only in Russia, from the mouth of the Khatanga River to Kamchatka and the borders of the Amur Oblast. Winters mainly in South Korea, with smaller numbers in Japan, North Korea and around Shanghai, China[675], and even fewer in the valley of the Yangtze Kiang, China. Rare migrant in N & E Mongolia. Scarce visitor elsewhere in China. Rare to occasional in S Asia, to Bangladesh and N India. Accidental along Pacific coast of North America, south to California, and to W Europe, where natural origin of some birds at least recently proven[533] in England and Denmark, on basis of stable isotope analysis[399]. However, most North American and W European records are still considered to involve escapees.

One of the most numerous waterfowl species in E Asia a century ago, the species declined sharply in the 1960s and 1970s. The Korean population, discovered in the 1980s, rose to 75,000 birds in 1994, 105,000 in 1997, 300,000 in 2002 and 500,000 in 2006[757,1095], and peaked at 1,060,000 birds in Jan 2009[874]. However, the most recent censuses recorded closer to 300,000 birds. Just under 100,000 birds were recently estimated in China[222,675] and several thousand in Japan[757]. The main reasons for the decline in the second half of 20th century are over-hunting (which has apparently declined recently[874]), pesticide pollution and grain poisoning[291]. Destruction or draining of wetlands for agriculture or urbanisation also poses serious problems in China and South Korea[145,874]. Finally, the species is particularly vulnerable because of the high concentration of the vast majority of its world population at just a few sites.

CAPTIVITY Widely imported and frequent in captivity until the 1960s. Harder to find now, mainly because it is difficult to breed in captivity. Generally sold at prices approximately twice those of other teals in Europe and up to five times in North America. The scarcity of captive breeding, along with its rather high value, make it less likely to escape from captivity than many other waterfowl species.

REFERENCES BirdLife International (2014)[145]; Boetticher (1952)[158]; Brazil (2009)[182]; Cao et al. (2010)[222]; Chiba et al. (2007)[226]; Degtyarev et al. (2006)[291]; Delacour (1956)[295]; Delacour & Mayr (1945)[297]; Eldridge & Harrop (1992)[353]; Fox et al. (2007)[399]; Garner (2013)[424]; Garner et al. (2008)[427]; Gillham & Gillham (1996)[439]; Gillham & Gillham (2000)[442]; Gombobaatar et al. (2003)[452]; Gray (1958)[465]; Harrop & McGowan (2009)[533]; Johnsgard (1960)[639]; Johnson & Sorenson (1999)[654]; Kejia & Qiang (2007)[675]; Li et al. (2009)[757]; Livezey (1991)[767]; McCarthy (2006)[817]; Moores in Kear (2005)[871]; Moores et al. (2010)[874]; Palmer (1976)[945]; Rose & Scott (2006)[1095]; Sibley (1938)[1190].

BAIKAL TEAL (continued)

353. Adult ♂ (definitive basic). Netherlands, Feb (Vincent Legrand).

354. First-winter ♂ (formative); at this time, most adults are in full or nearly full definitive basic plumage – also note thin head shape, pale bluish bill base, narrow, pointed, pale brown-edged upper flank feathers and scapulars, all typical of this age. Arizona, USA, Dec (Steve Mlodinow).

355. Group; note wing pattern close to that of Northern Pintail *A. acuta* (buff wingbar on greater coverts and white trailing edge); the bird with a whitish bar on greater coverts, dull speculum and blurred rear flanks is probably young ♀ (bottom, middle). South Korea, Oct (Aurélien Audevard).

356. Adult ♀ (definitive basic); diagnostic head and wing patterns; broad, rounded tertial coverts, as well as warm buff tips to greater coverts are adult features. Captivity (Harold Stiver).

EURASIAN TEAL
Anas crecca

Plates 37, 38

TAXONOMY *Anas Crecca* Linnaeus, 1758, *Syst. Nat.*, edn. 10, p.126. Phylogenetically, forms a clade with Green-winged Teal *A. carolinensis* and Speckled Teal *A. flavirostris*, which two species appear closer to each other than to Eurasian Teal[654]. Other studies place this species and Green-winged Teal near Baikal Teal *A. formosa* and Garganey *A. querquedula*[767]. Eurasian and Green-winged Teals are generally considered conspecific in North America, but are split in Eurasia. The latter position is adopted here (see Taxonomy of Green-winged Teal).

Under the system adopted here, *A. crecca* has two subspecies, the nominate over almost all of Eurasia, and *A. v. nimia* Friedmann, 1948, which is restricted to the Aleutian Is. The validity of this taxon, described as larger than the nominate subspecies, has been questioned several times, and few differences were found by Johnson & Sorenson[654]. More recently, a study of nuclear and mitochondrial DNA of *nimia*, *crecca* and *carolinensis* revealed that divergence occurred *c*.1.1 million years ago between *crecca* and *carolinensis*, but just 83,000 years ago between *crecca* and *nimia*[1370], although the authors of the study consider differentiation of *nimia* as valid due significant genetic divergence, low gene flow (with both *crecca* and *carolinensis*) and rather large population.

IDENTIFICATION The main identification problem involves Green-winged Teal. In ♂♂ in definitive basic and formative plumages, identification is complicated by the existence of rather frequent hybrids between the two species. In all other plumages, distinction is very difficult (see Green-winged Teal). In Asia, the risk of confusion with Baikal Teal must also be considered in any plumage other than definitive basic and formative adult ♂ (see Baikal Teal).

PLUMAGES Strong sexual dimorphism from first winter onwards. Complex alternate moult strategy (two plumages per definitive cycle, three in first cycle). Ageing ♂♂ relatively easy until late autumn and possible until first summer in the hand. Ageing ♀♀ harder from first winter onward, based on a thorough inspection of the upperwing.

Adult ♂

Definitive basic plumage (Oct–Nov/May–Jul). Head and upper neck reddish, with broad black eye-bands

strongly glossed green, meeting on nape. The eye-bands are bordered by a contrasting yellow-ochre line, which from above the eye-band extends to the chin. Bill dark grey. Iris hazel. Breast whitish more or less tinged pink, peach or pale yellow, with regular small round dark spots (more obvious with wear of pale fringes in late winter and spring). Belly whitish. Flank feathers whitish with dark grey vermiculations. Upper scapulars also vermiculated, the longest ones plainer with dark diffuse lines around shafts, forming sharp 'arrows'. Outer row of scapulars forms a double black-and-white horizontal line between flanks and upperparts. Tertials long, pointed, dark grey centred darker (like longest scapulars), except outermost, whose inner web is fringed by a broad black band, with a very thin pale buff margin, more obvious near tip and a diffuse whitish area between the black bar and rachis (Fig. 14 on p. 424). Feathers of back and rump grey fringed paler. Last row of uppertail-coverts long, centred black and fringed whitish-yellow. Rectrices dark fringed pale. Undertail-coverts form a bright yellow triangle framed black in profile. Upperwing dark grey with greater coverts forming a white wingbar variably tinged reddish on its inner part, broader toward its distal end, and inconspicuous on innermost part, but of even width and extends obviously onto tertial coverts in ♀. Thin white tips to secondaries form a rather narrow white trailing edge (Fig. 13 on p. 418). Black secondaries are strongly glossed green on almost all outer webs of four inner secondaries (sometimes three or five), but gloss limited to base of next two. Underwing grey, darker on leading edge, and axillaries and median coverts whitish. Legs grey.

Definitive alternate plumage (Jun–Jul/Oct–Nov). Similar to alternate plumage of ♀ but plainer face with eyestripe often interrupted in front of eye, scapulars dark brown with finer pale fringes and usually without inner marks. Bill usually all dark. Wing as basic plumage, with tips of inner greater coverts more reddish than ♀. Note that pre-basic moult is quite protracted but starts early, so that traces of basic plumage are visible (e. g. on head) during much of summer.

Adult ♀

Definitive basic plumage (Nov-Dec/Feb-Apr.). Overall mottled brown. Head beige with dark vermiculations on cheeks and supercilium, darker brown on forehead,

adult ♂   adult ♀   juvenile ♂   juvenile ♀

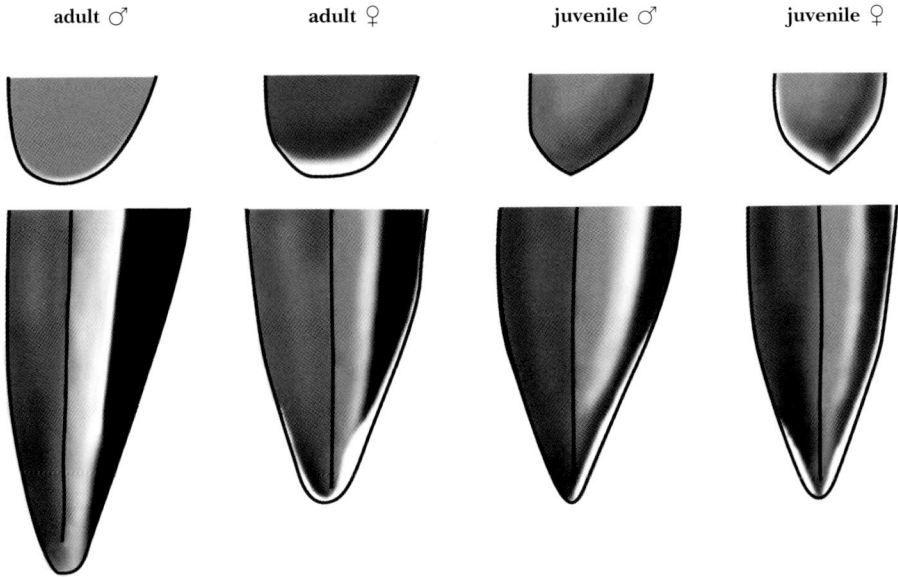

Fig. 14. Shape and pattern of the tertial coverts and outermost tertial in Eurasian Teal *Anas crecca* and Green-winged Teal *A. carolinensis*.

crown, nape and eyestripe (especially behind eye). Throat whitish. Bill dark grey with yellowish to pale orange variably extending from gape along tomium, sometimes its entire length. Dark spotting variable, but often has obvious dark spots on sides of bill, not shown by the juvenile. Iris brown. Rest of body yellowish to pale brown, with dark centres forming longitudinal stripes on breast. Scapulars fringed whitish with pale brown inner marks. Tertials grey with sharp white fringes. Outermost tertials useful to assess age (Fig. 14), with broad whitish to cream fringes, broader near tip of inner web and extending on outer web, pale area between rachis and longitudinal dark bar is browner and less sharply defined than ♂. Flank feathers have neat whitish fringes and obvious inner marks. Belly and undertail whitish to beige with dark spots. Large white horizontal patch under basal tail-sides. Upperwing similar to ♂ but tips of greater coverts less pale reddish on average, this colour being absent or, at most, limited to inner half of the wingbar, which is also of more even width. Lesser and median coverts variably marked with pale fringes (sometimes not at all). Tertial coverts broadly fringed white (plain or very faintly pale-fringed in ♂). The number of inner secondaries with green gloss over their length is usually limited to three, the fourth being often only partially

glossy. Tips of secondaries broader than in ♂. Legs greyish often with greenish or brown tones.

Definitive alternate plumage (Mar–Apr/Nov–Dec). Very similar to basic plumage, but darker and colder ground colour. Plainer appearance overall, because of browner (buff or reddish) fringes and inner marks to flank feathers and scapulars. Tertials shorter and round-tipped, browner and barred. Centres more obviously and irregularly mottled dark.

Juvenile

First basic plumage (until Oct–Dec). Very like ♀, but slightly darker, duller and less clearly marked, with fringes thinner and browner, and only faint inner marks on flank feathers and scapulars. Belly more strongly mottled brown. The bill often has a yellowish or orange tinge at the base and along the tomium, with smaller dark spots at sides, often concentrated towards culmen. These spots, if present, disappear quickly in young ♂. Legs usually grey-brown with a more or less marked olive tone. Distinction from adult ♀ nevertheless difficult on this basis and it is better to rely on shape and coloration of tertials and upperwing, even in the hand. Juvenile tertials are shorter and narrower, with a clear pale fringe, narrow but of fairly even width (vs. adult ♀). Tertial coverts distinctly fringed pale yellowish in juvenile ♀ and faintly fringed (often interrupted at tip) in young ♂. The black band on the inner web of the outermost tertial is thin and brown, slightly marked (♀) or blackish and better marked (♂) (Fig. 14). Tertials generally retained by ♂ until late autumn, but often until spring by ♀. Tertial coverts and upperwing-coverts visibly narrower, less round-tipped and fringed pale brownish. The green gloss of the speculum extends over two (♀) or 3–4 (♂) inner secondaries, with green sheen restricted to bases of one or more subsequent secondaries.

First-winter ♂

Formative plumage (Nov–Jan/May–Jul). After pre-formative moult, difficult to distinguish from definitive basic plumage ♂. Ageing will be easier in birds in which moult is reduced in extent (juvenile feathers visible on back or rear body, among rectrices, tertials or tertial coverts, e.g. juvenile tertial coverts narrower, more pointed, paler and pale-fringed at sides). The upperwing should also be checked (in the hand) until the second pre-basic moult: the shape of the median and greater coverts (the innermost may have been replaced), extent of green gloss on the speculum and slightly larger white tips to secondaries.

First-winter ♀

Formative plumage (Nov–Jan/Feb–Apr). Usually identical to adult ♀ in body coloration once pre-formative moult completed, even if the bill is on average less spotted at its sides and the base more strongly tinged yellow-orange. Ageing only possible using pattern of the tertials (one or more generally retained until midwinter) and upperwing-coverts, especially the greater coverts, as described under juvenile, and until second pre-basic moult.

GEOGRAPHIC VARIATION Two subspecies recognised (see Taxonomy), which differ only in measurements. Separating the two subspecies in the field is probably impossible. It has been suggested that the size of *crecca* increases along a cline from west to east, *nimia* representing only its eastern end[295], but this hypothesis is not necessarily supported by the available measurements (see, especially, Friedmann[406]).

MEASUREMENTS and MASS ♂ slightly larger and heavier than ♀. Subspecies *nimia* differs from *crecca* in length of wing, tail, middle toe and tarsus, which are on average 5–10% longer. Culmen length, however, does not seem different[406].

A. c. crecca. ♂: wing chord 179–200 (adult, 186, $n=36$) and 173–192 (juvenile, 181, $n=25$); ♀: wing chord 172–183 (adult, 178, $n=14$) and 170–180 (juvenile, 175, $n=17$)[1122]; ♂: wing chord 181–196 (adult, 187, $n=34$) and 176–192 (juvenile, 184, $n=63$), bill from tip of feathers 34–40 (36.4, $n=85$), tarsus 29–32 (30.4, $n=38$); ♀: wing chord 175–184 (adult, 180, i=22) and 166–185 (juvenile, 177, $n=30$), bill from tip of feathers 32–38 (34.9, $n=50$), tarsus 28–31 (29.8, $n=32$)[267]; ♂: wing chord 187 (adult, $n=1,001$) and 184.2 (juvenile, $n=3,582$), tarsus 31.1 (adult, $n=326$) and 31.0 (juvenile/first-winter, $n=886$), mass in winter 320.4 (adult, $n=999$) and 303.6 (juvenile/first-winter, $n=3,577$); ♀: wing chord 178.8 (adult, $n=499$) and 177.3 (juvenile, $n=2,295$), tarsus 30.0 (adult, $n=205$) and 30.0 (juvenile/first-winter, $n=557$), mass in winter 290.6 (adult, $n=498$) and 280.4 (juvenile/first-winter, $n=2,295$)[393].

A. c. nimia. ♂ ($n=13$): wing chord 182–204 (193.1), tail 65.1–76.0 (71.0), culmen 33.2–37.4 (35.8), tarsus 29.2–34.1 (31.4), middle toe (excluding nail) 33.1–39.1 (35.7); ♀ ($n=3$): wing chord 185–189 (186.7), tail 65.6–66.6 (66.1), culmen 34.2–36.1 (35.1), tarsus 30.4–31.2 (30.9), middle toe (excluding nail) 33.1–34.1 (33.8)[406]. Wing chord and middle toe length can be compared to those from same author for *crecca* in E Asia. ♂ ($n=25$): wing chord 174–187 (179.5), middle toe (excluding nail): 31.1–36.4 (33.0); ♀ ($n=21$): wing chord 166–182 (173.7), middle toe (excluding nail) 28.1–34.1 (32.1)[406]. ♂: mass in Jun 310–440 (392, $n=15$); ♀: mass in Jun 338–418 (378, $n=4$)[945]; length of nail on bill, averaging 6 mm in *crecca* and 7 mm in *nimia*, has been considered one of the most useful distinguishing features between the two subspecies[362].

VOICE ♀ gives a *quek*, rather nasal, shrill and high-pitched, recalling flight call of a snipe *Gallinago gallinago/delicata* and a rapid series of four notes, in decrescendo, like a false laugh. ♂ gives a characteristic *kreek*, sometimes more disyllabic, *dl-lik*. Various variations of these calls reported, and several types of whistles when birds 'chatter' at rest in compact flocks.

MOULT Complex alternate moult strategy. An auxiliary pre-formative moult is reported between Jul and Sep in young involving an unknown number of head and body feathers, possibly some inner upperwing-coverts and rectrices (see Introduction). Pre-formative moult occurs between Sep and Dec–Jan. It includes many head and body feathers (small proportion of feathers on belly, back and rear body), plus some inner upperwing-coverts, tertials and tertial coverts and none to all rectrices. Definitive pre-alternate moult occurs in Feb–Apr in ♀ and May–Aug in ♂. It includes some feathers mentioned above, and a variable number of inner primary coverts, rectrices and tertials. Definitive pre-basic moult starts with the wings in Jul–Aug in ♂ and *c*.1 month later in successful ♀♀. It ends in Oct–Dec on wintering grounds.

HYBRIDISATION Hybrids with Green-winged Teal regularly reported in North America, W Europe and E Asia (see that species). Other than with this cross, hybridises rarely in the wild, although hybrids with Mallard *A. platyrhynchos* are reported occasionally, and hybrids with Eurasian Wigeon *A. penelope*, Baikal Teal and Northern Pintail *A. acuta* even less frequently, but still regularly (see below and Hybridisation under Northern Pintail). Other natural hybrids mentioned, albeit very rarely, with Northern Shoveler *A. clypeata*[439], Garganey[465,817,947], Gadwall *A. strepera*[947] and Common Pochard *Aythya ferina*[465,817]. In captivity, hybrids described with Blue-winged Teal *Anas discors*[439], Falcated Duck *A. falcata*[439] and Hottentot Teal *A. hottentota*[439,1099]. In the case of hybrids with Wood Duck *Aix sponsa*[439], Chestnut Teal *Anas castanea*[1190] and Speckled Teal[439], it is unclear whether *A. crecca* or *A. carolinensis* was involved.

Eurasian Teal × Eurasian Wigeon. Rare in nature, but reported in at least Europe, Africa and Japan. Definitive basic ♂ generally has head like that of Eurasian Teal albeit with the yellowish line around the green band less pronounced. Bill intermediate, black except a bluish triangular patch at sides, recalling bill of Northern Pintail. Breast pale pink slightly mottled dark. Flanks, scapulars and upperparts pale grey vermiculated blackish, with a black horizontal band formed by lower row of scapulars, inherited from Eurasian Teal. Dark centres to longest scapulars more pronounced than in Eurasian Wigeon. White vertical stripe on femoral coverts varies in width. Belly whitish. Rear body close to that of Eurasian Wigeon. The call of one of these hybrids was described as similar to Eurasian Wigeon[439]. The ♀ from this cross has been described as like a small ♀ American Wigeon[441].

Eurasian Teal × Mallard. This hybrid has been known for a long time, was once even considered as a full species, and has also mistaken for Baikal Teal[1240]. Reported occasionally in the wild, the ♂ in definitive basic plumage is intermediate in size, tinged dark reddish-brown on crown and cheeks, with a glossy green eye-patch. However, the head is quite variable, with a bimaculated pattern sometimes pronounced and sometimes absent. A bright patch can be present at the bill base, and another, whitish or reddish, on rear cheeks. Bill has culmen, nail and tomium black with yellow, greenish or yellow-brown sides, sometimes reduced to diffuse spots at base and near tip. Iris brown-hazel. Breast deep pinkish-brown, clearly demarcated and finely mottled dark. Upperparts pale and vermiculated blackish, usually appearing burnished. Some hybrids show a horizontal black bar formed by the outer scapulars, sometimes topped by a paler band. Tertials pale grey-brown, rather broad. Sides whitish vermiculated blackish. Vertical white band on femoral coverts, and often a long white patch under basal tail-sides.

Eurasian Teal × Baikal Teal. Reported very occasionally in the wild and well known in captivity, where it is often recommended not to keep these two species together if they are to breed, as reproduction of Baikal Teal is notoriously hard. ♂ in definitive basic plumage recalls both species, with crown and cheeks reddish, a broad green eye-band behind the eye bounded by a broad white line recalling that of Eurasian Teal, plus another line running vertically across the cheeks, like a white 'Y' below the eye. Breast pale pink mottled dark. Flanks pale grey vermiculated blackish, scapulars apparently variable, largely grey and centred dusky, closer to Eurasian Teal, or with a clear-cut black line and fringed yellow-ochre, recalling Baikal Teal. A thin white band is (always?) visible at the front of the flanks and another on the femoral coverts. An orange-yellow triangular patch is visible under the tail-sides, intermediate in extent between the parent species. ♀ from this cross is apparently undescribed in the literature and probably very difficult to detect.

HABITAT and LIFE-CYCLE Migration and breeding timing are linked to latitude. Migratory movements are intense between Feb and Apr. Eggs are laid mostly from early Apr in south of range until mid-Jun in tundra. Occurs in a variety of habitats across a wide range from the Mediterranean to tundra marshes, through different types of lowland and highland swamps, steppes and taiga. Favours bogs and permanent marshes, in wooded areas, bordered by grassy vegetation such as sedges, with scattered small shallow waterbodies[144,393]. Once incubation is underway, ♂♂ abandons ♀♀ and gather to perform an often significant moult migration[794]. Other ♂♂ however, remain close to ♀♀, especially where pairs nest alone. Southbound migration starts once birds can fly again. Autumn migration peaks between Sep and Nov. In winter, inhabits a wide variety of habitats, often using smaller waterbodies than other ducks, with extensive riparian vegetation. Also uses large slightly flooded mudflats. Resting flocks generally use small sheltered ponds rather than open water. Large concentrations winter mostly at huge coastal wetlands (deltas, estuaries), including flooded meadows, grasslands and crops, mudflats in fresh, brackish or salt water (often intertidal)[144]. *A. c. nimia* occurs in shallow coastal wetlands, often with much aquatic vegetation, as well as on sandy or rocky shores in Aleutians, where it is sedentary[897].

RANGE and POPULATION Present over the entire Palearctic region.

A. c. crecca. Many small and isolated populations, often decreasing, south of mapped range, usually in mountainous regions, south to Spain, Italy and Turkey. Occasional out-of-range breeding may be linked to birds injured by hunting. Vagrant south of its winter range, and in North America, mainly on Pacific and Atlantic coasts. Total population estimated at 3,650,000–4,650,000 individuals[305], including 400,000 in W Europe, 750,000–1,350,000 in Black Sea, Mediterranean and W Africa[1154], 1,500,000 in SW Asia and E Africa[965], 400,000 in S Asia (mainly India) and 600,000–1,000,000 in E & SE Asia. General trend towards slight decrease, most pronounced in Asia[757]. The main factors are habitat destruction, increasing disturbance due to human activities[960], over-hunting[183] and ingestion of lead shot[863].

A. c. nimia. Breeds in Aleutian Is, west of Akuta I[645], where sedentary. Population estimated at close to 10,000 birds in 1990s and 2000s[1095 1348], but more recently 80,000 birds reported[1370]. No indication of population trends. Probably occasional nearby in W Alaska. There is one record, based on measurements, of an individual collected in Humboldt Bay, N California[362].

CAPTIVITY Quite frequently kept in captivity in Eurasia, especially where used as decoys for hunting. Usually inexpensive and breeds readily. Might escape from captivity in North America, although it is much less commonly kept there than Green-winged Teal.

REFERENCES Baker (1993)[56]; BirdLife International (2004)[139]; BirdLife International (2013)[144]; Bregnballe *et al.* (2004)[183]; Cramp & Simmons (1977)[268]; Delacour (1954)[295]; Delany & Scott (2006)[305]; Engelis (2003)[362]; Fox *in* Kear (2005)[393]; Friedmann (1948)[406]; Gillham & Gillham (1996)[439]; Gillham & Gillham (1999)[441]; Gillham & Gillham (2002)[443]; Gray (1958)[465]; Johnsgard (1975)[645]; Johnson (1995)[653]; Johnson & Sorenson (1999)[654]; Li *et al.* (2009)[757]; Livezey (1991)[767]; Madge & Burn (1988)[794]; McCarthy (2006)[817]; Mondain-Monval *et al.* (2002)[863]; Murie (1959)[897]; Palmer (1976)[945]; Panov (1989)[947]; Pease *et al.* (2005)[960]; Perennou *et al.* (1994)[965]; Rose & Scott (1997)[1095]; Roy (1995)[1099]; Salminen (1983)[1122]; Scott & Rose (1996)[1154]; Sibley (1938)[1190]; Suchetet (1894)[1240]; Wetlands International (2013)[1348]; Winker *et al.* (2013)[1370].

357. *A. c. crecca*, ♀ (first alternate); pre-alternate moult included tertials, some tertial coverts and scattered inner secondary coverts. France, Apr (Sébastien Reeber).

358. *A. c. crecca*, group; white wingbar on greater coverts is typically much broader than white trailing edge (vs. Green-winged Teal *A. carolinensis*), while in ♂ the wingbar typically broadens outwards. France, Feb (Jean-Luc Pinaud).

359. *A. c. crecca*, first-winter ♀ (formative); note juvenile tertials, narrower, pointed and with duller pattern on inner web of outermost, while lower scapulars and many flank feathers are also juvenile. France, Dec (Aurélien Audevard).

360. *A. c. crecca*, adult ♂ (definitive basic). England, Feb (Sébastien Reeber).

361. *A. c. crecca*, adult ♂ (definitive basic); differs from Green-winged Teal *A. carolinensis* mainly in white horizontal bar on lower scapulars and head pattern. India, Mar (Anand Arya).

362. *A. c. crecca*, juvenile ♂ (first basic); outer tertial typical, with broad black bar on outer half of inner web, paler bar towards centre and the whitish edge reduced to distal part, and note faint pale edges to tertials. Netherlands, Aug (Seraf van der Putten).

363. *A. c. crecca*, ♀ (formative/definitive basic); note white wingbar on greater coverts, broader than trailing edge. Denmark, Oct (Nis Lundmark Jensen).

364. *A. c. crecca*, adult ♂ (definitive basic); Eurasian Teal (especially adult ♂) may also show rufous tinge to wingbar, but usually much less marked than in Green-winged Teal *A. carolinensis*. France, Feb (Sébastien Reeber).

365. *A. c. crecca*, first-winter ♂ (formative); this plumage is almost definitive basic-like, but some juvenile feathers are retained among outer scapulars and tertial coverts, which are narrow and pale-fringed, while black and white horizontal bar does not appear on body. France, Dec (Aurélien Audevard).

366. *A. c. crecca*, adult ♂ (definitive basic); another variant, almost without rufous tinge to greater coverts. Denmark, Jun (Nis Lundmark Jensen).

367. *A. c. crecca*, adult ♀ (definitive basic), aged by broad, dark and bluntly pointed tertials, the outermost with a whitish area bordering the clear-cut blackish bar, along the inner web's white edge. France, Dec (Aurélien Audevard).

GREEN-WINGED TEAL
Anas carolinensis

TAXONOMY *Anas carolinensis* J. F. Gmelin, 1789, *Syst. Nat.*, 1, p. 533. Phylogenetic position somewhat controversial (see Taxonomy of Eurasian Teal), and sometimes considered closer to Speckled Teal *A. flavirostris* than Eurasian Teal *A. crecca*[654]. Initially described as species, Green-winged and Eurasian Teals were subsequently generally regarded as subspecies[968] until recently. In 2001, Sangster *et al.*[1132] summarised the reasons for the AERC-TAC's decision to treat them specifically[1133], namely the diagnostic plumage differences between adult ♂♂ in basic plumage, differences in behaviour during courtship[734] and the results of phylogenetic analyses showing that the closest relation of Green-winged Teal is Speckled Teal of South America[654]. The latter also revealed high genetic divergence (mitochondrial DNA) between *crecca* and *carolinensis* (5.8%), equivalent to that separating Mallard *A. platyrhynchos* and Northern Pintail *A. acuta* (5.7%). Another study of mitochondrial DNA found sharp divergence between the two taxa, but also shared haplotypes, suggesting shared ancestry or recent gene flow[1394].

More recently, new studies based on both mitochondrial and nuclear DNA of many populations of the two taxa have concluded their differentiation with, for mitochondrial DNA, a sharp break at the Bering Sea, thus corresponding to their geographical distribution. Regarding the nuclear DNA, however, the transition is more gradual and linked to gene flow, almost exclusively directed from the Palearctic to Nearctic. This logically corresponds to gene flow carried by ♂♂, which are more prone to erratic movements than ♀♀[973]. Another study of genetic differentiation between *crecca*, *nimia* and *carolinensis* showed that if *crecca/nimia* diverged c.83,000 years ago, the event separating *crecca* and *carolinensis* can be estimated at 1.1 million years[1370]. While *crecca* and *carolinensis* are considered conspecific in North America (AOU), they are recognised as separate species in the Old World by various recent authors[182,393] and the latter position has been adopted here.

IDENTIFICATION The identification of this species from most other dabbling ducks is usually not difficult given its small size, and, in juvenile and ♀ plumage, a pale horizontal patch under the tail-sides. Confusion problems start with Baikal Teal *A. formosa*, at least in

'♀-type' plumages (see that species) and the distinction is much more difficult with Eurasian Teal, although for ♂♂ in definitive basic (adult) and formative (first-winter) plumages, the problems mainly concern hybrids between them (see Hybridisation below). The distinguishing features are,

- A white vertical bar between the flanks and breast is visible in *carolinensis* (more obvious at favourable angles), which is completely absent in *crecca*.

- A white horizontal bar above the black bar that separates the flanks from the upperparts is obvious in *crecca* once pre-basic moult is completed. These two bars are formed by the outer row of scapulars, whose outer web is black in both species, whereas the inner web is white in *crecca* and grey in *carolinensis*.

- The green eye-band is bounded by a clear golden-yellow line in *crecca*. This line is much less pronounced or absent in *carolinensis*, being often reduced to a vague line below the eye and a comma at the base of the bill.

- The wingbar formed by tips to the greater coverts is often reddish inwards, becoming pale reddish to whitish on outermost greater coverts in *carolinensis*. In *crecca*, the outer half is mostly whitish (see ♀ below). The width of the wingbar is more even in *carolinensis*, whereas it clearly increases outwards in *crecca*.

- The vermiculations on the flanks and upperparts are narrower (<0.5 mm wide[1014]) and tighter in *carolinensis*, thus overall colour is slightly darker and browner. The vermiculations are wider and more clearly visible over a reasonable distance in *crecca*, for example on the upper flanks.

- The breast is on average more strongly tinged peach-pink in *carolinensis*.

- The scapulars and tertials have diffuse dark grey shafts in *crecca*, whereas *carolinensis* usually has a plainer grey pattern.

- The head, especially chin and forehead, are on average darker in *carolinensis*. Not always useful for identification of lone birds, this feature is nevertheless often visible in direct comparison.

- The vermiculated rear flanks are often separated

from the undertail-coverts by a pale diffuse stripe, often visible in *crecca* but averaging less pronounced in *carolinensis*.

- The yellow triangle on the sides of the undertail is usually tinged pale lemon in *crecca* but often shows a buff-yellowish or orangey tone in *carolinensis*.

Juvenile and definitive alternate plumages of ♂ are generally kept until mid- and late autumn, respectively, and their identification is obviously much more difficult. Distinction relies on upperwing pattern, but only some individuals of both species can be identified on this basis alone, and even then, only if the sex and age are known.

Adult ♀♀ of both species have long been deemed to be identical, and they are undoubtedly a real identification challenge. It is sometimes possible to try though, especially if faced with a ♀ accompanying a ♂ Green-winged Teal in Eurasia or a ♂ Eurasian Teal in North America for example. The identification of a ♀ teal primarily rests on the upperwing pattern. Overall, Green-winged Teal has the wingbar (tips to greater coverts) rather narrow, of even width and coloured reddish, and a broad white trailing edge to the secondaries. This results in a dark speculum bordered by two pale bars equivalent in width. In Eurasian Teal, the wingbar is whiter, wider and broadens distally, while the white trailing edge is slightly narrower. This results in an upperwing pattern in which the wingbar is usually much more obvious than the trailing edge. A few other features are important but secondary.

The colour of the wingbar is usually reddish on the inner part and white on the outer part in *carolinensis*, and usually mostly white in *crecca*. This feature has long been known, and was even considered sufficient to positively identify 90% of individuals[988]. The information presented here was based on a review of the greater coverts on 93 *carolinensis* (14 adult ♂♂, 20 young ♂♂, 37 adult ♀♀, 22 young ♀♀) and 104 *crecca* (19 adult ♂♂, 23 young ♂♂, 38 adult ♀♀, 24 young ♀♀). It should be borne in mind that a careful examination is needed. On a folded wing, the part that is visible usually corresponds to the inner third, in contact with the tertial coverts, which part of the wingbar is most likely to be tinged reddish in both species, and for all sexes and age groups. In both species, the wingbar is slightly more colourful on average in adult ♂♂ than young ♂♂. In *carolinensis*, adult ♂ has a clearly reddish wingbar on the inner part. The reddish hue is always pronounced at least up to the middle of the wingbar and reddish tones are usually visible on the outermost third.

Only two of 14 birds tested here had the two outermost greater coverts entirely white. Young ♂ has a wingbar on average slightly paler, the third outermost greater coverts being sometimes all white, and one outermost greater covert being all white in half (*n*=10). In adult ♂ *crecca*, the inner part of the wingbar is often reddish, but the third innermost greater covert is sometimes already largely white. A distinct reddish tinge reaches the middle of the wingbar in one quarter of birds, the middle being whitish or washed pale reddish in three-quarters. The outermost part of the wingbar is normally white with, at most, a reddish tone restricted to the fringe. The outermost greater covert is completely white in three-quarters of birds. Young ♂ pattern is quite similar, slightly less reddish on average, but with much overlap.

In the ♀♀, the adult has the wingbar slightly more reddish on average, especially on the inner half. ♀ *carolinensis* has the wingbar similar in colour to that of adult ♂ *crecca*, even if the reddish tone is a little deeper on average over the inner half. A distinct reddish tinge extends to at least the middle of the wingbar in more than half. The outermost greater covert is completely white in 90% of birds (and almost all young ♀♀). The second is white in half of ♀♀ and the fourth white in one-quarter. In *crecca*, the reddish tinge is usually restricted to the three innermost greater coverts. The outer half of the wingbar is completely white in almost all young ♀♀ and in 75% of adult ♀♀ (a reddish tinge exists in the other 25%).

Among ♀♀, there are undoubtedly birds with a pattern that could match either species. In particular, some adult ♀ *crecca* are more colourful than some young ♀ *carolinensis*. Knowledge of age is thus important to use this feature for specific identification, when it will be necessary to determine the precise colour of the greater coverts. For example, the eighth feather (from outside) is clearly reddish in *carolinensis*, and is almost never white or just washed reddish, whereas that is the case for 75% of ♀ *crecca*. The sixth feather (from outside) has a clear or strong reddish coloration in 75% of ♀ *carolinensis* (and is very rarely white), whereas 50% of ♀ *crecca* have this greater covert only slightly reddish and the other half white. The third outermost feather is completely white in virtually all ♀ *crecca*, while almost half of ♀ *carolinensis* show a slight reddish tinge.

- ***Width of the wingbar***: This feature was suggested recently[427]. While *carolinensis* has a fairly even-width wingbar, in *crecca* the white tips to the outer half of the greater coverts (except the outermost) are twice as wide as those of the inner coverts. The width of the white tip is also greater in adults (both sexes and both species).

- **White trailing edge**: Formed by the tips to the secondaries, in both species it is broader in ♀ than ♂ and on average barely wider in juvenile than adult. In *carolinensis*, its width is greater than half the width of the wingbar, and they often appear almost equally wide. This is even truer in young ♀, in which the wingbar is narrower than in young ♂ and adult ♀. In *crecca* the width of the trailing edge is typically less than half that of the wingbar (♀), and does not exceed one-quarter of it in most ♂♂[427, 1156].

- **Head pattern**: More contrasting in *carolinensis*, often including a distinct pale round patch at the bill base. The pale supercilium and dark patch on the rear cheeks are more sharply defined in *carolinensis*, while *crecca* typically has a plainer, warmer head. However, the head of *carolinensis* is more variable, and many birds do not really differ from typical *crecca* (the reverse does not seem true).

- **Bill**: A supportive feature, with much overlap. Young ♀ of *crecca* usually has a clear pale yellowish-orange area at the base of the mandible and tomium. This is on average less extensive in adult ♀, and sometimes completely lacking. In young ♀ *carolinensis*, the pale area is often present, but restricted, and disappears in many adult ♀♀.

- **Breast**: This feature, described by Scott[1156] may prove indicative. The breast of ♀ *carolinensis* is slightly darker and warmer, with a thinner and tighter dark spotting.

- **Overall coloration**: Overall, *carolinensis* shows slightly less reddish or warm tones than *crecca*.

- **Undertail patch**: Both species show a broad horizontal comma under the basal tail-sides, but in *carolinensis*, this area is frequently washed orange, buff or yellowish, whereas it is usually cream-coloured in *crecca*.

PLUMAGES Similar to Eurasian Teal, other than the details mentioned above. Features for sexing and ageing birds are the same as those for the latter species[56,224,1014].

GEOGRAPHIC VARIATION None described within the North American range of the species.

MEASUREMENTS and MASS ♂ slightly larger (all measurements) and heavier than ♀. ♂: wing chord 185.4 (adult, n=86) and 182.2 (juvenile, n=66), mass

322.1 (adult, n=113) and 326.6 (juvenile/first-winter, n=332); ♀: wing chord 177.8 (adult, n=51) and 175.3 (juvenile, n=71), mass 308.5 (adult, n=79) and 290.1 (juvenile/first-winter, n=265)[87]. ♂: wing chord 180–193 (186.3), bill from tip of feathers 36–40 (36.2), tarsus 30–34 (31.7); ♀: wing chord 173–187 (179), bill from tip of feathers 35–38 (36.5), tarsus 30–32 (30.8)[945]. ♂ (n=30): wing chord 173–194 (adult) and 171–190 (juvenile), culmen 34–40, bill depth at tip of forehead feathers 13.2–15.6, tarsus 29–34; ♀ (n=30): wing chord 168–188 (adult) and 162–185 (juvenile), culmen 32–38, bill depth at tip of forehead feathers 12.1–14.4, tarsus 28–33[1014]. Measurements very similar to those for Eurasian Teal, including those presented for both species by same authors[1014].

VOICE Seemingly identical to Eurasian Teal, but comparative study of sonograms would be useful.

MOULT Complex alternate moult strategy. Seemingly identical to Eurasian Teal (which see) and no difference in timing or extent of different moults described in the literature[653,1014] or observed in captivity. Like Eurasian Teal, pre-formative moult of young ♂ often ends in Jan, with juvenile feathers often still visible on upper flanks, whereas adult pre-basic moult in ♂ is often completed between mid-Oct and mid-Nov. Ageing is frequently easy during this period.

HYBRIDISATION Hybrids with Eurasian Teal reported occasionally in North America, W Europe and E Asia (see below). Natural hybrids reported occasionally in Eurasia and North America with Northern Pintail *A. acuta* (which see), Mallard *A. platyrhynchos* (see below) and in New World with American Wigeon *A. americana* (see below) and Blue-winged Teal *A. discors* (which see). Hybrids with Northern Shoveler *A. clypeata*[639] and Cinnamon Teal *A. cyanoptera*[782] are much rarer in the wild. In captivity, hybrids described with, among others, Wood Duck *Aix sponsa*[1190] and Ring-necked Duck *Aythya collaris*[1190]. Other hybrids reported in captivity with Eurasian Teal most likely also involve this species, because many old references do not indicate whether Eurasian Teal or Green-winged Teal is involved.

Green-winged Teal × American Wigeon[639,1190]. Size intermediate between those of its parents, this hybrid is very rare in North America. Like Eurasian Wigeon × Eurasian Teal, adult ♂ in basic plumage appears closer to the teal, with a reddish head (sometimes more beige), large dark glossy green eye-band that extends down hindneck, pale pink breast finely mottled dark, pale reddish vertical bar on fore flanks and upperparts strongly vermiculated dark grey. The rear body can be similar to American Wigeon, with undertail mostly black or recalling Green-winged Teal, with a horizontal whitish triangle on the basal tail-sides. The tail is long and pointed. The bill is black with a pale blue triangle at the sides.

Green-winged Teal × Mallard. Similar to Eurasian Teal × Mallard (see Eurasian Teal). Definitive basic plumage of ♂ of this hybrid is especially variable in the head coloration (with or without bimaculated pattern, ranging between both parents) and bill (variably yellow and black). It is unclear if any of this variability is related to the taxon involved (*crecca* or *carolinensis*), but at least some hybrids show a hint of the typical pale vertical bar on the fore flanks[443].

Green-winged Teal × Eurasian Teal. These hybrids are not very common, but are reported with a frequency close to that of Green-winged Teal in Europe or Eurasian Teal in North America[1204]. The identification problems raised by these hybrids are long known[446,1204,1319] and identification of Green-winged Teal in Eurasia or Eurasian Teal in North America must inevitably take into account their existence. They show a wide variety of appearances, often with a clear white vertical bar on fore flanks and a whitish horizontal stripe between the flanks and upperparts (make sure that pre-basic moult is completed to assess the horizontal bar on the lower scapulars, which is not visible if these feathers are definitive alternate or first basic). Each of these bars is often thinner and shorter than in the parent species from which it is inherited. However, other hybrids (backcrosses?) clearly show one of these two bars alone and a hint of the other. Other birds do not show either. The characters of both parents can be shown simultaneously or be intermediate, which is often the case of the facial pattern, with a pale crescent at the base of the bill and a clear pale line below the eye. In a North American context, a hybrid with a diffuse or interrupted stripe on the fore flanks, and a whitish horizontal bar can be a real pitfall. Faced by a presumed Eurasian Teal, the observer should ensure the complete absence of a pale vertical bar on the fore flanks and the presence of pale lines around the eye-band. Conversely, in Eurasia, a hybrid with a pronounced vertical white bar on the fore flanks and a faint whitish stripe on the lower scapulars will probably cause confusion. A

Green-winged Teal with a horizontal bar above the grey flanks barely paler than the rest of the plumage fits the normal variation of the taxon. The same is true for some birds (c.10%[1204]) with a vertical bar on the fore flanks that is slightly marked. In such cases, however, ensure that other features are normal, eliminating birds that exhibit both a very pronounced vertical bar and a pale grey horizontal one.

HABITAT and LIFE-CYCLE Habitat, behaviour, migration and breeding timing are like those of Eurasian Teal. Migrates fairly early, mostly between Feb and Apr, arriving on nesting grounds between late Mar, in south of range, and late May in north[653]. Wetlands favoured for breeding are often well wooded with deciduous species, including poplars[645], or conifers in taiga. Also present in tundra, especially near large estuaries. Favours tall herbaceous vegetation near water. Moult migrations poorly known, at least some ♂♂ leave nest sites early during incubation, gathering in flocks of a few to >100 birds, with ♀♀ that did not breed or failed. Pre-alternate moult begins in May in ♂♂ that mated early. ♀♀ that raise young moult their wings mainly between late Jul and Sep, usually close to nest sites, but sometimes after completing some of their post-nuptial migration[1092]. Like Eurasian Teal, departures southward are spread over late summer and autumn, arriving on wintering grounds in Aug–Dec, depending on latitude. There is a tendency towards a loop migration, with many birds using the Pacific flyway in autumn and migrating north in spring along the central and Mississippi flyways[862]. In the non-breeding season, uses various types of shallow wetlands, from flooded agricultural areas to brackish coastal marshes, backwaters, forested ponds and estuaries.

RANGE and POPULATION Strictly Nearctic, with a few isolated populations south of the mapped range, to California, New Mexico and Arizona[653]. In winter, the largest concentrations are reported in the Mississippi Valley and Louisiana. Also annual in Cuba, but smaller numbers farther east in the Caribbean and rare in the Lesser Antilles, Central America and N South America. Occasional visitor to W Europe and E Asia, where mainly reported in Japan. Population previously estimated at c.3,000,000 birds, with recent estimates of 3,586,000 in 2012 and 3,351,000 in 2013, following an increase over the last decade, compared to a mean 2,017,000 birds for the period 1955–2012[1294]. The demographic trend now appears to be favourable, but the species is heavily hunted, with the pressure having seemingly undergone a significant increase compared to the overall population. Harvests estimated at more than 2,000,000 birds in 2012 in USA[1028] and nearly 64,000 for Canada [432].

CAPTIVITY Quite frequently kept in captivity in North America, but also well represented and easy to find in Europe. Inexpensive and fairly easy to breed, perhaps even more readily bred than Eurasian Teal.

REFERENCES AOU (1998)[21]; Baker (1993)[56]; Bellrose (1980)[87]; Brazil (2009)[182]; Carney (1992)[224]; Fox *in* Kear (2005)[393]; Garner *et al.* (2008)[427]; Gendron & Smith (2013)[432]; Gillham & Gillham (1996)[439]; Gillham & Gillham (2002)[443]; Gillson (2004)[446]; Johnsgard (1960)[639]; Johnsgard (1975)[645]; Johnson (1995)[653]; Johnson & Sorenson (1999)[654]; Kessler & Avise (1984)[685]; Laurie-Ahlberg & McKinney (1979)[734]; Lockwood & Cooper (1999)[782]; Millington (1998)[848]; Millington (2007)[849]; Moison *et al.* (1967)[862]; Palmer (1976)[945]; Peters (1931)[968]; Peters *et al.* (2012)[973]; Phillips (1922–26)[988]; Pyle (2008)[1014]; Raftovich & Wilkins (2013)[1028]; Rogers (1967)[1092]; Sangster *et al.* (2001)[1132]; Sangster *et al.* (2002)[1133]; Scott (1999)[1156]; Sibley (1938)[1190]; Sibley (2013)[1204]; USFWS (2013)[1294]; Vinicombe (1994)[1319]; Winker *et al.* (2013)[1370]; Zink *et al.* (1995)[1394].

368. Adult ♂ (definitive basic). California, USA, Nov (Sébastien Reeber).

369. Adult ♂ (definitive alternate/definitive basic); note adult tertials. California, USA, Oct (Tom Grey).

370. Adult ♂ (definitive basic); vertical bar on fore flanks varies in prominence according to angle of view. California, USA, Nov (Sébastien Reeber).

371. Adult ♀ (definitive basic); the unflecked patch at the bill base and yellowish wash to the white undertail are good identification features. California, USA, Nov (Sébastien Reeber).

371. Adult ♂ (definitive basic); compared to Eurasian Teal *A. crecca*, note rufous tinge to tips of greater coverts. California, USA, Nov (Sébastien Reeber).

373. Adult ♀ (definitive basic), showing yellowish-buff tinge to undertail. California, USA, Nov (Sébastien Reeber).

374. First-winter ♂ (first basic/formative), with outermost tertials and vermiculations on rump, lower breast and mantle typical of ♂; note narrow, pointed flank feathers, short, frayed tertials and juvenile tertial coverts and rectrices. California, USA, Nov (Sébastien Reeber).

375. ♀ (formative/definitive basic); compared to Eurasian Teal *A. crecca*, note wingbar and trailing edge are of same width. Texas, USA, Feb (Greg Lavaty).

376. Adult ♀ (definitive basic), with adult tertial pattern; this bird shows pale spot at bill base typical of the species. California, USA, Nov (Sébastien Reeber).

MARBLED TEAL
Marmaronetta angustirostris

Plate 36

TAXONOMY *Anas angustirostris* Ménétriés, 1832, *Cat. Raisonné Objets Zool. Recueillis Voyage Caucase*, p. 58. Atypical species, the only member of its genus, with characteristics of both dabbling ducks (Anatini) and scaups (Aythyini). Formerly included in the Anatini, but now often placed in the Aythyini[321,773], although phylogenetically, Marbled Duck is rather distant from typical *Aythya*. Livezey[773] considered *Marmaronetta* to be the first species to have diverged from the ancestor common to all Aythyini and Mergini. No geographical variation or subspecies.

IDENTIFICATION Smallish duck, pale sandy-brown, neatly mottled whitish and remarkably uniform in flight. Usually unmistakable. Can recall Eurasian Teal *A. crecca* and Garganey *A. querquedula* in size, or ♀ Northern Pintail *A. acuta* by its dark diffuse eye-patch, but the more slender silhouette and much larger size should permit easy distinction. See also Crested Duck *Anas (Lophonetta) specularioides*, from South America which could possibly escape from captivity in the Holarctic.

PLUMAGES Weak sexual dimorphism from first winter onwards. Complex alternate moult strategy (two plumages per definitive cycle, three in first cycle) but timing poorly known. All plumages are very similar. Ageing possible until first winter, often more difficult thereafter, unless in the hand. Sexing possible from first winter, but easier in adults during the breeding period.

Adult ♂

Definitive basic plumage. Overall beige-brown, can appear grey-brown or sandy-grey depending on the light, but usually pale. Crown, forehead, lores, chin, throat and cheeks whitish-beige with dark vermiculations, obvious at front of head, more freckled or scaly at rear. Striking dark brown to blackish eye-patch extending rearwards. The long spotted feathers of the back of the head form a drooping rounded crest. Mainly when breeding, and in some postures, the feathers of the forehead and nape are erected, giving the head a unique rectangular profile. Iris brown to dark brown. Bill glossy black with blue area at the sides of the base, extending along the tomium to blend into a pale subterminal bar behind the black nail. Close up, this coloration is well demarcated. Feathers of breast white to beige with grey-brown bases forming irregular dark stripes. Feathers of mantle and

scapulars (the latter narrow and elongated, blunt at tips) grey-brown, darker on their centres, with distal parts showing large rounded whitish patches. The upperparts thus appear rather dark brown with whitish spots. Tertials broad, and pointed, beige to buff-brown, and may appear very pale at a distance. Flank feathers tipped with large round white or beige patches as are scapulars, but otherwise paler grey-brown. Feathers of femoral coverts, undertail-, uppertail-coverts and rump dark grey-brown at base, broadly tipped beige, appearing as dark stripes on a pale background. Plainer pale belly. Rectrices centred dark grey-brown with broad whitish diffuse fringes. Upperwing uniformly grey-beige with lesser coverts and remiges pale sandy-grey (tips of primaries with blackish inner webs and white outer webs, secondaries paler), median, greater and primary coverts slightly duskier. Underwing whitish, except pale grey-brown leading edge and dark tips to primaries. Legs and feet variable, usually dark grey to dull yellowish-olive. Webs dark grey.

Definitive alternate plumage. Very similar to basic plumage, but crest less obvious (often barely visible) and black eye-patch less contrasting. Bill duller with blue parts less clearly demarcated, turning grey.

Adult ♀

Definitive basic plumage. Very similar to adult ♂ and often indistinguishable at distance. Within a nesting pair, head shape is often the most obvious sexing feature. ♀ has a much less marked crest and does not inflate the crest or the feathers of the forehead, unlike the ♂. Close up, the bill has a large triangular olive-yellow diffuse patch at the sides of the bill base, without the ♂'s pale subterminal band behind the nail. Several other features, more tenuous and sometimes subjective, may be useful: slightly shorter bill, dark eye-patch less black and less extensive, vermiculations and streaks on fore cheeks and forehead less clearly defined, centres to scapulars browner, less dark (contrast slightly reduced with round whitish patches at tips), more even brown tertials (outer parts paler in ♂) and tips of primaries more clearly marked black.

Definitive alternate plumage. Seemingly identical to basic plumage. Bill with olive-yellow patch at base becomes greyish, making the sexing much more difficult than in breeding season.

Juvenile

First basic plumage. Similar to adult ♀ but pale tips to scapulars and flank feathers narrower and pale buff, thus less contrasting. Pale patches at tips of scapulars like thin bars rather than round, while pale fringes to the flanks extend onto sides of feathers, creating scalier, ill-defined and 'messy' appearance, very different from adult. Among other features, note that the head seems thinner without any trace of crest, the eye-patch is browner than adult (eye usually more discernible at distance), the bill dull blackish and feathers of back and rump lack clear pale fringes of adult (creating a finely streaked appearance). The breast, lower flanks and belly are more neatly and regularly streaked dark brown (pale grey-brown on belly). Upperwing-coverts darker[479] and browner, especially visible on primary coverts. Outer primaries also darker, with larger black tips.

First-winter

Formative plumage. Formative and first alternate plumages poorly described in the wild, but much closer to those of adult. In the hand, close scrutiny of the upperwing will usually permit ageing (shape of the tertial coverts, greater coverts and primaries, moult contrast among secondary coverts). The bill reaches adult coloration in both sexes before the age of six months.

GEOGRAPHIC VARIATION None despite huge, highly fragmented distribution.

MEASUREMENTS and MASS ♂ marginally larger than ♀. ♂ (*n*=10): wing chord 194–210 (age unknown, 202), tail 65–76 (70), bill 43.2–47.3 (45.0), tarsus 33.6–37.8 (36.2); ♀ (*n*=10): wing chord 192–202 (age unknown, 197), tail 59–74 (67), bill 40.5–44.0 (42.5), tarsus 34.2–37.8 (36.1). Birds from Spain bred in wild and reared in captivity: ♂ (*n*=10): mass 391–458 (420); ♀ (*n*=10): 367–438 (402). Adult (Spain): ♂ (*n*=3): mass 415–510 (465); ♀ (*n*=2): mass 375–469 (422)[479].

VOICE Usually silent. During courtship, ♂ (and occasionally ♀[479]) gives a nasal *weeep*.

MOULT Very few data available from the wild concerning extent and timing of different moults, especially pre-formative moult, and the first and definitive pre-alternate moults of ♀. In captivity at least, the available information matches that for *Anas* and *Aythya*, but this subject merits further study.

HYBRIDISATION Apparently no hybrids reported in the wild. In captivity, has hybridised with Ferruginous Duck *Aythya nyroca*[439,817,1175], while photographs of a captive hybrid with Wood Duck *Aix sponsa* have been published online[106].

HABITAT and LIFE-CYCLE Undertakes erratic and irregular movements, depending on regional variation in rainfall. Inhabits temporary, shallow, fresh or brackish wetlands, with much submerged and riparian vegetation[479], in dry Mediterranean, steppe and semi-desert regions. Also frequents floodplains of rivers and deltas and more permanent wetlands, such as coastal lagoons, slow-flowing streams or even ponds and reservoirs. Pairs form in late winter and early spring. Breeds in lone pairs, although nests can be close to one another where species is numerous. Laying reported Apr–Jun, and broods from mid-Apr to mid-Sep[479]. ♂ sometimes remains with ♀ and brood, defending them[474], but most ♂♂ abandon ♀♀ shortly after hatching[479]. Moult poorly known. Very gregarious in non-breeding season, when can form flocks of up to 2,000 individuals[484], using same habitats as nesting period.

RANGE and POPULATION Very fragmented Eurasian distribution. Tends to vacate northernmost sites to winter in south, where it does not breed, including the Sahel. Rare visitor to coasts of N Mediterranean, where it nested more regularly in past, and east to NW India and Bangladesh. Records from continental Europe often pose questions as to origin, the species being frequently kept in captivity. Global population estimated at 55,000–61,000 individuals[1348], with 44,000 in marshes of lower Euphrates Valley, SE Iraq in early 2010[1121]. The world population was previously estimated at 14,000–26,000 birds in 2002, but this difference probably does not reflect a real increase. The restoration of the Iraqi marshes area since 2002[1121] has probably resulted in a local improvement in conservation status, but also by concentration there of much of SW Asian population[145], part of which was overlooked. Considered Vulnerable by the IUCN, due to a steep decline and massive habitat loss over much of its range (*c*.50% of its favoured habitats were probably destroyed during the 20th century[145]), due to drainage for agriculture, use of water resources for agriculture, domestic reasons and large-scale development, including dams intended to regulate water levels, which is incompatible with temporary wetlands. Other reasons for decline include hunting, illegal or not, especially in Iraq, but probably elsewhere, where the species can be a collateral victim of hunting. Finally, agricultural and domestic water pollution contributes to alter remaining habitats.

CAPTIVITY Reportedly easy to maintain and breed in captivity, where it can even be rather prolific. Easily found for sale, and generally among the cheapest dabbling ducks. Thus very common in captivity, and regularly reported as an escapee, although a natural origin should not always be eliminated, as this species is probably capable of long-distance vagrancy. Without doubt it is extremely difficult to establish the origin of many birds reported in temperate countries of Europe.

REFERENCES Bird Hybrids Flickr forum (2008)[106]; BirdLife International (2014)[145]; Donne-Goussé *et al.* (2002)[321]; Gillham & Gillham (1996)[439]; Green (1997)[474]; Green (1998)[475]; Green (2000)[476]; Green (2000)[477]; Green (2001)[478]; Green *in* Kear (2005)[479]; Green *et al.* (2002)[484]; Iñigo *et al.* (2008)[618]; Livezey (1996)[773]; McCarthy (2006)[817]; Salim (2010)[1121]; Seth-Smith (1911)[1175]; Wetlands International (2014)[1348].

377. Pair (definitive basic); note differences in bill and tertials coloration, with ♂ on left. Turkey, Apr (Vincent Palomares).

378. ♂ (formative/definitive basic); bill coloration is typical of adult ♂, but the short tertials could indicate a second-calendar-year ♂. Tunisia, Apr (Stefano Guiducci).

379. Adult; note unique plain upperwing pattern. Spain, May (Christopher J. G. Plummer).

380. Adult ♂ (definitive alternate). France, Aug (Aurélien Audevard).

381. Adult, showing plain underwing pattern. Spain, Jul (Nis Lundmark Jensen).

RED-CRESTED POCHARD
Netta rufina

Plate 41

TAXONOMY *Anas rufina* Pallas, 1773, *Reise Verschiedene Provinzen Russischen Reichs*, 2, p. 713. Part of the Aythyini, the genus *Netta* includes Red-crested Pochard, a migrant breeder that is discontinuously distributed across temperate Europe and C Asia, and two other species in the S Hemisphere. These three and the presumed extinct Pink-headed Duck *Rhodonessa caryophyllacea* form a clade sister to the genus *Aythya*, and the whole sister to Marbled Duck *Marmaronetta angustirostris*[773]. Thus, Red-crested Pochard and Marbled Duck sit at the 'interface' between dabbling ducks (genus *Anas*) and diving ducks (genus *Aythya*). It is interesting to note that *Marmaronetta* hybridises very rarely, even in captivity, whereas Red-crested Pochard does so readily with both dabbling and diving ducks, in captivity and the wild.

IDENTIFICATION Unmistakable in all plumages.

PLUMAGES Strong sexual dimorphism from first winter onwards. Complex alternate moult strategy (two plumages per definitive cycle, three in first cycle). Ageing ♂♂ relatively easy until the beginning of the first summer. ♀ and juvenile more difficult to distinguish from first autumn onwards.

Adult ♂

Definitive basic plumage (Oct–Nov/May–Jun). Head rounded, with cheeks and throat purplish-brown, merging into reddish-orange upper and rear head, then yellow on rear crown. Lores often appear black. Iris vermilion. Bill bright coral-red, with nail whiter. Neck, nape, breast, belly, flanks and femoral coverts black. Flanks white except a few brown crescents at edge of folded wing. Mantle and scapulars hazelnut-brown with a white patch formed by leading edge of folded wing, visible at shoulders. Tertials colder and paler grey-brown. Back and rump brown, uppertail-coverts blackish. Tail grey. Upperwing-coverts uniform brown with scapulars, and broad white wingbar bordered by blackish tips to outer secondaries and primaries. Outer webs of outer primaries dark. Humeral and marginal coverts (leading edge) white. Underwing whitish, with coverts washed pale brown and dark tips to remiges. Legs dull orange with webs blackish-brown.

Definitive alternate plumage (Jun–July/Sep–Oct.). Plumage very similar to definitive basic plumage of ♀

(see below), but adult ♂ differs from ♀ and juvenile by bill and iris always being bright red (sometimes with dark smudges on culmen in summer/autumn) and by slightly brighter-coloured legs and broad white leading edge to wing.

Adult ♀

Definitive basic plumage (Oct–Dec/Feb–Apr). Head bicoloured, with forehead, crown, lores, nape and hindneck brown (blackish around eye) contrasting with cheeks, and sides of neck pale grey. Diffuse vertical bar at base of bill, chin, throat and foreneck white. Iris brown, sometimes reddish (age-related?). Bill lead-grey with yellowish to orange patch from around black nail extending until about mid-length of tomium and fading gradually. Breast and flanks pale brown, darker on sides of breast, paler on centre of breast and belly, without clear contrast. Undertail-coverts whitish. Tail grey-brown. Mantle, back, rump and scapulars plain brown, slightly darker than flanks. Upperwing like ♂, but no white leading edge and less white on outer primaries, which are washed pale brown. Underwing has leading edge (marginal/lesser coverts) brown, axillaries and median coverts whitish, greater coverts and remiges slightly darker grey. Trailing edge of primaries black, and trailing edge of secondaries white (subterminal blackish bands on outer secondaries). Legs dull yellowish-brown with dark webs.

Definitive alternate plumage (Feb–Apr/Oct–Dec). Seemingly identical to definitive basic plumage.

Juvenile

First basic plumage (until Sep–Jan). Similar to adult ♀, but distinguished by duller and less contrasting appearance. In particular, the crown is greyer without the blackish eye-patch, which makes the eye more obvious at a distance, which is generally not the case in adult ♀. Upperparts greyer too. Iris pale brown, paler than in adult ♀, quickly becoming reddish in young ♂. Bill is initially completely dark, with a small yellowish patch (♀) at the tip or a longer, pink and rapidly spreading patch (♂). Legs yellowish or dull pinkish, slightly brighter in ♂[794]. In the hand, juvenile rectrices are retained until at least Sep and sometimes until Dec[56], and greater coverts are narrower with rounded tips, whereas they are square-tipped in adult.

First-winter ♂

Formative plumage (Nov–Jan/May–Jul). Acquisition of formative plumage, which largely resembles that of adult, rapid in ♂. From Sep, the first adult-type feathers appear and cover most of the body by Nov–Dec. From Jan, many are very similar to adult. Some brown juvenile feathers are often still visible in the black breast and rear body, and the head shape is typically slightly thinner and squarer (less swollen) than adult. At distance, the best ageing feature is the belly, largely stained pale grey-brown in young ♂ (especially contrasting with chest), but black in adult. ♂. In early autumn, the bill is still largely grey with pink patches on the sides of distal half, and rose-orange covering about half of the bill in Oct. In Jan, it usually still has some dark marks on the proximal half of the culmen. The iris becomes reddish during first autumn and is like that of adult early in first winter. Finally, the upperwing remains juvenile, with a thinner white leading edge (white humeral spot still visible), the outer primaries washed pale grey-brown (in hand) and tips of greater coverts rounded.

First-winter ♀

Formative plumage (Nov–Jan/Feb–Mar). Pre-formative moult slower and less extensive in ♀, so that many remain much like juvenile until beginning of first winter. The distinction remains difficult and will require close observation. The yellow patches on the sides of the distal half of the bill are smaller than in adult ♀, and the iris remains pale brown at its outer edge and dark brown at the centre, often until the middle of the first winter at least. Tertials and retained tertial coverts slightly thinner, more pointed and appear visibly frayed at the tips (round-tipped in adult) until the beginning of the second pre-basic moult.

First-summer ♂

First alternate plumage (May–Jul/Sep–Dec). Difficult to distinguish from adult ♂ but at least some birds have blackish marks on upper culmen until first summer (adult ♂ can also show these in non-breeding season). The most reliable feature is the upperwing, still juvenile until second pre-basic moult.

GEOGRAPHIC VARIATION None described.

MEASUREMENTS and MASS ♂ and adult slightly larger than ♀ and young, respectively. ♂: wing chord 255–273 (adult, 264, n=16) and 250–264 (juvenile, 257, n=7), bill 45–52 (48.2, n=25), tarsus 42–47 (44.1, n=25), mass in Mar (Kazakhstan) (n=17) 990–1,300

(1,130) and Oct (n=11) 1,200–1,420 (1,320); ♀: wing chord 251–275 (adult, 260, n=14) and 237–259 (juvenile, 248, n=10), bill 42–50 (46.6, n=26), tarsus 40–45 (42.2, n=26), mass in Mar (Kazakhstan) (n=12) 1,000–1,200 (1,100) and Oct (n=6) 1,100–1,400 (1,220)[267].

VOICE Usually quiet, most frequently heard during courtship. ♂ gives short, repeated *seerr*, sometimes longer and often descending *see-urr* with an asthmatic and raspy tone, ending in a thin metal trill. ♀ gives a repeated *gurrr*, more like ♀ *Aythya*.

MOULT Complex alternate strategy. Pre-formative moult involves most head and body feathers, except some of the belly and back, usually all rectrices and a variable number of inner upperwing-coverts. It occurs between Sep and Dec in ♂ but until at least Feb in ♀, in which it is less extensive and probably merges into first pre-alternate moult. Definitive pre-alternate moult occurs in May–Jun in ♂[56]. Less well described in ♀ in the wild, but in captivity at least some head and body feathers are replaced prior to nesting, in Feb–Apr, resembling the moult timing in the genera *Anas* and *Aythya*. Definitive pre-basic moult begins in Jun–Jul and usually ends in Oct. It finishes approximately one month later in ♀.

HYBRIDISATION Hybridises frequently and with a large number of species. Natural hybrids regularly reported with Mallard *Anas platyrhynchos*, Northern Pintail *A. acuta*, Common Pochard *Aythya ferina* (see below for descriptions of these three hybrids), Ferruginous Duck *A. nyroca*, Tufted Duck *A. fuligula* (see these two species respectively), and possibly Baikal Teal *Anas formosa*[1097]. In captivity, hybridisation also reported with Common Shelduck *Tadorna tadorna*[1148], Wood Duck *Aix sponsa*[439,817], American Wigeon *Anas americana*[465], Eurasian Wigeon *A. penelope*[587,817], Chiloe Wigeon *A. sibilatrix*[619], African Black Duck *A. sparsa*[817], Yellow-billed Duck *A. undulata*[439,465], Pacific Black Duck *A. superciliosa*[465,585,817,988], Indian Spot-billed Duck *A. poecilorhyncha*[439,465,817], Yellow-billed Pintail *A. georgica*[439,465], Southern Pochard *Netta erythrophthalma*[439], Rosy-billed Pochard *N. peposaca*[439,465,817,988], Redhead *Aythya americana*[439,46,1190], Canvasback *A. valisineria*[439], Ring-necked Duck *A. collaris*[1190] and Greater Scaup *A. marila*[97,639].

Red-crested Pochard × Mallard. A rather common hybrid, at least locally in W & C Europe, and quite variable in overall appearance, meaning that it is not always possible to determine the sex. Head profile often reminiscent of Red-crested Pochard, being strong, rounded and with a relatively thin bill similar to Red-crested Pochard (more rarely closer to that of Mallard). ♂ (definitive basic) can have head uniformly dark, often with purple or violet sheen, or has bimaculated pattern with two pale patches on cheeks. The bill can be almost all reddish-pink, with or without dark marks on proximal half, or closer to ♀ Red-crested Pochard, dark grey with a yellow subterminal patch, including in ♂-plumaged birds. In all cases, the nail appears blackish. Breast very variable, blackish-brown to reddish, but also light brown paler than in either parent (intersex?). Brown to pale brown upperparts, sometimes grey and vermiculated, generally darker at border with flanks, which are usually pale grey (whitish finely vermiculated dark grey) to grey-beige or pale grey-brown. Tertials broad, pale grey. Rear body often recalls Mallard, black tail fringed white, sometimes with two central tertial coverts slightly up-curved. Upperwing intermediate. Legs yellow-orange. ♀ also varies, but usually is generally pale caramel, slightly darker on the upperparts with head similar to Red-crested Pochard in pattern and coloration. However, a blackish eyestripe is often visible, sometimes with a whitish supercilium[443] and grey area on rear cheeks. Bill mostly grey with yellowish at tip. Tertials broad and greyish. Tail dark-centred, white at edges. Legs yellowish-orange. See Gillham & Gillham[439,443] for further details of variation.

Red-crested Pochard × Northern Pintail[439,443,528]. Rarer than previous hybrid, which it resembles by obvious mix of characters inherited from dabbling ducks and Red-crested Pochard. Like the previous hybrid, appearance varies and gynandromorphy is frequent. Adult ♂ in basic plumage appears uniform grey-brown. All-dark head with reddish-brown hue. Bill pale pinkish at tip, greyer basally, with well-defined black nail and (proximal) part of the tomium and culmen. Grey body (pale vermiculated dark), browner and darker in places with little contrast between breast, flanks and upperparts. Legs dull yellowish. Some have body closer to ♀ Red-crested Pochard with contrast between cheeks and upper head, and hint of white vertical line on neck of Northern Pintail. Bill shows mixed characters between ♂ Northern Pintail (grey-blue surrounded by black in profile) with yellow patches at tip like ♀ Red-crested Pochard. Tail can be clearly pointed and elongated[528] or not. Upperwing usually has a dark brownish rectangle on the secondaries (speculum) bordered white.

Red-crested Pochard × Common Pochard. Reported quite frequently in Europe. Adult ♂ easily recognised in basic plumage, which can recall Redhead *Aythya americana*, including head shape and size. Head usually strong, rounded and reddish. Iris red. Bill variable, pale blue-grey with blackish marks at the base, on tomium, upper culmen and at tip, sometimes covering the nostrils. Part may be pinkish. Usually has two yellowish patches on the bill either side of the black nail. Breast and rear body black. Flanks whitish vermiculated pale grey, with or without hint of pale brown crescents beside the wing. Upperparts vary, sometimes brown recalling Red-crested Pochard, sometimes vermiculated pale grey becoming dark grey at rear and at border with flanks. Legs yellowish. ♀ in basic plumage fairly uniform pale brown (belly and rear flanks more whitish), with clear-cut whitish undertail-coverts. Head more variegated, with crown and nape dark brown, cheeks paler with whitish oval patch at base of bill and sometimes a pale bridle behind eye. Throat whitish. Bill can be entirely dark grey with two diffuse yellow patches either side of the nail, but sometimes has diffuse, broad, pale blue-grey subterminal band like Redhead.

HABITAT and LIFE-CYCLE Medium to long-distance migrant in Asia, but undertakes only short-range movements on coasts and in Europe, provided waters remain clear in winter. Inhabits deltas, slow-moving streams, ponds and lakes, of fresh or brackish water, rather deep and with extensive reedbeds. Pairs often solitary, but nests can be just 30 m apart[303]. Eggs laid mainly between mid-Apr and early Jun[794], in nests under dense vegetation on ground or on floating vegetation, especially in reedbeds. ♂ abandons ♀ during incubation and performs moult migration, often over long distances, with non-breeding ♀♀. Leaves moulting grounds late in season, and arrive in wintering areas from Oct, often well advanced in pre-basic moult (many Anseriformes leave moulting grounds as soon as they can fly again, before moulting the body feathers). Gregarious in winter, and can form large roosts especially in heavily hunted areas. Uses same habitats as in breeding season.

RANGE and POPULATION Eurasia, from Mongolia and NW China to Black Sea, with scattered populations in Turkey, Europe and NW Africa. Asian population is migratory, but partially sedentary in Europe. Wintering population estimated at 50,000 individuals in C & W Europe, 20,000–43,500 in the Black Sea and E Mediterranean, 250,000–400,000 in C & SW Asia and 100,000 in S Asia[1348]. The first-named population is increasing, while trends are unknown or unclear for the others. Introduced in UK, where several dozen pairs nest and numbers were estimated at 250 individuals in the early 2000s[62], making it virtually impossible to identify natural vagrants there. Threatened, at least locally, especially by hunting and habitat loss[145,289].

CAPTIVITY Probably one of the most frequently kept species in captivity, especially in Europe. Readily bred and regularly offered for sale, usually for some of the lowest prices among Anseriformes. Very likely to escape and many out-of-range birds are automatically considered to have done so.

REFERENCES Baker (1993)[56]; Banks *et al.* (2008)[62]; Bird Hybrids database (2014)[97]; BirdLife International (2014)[145]; Cramp & Simmons (1977)[268]; Defos du Rau (2002)[289]; Delany *in* Kear (2005)[303]; Gillham & Gillham (1996)[439]; Gillham & Gillham (2002)[443]; Gray (1958)[465]; Harrop (1993)[528]; Hopkinson (1933)[585]; Hopkinson (1935)[587]; IZY (1973)[619]; Johnsgard (1960)[639]; Keller (2006)[676]; Livezey (1996)[773]; Madge & Burn (1988)[794]; McCarthy (2006)[817]; Phillips (1922–26)[988]; Rothschild (1921)[1097]; Schmitz (1987)[1148]; Sibley (1938)[1190]; Wetlands International (2014)[1348].

382. Adult ♂ (definitive basic). India, Jan (Amit Thakurta).

383. Pair. Italy, Apr (Stefano Guiducci).

384. Adult ♀ (definitive basic). Switzerland, Feb (Aurélien Audevard).

385. First-winter ♀ (formative), with iris still reddish-brown on its outer part, as well as narrower and visibly frayed tertials. Switzerland, Feb (Aurélien Audevard).

386. Adult ♂ (definitive alternate); like ♀ and juvenile at this time, but easily distinguished by its red iris and bill. Netherlands, Aug (Otto Plantema)

387. ♀ (formative/definitive basic). India, Dec (Amit Thakurta).

388. Adult ♀ (definitive basic); inner secondaries (without white fringes) and broad square-tipped, blackish greater coverts suggest an adult. ♀. Netherlands, Jun (Seraf van der Putten).

389. Juvenile (first basic); resembles adult ♀, but iris pale brown (becoming reddish in ♂), shorter head feathers, juvenile rectrices, and dull bill (already reddish in young ♂ behind). Spain, Jul (Nis Lundmark Jensen).

390. Adult ♂ (definitive basic); in all plumages, very broad white wingbar is typical. India, Dec (Amit Thakurta).

CANVASBACK
Aythya valisineria

TAXONOMY *Anas valisineria* Wilson, 1814, *Amer. Orn.*, 8, p. 103, pl. 70, fig. 5. The genus *Aythya* is sister to the clade comprising the genus *Netta* (which also includes Pink-headed Duck *Rhodonessa caryophyllacea*). Both genera and Marbled Duck *Marmaronetta angustirostris* constitute the Aythyini. The genus *Aythya* comprises three subgenera: *Nyroca* for the four brown-plumaged species with white irides, *Aythya* for the five black-headed species, and *Aristonetta* for the three red-headed species (in adult ♂♂). Of these three, Redhead *A. americana* and Common Pochard *A. ferina* are sometimes considered sister species, beside Canvasback[773], but the latter is sometimes considered closer to Common Pochard[647]. No geographic variation or subspecies.

IDENTIFICATION In North American range, generally unmistakable. Compared to other diving ducks, has distinctive head profile, with flat crown and forehead prolonged by long straight culmen. Bill uniquely thin-tipped and entirely blackish. Also note large size. In very good views or in the hand, size of the nail is diagnostic, 4–6 mm wide and 6–8 mm long, vs. 3–5 mm wide and 4–6 mm long in Common Pochard and 7–9 mm wide and 8–10 mm long in Redhead[1014]. Redhead is the only other Nearctic duck with similar coloration, but has a different shape (shorter bill, high and steep forehead, rounded head). Canvasback also distinguished (in adult ♂) by flanks and upperparts, including tertials, appearing almost whitish, darker red head and red iris (vs. yellow). Other plumages of Canvasback are greyer and paler.

Distinction from Common Pochard is a little trickier. Although they rarely meet, the identification of a Common Pochard in North America, or a Canvasback in Eurasia requires meticulous care. However, a vagrant on the 'wrong' continent will nearly always join flocks of the 'other' species, permitting useful size comparisons, Canvasback being nearly a third heavier than Common Pochard. In all plumages, head profile is decisive: crown rather flat almost without any angle between the forehead and culmen, which is long and straight. In Common Pochard, the crown is higher and rounded and the culmen is clearly concave in profile. Note also that Canvasback often holds its tail raised at rest. Adult ♂♂ in basic plumage are easily separated using bill colour (all black in Canvasback, but with large pale blue-grey

area on the central bill in Common Pochard), head colour (red with cap, around eyes and lores blackish vs. entirely red), the brighter red iris of Canvasback, the black breast (small and oblique profile in Canvasback vs. extensive and vertically delineated in profile) and upperparts, flanks and tertial coloration (whitish vs. light grey). ♀♀ of the two species are difficult to separate as they are similarly coloured, even if the undertail-coverts average whiter and the body (flanks and upperparts) slightly paler, sometimes appearing almost whitish, in Canvasback. The other distinguishing features of head shape and overall size are like those for ♂♂, as well as bill coloration: entirely blackish in Canvasback and dark grey basally with a broad, diffuse subterminal pale blue-grey mark contrasting with the nail in Common Pochard.

Finally, hybrids between Canvasback and Common Pochard are occasionally reported in W Europe. They are very tricky to identify, but must be considered when faced with a potential vagrant of either species (see Hybridisation under Common Pochard).

PLUMAGES Strong sexual dimorphism from first winter onward. Complex alternate moult strategy (two plumages per definitive cycle, three in first cycle). Ageing can be difficult from beginning of second calendar year.

Adult ♂

Definitive basic plumage (Nov–Dec/May–Jun). Essentially tricoloured. Head and neck reddish, becoming blackish on crown and fore face including around eye and chin. Iris red. Bill long, narrowing at tip, all black. Upper breast black. Mantle, scapulars, tertials and flanks white with thin grey vermiculations, appearing whitish at distance. Lower breast and belly whitish. Back, rump, upper- and undertail-coverts blackish. Tail grey-brown. Upperwing fairly uniform, with secondary coverts, tips of primary coverts and alula vermiculated whitish-grey, primary coverts and bases of greater coverts forming darker bar on wing. Remiges pale grey-brown with blackish tips to primaries and outer secondaries. Outer webs of outer primaries dark. Underwing has coverts and axillaries whitish (centres to feathers on leading edge browner), remiges pale grey with darker trailing edge. Legs bluish-grey with darker webs.

Definitive alternate plumage (May–Jun/Oct–Nov). Similar to previous plumage, especially in older birds, though duller, more reminiscent of ♀, but still easily distinguished from latter and juvenile. Head reddish-brown, possibly with pale spots at bill base and around eye. Breast finely streaked brown (feathers with pale fringes and blackish bases) with a variable number of dusky feathers. Feathers of flanks, mantle and scapulars vermiculated or more obviously brown than basic plumage. Whole appearance dirtier grey-brown than basic plumage. Lower breast, belly and undertail with diffuse brownish patches. Back and rear body dull blackish (sometimes, pale tips to feathers visible).

Adult ♀

Definitive basic plumage (Nov–Dec/Mar–Apr). Head, neck and breast cinnamon-brown, darker on nape and crown, paler on throat and foreneck, with a pale line surrounding the eye and extending as a bridle across the upper cheeks. Iris blackish-brown. Bill dark grey to blackish. Mantle, scapulars and flanks appear uniformly pale grey at a distance. Up close, feathers whitish with dark grey-brown vermiculations and diffuse brownish crescents. Longest tertials dark grey. Back and rump dark brown possibly with fine vermiculations in places. Uppertail dark grey-brown. Belly creamy-whitish with brown patches increasing posteriorly. Undertail-coverts whitish. Upperwing like ♂, but more grey-brown and slightly darker: all coverts have tips largely vermiculated white, the darkest part of the wing being the greater primary coverts and trailing edge to primaries and outer secondaries. Underwing and legs like ♂.

Definitive alternate plumage (Apr–May/Oct–Nov). Similar to previous plumage, but browner and less uniform, with contrast between the breast and neck, and upperparts and flanks. Head usually plainer, often with the pale eye-ring and dark loral stripe the most contrasting elements. Bill dark grey, possibly with a diffuse paler subterminal band. Breast reddish-brown finely striped pale. Feathers of mantle and scapulars have large dark grey-brown bases and are distally vermiculated whitish, appearing overall rather darker and mottled dusky. Flank feathers have bases brown like breast, with whitish tips vermiculated whitish. Belly and undertail mottled or speckled grey.

Juvenile

First basic plumage (until Oct–Nov). Like definitive alternate plumage of ♀, but slightly darker brown and more uniform, especially on head and upperparts, usually without white and grey vermiculations. Relatively uniform brown head, darker and washed reddish in ♂, paler and yellowish in ♀. Bill dark grey. Iris initially dull orange in young ♂, already showing first signs of adult scarlet colour at age of three months[885]. Iris pale brown in ♀. Mantle feathers and scapulars dark grey-brown with at most a few buff freckles on fringes. Longest tertials grey, with a few pale vermiculations at the tips (♀) or with more obvious white vermiculations and speckles (♂)[224]. Tertial coverts with few to strong (♂) or none to very few (♀) white speckles (clear white speckles in adult ♀ but concentrated towards tip). Breast and flanks pale grey-brown with paler fringes forming vague crescents. Lower flanks, belly and undertail striped or mottled grey-brown. Distinguished from definitive plumages of both sexes by upperwing pattern, especially the primary- and median coverts narrower and more pointed in juvenile. Also grey-brown heavily speckled pale grey in adult ♀ but speckles more concentrated at the tip. In young ♀, secondary coverts are plain grey-brown or lightly speckled, while in young ♂, the pale grey speckles and vermiculations are stronger and more evenly distributed throughout[224].

First-winter ♂

Formative plumage (Oct–Mar/May–Jun). Following pre-formative moult, very similar to adult ♂ in basic plumage, and can be difficult to age. From early winter, the iris is red, with at most a few yellow or brown spots. The dark vermiculations on the mantle, scapulars and flanks are on average a little more strongly marked[1173], and some juvenile tertials (dark grey and rather uniform) and rectrices (brown and worn) are often retained. The best ageing feature, however, remains the upperwing pattern, useful until the second pre-basic moult. The wing of adult ♂ appears quite uniform pale grey and the primary- and median coverts almost whitish, offering no contrast with the scapulars and mantle. In young ♂, there is a clear contrast, usually between adult-type scapulars/tertial coverts and juvenile secondary coverts (speckled pale, but substantially darker grey-brown). Furthermore, the greater and primary coverts are almost entirely dark grey-brown. Note this moult limit can be located differently: pre-formative moult may include no tertial coverts in some, but many inner secondary coverts in others.

First-winter ♀

Formative plumage (Nov–Mar/Mar–May). Appearance gradually like that of basic plumage adult ♀ and generally cannot be aged without close check of upperwing pattern, useful until second pre-basic moult. In adult ♀, all secondary- and tertial coverts, as well as tertials, show pale grey flecks towards the tips, which are also broad and rounded. In young ♀, the speckles are more discreet or absent and less concentrated at the tips, which are sharper and more rapidly worn. At long range, the speckled tips to the median and posterior lesser coverts produce two pale wingbars in adult, whereas young ♀ shows a plainer upperwing.

GEOGRAPHIC VARIATION None.

MEASUREMENTS and MASS ♂ and adult slightly larger than ♀ and young, respectively. ♂ (*n*=12): wing chord 229–248 (235), tail 56–60 (57.1); ♀ (*n*=12): wing chord 221–234 (229), tail 56–59 (57.9)[945]. ♂ (*n*=18): culmen 60.0 (σ ± 0.6), tarsus 46.0 (σ ± 0.3); ♀ (*n*=9): culmen 56.2 (σ ± 0.6), tarsus 44.1 (σ ± 0.4)[337]. ♂ (*n*=30): wing chord 224–243 (adult) and 219–238 (juvenile), culmen 57–66, bill depth at tip of forehead feathering 23.6–28.1, tarsus 44–47, tail 54–61; ♀ (*n*=30): wing chord 216–234 (adult) and 211–228 (juvenile), culmen 55–63, bill depth at tip of forehead feathering 22.1–26.1, tarsus 43–46, tail 53–60[1014]. ♂: mass in autumn 1,482 (adult, σ ± 10, *n*=506) and 1,351 (first-winter, σ ± 30, *n*=78); ♀: mass in autumn 1,348 (adult, σ ± 17, *n*=187) and 1,229 (first-winter, σ ± 29, *n*=44)[1174]. ♂: mass in winter 850–1,600 (adult, 1252, σ ± 9, *n*=191) and 1,020–1,510 (first-winter, 1,250, σ ± 11, *n*=57); ♀: mass in winter 900–1,530 (adult, 1,154, σ ± 14, *n*=54) and 950–1,390 (first-winter, 1,149, σ ± 29, *n*=26)[1113].

VOICE ♂ in courtship produces a slightly squeaky chatter, with obviously louder notes, like *weee-whoo-o-o*. ♀ gives an *errr* similar to that of other *Aythya*.

MOULT Complex alternate moult strategy. Pre-formative moult occurs in Sep–Mar, possibly slowing down (♂) or even suspended (♀) during coldest months of winter[785] and includes a variable number of body feathers, with few or none replaced on belly, rear body and rump, and (often) 1–3 tertials and 1–5 tertial coverts[224,1014], sometimes a few inner upperwing-coverts and variable number of rectrices (sometimes all). This moult is faster and on average more extensive in young ♂♂ than young ♀♀[785]. Definitive pre-alternate moult occupies Mar–May in ♀♀ (during spring migration and arrival on breeding grounds) and May–Jul in ♂♂ (on moulting grounds). It includes a variable number of upperparts and breast feathers, few or no inner upperwing-coverts and up to two rectrices and tertials. This moult is more extensive on average in ♀♀ than ♂♂, and even more so in breeding ♀♀ than non-breeding ♀♀[785], while its extent possibly decreases with age in ♂♂[1014]. Definitive pre-basic moult occurs in both sexes between Jul and Nov, is complete, and begins with the simultaneous loss of the remiges[1263]. Nevertheless, this moult is perhaps sometimes protracted until the following spring, so as not to compromise the energy costs of spring migration, mating and even egg formation[785].

HYBRIDISATION Natural hybridisation reported occasionally with Redhead *A. americana*, Ring-necked Duck *A. collaris* and Common Pochard *A. ferina* (see these three species, respectively). Even more occasional cases mentioned in 19th century with Mallard *Anas platyrhynchos*[817,988] and Lesser Scaup *Aythya affinis*[817], or more recently with Tufted Duck *A. fuligula*[442], Greater Scaup *A. marila*[465,584,1195] and possibly American Wigeon *Anas americana*[345]. In captivity, hybrids also described with Wood Duck *Aix sponsa*[439], Rosy-billed Pochard *Netta peposaca*, Southern Pochard *N. erythrophthalma* and Red-crested Pochard *N. rufina*[439].

HABITAT and LIFE-CYCLE Migratory, with spring movements towards nesting grounds between early Mar and mid-Apr[885], when pairs form[573]. Breeds in various semi-permanent or permanent wetlands: ponds, lakes, shallow bays within large waterbodies, marshes and swamps with some deeper areas, backwaters and slow-moving streams. Appreciates the proximity to, provided there are shallow areas, helophytes (*Scirpus*, *Typha*, etc.) for nesting. Eggs laid mainly early May to mid-Jun. ♂ abandons ♀ in early incubation and heads to moulting grounds, usually further north[885], gathering to moult their flight feathers at large wetlands in company of non-breeding ♀♀ and second-calendar-year ♂♂, which usually do not breed[573]. Breeding ♀♀ usually moult their wings near nest sites, with their young, at most moving to more open water[945]. Migrates to wintering sites in stages over long period, with peak movements from mid-Oct to mid-Nov. In winter and on migration, more gregarious like all *Aythya*, lone birds or vagrants tending to join flocks of congenerics. Winters mainly along coasts, frequenting bays and brackish or saltwater lagoons, including sheltered coasts with muddy bottoms, estuaries, lakes and deep artificial reservoirs.

RANGE and POPULATION Strictly Nearctic. Scarce breeder in south and east of mapped range, from

Central Valley of California, C New Mexico, Kansas, Wisconsin, Michigan and C New York[885]. Winters mainly on coasts but extends via Mississippi Valley to Great Lakes. Mainly irregular visitor to interior of S USA and south to near Mexico City, Mexico. Strong annual fluctuations in most regions, depending on winter weather, with large numbers overwintering further north during mild weather. Rare visitor to the Aleutians, in far NE USA, N & E Canada, and south to Guatemala and Honduras[885]. Occasional or accidental in Greater Antilles, Hawaii, along Russian Pacific coast, Japan (annual), South Korea, Taiwan, NE China [182], Iceland, with a few reports in NW Europe, although the origin of these birds is often discussed (especially given the lack of records in the Azores to date). Mean breeding population in 1955–2012 estimated at 576,000 individuals, with a slight increase during last 20 years. Recent estimates of 760,000 birds in 2012 and 787,000 in 2013[1294].

CAPTIVITY Uncommon. The species is very demanding regarding the size and depth of its ponds, and is rather difficult to breed. It is usually sold at medium to high prices, and is often one of the most expensive species of Holarctic *Aythya*.

REFERENCES Brazil (2009)[182]; Carney (1992)[224]; Dzubin (1959)[337]; Edscorn (1974)[345]; Fournier & Hines (1998)[389]; Gillham & Gillham (1996)[439]; Gillham & Gillham (2000)[442]; Gray (1958)[465]; Hohman *in* Kear (2005)[573]; Hopkinson (1933)[584]; Howell & Webb (1995)[592]; Johnsgard (1979)[647]; Kessler & Avise (1984)[685]; Lagerqvist & Ankney (1988)[723]; Livezey (1996)[773]; Lovvorn & Barzen (1988)[785]; McCarthy (2006)[817]; Mowbray (2002)[885]; Palmer (1976)[945]; Phillips (1922–26)[988]; Pyle (2008)[1014]; Ryan (1972)[1113]; Serie *et al.* (1982)[1173]; Serie & Sharp (1989)[1174]; Sibley (2000)[1195]; Thompson & Drobney (1995)[1263]; USFWS (2013)[1294].

391. Adult ♂ (definitive basic). California, USA, Nov (Sébastien Reeber).

392. Adult ♂ (definitive basic). California, USA, Nov (Sébastien Reeber).

393. First-winter ♂ (formative); juvenile feathers still present on breast and head (duller), and rump, while tertials are still growing at end of pre-formative moult. California, USA, Apr (Sébastien Reeber).

394. Adult ♂ (definitive basic), showing clear pale patch on lower culmen, which is relatively frequent in captive birds in W Europe, probably as result of ancient hybridisation. Captivity (England), Feb (Sébastien Reeber).

395. ♀ (first alternate/definitive alternate); plainer, creamy-brown plumage. Montana, USA, Jul (Ron Bielefeld).

396. Adult ♀ (definitive basic); aged by adult tertials and white freckles on tips of greater coverts. California, USA, Nov (Sébastien Reeber).

REDHEAD
Aythya americana

TAXONOMY *Fuligula americana* Eyton, 1838, *Monogr. Anatidae*, p. 155. Within the genus *Aythya*, most closely related to Common Pochard *A. ferina* and Canvasback *A. valisineria*[685,773] (see Taxonomy of the latter).

IDENTIFICATION In a North American context, adult ♂ Redhead in basic plumage has a superficial resemblance to Canvasback in the same plumage, as it is the only other Nearctic duck with a grey body, black breast and rear body, and reddish head. ♀ and juvenile Redhead are more reminiscent of Ring-necked Ducks *A. collaris*, both in colour and shape, but are much larger (see Identification under latter). See Hybridisation for descriptions of similar-looking hybrids.

In Eurasia, where Redhead is an accidental visitor (W Europe and Asia), Common Pochard is the obvious problem. In all plumages, Redhead is clearly larger and *c.*25% heavier, and further differs in having a large round head rather like that of Red-crested Pochard *Netta rufina*. Adult ♂ in basic plumage differs by its bright yellow iris (vs. red in Common Pochard), largely pale blue-grey bill with a white subterminal band and black tip bordered vertically in profile (vs. largely black at base, with a pale blue-grey mark on the distal half and a black tip demarcated obliquely in profile) and body strongly vermiculated dark grey, being darker overall than Common Pochard. ♀♀ in formative and basic plumages differ from Common Pochard by being warmer and plainer brown, with almost no contrast between the breast and flanks, for example, and by the vertically delineated black tip to the bill in profile. The pale pattern on the head also differs somewhat: more contrasting in Common Pochard, which shows a clear pale line sloping behind the eye, while in Redhead the whitish eye-ring is generally the most striking feature. In Eurasia, other identification issues arise from the existence of hybrids, some of which are like this species, even when resulting from crosses between two other species. To identify a Redhead, first eliminate the possibility of hybrids involving Common Pochard on the one hand, and Red-crested Pochard or Ferruginous Duck *A. nyroca* on the other (see Hybridisation under these species).

PLUMAGES Strong sexual dimorphism from first winter onwards. Complex alternate moult strategy (two plumages per definitive cycle, three in first cycle).

Ageing can be tricky from the beginning of the second calendar year.

Adult ♂

Definitive basic plumage (Oct–Nov/Jun–Jul). Tricoloured. Head and neck reddish-orange. Iris bright yellow-orange. Bill blue with clear-cut white subterminal band and broad black tip. The black gape runs up along the bill base as a thin black line, visible when close. The bill colours become more vivid with age[1374]. Lower neck and breast black. Mantle, scapulars and flanks pale grey with tight dark grey vermiculations, appearing grey from afar, slightly darker posteriorly. Tertials rather uniform dark grey. Belly white. Back, rump and uppertail-coverts blackish. Tail grey-brown. Upperwing has grey secondary coverts variably speckled pale and primary coverts marginally darker. Broad pale grey wingbar (slightly paler on secondaries), with blackish terminal (primaries) or subterminal (secondaries) marks, forming a dark trailing edge, diffuse on the inner secondaries. The white-fringed tips to the secondaries form a thin trailing edge. Outer webs of outermost few primaries dark. Underwing-coverts and axillaries whitish (pale grey-brown on leading edge), centres to greater coverts and flight feathers pale grey with dark trailing edge more obvious on primaries. Legs brownish-grey with darker webs.

Definitive alternate plumage (Jun–Jul/Oct–Nov). Overall a duller and less contrasting version of definitive basic plumage, and easily distinguished from adult ♀ and juvenile. Brownish-orange head and blackish breast (or faintly streaked brown). Iris duller in non-breeding season. Bill also duller. Flanks, mantle and scapulars vermiculated with diffuse brownish patches, and have a messy, uneven appearance. Lower breast and belly irregularly marked with brown patches. Back and rear body dull blackish mottled pale.

Adult ♀

Definitive basic plumage (Nov–Dec/Apr–May). Head, neck and breast hazel-brown, darker on crown (including eye) and nape, and slightly paler to whitish at base of bill, chin and throat. Contrasting white eye-ring extends as a short bridle to rear. Adult ♀ peculiarly shows quite frequent scattered white feathers on the rear cheeks, neck-sides and nape. Iris brown, sometimes pale brown or yellowish. Bill pale grey with broad black tip and thin pale subterminal band, with same pattern as ♂, but significantly less obvious. Feathers of mantle, flanks and scapulars hazelnut-brown with broad pale grey fringes and dark grey vermiculations, forming vague pale crescents. Tertials round-tipped, dark grey-brown and uniform, without vermiculations. Back and rump grey-brown, with feathers barely fringed paler and uppertail slightly darker. Belly whitish, heavily stained brownish-grey lower down. Undertail grey-brown, often with white patch under tail-sides (tips to undertail-coverts). Tail grey-brown. Upperwing like ♂, but tinged browner overall, with subterminal blackish bars often more marked on secondaries. Coverts at most slightly speckled whitish towards the tips (variable in ♂). Underwing and legs like ♂.

Definitive alternate plumage (Apr–May/Oct–Nov). Similar to previous plumage, but has stronger brown and buff to reddish hues, e.g. on breast and upper flanks. The head is rather plain, albeit with bill base, chin and foreneck whitish and a conspicuous pale eye-ring. Upperparts, nape and upper head darker brown, also fairly uniform. Belly and undertail mottled brown. The bill also becomes very dark grey with an often barely visible pale subterminal band.

Juvenile

First basic plumage (until Sep–Nov). Like definitive alternate plumage of ♀ but irregularly stained brown, and head and upperparts uniform dark brown. Head dark brown with reddish tones and pale pattern barely noticeable in ♂, or paler brown, without red and clear pale pattern in ♀. Bill uniformly dark, dull grey, the pale subterminal band appearing at *c.*2 months in ♂, thereafter differences in the bill increase between the sexes. Iris initially pale yellowish-brown and dull, becoming brown centrally in young ♀, and yellow in ♂ at 3–4 months. Upperparts feathers fairly uniformly grey-brown, with subtle paler fringes. Tertials quickly fray at tips. Tertial coverts narrower, more pointed and frayed. Breast and underparts brownish-buff with poorly delineated whitish belly, diffuse and coarse brown patches, and juvenile feathers forming neat regular brownish streaks. Undertail-coverts whitish mottled brown. Juvenile rectrices retained until Nov–Feb at least. Secondary upperwing-coverts more pointed, faintly to strongly marked with pale vermiculations or speckles (♂) or all brown (♀)[224]. Greater coverts fringed pale at tips (♀). Legs greenish or brownish-grey with darker webs.

First-winter ♂

Formative plumage (Nov–Feb/May–Jun). Following pre-formative moult, much like adult ♂ in basic plumage, but slightly duller. From early winter, iris is yellow, albeit often less brightly coloured than adult. Head reddish, less bright or shiny, sometimes even dull dark brown. Bill similar to adult but less colourful and less well demarcated (often some black smudges on culmen until midwinter at least). The dark vermiculations on the scapulars and flanks are slightly less sharply defined. Traces of juvenile plumage also often visible on belly, which is ill-defined (especially vs. the black breast), and undertail, sometimes visibly spotted brown or whitish. In good conditions or the hand, check the upperwing. In some birds, no feathers are replaced, and thus as juvenile, including the narrow, pointed and frayed tertials and tertial coverts, without vermiculations or speckles. In others, there is moult contrast between the inner tertial and secondary coverts (which are adult-type, broader, rounded and vermiculated or speckled pale grey) and the rest of the wing (juvenile). The same birds may also retain juvenile tertials, and have primary coverts (and outer web of alula) devoid of flecks, narrow and visibly browner than the moulted inner wing.

First-winter ♀

Formative plumage (Nov–Jan/Apr–May). Pre-formative moult is protracted and merges into first pre-alternate moult, with an initially juvenile appearance becoming close to that of adult ♀ during winter. Some birds are fairly easy to separate at least until midwinter, with worn juvenile plumage. Subsequently, once juvenile plumage is largely replaced they become more difficult to distinguish. Nevertheless, note absence of white spots on back of head (also the case in many adult ♀♀) and the less developed whitish speckles or vermiculations on scapulars and flanks (sometimes almost absent). Undertail-coverts mottled pale brown and the pale belly is poorly demarcated. Often one to all tertials and tertial coverts still juvenile, with tips pointed and frayed. The upperwing is the feature for ageing, from late winter until the second pre-basic moult, either being fully juvenile (see above), or by showing contrast between most of the juvenile outer coverts and the innermost coverts, which are moulted, larger, rounded and fresh, with few or no pale speckles.

GEOGRAPHIC VARIATION None.

MEASUREMENTS and MASS ♂ and adult very slightly larger than ♀ and young, respectively. ♂: wing chord

212–256 (adult, 235, *n*=1,418) and 210–249 (juvenile, 231, *n*=711), culmen 41–62 (adult, 47.7, *n*=1,396), tarsus 44–60 (adult, 51, *n*=1,395); ♀: wing chord 206–243 (adult, 226, *n*=691) and 206–242 (juvenile, 222, *n*=520), culmen 41–57 (adult, 46.1, *n*=686), tarsus 43–57 (adult, 49.6, *n*=682)[1374]. ♂ (*n*=100): wing chord 221–237 (adult) and 216–232 (juvenile), culmen 45–51, bill depth at tip of forehead feathering 18.8–22.4, tarsus 40–45, tail 54–63; ♀ (*n*=100): wing chord 213–227 (adult) and 208–222 (juvenile), culmen 43–49, bill depth at tip of forehead feathering 18.0–21.7, tarsus 38–43, tail 53–61[1014].

VOICE ♂ in courtship gives a repeated *hukk*, and a unique and characteristic cat-like *meow*, or loud and rather nasal *wee-oo-oow*. ♀ gives an *errr* similar to that of other ♀ *Aythya*, or a *kerk*, slightly lower pitched and more reminiscent of a ♀ Mallard *Anas platyrhynchos* when taking off from the water.

MOULT Complex alternate moult strategy. Pre-formative moult occurs between Sep and Feb–Mar and includes a variable number of body feathers, sometimes 1–3 tertials and tertial coverts, plus some inner coverts and a variable number of rectrices (sometimes all). This moult averages faster and more extensive in young ♂♂ than young ♀♀. Definitive pre-alternate moult occurs Mar–May in ♀♀ and Jun–Jul in ♂♂ (on moulting grounds). It includes a variable number of upperparts and breast feathers[1014], few or no inner upperwing-coverts[1374], up to two rectrices and few tertials. Definitive pre-basic moult occurs in both sexes between Jul and Nov, is complete, and begins with the simultaneous loss of remiges and rectrices. It usually lasts until Nov with body feathers, often ending with tertials.

HYBRIDISATION In the wild (North America), hybridisation is occasionally reported with Ring-necked Duck, rarely with Greater Scaup *A. marila*, Lesser Scaup *A. affinis* (which see), and even more occasionally with Canvasback (see below). Other hybrids, potentially natural but exceptional, are mentioned with Wood Duck *Aix sponsa*[817,988] and Northern Pintail *Anas acuta*[817,1190]. In captivity, hybridisation has been reported with Mandarin Duck *Aix galericulata*[817,1008], American Wigeon *Anas americana*[131,1190], Mallard *A. platyrhynchos*[817,1190], Rosy-billed Pochard *Netta peposaca*[465], Red-crested Pochard[439,465,1190], Baer's Pochard *Aythya baeri*[948], Common Pochard[619], Tufted Duck *A. fuligula*[619,817], Hooded Merganser *Lophodytes cucullatus*[752,817] and Goosander *Mergus merganser*[443].

Redhead × Canvasback. Adult ♂ in basic plumage recalls Common Pochard, but can also suggest either parent. Occasionally reported in North America, this hybrid can be a real identification pitfall vs. Common Pochard, which is an accidental visitor there. Among features suggesting that species, the rounded head, which can be slightly conical, and grey body (white vermiculated dark grey) are intermediate between those of the parents (thus matching Common Pochard). Even the bill can be misleading, with a largely black tip with an oblique demarcation in profile, and a black tomium and base reaching the nostrils or covering much of the culmen. Sometimes, a thin pale subterminal band is visible. Identification is reliant on detailed observation of the bill and iris, whose colour ranges from yellow-orange to orange-red (vs. red). Also note the significantly larger size than Common Pochard. ♀ of the same cross has also been reported, and poses the same identification problems[439,440,1342]. It is mainly distinguished by its size, darker body colour (definitive basic plumage) and coloration of the bill. Note that, like most hybrids within this genus, such birds are apparently fertile[639].

HABITAT and LIFE-CYCLE Medium- to long-distance migrant whose breeding range barely overlaps the wintering range. Spring migration peaks between mid-Apr and mid-May, the eggs mainly being laid between mid-May and mid-Jul. Nests mainly from the Rockies and prairies north to the taiga. Rather generalist and opportunistic, it mostly uses temporary or semi-permanent wetlands subject to considerable fluctuations in water levels, with helophytic or tall herbaceous belts in which to nest[843]. Parasitises the nests of several other duck species, including dabblers[1343]. Favours medium- to large-sized ponds and lakes (>4 ha)[843], especially with alkaline waters and close to larger waterbodies used by the broods after hatching. Also inhabits various other wetlands, including artificial reservoirs. Pairs form between midwinter and spring migration, and ♂ abandons ♀ in late Jun to Jul, and heads to moulting sites. ♀♀ stay with their broods until the ducklings are 6–8 weeks old, i.e. before fledging, then also depart for moulting sites[1374]. Autumn migration mainly between mid-Oct and late Nov. Much more specialised in choice of habitat in winter, using shallow, sometimes hypersaline, coastal lagoons, whose bottoms are covered with beds *Halodule wrightii*, *Syringodium filiforme* or *Thalassia testudinum*[1374]. Present at a limited number of sites and forms huge monospecific flocks. Also observed alone or in small numbers at other coastal waterbodies, especially if droughts have led to increased salinity at their main wintering sites.

RANGE and POPULATION Strictly Nearctic, breeding over the north-west quarter of the USA. Sporadically breeds further south, primarily around the Great Lakes (even in New Brunswick in east), N & W Texas, New Mexico, Arizona and California's Central Valley (and south to Lake Salton) and into C Mexico. Most of the wintering population uses a relatively small number of sites on coasts of Gulf of Mexico from NW Florida to N Mexico, as well as large coastal lagoons in Sinaloa, Gulf of California. Laguna Madre, S Texas and N Tamaulipas, Mexico, are major sites at this season. Some may remain farther north during mild winters, or desert favoured coastal lagoons if their salinity increases or sea-grasses disappear, especially as a consequence of droughts[1374]. Rare in S Florida, the Great Antilles, accidental in E Siberia, Japan, Iceland and UK (rare sightings elsewhere in Europe considered to be escapees). Population 400,000–700,000 birds in 1950–80, increasing (irregularly) since, with 1,270,000 in 2012 and 1,202,000 in 2013[1294,1391]. Some 160,000–200,000 birds are harvested by hunters annually[648,843],

which, combined with loss of breeding habitats to agriculture and decline in the quality of certain coastal habitats in the Gulf of Mexico, could represent a threat to the species.

CAPTIVITY Easily found for sale and is inexpensive in North America, but rarer in Eurasia, where prices are often much higher than for Common Pochard. Quite uncommon in captivity in Europe, but presence is still sufficient to cast doubt on the origin of any birds seen in the wild.

REFERENCES Bird Hybrids Flickr Forum (2011)[131]; Bolton *et al.* (1999)[161]; Carney (1992)[224]; Gillham & Gillham (1996)[439]; Gillham & Gillham (1998)[440]; Gillham & Gillham (2002)[443]; Gray (1958)[465]; Haramis (1982)[513]; IZY (1968, 1971)[619]; Johnsgard (1960)[639]; Johnsgard (2010)[648]; Kessler & Avise (1984)[685]; Leverkühn (1890)[752]; Livezey (1996)[773]; McCarthy (2006)[817]; Michot & Woodin *in* Kear (2005)[843]; Patrick (1932)[948]; Phillips (1922–26)[988]; Prestwich (1960)[1008]; Pyle (2008)[1014]; Schmidt (1989)[1146]; Sibley (1938)[1190]; USWFS (2013)[1294]; Weller (1957)[1342]; Weller (1959)[1343]; Weller (1970)[1344]; Woodin & Michot (2002)[1374]; Zimpfer *et al.* (2011)[1391].

397. Adult ♂ (definitive basic). Texas, Dec (Alan D. Wilson).

398. Adult ♂ (definitive alternate); this plumage is duller than basic, but still very different from ♀. California, USA, Jun (Tom Grey).

399. Adult ♂ (definitive basic). Texas, USA, Feb (Greg Lavaty).

400. First-winter ♂ (formative) is like adult ♂, but note worn juvenile tertials and rectrices, as well as many brown juvenile feathers on belly and rear body. Texas, USA, Feb (Sébastien Reeber).

401. Adult ♀ (definitive basic). California, USA, Nov (Sébastien Reeber).

402. First-winter ♀ (formative); tertials and tertial coverts still juvenile with very frayed tips, while scapulars and flank feathers show fewer white speckles than adult ♀. Texas, USA, Feb (Sébastien Reeber).

COMMON POCHARD
Aythya ferina

TAXONOMY *Anas ferina* Linnaeus, 1758, *Syst. Nat.*, edn. 10, p. 126. Within the genus *Aythya*, constitutes a distinct sub-genus (*Aristonetta*) with the only two other red-headed species, Canvasback *A. valisineria* and Redhead *A. americana*. Relationships between these three species are not clearly established, some authors considering Common Pochard closer to the former[773] and others to the latter[647]. No geographic variation or subspecies.

IDENTIFICATION In Eurasia, usually identified easily, as the ♂ is the only red-headed duck, apart from Red-crested Pochard *Netta rufina*, which has a red bill, white flanks and brown upperparts. Both sexes, however, are closer to Canvasback and Redhead, two Nearctic species that very occasionally wander to the range of Common Pochard (see these two species). The main pitfall is the occasional Canvasback × Common Pochard hybrid (see below).

PLUMAGES Strong sexual dimorphism from first winter onwards. Complex alternate moult strategy (two plumages per definitive cycle, three in first cycle). Ageing can be difficult from beginning of second calendar year.

Adult ♂

Definitive basic plumage (Nov–Dec/May–Jun). Typical tricoloured appearance, red/black/grey. Head and neck reddish, slightly darker in front of the eye. Iris red, rather dusky. Bill has culmen slightly concave, blackish with broad pale blue-grey patch (becoming whitish forward) from behind nail, along sides to below nostrils and centre of culmen. In profile, the demarcation of the black tip is oblique. Breast black. Mantle, scapulars, tertials and flanks whitish with grey vermiculations, appearing uniform pale grey from afar. Belly white. Back dark grey, rump and uppertail-coverts blackish. Tail grey. Upperwing fairly uniform, with secondary coverts, tips of primary coverts and alula vermiculated whitish-grey (as upperparts), centres to greater coverts slightly darker. Primary coverts dark grey. Remiges pale grey with diffuse tips to primaries and subterminal marks on outer secondaries blackish, and white trailing edge to secondaries. Outer webs of 3–5 outermost primaries dusky. Underwing-coverts and axillaries whitish, leading edge browner, remiges pale grey with dark trailing edge on primaries. Legs bluish-grey with darker webs.

Definitive alternate plumage (May–Jun/Oct–Nov). Appearance intermediate, similar to basic plumage but duller and washed out, slightly closer to ♀. Head dull reddish, sometimes paler at bill base. Bill duller, with pale blue-grey area narrower and less clear-cut. Breast finely streaked brown (feathers with pale fringes and blackish bases) and irregular black patches. Feathers of flanks, mantle and scapulars more coarsely vermiculated or washed brown than basic plumage. Belly and undertail with irregular brown patches. Back and rear body dull blackish (pale tips to feathers).

Adult ♀

Definitive basic plumage (Nov–Dec/Mar–Apr). Head, neck and breast cinnamon-brown, darker on crown and nape, with pale brown to beige areas at the base of the bill, chin, throat and foreneck, and a pale bridle extending behind the thin eye-ring and broadening and fading on the rear cheeks. Iris warm or hazel-brown. Bill like ♂ but less contrasting: dark grey with smaller and less clear-cut blue-grey patch (though becomes more marked with age), sometimes reduced to a fine pale subterminal band. Mantle, scapulars and flanks appear uniform grey (light grey vermiculated dark) with diffuse darker grey-brown crescents, formed by bases to feathers. Longest tertials have pointed tips, dark grey becoming light grey on inner webs, with narrow black line on fringes. Back and rump dark brown with paler fringes. Uppertail dark grey-brown. Belly cream dappled light brown and poorly defined, with brown patches posteriorly. Undertail-coverts whitish irregularly marked brownish. Upperwing like ♂, but browner and darker, highlighting pale grey wingbar. Coverts vermiculated white at tips, greater coverts (and especially primary coverts) darker. Dark trailing edge to primaries and outer secondaries. Underwing and legs like ♂.

Definitive alternate plumage (Apr–May/Oct–Nov). Like previous plumage, but warmer and plainer brown, with almost no contrast between breast, upperparts and flanks. Head slightly plainer brown, the pale areas reduced and less marked. Bill dark grey with pale subterminal band reduced or absent. Breast reddish-brown finely streaked pale. Alternate feathers of mantle and scapulars have large dark grey-brown bases and buff fringes, possibly with pale grey vermiculations. Alternate flank feathers have dark brown bases, pale reddish-brown, beige or vermiculated whitish tips. Belly and undertail more strongly mottled or spotted grey than basic plumage.

Juvenile

First basic plumage (until Oct–Nov). Like alternate plumage of adult ♀, but duller brown overall. Head has diffuse or no pale markings, more tinged reddish-brown in young ♂. Bill dull dark grey. Iris warm brown, quickly becoming reddish in young ♂. Feathers of mantle and scapulars dark grey-brown broadly fringed pale brown, sometimes with pale grey vermiculations. Breast brown and finely streaked. Tertials rather uniform dark grey. Flanks pale grey-brown with paler fringes, forming vague dusky crescents. Belly has diffuse and irregular grey-brown patches and streaks. Lower belly and undertail strongly stained brown-grey. Upperwing has primary- and median coverts narrow and quickly frayed (vs. larger and rounded in adult) and greater coverts narrow and round-tipped (vs. broad and almost square-tipped), dark grey-brown (♀) or grey with pale flecks (♂). In adult, greater coverts are grey-brown with pale vermiculations concentrated at the tip (♀) or entirely pale grey strongly vermiculated (♂). Legs grey-brown or olive-grey.

First-winter ♂

Formative plumage (Oct–Mar/May–Jun). Following pre-formative moult, like adult ♂ in basic plumage. From early winter, iris largely red (pupil often rimmed dark brown) and bill similar to adult (blue-grey area partially brown). Look for any retained rectrices or tertials (plain dark grey becoming paler, and frayed). Some birds (especially in E Asia) suspend or protract their pre-formative moult into Jan–Feb, and show clear signs of immaturity throughout this period (retained lower scapulars, flanks and tertials for example). In advanced individuals, the best age feature remains the upperwing pattern until second pre-basic moult. Tertial- and secondary coverts uniform pale grey and vermiculated in adult ♂, without contrast with scapulars. In young ♂, the retained juvenile feathers are dark grey-brown speckled pale, and contrast with the innermost replaced coverts (adult-type). Greater and primary coverts usually dark grey-brown with few or no white speckles, vs. strongly speckled white at tips in adult. See also shape of coverts for ageing, as described under juvenile.

First-winter ♀

Formative plumage (Nov–Mar/Mar–May). Appearance gradually becomes like that of basic plumage adult ♀ by end of first winter, the pre-formative moult being generally less extensive (and/or slower) than in young ♂. However, ageing requires good views and usually requires a close check of the upperwing pattern until the second pre-basic moult. In adult, all secondary- and tertial coverts shows clear pale grey flecks or vermiculations towards the tips. In young ♀, the speckles are much more discreet or even lacking. At distance the speckled tips to the median and lesser coverts form faint wingbars, whereas the upperwing is plainer in young ♀. See also shape of coverts for ageing, as described under juvenile.

GEOGRAPHIC VARIATION None.

MEASUREMENTS and MASS ♂ and adult slightly larger than ♀ and young, respectively. ♂: wing chord 212–223 (adult, 217, *n*=19) and 202–220 (juvenile, 213, *n*=41), culmen 43–52 (47.1, *n*=62), tarsus 37–42 (39.5, *n*=52), mass in winter 585–1,240 (849, *n*=119); ♀: wing chord 200–216 (adult, 206, *n*=22) and 185–215 (juvenile, 206, *n*=23), culmen 42–48 (44.9, *n*=47), tarsus 36–41 (38.8, *n*=47), mass in winter 467–1,090 (807, *n*=202)[267]. ♂: wing chord 204–222 (adult, 215, *n*=56) and 203–218 (juvenile, 211, *n*=42), culmen 43–52 (46.9, *n*=62); ♀: wing chord 202–216 (adult, 207, *n*=40) and 199–212 (juvenile, 207, *n*=31), culmen 41-48 (44.8, *n*=41)[1122].

VOICE In courtship, ♂ gives a complex hissing sigh *ha-ha-haoow*, the first two syllables (sometimes just one) very brief and higher pitched, the third falling and drawn out, more audible, with an asthmatic cooing quality. During courtship, ♀ produces different squeaky calls, e.g. *ee-ee-ee-hew* (of 3–6 syllables). Both sexes produce an *errr* or *rraa*, especially when taking off.

MOULT Complex alternate moult strategy. Pre-formative moult occurs between Sep and Mar–Apr, often slowing in Jan–Feb, at least in birds that did not complete their moult in Dec–Jan. It involves, until Nov–Dec, a variable number of head and body feathers (smaller numbers on the rear body and belly) and rectrices (sometimes all). Pre-formative moult ends with the upper flanks and lower scapulars, often all tertials and tertial coverts, and some inner secondary coverts. More rarely, a few inner secondaries are replaced as well[56]. This moult averages faster and more extensive in young ♂♂ than young ♀♀. Definitive pre-alternate moult occurs between Feb and Apr in ♀♀ and Jun–Jul in ♂♂. It includes a variable number of head, breast, upperparts and flanks feathers, and few or no inner coverts, sometimes two rectrices, and one or more tertials. Definitive pre-basic moult occurs in both sexes between Jul and Nov, and is complete. ♀♀ moult 2–4 weeks later. The feathers of the head and body are replaced by Nov, usually ending with tertials.

HYBRIDISATION Hybridises regularly in the wild, especially with Tufted Duck *A. fuligula* and Ferruginous Duck *A. nyroca*, these hybrids being the most regularly reported in the wild in Europe among Anseriformes. Hybrids are also reported regularly with Red-crested Pochard, but much more rarely with Baer's Pochard *A. baeri*, Ring-necked Duck *A. collaris* and Greater Scaup *A. marila* (see these six species, respectively). The closest hybrid in appearance is undoubtedly that with Canvasback, which has been reported several times in W Europe (see below). Also in the wild, hybrids have been reported very occasionally with Eurasian Wigeon *Anas penelope*[130,442], Mallard *A. platyrhynchos*[260,465,988,1190,1241], Northern Pintail *A. acuta*[465,988], Eurasian Teal *A. crecca*[1241], Lesser Scaup *Aythya affinis*[465,587,1120], and possibly with Garganey *Anas querquedula*[752,1241] and Goldeneye *Bucephala clangula*[582,752]. In captivity, cases reported with many other species, e.g. Common Shelduck *Tadorna tadorna*[439], Wood Duck *Aix sponsa*[439,465,582,817,988], Brazilian Duck *Amazonetta brasiliensis*[223], African Black Duck *Anas sparsa*[187], Chiloe Wigeon *A. sibilatrix*[1176], Meller's Duck *A. melleri*[260], Redhead *Aythya americana*[619], New Zealand Scaup *A. novaeseelandiae*[439,465], Southern Pochard *Netta erythrophthalma*[439] and Rosy-billed Pochard *N. peposaca*[439,587,817].

Common Pochard × Canvasback. Hybrids resulting from this cross reported in W Europe and E Asia[116,439]. In particular, in England, a captive ♀ Canvasback mated with a wild ♂ Common Pochard producing two broods[189,1322]. In addition, many captive Canvasbacks there and also in France show characters probably of hybrid origin (obviously not first-generation). ♂ in basic plumage quite variable, but more often recalls Canvasback and constitutes a genuine identification pitfall in Eurasia. Many show intermediate size, structure (neck length in particular), head shape and body colour (width of dark grey vermiculations). The head often seems more rounded, like Common Pochard, but the front of the head is very dark red,

like Canvasback, especially as the iris is brighter red and more obvious. The bill is also intermediate, clearly recalling the long thin bill of Canvasback, but with a more concave culmen and clear pale blue-grey mark inherited from Common Pochard. This mark can be restricted to a small spot at the base of the culmen, resulting in a clear subterminal bar or be slightly more extensive on the sides. Nevertheless, this pale area is smaller than in hybrid Canvasback × Redhead, which often also shows at least some yellow-orange in the iris (often around the pupil). Adult ♂ Canvasback never has a pale mark on the bill, making coloration of the latter important for identifying hybrids (especially other than first-generation), but it will be very difficult to do so in alternate plumages (both sexes and juvenile). As for definitive basic plumage of ♀, it appears that some hybrids have a uniformly dark bill[1322] and others a clear pale mark.

HABITAT and LIFE-CYCLE Northern populations migratory, while those breeding at temperate latitudes are mainly sedentary, with winter movements being linked to temperatures at this season. Spring migration occurs between mid-Feb and mid-Apr, birds occupying their nesting sites from early Mar to early May, depending on latitude. Eggs are laid mainly in Apr–May. Favours large wetlands with eutrophic, alkaline or even brackish waters[1213]. Prefers lakes and ponds, rather shallow (<6 m), with floating macrophytes and helophytic belts, as well as areas of open water. Also inhabits slow-moving streams and artificial waterbodies, including sewage lagoons. Nests under dense vegetation, often on floating piles of debris and always close to the water, preferably where floating vegetation is dense. Most ♂♂ abandon ♀♀ shortly after laying, gather with non-breeding ♀♀ or those that failed, and then moult either near the nesting sites or after a short migration to sometimes massive gathering sites (up to 50,000 ♂♂ in W Europe[267]). ♀♀ moult at their nesting sites or nearby. Autumn migration peaks from late Sep to Nov, ♀♀ tending to migrate later (due to their later pre-basic moult) and further south than ♂♂[1213]. In winter, inhabits large lakes and ponds, artificial reservoirs, gravel and sand pits, and wide slow-moving rivers, and can form remarkably dense flocks. Feeds by diving, often up to 1–3 m[646].

RANGE and POPULATION Confined to Eurasia, with isolated populations south of mapped range in Japan, Tibet, Afghanistan[394], Armenia, NW Iran, Turkey and the Mediterranean (including Morocco and Tunisia). Rare in Iceland. Few in winter to Indochina,

Saudi Arabia and Equatorial Africa. Accidental North America. Total population estimated at 2,200,000–2,500,000 individuals[305], declining in the west, stable in S Asia, and regional trends unknown elsewhere[1348]. The decline in the west is attributed mainly to disturbance from hunting, to hyper-eutrophication of waters especially related to use of agricultural fertilisers, and widespread habitat loss[145,394].

CAPTIVITY Easy to keep and breed in captivity, and usually offered at very affordable prices in Eurasia (slightly rarer in North America). However, it is not among the commonest species in captivity. In North America, the species is obviously more likely to escape than to arrive there naturally.

REFERENCES Baker (1992)[56]; Bird Hybrids Flickr Forum (2009)[116]; Bird Hybrids Flickr Forum (2011)[130]; BirdLife International (2014)[145]; Brickell & Frandsen (1988)[187]; Bristow (1992)[189]; Carboneras (1992)[223]; Costa-Perez & Rodriguez-Parada (1981)[260]; Cramp & Simmons (1977)[268]; Delany & Scott (2006)[305]; Fox *in* Kear (2005)[394]; Gillham & Gillham (1996)[439]; Gillham & Gillham (2000)[442]; Gray (1958)[465]; Hopkinson (1926)[582]; Hopkinson (1935)[587]; IZY (1968, 1971)[619]; Johnsgard (1978)[646]; Johnsgard (1979)[647]; Leverkühn (1890)[752]; Livezey (1996)[773]; McCarthy (2006)[817]; Phillips (1922–26)[988]; Sage (1962)[1120]; Salminen (1983)[1122]; Severin (1981)[1176]; Sibley (1938)[1190]; Snow & Perrins (1998)[1213]; Suchetet (1897)[1241]; Vinicombe (1998)[1320]; Vinicombe (2003)[1322]; Wetlands International (2014)[1348].

403. Pair; note rather uniform grey wingbar in this species. England, Feb (Sébastien Reeber).

404. Adult ♂ (definitive basic). India, Dec (Sunil Singhal).

405. First-winter ♂ (first basic/formative); note juvenile (brown) traces on breast, rump, lower scapulars and upper flanks, as well as blurred bill pattern and brown, heavily frayed tertials. Japan, Nov (Stuart Price).

406. Adult ♀ (definitive basic). France, Feb (Sébastien Reeber).

407. First-winter ♀ (formative). India, Dec (Sunil Singhal).

408. First-winter ♀ (formative); note plain back and mottled brown body, while the tertials are being replaced (at end of pre-formative moult) and bill coloration is not fully adult (narrow pale subterminal band). Japan, Mar (Ayuwat Jearwattanakanok).

FERRUGINOUS DUCK
Aythya nyroca

Plate 45

TAXONOMY *Anas nyroca* Güldenstädt, 1770, *Novi Commentarii Acad. Sci. Imp. Petropolitanae*, 14 (1769), p. 403. Closely related to Hardhead *A. australis* in Australia, Madagascar Pochard *A. innotata* in Madagascar (considered extinct until rediscovered in 2006[1064]) and Baer's Pochard *A. baeri* in E Asia. Together, they form the subgenus *Nyroca* Fleming, 1822. No subspecies or geographical variation.

IDENTIFICATION Easily mistaken for Tufted Duck *A. fuligula* in ♀ and especially juvenile plumages, and with same plumages of Baer's Pochard. However, the main pitfalls are hybrid ♂ and ♀ emanating from several crosses, which are relatively frequent in the wild. In W Europe, hybrid-like Ferruginous Ducks are commoner than pure individuals.

Firstly, confusion with ♀ Tufted Duck must be eliminated. Some ♀♀ show an extensive white undertail and overall dark plumage with little contrast. Tufted Duck differs in head shape (stronger and squarer, usually with a short pointed crest), thicker bill, often with a variable amount of white at the base, usually stronger contrast between the breast and flanks, and undertail at least stained dark. Also note that most ♀ Tufted Ducks have a striking yellow iris. In juvenile plumage, however, Tufted Duck and Ferruginous Duck can be very difficult to distinguish using plumage alone. The overall coloration is duller with undertail-coverts stained brownish-grey in the latter, while Tufted Duck often shows only a hint of crest, plainer plumage and a dark bill and iris. Separation will rely on shape, size and the wingbar, and may be possible only under good viewing conditions.

Compared to Baer's Pochard, which is locally sympatric with Ferruginous Duck in Asia, note the absence of white on the fore flanks (often obvious in Baer's Pochard when swimming). Also note the larger size of the latter, its stronger bill, flatter head and thicker neck. In Baer's Pochard, the adult ♂ has a green sheen to the head-sides, and the ♀ a pale reddish-brown loral patch on an otherwise blackish head. See Baer's Pochard for further details.

The toughest problems arise from the frequent hybrids that occur in the wild, especially those involving Ferruginous Duck on one hand, and Tufted Duck or Common Pochard on the other (see Hybridisation).

Especially ♀ hybrids cause many misidentifications, let alone hybrids backcrossed with Ferruginous Duck, which are probably impossible to identify in the wild, at least ♀♀ and juveniles. To identify Ferruginous Duck, especially in areas where it is a rare visitor, the possibility of hybrids should be eliminated by considering the features listed below.

- *Size and shape*: Ferruginous Duck is small compared to Common Pochard, Tufted Duck or Baer's Pochard. Any bird close in size to, or larger than, Tufted Duck could be a hybrid.

- *Head*: Tall and oval-shaped, peaking above or just behind the eye, without any crest or notch on nape, which are standard in hybrids involving Tufted Duck. As in all *Aythya*, head profile should be assessed at rest, because it is directly affected by the position of the crown's longest feathers, which depends on the bird's behaviour.

- *Iris*: White in adult ♂ (from end of first winter), brown in ♀ and slightly sepia in juvenile (becoming distinctly paler by late summer in young ♂). Clear yellowish, orange or reddish tones are indicative of hybridisation.

- *Bill*: Proportionately long, thin and almost straight-edged in profile. Typically, the black tip is limited to the nail, but can extend slightly on the sides. This is commoner in ♀♀ and typical for immatures. A wide black tip like Tufted Duck, and the presence of black at the bill base, imply a hybrid.

- *Flanks*: In formative and definitive basic plumage, usually plain without any clear contrast vs. the breast. The absence of the dark brown (♀/immature) or black (adult ♂) bar behind the flanks (femoral coverts), or the presence of vermiculations, must be considered odd and probably inherited from Common Pochard. Also, when resting on the water, the rear flank feathers often extend further up over the folded wings, and form a flattened horizontal 'S', like Ring-necked Duck *A. collaris*. The white inner secondaries are thus usually hidden (visible in Tufted Duck and Baer's Pochard).

- *Undertail*: In adult plumage, they are pure white, surrounded by black, sharply defined and contrasting, especially when tail is raised. In first-calendar-year birds (until late autumn), they show some dark smudges, especially near the centre of the lower belly, which progressively disappear.

- **Wingbar**: White and broad in all sexes/ages, especially adult ♂, and always more striking than in Tufted Duck and hybrids.

- **Belly**: In adult, forms a characteristic pure white, well-defined, oval. At this age, the presence of dark smudges or bars, as well as a diffuse demarcation to the belly, are usually signs of a hybrid.

Finally, the white spot on the chin and black collar of the adult alternate ♂ are sometimes visible at close range. Their absence must be considered strange.

PLUMAGES Slight sexual dimorphism from juvenile plumage onwards. Complex alternate moulting strategy (two plumages per definitive cycle, three in first cycle). Ageing relatively easy until first winter, and possible until the end of first summer, especially for ♂♂. The extent of white on the primaries (and thus the wingbar) is on average more in ♂ than in ♀, and more extensive in adults than in young.

Adult ♂

Definitive basic plumage (Oct–Nov/May–Jun). Plain reddish-brown head, neck, breast and flanks, without vermiculations, which can appear very dark brown on poor light, or bright rusty or mahogany-brown in sunlight. Any contrast between these parts is only faint, the breast being slightly richer rufous. The flanks are rather uniform rufous, with faint pale vertical crescents on the feather edges. In close views, a narrow black collar and white dot on the chin are visible. Iris white. Bill lead-grey, slightly paler than in other sexes/ages. An indistinct subterminal pale band is visible just behind the nail, which is blackish and often contrasting. The pale subterminal area extends variably over the cutting edges towards the gape. The base is often pale than its centre (and compared to other plumages), showing a stronger contrast with the head feathers. Black is restricted to the nail in most adult ♂♂, but can slightly extend along both sides[438,1050]. Upperparts blackish-brown. Belly white, becoming roughly mottled blackish lower down and a vertical black bar separates the rear flanks from the pure white undertail-coverts, which extend slightly above the outer tail feathers at their base. When tail lowered on water, when feeding for example, the white is barely visible. Tail and rump blackish. Tertials and innermost secondaries blackish-brown, often with a green-and-bronze sheen. Large white wingbar, longer and broader

than in Tufted Duck, especially on primaries, almost reminiscent of Red-crested Pochard *Netta rufina*. The inner webs of the primaries are white (apart from black tips), except outermost primaries, where white is reduced to inner edge. Rest of wing blackish-brown, except broad white leading edge (shown by all ages/sexes, but much more prominent in adult ♂♂). Underwing whitish, except pale brown leading edge and dark trailing edge. Legs and feet grey.

Definitive alternate plumage (until Oct–Nov). Similar to basic male, but duller and more ♀-like. Head shape often differs slightly, being more rounded, as the feathers are shorter in this plumage. The head is darker, albeit with more reddish tones than ♀, and white iris remains striking. A hint of pale at the base of the bill is typical. The breast and flanks are duller brown, with more obvious dark streaks or crescents, contrasting with the white undertail-coverts. At a distance, the breast can be paler than both the head and flanks. The latter appear roughly barred as in alternate ♀, while the belly is still white but can show greyish smudging. Like many other pochards, there is some slight individual variation in the extent of pre-alternate moult. Some ♂♂ are browner and more streaked, while others are neater and more rufous. This is probably age-related, duller ♂♂ being first-summer[1321]. Bill generally darker than in winter, even blackish at distance, with pale subterminal band obscure or lacking, making the tip appear more diffuse.

Adult ♀

Definitive basic plumage (Oct–Nov/Mar–May). Similar to basic adult ♂, but browner, darker and duller, with fewer rufous tones. The head often shows two diffuse pale patches, at the bill base and on the rear cheeks. The iris is medium to dark brown. The bill is duller and slightly darker grey than in ♂, with the pale bluish subterminal bar narrower than in adult ♂, but more clear-cut. The black tip is larger, more diffuse and less contrasting. The base is also darker, generally showing only faint contrast with the head feathers. The flanks are variably marked with slightly paler and indistinct crescents, always more obvious than in ♂, and separated from undertail-coverts by a dark vertical bar, which is browner than in ♂. Like alternate ♂, the white upper belly often appears slightly smudged. Upperwing as adult ♂, but white leading edge less obvious and white wingbar somewhat thinner (broader black tips to remiges) and shorter, as outer 3–5 primaries have inner webs washed pale grey. Legs and feet as ♂.

461

Definitive alternate plumage (Apr–May/Oct–Nov). Head appears slightly capped due to darker crown and generally more obvious patches on ear-coverts and at bill base, sometimes extending towards the chin, throat and even upper foreneck, or via lores to forehead. Flanks have more obvious vertical pale and dark crescents, often contrasting with the upperparts. As in ♂, bill darker in breeding season, with an inconspicuous (or almost absent) pale line behind the nail.

Juvenile

First basic plumage (until Sep–Nov). Similar to adult ♀, but typically slightly smaller with a thinner and flatter head. Overall duller with slightly more yellowish or greyish-brown plumage. Head has typical bimaculated pattern with diffuse pale patches at the base of the bill and on ear-coverts, and an obvious capped appearance due to the dark crown. Iris dull grey-brown in juvenile, but quickly becomes paler in young ♂. Bill often entirely dark grey, without any clear pattern, lacking pale subterminal band, as well as contrasting black tip. The bill may appear shorter and relatively thicker than in adult during first three months, as full width and height are gained well before full length. Upperwing has less contrasting white wingbar, due to less clear-cut dark tips to secondaries, and inner webs to outermost primaries washed pale grey-brown. Undertail-coverts partly obscured by dirt stains, and belly pale buff neatly marked with dark spots, contrasting with the white underwing-coverts if seen in flight, and perhaps the most reliable feature to age the species after late summer. Tail slightly shorter, with rectrices more pointed and notched at tip.

First-winter ♂

Formative plumage (Oct–Mar/May–Jun). As pre-formative moult can be more extensive in ♂♂ than ♀♀, adult-like plumage is more quickly acquired by the former, despite significant individual variation in timing. Juvenile body feathers are usually replaced from Sep to Dec–Mar, the earliest birds having adult-looking plumage by early winter and others 1–2 months later. Between Nov and Jan at least, ageing should be rather easy, by variable mix of retained juvenile feathers and new, pre-formative, adult-like ones. Especially the flanks, breast and upperparts can look quite 'messy', vs. the clean new plumage of adult ♂♂ at same time. The undertail-coverts quickly become white, but close inspection should reveal brownish juvenile feathers still present. The head usually is adult-like, but often

retains (through winter and spring) a more flattened or rounded shape, as well as a hint of pale at the base of the bill. The iris becomes pale grey-brown by Sep, and some juvenile can be sexed as early as mid-Aug. By Oct, the iris is usually pale greyish, then whitish by midwinter and all white by Mar–Apr. The bill coloration changes gradually from all dull grey (juvenile), then paler from midwinter, but usually has a larger black tip and darker overall colour than adult ♂, even when plumage is adult-like.

First-winter ♀

Formative plumage (Oct–Mar/Mar–Apr). Like other pochards, pre-formative moult is less extensive (often protracted) in ♀♀ vs. ♂♂, the first pre-alternate moult being more extensive in the former. Thus, a young ♀ usually looks intermediate between juvenile and adult ♀ until midwinter, with many juvenile characters still obvious: belly extensively mottled (often more than in formative ♂), bill dark with ill-defined pattern and broad blackish tip, flanks irregularly and coarsely barred with pale crescents, head flatter and slightly paler, upperparts browner and more scalloped. Pre-alternate moult occurs thereafter (timing varies), and young ♀ is difficult to distinguish from adult ♀ by early spring. However, the belly and upperwing still present some juvenile features.

GEOGRAPHIC VARIATION None.

MEASUREMENTS and MASS ♂ and adult slightly larger and heavier than ♀ and young, respectively. ♂: wing chord 180–196 (adult, 188, $n=31$) and 177–192 (juvenile, 185, $n=27$), culmen 38–43 (40.3, $n=58$), tarsus 31–35 (32.7, $n=58$), tail 50–60 (54.0, $n=31$), mass 470–730 (589, $n=5$); ♀: wing chord 178–185 (adult, 182, $n=8$) and 171–183 (juvenile 177, $n=21$), culmen 36–40 (38.2, $n=28$), tarsus 30–34 (32.2, $n=29$), tail 50–55 (52.7, $n=31$), mass 464–727 g (558, $n=5$)[267].

VOICE Generally silent outside breeding season, with calls similar to other *Aythya*, and thus not very useful for identification. Associated with courtship, ♂ gives three[1230] or four[646] different calls and whistles: *weck*, a hoarser *wruck* and a low *witt*. Female calls similar to Common Pochard: *errr* and a repeated *gek*.

MOULT Complex alternate strategy. Not fully understood and merits further research. Pre-formative moult starts in Aug and is completed in Jan–Mar, sometimes slowed down or suspended during coldest parts of winter. It involves many to most head and body feathers, many to all rectrices, some to all tertials and tertial coverts, and sometimes some inner upperwing-coverts. Subsequent moults as adult. Definitive pre-alternate moult occurs between Feb and May in ♀, and May–Jul in ♂. It includes some to most head and body feathers, no to some tertials, tertial coverts and rectrices, and occasionally some innermost upperwing-coverts. Definitive pre-basic moult is complete and occurs in Jul–Oct (♂) or Aug–Nov (successful ♀♀), with all remiges shed synchronously in Jul–Aug. Many seem to shed their remiges near the breeding sites, and gather in large flocks to moult their body feathers once able to fly again[750].

HYBRIDISATION In the wild reported fairly frequently with Common Pochard, Tufted Duck and Red-crested Pochard, the two former being the second and fourth commonest hybrids in the wild in Europe among Anseriformes[1040]. The hybrid with Common Pochard was even described as a species, Paget's Pochard *Fuligula homeyeri* Bädeker, 1852, and *F. ferinoides* Bartlett, 1855. In Europe, rather frequent hybridisation has been suggested as contributory factor to the decline of Ferruginous Duck[1032]. One hybrid seen in the wild was thought to involve Canvasback *A. valisineria*, but natural hybridisation highly unlikely[439]. Natural crosses with Baer's Pochard have been reported recently in the wild, and may even represent an additional threat to that Critically Endangered species. In captivity, known to have hybridised with Wood Duck *Aix sponsa*, Mallard *Anas platyrhynchos*, Northern Pintail *A. acuta*, Northern Shoveler *A. clypeata*, Red Shoveler *A. platalea*, Speckled Teal *A. flavirostris*, Marbled Duck *Marmaronetta angustirostris*, Southern Pochard *Netta erythrophthalma*, Rosy-billed Pochard *N. peposaca*, Ring-necked Duck *Aythya collaris*, Madagascar Pochard *A. innotata*, Greater Scaup *A. marila*, New Zealand Scaup *A. novaeseelandiae* and Common Goldeneye *Bucephala clangula*[97,817].

Ferruginous Duck × Common Pochard. ♂ in definitive basic plumage rather variable, partly depending on the species to which each parent belongs. Differs from Ferruginous Duck by larger size, and head and bill shape closer to Common Pochard (culmen slightly concave and forehead more sloping). Bill thicker and appears slightly up-curved, with more black at tip, and larger pale subterminal band more like Common Pochard. The base often shows a black vertical band. Head and breast mahogany-brown, the head often clearly paler than Ferruginous Duck, contrasting with the beige-brown flanks that appear slightly barred or vermiculated at close range. The undertail-coverts are highly variable, ranging from almost white to black. Often they only show a white horizontal mark at the sides of the tail. The upperparts are medium grey-brown, slightly vermiculated, darker than the flanks. The wingbars are generally grey on the primaries and white on the secondaries[439] (sometimes grey over the entire length, and never as white as Ferruginous Duck). Iris colour ranges from pale yellow to light red, or almost white with a yellow/orange tone, especially on the outer half, but can easily appear whitish in the field. This hybrid could be mistaken for a first-winter ♂ (pre-formative) Ferruginous Duck, as many features resulting from hybridisation could be assigned to immaturity: intermediate iris and bill coloration, smudged undertail-coverts and belly, less well-marked wingbar and contrast between flanks and breast. Mostly, the latter at least is too strong for pure Ferruginous Duck, and one or more other features will not match pure Ferruginous Duck.

♀ also frequently encountered, representing one-third of reports of this cross[1034], despite being more likely to go unnoticed, and represents a much more serious identification pitfall with Ferruginous Duck. Size intermediate between those of the parents, but shape often close to that of Ferruginous Duck, generally with a rounder head. The bill is often stronger, dark grey with a broad black tip and pale subterminal band along the edges, forming a 'U' if seen from above. The iris is dark brown. The head is marked by two pale brown patches, at the bill base and on the rear cheeks. The upperparts are usually dark grey-brown, but on average paler than Ferruginous Duck, often with fine grey vermiculations. The flanks vary from warm brown to pale brown with dark crescents, depending on the individual and plumage, basic or alternate. Most show obvious contrast between the breast and flanks. The dark brown bar between the flanks and femoral coverts is sometimes absent, which is never the case in Ferruginous Duck. The undertail-coverts are usually white, little or unmarked with dark spots on the sides and lower abdomen. The belly is often tinged, streaked or mottled grey-beige. These patches are often more pronounced than in either parents, which has been suggested to be a character of their common ancestor, just as, for example, the bimaculated head pattern in many hybrid Anatinae. Upperwing as ♂. More than ♂ in basic plumage, it is important separate features linked to hybridisation and those with immaturity, and base identification on the maximum number of characters (see Identification).

Ferruginous Duck × Tufted Duck. The 'Ferruginous Duck-type' has a dark brown head with red sheen and tan-mahogany breast, duller dark brown upperparts, brown-cinnamon to beige flanks, paler than the breast, with a hint of a pale line bordering the upper flanks, as well as undertail variably stained white. These hybrids often also have a short, but sharply drooping crest, and a broad white wingbar. The 'Baer's Pochard-type' has head, breast and upperparts blackish-brown, with gloss of two colours visible simultaneously: green on the rear cheeks and reddish on the crown, but sometimes the opposite or only one of the two. The crest can be short, sharp and drooping, or broad and forming a bump like Ring-necked Duck, especially in courtship[439]. The flanks are grey with a more or less pronounced brown-beige tone, and often show a distinctly rounded shape in contact with the folded wing, with even a faint demarcation (as in Ring-necked and Ferruginous Ducks). The undertail can be broadly stained white or forms a white triangular patch. The iris is pale yellow and the bill intermediate between those of the two parents, often with a conspicuous white subterminal band. The white belly often extends onto the fore flanks above the waterline, which, along with the reddish breast, white iris and green sheen to the head, can suggest Baer's Pochard, but also Ring-necked Duck if the flanks are greyish. In alternate plumage, this hybrid looks much like a Ferruginous Duck[439].

♀ in definitive basic plumage is poorly known and surely easily missed in the wild. A description was given by Sage[1119] but subsequently contradicted by Gillham & Gillham[439]. Plumage coloration is not very useful for separating this hybrid from the highly variable ♀ of Tufted Duck, which can show a brownish breast, flanks and head, and almost all-white undertail-coverts. Attention should be paid to ♀♀ with a smallish rounded head, thin and longish bill with restricted black tip, a dark brown iris, broad white wingbar, and lack of contrast between breast and flanks, which in combination may indicate a hybrid. A juvenile of this cross would be barely identifiable.

Ferruginous Duck × Baer's Pochard. A hybrid resulting from this cross was described by Gillham & Gillham[439]. It resembled a Ferruginous Duck, with upperparts dark brown, flanks hazelnut-brown, slightly paler than the tan breast (which was marked with white spots on its lower half), white undertail, belly mottled brown

and a white spot on the chin. Recent descriptions and photographs[1278] show different types of intermediates. It is also reported that birds showing obvious signs of hybridisation are more numerous than 'pure' Baer's Pochards in South Korea and Japan[1278]. Finally, the recent sharp decline of Baer's Pochard could lead to an increase in hybrids, due to a lack of conspecific partners. In size and structure, some are close to Ferruginous Duck, but have a stronger bill, flat forehead and angular nape, but rather tall head, green sheen on the cheeks and slight reddish sheen on the crown, bright reddish breast, contrast between the breast and flanks and limited white in front of the flanks, including adult ♂♂ identified by their white iris. Others are closer to Baer's Pochard in overall structure, but have the head tall and rounded, thin bill with white subterminal bar stretching back along the edges, flanks as reddish as breast, and meeting above the whitish fore flanks. These hybrids are very close to 'Baer's Pochard-type' hybrid of Ferruginous Duck × Tufted Duck when they flatten their short crest. These birds, including adult ♂ in winter, often show obvious dark spots on the white belly, which could correspond to characters of the common ancestor. ♀♀ and juvenile of both parent species are probably too alike to permit detection of a hybrid of the same sex or age in the field. Other descriptions, especially from captivity, are needed to improve our knowledge of this hybrid.

Ferruginous Duck × Red-crested Pochard. ♂ well known and regularly observed in C Europe at least. The head is strong, high-crowned and reddish-brown. The bill is thin with straight edges in profile, bluish-grey with a variably extensive pink tones. The edges of the tip, either side of the black nail, show a peach-orangey tint. The iris is pale yellowish-brown. Breast dark brown to blackish with mahogany tones, darker than the head. Flanks pale grey, strongly vermiculated dark grey. Belly whitish at junction with the breast, becoming duskier lower. Undertail-coverts variable, sometimes almost all black, sometimes whitish and partially reddish-toned. Upperparts uniform dark brown with anterior scapulars often finely vermiculated grey. Tertials often exhibit a bronze sheen. Some birds at least show a broad white wingbar reaching the outer primaries, but Sage[1118] and Gillham & Gillham[439] stated that it is greyish on the primaries. Legs grey. Hybrids backcrossed with Ferruginous Duck differ from the latter mainly by the strongly mottled or barred belly[439,465].

HABITAT and LIFE-CYCLE Pair formation occurs

from Jan, with birds arriving on breeding grounds between Feb (in S Europe) and May (further north). During breeding season, favours shallow marshes with much aquatic vegetation and helophytes, such as small pockets of water in flooded reedbeds. Compared to other pochards, prefers more enclosed habitats and avoids open, flowing or brackish waters. Furthermore, less gregarious, often breeding in lower densities. Eggs laid between Feb and Jun. depending on latitude[216], but mostly in Apr–May. ♂ abandons ♀ during incubation to form small flocks and begin pre-alternate moult, usually near breeding sites. ♀ starts pre-basic moult at same time as young fledge, 1–2 months after ♂. Leaves moulting grounds between Aug and Oct for their wintering sites. More gregarious during migration and in winter, forming smaller flocks than other pochards, though up to 1,000–2,000 recorded in Africa[985]. Often in small groups of up to a few tens of birds or alone, often with Tufted Ducks or Common Pochards.

RANGE and POPULATION Breeds from C Europe through Eurasia, to W Mongolia, NW & C China (from Xinjiang and N Sichuan). More scattered populations in N Africa (Morocco to Libya), Turkey, Iran, Pakistan (Baluchistan, rare), Afghanistan, Kashmir and E China. Very scarce or former breeder in SW Europe. Chiefly migratory, but both wintering and breeding ranges, as well as local abundance, can fluctuate considerably between years. Migration routes poorly understood. Many wetlands where the species breeds freeze in winter, and at this season range extends from south of breeding range, south to the sub-Saharan belt, the Arabian Peninsula, much of the Middle East, Pakistan, the Indian Subcontinent and east to Thailand and S China. Rare but regular visitor to Japan and W Europe, chiefly in Oct–Mar. The current world population is estimated at c.163,000–257,000 individuals[141], including 36,000–54,000 in Europe[139], mainly in Romania, Croatia, Azerbaijan and Turkey (now uncommon), a few hundred in N Africa, mainly in Algeria[621], 25,000–100,000 in SW Asia, wintering in Africa, and c.100,000 in S & SE Asia[141], including 90,900 in NE Bangladesh (Tanguar Haor) in 2002[757]. Numbers fluctuate widely, and accuracy of some censuses have been questioned. Reportedly numerous in breeding season in Inner Mongolia, on Tibetan Plateau, China, and in Kazakhstan. Has declined massively over past two centuries in Europe, where it is now considered Vulnerable. Trends in Asia unclear. Drainage of shallow wetlands for agriculture is main reason for decline. Eutrophication due to nutrient pollution, resulting in loss of aquatic vegetation and increase in water turbidity, is also a contributory factor, as well as over-hunting by foreign hunters, especially in Africa[216].

CAPTIVITY Frequently held in captivity in Eurasia, where it breeds readily and is sold at a very affordable prices, often lower than those of most diving ducks. Rarer in North America. Regularly escapes from captivity in W Europe, but majority of birds reported are genuine vagrants.

REFERENCES Baker (1993)[56]; BirdLife International (2004)[139]; BirdLife International (2012)[141]; Callaghan & Green *in* Kear (2005)[216]; Cramp & Simmons (1977)[268]; Gillham (1987)[438]; Gillham & Gillham (1996)[439]; Gray (1958)[465]; Harrison & Harrison (1962)[521]; Isenmann & Moali (2000)[621]; Johnsgard (1965)[642]; Leuzinger & Schuster (2005)[750]; Li *et al.* (2009)[757]; Livezey (1996)[773]; McCarthy (2006)[817]; Petkov *et al.* (2003)[985]; Randler (2000)[1032]; Randler (2001)[1034]; Randler (2008)[1040]; Reeber (2001)[1050]; René de Roland *et al.* (2007)[1064]; Sage (1962)[1118]; Sage (1962)[1119]; Steinbacher (1960)[1230]; Townshend (2013)[1278]; Townshend (2014)[1279]; Vinicombe (2000)[1321].

409. Adult ♂ (definitive basic); note clear-cut white undertail-coverts, white iris and black on bill tip confined to nail, all typical of adult. France, Dec (Aurélien Audevard).

410. Adult ♂ (definitive basic), Italy, Mar (Stefano Guiducci).

411. Adult ♂ (definitive basic); note small size compared to Common Pochard *A. ferina* and typical pear-shaped head. France, Dec (Vincent Palomares).

412. Adult ♂ (definitive alternate/definitive basic) in pre-basic moult, still showing some dull alternate head and body feathers, a somewhat dusky bill, and replaced tertials. Switzerland, Oct (Christopher J. G. Plummer).

413. Adult ♂ (definitive basic); in flight, note contrasting, broad white wingbar. Turkey, May (Yann Kolbeinsson).

414. ♀ (formative/definitive basic); very worn inner tertials could indicate a first-winter, while the dark iris and clear-cut bluish bill-band sex this bird; the black bill tip seems broad, but no other visible signs of hybridisation (first-generation at least). Netherlands, Mar (Rick Van der Weijde).

415. ♀ (first alternate/definitive alternate); the rather dusky wingbar on primaries and faintly streaked belly could indicate ancient hybridisation or immaturity. Turkey, May (Yann Kolbeinsson).

BAER'S POCHARD
Aythya baeri

Plate 47

TAXONOMY *Anas (Fuligula) Baeri* Radde, 1863, *Reisen Süden Ost-Sibirien*, 2, p. 376, pl. 15. Forms a clade with the other three white-eyed pochards: Hardhead *A. australis*, Madagascar Pochard *A. innotata* and Ferruginous Duck *A. nyroca*[773], all four together comprising the subgenus *Nyroca* Fleming, 1822.

IDENTIFICATION Shows a superficial resemblance to Tufted Duck *A. fuligula* in juvenile plumage, but especially with Ferruginous Duck and their hybrids, which are the main identification pitfalls (see Hybridisation below). Ferruginous Duck shows obvious differences in size and shape in direct comparison. Baer's Pochard is significantly stronger, with a more elongated body, less tall and longer head, and, according to posture, rounded, rather peaked or flattened. Forehead typically less steep than Ferruginous Duck and nape often forms a sharper angle when feathers of crown held flat. The bill is significantly stronger than in Ferruginous Duck, much thicker at the base but also at tip. The feathers of the rear flanks extend less far on the upperparts, the flank delineation not forming the flattened 'S' shape typical of Ferruginous Duck. For the same reasons, these feathers rarely conceal the white inner secondaries on the folded wing, which are usually visible in Tufted Duck as well, but more rarely in Ferruginous Duck on the water. In terms of coloration, adult ♂ in basic plumage is distinguished from Ferruginous Duck by its black head with green hues contrasting with dark red-brown breast and white of belly extending over fore flanks, often reaching the wing when on water. In adult ♀, this white extends less far on the flanks but usually remains visible above the waterline when swimming. The same is true of juvenile plumage, but the white belly is variably marked with pale brown spots, and often less obvious when swimming. In same sex/age, the white is less extensive on the wing of Baer's Pochard than on Ferruginous Duck. Finally, note the presence of a pale face patch, often orangey, clearly visible in ♀ in all plumages and usually more so than in Ferruginous Duck. To identify a juvenile or ♀, one should primarily take into account general size and shape, and especially the shape of the head and bill.

PLUMAGES Slight sexual dimorphism from juvenile plumage onwards. Complex alternate moult strategy (two plumages per definitive cycle, three in first cycle). Ageing relatively easy until first winter, and possible until end of subsequent summer especially in ♂♂. The extent of the white on the primaries (and thus the wingbar) averages greater in ♂ than ♀, and in adult vs. young. A dark brown-coloured and medium-sized diving duck, characterised by a rounded or angular, fairly flat and crestless head, often without obvious angle between the forehead and culmen in profile. Bill rather strong and thick-based.

Adult ♂

Definitive basic plumage (Oct–Dec?/Jun–Aug?). Head and neck black with green sheen on cheeks and crown-sides, with white dot on the chin. The iris is white, often slightly yellowish. The bill is quite thick-based and almost straight-edged in profile, dark blue-grey to lead-grey on the proximal half, gradually becoming paler, even whitish near the nail, which is black. Breast reddish-brown with slight mahogany sheen. Upper flanks duller hazelnut-brown, with fringes forming pale crescents. Clear-cut, broad black vertical bar separating flanks from undertail-coverts. White of belly extends over fore flanks to the folded wing, forming an obvious broad white area above the waterline when on the water. Large white ventral patch also clearly defined. Lower belly grey-brown spotted pale and white undertail well demarcated (as in Ferruginous Duck). Upperparts dark brown to blackish, with subtle cinnamon vermiculations on the mantle and scapulars. Upperwing has lesser and median coverts cold dark brown often subtly vermiculated grey at the tips, greater and primary coverts blackish-brown. Broad white wingbar formed by bases to secondaries and extending on primaries, becoming pale grey on their outer half. Outermost primaries have outer webs dusky. Thick blackish trailing edge clearly defined on secondaries, diffuse on primaries. Underwing largely white except darker trailing and leading edges. Legs and feet grey, webs darker.

Definitive alternate plumage (Jul–Aug?/Oct–Dec?). Similar to definitive basic plumage but duller overall, especially the head, devoid of beautiful green gloss, and browner breast. White on fore flanks much reduced. Bill more uniformly dusky and duller. Essentially differs from adult ♀ by white or whitish iris.

Adult ♀

Definitive basic plumage (Nov–Dec?/Mar–May?). Appearance similar to ♂, but browner, duller and plainer overall, recalling alternate plumage. Head blackish-brown with brown to reddish oval patch at the base of the bill. Chin whitish. Iris brown to dull grey-brown. Bill greyer and darker than ♂ with pale blue subterminal band thinner but better defined than ♂. The black tip of the bill is often larger. The breast is reddish-brown to mahogany with numerous small black streaks (feather bases), barely darker than the flanks, which are brown with dark vertical crescents. Lower flanks (visible above waterline) and belly white. A blackish-brown bar (femoral coverts) separates the pure white flanks and sharply defined undertail. Lower belly has diffuse grey patches. Upperwing similar to ♂ but secondary coverts browner and lack vermiculations. Outer primaries average slightly paler grey-brown (white wingbars appear shorter). Legs like ♂.

Definitive alternate plumage (Apr–May?/Nov–Dec?). Head shows more obvious pale markings at base of bill, on throat (or upper neck) and also behind eye and on upper cheeks. Often a pale eye-ring is visible. Bill dark blue-grey with pale subterminal band much reduced or wholly absent. Otherwise very like basic plumage.

Juvenile

First basic plumage (until Oct–Nov?). Similar to adult ♀ in alternate plumage, but less reddish-brown, duller or even has yellowish tones to head- and neck-sides. Upper head and nape blackish giving somewhat capped effect. Iris dark brown. Bill dull dark grey without pale subterminal band, and barely duskier tip (nail not contrasting). Rest of plumage brown, duller than ♀, with white undertail often sullied brown, especially beside black vertical bar on femoral coverts. The belly is finely streaked pale brown and its contours are less clearly defined than adult (white belly often barely visible above water).

First-winter ♂

Formative plumage (Nov–Mar?/Jun–Jul?). Acquires plumage similar to adult during first winter. In young ♂ iris becomes paler from the first autumn and is almost whitish by the first winter. Resembles adult ♂ after pre-formative moult. Only distinguished by iris being not entirely white (especially around the pupil), reduced gloss on head, some brownish spots on white undertail and some pale grey-brown patches or streaks on belly. In the hand, look for moult contrast among secondary coverts (juvenile coverts juvenile are browner, narrower, rather pointed and frayed, without pale vermiculations), tertials, tertial coverts or rectrices.

First-winter ♀

Formative plumage (Nov–Mar?/Mar–May). Like other pochards, pre-formative moult seems less extensive and more protracted in young ♀ vs. young ♂. Indeed, some appear very like adult ♀ but are slightly duller until midwinter. Especially the head appears plainer dark brown (brown patch at base of bill scarcely noticeable), the scapulars show quite visible brown fringes and contrast between them, the flanks and breast is reduced, with little or no white above waterline. The belly flecked with pale grey-brown is generally the best feature for ageing, even if the bill is plainer dark grey until early winter at least, without a pale subterminal band and blackish nail barely discernible at any distance.

GEOGRAPHIC VARIATION None.

MEASUREMENTS and MASS ♂ (*n*=9): wing chord 206–215 (212), tail 54–64 (59.3), culmen 44–46 (45), tarsus 36–37 (36.4), mass *c*.880; ♀ (*n*=7): wing chord 196–209 (201), tail 57–60 (58.5), bill 40–45 (43), tarsus 34–36 (34.6), mass *c*.680[945].

VOICE Generally silent outside breeding season. Emits a *garrk* like other *Aythya* but higher pitched. ♂ and ♀ also produce some other rough or harsh sounds during courtship[182,214].

MOULT Complex alternate moult strategy. Few data published on moult in the wild, but like that of other pochards in captivity (see Ferruginous Duck). Nevertheless, it appears that the different moults may occur slightly later, with ♂♂ in breeding plumage reported until early Aug[903]. Similarly, pre-formative moult in Asian species seems more protracted through winter than in Europe and North America.

HYBRIDISATION The only cases suspected in the wild involved Common Pochard *A. ferina* (see below), but are very rare. Hybridisation with Ferruginous Duck is probably more frequent than published records suggest (see that species). In captivity, hybridisation recorded on single occasions with Wood Duck *Aix sponsa*[619], Chestnut Teal *Anas castanea*[619], Redhead *Aythya americana*[948] and New Zealand Scaup *A. novaeseelandiae*.

Baer's Pochard × Common Pochard. Hybrids (or suspected hybrids) from this cross are occasionally reported in E Asia, especially South Korea and Japan[99,872]. Unsurprisingly, adult ♂ in basic plumage strongly recalls hybrid Ferruginous Duck × Common Pochard, including reddish breast, largely white undertail and flanks, and greyish upperparts (vermiculated). Several features may indicate a hybrid, but available information is insufficient to determine their utility: hybrid involving Baer's Pochard (vs. those involving Ferruginous Duck) has a darker head (dark reddish, at least sometimes with strong green gloss on rear cheeks), a pale belly extending to the fore flanks, a rather pale iris appearing whitish or bright yellow (vs. often pale orangey), a slightly less pear-shaped and flatter head, and a more contrasting bill, with a pale blue-grey subterminal area virtually as obvious as in Common Pochard. Size is likely to be larger, close to Common Pochard.

HABITAT and LIFE-CYCLE Migratory, but biology poorly known, particularly due to its rarity. Arrives on breeding grounds between mid-Mar and mid-May (especially Apr)[214]. Like other pochards, favours lakes, ponds and marshes with abundant floating vegetation, surrounded by reeds or tall herbaceous vegetation, usually in open areas[214]. May nest among gull colonies. Brood care and pre-basic moult poorly described in the wild. Autumn migration occurs in Sep–Oct. In non-breeding season, found in small groups or alone (perhaps due to its decreasing numbers) and uses different types of freshwater lakes and reservoirs, brackish lagoons or estuaries.

RANGE and POPULATION Critically Endangered[145]. Former breeding range restricted to Manchuria (extreme SE Russia and NE China), with extensions into Mongolia and perhaps North Korea[214]. In recent years, breeding confirmed in Hebei (four pairs in 2012[1278]) and suspected in provinces of Henan and Shandong, E China, south of former known range. In winter, historically reported from E & S China, Thailand, Myanmar, Bangladesh and India, but since 2010/2011 probably winters regularly only in China[145]. It was formerly uncommon but is now very rare in Japan, North Korea, South Korea, Hong Kong, Taiwan, Nepal, Bhutan, Vietnam and Mongolia at this season. The decline in numbers has been very obvious in recent years. A maximum of 17 wintering birds was reported in Bangladesh recently, whereas 1,000–2,000 wintered

there two decades ago[230], while just 4–5 wintered at Bung Boraphet, Thailand, vs. >420 in 1988[145], and none was found breeding at Lake Khanka, on the Russia/China border, in the heart of the historical breeding range, in 2012[343,1278]. The overall population was estimated at >10,000–20,000 birds in the early 1990s, with concentrations of 2,500 at Tanguar Haor, Bangladesh, in 2001, 2,000 in Jiaozhou Bay, Shandong, E China, in 1991, and 1,530 at various locations in Assam, India, in 1997[757]. However, in 2012, the total population was estimated at probably <1,000 individuals[145]. Censuses of its main wintering sites in China during winter 2012/2013 yielded just 45 birds[343,1278]. The species appears to be on the brink of extinction, with a total population perhaps numbering just a few hundred individuals[343]. Threats are not completely understood, but indiscriminate hunting and widespread destruction of wetlands are certainly the primary reasons for the decline. Hybridisation with Ferruginous Duck, which has increased within the historical range of Baer's Pochard, might also be a contributory factor[343,1278]. In addition to the urgently needed protective measures at known sites, knowledge is required to establish specific management guidelines[145,343], while measures should also be taken to develop a captive stock of birds of proven 'genetic quality'[1278]. An international team is currently developing an action plan to aid the species' conservation[343].

CAPTIVITY Relatively uncommon in captivity, although it is quite easy to find on sale, and, in Europe at least, at similar prices to other pochards. Reportedly easy to keep and breed in captivity. The highly worrying conservation status in the wild, however, necessitates better management of the 'genetic quality' of captive birds, and increase exchange between collections, to avoid the effects of inbreeding.

REFERENCES Bird Hybrids Flickr Forum (2007)[99]; BirdLife International (2014)[145]; Brazil (2009)[182]; Callaghan *in* Kear (2005)[214]; Chowdhury *et al.* (2012)[230]; East Asian-Australasian Flyway Partnership (2014)[343]; IZY (1974, 1977)[619]; Li *et al.* (2009)[757]; Livezey (1996)[773]; McCarthy (2006)[817]; Moores & Moores (2003)[872]; Nechaev & Gluschenko (1993)[903]; Palmer (1976)[945]; Patrick (1932)[948]; Rahmani & Islam (2008)[1029]; Townshend (2013)[1278]; Wang *et al.* (2012)[1332].

BAER'S POCHARD (continued)

416. Adult ♂ (definitive basic). Japan, Feb (Mark Curley).

417. Adult ♂ (definitive basic). Japan, Feb (Mark Curley).

418. ♀ (formative/definitive basic). Hong Kong, China, Feb (Michelle & Peter Wong).

419. ♀ (formative/definitive basic); compare the Tufted Duck *A. fuligula* (rear left). Hong Kong, China, Feb (Michelle & Peter Wong).

RING-NECKED DUCK
Aythya collaris

Plates 48, 49

TAXONOMY *Anas collaris* Donovan, 1809, *British Birds*, 6, pl. 147. Closely related to Greater Scaup *A. marila*, Lesser Scaup *A. affinis* and Tufted Duck *A. fuligula* with which it forms a clade[773]. No subspecies or geographical variation described.

IDENTIFICATION No real identification problems, although hybrids can be misleading, either in North America or Eurasia. Adult ♂ in basic plumage can recall Tufted Duck, but easily distinguished by absence of long drooping crest, bill pattern, grey wingbars and grey flanks with white at their front. Hybrid ♂ Ring-necked Duck × Tufted Duck (see the latter) can offer a pitfall to observers unfamiliar with one species or the other, and must be taken into account when attempting identification. ♀ is like no other *Aythya*, except perhaps ♀ Redhead *A. americana*, especially during the breeding season (alternate plumage) and in juvenile plumage. Their distinction can be surprisingly tricky when faced with a lone bird and no comparison for size. If size cannot be assessed (Ring-necked Duck being much smaller), focus on head shape with typical bump on nape (vs. distinctly rounded in Redhead), an often conspicuous whitish patch at the bill base, orangey-brown iris in adult ♀ (vs. dark brown) and darker upperparts, accentuating contrast with the flanks (vs. plainer in Redhead). Finally, the innermost secondaries are blackish in Ring-necked Duck, but pale grey in Redhead, often visible as a pale grey patch above the rear flanks. Hybrid Ring-necked Duck × Redhead could also cause confusion, especially ♀♀, which seem quite rare (or are rarely detected) in the wild. Overall, hybrid ♀♀ recall a grey ♀ Ring-necked Duck[439] (see Hybridisation below). In North America, one could also encounter a Ring-necked Duck × Lesser Scaup hybrid (see the latter).

PLUMAGES Strong sexual dimorphism from first winter onwards. Complex alternate moult strategy (two plumages per definitive cycle, three in first cycle). Ageing relatively easy until first winter, and possible until end of subsequent summer, especially for ♂♂.

Adult ♂

Definitive basic plumage (Oct–Dec/Jun.). Small diving duck, with a rather stocky body, a long tail often held slightly raised, a large oval head with a long straight nape and broad, bump-shaped crest. Head, neck, upperparts, breast and rear body black. Head has soft purple sheen, sometimes green depending on the light. Iris bright yellow to orange-yellow, with orange often on the periphery of the iris. Can appear bright yellow especially when the pupil is constricted, particularly during courtship. Bill has clear-cut coloration, lead-grey with a thin white line surrounding the bill base, running along the tomium and merging into a broad white subterminal band, which is especially contrasting. The nostrils are also circled white. The nail is very broad and somewhat flattened, and the black tip extends about one-quarter of the total length of the culmen. A brown to purple collar (interrupted on hindneck) separates the head and breast, whose black coloration extends less far onto the belly than in other scaups. Seen in profile, the limit of the black breast is typically oblique. The white lower breast (or fore flanks) forms a characteristic sharp white point in front of the folded wing, and the thin white triangle between the black breast and uniformly pale grey flanks bounded by a white line are distinctive of the species. Moreover, the rear flank feathers extend further on the folded wing than other *Aythya*, creating a gently curved limit to the upper flanks. Belly white. Secondary upperwing-coverts, primary coverts and alula blackish. Remiges entirely grey except black subterminal marks and thin white tips, creating a broad greyish wingbar, with a dark trailing edge that fades gradually over the inner secondaries. The trailing edge is much less marked than in Tufted Duck and both scaups, and is slightly more pronounced in adult than juvenile. Underwing pale grey without marked trailing edge, and median coverts and axillaries whitish. Darker grey leading edge and finely vermiculated white. Legs and feet grey.

Definitive alternate plumage (Jun–Jul/Oct–Nov). Same overall pattern, but black parts of basic plumage are dull blackish-brown finely streaked or mottled pale, especially the breast and undertail. Also shows variable whitish patch around base of bill. Crest less pronounced. The flanks are entirely beige to reddish-brown, whiter at border with dark breast. Belly white. The bill is dark grey with a white subterminal bar, diffuse and less extensive, with a black tip. Iris often orange.

Adult ♀

Definitive basic plumage (Oct–Dec/Apr). Stocky shape

471

of ♂, with strong oval head, peaking well behind eye. Colour of head closer to that of ♀ Redhead, with forehead, crown and nape dark grey-brown (blackish around eye) and grey cheeks. Prominent white eye-ring extends as a line (or bridle) around the ear-coverts and then blends into a whitish area over the upper neck, throat, chin and base of the bill. As in Redhead, the nape has a variable number of white dots, which increase with age[576]. Iris pale orange-brown circled dark. Bill dark grey with broad black tip and slightly thinner white subterminal band. Breast reddish-brown vaguely streaked whitish (more clearly in fresh plumage). Upperparts (tertials included) and rear body uniform dark brown. Undertail-coverts variably stained white. Flanks cinnamon-brown vaguely marked with dark crescents, paler than breast, often almost whitish at junction with latter. Belly whitish, but limits with flanks and breast diffuse. Upperwing like adult ♂ but coverts dark brown. Underwing grey or whitish, rather variable. Legs and feet grey.

Definitive alternate plumage (May–Jun/Oct–Nov). Like basic plumage, but overall browner, duller and less contrasting. Head often seems more rounded at rear. Facial patch sullied with brownish spots, while upper neck, throat and rear cheeks are stained whitish, sometimes coarsely. Breast and flanks less reddish-brown and upperparts slightly paler, making whole body more uniform. The belly is mottled brownish, sometimes heavily. The bill is more uniform dark grey with a less contrasting black tip and the pale subterminal band is often barely visible.

Juvenile

First basic plumage (until Sep–Oct). Similar to alternate plumage of adult ♀ with head and neck thinner. Overall duller, with tones more yellowish than reddish. Crown dark, rest of head grey-brown, with pale pattern of adult ♀ subdued. Little contrast between head, neck, breast and flanks. The breast is often finely streaked dark, and becomes distinctly darker than fore flanks in young ♂. The belly is stained pale brown. Undertail-coverts well marked with white. Iris yellowish-brown to dark brown. Bill usually all dark and dull grey, with darker tip but pale subterminal band absent or barely visible (see below). Upperwing as adult ♀ but dark tips to outer secondaries less marked and contrasting, with a less distinct dark trailing edge than in adult. Sexing sometimes possible at this age, the ♂ having the crown, neck, breast and flanks darker[1098], making the paler fore flanks more contrasting. Note that the iris begins to

turn yellow early in ♂, with the difference noticeable in the hand at 35 days[836]. The bill acquires a diffuse subterminal bar before the first winter, while young ♀ often lacks this throughout the first year.

First-winter ♂

Formative plumage (Sep–Mar/Jun). Formative plumage is acquired between Sep and Mar, often beginning with head (crown, lores and around eye) and breast, then the upperparts. Sheen on head usually barely marked. The rear crown has a less obvious bump than adult ♂. Pre-formative moult usually ends with the flanks and rear body, the former then being variegated with white (front), grey and brown feathers. Following pre-formative moult in late winter, similar to adult ♂, with a variable number of juvenile feathers retained on belly and rear body (undertail, back to uppertail-coverts). The white area in front of the folded wing often has dark vermiculations[836] and the sides are not normally bordered by a whitish line at the top. The reddish collar is less visible or not at all. Tertials often replaced, but some birds retain one to several juvenile tertials, which are brown. The wing is still largely to wholly juvenile (until second pre-basic moult) and under good viewing conditions clearly contrasts with the black scapulars and tertials (or inner wing if moulted). The pattern on the bill is initially diffuse but gradually becomes more obvious during the first winter. Iris yellow-brown in autumn, then yellow during early winter.

First-winter ♀

Formative plumage (Oct–Mar/Apr). Pre-formative moult takes place until Feb–Mar and is on average less extensive than in ♂. It is therefore common to see ♀♀ still looking very similar to juveniles until midwinter, including head shape, overall coloration and belly mottled or streaked brown. The facial pattern is less marked than in adult ♀ and pale patch at the base of the bill is often spotted in its upper part[836]. In the hand, use the upperwing pattern (until the second pre-basic moult) and any juvenile rectrices. Iris often still dark brown and pale subterminal band to bill is still barely obvious.

GEOGRAPHIC VARIATION None.

MEASUREMENTS and MASS ♂ (*n*=100): wing chord 189–205 (adult) and 185–201 (juvenile), tail 49–63, culmen 44–50, bill depth at tip of forehead feathering 19.3–22.3, tarsus 33–37; ♀ (*n*=100): wing chord 180–196 (adult) and 176–192 (juvenile), tail 47–61, culmen

42–48, bill depth at tip of forehead feathering 18.0–20.9, tarsus 31–36[1014]. ♂: wing chord 191–220 (adult, 206, *n*=200) and 195–215 (juvenile, 203, *n*=51) (juvenile), bill from gape 46.0–52.2 (49.1, *n*=264), tarsus 40.5–46.8 (43.8, *n*=237); ♀: wing chord 178–210 (adult, 196, *n*=196) and 189–202 (192, *n*=57) (juvenile), bill from gape 44.5–50.2 (47.1, *n*=158), tarsus 40.0–45.9 (43.0, *n*=214)[576]. ♂: mass 542–910 (*n*=624)[574], with strong variation throughout year (821, *n*=69 in autumn[557], 667, *n*=71 in Aug during wing moult[576]) and by age: 768, *n*=42 in winter (adult) and 689, *n*=47 in winter (first-winter)[576]; ♀: mass: 490–894, *n*=685[574] with strong variation throughout year: 789, *n*=24 in May–Jun and 580, *n*=96 in Jul, and by age: 686, *n*=57 in winter (adult) and 651, *n*=36 in winter (first-winter)[576].

VOICE Usually quiet. Calls similar to other *Aythya* but rather high-pitched. ♀ gives a *wurrr* or *kerrr* in alarm, when calling to young or taking off. ♂ utters a low *wow* during courtship[574], and a *kerrr* like that of ♀. Also gives a soft hiss, in courtship or as contact calls when feeding.

MOULT Complex alternate moult strategy. Pre-formative moult more extensive in ♂ than ♀, and occurs between Sep and Mar, including most body feathers, with a smaller proportion on the belly (often few or none), rump and back, up to 2–3 tertials, two to all rectrices and some inner upperwing-coverts. Definitive pre-alternate moult occurs in Apr–May in ♀ (during spring migration and arrival on breeding grounds) and Jun–Aug in ♂ (on moulting grounds). As in other scaups, it includes most head feathers and scapulars, a variable number of breast and flank feathers, and sometimes the central rectrices. Definitive pre-basic moult starts in late Jul or Aug in ♂ with the wings and tail, on moulting grounds. Brood-rearing ♀ moults the same feathers near the nest site. The body feathers are often moulted later, until Dec, partly on wintering grounds. Moult may be slowed or suspended during migration.

HYBRIDISATION In the wild, hybridisation is reported regularly with Lesser Scaup *A. affinis* and Tufted Duck *A. fuligula* (see these species, respectively), sometimes with Redhead *A. americana* and more rarely with Wood Duck *Aix sponsa*, as well as Greater Scaup *Aythya marila* and Canvasback *A. valisineria* in North America, and Common Pochard *A. ferina* in Eurasia (see below). Hybridisation also reported in captivity with Green-winged Teal *Anas carolinensis*[1190], Mallard *A. platyrhynchos*[817], Ferruginous Duck *Aythya nyroca*[442]

and Red-crested Pochard *Netta rufina*[1190]. A hybrid with New Zealand Scaup *Aythya novaeseelandiae* has been reported[546,817], but its parentage does not seem certain.

Ring-necked Duck × Wood Duck. The ♂ has dark upperparts, breast streaked reddish and blackish, flanks and underparts pale vermiculated dark, secondaries brown with soft green sheen and brown underwing (different from both parents) or streaked like Wood Duck. The iris is orange-yellow with a yellow-brown orbital ring and the legs are closest to Wood Duck[314,439]. There is short crest on the lower nape, which is completely dark with a purple sheen. The bill is pinkish-red at the base, fading on the sides towards the tip, with a dark grey culmen, broad black tip and pale grey subterminal band.

Ring-necked Duck × Greater Scaup. Difficult to distinguish from hybrid with Lesser Scaup[439], especially in overall coloration, the extent of black on breast, lack of white in front of folded wing and head profile (see Lesser Scaup). Winter[1371] described a ♂ with a strong bill clearly like Ring-necked Duck, with a thin white line at the base, broad white subterminal band and black tip intermediate in extent. Another type is described as closer to Ring-necked Duck, with dark upperparts and white fore flanks[457].

Ring-necked Duck × Canvasback. A bird described by Elliott[354] and cited by Gillham & Gillham[439] had profile and head coloration close to those of Canvasback. The bill was blackish with a clear white subterminal band. The black of the breast was reduced, not extending far towards the belly and flanks, leaving a thin white band in front of the folded wing.

Ring-necked Duck × Common Pochard. Adult ♂ closely resembles that of hybrid Tufted Duck × Common Pochard, including the finely vermiculated upperparts and russet-toned head-sides. It differs in that the bill recalls Ring-necked Duck (proximal two-thirds darker grey, broad black tip with vertical limit in profile, clear white subterminal band and, at least sometimes, white around the nostrils), by the flanks clearly and finely vermiculated grey, and head without the short sloping crest. A bird described by Gantlett[414], first identified as a Tufted Duck × Common Pochard, fits that description. It probably involved Ring-necked Duck in its parentage, as postulated by Gillham & Gillham[439], who compared this bird with that described by Rigbäck[1071], which was also supposed to result from this cross.

Ring-necked Duck × Redhead. Shows similarities with hybrid ♂ Tufted Duck × Common Pochard and especially with Lesser Scaup × Redhead. The head is rounded and dark reddish-brown, sometimes with a green sheen[439]. The flanks are light grey, and contrast quite sharply with the darker upperparts. Many show rounded rear flanks, fringed by a whitish line at the top, like Ring-necked Duck. The iris is orange. The bill is similar to Redhead, but with a much more pronounced white subterminal band, the white extending along the tomium. The grey secondaries are tipped white with black subterminal bands more marked than in Redhead. Weller[1342] described a ♀ as close to Redhead, but greyer and having an eye-ring and bridle as white as Ring-necked Duck. The same author described both sexes of this hybrid as being intermediate in size and vocalisations.

HABITAT and LIFE-CYCLE Most leave their wintering grounds between late Feb and Apr. In breeding season, favours marshes, bogs and shallow ponds, with much submerged and floating vegetation. Typically in fresh water, with acidic to neutral PH. Nests are sited in tall herbaceous or helophytic vegetation, including sedges *Carex* spp.[574,1098]. Also on smaller waterbodies and artificial reservoirs, as well as temporary flooded areas. Eggs laid primarily between early May and mid-Jun. Only some second-year birds attempt to breed[569,570]. ♂♂ leave nest sites early during incubation for the moulting grounds, usually in north, where they gather in smaller flocks than other scaups (usually <300 birds[1098]) to moult. ♀♀ moult mainly at nest sites or nearby. Movements to wintering grounds occur mainly in Oct–Nov. Tends to migrate in smaller flocks than other scaups, usually 10–75 birds[1098]. On migration as in winter, inhabits shallow wetlands (usually <1.5 m deep) of variable size, with sheltered areas and abundant aquatic vegetation. Shuns the open waters favoured by other scaups, and avoids even slightly brackish waters.

RANGE and POPULATION Breeds in North America along taiga belt, from interior Alaska (where uncommon[1098]) to N Quebec (where rare[745]), Newfoundland and Labrador. More sporadic or isolated populations in Oregon and montane NE California, Nevada, Arizona and Colorado. Winters south of this range, where waters usually do not freeze. Uncommon or rare in Caribbean and on Bermuda. Occasional to Lesser Antilles, Central America to Panama, and N South America. The commonest Nearctic diving duck in Europe, where dozens are reported annually. Also rare visitor to Japan and E Asia. ♂♂ winter on average slightly further north than ♀♀[10]. Estimated global population 1,470,000 birds in 2005[1290], and averaged just over one million birds in 1990s and 2000s [1098], following an increase over the previous two decades, especially in E North America, where there were 501,000 breeding individuals on average between 1990 and 2012, and 630,000 in 2013[1294]. No clear long-term trend, despite that the species seems heavily hunted (545,000 and 651,000 birds in 2011 and 2012 in the USA[1028] and 21,000–38,000 birds per annum in Canada in 2000–2012[363]).

CAPTIVITY Encountered occasionally in captivity, primarily in North America. Quite uncommon due to rather unattractive plumage, relatively highly priced compared to other diving ducks, and comparatively difficult to breed.

REFERENCES Alexander (1983)[10]; Campbell *et al.* (1990)[219]; De Rouck (1982)[285]; Di Labio & Gosselin (1994)[314]; Elliot (1892)[354]; Environment Canada (2014)[363]; Gantlett (1985)[414]; Gillham & Gillham (1996)[439]; Gillham & Gillham (2000)[442]; Gosselin (1979)[457]; Heinzel *et al.* (1995)[546]; Hier (1989)[557]; Hohman (1984)[569]; Hohman (1986)[570]; Hohman *in* Kear (2005)[574]; Hohman & Crawford (1995)[575]; Hohman & Cypher (1986)[576]; Lepage & Doyon (1996)[745]; Livezey (1996)[773]; McCarthy (2006)[817]; Mendall (1958)[836]; Pyle (2008)[1014]; Raftovich & Wilkins (2013)[1028]; Rigbäck (1986)[1071]; Roy *et al.* (2012)[1098]; Sibley (1938)[1190]; USFWS (2005)[1290]; USFWS (2013)[1294]; Weller (1957)[1342]; Winter (1977)[1371].

420. Adult ♂ (definitive basic), with ♀ (left) and ♂ (rear) Tufted Duck *A. fuligula*. Iceland, Apr (Yann Kolbeinsson).

421. Adult ♀ (definitive basic). California, USA, Nov (Sébastien Reeber).

422. First-winter ♂ (formative); like adult, but some juvenile feathers still visible on upper and fore flanks, lower scapulars and rear body, and bill has not acquired fully adult pattern. Denmark, Jan (Nis Lundmark Jensen).

423. Adult ♂ (definitive basic); note purplish collar, visible only at a close range. California, USA, Jan (Tom Grey).

424. ♀ (formative/definitive basic). California, USA, Jan (Alan D. Wilson).

425. Adult ♂ (definitive basic); the only dark-headed *Aythya* with an all-grey wingbar. Florida, USA, Feb (Ron Bielefeld).

426. First-winter ♀ (first basic/formative); note thinner head, duller yellowish iris, dirty-looking head pattern and blurred bill pattern at this age. New York, USA, Nov (Sébastien Reeber).

TUFTED DUCK
Aythya fuligula

Plates 48, 49

TAXONOMY *Anas Fuligula* Linnaeus, 1758, *Syst. Nat.*, edn. 10, p. 128. Closely related to Greater Scaup *A. marila*, Lesser Scaup *A. affinis* and Ring-necked Duck *A. collaris*, with which it forms a clade[773]. No subspecies or geographical variation described.

IDENTIFICATION ♂ in basic plumage is unmistakable, even if it bears a superficial resemblance to Ring-necked Duck. Other plumages, brown and darker overall, are often more problematic because of their huge variability and resemblance to same plumages of ♀♀ and juveniles of other species. Natural hybrids, which are especially numerous in the genus *Aythya*, also pose serious identification pitfalls.

In Eurasia, Tufted Duck outnumbers all similar species almost everywhere, including Greater Scaup in freshwater areas outside breeding season. Except basic plumage of adult ♂, many have undertail-coverts broadly marked with white, which can cause confusion with Baer's Pochard *A. baeri* and Ferruginous Duck *A. nyroca* (see these two species). A hybrid Tufted Duck × Ferruginous Duck can also be very misleading, if not virtually impossible to distinguish from a pure Tufted Duck in juvenile plumage (see Hybridisation under Ferruginous Duck).

Other species may suggest Tufted Duck, including in North America, where it is a rare but regular visitor. ♂ in basic plumage can be mistaken for Ring-necked Duck, but is easily distinguished by its long, drooping crest, white flanks (not grey), blue-grey and pointed black bill, without any distinctive pattern, and its white wingbar (not grey). In alternate plumage (eclipse), adult ♂ is distinguished by same bill pattern (although washed out), the shape of the crest, the wingbar, and the usually grey flanks (vs. reddish-brown, paler in front, of Ring-necked Duck). Note also that Tufted Duck normally lacks a white facial mask, unlike Ring-necked Duck in the same plumage. A hybrid ♂ Tufted Duck × Ring-necked Duck is a serious pitfall when trying to identify a Tufted Duck in North America or a Ring-necked Duck in Eurasia (see below). In both cases, be wary of a bird that looks different from those around them, but does not show all the typical features of the species it resembles.

Problems with Greater and Lesser Scaups concern ♀ and juvenile plumages. Adult ♀ Tufted Duck can show a very large white facial patch, frequently matching that of Lesser Scaup, more rarely that of Greater Scaup. However, always has short crest on nape, strong square-shaped head, extensive black bill tip, darker brown breast (usually), white wingbar reaching the central primaries and plain dark brown upperparts, strongly contrasting with the flanks. The shape of Tufted Duck is often quite characteristic, with a rather short body, tail usually held upwards at rest, which is rarely the case in other scaups, especially in Greater Scaup. Juvenile plumage is probably the most confusing, as Greater and Lesser Scaups also show plain upperparts in this plumage. Moreover, bill pattern is not straightforward at this age and Tufted Duck has a much-reduced crest. Identification will thus rely mainly on size (vs. Greater Scaup), structure, shape and wingbar (vs. Lesser Scaup). Finally, note the more determined 'jump' just before diving by Greater Scaup, which can be a useful feature at a distance.

Adult ♂ hybrid Tufted Duck × Greater Scaup (see latter) in basic plumage differs mainly from Tufted Duck in finely vermiculated upperparts appearing grey and contrasting with the black head from a distance, and a hint of a short, triangular and prominent crest on the top of the head. In alternate plumage (eclipse), Tufted Duck shows no white facial patch, which is the case for at least some hybrids resulting from this cross. The ♀ is variable and can also recall Greater Scaup. When identifying a ♀ Tufted Duck, be wary of birds with an elongated shape, rounded back, rather plain dark brown upperparts, strong contrast between flanks and upperparts, tail held flat on the water at rest, or with a rounded head lacking even a hint of a crest.

Finally, two features often shown by hybrids, the extensive white facial patch and pale patch on the ear-coverts, are often completely absent in Tufted Duck. Juvenile plumage is probably the most difficult, especially ♀ in its first summer, because head shape and overall colours may be affected by ongoing moult or heavy wear. These plumages always have dark upperparts, a bill often heavily stained with black and a barely distinguishable nail. Hybrid Tufted Duck × Lesser Scaup (see the latter) presents similar problems, but the ♀ resulting from this cross is insufficiently known. Adult ♂ in basic plumage has a broad, truncated or rounded crest visible on the nape, and its upperparts are darker, with pale vermiculations visible only when close. Size and the shape are closer to those of Tufted Duck.

One should also consider the risks associated with backcrosses of the following hybrids with Tufted Duck, especially as these are rather numerous in the wild. Adult ♂♂ of these backcrosses in basic plumage can generally be identified under very good viewing conditions: Tufted Duck × Common Pochard, Tufted Duck × Greater Scaup, Tufted Duck × Ferruginous Duck, all of which are very similar to Tufted Duck.

PLUMAGES Strong sexual dimorphism from first winter onwards. Complex alternate moult strategy (two plumages per definitive cycle, three in first cycle). Ageing relatively easy until first winter, and possible until end of first summer, especially for ♂♂ using upperwing pattern (until second pre-basic moult). The extent of the white towards the outer primaries (and thus the wingbar) averages greater in ♂ than in ♀, and very slightly more in adult vs. young birds.

Adult ♂

Definitive basic plumage (Nov/May–Jun.). Small to medium-sized diving duck, rather short-bodied, with a stocky shape, a short tail often held raised, and a large round head with long, unique, drooping crest. Head, neck, upperparts, breast and rear body black. Head usually has violet or purple gloss, often barely visible, and can appear green under certain lights. Iris bright yellow. Bill pale blue-grey with a poorly defined whitish subterminal band and black tip largely encompassing the nail. Belly and flanks white, without vermiculations. Secondary upperwing-coverts, primary coverts and alula plain blackish (primary and median coverts sometimes faintly speckled grey. A white wingbar is formed by the remiges, which are broadly tipped blackish. This bar is completely white on secondaries and inner primaries (outer webs), becoming gradually grey-brown towards the outer primaries. Underwing mostly very pale grey, white on median coverts and axillaries. Legs and feet grey.

Definitive alternate plumage (Jun–Jul/Oct–Nov). Rather like basic plumage, but black parts replaced with dull blackish-brown, the white flanks are grey-brown with broad diffuse pale crescents, and the undertail-coverts are frequently streaked white. Does not usually show a white facial patch at the base of the bill. Belly largely white. In addition, the crest is much shorter and dishevelled, and the bill darker, less blue-grey.

Adult ♀

Definitive basic plumage (Nov/Mar–May). Compact structure of ♂, with strong and square-shaped head, and the darkest overall colour among Holarctic *Aythya*, except Ferruginous Duck. Head dark chocolate-brown to blackish with a short crest and variable white facial patch (often poorly defined and limited to the base of the bill, sometimes absent, but can extend below the gape and on forehead). Pale ear-coverts patch normally absent. Iris yellow to yellow-brown, often duller than ♂ (age-related?). Bill like that of ♂, but dark grey with a diffuse pale subterminal band. Breast dark chestnut-brown. The upperparts (including tertials) are uniform dark brown. Flanks grey-brown, paler than rest of body when bird is on the water, marked with dark crescents. Rear body blackish-brown with usually some white patches on undertail-coverts, sometimes almost completely white as in adult ♀ Ferruginous Duck. The extent of white is more pronounced in late autumn when the feathers are fresh, and tends to decrease with wear. Belly white, occasionally heavily stained dark, which plumage was once considered a variant[519,520]. Upperwing like adult ♂ but coverts dark brown. Legs and feet grey.

Definitive alternate plumage (Apr–Jun/Oct–Nov). Similar to basic plumage, but a variable number of body feathers are replaced in Mar–May. The facial patch is often sullied with brown spots, the crest is shorter or virtually absent (especially in alarm postures), the head and upperparts are blackish-brown, while the flanks show warmer brown, almost similar to the breast. The belly is variably marked with diffuse dark patches. Bill darker, with black tip barely discernible.

Juvenile

First basic plumage (Jun/Sep–Oct). Similar to adult ♀ but overall coloration slightly paler and duller, with crest reduced or virtually absent. Head dark brown (paler than adult ♀), with blackish crown and hint of a pale facial patch. Iris olive-brown (♀) to yellowish-brown (♂). Bill dark grey, blackish towards the tip, with indistinct nail. Upperparts and rear body dark brown like head, with a fine scaly pattern due to yellowish fringes to scapulars. Tertials rather short, brown and washed out at tips, without soft bronze or green sheen of adult. Tertial coverts brown (no bronze sheen), narrow, rounded or pointed (almost square in adult) and frayed at tip. Breast and flanks slightly paler yellowish-brown. Belly pale, neatly streaked brown and ill-defined (a very useful feature for ageing in flight), sometimes with stronger patches. Wing similar to ♀ but coverts browner, narrower and quickly fray at tips, with faint (♂) or no (♀) pale grey speckling, primaries and even 1–2 outer secondaries not white (washed pale grey-brown), and blackish trailing edge to secondaries less clear-cut. Legs dull grey.

First-winter ♂

Formative plumage (Oct–Mar/Jun.). Like other *Aythya*, acquisition of formative plumage is protracted, from Oct to Mar, often suspended during coldest part of winter, and is quite variable in extent. The first signs of formative plumage usually appear on the head and scapulars, then flanks, breast and rear body. Until the beginning of the first winter, young ♂♂ are easy to age by the clear remnants of juvenile plumage. Once pre-formative moult completed (in Feb–Mar), very similar to adult ♂ in basic plumage, usually with a shorter crest. Age can be assessed by retained juvenile feathers (brown) on the belly, undertail and rump. The tertials are often replaced, but some birds retain one to several juvenile tertials, brown, faded and frayed at tips. Wing still largely juvenile and, under good viewing conditions, clearly contrast with the upperparts and black tertials (until second pre-basic moult). Iris yellow-brown at beginning of first winter, turning yellow by spring.

First-winter ♀

Formative plumage (Oct–Mar/Apr). Pre-formative moult is protracted, until Feb–Mar, but less extensive on average than in ♂. Nevertheless, good viewing conditions are required to detect the retained juvenile feathers, paler, washed yellowish and duller, especially on the breast and flanks. The belly is still juvenile, as well as most tertials and tertial coverts, during the first winter (see above). The bill is still often irregularly marked black during the same period. The iris is normally dull brown throughout the first winter and does not turn bright yellow until later in the second calendar year.

GEOGRAPHIC VARIATION None.

MEASUREMENTS and MASS ♂: wing chord 198–215 (206, *n*=46), tail 49–58 (54, *n*=44), bill 37–44 (40, *n*=66), tarsus 34–37 (36, *n*=40); ♀: wing chord 193–205 (199, *n*=40), tail 48–57 (53, *n*=39), bill 36–41 (39, *n*=73), tarsus 32–37 (35, *n*=40)[1086]. ♂ (*n*=70): wing chord 193–209 (adult) and 189–205 (juvenile), tail 47–59, culmen 37–44, bill depth at tip of feathering 16.5–20.1, tarsus 34–38; ♀ (*n*=80): wing chord 186–202 (adult) and 182–198 (juvenile), tail 45–58, culmen 36–42, bill depth at tip of feathering 15.5–18.8, tarsus

34–37[1014]. ♂: mass in Dec–Mar 600–1,020 (813, *n*=92)[79]; in Jan 765–1,015 (868, *n*=27)[686]; ♀: in Dec–Mar 560–930 (718, *n*=58)[79], in Jan 730–815 (778, *n*=5)[686].

VOICE ♂ is usually quiet, and mostly heard during courtship, giving low quacks and whistles that can recall Eurasian Wigeon *Anas penelope*, but weaker and shorter. ♀ gives different kinds of guttural calls typical of *Aythya*, e.g. *karrr* or *brre*, repeated, either in alarm or contact call, or when taking off.

MOULT Complex alternate moult strategy. Pre-formative moult more extensive in ♂ than ♀, occurs between Sep and Mar, primarily on wintering grounds, and includes most body feathers, with a smaller proportion (to almost none) replaced on the belly, rear body, rump, tertials and upperwing-coverts. Definitive pre-alternate moult occurs from Mar to May in ♀ (during spring migration and on arrival at nest sites) and in Jun–Jul in ♂ (on moulting grounds). Definitive pre-basic moult occurs in Jul–Nov, is complete and begins with simultaneous loss of the remiges in Jul–Aug in ♂, or 1–2 months later in ♀♀ that breed successfully.

HYBRIDISATION Those hybrids most problematic with respect to identification are also those most frequently reported in the wild. Those with Greater and Lesser Scaups are especially tricky in ♀ and juvenile plumages (see those species). Hybridisation with Ferruginous Duck (which see) produces birds potentially resembling several other *Aythya*, both ♂♂ and ♀♀. Hybrids with Common Pochard and Ring-necked Duck are described below. Hybrids with Red-crested Pochard *Netta rufina* are sometimes reported in Europe. They have a dark head with red tones, a long blue-grey bill with diffuse pinkish patches especially near the tip, an orange to pale yellow iris, a black breast extending to the hindneck (like many hybrids involving Red-crested Pochard), white flanks and blackish-brown upperparts. Other hybrids reported very occasionally in the wild, with Cape Teal *Anas capensis* in Africa[187], Mallard *A. platyrhynchos*[439,817], Garganey *A. querquedula*[439] and Canvasback *Aythya valisineria* in North America[442]. Hybrids with Wood Duck *Aix sponsa* are mentioned primarily in captivity, but have also been reported in the wild, at least in Europe, but it is not always easy to rule out captive origin. These hybrids show obvious characters of both species, including a pink-based bill highlighted with a yellow line, indicating Wood Duck, and grey flanks contrasting with the rest of the dark body, like Tufted Duck (see Gillham & Gillham[439] for

a complete description). Logically, this cross would be difficult to differentiate from hybrid Wood Duck × Ring-necked Duck, which has occurred in North America (see under Ring-necked Duck). Occasional hybridisation occurs in captivity with Northern Pintail *Anas acuta*[588], American Wigeon *A. americana*[1190], Eurasian Wigeon *A. penelope*[588,817], Redhead *Aythya americana*[619] (including recent cases, documented with photographs), New Zealand Scaup *A. novaeseelandiae*[439], Bufflehead *Bucephala albeola*[1190], Common Goldeneye *B. clangula*[38], Southern Pochard *Netta erythrophthalma*[439] and Rosy-billed Pochard *N. peposaca*[439,817].

Tufted Duck × Common Pochard. This hybrid is the most frequently reported in the wild in Eurasia among Anseriformes. This cross produces different types of hybrids, which can suggest many other species of *Aythya,* but most resemble Lesser Scaup, especially if the parents are a ♂ Tufted Duck and ♀ Common Pochard. Gillham & Gillham[439] stated that 75% of these hybrids can be considered 'Lesser Scaup-type', which are slightly larger than Tufted Duck with a slightly less compact shape and a short rounded crest (often close to that of Lesser Scaup). Some, however, show no trace of a crest[94,310]. The bill is often longer than Lesser Scaup, but also less spatulate, and blue with a black area at the base, which can extend to the nostrils, is limited to a few traces or merges gradually into the paler distal half of the bill. The broad black tip extends along the tomium, in a pattern often like Common Pochard, but can also be similar to Tufted Duck[440]. A vague subterminal band inherited from Tufted Duck is often visible in winter. The iris can be yellow, amber, orange or reddish, but can also change seasonally and, moreover, differ in the eyes of the same bird. The dark head is generally warm brown with purple reflections, but can be green or conversely paler reddish-brown, and also varies greatly seasonally[439]. The breast is black, sometimes obliquely demarcated from the flanks in profile like Ring-necked Duck[936]. Flanks whitish with very fine and tight grey-brown vermiculations that are barely discernible. The wingbar is usually white on the secondaries and grey on the primaries (recalling Lesser Scaup), but can be all grey. The dark trailing edge to the secondaries is often less marked or absent on the inner half. The innermost secondaries, tertials and longest scapulars are also paler grey than Lesser and Greater Scaups, often visible on the folded wing, as the inner wing forms a pale grey patch above the rear flanks. The rest of the upperparts are whitish very finely vermiculated dark grey, appearing very uniform.

Hybrid Common Pochard × Ring-necked Duck is rather similar (see Ring-necked Duck). Some hybrids of this type have paler upperparts, a rounded head without any crest and markedly reddish, a red-orange iris, wingbar whitish on the secondaries and grey on the primaries, and recall Redhead[678,1031,1050]. These birds could be backcrosses with Common Pochard.

♀♀ from this cross are also rather variable, and can resemble ♀ Common Pochard, Tufted Duck, Lesser Scaup, Greater Scaup and even Ring-necked Duck. The first type resembles Greater Scaup, being fairly large, massive-headed with or without a short pointed crest and a dark brown head with a large white face patch. However, they also have a very dark bill base and extensive black tip extending along the tomium, a brown iris, clear contrast between dark greyish-brown upperparts and paler flanks, and undertail-coverts marked with white. The wingbar can be grey or white[439]. Another well-known type is slightly shorter and stockier, often with a raised tail and large head, with a hint of very angular crest on the neck, a dark iris, a dark lead-grey base to the bill, with a broad black tip, and a paler body than the previous hybrid. The crown and area around the eyes are dark brown, contrasting with the white bill base and throat, and the paler brown cheeks. The breast is reddish-brown, the upperparts brown with broad grey fringes, and flanks pale brown. Finally, the central undertail-coverts are whitish, often contrasting sharply with the brown lateral coverts. The wingbar is usually grey. This type is like a ♀ Ring-necked Duck.

Tufted Duck × Ring-necked Duck. These hybrids can be very misleading, both in North America and Eurasia. They can show a short, drooping crest, closer to Tufted Duck, or a truncated crest very like Ring-necked Duck, but more often a broad rounded crest. The bill is dark grey and intermediate in length, with a white subterminal band less pronounced than Ring-necked Duck, but more so than Tufted Duck. A white line sometimes surrounds the top of the bill base and partially its sides. The flanks are like those of Ring-necked Duck, with their shape forming a flattened horizontal 'S', pale grey becoming whiter on the fore flanks in front of the folded wing. The wingbar is white on the secondaries and grey on the primaries, but can be completely white. The ♀ is less well known, and has intermediate characters, overall usually closer to Tufted Duck, but with a bill clearly like Ring-necked. The head shape is reminiscent of Lesser Scaup, with a rather long bill, dark grey with a broad black tip and a clear-cut pale subterminal band. A large whitish patch is visible at the bill base and onto the throat, and the iris is orangey. The demarcation on the upper flanks is intermediate in shape with a slightly paler area on the fore flanks. Breast intermediate. Other birds seen in the wild have the same bill pattern including clear white subterminal bar and some white on the tomium and around the nostrils, a blackish head with a short erect crest, a white facial patch slightly mottled brown, orange iris, breast reddish streaked blackish, flank feathers pale brown with whitish vermiculations, and an undertail stained pale.

HABITATS and LIFE-CYCLE Breeds from plains and mountains at temperate latitudes to steppes of C Asia and Arctic tundra, as well as across almost the entire Eurasian taiga belt. Inhabits a variety of habitats for breeding, including shallow lakes, reservoirs, gravel and sand pits, ponds and slow-moving streams, usually with abundant riparian and aquatic vegetation[143,1086]. Favours eutrophic waters with small islets safe from terrestrial predators, including within colonies of gulls. Pairs arrive at their nesting sites between early Apr and early Jun, depending on latitude. Breeds alone or at rather high densities (with nests a few metres apart), but not truly colonial. Like other *Aythya*, ♂♂ depart nesting sites shortly after egg laying, and gather to moult, usually on large, still waterbodies. ♀♀ moult later, usually at their nesting grounds or nearby. Autumn migration varies among populations, birds breeding in W Europe making only short migrations, but exclusively migratory over most of its Eurasian breeding range. In winter, forms huge gatherings on large lakes, broad rivers and reservoirs, but also on brackish or salt water if they are sufficiently sheltered. The segregation of the sexes, which begins during moult, lasts throughout the winter, with largely unbalanced sex ratios over many parts of the winter range. Pairs form from midwinter. Returns to breeding grounds from Feb.

RANGE and POPULATION Breeds at scattered localities south of mapped range, including occasionally in its Asian and African wintering grounds (sometimes birds wounded by hunters). Global population estimated at 2,600,000–2,900,000 birds in winter[305] and 730,000–880,000 pairs, in moderate decline[139], with 530,000–560,000 pairs in Russia[278]. Birds breeding in W Europe winter largely near their breeding sites. Further north, those breeding in Iceland, Fennoscandia to W Russia winter between the S Baltic Sea, North Sea, British Isles and Atlantic coasts of Europe south to W Africa. European wintering population estimated at 1,200,000 birds, in moderate decline[139]. Birds breeding in NE Europe and W Russia winter in C Europe, the Mediterranean and Black Sea (600,000 individuals), and NE Africa (200,000[965]). Breeders in Asia and C Siberia winter between the Red Sea and Caspian Sea to China, and south of the Himalayas, with a population estimated at 100,000–1,000,000 birds[1086], but 300,000 birds alone estimated in India[305]. Breeding birds in E Siberia winter in China and N Philippines, to South Korea and Japan. This population is currently estimated at 200,000–300,000 birds[222]. Conflicting estimates available for China, with 500,000 birds at the start of the present century[858], but only a few thousand birds along the Yangtze since[71,222]. Overall stable or slightly decreasing, but trends poorly known in east of range. Rare but more regular visitor recently to North America, mainly along Pacific coast from the Aleutians to California, along coasts of E Canada and NE USA, and on the Great Lakes.

CAPTIVITY Encountered fairly regularly in captivity, especially in Europe, although its black-and-white plumage does not make it sought-after. Breeds easily, and is usually inexpensive.

REFERENCES Astley (1921)[38]; Barter *et al.* (2004)[71]; Bauer & Glutz von Blotzheim (1968–69)[79]; Bezzel (1960)[94]; BirdLife International (2004)[139]; BirdLife International (2013)[143]; Brickell & Frandsen(1988)[187]; Cao *et al.* (2010)[222]; Database on Waterfowl Resources of Russia (2001)[278]; Delany & Scott (2006)[305]; Demongin (1995)[310]; Gantlett (1985)[414]; Gillham & Gillham (1996)[439]; Gillham & Gillham (1998)[440]; Gillham & Gillham (2000)[442]; Harrison & Harrison (1960)[519]; Harrison & Harrison (1961)[520]; Hopkinson (1935)[588]; IZY (1968)[619]; Kemp (1991)[678]; Kestenholz (1994)[686]; Livezey (1996)[773]; McCarthy (2006)[817]; Miyabayashi & Mundkur (1999)[858]; Osborne (1972)[936]; Perennou *et al.* (1994)[965]; Pyle (2008)[1014]; Randler (2000)[1031]; Reeber (2001)[1050]; Rigbäck (1986)[1071]; Robinson *in* Kear (2005)[1086]; Scott & Rose (1996)[1154]; Sibley (1938)[1190].

TUFTED DUCK (continued)

427. First-winter ♀ (formative), best aged by blurred dusky traces on culmen (variably marked, but usually blacker and more clear-cut in adult), dark iris and old tertials (pale brown and very frayed at tips). England, Feb (Sébastien Reeber).

429. Adult ♀ (definitive basic); aged by pale blue bill, bright yellow iris and long tertials with a soft green or bronze sheen. England, Feb (Sébastien Reeber).

428. Adult ♂ (definitive basic). England, Feb (Sébastien Reeber).

430. Adult ♂ (definitive basic); tertial coverts are broad-tipped, not worn and show slight bronze sheen, typical of this age. Denmark, Mar (Nis Lundmark Jensen).

431. Adult ♂ (definitive basic); compared to both scaups, note parallel-sided bill and extensive black bill tip. England, Feb (Sébastien Reeber).

432. First-winter ♂ (formative); much like adult, but note old juvenile or growing tertials (end of pre-formative moult), and brown juvenile feathers on back and mantle, rather short crest and dusky traces on culmen. England, Feb (Sébastien Reeber).

GREATER SCAUP
Aythya marila

Plates 50, 51, 52

TAXONOMY *Anas Marila* Linnaeus, 1761, *Fauna Svecica*, edn. 2, p. 39. Polytypic. Very closely related to Lesser Scaup *A. affinis*. These sister species form a clade with Tufted Duck *A. fuligula* and Ring-necked Duck *A. collaris*[773]. Two subspecies are currently recognised: the nominate occurs in Europe and W Asia, while *A. m. nearctica* Stejneger, 1885, is found in E Asia and North America. *A. mariloides* Vigors, 1839, was initially applied to birds of the Bering Sea and is sometimes still used for all Nearctic birds[236,1022]. However, this name was invalidated[63] being previously associated with Lesser Scaup. Another issue concerns the identity of E Asian birds, sometimes considered within *nearctica*[182,928] and sometimes *marila*[684,1014], although their appearance is much closer to *nearctica* (see Geographic Variation), but further study including of DNA is required.

IDENTIFICATION Sometimes problematic because of its strong resemblance to Lesser Scaup and the presence in the wild of relatively numerous hybrids. In North America, where both species are common, these problems even affect perceptions of their status and many censuses do not distinguish between them. The two species are generally not numerous in the same places, though, due to differences in their distributions (Greater Scaup being more northerly at all seasons) and habitat preferences (Greater Scaup prefers coastal waters, often salt or brackish). In Europe and Asia, where only Greater Scaup is locally common, identification issues mainly focus on some ♀ Tufted Ducks and hybrids between this species and Greater Scaup, especially ♀♀. Such hybrids are not uncommon in the wild, especially inland where Greater Scaup is usually quite rare. For example, Smallshire[1208] estimated that 20% of Greater Scaups seen inland in Britain were hybrids.

Separation of Greater Scaup and Lesser Scaup is based on a series of rather subtle features, and it is necessary to consider several in combination. It is also useful to mention that the distinction between these two species is tougher in North America and E Asia, given that the subspecies *nearctica* is actually intermediate between *marila* and *affinis*. Greater Scaup is distinguished by its significantly larger size (Lesser Scaup is similar to Tufted Duck) with a more rounded silhouette, rounded back, thick neck, large and chubby

head, and strong bill. The shape is different and can be the easiest feature to use with practice: Lesser Scaup has a small head, taller than it is long, with a distinct angle between the crown and nape, which forms an almost straight, vertical line with the hindneck. The head peaks often well behind the eye. In Greater Scaup, the head profile is elongated and rounded, without any distinct angle with the hindneck. The head peaks above the eye. However, the head profile of *nearctica* differs substantially, being more angular with a typically 'bumpy' forehead, and the head peaks slightly in front of the eye. Note also that head shape varies depending on the bird's behaviour[748]. After feeding underwater, the feathers are tightly flattened against the skull, which greatly affects head shape and makes the bill appear longer. A more relaxed posture is necessary to assess shape correctly. Seen from the front, the head has a very different shape between the two species: Greater Scaup has 'swollen' cheeks, creating a sharp angle (near the eye) with the crown-sides; in Lesser Scaup, the cheeks are less prominent and the angle with the sides flatter. Two other subtle differences may be useful: in profile and at rest, Greater Scaup has a regularly rounded back, whereas Lesser Scaup has a more angular back that peaks closer to the head. Furthermore, Lesser Scaup more frequently holds its tail out of the water and slightly raised at rest[177].

Other important features are the precise shape of the black nail, rounded when viewed from the front in Greater Scaup (vs. much thinner, longish and parallel-sided in Lesser Scaup) and the bill is thicker at the base, longer, more spatulate-tipped[907] with an almost straight culmen in profile (vs. thinner and parallel-sided from the front and culmen slightly concave). In profile, the nail of Greater Scaup appears broad, almost ball-shaped, while that of Lesser Scaup is significantly thinner, like a small claw. Note that the black of the nail frequently overflows onto the sides in Greater Scaup, which is much rarer in Lesser Scaup. The white wingbar on the secondaries and inner primaries also distinguishes Greater Scaup (but more so in *marila* than *nearctica*) vs. white on secondaries and pale grey-brown on primaries, with a clear demarcation, in Lesser Scaup. The underwing-coverts are mostly white or pale grey in Greater Scaup, while white is restricted to the median coverts, lower lesser coverts and axillaries in

Lesser Scaup (more contrasting underwing, especially in ♀♀[422]). These features are only useful to separate alternate adult ♂♂, immatures and juveniles from the equivalent plumages of Lesser Scaup.

Adult ♂ in basic plumage is also distinguished by the black vermiculations on the upperparts significantly (*marila*) or slightly (*nearctica*) thinner than Lesser Scaup, thus reducing the contrast with the flanks. The latter are usually white or nearly so in Greater Scaup (vs. vermiculated grey, at least at their extremes in Lesser Scaup). Finally, the sheen of the head is usually green in Greater Scaup, but more frequently purple in Lesser Scaup, although the angle of the light can suggest the reverse is true. In adult ♀ the pale ear-coverts are more pronounced, whatever the season, in Greater Scaup, with the ground colour of the head paler brown, usually barely darker than the rest of the body, whereas it is blackish-brown in Lesser Scaup. Also, the white patch at the base of the bill is larger and more rounded in Greater Scaup, whereas the white is rather thin on the forehead, strongly tapers at the gape and often forms a wedge towards the eye in profile in Lesser Scaup. Young ♀♀ in late winter and spring simultaneously exhibit two or three generations of feathers, which affects both the coloration and head shape features, making identification more complicated.

Hybrid Greater Scaup × Lesser Scaup is much more problematic. Surprisingly, it is very little described in the literature, even in captivity (see Hybridisation). It is probable that natural hybrids occur regularly and go mostly unnoticed. Clearly, some birds in North America are difficult to assign with certainty to one species, even adult ♂♂. An in-hand study of the wingbars of 365 birds concluded that 9% of birds showed intermediate characters, and could not be identified using this feature alone[1369]. Finally, it would be interesting to know to what extent the differences between *marila* and *nearctica* (in measurements, head shape, vermiculations on upperparts and wingbars), which make the latter closer to *affinis*, are explained by ancient or ongoing gene flow from the latter, although reproductive barriers between the two species are clearly sufficiently strong to maintain them, despite considerable phenotypic similarity and broad sympatry. A genetic study of Greater Scaups in Long Island Sound, New York and Connecticut, also concluded that hybrids were rare[381].

Tufted Duck *A. fuligula* is much less problematic, although some ♀♀ show a vague resemblance to ♀ Greater Scaup, mainly because the white facial patch is particularly broad at the bill base (see Identification).

Hybrid Greater Scaup × Tufted Ducks are misleading (see Hybridisation) and also within a Eurasian context, hybrid Tufted Duck × Common Pochard can also represent a serious pitfall (for ♀♀) (see under Tufted Duck).

PLUMAGES Nominate subspecies. Strong sexual dimorphism from first winter onwards. Complex alternate moult strategy (two plumages per definitive cycle, three in first cycle). Ageing relatively easy until the first winter, and possible until the end of the subsequent summer especially for ♂♂. The extent of white on each web of the innermost primaries, which makes the wingbar appear more or less white and reach towards the wingtip, exhibits strong individual variation[177,1014,1369], but is on average substantially greater in the ♂ vs. the ♀, slightly so in adult vs. juvenile and, finally, on average greater in *marila* than *nearctica*.

Adult ♂

Definitive basic plumage (Nov/June). Head, neck, upper mantle and breast black with beautiful green gloss on the head-sides, which can appear violet or purple according to the light. Iris yellow to slightly orange. Bill pale blue-grey with black tip limited to the nail. Some birds, including adults, can have black faintly extending on both sides of the nail. Exceptionally, the bill can even be partially or entirely black[441]. Belly and flanks all white, clearly demarcated from the black breast and lower belly and rear body. Some fine pale grey vermiculations are sometimes visible on the rear flanks. Back white vermiculated black, lower mantle and scapulars white vermiculated dark grey. Tertials blackish vermiculated or speckled white, especially at tips. Upperwing has lesser and median coverts blackish largely vermiculated white (slightly darker than scapulars in flight), greater coverts, primary coverts and alula blackish. A broad wingbar is formed by the white secondaries, with large black tips, and 5–7 inner primaries with white outer webs. The wingbar gradually becomes greyish on the outer primaries. Underwing pale grey with tips of greater and median coverts and axillaries white. Legs and feet grey.

Definitive alternate plumage (Jun–Jul/Oct–Nov). More similar to definitive basic plumage than other species of *Aythya*. The black parts of the basic plumage of adult ♂ are still very dark, but duller and faintly streaked pale brown or grey. The breast is often distinctly streaked and paler than the head. A white facial patch recalling that of ♀ is often visible, although it is usually limited to a small whitish area at the base of the bill. Flanks and upperparts variegated with basic-type (white vermiculated dark grey) and brownish feathers. The basic wing is retained, sometimes with the exception of a small number of inner lesser coverts. Bill shows dark marks.

Adult ♀

Definitive basic plumage (Nov/Apr). Head dark brown with a broad white facial patch extending well beyond the gape towards the chin, and a large pale auricular patch, both of which can be obscured by dark tips to the feathers when fresh. Iris yellow, often slightly less bright than ♂. Birds with a bright yellow iris considered second-summer or older[1281], but adult ♀♀ can also have a yellow-brown iris[748]. Bill like ♂, but darker and greyer, making the nail less distinct. Breast reddish to hazel-brown. Flanks, mantle and scapulars uniform, with brown feathers paler grey distally and vermiculated dark brown. Generally grey-brown, overall much paler than fore and rear body, with diffuse dark crescents. Tertials dark brown, often faintly speckled pale grey. Rear body blackish marked with brown. Belly whitish. Wing like adult ♂ but dark brown coverts with few or no pale grey speckles at the tips. Legs and feet grey.

Definitive alternate plumage (May–Jun/Oct–Nov). Similar to basic plumage, but a variable number of head and body feathers are moulted in Apr–May, especially the scapulars, which are mostly replaced. Entire plumage brown with darker upperparts. New feathers on upperparts and flanks are brown, with few or no pale grey vermiculations. The breast, head, upperparts and flanks are rather uniform and evenly coloured, slightly darker around the eyes. The white facial and auricular patches are prominent, even whitish in summer, and the foreneck is often also pale. Bare parts as basic plumage, but bill often darker (variable) or even blackish on culmen.

Juvenile

First basic plumage (Jun/Sep–Oct). Overall dull brown with dark brown head, pale brown facial patch generally not extending to the forehead, pale ear-coverts patch reduced or scarcely marked, and foreneck slightly paler. Iris dull dark brown (♀) or yellow-brown (♂). Bill dark grey with many diffuse black smudges on the culmen and around the nail, on average slightly more pronounced in ♀. Breast dark brown with paler streaks gradually blending into the belly, without contrast. Flanks dull hazel-brown with slightly darker centres

often typically arranged in horizontal lines. Upperparts uniform blackish-brown without vermiculations and visibly darker than flanks. Belly beige finely streaked pale brown. Rear body dark brown stained and streaked pale brown. Upperwing like adult ♀ but median and lesser coverts brown with few pale vermiculations at the tips (♂) or none (♀). The white wingbar on average extends less far onto the inner primaries than in adults, in both sexes. Trailing edge of wing less black, less contrasting and less clearly defined than in adult. Legs dull grey.

First-winter ♂

Formative plumage (Oct–Mar/Jun). Acquisition of formative plumage is protracted over several months, but is quite variable in extent and speed of development, so it is normal to see first-winter ♂♂ at different stages side by side. The adult-type formative feathers appear firstly on the head (black with moderate green sheen), anterior scapulars (white vermiculated dark grey, slightly more strongly than in ad[670]) and upper flanks (white). Until Feb, first-winter ♂♂ typically show a mix of juvenile and formative feathers. In early spring, those birds whose moult was less extensive still look variegated, but others are close to adult. Some brown juvenile feathers are still visible on the belly, undertail and uppertail. One to three tertials are sometimes replaced, but many birds retain some (or even all their) juvenile tertials, which are uniform brown. The rectrices are usually still juvenile, worn and very pale during first spring. The wing is still mainly juvenile as well until the second pre-basic moult, with mostly brownish-black coverts, which contrast sharply with the scapulars in flight. Iris yellow-brown from the beginning of the first winter, turning bright yellow in spring.

First-winter ♀

Formative plumage (Oct–Mar/Apr). Pre-formative moult can be relatively slow in ♀ too, and averages less extensive than in ♂ of same age. Until Feb, under good viewing conditions, it is usually quite easy to distinguish the presence of juvenile feathers, paler, duller and not vermiculated, among the replaced adult-type feathers of the flanks, breast and upperparts. The belly usually is of juvenile appearance, typically finely streaked pale brown. The upperwing-coverts appear worn and uniform brown, without speckles (until the second pre-basic moult). The iris remains dull yellowish-brown throughout the first winter, whereas it is already much yellower in ♂ of same age.

GEOGRAPHIC VARIATION Subspecies *nearctica* is marginally smaller than *marila*, but Pacific birds seem to be smallest[56,928]. The head profile is a little different with, in *nearctica*, a prominent and slightly 'bumped' forehead, often vertical where it meets the bill. The crown often peaks a little in front of the eye and the centre of the crown is often flat or even forms a slight hollow, while another angle is formed between the crown and nape. The frontal bump is also visible if the bird is sleeping. In relaxed posture, the head profile of *marila* forms a smooth and more neatly rounded curve between the bill base and the hindneck. In adult ♂ basic plumage, *nearctica* is distinguished more easily by its coarser vermiculated upperparts. Thus, the difference in this feature between Greater and Lesser Scaup is evident in Europe, the latter showing obvious contrast between the under- and upperparts even from afar. In North America, the difference is barely useful for distinguishing them, as the width of the black vermiculations on the scapulars is generally <1 mm in *marila* and >1 mm in *nearctica*[1014]. In *nearctica*, the upperparts gradually darken from the front to back, whereas in *marila* the scapulars appear whiter, the posterior scapulars contrasting sharply with the dark tertials. Finally, the white in the primaries averages more extensive in *marila*, resulting in a wingbar slightly whiter and longer towards the wingtip. In *nearctica*, its extent is more variable but slightly more restricted, making *nearctica* again somewhat intermediate between *marila* and Lesser Scaup.

MEASUREMENTS and MASS ♂ slightly larger (all measurements) and heavier than ♀. The data available for North America suggest that birds in the east are larger, and birds on Pacific coasts smaller.

A. m. marila. ♂: wing chord 219–237 (227, *n*=45), tail 52–61 (56.3, *n*=45), bill 41–47 (44.0, *n*=46), tarsus 38–42 (39.9, *n*=56), middle toe 61–72 (65.9, *n*=58), mass 972–1,372 (1,219, *n*=17); ♀: wing chord 211–225 (217, *n*=35), tail 51–60 (55.7, *n*=34), bill 40–45 (42.9, *n*=36), tarsus 37–41 (38.6, *n*=45), middle toe 61–68 (64.3, *n*=40), mass 1,037–1,312 (1183, *n*=12)[267].

A. m. nearctica. S Ontario. ♂ (*n*=81): wing chord 217.8 (±5.7), culmen 45.3 (±1.7), tarsus 38.3 (±1.6); ♀ (*n*=61): wing chord 211.8 (±3.9), culmen 44.8 (±1.4), tarsus 37.4 (±1)[1369]. Long Island Sound. ♂ (*n*=283) wing chord 228.0 (±5.0), culmen 44.6 (±1.5), tarsus 40.1 (±2.1); ♀ (*n*=103): wing chord 220.0 (±6.0), culmen 43.5 (±1.8), tarsus 39.0 (±2.2)[684]. Alaska (May–Jun). ♂: mass 844–

1,046 (932, *n*=17); ♀: mass: 856–1117 (988, n=10)[620]. New York (Jan–Mar). ♂: mass 850–1,350 (1,054, *n*=44); ♀: mass 740–1260 (976, *n*=23)[1113]. Long Island Sound (Oct–Jan). ♂: mass 657–1,316 (1054, n=345); ♀: mass 688–1,210 (959, *n*=104)[684].

VOICE Generally silent away from breeding grounds, although vocalisations associated with courtship may be given on wintering grounds or during spring migration. ♂, rarely heard, emits a series of low, fluted sounds, including a cooing *koo-whooo*. ♀ gives a repeated *arrr* similar to other ♀ *Aythya*, either in alarm or when taking off.

MOULT Complex alternate moult strategy. Preformative moult occurs between Sep and Mar, and includes a variable number of head and body feathers, with few or no feathers replaced on the belly, rear body and rump, possibly one to all tertials, occasionally two to all rectrices, and some inner upperwing-coverts. Definitive pre-alternate moult occurs in Apr–May in ♀♀ and Jun–Aug in ♂♂ (at moulting sites). Definitive pre-basic moult occurs in both sexes between Jul and Nov.

HYBRIDISATION In Eurasia, natural hybridisation involving this species is relatively common with Tufted Duck, much rarer with Common Pochard *A. ferina* and exceptional with Ferruginous Duck *A. nyroca*[582]. Cases have been reported in Europe and North America with Lesser Scaup[817], but their frequency is completely unknown. In North America, Greater Scaup seems to hybridise more rarely, hybrids having been reported occasionally in the wild with Redhead *A. americana* (see below), Ring-necked Duck (see that species) and exceptionally Canvasback *A. valisineria*[465,584,684,817,1195]. Finally, natural hybridisation has been reported exceptionally on both continents with Goldeneye *Bucephala clangula*[817]. In captivity, very occasional cases reported with Yellow-billed Duck *Anas undulata*[660], Southern Pochard *Netta peposaca* and Ruddy Duck *Oxyura jamaicensis*[817].

Greater Scaup × Tufted Duck. This hybrid is among the commonest in W Europe after Tufted Duck × Common Pochard and Ferruginous Duck × Common Pochard, and ♀♀, in particular, pose a considerable identification challenge. The ♂ from this cross is quite variable; Gillham & Gillham[439] assigned the 24 ♂♂ they analysed to four different types, one suspected of being a backcross with Greater Scaup and two others that might have actually involved Lesser Scaup in their parentage.

It is also worth mentioning that this hybrid's appearance can vary depending on the subspecies of Greater Scaup involved. Size intermediate between those of the parents (often closer to Tufted Duck), usually with a distinct triangular crest that peaks on the top of the head. The head's sheen is usually green, sometimes purple or both colours[439]. The bill is closer to Greater Scaup in shape, pale blue-grey with a black tip often reduced to the nail and its immediate surroundings. The flanks are white with occasional grey vermiculations, which are difficult to see in the field. The upperparts are darker than in Greater Scaup, with vermiculations broader and tighter. Iris yellow and white wingbar like those of the parents. ♀ variable and can resemble ♀ Greater Scaup, Lesser Scaup or Tufted Duck, with colour, shape and size similar to those of one or other of these three species. The crest can be sharp and pointed above the nape (as Tufted Duck), rounded and bumped (as Lesser Scaup) or absent (as Greater Scaup). The bill varies in size and shape between those of the parents, but usually approaches Greater Scaup. The black tip overflows the nail, but it is not always easy to see, the tip often being dark grey and diffuse. The white face patch is often more extensive than in ♀ Tufted Duck. The upperparts are rather dusky, reminiscent of ♀ Tufted Duck but can also match first-winter ♀ Greater Scaup. A few birds have partially white undertail-coverts[1031].

Greater Scaup × Common Pochard. This hybrid (♂) occasionally shows up in Europe and Asia, and was even described as a species, *Fuligula marloides*[582,817]. This cross produces quite variable hybrids that recall both Greater Scaup and Redhead. Note that a captive ♂ hybrid detailed by Gillham & Gillham[439] changed the colour of the head and neck during its second year, from blackish to deep reddish. These hybrids have a head profile closer to Common Pochard, with a sloping forehead and long bill. The latter is pale blue-grey with a broad black tip (sometimes as Tufted Duck, sometimes reaching further along the tomium) and black basally. The head is usually dark reddish-brown, which may appear blackish at a distance, but with a purple sheen (or sometimes green on cheeks[439]) or almost as red as a Redhead. The iris is orange-red to yellow-orange, often paler in the centre than at the periphery. The flanks and upperparts are white with variably dense vermiculations. Tertials often grey vermiculated dark. Alternate plumage (eclipse) is like that of Greater Scaup with a dark brown head and white mask[439]. Distinguished by iris colour and the extent of black at the base and tip of the bill.

Greater Scaup × Lesser Scaup. Very little accurate information in the literature. Delacour[295] described a captive hybrid pair as having characteristics intermediate between the parents.

Greater Scaup × Redhead. Few descriptions in the literature[817], but some ♂♂ have been reported in North America and in captivity. These had a shape rather closer to Greater Scaup (*marila*) with a large round head, blue-grey bill with a slightly concave culmen and a vertically demarcated black tip in profile, intermediate between the two parents, a bright golden-yellow iris, black head with green sheen on cheeks and purple on nape and crown, pale grey flanks visibly vermiculated dark grey, upperparts also vermiculated but darker than flanks and tertials brown barely speckled pale. From a distance, seems much closer to Greater Scaup than Redhead.

HABITAT and LIFE-CYCLE Spring migration occurs Feb–May. Breeds on ponds, slow-flowing streams and small freshwater lakes in the Arctic tundra, northern taiga, in upland moorlands and along coasts. Usually prefers shallow water (<2 m deep[684,1022]) with grassy shores, devoid of trees. In lone pairs or loose colonies, sometimes near colonies of gulls[684]. Eggs laid mainly from late May to mid-Jun (until mid-Aug) in Arctic, but earlier further south along Baltic Sea. From the beginning of incubation, ♂ abandons ♀ to gather (up to 4,000 together in Iceland[1154]) on their moulting grounds, usually huge lakes in the immediate vicinity of the nesting sites or relatively nearby[684,794]. ♀♀ usually moult on their nesting sites, although large groups have also been reported far from breeding areas[1154]. Autumn migration starts once able to fly again, from mid-Aug. Adult ♂♂ winter significantly further north than ♀♀ and imm[794]. Very gregarious in winter, forming compact flocks of up to several thousand birds, on coastal, salt or brackish, usually shallow and sheltered, waters. Prefers coastal areas near outlets of nutrient-rich fresh water. Winters in smaller numbers on some large inland freshwater lakes (where more frequent on migration).

RANGE and POPULATION Breeds in the Holarctic tundra and winters almost exclusively south of its breeding range, mainly on coasts. Global population estimated at 1,200,000-1,400,000 individuals[305], but probably closer to one million birds at the start of the present decade.

A. m. marila. Breeds from Iceland to around the Lena River in E Siberia, where replaced by the subspecies *nearctica*. Besides the mapped range, winters locally in the Adriatic Sea and N Mediterranean. Uncommon to casual visitor throughout interior of Europe, N Africa, Arabia and India. Populations estimated in 1990s at 100,000–200,000 individuals for the Caspian Sea, Black Sea and Mediterranean[1154] and more than 120,000 in W Europe[139] in the early 2000s (310,000 in early 1990s[735]). Casual visitor to the Aleutians where this subspecies has even been reported breeding[63].

A. m. nearctica. Two apparently separate populations. The Asian population nests east of the Lena River. Apart from the mapped range, winters locally south to Taiwan and Hong Kong[182,222,757]. In winter this population has been estimated at 200,000–300,000 individuals. The North American population is largely concentrated in Alaska and W Canada, locally further east (including Great Slave Lake, Northwest Territories) and uncommon to sporadic in Newfoundland and the Gulf of St. Lawrence[684] (except Ungava Peninsula, N Quebec); 60–70% of North American birds winter on the Atlantic coast, with the largest concentrations off Long Island, New York. The Pacific coast hosts *c.*20%, with major concentrations between British Columbia, Canada, and Washington State, USA on the one hand, and in San Francisco Bay, California, on the other[684]. Small numbers winter in the Gulf of Mexico between W Florida and S Texas, and on the Great Lakes. Estimated population 560,000[305].

Declines reported in Europe and North America, for unknown reasons, although speculated to be due to oil spills, including in the Caspian Sea, organo-chlorine contaminants, destruction linked to gill-nets for fishing[1022] and excessive hunting pressure, at least in North America[1147].

CAPTIVITY Fairly little sought-after and rather expensive, although relatively easy to keep. Rarely kept outside a few specialised collections.

REFERENCES Baker (1993)[56]; Banks (1986)[63]; Billard & Humphrey (1992)[96]; BirdLife International (2004)[139]; BirdLife International (2013)[144]; Bishop (1895)[148]; Bradshaw (2005)[177]; Brazil (2009)[182]; Cao *et al.* (2010)[222]; Clements *et al.* (2013)[236]; Cramp & Simmons (1977)[268]; Delacour (1954–64)[295]; Delany & Scott (2006)[305]; Fish (1999)[381]; Garner (2002)[422]; Gillham & Gillham (1996)[439]; Gillham & Gillham (1999)[441]; Gillham & Gillham (2000)[442]; Gray (1958)[465]; Hopkinson (1926)[582]; Hopkinson (1933)[584]; Irving (1960)[620]; Johnstone (1955)[660]; Kaufman (2011)[670]; Kessel *et al.* (2002)[684]; Laursen (1992)[735]; Leukering (2011)[748]; Li *et al.* (2009)[757]; Livezey (1996)[773]; Madge & Burn (1988)[794]; McCarthy (2006)[817]; Nelson (1996)[907]; Ogilvie & Young (1998)[928]; Pyle (2008)[1014]; Pyle & Pyle (2009)[1016]; Quinn in Kear (2005)[1022]; Randler (2000)[1031]; Ryan (1972)[1113]; Sangster *et al.* (2005)[1135]; Schmidt (2006)[1147]; Scott & Rose (1996)[1154]; Sibley (2000)[1195]; Smallshire (1986)[1208]; Trauger (1974)[1281]; Wilson & Ankney (1988)[1369]; Zimpfer *et al.* (2011)[1391].

433. *A. m. marila*, adult ♂ (definitive basic). Switzerland, Dec (Christopher J. G. Plummer).

434. *A. m. marila*, adult ♂ (definitive basic). Iceland, May (Yann Kolbeinsson).

435. *A. m. marila*, adult ♂ (definitive alternate/definitive basic); note mix of alternate and basic feathers, and adult bare-parts coloration. France, Nov (Sébastien Reeber).

436. *A. m. marila*, adult ♂ (definitive alternate/definitive basic); pale grey (freckled white) secondary upperwing-coverts, not contrasting with scapulars, are typical of adult ♂. Poland, Oct (Zbigniew Kayzer).

437. *A. m. marila*, ♀ (first alternate/definitive alternate); when relaxed, note typically rounded head of this subspecies. Denmark, May (Nis Lundmark Jensen).

438. *A. m. marila*, ♀ (first alternate/definitive alternate). Iceland, May (Yann Kolbeinsson).

439. *A. m. nearctica*, first-winter ♀ (first basic/formative), in mostly juvenile plumage (including tertials and at least some rectrices). Japan, Feb (Aurélien Audevard).

440. *A. m. nearctica*, first-winter ♀ (first basic/formative); many head, some scapulars and flank feathers are formative, but juvenile feathers obvious on breast, rear body and tertials. Japan, Mar (Ayuwat Jearwattanakanok).

441. *A. m. nearctica*, adult ♂ (definitive basic); note head shape in this subspecies, with typical forehead 'bump'. California, USA, Nov (Sébastien Reeber).

442. *A. m. nearctica*, adult ♀ (definitive basic); this bird has completed its pre-basic moult; note same head shape as adult ♂ (previous image). California, USA, Nov (Sébastien Reeber).

443. *A. m. nearctica*, first-winter ♂ (first basic/formative); head, upperparts and rear flanks have been partly moulted, but many juvenile feathers have been retained here, while iris is adult colour but the bill's pattern is still blurred. Japan, Mar (Ayuwat Jearwattanakanok).

444. *A. m. nearctica*, first-winter ♂ (first basic/formative); a few formative (adult-type) feathers have appeared (e.g. on head and scapulars), but plumage still largely juvenile, and note ill-defined bill pattern and rather dark iris. California, USA, Nov (Sébastien Reeber).

LESSER SCAUP
Aythya affinis

TAXONOMY *Fuligula affinis* Eyton, 1838, *Monogr. Anatidae*, p. 157. Monotypic. Very closely related to Greater Scaup *A. marila*.

IDENTIFICATION Lesser Scaup is the most common scaup in North America, but in Eurasia it is only an occasional visitor. The closest species is Greater Scaup, which is reasonably common on both continents and in North America this species poses the principal identification challenge (see that species). Other pitfalls involve hybrids, some of them very similar to Lesser Scaup. In North America, some hybrids, especially Lesser Scaup × Tufted Duck *A. fuligula* and Lesser Scaup × Ring-necked Duck *A. collaris*, which are rare but regular in the wild, can closely resemble this species. Both show significantly darker upperparts, which contrast obviously with the flanks (see Hybridisation). In Eurasia, hybrids reminiscent of Lesser Scaup are much more frequent than the species itself. Hybrid Lesser Scaup × Tufted Duck is reported occasionally and can be confusing, while two other hybrids also represent pitfalls, either for ♂♂ or ♀♀: Common Pochard *A. ferina* × Tufted Duck (see Tufted Duck) and Greater Scaup × Tufted Duck (see Greater Scaup). It is necessary to identify Lesser Scaup using several features, and especially to ensure that head shape, bill shape and colour, width of the dark vermiculations on the upperparts and wingbar are all consistent with the norm.

PLUMAGES Strong sexual dimorphism from first winter onwards. Complex alternate moult strategy (two plumages per definitive cycle, three in first cycle). Ageing relatively easy until the first winter, and possible until the end of the subsequent summer, especially for ♂♂.

Adult ♂

Definitive basic plumage (Nov/Jun). Small to medium-sized diving duck, with an elegant shape, and small head with a rather short bill. Head, neck, upper mantle and breast black, with sheen on the cheeks generally purple, sometimes green, depending on the light. Iris bright yellow. Bill pale grey with a variable bluish hue and black limited to the nail (rarely overflowing, vs. Greater Scaup). Seen front-on, the nail is shaped like a bean; in profile, it is often barely visible. Belly and flanks all white. Lower abdomen and rear body black. Some dark grey vermiculations are usually visible on the upper and rear flanks. Back white vermiculated black, lower mantle and scapulars white coarsely vermiculated dark grey. Tertials blackish vermiculated or speckled white at tips and along shafts. Upperwing lesser and median coverts blackish largely vermiculated white (slightly darker than the scapulars in flight), greater coverts, primary coverts and alula blackish. Wingbar formed by white secondaries and primaries with bases pale grey-brown, typically two-toned with a clear demarcation between the two colours. Broad and clear-cut blackish trailing edge. Some adult ♂♂ can show a limited amount of white on the inner primaries[1369]. Underwing slightly more greyish than Greater Scaup with median covert tips and axillaries forming a diffuse white bar. Legs and feet grey.

Definitive alternate plumage (Jun–Jul/Oct–Nov). This plumage shows a few more blackish or brownish feathers (not vermiculated) than the alternate plumage of Greater Scaup. Head, neck, breast and back dull blackish streaked brownish. A diffuse whitish crescent is visible at the bill base. Flanks and upperparts often show a mix of basic-type (white vermiculated blackish) and alternate-type feathers (plainer, brown or blackish). Wing as definitive basic plumage, but bill darker and duller blue-grey, with less contrasting nail.

Adult ♀

Definitive basic plumage (Nov/Apr). Head dark brown to blackish, often the darkest part of the body. White face patch (stained brown when plumage fresh) at the bill base, broader in front of the eye than on the forehead, encompassing the gape as a thin line. Iris yellow or amber, probably partly age-related[1281], changing from dull brown to bright yellow primarily in the second calendar year. However, some ♀♀ have a yellow iris during their first winter and others retain an amber-coloured iris for life. Bill pale blue-grey with black nail usually distinct. Breast reddish-brown and rather bright, contrasting with the head. Mantle and scapulars whitish with dark vermiculations and brownish patches. Flanks similar but paler with diffuse brown crescents. Tertials uniform dark brown. Rump and uppertail-coverts blackish streaked pale. Belly whitish. Upperwing like adult ♂ but lesser and median coverts dark brown with pale grey speckling distinctly concentrated at the tips. Legs and feet grey.

Definitive alternate plumage (May–Jun/Oct–Nov). A variable number of head and body feathers are replaced, giving an overall browner, darker and more evenly coloured plumage. Head dark brown, blackish around eye, with facial patch stained or speckled brown and a pale crescent on the ear-coverts. Breast dark reddish-brown, almost similar to the rest of the body. Scapulars and flank feathers replaced (usually most), centred blackish with broad pale brown to beige fringes, and upperparts darker. Bare parts as basic plumage, but bill often darker lead-grey.

Juvenile

First basic plumage (until Sep–Oct). Plumage duller brown, plainer and paler than adult ♀ with dark brown head and pale facial patch reduced to a vague crescent at the base of the bill. Iris dull dark brown (♀) or yellowish-brown (♂). Bill dark grey irregularly marked with diffuse dark patches and nail barely discernible. Rest of body close to adult ♀ in alternate plumage, drab olive and plainer overall, without the pale greyish patches of adult ♀ in basic plumage. The pale belly is marked with brown spots forming faint but neat streaking. The belly patch is ill-defined. Upperwing like adult ♀ but lesser and median coverts blackish with some pale speckling well distributed over (♂) or dark brown without speckling (♀). Trailing edge less black, less contrasting and less clear-cut than in adult. Legs dull grey.

First-winter ♂

Formative plumage (Oct–Mar/Jun.). Formative plumage is acquired over a long period and progress varies individually. During most of autumn and winter, young ♂ shows a mix of juvenile and formative (adult-type) feathers. Adult ♂ is already in full basic plumage between mid-Nov and mid-Dec. Following pre-formative moult and during the subsequent spring, some retain a fairly large number of juvenile feathers, but the majority are almost adult-like. Ageing necessitates searching for juvenile feathers (brown, worn and plain) on the belly, under- and uppertail coverts, tertial coverts (narrower, slightly pointed and frayed) and tertials. From afar, the best feature is often the lesser and median coverts being still juvenile, appearing all dark (at most with faint pale speckling), contrasting strongly with the pale grey scapulars (until second pre-basic moult). The iris is yellow from the first winter, but usually not bright yellow until spring.

First-winter ♀

Formative plumage (Oct–Mar/Apr). Very similar to adult ♀ at the same time, but usually retains a variable number of juvenile feathers, which are duller and plainer, until midwinter, thus plumage appears 'messy'. The pale belly is still juvenile, faintly streaked pale brownish and ill-defined. The iris is usually dull brown throughout the first winter, yellowish-amber during the first summer, and yellow from the subsequent autumn. In the hand, aged by the upperwing pattern (lesser and median coverts not speckled vs. speckled at tips in adult) until the second pre-basic moult.

GEOGRAPHIC VARIATION None.

MEASUREMENTS and MASS ♂ slightly larger than ♀ and adult a little larger than first-winter. ♂ (*n*=40): wing chord 193–226 (204.8), tail 47–59 (52.3), culmen 47–54 (50), tarsus 30.3–37.5 (35.1); ♀ (n=47): wing chord 184–205 (195), tail 48–56 (52.0), bill 46–54 (49.7), tarsus 32.0–36.8 (34.3)[41]. ♂: mass 546–1,156 (*n*=1,718), with seasonal variation, 959.0 in Oct (*n*=38), 721.3 in May–Jul (*n*=40) and 721.4 in Jan (*n*=28); ♀: mass 517–1,037 (*n*=1,252), with seasonal variation, 868.1 in Oct (*n*=36), 647.5 in Mar (*n*=22)[41]. Adult ♂: wing chord 208 (*n*=381), tail 52.3 (*n*=131), culmen 41.4 (*n*=290), tarsus 35.2 (*n*=322); first-winter ♂: wing chord 206 (*n*=115), culmen 41.5 (*n*=94), tarsus 35.7 (*n*=99); adult ♀: wing chord 203 (*n*=184), tail 52 (*n*=70), culmen 40.3 (*n*=140), tarsus 34.9 (*n*=135); first-winter ♀: wing chord 199 (*n*=105), culmen 40.6 (*n*=92), tarsus 34.8 (*n*=98)[27].

VOICE ♂ generally quiet and heard almost only during courtship, when soft whistles are given. ♀ utters an *arrr* or *errr*, both rather sharp and similar to other ♀ *Aythya*, mainly when alarmed, disturbed or taking off.

MOULT Complex alternate moult strategy. Extent and timing of different moults seemingly identical to those of Greater Scaup[1014].

HYBRIDISATION Hybrids regularly reported in the wild with Tufted and Ring-necked Ducks in North America, but also (rarely) in Europe with the first-named. Apparently rarer, hybrids with Redhead *A. americana* have also been reported (see below). A case of hybridisation with Common Pochard *A. ferina* produced a ♂ and a ♀, described as having characteristics of both parents[1120]. Hybrids with Greater Scaup are poorly described and their frequency unknown (see Identification of that species). Single cases reported in captivity with Wood Duck *Aix sponsa*[1190] and American Wigeon *Anas americana*[619].

Lesser Scaup × Tufted Duck. ♂♂ of this hybrid regularly observed in the wild. The head has a short, broad and rounded crest, drooping on the upper neck. The head's sheen is often purple but can be green[439], or green on the cheeks and purple on the upper head. The flanks are white with quite obvious thin pale grey vermiculations. The iris is bright yellow. The bill is paler blue-grey towards the tip and the black tip is reduced, intermediate between the two parents. The scapulars show white and black vermiculations of near-equal width, the upperparts becoming darker posteriorly. Looks rather dark from afar and contrasts with the largely white flanks. The wingbar seems intermediate between the two species, with white extending over the inner primaries. ♀♀ from this cross are poorly described, and need to be distinguished from hybrid ♀ Tufted Duck × Greater Scaup, which is not easy (see Greater Scaup). Focus on the shape of the crest, the tip of the bill, coloration of the undertail and the wingbar.

Lesser Scaup × Ring-necked Duck. Rather variable, most hybrids show features of both parents and are rather like the previous hybrid, from which best distinguished by the shape of the crest. Two ♂♂ described by McIlhenny[828] had a head shape and iris close to those of Lesser Scaup, but bill, tail and breast like Ring-necked Duck. Another bird described in Gillham & Gillham[439] had a head like that of Ring-necked Duck, including a reddish collar, and bill, upperparts and flanks closer to Lesser Scaup. It seems that these hybrids are fairly regular in North America and show a tall head that peaks at the rear and a straight nape, recalling Ring-necked Duck. The bill is often bluish-grey without white on the tomium and a variable pale subterminal bar, the black tip being intermediate in extent. The sheen of the head has been reported as bluish or purple, but can be green as well. The upperparts are pale grey with well-marked blackish vermiculations, the whole appearing mid- to dark grey. The flanks are white with pale grey vermiculations. The ♀ has the same head profile, a brown iris (needs confirmation in adult), a whitish facial patch restricted to the base of the bill and partially sullied brown, a lead-grey bill with a clear pale subterminal bar and a black tip like ♂ (pale grey tomium on upper mandible typically reaches the black tip). The breast is reddish, much paler than the head and barely darker than the flanks, without clear demarcation. Mostly grey flanks with diffuse brownish patches. Upperparts intermediate. The wingbar is also intermediate between

the parents, but is much whiter on the secondaries than the primaries. Also note that separating this hybrid from a Greater Scaup × Ring-necked Duck is undoubtedly difficult, and some descriptions in the literature[25,285,439] could relate to either.

Lesser Scaup × Redhead. Old reports of hybridisation in captivity exist, but its occurrence in the wild remains hypothetical according to McCarthy[817]. Photographs published on the internet, however, show ♂♂ that probably stem from this cross. The head profile is rather close to that of Lesser Scaup with a tall crown, a notch on the nape and a steep forehead. Head blackish with a reddish hue on the crown-sides. Bill pale blue-grey with diffuse whitish subterminal band and black tip intermediate between those of the two presumed parents. Iris yellow-orange close to Redhead. Upperparts finely vermiculated and appear grey, flanks paler but also vermiculated, rear body and breast black, tertials appearing plain grey. The wingbar is white on the secondaries and grey on primaries. This type of bird is very close to hybrid Ring-necked Duck × Redhead (see the first-named); however, the latter seems to show stronger contrast between the flanks and upperparts, which are demarcated like in Ring-necked Duck, and a bill with a broad black tip and sharp white subterminal band.

HABITAT and LIFE-CYCLE One of the latest spring migrants among North American wildfowl, and many pairs only form between Apr and early May, at stopover sites. Most pairs arrive on breeding grounds in May[40]. Breeds in marshes, ponds, shallow lakes and fresh or slightly brackish lagoons, permanent or temporary, with abundant submerged or floating aquatic vegetation, and fringing vegetation (*Scirpus*, *Typha*)[40,42]. Eggs are laid between late May and late Jul. The ♂ abandons the ♀ during early incubation, to gather and moult on larger waterbodies, especially in the boreal taiga. Especially large gatherings recorded at lowland lakes in Saskatchewan, Canada, with up to 300,000 on Lake MacCallum[40]. Non-breeders and ♀♀ that failed join ♂♂, whereas successful ♀♀ usually moult at their breeding sites or in immediate vicinity[40]. Also a late migrant in autumn, when many depart their moulting grounds only with onset of winter weather[563]. In winter, forms flocks on large lakes and reservoirs, fresh and brackish coastal lagoons and estuaries, and locally along coasts, but much more numerous than Greater Scaup inland and on fresh water.

RANGE and POPULATION Strictly Nearctic, most of the population breeding in the boreal taiga. The winter range hardly overlaps the breeding distribution, with the main wintering areas in Florida, Louisiana and along both coasts of Mexico[40]. Uncommon or rare to Honduras and N Caribbean. Rare or occasional in South America, Europe and E Asia. Lesser and Greater Scaups are generally not distinguished by many censuses, but the proportion of Lesser Scaups in the following totals was estimated at 89%[40,87]. Over the period 1955–2012, the population averaged c.5,048,000 breeding birds[1294]. The most recent surveys show a slight decrease, with 5,240,000 in 2012 and 4,166,000 in 2013, compared to the fluctuating population of 6,000,000–8,000,000 in 1970–85[1294], although just 2,950,000 were counted in 2005, suggesting a recent increase[1290]. The decrease in both breeding and wintering populations is perhaps mainly noticeable in the southernmost parts of both respective ranges[42,209].

CAPTIVITY Uncommon in captivity and generally rather expensive (slightly more so than Greater Scaup) in Europe and North America, and considered rather unattractive presumably due to its drab coloration. Most birds reported in Europe and E Asia are considered to be genuine vagrants.

REFERENCES Anderson & Timken (1969)[25]; Anderson *et al.* (1969)[27]; Austin *et al.* (1998)[40]; Austin *et al.* (1998)[41]; Austin *et al. in* Kear (2005)[42]; Bailey (1983)[48]; Bellrose (1980)[87]; Butcher & Niven (2007)[209]; De Rouck *et al.* (1982)[285]; Gillham & Gillham (1996)[439]; Hochbaum (1955)[563]; IZY (1959)[619]; Kaufman (2011)[670]; Leukering (2011)[748]; McCarthy (2006)[817]; McIlhenny (1937)[828]; Nelson (1996)[907]; Nudds & Cole (1991)[921]; Pyle (2008)[1014]; Sage (1963)[1120]; Sibley (1938)[1190]; Trauger (1974)[1281]; USFWS (2005)[1290]; USFWS (2013)[1294]; Wilson & Ankney (1988)[1369].

445. First-winter ♂ (formative), with numerous brown juvenile feathers scattered over head and breast, more obvious on upper and rear flanks, and lower scapulars. Texas, USA, Feb (Joe Fischer).

446. Adult ♂ (definitive basic); note lesser and median coverts heavily flecked white, offering no contrast with scapulars, typical of adult ♂. California, USA, Nov (Sébastien Reeber).

447. Adult ♀ (definitive basic); compared to Greater Scaup *A. marila*, note same differences in head and bill shape as ♂♂. California, USA, Nov (Sébastien Reeber).

448. First-winter ♂ (formative); note plain dark secondary upperwing-coverts, as well as uniform dark brown rump, back and mantle, while the wingbar is white on secondaries, and pale grey-brown on primaries (useful for species identification). Texas, USA, Mar (Greg Lavaty).

449. Adult ♂ (definitive basic). California, USA, Nov (Sébastien Reeber).

450. Adult ♀ (definitive basic); compared to Greater Scaup *A. marila*, note clear contrast in wingbar between secondaries and primaries. Texas, USA, Nov (Greg Lavaty).

STELLER'S EIDER
Polysticta stelleri

Plates 55, 56

TAXONOMY *Anas Stelleri* Pallas, 1769, *Spicilegia Zool.*, fasc. 6, p. 35, pl. 5. Monotypic. Steller's Eider is the sole member of the genus *Polysticta*, which along with the genus *Somateria* forms a monophyletic group sister to all other sea ducks (tribe Mergini)[771].

IDENTIFICATION Does not usually pose any identification problems, given distinctive plumage of ♂♂ and relative lack of other species within its Arctic range and coastal habitats. Has a peculiar bill shape, with small extensions along the edges of the upper mandible towards the tip and orientated obliquely downwards.

PLUMAGES Strong sexual dimorphism from first winter onwards. Complex alternate moult strategy (two plumages by definitive cycle, three in first cycle). Ageing ♂♂ is relatively easy until the first summer and possible until the second summer. Ageing ♀♀ is fairly easy until the first summer.

Adult ♂

Definitive basic plumage (Oct–Dec/May–Jul). Contrasting plumage with buff to pale ochre tones, appearing bright white in the sun. Head mainly pale grey (crown and cheeks), and white with black chin and throat linked to a black collar glossed purple, broader on the hindneck, and black mantle. A round black patch surrounds the eye, another dark and diffuse grey-green patch is visible on the lores and a short, ruffled puff of green black-tipped feathers adorns the neck. Iris dark brown, sometimes warmer brown[267]. Bill grey-blue with nail slightly paler. Upper breast (at border with black collar) and upper flanks white, merging into yellow-ochre of rest of breast and orange-buff flanks, becoming darker towards the belly, which is dark ochre-brown, merging into black lower abdomen. A broad white band separates the coloured breast and sides, and ends with two black spots (sometimes concealed) on the breast-sides, just above the waterline on resting birds. Back, rump and uppertail-coverts black. Tail dark grey, sometimes with white markings at the tips of the outer webs of the outer rectrices. Sides of mantle and inner scapulars white. Median scapulars long and drooping. Tertials curved, with inner webs blackish glossed purple-blue and outer webs form long white lines, which broaden into thin triangles that cover the tips. Upperwing black

and white with secondary- and tertial coverts white. Secondaries blackish with broad white tips (up to 15 mm on central feathers, 6–8 mm on outermost) and a clear purple-blue sheen, paler outwards. Remiges and lesser coverts dark grey-brown with outer webs and tips blackish. Secondary underwing-coverts and axillaries whitish, greater coverts and primary coverts pale grey, remiges grey except trailing edge of secondaries. Legs and feet grey with blackish webs.

Definitive alternate plumage (Jun–Jul/Sep–Nov). Closer to basic plumage of ♀ in overall grey-brown coloration, but usually easily separated using head and upperwing pattern. Head dark grey-brown with a variable number of small pale grey streaks and dots, black on chin and nape. A pale eye-ring is often visible. Iris, bill and legs as basic plumage. A 'ghost' of the black collar is usually visible. Scapulars, mantle, back, rump and uppertail-coverts blackish-brown with pale grey-brown fringes. The scapulars, significantly shorter and more round-tipped than in basic plumage, often reveal the white part of the folded wing. Some scapulars show a slight purple-blue sheen. Basic tertials often retained. Breast grey-brown with irregular ochre, cinnamon and blackish streaks. Rest of underparts brown irregularly streaked black, becoming blackish towards the belly (feathers often still mainly basic).

Adult ♀

Definitive basic plumage (Oct–Dec/Feb–Mar). Appears uniformly dark brown from afar, the only distinguishing features being the two white wingbars framing the speculum and the whitish underwing. Head reddish-brown finely streaked or mottled blackish. Broad pale grey-brown to whitish eye-ring, often visible at some distance. Iris dark brown. Bill pale and dull blue-grey. A large black collar similar to ♂ is visible when the bird stretches its neck. Breast ochre to hazelnut-brown heavily mottled or streaked blackish. Flanks more uniform brown, with less pronounced streaks. Belly and under- and uppertail-coverts very dark reddish-brown to blackish. The number of dark streaks on the lower breast and upper belly varies individually and perhaps with age[404]. Tail dark grey-brown. Upperparts blackish fringed hazelnut to reddish-brown, giving a faint scaly appearance to scapulars, but back more distinctly streaked. The fringes to the scapulars tend to fade with wear[404], and the posterior scapulars, elongated and pointed, often show a slight bluish or purple sheen. Tertials elongated and curved, like those of ♂, with a more or less well-defined central whitish or pale grey stripe that broadens towards tip. Inner webs have strong bluish sheen. Upperwing entirely dark brown with subtle hazelnut-brown fringes, slightly paler on lesser and median coverts. Tips of primaries blackish. Two large white bars formed by tips to the greater coverts (12–20 mm on central feathers, often with small dark spots at the tip) and secondaries (8–12 mm). These two bars border the blackish speculum with blue gloss fading outwards, often without any gloss on the three outermost secondaries. Underwing largely white with leading edge mottled brown and grey remiges (outer primaries silvery-grey). Trailing edge to secondaries white, blackish on primaries. Legs and feet grey with black webs.

Definitive alternate plumage (Feb–Mar/Oct–Dec). Similar to basic plumage, except that ground colour of the head is pale cinnamon-grey, streaked dark. The pale eye-ring is faded, but a paler loral patch is usually visible. The breast appears more spotted or streaked too. Feathers of upperwing still basic, the fringes to the lesser and median coverts becoming greyer and more visible with wear.

Juvenile

First basic plumage (until Sep–Jan). Very like basic plumage of adult ♀ with head and breast brown faintly mottled blackish (rather than regularly streaked), and pale patches on the lores and around eye. Throat paler and not mottled. Scapulars shorter and rounded, centred duller dark grey than adult. The tail is shorter and more rounded, less wedge-shaped. However, the two main ageing features are the juvenile tertials (short, straight and round-tipped, without white central lines of adult ♀), and upperwing pattern showing thin and inconspicuous white wingbars bordering the speculum. The tips of the greater coverts and secondaries show less white (6–7 mm wide[224], sometimes almost none on former). The bluish sheen to the speculum is less marked than in adult ♀. ♂ distinguished from ♀ at this age by presence of two white spots on breast, by its tertials (brown fringed pale buff in ♀, dull grey with traces of white or bluish in ♂) and tips to the inner secondaries (white tips to ss8–12 especially on outer webs in ♀, on both webs in ♂)[1014].

First-winter ♂

Formative plumage (Nov–Mar/May–Jul). Pre-formative moult slow and the resulting plumage is often not complete until Mar–Apr. Until midwinter, appearance is fairly close to adult ♀ and thereafter remains mainly grey-brown. Once complete, formative plumage vaguely recalls a very much duller version of the basic adult ♂. The head and breast are pale grey-brown finely freckled or mottled blackish, sometimes with a broad blackish collar. The puff of feathers on the nape develops gradually, while the chin and throat are often blackish. A variable number of white or pale ochre feathers are visible, especially at the base of the bill, on the hindneck, upper breast and flanks. Formative scapulars similar to definitive basic plumage, but shorter and duller, with less white on inner webs. Many birds perform a reduced pre-formative moult, and appear more intermediate between the above description and that of juvenile.

First-winter ♀

Formative plumage (Nov–Mar/May–Jul). Following pre-formative moult, strongly resembles adult ♀, except for juvenile feathers in tail (rectrices shorter, brown, worn and have bare rachis at tip), belly (more mottled light brown) and wing (thin white wingbars framing speculum with moderate gloss). Like ♂, many ♀♀ undertake a limited pre-formative moult, and clearly show a mix of juvenile and formative (adult-like) feathers, giving an overall 'messier' appearance.

First-summer ♂

First alternate plumage (Jun–Jul/Sep–Dec). First pre-alternate moult is on average limited and produces feathers closer to those of definitive alternate plumage, i.e. duller. Appearance remains close to that of formative plumage, but the head is often pale grey-brown, with a white area around the eye and extending rearwards, and the mantle is dark grey-brown. Distinction from adult in alternate plumage is simple, by the overall paler plumage, and the upperwing pattern still juvenile, paler brown (due to wear) with two irregular white bars framing the speculum until the second pre-basic moult around Sep.

First-summer ♀

First alternate plumage (Jun–Jul/Sep–Dec). Very like definitive alternate plumage, but retains juvenile wing and rectrices until the second pre-basic moult around Sep.

Second-winter ♂

Second basic plumage (Nov–Dec/Jul). Similar to

definitive basic plumage, but generally a little less bright. Easily distinguished from adult by upperwing pattern, especially the variable number of blackish-brown or white sullied dusky lesser and median coverts, and more or less well-marked dark patches on greater coverts. In birds with a largely white upperwing, the dark traces are generally concentrated at the 'wrist' and on inner median coverts, while the white central line on the inner web of the tertials is usually narrower and less clear-cut[1014], and the underwing-coverts less white[404].

Third-winter ♂

Third basic plumage (Oct–Dec/May–Jul). Distinguished from adult ♂ by the presence of a larger number of dark spots in the white part of the upperwing. However, further research is needed to determine if this could be within the normal variation of adult ♂♂[1014].

GEOGRAPHIC VARIATION None described. Pearce et al.[957] compared different populations (Siberian–Atlantic/Siberian–Pacific/Alaska) and found slight differences in mitochondrial DNA but none in nuclear DNA, indicating that there is probably sufficient gene flow between ♂♂ of different populations to prevent differentiation.

MEASUREMENTS and MASS Almost no differences between sexes. Adult slightly larger than young. Western populations. ♂: wing chord 220 (adult, $n=45$) and 203 (juvenile, $n=2$), bill 38.6 (adult, $n=48$), mass in winter 850 (adult, $n=10$); ♀: wing chord 217 (adult, $n=39$) and 210 (juvenile, $n=32$), bill 40.2 (adult, $n=37$), mass in winter 838 (adult, $n=13$); Eastern populations. Adult ♂: wing chord 223 ($n=50$), bill 39.9 ($n=46$), tarsus 37.9 ($n=41$), mass in Sep 690–1,010 (848, $n=100$); adult ♀: wing chord 219 ($n=35$), bill 40.2 ($n=33$), tarsus 38.8 ($n=26$), mass in Sep 700–970 (834, $n=100$)[855]. NE Yakutia. ♂ ($n=19$): wing chord 212–238 (223), bill 36–43 (39.7); ♀ ($n=14$): wing chord 208–235 (227), bill 37–48 (43.8)[945]. ♂ ($n=46$): wing chord 204–223 (adult) and 199–218 (juvenile), tail 79–94, bill length from proximal end of nostrils 22–28, bill depth at proximal end of nostrils 13.4–15.6, tarsus 37–42; ♀ ($n=38$): wing chord 199–218 (adult) and 194–214 (juvenile), tail 74–89, bill length from proximal end of nostrils 20–25, bill depth at proximal end of nostrils 13.2–15.3, tarsus 36–41[1014].

VOICE Usually quiet, but more regularly heard during courtship. ♂ gives short whistling sounds, quite low and plaintive, against background of long low grunts. Similar sounds, more quacking and 'chatty', given by ♀. The wings produce a slight hiss, easily audible at close range, particularly on take-off.

MOULT Complex alternate moult strategy. Pre-formative moult in Oct–Mar includes a variable proportion of head and body feathers, but usually no belly feathers, rectrices, tertials or wing feathers. Some perform a limited pre-formative moult, not including, for example, the rump, scapulars and some flank feathers. First pre-alternate moult involves only some of the preceding feathers, in May–Jul. The second pre-basic moult occurs from Jul–Aug to Oct–Nov, is complete, a little earlier and more protracted than in adults. Definitive pre-alternate moult involves many to most head and body feathers but few or no tertials and rectrices[1014] and occurs in Apr–Jun in ♀ and Jul–Aug in ♂[404]. Definitive pre-basic moult occurs quite late, starts with the remiges and rectrices between mid Aug and late Sep, and ends with the body feathers in Dec.

HYBRIDISATION Natural hybridisation is highly exceptional but has been reported once with Mallard *Anas platyrhynchos*[817] and several times with Common Eider *Somateria mollissima*[388,493,564].

Steller's Eider × Common Eider. An adult ♂ in definitive basic plumage from this cross was reported in Norway between Apr 1995 and spring 1999[388,443], which exhibited, among other odd characters, a size smaller than King Eider *Somateria spectabilis*, as well as large white 'goggles' surrounded by green. The head profile recalled Steller's Eider in its angular appearance, as did the fairly long tail. The head was mainly white with a green patch in front of the eye and pale green neck-sides. The bill was pale grey, and its shape similar to Steller's Eider, with rounded feathering at the bill base. The pale orange-brown breast merged gradually into the blackish underparts. Tertials dark with an inconspicuous pale rachis, and scapulars also dark, with paler grey centres. The back and rear body were black, without the large white patches on the femoral coverts visible in ♂ *Somateria*. The lesser and median coverts were pure white, and greater coverts and secondaries dark with broad white tips, forming two wingbars. Another hybrid resulting from this cross in Germany[564] was reportedly quite different, but a detailed description is lacking[443].

HABITAT and LIFE-CYCLE Migratory, moving to its

nesting grounds between mid-Apr and early Jun, most wintering sites being abandoned by mid-May. Birds continue arriving at their nesting sites until mid-Jun, the eggs being laid over the next month[404]. Inhabits low coastal tundra with many streams, backwaters and ponds of various sizes, usually a few km from the coast itself[855], sometimes up to 150 km[167,404,1216], i.e. much further than other species of eiders[1301]. Breeds alone or in small colonies of up to 60 nests[855], often in vicinity of nesting Pomarine Skuas *Stercorarius pomarinus*, which offer some protection from predators[855]. In years with low densities of lemmings, ducklings and adults are subject to increased predation (especially by Arctic Fox *Alopex lagopus*, Snowy Owls *Bubo scandiacus* and skuas[145]) and may even not attempt to nest[855,1217]. ♂♂ gather along the coast, near the breeding areas, and post-hatching the ♀ leads the ducklings to the coast too, where they form crèches[646]. At the same time, non-breeders summer in flocks on Arctic coasts between the wintering and nesting sites. Migration to moulting grounds, which can be up to 3,000 km away, occurs from mid-Jul to early Sep. They then form large gatherings, of up to 50,000 birds[733,855]. In winter, usually in small flocks, along shallow rocky coasts, favouring sheltered areas such as bays, harbours and fjords, mainly where fresh water enters the sea. Feeds by up-ending like dabbling ducks. Highly philopatric to wintering and moulting sites[282,404,661].

RANGE and POPULATION Breeds in the Arctic, where it is never numerous between the Lena River and Yamal Peninsula[1379] and very patchy further west to the Kola Peninsula[167,923,1216]. In Alaska, now breeds in fairly large numbers only around Barrow, whereas the species used to breed commonly south to the Yukon-Kuskokwim Delta, until a few decades ago[683]. Rare visitor to British Columbia, with a few reports south to California. Rare in Hokkaido, Japan, and accidental further south to NE China[182]. Uncommon in Iceland and rare or accidental in the North Sea or further south, as well as extreme NE USA, Quebec and Baffin I. The most pessimistic of recent estimates indicates a global population of 110,000–125,000 birds[145]. The European population was

estimated at just 10,000–15,000 birds[1396], or fluctuating between 7,700 and 20,800[139] in the early 2000s, or 27,000 subsequently[3], vs. 30,000–50,000 in the early 1990s[1396]. In N Pacific, population estimated at 180,000 birds[1348]. Irrespective of the conflicting data, it is clear that the overall population has undergone a severe decline over recent decades, as the world population was estimated at 400,000–500,000 birds in the 1960s and 220,000 in the late 1990s[990]. The decline is estimated at 13% per year in the Baltic (1994–2003), and 8% per year (1985–2003)[1396] or 9% per year (1992–2010)[727] in Norway. A possible shift in the wintering grounds linked to the reduction in Arctic pack ice is also mentioned. Among the causes of the decline are hunting, legal and illegal, ingestion of lead shot and the impact of gas and oil exploitation. Years with very low breeding success seem increasingly frequent.

CAPTIVITY Very rare in captivity, where it breeds only rarely, although the formation of a captive stock is proposed as a conservation action, in order to support re-introduction schemes[145]. Observations outside the normal range are very unlikely to involve escapees.

REFERENCES Aarvak *et al.* (2013)[3]; BirdLife International (2004)[139]; BirdLife International (2014)[145]; Bowler *et al.* (1997)[167]; Brazil (2009)[182]; Carney (1992)[224]; Cramp & Simmons (1977)[268]; Dau *et al.* (1985)[282]; Forsman (1995)[388]; Fredrickson (2001)[404]; Gillham & Gillham (2002)[443]; Gudmundsson (1932)[493]; Hoff & Eggert (1995)[564]; Johnsgard (1978)[646]; Jones (1965)[661]; Kertell (1991)[603]; Larned (2012)[727]; Larned *et al.* (2011)[728]; Laubhan & Metzner (1999)[733]; Livezey (1995)[771]; McCarthy (2006)[817]; Mitchell & Pihl *in* Kear (2005)[855]; Morse (2009)[880]; Nygård *et al.* (1995)[923]; Palmer (1976)[945]; Pearce *et al.* (2005)[957]; Petersen (1981)[975]; Petersen *et al.* (2006)[982]; Pihl (2001)[990]; Portenko (1952)[1001]; Pyle (2008)[1014]; Quakenbush & Suydam (1999)[1017]; Quakenbush *et al.* (2002)[1018]; Safine (2011)[1116]; Solovieva (1997)[1216]; Solovieva *et al.* (1998)[1217]; USFWS (2002)[1289]; Uspenski (1972)[1301]; Wetlands International (2014)[1348]; Yésou & Lappo (1992)[1379]; Zydelis *et al.* (2006)[1396].

451. Adult ♂ (definitive basic). Norway, Apr (Tormod Amundsen/ Biotope).

452. Adult ♀ (definitive basic); the tertials and two broad white wingbars are typical of this age. Norway, Apr (Tormod Amundsen/ Biotope).

453. Adult ♂ (definitive basic). Norway, Apr (Tormod Amundsen/ Biotope).

454. Adult ♂ (definitive alternate). Iceland, Jul (Yann Kolbeinsson).

455. Adult ♀ (definitive basic); note width of white wingbars and strong blue gloss to secondaries and tertials. Norway, Mar (Ingo Waschkies).

456. First-summer ♂ (formative/first alternate); head already shows hint of definitive basic pattern. Norway, Jun (Eva Foss Henriksen).

501

SPECTACLED EIDER
Somateria fischeri

Plates 55, 56

TAXONOMY *Fuligula (Lampronetta) Fischeri*, J. F. Brandt, 1847, *Novam Rossicarum Avium Specimen*, p. 18, pl. 1. Monotypic, with no geographic variation.

IDENTIFICATION Easy to identify under reasonable conditions, irrespective of plumage. Considerably smaller than Common Eider *S. mollissima*, and just smaller than King Eider *S. spectabilis*. In all plumages, the presence of 'goggles' (broad pale circles around the eyes) and feathering on bill are characteristic, the latter covering the culmen beyond the nostrils and then running as a straight line back to the gape, in a very different pattern from the other two species. In flight, the black rump extends further onto the back than in Common Eider. During the first winter and following spring, has a variable amount of white on the neck and upperparts with a dark breast (vs. the other two eiders at the same age, in which the breast is usually the whitest part of the body). Also in all plumages, the 'sails' formed by the longest scapulars are not very obvious in the adult ♂ and hardly at all in ♀, which shows a regularly rounded back. However, a hybrid Common Eider × Steller's Eider reported in Norway between 1995 and 1999[388] superficially resembled this species (see Steller's Eider).

PLUMAGES Strong sexual dimorphism in first winter. Complex alternate moult strategy (two plumages per annual cycle, three in first cycle). ♂♂ are easy to age until the second winter, ♀♀ until first summer. Note that the only regularly observed plumages on the coasts of inland Alaska and Russia are adult breeding (♂ in basic plumage and ♀ in alternate plumage) and possibly juvenile, just before their departure. Most moulting and immature birds only occur at sea.

Adult ♂

Definitive basic plumage (Nov–Dec/Jun–Jul). Medium-sized sea duck, mostly black and white. Head green on the nape, crown, lores and forehead, with the exception of two large round white patches around the eyes, encircled by a black line, and a white band at the base of the bill. Cheeks, throat, neck, breast-sides, upperparts and tertials white. Rest of breast, belly, flanks, under- and uppertail-coverts, tail, rump and lower back black, with pale grey streaks often clearly visible on the breast. The iris is dark brown around the pupil with a bright blue rim visible up close. The bill is bright orange at the base, paler at the tip. Legs dull yellow with brown webs. Upperwing like equivalent plumage of Common Eider, with remiges, greater and primary coverts, and alula blackish, lesser and median coverts white. Underwing, including axillaries, washed greyish, making the whole darker than in other *Somateria*.

Definitive alternate plumage (Jun–Jul/Oct–Nov). The head has a pattern similar to basic plumage, but the white parts are pale grey-brown and the dark parts finely streaked dark grey-brown. The 'goggles' are still easily visible, especially as they are surrounded by a black line. The bill is duller pinkish-orange. The underparts, rear body, rump and lower back are blackish with diffuse brown streaks. The breast is slightly paler and also streaked. The scapulars are dark grey, while the mantle is white. The wings were not moulted during pre-alternate moult and thus remain white and black. Before being replaced early in pre-basic moult, the white tertials can look heavily worn.

Adult ♀

Definitive basic plumage (Nov–Dec/Apr). At this season, birds are grouped on the ice and unlikely to be seen from land. Nape, central crown, forehead and lores quite dark cinnamon-brown. Neck, throat, cheeks and 'goggles' pale brown-beige, the latter surrounded by a fuzzy dark line on the top and the sides. Head and neck tinged ochre, contrasting slightly with the beautiful warm reddish-brown body, strongly and regularly streaked black. Tertials blackish fringed tan. Iris dark brown with blue rim. Bill blue-grey with nail slightly darker. Lesser and median coverts brown fringed paler, with blackish remiges and greater coverts. Pale tips to the inner greater coverts and secondaries variably marked, but usually less than in Common Eider and substantially less than King Eider in same plumages. Underwing has axillaries and median coverts pale grey, not white like the other species. Legs yellowish-brown.

Definitive alternate plumage (May–Jun/Oct–Nov). Like basic plumage but ground colour markedly paler, ranging from grey-beige to pale caramel, thus black streaks more obvious on the breast, flanks and scapulars. The 'goggles', cheeks and throat are usually pale grey, and the front of the 'goggles' can be very dark and contrasting. Tertials either basic (dark, sharp and relatively worn) or alternate (new, long, curved, paler and coppery-reddish). Bill generally darker than in winter.

Juvenile

First basic plumage (until Oct–Nov). Similar to adult ♀ alternate plumage in its overall colour, but greyer and drabber, with upperparts slightly darker and rest of body marginally paler, the breast and belly being finely and neatly streaked. The bars on the flanks are ill-defined and less regular, and appear as dusky patches. Scapulars small, round, black centred with thin reddish-brown fringes, appearing faintly scaly, unlike the barred pattern of adult ♀. The 'goggles' are slightly less contrasting and smaller than in subsequent plumages, but still obvious. The feathering on the upper bill is less than in adult, giving the forehead a more concave profile. Iris dark brown. Bill dark pinkish-brown. Can be sexed in the hand or in excellent views, mainly based on the presence of pale brown fringes to the inner greater coverts and secondaries, forming a hint of double wingbars. These fringes are virtually absent in ♂♂ at all ages.

First-winter ♂

Formative plumage (Nov–Mar/May–Jun). ♂ retains a variable number of juvenile feathers, brown and vaguely barred, especially on belly, rump, and under- and uppertail-coverts. The head, initially juvenile, slowly acquires more or less adult-type feathers, grey-green (nape, central crown and forehead) and whitish-grey (cheeks and 'goggles'). The bill quickly becomes pink to dull yellow-orange. Iris bluish around the edge. The breast and flanks become partially dull blackish, and new scapulars are largely whitish with greyish tips. Upperwing identical to juvenile, uniform brown and dark. Legs pale yellow-brown.

First-winter ♀

Formative plumage (Nov–Mar/May–Jun). Differs from adult ♀ by juvenile feathers on belly, rear body and especially rump, with some on flanks, breast and upperparts. Overall greyer and duller, more variegated and irregularly barred than adult ♀. Tips to inner greater coverts and secondaries barely marked pale brown. Tertials brown, rather short, round-tipped and slightly curved. Bill dark grey.

First-summer ♂

First alternate plumage (Jun–Jul/Sep–Oct). Similar to adult alternate plumage, but has dark grey-brown tertials and upperwing is still mainly (at least) juvenile and dark brown. In early first summer, just before second pre-basic moult, the rectrices and remiges often appear very washed out, worn and frayed.

First-summer ♀

First alternate plumage (Jun–Jul/Sep–Oct). Similar to adult ♀, especially young ♀♀ that have undergone an extensive pre-formative and/or pre-alternate moult. Look for retained juvenile feathers especially on the belly, rear body and rump, and juvenile tertials (shorter, straighter, dark brown and round-tipped).

Second-winter ♂

Second basic plumage (Oct–Nov/Jun–Jul). Similar to adult in equivalent plumage, except that tertials have faded dark grey tips (vs. white in adult.). In flight, a variable number of marginal, lesser and median coverts are stained brown, producing an upperwing pattern ranging from dark brown with a large white oblong patch to a white upperwing with some brownish smudges.

Second-summer ♂

Second alternate plumage (Jun–Jul/Sep–Nov). Same as adult in equivalent plumage, except retained tertials and upperwing as described under second basic plumage.

Third-winter ♂

Third basic plumage (Nov–Dec/Jun–Jul). ♂♂ in adult-type basic plumage with all-white tertials but some brown spots on the lesser coverts are probably third-winter birds. However, some birds at this age can show perfectly white lesser and median coverts.

GEOGRAPHIC VARIATION None.

MEASUREMENTS and MASS ♂ (*n*=30): wing chord 251–266 (adult) and 238–260 (juvenile), tail 74–87, bill length from proximal end of nostrils 30–34, bill depth at proximal end of nostrils 14.9–17.6, tarsus 46–51; ♀ (*n*= 30): wing chord 246–259 (adult) and 233–254 (juvenile), tail 72–85, bill length from proximal end of nostrils: 31–35, bill depth at proximal end of nostrils: 14.8–17.5, tarsus 45–49[1014]. Culmen length from tip of feathers 22–28 in Spectacled Eider, 28–36 in King Eider and 43–60 in Common Eider[1014]. ♂: mass in spring 1,275–1,750 (1,494, *n*=53); ♀: mass in spring 1,300–1,850 (1623, *n*=53)[267]. ♂: mass in early summer 1,325–1,540 (1,417, *n*=11); ♀: mass in early summer 1,125–1,450 (1,247, *n*=15)[279].

VOICE ♂ gives a cooed *aa-hooo*, barely audible at any distance[794,928]. ♀ utters a soft repeated chuckle when alarmed or when calling its brood[279].

MOULT Complex alternate moult strategy. The small population and range, which is exclusively marine, make it difficult to obtain information on the species' moult, which are probably similar to those of King Eider (which see).

HYBRIDISATION No cases of hybridisation reported in the literature, but photographs published on the internet unequivocally show two captive hybrids between Spectacled Eider and King Eider (see the latter).

HABITAT and LIFE-CYCLE Undoubtedly among the most remarkably adapted species to extreme Arctic conditions and life at sea, where it spends most time. Arrives at breeding sites between mid-May and mid-Jun depending on the thaw in the coastal tundra, where the species favours grassy marshes dotted with numerous shallow ponds. In E Siberia, sometimes breeds up to 120 km from the sea[279]. The birds arrive in pairs, and breed singly or in loose colonies like King Eider. Peak egg laying occurs 12 days after arrival[279]. ♂♂ leave early in incubation and gather at moulting sites, generally near coasts[1167]. ♀♀ and their broods remain on the nesting sites until fledging in early Sep. All then leave the breeding grounds and adult ♀♀ begin their wing moult. Once able to fly again, in Sep–Oct, the ♂♂ move to the species' only known wintering site, where joined soon after by ♀♀. From Nov, almost the entire world population spends the winter in dense flocks, near holes in the sea ice covering the Bering Sea[978,983]. In Apr–May, the birds gradually leave, and follow the sea ice thaw to their breeding grounds.

RANGE and POPULATION Range, centred on the Bering Sea, has shrunk in recent decades in Alaska, where the species is now mainly found in the Yukon-Kuskokwim Delta and along the Arctic coast, principally between Barrow and Prudhoe Bay. These two populations number *c.*5,000 and 3,000–4,000 pairs[144,1167], the rest of the population breeding in Siberia, where aerial surveys conducted in 1993–95 estimated 146,245 birds[346]. Moult gatherings are reported off the major river deltas of E Siberia, which holds the bulk of the Russian breeding population[279], as well as off the Chukchi Peninsula and NW Alaska. The winter range was only discovered recently, using satellite transmitters attached to breeding birds[58,978], which also revealed frequent exchanges between populations[279]. Almost all of the global population winters in a single area between St. Lawrence I and St. Matthew I, in the Bering Sea, where censuses have reported 330,000–390,000 birds[305] vs. close to 400,000 estimated in the 1970s[144]. The demographic trends of the different populations are dissimilar. The Yukon-Kuskokwim declined by almost 95% between 1970 and 1992, from 47,700–70,000 pairs to 1,700–3,000 pairs[1229], then increased to *c.*5,000 pairs in 2008[346]. A dramatic decrease was also reported at Prudhoe Bay, N Alaska, estimated at 80% in 1981–91[144,346]. Very casual outside its normal range, with a few scattered reports from Northwest Territories, British Columbia, Svalbard and Norway. Because the entire population is extremely concentrated in the non-breeding season, associated with sea ice and requiring abundant shellfish resources to survive extremely harsh environmental conditions[979], this species is likely to be threatened by global warming and ongoing habitat destruction, and disturbance linked to inshore and offshore petroleum extraction, maritime traffic and the resultant risk of pollution[144,786,979]. Egg harvesting and hunting by native people is locally unsustainable[279].

CAPTIVITY Very rarely kept in captivity, difficult to breed, requires special care and very expensive, which makes it unlikely to escape.

REFERENCES Balogh (1996)[58]; BirdLife International (2013)[144]; Dau & Kistchinski *in* Kear (2005)[279]; Delany & Scott (2006)[305]; Edwards (2010)[346]; Forsman (1995)[388]; Lovvorn *et al.* (2009)[786]; Madge & Burn (1988)[794]; Ogilvie & Young (1998)[928]; Petersen (1996)[978]; Petersen & Douglas (2004)[979]; Petersen *et al.* (1999)[983]; Pyle (2008)[1014]; Sea Duck Joint Venture (2004)[1167]; Stehn *et al.* (1993)[1229].

457. Adult ♂ (definitive basic). Alaska, Jun (William Price).

458. Adult ♂ (definitive basic). Alaska, Jun (William Price).

459. Group (adult); at this time, adult ♂♂ are in basic plumage and ♀♀ in alternate plumage. Alaska, Jun (William Price).

460. First-spring ♀ (formative/first alternate), showing many juvenile feathers, including belly and very worn primaries. Alaska, Jun (Anders Blomdahl).

461. Adult ♀ (definitive alternate). Alaska, Jun (Otto Plantema).

462. Adult ♂ (definitive basic). Alaska, Jun (Anders Blomdahl).

KING EIDER
Somateria spectabilis

TAXONOMY *Anas spectabilis* Linnaeus, 1758, *Syst. Nat.*, edn. 10, p. 123. Monotypic. No geographic variation described.

IDENTIFICATION ♂♂ unmistakable after first summer, but young ♂ and ♀♀ are more like Spectacled Eider *S. fischeri* and Common Eider *S. mollissima*. Differs from Common Eider by smaller size, more compact shape with a thicker neck, shorter bill and clearly rounded head. Can be surprisingly difficult to spot among Common Eiders, especially in flight. Look for the shorter and stockier shape, while the frequency of the wingbeats, usually faster, can imitate that of Common Eiders[152]. Adult ♂ normally unmistakable; its mostly black plumage and peach-pink breast are often the first features to attract attention within a mixed flock of eiders. In flight, the black scapulars and leading edge make the upperparts appear much darker. In alternate plumage, appears very dark like other eiders, but differs in its black tertials. Young ♂♂ have a succession of mostly brown, black and white plumages, similar to those of Common Eider, being distinguished mainly by head, bill, size and shape at these stages. The diagnostic orange base to the bill is evident in the first autumn, when the plumage is still entirely dark brown. Adult ♀ also identified by its smaller size and more compact and stocky shape. The feathering protrudes significantly less on the bill sides than Common Eider and also extends further on the culmen than on the sides. The bill is much shorter, and darker than the head, especially as a diffuse pale patch near the base of the bill accentuates the contrast. This contrast is usually reversed in Common Eider, where the bill is paler than the head. This pale patch emphasises the dark gape, which is up-curved, giving a typical 'smiling' impression to ♀ King Eider. The forehead is slightly rounded, and the head shape oval and elongated in profile, with the top fairly flat, often peaking well behind the eye. The overall colour is warmer in winter, ochre-reddish, and often noticeable among flocks of Common Eider. Note the dark pattern of the scapulars and flank feathers, which are 'U-shaped', but flatter, forming vertical stripes in Common Eider. In flight, axillaries and underwing median coverts whiter and more contrasting than Common Eider. Juvenile differs from Common Eider much like adult ♀, but some characters are less marked (generally greyer and duller, flanks more barred or mottled dusky than 'U-shaped' marks, etc.). Size and shape are the most important features.

PLUMAGES Strong sexual dimorphism from first winter onwards. Complex alternate moult strategy (two plumages per definitive cycle, three in first cycle). Ageing ♂♂ is relatively easy until the second summer, and ♀♀ until the first summer.

Adult ♂

Definitive basic plumage (Dec/Jul). Crown and nape pale blue-grey, highlighted by white orbital patch above the eyes, extending as a white bridle across the cheeks. The base of the culmen is outlined in black, prolonged by an eyestripe that runs alongside the white bridle. The cheeks are washed green near the eye, blending into the white chin and throat. A well-marked black 'V' adorns the chin, but is usually visible only when the bird raises its bill (in stretching for example). The sides of the forehead are adorned by two huge, rounded and orange frontal lobes, separated by a thin band of feathers on the forehead. The bill is short, bright coral-red with a white nail. Iris dark brown. The breast is peach-pink. Mantle white, as well as two large round patches on the femoral coverts. Back, scapulars, central rump, uppertail-coverts, tail and underparts black. Tertials black, long and drooping. The longest scapulars show sharp extensions on their outer webs that form often very visible pointed 'sails' when not held tight against the body, e.g. when diving. In flight, upperwing all black except median and lower lesser coverts, which form a long white oval patch. The black tips to the greater coverts also show small white spots visible when close. Underwing grey with a paler area formed by the white median coverts and axillaries. Legs yellow-orange.

Definitive alternate plumage (Jul/Nov). Entirely blackish-brown body, almost matt black on cheeks, scapulars, tertials, flanks and belly, overall darker than ♀. Retains partially white mantle with a variable number of small white spots on breast. The sharp 'sails' formed by the longest scapulars remain visible. Bill duller red, topped by pale orange frontal lores, reduced and less bright than during rest of year. Nail often quite dusky. Upperwing still basic, which is also evident by the presence of a large horizontal white line between the flanks and upperparts. Legs yellow-orange.

Adult ♀

Definitive basic plumage (Dec/Apr–May). Overall reddish ochre-brown plumage, rather bright. Head and neck finely streaked black, with a diffuse pale patch at the base of the bill, a pale crescent above the eye that extends as a vague bridle over the cheeks towards the whitish throat. Feathering extends far onto the culmen, and sometimes forms a small bulge at the front. Bill lead-grey with a blackish nail and a pale grey subterminal band. Iris dark brown. Breast reddish-brown with small dark crescents, which become much more visible on the fore flanks, and large black 'U-shaped' marks further back. Scapulars centred black with pale reddish fringes, the longest scapulars with small rounded 'sails' on their outer webs. Tertials broad, drooping, black with diffuse reddish fringes. Back and rump black finely streaked reddish-brown. Belly dark and rather uniform reddish-brown, undertail slightly paler with coarse speckles. Upperwing dark, with lesser and median coverts blackish fringed tan, usually duller than body colour. Inner half of greater coverts blackish, broadly tipped white, forming a short wingbar. The secondaries are also tipped white, the trailing edge being broader inwardly. Underwing all grey, except white area on axillaries and part of median coverts. The leading edge is usually the darkest part of the underwing. Legs and feet grey.

Definitive alternate plumage (May–Jun/Nov). Like basic plumage, but ground colour of entire body paler, usually light reddish to beige. The breast feathers are more clearly marked with black crescents, which added to the paler ground colour, makes the whole plumage typically appear scalier. When they were replaced as part of pre-alternate moult, which is true for only some ♀♀, the tertials are buff to pale reddish, more whitish at the tips, with a wide black rachis, which thickens towards the tip. Bill usually uniformly dark without pale subterminal bar. Legs grey.

Juvenile

First basic plumage (until Oct–Nov). Like adult ♀, but colder grey throughout. Shows a pale diffuse eye-ring, broader above the eye, and rather contrasting pale base to the bill, chin and throat. The bill is dark grey with just a hint of pale subterminal band. The breast and belly are slightly paler, very finely dotted, but appear plainer than in adult. The dark marks on the flanks and scapulars are dull brown, less well defined and coarser,

not forming the characteristic 'U-shape' of adult. The scapulars are also more uniform dusky and shorter than adult. Finally, in flight, shows only a vague trace of wingbars, formed by tips to inner greater coverts and inner secondaries. ♂ separated from ♀ by presence of small white dots in centre of breast feathers, by colour and shape of frontal lobes (pale yellow-pinkish), lack of bulge (or small 'sails') on longest scapulars, and lack of pale tips to inner greater coverts.

First-winter ♂

Formative plumage (Nov–Mar/May–Jul). Easily distinguished from ♀ at same age. In Nov–Dec, completely brown with breast finely dotted with white and bill base already largely pale yellowish-pink. Pre-formative moult then continues during much of the winter, with first-winter ♂ being variable in appearance. Most have a brown head with blackish-brown cheeks, clear eye-ring, breast largely stained white, mantle variegated blackish-brown and white, and scapulars and flanks mainly blackish. After moult, during the subsequent spring, the crown and nape are often variegated pale blue-grey and blackish-brown, the latter generally more numerous on the lower hindneck. The white cheeks are variably marked blackish (sometimes entirely), and an often-complete white collar highlights the whitish breast, often washed pale pinkish. The bill is dull red with pale orange frontal lobes. The flanks and scapulars are black, while the two round patches on the femoral coverts are either white, blackish or white mottled brown. The rump, belly, upper- and undertail-coverts often show a mix of juvenile (whitish and spotted) and formative (blackish) feathers. In birds which undertook extensive pre-formative moult, traces of juvenile plumage are limited to the central belly and scattered on the back, as well as the upperwing. In late spring, these feathers are generally heavily worn and then appear pale brown or even bleached in birds that wintered well south of their usual range.

First-winter ♀

Formative plumage (Nov–Mar/May–Jul). Duller than adult ♀, including new formative feathers. Often shows clear contrast between the new feathers that cover a variable part of the head, flanks and upperparts, and the belly and rear body, which are covered with juvenile feathers, whitish with fine dark streaks. In flight, the fine wingbars formed by the tips to the inner greater coverts and secondaries are barely visible (much less so than adult ♀, but more than in first-winter ♂).

First-summer ♂

First alternate plumage (Jun–Jul/Sep–Oct). The first pre-alternate moult involves some of the same feathers as pre-formative moult and results in a body plumage close to definitive alternate plumage (eclipse adult ♂). Best distinguished by the variable traces of juvenile body plumage (especially the belly), by the less developed pale yellowish-pink frontal lobes and all-dark juvenile upperwing until the subsequent pre-basic moult.

First-summer ♀

First alternate plumage (May–Jul/Sep–Oct). Very like adult ♀, especially ♀♀ that undertook extensive pre-formative and/or pre-alternate moults. Distinguished by being generally a little greyer and duller, and retained juvenile tertials, which are shorter, uniform dark brown, round-tipped and easily distinguished from adult tertials (especially new alternate feathers) which are long, curved and pointed. The bill usually shows a pale subterminal band more marked than adult ♀ (variable) and features of upperwing are the same as juvenile until the subsequent pre-basic moult.

Second-winter ♂

Second basic plumage (Oct–Nov/May–Jul). Resembles definitive basic plumage (adult ♂), but distinguished by variable presence of dark or blackish speckles on head, especially the upper cheeks (where they can replace green of adult), crown and nape. The frontal lobes form a bulge slightly less marked than in adult at the base of the bill, and are more yellowish-orange than bright orange. The bill is also slightly pinker with a paler tip. The breast is often reported to be whiter without the pink wash of adults[1242]. A good ageing feature that is often visible is the wide oval white patches on the upperwing, which are smaller, less sharply defined and/or partially concealed by partly blackish coverts. Like other eiders, in Nov, second-winter ♂♂ typically look more like definitive basic plumage than adult ♂♂, which are still in alternate plumage (eclipse) at this time.

Second-summer ♂

Second alternate plumage (Jun–Jul/Nov). Similar to adult ♂, except upperwing, which is not or almost not replaced during second pre-alternate moult, and is similar to second basic plumage (first-winter ♂). However, this feature is not always reliable, and some second-summer birds show a pattern very similar to adult[1242].

Third-winter ♂

Third basic plumage (Nov–Dec/Jul). Distinguished from adult ♂ by presence of larger number of dark spots in white upperwing, and smaller bulge at the base of the bill (measured in the hand). However, further research is needed to determine the normal variation of adult ♂♂[1014].

GEOGRAPHIC VARIATION None.

MEASUREMENTS and MASS ♂ (*n*=90): wing chord 260–286 (adult) and 250–278 (juvenile), tail 76–89, bill length from proximal end of nostrils 32–35, bill depth at proximal end of nostrils 16.1–18.2, tarsus 46–51; ♀ (*n*=80): wing chord 251–279 (adult) and 243–272 (juvenile), tail 75–87, bill length from proximal end of nostrils 32–36, bill depth at proximal end of nostrils 15.8–18.5, tarsus 44–49[1014]. Culmen length from tip of feathers 22–28 in Spectacled Eider, 28–36 in King Eider and 43–60 in Common Eider[1014]. ♂: mass in Jun 1,367–1,954 (1,655, *n*=39); ♀: mass in Jun 1,213–1,923 (1,569, *n*=139)[267].

VOICE ♂ produces a cooing faster and higher-pitched than Common Eider. ♀ gives a quacked *gog-gog-gog*. The species is generally less often heard than Common Eider, and its sounds are less audible.

MOULT Complex alternate moult strategy. The question of an auxiliary pre-formative moult in first-year ♂ is often raised, leading from juvenile plumage to body feathers mainly blackish-brown and uniform[1242], but was rejected by Pyle[1014]. Pre-formative moult occurs in Oct–Mar, often including a high proportion of feathers on the head, neck, breast and scapulars. Only some birds replace a variable number of upper- and undertail-coverts, flanks and mantle feathers. Most moult few or no feathers on rump, belly, tertials, inner upperwing-coverts and rectrices. First pre-alternate moult generally involves some of the previous feathers, in May–Jul. Second pre-basic moult lasts from Jul to Oct, 1–2 months earlier than adult. It is complete, although a few alternate or juvenile feathers may be retained, especially on belly. Definitive pre-alternate moult includes many to most head and body feathers and occurs in Apr–May in ♀, en route to nesting sites, and Jun–Jul in ♂ on moulting sites. Occasionally, some inner upperwing-coverts are replaced by ♀, which then lacks the typical white tips to the basic inner greater coverts[1014]. Definitive pre-basic moult is consecutive to pre-alternate moult in ♂ and starts with the remiges and rectrices in Aug–Sep. ♀ begins pre-basic moult after its offspring fledge and migration to moulting sites, 1–2 months after ♂. Many birds leave the moulting sites as soon as they can fly again.

HYBRIDISATION Apart from a hybrid ♂ reported in captivity with Tufted Duck *Aythya fuligula*[443], the species regularly hybridises with Common Eider in the wild. Such hybrids, almost all ♂♂, are reported annually, in North America and N Europe. In Iceland, it has been assumed that hybridisation is often due to ♂ King Eiders mating with ♀ Common Eiders in colonies of the latter[439].

King Eider × Common Eider. Adult ♂♂ of this cross have the underparts and rear body common to both species, but the scapulars and tertials are medium grey with obvious 'sails', a rounded head with an arched forehead, a yellow-orange bill, paler at the tip, two broad frontal lobes (slightly wider than adult ♂ of *S. m. dresseri* if *S. m. borealis* is the subspecies of Common Eider involved in the parentage), nape, crown and forehead pale grey-blue, a black line at the base of the bill (on sides and above), and a longish eye-patch above and behind the eye. A white line runs across the rear cheeks and more or less into this black patch, sometimes to above the eye. The upper and rear cheeks are variably green. Many birds show a clear black 'V' on the chin, which can be almost absent or partial[439]. The wing on the other hand is more often like that of Common Eider, with white or very pale grey wing-coverts. Some features vary depending on the subspecies of Common Eider involved, including the head profile and shape of the frontal lobes, and bill colour, which also varies with age and season. For example, a hybrid involving *S. m. v-nigrum* caught in Nunavut[1283] showed, among other features, a bright orange bill with reddish edges and frontal lobes framed by a broad black line, a rather large black eye-patch and much green on the upper cheeks. Several sources claim that these hybrids are sterile[463,987], but a bird in Norway had very pale grey scapulars, pinkish breast, black band extending from the bill to the nape (albeit significantly less broad and less extensive than Common Eider), nape and crown pale greyish-green, sharply pointed feathering at the base of the bill and a brightly coloured bill. These features correspond to what one might expect from a backcross with Common Eider. The ♀ resulting from this cross is very rarely reported or described in the literature, but is said to be close to ♀ King Eider with atypical characters[439,1305].

King Eider × Spectacled Eider. Hybrid reported in captivity in Germany, from where photographs of a ♀ and ♂ have been published on the internet. The ♂ has black flanks and rear body, with two white patches on the femoral coverts like both parent species, slate-grey scapulars with two rounded 'sails', and white foreneck and throat. The breast is brownish-pink, much darker than King Eider. The nape, crown and forehead (with pattern close to King Eider) are pale blue-grey, cheeks are partly tinged green and a large black spot surrounds the eye. The bill is pale orange-red, paler over its distal half, with a slightly brownish nail. The sides of the bill are feathered like King Eider with a clear bulge on the forehead, but the feathers cover the culmen only above the nostrils, and there are no frontal lobes. The legs are orange. The ♀ has a rather dark reddish-brown body, streaked like ♀ Spectacled Eider, neck and head more ochre-yellow to cinnamon, head profile intermediate between those of the two species with a fairly deep forehead, feathers covering the culmen above the middle of the nostrils and forming a right-angle with the base of the bill, which is almost vertical. A pale semicircle is visible above the eye, intermediate in size between that shown by the parents. The bill is dark greyish-blue, blackish at the base and on the nail.

HABITAT and LIFE-CYCLE During the breeding season, inhabits different lakes, ponds, bogs and small rivers in the Arctic tundra, usually up to 50 km from the coast, rarely up to 100 km[927]. For laying and early growth stages of the ducklings, the species prefers small shallow ponds with emergent aquatic vegetation. The families then swim and walk towards more open waters, either brackish or salt[1213], where they are protected from early frosts. Does not form dense colonies like Common Eider[1245] (although sometimes forms loose colonies[794]), breeding for example at a density of 1.2 nests per km² along coasts of the Beaufort Sea. Most arrive at the breeding sites by late May to mid-Jun, depending on the freshwater thaw[1213], with eggs being laid in Jun[677]. ♂♂ leave the nest sites early during incubation[318,927] and form huge gatherings (e.g. up to 100,000 off coast of W Greenland[794]) to moult between mid-Jul/Aug and Oct, joining non-breeding second-calendar-year birds, which moult at the same time or earlier. ♀♀ remain with their offspring, sometimes in crèches, for up to 50 days after hatching, then fly to the moulting sites, which are usually in sheltered fjords, rich in benthic fauna[927]. Winters at sea or off coasts, often near pack ice, forming compact 'rafts' sometimes of thousands of birds.

RANGE and POPULATION In addition to the mapped range, nests locally or irregularly in N Scandinavia, S Hudson Bay[1127] and N Quebec, with a total population estimated at 790,000–930,000 birds[305]. The main moulting grounds of North American breeders lie off the Chukchi Peninsula and Greenland[1166]. Winters to the south of the breeding range, many birds nevertheless do not move below the Arctic Circle in winter. The wintering population in N Pacific includes breeders from the Beaufort Sea and W Canadian Arctic, with 300,000–400,000 birds[318,1166]. In N Atlantic, population estimated at 280,000 individuals[1166], although the Greenland population has been separately estimated at 300,000–500,000 birds. Few recent data available for the Russian Arctic, but the wintering population in Norway is estimated at 50,000–100,000 birds[139]. Small numbers regularly venture south in the Pacific to California or E Hokkaido, Japan. In N Atlantic, regular from Iceland to Scotland and in Baltic Sea. Wanders via Florida to the Gulf of Mexico, and also to France, Spain and exceptionally the Mediterranean (Italy). Very casual inland, except on the Great Lakes, Canada/USA. Demographic trends reveal a significant decrease in the North American population at least. Spring censuses conducted at Point Barrow, Alaska, where most of NW American Arctic population passes, produced 802,556 birds in 1976, 350,835 birds in 1996[1245], 304,966 birds in 2003 and 591,961 birds in 2004[1019], suggesting a certain stability over the past 15 years, following a sharp decline. The most serious threats are related to increasing petroleum extraction, both inshore and offshore in the Arctic Ocean, facilitated by the decline in pack ice in recent decades[912]. Among other threats are unsustainable hunting in Greenland[927] and the massive use of gill-nets that drown many birds[839].

CAPTIVITY Very rarely kept in captivity for ornament and thus unlikely to escape. The species requires special care, is difficult to breed and usually only sold at prohibitive prices.

REFERENCES BirdLife International (2004)[139]; BirdLife International (2013)[144]; Blomdahl *et al.* (2002)[152]; Cramp & Simmons (1977)[268]; Delany & Scott (2006)[305]; Dickson (2012)[318]; Gillham & Gillham (1996)[439]; Gillham & Gillham (2002)[443]; Goudie *et al.* (2000)[463]; Kellett & Alisauskas (2000)[677]; Madge & Burn (1988)[794]; Merkel (2004)[839]; Nikolaeva *et al.* (2006)[912]; Ogilvie *in* Kear (2005)[927]; Palmer (1977)[946]; Pettingill (1959)[987]; Pyle (2008)[1014]; Quakenbush *et al.* (2009)[1019]; Raven & Dickson (2009)[1049]; Sandilands (2005)[1127]; Sea Duck Joint Venture (2004)[1166]; Snow & Perrins (1998)[1213]; Suddaby *et al.* (1994)[1242]; Suydam *et al.* (2000)[1245]; Trefry *et al.* (2007)[1283]; van den Berg (2002)[1305].

463. Adult ♂ (definitive basic). Norway, Mar (Tormod Amundsen/ Biotope).

464. Adult ♂ (definitive basic); black 'V' on throat typical of this species and some subspecies of Common Eider *S. mollissima*. Norway, Mar (Tormod Amundsen/Biotope).

465. Adult ♂ (definitive basic); in flight, extent of white patch on median and lesser coverts, and white tips to greater coverts probably age-related, including after second winter. Norway, Mar (Tormod Amundsen/Biotope).

466. First-winter ♂ (formative); like other *Somateria*, young ♂♂ are dark brownish with a whitish breast, but the bill pattern is diagnostic. Norway, Apr (Tormod Amundsen/Biotope).

467. First-summer ♂ (first alternate); the juvenile upperwing (including tertials) is brown and very worn, distinguishing this plumage from all subsequent ones. Iceland, Jul (Yann Kolbeinsson).

468. Second-winter ♂ (second basic), resembles adult ♂, but has variable dusky spotting on head, not fully developed swollen bill. and shorter tertials and 'sails'. Norway, Apr (Tormod Amundsen/ Biotope).

469. Adult ♀ (definitive basic); head and bill shape, pattern of feathering on the bill base, 'sails' and U-shaped black markings on flanks are all distinctive. Norway, Mar (Tormod Amundsen/ Biotope).

470. Adult ♀ (definitive basic); note short bill with concave culmen, pale subterminal band, short, wide and rounded lobes, and slightly up-curved gape. Norway, Mar (Tormod Amundsen/Biotope).

471. First-winter ♀ (formative); this bird has not moulted its belly feathers and has faint pale trailing edge to secondaries and greater coverts. Norway, Mar (Ingo Waschkies).

472. Adult ♀ (definitive alternate); paler and less rufous than definitive basic plumage (sometimes even greyish), the long drooping tertials often being the warmest part. Svalbard, Jun (Vincent Legrand).

COMMON EIDER
Somateria mollissima

TAXONOMY *Anas mollissima* Linnaeus, 1758, *Syst. Nat.*, edn. 10, p. 124. Polytypic species with six subspecies generally recognised: *mollissima* in NW Europe, *faeroeensis* C. L. Brehm, 1831, in the Faeroe Is, *borealis* C. L. Brehm, 1824, in N Atlantic Ocean, *sedentaria* Snyder, 1941, in Hudson Bay, *dresseri* Sharpe, 1871, in E North America and *v-nigrum* (initially *S. m. v-nigra*) Bonaparte, 1855, in N Pacific between Canada and E Siberia. Intergradation between these taxa exists especially in N Atlantic. For example, birds in the Shetland Is and Orkneys, Scotland, are treated within *faeroeensis* but show intermediate characters between *faeroeensis* and *mollissima*. Elsewhere in Britain, Ireland and SW Norway, birds are attributed to the nominate subspecies, but also show intermediate characters[794,928]. Similarly, birds in SE Greenland and Iceland, considered to belong to *borealis*[267] or sometimes to *mollissima*[771], are actually intermediate between these two, and have even been named *S. m. islandica* C. L. Brehm, 1831. These regions were perhaps colonised at the end of the last ice age by both western birds (*borealis*) and south-eastern birds (*mollissima*)[1264]. Finally, the subspecies *sedentaria* appears only marginally different from *dresseri*, and intergrades with *borealis* in the north of its range[838,945,1082]. In consequence, Garner & Millington[426] elected to recognise only four subspecies: *mollissima* (including *faeroeensis*), *borealis* (including *islandica*), *dresseri* (including *sedentaria*) and *v-nigrum*, partly based on the phylogenetic study of Livezey[771], who even assigned specific rank to *v-nigrum*. Indeed, the range of *v-nigrum* is wholly disjunct year-round and this taxon possesses several distinctive features[426,771]. This conclusion was also supported by a recent genetic study[1226], which found that differences between 15 different populations of eiders in North America and Scandinavia do match the six different subspecies generally accepted. However, pending further work, and given that the major taxonomic committees unanimously accept the aforementioned six subspecies, this position has been adopted here.

IDENTIFICATION The largest sea duck in N Hemisphere, with distinctive head profile and plumage, usually found in coastal waters. Adult ♂ unmistakable. Immature and ♀ plumages are closer to those of King Eider *S. spectabilis* and Spectacled Eider *S. fischeri*

(which see). Distinction of the different subspecies of Common Eider is more complex and discussed below (see Geographic Variation).

PLUMAGES Nominate subspecies. Strong sexual dimorphism from first winter onwards. Complex alternate moult strategy (two plumages per definitive cycle, three in first cycle). Ageing ♂♂ relatively easy until the second summer. Ageing ♀♀ fairly easy until the first summer.

Adult ♂

Definitive basic plumage (Nov–Dec/Jun–Jul). Large head with two black bands from base of bill to nape, meeting on the forehead but divided on the central crown and nape by a white line. Large green patches on rear cheeks and neck-sides, each crossed by an oblique white line. Rest of head, chin, neck, breast, upperparts and upper rump white. In fresh plumage, breast is often washed pale peach-pink. Tertials long, drooping and white. Bill typically thick and conical, usually olive-green at base, more greyish in centre with a strong grey-green to pale ivory nail. However, the bill's coloration is quite variable individually and more yellow or orange pre-breeding. The feathering at the bill base extends remarkably far over the sides of the bill, forming a rounded tip beyond the nostrils. The edges of the culmen base, known as process or frontal lobes, form two tips of bare skin in the black feathers either side of the forehead. Iris dark brown. Underparts (belly, flanks and undertail), tail, uppertail-coverts and lower rump black. Two large white patches visible on the femoral coverts. Upperwing white with alula, primary- and greater coverts black (the outermost faintly tipped white), primaries blackish-grey and secondaries black. Underwing has axillaries, lesser and median coverts white, primary coverts, greater coverts and remiges grey. Legs and feet greyish-olive, fairly close to the bill colour.

Definitive alternate plumage (Jun–Jul/Oct–Nov). Body uniform blackish-brown, darker than ♀ and unstreaked. The head has a vague pale yellowish-grey supercilium and the crown is paler than the cheeks. Bill pale bluish-grey. Breast and mantle has scattered white feathers. Tertials, upper- and underwing usually not moulted, so identical to basic plumage. Legs grey more or less tinged olive-green.

Adult ♀

Definitive basic plumage *(Nov–Dec/Apr).* Head, neck and breast grey-brown finely streaked dark, with a paler supercilium, broad especially above the eye. Head shape and feathers at base of bill as in ♂. Bill grey-blue to pale olive-grey with light grey to ivory nail. Iris dark brown. Flanks, mantle and scapulars reddish-brown to pale greyish-brown with broad black bars. Tertials broad, drooping, centred blackish with diffuse reddish fringes. Back and rump usually brighter reddish-brown finely streaked black. Belly brown, darker and plainer, lower belly and undertail pale brown with speckles. Tail brown. Upperwing dark brown with lesser and median coverts broadly fringed pale tawny, secondaries and greater coverts tipped white (mainly outer webs), forming a double wingbar framing the speculum, the latter sometimes with soft purple sheen. However, these white tips are very variable (clearer inwards), perhaps linked to age but seemingly not to the general condition of the bird, as is often reported[511,512,742]. Underwing completely grey, except for a white area on the axillaries and some median coverts. Legs grey-brown to dull greyish-green, less clearly olive than ♂. Senescent ♀♀ frequently show ♂ characters, especially a variable number of white specks, mainly on the breast, but also the upperparts, neck, throat and cheeks (often above the eye). The flanks are more or less blackish.

Definitive alternate plumage *(May/Oct–Nov).* Very similar to basic plumage but ground coloration averages greyer and paler, often devoid of reddish or warm colours. Tertials are replaced during pre-alternate moult in some ♀♀. Alternate tertials are centred black with large coppery-buff fringes, usually with a black anchor-shaped pattern at the tips and are often the most brightly coloured part of the plumage. The blackish bars on the scapulars and flanks are broader, generally making the entire plumage slightly darker. Bare parts similar to basic plumage.

Juvenile

First basic plumage *(until Oct–Nov).* Like adult ♀ but duller, with dark grey bars more diffuse on the flanks, rear body, rump and back. The flanks often show juvenile feathers, grey and uniform, until the beginning of the first winter. Belly finely streaked dark, less uniform than adult. Scapulars uniformly dark brown, vaguely fringed pale brown. Head has a more obvious supercilium, especially above the eye. Bill mid-grey to dull grey-brown, differing from adult ♀ by tip and nail duskier. Tertials shorter, straight, round-tipped, entirely dark brown except paler fringe towards the tip. Upper- and underwing as adult ♀ but white tips to greater coverts and secondaries often poorly marked or lacking. Lesser and median coverts sepia-brown with thin and poorly marked pale fringes. ♂ differs from ♀ in same plumage by presence of white spots on the breast and by greater coverts and secondaries uniform dark brown, without pale wingbars shown by young ♀. Bill becomes yellowish or greenish from Oct, often before white or black formative feathers appear.

First-winter ♂

Formative plumage *(Nov–Mar/May–Jun).* Early in pre-formative moult, like ♀, especially as some ♂♂ begin to acquire white and black feathers only from Mar. Highly variable appearance as pre-formative moult very protracted, variable in extent, and moreover formative feathers vary in colour. Retains most to all juvenile feathers in the wing (rarely a few inner lesser and median coverts are moulted, white), back, rump, belly and tail until second pre-basic moult, in Jul–Aug. The feathers of the upper head, mantle and scapulars are not moulted at all, or completely replaced. Initially dark grey-brown vaguely barred black, these body parts become progressively paler and washed out with wear. Following pre-formative moult, the new feathers on the white parts of the adult (cheeks, neck, breast, mantle and scapulars) are either black or white. Thus, the cheeks of some birds are all black, whereas others are variegated black and white. Similarly, if the breast is usually largely white, even with a pinkish hue like that of adult, black feathers can sometimes be numerous as well. All this means that in a flock of eiders, it is sometimes difficult to find two young ♂♂ that are alike! Easy to distinguish from adult ♂ during first year of life by dark upperwing and blackish tertials becoming pale brown when worn.

First-winter ♀

Formative plumage *(Nov–Mar/May–Jun).* Overall coloration paler than adult ♀ with a variable number of juvenile feathers, greyer and vaguely barred blackish. Distinguished from adult ♀ by less visible and regular black bars on flanks and upperparts. Bill slightly darker than ♀, particularly the nail, which is often dusky until early winter. White wingbars inconspicuous (see Juvenile).

First-summer ♂

First alternate plumage *(Jun–Jul/Sep–Oct).* Dark, like definitive alternate plumage, except the tertials and upperwing, which are all dark until the second pre-basic moult in Aug–Sep. The extent of the first alternate moult, however, is very variable, and often many of the formative black and white feathers are retained, especially on the breast, flanks and upperparts. The other formative feathers are moulted for matt blackish-brown feathers. Overall, this plumage is usually chocolate-brown with a variable number of white spots on the breast and scapulars.

First-summer ♀

First alternate plumage (Mar–May/Sep–Oct). Very like adult ♀, but differentiated quite easily even from afar by its juvenile tertials (shorter than those of adult, compared to secondaries), worn, fairly straight, dark and round-tipped, with diffuse pale fringes. The nail is usually dark and does not contrast with the rest of the bill, and the pale wingbars on the greater coverts and secondaries are barely marked. Also the area covered by the scapulars is smaller, often revealing a larger portion of the folded wing. The retained juvenile feathers on the flanks are less regularly barred than adult. Difficult or impossible to distinguish from adult ♀ after second pre-basic moult, although the extent of white fringes to greater coverts and secondaries might be marginally thinner in young ♀♀ (more study needed).

Second-winter ♂

Second basic plumage (Oct–Nov/Jun–Jul). This plumage is attained earlier in the season than in three-year-old birds or older, with largely white plumage by Nov, while adult is still largely in alternate plumage (eclipse). Resembles definitive basic plumage (adult ♂), but differs primarily by shorter tertials, pale grey to whitish at the base, gradually becoming blackish towards the tip (vs. white in adult ♂). Shows a variable number of diffuse black-brown tips especially on the back and rump, but often on the scapulars and cheeks as well. The white stripe on the crown is often diffuse or partially obscured with brown. The upperwing is variably white, usually with some lesser and median coverts whitish mottled dark brown. The leading edge and distal median coverts are often completely brown, resulting in a large, pale and diffuse oval spot on the upperwing, very different from that shown by adult ♂♂.

Second-summer ♂

Second alternate plumage (Jun–Jul/Sep–Nov). Similar to adult with exception of upperwing and tertials, which are not or almost not moulted, like second basic plumage (second-winter ♂).

Third-winter ♂

Third basic plumage (Nov–Dec/Jun–Jul). Very similar to definitive basic plumage, with the exception of a (variable) small number of marginal (leading edge) and distal median coverts (near the 'wrist') stained dark brown on upperwing. Note dark marks on tips of tertials. These feathers are all white in ♂ from fourth winter. It would be interesting to study colour variation in the tips of primary coverts, greater coverts and secondaries, where the extent of the white tips could be age-related too.

GEOGRAPHIC VARIATION Huge variation, partly clinal, throughout range, mainly visible in the structure, size, size and shape of the bill, shape of the frontal lobes, extent of green on the cheeks, presence of 'sails' on the longest scapulars and black 'V' on the chin in adult ♂, as well as overall colour tone in ♀. The following features should be assessed when attempting subspecific identification, but it is important to precisely assess the age first.

- The bill colour varies individually within a population, seasonally and depending on the bird's sexual condition, and the colour of the bill is often reflected in the legs.

- The black 'V' on the throat from which *v-nigrum* takes its name can be shown by all subspecies[1207]. It may be diffuse or reduced to a dark spot at the tip of the 'V'. Its presence in some subspecies may be related to immaturity, corresponding to a common ancestral character.

- The shape of the frontal lobes varies with the angle of view, which is easily assessed under field conditions, but can be misleading on a single photograph.

- The length of the frontal lobes is an important feature and can be assessed by comparing the distances between the proximal edge of the nostril to the tip of the bill, and to the tip of the lobe. It is also important to assess the distance between the eye and the tip of the lobe.

- The 'sails' on the lower back in a bird on the water are held erect when the scapulars slightly rotate on their axis. They are highly developed in King Eider and also present in all Arctic and Nearctic Common Eiders. Depending on the bird's behaviour, they can be raised or flattened.

- The extent of the feathering at the base of the bill is often difficult to assess other than on photographs or in the hand, but its shape is a diagnostic feature, including for immatures and ♀♀.

- Coloration of ♀♀ varies between populations, from pale grey (especially in *sedentaria*) to warm reddish-brown. This colour relates to definitive alternate plumage, basic plumage being redder and warmer in all subspecies (and species) of eiders. Plumage also becomes paler with age[837].

S. m. faeroeensis. Birds of the Faeroe Is differ only marginally from *mollissima*. About 10% smaller, including bill length, with little overlap. Frontal lobes are shorter and taper to a sharp point. In adult ♂, the bill is greyish-green with frontal lobes olive, averaging less yellow. Adult ♀ is darker overall, and more strongly barred black[794,928]. These differences are subtle, and identification of this subspecies outside its usual range is probably impossible apart from typical individuals measured in the hand. To complicate matters, birds on the Orkneys and Shetlands, assigned to *faeroeensis*, are intermediate between those of the Faeroes and *mollissima*.

S. m. borealis. Populations vary from east to west across its range, due to intergradation, perhaps old, with all neighbouring taxa. Slightly smaller than *mollissima* in Arctic Canada, but larger in contact zones with *dresseri*, *sedentaria* and in east of its range, with the largest birds on Spitsbergen. Adult ♂♂ in the Canadian Arctic and W Greenland have bright yellow and relatively short frontal lobes. The lobes are rather mustard-yellow to olive-grey, longer and slightly round-tipped in birds from SE Greenland, and even more clearly so in Iceland and Svalbard[928]. The shape and colour of the frontal lobes and bill vary individually within *borealis*, with more birds similar to *mollissima* in the east of the range. The feathering at the base of the bill is moderately long, narrow and barely round-tipped, usually not reaching the nostrils (vs. *dresseri* and *mollissima*). The head has a rather characteristic shape, with a taller and flat crown, forming sharper angles with the nape and forehead (which appears steeper). The longest scapulars form visible 'sails' on the back, which is a useful distinction from *mollissima*, whatever the plumage. In addition, the lower edge of the black eye-band is generally straight and the breast tinged pale pink[426]. ♀♀ hardly differ in plumage, averaging more reddish-brown and more buff in Iceland. However, much variation in the shape and length of the frontal lobes in this taxon makes

the subspecific identification of ♀♀ very difficult or impossible, although the presence of 'sails' is an important feature.

S. m. dresseri. Medium to large (like *mollissima*), with slight clinal variations as between birds of Labrador and those, larger ones, from Maine[837]. Distinguished mainly by its characteristic head and bill profile. The bill seems less massive and thinner tipped, with large and swollen frontal lobes (forehead appears 'bumped' and prolonged by the rounded upper head). Other subspecies show a slight break between the base of culmen and forehead in profile, and thus the head appears more angular. The frontal lobes are long, reaching almost to the eye, the nostrils being located much closer to the tip of the bill than to the lobes. They are also very broad and round-tipped, which is usually sufficient to distinguish this subspecies from all others. The great width of these frontal lobes also decreases the thickness of the black line of feathers underlining them. The feathering at the base of the bill is long, thin and pointed, ending below the nostrils (as in *mollissima*). The bill is dull grey-green, with yellow-green to yellow-orange lobes. Typically, the green patches on the rear cheeks extend as a diffuse band under the black eye-band, a feature shared only by *sedentaria* and *v-nigrum*. The black eye-band tends to taper into a sharper point on the nape than other subspecies[426] and their lower edge appears straight in profile. The scapulars form obvious 'sails' that distinguish it from *mollissima*. These features, especially the shape of the frontal lobes and head profile are visible in the ♂ from first winter onward. They are less pronounced in ♀, but should be sufficient to distinguish *dresseri* from the other taxa in good views. Also note that ♀♀ usually have pale brown plumage barred dark reddish-brown rather than black[928].

S. m. sedentaria. Intermediate between *borealis* and *dresseri* in many respects, but closer to latter[426,771], albeit a little larger. Feathering at the base of the bill rather short and pointed, frontal lobes like those of *dresseri*, but slightly shorter, narrower and less round-tipped, and yellowish (greener in young ♂). The green hue on the neck-sides extends under the black eye-band (however, less than in *dresseri*). Usually, no black 'V' on throat. Adult ♀ in alternate plumage averages greyer (sometimes even silver-grey) and paler than all other subspecies, streaked brown. In basic plumage, more caramel-beige compared to reddish hue of same plumage in other subspecies. However, *borealis* can also show quite grey and pale plumage. Typical females are distinguished by the shape of the frontal lobes and the feathering at the base of the bill, which differ from those of *borealis* and *dresseri* in the same way as the ♂.

S. m. v-nigrum. This large subspecies is well distinguished from the others. Adult ♂ has a long bright orange bill, more yellow-orange at tip. The frontal lobes are short and taper to a sharp point, the proximal edge of the nostril being located approximately halfway between the bill tip and that of the lobe. The thin lobe reveals a broad black line below it (vs. *dresseri*) and the feathering at the base of the bill ends in front of the nostril in a broad rounded tip, very different to *borealis* and *dresseri*. As in the latter, the green on the rear cheeks extends as a diffuse line under the black eye-band. The lower edge of that band forms a smoothly curved and strongly concave line, while it is straighter, horizontal and forms a sharp angle with the black line below the frontal lobe in *dresseri* and *borealis*. The throat has a black 'V', often difficult to see in the field. Obvious 'sails' are normally visible when erect. Finally, note that when the neck is stretched, its shape is characteristic, with the bill often held pointing down. First-winter ♂♂ soon show a characteristic bright yellow bill combined with typical-length frontal lobes and feathering at the base of the bill. The ♀ is the most distinctive of the different taxa, because of its short, sharp frontal lobes, and feathering at the base of the bill forming a very characteristic oval swelling. Its plumage is generally pale beige to pale buff, streaked blackish-brown.

In a European context, *faeroeensis* and *mollissima*, the local subspecies, are probably indistinguishable, at least under field conditions. Recent attention towards eiders in N British Isles has shown that *borealis* regularly occurs in small numbers[427,426], and produced the first W Palearctic record of *dresseri* in Jan 2010[379]. The subspecies *v-nigrum* was observed in Varangerfjord, Norway, in early 2014, for the first time in Europe. Compared to the local taxa, the presence of 'sails' on the back of adult ♂♂ distinguishes it from all other subspecies (present to a lesser extent in young ♂♂ from first winter and in adult ♀♀, but hardly ever in first-winter ♀♀). Checking the head should quickly reveal the yellow-orange bill of an Arctic eider (*v-nigrum* or *borealis*) or the peculiar shape of the frontal lobes of *dresseri*. Note that while detecting *borealis* in W Europe cannot be considered easy, an adult ♂ *v-nigrum* or *dresseri* would be easier to spot within a flock of local eiders. Identification in Europe of a ♀ *v-nigrum* or *dresseri* requires close

examination of the head, but *borealis* probably cannot be identified unless measured.

Identification of the various taxa in a North American context has been discussed in detail, by Mendall[837,838] and Palmer[945], who reported intergradation between *dresseri* and *borealis* on the coast of Labrador and between *sedentaria* and *borealis* in NW Hudson Bay. Much rarer mixed pairs have been reported between *v-nigrum* and *borealis*[817]. However, among the three subspecies in E North America, Mendall estimated at 95% those birds (all sexes and ages) that can be identified with a satisfactory degree of certainty, on the basis of measurements. It seems that the various North American taxa are all occasionally seen outside their respective ranges, as evidenced by reports of *v-nigrum* in Minnesota[316] or *borealis* at Point Barrow, Alaska. A lack of green under the black eye-band points to *borealis* while, apart from intermediate individuals, *v-nigrum*, *dresseri* and *borealis* are sufficiently distinctive to be identified outside their respective ranges, even ♀♀, if conditions permit. An out-of-range observation of *sedentaria* would be more difficult to confirm, due to its variability and the occurrence of intermediates.

MEASUREMENTS and MASS In all subspecies and for all measurements, ♂ is *c*.10–15% larger than ♀.

S. m. mollissima. ♂: wing chord 289–315 (304, *n*=20), tail 90–104 (96, *n*=17), bill 53–61 (57.2, *n*=22), tarsus 52–57 (54.2, *n*=21), mass in summer 1,384–2,800 (2,218, *n*=22), mass in winter 1,965–2,875 (2,315, *n*=22); ♀: wing chord 286–312 (301, *n*=21), tail 90–98 (94.7, *n*=21), bill 51–59 (54.4, *n*=23), tarsus 50–56 (52.8, *n*=23), mass in summer 1,192–2,895 (1,915, *n*=32), mass in winter 1,864–2,595 (2142, *n*=18)[267].

S. m. faeroeensis. ♂: wing chord 260–284 (270, *n*=22), bill 48–56 (49.4, *n*=22); ♀: wing chord 257–271 (264, *n*=7), bill 45–50 (48.0, *n*=7); mass in summer 1,703–2,223 (1847, *n*=6)[267].

S. m. borealis. ♂: wing chord 284–302 (291, *n*=15), bill 47–56 (51.1, *n*=17), tarsus 48–53 (50.2, *n*=17), mass in summer 1,560–2,710 (2,000, *n*=12); ♀: wing chord 278–287 (282, *n*=5), bill 46–52 (47.6, *n*=5), tarsus 47–51 (49.1, *n*=5); mass in summer, E Greenland 1,575–2,165 (1,810, *n*=11), mass in summer, Southampton I, Canada 1,300–2,100 (1,648, *n*=28)[267,463]. ♂ (*n*=71): wing chord 272–297 (adult) and 265–288 (juvenile), tail 81–95, bill depth at proximal end of nostrils 18.6–20.5, bill length from proximal end of nostrils 34–42, tarsus 48–54.

♀ (*n*=86): wing chord 261–289 (adult) and 254–280 (juvenile), tail 76–91, bill depth at proximal end of nostrils 19.7–22.2, bill length from proximal end of nostrils 33–41, tarsus 47–53[1014]. Adult ♂ (*n*=26): bill from tip to end of right frontal lobe 64–71.5 (68.23), bill length from proximal end of nostrils 27.5–36.0 (32.4), frontal lobe from proximal end of nostrils 17–22 (18.87). Adult ♀ (*n*=86): bill from tip to end of right frontal lobe 59–71 (63.40), bill length from proximal end of nostrils 22.5–32.5 (28.27), frontal lobe from proximal end of nostrils 13.5–21.0 (17.12)[838].

S. m. dresseri. ♂: wing chord 287–300 (293, *n*=12), bill 56–60 (57,8, *n*=12), tarsus 51–55 (52,7, *n*=12), mass in summer 1,700–2,450 (*n*=119); ♀: wing chord 274–298 (282, *n*=12), bill 49–53 (50.8, *n*=12), tarsus 49–53 (50.7, *n*=12); mass in summer 1,850–2,560 (*n*=143)[945]. ♂ (*n*=37): wing chord 279–299 (adult) and 271–290 (juvenile), tail 82–96, bill depth at proximal end of nostrils 16.9–20.8, bill length from proximal end of nostrils 34–39, tarsus 49–55. ♀ (*n*=45): wing chord 268–288 (adult) and 260–280 (juvenile), tail 78–92, bill depth at proximal end of nostrils 16.6–20.4, bill length from proximal end of nostrils 31–36, tarsus 47–53[1014]. Adult ♂ (*n*=49): bill from tip to end of right frontal lobe 75–90 (81.96), bill length from proximal end of nostril 40–51 (45.12), frontal lobe from proximal end of nostrils 23.0–34.5 (28.03). Immature ♂ (*n*= 38): bill from tip to end of right frontal lobe 69–86 (78.12), bill length from proximal end of nostrils 35–46 (41.37), frontal lobe from proximal end of nostrils 19–32 (24.08). Adult ♀ (*n*=163): bill from tip to end of right frontal lobe 68–80 (72.66), bill length from proximal end of nostrils 32.0–41.5 (36.96), frontal lobe from proximal end of nostrils 17.5–27.0 (22.16)[838].

S. m. sedentaria. ♂: wing chord 305–315 (311, *n*=5), bill 55–60 (57.8, *n*=5), mass in summer 2,200–2,350 (2,276, n=4); ♀: wing chord 293–325 (303, *n*=18), bill 47–60 (51.5, *n*=18), mass in summer 1,680–2,500 (*n*=18)[463]. ♂ (*n*=30): wing chord 296–320 (adult) and 289–315 (juvenile), tail 89–100, bill depth at proximal end of nostrils 19.1–21.0, bill length from proximal end of nostrils 36–40, tarsus 49–56. ♀ (*n*=46): wing chord 285–315 (adult) and 278–305 (juvenile), tail 85–97, bill depth at proximal end of nostrils 18.7–20.6, bill length from proximal end of nostrils 34–37, tarsus 48–55[1014]. Adult ♂ (*n*=11): bill from tip to end of right frontal lobe 75–82 (78.23), bill length from proximal end of nostrils 38–44 (40.96), frontal lobe from proximal end of nostrils 20.0–24.5 (22.82). Adult ♀ (*n*=22):

bill from tip to end of right frontal lobe 67.5–74.0 (70.48), bill length from proximal end of nostrils 31–39 (34.80), frontal lobe from proximal end of nostrils 19–23 (20.07)[838]. Using comparable methodology, significant differences were found between populations of E & W Hudson Bay[1082], with head and tarsi longer in eastern populations, and bill (from nostrils) shorter. Measurements as follows for eastern populations. Adult ♂ (*n*=10): bill from tip to end of right frontal lobe: 79.7 (±3.3), bill length from proximal end of nostrils 40.5 (±2.7), tarsus 68.6 (±1.3). Adult ♀ (*n*=30): bill from tip to end of right frontal lobe: 71.4 (±2.8), bill length from proximal end of nostrils 34 (±2.0), tarsus 66.4 (±2.0). For populations of W Hudson Bay. Adult ♂ (*n*=9): bill from tip to end of right frontal lobe 82.8 (±2.3), bill length from proximal end of nostril 45.3 (±2.2), tarsus 66.2 (±2.0). Adult ♀ (*n*=79): bill from tip to end of right frontal lobe 71 (±2.4), bill length from proximal end of nostrils 35.9 (±1.6), tarsus 62.8 (±2.0).

S. m. v-nigrum. ♂: wing chord 290–315 (303, *n*=20), bill 48–56 (52.7, *n*=20), tarsus 50–55 (52.7, *n*=20); ♀: wing chord 270–295 (289, *n*=13), bill 44–53 (48.9, *n*=13), tarsus 49–54 (51.3, *n*=13)[945]. ♂ (*n*=82): wing chord 292–319 (adult) and 282–309 (juvenile), tail 89–102, bill depth at proximal end of nostrils 16.6–19.8, bill length from proximal end of nostrils 35–41, tarsus 50–57. ♀ (*n*=88): wing chord 281–308 (adult) and 271–298 (juvenile), tail 87–100, bill depth at proximal end of nostrils 16.0–19.1, bill length from proximal end of nostrils 30–37, tarsus 49–55[1014].

Mendall[838] gave bill measurements of birds with intermediate characteristics between *borealis* and *dresseri* Adult ♂ (*n*=10): bill from tip to end of right frontal lobe 66–73 (70.95), bill length from proximal end of nostrils 31.0–34.5 (33.0), frontal lobe from proximal end of nostrils 18–22 (20.5). Adult ♀ (*n*=47): bill from tip to end of right frontal lobe 62–72 (66.40), bill length from proximal end of nostrils 27.5–36.0 (31.48), frontal lobe from proximal end of nostrils 14–23 (18.25).

VOICE Song of ♂ an impressive very low moaning cooing, *oh-aaoow-hooo*, the middle syllable being loudest and higher pitched, usually issued by flocks of ♂♂ during courtship, including at night, when audible far away over calm water. Simultaneously, ♀♀ give a hoarse, low cackling, usually of 3–5 notes, *gok-gok-gok-gok*, continuously emitted during courtship, or when alarmed.

MOULT Complex alternate moult strategy, similar to King Eider (which see). Pre-formative moult in Oct–Mar. First pre-alternate moult in May–Aug, sometimes much reduced. Second pre-basic moult occurs earlier than in adult, completed Oct–Nov. Definitive pre-alternate moult between mid-Jun and early Aug in ♂♂, although varies according to latitude in ♂, and apparently even more in ♀, Mar–Apr in south and until May in north. Definitive pre-basic moult between mid-Jul and late Aug in ♂, c.1 month later in ♀ and earlier in non-breeders. Completed Nov–Dec in ♂, slightly later in ♀, for which Baker[56] indicated moult can be protracted until Mar.

HYBRIDISATION Hybridises regularly with King Eider (which see). Hybrids with other species exceptional in the wild and generally distinctive: Some reports with Common Shelduck *Tadorna tadorna*[722], including in the Netherlands and England, and others with Mallard *Anas platyrhynchos* but Gillham & Gillham mentioned just one ♂ in the wild[439,817]. On one or a few occasions, hybridisation has been reported with Northern Pintail *Anas acuta*[996], Steller's Eider *Polysticta stelleri*[388] (which see) and Goosander *Mergus merganser*[442]. Finally, a ♀ Common Eider paired with a ♂ Velvet Scoter *Melanitta fusca* was mentioned as having three eggs in Iceland, but no information on the outcome[493].

HABITAT and LIFE-CYCLE Many winter close to the breeding sites, but short- to medium-range migrations occur. Almost exclusively coastal, inhabiting rocky coasts, pebble beaches, sandy islets and estuaries. Rarer up to a few kilometres inland[926], but the species regularly nests on some large inland lakes of C Europe, west to France[951]. Nests are preferably sited under low vegetation, small rocks and beach debris, sometimes benefiting from protection of gull colonies[320,459,926], whose nests are sometimes 'usurped' by eiders to lay their own eggs[967]. Can also form dense colonies, especially in far north of range, where sheltered habitats safe from predators are rare. These colonies hold up to 10,000–15,000 birds, in densities of up to 250 nests per ha[267,463] or even 1,500 nests per ha in the Gulf of St. Lawrence, Quebec[492]. Eggs are laid mainly between Apr in south of range and in May–Jun in the north. Most ♂♂ abandon ♀♀ a few days after hatching, and gather with non-breeding immatures at moulting sites. ♀♀ are split between those that raise their offspring alone, and those who entrust their ducklings to crèches in the care of other ♀♀. In their study in Finland, Kilpi *et al.*[687] found that these three categories account for 23%, 31% and 46% of ♀♀, especially depending on their physical condition. Overwintering occurs in the same coastal habitats, especially those well stocked with shellfish. In C Europe, the species' regular presence is permitted by the invasive zebra mussel *Dreissena polymorpha*. In areas where it is abundant, forms very dense rafts at sea.

RANGE and POPULATION Distributed along coasts of N Holarctic, with an estimated population of 3,100,000–3,800,000 individuals[139]. Demographic trends contrasting, some populations being subject to unsustainable heavy hunting for a long-lived species. It is also particularly affected by oil spills and outbreaks of avian cholera[492].

S. m. mollissima. Breeds on coasts of N Europe from British Isles (except Orkney and Shetland), east to Vaygach I and north to Novaya Zemlya. Breeding sporadic/irregular further south, to France, as well as in C Europe (south to Italy). An isolated and largely sedentary population occurs on Ukrainian coast of Black Sea (nearly 1,000 pairs in mid-1990s[36] and 1,800 in the early 2000s[305]). Winters in same regions and slightly further south, more sporadically to Bay of Biscay, N Mediterranean and some lakes in C Europe. Between 1,300,000 and 1,700,000 individuals counted in winter (especially in the Baltic, North Sea and coasts of Norway to Russia). Breeding population estimated at 600,000–785,000 pairs, with a notable increase in the 1970s to 1990s, and currently stable or slightly increasing[139].

S. m. faeroeensis. Total population estimated at 18,000–25,000 individuals, of which 6,000–12,000 in the Faeroes and 12,000–13,500 in Orkney and Shetland[926].

S. m. borealis. Breeds in the Arctic north of *mollissima* and *dresseri* (Franz Josef Land, Svalbard, Iceland, Greenland, west to Queen Elizabeth Is, and south to coast of C Labrador, Canada). Disperses and winters usually north to pack ice and further south on coasts of Labrador, Newfoundland and Gulf of St. Lawrence, mainly on the Mingan Is. Rarer south to British Isles and NE USA. Breeding populations estimated at 200,000 pairs for Nunavik and Nunavut in Canadian Arctic[492], 15,000–25,000 pairs in Greenland, 200,000–350,000 in Iceland and 13,500–27,500 pairs on Svalbard[139]. Estimates of wintering populations sometimes contradictory: 350,000–630,000 in Greenland and 100,000–1,000,000 in Iceland[139], but 30,000–300,000 for Greenland, 600,000–900,000 for Iceland, 40,000–80,000 for Svalbard[926], and total population 1,450,000 individuals[305]. An estimate was also made for wintering populations of E Canada and Greenland, of 400,000–500,000 birds[1165]. Overall declining, especially the Greenlandic population[502,840].

S. m. dresseri. Breeds from E Labrador, SE Quebec, New Brunswick, Nova Scotia to Maine and further south. Range meets *borealis* in the north. Regular in winter south to New Jersey, with vagrants even further south. Population estimated at 280,000 birds wintering in E Canada and 57,000 in NE USA (mostly Maine and Massachusetts)[1165], and just over 100,000 breeding pairs, including 32,000 in St. Lawrence estuary, 3,200 pairs in Newfoundland, 8,800 in Labrador, 10,000 on coasts of NE Quebec, 10,000 in New Brunswick, 15,000 in Nova Scotia, 28,000 in Maine and 200 in Massachusetts[492].

S. m. sedentaria. Restricted to Hudson Bay and James Bay, Canada, north-west to near Chesterfield Inlet, where intergrades with *borealis*. Winters mainly in open water west of Belcher Is and along coast of W Quebec. Population estimated at 200,000 individuals, following heavy losses during winter 1991–92[1165], while another estimate is of 75,000 pairs[492].

S. m. v-nigrum. Breeds along E Siberian Arctic coast from near the Lena River, New Siberian Is, in N Pacific (northern third of Kamchatka Peninsula), east to Kodiak I, and north along coast of Alaska and Canada to the Boothia Peninsula, Nunavut and southern and western coasts of Victoria and Banks Is. Winters in ice-free areas of Bering Sea, with major concentrations off the Chukchi Peninsula, Russia[1165]. Overall population estimated at 100,000 birds[1165], or 150,000 birds of which 80,000 in Canada, 25,000 in Alaska and 20,000 in E Russia[1095], and 130,000–200,000 birds[858]. The most recent census is of 38,000–53,000 birds in Alaska[1331]. Until the 1960s, bred on coasts of S & SE Alaska, including Homer Spit. Decreased sharply, with a decline of 50.6% between 1995 and 2008[1042] in Bathurst Inlet, Nunavut, where one-quarter of Canadian eiders breed. Same trend for birds migrating off Barrow Point, Alaska

(breeding in Beaufort Sea and Arctic Canada): 156,081 in 1976, vs. 72,606 in 1996[1245] and 115,000 and 110,000 in 2003 and 2004[1019]. The population of Yukon-Kuskokwim Delta and W Beaufort Sea, following decline of 50–90% in 1957–92[823], now appears stable at a low level[980] or is slightly increasing[280,1019,1364].

CAPTIVITY Quite rarely kept in captivity for ornament, like many sea ducks, except in a few specialised collections, because they require special conditions, care and feeding.

REFERENCES Ardamatskaya (2001)[36]; Baker *et al.* (1997)[52]; Baker (1993)[56]; BirdLife International (2004)[139]; Brewster (1885)[185]; Cramp & Simmons (1977)[268]; Dau & Larned (2005)[280]; Delany & Scott (2006)[305]; Dickerman & Lee (1961)[316]; Dickson *et al.* (2009)[319]; Donehower & Bird (2008)[320]; Farelly & Charles (2010)[379]; Forsman (1995)[388]; Garner & Millington (2010)[426]; Garner *et al.* (2008)[427]; Gillham & Gillham (1996)[439]; Gillham & Gillham (2000)[442]; Götmark (1989)[459]; Goudie *et al.* (2000)[463]; Groupe conjoint de travail sur la gestion de l'Eider à duvet (2004)[492]; Gudmundsson (1932)[493]; Hansen (2002)[502]; Hanssen *et al.* (2006)[511]; Hanssen *et al.* (2008)[512]; Kilpi *et al.* (2001)[687]; Lack (1974)[722]; Lehikoinen *et al.* (2010)[742]; Livezey (1995)[771]; Lock (1986)[780]; Madge & Burn (1988)[794]; McCarthy (2006)[817]; McCracken *et al.* (2006)[823]; Mendall (1980)[837]; Mendall (1986)[838]; Merkel (2004)[840]; Miyabayashi & Mundkur (1999)[858]; Norton (1897)[916]; Ogilvie & Young (1998)[928]; Ogilvie *in* Kear (2005)[926]; Palmer (1976)[945]; Paul & Crouzier (2009)[951]; Perry (1982)[967]; Petersen & Flint (2002)[980]; Pitt (1944)[996]; Pyle (2008)[1014]; Quakenbush *et al.* (2009)[1019]; Raven & Dickson (2009)[1049]; Robertson *et al.* (2001)[1082]; Rose & Scott (1997)[1095]; Sea Duck Joint Venture (2004)[1165]; Smalley (1907)[1207]; Sonsthagen (2006)[1224]; Sonsthagen *et al.* (2007)[1225]; Sonsthagen *et al.* (2011)[1226]; Suydam *et al.* (2000)[1245]; Tenovuo & Tenovuo (1983)[1259]; Tiedemann & Noer (1998)[1264]; Walton *et al.* (2012)[1331]; Wilson *et al.* (2007)[1364].

473. *S. m. borealis*, adult ♂ (definitive basic). Svalbard, Jun (Vincent Legrand).

474. *S. m. borealis*, adult ♂ (definitive basic). Iceland, Apr (Yann Kolbeinsson).

475. *S. m. borealis*, adult ♂ (definitive basic); note small 'sails', usually absent in nominate race. Iceland, Feb (Yann Kolbeinsson).

476. *S. m. borealis*, adult ♀ (definitive alternate). Iceland, Jun (Yann Kolbeinsson).

477. *S. m. borealis*, adult ♀ (definitive alternate), showing rather small bill with rounded feathers at its base, thus head somewhat like ♀ King Eider *S. spectabilis*. Svalbard, Jun (Vincent Legrand).

478. *S. m. dresseri*, adult ♂ (definitive basic); note distinctive head and bill shape of this subspecies. Quebec, Canada, Apr (Mikaël Jaffré).

479. *S. m. dresseri*, adult ♂ (definitive alternate); white upperwing and tertials typical of adult, whereas at same time most second-calendar-year birds have much more advanced basic plumage. New York, USA, Nov (Sébastien Reeber).

480. *S. m. dresseri*, second-winter ♂ (second basic); note blackish tips to tertials and dull bill coloration at this age, while the lobes are already distinctive in this subspecies, as is green tinge extending below eye. New York, USA, Nov (Sébastien Reeber).

481. *S. m. dresseri*, first-winter ♂ (first basic/formative), with some black or white formative feathers visible (♂), while dark tertials distinguish this age from any other. New York, USA, Nov (Sébastien Reeber).

482. *S. m. dresseri*, adult ♀ (definitive alternate/definitive basic). New York, USA, Nov (Sébastien Reeber).

483. *S. m. faeroeensis*, adult ♂ (definitive basic); compared to nominate, note marginally shorter head and bill, especially noticeable on the lobes. Faeroe Is, May (Silas Olofson).

484. *S. m. faeroeensis*, adult ♂ (definitive basic). Faeroe Is, May (Silas Olofson).

485. *S. m. mollissima*, adult ♂ (definitive basic). Norway, Jun (Sébastien Reeber).

486. *S. m. mollissima*, adult ♂ (definitive basic). Sweden, Apr (Johannes Rydström).

487. *S. m. mollissima*, group; in winter, eiders often form compact rafts at sea. Norway, Feb (Tormod Amundsen/Biotope).

488. *S. m. mollissima*, adult ♂ (definitive alternate); note unique combination of mostly dark body and white upperwing and tertials, which age/sex this bird. Netherlands, Oct (Rick Van der Weijde).

489. *S. m. mollissima*, adult ♀ (definitive basic); note two white wingbars at this age. Norway, Feb (Tormod Amundsen/Biotope).

490. *S. m. mollissima*, adult ♀ (definitive alternate); like other ♀ *Somateria*, this plumage is paler, usually greyer, the tertials being the most coloured part. Norway, Jun (Sébastien Reeber).

491. *S. m. mollissima*, juvenile (first basic). Italy, Oct (Stefano Guiducci).

492. *S. m. mollissima*, first-winter ♂ (formative); pre-formative moult is variable and lasts until late winter, producing wide range of appearance, but always has dark tertials. Netherlands, Dec (Rick Van der Weijde).

493. *S. m. mollissima*, first-winter ♂ (formative). Scotland, Mar (Dennis Morrison).

494. *S. m. mollissima*, first-summer ♀ (first alternate); note reduced scapular area and juvenile wing (brown, worn, no white wingbars) and tertials (short, straight, brown and worn). Norway, Jun (Sébastien Reeber).

495. *S. m. mollissima*, second-winter ♂ (second basic); much like adult ♂, but has blackish tertial tips. France, Dec (Vincent Palomares).

496. *S. m. v-nigrum*, adult ♂ (definitive basic), showing distinctive bill colour, short pointed lobes, rounded feathering at bill base and green colour extending well below eye of this race. Captivity, Nov (Sébastien Reeber).

497. *S. m. v-nigrum*, adult ♂ (definitive basic). Alaska, USA, Jun (William Price).

498. *S. m. v-nigrum*, adult ♂ (definitive basic). Alaska, USA, Jul (Bob Steele).

499. *S. m. v-nigrum*, adult ♀ (definitive basic); the short lobes and round feathering at the bill base impart a very distinctive appearance to this subspecies. Captivity, Nov (Sébastien Reeber).

500. *S. m. sedentaria*, adult ♀ (definitive alternate). Hudson Bay, Canada, Jul (Philippe J. Dubois).

501. *S. m. v-nigrum*, adult ♀ (definitive alternate). Chukotka, Russia, Jul (Anders Blomdahl).

502. *S. m. sedentaria*, adult ♀ (definitive alternate). Hudson Bay, Canada, Jul (Mikaël Jaffré).

HARLEQUIN DUCK
Histrionicus histrionicus

Plate 59

TAXONOMY *Anas histrionicus* Linnaeus, 1758, *Syst. Nat.*, edn. 10, p. 127. Within the Mergini, Harlequin Duck constitutes a monotypic genus and forms a clade including the eiders *Somateria* and *Polysticta*. Within this clade, *Histrionicus* diverged first and is thus considered sister of a monophyletic group including all other species[771]. Weak geographic variation (see below).

IDENTIFICATION Usually unmistakable given plumage, behaviour and habitats. Definitive basic and formative plumages of ♂ are typically variegated, but other plumages are uniformly dark.

PLUMAGES Strong sexual dimorphism from first winter onwards. Complex alternate moult strategy (two plumages per definitive cycle, three in first cycle). Ageing relatively easy until middle of first winter (♂) and possible until end of subsequent summer (♂ and ♀). A rather small sea duck, with a tall rounded head, a small bill and a rather long tail. Often holds head and neck slightly raised in flight, which is almost always over water, very rarely over land, even avoiding islands, dams and rocks.

Adult ♂

Definitive basic plumage (Sep–Oct/Jun–Jul). Head, neck and breast dark blue-grey with large white semi-circular patch at the base of the bill extending as an orange to reddish line on crown-sides. Four other characteristic white patches: the first, small and round on the rear cheeks, the second, oval, vertical and elongated, on the neck-sides, and the last two, long and framed in black, separating the neck from the breast and the breast from the flanks. Black forehead continues as longitudinal black and yellow-ochre stripes on the crown. Iris dark reddish-brown. Bill small, dark grey basally, becoming pale blue-grey at tip, with nail and around nostrils whitish. Fore flanks and belly dark blue-grey, with broad reddish patches covering part of the centre and rear flanks. Lower belly and undertail blackish with two round white spots on the basal tail-sides. Mantle blue-grey, merging into black back, rump and uppertail. Rectrices blackish, long and pointed. Inner (smaller) scapulars black, outer scapulars slightly elongated and pointed, white, forming a broad longitudinal line just above the folded wing. The longest tertial is blackish with a broad white line along the shaft and the

outermost tertials broad and truncated, largely white on the inner webs with clear black line on the inner fringes. Upperwing entirely blackish, with soft bluish or purple sheen on coverts and secondaries (except outermost 1–3 secondaries). Some round white spots, variable in size, on 2–3 inner greater and 1–3 central median coverts. Underwing all dark, blackish lesser coverts and secondaries, with more silvery highlights on tips of median and greater coverts, on lesser coverts and at base of outer primaries. Legs grey with black webs.

Definitive alternate plumage (Jun–Jul/Sep–Oct). Like definitive basic plumage of ♀ in its uniform dark brown appearance. Distinguished by head and mantle blacker with bluish sheen, white patches at base of bill often smaller but more clear-cut and contrasting, and white areas of retained basic or alternate tertials (the latter narrower and more pointed, with smaller patches). Basic upperwing retained, with blue gloss and white spots (usually worn) on median and greater coverts. Belly and rear body blackish. Many ♂♂ retain some typical basic feathers (traces of white on breast, reddish on flanks, etc.).

Adult ♀

Definitive basic plumage (Oct–Nov/May–Jul). Fairly uniformly dark brown, the only noticeable feature being the white face markings. Rather variable in overall colour, some ♀♀ being brown, others darker (blackish head and upperparts) and others more reddish. Head brown with variable white area at base of the bill, reminiscent of ♂, but smaller, more diffuse and partially concealed with pale brown. This patch is often divided by a dark loral stripe and linked to a white crescent underlining the eye. Another round white spot is present on the rear cheeks, which is also more diffuse than in ♂. Some ♀♀ show whitish streaks on the rear head[1080]. Iris brown. Bill like ♂. Chin and foreneck paler brown. Large oval, whitish ventral patch, largely stained brown at sides, and barred pale brown in centre. Upperparts blackish-brown, sometimes with velvety sheen. Breast and flanks paler brown. Back, rump and undertail-coverts dark brown to blackish. Tertials broad, the two outermost truncated at tip, entirely blackish with possibly a trace of pale stripe along shaft on inner web. Upperwing blackish-brown (darker on secondary coverts) with slightly paler marks on tips of inner webs to greater coverts, often barely visible. Occasionally, very small pale speckles visible in hand. Underwing like ♂ but lesser coverts more speckled pale. Legs grey with black webs.

Definitive alternate plumage (May–Jul/Oct–Nov). Seemingly identical to basic plumage, but described as slightly more slate-grey[945].

Juvenile

First basic plumage (until Sep–Jan). Similar to basic plumage of adult ♀, but slightly more grey-brown, duller and paler overall, especially head and upperparts. Distinction from adult ♀ depends on close check of the belly, tertials, rectrices and some other more subjective features. The pale belly shows retained juvenile feathers, which produce neat pale brown-grey streaking instead of the more roughly mottled belly of ♀. The pale belly is usually better demarcated in young birds. The tertials are shorter and pointed, brown and quickly worn at tips, with a vague pale stripe on the rachis[224], more marked in the young ♂ than ♀[1014]. Upperwing is brown, visibly paler than adult ♀, the coverts and secondaries being narrower and quickly worn at tips. The secondaries show no sheen. The rectrices are also browner than in adults, with notched tips. Pale patches on head more or less concealed by brownish tones. Breast feathers fringed pale, producing a finely streaked appearance. The legs are grey tinged yellowish, brownish or olive.

First-winter ♂

Formative plumage (Oct–Jan/Jun–Jul). Acquisition of formative plumage is slow and protracted, the first signs of adult plumage often appearing as early as Oct (but sometimes much later), especially on the head. Following pre-formative moult, more similar to adult, but a little duller (brown tones to blue moulted feathers). Distinguished mainly by retained juvenile parts: belly with broad whitish oval patch finely streaked grey-brown (very different from adult) and contrast between new and retained feathers on back and rump. Upperwing like juvenile. Some to all tertials moulted (formative tertials close to those of adult). The rectrices are also a good ageing character, as at least most are still juvenile, brown, worn and notched at tips. Among more subtle features, the white patches on face and neck can show more brownish flecks and ill-defined black contours. Formative scapulars form a white area much less extensive than on adult. Pre-formative moult sometimes less extensive, leading to a more variegated appearance with juvenile feathers[1209].

First-winter ♀

Formative plumage (Oct–Jan/Jun–Jul). Like adult ♀. Age can be determined primarily by presence of juvenile feathers, e.g. the belly, white finely streaked grey-brown, contrasting markedly with the moulted lower flanks. Note also a generally clear contrast between the moulted mantle and scapulars (blackish-brown with pale sheen) and the juvenile wing, paler and duller brown. Adult ♀ shows no noticeable contrast between these parts. The juvenile tertials show no pale area along the shaft, are shorter, paler and frayed at tips. The tertial- and secondary coverts are narrower, plain and worn at tips. The juvenile rectrices are heavily worn in late winter and spring.

First-summer ♂

First alternate plumage (Jun–Jul/Sep–Oct). First pre-alternate moult seems limited in extent, and usually does not include retained juvenile feathers (wings, belly, and all or part of back, tertials and rectrices), producing stronger contrast until second pre-basic moult (especially between wing and body).

First-summer ♀

First alternate plumage (Jun–Jul/Sep–Oct). As in ♂, first pre-alternate moult seems limited and does not generally involve retained juvenile feathers. With wear, the contrasts described for formative plumage are emphasised.

Second-winter ♂

Second basic plumage (Sep–Oct/Jun–Jul). The question of a second basic plumage distinguishable from definitive basic plumage in ♂ has often been suggested[267,309,945,1080]. Some show reddish flanks washed brown, possibly due to individual variation or related to the general condition during previous pre-basic moult[1084].

GEOGRAPHIC VARIATION Separate subspecies have been named for populations of the Pacific (*H. h. pacificus*) and Atlantic (*H. h. histrionicus*) respectively[193], but many believe that the evidence to support this treatment is insufficient[347,945,1014,1080]. Pacific birds have been described as being slightly smaller with a stronger bill, more reddish on the crown-sides and smaller reddish patches on the flanks (adult ♂ in basic plumage), but these differences are masked by variability between individuals and/or populations. Many allopatric populations exist with very limited gene flow between them, especially as immature fidelity to moulting and wintering sites is 89–93%, rising to 96–98% in adults in British Columbia[1060]. Studies of the level of differentiation between populations in Prince William Sound and Kodiak I[725], or Washington, Oregon and Montana[725] or populations in NW Atlantic[1080,1085] all uncovered subtle variation, indicating a probably still low level of divergence[1085].

MEASUREMENTS and MASS ♂ and adult slightly larger than ♀ and young, respectively. SW Alberta, Canada. Adult ♂ (*n*=82): wing chord 188–217 (adult, 205) and 157–195 (juvenile, 182, *n*=32), culmen 24.3–30.4 (27.6), tarsus 36.2–40.2 (38.2), mass **breeding** 520–680 (610); adult ♀ (n=63): wing chord 172–211 (196), culmen 23.2–27.8 (25.4), tarsus 34.3–39.2 (36.6), mass **with ducklings** 480–571 (517); ♀ juvenile (*n*=44): 145–193 (177)[1080]. NW Montana. Adult ♂ (*n*=12): wing chord 180–201 (195.7), tail 92–106 (99.1), culmen 25.7–29.9 (28.8), tarsus 35–42 (38.1), mass **breeding** 660–710 (684.2); adult ♀ (*n*=7): wing chord 181–198 (187.0), tail 84–93 (87.0), culmen 24.9–28.0 (26.3), tarsus 36–40 (38.1), mass **breeding** 545–660 (626.5, *n*=10)[714]. Isle au Haut, Maine. Adult ♂: wing chord 181–216 (adult, 206, *n*=57) and 191–202 (juvenile, 196, *n*=12), tail 91–110 (101, n=64), culmen 24.1–27.9 (26.2, *n*=64), tarsus 34.8–42.9 (38.4, *n*=62), mass **breeding** 520–760 (672, *n*=63); ♀: wing chord 177–210 (194, *n*=49), tail 72–96 (84.0, *n*=48), culmen 23.2–26.8 (25.1, *n*=53), tarsus 34.0–41.5 (37.2, *n*=51), mass **breeding** 500–660 (592, *n*=52)[1080]. ♂ (*n*=100): wing chord 193–210 (adult) and 183–200 (juvenile), culmen 25–31, bill depth at tip of forehead feathers 14.5–16.9, tail 90–107, tarsus 35–42; ♀ (*n*=100): wing chord 182–201 (adult) and 173–191 (juvenile), culmen 23–29, bill depth at tip of forehead feathers 13.1–15.4, tail 78–89, tarsus 34–40[1014]. A complete set of biometric data from several North American localities was presented by Robertson & Goudie[1080].

VOICE ♂ gives different high-pitched squeaky and tinny calls during courtship, e.g. *hig hig hig* or *hik-heeek* ..., which are repeated more or less rapidly, at varying pitch and volume, depending on level of excitement. Choruses of several ♂♂ in courtship sound like toys. ♂ also sometimes utters a similar sound in flight, but more reminiscent of a low bark. ♀ is even quieter, but produces a fast, nervous *ek-ek-ek-ek*, or a soft *gook*.

MOULT Complex alternate strategy. Pre-formative moult occurs between Sep and Mar–Apr, is quite variable in extent and timing, depending especially on hatch date (breeding season protracted and varies regionally)[1209]. It has also been suggested that formative plumage is more adult-like in captive birds than in the wild[1080]. This moult includes a variable number of body feathers (smaller proportion on belly and back), but not the wings. Up to three tertials are moulted[224,1014], and sometimes two to several central rectrices, rarely all[1014]. First pre-alternate moult is limited, in early summer, with usually a small number of body feathers. Definitive pre-basic moult starts late Jul to mid-Aug in most ♂♂ and non-breeding ♀♀[6,255], and 4–6 weeks later in ♀♀ that breed successfully, and is complete, beginning with the wings and tail, and ends early Oct for the earliest adult ♂♂ and Nov in most ♀♀[1080]. Definitive pre-alternate moult varies depending on breeding timing[1083,1080] and starts late Jun or early Jul in Alaska and SW British Columbia[255,336] but up to one month later in Labrador[6]. It includes some body feathers, sometimes up to 4 tertials, occasionally some inner upperwing-coverts and none to a few rectrices[1014].

HYBRIDISATION One of the few Holarctic Anseriformes for which no hybridisation has been reported in the literature, either in the wild or in captivity.

HABITAT and LIFE-CYCLE Spring migration occurs mostly between early Apr and mid-May, possibly partly overland, although there does not appear to be any direct evidence of this[1080]. Depending on locality (altitude, latitude) eggs are laid between mid-Apr and late Jul (late Apr–late May in British Columbia[1080], mid-May to late Jul in Newfoundland, first half of Jun in Iceland[347]). For nesting, the species inhabits streams and rivers with fast, turbulent flow, and calmer areas to rest and feed. ♂♂ abandon ♀♀ shortly after laying to form small flocks, often at coastal moulting sites, despite pair-bond being generally life-long[1210]. Immature ♂♂ often migrate north but do not usually reach the rivers used for breeding[347]. ♀♀ head to moulting sites with their ducklings and moult their remiges later. Autumn migration involves moving to the nearest suitable coastal area, often descending streams (♀♀ sometimes swimming with their broods[274,336,1061]). In non-breeding season, frequently found along exposed rocky shores, in small flocks that are often very compact at rest. Often feeds among rocks or artificial piers subject to the action of waves and tides. Frequently perches on rocks to rest.

RANGE and POPULATION Several disjunct breeding populations. Those of Greenland and Iceland winter along nearby coasts, whereas the rather small E

Canadian population winters on the Atlantic coast, south to New Jersey. Populations of E Russia winter between the Aleutians and Honshu, Japan. The W American breeding population winters along the Pacific coast from the Aleutians to Oregon (few in California). Rare or occasional elsewhere in USA (Great Lakes, Gulf of Mexico, etc.) and in C Canada. Population estimated at 1,800 individuals in NE America, 8,250–16,500 in Greenland, 9,000–15,000 in Iceland, 25,000–100,000 in E Asia and 150,000–250,000 in NW North America[1348], or a global population of 190,000–380,000 individuals[305]. Trends stable or unknown among different populations, but increasing in E North America[1348]. Hunting and construction of hydroelectric dams have a negative impact locally[347].

CAPTIVITY Rarely kept in captivity, although slightly more frequently offered for sale recently, but prices generally remain prohibitive. Rarely bred, probably because of its preference for cold, clear, flowing and sufficiently deep water. Nevertheless, some observations in NW Europe are considered to relate to escapes from captivity.

REFERENCES Adams (1999)[6]; Bengtson (1972)[92]; Boertmann & Mosbech (2002)[157]; Brodeur *et al.* (2002)[190]; Brooks (1915)[193]; Brown (1998)[198]; Carney (1992)[224]; Chubbs *et al.* (2001)[231]; Cooke *et al.* (1997)[255]; Cramp & Simmons (1977)[268]; Crowley (1994)[274]; Delany & Scott (2006)[305]; Dementiev & Gladkov (1967)[309]; Dzinbal (1982)[336]; Einarsson *in* Kear (2005)[347]; Iverson & Esler (2006)[623]; Kuchel (1977)[714]; Lanctot *et al.* (1999)[725]; Livezey (1995)[771]; Palmer (1976)[945]; Pyle (2008)[1014]; Regehr (2011)[1060]; Regehr *et al.* (2001)[1061]; Robert *et al.* (2008)[1078]; Robertson & Goudie (1999)[1080]; Robertson *et al.* (1997)[1083]; Robertson *et al.* (1998)[1084]; Robertson *et al.* (2008)[1085]; Smith *et al.* (1998)[1209]; Smith *et al.* (2000)[1210]; Thomas *et al.* (2008)[1261]; Wetlands International (2014)[1348]; Wright & Clarkson (1998)[1375].

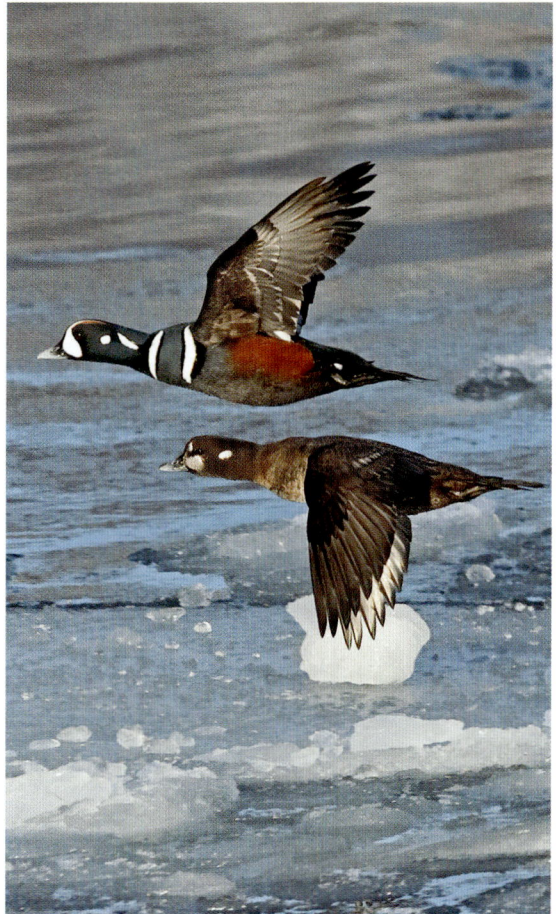

503. Pair (definitive basic). Japan, Feb (Mark Curley).

504. Adult ♂ (definitive basic). Iceland, Jun (Otto Plantema).

505. Adult ♂ (definitive basic). New Jersey, USA, Nov (Sébastien Reeber).

506. Adult ♀ (definitive basic/definitive alternate). Iceland, Jun (Seraf van der Putten).

507. First-summer ♀ (first alternate); like adult ♀, but has heavily worn retained juvenile feathers (wing, tertials, some rectrices, etc.). Iceland, Jul (Alain Verneau).

508. First-winter ♂ (formative); initially resembles adult ♀, but young ♂ acquires adult coloration between first winter and subsequent summer. Japan, Feb (Stuart Price).

SURF SCOTER
Melanitta perspicillata

Plate 60

TAXONOMY *Anas perspicillata* Linnaeus, 1758, *Syst. Nat.*, edn. 10, p. 125. The genus *Melanitta* forms a rather tight clade within the Mergini close to the extinct Labrador Duck *Camptorhynchus labradorius*[771]. Depending on taxonomy, this clade comprises 3–6 species: Surf Scoter, which is monotypic, the 'black' scoters (*nigra* and *americana*) and the 'white-winged' scoters (*fusca*, *deglandi* and *stejnegeri*). Within *Melanitta*, Surf Scoter is more closely related to the latter three[771].

IDENTIFICATION Usually not difficult to identify, with most problems arising from the huge distances often involved with observing sea ducks. Their inter- and intra-specific gregariousness means that a 'lost' Surf Scoter in E Asia or W Europe will almost certainly join the local scoters, permitting useful comparisons. In all plumages, Surf Scoter differs from Common and Black Scoters (which are very similar to each other) by its slightly greater size, proportionately larger and more angular head with prominent forehead and continuation via the culmen, thick-based bill, short, thick neck and slightly shorter tail. Diving technique is also useful: Surf Scoter dives from the surface by spreading its wings (like 'white-winged' scoters), while usually both 'black' scoters perform a quick jump above the surface and dive with their wings tight against the body. In the latter species, the birds often exercise their wings or shake water from the plumage, lowering the neck to the surface, in a characteristic posture. In terms of plumage, Common and Black Scoters (adult ♂) are all black without any white, while other plumages exhibit a broad pale patch over the cheeks and throat, very different from Surf Scoter. Differs from the three species of 'white-winged' scoters in being slightly smaller and, moreover, by the absence of large white patches on the tips to the greater coverts and secondaries, which in all three species forms an obvious patch in flight, when flapping its wings on the water or diving with slightly open wings, and even at rest a white bar is often visible. Head shape also differs from Velvet Scoter, but is closer to White-winged and Siberian Scoters.

PLUMAGES Clear sexual dimorphism from first winter onwards. Simple alternate moult strategy (two plumages in the first and definitive cycles). Ageing ♂♂ relatively easy until first summer and possible until second summer in good conditions or in the hand. Ageing ♀♀ harder after second pre-basic moult (second autumn).

Adult ♂

Definitive basic plumage (Nov/Apr). Plumage entirely matt black or has velvety sheen, with a large white patch covering the nape and another on the forehead, not reaching the top of the bill, but extending close to the eyes. Iris white. Bill thick-based and triangular, with black feathering on the upper culmen tapering to a point over the nostrils. Characteristic coloration with distal half yellow, upper culmen reddish and basal sides whitish with a clear-cut and strong black patch with rounded corners. Wings all black, but the remiges appear greyish in flight. Legs bright pinkish-red, sometimes pink or orange, with black webs.

Definitive alternate plumage (Apr–May/Oct–Nov). Pre-alternate moult limited or absent, with little seasonal change in appearance. In summer, the belly generally seems slightly browner and the plumage duller, paler and 'messier'.

Adult ♀

Definitive basic plumage (Nov/Apr). Overall uniform dark grey-brown with remiges appearing slightly paler grey in flight. The only noticeable features are the black crown, cheeks slightly paler grey, a vertical oblong pale patch at the bill base and another round patch or crescent on the ear-coverts. A third whitish patch is sometimes visible on the nape, with the same pattern as ♂ but less well defined (clearer with age?). Iris usually pale grey-brown, sometimes yellowish or pale grey. The paleness of the iris is probably related to age (older than three years?). Bill slightly less swollen basally than in ♂, all dark grey, but slightly paler at the base, with two round, variable, blackish spots on the sides. Nail often tinged yellow-ochre on the sides. Legs orange-yellow to dull yellow-brown with dark marks and webs.

Definitive alternate plumage (Apr–May/Oct-Nov). Pre-alternate moult limited at most, perhaps absent. In summer, appears a little paler, worn and messier. Patches on face often more strongly marked.

Juvenile

First basic plumage (until Nov). Similar to ♀ but browner and paler, with a broad pale brownish oval patch on the belly (black in adult ♀). Facial pattern more pronounced: cheeks paler grey, contrasting more with blackish crown and nape, facial patches whitish larger and more obvious, sometimes even joining under eye. Iris dark brown. Bill dark grey. Legs dull yellowish-brown, webs darker. Sexes identical, but tertials average slightly longer and more curved in young ♂♂[1014].

First-winter/first-summer ♂

Formative plumage (Oct/Jun). Acquisition of formative plumage is slow and protracted, often not completed until the end of the first winter. After the initial stages (Oct–Nov), the bill coloration readily permits sexing. Thereafter, young ♂ shows a succession of intermediate appearances between juvenile and formative plumages, the latter closer to that of adult ♂. Distinguished by being more brown and matt, with a variable number of scattered juvenile feathers on the upperparts, flanks and rear body. The belly is pale, with wear becoming whitish in spring. Tertials often still juvenile, as are a variable number of rectrices, which appear faded and worn by late winter. Moult contrast also evident in the wing, with juvenile secondary coverts contrasting with black formative scapulars, tertial coverts and, often, innermost lesser coverts. Among other features of a young ♂ are the lack of white patch on forehead, vague greyish patch on nape, feathering of upper culmen not reaching above nostrils and bill less intensely coloured with blackish stains on culmen and tomium. The greyish iris gradually becomes whitish by the end of the second calendar year (variable) and the legs, initially dull orange, become pinker or reddish after first summer.

First-winter/first-summer ♀

Formative plumage (Oct/Jun). Similar to adult ♀, but juvenile plumage, initially slightly paler and more grey-brown than adult ♀, tends to fade even more by first summer. Differs from adult ♀ mainly by its pale belly, becoming white in spring. Face pattern slightly paler too, the whitish patches often meeting and strongly demarcated from blackish crown. Iris dark brown in winter, becoming greyish like adult ♀ between first summer and second winter. Bill is on average tinged more olive than adult ♀. In spring of second calendar year, the rectrices, tertials and primaries are mostly or all juvenile, short, narrow, pale and heavily worn.

Second-winter ♂

Second basic plumage (Oct/Sep). Very like definitive basic plumage, but belly generally more brownish,

becoming paler in spring of third year, sometimes with whitish juvenile feathers[1014]. The bill is slightly less swollen at the base than in adult, and marginally less brightly coloured. The black feathering extends slightly less far onto the culmen than adult ♂ (not reaching above nostrils). The white patches on the forehead and nape are smaller and/or partially stained greyish (or even lacking on the forehead).

GEOGRAPHIC VARIATION None.

MEASUREMENTS and MASS ♂ and adult slightly larger than ♀ and young, respectively. ♂ (*n*=21): wing chord 244.0 ± 5.0, culmen 35.8 ± 2.2, tarsus 53.4 ± 2.4, mass 1,059.3 ± 133.7; ♀ (*n*=15): wing chord 228.7 ± 6.0, culmen 38.8 ± 2.2, tarsus 50.7 ± 3.4, mass 985.3 ± 118.6[246]. ♂ (*n*=12): wing chord 233–252 (245), culmen 36–40 (37.0), tail 79–84 (82.0); ♀ (*n*=12): wing chord 215–240 (228), culmen 37–40 (38.8), tail 68–74 (72.0)[945]. ♂: wing chord 240.7 ± 6.7 (*n*=6), culmen 36.6 ± 2.1 (*n*=9), tarsus 53.8 ± 2.7 (*n*=9), tail 78.6 ± 10.2 (*n*=8), mass 1,000 ± 15 (*n*=9); ♀: wing chord 224.4 ± 3.3 (*n*=29), culmen 36.2 ± 1.2 (*n*=29), tarsus 51.5 ± 1.5 (*n*=29), tail 81.2 ± 6.3 (*n*=21), mass 854 ± 24 (*n*=29)[879]. ♂ (*n*=100): wing chord 233–251 (adult) and 225–244 (juvenile), culmen length from proximal end of nostrils 32–37, tail 73–90, tarsus 41–47; ♀ (*n*=100): wing chord 218–235 (adult) and 210–227 (juvenile), culmen length from proximal end of nostrils 27–32, tail 66–82, tarsus 38–45[1014]. Pyle[1014] also gives bill depth at proximal end of nostrils ♂: 20.8–24.7 (adult, three years or more), 19.6–22.1 (immature, 1–2 years) and 18.2–21.3 (juvenile, up to one year old); ♀: 15.1–19.3.

VOICE Usually silent. ♂ gives a *puk*, *pyuk* or *gok* and a quite low whistle, sometimes plaintive-sounding. The wingbeats produce a low whistling, heard most frequently when the birds pursue each other low over the water. ♀♀ gives a raucous croak, *krraaah*, especially at nesting sites.

MOULT Simple alternate strategy (?). The extent of definitive pre-alternate moult is still unclear, described as extensive in older adults of both sexes in spring, with moult almost continuous between Apr and Jan, more active in summer[1138]. Other authors found it limited (neck, back, breast and flanks) or absent[1014]. If it is absent, moult strategy would be complex basic. Pre-formative moult occurs between Oct and Mar–May, appears more extensive in ♂ than in ♀[1012], and includes many feathers of the head and neck, and a variable number on the mantle, back, breast, scapulars and flanks. The rump, upper- and undertail-coverts are largely not replaced, while the lower breast and belly are usually not moulted at all. Occasionally 1–3 tertials and often two (sometimes all) rectrices are replaced[1012]. No pre-alternate moult during first cycle. Definitive pre-basic moult is complete, starts with the wings and occurs in Aug–Nov, continuing possibly at low rate until Jan. Adult ♂♂ arrive first at the moulting sites (departing from Jun), followed by ♀♀ that failed in their breeding attempt (up to one month later) and finally those that raised young[81,1139], which sometimes do not start to moult their wings until Oct.

HYBRIDISATION A hybrid was long ago described with White-winged Scoter[49], but it could have been an aberrant Surf Scoter[697,1142,1273]. Apparently no other cases of hybridisation reported in captivity or in the wild[97,817].

HABITAT and LIFE-CYCLE Migration to breeding grounds occurs between Mar and May. Eggs are laid mainly in Jun–Jul. Breeds from the taiga to the Arctic tundra, on small shallow lakes and ponds (often <20 ha), often slightly acidic with low mineral content, and rocky shores often devoid of tall vegetation[288,1051,1138]. Like eiders, ♂♂ depart nesting sites during incubation, often spending <3 weeks on the nesting grounds[1139]. ♀♀ with broods leave the nest sites after fledging for the moulting sites, usually from mid-Aug. Arrives on wintering grounds from late Sep (especially adult ♂♂ and non-breeders). Overwinters largely in shallow coastal waters, especially with sandy or pebble substrates[462], but also on rocky coasts. Favours areas rich in bivalves. Searches for food even in quite rough seas with high waves, hence its name[1051].

RANGE and POPULATION In addition to mapped range, uncommon but regular visitor to N Gulf of Mexico. Regular visitor to Great Lakes (especially on migration), but rarer elsewhere throughout inland North America. Rare in W Europe (albeit the most frequently reported Nearctic scoter), much rarer in NW Pacific, south to Honshu, Japan. Censuses difficult because all three North American species of scoter form huge mixed flocks often far from the coast: 765,000 birds[1095] in the early 1990s, or >500,000 breeding birds and >1,000,000 in winter more recently[1051], and estimates of 200,000–250,000 in E North America and 150,000–200,000 in W North America[1348]. Between 64,050 and 212,008 birds (mean 147,110) recorded during autumn migration, off Avalon, New Jersey, in 1993–2011[908], and the species also commonly winters north of here. The wide estimate given by Wetlands International[305] (250,000–1,300,000 birds) reflects these uncertainties. Appears to be declining[209,1051,1348], probably mainly because of oil spills and overhunting on the breeding grounds.

CAPTIVITY Very rarely kept and even more rarely bred in captivity, particularly due to the fact that the species requires very special conditions. Very unlikely to escape from captivity.

REFERENCES Baird *et al.* (1884)[49]; Bédard *et al.* (1997)[81]; Bird Hybrids database (2014)[97]; Brown (1992)[194]; Butcher & Niven (2007)[209]; Consortium Gauthier Guillemette-Grebe (1993)[246]; Décarie *et al.* (1995)[288]; Delany & Scott (2006)[305]; Goudie *et al.* (1994)[462]; Iverson *et al.* (2003)[622]; Kolbe (1979)[697]; Livezey (1995)[771]; McCarthy (2006)[817]; Morrier *et al.* (1997)[879]; New Jersey Audubon Society (2014)[908]; Palmer (1976)[945]; Pyle (2008)[1014]; Reed *in* Kear (2005)[1051]; Rose & Scott (1997)[1095]; Savard *et al.* (1998)[1138]; Savard *et al.* (2007)[1139]; Scherrer & Hilsberg (1982)[1142]; Todd (1979)[1273]; Wetlands International (2014)[1348].

509. Adult ♂ (definitive basic). California, USA, Mar (Sébastien Reeber).

510. Adult ♀ (definitive basic). New York, USA, Nov (Sébastien Reeber).

511. Adult pair (definitive basic). New York, USA, Nov (Sébastien Reeber).

512. Adult ♀ (definitive basic). New York, USA, Nov (Sébastien Reeber).

513. First-winter ♀ (first basic/formative); note mix of juvenile and formative feathers, some juvenile rectrices and brown iris. California, USA, Nov (Tom Grey).

514. Second-winter ♂ (second basic); the white forehead is reduced at this age and sometimes absent (as here). California, USA, Nov (Bob Steele).

VELVET SCOTER
Melanitta fusca

Plates 61, 62

TAXONOMY *Anas fusca* Linnaeus, 1758, *Syst. Nat.*, edn. 10, p. 123. Besides *fusca* in W Eurasia, two taxa other related have been described, *deglandi* Bonaparte, 1850, in North America, and *stejnegeri* Ridgway, 1887, in E Asia. Initially considered specifically until Dwight[335], the three taxa were then considered conspecific. More recently, their status has been discussed again, sometimes being treated as three species again[142,428], or to split *fusca* and *deglandi*, the latter including *stejnegeri*[1233]. This position is accepted in Europe, pending additional data that might eventually permit the splitting of *stejnegeri* and *deglandi*[240,273], but all are considered conspecific by the AOU. These three scoters, largely allopatric, can be distinguished on the basis of their appearance, in all ages and sexes, with differences in plumage, bill coloration, head and bill shape, and vocalisations. Clinal variation is unknown, and there is apparently no published report of hybrids between the various taxa, which further argues for their separate treatment[428,548], which has been followed here.

IDENTIFICATION Confusion with Black *M. americana*, Common *M. nigra* and Surf Scoters *M. perspicillata*, the only other uniformly dark or blackish sea ducks, is generally prevented by the large white patch on the secondaries, obvious in flight and also often visible on the folded wing, especially between dives, when the wings are held slightly open (see Surf Scoter). Separation of the three 'white-winged' scoters requires more attention, although adult ♂♂ are fairly easy to identify. With sufficient views, detection of *stejnegeri* or *deglandi* in Europe should not be very difficult, given the pink or reddish bill, distinctive head profile and white eye-patch behind the eye. Similarly, identifying a ♂ *fusca* in North America or E Asia should be rather easy by the partially bright yellow bill. The main distinguishing features of adult ♂♂ are as follows.

- Head shape is very important, the head of *fusca* being rather rounded without salient angles, even if the crown is fairly flat. The forehead/culmen line is regularly curved and slightly concave. In *stejnegeri*, the nape is thicker, the head profile being pear-shaped and regularly curved from the back of the crown (the highest point of the head) to the tip of the bill, with a prominent knob at the base of culmen. In *deglandi* the head is much more angular,

with a tall, slightly bumped forehead (the highest point of the head is above the eye or in front of it) and a square bump at the base of culmen, like 'steps' from the forehead to the bill tip.

- The bill's shape is mainly affected by the basal knob. In *fusca*, it forms a slight bulge, barely salient in the culmen line. In *deglandi*, it is stronger and provides an angular look in profile. The nasal cavity appears oval-shaped or semi-circular in profile (scarcely visible in *fusca* and round in *stejnegeri*). In *stejnegeri*, the knob is more salient in the otherwise oval-shaped profile, and the knob has a small, flattened and often overhanging protuberance, which varies individually and size is probably age-related. In the non-breeding season, the bulge is often less marked in all taxa.

- Bill coloration is also very useful in the field, but requires close scrutiny. *M. fusca* has a yellow-and-black bill, the yellow extending broadly on the sides of the maxilla, and from the base of the knob to the bill tip. In the other two taxa, the bill is black, pink or reddish with a little yellow, but the pattern differs. In *deglandi*, the pinkish-red extends from the orange nail along the maxilla sides, and tapers to a point below the nostrils. The culmen below the knob is whitish, with a small yellow area just below the nostrils. The black bill base extends from the gape along the tomium to the nail (as in *fusca*). In *stejnegeri*, the bill is mainly blackish and orange-red. The black base does not extend along the tomium in full adult ♂♂ (vs. *deglandi*), the red area being outlined by a yellow line along the tomium and is generally obvious at reasonable distance. The distal culmen, just under the bill's knob, is usually white in adults, but may show a variable amount of black, often with a forked pattern encircling the nail.

- The black feathering at the bill base differs significantly between the three taxa in shape and extent. The feathering forms an obtuse angle in *fusca*, the wedge located above the nostrils. In *deglandi*, the black feathering forms a typical right angle, projecting below the nostrils. Half of the knob appears feathered. In *stejnegeri*, the feathering forms a slightly acute angle, although the pattern can match *deglandi*.

- A white sub-ocular patch partly surrounds the eye, starting at its front, continuing below and extending slightly behind it in *fusca*. In *deglandi* and *stejnegeri*, this white patch usually extends much further towards the rear crown, reaching well above the eye in profile. This white 'comma' often seems longer and thinner in *stejnegeri* than *deglandi*. These two taxa sometimes show a pattern like *fusca* (*c.*1% of ♂♂[421]), perhaps age-related. On the other hand, *fusca* can show a slightly longer white patch, but this does not match the usual pattern of *deglandi* and *stejnegeri*. Finally, a thin white line surrounds the top of the eye, usually complete in the latter two taxa, usually partly obscured or interrupted in *fusca*, but with much overlap.

- The flanks are stained rusty-brown in *deglandi*, especially at the front where the black breast appears clear-cut, but are all black in *fusca* and *stejnegeri*, visible even at a distance (appearing slightly mottled paler grey in summer).

Between first winter and first summer, formative plumage gradually replaces juvenile plumage. The young ♂ then passes through a succession of different appearances, varying between individuals. The flank colour, bulge at the base of the bill and white sub-ocular patch are generally less useful at this age. However, the first signs of the bill colour can appear quite quickly during the first winter. Head shape and the feathers at the bill base remain useful for identification at this age.

♀♀ of the three taxa are more difficult to separate, but it is generally possible at close range. Correctly identifying a ♀ *stejnegeri* or *deglandi* on the 'wrong' side of N Pacific would require very thorough scrutiny.

- Head profile differs between ♀♀ of the different taxa, like ♂♂. *M. fusca* has a quite rounded head, with a regular, unbroken and concave line from the forehead to the bill tip. The basal two-thirds of the culmen are usually straight or only very slightly swollen, whereas the tip typically appears slightly snub, which is accentuated when the birds hold their bill slightly upwards in alarm. In *deglandi*, the profile appears stockier and squarer, and can be reminiscent of Surf Scoter *M. perspicillata*. Like ♂♂, the forehead/bill profile is typically 'stepped' with a prominent, steeper forehead and a swollen, partly feathered, culmen. The angle between the forehead and culmen is more pronounced in *deglandi* than the two other taxa. Moreover, this angle is sited well within the feathered part in *deglandi* (vs. just above

the bill base in *fusca* and *stejnegeri*). In *stejnegeri*, the forehead/bill profile is usually straighter, more like Common Eider *Somateria mollissima*. The forehead is less prominent, as is the bulge at the base of the culmen.

- The feathering at the bill base is the most objective feature, but requires close scrutiny. It varies between the three taxa as in ♂♂. In *fusca*, the angle formed by this feathering is obtuse and located at the same horizontal level as the nostril, which is 6–8 mm from the nearest feathers[267,428]. In *deglandi*, the feathering forms a straight angle, the wedge being sited below the level of the nostrils, and 1–4 mm from the latter. Front on, the forehead feathers extend to the culmen usually forming a sharp 'V', whereas this limit is rounded and flatter in the other taxa. *M. stejnegeri* is usually very like *deglandi*, but the feathering forms a slightly acute angle.

- On average, *deglandi* and *stejnegeri* show more obvious pale face patches than *fusca* by age-group (first-winter of all three taxa have more prominent patches than adults).

PLUMAGES Clear sexual dimorphism from first winter onwards. Simple alternate moult strategy (two plumages in first and definitive cycles). Ageing ♂♂ relatively easy until first summer and possible until second summer in good views or in the hand. Ageing ♀♀ harder after second pre-basic moult (second autumn). See also above.

Adult ♂

Definitive basic plumage (Nov/Apr). All-black plumage, except the wing (secondaries and tips to greater coverts white, underwing greater and median coverts grey) and head, which has a white sub-ocular patch that surrounds the eye below it. More rarely an incomplete, thin white line runs around the top of the eye. Iris whitish to pale blue-grey. Bill-sides largely bright yellow, lower culmen yellowish or whitish, nail ivory, all contrasting with the base, periphery of nostrils, upper culmen and tomium, which are black. Legs reddish and feet with black webs.

Definitive alternate plumage (Apr–May/Oct–Nov). Pre-alternate moult, at most, limited. Most feathers remain largely basic, and often appear more worn and duller, possibly with some scattered black alternate feathers.

Adult ♀

Definitive basic plumage (Nov/Apr). Similar to ♂, but browner and duller, without soft velvety purple sheen.

Head distinctly different as lacks any white sub-ocular patch, but there are two diffuse pale areas, at the bill base and on the ear-coverts. Iris dark brown, sometimes slightly paler grey (probably older ♀♀). Bill dark grey, often with slight yellowish or orange tint at the nail, and more rarely (older ♀♀?) on the sides. Legs and feet grey-brown with dull yellowish or orange tones.

Definitive alternate plumage (Apr–May/Oct–Nov). Like ♂, pre-alternate moult is absent or limited and, if any, causes no noticeable change in appearance. All plumage slightly more dappled, pale and 'messy'. The pale spots on the head-sides are more marked, often whitish.

Juvenile

First basic plumage (until Nov). Very similar to adult ♀ but marginally paler and browner overall, with a broad oval pale to whitish patch on the belly, and better-marked pale spots on the head-sides. Up close, note the pale fringes to the scapulars and upperwing-coverts forming neat lines. Legs and feet yellowish-grey or dull yellow-brown with darker webs. Tips to greater coverts dark or have small white spots (outer webs), vs. largely white in ad[56], pointed in young, broader and square in adult. The outermost secondaries with inner webs white in adult (outer black), whitish and ill-defined in young ♂ (outer web blackish-brown), and pale grey-brown and diffuse in young ♀ (outer web grey-brown).

First-winter /first-summer ♂

Formative plumage (Oct/Jun). Pre-formative moult occurs from Oct until late winter, is slow and quite variable in extent. Young ♂♂ can show a wide variety of appearances between juvenile plumage (until Oct–Nov) and plumage more similar to adult in subsequent spring. The yellow bill-sides are often first obvious sign of ♂, appearing from Nov in many, concurrently with several black feathers on the head. Black formative feathers become more numerous thereafter, especially on head, breast, flanks and scapulars, affording variegated brownish and black plumage. By the end of pre-formative moult, birds that moulted extensively are much more like adult ♂ but duller blackish with a whitish belly. Some pale brown juvenile feathers are often visible. Bill has dull yellow pattern, often with culmen and nail at least partly dusky. Iris dark brown during first winter, becoming pale grey-brown during subsequent summer and resembles adult by second autumn (individual variation is evident though). The sub-ocular patch is greyer, smaller and usually not obvious. Up to three tertials are moulted, therefore

like those of adult (black, long, pointed and curved), but most retain several to all juvenile tertials (shorter, browner, rounded and frayed). Most to all rectrices are juvenile, pointed, pale and worn, becoming heavily worn in spring. Legs and feet gradually acquire adult colours during second calendar year.

First-winter/first-summer ♀

Formative plumage (Oct/Jun). By end of pre-formative moult, very like adult ♀ in which moult was extensive. The best ageing feature remains the largely whitish belly. White spots on the head-sides are on average more visible, but this is useful only in direct comparison. Bill like adult ♀, but usually all dark or blackish-grey. Iris dark brown.

Second-winter ♂

Second basic plumage (Oct/Sep). Identical to adult ♂, but some distinguished by presence of juvenile feathers on the belly, which often appears more mottled brown until second spring. The white sub-ocular mark is often smaller, the iris marginally darker and the lower culmen and nail variably marked dusky.

GEOGRAPHIC VARIATION None described.

MEASUREMENTS and MASS ♂ and adult slightly larger than ♀ and young, respectively. ♂: wing chord 269–286 (adult, 280, *n*=31) and 260–282 (juvenile, 268, *n*=17), bill 41–51 (44.9, *n*=47), tarsus 46–53 (48.8, *n*=43), mass in winter 1,517–1,980 (adult, 1,726, *n*=9); ♀: 255–271 (adult, 263, *n*=7) and 232–262 (juvenile, 251, *n*=22), bill 37–44 (40.8, *n*=27), tarsus 43–49 (45.8, *n*=27), mass in winter 1,360–1,895 (1,658, *n*=11)[267]. ♂: wing chord 267–293 (adult, 279, *n*=66) and 252–278 (juvenile, 266, *n*=26), bill 40–48 (adult, 44.9, *n*=66); ♀: 239–263 (263, *n*=40) and 233–263 (juvenile, 251, *n*=24), bill 39–45 (41.1, *n*=48)[1122].

VOICE Usually silent, most frequently heard during courtship, but sometimes in winter, especially in flocks on a calm sea. The male gives a *warr-err* and *wak wak* during courtship, while ♀ utters a harsh *braaarr* or *kerrr*, most often heard near the nest.

MOULT Simple alternate strategy (?). Seemingly very like that of Surf and White-winged Scoters (which see). The precise extent of definitive pre-alternate moult remains to be established. It seems variable in ♂ and almost absent in ♀. Several authors indicate a moult in ♂♂ involving some feathers of the flanks and mantle, scapulars and none to a few rectrices[56]. Pre-formative moult between mid-Oct and Mar–Apr. Apparently no pre-alternate moult during second calendar year, at least in *deglandi*[1014]. Definitive pre-alternate moult uncertain. Definitive pre-basic moult begins between mid-Jul and Sep, until Oct–Nov.

HYBRIDISATION Natural hybridisation reported very occasionally, and historically, with Common Goldeneye *Bucephala clangula*[49,947,1194] and Common Eider *Somateria mollissima*[493,947].

HABITAT and LIFE-CYCLE Breeders arrive near nesting sites in Apr–May, depending on the thawing. Frequents sandy or pebble shores, freshwater lakes, ponds and large rivers in the taiga to southern tundra and, locally, lakes in the alpine zone of the Caucasus. Regularly nests in gull colonies[992]. Eggs usually laid from mid-May[992]. Shortly afterwards, ♂♂ abandon ♀♀ and head to moulting sites, where they join non-breeders from Jun. ♀♀ do not usually moult until Aug, either gathering at moulting sites or on nesting sites. In non-breeding season, spends most time at sea, favouring huge shallow bays with plentiful mussels[144]. Less frequent but regular on freshwater bodies, mainly on large lakes in C Europe, where it is much more regular than Common Scoter and takes advantage of the presence of zebra mussels *Dreissena polymorpha*.

RANGE and POPULATION In Siberia, nests east as far as the Yenisey, where it is replaced by Siberian Scoter. The precise boundaries of their respective ranges and the possible existence of a sympatric zone remain unknown. A geographically highly disjunct population breeds on some lakes in the Caucasus and environs, between NE Turkey, Georgia, Armenia and Turkmenistan. In winter, largely concentrated in the Baltic, with smaller numbers in North Sea and English Channel. Much rarer elsewhere along Atlantic coast south to Spain, locally in N Mediterranean Sea and on some large lakes in C Europe. Very rare or accidental further south to NW Africa, Israel, Afghanistan, Iceland and Greenland, thus future occurrence in NE North America possible[1206]. The Baltic Sea population was estimated at 933,000 birds in 1992–93[1206], leading to a global estimate of *c*.1,000,000 in the mid-1990s[991]. In 2007–09, a total of 373,000 was reported there, suggesting a serious decline in the main stronghold[1206]. The decline has been confirmed in other wintering or breeding populations[144,328,514,580,1045]. The Caucasian population winters primarily in S & E Black Sea and numbers *c*.1,500 birds[305]. The decline in the Baltic could partly reflect a shift in the wintering range towards the White or Barents Sea (?), as it had already shifted towards N Baltic Sea previously[1206]. However, this remains to be confirmed, and the apparent decrease has led to it being classified as Endangered by BirdLife International[142].

CAPTIVITY Very rarely kept in captivity (even more rarely bred) and occurs only in a few specialised collections, like many sea ducks. All scoters require cold, clear and clean waters, and a special diet. Moreover, they are prone to respiratory fungal diseases and frequently develop deformations of their legs if standing for too long. These problems also often occur in care centres for oiled birds.

REFERENCES Baird *et al.* (1884)[49]; Baker (1993)[56]; BirdLife International (2012)[142]; BirdLife International (2013)[144]; Collinson *et al.* (2006)[240]; Cramp & Simmons (1977)[268]; Crochet *et al.* (2010)[273]; Delany *et al.* (2006)[305]; Dubois *et al.* (2008)[328]; Dwight (1914)[335]; Garner (1999)[421]; Garner *et al.* (2004)[428]; Gudmundsson (1932)[493]; Hario & Rintala (2011)[514]; Helbig *et al.* (2002)[548]; Holt *et al.* (2011)[580]; Kolbe (1979)[697]; Panov (1989)[947]; Pihl & Laursen (1996)[991]; Pihl & Fox *in* Kear (2005)[992]; Pyle (2008)[1014]; Rassi *et al.* (2010)[1045]; Salminen (1983)[1122]; Scherrer & Hilsberg (1982)[1142]; Sibley (1994)[1194]; Skov *et al.* (2011)[1206]; Stepanyan (2003)[1233]; Todd (1979)[1273]; Witherby *et al.* (1944)[1373].

515. Adult ♂ (definitive basic); extent of white eye-patch, partially black nail and grey traces to tips of greater coverts suggest a second-winter ♂. Denmark, Oct (Eva Foss Henriksen).

516. Adult ♂ (definitive basic). Sweden, May (Ingo Waschkies).

517. Adult ♂ (definitive basic). Sweden, May (Ingo Waschkies).

518. First-winter ♂ (formative), with Common Scoter *M. nigra* (left); still resembles juvenile, but bill already shows a hint of adult coloration. Netherlands, Jan (William Price).

519. First-spring ♂ (formative/perhaps first alternate); like adult ♂, but bill has black nail, with dull grey iris and lacks white patch below eye. France, May (Sébastien Reeber).

520. Adult ♀ (definitive basic); probably adult, given long tertials and pinkish hue to sides of bill; note species diagnostic shape of feathering at bill base. Sweden, May (Ingo Waschkies).

WHITE-WINGED SCOTER
Melanitta deglandi

TAXONOMY *Oidemia deglandi* Bonaparte, 1850, *Revue critique de l'Ornithologie européenne de M. le Docteur Degland (de Lille): Lettre à M. de Selys-Longchamps*, p.108. See Taxonomy of Velvet Scoter. The subspecies *Oidemia deglandi dixoni* W. S. Brooks, 1915, was described from Alaska, but differs only marginally (see Geographic Variation).

IDENTIFICATION In North America, observed in the company of Black *M. americana* and Surf Scoters *M. perspicillata*, but usually easily distinguished by its larger size and usually easily visible white secondaries, even on the water. Adult ♂ also has a white patch below and behind the eye, and a distinctive hazelnut-reddish tone to the flanks. ♀♀ and juveniles have a head pattern very different from that of other scoters (see Surf Scoter). Distinction from Siberian Scoter *M. stejnegeri* and Velvet Scoter *M. fusca* is detailed under the latter.

PLUMAGES Clear sexual dimorphism from first winter onwards. Simple alternate moult strategy (two plumages in first and definitive cycles), without obvious seasonal changes. Ageing ♂♂ relatively easy until first summer and possible until second summer in good views or in the hand. Ageing ♀♀ harder after second pre-basic moult (second autumn). Large, entirely black or dark sea duck, the top of the bill with a distinct lump. The large white rectangle formed by the secondaries on an otherwise dark duck is unique in North America. See also Velvet Scoter for further details, especially those permitting distinction from Velvet and Siberian Scoters.

Adult ♂

Definitive basic plumage (Nov/Apr). Entirely black plumage, except hazel to rusty-reddish flanks (more pronounced on fore flanks and visible especially in good light), long white sub-ocular patch (very elongated towards rear crown, often with a fine line encircling the eye) and wing (white secondaries except outermost and tips to greater coverts, underwing median and greater coverts grey). Iris whitish to pale blue-grey. Bill has clear square bulge between forehead and culmen, with pinkish patches on sides (yellow below nostril), lower culmen whitish and nail yellow-orange to red. Legs and feet bright pink to reddish with blackish webs.

Definitive alternate plumage (Apr–May/Oct–Nov). Similar to basic plumage, but somewhat browner and duller, due to alternate feathers and/or wear to basic feathers. Many adult ♂♂ clearly show two generations of feathers (brown and black) simultaneously.

Adult ♀

Definitive basic plumage (Nov/Apr?). Similar to ♂, but browner and duller, without velvety sheen. The head has two pale and diffuse spots, at the bill base and on the ear-coverts. Iris dark grey-brown, sometimes slightly paler grey (probably older ♀♀). Bill dark grey to blackish often with a slight yellowish or orange tinge at the nail, and rarely, vague pinkish spots on the sides like pattern of ♂ (older ♀♀ only?). Legs and feet grey-brown with dull yellowish or orange tones.

Definitive alternate plumage (Apr–May/Oct–Nov?). Like ♂, pre-alternate moult is at most limited. The plumage is browner and worn, and looks 'messier'. The pale spots on the head-sides are more marked, often whitish.

Juvenile

First basic plumage (until Nov). Like adult ♀ but slightly paler and more greyish, with a pale belly and pale facial spots. The head shape is also distinguished by the near-lack of culmen bulge. Close up, the pale fringes to the scapulars and upperwing-coverts form faint delicate lines. Bill all dark. Legs and feet yellow-grey or dull yellow-brown with darker webs. Juvenile can be sexed in the hand by pattern of the outermost secondaries (inner web white and outer web black in adult, inner web partly whitish and diffuse in young ♂ and pale grey-brown with outer web dark brown in young ♀[1014]).

First-winter/first-summer ♂

Formative plumage (Oct–Nov/Jun). Between Oct and Mar slowly develops plumage like that of adult. A hint of adult bill coloration and pattern appears from Nov. The proportion of black formative feathers increases thereafter, especially on the head, breast, flanks and scapulars, going through a succession of plumages more or less variegated black and dark brown. Following pre-formative moult, distinguished from adult ♂ by variable number of juvenile feathers (brown and paler), belly becoming white by first summer and bill coloration duller and ill-defined (lower culmen and nail usually dusky). The iris, initially dark brown, gradually acquires adult colour between spring and the end of second calendar year. Sub-ocular patch poorly defined, pale greyish and incomplete, especially behind the eye. The tips of the moulted inner greater coverts (broad, square and white) contrast with those of the juvenile greater coverts, which are narrower, pale and diffuse. Two to all tertials juvenile (shorter, brown, rounded and frayed), the others formative or adult. Tertials elongated, pointed and curved. Most to all rectrices are still juvenile, being narrow, pale and worn, to heavily worn in spring. Legs and feet gradually acquire their adult colours during the second calendar year.

First-winter / first-summer ♀

Formative plumage (Oct–Nov/Jun). By end of pre-formative moult, like adult ♀. Readily distinguished by largely white belly. The white spots on the head-sides are on average more pronounced. Bill like that of adult ♀, but usually completely dark grey to blackish, with bulge at base of culmen less marked. Iris dark brown. The rest of the body often distinctly shows feathers of two generations. Also distinguished from adult ♀ by juvenile tertials and rectrices (often all), narrow, short and increasingly worn and faded by summer.

Second-winter ♂

Second basic plumage (Oct–Nov/Sep). Very like adult ♂ after second pre-basic moult and some indistinguishable. Others can be aged (more easily in the hand) by presence of brown and pale feathers on belly, sub-ocular patch on average less contrasting and slightly shorter behind the eye, and/or bill more marked dusky. The culmen bulge is also less pronounced on average, the bill depth at the proximal end of the nostrils 21.5–22.9 mm in ♂♂ at this age, vs. 22.1–24.5 mm in adult ♂♂[1014].

GEOGRAPHIC VARIATION Weak geographical variation reported; populations of Alaska have bill on average a little broader and shorter, and named *dixoni*[193]. These differences, if real, appear insufficient to support subspecific status[549,1014].

MEASUREMENTS and MASS ♂ and adult slightly larger than ♀ and young, respectively. ♂: wing chord 282 (adult, *n*=85) and 274 (juvenile, *n*=41), mass 1,361–1,769 (1,588, *n*=7); ♀: wing chord 267 (adult, *n*=32) and 259 (juvenile, *n*=39), mass 953–1,406 (1,179, *n*=15)[87]. ♂ (*n*=14): wing chord 271–292 (283.5), culmen 37–43 (40.8), tarsus 49–64 (52.9); ♀ (*n*=34):

wing chord 259–285 (264.0), culmen 37–41 (38.3), tarsus 45–50 (48.6)[200]; ♂ (*n*=12): wing chord 272–289 (279.2), culmen 36–47 (41.2), tarsus 46–52 (49.3), tail 69–87 (81.4); ♀ (*n*=12): wing chord 258–274 (268.0), culmen 35–41 (38.2), tarsus 45–50 (48.2), tail 75–88 (79.0)[945]; ♂ (*n*=100): wing chord 270–289 (adult) and 261–279 (juvenile), tail 74–88, culmen length from proximal end of nostrils 35–40, bill depth at proximal end of nostrils 19.5–24.5, tarsus 48–55; ♀ (*n*=100): wing chord 255–273 (adult) and 246–263 (juvenile), tail 70–84, culmen length from proximal end of nostrils 32–37, bill depth at proximal end of nostrils 17.3–20.6, tarsus 45–52[1014]. Mass may be lower than Velvet Scoter, as indicated in some literature[223], with means of 1,720 g and 1,630 g for ♂ and ♀, respectively, vs. 1,540 g and 1,220 g, respectively, for *deglandi*. This requires support from comparison of equivalent samples (age/sex groups, season). Indeed, the available data show wide fluctuation throughout the year, i.e. 1,388–2,128 (1,917, *n*=29) for ♂ and 1,566–1,946 (1,732, *n*=10) for ♀ in Dec–Apr, Alaska[1128]. See Brown & Fredrickson[200] for other mass data.

VOICE Rather silent. ♂ gives a double whistle *wieurr-wir*, while ♀ utters a shrill whistle and harsh croak. These vocalisations are different from those of Velvet Scoter, which may be related to differences in trachea structure and has been considered a supporting character for considering them species[240].

MOULT Simple alternate strategy (?), like that of Surf Scoter (which see). Extent of pre-alternate moult (all ages and sexes) unclear and controversial. Some authors report a definitive pre-alternate moult in ♂ from Mar to May[335,945]. In contrast, Pyle[1012], detailing 29 skins of *Melanitta* sp. taken just before wing moult, found traces of pre-alternate moult in just one ♂ and one ♀ Surf Scoter. These had replaced some nape feathers, and a few others on the upper back, upper breast and flanks. If definitive pre-alternate moult is absent in White-winged Scoter, moult strategy would be complex basic. Pre-formative moult occurs between mid-Oct and early spring, and appears more extensive in ♂ than in ♀[1012]. Of 47 individuals examined, 21% replaced at least one tertial, and two-thirds replaced some to all rectrices[1012]. Pre-basic moult occurs somewhat later in breeders, in Aug–Nov.

HYBRIDISATION Very rarely reported, either in wild or captivity, including with the other 'white-winged' scoters. In North America, several reports with Surf

Scoter[697,1142,1273] stem from the same reference[49], and may in fact have pertained to an aberrant Surf Scoter[945]. In Iceland, an old report involved a ♂ paired with a ♀ Common Eider *Somateria mollissima*[698].

HABITAT and LIFE-CYCLE Pair formation probably occurs mainly during spring migration[200], the species being a late breeder, with eggs predominantly laid in Jun–Jul. Inhabits varied nesting habitats near fresh, brackish or salty, still or flowing water, from taiga to Arctic tundra. Favours islands with low, dense vegetation, either along the coast, in deltas or large inland lakes. ♂♂ abandon ♀♀ during incubation and head to moulting sites on the coast (sheltered bays, estuaries) or large inland lakes. ♀♀ seem to moult at least partly at their nesting sites, along with their offspring[200]. In migration and winter, mainly found in coastal habitats rich in shellfish, especially on sandy substrates[1236]. Of the three North American scoters, it is nevertheless the least rare inland, with significant numbers on the Great Lakes.

RANGE and POPULATION Outside mapped range, small scattered populations in N Alberta, Saskatchewan and Manitoba. Rare or extirpated further south to US border, where it formerly bred in North Dakota. Regular in small numbers on large inland lakes in N USA and E Canada. These are mainly migrants, but a few thousand overwinter there. On the Great Lakes, numbers increased following the invasion of zebra mussels *Dreissena polymorpha*[199]. Occasional visitor to Europe, with a dozen records since 1993 (especially in Iceland, with some in Ireland, Faeroes and Denmark). More regular and long known in NE Asia[309]. The wintering population has been subject to conflicting estimates, due especially to difficulties of distinguishing scoter species in huge mixed flocks. An estimate of 1,000,000 birds has been given[1095], as well as 555,000–675,000 individuals[87] or 140,000–240,000 individuals[355,1354,1348]. The species has decreased substantially in part of its range[1292] and has been extirpated in the south, including the prairies. However, a shift in both breeding and wintering ranges could affect perceptions of trends.

CAPTIVITY Very rare in captivity and unlikely to escape (see Velvet Scoter).

REFERENCES Alberta Sustainable Resource Development (2002)[7]; Baird *et al.* (1884)[49]; Bellrose (1980)[87]; Brooks (1915)[193]; Brown & Fredrickson (1997)[199]; Brown & Fredrickson (1997)[200]; Carboneras (1992)[223]; Collinson *et al.* (2006)[240]; Dementiev & Gladkov (1967)[309]; Dwight (1914)[335]; Ellis-Joseph *et al.* (1992)[355]; Hellmayr & Conover (1948)[549]; Kolbe (1979)[697]; Kolbeinsson *et al.* (2001)[698]; Palmer (1976)[945]; Pyle (2005)[1012]; Pyle (2008)[1014]; Rose & Scott (1997)[1095]; Sanger & Jones (1984)[1128]; Scherrer & Hilsberg (1982)[1142]; Stott & Olson (1972)[1236]; USFWS (2011)[1292]; Wetlands International (2014)[1348]; Wilkins & Otto (2003)[1354].

521. Adult ♂ (definitive basic); vs. Velvet Scoter *M. fusca*, note warm brown flanks, bill coloration, culmen shape and elongated white eye-patch. British Columbia, Canada, Dec (Alan D. Wilson).

522. Adult ♂ (definitive alternate); diagnostic head and bill shape and coloration. Canada, Aug (Zbigniew Kayzer).

523. Adult ♂ (definitive basic/definitive alternate). Iceland, Jun (Yann Kolbeinsson).

524. First-winter ♂ (first basic/formative); note the blackish (moulted) head. Also aged by the lack of white on the greater-coverts. British Columbia, Canada, Dec (Alan D. Wilson).

525. ♀; apart from head and bill shape, and feathering to base of bill, also note that in same plumage and at same time, white face patches are more obvious vs. Velvet Scoter *M. fusca*. Iceland, Jun (Yann Kolbeinsson).

SIBERIAN SCOTER
Melanitta stejnegeri

TAXONOMY *Oidemia stejnegeri* Ridgway, 1887, *Manual N. Amer. Birds*, p.112. See Taxonomy of Velvet Scoter. Considered a full species[142,428], as a subspecies of White-winged Scoter *M. deglandi*[240,273,1233] or as a subspecies of Velvet Scoter *M. fusca* (also including *deglandi*)[22]. The former position has been adopted here. Also called Stejneger's Scoter or Asian White-winged Scoter.

IDENTIFICATION In Asia, often in the company of the only other sympatric scoter, Black Scoter *M. americana*, which is readily distinguished by the absence of white on the rear wing, its all-black plumage (adult ♂) or blackish-brown with broad pale patch covering the head-sides up to the eye (other plumages). Distinction from Velvet and White-winged Scoters is discussed under the former.

PLUMAGES Clear sexual dimorphism from first winter onwards. Simple alternate moult strategy (two plumages in first and definitive cycles), no significant seasonal change in appearance. Ageing ♂♂ relatively easy until first summer and possible until second summer in good views or in the hand. Ageing ♀♀ harder after second pre-basic moult (second autumn). See Identification under Velvet Scoter for further details, especially those permitting distinction from Velvet and White-winged Scoters.

Adult ♂

Definitive basic plumage (Nov/Apr). Black plumage with velvety sheen, except sub-ocular white patch (continuing as a long point towards the rear crown, often with a thin line encircling the eye). The wing has a broad white rectangle on the secondaries and tips of greater coverts. The underwing median and greater coverts are grey. Iris whitish to pale blue-grey. Bill has obvious bulge or knob on upper culmen and small (variable) protuberance overhanging its tip. The knob, nostrils (rounded in profile) and proximal third of the bill are black. Lower culmen white, nail orange-red, sometimes edged black. The red on the sides of the bill extends to below the nostrils. Clear bright yellow line on distal half of tomium reaching the nail. Legs and feet pink to reddish with black webs.

Definitive alternate plumage (Apr–May/Oct–Nov). Extent of pre-alternate moult not well known, but appearance does not actually change throughout the year (slightly duller in summer).

Adult ♀

Definitive basic plumage (Nov/Apr?). Overall coloration browner, more matt and duller than ♂. Two pale patches are visible, at the bill base and on ear-coverts. Iris dark grey-brown (possibly paler, like *deglandi*?). Bill dark grey to blackish, often with a slight yellowish or orange tint at the nail and vague reddish patches on the sides, recalling ♂ pattern, and more frequent than in *deglandi* and *fusca*. These patches may increase in size with age. Legs and feet grey-brown with dull yellowish or orange tones.

Definitive alternate plumage (Apr–May/Oct–Nov?). Extent of pre-alternate moult unknown. Plumage seems browner, more worn and 'messy'. The pale spots on head-sides are more marked, often whitish.

Juvenile

First basic plumage (until Nov). Like adult ♀ but slightly paler and more greyish. Mainly characterised by its entirely pale brownish belly. Up close, note the narrow pale fringes to the upperwing-coverts. Bill all dark. Legs and feet grey-brown to dull yellowish with dark webs.

First-winter/first-summer ♂

Formative plumage (Oct/Jun). Acquisition of formative plumage protracted throughout first winter. The reddish sides to the bill tip, however, appear early and permit sexing by late autumn. Following pre-formative moult, more like adult ♂, apart from predominantly white belly, nail and culmen still marked dusky, iris darker grey until at least early spring (to early second winter) and grey sub-ocular patch incomplete behind eye. Also look for presence of juvenile rectrices and tertials, which are usually pale, brown and heavily worn in spring. Legs and feet become pink to reddish during second calendar year.

First-winter/first-summer ♀

Formative plumage (Oct/Jun). Similar to adult ♀, and distinguished especially by pale to whitish belly. Pale facial spots slightly more pronounced. Up close, useful for ageing are the presence of two generations of feathers, some rather new and blackish-brown (formative) and others brown, faded and worn (juvenile), as well as juvenile tertials and tertial coverts, which are shorter, paler brown and frayed. In addition, those with a pale iris (not dark brown) and/or diffuse orange or reddish patches on the bill-sides are generally adult ♀♀.

Second-winter ♂

Second basic plumage (Oct/Sep). Few reliable ageing features known, but it is probable that those useful for *fusca* and *deglandi* are also valid (presence of brown feathers on belly, dusky traces on the lower culmen and nail, less developed bulge on the upper culmen and no overhanging protuberance, and on average smaller sub-ocular patch.

GEOGRAPHIC VARIATION None.

MEASUREMENTS and MASS Very few data published[992]. Some data on mass (♀ in summer: 957 g, ♂♂ in spring 1,020–1,437 g, ♂ in Nov 1,300 g and ♀ in Oct 1,030 g[308,992]) suggest that it is lower than in the other two taxa. However, huge seasonal variation in mass make larger samples necessary.

VOICE Rather silent. Little published information, ♂ giving a *weee-err* and *aah-er*, and ♀ repeated hoarse croaks[182]. A comparative analysis of the vocalisations of the three 'white-winged' scoters is probably needed for a better understanding of their phylogenetic relationships.

MOULT Simple alternate strategy (?). Probably like that of Surf Scoter (which see). No details on the timing and extent of moults in this species.

HYBRIDISATION None reported, either in captivity or in the wild.

HABITAT and LIFE-CYCLE Again, few published data for this species compared to Velvet and White-winged Scoters, but habitats and general habits apparently similar. This scoter inhabits wetlands in the taiga, as well as wooded and open tundra[182] and winters mainly in coastal waters and on large freshwater bodies.

RANGE and POPULATION Breeds in E Siberia, west to the Yenisei[428,992] or Lena Rivers[182] (limits of range and possible zone of sympatry with Velvet Scoter remain to be established). The bulk of the population overwinters off the coasts of N Japan, the Kuril Is and south of the Sea of Okhotsk. Occasional in Alaska and Europe, in France (Dec 1886[635]), Iceland, Ireland, Poland and Finland. Global population estimated at 600,000–1,000,000 birds[858], with trend unknown.

CAPTIVITY Very rarely kept, thus out-of-range reports almost certainly involve wild birds.

REFERENCES AOU (2010)[22]; BirdLife International (2012)[142]; Brazil (2009)[182]; Butcher & Niven (2007)[209]; Collinson *et al.* (2006)[240]; Crochet *et al.* (2010)[273]; Dementiev & Gladkov (1952)[308]; Garner *et al.* (2004)[428]; Jiguet (2007)[635]; Miyabayashi & Mundkur (1999)[858]; Pihl & Fox *in* Kear (2005)[992]; Stepanyan (2003)[1233].

526. Adult ♂ (definitive basic/definitive alternate) showing diagnostic head and bill shape and coloration. Chukotka, Russia, Jul (Anders Blomdahl).

527. First-winter ♀ (first basic/formative); feathering at base of bill forms a slightly sharp angle, and culmen/forehead line is remarkably straight; aged by tertials having typically pointed and frayed tips. Japan, Dec (Stuart Price).

COMMON SCOTER
Melanitta nigra

Plate 63

TAXONOMY *Anas nigra* Linnaeus, 1758, *Syst. Nat.*, edn. 10, p. 123. Among the six taxa of *Melanitta*, Common Scoter and Black Scoter *M. americana* are sister (subgenus *Oidemia*) and to a clade including all other scoters (subgenus *Melanitta*)[771]. Until the early 20th century, Black and Common Scoters were treated as species[335], then widely regarded as two subspecies of Common Scoter[19,1324]. Their status was recently revised[240,771,1232], and they are now considered species again, based on their allopatric distributions, absence of known hybrids or intermediates, differences in bill structure and colour, and significant differences in the courtship vocalisations of ♂♂[1129]. This decision as much reflects changes in definition of species than new knowledge of the taxa involved[427], and has been adopted almost unanimously, including by taxonomic committees in North America[22] and Europe[273].

IDENTIFICATION Separation from 'white-winged' scoters and Surf Scoter usually not difficult, adult ♂♂ being the only all-black scoters and ♀♀ showing large distinctive pale cheeks. In flight, Common and Black Scoters show typical silvery-whitish 'flashes' on the 'hand' of the underwing. Similarly, these species have the outermost primary (p10) shorter than the eighth (p8), while the reverse is true in all other scoters. Separating Common and Black Scoters is more difficult, especially plumages other than adult ♂. For the latter, the key features are detailed below.

- *Bill shape*: Common Scoter has a short, steep knob at the base of culmen, often like a small ball or square, and largely black. Its top often forms a right angle with the forehead and the distal edge reaches the nostrils or just before (less than the mid-length on the bill), forming a distinct angle with the rest of the culmen. In profile, the distal culmen is almost straight, with a very flat nail. Black Scoter has a broad, elongated bump, smoothly curved and forming an obtuse angle with the forehead, its distal edge clearly falling beyond the nostrils, i.e. over halfway along the bill. It does not form a sharp angle with the lower culmen. In profile, the distal culmen is visibly concave, with the nail slightly but distinctly downcurved. On average, the bill of Common Scoter is slightly longer (*c*.10%) than in Black Scoter.

- *Culmen coloration*: Black with yellow on top in both species, in Common Scoter the yellow covers the central culmen, broadens to encompass the nostrils and then narrows to form a line to the forehead, which is often visible only from in front, the yellow being sometimes barely visible in profile, and the sides of the knob are black. In Black Scoter, the yellow (often clearly orangey) covers the entire bulge and reaches the black feathers. It encompasses the nostrils but often extends a little less towards the nail than Common Scoter. In some ♂ Common Scoters (usually second calendar year?[267]), the yellow extends a little more either side of the knob, to cover its distal half. Seen from in front and afar, such birds can suggest Black Scoter, but the bill shape remains the same. In profile, the yellow is thus less extensive in Common Scoter, with the black vertical base to the bill separating the yellow from the feathers.

- *Position and shape of nostrils*: This feature requires close scrutiny, at a distance where the colour and shape of the bill are generally obvious. The nostrils are oval and their distal edge is halfway between the gape and bill tip in Common Scoter. In Black Scoter, the nostril's shape recalls a rice grain and its proximal edge is sited halfway between the gape and bill tip.

- *Orbital ring*: Generally yellow in Common Scoter and bluish-grey to blackish in Black Scoter.

- *Head colour*: Black in both species, with feather tips flame or pencil-shaped and show a velvety blue hue to the head-sides in Black Scoter. In Common Scoter, a matt black and ruffled mask encircles the bill base, which in profile forms a vertical black bar between it and the rest of the head, which is slightly paler and shinier.

- *Head shape*: In Common Scoter it is usually more angular, with a rather square forehead, which is very steep, often vertical and forms a right-angle with the bill knob, and also a clear angle with the crown. In profile, the latter is often flattened or angular when the feathers are erect. Usually, Black Scoter has a regularly rounded head profile between the bill base and the nape. The neck is often distinctly thicker[427].

- **Tail length**: On average longer (in direct comparison) in Common Scoter.

Finally, Garner[427] also indicated that, in direct comparison, Black Scoter seems to float higher on water, making it appear taller, and tends to feed closer inshore, even in the breakers, which Common Scoter almost never does. Indeed, Black Scoter is often seen much closer to shore (thereby affording much better views) than Common Scoter on their usual wintering grounds.

In first-winter ♂♂, distinction is often possible from Nov. Indeed, identification of adult ♂♂ is largely based on bill colour, which begins to appear in young ♂♂ when plumage is still largely juvenile. The patch coloration is initially olive, brownish or yellowish, but apart from colour has the same characteristics as the yellow patch in adults. Position and shape of the nostrils and head shape are also reliable at this age, but the orbital ring and knob acquire their definitive appearance between first summer and second winter.

♀♀ can be separated, although this requires much better views, and preferably good photographs. Even then, some individuals appear impossible to identify. Given bill shape is the most useful character, juveniles (especially ♀♀) will be even more difficult to identify.

- **Bill shape**: The bill of Common Scoter averages slightly longer, with a fairly straight culmen in profile (at most, a slight bump at the forehead) and very flat nail. In Black Scoter, the upper culmen shows a slight and elongated swelling that reaches beyond the nostrils, reminiscent of ♂ but less pronounced. The rest of the culmen is concave, with nail slightly downcurved (variable in both taxa though). The tip of the bill appears slightly snub.

- **Feathering at base of bill**: In Common Scoter, in profile the limit of the feathering on the base of the bill forms a straight or slightly convex line, and then becomes rounded to the gape. In Black Scoter, the limit of the feathers is often slightly concave and forms a right-angle with the gape, which is often more prominent. However, this feature is rather variable (especially in *americana*) and is no more than contributory.

- **Bill coloration**: Both taxa have a dark grey to blackish bill with a variable number of yellow spots around the nostrils and central culmen. Their absence is frequent in both taxa, and their extent may be age-related. These spots are usually absent or reduced in Common Scoter, whereas in Black Scoter, they can almost reach the extent of the yellow spot in ♂♂. Waring[1337] indicated that 10% of ♀ Black Scoters show more yellow than Common Scoter.

- **Head shape**: That of Common Scoter is regularly rounded, with a forehead forming a moderate angle with the culmen. Black Scoter often shows a bulging forehead, marking a right-angle with the upper culmen and the flatter crown. The whole head thus appears more squared.

- **Nape colour**: The dark crown continues along the nape in both species, but in Black Scoter it forms a rectangular, blunt-tipped stripe. In Common Scoter, it tapers to a long point[427].

- **Cheeks colour**: Averages more marked with brown (fore cheeks in contact with bill and vertical crescent behind eye) in Common Scoter. The cheeks of Black Scoter average greyer, paler and more clear-cut.

PLUMAGES Clear sexual dimorphism from first winter onwards. Simple alternate moult strategy (two plumages in first and definitive cycles). Ageing ♂♂ relatively easy until first summer and possible until second summer in good views or in the hand. Ageing ♀♀ possible until second pre-basic moult (second summer).

Adult ♂

Definitive basic plumage (Nov/Apr). All-black plumage, except underwing (remiges) paler, and inner webs of primaries pale grey forming silvery flashes on flying birds in good light. The tips of the cheek feathers are pencil-shaped and form small regular stripes. These feathers also show a bluish velvety sheen. Iris dark brown with a yellow orbital ring visible up close. Bill black with a prominent knob on upper culmen and variable yellow mark. In most birds, yellow covers the top of culmen, encompasses the nostrils and extends as a line to the forehead. Others show more yellow, covering the entire width of the knob from the front, and extending to the upper nail. Exceptionally, the bill is almost all yellow, but keeps its characteristic shape. Legs blackish-grey.

Definitive alternate plumage (Apr–May/Oct–Nov). Extent of pre-alternate moult debated, but in summer appears duller, often with a 'messy' mix of black and more worn, grey-brown feathers. The general appearance remains similar though.

Adult ♀

Definitive basic plumage (Nov/Apr). Overall dark brown with broad, barely paler, fringes to scapulars and flank feathers, giving a hint of scaly appearance, clearly accentuated by wear. The only contrasting feature, a pale grey vermiculated dark area on the cheeks and upper neck to the nape is highlighted by the dark crown that reaches the eye. The fore part of this area, in contact with the bill, is often tinged darker brown, and a vague vertical crescent runs over the cheeks behind the eye. Underwing has silvery 'flashes' on primaries like ♂ but less prominent. Iris brown to dark brown (sometimes hazel-brown). Bill dark grey to blackish, often with yellow around the nostrils and sometimes scattered yellow spots elsewhere on the culmen. Occasionally, the yellow area is larger, including part of the tomium. Legs dark grey with yellow tones in places, webs blackish.

Definitive alternate plumage (Apr–May/Oct–Nov). No real change in seasonal appearance, even if the entire plumage appears duller and paler (more grey-beige).

Juvenile

First basic plumage (until Nov). Like adult ♀ but paler overall with warmer brown plumage, cheeks and upper neck pale grey, more contrasting with the rest of the body, and whitish belly, neatly streaked brown. Tertials short, straight and round-tipped. The outermost primary is slightly (♂) or not (♀) notched, whereas in adult it is strongly (♀) to very strongly (♂) notched.

First-winter/first-summer ♂

Formative plumage (Nov/Jun). Pre-formative moult varies in extent, is usually slow, with more or less active phases. Between Oct and May, young ♂♂ thus show a great variety of appearances between juvenile and formative plumages. When pre-formative moult is extensive, the plumage is close to adult ♂, albeit with a pale brown belly becoming whitish in first spring. A variable number of juvenile feathers (brown, worn and faded) are often visible on the undertail and rump. Most (or all) upperwing-coverts, usually some to all rectrices and often the tertials are still juvenile until first summer. Typically, during first spring, the scapulars only partially cover the folded wings, which show clear contrast (brownish and faded wing vs. blackish scapulars and flanks). The orbital ring becomes visible, but is initially pale, not yellow before the end of second calendar year. Similarly, if the bill fairly quickly acquires adult-type coloration (yellow appears early in first winter), it achieves its final shape between first summer and second winter.

First-winter/first-summer ♀

Formative plumage (Nov/Jun). Like adult ♀, but most

birds clearly show two generations of feathers, the juvenile feathers, brown fading until first summer, and formative feathers, dark brown close to those of adult ♀. In spring, ♀♀ with reduced pre-formative moult can be surprisingly pale, even brown-beige. The best ageing feature is the pale belly becoming whitish towards first summer. Cheeks on average paler and more contrasting. Finally, note the (usual) presence of juvenile tertials and rectrices, short and heavily worn in spring.

Second-winter ♂

Second basic plumage (Oct/Sep). Very like adult ♂, but at least some birds can be distinguished by bill knob much less prominent, orbital ring not yellow until second winter and belly dark brown, fading until subsequent summer. Outermost primaries sometimes only slightly notched.

GEOGRAPHIC VARIATION None described.

MEASUREMENTS and MASS ♂ and adult slightly larger than ♀ and young, respectively. ♂: wing chord 227–243 (adult, 234, $n=40$) and 216–234 (juvenile, 224, $n=34$), bill 44–51 (adult, 47.2, $n=40$); ♀: wing chord 215–234 (adult, 227, $n=40$) and 207–227 (juvenile, 218, $n=28$), bill 40–47 (adult, 43.5, $n=40$)[1122]. ♂: wing chord 224–247 (adult, 234, $n=91$) and 217–241 (juvenile, 226, $n=30$), bill 43–51 (47.5, $n=47$), tarsus 43–48 (45.4, $n=69$); ♀: wing chord 216–239 (adult, 226, $n=31$) and 206–226 (juvenile, 218, $n=30$), bill 41–46 (43.4, $n=32$), tarsus 41–46 (43.5, $n=55$)[267]. ♂: mass in winter 964–1,339 (1,165, $n=14$); ♀: mass in winter 973–1,233 (1,059, $n=10$)[267].

VOICE Usually quiet. During courtship, ♂ gives a succession of quick whistles, *piew-piew-piew-piew-piew...*, a few seconds long, audible especially in small groups of ♂♂ accompanying one or more ♀♀. Note that these vocalisations differ significantly from those of Black Scoter, as each note lasts on average one-tenth of a second (75–170 ms, $n=202$), while these same notes last seven-tenths of a second (309–1,089 ms, $n=290$) in Black Scoter, with very little variability among populations of each species[1129]. Also gives, including while migrating at night, a fluting *gup* or *giu*. The ♀ gives hoarse *krerr* or *kraaa*, particularly near nest sites.

MOULT Simple alternate strategy (?). Pre-formative moult, protracted and variable in extent, occurs in Sep–May, often slowing down in midwinter. It includes a variable number of (sometimes all) feathers of head, flanks and scapulars, with often smaller numbers on the breast, back, rump, inner upperwing-coverts, undertail-coverts and rectrices. Belly hardly replaced, like rest of wing and (usually) tertials. No pre-alternate moult during first cycle (?). Extent of definitive pre-alternate moult not unanimously accepted, Baker[56] indicated moult of the rectrices and a small number of feathers of mantle and scapulars, in Mar–May, adding that rectrices are moulted in autumn as well, and the feathers of the neck and head twice a year in ♀ (Oct and Apr–May) or three times in ♂ (Sep–Oct, Dec–Jan and Apr–May). In Black Scoter, Pyle[1014] indicated pre-alternate moult to be limited or absent, in Jun–Aug, with no active moult in Dec–May[1012]. Definitive pre-basic moult starts with the wings, from mid-Jul to mid-Sep in ♂ and Sep–Oct in ♀[56], and ends in Nov–Dec, and Feb in some ♀♀.

HYBRIDISATION Reported just once, with Eurasian Wigeon *Anas penelope*[752] of uncertain origin (captive or not). Very rare reports of atypical individuals may suggest hybrids with Black Scoter *M. americana*[427,1325], but thorough descriptions of such birds are still lacking.

HABITAT and LIFE-CYCLE Migrates to breeding grounds in Mar–May, with eggs laid between end of May and early Jul. Usually breeds in lone pairs in boreal habitats, from the tundra, including mountains north of the taiga, occupying bogs, lakeshores or slow-moving streams, preferably of fresh water. Favours islands and/or dense vegetation on banks, including tall grass, birches and willows, although it avoids heavily wooded habitats. Soon after egg-laying, ♂♂ perform long-distance migration to moulting sites, mainly at sea, which are also used for wintering. Second-calendar-year birds can over-summer (and moult their remiges) at the wintering sites or on the breeding grounds. ♀♀ whose nests fail may also migrate to moult, but at least some successful ♀♀ moult their flight feathers near the nest sites, often in small groups. Very gregarious in non-breeding season, inhabiting marine habitats, coastal bays and continental shelf waters <20 m deep[396], preferably of 5–15 m[665], usually <2 km from the coast[1213]. Generally uncommon inland, but regularly migrates overland, by night and at high altitude.

RANGE and POPULATION The eastern limit of the breeding range is in C Siberia, around the Lena and Olenek Rivers[396,1253]. Uncommon breeder in Iceland, Ireland, Scotland and Svalbard. Uncommon in winter in Mediterranean (especially the north-west) and C Europe. Rare in Black Sea and vagrant to Middle East. Apparently no reports from North America, where it could occur (rare but regular in Greenland). Global population estimated at 1,600,000 birds[305] in sharp decline[1206]. In Baltic Sea, a decrease of 47.4% reported between 1988–93 and 2007–09, with 783,000 and 412,000 birds counted, respectively[1206], but monitoring of passage through Gulf of Finland revealed that the apparent decline could be at least partly due to the wintering population shifting to the North Sea[991]. Like other sea ducks, prone to high mortality as a result of marine pollution caused by oil spills, especially as the population is highly concentrated at a few sites. Also reportedly affected by over-exploitation of the seabed and high-speed ferries (especially on moulting grounds)[145,396]. Could also be threatened by offshore wind farms in shallow coastal areas[665].

CAPTIVITY This species requires special conditions in captivity (deep, cold and clear water, natural food, etc.) and rarely breeds. Moreover, being rather colourless, it is unlikely that a bird outside the normal range will have escaped from captivity.

REFERENCES Alderfer (1992)[8]; AOU (1957)[19]; AOU (2010)[22]; Baker (1992)[56]; BirdLife International (2014)[145]; Bordage & Savard (2011)[162]; Chesser *et al.* (2010)[22]; Collinson *et al.* (2006)[240]; Cramp & Simmons (1977)[268]; Crochet *et al.* (2010)[273]; Dean (1989)[286]; Delany & Scott (2006)[305]; Dwight (1914)[335]; Fox & Pihl *in* Kear (2005)[396]; Gantlett *et al.* (1996)[417]; Garner (1989)[418]; Garner *et al.* (2008)[427]; Hoffman & Bancroft (1984)[565]; Kaiser *et al.* (2006)[665]; Leverkühn (1890)[752]; Livezey (1995)[771]; Pyle (2005)[1012]; Pyle (2008)[1014]; Salminen (1983)[1122]; Sangster (2009)[1129]; Skov *et al.* (2011)[1206]; Snow & Perrins (1998)[1213]; Stepanyan (1990)[1232]; Syroechkovski & Koblik (2011)[1253]; Voous (1960)[1324]; Voous (1972)[1325]; Waring (1993)[1337].

COMMON SCOTER (continued)

528. Adult ♂ (definitive basic) and one ♀. Poland, Apr (Zbigniew Kayzer).

529. Adult ♂ (definitive basic); vs. Black Scoter *M. americana*, note very different bill shape and coloration, black area at contact of bill and yellow orbital ring. Germany, Dec (Ingo Waschkies).

530. Adult ♀ (definitive basic); note flat nail, much shorter bump on culmen, and vertical feathering at base of bill. Denmark, Dec (Eva Foss Henriksen).

531. Adult ♂♂ (definitive basic) and one ♀; posture, with bill held slightly up, and thin neck are typical. Poland, Apr (Zbigniew Kayzer).

532. Adult ♀ (definitive basic); a dusky trace on cheeks below the eye is frequent; again, note the flat nail to the bill. France, Feb (Sébastien Reeber).

BLACK SCOTER
Melanitta americana

Plate 63

TAXONOMY *Oidemia americana* Swainson, 1832, *Fauna Bor. Amer.*, 2, 1831 [1832], p. 450. Within the genus *Melanitta* very close to, and often considered conspecific with, Common Scoter *M. nigra* (which see).

IDENTIFICATION Dark (♀) or black (♂) sea duck, distinguished quite readily from Surf Scoter *M. perspicillata*, White-winged Scoter *M. deglandi* and Siberian Scoter *M. stejnegeri* under reasonable viewing conditions. Separation from Common Scoter is much more difficult (which see).

PLUMAGES Clear sexual dimorphism from first winter onwards. Simple alternate moult strategy (two plumages in first and definitive cycles). Ageing ♂♂ relatively easy until first summer and sometimes possible until second summer in good views or in the hand. Ageing ♀♀ harder after second pre-basic moult (second autumn). See also Identification under Common Scoter for further details.

Adult ♂

Definitive basic plumage (Nov/Apr). Entirely black plumage, but primaries visibly paler in flight, especially on underwing (producing typical silvery reflections in flight). The feathers on the head-sides have pencil-shaped tips, forming short grooves, with blue-grey velvety hue often making head paler than black gape. Iris dark brown with dark grey orbital ring. Bill black with broad bump covering more than half the culmen reaching in front of nostrils, bright yellow with orange tone to its lower part. Legs blackish-grey.

Definitive alternate plumage (Apr–May/Oct–Nov). Depending on extent of pre-alternate moult (limited at most), overall plumage duller and can look 'messy', with two generations of feathers visible (basic, worn and faded, and alternate, matt black). The general appearance remains similar.

Adult ♀

Definitive basic plumage (Nov/Apr). Dark brown overall, the only noticeable feature is a large paler grey area, vermiculated dark, on the cheeks, throat and upper neck. Iris dark brown. Bill dark grey to blackish, sometimes with a slight bump like that of ♂ on inner culmen. Inside nostril yellow, sometimes with yellow

spots on central culmen and elsewhere within area covered by yellow patch of ♂. Rarely, the same patch appears in ♀ (older individuals?). Legs dark grey to blackish, with a yellowish-brown tone on toes and tarsi.

Definitive alternate plumage (Apr–May/Oct–Nov). Plumage similar but duller and slightly paler.

Juvenile

First basic plumage (until Nov). Like adult ♀ but cheeks and upper neck slightly paler and belly white showing as a large oval neatly streaked brownish. Bill usually all dark grey. Tertials short, straight and round-tipped. The outermost primary is slightly (♂) or not (♀) notched, whereas in adult it is strongly (♀) to very strongly (♂) notched.

First-winter/first-summer ♂

Formative plumage (Nov/Jun). From Oct, young ♂♂ pass through a succession of intermediate appearances until formative plumage in Apr–May. This is like definitive basic plumage, but wings and belly mainly to completely juvenile, the latter being pale brown in winter, becoming white in summer. Juvenile feathers (brown, worn and faded) are also visible to a variable extent on the undertail, rump, among the tertials (often all) and rectrices (sometimes none). The bill begins to show a yellow tint from Nov, and most have a clearly defined yellow patch like that of adult ♂ in Jan. The bump at the culmen base appears much more slowly, and is usually barely visible during first winter.

First-winter/first-summer ♀

Formative plumage (Nov/Jun). Like adult ♀ but two generations of feathers usually clearly visible (juvenile, brown becoming beige-brown in spring, and formative, dark brown) on body. When pre-formative moult is reduced, the plumage can be surprisingly pale in late spring. In the reverse case, appearance is very similar to adult ♀, but pale belly becoming white, contrasting strongly with rest of body. Note presence of juvenile tertials and (sometimes) rectrices, shorter and heavily worn in spring.

Second-winter ♂

Second basic plumage (Oct/Sep). Very like adult ♂, but differs (in very good views or the hand) by chin, throat and belly having brownish tones, the latter becoming paler until summer[1014]. Sometimes, the outermost primary is only slightly notched.

GEOGRAPHIC VARIATION Apparently none, but possible differences between Asian and American populations should be evaluated further.

MEASUREMENTS and MASS ♂ and adult slightly larger than ♀ and young, respectively. ♂ (*n*=34): wing chord 228.4 (±7.8), bill 43.7 (±2.4), tarsus 55.6 (±3.5), mass 1,117.0 (±101.6); ♀ (*n*=21): wing chord 218.8 (±7.7), bill 40.9 (±2.8), tarsus 52.4 (±4.0), mass 987.4 (± 110.1)[246]. ♂ (*n*=12): wing chord 229–241 (234), bill 40–47 (43.3), tail 82–100 (91.0); ♀ (*n*=11): wing chord 206–230 (222), bill 39–44 (42.2), tail 69–82 (73.0)[945]. ♂ (*n*=60): wing chord 223–240 (adult) and 214–232 (juvenile), bill length from proximal end of nostrils 29–32, bill depth at proximal end of nostrils 15.8–17.3, tarsus 43–50, tail 83–99; ♀ (*n*=50): wing chord 213–231 (adult) and 205–222 (juvenile), bill length from proximal end of nostrils 25–29, bill depth at proximal end of nostrils 14.2–15.7, tarsus 40–47, tail 65–82[1014].

VOICE More often heard than other scoters. ♂ gives a rather long piping, plaintive whistle *geeeew*. See also Common Scoter. ♀ utters a hoarse *kraaa* especially near nesting sites.

MOULT Simple alternate strategy (?). Apparently identical to that of Common Scoter (which see). Pre-formative moult is protracted from Sep to May. Definitive pre-basic moult starts from mid-Jul to mid-Sep (♂) or Sep–Oct (♀)[56,162] and ends in Nov–Dec, or even Feb in some ♀♀.

HYBRIDISATION Rare reports of birds with intermediate characters may be result of hybridisation with Common Scoter[427,1325].

HABITAT and LIFE-CYCLE Pairs arrive at nesting sites mainly in May, eggs being laid between late May and early Aug[162]. Inhabits small-sized (often <40 ha) and shallow (<5 m) lakes, with clear acidic water, often on rocky substrates, in the tundra and northern taiga. Also uses large rivers and backwaters, but avoids wooded areas and large lakes[162,246]. Favours islands with low vegetation to conceal the nest, and shores with helophytic vegetation, where ♀ can hide with brood in the water. Breeds at age of two years, the young

spending the summer at sea, anywhere between the wintering and breeding grounds. ♂♂ abandon ♀♀ shortly after laying and form large flocks to moult, often following a long migration. Successful ♀♀ moult once their offspring fledge. During moult of remiges, as in winter, uses marine habitats, mainly on sand or pebble substrates, or around rocky points[162,460]. Compared to Common Scoter, seems to remain closer to shore, often in small scattered flocks. Capable of long migrations overland, though rarely seen on inland waters (except Great Lakes).

RANGE and POPULATION Three disjunct populations. E Canadian breeders (especially NC Quebec) winter on the Atlantic coast, centred on New Jersey. Uncommon but regular in Gulf of Mexico. Breeders in Alaska (rare along Arctic coast east to Canada) winter on Pacific coast, with most off S Alaska and Canada. The Asian population breeds east of the Lena River and winters from Kuril Is to Japan, with smaller numbers south to Yellow Sea and E China Sea. Total population estimated at 530,000–830,000[305], with 250,000 in E North America, 160,000 in W North America and 300,000–500,000 in E Asia[1348], but problems exist due to scoters being difficult to identify within huge mixed flocks at sea. Other estimates indicate 388,000 in 1992 in Alaska[243], or totals of 69,242–256,633 migrants per year (mean 150,481) at Avalon, New Jersey, in 1995–2011[908], although much of the Atlantic population winters north of there. Trend uncertain, unknown in Asia, but reported as slightly increasing in Alaska[1168] and E North America[1164], and generally considered to be in marked decline[145].

CAPTIVITY Requires specific conditions in captivity (large deep ponds, with clear, clean and rather cold water, natural food, etc.), and thus very rarely kept, much less bred. Very unlikely to escape.

REFERENCES Baker (1992)[56]; BirdLife International (2014)[145]; Bordage & Savard (2011)[162]; Conant & Groves (1992)[243]; Consortium Gauthier & Guillemette-Grebe (1993)[246]; Consortium Gauthier & Guillemette-Dwight (1914)[335]; Delany & Scott (2006)[305]; Garner *et al.* (2008)[427]; Goudie (1984)[460]; New Jersey Audubon Society (2013)[908]; Palmer (1976)[945]; Pyle (2005)[1012]; Pyle (2008)[1014]; Sea Ducks Joint Venture (2003)[1164]; Sea Ducks Joint Venture (2012)[1168]; Voous (1972)[1325]; Wetlands International (2014)[1348].

533. Adult ♂ (definitive basic). Japan, Jan (Stuart Price).

534. Adult ♂ (definitive basic). Japan, Dec (Stuart Price).

535. Adult ♂ (definitive basic). Japan, Mar (Stuart Price).

536. Adult ♀ (definitive basic); note rather swollen culmen and forehead bump, as well as salient gape, typical of this species. Japan, Dec (Stuart Price).

537. Adult; note typical thick neck and long pointed tail of ♂♂, as well as extensive yellow patch on bill of ♀. Japan, Feb (Aurélien Audevard).

538. Juvenile/first-winter ♀ (first basic/formative); the easiest way to distinguish birds in their first year from adult is whitish belly (true of all scoters). New York, USA, Nov (Sébastien Reeber).

LONG-TAILED DUCK
Clangula hyemalis

Plate 64

TAXONOMY *Anas hyemalis* Linnaeus, 1758, *Syst. Nat.*, edn. 10, p. 126. Member of the Mergini, and a monotypic genus. The cladistic analysis proposed by Livezey[771] places this species in a monophyletic group sister to scoters, and including mergansers and goldeneyes. No geographical variation or subspecies.

IDENTIFICATION Generally does not pose identification problems. A medium-sized sea duck, characterised by long tail (very long in adult ♂), a high, rounded head, and short and stocky bill. The different plumages are mainly dark brown and blackish in spring and summer, more variegated with white over rest of year. This species does not completely fold its wings between dives, thus the dark upperwing covers the white flanks, making the bird appear darker while it is feeding.

PLUMAGES Sexual dimorphism appears during first winter, and is strong in adults at all seasons. Complex alternate moult strategy (two plumages per year in definitive cycle, three in first cycle). However, it appears that both definitive moults are protracted and often suspended, leading to various plumages often placed into four types. Indeed, a flock of Long-tailed Ducks often presents as many different appearances as individuals! These are sometimes considered to be the product of pre-supplemental moults (see Moult). Ageing relatively easy until first summer.

Adult ♂

Definitive basic plumage (Sep–Oct/Mar–May). Beautiful plumage mainly white, pale grey and black. Head shows two successive aspects (see Moult), the first in Sep–Oct being white, pale grey around the eye with a dark grey patch on lower cheeks. Assuming that this resulted from a plumage (and moult) different from the next, it has been reported that the white head feathers are shorter than those in winter[945,1081]. In late autumn/early winter, a large round, pale olive-grey patch appears, almost from the bill base to around the eye (except the white eye-ring). It extends as a large black oval spot on the lower cheeks and brown on the sides of the upper neck. A pale yellow wash often covers the forecrown. Iris hazel. Bill bicoloured, basal half slate-black with clear-cut pale pink distal half (rarely yellow), except blackish nail. Neck and upper breast white. Large black pectoral band covers lower breast and upper belly, extending as complete collar onto mantle, the black then continuing over the back, central rump, uppertail-coverts and central rectrices. The latter are very long (17–24 cm[1081], or 13–18.5 cm longer than the next outermost pair[1014]). Rest of rectrices show more white outwards. Sides of rump, undertail to belly white. Flanks pale grey. Scapulars elongated, pointed and pale grey, the longest largely white and falling over the rear flanks. Inner tertials black, central tertials to innermost secondaries with a clear rusty hue. Upperwing entirely dark brown with tertial coverts, lesser and median coverts blackish. Underwing dark grey with lesser and median coverts blackish-brown, and greater coverts and remiges with silvery tones. Legs and feet pale blue-grey with blackish webs.

Definitive alternate plumage (Mar–Jul/Sep–Nov). Head and neck black, with broad grey/olive-brown patch in front and around eye, with a large white eye-ring extending as short eyestripe. During breeding, a variable number of retained basic white feathers are often visible on nape. Bill of breeding ♂ has pinkish distal band, becoming greyish or is lost, the bill then being entirely dark grey. This pink band is strongly marked in non-breeding adult ♂♂[1081]. Small pale or reddish bars on upper mantle and shoulders. Rest of mantle, breast and upper belly blackish. Scapulars buff to pale reddish with black triangle in centre. Posterior scapulars very elongated and sharply pointed (11–14 cm[1081]), white, pale ochre or buff with a black rachis stripe tapering at the tip. These scapulars can be replaced by shorter and rounded feathers, usually yellow-ochre to deep reddish, and are often said to result from pre-supplemental moult (see Moult), but their appearance is more probably related to the time they were grown[1014]. Flanks grey. Back and rump blackish-brown. Belly white. Basic tail and wings retained.

Adult ♀

Definitive basic plumage (Oct–Dec/Mar–May). Plumage very variable. Head and neck white more or less mottled pale grey, and crown, nape, hindneck and broad ear-patch dark (brown, grey or blackish). Besides patch on lower cheeks, this dark tone is sometimes much reduced on top and back of head, e.g. just a short bar on forecrown, the rest being irregularly spotted pale grey. Iris brown. Bill dark grey, with blue or greenish tones more or less marked, but no subterminal patch. Breast dark reddish-brown, black, or grey, sometimes paler in front, but usually clearly demarcated from neck and flanks. Belly, flanks, lower belly, undertail and rump-sides white. Back, central rump and central rectrices dark brown or blackish, with variably marked grey-brown to pale reddish fringes. Outer rectrices with white outer webs. Mantle and scapulars very variable too, centred with black arrows and fringed chestnut-brown, dull grey-brown or pale grey. Posterior scapulars variably long and pointed. Reportedly second basic plumage of ♀ (second winter) has shorter and greyer scapulars[984]. Tertials (long, broad and pointed) and inner secondaries rusty with often subtle pale fringes. Upperwing dark grey-brown, darker on lesser and median coverts (often with soft bronze sheen). Underwing, legs and feet like ♂.

Definitive alternate plumage (Mar–Jul/Oct–Dec). Much darker than basic plumage. Base of bill, forehead, crown, cheeks, chin, throat, foreneck and lower neck dark brown to blackish. Large half-collar pale or whitish under cheeks and broad grey-brown to olive patch in front of eye. Broad white eye-ring (interrupted in front) extending as thin whitish line behind eye. Iris brown. Bill has stronger blue tones than in basic plumage. Breast brown to dark or dull grey-brown, more or less barred whitish especially where meets flanks. Scapulars rather short, blackish-centred with pale grey or pale brown fringes. By end of pre-alternate moult, flanks washed pale grey-brown. Rest of body similar to basic plumage.

Juvenile

First basic plumage (until Sep–Jan). Resembles basic plumage ♀ but duller and less white. Head, neck and breast more evenly dark. Head dark grey-brown with dark ear-patch initially poorly marked and whitish patch often reduced to around eye. A vague pale area recalling that of alternate ♀ runs from upper cheeks, bypasses the rear cheeks and joins throat. However, some birds have an almost all-dark brown head. Iris dark brown. Bill dark grey. Breast and upper belly dark grey-brown to dark buff. Flanks buff, pale brown or pale grey. Belly white. Tail brown, white on sides (narrow fringes to outer rectrices). Juvenile rectrices have rachis quickly bare at tips. Back and central rump dark brown. Scapulars brown to dull grey-brown with dark centres. Tertials short, narrow, truncated at tips, dark brown with rusty tone, often quickly worn at the tips. Upperwing all dark and dull brown (without bronze sheen). Underwing

dark brown, with greyer remiges. Legs and feet initially tinged olive-grey. Sexing possible in hand, by comparing length of central rectrices: the longest ones exceed the third pair (from centre) by 8–16 cm in ♂, and 3–6 cm in ♀[1014]. The pale subterminal bill band appears from Oct–Nov in young ♂.

First-winter ♂

Formative plumage (Oct–Mar/May–Aug.). Plumage variable and acquired slowly, over relatively long period. Pre-formative moult variable in extent, some birds showing obvious signs of juvenile plumage until winter. First-winter ♂ distinguished quite easily from ♀♀ of all ages by presence of pale or pink patch on bill. However, bill coloration is quite variable individually. Many young ♂♂ have a grey-pinkish spot barely discernible by Oct–Nov, which usually becomes more obvious in Dec–Feb, but even in midwinter some still show an unclear pinkish subterminal band. Also note some pale grey to whitish scapulars growing at same time. Overall, young ♂ still rather closely resembles ♀ in autumn, but is more like basic plumage adult ♂ (albeit slightly patchier) by Jan–Mar. In these birds with near-adult coloration, the peri-ocular patch is browner or pale grey (vs. olive-grey in adult ♂), often with a trace of black line on crown-sides. The patch on ear-coverts is blackish or brown, and ill-defined. Blackish breast-band, less extensive towards belly with scattered whitish or brownish feathers. Scapulars partly pale grey or white, the longest sometimes being considerably elongated and resembling those of basic adult ♂. Other scapulars, often innermost, are speckled or tinged brown. Flanks pale grey. In intermediate birds, it is safer to determine age on the basis of the usually retained juvenile tertials, shorter and worn at tips, but sometimes partly replaced (then adult-type). Juvenile rectrices are generally retained, thereby having a short tail typical of this age when other ♂ features (pink patch on bill, white scapulars, etc.) are also visible. Central rectrices can be moulted and then contrast with the outer juvenile rectrices. When moulted these rectrices are shorter than adult – difference between central rectrices and third pair from centre 8–13 cm (13–18.5 cm in adult)[1014]. Finally, note secondary upperwing-coverts, browner than in adult ♂, often contribute to the duller appearance.

First-winter ♀

Formative plumage (Oct–Mar/May–Aug.). Like young ♂, pre-formative moult is slow, protracted and variable in extent, some ♀♀ appearing largely juvenile until midwinter, sometimes even until spring. During autumn/early winter, many young ♀♀ generally have an appearance intermediate between juvenile and basic plumage adult ♀. Head less marked with white, more sullied pale grey-brown, with dark marks less clearly defined. Scapulars usually appear dull brown and typically short, round-tipped and grey with black centres. Whatever their colour, the pale fringes are less clearly defined than in adult ♀. White belly appears finely streaked pale brown up close. The bill, dark grey at first, quickly acquires adult-type coloration, frequently greyish-turquoise and pale-based. Ageing ♀♀ in winter can nevertheless be difficult, so check for juvenile rectrices and tertials (shorter, brown or faded, and frayed at tips).

First-summer ♂

First alternate plumage (May–Aug?/Oct–Dec). Plumage poorly known and highly variable, suggesting an incomplete definitive alternate plumage. Young ♂ usually easily distinguished from adult ♀ at this time and distinguished from adult ♂ by mix of alternate and formative or juvenile feathers. Note especially the juvenile rectrices (evenly worn, short and faded), or formative in case of central ones (shorter than adult ♂), tertials all or partly juvenile (short, dull brown, faded and frayed at tips) and upperwing (secondaries dull and frayed).

First-summer ♀

First alternate plumage (May–Aug?/Oct–Dec). Like ♂, this plumage is poorly described and appears variable. Generally darker and less contrasting than adult ♀ with whitish marks of face sullied brown and diffuse. Scapulars similar to those of formative plumage, rather short, round-tipped, often greyish with black centres. However, age safely determined only on basis of pattern of rectrices, tertials and upperwing, as in formative and juvenile plumages, but feathers very worn and faded.

Second-winter ♂

Second basic plumage (Sep–Oct/Mar–May). Identical to definitive basic plumage, but extent of olive-grey colour on face, presence of juvenile feathers (lesser and median coverts, tertials, belly feathers) and length of central rectrices can help identify second-winter birds[56,1014].

Second-winter ♀

Second basic plumage (Sep-Oct/Mar-May). As ♂, identical to definitive basic plumage, but presence of juvenile feathers (lesser and median coverts, tertials, belly) distinguishes second-winter birds[56,1014].

GEOGRAPHIC VARIATION None described.

MEASUREMENTS and MASS ♂ and adult slightly larger than ♀ and young, respectively. ♂: wing chord 218–241 (adult, 228, n=45) and 205–227 (juvenile, 214, n=14), tail 188–254 (adult, 215, n=43) and 61–74 (juvenile, 66.1, n=14), tarsus 34–38 (35.8, n=70); ♀: wing chord 204–220 (adult, 212, n=20) and 192–211 (juvenile, 202, n=16), tail 64–78 (adult, 70.4, n=17) and 51–64 (juvenile, 56.8, n=17), tarsus 32–37 (34.1, n=36)[267]. ♂: wing chord 210–236 (adult, 224, n=95) and 198–224 (juvenile, 212, n=36), bill 24–30 (27.2, n=97); ♀: wing chord 202–220 (adult, 211, n=42) and 183–210 (juvenile, 201, n=43), bill 24–29 (25.9, n=36)[1122]. Adult ♂ (n=15): wing chord 223.2 ± 1.1, culmen 27.1 ± 0.3, tarsus 35.6 ± 0.3, mass in Oct 862.8 ± 17.9; adult ♀ (n=12): wing chord 210.2 ± 1.1, culmen 26.5 ± 0.4, tarsus 34.7 ± 0.3, mass in Oct 733.6 ± 17.9 (n=10)[737]. ♂ (n=100): wing chord 208–232 (adult) and 196–220 (juvenile), culmen 25–30, bill depth at tip of forehead feathers 14.9–17.7, tail 180–265, tarsus 33–38; ♀ (n=100): wing chord 195–216 (adult) and 185–206 (juvenile), culmen 24–28, bill depth at tip of forehead feathers 13.3–16.1, tail 58–74, tarsus 32–36[1014].

VOICE Usually quiet outside breeding season, during which it may be quite noisy. ♂♂ give a strong, trisyllabic, nasal *aw aw-aaow-lik* or *urr urr-u-ooh-lip*, most often in contact with other territorial ♂♂. Sometimes utters various other barked calls or chattering sounds. ♀ has rapid series of guttural calls, like *err*, a repeated *gak gak gak* or a softer *egg*.

MOULT The species' moult has been and remains the subject of much debate, although many authors[56,945,1081,1123] agree over four plumages, resulting from four annual moults, but this variability has also been assumed to be the result of just two annual moults[928,1014], which is compatible with the approach of Humphrey & Parkes (see Introduction). Indeed, if the shape and coloration of the feathers are controlled by a hormonal activity independent of the process responsible for the moult, there is no need for additional moults to explain differences between individuals of the same sex and age, at the same season. Thus, scapulars worn in spring and summer by adult ♂♂, derived from a single moult, could be long, pointed, fringed yellow-ochre to white when acquired early in the season, and short, rounded and reddish if grown later[1014]. To assign these appearances to different moults, it must be ascertained that the same follicles were activated twice, or that these feathers are worn consecutively by a single individual. In addition, four annual moults should lead to many transient stages during which feathers of different types are visible side by side on the same individual.

Considering homologies between related species, the hypothesis of two annual moults is adopted here. An additional moult is inserted in the first cycle, thus making an alternate complex strategy. The great variability in appearance is thus linked to the fact that both annual moults are very protracted, so that the species is in moult almost ten months a year. In addition, pre-formative and pre-alternate moults are clearly very variable in extent, duration and speed between individuals, perhaps depending on age[1014]. This succession of slow and variable moults may be an adaptation to constantly needing well-insulated and watertight plumage, for diving in cold water[1383].

Pre-formative moult occurs Oct–Mar, and includes a variable number of body feathers, few or no tertials, tertial coverts or inner secondary upperwing-coverts, and 1–3 pairs of central rectrices[1014]. This moult varies in extent, some (mainly ♂♂) achieving an appearance much like definitive basic plumage (except the belly, wings and outer rectrices), whereas others retain plumage largely juvenile until spring[56]. First pre-alternate moult is not well known, sometimes considered identical in extent and timing to equivalent moult in adults[56,945,1081], or presumed to be reduced (or almost lacking) and occurring in Jun–Aug[1014]. Definitive pre-basic moult is complete, begins between late July and Aug with the wings (on average three weeks later in ♀♀, breeding or not[658]) and then the tail and body until Nov–Dec. Definitive pre-alternate moult is variable and very protracted, from Mar to Aug in both sexes. It includes the head, neck and scapulars before breeding, and flanks and rear body afterwards.

HYBRIDISATION Exceptional in captivity, where reported with Mandarin Duck *Aix galericulata*[639] and Chestnut Teal *Anas castanea*[295]. No hybrids recorded in the wild.

HABITAT and LIFE-CYCLE Medium-distance migrant, but locally simply moves to coasts close to nesting grounds. Spring migration occurs between late Feb and late May, peaking between mid-Apr and mid-May. At this time, the species forms huge migratory flocks, from which groups of already-formed pairs disperse to nesting sites. Inhabits Arctic tundra, typically favouring tundra and other habitats with maze of small ponds and rivers, and small islets and hummocks for nesting. Also uses coastal habitats (offshore islands) and shores of large lakes, south to the willow and dwarf birch zone, but less frequent in wooded tundra. Nests in lone pairs, but sometimes at relatively high density, with frequent territorial conflicts early in season. Eggs are laid late May to late Jun. ♂♂ abandon ♀♀ during early incubation, and head to nearby coasts (but sometimes up to 1,000 km[794]) where they form small moulting flocks. ♀♀ often leave their flightless offspring, the latter forming groups without any parental care[646]. Other adults stay with their young, but in all cases wing moult is performed near the nest sites. Migration south occurs after wing moult and until Dec[1081], depending on the population. Very gregarious in non-breeding season, forming huge flocks of up to tens of thousands of birds. At this time, found mainly at sea, sometimes far offshore, in water 10–35 m deep[1154]. Feeds by day, usually at 3–10 m (up to 50–60 m[1383]). Rare inland, where the species favours large deep lakes.

RANGE and POPULATION Continuous circumpolar breeding range. Outside mapped range, winters in small numbers in Black and Caspian Seas, in E Asia south to South Korea (few), along US Pacific coast to California and along Atlantic coast to Florida, as well as north, usually to the pack ice and prone to mass movements in face of hard weather conditions. Uncommon to occasional visitor far south of its usual range, including inland (most of Europe to Mediterranean, Iran, Kuwait, Israel, India, E China and the inland USA to Gulf of Mexico). Total population estimated at 6,200,000–6,800,000 individuals, declining and classified as Vulnerable[145,1154]. Has sharply decreased recently, with regional population estimated at 1,600,000 birds in NW Europe, compared to 4,272,000 in the Baltic in 1992–93[1206], with 500,000–1,000,000 in E Asia[858] and 1,000,000 in North America[305,1348]. The latter population was previously estimated at 2,700,000 birds during the 1990s[1154]. Evidence for a sharp decline in the Baltic and North America (-1.9% per year in 1965–2005[209]) are consistent, with no suggestion of a northward shift in range[145,1206]. Threats include destruction of its breeding habitats due to oil pollution (especially in Russia) and mortality in fishing nets. The main threat, as for other Arctic birds, seems to come from disruptions to cyclic abundance of lemmings[515], the scarcity of the later increasing the predation of eggs, chicks and even adult wildfowl and waders. It is also possible that other factors may affect the general condition of ♀♀, which can even elect not to breed[145].

CAPTIVITY Rarely kept in captivity and even more rarely bred, mainly because of its requirements (needs cold, deep clear water and some natural food). Rarely offered for sale, usually at prohibitive prices. Thus very unlikely to escape, with most out-of-range reports being considered natural vagrants.

REFERENCES Alison (1975)[15]; Baker (1993)[56]; BirdLife International (2014)[145]; Butcher & Niven (2007)[209]; Cramp & Simmons (1977)[268]; Delacour (1954)[295]; Delany & Scott (2006)[305]; Hario *et al.* (2009)[515]; Howell *et al.* (2003)[589]; Johnsgard (1960)[639]; Johnsgard (1978)[646]; Johnson (1985)[658]; Leafloor *et al.* (1996)[737]; Livezey (1995)[771]; Madge & Burn (1988)[794]; Miyabayashi & Mundkur (1999)[858]; Ogilvie & Young (1998)[928]; Palmer (1976)[945]; Peterson & Ellarson (1978)[984]; Ploeger (1968)[998]; Pyle (2008)[1014]; Robertson & Savard (2002)[1081]; Salminen (1983)[1122]; Salomonsen (1941)[1123]; Salomonsen (1949)[1124]; Scott & Rose (1996)[1154]; Skov *et al.* (2011)[1206]; Vahatalo *et al.* (2004)[1302]; Wetlands International (2014)[1348]; Young & Kear *in* Kear (2005)[1383].

539. Adult ♂ (definitive basic). Norway, Feb (Tormod Amundsen/ Biotope).

540. Adult ♂ (definitive alternate), in almost full alternate plumage. Norway, Jun (Sébastien Reeber).

541. Adult ♂ (definitive alternate); note basic feathers still retained, as well as the much longer alternate scapulars. Norway, Jun (Sébastien Reeber).

542. Adult ♂ (definitive alternate/definitive basic) in pre-basic body moult. France, Oct (Aurélien Audevard).

543. Adult ♂ (definitive alternate) in territorial display-flight. Norway, Jun (Sébastien Reeber).

544. First-winter ♂ (formative); note bill pattern still blurred (although permits sexing), as well as juvenile breast, fore flanks and some scapulars retained. Iceland, Feb (Yann Kolbeinsson).

545. Adult ♀ (definitive basic). Iceland, Nov (Yann Kolbeinsson)

546. Adult ♀ (definitive basic). Norway, Feb (Tormod Amundsen/ Biotope).

547. First-winter ♀ (formative). Iceland, Nov (Yann Kolbeinsson).

548. Adult ♀ (definitive alternate). Norway, Jun (Sébastien Reeber).

549. Adult ♀ (definitive alternate). Iceland, May (Yann Kolbeinsson).

550. Adult ♀ (definitive alternate). Iceland, May (Yann Kolbeinsson).

BUFFLEHEAD
Bucephala albeola

Plate 67

TAXONOMY *Anas Albeola* Linnaeus, 1758, *Syst. Nat.*, edn. 10, p. 124. See Taxonomy of Common Goldeneye *B. clangula*. Weak geographical variation, monotypic.

IDENTIFICATION Small diving duck unlikely to be confused with other species, due to its size, active behaviour and distinctive plumage. Significantly smaller than the other goldeneyes, and does not produce the characteristic sound of their wingbeats.

PLUMAGES Strong sexual dimorphism in definitive basic plumage. Complex alternate moult strategy (two plumages per definitive cycle, three in first cycle). Plumages of ♀♀ and formative (first winter) and alternate (eclipse) plumages of ♂♂ rather similar.

Adult ♂

Definitive basic plumage (Oct/Jun–Jul). Mainly black and white. Large rounded head with large round white patch covering top and back of head reaching behind eye. Rest of head black with strong gloss, often purple at front, and blue or green at its base and back, but varies depending on light. Iris dark brown. Small pale blue-grey bill, often blackish at base, whitish towards tip. Mantle, inner scapulars and tertials black. Upper back and rump black in centre, merging into paler grey coloration on sides and uppertail-coverts. Tail dark grey. Neck, breast, belly, flanks and belly white. Upperwing blackish with large white area covering the visible part of six innermost secondaries, the corresponding greater coverts, median coverts and part of primary coverts. Marginal coverts black with white fringes. Underwing largely dark grey, with lesser, median coverts and secondaries appearing pale grey to whitish. Axillaries dark grey tipped white. Legs bright pink.

Definitive alternate plumage (Jun–Jul/Oct). Similar to adult ♀, but overall coloration more contrasting, with head blacker and white spot on rear head much larger and rounder. Upperparts blackish and flanks and rump pale grey, almost devoid of brown tones. Some basic feathers, black (head and upperparts) or white (breast and flanks), often retained. Basic upperwing pattern retained, very easy to distinguish from that of ♀, often visible even on water, and by large white bar between sides and upperparts.

Adult ♀

Definitive basic plumage (Nov/Jun–Aug). Plumage overall dark and dull grey-brown, with only notable marking a large elongated white spot on upper cheeks. Rest of head blackish-brown, slightly paler on throat and upper neck. Iris dark brown. Bill dark grey, blackish at base. Mantle feathers blackish brown fringed slightly paler. Scapulars, back, rump blackish almost uniform, the outer scapulars being tinged slightly greyer, appearing more glossy. Uppertail grey. Sides of breast, flanks and undertail pale grey with brownish tones. Breast centre and belly pale to whitish. Tail grey-brown. Upperwing dark brown to blackish (frequent sheen on lesser and median coverts) with 5–6 innermost secondaries largely white, s5 with little or no white, and a variable number of central greater coverts having a white patch near tip. In some ♀♀, greater coverts have a white distal half, with dark tips forming a thin bar[224]. Tertial coverts broad, rounded and black. Tertials black slightly curved and round-tipped. Underwing like ♂. Legs dull greyish-pink, webs darker.

Definitive alternate plumage (Jul–Aug/Nov). Similar to basic plumage, but often seems somewhat plainer and browner overall.

Juvenile

First basic plumage (until Oct–Nov). Similar to adult ♀ but several subtle plumage features are especially useful for ageing in direct comparison or with practice: throat paler brown, white patch on rear cheeks smaller (with individual variation and note influence of head posture) and belly neatly marked grey-brown, less whitish. Upperparts browner and duller, less blackish, partly because of long narrow scapulars, with pointed tips (square and broader in subsequent plumages), brown and dull. Tertials shorter, straighter, quickly becoming brown and frayed at tips. Rump pale grey-brown in young ♂♂, contrasting with back and blackish-brown tail, the latter darker than in subsequent plumages. In the hand, note dark brown to blackish tertial coverts, narrow and quickly worn, the lesser and median coverts narrow and round-tipped, brown and without sheen. Upperwing pattern useful for sexing: young ♀♀ show few or no white spots on greater coverts and usually no white on s5. Moreover, the white areas on the inner secondaries generally far from cover the entire outer web. Young ♂ usually has some white oval spots towards tips of greater coverts, and s5 shows a clear white patch on outer web. White areas of inner secondaries cover most of outer webs and extend onto inner webs. Sex of juvenile can also be determined by length of folded wing (♂ > 159 mm, ♀ <159 mm [1014], or for 97% of young ♀♀ < 160 mm and 98% of young ♂♂ >160 mm [224]).

First-winter ♂

Formative plumage (Nov–Jan/Jun–Aug). Formative feathers intermediate or more similar to those of adult appear as early as Nov but are rarely obvious until midwinter. Before then, appearance very similar to that of adult ♀, but soon the front and base of the head turn black (with metallic sheen) and white feathers appear above white ear-patch. Formative scapulars longer (more square-tipped, different from juvenile scapulars) and variable, between grey tone of ♀ and broadly whitish [1014]. Some white feathers often mixed in grey breast and flanks, often with large white area on fore flanks. Lower rump remains quite pale and grey contrasting sharply with black back. Juvenile upperwing pattern retained, and thus similar to adult ♀, but with narrower, worn secondary- and tertial coverts, browner without sheen, and often a large white patch on s5.

First-winter ♀

Formative plumage (Nov–Jan/Jun–Aug). During first winter, gradually shifts from juvenile appearance to adult appearance, which are close to one another. Head paler grey-brown than young ♂ and adult ♀ at same season. Contrast between back and rump less pronounced than in young ♂, close to ♀. Therefore differs from adult ♀ mainly by upperwing pattern (white spots reduced or absent on central greater coverts, white patch absent on s5 and reduced on s6, secondary- and tertial coverts narrower, pointed or round-tipped (vs. square in adult ♀), frayed at tips, brown and lack sheen.

First-summer ♂

First alternate plumage (Jun–Aug/Oct–Nov). Close to definitive alternate plumage of ♂ but formative plumage usually still easily visible, so easily distinguished from ♀♀ of all ages. Upperwing pattern useful for ageing until second pre-basic moult.

First-summer ♀

First alternate plumage (Jun–Aug/Nov–Dec). Largely identical to formative plumage. Upperwing pattern useful for ageing until beginning of second pre-basic moult.

Second-winter ♂

Second basic plumage (Oct/Jun–Jul). Identical to adult ♂ in same plumage, but throat washed dusky or brown, and upperwing has outer lesser and inner median coverts mottled dusky [1014]. Extent of white on greater coverts is less in some birds, with dark bars formed by bases and tips to feathers, across white area of upperwing.

GEOGRAPHIC VARIATION No subspecies or strong geographical variation, but birds west of Rockies (British Columbia to N California) show, in adult ♀♀ and formative plumages, a browner tone to dark areas of plumage, whereas they are more blackish and grey in Alberta, Yukon and Alaska [367], but these differences may also reflect bleaching [1014].

MEASUREMENTS and MASS ♂ noticeably larger and heavier than ♀, and adult slightly larger than young. Adult ♂ (*n*=12): wing chord 169–175 (173), culmen 27–30 (28.7), tail 70–78 (74.7), tarsus 32–35 (33.7); adult ♀ (*n*=12): wing chord 152–161 (156), culmen 24–27 (25.1), tail 59–70 (65.7), tarsus 30–31 (30.0) [945]. ♂ (*n*=90): wing chord 164–176 (adult) and 159–170 (juvenile), culmen 26–30, bill depth at tip of forehead feathers 13.6–15.8, tail 69–80, tarsus 32–35; ♀ (*n*=100): wing chord 146–160 (adult) and 143–156 (juvenile), culmen 23–27, bill depth at tip of forehead feathers 12.6–14.6, tail 60–71, tarsus 30–33 [1014]. ♂: mass in winter (Oregon) 473 ± 33 (adult, *n*=29) and 450 ± 27 (first-winter, *n*=23); ♀: mass in winter (Oregon) 334 ± 23 (adult, *n*=16) and 315 ± 23 (first-winter, *n*=16) [551].

VOICE Usually silent, heard especially during courtship, when ♂ gives (rarely) squeaky rasping sounds. ♀ heard more frequently, and gives rapid and prolonged series of *kek-kek-kek* notes during courtship or when searching for nest sites. Different social and alarm calls like *err*, *brep* or a longer *brerr*, with a quality recalling a female *Aythya* species.

MOULT Complex alternate strategy. Pre-formative moult protracted, between Aug–Sep and Mar, involving some to most head and body feathers, sometimes a few tertials and inner secondary upperwing-coverts, and generally all rectrices (latter from Oct [429]). First pre-alternate moult seems limited, in Jun–Aug, perhaps even occurring only in some ♂♂ [71,1014]. Includes head feathers and some feathers on the flanks, upper breast [429] and/

or upperparts[1014]. Definitive pre-basic moult starts with wings and rectrices between mid-Jul and mid-Aug in ♂, or mid-Aug in ♀ and second-year birds. It is completed in Oct (often at the beginning of the month) in ♂ and from mid-Nov in ♀. Definitive pre-alternate moult in May–Jul in ♂ and one month later in ♀, including most head and body feathers, but probably few or no tertials and rectrices[1014].

HYBRIDISATION Very rarely mentioned in wild, there are nevertheless rare reports of hybrids involving Common Goldeneye (or perhaps Barrow's Goldeneye *B. islandica*) and, occasionally, Hooded Merganser *Lophodytes cucullatus* (see below). In captivity, a case was mentioned with Tufted Duck *Aythya fuligula*[1190].

Bufflehead × Common Goldeneye. ♂ in definitive basic plumage is distinctive, with a substantially smaller size than Common Goldeneye, a short, triangular and dark grey (intermediate) bill, large head with short tuft often forming a distinct angle on rear crown and black coloration from the chin, the basal bill-sides, the entire crown including the eyes, and the nape and hindneck, with a long white patch from the lower lores across the upper cheeks. Lower cheeks can be pale grey to blackish. Iris amber. Longest scapulars white and rear body blackish (always?). Rest of body as in both species. Legs peach-pink.

Bufflehead × Barrow's Goldeneye. Different authors have indicated the possibility of this cross based on a wing taken by a hunter with biometrics and appearance intermediate between those of Bufflehead and one of the goldeneyes[439,817,945]. It is also possible that such hybrids could be mistaken for the previous one, although one might expect darker scapulars. In any case, a hybrid of this type among a flock of Barrow's Goldeneyes should be carefully scrutinised.

Bufflehead × Hooded Merganser. Exceptional in the wild[111,804,1195]. Its size is reportedly similar to Bufflehead, with a black head and large white patches behind the eye[804,76], a white breast with black vertical stripes on fore flanks, the latter being grey vermiculated dark. The bill appears to be either close to Hooded Merganser[111,76] or to Bufflehead[804]. Upperwing pattern has only the inner secondaries white (as ♀ Bufflehead[804]), or closer to ♂ Hooded Merganser, but with lesser coverts partly white[111].

HABITAT and LIFE-CYCLE Almost exclusively migratory. Most migrate north in Mar–Apr with eggs mainly laid in May–Jun[429]. Breeding habitats comprise small to mid-sized ponds (<100 ha) in wooded taiga, shunning both large lakes and ponds with abundant helophytic vegetation. Requires presence of trees along banks, especially poplars *Populus* spp. and some conifers, where it favours above all old cavities of Northern Flicker *Colaptes auratus* to nest, often less than 10 m from the water[368]. ♂♂ leave the breeding sites shortly after egg laying, and gather at moulting sites either close or far away[429], where they are joined by second-year birds, by ♀♀ that failed to breed and those that left their offspring with other ♀♀. Moulting sites are usually on large inland lakes with sparsely wooded shores[368]. Migratory movements related to moult of different age and sex groups are noticeable between Jun and mid-Sep[429]. Autumn migration often occurs late, triggered by the freeze and peaks from mid-Oct and late-Nov. In winter, mainly in small flocks in salt or brackish water, but often in more sheltered habitats than other *Bucephala*. Occurs in smaller numbers on freshwater lakes, reservoirs and large, slow-moving inland rivers.

RANGE and POPULATION Apart from main range, a few disjunct populations in states of Washington, Oregon, California, Idaho, Montana and Wyoming. Birds breeding west of the Rockies winter on the Pacific coast. Those from C & E Canada winter from Great Lakes and SW USA to Atlantic coast. Birds nesting in Alberta can overwinter either in the west, south or east. In winter, the bulk of the population is located on the coast from C British Columbia to California, and between New Jersey and North Carolina[429]. Uncommon visitor in Japan (a few dozen each winter) and Russian Far East. Accidental in Greater Antilles, the Azores and several countries of W Europe. Population estimated at 1,200,000 individuals in the early 2000s[1154] and 1,000,000 birds in 2011[1292], when stable or slightly increasing, following a sharp increase from 500,000 birds estimated in 1960[367,945]. However, this increase probably followed a severe decrease, due to over-hunting, until the early 20th century[368]. Game harvesting is relatively high at present, with slightly more than 200,000 birds taken annually in Canada and USA[648].

CAPTIVITY Said to be quite demanding as to its requirements (preferably fairly deep, clear and flowing water), and rather difficult to breed if these conditions are not met. Generally offered for sale at a price up to twice that of other *Bucephala*, and three or four times the price of Hooded Merganser for example. Therefore, quite rare in captivity (especially in Eurasia) and unlikely to escape. Nevertheless, individuals seen in the wild in Europe, but banded in captivity, show that some do so.

REFERENCES Battagin (2006)[76]; Bird Hybrids Flickr Forum (2009)[111]; Butcher & Niven (2007)[209]; Carney (1992)[224]; Erskine (1972)[367]; Erskine *in* Kear (2005)[368]; Gauthier (1993)[429]; Gillham & Gillham (1996)[439]; Henny *et al.* (1981)[551]; Johnsgard (2010)[648]; Marcisz (1981)[804]; McCarthy (2006)[817]; Palmer (1976)[945]; Pyle (2008)[1014]; Scott & Rose (1997)[1154]; Sibley (1938)[1190]; Sibley (2000)[1195]; USFWS (2011)[1292].

551. Adult ♂ (definitive basic). California, USA, Apr (Sébastien Reeber).

552. Adult ♂ (definitive basic). California, USA, Nov (Sébastien Reeber).

553. First-winter ♂ (formative); like very dull adult basic ♂, with white and glossy black feathers on head, greyer breast and flanks paler than adult ♀, but usually at least some juvenile scapulars and tertials (browner, pointed and frayed at tips). British Columbia, Canada, Jan (Alan D. Wilson).

554. Adult ♀ (definitive basic); best separated from juvenile by more contrasting head, blackish throat, slight sheen on upperparts, blunt-tipped scapulars and tertials, and adult rectrices. New York, USA, Nov (Sébastien Reeber).

555. First-winter ♀ (formative); compared to adult ♀ and young ♂, note lack of white on greater coverts. Texas, USA, Feb (Greg Lavaty).

556. Adult ♀ (definitive basic); wing pattern (greater coverts) shared by first basic ♂, although latter often has a little less white on average. Texas, USA, Feb (Greg Lavaty).

COMMON GOLDENEYE
Bucephala clangula

TAXONOMY *Anas Clangula* Linnaeus, 1758, *Syst. Nat.*, edn. 10, p. 125. There are three species in the genus *Bucephala*, all endemic to the Holarctic, Common Goldeneye being the only one that breeds in Eurasia, excluding Iceland. The genus *Bucephala* is part of the Mergini, the goldeneyes being closest to the mergansers. Within the genus, Common Goldeneye is close to Barrow's Goldeneye *B. islandica*[771], which are closer to one another than Bufflehead *B. albeola*. There are two subspecies, the nominate in Eurasia, and *B. c. americana* Bonaparte, 1838, in the Nearctic.

IDENTIFICATION Medium-sized diving duck, whose wingbeats produce a typical noise in adult ♂ (on which the species' scientific name is based), less marked in adult ♀ and absent in juvenile. Generally easy to identify, except vs. Barrow's Goldeneye (see below). Can superficially resemble Bufflehead and Smew *Mergellus albellus*, both of which are smaller and whose ♀-type plumages are mostly grey with darker head and white on upperwing. Separation of Barrow's and Common Goldeneyes is not difficult with ♂♂ in definitive basic plumage, but requires more care in other plumages, especially juvenile. Also bear in mind that hybrids are reported occasionally and show intermediate characters (see Hybridisation). The distinguishing features for adult ♂♂ (basic plumage) are as follows.

- *General appearance*: Blacker, and size visibly stronger, shape stockier in Barrow's Goldeneye.

- *Head shape*: Barrow's Goldeneye has the head overall oval, tall, with very steep and even forehead, and a rather flat crown peaking above the eye in profile. Lower nape distinctly swollen. Common Goldeneye has a rounder or conical head, peaking sharply behind the eye, the 'swell' of the nape located higher. Note that the head profile changes with the position of the feathers and the bird's behaviour (tighter between dives, erected during courtship or interactions with other birds, for example).

- *Bill shape*: In profile, the bill of Barrow's Goldeneye is slightly thicker and relatively shorter, triangular. Its lower mandible is slightly convex, giving the bill a snub appearance. From the front, the bill of Barrow's Goldeneye is narrower, while the nail (often difficult to see) is significantly larger and round, covering almost the entire width of the tip.

- *Head sheen*: Purple or violet, barely visible, in Barrow's Goldeneye, and green and obvious under appropriate light in Common Goldeneye.

- *White patch at base of bill*: In Barrow's Goldeneye it is the shape of a reversed comma, tapering to a point above the eye. In Common Goldeneye, the patch is rounded or slightly oval. In formative (first-winter) or alternate (eclipse) plumage, the white is partially obscured and often takes the shape of a small crescent.

- *Scapulars*: Black with successive elongated white patches in Barrow's Goldeneye. The black tips to the scapulars reach the black upper flanks. In Common Goldeneye, the longest row of scapulars is largely white, with oblique and parallel black streaks, the white meeting the white flanks.

- *Upper and rear flanks*: Barrow's Goldeneye presents a broad black line framing the white flanks at the rear, above and across the sides of the breast. Common Goldeneye has all-white flanks, often with a visible black spot in front of the folded wing.

- *Upperwing pattern*: Both species have a large white area on the proximal half of the wing, but Barrow's Goldeneye shows 5–6 white secondaries. The corresponding greater coverts have black spots at tip and broad black bases, forming two lines, one thin, discontinuous or almost absent and the other thick. Median coverts are white, except the four outermost, which are largely centred black. Finally, lesser coverts are largely black. The whole forms three distinct white patches. In Common Goldeneye, the white is much broader, forming a large single patch covering the seven inner secondaries, and the corresponding greater, median and posterior lesser coverts.

Identifying ♀♀, juveniles and, to a lesser extent, ♂♂ in definitive alternate plumage is much more difficult, and must be partly based on subjective features such as head shape, and shape and size of the bill, which are easy to assess with some practice. In all cases, first sex and age the bird and base the identification on multiple features. Again, be wary of hybrid ♀♀ (see Hybridisation). The distinguishing features of ♀♀ and juveniles are:

- *Size and structure*: In same age and sex, Barrow's

Goldeneye is larger and stockier on average, but with some overlap (especially if sex and age unspecified). Size differences are greater in Eurasia (nominate Common Goldeneye) than in North America (subspecies *americana*).

- **Head shape**: In both species, head shape varies constantly depending on behaviour. Thus, on diving, the crown feathers are tightened, the head profile being flatter and thinner, and the bill more prominent. In contrast, at rest or during interactions with congeners, the crown feathers can be erect. To acquire a precise idea of head shape, it is necessary to spend time with the bird, and not to assess this feature on a single photograph for example. It is best to directly compare the bird with others nearby. Also note that juvenile (up to early first winter at least) of both sexes have shorter head feathers, making these subtle differences even more difficult to assess. At rest, Barrow's Goldeneye has a steeper, more bumped forehead, peaking above the eye, and extending in a flat cap and long nape, also flat. In profile, Common Goldeneye has the forehead more in continuation of the culmen, a conical crown peaking behind the eye and nape appearing shorter, forming a hump behind the cheeks, much higher than Barrow's Goldeneye. When sleeping, ♀♀ are identifiable by their head shape, and it is often easier because the shape is more constant[1203].

- **Head colour**: Adult ♀ Barrow's Goldeneye is deeper brown, more chocolate and darker. ♀ Common Goldeneye is brown with a more cinnamon or hazelnut tone, and paler. In direct comparison, and having ascertained sex and age, this feature can be useful. Juveniles of both species have duller, slightly greyer heads, quickly becoming darker in young ♂♂, which is of no use for identification. Also note that when neck is stretched, the brown extends slightly further down the upper neck in Barrow's, but not in Common, where the limit of the brown is at the base of the head.

- **Bill size**: Firstly, it is important to note that perception of bill size in goldeneyes is largely influenced by the position of the head feathers. When flattened (between dives), the bill seems long and strong, but when feathers erect it seems smaller. On average, the bill of Barrow's is shorter and thicker based, giving it a stockier appearance. Nevertheless, there is much overlap (see Measurements and Mass) and Fjeldså[383], for example, stated that 50% of ♀♀ of

both species were in the 'overlap zone'. Differences in bill size between subspecies of Common Goldeneye complicate using this feature: in North America, Barrow's has a very slightly thicker bill at base (<5%) and shorter (*c.*10%) on average. Compared to Eurasian Common Goldeneye, Barrow's has a bill of same length, but *c.*15% thicker based on average. Finally, one should also consider that if the bill is marginally shorter and thicker in Barrow's, this impression is enhanced by the bird's general size and more massive head shape.

- **Bill shape**: In Barrow's Goldeneye, the nail is larger, broader, on a bill narrower-tipped (width at distal edge of nostrils 16.1–19.1 mm in *americana* Common Goldeneye vs. 12.8–16.1 mm in Barrow's[1014]), thus the nail covers almost the whole tip. The differences are already visible in ducklings[905]. From the front, the bill of Barrow's is wider-based and steadily tapers towards the tip. In Common, bill width is much more constant over its length. In profile, Barrow's has nail and tip more snub, with a markedly convex lower mandible (vs. almost straight in Common).

- **Bill colour**: Adult ♀♀ of both species have a largely blackish bill in summer. Between Nov and Jun, in Common Goldeneye, a small yellow spot covers the bill tip and rarely reaches the nostrils. In some, it extends further over nostrils and, very rarely, it extends over much of the bill. Barrow's Goldeneye usually has a largely yellow-orange bill with a dark nail (most birds in North America) or a yellow spot on the distal half, from the nail to just below the nostril and along the tomium (most birds in Iceland). Rarely, North American Barrow's Goldeneye shows only a small yellow spot at the bill tip, like most Common Goldeneyes. In juvenile this appears as a brownish, dull orange or diffuse olive stain in ♀♀ and may cover the entire bill in Common Goldeneye, both in North America[1198] and Eurasia. Lastly, note that this patch is more orange on average in Barrow's Goldeneye, and more yellow in Common Goldeneye.

- **Chest**: Often slightly greyer and plainer in Barrow's Goldeneye, more evenly coloured with the flanks (vs. usually whitish in front in Common Goldeneye). Combined with brown head extending further down neck, it makes the large white collar of Common less visible in Barrow's.

- **Upperwing pattern**: Useful once age known. In adult

♀, Common Goldeneye has seven white inner secondaries and two elongated white areas (bases to greater coverts and tips of median coverts on one hand, posterior lesser coverts on the other) separated by broad black bands (tips of greater and median coverts). Barrow's Goldeneye usually has 4–5 white secondaries and less white on the posterior lesser coverts, often restricted to a broad whitish or pale grey line. Moreover, the white bar of the greater coverts is narrower, the black bases being more visible and a thin line formed by white tips to median coverts. In young ♀♀ of both species, there is generally no black bar on the base of secondaries, all the white secondaries and greater coverts forming a square. Lesser coverts show a diffuse pale grey area in Barrow's, and a wider and whiter patch in Common.

PLUMAGES Nominate subspecies (subspecies differ only in measurements). Strong sexual dimorphism in definitive basic plumage. Complex alternate moult strategy (two plumages per definitive cycle, three in first cycle). Plumages of ♀♀ and formative (first-winter) and, to lesser extent, alternate (eclipse) plumages of ♂♂ rather similar. See also previous section.

Adult ♂

Definitive basic plumage (Oct–Nov/Jun). Often seems bright white overall. Head black with strong green metallic gloss, with oval or round white spot at base of bill. Iris bright yellow to golden-yellow. Bill triangular, slate-grey to blackish, and shiny. Neck, breast, belly to undertail pure white, sometimes slightly washed pink or pale ochre. Mantle, inner scapulars, back, rump and rear body blackish. Lower scapulars with black fringe on outer web (the shortest) or on both webs (the longest). Tail dark grey. Upperwing blackish except 6–7 inner secondaries, corresponding greater, all median and posterior lesser coverts white. Underwing dark grey with leading edge blackish and visible part of inner secondaries white (greater coverts grey, concealing the secondaries, much longer than upperwing greater coverts). Legs bright yellow-orange, webs dark.

Definitive alternate plumage (Jun/Oct–Nov). Similar to definitive alternate plumage of ♀ (including dark bill), but has head darker and colder brown and often shows traces of basic plumage (e.g. hint of pale crescent at base of bill, white feathers on breast, fore flanks and/ or among anterior scapulars). Basic upperwing pattern retained, easily distinguishing it from ♀.

Adult ♀

Definitive basic plumage (Nov–Dec/May–Jun). Head pale chocolate- to hazelnut-brown, with a yellow-ochre hue when well lit. Iris whitish to pale yellow. Bill blackish with yellow spot surrounding nail and usually not reaching nostrils, but some have a larger yellow-orange patch (to above nostrils) and, very rarely, an entirely yellow-orange bill. Large white collar separating head from pale ash-grey breast and flanks, where paler fringes to feathers form subtle stripes and/or pale crescents. All upperparts evenly coloured, slightly darker. Tips of longest scapulars fringed whitish. Belly whitish. Tail grey. Upperwing grey-brown, like upperparts (secondary coverts broad and rather square-tipped), except large white area (6–7 inner secondaries, corresponding greater coverts and posterior lesser coverts) divided in three by two dark bars that are usually sharp and continuous (tips of greater and median coverts). Underwing like ♂. Legs yellow slightly orange, webs darker.

Definitive alternate plumage (May–Jun/Nov–Dec). Very similar to basic plumage, but slightly browner and darker overall, including head and flanks. White collar often less distinct. Bill all black, usually not acquiring its yellow spot until Nov.

Juvenile

First basic plumage (until Oct–Nov). Similar to adult ♀ but duller overall, with a greyer-brown head, and body with a browner-grey tinge. Like mergansers, the head looks smaller and thinner, the feathers of the crown and nape shorter. White collar thinner and poorly defined. Iris olive-brown to yellowish-brown, gradually becoming whitish at the periphery. Bill entirely brownish-grey or olive. Tips of longest scapulars lack white tips. Tertials short and matt black, quickly frayed at tips. Upperwing pattern differs from adult ♀, with secondary coverts narrower and round-tipped. Young ♀ has white greater coverts with poorly marked dark tips (often a small spot), grey-brown median coverts (not blackish) and pale grey posterior lesser coverts (not white). This results in a large white square with a diffuse greyish area on lesser coverts, instead of three separate, clear-cut, white patches in adult ♀. In young ♂, upperwing similar, but dark spots at tips of greater coverts often more marked, usually forming dotted line between greater coverts and secondaries. Furthermore, some young ♂♂ distinguished by darker head and pale fringes to feathers of breast and flanks[1014], but sexing often relies on measurements (bill and wing chord). Legs dull yellow-brown.

First-winter ♂

Formative plumage (Nov–Jan/Jun–Aug.). Until early winter, much like adult ♀, and often distinguished only by upperwing pattern, yellow iris remaining dark around pupil much of winter at least, and by bill often entirely blackish before first adult-type feathers appear. Formative feathers grown in Dec–Feb (individually variable) show adult-type coloration. This results in a dark head (mix of brown and black feathers) with a more or less complete white patch at the bill base, a partly or largely white breast, white feathers on the flanks (especially fore and upper flanks), mantle and posterior scapulars blackish, and anterior scapulars centred white.

First-winter ♀

Formative plumage (Nov–Jan/Jun–Aug.). Similar to adult ♀, but differs by juvenile upperwing pattern retained (see above). Signs of juvenile plumage (tertials shorter and frayed, head duller looking smaller and thinner than adult) often visible until early winter, and iris centred brown (often until subsequent spring). Bill coloration acquired slowly: in early winter, often dark olive-brown with a diffuse orange patch near tip.

First-summer ♂

First alternate plumage (Jun–Aug/Oct–Nov). As ♂ in formative plumage (first pre-alternate moult limited at most) but generally plainer and browner head. Distinguished from adult ♂ in pre-alternate moult by upperwing pattern retained until second pre-basic moult (Jul–Aug).

First-summer ♀

First alternate plumage (Jun–Aug/Nov–Dec). Very similar to adult ♀ but upperwing pattern retained until second pre-basic moult. Early in first summer, often still has iris centred grey or brown (dark inner ring frequently merging into black pupil), and worn brown feathers (scattered to most) on mantle and rear body for example. Tertials and tertial coverts often very heavily worn and faded. Blackish bill with vague traces of brown or orange towards tip.

Second-winter ♂

Second basic plumage (Oct–Nov/Jun). Virtually identical to definitive basic plumage, but head often duller, with brown feather bases partially visible, less strong green gloss, dark marks on tips of some greater coverts,

blackish median coverts and fewer all-white lesser coverts, all indicative of this age[56,1014].

GEOGRAPHIC VARIATION Two subspecies generally recognised, which differ mainly in measurements, *B. c. americana* being substantially stronger, with a thicker, longer bill. Apparently no other distinguishing characters.

MEASUREMENTS and MASS ♂ noticeably larger than ♀ (wing chord discriminates subspecies), and adult slightly larger than young.

B. c. clangula. ♂: wing chord 209–231 (adult, 220, n=31) and 202–224 (juvenile, 214, n=21), bill 30–36 (33.3, n=57), tarsus 37–41 (38.8, n=40); ♀: wing chord 197–207 (adult, 203, n=24) and 186–200 (juvenile, 195, n=16), bill 28–31 (29.4, n=48), tarsus 33–37 (35.1, n=46)[267]. ♂: wing chord 214–231 (adult, 222, n=35) and 207–217 (juvenile, 212, n=21), bill 32–37 (34.3, n=39); ♀: wing chord 195–209 (adult, 202, n=22) and 188–203 (juvenile, 196, n=17), bill 28–32 (30.3, n=25)[1122]. ♂ (n=100): 205–232 (adult) and 198–224 (juvenile), culmen 31–38, bill depth at tip of forehead feathers 18.2–22.0, tail 77–91, tarsus 36–41; ♀ (n=100): 183–222 (adult) and 177–205 (juvenile), culmen 28–35, bill depth at tip of forehead feathers 16.0–18.5, tail 69–82, tarsus 33–37[1014]; compared with measurements by Pyle for *americana* (below) and Barrow's Goldeneye. ♂: mass in winter 966–1,245 (966, n=9); mass in summer 888–1,180 (982, n=4); ♀: mass in winter 707–860 (787, n=9); mass in summer 500–650 (583, n=3)[267].

B. c. americana. Adult ♂ (n=12): wing chord 223–239 (232), bill 36–40 (38.6), tarsus 37–42 (40.9); adult ♀ (n=12): wing chord 199–220 (209), bill 33–35 (33.5), tarsus 37–39 (38)[945]. ♂ (n=100): 215–239 (adult) and 208–231 (juvenile), culmen 33–41, bill depth at tip of forehead feathers 19.8–23.6, tail 83–98, tarsus 37–42; ♀ (n=100): 193–219 (adult) and 187–212 (juvenile), culmen 31–37, bill depth at tip of forehead feathers 17.4–19.6, tail 74–88, tarsus 34–39[1014]; compared with measurements by Pyle for *clangula* (above) and Barrow's Goldeneye. ♂: mass in winter 938–1,275 (1,108, n=26); ♀: mass in winter 710–880 (820, n=9)[945]. ♂: mass in winter 910–1,329 (adult, 1,143, n=33) and 808–1,168 (first-winter, 1,040, n=23); ♀: mass in winter 722–930 (adult, 836, n=14) and 600–847 (first-winter, 745, n=10)[340].

VOICE Mostly silent, except ringing sound of wingbeats. In courtship, ♂ gives a croak-like *hun-hurrrr*, very nasal and ending in weak rattle, sometimes prolonged, sometimes quickly repeated (interactions between ♂♂). On taking off, utters a low, discreet rattle *anrrr*. Sometimes a *krek* in alarm. ♀ gives an *errr* like those of ♀♀ *Aythya*, as well as a *kek* or *krek* singly or repeated.

MOULT Complex alternate strategy, similar to mergansers of the genus *Mergus* (see Red-breasted Merganser). Pre-formative moult is protracted between Aug–Sep and Mar–Apr, involving up to four tertials, at most a few inner upperwing-coverts and six to all rectrices. First pre-alternate moult is limited or even absent in Jun–Aug, perhaps only in ♂[1014]. Definitive pre-basic moult starts between mid-Jul and mid-Sep and ends between late Oct and mid-Nov in ♂, 3–4 weeks later in ♀. Definitive pre-alternate moult occurs Jun–Aug (sometimes from May in ♀♀), including few or no tertials or rectrices[56,1014].

HYBRIDISATION In the wild, hybrids with Barrow's Goldeneye are encountered occasionally, especially in North America, and constitute real identification pitfalls (see below). Other natural cases are reported with Bufflehead, Hooded Merganser *Lophodytes cucullatus* and Smew (see these three species). Also in the wild, hybridisation mentioned very occasionally with Wood Duck *Aix sponsa*[817], Greater Scaup *Aythya marila*[97,817], Velvet Scoter *Melanitta fusca*[49,947,1194], Goosander *Mergus merganser*[465,817,1190] and possibly Red-breasted Merganser *Mergus serrator*[947] and Common Pochard *Aythya ferina*[97,817]. There is only one report with Mallard *Anas platyrhynchos*, but involving nearly 90 hybrids reported in Moscow in 1989–92[703]. Finally, an old report exists with Garganey *A. querquedula* but is apparently dubious[817]. In captivity, hybridisation also described with Tufted Duck *Aythya fuligula*[38,465] and Ferruginous Duck *A. nyroca*[1190].

Common Goldeneye × Barrow's Goldeneye. Reported annually in North America[69,450,624,811,812,1194,1199,1215] and Iceland[91], much more occasionally in W Europe and E Asia. ♂ in definitive basic plumage can be quite difficult to spot within a flock of Barrow's Goldeneye, which it more closely resembles compared to Common Goldeneye. Head shape can easily recall either parent, and its sheen is usually brown, reddish or purplish. The white patch at the bill base is variable and often difficult to assess depending on the angle. It is sometimes quite rounded[91,624,1215], closer to Common Goldeneye, often oval or pear-shaped, unlike either parent species. The black line on the fore flanks is absent in most birds, and

at most, half as long as shown in Barrow's Goldeneye[439]. The extent of white on the scapulars is typically intermediate between those of the parents. ♀ hybrids are reported much less frequently, unsurprisingly considering the difficulties in distinguishing their parents in this plumage. Whatever their real frequency in the wild, it is probable that they go largely unnoticed. Knowledge of this hybrid is reduced to a few descriptions of ♀ goldeneyes showing intermediate features that cannot be assigned to either species with certainty. Especially, questions arise concerning ♀♀ with largely yellow bills, and whose head shape does not match either species. Any attempt to identify a hybrid ♀ requires a very detailed examination of the bird.

HABITAT and LIFE-CYCLE Mainly migratory (some sedentary populations in NW Europe), arriving at its nesting sites between early Mar and mid-May depending on latitude, initially gathering on major rivers then moving to nearby wetlands. Breeds mainly in taiga, always close to water. Prefers oligotrophic fishless ponds[1390] in wooded areas, but also occurs on deep lakes and slow-flowing streams a few metres deep within riparian deciduous woodland. Pairs breed alone, the ♀ laying its eggs in a tree hollow or cavity. The density of breeding pairs, naturally limited by availability of nest sites, can be strongly enhanced by nestboxes, as is the case across much of Scandinavia, for example[311,1005]. Egg laying takes place mainly between mid-Apr and mid-June[315], the ♂♂ departing around midway through incubation[1005], undertaking a short migration, often northward, to moulting sites (lakes, broad rivers or coasts). Gregarious outside breeding season, but prefers to feed alone or in small groups. In winter, mainly found along coasts, using large sheltered bays or fjords, coastal lagoons or estuaries, to a lesser extent large bodies of fresh water, favouring depths of around 4 m[1213]. Leaves the breeding or moulting sites very late, with autumn migration in full swing from mid-Nov to mid-Dec. ♀♀ and young tend to migrate further south.

RANGE and POPULATION Huge Holarctic range, with an estimated total population of 2,500,000–4,600,000 individuals[1203]. The northern limit of the range is delimited by those of the trees it uses to nest. Winters as far north as conditions permit. Prone to mass influxes southward or to coasts during harsh winter weather.

B. c. clangula. Breeds in Palearctic boreal forest, with small populations or isolated pairs further south (Scotland, C Europe, Dnieper Valley, Ukraine, lower Volga, etc.). Rare or uncommon winter visitor to Spain, N Africa, Middle East, south of the Himalayas or Myanmar. European population 1,200,000–1,500,000 birds, *c.*60,000 individuals in Black Sea and 100,000–1,000,000 birds in Caspian Sea[1348]. E Asian population also estimated at 100,000–1,000,000 birds, but probably closer to lower limit of this range[182,757,1348]. Trend apparently stable.

B. c. americana. Breeds in Nearctic boreal forests, south to Maine, Great Lakes, Minnesota and Montana. Major wintering areas along US Atlantic coast (south to Virginia) and SE Alaska to British Columbia. Further south, uncommon to N Mexico. Occasional in Central America and Greater Antilles. Population estimated at 1,200,000 birds[1348] or 1,500,000 birds[1390], with 369,000 estimated in E North America[1291]. The population has probably increased slightly over the last *c.*40 years[209,648].

CAPTIVITY Uncommon overall, especially due to its requirements (needs fairly large ponds of rather deep, clear and cold water, preferably flowing). Said to breed quite readily if these conditions are met. Usually relatively expensive, much more so than most dabblers. Unlikely to escape from captivity.

REFERENCES Astley (1921)[38]; Baird *et al.* (1884)[49]; Baker (1993)[56]; Bannon (1978)[69]; Bengtson (1972)[91]; Bird Hybrid database (2014)[97]; BirdLife International (2014)[145]; Brazil (2009)[182]; Butcher & Niven (2007)[209]; Cramp & Simmons (1977)[268]; Delany & Scott (2006)[305]; Dennis (1987)[311]; Di Labio *et al.* (1997)[315]; Eadie *et al.* (1995)[340]; Fjeldså (1973)[383]; Gillham & Gillham (1996)[439]; Gochfeld & Tudor (1976)[450]; Gray (1958)[465]; Jackson (1959)[624]; Johnsgard (2010)[648]; Korbut (2001)[703]; Li *et al.* (2009)[757]; Livezey (1995)[771]; Martin & Di Labio (1994)[811]; Martin & Di Labio (1994)[812]; McCarthy (2006)[817]; Moores & Moores (2003)[873]; Nelson (1993)[905]; Palmer (1976)[945]; Panov (1989)[947]; Pöysä & Pöysä (2002)[1005]; Pyle (2008)[1014]; Salminen (1983)[1122]; Sibley (1938)[1190]; Sibley (1994)[1194]; Sibley (2010)[1198]; Sibley (2010)[1199]; Sibley (2012)[1203]; Snow & Perrins (1998)[1213]; Snyder (1953)[1215]; USFWS (2009)[1291]; Wetlands International (2014)[1348]; Zicus *in* Kear (2005)[1390].

557. *B. c. clangula*, adult ♂ (definitive basic). France, Mar (Aurélien Audevard).

558. *B. c. clangula*, adult ♂ (definitive basic); vs. Barrow's Goldeneye *B. islandica*, note white band on scapulars and absence of black line between white median and greater coverts. Japan, Apr (Stuart Price).

559. *B. c. clangula*, adult ♀ (definitive basic). Scotland, Jan (Dennis Morrison).

560. *B. c. clangula*, adult ♀ (definitive basic); in breeding season, note all-blackish bill. Finland, Jun (Sébastien Reeber).

561. *B. c. clangula*, adult ♀ (definitive basic); note typical upperwing pattern at this age, with three distinct white patches separated by black lines. Sweden, Apr (Johannes Rydström).

562. *B. c. clangula*, adult ♀ (definitive basic). Poland, Jan (Zbigniew Kayzer).

563. *B. c. clangula*, first-winter ♀ (formative); aged by bill and iris colours. Netherlands, Jan (Rick Van der Weijde).

564. *B. c. americana*, adult ♂ (definitive basic); compared to nominate, note slightly (but variably) longer and thicker bill. California, USA, Nov (Sébastien Reeber).

565. *B. c. clangula*, first-winter ♂ (formative); note mixture of juvenile and formative adult-like feathers, as well as dull yellow-brown iris. France, Dec (Vincent Palomares).

566. *B. c. americana*, adult ♀ (definitive basic), developing yellow patch on bill by Nov. California, USA, Nov (Sébastien Reeber)

567. Common Goldeneye *B. clangula* × Barrow's Goldeneye *B. islandica*, adult ♂ (definitive basic); note many intermediate features in head shape and coloration. Washington, USA, Mar (Steve Mlodinow).

BARROW'S GOLDENEYE
Bucephala islandica   **Plates 65, 66**

TAXONOMY *Anas islandica* J. F. Gmelin, 1789, *Syst. Nat.*, 1, p. 541 (Iceland). Member of the tribe Mergini, most closely related to Common Goldeneye *B. clangula* (which see). Monotypic with weak geographical variation.

IDENTIFICATION Unlikely to be mistaken for any other species, except Common Goldeneye. Adult ♂♂ in basic plumage are rather similar, and other plumages are even harder to separate, being further complicated by the existence of relatively frequent hybrids (see Common Goldeneye).

PLUMAGES Strong sexual dimorphism in definitive basic plumage. Complex alternate moult strategy (two plumages per definitive cycle, three in first cycle). Plumages of ♀♀ and formative (first-winter) and alternate (eclipse) plumages of ♂♂ rather similar. See also Identification under Common Goldeneye.

Adult ♂

Definitive basic plumage (Oct–Nov/Jun). Black and white overall. Head black with purple sheen and an oval white patch at the bill base appears as tapering crescent above the eye. Iris bright yellow to pale yellow, sometimes white. Bill short and stocky, slate-grey to black, and shiny. Neck, breast, flanks and belly pure white, except broad black line between the fore flanks and breast. Upper and rear flanks black. Mantle, inner scapulars, back, rump and rear body blackish. Longest scapulars with white centres forming series of 6–7 rectangular white spots on black upperparts. Tail dark grey. Upperwing blackish except innermost 5–6 secondaries, the corresponding greater coverts, median (except outermost few, centred black) and adjacent lesser coverts. The black bases to the greater coverts form a broad band and their tips with variable black spots form a second line, dotted, broken or even lacking. Underwing dark grey with dark brown to blackish lesser coverts and visible inner secondaries are white (the grey greater underwing-coverts, which overlay the secondaries, are much longer than the greater upperwing-coverts). Legs bright yellow-orange with dark webs.

Definitive alternate plumage (Jun/Oct–Nov). Similar to alternate plumage of ♀ (including dark bill), but head darker brown or mixed blackish. Traces of basic plumage (hint of white crescent at base of bill,

white feathers on breast, fore flanks and/or anterior scapulars) are often clearly visible. Basic upperwing pattern retained, easily distinguished from ♀.

Adult ♀

Definitive basic plumage (Nov–Dec/May–Jun.). Head chocolate-brown with a reddish hue. Iris whitish to pale yellow. Bill has blackish base and nail and an orange patch from behind the nail to just below nostril (most in Iceland) or covering most of bill (most in North America). A white collar separates the brown head and upper neck from the breast (paler in centre) and flanks ash-grey, with fringes of feathers forming pale crescents. All upperparts uniform, but a little darker, with indistinct pale fringes. Tips of longest scapulars fringed white. Belly whitish. Tail grey. Upperwing grey, like upperparts (secondary coverts broad and quite square-tipped), except 5–6 innermost secondaries and corresponding greater coverts. Tips and bases of greater coverts black forming two broad bars. Tips of median and posterior lesser coverts white and form a variably marked whitish area. Underwing like ♂ but lesser coverts slightly paler. Legs yellow slightly orange, webs darker.

Definitive alternate plumage (May–Jun/Nov–Dec). Apparently identical to basic plumage, but looks slightly darker. Completely black bill, not acquiring orange patch until Oct–Nov.

Juvenile

First basic plumage (until Oct–Nov). Similar to adult ♀ but duller, more brownish and overall plainer, with a thinner head shape (forehead and nape less swollen). Iris initially grey-brown to bluish[904] with dark-brown ring around pupil, gradually becoming paler inwards. Bill entirely dark, dull grey, nail initially tinged reddish. Tertials short and matt blackish, quickly frayed at tips. Upperwing pattern distinctly different from adult ♀, with secondary coverts narrower and more round-tipped, but few or no differences between sexes at this age. The 5–6 innermost secondaries and corresponding greater coverts are virtually all white without black bar formed by bases of secondaries and tips of greater coverts. At most, dark and diffuse spots on tips of latter form a vague dotted line, on average somewhat more marked in young ♂. Median and posterior lesser coverts have variably marked whitish fringes, forming a vague pale greyish area at front of upperwing, less visible than in adult ♀. These variations do not appear sex-dependent, or at best exhibit strong overlap. Legs dull yellow-brown.

First-winter ♂

Formative plumage (Nov–Jan/Jun–Aug.). Until early winter at least, similar to adult ♀. Distinguished especially by juvenile upperwing pattern, the iris becoming whitish or pale yellow-green outwards, but still brown around pupil and often has entirely blackish bill (or with vague yellowish-grey band behind nail), even before first adult-type formative feathers, which usually appear in Dec–Feb, varying individually. Overall gradually approaches basic plumage of adult ♂, but even in best-marked birds head remains dull blackish, the white crescent shorter and stained dusky, dark feathers often mixed with white feathers of breast and flanks, and scapulars shorter with white spots smaller and not forming regular patches of adult.

First-winter ♀

Formative plumage (Nov–Jan/Jun–Aug.). Very similar to adult ♀ and separated from latter especially by juvenile upperwing (see above). Some signs of juvenile plumage (tertials and tertial coverts brown and frayed at tips) and iris with fine diffuse brown ring around pupil are often visible. The orange of bill initially appears dirty brown-olive and less extensive, usually not achieving bright colour of adult by late winter.

First-summer ♂

First alternate plumage (Jun–Aug/Oct–Nov). Intermediate between formative plumage of ♂ and adult ♀ (first pre-alternate moult limited). Distinguished from adult of both sexes by juvenile upperwing pattern, retained until second pre-basic moult (Jul–Aug) and from ♀ at same age by some ♂-type formative feathers.

First-summer ♀

First alternate plumage (Jun–Aug/Nov–Dec). Very similar to adult ♀ but upperwing retained until second pre-basic moult. Tertials, tertial coverts and often many upperparts feathers (among others) appear brown and heavily worn.

Second-winter ♂

Second basic plumage (Oct–Nov/Jun). Very like definitive basic plumage, but head often lacks gloss, white crescent

somewhat less extensive and less clear-cut, dark marks at tips of some greater coverts and fewer white lesser coverts may all be indicative of this age[1014].

GEOGRAPHIC VARIATION The bill coloration of adult ♀♀ between Oct–Nov and May–Jun varies between North American and Icelandic populations. The bill has a yellow-orange patch from the nail to below the nostril in most Icelandic ♀♀, whereas bright orange covers most of the bill in North American birds. It has been claimed that birds in E North America are intermediate in colour[928], but this has since been invalidated[315,341].

MEASUREMENTS and MASS ♂ noticeably larger and heavier than ♀ and adult slightly larger than young. Iceland. ♂: wing chord 236–253 (244, $n=21$), culmen 31–37 (34.6, $n=41$), tail 86–91 (88.9, $n=8$), tarsus 40–48 (43.0, $n=40$), mass 1,000–1,387 (1,167.1, $n=163$); ♀: wing chord 198–231 (214, $n=50$), culmen 28–34 (31.2, $n=101$), tail 81–88 (85.0, $n=5$), tarsus 32–43.2 (38.3, $n=103$), mass 638–1,056 (823.2, $n=332$)[348]. North America. Adult ♂ ($n=12$): wing chord 230–245 (239), culmen 32–36 (34.3), tarsus 40–43 (42.0); adult ♀ ($n=12$): wing chord 210–223 (218), culmen 30–33 (31.7), tarsus 37–40 (38.0)[945]. ♂: mass in winter (Washington state) 980–1,315 (adult, 1,130.5, $n=18$) and 832–1,113 (first-winter, 977.8, $n=4$); ♀: mass in winter (Washington state) 577–857 (adult, 750.7, $n=10$) and 609–818 (first-winter, 736, $n=5$)[382]. ♂ ($n=66$): 228–248 (adult) and 220–237 (juvenile), culmen 32–36, bill depth at tip of forehead feathers 20.9–24.5, tail 83–93, tarsus 39–44; ♀ ($n=100$): 202–224 (adult) and 196–213 (juvenile), culmen 29–33, bill depth at tip of forehead feathers 18.4–20.8, tail 79–89, tarsus 37–41; compared with measurements by Pyle[1014] of both subspecies of Common Goldeneye.

VOICE Generally silent other than in courtship, during which ♂ gives series of weak rattles and nasal sounds *gra-graa*, amid asthmatic clicking sounds in background. ♀ utters a repeated *gak gak-gak...* on breeding grounds, or *werr* or *brer* in alarm. As in Common Goldeneye, the wingbeats of adult (especially ♂) produce a quite loud and characteristic ringing sound.

MOULT Complex alternate strategy, similar to that of *Mergus* (see Red-breasted Merganser *M. serrator*). Pre-formative moult is protracted, between Aug–Sep and Mar, involving up to four tertials, at most a few inner upperwing-coverts and two to all rectrices. First pre-alternate moult limited (or absent), in Jun–Aug, perhaps only in ♂[1014]. Definitive pre-basic moult starts with wings and rectrices between mid-Jul and late Aug in ♂, 2–4 weeks later in ♀[341] and completed by late Oct in ♂ and mid-Dec in ♀. Definitive pre-alternate moult between mid-May and mid-Jul includes few or no tertials or rectrices[341].

HYBRIDISATION Very rarely reported in the wild, but hybrids with Common Goldeneye are mentioned regularly in North America (see latter species). Much rarer cases reported with Hooded Merganser *Lophodytes cucullatus* (which see) and perhaps Bufflehead *B. albeola*[817].

HABITAT and LIFE-CYCLE Migration to the breeding grounds peaks between mid-Mar and mid-Apr, the eggs being laid mainly from mid-Apr to late Jun. Favours lakes with alkaline water, low densities of fish, few helophytes, an abundant invertebrate fauna, on plains as well as in mountains (up to 1,850 m, exceptionally 3,000 m in North America[145,219]). Also on ponds, rivers, backwaters or beaver dams[341]. In North America, ♀♀ often nest in tree hollows and cavities dug by woodpeckers. Readily uses nestboxes as well. In Iceland, uses holes in volcanic rock or soil, under dense low vegetation. ♂♂ depart nest sites during incubation, and move (sometimes >1,000 km[341,1140]) to moulting sites, where they gather to replace their flight feathers (up to 5,000–7,000 birds, mainly adult ♂♂, at two sites in Alberta, Canada[568]). Some ♀♀ also leave their broods in care of other ♀♀, to moult their remiges (on site or same moulting grounds as ♂♂). Late migrant, arriving on its wintering grounds mainly between early Nov and mid-Dec. In winter, mainly favours sheltered rocky shores well stocked with mussels. Does not regularly join Common Goldeneye in winter in Gulf of St. Lawrence and forms on average larger flocks (20.3 vs. 9.8 birds[164]). Icelandic population largely sedentary on inland lakes.

RANGE and POPULATION Three distinct populations,

the most important breeding in the American north-west (rare in Colorado, and extirpated/occasional in California[341]) wintering south to Washington state (fewer south to San Francisco Bay, California, and inland). In NE America, breeds on plateaux along NW Gulf of St. Lawrence, Quebec (possibly in N & NE Labrador, Hudson Bay and Newfoundland, but apparently unconfirmed[283,341,1076,1077,1137]). Winters chiefly in Gulf of St. Lawrence[1075], more sporadically south to Maine and exceptional south to New Jersey and Great Lakes region. In Iceland, located especially around Lake Mývatn and the Laxá River, and essentially sedentary. Bred occasionally during 19th century in SW Greenland[1125]. Estimates of American north-west population are of 123,000–179,000 individuals[348] and 200,000–250,000 birds[1348], having increased significantly in recent decades[209]. In NE America, population estimated at 4,000–6,000 birds[1348] or *c.*6,200 birds[1075] with 1,500–1,800 birds in Iceland[1348], where considered stable.

CAPTIVITY Rare in captivity because of their generally high price, highly specific requirements (clear, deep and cold waters, preferably flowing, with some natural food) and unwillingness to breed. Unlikely to escape from captivity.

REFERENCES BirdLife International (2014)[145]; Bourget *et al.* (2007)[164]; Butcher & Niven (2007)[209]; Campbell *et al.* (1990)[219]; Daury & Bateman (1996)[283]; Di Labio *et al.* (1997)[315]; Eadie *et al.* (2000)[341]; Einarsson *in* Kear (2005)[348]; Fitzner & Gray (1994)[382]; Hogan *et al.* (2011)[568]; McCarthy (2006)[817]; Nelson (1983)[904]; Ogilvie & Young (1998)[928]; Palmer (1976)[945]; Pyle (2008)[1014]; Robert & Savard (2006)[1075]; Robert *et al.* (1999)[1076]; Robert *et al.* (2000)[1077]; Salomonsen (1950)[1125]; Savard (1996)[1137]; Savard & Robert (2013)[1140]; Tobish (1986)[1272]; Van De Wetering (1997)[1304]; Wetlands International (2014)[1348].

568. Adult ♂ (definitive basic). Iceland, Apr (Yann Kolbeinsson).

569. Adult ♀ (definitive basic); many in North America have mostly yellow bill. California, USA, Dec (Tom Grey).

570. Adult ♀ (definitive basic); most ♀♀ in Iceland have yellow patch on bill (vs. North America), but unlike Common Goldeneye *B. clangula*, this patch is more extensive under the nostril than above it. Iceland, May (Yann Kolbeinsson)

571. First-summer ♀ (formative/first alternate); much like adult ♀ but iris not fully coloured toward centre in second summer, and note brown, worn and frayed tertial coverts. Iceland, Jul (Vincent Legrand).

572. First-winter ♂ (formative); some formative feathers are obviously like those of adult ♂ but confusion impossible until second summer. Iceland, May (Yann Kolbeinsson).

573. First-winter ♀ (formative) and adult ♀ (definitive basic); in adult (behind), note white patches on median coverts, brighter iris and bill coloration, the latter's being more clear-cut. Iceland, May (Yann Kolbeinsson).

SMEW
Mergellus albellus

Plate 67

TAXONOMY *Mergus Albellus* Linnaeus, 1758, *Syst. Nat.*, edn. 10, p. 129. Monotypic, this species, along with Hooded Merganser *Lophodytes cucullatus*, is phylogenetically somewhat intermediate between mergansers (genus *Mergus*) and goldeneyes (*Bucephala*)[771]. It has also been suggested that Smew and Hooded Merganser are closer to each other than either is to *Mergus* or *Bucephala*[321]. Treatments are varied: all species placed in *Mergus*, splitting Smew and Hooded Merganser as their own genus, *Mergellus* Selby, 1840, or placing the latter two species in separate genera, *Mergellus* and *Lophodytes*, Reichenbach, 1853. This third position is currently accepted by most authorities[20,142,236,437].

IDENTIFICATION May suggest Common Goldeneye *Bucephala clangula* in many ways, but easily distinguished. Flight is fast and vigorous, with a relatively short rear body, rather long, pointed wings and a long neck. Often shy and easily alarmed.

PLUMAGES Strong sexual dimorphism in definitive basic plumage. Complex alternate moult strategy (two plumages per definitive cycle, three in first cycle). Plumages of ♀♀ and formative (first-winter) and, to a lesser extent, alternate (eclipse) plumages of ♂♂ rather similar.

Adult ♂

Definitive basic plumage (Nov–Dec/Jun–Jul). Mainly white, with some grey and black, and unmistakable. Drooping crest and elongated erectile feathers on forehead. Head white, except clear-cut rounded black face patch from sides of bill base and encircling the eye. Sides and base of crest black, but only visible depending on position of crest. Iris brown-hazel, becoming grey or even whitish with age. Bill more triangular and much shorter than *Mergus*. Neck, breast, belly and undertail white, except for two thin, sharp black lines, the first from the mantle towards the centre of the breast and the other on the fore flanks. The latter are white finely vermiculated grey to blackish (appearing pale grey from afar). Mantle and inner scapulars black, outer scapulars white. Tertials pale grey with white fringes and dark shafts. Tertial coverts white. Back, rump, uppertail-coverts and tail grey. Upperwing has distal half blackish-grey, large oval white patch on lesser and median coverts (leading edge and innermost coverts black), and greater coverts and secondaries black with white tips, forming two lines framing speculum. Underwing grey with axillaries, lesser and median coverts, and tips of greater coverts whitish, and darker streaking on posterior lesser coverts and leading edge. Legs bluish-grey with blackish webs.

Definitive alternate plumage (Jun–Jul/Oct–Nov). Like ♀ but upper head and around eye brown often washed blackish, not contrasting with face patch, crown often flecked white (retained basic feathers), and mantle dark or blackish. Basic feathers are also often retained and visible on the flanks or scapulars (alternate scapulars darker than those of ♀ or with dusky centres). Wing still basic (white patch on lesser median coverts more extensive, leading edge and inner secondary coverts blackish, not grey like ♀).

Adult ♀

Definitive basic plumage (Dec–Jan/Jun–Jul). Overall greyish with head and hindneck dark reddish-brown, blackish lores (face patch same shape as in ♂) and white area covering lower cheeks, throat, chin and upper neck. Long erectile feathers of rear crown form a shaggy bump. Iris warm brown. Bill grey and uniform, similar to ♂. Breast, flanks and lower belly grey more or less vaguely mottled dark. Belly whitish. Mantle, scapulars, back, rump and tail also grey, but often slightly darker than breast and flanks. Tertials dark grey, rounded and fringed with white at tips. Outermost tertial has whitish inner web finely fringed dark. Tertial coverts blackish, the outermost with a large diffuse pale centre. Upperwing like ♂ but white patch on lesser and median coverts smaller, less clear-cut and contrasts less strongly with leading edge, and innermost secondary coverts, grey and not blackish. Thin white tips to greater coverts and secondaries form two narrow wingbars. Underwing and legs like ♂.

Definitive alternate plumage (Jun–Jul/Nov–Dec). Identical to basic plumage, but lores paler grey-brown and bill slightly darker.

Juvenile

First basic plumage (until Oct–Dec). Very like adult ♀, distinction generally requiring good views. Note different head shape, smaller, thinner, squarer and almost lacks any crest. Among other important features, the white tips to greater coverts and secondaries form two wingbars visibly larger than in adult ♀. In latter, the white bar on greater coverts is more irregularly thick or appears as a dotted line. Moreover, the white lesser and median coverts show brownish crescents at tips (all white in adult ♀). Whitish to cream-coloured belly often spotted, or neatly but faintly streaked grey. Finally, has dull grey-brown iris (warmer in adult).

First-winter ♂

Formative plumage (Nov–Jan/Jun–Aug). Different from adult ♂, which achieves basic plumage late (Nov–Dec), by appearing largely juvenile until midwinter at least. Provided adult-type feathers are not visible, young ♂ can be distinguished from adult ♀ like juvenile, but sexed only using measurements. Juvenile tertials are grey, pointed, brown and frayed at tips, whereas formative tertials, often present alongside previous ones, are paler grey, longer and slightly curved. As early as Jan, a few white feathers usually appear on the reddish-brown head or behind the eyes, while the breast quickly becomes whiter. Later, the lores turn black, the flanks white and black lines on the breast appear.

First-winter ♀

Formative plumage (Nov–Jan/Jun–Aug.). Very like juvenile plumage and differs from adult ♀ in same way, i.e. by upperwing pattern (width of white wingbars, dark marks on tips of white lesser and median coverts), by belly spotted or appearing vaguely streaked grey, by sparse crest (smaller, fine and squarer head) and browner lores (vs. blackish). Tertials grey with brownish hue, frayed at tips from early winter. Juvenile tertial coverts blackish, rather pointed and worn at tips.

First-summer ♂

First alternate plumage (Jun–Aug/Nov–Dec). Plumage poorly described in the wild (as is precise extent of first pre-alternate moult). Like definitive alternate plumage ♂ (see Moult), but essentially distinguished by tertials, wing and often at least some rectrices still juvenile until second pre-basic moult. Juvenile tertials, primaries and rectrices are brown (or bleached), narrow and heavily worn. White fringes to greater coverts and secondaries often scarcely visible due to wear, as well as brown fringes to white lesser and median coverts. However, the leading edge is usually brown and ill-defined in young ♂, sometimes with clear moult contrast with innermost secondary- and tertial coverts if they have been replaced during pre-formative moult. Retained juvenile tertials and tertial coverts are dark grey, pointed and heavily worn, distinctive from adult ♂ at this time.

First-summer ♀

First alternate plumage (Jun–Aug/Nov–Dec?). Even more than in ♂, first pre-alternate moult is poorly known in the wild. Easily distinguished from adult ♀ at same season, using same features as detailed for ♂ in first alternate plumage. Features of upperwing less useful because of wear, and loral patch brown in both age groups. However, the retained juvenile tertials and tertial coverts are blackish-brown, short, narrow and heavily worn (these feathers can also be partly replaced by formative feathers, closer to adult).

Second-winter ♂

Second basic plumage (Nov–Dec/Jun–Jul). Identical to definitive basic plumage, but often has some brown spots around eye and tips of longest scapulars tinged grey. Birds showing all-white scapulars (in the hand) are generally in their third winter at least[56].

GEOGRAPHIC VARIATION None.

MEASUREMENTS and MASS ♂ noticeably larger and heavier than ♀ and adult slightly larger than young. ♂: wing chord 197–208 (adult, 202, $n=25$) and 188–202 (juvenile, 196, $n=20$), bill 27–32 (29.6, $n=46$), tarsus 31–36 (34.0, $n=46$); ♀: wing chord 181–189 (adult, 184, $n=10$) and 171–184 (juvenile, 177, $n=24$), bill 25–29 (26.8, $n=33$), tarsus 29–32 (30.6, $n=33$)[267]. ♂: wing chord 194–211 (adult, 202, $n=54$) and 185–203 (juvenile, 194, $n=33$), bill 27–32 (29.7, $n=54$); ♀: wing chord 179–191 (adult, 184, $n=11$) and 172–181 (juvenile, 176, $n=28$), bill 25–28 (25.8, $n=11$)[1122]. ♂ (sample unknown): mass in Apr 590–795 (700), mass in Oct 540–825 (adult, 652) and 500–760 (juvenile, 630), mass in Nov 720–935 (adult, 814) and 645–920 (juvenile, 882); ♀ (sample unknown): mass in Apr 510–670, mass in Oct 515–630 (adult, 568) and 500–680 (juvenile, 556), mass in Nov 550–650 (adult, 572) and 535–670 (juvenile, 588)[308,930].

VOICE Usually quiet, most frequently heard during courtship and when alarmed. ♂ in courtship gives a slow rattle, becoming faster and followed by a nasal sound, *k-k-k-krrr-anh-hun*. Heard from distance, sounds rather like Garganey *Anas querquedula* or Ruddy Duck *Oxyura jamaicensis*. During courtship, ♀ utters a tinny rattle, *krrr*. The alert call of both sexes is a harsh and rather high-pitched *eerr*.

MOULT Complex alternate strategy, presumably similar to genus *Mergus* (see Red-breasted Merganser). Pre-formative moult protracted, between Sep and Mar–Apr, involving 1–4 tertials and two to all rectrices. First pre-alternate moult poorly studied in wild, but apparently limited or even absent, in Jun–Aug. Baker[56] did not distinguish this moult from definitive pre-alternate in extent. Definitive pre-basic moult starts with the wings and rectrices between mid-Jul and Sep in ♂, slightly later in ♀, and ends between mid-Nov and mid-Dec in ♂, fractionally later in ♀. Definitive pre-alternate moult partial, in Jun–Aug (usually no tertials or rectrices replaced).

HYBRIDISATION Exceptional, except with Common Goldeneye, with which it is reported occasionally (see below). Furthermore, a hybrid with Hooded Merganser has been described in the wild, but had possibly escaped from captivity[439], where others reported[120]. Finally, a single hybrid with Goosander *Mergus merganser* was described from the wild too[439].

Smew × Common Goldeneye. Most frequently reported in N Europe. Adult ♂ in basic plumage mainly white with some black on crown, neck, cheeks and base of bill, generally with two white stripes, the first across the rear cheeks and the second on the lores. The head shape (with a short crest) and coloration pattern varies, however, and may suggest either species. Iris brown. Mantle, back, rump and tail blackish. Neck, breast, scapulars and underparts all white with fine grey vermiculations on upper and rear flanks. Upperwing pattern intermediate between those of the parents (inner wing largely white with two large black bars at base of greater coverts and secondaries). Legs dark yellow-brown.

HABITAT and LIFE-CYCLE Exclusively migratory, Smew arrive on their breeding grounds between mid-Apr and mid-May, and lay eggs from mid-May, mostly in isolated pairs. Nests around lakes, ponds, bogs, backwaters, slow-flowing rivers in mixed forest or dominated by conifers, from lowlands to low mountains with trees (deciduous mostly), nesting in holes, including old cavities of Black Woodpecker *Dryocopus martius*. Readily accepts nestboxes. Prefers shallow oligotrophic waters, up to 4–6 m deep[930,1213]. ♂♂ abandon ♀♀ shortly after hatching, and head to moulting sites. Migration south starts early Sep or Oct, but does not arrive at southern wintering sites before mid-Nov to mid-Dec. Outside breeding season, mostly in small groups, but can form flocks of up to 10,000 birds[930]. Notoriously prone to movements during winter, depending on weather conditions. At this season, occurs on ponds, lakes, reservoirs, gravel pits, coastal lagoons and brackish estuaries, but rarely at sea.

RANGE and POPULATION Breeds in Eurasian taiga. Outside mapped wintering range, very patchy, rare or occasional further south, especially during cold spells, to Mediterranean Sea, in most countries of Middle East, from Aral Sea to Indus Valley, Pakistan, and south of the Himalayas to Myanmar. Rare visitor to W & C Aleutian Is, and very occasional along US Pacific coast south to California[648]. Total population small, despite huge range, with an estimated 130,000 individuals: 40,000 in NW & C Europe, 35,000 in E Europe, 30,000 in SW Asia and 25,000 in E Asia[305,1348]. Perhaps slightly increasing in W Europe, but trend stable or unknown elsewhere.

CAPTIVITY Reportedly easier to keep in mixed collections and to breed than mergansers (*Mergus*). Quite expensive and usually priced significantly higher than Hooded Merganser. Relatively rare outside major collections and thus unlikely to escape.

REFERENCES AOU (1983)[20]; Baker (1993)[56]; Bird Hybrids Flickr Forum (2009)[120]; BirdLife International (2012)[142]; Clements *et al.* (2013)[236]; Cramp & Simmons (1977)[268]; Crochet & Joynt (2012)[272]; Delany & Scott (2006)[305]; Dementiev & Gladkov (1952)[308]; Donne-Goussé (2002)[321]; Gill & Donsker (2014)[437]; Gillham & Gillham (1996)[439]; Johnsgard (2010)[648]; Livezey (1995)[771]; Olney *in* Kear (2005)[930]; Salminen (1983)[1122]; Snow & Perrins (1998)[1213]; Wetlands International (2014)[1348].

574. Adult ♂ (definitive basic). Japan, Jan (Stuart Price).

575. Adult ♂ (definitive basic). Japan, Jan (Stuart Price).

576. Adult ♂ (definitive basic). Japan, Feb (Stuart Price).

577. Adult ♀ (definitive basic); separated from juvenile (first basic) and first-winter ♀ (formative) by blackish lores, thin white wingbars (tips to greater coverts and secondaries) and pure white wing patch. Switzerland, Feb (Christopher J. G. Plummer).

578. First-winter ♂ (formative); some formative (adult-like) feathers obvious here, but most birds are closer to adult ♀ than adult ♂ until first summer. Hong Kong, China, Dec (Michelle & Peter Wong).

579. First-winter ♀ (formative); compared to adult ♀, note paler lores, broad white wingbars and wing patch with brownish traces. Denmark, Feb (Nis Lundmark Jensen).

HOODED MERGANSER
Lophodytes cucullatus

Plate 68

TAXONOMY *Mergus cucullatus* Linnaeus, 1758, *Syst. Nat.*, edn. 10, p. 129. See Taxonomy of Smew. Monotypic.

IDENTIFICATION Diving duck with shape close to that of *Mergus* mergansers, but smaller, with narrower wings and long, broad tail. Definitive basic plumage of ♂ unmistakable. Shape longish and low on water, combined with head shape, usually distinctive. In flight, shows little white on secondaries.

PLUMAGES Strong sexual dimorphism in definitive basic plumage, from second pre-basic moult onwards. Complex alternate moult strategy (two plumages per definitive cycle, three in first cycle). Sexing young birds tricky before first winter, and sometimes until end of first summer. Ageing easy in ♂ until first summer, but requires reasonable views in ♀♀.

Adult ♂

Definitive basic plumage (Oct/May–Jun). Mainly black, white and reddish, very distinctive and shape changes dramatically depending on position of crest. Head and neck black with a white area from behind the eye covering the sides of the crest. When held flattened (especially in flight), it forms a large bump on the nape, while the white area then forms a broad stripe. When crest is held erect, the rear and top of the head form a large round patch, largely white. Iris pale yellow to bright yellow. Bill black. Breast and belly white with two broad vertical black lines separated by a white line on the fore flanks. The latter appear copper to orangey, more greyish in front and significantly vermiculated blackish. Femoral coverts stained pale brown-yellowish. Mantle and scapulars blackish. Tertials elongated, drooping, black with broad white rachis. Back and rump dark grey-brown to blackish with feathers fringed pale. Rectrices dark grey-brown. Upperwing mainly blackish, with posterior lesser and median coverts forming a pale grey oval, inner greater coverts with black bases and clear-cut white tips (five outermost greater coverts blackish) forming two broad bars. Inner secondaries blackish with broad white line on outer half of outer web, and black base. Four outermost secondaries all dark. Underwing dark grey except whitish axillaries and median coverts. Legs yellow with dark brown areas and dark webs.

Definitive alternate plumage (Jun–Jul/Sep–Oct). Appearance similar to ♀; however, often with distinctive basic feathers retained on the body (e.g. around eye, traces of black on mantle or/and scapulars, white on breast and reddish vermiculated feathers on flanks). Other birds undertake extensive pre-alternate moult and show virtually no basic feathers on the body. Easily distinguished from juvenile and adult ♀ by upperwing pattern (pale grey patch on lesser and median coverts), bright yellow iris (beware senescent ♀♀) and long black tertials with white rachis. Bill dark with base and tomium of lower mandible pinkish or orange.

Adult ♀

Definitive basic plumage (Oct/May–Jun). Plumage overall dull greyish-brown. Head bicoloured with broad crest, strongly affecting head profile as in ♂, reddish to coppery, more yellowish to whitish towards tips of feathers. Iris quite variable, especially depending on lighting, usually amber, sometimes brown, hazelnut or more yellow. Bill dark grey with yellow or bright orange at base running along tomium up to three-quarters of length. Cheeks, neck, breast and flanks pale grey-brown (centres of flank feathers darker) and dull. Throat, foreneck and centre of breast paler, blending into white belly clearly demarcated at its sides. Lower belly and undertail loosely barred or mottled pale brown and beige. Mantle and scapulars dark blackish grey-brown. Feathers of back and rump grey-brown centred blackish. Upperwing like adult ♂ but overall browner, lesser and median coverts square-tipped, uniform blackish with soft sheen and paler fringes on outermost. Black bases to greater coverts and inner secondaries broader, forming two black bars, more pronounced and more regular in width than ♂. White tips to inner greater coverts reduced. Tertials sharp, shorter and straighter than ♂, including formative plumage (first winter), with white rachis slightly narrower and somewhat diffuse on three outer tertials. Underwing like ♂. Legs dull yellow-brown with dark webs.

Definitive alternate plumage (Jun–Jul/Sep–Oct). Very like basic plumage. At most, brown fringes to scapulars and pale fringes to flanks feathers appear more pronounced on average. Head usually more evenly brown.

Juvenile

First basic plumage (until Aug–Dec). Similar to adult ♀, with crest shorter, less prominent and more shaggy, and overall coloration a little greyer, duller and more uniform (paler upperparts). Also distinguished by beige belly mottled pale brown (white in adult), and tertials short, straight, narrow and generally frayed at tips, with or without hint of white shaft stripe. Bill colour less clear-cut and less bright. In the hand, note secondary coverts more rounded, brown and often worn at tips (rather square and blackish in adult ♀). Sexing juvenile generally possible only in hand and not for all birds, based on measurements (see below), and white perhaps slightly more extensive on greater coverts in young ♂♂[1014]. White of central greater coverts significantly larger in adult ♀♀ than young ♀♀.

First-winter ♂

Formative plumage (Oct–Jan/Sep–Oct). Similar to juvenile until Oct–Nov (sometimes Dec), adult-type formative feathers then appearing, for example behind eye, on breast or upper flanks. Young ♂♂ usually retain obvious signs of immaturity until second pre-basic moult. The age of the birds with largely adult-type coloration may be assessed using upperwing pattern: at most a few, new, pale grey lesser and median coverts among darker juvenile feathers and narrower central greater coverts with white at tip limited or divided in two, or with dark spot at tip. Formative tertials also shorter, less curved, with whitish shafts less clear-cut and usually at least some juvenile tertial coverts narrower, brown and worn at tips. In late autumn/early winter, bill is yellow- to greenish-brown, often darker on sides than on culmen. It becomes blackish in spring. Iris warm brown initially, then orange to pale yellow by midwinter, and bright yellow in first summer. First alternate plumage identical (see Moult).

First-winter ♀

Formative plumage (Oct–Jan/Sep–Oct). Intermediate between juvenile and adult ♀, themselves rather similar. Note rounded crest longer than juvenile and often a mix of two generations of feathers: juvenile feathers, brown and fading in spring, and adult-type feathers, more blackish on upperparts and browner on flanks and breast. Central greater coverts show very little white at tips, and usually two whitish spots either side of shaft. Juvenile tertial coverts brown and pointed, visibly frayed at tips. Formative tertials broad, short, straight, often with white rachis stripe. Iris and bill colours close to adult from first winter. First pre-alternate moult is limited to absent (see Moult), but at least some show brown feathers on adult-like parts of head, breast and upperparts[332].

GEOGRAPHIC VARIATION None. The two North American populations were separated 57,000 years ago (between 10,000 and 357,000 years) and have been disjunct for 16,000 years. However, genetic analysis suggests continued gene flow between the populations[332,959].

MEASUREMENTS and MASS ♂ and adult noticeably larger than ♀ and young, respectively. ♂ (n=12): wing chord 191–207 (198), tail 86–96 (90), culmen 37–41 (39.6), tarsus 30–34 (32.4); ♀ (n=12): wing chord 180–191 (185), tail 81–93 (87), culmen 35–40 (38.3), tarsus 30–32 (31.3)[945]. ♂ (n=40): wing chord 185–203 (adult) and 175–194 (juvenile), culmen 37–42, bill depth at tip of forehead feathers 11.6–13.2, tail 85–96, tarsus 30–34; ♀ (n=40): wing chord 173–187 (adult) and 163–178 (juvenile), culmen 35–40, bill depth at tip of forehead feathers 11.1–12.6, tail 80–91, tarsus 29–33[1014]. ♂ (i=19): mass 595–879 (680); ♀ (n=12): mass 453–652 (554)[704].

VOICE Usually silent. In courtship, ♂ gives a loud croaking *kror-cro-arrrr* that slows. ♀ utters *rrra* or *kerr*, more usual among mergansers.

MOULT Complex alternate strategy. Pre-formative moult protracted, in Aug–Mar, involving a variable number of head and body feathers, 1–4 tertials, at most a few inner secondary coverts and two to all rectrices[1014]. First pre-alternate moult limited to absent, in Jun–Aug, including feathers of head and mantle in young ♂ (precise extent in young ♀ unknown). Definitive pre-basic moult occurs just after, in Aug–Oct. It starts with the remiges, upperwing-coverts and rectrices. Definitive pre-alternate moult occurs in May–Jul, including many to most head and body feathers, but few or no tertials and upperwing-coverts. On average perhaps more extensive in ♂ than ♀[332].

HYBRIDISATION In the wild, reported occasionally with Common Goldeneye *Bucephala clangula*, Barrow's Goldeneye *Bucephala islandica* (see below), and even more rarely Wood Duck *Aix sponsa* and Bufflehead *Bucephala albeola*[122,439,804] (see these two species). Natural hybridisation has also been reported once or on very few occasions with Red-breasted Merganser *Mergus serrator*[365,817], Gadwall *Anas strepera*[1194] and Smew

Mergellus albellus[118,439], the latter perhaps involving escapees. In captivity, hybridisation also mentioned with Redhead *Aythya americana*[752,817] and Goosander *Mergus merganser*[660].

Hooded Merganser × Common Goldeneye[57,845]. There is a risk of confusion between this hybrid and that involving Barrow's Goldeneye (see below). In definitive basic plumage, ♂ usually shows typical features of both parents. It is characterised by an usually long thin bill, inherited from Hooded Merganser, and a high, rounded or more conical head closer to Common Goldeneye, a blackish head with faint green sheen and white marks in front of and behind eye, sometimes onto cheeks, which is not the case in either parent. Some also show an all-black head, but it is possible that some at least actually involve Barrow's Goldeneye in their parentage. The breast is white with the two black lines of Hooded Merganser (sometimes absent[439]), but greyer and/or thinner, and grey flanks (white vermiculated blackish). The white pattern on the longest scapulars can suggest Barrow's Goldeneye. In flight, upperwing shows large white patches, the first on the posterior lesser and median coverts, and the other on the greater coverts and secondaries, with a thin black bar at the base of the greater coverts separating them. Iris bright yellow. Legs yellow-brown. Gillham & Gillham[439,443] also described an adult ♂ in alternate plumage, a ♀ and a juvenile, all captive.

Hooded Merganser × Barrow's Goldeneye. Similar to previous hybrid but the gloss on the head is purple, not green, the white of the longest scapulars is reduced to more or less rounded spots surrounded by black, and the flanks appear darker grey, more contrasting with the breast. At least some birds have the head completely black, with shape recalling that of Barrow's Goldeneye[877].

HABITAT and LIFE-CYCLE Low to medium-distance migratory species, wintering over much of its breeding range (except where waterbodies freeze). Spring migration occurs very early, from mid-Jan to late Mar, peaking in Feb. Pair formation occurs in late autumn or winter, i.e. much earlier than in genus *Mergus*[261]. Eggs are laid between Feb and early May (mainly early Mar to mid-Apr)[332]. Inhabits marshes, lakes, ponds, oxbows, slow or moderately rapidly flowing streams in forested areas, shallow (<70 cm[332,1269]) and substrates often covered with stones or pebbles. Unlike genus *Mergus*, favours smaller and/or fishless ponds[332]. Prefers to nest in natural tree cavities and hollows, in the immediate

vicinity of water. The installation of nestboxes favours the species locally, including in wet areas devoid of trees. ♂♂ abandon ♀♀ and nesting sites just after egg laying, and head to moulting sites, sometimes distant and much further north[959]. ♀♀ can moult their remiges on their nesting sites, but most gather at moulting sites, permitted by the early breeding season. Migration to wintering sites occurs late in the season, mainly from mid-Nov to mid-Dec, often triggered by freezing conditions. During migration and winter, found at various types of shallow wetlands, with fresh or brackish water, often lined with trees, where the species often occurs alone or in small flocks of fewer than a dozen birds.

RANGE and POPULATION Besides the mapped area, rare or occasional breeder from C Alaska to New Mexico and in coastal states from N Florida to Nova Scotia[332]. Uncommon to rare visitor inland in SW USA and N Mexico. Some winter records in W Europe probably natural, as evidenced by reports in Azores. Population initially estimated at 76,000 birds in 1970s[85], but this appears to be a massive under-estimate, given annual hunting harvest (*c.*100,000 birds for Canada and USA in the early 2000s[363,648]). Current estimates, made difficult by the species' habitats and solitary behaviour, of 1,100,000 individuals[1348], and increasing.

CAPTIVITY More easily kept and much more readily bred than the genus *Mergus*. Also much more affordable than other mergansers and goldeneyes, and found regularly in captivity, thus could escape and survive at temperate latitudes in Eurasia. Most individuals observed in continental Europe are presumed to be of captive origin, although there are no records of breeding yet[62].

REFERENCES AOU (1983)[20]; Ball (1934)[57]; Banks *et al.* (2008)[62]; Bellrose (1976)[85]; Bird Hybrids Flickr Forum (2009)[118]; Bird Hybrids Flickr Forum (2010)[122]; BirdLife International (2012)[142]; Clements *et al.* (2013)[236]; Coupe & Cooke (1999)[261]; Donne-Goussé *et al.* (2002)[321]; Dugger *et al.* (2009)[332]; Environment Canada (2014)[363]; Erickson (1951)[365]; Gillham & Gillham (1996)[439]; Gillham & Gillham (2002)[443]; Johnsgard (2010)[648]; Johnstone (1955)[660]; Kortright (1942)[704]; Leverkühn (1890)[752]; Livezey (1995)[771]; Marcisz (1981)[804]; McCarthy (2006)[817]; Millard (1994)[845]; Morlan (2005)[877]; Palmer (1976)[945]; Pearce *et al.* (2008)[959]; Pyle (2008)[1014]; Sangster *et al.* (1997)[1131]; Sibley (1994)[1194]; Titman *in* Kear (2005)[1268]; Wetlands International (2014)[1348]; Wood (2010)[122].

580. Adult ♂ (definitive basic). New York, USA, Nov (Sébastien Reeber).

581. Adult ♀ (definitive basic); note adult tertials with whitish shafts. New York, USA, Nov (Sébastien Reeber).

582. Adult ♀ (definitive basic); in flight, best aged by broad white tips to central and inner greater coverts. Florida, USA, Jan (Ron Bielefeld).

583. First-winter ♂ (first basic/formative); some ♂-type formative feathers have appeared on head and upper flanks, and bill already has black sides; the brownish tertials and tertial coverts with frayed tips age this bird. New York, Nov (Sébastien Reeber).

584. First-winter ♀ (first basic/formative); tertials and tertial coverts (only partly visible here) are brownish, pointed and frayed at the tips. New York, Nov (Sébastien Reeber).

585. Adult pair (definitive basic); adult ♂ has pale grey wing patch on median and lower lesser coverts, and both sexes have broad white tips to central and inner greater coverts. Texas, USA, Dec (Greg Lavaty).

GOOSANDER (COMMON MERGANSER)
Mergus merganser

Plate 70

TAXONOMY *Mergus Merganser* Linnaeus, 1758, *Syst. Nat.*, edn. 10, p. 129. See Taxonomy of Red-breasted Merganser *M. serrator* concerning the systematic position of *Mergus* and its organisation. Three subspecies are often listed, but the literature is not unanimous on their definition. The nominate subspecies occurs over much of the Palearctic, while *M. m. americanus* Cassin, 1852, which is reasonably distinct, is its Nearctic counterpart. Confusion concerns two other named taxa: *comatus* Salvadori, 1895, of C & S Asia, and *orientalis* Gould, 1845 in E Asia. Several authors restrict *orientalis* to Central Asia[236,437,798], but this seems questionable, as its type was taken in SE China in Fujian (*Proc. Zool. Soc. London* 1845, p. 1), i.e. outside the range of *comatus*, but within that occupied by the E Asian population in winter, recognised by Brazil[182] under the name *orientalis*. Other authors consider *comatus* and *orientalis* synonyms[1269], in which case, however, the former is junior to *orientalis*. Finally, several authors correctly use *comatus* for the population of C Asia, but consider E Asian birds within the nominate subspecies[794,928,1044], which treatment is adopted here (see Geographic Variation) in the absence of precision as to the diagnosability of the E Asian population (*orientalis sensu* Brazil[182]).

IDENTIFICATION Large diving duck with an elongated body and long thin bill, its shape typical of *Mergus*. Could be confused with Red-breasted and Scaly-sided Mergansers *M. squamatus*, especially in plumages other than basic plumage adult ♂ (see Red-breasted Merganser).

PLUMAGES Nominate subspecies. Little sexual dimorphism in juvenile plumage, becoming stronger during first spring and obvious after first summer. Complex alternate moult strategy (two plumages per definitive cycle, three in first cycle). Ageing relatively easy until end of first summer. See Geographic Variation.

Adult ♂

Definitive basic plumage (Nov–Dec/Apr–May). Essentially bicoloured; head and upper neck black with green sheen and a long flattened crest forming a bump on hindneck. Iris brown. Bill bright red with culmen and nail blackish, lower mandible blackish with red tomium. Lower neck, breast, flanks and belly to undertail white, more or less

strongly tinged cream to pink, perhaps depending on diet[794]. Uppertail-coverts, rump and back white with thin blackish crescent-shaped streaks, sometimes also visible on upper and rear flanks. Mantle and inner scapulars black. Outer scapulars, tertial coverts and tertials white, latter with thin black fringe on inner webs. Rectrices blackish-grey. Upperwing has distal half blackish, as are four outermost secondaries (outer webs), corresponding greater coverts, inner two-thirds of leading edge and innermost upperwing-coverts to shortest tertial. Rest of wing (most secondary coverts and secondaries) white. Underwing dark grey and whitish. Legs and feet red-orange.

Definitive alternate plumage (May–Jun/Oct–Nov). Closer to ♀ but readily distinguished by basic upperwing and tertials not replaced. The whole forms a large white area, as the grey alternate scapular region is smaller and does not cover the folded wing. Rest of plumage as adult ♀, but head darker around eye and on crown, upperparts slightly darker (and browner), and flanks more clearly marked with pale crescents. Also note darker red bill.

Adult ♀

Definitive basic plumage (Nov–Dec/Apr–May). Head and upper neck a beautiful reddish-brown, with a greyish-white lower neck and chin. Crest longer, more drooping and 'dishevelled' than ♂. Iris brown often surrounded by yellowish (age-related?). Bill like ♂ but duller red. Sides of neck and breast as well as flanks grey, subtly streaked pale. Centre of breast paler, turning creamy-white on belly, often vaguely mottled dark posteriorly. Mantle and scapulars slightly darker grey than flanks, with neat blackish shafts. Back, rump and uppertail-coverts slightly paler grey than scapulars. Upperwing as ♂ but lesser and median coverts have dark grey shafts, tertial coverts and tertials grey with darker fringes in latter, thus white area is reduced to greater coverts and secondaries (except four outermost), with dark spots at tips of greater coverts, forming a fine line, more or less obvious between latter and secondaries. Underwing as adult ♂ but lesser and median coverts on average greyer. In the hand, wing length almost discriminates the sexes in adult (see Measurements and Mass), once subspecies is known[26,56,224,1014].

Definitive alternate plumage (May–Jun/Oct–Nov). Very

like basic plumage, but less swollen crest and often shows pale line between base of bill and eye, while rest of lores and crown are darker. Scapulars more grey-brown (bluish-grey in basic plumage). Flanks and breast-sides more distinctly streaked pale (feather fringes) and lower belly often irregularly sullied dark.

Juvenile

First basic plumage (until Aug–Sep). Like basic-plumage adult ♀ but duller (head less warm reddish-brown, more tinged ochre, upperparts and flanks browner grey). Pale chin less clear-cut. Pale line from base of bill to just below eye is sharper and surrounded by two dark lines. Iris dull yellowish. Tertials and tertial coverts uniform grey with sharper tips (quickly frayed). Median coverts (especially outermost) slightly paler grey in young ♂ than ♀ at any age. Greater coverts white and narrower than adult, often with vague traces of grey at tips, unlike clear blackish spots of adult ♀. In the hand, wing length (if fully grown) discriminates the sexes (see Measurements and Mass)[26,56,224,1014].

First-winter ♂

Formative plumage (Aug–Sep/Jul–Aug). Pre-formative moult protracted and variable in extent. Juvenile appearance is generally kept until at least late autumn and often until second pre-basic moult, thus difficult to distinguish from adult ♀♀, which is less frequently true of Red-breasted Merganser. Other birds acquire a more colourful plumage, suggesting adult ♂. Intermediate- or adult-type feathers often appear gradually around eye, on chin, mantle, inner scapulars (often largely centred black), some outer scapulars (grey) and flanks (sometimes white, vermiculated grey or largely centred white) in Dec–Apr. Frequently, the breast appears whiter than in ♀. Lesser and median coverts remain grey (mostly white in adult ♂), and are generally paler, especially towards 'wrist', than in ♀ at all ages. Formative tertials (1–4 usually present) are variably whitish, sometimes suggesting adult ♂, or pale grey with a blackish line on the inner fringe, or uniform darker grey. Bill and legs acquire adult colour progressively during first winter. First pre-alternate moult limited to head and mantle in some birds (perhaps only ♂♂[1014]).

First-winter ♀

Formative plumage (Aug–Sep/Jul–Aug.). Juvenile characters (especially striped lores, chin faintly contrasting, head more ochre, crest less thick, bill colour duller, etc.) disappear gradually during first winter.

Following pre-formative moult (Feb–May), very like adult ♀, and usually difficult to separate, many body feathers showing adult-type coloration. Distinction possible only in very good views or in the hand, except in those birds that undertook a limited pre-formative moult, still with many juvenile feathers (worn, brown, frayed or bleached in spring). Close up, note juvenile tertials retained (one to all), plainer grey, narrow, pointed and frayed. Formative tertials are usually difficult to distinguish from those of adult. Similarly, lower belly and undertail are generally uniformly pale (often sullied dark in adult ♀). In the hand, the shape of the upperwing-coverts and tertial coverts, narrower, pointed and worn at tips, is useful, as is wing length. The inner greater coverts show a little more grey at tips than in young ♂, forming a different pattern from the black clear-cut line of adult ♀.

GEOGRAPHIC VARIATION Three subspecies (see Taxonomy), but differences between populations wintering in E Asia and Europe still unclear.

M. m. americanus. Could occur in W Europe and E Asia. Distinguished from nominate subspecies in all plumages, in adult ♂♂ as follows.

- *Upperwing*: Black bases to greater coverts broader and not entirely covered by white median coverts, (vs. *merganser*). In latter, the white area covers the entire inner wing. In *americanus*, a black bar 5–10 mm wide, formed by the bases of the greater coverts, partly divides the white into two. This bar is very obvious in flight (beware, nominate *merganser* can show traces of blackish), and usually visible on the folded wing, above the rear flanks.

- *Shape of nail*: Often well hooked, almost downward-pointing in *merganser*. In profile, the nail encompasses the lower mandible over a length equivalent to the thickness of the bill at its tip. The nail is slightly flatter and shorter in *americanus*, often barely encompassing the lower mandible.

- *Shape of culmen*: In profile, *merganser* has a concave culmen. Slightly straighter in *americanus*, thus bill is thicker over its middle portion, and overall more triangular. In *merganser*, the bill narrows quickly over its proximal half and is of constant thickness distally.

- *Colour of bill*: Deep vermilion-red in *merganser*, whereas it is paler and brighter in *americanus*. The lower mandible appears largely red in *americanus*, even from below, whereas red is almost restricted to the tomium in *merganser* (underside black).

- **Feathering at base of bill**: In profile, feathers cover the sides of the base of the maxilla and taper to a point. This point is sharper (angle *c.*60°) in *merganser* than *americanus* (nearer 90°). The frontal lobe is thus narrower and sharper in *merganser* (*c.*45°). Another way to interpret the same feature is to judge the tip of the feathering vs. the distance of gape to proximal edge of nostrils: the feathering reaches half this distance in *merganser* (gape more salient), but usually one-quarter in *americanus*. Finally, the less extensive feathering in *americanus* reveals a broad pinkish-red bill base which, along with its brighter colour, makes the bill much more visible from afar.

- **Head shape**: In *merganser*, more angular: the front is slightly steeper, the crown flatter and forms an angle with the nape, the crest forming a long bump on the hindneck. The chin often appears rounded. In *americanus*, the head is thinner, rounded, often devoid of sharp angles. The crest is the same length but appears less swollen and tighter. The head is barely wider than the neck and tapers at the front to merge into the bill, which is thicker at the base.

A few other features have been described[308,420,1200]: leading edge of the underwing whiter in *merganser* but stained grey in *americanus*, and grey rump slightly paler in *merganser*. The pinkish-coloured breast and lower parts are reportedly more striking on average and appear earlier in winter in *merganser*. Separating ♂♂ in definitive alternate plumage is based on same features, except head profile. Subspecific identification of ♀♀ is trickier, and based on feathering at base of bill, as in ♂, but less marked. The upperparts are plainer and paler grey in *merganser*, with darker centres and paler fringes giving a scalier appearance in *americanus*. As in ♂, the underwing's leading edge averages whiter in *merganser*.

M. m. comatus. Apparently no intermediates described with *M. m. merganser*[928]. *M. m. comatus* is reportedly slightly larger, with bill averaging 8% shorter, wings 5% longer and legs perhaps shorter[928]. Morphological distinction from the nominate subspecies less well described in the literature and their variability unknown.

- **Feathering at base of bill**: Like that of *americanus* and does not form tipped end towards the nostril. As *americanus*, in profile the frontal lobes run slightly further beyond the gape, which are barely prominent, quite unlike *merganser*. Like *americanus*, the tip of the feathering reaches approximately one-quarter of the distance between gape and proximal edge of the nostrils (half this in *merganser*).

- **Nostril position**: The nostrils are located closer to the feathers than in *merganser*, and perhaps even *americanus*, i.e. clearly less than half the distance between the gape and bill tip.

- **Bill shape**: Culmen markedly concave, which appears even more obvious than in *merganser* due to shorter bill, and a thinner distal half. The nail appears hooked like *merganser*.

- **Colour of bill**: Lower mandible appears almost or wholly black (variable?) in *comatus*, whereas its tomium is red in *merganser*. The lower mandible is largely red in *americanus*.

- **Head shape**: Appearance at least as angular as *merganser*, with a steep forehead prolonging the highly concave culmen, a tall flat crown and a marked angle with the nape. The crest is long (almost reaching the limit of the white hindneck in adult ♂ in basic plumage), but appears less swollen, flatter and forms a notch at its tip, rather than a bump on hindneck like *merganser*. ♀♀ often show a shaggier crest than *merganser*, even if it is more difficult to quantify.

Three other features relate to adult ♂ in basic plumage. The white tertials with a black line on the fringe of the inner web averages thicker in *comatus*. The black of the upperparts is visibly more extensive, including the shoulders (broad black line down to breast-sides) and black posterior scapulars visibly longer and often drooping. Lower back and rump appear pale grey, with marked white speckles. Apparently, no difference between *merganser* and *comatus* in upperwing pattern. Finally, note head colour of ♀ reported as slightly paler on average[928].

MEASUREMENTS and MASS ♂ and adult noticeably larger than ♀ and young, respectively, with wing length permitting sexing by age-class.

M. m. merganser. ♂: wing chord 275–295 (adult, 285, *n*=30) and 263–291 (juvenile, 275, *n*=27), tail 100–111 (adult, 105.0, *n*=24), bill 52–60 (55.8, *n*=58), tarsus 49–55 (51.7, *n*=58); ♀: wing chord 255–270 (adult, 262, *n*=23) and 242–260 (juvenile, 252, *n*=20), tail 95–109 (adult, 100, *n*=23), bill 44–52 (48.7, *n*=43), tarsus 44–51 (47.4, n=43)[267]. ♂: wing chord 279–299 (adult, 286, n=44) and 262–280 (juvenile, 272, n=10), bill 52–60 (56.4, n=47); ♀: wing chord 251–273 (adult, 261, n=18) and 244–258 (juvenile, 251, n=7), bill 46–53 (48.8, n=21)[1122].

M. m. americanus. Adult ♂: wing chord 260–283 (n=57), culmen 49–60 (n=59), tarsus 47–60 (n=60), mass (year-round) 1,264–2,054 (1,589, n=60); juvenile/first-winter ♂: wing chord 239–277 (n=75), culmen 47–57 (n=73), tarsus 45–55 (n=77), mass 1,162–1,809 (1,417, n=76); adult ♀: wing chord 230–259 (n=55), culmen 45–52 (n=56), tarsus 40–48 (n=58); mass 898–1,397 (1,185, n=63); juvenile/first-winter ♀: wing chord 239–277 (n=75), culmen 42–51 (n=94), tarsus 41–49 (n=105), mass 860–1,440 (1,137, n=102)[366]. Adult ♂ (n=12): wing chord 269–285 (278), culmen 54–59 (55.8), tail 96–102 (100); adult ♀ (n=12): wing chord 246–259 (253), culmen 47–54 (49.2), tail 90–98 (93)[945]. ♂ (n=100): 261–284 (adult) and 252–274 (juvenile), culmen 50–59, bill depth at tip of forehead feathers 15.2–18.3, tail 94–106, tarsus 47–54; ♀ (n=100): 236–257 (adult) and 226–248 (juvenile), culmen 44–52, bill depth at tip of forehead feathers 12.5–14.3, tail 87–99, tarsus 42–49[1014].

M. m. comatus. Few data published. ♂: wing chord 286–305 (295), bill 48–56 (51.5); ♂: head: 120–128; tail 105–120; ♀: head: 109–120; tail 95–100[1044].

VOICE In courtship, ♂ gives a *kh-kh-koh-kroooh*, with drawled last syllable, and a strange croaking nasal tone like an amphibian. Number of syllables and pitch can vary depending on intensity of courtship and interactions between different ♂♂. Up close, various low, muted sounds are uttered simultaneously. At same time, ♀ emits phrases of harsh notes, variable in number, e.g. *arr-kre-kre-kre-kre* at slow pace. At other times, ♀ gives short croaks, *ga-rrk*, most frequently heard if alarmed or taking off. Vocalisations apparently similar between subspecies, but detailed studies lacking.

MOULT Complex alternate strategy. See Red-breasted Merganser. Pre-formative moult in Aug–Apr or even later, sometimes slowed or suspended in Dec–Mar[56]. First pre-alternate moult limited (sometimes absent?) in Jun–Aug, continuing as second pre-basic moult in Jul–Oct in second-year birds[1014]. Definitive pre-alternate moult partial in May–Jul. Definitive pre-basic moult from early Jun to Dec starting with the remiges and rectrices, slightly later in ♀.

HYBRIDISATION Natural hybridisation seems exceptional and has been reported with Common Goldeneye *Bucephala clangula*[465,817,1190], Red-breasted Merganser[151], Smew *Mergellus albellus*[439] and possibly Mallard *Anas platyrhynchos*[442,817,1145,1190]. In captivity, cases reported with Common Shelduck *Tadorna tadorna*[439,465,763], Redhead *Aythya americana*[442], Common Eider *Somateria mollissima*[129,442,443] (perhaps in the wild as well) and Hooded Merganser *Lophodytes cucullatus*[660].

HABITAT and LIFE-CYCLE Breeds at various latitudes, with southern populations (temperate and montane regions) being sedentary or short-distance migrants. Arrives on breeding grounds in Mar–May[1154], with eggs laid from late Mar in south of range[267], but mainly Apr–May in Scandinavia or until Jun in northernmost Eurasia and North America[798]. Inhabits lakes, ponds and rather fast-flowing parts of rivers, usually in deep, clear, oligotrophic water, well stocked with fish. Although the species can also nest on the ground (burrows, hollows between rocks, tree roots, etc.), it prefers holes in trees, often >15 m above ground[1269], meaning that its northern range limit largely matches that of boreal forest[798]. Populations strongly enhanced locally by nestbox schemes. ♂♂ abandon ♀♀ early during incubation and gather in small flocks along sea coasts and lakeshores, including north to the Arctic Ocean. ♀♀ generally moult on breeding grounds or nearby, along with their offspring. Departs for wintering grounds rather late in season, in Oct–Dec, often triggered by freezing of moulting or breeding areas[1213]. In winter, on large freshwater bodies, often several metres deep at least, e.g. lakes, gravel pits, reservoirs and rivers, particularly depending on availability of fish. Prone to large-scale movements to coastal waters if inland waters freeze[145].

RANGE and POPULATION Three essentially allopatric populations in Holarctic. Total population estimated at 1,700,000–2,400,000 birds[305], and increasing[145] although trend less well known in E Asia. Geographically isolated populations may be genetically distinct, given strong philopatry of ♀♀[543].

M. m. merganser. Palearctic range from Iceland to W Aleutians. Several isolated breeding populations in E & C Europe. Transition or zone of sympatry with *comatus* not well known, in NW China and E Kazakhstan, both subspecies sometimes said to winter in N India[1044]. Two wintering populations (division unknown on Siberian breeding grounds): the first (*c*.300,000 birds[1348]) winters in Europe and the second (50,000–100,000 birds[757,858]) in E Asia.

M. m. americanus. Nearctic range, and as for *merganser*, southernmost breeding locations are generally montane (Rockies). In winter, uncommon in SE USA and N Mexico. Population *c.*300,000–500,000 birds in W North America, and 1000,000–1,500,000 individuals in E North America[1348].

M. m. comatus. Breeds in C Asia, from Uzbekistan and Kyrgyzstan to Tibet and SW China to Sichuan. Northern limit of range poorly defined. Partially sedentary where waters do not freeze, but overwinters south to Pakistan, N India and Myanmar. Population estimated at 2,500–10,000 individuals[215].

CAPTIVITY Has special requirements in captivity – large deep ponds, clear water and some live food. The species is also said so be aggressive towards other species. Quite difficult to breed, generally expensive and typically scarce in captivity, so unlikely to escape.

REFERENCES Anderson & Timken (1972)[26]; Baker (1993)[56]; Bird Hybrids Flickr Forum (2011)[129]; BirdLife International (2014)[145]; Blaser (1978)[151]; Brazil (2009)[182]; Callaghan & Green (1993)[215]; Carney (1992)[224]; Clements *et al.* (2013)[236]; Cramp & Simmons (1977)[268]; Delany & Scott (2006)[305]; Dementiev & Gladkov (1952)[308]; Erskine (1971)[366]; Garner (1999)[420]; Gill & Donsker (2014)[437]; Gillham & Gillham (1996)[439]; Gillham & Gillham (2000)[442]; Gillham & Gillham (2002)[443]; Gray (1958)[465]; Hefti-Gautschi *et al.* (2009)[543]; Johnstone (1955)[660]; Li *et al.* (2009)[757]; Lind & Poulsen (1963)[763]; Madge & Burn (1988)[794]; Mallory & Metz (1999)[798]; McCarthy (2006)[817]; Miyabashi & Mundkur (1999)[858]; Ogilvie & Young (1998)[928]; Palmer (1976)[945]; Pearce & Petersen (2009)[955]; Peters *et al.* (2012)[972]; Pyle (2008)[1014]; Rasmussen & Anderton (2005)[1044]; Salminen (1983)[1122]; Schlüter (1891)[1145]; Scott & Rose (1996)[1154]; Sibley (1938)[1190]; Sibley (2011)[1200]; Snow & Perrins (1998)[1213]; Titman *in* Kear (2005)[1269]; Wetlands International (2014)[1348].

586. *M. m. merganser*, adult ♂ (definitive basic). France, Mar (Vincent Palomares).

587. *M. m. merganser*, adult ♂ (definitive basic); vs. other subspecies, note diagnostic pointed feathering at base of bill and long nail. Netherlands, Feb (Seraf van der Putten).

588. *M. m. merganser*, adult ♂ (definitive basic); note upperwing pattern without dark bar at base of greater coverts (vs. *americanus*). Denmark, Jan (Nis Lundmark Jensen).

589. *M. m. merganser*, adult ♂ (definitive alternate); vs. ♀, note white upperwing and tertials, and duskier head. Sweden, Aug (Nis Lundmark Jensen).

590. *M. m. merganser*, adult ♀ (definitive basic); for ageing, note long, thick crest, and broad, round-tipped, fresh and pale grey-centred tertials. Scotland, Jan (Dennis Morrison).

591. *M. m. merganser*, first-winter (formative); aged by upperwing pattern, with barely visible dusky patches at tips of greater coverts (vs. well-marked black tips in adult ♀), while pale grey median and lesser coverts suggest a ♂. Japan, Jan (Stuart Price).

592. *M. m. merganser*, first-winter ♂ (formative); aged by tertials being rather pointed, frayed and brown at tips, while some feathers on head (blacker) and flanks (vermiculated) indicate a ♂. France, Feb (Vincent Palomares).

593. *M. m. comatus*, adult ♂ (definitive basic); note head shape, as well as thin bill, with almost no red on lower mandible and feathering at base without sharp angle. India, Dec (Jainy Kuriakose).

594. *M. m. comatus*, adult ♀ (definitive basic); identified like ♂ (using bill pattern). India, Dec (Jainy Kuriakose).

595. *M. m. americanus*, adult ♂ (definitive basic); note much narrower head whose profile merges into that of bill, which is deeper at base, and feathers do not extend onto bill base as in nominate. California, USA, Nov (Tom Grey).

596. *M. m. americanus*, adult ♂ (definitive basic); in flight, broad black bar at base of greater coverts is unique to this subspecies. British Columbia, Canada, Apr (Alan D. Wilson).

597. *M. m. americanus*, adult ♀ (definitive basic); the same bill features as ♂ can be applied in ♀, but are usually less obvious. British Columbia, Canada, Feb (Alan D. Wilson).

SCALY-SIDED MERGANSER
Mergus squamatus

Plate 69

TAXONOMY *Mergus squamatus* Gould, 1864, *Proc. Zool. Soc. Lond.*, p. 184. See Taxonomy of Red-breasted Merganser *M. serrator*. Monotypic.

IDENTIFICATION Can only be confused with either of the other two *Mergus*, both of which are sympatric, Goosander *M. merganser* and Red-breasted Merganser, especially in plumages other than basic plumage adult ♂. Identification is sometimes complex because it is, in many ways, intermediate between the other *Mergus*. See Identification under Red-breasted Merganser.

PLUMAGES Little sexual dimorphism in juvenile plumage, becoming clearer during first spring and strong after first summer. Complex alternate moult strategy (two plumages per annual cycle, three in first cycle). Ageing rather easy until end of first summer.

Adult ♂

Definitive basic plumage (Oct–Nov/Apr–May). Mainly black and white. Head and neck black with green sheen, crest formed by numerous very long feathers, affording a much shaggier look than in Red-breasted Merganser. Iris usually dark brown, sometimes paler and greyer. Bill dark red with culmen spotted black and nail usually pale yellow. Black hindneck reaches mantle and inner scapulars. Lower scapulars and tertials white, the latter with thick black line on inner webs. Entire underparts white to creamy (sometimes also stripe on foreneck). Flank feathers marked by two black lines: the first, innermost, forming a chevron and the second, rounded at the edge, forming a beautiful scaly pattern. Some similar crescents and stripes, smaller and thinner, cover the back, rear body and the lower belly. Longer uppertail-coverts tinged plainer grey. Rectrices grey (paler outwards). Upperwing has distal half blackish, all secondary coverts and secondaries white (except four outer greater coverts and secondaries), except the leading edge, innermost secondary coverts, base of greater coverts and secondaries, which are black, the latter forming two black lines in the white area. Underwing whitish (axillaries and median coverts) and pale grey, darker on outer half. Legs orange-red with webs darker.

Definitive alternate plumage (May–Jun/Sep–Oct). Closer to adult ♀ but often retains an almost basic appearance, with reddish-brown head and neck. Retained basic feathers make head darker, while mantle often variegated grey and black. Breast and flanks show a mix of basic and alternate feathers, the latter with broad, vague grey and white stripes. The upperwing is basic, with a long white patch clearly defined on the lesser and median coverts. In adult ♀, this patch is pale grey to whitish, but diffusely delineated, and the black bar on the greater coverts is smaller and less clearly marked than that at base of secondaries. Similarly, the basic tertials, white fringed black, differ from those of adult ♀.

Adult ♀

Definitive basic plumage (Oct–Nov/Apr–May?). Head and neck pale reddish-brown, with long, very shaggy crest, darker around eye and small pale ill-defined patch on chin and throat. Iris dark brown. Bill red with black culmen and variable dark spots on sides, nail paler and yellow. Contrast between head/neck and breast stronger than Red-breasted Merganser, but less marked than Goosander. Centre of breast and belly whitish. Sides of breast, flanks, back, rump and rear body to undertail-coverts pale grey with many crescent-shaped marks, white on grey background or blackish on pale grey background, like those of ♂ but less neatly defined. Mantle, scapulars and tail slightly darker grey than flanks. Tertials pale grey in centres (whitish on outermost tertials), with black fringe on inner webs. Outermost tertial coverts have large white subterminal spot. Upperwing like ♂, albeit with lesser and median coverts pale grey with whitish fringes, producing a patch like ♂, but greyer and diffusely marked. Greater coverts have tips finely marked black. Underwing like ♂, but more marked with grey. Legs and feet orange-red, with dark webs.

Definitive alternate plumage (May–Jun/Sep–Oct?). Very like basic plumage, but alternate feathers on flanks (especially upper flanks) show broader, greyer and less clearly defined crescents.

Juvenile

First basic plumage (until Aug–Sep). Like adult ♀ but duller and more likely to be confused with other mergansers. Head and neck reddish-brown with darker crown and nape, poorly-defined whitish foreneck and throat, and clear pale stripe from base of bill to just below eye. Another pale mark is often visible above the eye. Crest shorter. Iris pale greyish or yellowish, especially outwards. Bill initially pale, dull orange with dusky coloration on culmen extending further onto sides of upper mandible. Nail whitish. Flanks, rear body, back and rump uniformly grey, without blackish crescents or bars, but faint whitish fringes and grey chevrons. Legs dull brownish-yellow.

First-winter ♂

Formative plumage (Aug–Sep/Jul–Aug). Plumage poorly described in the wild, including its variability, but clear similarities with other *Mergus* during pre-formative moult and resultant plumage. Following pre-formative moult (in Mar–Jul), young ♂♂ can recall alternate plumage of adult ♂ and adult ♀, with a usually brownish head (blackish around eye, on lores and, variably, the crown). On the other hand, has a fairly short crest, a mix of grey and blackish feathers on mantle and scapulars, and flanks often like those of adult ♂, but with juvenile feathers mixed (grey with broad dark grey crescents). Rear body and back similar to those of ♀ with tertials rather pointed, grey, centred whitish with diffuse black fringes. Juvenile wing is retained. Iris initially circled grey or pale yellowish, but like that of adult apparently from first spring. Legs orange-yellow, paler than adult, becoming pink or orange from midwinter.

First-winter ♀

Formative plumage (Aug–Sep/Jul–Aug.). Few detailed data published on this plumage. Juvenile features (striped lores, iris largely circled pale grey, legs more yellow than orange, and short crest) often discernible until early first winter at least. Following pre-formative moult, probably very like adult ♀, but at least some birds identifiable, in particular by presence of grey juvenile feathers, uniform and fringed whitish on upper flanks, and from back to uppertail. Also note juvenile tertials retained, more uniform than adult ♀, sharper and clearly frayed at tips from early winter. Retained tertial coverts narrower, pointed at tips and more worn than adult ♀. Presence of whitish spot on outermost tertial coverts, as in adult ♀, undescribed.

GEOGRAPHIC VARIATION None.

MEASUREMENTS and MASS

♂ and adult noticeably larger than ♀ and young, respectively. Few data published from the wild. Hughes[601] gave an overview of various references, all based on limited samples: ♂: wing chord 250–265, culmen 52–57, tarsus 46–48, mass in Apr (*n*=3) 1,125–1,400 (1,232); ♀: wing chord 220–250, tail 100–127, mass in Apr (*n*=3) 870–1,100 (956). Other mass data have been published for the breeding season: ♀ (*n*=8): 930–1,070 (977)[1218].

VOICE

Usually quiet. ♀ gives a harsh *grrek*, like Goosander, but weaker and less hoarse[1218]. Adult of both sexes also utters calls comparable to Red-breasted Merganser[182], as well as asthmatic wheezing sounds.

MOULT

Very few data published on extent and timing of various moults in the wild (see Moult of Red-breasted Merganser). Pre-alternate moult in adult ♂ starts mid-Apr, together with non-breeding, second-calendar-year birds[700] and consecutive pre-basic moult virtually finished by Nov[331,700] (some in complete basic plumage by mid-Oct).

HYBRIDISATION No reports published.

HABITAT and LIFE-CYCLE

Arrives on nesting grounds by late Mar or early Apr, generally as rivers start to thaw. To nest, uses fast-flowing montane rivers with many emergent rocks and islets, preferring large sections (20–60 m wide) rather than narrow sections with wooded banks[331,1388]. Pairs hold territories along a stretch of river between 500 m and 3–4 km long[156,699], and nest in a tree cavity on the shore or up to 120 m from the water, including nestboxes where available. Like other mergansers, adult ♂♂ start pre-alternate moult early in incubation, at the nesting sites[700] then form small flocks and move to moulting sites. ♀♀ moult their remiges on their nesting grounds, with their offspring[1219]. Southbound migration mainly occurs between mid-Sep and mid-Oct, and can be triggered by the onset of freezing conditions. In non-breeding season, prefers large, ice-free rivers (often downstream from their breeding sites), estuaries and even coastal waters, where *c.*10% of birds apparently overwinter[145]. Mostly found in small groups up to 20 birds.

RANGE and POPULATION

Breeding range restricted to far SE Russia, extreme NE China and North Korea. Winters mainly in inland SE China (major concentration in Jiangxi[72]) and to lesser extent along coast of Yancheng (Jiangsu, China) and South Korea. Rare in Japan, with vagrants reaching Myanmar, Taiwan and N Thailand. The population is widely dispersed, nowhere abundant, and some wintering sites probably remain undiscovered. Recent estimates suggest 2,400–4,500 mature individuals (3,600–6,800 birds in total)[764] and 4,600 pairs[72]. The known breeding population is estimated at 1,575 breeding pairs in Sikhote-Alin' Mts,

Russia (Khabarovsk Kray and Primorskiy Kray), 150–200 pairs in Changbai Mts, China, close to North Korea, 30–40 pairs in the Little Khingan (NE Heilongjiang, China), where probably extirpated[764], and probably <200 pairs in North Korea[764,1219]. In winter, recent surveys have produced 370–770 birds, confirming the weak knowledge of its distribution at this season, but also raises concern of an ongoing rapid decline[72]. The decrease is well known globally, even if regional increases have occurred recently[1185]. However, the species' low genetic diversity suggests that it has probably not been numerous for a very long time[1219]. The main threats identified are the large-scale destruction and modification of its nesting and, especially, wintering habitats, including the construction of dams, extraction of sand and gravel, domestic and industrial pollution[72], mortality in fishing nets, and disturbance due to recreational activities[331]. In consequence, the species is classified as Endangered[145]. The main nesting sites are protected in North Korea, but only locally in China and Russia. Nestbox schemes in Russia have resulted in increased density in some suitable areas, in tandem with public information initiatives[269]. An international team has recently been established to work for the species' conservation.

CAPTIVITY Very rare in captivity and usually very expensive when offered for sale. Like other mergansers, very demanding in its requirements, especially for breeding. Bred by some specialised zoos and collections, and very unlikely to escape from captivity.

REFERENCES Barter *et al.* (2013)[72]; BirdLife International (2014)[145]; Bocharnikov & Shibnyev (1994)[156]; Brazil (2009)[182]; Cao & Barter (2008)[220]; Cranswick (2010)[269]; Duckworth & Chol (2005)[331]; He *et al.* (2002)[542]; Hughes *in* Kear (2005)[601]; Hughes & Bocharnikov (1992)[603]; Kolomiitsev (1992)[699]; Kolomiitsev (1995)[700]; Lin *et al.* (2008)[762]; Liu *et al.* (2010)[764]; Shokhrin & Solovieva (2003)[1185]; Solovyeva & Pearce (2011)[1219]; Solovyeva & Shokhrin (2008)[1218]; Solovyeva *et al.* (2014)[1221]; Wang *et al.* (2010)[1335]; Zhao & Pao (1998)[1388].

598. Adult ♂ (definitive basic). Japan, Nov (Mark Curley).

599. Adult ♂ (definitive basic) completing pre-basic moult with the tertials. Jilin, China, Sep (Peiqi Liu).

600. Adult ♂ (definitive basic). South Korea, Dec (Philippe J. Dubois).

601. Adult ♀ (definitive basic); note long crest for ageing. Japan, Nov (Mark Curley).

602. First-winter ♀ (first basic/formative); note iris circled pale brownish-yellow and juvenile tertials (uniform dark grey-brown). Jilin, China, Oct (Peiqi Liu).

603. Adult ♀ (definitive basic/definitive alternate). Jilin, China, Jun (Peiqi Liu).

RED-BREASTED MERGANSER
Mergus serrator   **Plate 69**

TAXONOMY *Mergus Serrator* Linnaeus, 1758, *Syst. Nat.*, edn. 10, p. 129. Within the tribe Mergini, which includes all sea ducks, the genus *Mergus* forms a clade with Hooded Merganser *Lophodytes cucullatus*, close to Smew *Mergellus albellus* on the one hand, and the genus *Bucephala*[771]. These are highly specialised ducks with several distinct morphological and ecological characters[766]. In particular, the long thin bill has sharp, forward/backward 'teeth' for catching fish underwater. *Mergus* contains five species (one extinct, Auckland Merganser *M. australis*), including three in N Hemisphere, among which Red-breasted Merganser is either placed alongside Goosander *M. merganser*[640,1219] or considered closer to Scaly-sided Merganser *M. squamatus*[766,771]. Monotypic, but Greenland birds were named *M. s. schioleri* Salomonsen, 1949, a treatment since rejected[267,1014,1270,1267].

IDENTIFICATION Mergansers are very distinctive ducks, rarely mistaken for other wildfowl. Within the present species' range, Goosander and Scaly-sided Merganser also occur. ♀♀ and young of these species can pose identification problems, albeit usually quickly solved with reasonable views. In definitive basic plumage, ♂ not difficult to identify, being the only species with a broad ochre and streaked breast-band, black fore flanks with a vertical line of white spots, and vermiculated flanks. The breast and flanks are white to pale pink in the other two species, with black crescents producing a scaly pattern in Scaly-sided Merganser. In definitive alternate plumage, adult ♂♂ are more like ♀♀, except the upperwing pattern, still basic, which can be used for specific identification. The nominate subspecies of Goosander has a uniform white patch on the secondaries and secondary coverts, while the North American subspecies, *M. m. americanus*, shows a clear black bar formed by the bases to the greater coverts. Red-breasted and Scaly-sided Mergansers show two black bars, at the bases of the greater coverts and the secondaries. The wing of the former has a broad dark leading edge, while in the latter the white patch meets the leading edge near the 'wrist', and the black head and neck reaches the black mantle.

In all other plumages, distinction from Goosander at long range relies on observation of the transition between the reddish-brown head/upper neck and pale grey breast. It is clear-cut in Goosander, but diffuse and gradual in Red-breasted Merganser. Among other features, note the greater size of Goosander, more massive shape, with a thicker head, more swollen crest generally forming a bump on the hindneck (vs. long shaggy crest, often two separate tufts, in Red-breasted Merganser), its stronger neck and relatively thicker based bill (vs. bill longer, of more constant thickness and slightly snub in Red-breasted Merganser). Also note well-demarcated white throat of Goosander, whereas it is whitish and diffuse in Red-breasted Merganser. Furthermore, the position of the nostrils is different: their distal edge reaches halfway between the gape and bill tip in Goosander, while they are located approximately one-quarter of this length in Red-breasted Merganser. Close up, a pale streak surrounded by two diffuse dark streaks are more or less visible on the lores in Red-breasted Merganser (and juvenile Goosander). The shape of the feathering at the base of the bill also differs: in profile, the gape is very prominent, extending much further into the feathers in Red-breasted Merganser. This is even more obvious compared to the Nearctic subspecies of Goosander. Note also, in adult, iris reddish (♀) to red (♂) in Red-breasted Merganser, but dark brown in Goosander. The feathers of the mantle and scapulars show neat blackish shafts in Goosander, absent in Red-breasted Merganser. Finally, the overall colour is a little different, Goosander having the body slightly bluish-grey with a reddish-brown head. The body of Red-breasted Merganser is more brownish-grey, and its crest more yellowish-brown and duller. Added to the contrast between head and breast, this makes Goosander look more two-toned. In flight, the slightly darker flanks of Red-breasted Merganser contrast more with the belly and whitish axillaries.

Distinction from Scaly-sided Merganser is trickier, because, in many ways, its ♀ is intermediate between those of the two other species, including in size and structure. It is essentially characterised by its longer and shaggier crest, and dark crescents on the flanks that give a distinctive scaly appearance. The colour of the head, head/neck contrast and head/throat contrast are intermediate between those of Goosander and Red-breasted Merganser. The shape of the bill (relatively thick-based) and position of the nostrils (distal edge midway along the bill) are closer to those of Goosander, but the two features are useful for identification, including in flight given good views[603], the bill and head appearing elongated and thin. The nail is not as bent as Goosander, but is pale yellow, unlike the other two species. In flight, the median and lower lesser coverts of Red-breasted Merganser are grey-brown, while those of Goosander are mid-grey, and ♀ Scaly-sided Merganser pale grey to whitish.

Also, nesting habitat of Scaly-sided Merganser is like that of Goosander, but different from Red-breasted Merganser. Therefore juveniles of both former species are likely to be seen together, and can be difficult to distinguish. Juvenile Scaly-sided Merganser lacks clean crescents of ♀ on its flanks, but white and grey markings are variably pronounced. Identification relies on size, shape (especially thinner head and bill) and upperwing pattern (presence of black bar at base of secondaries). Other useful differences between juvenile are the face being more marked in Goosander, in which the loral stripe is paler on a darker brown ground. In Scaly-sided Merganser, this stripe is more buff on a slightly paler head[603]. Details of the bill are discriminatory (blackish concave culmen with long hooked nail in Goosander vs. culmen straighter, pale nail slightly curved and not reaching further down than the tip of the lower mandible in profile).

PLUMAGES Little sexual dimorphism in juvenile plumage, becoming gradually stronger and obvious after first summer. Complex alternate moult strategy (two plumages per final year cycle, three in first cycle). Ageing ♂♂ relatively easy until first summer; ♀♀ harder from beginning of second calendar year.

Adult ♂

Definitive basic plumage (Nov–Dec/Apr–May). Head, upper neck and crest black with green gloss, highlighted by broad white collar, interrupted only on hindneck by thin black line. Iris red. Bill pinkish-red, slightly duller, with blackish culmen and nail. Breast pale yellow-ochre with diffuse and irregular longitudinal blackish streaks that merge into a broad black band on lower breast and fore flanks, with a vertical line of white patches visible on the latter. Flanks, back, rump and uppertail-coverts white vermiculated grey. Belly and undertail white. Rectrices dark grey. Inner scapulars and mantle blackish, outer scapulars, tertial coverts and tertials mainly white, the latter with thin black fringe on inner web. Upperwing blackish-grey with large white patch on inner wing. Secondaries white with black bases forming a broad line visible in flight (the four outermost with outer webs entirely black), and greater coverts white with black base forming a second line (4–5 outermost greater coverts blackish). Median and posterior lesser coverts form a large white patch. Innermost secondary coverts, leading edge and outer half of wing blackish. Underwing mostly grey with diffuse white bars formed by fringes to coverts, and median coverts and axillaries whitish. Legs and feet red.

Definitive alternate plumage (May–Jun/Oct–Nov). Like adult ♀ with frequent scattered basic feathers retained, visible especially on the head, mantle, breast-sides and flanks. The best sexing feature is the upperwing: tertials all white with a thin line on the fringes of the inner webs (dark grey in ♀) and median coverts and posterior primary coverts white (not grey). These wing features are usually visible on folded wing and in flight, insofar as scapular area is much less extensive on wing than basic plumage.

Adult ♀

Definitive basic plumage (Nov–Dec/Apr–May). Head and upper neck pale reddish-brown, with very shaggy crest but often still has an unkempt or dishevelled appearance. Thin dark loral stripe, underlined by a paler to whitish stripe that extends in semi-circle below eye. Throat pale, but no clear contrast with rest of head. Iris reddish, sometimes brown. Bill reddish-pink, dark culmen and nail. Colour of head and upper neck merges gradually with breast, pale grey at front, brownish on sides. Flanks grey with pale crescents more or less well marked. Belly and undertail whitish. Mantle, scapulars, back, rump and tail slightly darker and browner than flanks. Tertials pale grey in centre with black fringe on inner web, except on outermost, which is white-centred. Upperwing lesser and median coverts brownish-grey as upperparts, outer wing slightly darker, greater coverts (except 4–5 outermost) and secondaries (except outer web of four outermost) white, separated by a black line formed by bases to secondaries. Inner greater coverts tips have dark grey fringes. Underwing like ♂. Legs and feet dull red, webs darker.

Definitive alternate plumage (May–Jun/Oct–Nov). Similar to basic plumage, but pale fringes to flanks, rump, back, mantle and scapulars more whitish, giving the bird a more streaked appearance.

Juvenile

First basic plumage (until Aug–Sep). As ♀ in basic plumage, but slightly browner overall (especially centre of breast and belly, not whitish), with denser and shorter crest (feathers of nape <40 mm). Dark and pale horizontal stripes on lores more contrasting than adult. Iris pale brown to yellowish. Bill dull brownish-pink. Legs dull yellowish-brown. Upperwing as adult ♀ but tertials more uniform grey, with broad, diffuse, dark fringes on inner webs of outer tertials. White inner greater coverts have very little grey (♂) to a small grey spot (♀) at tips[1014]. Outermost tertial has white inner web with broad black fringe. All upperwing-coverts narrower and round-tipped (broad and rather truncated or square-tipped in adult).

First-winter ♂

Formative plumage (Aug–Sep/Jul–Aug). Pre-formative moult proceeds slowly and is quite variable in extent. Following this, most birds appear similar to juvenile or ♀. Others show an appearance more reminiscent of adult ♂, but confusion not possible. Distinguished from afar by more variegated and duller plumage. Also, lesser, median and tertial coverts grey-brown and 1–4 juvenile tertials retained, grey (not white). Iris initially yellowish becoming orange then red by end of first winter. The bill and legs acquire adult coloration during the first winter. First pre-alternate moult limited to feathers of head and mantle in some (perhaps only ♂♂[1014]), with overall appearance and distinction from adult ♂ largely unchanged until second pre-basic moult.

First-winter ♀

Formative plumage (Aug–Sep/Jul–Aug). Very similar to adult ♀ but head duller pale cinnamon-brown, crest shorter (head appearing shaggier than tufted), bill and legs initially yellow-brown, becoming dull orange in winter. Iris initially pale yellowish-brown, gradually becoming darker during first winter. Inner greater coverts with slightly more grey at tips than in young ♂ (black bar in adult ♀). Longest tertials grey-brown, usually fairly uniform, with fringe of inner web dark and diffuse, rarely like adult, with whitish centres. Tertial coverts dark grey, rather pointed (glossy black with rounded tips in adult ♀)[224]. Outer tertials with inner webs averaging greyer than ♂ at same age, and blackish line on fringe of inner web broader and more diffuse.

GEOGRAPHIC VARIATION Weak and unconfirmed, but Greenland population reportedly larger.

MEASUREMENTS and MASS ♂ and adult slightly larger than ♀ and young, respectively. Netherlands, in winter. ♂: wing chord 235–255 (adult, 247, n=32) and 226–245 (juvenile, 236, n=12), culmen 56–64 (59.2, n=46), tail 76–87 (adult, 81.2, n=34) and 67–75 (juvenile, 70.8, n=10), tarsus 44–50 (47.0, n=45); ♀: wing chord 216–239 (adult, 228, n=14) and 208–221 (juvenile, 217, n=14), culmen 48–55 (52.1, n=28), tail 73–81 (adult, 76.4, n=14) and 57–70 (juvenile, 64.0, n=12), tarsus 40–45 (42.7, n=28)[267]. ♂ (n=12): wing chord 238–257 (adult, 248.5), culmen 57–60 (59), tail 78–86 (adult, 82), tarsus 45–48 (46.3); ♀ (n=12): wing chord 213–239 (adult, 224), culmen 50–58 (55), tail 69–78 (adult, 73.8), tarsus 42–49 (44)[945]. ♂ (n=79): wing chord 228–252 (adult) and 219–243 (juvenile), culmen 56–64, bill depth at tip of forehead feathers 13.6–15.9, tail 76–88, tarsus 44–50; ♀ (n=63): wing chord 207–227 (adult) and 198–218 (juvenile), culmen 59–57, bill depth at tip of forehead feathers 11.6–14.3, tail 68–81, tarsus 40–46[1014]. ♂: mass in breeding season (Iceland) 1,134 (n=18)[90], mass in winter (Netherlands and Denmark) 947–1,350 (1,197, n=11)[267], mass in winter (Texas) 1,157 (adult, n=16) and 1,039 (juvenile, n=8)[56]; ♀: mass in breeding season (Iceland) 998 (n=30)[90], mass in winter (Netherlands and Denmark) 900–1,100 (984, n=5)[267], mass in winter (Texas) 924 (adult, n=20) and 804 (juvenile, n=5)[56].

VOICE ♂ (mainly on breeding grounds) produces a harsh and rough *kok*, *krak* and a rapid whistled *pit-tik-kieew* in courtship. ♀ utters a repeated raspy *rrrek*, often when taking off or near the nest.

MOULT Complex alternate strategy. Pre-formative moult variable in extent and protracted (Aug–Apr) possibly slowed or suspended in midwinter, as is the case with many Anatidae that do not nest at the age of one year. It includes a variable number body feathers (sometimes few, sometimes most), 1–4 tertials[1014], possibly some inner upperwing-coverts and two to all rectrices. First alternate moult reduced (or possibly even absent), in Jun–Aug, and continues with second pre-basic moult, in Jul–Oct in second-year birds[1014]. The former includes some head and mantle feathers, at least in some birds, perhaps only ♂♂[1014]. Definitive pre-alternate moult occurs in May–Jul, including some head and body feathers, but few or no feathers on the rump, back, belly, tertials, tertial coverts and secondary upperwing-coverts. Moult has been reported from late Feb or Mar in ♀, including the head, neck, belly and more scattered feathers on the upperparts and flanks[1267]. This could suggest a similarity with the Anatini, where pre-alternate moult occurs before breeding (♀) or after breeding (♂) depending on sex. Such timing is not confirmed by all authors though[56,1014]. Definitive pre-basic moult is complete between mid-Jul and Dec, beginning with the remiges and rectrices (flightless period 30–33 days[266]), on average a month later in ♀ that raised young[56]. Replacement of the belly feathers occurs during the flightless period, while the greater coverts are shed along with the flight feathers, and the lesser and median coverts are replaced on average ten days after the remiges[266].

HYBRIDISATION Exceptional in the wild, reported with Goosander[151], probably Hooded Merganser[365], and possibly Mallard *Anas platyrhynchos*[407,465], Common Eider *Somateria mollissima*[1259] and Common Goldeneye *Bucephala clangula*[947]. In captivity, some rare or unique cases reported with Wood Duck *Aix sponsa* [439] and Goosander [642]

HABITAT and LIFE-CYCLE Migratory, but more sedentary on coasts. Migrants arrive on their breeding grounds by mid-Mar in south and on coast, but not until May in north and inland, with eggs mainly laid in Jun[1267,1270]. Breeds in lone pairs or loose colonies. Inhabits wide variety of habitats for breeding, usually preferring fjords, sheltered bays, inlets, sandy estuaries, coasts with many islands, islets, sandbars, and vegetated rocky reefs. Also found on banks of lakes (rather deep and oligotrophic), rivers in tundra and taiga, and locally further south in temperate zone. ♂♂ abandon ♀♀ shortly after laying and moult in small groups, usually on coasts. ♀♀ generally moult at nest sites, often with their offspring. Shortly after regaining flight, autumn migration starts, with arrivals on wintering grounds in Sep–Nov. In winter, usually in small flocks, sometimes up to 100 where conditions suitable. Frequents essentially coastal habitats (rocky coasts, estuaries, bays, brackish lagoons), preferring areas sheltered from wave action, but often with strong currents (channels and inlets). Rare inland, except at a few large, often deep lakes, where it shows up especially during migration.

RANGE and POPULATION Outside of mapped breeding range, nests locally further south, e.g. in Europe (isolated pairs to Switzerland and France). Some vagrants beyond southern wintering grounds too, even in W Mediterranean, Gulf of Oman or S Pakistan. Global population estimated at 510,000–610,000 birds[642], including 170,000 in NW & C Europe, 50,000 in Black and Mediterranean Seas, <10,000 in C Asia[1154], 25,000–100,000 in E Asia, 237,000 in North America[461] and 10,000–25,000 in Greenland[1348]. Trends stable or unknown[1348]. Potentially threatened by deliberate persecution by fishermen and fish farmers[1270], various types of fishing gear, destruction of breeding habitats and oil spills[145].

CAPTIVITY Uncommon and rarely bred in captivity, due to special requirements (size and depth of ponds, water quality, food, etc.). Generally expensive (much more so than Hooded Merganser, for example) and usually only maintained in specialised collections. Unlikely to escape from captivity.

REFERENCES Baker (1992)[56]; Bengtson (1972)[90]; BirdLife International (2014)[145]; Blaser (1978)[151]; Bowles (1980)[168]; Brazil (2009)[182]; Carney (1992)[224]; Craik *et al.* (2009)[266]; Cramp & Simmons (1977)[268]; Delany & Scott (2006)[305]; Erickson (1952)[365]; Fritsch (1905)[407]; Gillham & Gillham (1996)[439]; Goudie *et al.* (1994)[461]; Gray (1958)[465]; Grössler (1972)[491]; Hughes & Bocharnikov (1992)[603]; Johnsgard (1961)[640]; Johnsgard (1965)[642]; Livezey (1989)[766]; Livezey (1995)[771]; Palmer (1976)[945]; Panov (1989)[947]; Pyle (2008)[1014]; Scott & Rose (1996)[1154]; Solovyeva & Pearce (2011)[1219]; Tenovuo & Tenovuo (1983)[1259]; Titman (1999)[1267]; Titman *in* Kear (2005)[1270]; Vaurie (1965)[1316]; Wetlands International (2014)[1348].

604. Adult ♂ (definitive basic). Netherlands, Feb (Rick Van der Weijde).

605. Adult ♂ (definitive basic); starting pre-alternate moult with the head feathers; at same period, young ♂ (formative) is much more like ♀. Iceland, May (Yann Kolbeinsson).

606. First-winter male (formative); note pale iris and bill, and pointed tertials, while the blackish lores and whitish centres to outermost tertials indicate a male. California, USA, Nov (Sébastien Reeber).

607. Adult ♀ (definitive alternate); much more streaked than in basic plumage. Iceland, Jul (Vincent Legrand).

608. Juvenile/first-winter (first basic/formative); note pale yellowish-brown iris, grey-brown tertials, and greater coverts with reduced dusky tips, not forming a black bar between greater coverts and secondaries like adult. California, USA, Dec (Alan D. Wilson).

609. First-winter ♂ (formative); scattered formative feathers (fore flanks) indicate a ♂, while the pointed, worn and frayed tertials and greater coverts without dusky tips all indicate age. Japan, Mar (Stuart Price).

MASKED DUCK
Nomonyx dominica

Plate 72

TAXONOMY *Anas dominica* Linnaeus, 1766, *Syst. Nat.*, edn. 12, 1, p. 201. This species is placed in the tribe Oxyurini, which is centred on S Hemisphere, mainly comprising the six species of *Oxyura*, alongside the monotypic genera *Biziura*, *Heteronetta* and *Nomonyx*[770]. This tribe is sometimes even considered a sub-family distinct from the Anatinae, the Oxyurinae[649]. Black-headed Duck *Heteronetta atricapilla* diverged first, followed by Masked Duck, making it the closest neighbour to a monophyletic group comprising the genus *Oxyura*[820]. The species has also been included within *Oxyura*[223,649,1193,1237] but is now placed in its own monotypic genus[142,236,364,437]. The position of this tribe within the Anseriformes is also debated, some authors considering that it diverged early, after the geese[454,600], and others, including the AERC-TAC and AOU, placing stifftails at the end of the sequence[142,236,437].

IDENTIFICATION By its behaviour, size, shape and coloration, can be mistaken only for Ruddy Duck *Oxyura jamaicensis* in the Holarctic. Masked Duck is much smaller, more compact, with a proportionately large head and neck hardly visible. The bill is slightly shorter, broader and thicker, and the crown is flat. Basic and formative plumages of both sexes and alternate plumage of ♀ show cheeks strongly striped yellowish or whitish and blackish, recalling Ruddy Duck, but latter never has a clear supercilium like Masked Duck. In same plumages, the upperparts and flanks of Masked Duck are visibly spotted or streaked pale and, in adult, a white patch on the upperwing. Finally, Masked Duck inhabits wetlands heavily choked with submerged and floating aquatic vegetation, only rarely venturing into open water. Dives without leaping first, like other stifftails[351], and in taking off does not run for a long distance on water[600].

PLUMAGES Clear sexual dimorphism in alternate plumage, which appears gradually during first year of life. Complex or simple alternate moult strategy (two plumages per definitive cycle and two or three in first cycle, see Moult). Ageing requires good views. Moult cycle may be linked to that of breeding, but depending on locality and rainfall (intensity and timing), which provide temporarily suitable habitats, the species may breed throughout year and at different seasons between years. It is also possible that the moult schedule is more rigid and that it is the feathers' pigmentation (resulting from hormonal activity) which varies with the conditions. This would imply that either of the basic and alternate plumages may be the most colourful and used to breed in adult ♂. The subject is still insufficiently studied, as is the case for other tropical Anseriformes.

'Colourful' plumage has been reported every month of the year within the species' range[600], but in North America it is mentioned mainly in Jun–Oct[1195] (like the Caribbean [322]), or Feb–Sep[351] and, in Texas, from early summer to late autumn[945]. In Florida and Texas, there are undoubtedly records of this plumage until Dec. Hereafter, it is assumed, however, that this plumage in ♂ follows pre-alternate partial moult in spring, and that the complete pre-basic moult leads to more cryptic plumage. This arbitrary choice matches what is known for Ruddy Duck and was followed by Eitniear[351] for North America.

Adult ♂

Definitive basic plumage (year-round?). Plumage similar to adult ♀, but slightly brighter and rather more spotted or mottled than streaked. White patch on wing larger. Head pale reddish, becoming yellowish-beige on face and white on chin and throat, with three broad, clear-cut black horizontal stripes: the first on the crown, the second formed by the eyestripe and the third by a line from the gape to the rear cheeks. Two faint pale lines separate them, the supercilium being generally thinner but still contrasting. The overall contrast offered by these bands is less strong in adult ♂ than other plumages, due to the slightly wider dark bars and the more reddish background. The pale fringes and dark bases to the chin and upper throat create a finely streaked appearance[351]. Iris warm brown with contrasting yellow orbital ring less visible than alternate plumage. Bill dull blue-grey with dark tip and pinkish hue at base of tomium. Rest of body reddish-beige with inner blackish marks to individual feathers. Scapulars closer to those of ♀ than alternate plumage, with reddish-beige fringes more or less continuous and, frequently, hints of small pale indentations. Adult ♂ nevertheless frequently shows one or more alternate-type scapulars (among the longest) with a continuous reddish fringe (see Pyle[1014]). Breast has reddish tones often pronounced (visibly more than ♀

in direct comparison). Feathers of flanks have reddish-buff fringes and sharp black centres, creating a more clearly mottled appearance than other plumages. Back blackish-brown. Lower rump heavily streaked whitish and dark brown. Rectrices elongated, pointed and dark. Upperwing mostly blackish with a large white patch, unique among Holarctic Anseriformes, on the outer secondary coverts and secondaries. This patch covers at least the outer half of the greater coverts and the base of the outer secondaries. Of these, white covers the base and almost the entire outer web of s1[1014], but diminishes inwards, to small spots on the central secondaries. Inner greater and median coverts fringed reddish towards tip. Underwing blackish, but median coverts paler grey and axillaries white. Legs and feet grey.

Definitive alternate plumage (year-round?). Plumage mainly reddish and black. Large black area covering forehead, crown, cheeks and chin. Iris warm reddish-brown with a broad and contrasting white eye-ring. Bill bright pale blue like other stifftails in same plumage, with contrasting black tip, varying amount of black on lower culmen, and base variably marked greenish-yellow. Rest of head, neck, breast, mantle, scapulars and flanks reddish, appearing more or less orangey depending on light. Small round black spots visible on breast-sides, while upperparts and flanks feathers have large black inner marks. Belly and undertail striped white or mottled pale brown-reddish. Tertials blackish with reddish fringes. Back and uppertail-coverts blackish, rump feathers with reddish fringes. Rectrices darker and less pointed than in definitive basic plumage[351]. Legs and feet olive-brown to yellowish.

Adult ♀

Definitive basic plumage (year-round?). Overall coloration close to ♂ in basic plumage, but duller, washed more yellowish (less reddish) with darker upperparts. Head with more contrasting dark bars due to pale stripes being whitish or yellowish, that on cheeks broader than in ♂. Chin and lower cheeks whitish or creamy-white. Iris dark brown. Bill slate-grey, darker towards culmen and tip, pinkish on tomium. Base of bill variably washed green-yellow (depending on plumage or age?). Breast pale buff to greyish with dark speckles. Scapulars broadly blackish with small indentations on fringes and two pale spots at tips, separated by black shaft (vs. continuous pale bar at tip in young). Flank feathers dull blackish with irregular yellowish fringes. Belly whitish to pale buff. Undertail-coverts variably streaked dark

(bases of feathers). Upperwing close to ♂ but white patch reduced on inner wing and secondaries. Reddish fringes to median and inner greater coverts of adult ♂ replaced by whitish. On s1, no white on inner web and outer web is about half white (black tip >20 mm[1014]). Underwing like ♂. Legs grey-brown.

Definitive alternate plumage (year-round?). Differences between definitive plumages of ♀ poorly known. Alternate plumage seems slightly more colourful and uniform, less dark on upperparts. Fringes to scapulars, flanks and breast are broader, more continuous and tinged cinnamon or reddish. Head has dark areas (crown and eyestripe) more pronounced, almost black, the pale supercilium being sometimes barely visible in front of the eye.

Juvenile

First basic plumage (year-round?). Similar to basic ♀ but paler and less contrasting, the blackish parts of the adult being dull brown. Lateral indentations sometimes touching on shafts and continuous pale terminal bars on tips of scapulars produce an appearance more streaked than spotted. In adult ♀ lateral indentations are reduced or small, round, and terminal bar is divided by black central shaft. The flanks appear dull brown with dull buff bars, and no clear contrast with scapulars. In adult ♀ in basic plumage, the contrast between the upperparts and flanks is generally stronger. In hand or good views, note the juvenile rectrices, frayed at tips with bare rachis and lesser coverts narrow, rounded and worn at tips (new and square in adult), with a dull brown colour (blackish with slight sheen in adult). Median and inner greater coverts fringed pale buff. Outer primaries pointed at tips and lack slight sheen shown by adult. White upperwing patches smaller in young ♀ than young ♂, the adult ♀ having an intermediate pattern. On s1, young ♂ shows some white at base of inner web, and over more than half of outer web (black tip <20 mm[1014]). White pattern of s1 identical in young and adult ♀♀[1014].

Immature ♂

Formative plumage/first alternate plumage (year-round?). Insufficiently known. Pre-formative moult results in gradual replacement of juvenile feathers by formative feathers of definitive basic type[351]. Differs from adult by presence of mix of adult and juvenile feathers. Some juvenile feathers retained on wings (note extent of white patch and white on s1, the shape of lesser coverts and outer primaries), on back (feathers worn and brown) and belly (which seems vaguely barred or mottled dark) until second pre-basic moult. The longest scapulars also appear to be retained[1014].

Immature ♀

Formative plumage/first alternate plumage (year-round?). As formative ♂, distinguished from adult plumages by presence of retained juvenile feathers (wings, longest scapulars) visible in the hand or in very good views. Once age known, sexed by coloration of formative feathers (redder in young ♂) and upperwing pattern (extent of white on s1 as juvenile).

GEOGRAPHIC VARIATION None described.

MEASUREMENTS and MASS ♂ and adult marginally larger than ♀ and young, respectively. ♂ (*n*=12): wing chord 142–148 (145), tail 81–85 (82), culmen 31.0–33.9 (32.8), tarsus 26–29 (27.6); ♀ (*n*=12): wing chord 136–148 (143), tail 74–86 (80), culmen 32–35 (33.8), tarsus 27–28 (27.4)[945]. ♂ (*n*=5): wing chord 136–138 (137), tail 75–79 (77), culmen 31.1–33.9 (32.0), tarsus 26.1–27.6 (27.0), mass 359–449 (385, *n*=19); ♀ (*n*=5): wing chord 132–139 (136), tail 74–79 (77, n=4), culmen 30.8–34.2 (32.0), tarsus 25.7–27.9 (26.9), mass 275–445 (346, *n*=17)[649]. ♂ (*n*=30): wing chord 135–147 (adult) and 131–143 (juvenile), culmen 32–36, bill depth at tip of forehead feathers 15.8–16.8, tail 75–88, tarsus 26–29; ♀ (*n*=30): wing chord 132–144 (adult) and 128–139 (juvenile), culmen 31–35, bill depth at tip of forehead feathers 15.3–16.2, tail 73–86, tarsus 24–28[1014]. Venezuela. ♂: mass 372 (*n*=29); ♀: 358 (*n*=34)[453].

VOICE In courtship, ♂ gives characteristic cooing sounds, *wooo-kooroo-kooroo*, the first syllable longer and rising, followed by 2–4 syllables, transcribed *kooroo*, dropping and reduced, to point that only two first syllables are usually audible. Also a *woo-oo* that expires and falls, perhaps not vocal, when neck is inflated. ♀ produces an acute whistle, also short *gritt* or *brek* calls.

MOULT Requires further research (see Plumages). For North America, moult timing is uncertain and perhaps variable. Note that it is assumed that a double annual wing moult occurs in this species and Ruddy Duck[945], and that pre-formative moult is complete[572]. It is also possible that second pre-basic moult is 3–5 months ahead, and first pre-alternate moult is absent.

HYBRIDISATION Apparently not reported, either in the wild or captivity.

HABITAT and LIFE-CYCLE Little known and studied compared to other stifftails[649]. Frequently goes unnoticed due its discreet, secretive habits, low density and densely vegetated habitats. Reportedly sedentary over most of its range, but capable of moving long distances even outside its normal range. Such movements are irregular, erratic and primarily related to temporary appearance of suitable environments, linked to rainfall. Occurrence in North America also seems related to cyclonic events, which create a string of flooded areas along coast of Gulf of Mexico, favouring arrival of birds from the south[648]. Nesting is facilitated by favourable conditions, and appears to occur throughout year[351,600]. In North America, observations of nests and chicks suggest that breeding occurs mainly in Apr–Oct[306,351,924]. Inhabits freshwater wetlands, temporary or permanent, shallow, overgrown with helophytic or floating vegetation, the surface of the water often being invisible. In alarm, Masked Duck hides in the vegetation, with the body largely submerged, and dives to escape, rather than fly. Usually found alone, in pairs or small flocks, sometimes up to several tens of birds.

RANGE and POPULATION Mainly South America. Reaches northernmost limit in USA, primarily in Texas, the only state where breeding has been recorded[351]. Observed infrequently in Florida, rarely in Louisiana and exceptionally further north to Wisconsin and Massachusetts[351]. Total population estimated at just 10,000 birds[215] but also 25,000–100,000 individuals at end of the last decade[600,1348]. In USA, where its abundance seems cyclical, four major invasions have occurred since the 1880s[351]. A census that recorded 47 birds between Sep 1992 and Mar 1993, led to an estimate of 3,817 individuals for Texas[29], which seems too high[648]. Nevertheless, the species' very secretive behaviour, ability to use small waterbodies and fact that many potential sites in Texas are privately owned[351] probably result in many birds going unnoticed.

CAPTIVITY Very rarely encountered in captivity, even in specialised collections.

REFERENCES Anderson (1999)[28]; Anderson *et al.* (1998)[29]; BirdLife International (2012)[142]; Callaghan & Green (1993)[215]; Carboneras (1992)[223]; Clements *et al.* (2013)[236]; Delnicki (1975)[306]; Downer & Sutton (1990)[322]; Eitniear (2013)[351]; Eo *et al.* (2009)[364]; Gill & Donsker (2014)[437]; Gomez-Dallmeier & Cringan (1990)[453]; González *et al.* (2009)[454]; Hohman (1996)[572]; Hughes *in* Kear (2005)[600]; Johnsgard (2010)[648]; Johnsgard &

Carbonell (1996)[649]; Johnsgard & Hagemeyer (1969)[650]; Livezey (1995)[770]; Lockwood (1997)[781]; McCracken & Sorenson (2005)[818]; McCracken *et al.* (1999)[820]; Oberholser (1974)[924]; Palmer (1976)[945]; Pyle (2008)[1014]; Raikow (1970)[1030]; Sibley (2000)[1195]; Sibley & Monroe (1993)[1193]; Sraml *et al.* (1996)[1228]; Stotz *et al.* (1996)[1237]; Todd (1996)[1274]; Wetlands International (2014)[1348].

610. Adult ♂ (definitive alternate). Florida, USA, Feb. (Ron Bielefeld).

611. Adult ♂ (definitive alternate); in courtship, the neck is inflated. Texas, USA, Dec (Greg Lavaty).

612. Adult ♂ (moulting); head is basic-like, but rest of body seems mostly alternate (see text); bill and orbital ring typical of non-breeding birds. Texas, USA, Mar (Mike Danzenbaker).

613. Adult ♂? (definitive alternate?); plumage and bare parts suggest an adult ♂, but wing patch seems quite reduced and could match a young male. Texas, USA, Dec (Greg Lavaty).

614. Juvenile (first basic/formative); body appears typically streaked rather than spotted, with a brown ground colour, while the longest scapular has a broad whitish bar at its tip, typical of this age. Texas, USA, May (Greg Lavaty).

615. Immature ♀ (formative/first alternate); the body feathers, especially scapulars, are black and glossy, which can be acquired during pre-formative or first-pre-alternate moult; the longest scapulars are yet to be replaced, and are clearly browner with a whitish bar at tip (juvenile). Texas, USA, Mar (Mike Danzenbaker).

RUDDY DUCK
Oxyura jamaicensis

Plate 71, 72

TAXONOMY *Anas jamaicensis* J. F. Gmelin, 1789, *Syst. Nat.*, 1, p. 519. Ruddy Duck is a member of the tribe Oxyurini (see Taxonomy of Masked Duck *Nomonyx dominicus*), in which *Oxyura* is the only polytypic genus. Within this genus, Ruddy Duck was considered close to a monophyletic group comprising all other species[770] or as part of a clade comprising the New World taxa, similar to that grouping the three species from Eurasia, Africa and Australia[820]. Debate is ongoing concerning the status of the two South American taxa, Peruvian Ruddy Duck *O. (j.) ferruginea* Eyton, 1838, and Colombian Ruddy Duck *O. (j.) andina* Lehmann, 1946. These two are sometimes treated as a separate species together (*O. ferruginea*)[201,437,628,1070], but many authors and the AOU South American Checklist Committee (SACC) consider them as subspecies of Ruddy Duck[5,317,384,602,818,1063]. It was suggested that *ferruginea* is closer to Lake Duck *O. vittata*, of the Southern Cone[770,1205], but this has since been invalidated[818].

IDENTIFICATION Size, shape, coloration and behaviour makes its distinction from other species of Anseriformes easy, with the exception of the two other Holarctic stifftails, Masked Duck in North America and White-headed Duck *O. leucocephala* in Eurasia (which see). In W Europe, separation of this and the latter species may be complicated by relatively frequent hybrids (see White-headed Duck).

PLUMAGES Nominate subspecies. Strong sexual dimorphism in adult. Complex alternate or simple alternate moult strategy (two plumages per definitive cycle and two or three plumages in first cycle, see Moult). Sexual dimorphism appears gradually during first year of life. Note that 'colourful' plumage, worn for mating and breeding, results from a partial pre-alternate moult from late winter and is termed alternate plumage hereafter. This differs from the norm in ♂♂ Anatinae, which mostly mate on the wintering grounds or during spring migration, presumably as a response to boreal conditions. A paired ♀, protected by a ♂, may be able to more easily store the reserves needed for migration and breeding in habitats with low productivity[590], or is winter courtship simply to save time during short boreal summers? Originating mostly in tropical regions, stifftails usually mate on the breeding grounds, shortly before egg laying. A colourful plumage

is therefore of no use in 'winter'. A small diving duck with a proportionately strong head and long pointed tail often held upright at rest, showing the white undertail. Very short wings compared to its mass, which forces it to run for a long time on the water (and upwind) to take off. In flight, very fast wingbeats, on a straight trajectory and at high speed, much like an auk.

Adult ♂

Definitive basic plumage (Sep–Nov/Mar–Apr). Mainly grey-brown variably stained red, with black crown and white cheeks. Top of head, including eye, black merging into grey (whitish finely vermiculated black) of nape, and brown-beige foreneck and neck-sides. Cheeks white to base of bill and chin. Iris warm brown (appearing black at distance). Bill blackish-grey. Mantle, scapulars and rest of upperparts to uppertail-coverts dark grey-brown with thin whitish flecks or vermiculations, frequently flecked with reddish spots. Rectrices long, thin and pointed, dark grey-brown to blackish. Centre of breast and belly whitish (silvery), ill-defined, variably spotted or barred brown-grey (feather bases). Undertail-coverts whitish separated from belly by brown-grey stains. Feathers of breast-sides and flanks grey-brown at base and pale grey to beige at tips. Reddish patches often visible in places. Tertials dark grey-brown, shorter, straighter and wider-tipped than alternate tertials[201], speckled pale on fringes. Tertial coverts broad and round-tipped. Upperwing entirely dark grey-brown with thin pale grey flecks barely noticeable on secondary coverts, which are broad and round-tipped (in hand). Tips of secondaries slightly paler. Underwing has axillaries, median coverts and tips to greater coverts whitish, centres of greater coverts pale grey, leading edge and remiges darker grey. Underside of primaries can show silvery sheen, especially when flying over water. Legs and feet pale blue-grey with dark webs.

Definitive alternate plumage (Mar–Apr/Aug–Sep). Similar to basic plumage, but dark grey-brown body essentially replaced by reddish. Top of head and nape black (tapering on hindneck) with cheeks white to chin and base of bill. Rare variants have all-black head or variable black spots below eye, both in North America and Europe. Bill bright clear blue with an inconspicuous black nail in profile. Sides of tip of bill, either side of nail, often tinged pale pink. Feathers of upper neck and centre of breast have blackish bases, appearing initially streaked, then dark with wear. Lower neck, mantle, scapulars, breast-sides and flanks reddish-brown to bright reddish, possibly appearing cinnamon in places. Back and rump darker, streaked blackish. Belly silvery grey-beige variably stained or vaguely streaked grey-brown (feather bases). Tail dark brown. Tertials elongated, slightly curved and round-tipped. Upper- and underwing as basic plumage, but secondary upperwing-coverts usually strongly tinged red. Legs and feet grey with dark webs.

Adult ♀

Definitive basic plumage (Sep–Nov/Mar–Apr). Cold grey-brown appearance, with a pale brown face crossed by dark bar the only remarkable feature. Top of head (down to eyes) dark brown (feather tips paler than bases) extending as a vertical line on nape. Cheeks pale grey-brown (whitish speckled grey) with an ill-defined dark bar from the gape through the upper cheeks. ♀♀ without this dark bar reported[201] (senescence?). Base of bill and chin whitish. Iris brown. Bill lead-grey. Upperparts dark grey-brown with irregular pale flecks and vermiculations. Breast and flanks pale grey-brown to beige with more or less regular dark streaks. Central breast paler. Belly very pale grey-brown to whitish (silvery sheen) with darker spots and stripes (feather bases). Lower belly strongly sullied grey-brown. Undertail-coverts whitish. Tail dark grey-brown to blackish. Upperwing dark brown, tinged reddish in places, with thin pale flecks on tips of secondary coverts (and often on outer webs of secondaries, inner at least). Underwing like ♂. Legs and feet blue-grey with darker webs.

Definitive alternate plumage (Mar–Apr/Aug–Sep). Appearance similar to basic plumage, but browner, warmer and darker overall. Head less contrasting, with buff to pale reddish-brown cheeks and a larger dark bar than in basic plumage, but often less contrasting due to darker background. The base of the bill and chin are slightly paler than the cheeks. Mantle, scapulars, back, rump and flanks hazelnut-brown irregularly marked with dark stripes (appears more striped than pale-speckled). Breast more uniform tan with bases of feathers creating faint blackish bars, and appears overall darker brown, but little contrast between upperparts and flanks. Ochre, cinnamon or red flecks, or even patches, often visible on lower neck, and scapulars and flanks. Upperwing dark brown with few to many reddish spots on coverts. Legs slate-grey, sometimes with olive-brown tones.

Juvenile

First basic plumage (until Oct–Dec). Similar to definitive basic plumage ♀. Rather easy to distinguish from adult ♀ in alternate plumage, alongside which young are seen when fledging. Juvenile duller, paler and much greyer, often with a warmer light brown or pale reddish breast. Up close, feathers of the upperparts and rear flanks show irregular and coarser dark brown patches, but few or no pale flecks typical of basic adult ♀. The rear flanks, however, are often distinctly barred. Cheeks whitish with dark grey-brown flecks and slightly marked bar from gape. Tertials (often difficult to see) short, straight and quickly worn at tips. In the hand, tertial coverts, greater and median coverts narrower and slightly more pointed with a trapezoidal shape (well-rounded in adult). White axillaries rather narrow and pointed (rounded in ad[56]). Belly feathers white with pale grey bases, appearing less streaked or mottled than adult. In many cases, age determined from rectrices, which when erect, are visible at a reasonable distance. Juvenile rectrices narrower and whitish at tips, which are narrow and frayed, often with a bare rachis. Care should be taken, however, as unlike most other ducks, the rectrices are moulted in stages over a longer period in adults. In consequence, many birds can show different generations of rectrices in Jul–Apr. Birds with entirely juvenile-type rectrices until Apr are of this age.

Immature ♂

Formative plumage/first alternate plumage (Nov–Feb/Apr–Jun). Until Nov–Dec at least, greatly resembles ♀ in basic plumage and easily distinguished from adult ♂ (basic) by all-white cheeks of latter. Acquisition of formative plumage is slow and does not permit sexing until early winter. This plumage is characterised by whitish cheeks (the dark line gradually disappears in Dec–Jan), which instead show variably marked grey or blackish spots. Crown shows mix of brown and black feathers, whereas the neck-sides show traces of grey feathers. Upperparts and flanks brown tinged reddish with grey flecks to tips, often giving the body (upperparts especially) a barred appearance. Juvenile feathers of belly, wings, tertials and rectrices entirely or mostly retained. Note this plumage can be attained only in Mar and moulted again one month later.

Immature ♀

Formative plumage/first alternate plumage (Nov–Feb/Apr–Jun). Appearance intermediate between juvenile and adult ♀ in basic plumage, often with pale flecks on moulted upperparts feathers. Chin and throat white (pale grey in young ♂). Usually, it will be possible to determine age only based on rectrices, and in the hand, based on the unmoulted body parts (wings, tertials, tertial coverts and belly as juvenile).

GEOGRAPHIC VARIATION Besides the nominate subspecies, two others are recognised and sometimes even split (see Taxonomy), both in South America. Peruvian Ruddy Duck *O. j. ferruginea* (adult ♂ in alternate plumage) differs from nominate subspecies by some measurements and mass slightly greater, the almost completely black head (only white spots on and around chin in some birds) and a body slightly brighter red. ♀ in the same plumage differs from the nominate subspecies by plumage visibly more tinged reddish, including the cheeks, reducing the contrast with the dark line from the gape. Colombian Ruddy Duck *O. j. andina* is often considered to represent an intergrade (stable hybrid or ongoing hybrid) population between *ferruginea* and *jamaicensis*. Adult ♂ in alternate plumage has an intermediate and very variable head pattern[5,384], with white cheeks and a few dark patches below the eyes, or black cheeks with some white spots. Many have irregular lines of black spots from the eye and fading on the cheeks. ♀ described as having slightly darker cheeks than the nominate subspecies. North American populations sometimes regarded as subspecifically distinct (*O. j. rubida* Wilson, 1814[647,945]), nominate then being restricted to the Caribbean. Adult ♂♂ said to differ from North American birds by slightly shorter wing and, in alternate plumage, dark collar below white cheeks[201]. These differences are often considered insufficient to warrant subspecific rank[201,602,1014], the longer wing of North American birds probably the result of migrating to and from northerly latitudes.

MEASUREMENTS and MASS Nominate subspecies. ♂ and adult noticeably larger than ♀ and young, respectively. North America. Adult ♂: wing chord 147–161 (154.0, *n*=87), tail 65–82 (72.7, *n*=152), bill from gape 37.3–44.4 (40.8, *n*=157), tarsus 32.6–35.3 (33.9, *n*=87); adult ♀: wing chord 133–155 (148.2, *n*=78), tail 52–77 (69.5, *n*=150), bill from gape 36.4–44.5 (40.1, *n*=186), tarsus 30.8–34.6 (32.7, *n*=78)[201]. ♂ (*n*=100): wing chord 138–152 (adult) and 133–147 (juvenile), culmen 38–43, bill depth at tip of forehead feathers 18.0–21.2, tail 68–78, tarsus 32–37; ♀ (*n*=100): wing chord 133–147 (adult) and 129–140 (juvenile), culmen 36–42, bill depth at tip of forehead feathers 17.4–20.5, tail 64–74, tarsus 30–35. ♂: mass in winter 563 (±18,

n=19)[372], mass in spring 629 (±3, *n*=157)[201]; ♀: mass in winter 542 (±14, n=18)[372], mass during incubation 532 (± 4, *n*=93)[201].

VOICE Nominate subspecies. Usually silent except during courtship, during which ♂ produces a non-vocal sound by quickly patting the bill against the swollen breast, sending air bubbles through the water, transcribed *fif fif fif fififi wak-rrrr*. Although the sound is not very loud, it can be heard from surprisingly far. At same time, ♂♂ pretend to charge other birds by running on water, which produces a slamming sound of the legs. The bubbling sound is slightly different in the two South American taxa, and can be transcribed *fif fif fif fififi roo-ii-oorrr*, the last syllable lower and more nasal. A comparative study of sonograms might be useful to clarify any possible differences. ♀ utters various quacks or whistled calls, especially when pursued by several ♂♂.

MOULT The moult of this species (and probably other stifftails) is only poorly understood. The 'beautiful' plumage of the ♂ results from a partial pre-alternate moult in Feb–May. This is usually the case for breeding plumage of ♀ *Anas* and *Aythya*, for example, but ♂♂ of these species acquire this plumage mostly in autumn. This feature may be shared by Masked Duck (which see) and partly by Long-tailed Duck *Clangula hyemalis*, whose pre-alternate moult is very protracted, and starts well before the birds arrive on the nesting grounds, ending after departure towards moulting sites. A second singularity is the possible double annual complete moult, including the remiges[56,945], which is known to be more common in captivity than in the wild[572] (including by age and sex groups[632]). This double moult was reported in 6–12% of individuals in a sample of captive birds[561], but is apparently very rare in the wild, slightly more frequent in ♀♀ than ♂♂[632]. Thereafter, Pyle[1014] raised the possibility that the apparent double moult may actually reflect a highly advanced second pre-basic moult (in Apr–Jul, instead of Jul–Nov in adult). Young birds thus moult their flight feathers in spring, which could have been interpreted as a second annual moult of the remiges. The final originality is that the rectrices are moulted in two waves, the second part being shed only when the first are almost grown again[632]. The rectrices are moulted twice per year, so that two generations are visible for much of the year.

Pre-formative and first pre-alternate moults might constitute a single moult, as evidence of feathers being replaced at least twice before first complete moult seems to be lacking[1014]. This (these) moult(s) occur in Oct–Mar, and involve part to most body feathers (often except the belly), and few or no inner secondary upperwing-coverts, tertials and rectrices. At least some second-calendar year birds replace their feathers in Mar–May[1012], but the question of whether this wing moult forms part of a complete pre-formative/first pre-alternate moult, or of an early second pre-basic moult is unknown[1014]. Definitive pre-alternate moult occurs in Feb–May, and includes many head and body feathers and usually the rectrices. Definitive pre-basic moult starts with the wings in Jul–Sep, and continues with the head, body and tail. Rectrices are replaced gradually (see above).

HYBRIDISATION Apparently no cases reported in the species' natural range. The status of subspecies *andina*, however, raises questions, as this taxon is sometimes regarded as the result of large-scale hybridisation, past or ongoing, between *jamaicensis* and *ferruginea*[384]. In Europe, where Ruddy Duck is introduced, hybridisation with White-headed Duck is considered to be a potentially serious threat to the Iberian population of the latter (see White-headed Duck). Finally, a case, possibly of captive origin, has been reported with Greater Scaup *Aythya marila*[1190].

HABITAT and LIFE-CYCLE Northern populations migratory, others sedentary or short-distance migrants. Spring migration occurs mainly mid-Mar to late May. Breeds on lakes, reservoirs and freshwater ponds, usually requiring open water for take-off, abundant emergent aquatic vegetation, and preferably a helophytic belt. Eggs laid May–Aug[201], over a protracted period, especially in south of range (and European feral populations), perhaps permitting some ♀♀ to raise two broods per year[945], or could also be linked to the hypothesis of an early second pre-basic moult in Apr–Jul, young ♀♀ then breeding after this moult. Most ♂♂ abandon ♀♀ during incubation or shortly after hatching, but some apparently take care of the brood. However, this behaviour could also reflect ♂♂ attracted to a ♀ and showing aggressive behaviour towards any intruder, without actually fathering the brood. ♀ (or both parents) often leave young before they can fly, at 3–4 weeks old, to start pre-basic moult. However, the ♀ can also moult with its offspring. ♂♂ moult either at nesting sites or after short migration to moulting sites. An early migrant among North American diving ducks[201], movements peaking between mid-Sep and mid-Oct. In winter, sometimes forms huge gatherings, mainly on coasts (brackish lagoons, estuaries) and large inland lakes. Often in company of *Aythya* spp.

RANGE and POPULATION Outside mapped range, rare to EC Alaska and breeds more irregularly from south of Great Lakes to along St. Lawrence River and in coastal regions of E USA. Irregular or very scattered breeder further south to Texas, Louisiana, Florida and NE Mexico. Uncommon in West Indies. In winter, main concentrations reported in San Francisco Bay and Salton Sea, California, in Texas, and in Chesapeake Bay, Maryland/Virginia[201]. Population estimated at 485,000 individuals[1247] or 500,000 birds[304], and currently stable. South American *andina* estimated at 10,000 individuals and *ferruginea* at 25,000–100,000 birds[1247], both probably in decline due to habitat loss[602]. The species was introduced in the UK in the 1950s, where it increased to almost 6,000 birds by the early 2000s[62] and spread to France, Spain and the Netherlands in mid-1990s. The species was then reported in most countries in W & C Europe, as well as Morocco and Iceland. It is considered a serious threat to Spanish populations of White-headed Duck, already on the verge of extinction primarily due to massive habitat loss. Ruddy Duck readily hybridises with this species, ♂♂ (and hybrid ♂♂) being socially dominant over White-headed Ducks. An international action plan has been implemented, aiming to eradicate the European population of Ruddy Duck[270,604,608,1211]. In the early 2010s, UK population had been reduced to <100 birds, the French population was stable at *c*.150 wintering individuals, the species had been eradicated from Spain (including dozens of hybrids) and measures are being taken in Belgium, Denmark, Portugal, Sweden and Switzerland. However, in 2014, its numbers were still increasing in the Netherlands.

CAPTIVITY Deemed fairly easy to keep and breed, provided it has clear water and sufficiently deep ponds. Usually sold at higher prices than pochards for example. Its possession in captivity and trade are prohibited or controlled in several European countries. The first birds recorded in W Europe raised discussion as to possible transatlantic origin, but the source of introduced birds is known[891], and there is apparently no evidence of natural arrival in Europe. Icelandic birds are thought to originate from the British Isles[602] and the species has been reported just once in the Azores[1090].

REFERENCES Adams & Slavid (1984)[5]; Baker (1993)[56]; Banks *et al.* (2008)[62]; Brua (2002)[201];

Cranswick & Hall (2010)[270]; Delany & Scott (2002)[304]; Dickinson & Remsen (2013)[317]; Euliss *et al.* (1997)[372]; Fjeldså (1986)[384]; Gill & Donsker (2014)[437]; Henderson (2010)[550]; Hobson *et al.* (2000)[561]; Hohman (1993)[571]; Hohman (1996)[572]; Hohman *et al.* (1992)[578]; Howell (2010)[590]; Hughes *in* Kear (2005)[602]; Hughes *et al.* (1999)[604]; Hughes *et al.* (2006)[608]; Jaramillo (2003)[628]; Jehl & Johnson (2004)[632]; Johnsgard (1979)[647]; Livezey (1995)[770]; McCracken & Sorenson (2005)[818]; McCracken *et al.* (1999)[820]; McCracken *et al.* (2000)[821]; Muñoz-Fuentes *et al.* (2006)[891]; Muñoz-Fuentes *et al.* (2012)[894]; Palmer (1976)[945]; Pyle (2005)[1012]; Pyle (2008)[1014]; Remsen *et al.* (2014)[1063]; Ridgely & Greenfield (2001)[1070]; Rodebrand (2011)[1090]; Sibley (1938)[1190]; Siegfried (1976)[1205]; Smith *et al.* (2005)[1211]; Wetlands International (2014)[1247].

616. *O. j. jamaicensis*, adult ♂ (definitive alternate). France, Apr (Sébastien Reeber).

617. *O. j. jamaicensis*, adult ♂ (definitive basic); in autumn, this is the only plumage with pure white cheeks. New Jersey, USA, Nov (Sébastien Reeber).

618. *O. j. jamaicensis*, adult ♀ (definitive basic); best aged by the uniformly adult rectrices, and note whitish speckles on upperparts. New Jersey, USA, Nov (Sébastien Reeber).

619. *O. j. jamaicensis*, first-winter ♂ (first basic/formative); in autumn/winter, reliably aged by juvenile rectrices (thin, with bare rachis tip forming whitish shaft), but note here that outer rectrices have been replaced. New Jersey, USA, Nov (Sébastien Reeber).

620. *O. j. jamaicensis*, first-winter ♂ (first basic/formative), sexed by presence of a few reddish upperparts feathers, and note whitish cheeks with the dark bar somewhat blurred. New Jersey, USA, Nov (Sébastien Reeber).

621. *O. j. jamaicensis*, first-winter (first basic/formative); vs. adult ♀, note plainer upperparts (less marked/no white speckles) and bill tinged olive or brownish, while browner crown and speckled grey cheeks suggest a ♀. New York, Nov (Sébastien Reeber).

WHITE-HEADED DUCK
Oxyura leucocephala

Plates 71, 72

TAXONOMY *Anas leucocephala* Scopoli, 1769, *Annus I Hist.-Nat.*, p. 65. See Taxonomy of Masked Duck *Nomonyx dominicus*. Within the genus *Oxyura*, White-headed Duck is sometimes regarded as the closest relative of Maccoa Duck *O. maccoa*[770] or as part of a clade also including this species and Blue-billed Duck *O. australis*[818]. Minor differences have been described between populations of W Mediterranean and elsewhere (see Geographic Variation), but no subspecies described.

IDENTIFICATION Given its curious shape (large head held hunched, rounded back, long stiff tail often held upright) and coloration, unlikely to be mistaken for any other naturally occurring species in its range. The resemblance is much stronger with Ruddy Duck *O. jamaicensis*, which was introduced in the UK and occurs as a feral species in many countries in W Europe, and therefore liable to cause identification problems. The situation has also resulted in natural hybridisation and thus birds even more difficult to identify. Distinction from Ruddy Duck normally not problematic in adult ♂♂. White-headed Duck has more white on cheeks, the black crown not reaching the eye, the latter forming a small black spot visible from afar. Similarly, the white cheeks cover part or all of the nape, while the black nape is broad in Ruddy Duck, obvious in profile. The bill of the latter has a slightly concave culmen in profile, while that of adult ♂ White-headed Duck has a clear bulge on the top of the culmen. Ruddy Duck has a reddish body (alternate plumage) or grey-brown (basic plumage), while that of White-headed Duck is mostly ochre-yellow whatever the season. Finally, the belly of White-headed Duck is usually close in colour to that of sides or slightly paler, while Ruddy Duck has a large pale silvery ventral patch (and paler underwing). Courtship is very different between the two species (bill patting on breast and producing bubbles in water in Ruddy Duck, and, among others, the head and tail held high and right in White-headed Duck, the tail sometimes inclined towards the back, beyond the vertical; see Voice of both species).

Adult ♀♀ of the two species are more similar, but can be distinguished using the following features.

- Ruddy Duck is smaller, irrespective of age and sex, the size difference being obvious in direct comparison. Overall shape is much stockier in White-headed Duck, due to its stronger head, often held hunched down, and thick bill, with the back appearing swollen. From the front, White-headed Duck is significantly wider-bodied and appears rather 'flat' on the water, the difference between the two species being usually striking.

- At rest, White-headed Duck is distinguished by its longer body and rounded back, peaking far back behind the neck. Between dives or when swimming, White-headed Duck frequently holds its bill just above the water, the breast often being inconspicuous. Ruddy Duck more frequently stretches its neck, and seems to float higher on water.

- Head shape also differs significantly: Ruddy Duck has a rather tall crown (sometimes pear-shaped and peaking well behind the eye) with a relatively steep forehead, whose shape 'extends' the culmen via its concave appearance. White-headed Duck has a flattened head and a barely discernible forehead, mainly because the bill is much thicker-based.

- The bill is similarly shaped as in ♂♂ of both species: culmen is regularly concave in Ruddy Duck vs. culmen markedly bulging over its proximal half in White-headed Duck. This bulge at the bill base is very obvious in profile and in front. It is somewhat less pronounced than in adult ♂ during nesting period. It is also less marked in both sexes during first winter and barely marked in juvenile.

- Tail shorter in Ruddy Duck, which it also holds open more often than White-headed Duck, including at rest. In profile, in the latter, one or a few rectrices are often detached from the others, an impression accentuated by the feathers' length. In direct comparison, differences are obvious. Also note, close up, the tail tips are pointed in White-headed Duck, more rounded in Ruddy Duck.

- Feathering at the base of the bill is diagnostic. The feathering forms a regular convex curve between the base of culmen and gape in Ruddy Duck. This limit is straight (slightly wavy) in White-headed Duck.

- The head of White-headed Duck is more contrasting. The wide bar from the gape can cover a large part of the cheeks, leaving a whitish chin, throat and thin line separating the upper head from the cheeks. In Ruddy Duck, the bar on the cheeks is less marked, the dark parts of the head are dark brown (blackish in White-headed Duck) and the pale parts are pale grey-brown (vs. white).

- The tone of the breast and body is distinctive, pale ochre-brown in White-headed Duck, but dark grey-brown (basic plumage) or warm brown (alternate plumage) in Ruddy Duck. Close up, the plumage of White-headed Duck appears more distinctly and regularly striped blackish. There is usually visible contrast between the upperparts and flanks in Ruddy Duck, which is virtually absent in White-headed Duck.

- The undertail area is usually white in Ruddy Duck (vaguely striped or spotted dark in juvenile) but streaked dark or even completely dark in White-headed Duck.

- The belly of Ruddy Duck is pale, forming a silvery whitish oval, variably streaked or mottled dusky. In White-headed Duck it varies between a colour similar to the flanks or slightly paler (obviously barred dark), and dark brown.

Problems caused by hybrids trickier, especially as hybrids seem quite variable (see Hybridisation). First-generation hybrids can show a mix of features typical of both species, as well as intermediate features. The bill shape is often intermediate, with a slight bump on the upper culmen, which seems slightly curved and elongated in profile. Mostly, a careful examination will reveal features not shown by pure birds. Identification of a hybrid ♀ is more difficult, but possible if based on close scrutiny of as many features as possible among those mentioned above. However, identification of a juvenile will be even more difficult, especially as the bill shape is not yet definitive and the plumage is duller in both species.

PLUMAGES Clear sexual dimorphism from first winter onwards. Complex alternate or simple alternate moult strategy (two plumages per definitive cycle and 2–3 in first cycle, see Moult). Distinction of adult ♀ from young requires good views. Note that 'beautiful' plumage, for breeding, results from a pre-alternate moult in late winter and is called alternate plumage hereafter (see Moult of Ruddy Duck). Apart from usual plumages, there is a 'dark morph' in Spain, described recently[1299] and whose appearance could reflect the fact that

these populations passed through a tight bottleneck (a few dozen individuals), and to the resulting genetic impoverishment[605,875,889,893].

Adult ♂

Definitive basic plumage (Aug–Dec/Apr). The definitive plumages are closer to each other than those of Ruddy Duck. Basic plumage thus resembles alternate plumage (see below), but slightly duller, with warm hues less obvious. Head white with a larger black cap, usually reaching the eye, top of culmen and centre of nape. Black parts frequently dotted with brown and white. Dark grey collar fades on hindneck and nape, with a dark slash (often broad) across the rear cheeks. Neck (and lower nape) dark grey (not black). Breast reddish-brown finely striped blackish. Uppertail-coverts and rear flanks dull reddish-brown barred dark. Bill pale grey to blackish, becoming blue in winter.

Definitive alternate plumage (Apr–May/Aug–Sep). Head mostly white with black patches of varying extent[1277] on crown and around eye. The black patches can cover the cap (extending to eye), part of forehead, all or part of the central nape and possibly scattered on the cheeks in some (especially third-calendar-year birds). These black patches can also be reduced to centre of crown (barely visible in field), especially in socially dominant[605] or older ♂♂. Iris brown. Bill thick-based with a strong bulge on proximal half of upper mandible, bright azure-blue with dusky nail. Cheeks and centre of nape white, contrasting strongly with black lower hindneck and collar. Sometimes, a thin oblique line extends from the hindneck to the central cheeks. Breast dark reddish to mahogany-brown. Mantle, scapulars and tertials sandy-coloured with cinnamon, ochre or reddish tones, and fine blackish vermiculations more strongly marked at base of tertials. Flanks often similar in tone or are more reddish and darker, closer to the breast, sometimes clearly streaked blackish. Back and rump dark grey-brown with buff vermiculations. Uppertail- and femoral coverts dark reddish-brown to mahogany. Tail blackish. Belly pale brown or tan with dark transverse stripes. Undertail-coverts buff to pale ochre-brown with pale grey stripes. Upperwing dark grey with pale ochre vermiculations, remiges entirely dark grey-brown. Underwing has grey secondary coverts, crossed by a whitish to light grey area formed by axillaries and median coverts. Remiges and leading edge dark grey. Legs and feet pale grey-blue with dark webs.

Dark morph, described by Pereira & Urdiales[1299] in Spain, characterised by more black on head during first few years of life, belly dark brown with ochre hues and stronger dark grey transverse bars more pronounced, undertail dark reddish heavily striped blackish and underwing darker grey, with less white. However, the coloration of this species is quite variable, and many birds have characters of both forms described here.

Adult ♀

Definitive basic plumage (Aug–Dec/Apr). Similar to alternate plumage described below, but has a colder body and dark vermiculations less sharply defined[1299]. The main differences are on the face, with cheeks more white, making the dark bar appear stronger. This bar also seems thinner and of more even width. Bill blackish.

Definitive alternate plumage (Apr–May/Aug–Sep). Body mainly ochre- to reddish-brown, with upper head (to below eye and covering upper half of bill base) blackish-brown, nape marked grey-brown and a broad irregular bar from gape across white cheeks towards the nape. Chin and upper throat whitish, and cheeks (either side of dark bar) pale variably mottled brown (face can be almost entirely dark brown). Iris dark brown. Bill dark grey, sometimes with yellowish, olive or brownish at base. Mantle, scapulars, breast, flanks and belly rather evenly coloured, ochre-red (more grey, cinnamon or sandy-coloured individually) clearly striped blackish. Undertail-coverts pale grey marked whitish. Back and rump grey-brown streaked pale buff. Uppertail reddish-brown streaked black. Upperwing like ♂ but has duller secondary coverts. Underwing like ♂. Legs lead-grey with darker webs. Dark morph[1299] has darker head (upper head, nape and broad black bar across cheeks), with only chin and thin line through whitish upper cheeks (lower cheeks mottled dusky). Body deeper reddish (instead of paler cinnamon-red in light morph), streaked black (less obvious due darker ground colour). As ♂, underwing is described as greyer.

Juvenile

First basic plumage (until Sep–Mar?). Similar to basic plumage ♀ but greyer and paler face, highlighting the dark bars on the cheeks, vermiculations less sharply defined on body (often replaced by dark grey stripes) and breast is warmer (reddish-buff) than surrounding parts. Flanks often appear slightly paler than scapulars. Distinction is quite easy compared to alternate adult ♀, including the darker head-sides in the latter and warmer hazelnut-reddish hue on body. The most reliable features though are the bill which is significantly less swollen at base than in adult, and juvenile rectrices

(shorter, frayed and notched at tips, with bare-tipped rachis giving a typical pale or whitish colour to the tips).

First-winter ♂

Formative plumage/first alternate plumage (Nov–Mar/Apr–Jun). Rapidly during first autumn, cheeks of young ♂ become whiter and sexing becomes possible. Following pre-formative moult, i.e. by midwinter, young ♂ in basic plumage resembles adult ♂, but has bill even less swollen at base and duller grey-blue, with more blackish on head. Usually, a more or less continuous vertical black bar is visible on nape, and an oblique line runs from hindneck over cheeks, almost reaching eye. The body is slightly duller and irregularly coloured, and at least some rectrices are still juvenile (see above) until second pre-basic moult. It has been reported that some second-year birds have a yellow iris[18], which has also been wrongly described as the rule in adult ♂[308,794]. Extent and sequence of moults during second calendar year poorly understood (see Moult), but from first spring young ♂ has more black on head, sometimes even covering it completely, yet otherwise is closer to adult ♂ in alternate plumage, bill included.

First-winter ♀

Formative plumage/first alternate plumage (Nov–Mar/Apr–Jun). Like ♂, transition from juvenile to formative plumage recalls definitive basic plumage, is slow and lasts until at least midwinter. Until second pre-basic moult, probably distinguished from adult ♀ only by bill slightly less swollen at base and by retained juvenile rectrices.

GEOGRAPHIC VARIATION No subspecies recognised, but population of W Mediterranean has bill slightly stronger on average than those further east[18]. This western population also shows stronger variation in overall coloration, with dark morph recently described (see Plumages). Analysis of historical specimens (67 individuals collected 1861–1976) from different regions revealed no significant genetic differentiation across the species' range. Analysis of more recent samples from Spanish population, which declined to a tiny number (a few dozen birds in 1970–80), revealed a significant loss in diversity of mitochondrial DNA haplotypes[889]. Other similar analyses of wild populations and captive stocks dedicated to various reintroduction programmes have reached similar conclusions as to the poor genetic diversity of both Spanish populations and the two main captive stocks. This is a concern for reintroduction efforts, these studies highlighting the need for incorporating birds from other geographic origins in the captive stock for future operations[890,893].

MEASUREMENTS and MASS ♂ and adult slightly larger than ♀ and young, respectively. ♂ (*n*=37): wing chord 154–165 (159), tail 82–102 (98), culmen 42–50 (46), tarsus 34–43 (36)[605]. ♂ (*n*=10): 157–172 (162), tail 85–100 (92, *n*=9), culmen 43–48 (45.5, *n*=17), tarsus 35–38 (35.9, *n*=17); ♀ (*n*=6): wing chord 148–167 (159), tail 75–93 (86, *n*=5), culmen 43–46 (44.5, *n*=16), tarsus 33–37 (34.9, *n*=16)[267]. ♂ (*n*=9): mass 553–865 (717); ♀ (*n*=9): 510–900 (657, including birds during egg laying)[18,267,605].

VOICE Usually silent, except during courtship (♂♂) or when alarmed. Gives a rattling, raspy and low call, longish but varies in cadence. Also a *huu-luu*, fluting and fairly high-pitched, with a quality recalling that of Common Scoter *Melanitta nigra*[605]. Courtship consists of four main postures, including the ♂ swimming with head and tail erect or lying on the water exhibiting the flanks. ♀ can give whistled calls at predators or intruders. Other calls, transcribed *errr*, may also be uttered.

MOULT Very few data available on moult in the wild. Timing probably varies depending on nesting areas, many breeding sites in Turkey and further east being frozen in winter. Pre-formative moult occurs during the first winter, and probably ends in Mar–Apr, one month after pre-alternate of ad[649]. In Spain, definitive pre-alternate moult occurs in ♂ (at least) in Dec–Mar and definitive pre-basic moult is reported Aug–Sep[18]. No information on first pre-alternate moult. In captivity at Slimbridge, UK, two complete annual moults reported, corresponding to above-mentioned timing: the wings, tail (after remiges shed) and then the rest of the body in Jan–Mar and from Jul. Dominant ♂♂ begin pre-alternate moult one month before, and their pre-basic moult one month after other ♂♂[649]. These indications of two annual wing moults in captivity, do not necessarily prove their occurrence in the wild, as it has been shown in Ruddy Duck (which see) that this double moult is performed more frequently in captivity than in the wild[572,632]. It is worth mentioning though that flightless ♂♂ have been reported in Dec in India and Pakistan[34,605]. Finally, three annual wing moults were reported in five of 19 captives in Spain, in Apr, Dec and Aug[605].

HYBRIDISATION Reported only with Ruddy Duck, in the wild and captivity. This phenomenon has even been described as a contributing factor to the precarious status of White-headed Duck, through hybridisation and genetic 'pollution'. Indeed, ♂ Ruddy Ducks and hybrids (fertile) tend to be socially dominant over ♂ White-headed Ducks, by monopolising ♀♀[270,599,607,609,888,890,892].

White-headed Duck × Ruddy Duck. This cross has been reported particularly in Spain (68 hybrids collected[270]), Portugal[270] and France. A report from Turkey[689,963] has been invalidated since. They can be very misleading for identification, though first-generation ♂♂ are usually fairly easy to distinguish. Detailed work on the description of these hybrids, first-generation and more, on which much of the following information is based, was undertaken by Urdiales & Pereira[1299].

Adult ♂ in alternate plumage has intermediate characters, especially the long bill with fairly straight or slightly swollen basal culmen, whereas it is strongly swollen in adult ♂ *leucocephala*, and concave in ♂ *jamaicensis*. There are fairly large variations among first-generation hybrids, including depending on the sex of each parent species. Note that it is easier to assess the different features knowing the age and plumage of the bird. Size and structure variable, can approach *leucocephala*, even if the hybrid usually appears to float higher on the water, with a shorter body and tail. The head always appears whiter than *jamaicensis* (eye generally well distinct), often with as much white as dark-morph *leucocephala*. Upperparts closer to those of *jamaicensis* in their reddish to hazel-brown colour (darker) and in vermiculations lacking or visibly thinner than *leucocephala*. Back and rump intermediate, less black than *jamaicensis* but darker than *leucocephala*, with fine vermiculations. Belly shows a large white area variably barred dark, and silvery sheen, but can be pale ochre-brown or dark ochre-grey, closer to *leucocephala*. The flanks can suggest either species[1299]. Undertail-coverts vary from pure white (when ♂ parent is *jamaicensis*) or have a whitish to ochre hue streaked dark grey (when ♂ is *leucocephala*). Underwing variable between the two species. Adult ♂ in basic plumage is similar, except dark bill, more black and brown on head, upper neck greyer possibly streaked blackish, scapulars ochre (possibly pale grey at tips) and strongly marked blackish, and flanks pale ochre-brown to whitish vermiculated dark grey-brown. Another potentially interesting element is the courtship, which is very different between the two species (see relevant Voice sections). Hybrids seem to perform only courtship close to that of Ruddy Duck, but fewer patters on the breast[605,1299].

Adult ♀ of this hybrid obviously more problematic and can be very misleading, particularly difficult to distinguish from young White-headed Duck, which does not show the typical bulge. See ♂ above for differences in size, shape and bill shape. Head similar to dark-morph *leucocephala*, but nevertheless the throat and lower cheeks are less speckled brown, which strengthens the contrast in the face. Upperparts indistinguishable from dark-morph *leucocephala*. Back and rump intermediate. Belly, undertail and underwing may resemble both parents. Flanks paler ochre-brown than *jamaicensis*, vermiculated dark.

Second-generation hybrids (backcross with one of parent species) obviously even more difficult to detect, undoubtedly almost indistinguishable in ♀♀ and, especially, juveniles. Faced by a potential out-of-range White-headed Duck, be particularly wary of birds like latter in size, structure and/or head pattern, but with a bill slightly or not swollen basally, with upperparts reddish (♂) or dark ochre-brown (♀), vermiculations reduced or lacking, and a silvery or whitish patch or all-white undertail. Up close, the shape of feathering at the base of the bill is very useful to the extent that no first-generation hybrid known to Urdiales & Pereira [1299] has a pattern similar to *leucocephala*.

HABITAT and LIFE-CYCLE Northern populations are migratory, the others being sedentary or erratic, especially depending on water conditions. Eggs are laid between Apr and Sep (from Apr in Spain[18] and mid-May in C Asia[308]). Pairing behaviour poorly known, but probably monogamous and polygamous, with pairs forming just before arrival on nesting sites, or on the breeding grounds as in Ruddy Duck. Late acquisition of 'beautiful' plumage by pre-alternate moult, unlike other Holarctic ducks, might support this assumption. For breeding, inhabits semi-permanent or temporary wetlands, fresh or brackish, variable in size, generally with a wide helophytic belt (mainly *Phragmites* reeds), areas of open water and abundant aquatic vegetation (e.g. *Potamogeton* sp.). Favours large shallow lagoons[18,39,605,649,1169]. Post-breeding, performs pre-basic moult (few details on timing and precise location of moulting sites in relation to sex and age). Migratory population then performs autumn migration, arriving on wintering grounds in Sep–Oct [605]. In winter, much more gregarious, with gatherings of up to 11,000 birds reported[308,605]. Like rest of year, frequents habitats often heavily impacted by intensity of recent rainfall and liable to switch wintering sites from one year to next, depending on local conditions. In winter, frequents similar habitats but prefers large, brackish, coastal or inland lagoons and large open waterbodies, generally deeper than in nesting period.

RANGE and POPULATION Endangered[145]. Range strongly fragmented during 20th century, and estimated total numbers have declined by factor of ten. Species formerly bred but is considered extinct in France, Italy, Hungary, as well as most countries in Balkans, Israel, Egypt, Ukraine, and possibly other countries mentioned hereafter. Species is partially sedentary but vacates northernmost regions and those that freeze in winter, gathering on brackish waters and/or further south, locally in S & E Balkans, much of N Middle East (rare in Arabia), to Pakistan and India (rare)[12,145,225,605,754,788,1143]. Rare visitor to W Europe (where origin of birds, Iberian or eastern, not well established) and C Europe. Global population estimated at >100,000 in Asia in early 20th century[481] but has decreased sharply since, with just 8,000–13,000 currently[145,754]. Four distinct populations. Spanish population reached a minimum of 22 birds in 1977[605,875], then increased due to strong protection plus a huge reintroduction scheme, reached 4,500 birds in 2000, and has ranged between *c*.1,600 and 2,700 in the current decade[1276]; the species has recently re-colonised NW Morocco, presumably as a consequence of the recent increase of the Spanish population. The second population, of NE Algeria and Tunisia, was estimated at 400–600 birds in the early 2000s[1348]. The third population occurs in C Asia, E Mediterranean and Middle East, is partially migratory and numbered 5000–10,000 birds in the early 2000s, following a sharp decline, which is apparently ongoing[754]. Post-nuptial gatherings, including most of migratory population of steppes of C Asia, peak at 4,000–4,500 birds, currently in C Kazakhstan (Tengiz-Korgalzhyn region)[1143]. Last population breeds in Mongolia and China, and winters in Pakistan[605]. It currently numbers <50 birds[12], vs. >1,000 in 1960s[754].

Main threats are ongoing degradation of habitats and, locally in Asia, over-hunting. Semi-permanent or temporary habitats are by their nature very sensitive, and it is estimated that nearly 50% of suitable sites disappeared during 20th century[145], due to drainage and use of water for agriculture and domestic purposes. Disturbance by human activities (fish farming, hunting) and pollution also damage remaining habitats. The introduction and establishment of feral populations of Ruddy Duck also constitutes a serious threat (see this species). Other threats identified, such as ingestion of lead shot, mortality in fishing nets and climate change, which is suspected to be causing more frequent droughts in C Asia[145,605]. National and international action plans[482,609] are being implemented to counteract the effects of these factors, including population reinforcement in Spain. As such, genetic markers have been defined to identify hybrids and eliminate them from captive stocks used in reintroduction schemes[890].

CAPTIVITY Rather rarely kept in captivity (outside of captive stocks dedicated to reintroduction programmes), deemed rather easy to maintain but difficult to breed. In Europe, usually sold at lower prices than, for example, most sea ducks, mergansers and goldeneyes. Rarer in North America.

REFERENCES Ali & Akhtar (2005)[12]; Almaraz & Amat (2004)[17]; Amat & Sánchez (1982)[18]; Anstey (1989)[34]; Atiénzar *et al.* (2012)[39]; BirdLife International (2014)[145]; Chaudhry (2002)[225]; Cramp & Simmons (1977)[268]; Cranswick & Hall (2010)[270]; Dementiev & Gladkov (1952)[308]; Gantlett (1993)[416]; Gillham & Gillham (1996)[439]; Green & Anstey (1992)[480]; Green & Hughes (1996)[482]; Green & Hughes (2001)[483]; Green & Hunter (1996)[481]; Hohman (1996)[572]; Hughes (1996)[599]; Hughes & Green *in* Kear (2005)[605]; Hughes *et al.* (2006)[607]; Hughes & Yurlov (2006)[609]; Jehl & Johnson (2004)[632]; Johnsgard & Carbonell (1996)[649]; King (1999)[689]; Li & Mundkur (2003)[754]; Livezey (1995)[770]; Ma Ming (2007)[788]; Madge & Burn (1988)[794]; McCracken & Sorenson (2005)[818]; Moreno-Arroyo & Torres Esquivias (2000)[875]; Muñoz-Fuentes (2001)[888]; Muñoz-Fuentes *et al.* (2005)[889]; Muñoz-Fuentes *et al.* (2005)[890]; Muñoz-Fuentes *et al.* (2007)[892]; Muñoz-Fuentes *et al.* (2008)[893]; Peet (1998)[963]; Pyle (2008)[1014]; Schielzeth *et al.* (2003)[1143]; Sebastián-González *et al.* (2013)[1169]; Torres Esquivias (2009)[1276]; Torres Esquivias & Ayala Moreno (1986)[1277]; Urdiales & Pereira (1993)[1299]; Wetlands International (2014)[1348].

622. Adult ♂ (definitive alternate); note variation in extent of black on head between the three ♂♂ shown on this page. Spain, May (Ingo Waschkies).

623. Adult ♂ (definitive alternate). Spain, May (Ingo Waschkies).

624. Adult ♂ (definitive alternate), with rather pale upperparts. Spain, Feb (Sébastien Reeber).

625. Juvenile (first basic); note dull head pattern and culmen not swollen at its base. Spain, Aug (Dennis Morrison).

626. Adult ♀ (definitive basic); a dark-plumaged bird. Spain, Sep (Christopher J. G. Plummer).

627. ♀ (first/definitive alternate?); head can be quite dark when breeding. Spain, May (Ingo Waschkies)

REFERENCES

1. Aarvak, T. & Øien, I. J. (2003) Moult and autumn migration of non-breeding Fennoscandian Lesser White-fronted Geese *Anser erythropus* mapped by satellite telemetry. *Bird Conserv. Intern.* 13: 213–226.

2. Aarvak, T., Øien, I. J. & Nagy, S. (1996) *The Lesser White-fronted Goose Monitoring Programme: Annual Report 1996*. Norwegian Ornithological Society, Klaebu.

3. Aarvak, T., Øien, I. J., Krasnov, Y. V., Gavro, M. V. & Shavykin, A. A. (2013) The European wintering population of Steller's Eider *Polysticta stelleri* reassessed. *Bird Conserv. Intern.* 23: 337–343.

4. Abraham, K. F. & Jefferies, R. L. (1997) High goose populations: causes, impacts and implications. Pp. 7–72 *in* Batt, B. D. J. (ed.) *Arctic Ecosystems in Peril: Report of the Arctic Goose Habitat Working Group*. US Fish & Wildlife Service, Washington DC & Canadian Wildlife Service, Ottawa.

5. Adams, J. & Slavid, E. R. (1984) Cheek plumage pattern in Colombian Ruddy Duck *Oxyura jamaicensis*. *Ibis* 126: 405–407.

6. Adams, P. A. (1999) Time-activity budgets of Harlequin Ducks (*Histrionicus histrionicus*) moulting at the Gannet Islands, Labrador. B.Sc. thesis. Memorial Univ. Newfoundland, St. John's.

7. Alberta Sustainable Resource Development (2002) *Status of the White-winged Scoter (Melanitta fusca deglandi) in Alberta*. Alberta Sustainable Resource Development, Fish & Wildlife Division, & Alberta Conservation Association, Edmonton.

8. Alderfer, J. (1992) Immature Black Scoters. *Birding World* 5: 193–194.

9. Aldrich, J. W. & Baer, K. P. (1970) Status and speciation in the Mexican Duck (*Anas diazi*) *Wilson Bull.* 82: 63–73.

10. Alexander, W. C. (1983) Differential sex distributions of wintering diving ducks (Aythyini) in North America. *Amer. Birds* 37: 26–29.

11. Ali, S., Ripley, S. D. & Dick, J. H. (1987) *Compact Handbook of the Birds of India and Pakistan*. Oxford Univ. Press, Delhi.

12. Ali, Z. & Akhtar, M. (2005) Bird surveys at wetlands in Punjab, Pakistan, with special reference to the present status of White-headed Duck *Oxyura leucocephala*. *Forktail* 21: 43–50.

13. Alisauskas, R. T. (1998) Winter range expansion and relationship between landscape and morphometrics of mid-continent Lesser Snow Geese. *Auk* 115: 851–862.

14. Alisauskas, R. T., Leafloor, J. O. & Kellett, D. K. (2012) *Status of the Midcontinent Population of Lesser Snow Geese and Ross's Geese Following Special Conservation Measures*. US Fish & Wildlife Service, Washington DC & Canadian Wildlife Service, Ottawa.

15. Alison, R. M. (1975) Breeding biology and behavior of the Oldsquaw (*Clangula hyemalis* L.). *Orn. Monogr.* 18.

16. Alison, R. M. & Prevett, J. P. (1976) Occurrence of duck hybrids at James Bay. *Auk* 93: 643–644.

17. Almaraz, P. & Amat, J. A. (2004) Multi-annual spatial and numeric dynamics of the white-headed duck *Oxyura leucocephala* in southern Europe: seasonality, density dependence and climatic variability. *J. Anim. Ecol. 73 : 1013–1023.*

18. Amat, J. A. & Sánchez, A. (1982) Biología y ecología de la Malvasía (*Oxyura leucocephala*) en Andalucía. *Doñana Acta Vert.* 9: 251–320.

19. AOU (1957) *Check-list of North American Birds*. Fifth edn. American Ornithologists' Union, Baltimore.

20. AOU (1983) *Check-list of North American Birds*. Sixth edn. American Ornithologists' Union, Lawrence, KS.

21. AOU (1998) *Check-list of North American Birds*. Seventh edn. American Ornithologists' Union, Washington DC.

22. AOU (2010) Fifty-first supplement to the American Ornithologists' Union *Check-list of North American Birds*. *Auk* 127: 726–744.

23. Anderson, A. (2003) The reintroduction of the Lesser White-fronted Goose in Swedish Lapland – a summary for 2000–2003. *Fennoscandian Lesser White-fronted Goose conservation Project Report 2001–2003*: 51–52.

24. Anderson, B. W. (2010) *Evolution and Taxonomy of White-cheeked Geese*. Avvar Books, Blythe, CA.

25. Anderson, B. W. & Timken, R. L. (1969) A hybrid Lesser Scaup × Ring-necked Duck. *Auk* 86: 556–557.

26. Anderson, B. W. & Timken, R. L. (1972) Sex and age ratios and weights of Common Mergansers. *J. Wildl. Manag.* 36: 1127–1133.

27. Anderson, B. W., Ketola, T. E. & Warner, D. W. (1969) Spring sex and age ratios of Lesser Scaup and Ring-necked Ducks in Minnesota. *J. Wildl. Manag.* 33: 209–212.

28. Anderson, T. J. (1999) Habitat use by Masked Ducks along the gulf coast of Texas. *Wilson Bull.* 111: 119–121.

29. Anderson, T. J., Muehl, G. T. & Tacha, T. C. (1998) Distribution and abundance of waterbirds in coastal Texas. *Bird. Pop.* 4: 1–15.

30. Andersson, Å. & Larsson, T. (2006) Reintroduction of Lesser White-fronted Goose *Anser erythropus* in Swedish Lapland. Pp. 635–636 in Boere, G. C., Galbraith, C. A. & Stroud, D. A. (eds.) *Waterbirds around the World*. The Stationary Office, Edinburgh.

31. Ankney, C. D. (1984) Nutrient reserve dynamics of breeding and molting Brant. *Auk* 101: 361–370.

32. Ankney, C. D., Dennis, D. G., Wishard, L. N. & Seeb, J. E. (1986) Low genetic variation between Black Ducks and Mallards. *Auk* 103: 701–709.

33. Ankney, C. D., Dennis, D. G. & Bailey, R. C. (1987) Increasing mallards, decreasing American black ducks: coincidence or cause and effect?. *J. Wildl. Manag.* 51: 523–529.

34. Anstey, S. (1989) *The Status and Conservation of the White-headed Duck Oxyura leucocephala: A Report on a Joint Study Carried Out by the IWRB and the WWT*. Wildfowl and Wetlands Trust, Slimbridge.

35. Antonius, O. (1933) Bemerkungen über Bastarde und Bastardzucht. *Biologia generalis* 9: 39–47.

36. Ardamatskaya, T. B. (2001) The expansion of the Common Eider *Somateria mollissima* at Ukrainian coast of the Black Sea. *Acta Orn.* 36: 53–54.

37. Ashley, E. P., Petrie, S. A., North, N. R. & Bailey, R. C. (2007) Tertial and upper wing covert molt in young American Black Ducks. *Waterbirds* 30: 433–440.

38. Astley, H. D. (1921) Avicultural notes. *Avicult. Mag.* (3)12: 84–87, 97–99.

39. Atiénzar, F., Antón-Pardo, M., Armengol, X. & Barba, E. (2012) Distribution of the White-headed Duck *Oxyura leucocephala* is affected by environmental factors in a Mediterranean wetland. *Zool. Stud.* 51: 783–792.

40. Austin, J. E., Custer, C. M. & Afton, A. D. (1998) Lesser Scaup (*Aythya affinis*). *In* Poole, A. (ed.) The Birds of North America Online. Cornell Lab of Ornithology, Ithaca, NY. http://bna.birds.cornell.edu/bna/species/338

41. Austin, J. E., Custer, C. M. & Afton, A. D. (1998) Lesser Scaup (*Aythya affinis*) In Poole, A. & Gill, F. (eds.) The Birds of North America, no. 338. The Birds of North America Inc., Philadelphia.

42. Austin, J. E., Custer, C. M. & Afton, A. D. Lesser Scaup *Aythya affinis*. Pp. 679–685 *in* Kear, J. (ed.) *Ducks, Geese and Swans*. Oxford Univ. Press.

43. Austin, J. E. & Miller, M. R. (1995) Northern Pintail (*Anas acuta*). *In* Poole, A. (ed.) The Birds of North America Online. Cornell Lab of Ornithology, Ithaca, NY. http://bna.birds.cornell.edu/bna/species/163

44. Austin, O. L. & Kuroda, N. (1953) Birds of Japan: their status and distribution. *Bull. Mus. Comp. Zool.* 109.

45. Avise, J. C., Ankney, C. D. & Nelson, W. S. (1990) Mitochondrial gene trees and the evolutionary relationship of Mallard and Black Ducks. *Evolution* 1109–1119.

46. Avise, J. C., Alisauskas, R. T., Nelson, W. S. & Ankney, C. D. (1992) Matriarchal population genetic structure in an avian species with female natal philopatry. *Evolution* 46: 1084–1096.

47. Bacon, P. J. (1980) A possible advantage for the "Polish" morph of the Mute Swan. *Wildfowl* 31: 51–52.

48. Bailey, R. O. (1983) Use of southern boreal lakes by moulting and staging diving ducks. *Proc. West. Hemisphere Waterfowl and Waterbird Symp.* 1: 54–59.

49. Baird, S. F., Brewer, T. M. & Ridgway, R. (1884) *Water Birds of North America*. Little, Brown & Co., Boston.

50. Baker, A. J. (1998) Identification of Canada Goose stocks using restriction analysis of mitochondrial DNA. Pp. 435–443 *in* Rusch, D. H., Samuel, M. D., Humburg, D. D. & Sullivan, B. D. (eds.) *Biology and Management of Canada Geese*. Proc. Intern. Canada Goose Symp., Milwaukee, WI.

51. Baker, A. J. & Marshall, H. D. (1997) Mitochondrial control region sequences as tools for understanding evolution. Pp. 51–79 *in* Mindell, D. P. (ed.) *Avian Molecular Evolution and Systematics*. Academic Press, San Diego, CA.

52. Baker, A. J., Grapputo, A., Dickson, K., Wendt, S. & Schribner, K. (1997) Mitochondrial DNA control region sequence variation in Common Eiders reveals extensive mixing of subspecies. First North Amer. Duck Symp. & Workshop. Baton Rouge.

53. Baker, E. C. S. (1908) *Indian Ducks and their Allies*. Bombay Natural History Society, Bombay.

54. Baker, E. C. S (1929) *The Fauna of British India including Ceylon and Burma*. Vol. 6. Second edn. Taylor & Francis, London.

56. Baker, K. (1993) *Identification Guide to European non-Passerines*. BTO Guide 24. British Trust for Ornithology, Thetford.

57. Ball, S. C. 1934. Hybrid ducks, including descriptions of two crosses of *Bucephala* and *Lophodytes*. Publ. Peabody Mus. Nat. Hist. 3.

58. Balogh, G. (1996) Secret Spectacled Eider wintering grounds found. *WWF Arctic Bull.* 1: 14–15.

59. Banko, W. E. (1960) *The Trumpeter Swan: Its History, Habits, and Population in the United States*. N. Amer. Fauna 63. US Fish & Wildlife Service, Washington DC.

60. Banko, W. E. & Mackay, R. H. (1964) Our native swans. Pp. 155–164 *in* Linduska, J. P. (ed.) *Waterfowl Tomorrow*. US Fish & Wildlife Service, Washington DC.

61. Banko, W. E. & Schorger, A. W. (1976) Trumpeter Swan. Pp. 5–71 *in* Palmer, R. S. (ed.) *Handbook of North American Birds*. Vol. 2(1). Yale Univ. Press, New Haven, CT.

62. Banks, A. N., Wright, L. J., Maclean, I. M. D., Hann, C. & Rehfisch, M. M. (2008) *Review of the Status of Introduced Non-Native Waterbird Species in the Area of the African-Eurasian Waterbird Agreement: 2007 Update*. British Trust of Ornithology, Thetford.

63. Banks, R. C. (1986) Subspecies of the Greater Scaup and their names. *Wilson Bull.* 98: 433–444.

64. Banks, R. C. (2010) Proposal: Recognize *Anas diazi* as a species – again. In: AOU 2010. Proposals 2010-B.

65. Banks R. C. (2011) Taxonomy of the Greater White-fronted Geese (Aves: Anatidae). *Proc. Biol. Soc. Wash.* 124: 226–233.

66. Banks, R. C., Cicero, C., Dunn, J. L., Kratter, A. W., Rasmussen, P. C., Remsen, J. V., Rising, J. D. & Stotz, D. F. (2004) Forty-fifth supplement to the American Ornithologists' Union *Check-list of North American Birds. Auk* 121: 985–995.

67. Banks, R. C., Chesser R. T., Cicero, C., Dunn, J. L., Kratter, A. W., Lovette, I. J., Rasmussen, P. C., Remsen, J. V., Rising, J. D. & Stotz, D. F. (2007) Forty-eighth supplement to the American Ornithologists Union *Check-List of North American Birds. Auk* 124: 1109–1115.

68. Banks, R. C., Chesser, R. T., Cicero, C., Dunn, J. L., Kratter, A. W., Lovette, I. J., Rasmussen, P. C., Remsen, J. V., Rising, J. D., Stotz, D. F. & Winker, K. (2008) Forty-ninth supplement to the American Ornithologists' Union *Check-List of North American Birds. Auk* 125: 758–768.

69. Bannon, P. (1978) Garrot commun × de Barrow. *Bull. Orn. (Quebec)* 23: 43–63.

70. Barrett, V. A. & Vyse, E. R. (1982) Comparative genetics of three Trumpeter Swan populations. *Auk* 99: 103–108.

71. Barter, M., Chen, L., Cao, L. & Lei, G. (2004) *Waterbird Survey of the Middle and Lower Yangtze River Floodplain in Late January and Early February 2004*. China Forestry Publishing House, Beijing.

72. Barter, M., Cao, L., Wang, X., Lu, Y., Lei, J., Solovyeva, D. & Fox, A. D. (2013) Abundance and distribution of wintering Scaly-sided Mergansers *Mergus squamatus* in China: where are the missing birds? *Bird Conserv. Intern.* 24(04): 405-416.

73. Barthel, P. H. & Frede, M. (1989) Die Bestimmung von Gänsen der Gattung *Anser. Limicola* 3: 1–31.

74. Batbayar, N., Takekawa, J. Y., Newman, S. H., Prosser, D. J., Natsagdorj, T. & Xiao, X. (2011) Migration strategies of Swan Geese *Anser cygnoides* from northeast Mongolia. *Wildfowl* 61: 90–109.

75. Bateson, P., Lotwick, W. & Scott, D. K. (1980) Similarities between the faces of parents and offspring in Bewick's swan and the differences between mates. *J. Zool.* 191: 61–74.

76. Battagin A. (2006) [Photos]. http://fog.ccsf.edu/jmorlan/homexbuff120806.htm

77. Batty, C. & Lowe, T. (2001) Vagrant Canada Geese in Britain and Ireland. *Birding World* 14: 57–61.

78. Batty, C., Hackett, P. & Lowe, T. (2001) Vagrant Canada Geese in Britain: autumn 2001. *Birding World* 14: 515–519.

79. Bauer, K. M. & Glutz von Blotzheim, U. N. (1968–69) *Handbuch der Vögel Mitteleuropas*. Bd. 2–3. Akademische Verlagsgesellschaft, Frankfurt am Main.

80. Beacham, W. (ed.) (1997) Korean Crested Shelduck.

Pp. 88–90 *in The Official World Wildlife Fund Guide to Extinct Species of Modern Times*. Beacham Publishing, London.

81. Bédard, J. H., Nadeau, A. & Savard, J.-P. L. (1997) *Répartition et abondance de la Macreuse à front blanc dans le moyen estuaire du Saint-Laurent à l'automne*. Canadian Wildlife Service, Ottawa.

82. Beekman, J. H. (1997) International censuses of the North-west European Bewick's Swan population, January 1990 and 1995. *Swan Specialist Group Newsletter* 6: 7–9.

83. Beekman, J. H., Rees, E. C. & Bacon, P. J. (1994) Bewick's Swan *Cygnus columbianus bewickii*. Pp. 108–109 *in* Tucker, G. M. & Heath, M. F. (eds.) *Birds in Europe: Their Conservation Status*. BirdLife Conservation Series no. 3. BirdLife International, Cambridge, UK.

84. Bell, C. G. V. (1997) Field sexing of some monomorphic Zimbabwean ducks. *Honeyguide* 43: 76–79.

85. Bellrose, F. C. (1976) *Ducks, Geese and Swans of North America*. Second edn. Stackpole Books, Harrisburg, PA.

86. Bellrose, F. C. (1976) The comeback of the Wood Duck. *Wildl. Soc. Bull.* 4: 107–110.

87. Bellrose, F. C. (1980) *Ducks, Geese and Swans of North America*. Third ed. Stackpole Books, Harrisburg, PA.

88. Bellrose, F. C. (1990) History of Wood Duck management in North America. Pp. 13–20 *in* Frederickson, L. H., Burger, G. V., Havera, S. P., Graber, D. A., Kirby, R. E. & Taylor, T. S. (eds.) *Proc. 1988 N. Amer. Wood Duck Symp.*

89. Bellrose, F. C. & Holm, D. J. (1994) *Ecology and Management of the Wood Duck*. Stackpole Books, Harrisburg, PA.

90. Bengtson, S. A. (1972) Reproduction and fluctuations in the size of duck populations at Lake Mývatn, Iceland. *Oikos* 23: 35–58.

91. Bengtson, S. A. (1972) An apparent hybrid between Barrow's Goldeneye *Bucephala islandica* and Common Goldeneye *B. clangula* in Iceland. *Bull. Brit. Orn. Club* 92: 100–101.

92. Bengtson, S. A. (1972) Breeding ecology of the Harlequin Duck *Histrionicus histrionicus* (L.) in Iceland. *Ornis Scand.* 3: 1–19.

93. Bengtsson, K. (2007) Vitkindad gås – det rysk/baltiska beståndets expansion. *Anser* 46: 137–162.

94. Bezzel, E. (1960) Beobachtungen an wildlebendenbastarden Tafel × Reiherente (*Aythya ferina × Aythya fuligula*). *J. Orn.* 101: 276–281.

95. Bielefeld, R. R., Brasher, M. G., Moorman, T. E. & Gray, P. N. (2010) Mottled Duck (*Aythya fuligula*). *In* Poole, A. (ed.) The Birds of North America Online. Cornell Lab of Ornithology, Ithaca, NY. http://bna.birds.cornell.edu/bna/species/081

96. Billard, R. S. & Humphrey, P. S. (1992) Molts and plumages of the Greater Scaup. *J. Wildl. Manag.* 36: 765–774.

97. Bird Hybrids database (2014) http://www.bird-hybrids.com/

98. Bird Hybrids Flickr Forum (2007) [S. Mlodinow]. www.flickr.com/groups/hybridbirds/discuss/72157625941234626/

99. Bird Hybrids Flickr Forum (2007) [C. Police]. www.flickr.com/groups/hybridbirds/discuss/72157603578838545/

100. Bird Hybrids Flickr Forum (2008) [J. Lehmhus]. www.flickr.com/groups/hybridbirds/discuss/72157609387249583/

101. Bird Hybrids Flickr Forum (2008) [B. Olsen]. www.flickr.com/groups/hybridbirds/discuss/72157609386260598/

102. Bird Hybrids Flickr Forum (2008) [P. Mansfield & J. Lehmhus]. www.flickr.com/groups/hybridbirds/discuss/72157605262076961/

103. Bird Hybrids Flickr Forum (2008) [J. Lehmhus]. www.flickr.com/groups/hybridbirds/discuss/72157604116714102/

104. Bird Hybrids Flickr Forum (2008) [I. Weiß]. www.flickr.com/groups/hybridbirds/discuss/72157603990534924/

105. Bird Hybrids Flickr Forum (2008) [C. G. Gustavsson & H. Lehto]. www.flickr.com/groups/hybridbirds/discuss/72157606470242798/

106. Bird Hybrids Flickr Forum (2008) [I. Gereg & B. Olsen]. www.flickr.com/groups/hybridbirds/discuss/72157609386260598/

107. Bird Hybrids Flickr Forum (2009) [A. Nixon]. www.flickr.com/groups/hybridbirds/discuss/72157622934653737/

108. Bird Hybrids Flickr Forum (2009) [S. Yellseev]. www.flickr.com/groups/hybridbirds/discuss/72157601886415063/

109. Bird Hybrids Flickr Forum (2009) [C. G. Gustavsson]. www.flickr.com/groups/hybridbirds/discuss/72157622611270523/

110. Bird Hybrids Flickr Forum (2009) [D. Appleton]. www.flickr.com/groups/hybridbirds/discuss/72157616726711779/

111. Bird Hybrids Flickr Forum (2009) [C. Wood]. www.flickr.com/groups/hybridbirds/discuss/72157623022942883/

112. Bird Hybrids Flickr Forum (2009) [J. Lehmhus]. www.flickr.com/groups/hybridbirds/discuss/72157622611286979/

113. Bird Hybrids Flickr Forum (2009) [J. Lehmhus]. www.flickr.com/groups/hybridbirds/discuss/72157622631600615/

114. Bird Hybrids Flickr Forum (2009) [J. Lehmhus]. www.flickr.com/groups/hybridbirds/discuss/72157622611286979/

115. Bird Hybrids Flickr Forum (2009) [J. Lehmhus, C. G. Gustavsson & S. Mlodinow]. www.flickr.com/groups/hybridbirds/discuss/72157612791914423/

116. Bird Hybrids Flickr Forum (2009) [R. Andrews]. www.flickr.com/groups/hybridbirds/discuss/72157622755783324/

117. Bird Hybrids Flickr Forum (2009) [T. Smith & B. Cunningham]. www.flickr.com/groups/hybridbirds/discuss/72157603572995563/

118. Bird Hybrids Flickr Forum (2009) [D. Appleton]. www.flickr.com/groups/hybridbirds/discuss/72157619423054957/

119. Bird Hybrids Flickr Forum (2009) [D. Appleton]. www.flickr.com/groups/hybridbirds/discuss/72157616184880609/

120. Bird Hybrids Flickr Forum (2009) [D. Appleton]. www.flickr.com/groups/hybridbirds/discuss/72157619423054957/

121. Bird Hybrids Flickr Forum (2010) [A. Roberts]. www.flickr.com/groups/hybridbirds/discuss/72157623875551535/

122. Bird Hybrids Flickr Forum (2010) [C. Wood]. www.flickr.com/groups/hybridbirds/discuss/72157623022942883/

123. Bird Hybrids Flickr Forum (2010) [J. Lehmhus]. www.flickr.com/groups/hybridbirds/discuss/72157623258474553/

124. Bird Hybrids Flickr Forum (2011) [J. Lehmhus]. www.flickr.com/groups/hybridbirds/discuss/72157625908710309/

125. Bird Hybrids Flickr Forum (2011) [S. Mlodinow]. www.flickr.com/groups/hybridbirds/discuss/72157625713539799/

126. Bird Hybrids Flickr Forum (2011) [D. Appleton]. www.flickr.com/groups/hybridbirds/discuss/72157601790274011/

127. Bird Hybrids Flickr Forum (2011) [J. Lehmhus]. www.flickr.com/groups/hybridbirds/discuss/72157625908553139/

128. Bird Hybrids Flickr Forum (2011) [C. G. Gustavsson]. www.flickr.com/groups/hybridbirds/discuss/72157623781458225

129. Bird Hybrids Flickr Forum (2011) [D. Appleton]. www.flickr.com/groups/hybridbirds/discuss/72157625837786691/

130. Bird Hybrids Flickr Forum (2011) [J. Lansdell]. www.flickr.com/groups/hybridbirds/discuss/72157626012756569/

131. Bird Hybrids Flickr Forum (2011) [S. Mlodinow]. www.flickr.com/groups/hybridbirds/discuss/72157625713416817/

132. Bird Hybrids Flickr Forum (2011) [D. Appleton]. www.flickr. com/groups/hybridbirds/discuss/72157625896041211/

133. Bird Hybrids Flickr Forum (2011) [D. Appleton]. www.flickr. com/groups/hybridbirds/discuss/72157627931319698/

134. Bird Hybrids Flickr Forum (2012) [J. Lehmhus]. www.flickr. com/groups/hybridbirds/discuss/72157629376844639

135. Bird Hybrids Flickr Forum (2012) [Photos]. www.gobirding. eu/Photos/BrentGoosexRedbreastedGoose.php

136. Bird Hybrids Flickr Forum (2013) [Photos]. www.flickr.com/ groups/hybridbirds/discuss/72157626123932728/

137. Bird Hybrids Flickr Forum (2013) [Photo]. www.gobirding. eu/Photos/PinkfootedGoose.php

138. BirdLife International (2001) *Threatened Birds of Asia: the BirdLife International Red Data Book*. BirdLife International, Cambridge, UK.

139. BirdLife International (2004) *Birds in Europe: Population Estimates, Trends and conservation Status*. BirdLife Conservation Series no. 12. BirdLife International, Cambridge, UK.

140. BirdLife International (2009) *Dendrocygna javanica*. IUCN Red List of Threatened Species. Version 3.1. www.iucnredlist. org/apps/redlist/details/100600351

141. BirdLife International (2012) Species factsheets. www. birdlife.org

142. BirdLife International (2012) The BirdLife checklist of the birds of the world, with conservation status and taxonomic sources. Version 5. www.birdlife.info/im/species/checklist. zip

143. BirdLife International (2013) IUCN Red List for birds. www. birdlife.org

144. BirdLife International (2013) Species factsheets. www. birdlife.org

145. BirdLife International (2014) Species factsheets. www. birdlife.org

146. BirdLife International Cambodia Programme (2012) *The Biodiversity of the Proposed Western Siem Pang Protected Forest Stung Treng Province, Cambodia*. BirdLife International Cambodia Programme, Phnom Penh.

147. Birkhead, M. & Perrins, C. (1986) *The Mute Swan*. Croom Helm, London.

148. Bishop, L. B. (1895) *Aythya marila* or *A. m. nearctica*? *Auk* 12: 293–295.

149. Blair, M. J., McKay, H., Musgrove, A. J. & Rehfisch, M. M. (2000) *Review of the Status of Introduced Non-native Waterbird Species in the Agreement Area of the African–Eurasian Waterbird Agreement Research Contract CR0219*. British Trust for Ornithology, Thetford.

150. Blanford, W. T. (ed.) (1898) *The Fauna of British India Including Ceylon and Burma*. Vol. 4. Taylor & Francis, London.

151. Blaser, P. (1978) Ein Gansesager-Mittelsager-Bastard am Thunersee. *Orn. Beob.* 75: 275–276.

152. Blomdahl, A., Breife, B. & Holmström, N. (2002) Flight identification of Common Eider, King Eider and Steller's Eider. *Brit. Birds* 95: 233–239.

153. Bloomfield, A. (2004) Hybrid and aberrant geese in Britain. *Birding World* 17: 123–127.

154. Bloomfield, A. & McCallum, J. (2001) Changing fortunes of the Black Brant. *Birding World* 14: 66–68.

155. Blurton Jones, N. G. (1972) Moult migration of emperor geese. *Wildfowl* 23: 92–93.

156. Bocharnikov, V. N. & Shibnyev, Y. B. (1994) The Scaly-sided Merganser *Mergus squamatus* in the Bikin River basin, Far-

East Russia. Pp. 3–10 *in* Hughes, B. & Hunter, J. (eds.) *The Scaly-sided Merganser Mergus squamatus in Russia and China*. Wildfowl & Wetlands Trust, Slimbridge.

157. Boertmann, D. & Mosbillh, A. (2002) Molting Harlequin Ducks in Greenland. *Waterbirds* 25: 326–332.

158. Boetticher, H. (1952) *Gänse- und Entenvögel aus aller Welt*. Die Neue Brehm-Bücherei, Brehm. (In German)

159. Bolen, E. G., McDaniel, B. & Cottam, C. (1964) Natural history of the black-bellied tree duck (*Dendrocygna autumnalis*) in southern Texas. *Southwestern Naturalist* 1964: 78–88.

160. Bolen, E. G. (2005) Black-bellied Whistling-duck *Dendrocygna autumnalis*. Pp. 192–195 *in* Kear, J. (ed.) *Ducks, Geese and Swans*. Oxford Univ. Press.

161. Bolton, M., Foggitt, G., Archer, M., Tipper, R. & Wates S. (1999) A Redhead-like *Aythya* hybrid in Portugal. *Birding World* 13: 279–280.

162. Bordage, D. & Savard, J.-P. L. (2011) Black Scoter (*Melanitta americana*). *In* Poole, A. (ed.) The Birds of North America Online. Cornell Lab of Ornithology, Ithaca, NY. http://bna. birds.cornell.edu/bna/species/177

163. Bottjer, P. D. (1983) Systematic relationships among the anatidae: an immunological study, with a history of Anatid classification and a system of classification. Ph.D. thesis. Yale Univ., New Haven, CT.

164. Bourget, D., Savard, J.-P. L. & Guillemette, M. (2007) Distribution, dict and dive behavior of Barrow's and Common Goldeneyes during spring and autumn in the St. Lawrence Estuary. *Waterbirds* 30: 230–240.

165. Bourne, G. R. (1979) Weights and linear measurements of Black-bellied Whistling-ducks in Guyana. *First Welder Wildl. Found. Symp., Sinton, Texas*: 186–188.

166. Bowler, J. (2005 Whistling Swan *Cygnus columbianus columbianus*. Pp. 238–243 *in* Kear, J. (ed.) *Ducks, Geese and Swans*. Oxford Univ. Press.

167. Bowler, J., Quinn, J. & Hunter, J. (1997) Steller's Eiders breeding in western Taymir and northeast European Russia. *Threatened Waterfowl Specialist Group Newsletter* 10: 24–26.

168. Bowles, W. F. (1980) Winter ecology of Red-breasted Mergansers of the Laguna Madre of Texas. M.Sc. thesis. Corpus Christi State Univ.

169. Boyd, H. (2005) Pink-footed Goose *Anser brachyrhynchus*. Pp. 270–276 *in* Kear, J. (ed.) *Ducks, Geese and Swans*. Oxford Univ. Press.

170. Boyd, H. (2005) Brent Goose (Brant) *Branta bernicla*. Pp. 321–329 *in* Kear, J. (ed.) *Ducks, Geese and Swans*. Oxford Univ. Press.

171. Boyd, H. (2005) American Wigeon *Anas americana*. Pp. 503–506 *in* Kear, J. (ed.) *Ducks, Geese and Swans*. Oxford Univ. Press.

172. Boyd, H. & Dickson, K. (2005) Canada Goose *Branta canadensis*. Pp. 306–316 *in* Kear, J. (ed.) *Ducks, Geese and Swans*. Oxford Univ. Press.

173. Boyd, H. & Maltby, L. S. (1979) The brant of the western Queen Elizabeth Islands, N.W.T. Pp. 5–21 *in* Jarvis, R. L. & Bartonek, J. C. (eds.) *Management and Biology of Pacific Flyway Geese, A Symposium*. Oregon State Univ. Book Stores, Corvallis.

174. Boyd, H. & Maltby, L. S. (1980) Weights and primary growth of Brent geese *Branta bernicla* moulting in the Queen Elizabeth Islands, NWT, Canada, 1973–1975. Ornis Scand. 11: 135–141.

175. Boyd, H., Maltby, L. S. & Reed, A. (1988) Differences in the plumage patterns of Brant breeding in high Arctic Canada. *Can. Wildl. Serv. Prog. Note* 174: 1–9.

176. Boyd, W. S., Ward, D. H., Kraege, D. K. & Gerick, A. A. (2013) Migration patterns of western high Arctic (Grey-belly) Brant *Branta bernicla. Wildfowl*, spec. issue n°3: 3–25.

177. Bradshaw, C. (2005) Identification review – Lesser Scaup. *Brit. Birds* 98: 89–95.

178. Brazil, M. (1981) Geographical variation in the bill patterns of Whooper Swans. *Wildfowl* 32: 129–131.

180. Brazil, M. (1991) *Birds of Japan.* Helm, London.

181. Brazil, M. (2003) *The Whooper Swan.* T. & A. D. Poyser, London.

182. Brazil, M. (2009) *Birds of East Asia.* Christopher Helm, London.

183. Bregnballe, T., Madsen, J. & Rasmussen, P. A. F. (2004) Effects of temporal and spatial hunting control in waterbird reserves. *Biol. Conserv.* 119: 93–104.

184. Brewer G. L. (2005) Falcated Duck *Anas falcata.* Pp. 495–496 *in* Kear, J. *Ducks, Geese and Swans.* Oxford Univ. Press.

185. Brewster, W. (1885) The Eider Ducks of the New England coast. *Auk* 2: 111.

186. Brewster, W. (1902) An undescribed form of the Black Duck (*Anas obscura*) *Auk* 19: 183–188.

187. Brickell, N. & Frandsen, J. (1988) *Ducks, Geese and Swans of Africa and its Outlying Islands.* Frandsen Publishers, Sandton.

188. Brimley, H. H. (1927) Rare birds in North Carolina. *Auk* 44: 427–428.

189. Bristow, P. (1992) Pochard × Canvasback hybrids in Britain. *Birding World* 4: 437.

190. Brodeur, S., Savard, J.-P. L., Robert, M., Laporte, P., Lamothe, P., Titman, R. D., Marchand, S., Gilliland, S. & Fitzgerald G. (2002) Harlequin Duck *Histrionicus histrionicus* population structure in eastern Nearctic. *J. Avian Biol.* 33: 127–137.

191. Brodsky, L. M. & Weatherhead, P. J. (1984) Behavioral and ecological factors contributing to American Black Duck-Mallard hybridization. *J. Wildl. Manag.* 48(3): 846–852.

192. Brodsky, L. M., Ankney, C. D. & Dennis, D. G. (1988) The influence of male dominance on social interactions in black ducks and mallards. *Anim. Behav.* 36: 1371–1378.

193. Brooks, W. S. (1915) Notes on birds from east Siberia and arctic Alaska. *Bull. Mus. Comp. Zool.* 59: 361–413.

194. Brown, A. (1992) Identification pitfalls and assessment problems: 12. Surf Scoter. *Brit. Birds* 85: 437–439.

195. Brown, D. (2010) Wood Duck and Mandarin Duck: identification of females. *Birding World* 23: 154–155.

196. Brown, D. (2010) Identification and taxonomy of Bean Geese. *Birding World* 23: 110–121.

197. Brown, L. H., Urban E. K. & Newman K. (1982) *The Birds of Africa.* Vol. 1. Academic Press, London.

198. Brown, M. E. (1998) Population genetic structure, philopatry and social structure in three Harlequin Duck (*Histrionicus histrionicus*) breeding subpopulations. M.Sc. thesis. Univ. of California, Davis.

199. Brown, P. W. & Fredrickson, L. H. (1997) White-winged Scoter (*Melanitta fusca*). *In* Poole, A. & Gill. F. (eds.) The Birds of North America, no. 274. Academy of Natural Sciences, Philadelphia, PA & American Ornithologists' Union, Washington DC.

200. Brown, P. W. & Fredrickson, L. H. (1997) White-winged Scoter (*Melanitta fusca*). *In* Poole, A. (ed.) The Birds of North America Online. Cornell Lab of Ornithology, Ithaca, NY. http://bna.birds.cornell.edu/bna/species/274

201. Brua, R. B. (2002) Ruddy Duck (*Oxyura jamaicensis*). *In* Poole, A. (ed.) The Birds of North America Online. Cornell Lab of Ornithology, Ithaca, NY. http://bna.birds.cornell.edu/bna/species/696

202. Bruggers, R. L. (1978) Feather morphology as an age indicator in Mandarin Ducks. *Ohio J. Sci.* 78: 39–43.

203. Bruns, H. A. (1985) Von nichtheimischen Wildgansen und Artbastarden am Dummer (Niedersachsen) *Seevögel* 6 (suppl.): 176–177.

204. Buckley, P. A. & Mitra, S. S. (2002) Three geese resembling Gray-bellied Brant/Lawrence's Brant from Long Island, New York. *North Amer. Birds* 56: 502–507.

205. Buckley, P. A., Mitra, S. S. & Brinkley, E. S. (2004) Multiple occurrences of Dark-bellied Brant (*Branta* [*bernicla*] *bernicla*) in North America. *North Amer. Birds* 58: 180–185.

206. Bulgarell, M., Sorenson, M. D., Peters, J. L., Wilson, R. E. & McCracken, K. G. (2010) Phylogenetic relationships of *Amazonetta, Speculanas, Lophonetta,* and *Tachyeres*: four morphologically divergent duck genera endemic to South America. *J. Avian Biol.* 41: 186–199.

207. Burgers, J., Smit, J. J. & van der Voet, H. (1991) Origins and systematics of two types of the Bean Goose *Anser fabalis* (Latham, 1787) wintering in The Netherlands. *Ardea* 79: 307–316.

208. Burn, J. & Brickle, N. (1992) Status and notes on the ecology of *Cairina scutulata* (White-winged Wood Duck) and *Ciconia stormi* (Storm's Stork) in the Sumatran provinces of Riau and Jambi, Indonesia. Spirit of Sumatra 1992. Preliminary report. Wildfowl & Wetlands Trust, Slimbridg.

209. Butcher, G. S. & Niven, D. K. (2007) *Combining Data from the Christmas Bird Count and Breeding Bird Survey to Determine the Continental Status and Trends of North American Birds.* National Audubon Society, Ivyland, PA.

210. Callaghan, D. (2005) Swan Goose *Anser cygnoid.* Pp. 263–266 *in* Kear, J. (ed.). *Ducks, Geese and Swans.* Oxford Univ. Press.

211. Callaghan, D. (2005) South American Comb Duck *Sarkidiornis sylvicola.* Pp. 394–395 *in* Kear, J. (ed.) *Ducks, Geese and Swans.* Oxford Univ. Press.

212. Callaghan, D. (2005) Crested Shelduck *Tadorna cristata.* Pp. 439–441 *in* Kear, J. (ed.) *Ducks, Geese and Swans.* Oxford Univ. Press.

213. Callaghan, D. (2005) Mottled Duck (*Anas fulvigula*). Pp. 517–520 *in* Kear, J. (ed.) *Ducks, Geese and Swans.* Oxford Univ. Press.

214. Callaghan, D. (2005) Baer's Pochard *Aythya baeri.* Pp. 662–664 *in* Kear, J. (ed.) *Ducks, Geese and Swans.* Oxford Univ. Press.

215. Callaghan, D. & Green, A. J. (1993) Wildfowl at risk. *Wildfowl* 44: 149–69.

216. Callaghan, D. & Green, A. J. (2005) Ferruginous Duck *Aythya nyroca.* Pp. 659–662 *in* Kear, J. (ed.) *Ducks, Geese and Swans.* Oxford Univ. Press.

217. Callaghan, D. & Harshman, J. (2005) Taxonomy and systematics. Pp. 14–26 *in* Kear, J. (ed.) *Ducks, Geese and Swans.* Oxford Univ. Press.

218. Callaghan, D., Rees, E. & Harshman, J. (2005) The swans. Pp. 217–219 *in* Kear, J. (ed.) *Ducks, Geese and Swans.* Oxford Univ. Press.

219. Campbell, R. W., Dawe, N. K., McCowan, I., Cooper, J. M.,

Kaiser, G. W. & McNall, M. C. E. (1990) *The Birds of British Columbia*. Vol. 1. Royal British Columbia Museum, Victoria.

220. Cao, L. & Barter, M. (2008) *Non-breeding Season Survey for Scaly-sided Mergansers in Fujian, Guangdong and Jiangxi Provinces*. Univ. of Science & Technology of China, Hefei.

221. Cao, L., Barter, M. & Lei, G. (2008) New Anatidae population estimates for eastern China: implications for current flyway estimates. *Biol. Conserv.* 141: 2301–2309.

222. Cao, L., Zhang, Y., Barter, M. & Lei, G. (2010) Anatidae in eastern China during the non-breeding season: geographical distributions and protection status. *Biol. Conserv.* 143: 650–659.

223. Carboneras, C. (1992) Family Anatidae (ducks, geese and swans). Pp. 536–628 *in* del Hoyo, J., Elliott, A. & Sargatal, J. (eds.) *Handbook of the Birds of the World*. Vol. 1. Lynx Edicions, Barcelona.

224. Carney, S. M. (1992) *Species, Age and Sex Identification of Ducks Using Wing Plumage*. US Fish & Wildlife Service, Washington DC.

225. Chaudhry, A. A. (2002) *White-headed Duck Survey in Pakistan*. Wetlands International, Selangor.

226. Chiba, A., Honma, R. & Satoh, Y. (2007) Note on the external features and sexual behavior of a wild hybrid Baikal Teal × Northern Pintail male found at Hyo-ko Waterfowl Park, Niigata, Japan. *Orn. Sci.* 5: 221–225.

227. Childs, H. E. (1952) Hybrid between a Shoveler and a Blue-winged Teal. *Condor* 54: 67–68.

228. Choudhury, A. (2005) Lesser Whistling-duck *Dendrocygna javanica*. Pp. 207–209 *in* Kear, J. (ed.) *Ducks, Geese and Swans*. Oxford Univ. Press.

229. Choudhury, A. (2007) White-winged Duck *Cairina* (=*Asarcornis*) *scutulata* and Blue-tailed Bee-eater *Merops philippinus*: two new country records for Bhutan. *Forktail* 23: 153–155.

230. Chowdhury, S. U., Lees, A. C. & Thompson, P. M. (2012) Status and distribution of the endangered Baer's Pochard *Aythya baeri* in Bangladesh. *Forktail* 28: 57–61.

231. Chubbs, T. E., MacTavish, B., Oram, K., Trimper, P. G., Knox, K. & Goudie, R. I. (2001) Unusual Harlequin Duck *Histrionicus histrionicus* nest-site discovered in central Labrador. *Can. Field-Naturalist* 115: 177–179.

232. Ciaranca, M. A., Allin, C. C. & Jones, G. S. (1997) Mute Swan (*Cygnus olor*). In Poole, A. (ed.) The Birds of North America Online. Cornell Lab of Ornithology, Ithaca, NY. http://bna.birds.cornell.edu/bna/species/273

233. CISEH (2014) http://www.invasive.org/browse/subinfo.cfm?sub=56269

234. Clancey, P. A. (1967) *Gamebirds of Southern Africa*. Purnell, Cape Town.

235. Clark, A. (1974) Hybrid *Dendrocygna viduata* × *Dendrocygna bicolor*. *Ostrich* 45: 255.

236. Clements, J. F., Schulenberg, T. S., Iliff, M. J., Sullivan, B. L., Wood, C. L. & Roberson, D. (2013) The eBird/Clements checklist of birds of the world: Version 6.8. www.birds.cornell.edu/clementschecklist/download/

238. Coimbra-Filho, A. F (1965) Hybrids between *Dendrocygna autumnalis discolor* and *D. viduata* (Anatidae, Aves). *Rev. Bras. Biol.* 25: 277–280.

239. Collar, N. J. & Andrew, P. (1988) *Birds to Watch: The ICBP World Check-List of Threatened Birds*. International Council for Bird Preservation, Cambridge, UK.

240. Collinson, M., Parkin, D. T., Knox, A. G., Sangster, G. & Helbig, A. J. (2006) Species limits within the genus *Melanitta*, the scoters. *Brit. Birds* 99: 183–201.

241. Coluccy, J. M. (2001) Reproductive ecology, bioenergetics, and experimental removal of local Giant Canada Geese (*Branta canadensis maxima*) in central Missouri. Ph.D. thesis. Univ. of Missouri, Columbia.

242. Combs, D. L. & Fredrickson, L. H. (1995) Molt chronology of male Mallards wintering in Missouri. *Wilson Bull.* 107: 359–365.

243. Conant, B. & Groves, D. J. (1992) *Alaska-Yukon Waterfowl Breeding Population Survey, May 24 to June 21, 1992*. US Fish & Wildlife Service, Juneau, AK.

244. Cong, P., Wang, X., Cao, L. & Fox, A. D. (2012) Within-winter shifts in Lesser White-fronted Goose *Anser erythropus* distribution at East Dongting Lake, China. *Ardea* 100: 5–11.

245. Conroy, M. J., Barnes, G. G., Bethke, R. W. & Nudds, T. D. (1989) Increasing mallards, decreasing American black ducks: no evidence for cause and effect. A comment. *J. Wildl. Manag.* 53(4): 1065–1071.

246. Consortium Gauthier & Guillemette-Grebe (1993) Étude de l'avifaune et du castor: fréquentation et description des habitats de pré-nidification des macreuses, 1990. Complexe Grande-Baleine. Avant-projet phase II. Report for Hydro-Quebec, vice-présidence Environnement, Montréal.

247. Cooch, F. G. & Cooch, E. G. (2005) Snow Goose *Anser caerulescens*. Pp. 297–302 *in* Kear, J. (ed.) *Ducks, Geese and Swans*. Oxford Univ. Press.

248. Cooch, E. G., Lank, D. B., Dzubin, A., Rockwell, R. F. & Cooke, F. (1991) Body size variation in Lesser Snow Geese: environmental plasticity in gosling growth rates. *Ecology* 72: 503–512.

249. Cooch, E. G., Lank, D. B., Rockwell, R. F. & Cooke, F. (1991) Long-term decline in body size in a snow goose population: evidence of environmental degradation? *J. Anim. Ecol.* 60: 483–496.

250. Cooke, F. & Cooch, F. G. (1968) The genetics of the polymorphism in the goose *Anser caerulescens*. *Evolution* 22: 289–300.

251. Cooke, F. & Ryder, J. P. (1971) The genetics of polymorphism in the Ross's Goose (*Anser rossii*) *Evolution* 25: 483–490.

252. Cooke, F., Finney, G. H. & Rockwell, R. F. (1976) Assortative mating in lesser snow geese (*Anser caerulescens*) *Behav. Genetics* 6: 127–140.

253. Cooke, F., Parkin, D. T. & Rockwell, R. F. (1988) Evidence of former allopatry of the two color phases of Lesser Snow Geese (*Chen caerulescens caerulescens*) *Auk* 105: 467–479.

254. Cooke, F., Rockwell, R. F. & Lank, D. B. (1995) *The Snow Geese of La Pérouse Bay: Natural Selection in the Wild*. Oxford Univ. Press.

255. Cooke, F., Robertson, G. J., Goudie, R. I. & Boyd, W. S. (1997) Molt and the basic plumage of male Harlequin Ducks. *Condor* 99: 83–90.

256. Cooper, A., Rhymer, J., James, H. F., Olson, S. L. & McIntosh, C. E. (1996) Ancient DNA and island endemics. *Nature* 381: 484.

257. Cooper, J. A. (1979) Trumpeter Swan nesting behaviour. *Wildfowl* 30: 55–71.

258. Cope, D. R., Pettifor, R. A., Griffin, L. R. & Rowcliffe, J. M. 2003. Integrating farming and wildlife conservation: the Barnacle Goose Management Scheme. *Biol. Conserv.* 110: 113–122.

259. Cosgrove, P. (2003) Mandarin Ducks in northern Scotland and the potential consequences for breeding Goldeneye. *Scott. Birds* 24: 1–10.

260. Costa-Perez, L. & Rodriguez-Parada, P. (1981) Hibridos de anatidas en las marismas de Guadalquivir. *Doñana Acta Vertebrata* 8: 318–321.

261. Coupe, M. & Cooke, F. (1999) Factors affecting the pairing chronologies of three species of mergansers in southwest British Columbia. *Waterbirds* 22: 452–458.

262. Cox, C. & Barry, J. (2005) Aging of American and Eurasian Wigeons in female-type plumages. *Birding* 37: 156–164.

263. Cracraft, J. (1983) Species concepts and speciation analysis. Pp. 159–187 *in* Johnston, R. F. (ed.) *Current Ornithology*. Springer Verlag, New York.

264. Cracraft, J. (1989) Speciation and its ontology: the empirical consequences of alternative species concepts for understanding patterns and processes of differentiation. *Speciation and its Consequences*: 28–59.

265. Craigie, G. E. & Petrie, S. A. (2003) Moult intensity and chronology of Tundra Swans during spring and fall migration at Long Point, Lake Erie, Ontario. *Can. J. Zool.* 81: 1057–1062.

266. Craik, S. R., Savard, J.-P. L. & Titman, R. D. (2009) Wing and body molts of male Red-Breasted Mergansers in the Gulf of St. Lawrence, Canada. *Condor* 111: 71–80.

267. Cramp, S. & Simmons, K. E. L. (eds.) (1977) *The Birds of the Western Palearctic*. Vol. 1. Oxford Univ. Press.

269. Cranswick, P. (2010) Conservation of the Scaly-sided Merganser in Far East Russia. *WWT Conserv. Rep. 2008–2009*: 33.

270. Cranswick, P. A. & Hall, C. (2010) Eradication of the Ruddy Duck *Oxyura jamaicensis* in the Western Palaearctic: a review of progress and a revised Action Plan 2010–2015. https://wcd.coe.int/com.instranet.

271. Cranswick, P. A., Raducescu, L., Hilton, G. M. & Petkov, N. (2010) *International Single Species Action Plan for the Conservation of the Red-breasted Goose Branta ruficollis, 2011–2020*. Wildfowl & Wetlands Trust/BirdLife International, Slimbridge.

272. Crochet, P.-A. & Joynt, G. (2012) AERC list of Western Palearctic birds. December 2012 version. www.aerc.eu/tac.html

273. Crochet, P.-A., Raty, L., De Smet, G., Anderson, B., Barthel, P. H., Collinson, J. M., Dubois, P. J., Helbig, A. J., Jiguet, F., Jirle, E., Knox, A. G., Le Maréchal, P., Parkin, D. T., Pons, J.-M., Roselaar, C. S., Svensson L., van Loon, A. J. & Yésou P. (2010) AERC TAC's taxonomic recommendations. July 2010. www.aerc.eu/tac.html.

274. Crowley, D. W. (1994) Breeding habitat of Harlequin Ducks in Prince William Sound, Alaska. M.Sc. thesis. Oregon State Univ. Corvallis.

275. Csörgey, T. (1926) Bastard einer *Branta leucopsis* Bechst. und *Anser fabalis* Lath. *Aquila* 32/33: 277

276. Dale, J. J. & Thompson, J. E. (2001) Black-bellied Whistling-duck (*Dendrocygna autumnalis*). *In* Poole, A. (ed.) The Birds of North America Online. Cornell Lab of Ornithology, Ithaca, NY. http://bna.birds.cornell.edu/bna/species/578

277. Dalgety, F. C. & Scott, P. (1948) A new race of the White-fronted Goose. *Bull. Brit. Orn. Club* 68: 109–121.

278. Database on Waterfowl Resources of Russia (2001) [First results of implementation of the interregional program "Development of monitoring system and protection of waterfowl in Russia"]. Wetlands International & Centre for Studying Migratory Animals of Eurasia, Moscow. (In Russian.)

279. Dau, C. P. & Kistchinski, A. A. (2005) Spectacled Eider *Somateria spectabilis*. Pp. 693–698 *in* Kear, J. (ed.) *Ducks, Geese and Swans*. Oxford Univ. Press.

280. Dau, C. P. & Larned, W. W. (2005) Aerial population survey of common eiders and other waterbirds in near shore waters and along barrier islands of the Arctic Coastal Plain of Alaska, 24–27 June 2005. Unpubl. US Fish & Wildlife Service, Anchorage, AK.

281. Dau, C. P., Bolinger, K. S., Mallek, E. J. & Stehn, R. A. (2006) *Monitoring the Emperor Goose Population by Aerial Counts and Fall Age Ration – Fall 2006*. US Fish & Wildlife Service, Anchorage, AK.

282. Dau, C. P., Sarvis, J. E. & Jones, R. D. (1985) Temporal and spatial distribution of band recoveries of Steller's Eiders from Izembek Lagoon, Alaska. *In* Roth, T. C. (ed.) *Alaska Bird Conference: Program and Abstracts*. Anchorage, AK.

283. Daury, R. W. & Bateman, M. C. (1996) *The Barrow's Goldeneye (Bucephala islandica) in the Atlantic Provinces and Maine*. Canadian Wildlife Service, Ottawa.

284. Davies, G. (2005) Egyptian Goose *Alopochen aegyptiacus*. Pp. 401–407 *in* Kear, J. (ed.) *Ducks, Geese and Swans*. Oxford Univ. Press.

285. De Rouck, K., van Camp, I. & Colin, D. (1982) Cross between Ring-necked Duck *Aythya collaris* and Scaup *Aythya marila*. *Wielewaal* 48: 344.

286. Dean, A. R. & The Rarities Committee (1989) Distinguishing characters of American/east Asian race of Common Scoter. *Brit. Birds* 82: 615–616.

287. Dean, W. R. J. (1978) Moult seasons of some Anatidae in the western Transvaal. *Ostrich* 49: 76–84.

288. Décarie, R., Morneau, F., Lambert, D., Carrière, S. & Savard, J.-P. L. (1995) Habitat use by brood-rearing waterfowl in subarctic Quebec. *Arctic* 48: 383–390.

289. Defos du Rau, P. (2002) Elements for a red-crested pochard (*Netta rufina*) management plan. *Game & Wildl. Sci.* 19(2): 89-141.

290. Degtyarev, A. G. (1995) Localization and status of geese mass moult sites in northern Yakutia. *Goose Study Group Bull. Eastern Europe and Northern Asia* 1: 167–169.

291. Degtyarev, A. G., Germogenov, N. I., Heui-Young, K. & Hansoo, L. (2006) Baikal Teal wintering status and distribution in South Korea. *Threatened Waterfowl Specialist Group News* 15: 77–81.

293. del Hoyo, J. & Collar, N. J. (2014) *HBW and BirdLife International Illustrated Checklist of the Birds of the World*. Lynx Edicions, Barcelona.

294. Delacour, J. (1951) Taxonomic notes on the Bean geese, *Anser fabalis* Lath. *Ardea* 39: 135–142.

295. Delacour, J. (1954–64) *The Waterfowl of the World*. Vols. 1–4. Country Life, London.

297. Delacour, J. & Mayr, E. (1945) The family Anatidae. *Wilson Bull.* 57: 3–55.

298. Delacour, J. & Ripley, S. D. (1975) Description of a new subspecies of the White-fronted Goose, *Anser albifrons*. *Amer. Mus. Novit.* 2565: 1–4.

299. Delacour, J. & Zimmer, J. T. (1952) The identity of *Anser nigricans* Lawrence 1846. *Auk* 69: 82–84.

300. Delany, S. N. (1993) Introduced and escaped geese in Britain in summer 1991. *Brit. Birds* 86: 591–599.

301. Delany, S. (2005) Mute Swan *Cygnus olor*. Pp. 231–234 in Kear, J. (ed.) *Ducks, Geese and Swans.* Oxford Univ. Press.

302. Delany, S. (2005) Common Shelduck *Tadorna tadorna*. Pp. 420–423 in Kear, J. (ed.) *Ducks, Geese and Swans.* Oxford Univ. Press.

303. Delany, S. (2005) Red-crested Pochard *Netta rufina*. Pp. 631–633 in Kear, J. (ed.) *Ducks, Geese and Swans.* Oxford Univ. Press.

304. Delany, S. & Scott, D. (2002) *Waterbird Population Estimates.* Third edn. Wetlands International, Wageningen.

305. Delany, S. & Scott, D. (2006) *Waterbird Population Estimates.* Fourth edn. Wetlands International, Wageningen.

306. Delnicki D. (1975) The masked duck. *Ducks Unlimited* 41: 46–60.

307. Delnicki, D. & Reinecke, K. J. (1986) Mid-winter food use and body weights of Mallards and Wood Ducks in Mississippi. *J. Wildl. Manag.* 50: 43–51.

308. Dementiev, G. P. & Gladkov, N. A. (eds.) (1952) *Birds of the Soviet Union.* Nauka, Moscow.

309. Dementiev, G. P. & Gladkov, N. A. (1967) *Birds of the Soviet Union.* Vol. 4. Israel Prog. for Sci. Trans., Jerusalem.

310. Demongin, L. (1995) Des fuligules hybrides à Léry-Poses (Eure). *Le Cormoran* 9: 131–134.

311. Dennis, R. H. (1987) Boxes for goldeneyes: a success story. *RSPB Conserv. Review* 1: 85–87.

312. Dereliev, S. (2000) Dynamics of the numbers and distribution of the Red-breasted Goose (*Branta ruficollis*) in its main wintering grounds around the Shabla and Durankulak Lakes. *MSc thesis. Faculty of Biology, Sofia University 'St. Kliment Ohridski', Sofia, Bulgaria.*

313. Dersu & Associates (2008) *Baseline Inventory: Wildlife and Habitat Studies of the Nakai Plateau. C880: Consultancy Agreement for Wildlife Program Phase 1.* Nam Theun Power Company, Vientiane.

314. Di Labio, B. M. & Gosselin, M. (1994) A probable Wood Duck × Ring-necked Duck hybrid in Ontario. *Ontario Birds* 12: 119–122.

315. Di Labio, B., Pittaway, R. & Burke, P. (1997) Bill color and identification of female Barrow's Goldeneye. *Ontario Birds* 15: 81–85.

316. Dickerman, R. W. & Lee, F. B. (1961) *Somateria mollissima v. nigra* in Minnesota. *Auk* 78: 260–261.

317. Dickinson, E. C. & Remsen, J. V. (eds.) (2013) *The Howard and Moore Complete Checklist of the Birds of the World.* Vol. 1. Aves Press, Eastbourne.

318. Dickson, D. L. (2012) *Seasonal Movement of King Eiders Breeding in Western Arctic Canada and Northern Alaska.* Canadian Wildlife Service, Edmonton.

319. Dickson, D. L., Raven, G. & Bowman, T. (2009) Tracking the movement of Pacific Common Eiders from nesting grounds near Bathurst Inlet, Nunavut to moulting and wintering areas using satellite telemetry. 2006/2008 Progress Report. Unpubl. Canadian Wildlife Service, Edmonton.

320. Donehower, C. E. & Bird, D. M. (2008) Gull predation and breeding success of Common Eiders on Stratton Island, Maine. *Waterbirds* 31: 454–462.

321. Donne-Goussé, C., Laudet, V. & Hänni, C. (2002) A molecular phylogeny of anseriformes based on mitochondrial DNA analysis. *Mol. Phyl. & Evol.* 23: 339–356.

322. Downer, A. & Sutton, R. L. (1990) *Birds of Jamaica: A Photographic Field Guide.* Cambridge Univ. Press, UK.

323. Drewien, R. C. & Bouffard, S. H. (1994) Winter body mass and measurements of Trumpeter Swans *Cygnus buccinator. Wildfowl* 45: 22–32.

324. Drilling, N. (2000) White-winged Duck research in Way Kambas, Sumatra. *Threatened Waterfowl Specialist Group Newsletter* 12: 12.

325. Drilling, N. (2001) Ecology and conservation of the White-winged Duck in Sumatra. *Threatened Waterfowl Specialist Group Newsletter* 13: 14–15.

326. Drilling, N., Titman, R. & McKinney, F. (2002) Mallard (*Anas platyrhynchos*). *In* Poole, A. (ed.) The Birds of North America Online. Cornell Lab of Ornithology, Ithaca, NY. http://bna. birds.cornell.edu/bna/species/658

327. Dronneau, C. (2006) L'Oie des moissons *Anser fabalis*: taxonomie, identification et statut actuel en France. *Ornithos* 13: 33–47.

328. Dubois, P. J., Le Maréchal, P., Olioso, G. & Yésou, P. (2008) *Nouvel Inventaire des Oiseaux de France.* Delachaux & Niestlé, Paris.

329. Dubowy, P. J. (1987) Seasonal variation in the structure of North American waterfowl communities. Ph.D. thesis. Univ. of California, Davis.

330. Dubowy, P. J. (1996) Northern Shoveler (*Anas clypeata*). *In* Poole, A. (ed.) The Birds of North America Online. Cornell Lab of Ornithology, Ithaca, NY. http://bna.birds.cornell. edu/bna/species/217

331. Duckworth, J. W. & Chol, K. (2005) Scaly-sided Mergansers *Mergus squamatus* on the lower Chongchon River, central Korea. *Wildfowl* 55: 133–142.

332. Dugger, B. D., Dugger, K. M. & Fredrickson, L. H. (2009) Hooded Merganser (*Lophodytes cucullatus*). *In* Poole, A. (ed.) The Birds of North America Online. Cornell Lab of Ornithology, Ithaca, NY. http://bna.birds.cornell.edu/bna/ species/098

333. Duncan, D. C. (1985) Differentiating yearling from adult Northern Pintails by wing-feather characteristics. *J. Wildl. Manag.* 49: 576–579.

334. Dunn, J. L. (2005) Field impressions and other thoughts about Tule Geese (*Anser albifrons elgasi*). *Central Valley Bird Club Bull.* 8: 1–7.

335. Dwight, J. (1914) The moults and plumages of the scoters, genus *Oidemia* (*Melanitta*). *Auk* 31: 293–308.

336. Dzinbal, K. A. (1982) Ecology of Harlequin Ducks in Prince William Sound, Alaska, during summer. M.Sc. thesis. Oregon State Univ. Corvallis.

337. Dzubin, A. (1959) Growth and plumage development of wild-trapped juvenile Canvasback (*Aythya valisineria*). *J. Wildl. Manag.* 23: 279–290.

338. Dzubin, A. (1979) Recent increases of Blue Geese in western North America. Pp. 141–175 in Jarvis, R. L. & Bartonek, J. C. (eds.) *Management and Biology of Pacific Flyway Geese.* Oregon State Univ. Book Stores, Corvallis.

339. Dzubin, A. & Cooch, E. G. (1992) *Measurements of Geese: General Field Methods.* California Waterfowl Association, Sacramento, CA.

340. Eadie, J. M., Mallory, M. L. & Lumsden, H. G. (1995) Common Goldeneye (*Bucephala clangula*). *In* Poole, A. (ed.) The Birds of North America Online. Cornell Lab of Ornithology, Ithaca, NY. http://bna.birds.cornell.edu/bna/ species/170

341. Eadie, J. M., Savard, J.-P. L. & Mallory, M. L. (2000) Barrow's Goldeneye (*Bucephala islandica*). In Poole, A. (ed.) The Birds of North America Online. Cornell Lab of Ornithology, Ithaca, NY. http://bna.birds.cornell.edu/bna/species/548

342. Earnst, S. L. (1992) The timing of wing molt in Tundra Swans: energetic and non-energetic constraints. *Condor* 94: 847–856.

343. East Asian-Australasian Flyway Partnership (2014) www.eaaflyway.net/the-flyway/migratory-waterbirds-in-eaaf/the-flywaymigratory-waterbirds-in-eaafbaers-pochard/

344. Eda, M., Shimada, T., Amano, T., Ushiyama, K., Mizota, C. & Koike, H. (2013) Phylogenetic relationship of the Greater White-Fronted Goose *Anser albifrons* subspecies wintering in the Palaearctic region. *Orn. Sci.* 12: 35–42.

345. Edscorn, J. B. (1974) The fall migration: Florida region. *Amer. Birds* 28: 40–44.

346. Edwards, G. (2010) Endangered and threatened wildlife and plants; Spectacled Eider (*Somateria fischeri*): initiation of 5-year status review federal register. Federal Register 75, 66 (April 7, 2010), Notices.

347. Einarsson, A. (2005) Harlequin Duck *Histrionicus histrionicus*. Pp. 706–709 in Kear, J. (ed.) *Ducks, Geese and Swans*. Oxford Univ. Press.

348. Einarsson, A. (2005) Barrow's Goldeneye *Bucephala islandica*. Pp. 735–739 in Kear, J. (ed.) *Ducks, Geese and Swans*. Oxford Univ. Press.

349. Einarsson, O. (1996) Breeding biology of the Whooper Swan and factors affecting its breeding success, with notes on its social dynamics and life cycle in the wintering range. Ph.D. thesis. Univ. of Bristol.

350. Eisenhauer, D. I. & Kirkpatrick, C. M. (1977) Ecology of the emperor goose in Alaska. *Wildl. Monogr.* 57: 3–62.

351. Eitniear, J. C. (2013) Masked Duck (*Nomonyx dominicus*). In Poole, A. (ed.) The Birds of North America Online. Cornell Lab of Ornithology, Ithaca, NY. http://bna.birds.cornell.edu/bna/species/393

352. Elder, W. H. (1946) Age and sex criteria and weights of Canada geese. *J. Wildl. Manag.* 10: 93–111.

353. Eldridge, M. & Harrop, A. (1992) Identification and status of Baikal Teal. *Birding World* 5: 11.

354. Elliot, D. G. (1892) Hybridism and a description between *Anas boschas* and *Anas americana*. *Auk* 9: 160–166.

355. Ellis-Joseph, S., Hewston, N. & Green, A. (1992) *Global Waterfowl: Conservation Assessment & Management Plan.* Captive Breeding Specialist Group & Wildfowl & Wetlands Trust, Slimbridge.

356. Ely, C. R. & Dzubin, A. K. (1994) Greater White-fronted Goose (*Anser albifrons*). The Birds of North America Online (A. Poole, Ed.). Ithaca: Cornell Lab of Ornithology; Retrieved from the Birds of North America Online: http://bna.birds.cornell.edu/bna/species/131

357. Ely, C. R. & Scribner, K. T. (1994) Genetic diversity in arctic-nesting geese: implications for management and conservation. *Trans. North Amer. Wildl. Nat. Res. Conf.* 59: 91–110.

358. Ely, C. R. & Takekawa, J. Y. (1996) Geographic variation in migratory behavior of Greater White-fronted Geese (*Anser albifrons*). *Auk* 113: 889–901.

359. Ely, C. R., Fox, A. D., Alisauskas, R. T., Andreev, A., Bromley, R. G., Degtyarev, A. G., Ebbinge, B., Gurtovaya, E. N., Kerbes, R., Kondratyev, A. V., Kostin, I., Krechmar, A. V., Litvin, K. E., Miyabayashi, Y., Mooij, J. H., Oates, R. M., Orthmeyer, D. L., Sabano, Y., Gay Simpson, S., Solovieva, D. V., Spindler, M. A., Syroechkovsky, Y. V., Takekawa, J. Y., & Walsh, A. (2005) Circumpolar variation in morphological characteristics of Greater White-fronted Geese *Anser albifrons*. *Bird Study* 52: 104–119.

360. Ely, C. R., Nieman, D. J., Alisauskas, R. T., Schmutz, J. A. & Hines, J. E. (2013) Geographic variation in migration chronology and winter distribution of midcontinent greater white-fronted geese. *J. Wildl. Manag.* 77: 1182–1191.

361. Emelyanov, V. I. (2000) [*Morphometry Analyses of the Bean Goose (Anser fabalis Lath.) as a Basis of Protection and Rational Use of the Geese in Priyeniseiskaya Siberia*]. Krasnoyarsk State Univ. (in Russian)

362. Engelis, A. (2003) Specimens of Eurasian Green-winged Teal (*Anas crecca crecca*) from the Central Valley of California. *Central Valley Bird Club Bull.* 6(2): 34–36.

363. Environnement Canada (2014) [Résultats des prises estimées]. www.ec.gc.ca/reom-mbs/default.asp?lang=Fr&n=CFB6F561-1

364. Eo, S. H., Bininda-Emonds, O. R. P. & Carroll, J. P. (2009) A phylogenetic supertree of the fowls (Galloanserae, Aves). *Zool. Scripta* 38: 465–481.

365. Erickson, J. G. (1952) A possible hybrid between the Hooded Merganser and the Red-breasted Merganser. *Wilson Bull.* 64: 167.

366. Erskine, A. J. (1971) Growth, and annual cycles in weights, plumages and reproductive organs of Goosanders in eastern Canada. *Ibis* 113: 42–58.

367. Erskine, A. J. (1972) *Buffleheads*. Canadian Wildlife Service, Ottawa.

368. Erskine, T. (2005) Bufflehead *Bucephala albeola*. Pp. 726–730 in Kear, J. (ed.) *Ducks, Geese and Swans*. Oxford Univ. Press.

369. Esler, D. & Grand, J. B. (1994) The role of nutrient reserves for clutch formation by Northern Pintails in Alaska. *Condor* 96: 422–432.

371. Ethiopian Wildlife and Natural History Society (2001) Ethiopia. Pp. 291–336 in Fishpool, L. D. C. & Evans, M. I. (eds.) *Important Bird Areas in Africa and Associated Islands: Priority Sites for Conservation*. BirdLife International, Cambridge, UK.

372. Euliss, N. H., Jarvis, R. L. & Gilmer, D. S. (1997) Relationship between waterfowl nutrition and condition on agricultural drainwater ponds in the Tulare Basin, California: waterfowl body composition. *Wetlands* 17: 106–115.

373. Evans, M. E. (1977) Recognizing individual Bewick's Swans by bill pattern. *Wildfowl* 28: 153–158.

374. Evans, M. E. & Kear, J. (1978) Weights and measurements of Bewick's Swans during winter. *Wildfowl* 29: 118–122.

375. Evans, M. E. & LeBret, T. (1973) Leucistic Bewick's Swans. *Wildfowl* 24: 61–62.

376. Evans, M. E. & Sladen, W. J. L. (1980) A comparative analysis of bill-markings of Whistling and Bewick's Swans and out-of-range occurrences of the two taxa. *Auk* 97: 697–703.

377. Evans, T. D., Robichaud, W. G. & Tizard, R. J. (1996) The White-winged Duck *Cairina scutulata* in Laos. *Wildfowl* 47: 81–96.

378. Evarts, S. (2005) Cinnamon Teal *Anas cyanoptera*. Pp. 549–553 in Kear, J. (ed.) *Ducks, Geese and Swans*. Oxford Univ. Press.

379. Farelly, W. & Charles, D. (2010) The Dresser's Eider in County Donegal – a new Western Palearctic bird. *Birding World* 23: 62–64.

380. Finn, F. (1915) *Indian Sporting Birds*. Edwards, London.

381. Fish, S. M. (1999) Genetic differences in Greater Scaup wintering in the Long Island Sound region. M.Sc. thesis. Univ. of Connecticut, Storrs.

382. Fitzner, R. E. & Gray, R. H. (1994) Winter diet and weights of Barrow's and Common goldeneye in southcentral Washington. *Northwest Sci.* 68: 172–177.

383. Fjeldså, J. (1973) Possible female hybrids between *Bucephala islandica* and *clangula*. *Bull. Brit. Orn. Club* 93: 6–9.

384. Fjeldså, J. (1986) Color variation in the Ruddy Duck (*Oxyura jamaicensis andina*). *Wilson Bull.* 98: 592–594.

385. Flint V. E. & Anzigitova N. V. (1993) On collecting a hybrid between Wigeon (*Anas penelope*) and Falcated Duck (*Anas falcata*) on the Yenesei River [*in Russian*]. *Sbornik trudov Zoologicheskogo Muzeia* 30: 212–213.

386. Flint, V. E., Boehme, R. L., Kostin, Y. V. & Kuznetsov, A. A. (1984) *A Field Guide to Birds of the USSR*. Princeton Univ. Press.

387. Fooks, H. A. (1966) Whistling Teal [*Dendrocygna javanica* (Horsfield)] and other memories of Alipore Zoo, Calcutta. *J. Bombay Nat. Hist. Soc.* 63: 200–202.

388. Forsman, D. (1995) A presumed hybrid Steller's Eider × Common Eider in Norway. *Birding World* 8: 138.

389. Fournier, M. A. & Hines, J. E. (1998) Productivity and population increase of subarctic breeding Canvasbacks. *J. Wildl. Manag.* 62: 179–184.

390. Fox, A. D. (2005) Bean Goose *Anser fabalis*. Pp. 266–270 *in* Kear, J. (ed.) *Ducks, Geese and Swans*. Oxford Univ. Press.

391. Fox, A. D. (2005) Lesser White-fronted Goose *Anser erythropus*. Pp. 286–289 *in* Kear, J. (ed.) *Ducks, Geese and Swans*. Oxford Univ. Press.

392. Fox, A. D. (2005) Gadwall *Anas strepera*. Pp. 491–494 *in* Kear, J. (ed.) *Ducks, Geese and Swans*. Oxford Univ. Press.

393. Fox, A. D. (2005) Eurasian and American Green-winged Teal *Anas crecca / Anas carolinensis*. Pp. 609–613 *in* Kear, J. (ed.) *Ducks, Geese and Swans*. Oxford Univ. Press.

394. Fox, A. D. (2005) Common Pochard *Aythya ferina*. Pp. 651–654 *in* Kear, J. (ed.) *Ducks, Geese and Swans*. Oxford Univ. Press.

395. Fox, A. D. & Owen, M. (2005) White-fronted Goose *Anser albifrons*. Pp. 281–285 *in* Kear, J. (ed.) *Ducks, Geese and Swans*. Oxford Univ. Press.

396. Fox, A. D. & Pihl, S. (2005) Common Scoter *Melanitta nigra*. Pp. 719–723 *in* Kear, J. (ed.) *Ducks, Geese and Swans*. Oxford Univ. Press.

397. Fox, A. D. & Stroud, D. A. (2002) The Greenland White-fronted Goose *Anser albifrons flavirostris*. *BWP Update* 4: 65–88.

398. Fox, A. D., Gladhder, C., Mitchell, C. R., Stroud, D. A., Boyd, H. & Frikke, J. (1996) North American Canada Geese (*Branta canadensis*) in west Greenland. *Auk* 113: 231–233.

399. Fox, A. D., Christensen, T. K., Bearhop, S. & Newton, J. (2007) Using stable isotope analysis of multiple feather tracts to identify moulting provenance of vagrant birds: a case study of Baikal Teal *Anas formosa* in Denmark. *Ibis* 149: 622–625.

400. Fox, A. D., Ebbinge, B. S., Mitchell, C., Heinicke, T., Aarvak, T., Colhoun, K., Clausen, P., Dereliev, S., Faragao, S., Koffijberg, K., Kruckenberg, H., Loonen, M. J. J. E., Madsen, J., Mooij, J., Musil, P., Nilsson, L., Pihl, S. & van der Jeugd, H. (2010) Current estimates of goose population sizes in estern Europe, a gap analysis and an assessment of trends. *Ornis Svecica* 20: 115–127

401. Fox, A. D., Francis, I. S. & Walsh, A. J. (2011) Report of the 2010/2011 international census of Greenland White-fronted Geese. Greeland White-fronted Geese Study and National Parks and Wildlife Service.

402. Fox, A. D., Lei, C., Barter, M., Rees, E. C., Hearn, R. D., Hao, C. P., Xin, W., Yong, Z., Tao, D. S. & Fang, S. X. (2013) The functional use of East Dongting Lake, China, by wintering geese. *Wildfowl* 58: 3–19.

403. Frade, F. & Pinho, M. (1971) A brief note on breeding the Spur-winged Goose and on hybridisation between the Spur-winged Goose and the Egyptian Goose at Lisbon Zoo. *Intern. Zoo Yearbook* 11: 133.

404. Fredrickson, L. H. (2001) Steller's Eider *Polysticta stelleri*. *In* Poole, A. (ed.) The Birds of North America Online. Cornell Lab of Ornithology, Ithaca, NY. http://bna.birds.cornell.edu/bna/species/571

405. Friedmann, H. (1947) Geographic variations of the Black-bellied, Fulvous, and White-faced Tree-Ducks. *Condor* 49: 189–195.

406. Friedmann, H. (1948) The Green-winged Teals of the Aleutian Islands. *Proc. Biol. Soc.Wash.* 61: 157–158.

407. Fritsch, A. (1905) Über einen vermutlichen Enten-Säger Bastard. *Orn. Jahrb.* 16: 143.

408. Fullagar, P. (2005) Spot-billed Duck *Anas poecilorhyncha*. Pp. 538–540 *in* Kear, J. (ed.) *Ducks, Geese and Swans*. Oxford Univ. Press.

409. Fullagar, P. (2005) Cotton Teal (Cotton Pygmy-goose) *Nettapus coromandelianus*. Pp. 475–477 *in* Kear, J. (ed.) *Ducks, Geese and Swans*. Oxford Univ. Press.

410. Fullagar, P. (2005) Pacific Black Duck (Grey Duck) *Anas superciliosa*. Pp. 533–538 *in* Kear, J. (ed.) *Ducks, Geese and Swans*. Oxford Univ. Press.

411. Fuller, E. (2001) *Extinct Birds*. Revised edn. Comstock Publishing, Ithaca, NY.

412. Gale, R. S., Garton, E. O. & Ball, I. J. (1987) *The History, Ecology, and Management of the Rocky Mountain Population of Trumpeter Swans*. US Fish & Wildlife Service, Montana Cooperative Wildlife Research Unit, Missoula, MT.

413. Gammonley, J. H. (2012) Cinnamon Teal *Anas cyanoptera*. *In* Poole, A. (ed.) The Birds of North America Online. Cornell Lab of Ornithology, Ithaca, NY. http://bna.birds.cornell.edu/bna/species/209

414. Gantlett, S. J. M. (1985) Hybrid resembling Ring-necked Duck. *Brit. Birds* 78: 42–43.

415. Gantlett, S. J. M. (1989) Hybrid bird resembling Baikal Teal in Norfolk. *Birding World* 1: 426–427.

416. Gantlett, S. (1993) The status and separation of White-headed Duck and Ruddy Duck. *Birding World* 6: 273–281.

417. Gantlett S., Harrap, S. & Millington, R. (1996) Taxonomic progress. *Birding World* 9: 251–252.

418. Garner, M. (1989) Common Scoter of the nominate race with extensive yellow on bill. *Brit. Birds* 82: 616–618.

419. Garner, M. (1998) Brent crosses. *Birdwatch* 78: 29–32.

420. Garner, M. (1999) Identification of Common Merganser. *Birding World* 12: 31–33.

421. Garner, M. (1999) Identification of White-winged and Velvet Scoters – males, females and immatures. *Birding World* 12: 319–324.

422. Garner, M. (2002) Identification extra: Lesser Scaup – the underwing. *Birding World* 15: 506–508.

423. Garner, M. (2010) http://birdingfrontiers.com/2010/11/23/bean-goose-salton-sea-part-2

424. Garner, M. (2013) Baikal Teal at Southport: first winter or adult male? http://birdingfrontiers.com/2013/12/07/baikal-teal-at-southport-first-winter-or-adult-male/

425. Garner, M. & Millington, R. (2001) Grey-bellied Brent and the Dundrum conundrum. *Birding World* 14: 151–155.

426. Garner, M. & Millington, R. (2010) The forms of Common Eider: their identification, taxonomy and vagrancy. *Birding World* 23: 65–82.

427. Garner, M. & friends [*et al.*] (2008) *Frontiers in Birding.* BirdGuides Ltd., Sheffield, UK.

428. Garner, M., Lewington, I. & Rosenberg, G. (2004) Stejneger's Scoter in the Western Palearctic and North America. *Birding World* 17: 337–347.

429. Gauthier, G. (1993) Bufflehead *Bucephala clangula. In* Poole, A. (ed.) The Birds of North America Online. Cornell Lab of Ornithology, Ithaca, NY. http://bna.birds.cornell.edu/bna/species/067

430. Gavin, A. (1947) Birds of the Perry River District, Northwest Territories. *Wilson Bull.* 59: 195–203.

431. Geldenhuys, J. N. (1975) Waterfowl (Anatidae) on irrigation lakes in the Orange Free States. *Ostrich 46: 219–235.*

432. Gendron, M. H. & Smith, A. C. (2013) *Site web de l'Enquête nationale sur les prises. Surveillance des populations d'oiseaux. Centre national de la recherche faunique, Service canadien de la faune, Ottawa.*

433. Gerasimov, N. N. & Gerasimov, Y. N. (1995) Present status and perspectives for protection of geese in Kamchatka. *Goose Study* 9: 10–14.

434. Gibson, D. D. (2002) Correct type locality of the Emperor Goose (*Chen canagica*). *Proc. Biol. Soc. Wash.* 115: 706–707.

435. Gibson, D. D. & Byrd, G. V. (1973) Alaska region. *Amer. Birds* 27: 807–809.

437. Gill, F. & Donsker, D. (eds.) (2014) IOC World Bird List v. 4.1. http://www.worldbirdnames.org/

438. Gillham, E. 1987. *Tufted Ducks in a Royal Park.* Privately published.

439. Gillham, E. & Gillham, B. (1996) *Hybrid Ducks, a Contribution Towards an Inventory.* Privately published.

440. Gillham, E. & Gillham, B. (1998) *Updating – Hybrid Ducks, a Contribution Towards an Inventory.* Privately published, Lydd on Sea.

441. Gillham, E. & Gillham, B. (1999) *Updating – Hybrid Ducks, a Contribution Towards an Inventory.* Privately published, Lydd on Sea.

442. Gillham, E. & Gillham, B. (2000) *Updating – Hybrid Ducks, a Contribution Towards an Inventory.* Privately published, Lydd on Sea.

443. Gillham, E. & Gillham, B. (2002) *Hybrid Ducks, the 5th Contribution Towards an Inventory.* Privately published, Lydd on Sea.

444. Gillham, E. & Gillham, B. (2003) PhotoForum: Identification of hybrid ducks. *Birding World* 16: 58–68.

445. Gillissen, N., Haanstra, L., Delany, S., Boere, G. & Hagemeijer, W. (2002) *Numbers and Distribution of Wintering Waterbirds in the Western Palearctic and Southwest Asia in 1997, 1998 and 1999. Results from the International Waterbird Census.* Wetlands International, Wageningen.

446. Gillson G. (2004) Eurasian and American Green-winged Teal and hybrids: an identification challenge. http://thebirdguide.com/identification/Eurasian_Teal/teal_hybrid.htm

447. Ginn, H. B. & Melville, D. S. (1983) *Moult in Birds.* British Trust for Ornithology, Tring.

448. Girard, O. (2005) Garganey *Anas querquedula.* Pp. 601–605 in Kear, J. (ed.) *Ducks, Geese and Swans.* Oxford Univ. Press.

449. Click, B. (1983) Bursa of Fabricius. *Avian Biol.* 7: 443–500.

450. Gochfeld, M. & Tudor, G. (1976) An apparent hybrid goldeneye from Maine. *Wilson Bull.* 88: 348–349.

451. Godfrey, W. E. & Crosby, J. A. (1986) *The Birds of Canada.* National Museum of Natural Sciences, Montreal.

452. Gombobaatar, S., Tseveenmyadag, N. & Nyambayar, B. (2003) Current status of research and future trends of Swan Goose *Anser cygnoides* and Baikal Teal *Anas formosa* in Mongolia. *2003 Intern. Anatidae Symp. East Asia & Siberia Region, Seosan, Korea*: 79–82.

453. Gómez-Dallmeier, F. & Cringan, A. (1990) *Biology, Conservation and Management of Waterfowl in Venezuela.* Ed. Ex Libris, Caracas.

454. González, J., Düttmann, H. & Wink, M. (2009) Phylogenetic relationships based on two mitochondrial genes and hybridization patterns in Anatidae. *J. Zool.* 279: 310–318.

455. Goroshko, O. A. (2001) Swan Goose in the eastern Transbaikalia and Mongolia. *Casarca* 7: 68–98. (In Russian with English summary)

456. Goroshko, O. A. (2003) Swan Geese on Torey Lakes, Transbaikalia, in 2002. *Casarca* 9: 96–99. (In Russian with English summary)

457. Gosselin, M. (1979) Notes sur l'observation d'un oiseau du genre *Aythya. Bull. Orn. (Quebec)* 24: 40–41.

458. Gotfredson, A. B. (2002) Former occurrence of geese (genera *Anser* and *Branta*) in ancient west Greenland: morphological and biometric issues. *Acta Zool. Cracoviensa* 45: 179–204.

459. Götmark, F. (1989) Costs and benefits to Eiders nesting in gull colonies: a field experiment. *Ornis Scand.* 20: 283–288.

460. Goudie, R. I. (1984) Comparative ecology of Common Eiders, Black Scoters, Oldsquaws, and Harlequin Ducks wintering in southeastern Newfoundland. M.Sc. thesis. Univ. of Western Ontario, London.

461. Goudie, R. I., Brault, S., Conant, B., Kondratyev, A. V. & Petersen, M. R. (1994) *The Status of Sea Ducks in the North Pacific Rim: Toward Their Conservation and Management.* Canadian Wildlife Service, Delta, BC.

462. Goudie, R. I., Brault, S., Conant, B., Kondratyev, A. V., Petersen, M. R. & Vermeer, K. (1994) The status of sea ducks in the north Pacific rim: toward their conservation and management. *Trans. 59th North Amer. Wildl. Nat. Res. Conf.*

463. Goudie, R. I., Robertson, G. J. & Reed, A. (2000) Common Eider (*Somateria mollissima*) *In* A. Poole, & Gill, F. (eds.) The Birds of North America, no. 546. Academy of Natural Sciences, Philadelphia, PA.

464. Graham, R. S., Schulte, P. M., Egginton, S., Scott, A. L. M., Richards, J. G. & Milsom, W. K (2011) Molecular evolution of cytochrome c oxidase underlies high-altitude adaptation in the Bar-Headed Goose. *Mol. Biol. & Evol.* 28: 351–363.

465. Gray, A. P. (1958) *Bird Hybrids. A Check-list with Bibliography.* Commonwealth Agricultural Bureaux, Farnham.

466. Gray, G. R. (1841) *A List of the Genera of Birds.* R. & J. E. Taylor (eds.), London.

467. Gray, P. N. (1993) Biology of the southern Mallard, Florida's Mottled Duck. Ph.D thesis. Univ. of Florida, Gainesville.

468. Green, A. J. (1992) An action plan for the White-winged Wood Duck. *CBSG News* 3: 25–26.

469. Green, A. J. (1992) Conservation plan for the White-winged Wood Duck. *Threatened Waterfowl Res. Group Newsl.* 2: 3–4.

470. Green, A. J. (1992) *The Status and Conservation of the White-winged Wood Duck Cairina scutulata*. International Wetlands Research Bureau, Slimbridge.

471. Green, A. J. (1993) An action plan for the White-winged Wood Duck. *Oryx* 27: 3–5.

472. Green, A. J. (1993) The biology of the White-winged Duck *Cairina scutulata*. *Forktail* 8: 65–82.

473. Green, A. J. (1993) The status and habitat of the White-winged Duck *Cairina scutulata*. *Bird Conserv. Intern.* 3: 119–143.

474. Green, A. J. (1997) Brood attendance and brood care in the Marbled Teal, *Marmaronetta angustirostris*. *J. Orn.* 138: 443–449.

475. Green, A. J. (1998) Clutch size, brood size and brood emergence in the Marbled Teal *Marmaronetta angustirostris* in the Marismas del Guadalquivir, southwestern Spain. *Ibis* 140: 670–675.

476. Green, A. J. (2000) Sexual dimorphism in morphometry and allometry in the Marbled Teal *Marmaronetta angustirostris*. *J. Avian Biol.* 31: 345–350.

477. Green, A. J. (2000) The scaling and selection of sexually dimorphic characters: an example using the Marbled Teal. *J. Avian Biol.* 31: 345–350.

478. Green, A. J. (2001) The habitat requirements of the Marbled Teal *Marmaronetta angustirostris*, Ménétr., a review. Pp. 131–140 *in* Comín, F. A., Herrera, J. A. & Ramírez, J. (eds.) *Limnology and Aquatic Birds: Monitoring, Modelling and Management*. Univ. Autónoma del Yucatán, Mérida.

479. Green, A. J. (2005) Marbled Duck *Marmaronetta angustirostris*. Pp. 625–628 *in* Kear, J. (ed.) *Ducks, Geese and Swans*. Oxford Univ. Press.

480. Green, A. J. & Anstey, S. (1992) The status of the White-headed Duck *Oxyura leucocephala*. *Bird Conserv. Intern.* 2: 185–200.

481. Green, A. J. & Hunter, J. (1996) Declining White-headed Duck: a call for information. *Threatened Waterfowl Research Group News* 9: 19–21.

482. Green, A. J. & Hughes, B. (1996) *Action Plan for the White-headed duck (Oxyura leucocephala) in Europe*. BirdLife International, Cambridge, UK.

483. Green, A. J. & Hughes, B. (2001) *Oxyura leucocephala* White-headed Duck. *BWP Update* 3: 79–90.

484. Green, A. J., Hamzaoui, M. E., El Agbani, M. A. & Franchimont, J. (2002) The conservation status of Moroccan wetlands with particular reference to waterbirds and to changes since 1978. *Biol. Conserv.* 104: 71–82.

485. Green, A. J., Hughes, B. & Callaghan, D. (2005) White-winged Duck *Asarcornis scutulata*. Pp. 455–459 *in* Kear, J. (ed.) *Ducks, Geese and Swans*. Oxford Univ. Press.

486. Green, A. J., Callaghan, D. A. & Hughes, B. (in prep.) Taxonomic status of the White-winged Duck *Cairina scutulata*.

487. Greenway, J. C. (1967) Washington Island Gadwall. Pp. 171–172 *in Extinct and Vanishing Birds of the World*. Second edn. Dover Publications, New York.

488. Greenwood, P. J. (1980) Mating systems, philopatry, and dispersal in birds and mammals. *Anim. Behav.* 28: 1140–1162.

489. Grieb, J. R. (1970) The Shortgrass Prairie Canada Goose population. *Wildl. Monogr.* 22.

490. Grimmett, R., Inskipp, C. & Inskipp, T. (1999) *Pocket Guide to the Birds of the Indian Subcontinent*. Christopher Helm, London.

491. Größler, K. (1972) *Mergus serrator schioeleri*. *J. Orn.* 113: 111.

492. Groupe conjoint de travail sur la gestion de l'Eider à duvet (2004) *Plan Québequois de gestion de l'Eider à duvet Somateria mollissima dresseri*. Groupe conjoint de travail sur la gestion de l'Eider à duvet, Quebec, 44 p.

493. Gudmundsson, E. (1932) Beobachtungen an Isländischen Eiderenten (*Somateria m. mollissima*). *Beiträge zur Fortpflanzungs-biologie der Vögel mit Berücksichtigung der Oologie* 8: 85–93, 142–147.

494. Gustavsson, C. G. (2010) Coloured tail-coverts in *Anser × Branta* goose hybrids despite all-white coverts in both parent species. *Ornis Svecica* 20: 67–75.

495. Gyimesi, A. & Lensink, R. (2012) Egyptian Goose *Alopochen aegyptiaca*: an introduced species spreading in and from the Netherlands. *Wildfowl* 62: 128–145.

496. Hachisuka, M. (1928) *Variations Among Birds, Chiefly Game Birds: Heterochrosis, Gynandromorphs, Aberration, Mutation, Atavism and Hybrids*. Ornithological Society of Japan, Tokyo.

497. Haldane, J. B. S. (1922) Sex ratio and unisexual sterility in hybrid animals. *J. Genetics* 12: 101–109.

498. Hall, C., Glanville, J., Boland, H., Einarsson, Ó., McElwaine, G., Holt, C. A., Spray, C. J. & Rees, E. C. (2012) Population size and breeding success of Icelandic Whooper Swans *Cygnus cygnus*: results of the 2010 international census. *Wildfowl* 62: 73–96.

499. Hanby, A. M. (1986) Bewick's Swan with yellow legs. *Brit. Birds* 79: 206.

500. Handley, C. O. (1950) The Brant of Prince Patrick Island, Northwest Territories. *Wilson Bull.* 62: 128–132.

501. Hansen, H. A., Shepard, P. E. K., King, J. G. & Troyer, W. A. (1971) The Trumpeter Swan in Alaska. *Wildl. Monogr.* 26: 1–83.

502. Hansen, K. (2002) *A Farewell to Greenland's Wildlife*. Baere Dygtighed & Gads Forlag, Copenhagen.

503. Hansen, H. A. & Nelson, H. K. (1964) *Honkers Large and Small. Waterfowl Tmorrow*. US Government Printing Office, Washington DC.

505. Hanson, A. R. & Ankney, C. D. (1994) Morphometric similarity of Mallards and American black ducks. *Canadian J. Zool.* 72: 2248–2251.

506. Hanson, H. C. (1951) A morphometrical study of the Canada goose, *Branta canadensis interior* Todd. *Auk*, 164–173.

507. Hanson, H. C. (1997) *The Giant Canada Goose*. Rev. edn. Southern Illinois Univ. Press, Carbondale.

508. Hanson, H. C. (2006) *The White-cheeked Geese: Taxonomy, Ecophysiographic Relationships, Biogeography and Evolutionary Considerations*. Vol. 1. Avvar Books, Blythe, CA.

509. Hanson, H. C. (2007) *The White-cheeked Geese: Taxonomy, Ecophysiographic Relationships, Biogeography and Evolutionary Considerations*. Vol. 2. Avvar Books, Blythe, CA.

511. Hanssen, S. A., Folstad, I. & Erikstad, K. E. (2006) White plumage reflects individual quality in female eiders. *Anim. Behav.* 71: 337–343.

512. Hanssen, S. A., Hasselquist, D., Folstad, I. & Erikstad, K. E. (2008) A label of health: a previous immune challenge is reflected in the expression of a female plumage trait. *Biol. Lett.* 4: 379–381.

513. Haramis, G. M. (1982) Records of Redhead × Canvasback hybrids. *Wilson Bull.* 94: 599–602.

514. Hario, M. & Rintala, J. (2011) Population trends of the archipelago birds along the Finnish coasts during 1986–2010. *Linnut* 2010: 40–51.

515. Hario, M., Rintala, J. & Nordenswan, G. (2009) Dynamics of wintering long-tailed ducks in the Baltic Sea and the connection with lemming cycles, oil disasters, and hunting. *Suomen Riista* 55: 83–96.

516. Harrigal, D. & Cely, J. E. (2004) Black-bellied Whistling-ducks nest in South Carolina. *The Chat* 68: 106–108.

517. Harrison, J. M. (1959) Comments on a Wigeon × Northern Shoveler hybrid. *Bull. Brit. Orn. Club* 79: 142–151.

518. Harrison, J. M. (1964) Further comments on hybridisation between the European Wigeon and Northern Shoveler. *Bull. Brit. Orn. Club* 84: 30–39.

519. Harrison, J. M. & Harrison, J. G. (1960) On varieties of the Tufted Duck, with an account of an unrecorded type of variation. *Bull. Brit. Orn. Club* 80: 25–28.

520. Harrison, J. M. & Harrison, J. G. (1961) Variant winter plumage of the female Tufted Duck. *Bull. Brit. Orn. Club* 81: 103–105.

521. Harrison, J. M. & Harrison, J. G. (1962) Variant winter plumage in the Scaup. *Bull. Brit. Orn. Club* 82: 43.

522. Harrison, J. M. & Harrison, J. G. (1965) A Cinnamon Teal × Northern Shoveler hybrid. *Bull. Brit. Orn. Club* 85: 107–110.

523. Harrison, J. M. & Harrison, J. G. (1968) Wigeon × Chiloe Wigeon hybrid resembling American Wigeon. *Brit. Birds* 61: 169–171.

524. Harrison, J. M. & Harrison, J. G. (1968) Some wild-shot duck hybrids from the Indian subcontinent. *J. Bombay Nat. Hist. Soc.* 65: 670–676.

525. Harrison, J. M. & Harrison, J. G. (1969) Comments on a wildshot Pintail × Teal hybrid. *Bull. Brit. Orn. Club* 89: 100–103.

526. Harrison, J. M. & Harrison, J. G. (1971) Notes on a further Pintail × Teal hybrid. *Bull. Brit. Orn. Club* 91: 28–32.

527. Harrison, X. A., Dawson, D. A., Horsburgh, G. J., Tregenza, T. & Bearhop, S. (2010) Isolation, characterisation and predicted genome locations of Light-bellied Brent goose (*Branta bernicla hrota*) microsatellite loci (Anatidae, Aves). *Conserv. Genetics* 2: 365–371.

528. Harrop, A. H. J. (1993) Presumed Red-crested Pochard × Northern Pintail hybrid. *Brit. Birds* 86: 130–131.

529. Harrop, A. H. J. (1994) Field identification of American Wigeon. *Birding World* 7: 50–56.

530. Harrop, A. H. J. (1994) Photo-forum: a presumed hybrid American Wigeon in Grampian. *Birding World* 7: 116–117

531. Harrop, A. H. J. (1998) Successful hybridisation between Ruddy Shelduck and Egyptian Goose. *Brit. Birds* 91: 281–282.

532. Harrop, A. H. J. (2002) The Ruddy Shelduck in Britain: a review. *Brit. Birds* 95: 125–128.

533. Harrop, A. H. J. & McGowan, R. Y. (2009) Britain's first Baikal Teal. *Brit. Birds* 102: 691–696.

534. Harshman, J. (1996) Phylogeny, evolutionary rates, and ducks. Ph.D. thesis. Univ. of Chicago.

535. **Hartlaub, G. (1852) Descriptions de quelques nouvelles espèces d'oiseaux.** *Rev. Mag. Zool.* (2)4: 1–7.

536. Harvey, N. G. (1999) A hierarchical genetic analysis of swan relationships. Ph.D. thesis. Univ. of Nottingham.

537. Hatch, S. A. & Hatch, M. A. (1983) An isolated population of small Canada Geese on Kaliktagik Island, Alaska. *Wildfowl* 34: 130–136.

538. Hawkes, L. A., Balachandran, S., Batbayar, N., Butler, P. J., Chua, B., Douglas, D. C., Frappell, P. B., Hou, Y., Milsom, W. K., Newman, S. H., Prosser, D. J., Sathiyaselvam, P., Scott, G. R., Takekawa, J. Y., Natsagdorj, T., Wikelski, M., Witt, M. J., Yan, B. & Bishop, C. M. (2012) The paradox of extreme high-altitude migration in Bar-headed geese *Anser indicus*. *Proc. Roy. Soc. B: Biol. Sci.* 280: 1750.

539. Hawkes, L. A., Balachandran, S., Batbayar, N., Butler, P. J., Frappell, P. B., Milsom, W. K., Tseveenmyadag, N., Newman, S. H. & Scott, G. R. (2011) The trans-Himalayan flights of Bar-headed Geese (*Anser indicus*). *Proc. Natl. Acad. Sci. USA* 108: 9516.

540. Hawkins, G. (2011) Molts and plumages of ducks (Anatinae); an evaluation of Pyle (2005). *Waterbirds* 34: 481–494.

541. Hayashi, T. (1982) Bill patterns of Whistling Swans *Cygnus columbianus jankowskyi* wintering at Lake Suwa. *Tori* 31: 1–16.

542. He, F. Q., Melville, D., Gui, X. J., Hong, Y. H. & Liu, Z. Y. (2002) Status of the Scaly-sided Merganser wintering in mainland China in the 1990s. *Waterbirds* 25: 462–464.

543. Hefti-Gautschi, B., Pfunder, M., Jenni, L., Keller, V. & Ellegren, H. (2009) Identification of conservation units in the European *Mergus merganser* based on nuclear and mitochondrial DNA markers. *Conserv. Genetics* 10: 87–99.

544. Heinicke, T. (2009) Status of the Bean Goose *Anser fabalis* wintering in central Asia. *Wildfowl* 59: 77–99.

545. Heinicke, T., Yakushev, N. N. & Syroechkovski, E. E. (2009) The importance of the Kanchalan River, Chukotka, Russia, for the Lesser White-fronted Goose *Anser erythropus*. *Wildfowl* 59: 124–134.

546. Heinzel, H., Fitter, R. & Parslow, J. (1995) *Birds of Britain and Europe with North Africa and the Middle East.* Collins, London.

547. Heitmeyer, M. E. (1987) The prebasic moult and basic plumage of female Mallards (*Anas platyrhynchos*) *Canadian J. Zool.* 65: 2248–2261.

548. Helbig, A. J., Knox, A. G., Parkin, D. T., Sangster, G. & Collinson, M. (2002) Guidelines for assigning species rank. *Ibis* 144: 518–525.

549. Hellmayr, C. E. & Conover, B. (1948) Catalogue of birds of the Americas and the adjacent islands, pt. 1(2). *Publ. Field Mus. Nat. Hist. Zool. Ser.* 13(1).

550. Henderson, I. (2010) The eradication of ruddy ducks in the United Kingdom. *Aliens* 29: 17–24.

551. Henny, C. J., Carter, J. L. & Carter, B. J. (1981) A review of Bufflehead sex and age criteria with notes on weights. *Wildfowl* 32: 117–122.

552. Hepp, G. R. & Hair, J. D. (1983) Reproductive behavior and pairing chronology in wintering dabbling ducks. *Wilson Bull.* 95: 675–682.

553. Hepp, G. R. & Hines, J. E. (1991) Factors affecting winter distribution and migration distance of Wood Ducks from southern breeding populations. *Condor* 93: 884–891.

554. Hepp, G. R., Novak, J. M., Scribner, K. T. & Stangel, P. W. (1988) Genetic distance and hybridization of black ducks and mallards: a morph of a different color? *Auk* 105: 804–807.

555. Hepp, H. R. & Bellrose, F. C. (2013) Wood Duck (*Aix sponsa*). *In* Poole, A. (ed.) The Birds of North America Online. Cornell Lab of Ornithology, Ithaca, NY. http://bna.birds.cornell.edu/bna/species/169

556. Heusmann, H. W. (1974) Mallard–Black Duck relationships in the northeast. *Wildl. Soc. Bull.* 2: 171–177.

557. Hier, R. H. (1989) Fall weights of Redheads and Ring-necked Ducks in northern Minnesota. *Prairie Nat.* 21: 229–233.

558. Hillgarth, N. & Kear, J. (1982) Causes of mortality among whistling ducks in captivity. *Wildfowl* 33: 133–139.

559. Hines, J. E., Dickson, D. L., Turner, B. C., Wiebe, M. O., Barry, S. J., Barry, T. A., Kerbes, R. H., Nieman, D. J., Ray, M. F., Fournier, M. A. & Cotter, R. C. (2000) Population status, distribution, and survival of Shortgrass Prairie Canada Geese from Inuvialuit settlement region, western Canadian Arctic. *In* Dickson, K. M. (ed.) *Towards Conservation of the Diversity of Canada Geese (Branta canadensis).* Canadian Wildl. Serv. Occ. Pap. 103.

560. Hipes, D. L. & Hepp, G. R. (1995) Nutrient-reserve dynamics of breeding male Wood Ducks. *Condor* 97: 451–460.

561. Hobson, K. A., Brua, R. B., Hohman, W. L. & Wassenaar, L. I. (2000) Low frequency of "double molt" of remiges in Ruddy Ducks revealed by stable isotopes: implications for tracking migratory waterfowl. *Auk* 117: 129–135.

562. Hochbaum, H. A. (1942) Sex and age determination of waterfowl by cloacal examination. *Trans. North Amer. Wildl. Conf.* 7: 299–307.

563. Hochbaum, H. A. (1955) *Travels and Traditions of Waterfowl.* Univ. of Minnesota Press, Minneapolis.

564. Hoff, H.-J. & Eggert, B. (1995) Hybrid Scheckente × Eiderente *Polysticta stelleri × Somateria mollissima. Limicola* 9: 85.

565. Hoffman, W. & Bancroft, G. T. (1984) Molt in vagrant Black Scoters wintering in peninsular Florida. *Wilson Bull.* 96: 499–504.

566. Hoffman, W. & Elliott, W. P. (1974) Occurrence of intergrade Brant in Oregon. *Western Birds* 5: 91–93.

567. Hoffmann, E. (2005) Muscovy Duck *Cairina moschata.* Pp. 453–455 *in* Kear, J. (ed.) *Ducks, Geese and Swans.* Oxford Univ. Press.

568. Hogan, D., Thompson, J. E., Esler, D. & Boyd, W. S. (2011) Discovery of important postbreeding sites for Barrow's Goldeneye in the boreal transition zone of Alberta. *Waterbirds* 34: 261–288.

569. Hohman, W. L. (1984) Aspects of the breeding biology of Ring-necked Ducks (*Aythya collaris*). Ph.D. thesis. Univ. of Minnesota, St. Paul.

570. Hohman, W. L. (1986) Changes in body weight and composition of breeding Ring-necked Ducks (*Aythya collaris*). *Auk* 103: 181–188.

571. Hohman, W. L. (1993) Body composition dynamics of Ruddy Ducks during wing moult. *Canadian J. Zool.* 71: 2224–2228.

572. Hohman, W. L. (1996) Prevalence of double wing molt in free-living Ruddy Ducks. *Southwestern Natur.* 41: 195–198.

573. Hohman, W. L. (2005) Canvasback *Aythya valisineria.* Pp. 639–643 *in* Kear, J. (ed.) *Ducks, Geese and Swans.* Oxford Univ. Press.

574. Hohman, W. L. (2005) Ring-necked Duck *Aythya collaris.* Pp. 667–671 *in* Kear, J. (ed.) *Ducks, Geese and Swans.* Oxford Univ. Press.

575. Hohman, W. L. & Crawford, R. D. (1995) Molt in the annual cycle of Ring-necked Ducks. *Condor* 97: 473–483.

576. Hohman, W. L. & Cypher, B. L. (1986) Age-class determination of Ring-necked Ducks. *J. Wildl. Manag.* 50: 442–445.

577. Hohman, W. L. & Lee, S. A. (2001) Fulvous Whistling-duck (*Dendrocygna bicolor*). *In* Poole, A. (ed.) The Birds of North America Online. Cornell Lab of Ornithology, Ithaca, NY. http://bna.birds.cornell.edu/bna/species/562

578. Hohman, W. L., Ankney, C. D. & Roster, D. L. (1992) Body condition, food habits, and molt status of late-wintering Ruddy Ducks in California. *Southwestern Natur.* 37: 267–273.

579. Holmes, D. A. (1977) A report on the White-winged Wood Duck in southern Sumatra. *Wildfowl* 28: 61–64.

580. Holt, C. A., Austin, G. E., Calbrade, N. A., Mellan, H. J., Mitchell, C., Stroud, D. A., Wotton, S. R. & Musgrove, A. J. (2011) *Waterbirds in the UK 2009/10: The Wetland Bird Survey.* British Trust for Ornithology/Royal Society for the Protection of Birds/Joint Nature Conservation Committee, Thetford.

581. Hoogerwerf, A. (1950) De Witvlengeleend, *Cairina scutulata,* van de Grote Soenda eilanden. *Ardea* 38: 64–69.

582. Hopkinson, E. (1926) *Records of Birds Bred in Captivity.* H. F. & G. Witherby, London.

584. Hopkinson, E. (1933) Additions to breeding records: some corrections. *Avicult. Mag.* (4)11: 396–397.

585. Hopkinson, E. (1933) More additions to breeding records. *Avicult. Mag.* (4)11: 42–52, 79–85, 99–106, 131–137.

586. Hopkinson, E. (1934) More additions to breeding records. *Avicult. Mag.* (4)12: 310–324.

587. Hopkinson, E. (1935) Duck hybrids. *Avicult. Mag.* (4)13: 78–86.

588. Hopkinson, E. (1935) Duck-breeding records. Summary of records to date (August 1935) *Avicult. Mag.* (4)13: 173–176.

589. Howell, M. D., Grand, J. B. & Flint, P. L. (2003) Body molt of male Long-tailed Ducks in the near-shore waters of the north slope, Alaska. *Wilson Bull.* 115: 170–175.

590. Howell, S. N. G. (2010) *Molt in North American Birds.* Houghton Mifflin, New York.

591. Howell, S. N. G. & Corben, C. (2000) Molt cycles and sequences in the Western Gull. *Western Birds* 31: 38–49.

592. Howell, S. N. G. & Webb, S. (1995) *A Guide to the Birds of Mexico and Northern Central America.* Oxford Univ. Press, New York.

593. Howell, S. N. G., Corben, C., Pyle, P. & Rogers, D. I. (2003) The first basic problem: a review of molt and plumage homologies. *Condor* 105: 635–653.

594. Howell, S. N. G., Corben, C., Pyle, P. & Rogers, D. I. (2004) The first basic problem revisited: reply to commentaries on Howell *et al.* (2003) *Condor,* 106: 206–210.

595. Howell, T. R. (1959) A hybrid of the Pintail and Green-winged Teal. *Condor* 61: 226–227.

596. Huang, Z., Yang, C. & Ke, D. (2014) DNA barcoding and phylogenetic relationships in Anatidae. *Mitochondrial DNA* 0: 1–3.

597. Hubbard, J. P. (1977) The biological and taxonomic status of the Mexican Duck. *Bull. New Mexico Dept. Fish & Game* 16: 1–56.

598. Huey, W. S. (1961) Comparison of female Mallard with female New Mexican Duck. *Auk* 78: 428–431.

599. Hughes, B. (1996) The Ruddy Duck *Oxyura jamaicensis* in Europe and the threat to the White-headed Duck *Oxyura leucocephala. Oxyura* 8: 51–64.

600. Hughes, B. (2005) Masked Duck *Nomonyx dominicus.* Pp. 348–351 *in* Kear, J. (ed.) *Ducks, Geese and Swans.* Oxford Univ. Press.

601. Hughes, B. (2005) Scaly-sided Merganser *Mergus squamatus.*

Pp. 759–763 *in* Kear, J. (ed.) *Ducks, Geese and Swans.* Oxford Univ. Press.

602. Hugues B. (2005) Ruddy Duck. Pp. 351–355 *in* Kear, J. (ed.) *Ducks, Geese and Swans.* Oxford Univ. Press.

603. Hughes, B. & Bocharnikov, V. N. (1992) Status of the Scaly-sided Merganser *Mergus squamatus* in the Far East of Russia. *Wildfowl* 43: 193–199.

604. Hughes, B., Criado, J., Delany, S., Gallo-Orsi, U., Green, A. J., Grussu, M., Perennou, C. & Torres, J. A. (1999) *The Status of the North American Ruddy Duck Oxyura jamaicensis in the Western Palearctic: Towards an Action Plan for Eradication.* Council of Europe Publishing, Strasbourg.

605. Hughes, B. & Green, A. J. (2005) White-headed Duck. Pp. 364–369 *in* Kear, J. (ed.) *Ducks, Geese and Swans.* Oxford Univ. Press.

606. Hughes, B. & Green, A. J. (2005) Ruddy Shelduck. Pp. 426–429 *in* Kear, J. (ed.) *Ducks, Geese and Swans.* Oxford Univ. Press.

607. Hughes, B., Henderson, I. & Robertson, P. (2006) Conservation of the globally threatened white-headed duck, *Oxyura leucocephala*, in the face of hybridization with the North American ruddy duck, *Oxyura jamaicensis*: results of a control trial. *Acta Zoologica Sinica* 52: 576–578.

608. Hughes, B., Robinson, J. A., Green, A. J., Li, Z. W. D. & Mundkur, T. (2006) *International Single Species Action Plan for the Conservation of the White-headed Duck, Oxyura leucocephala.* AEWA Tech. Ser. no. 8. African-Eurasian Migratory Waterbird Agreement, Bonn.

609. Hughes, B. & Yurlov A. K. (2006) *International Single Species Action Plan for the Conservation of the White-headed Duck, Oxyura leucocephala.* UNEP/CMS Secretariat, Bonn.

610. Humphrey, P. S. & Parkes, K. C. (1959) An approach to the study of molts and plumages. *Auk* 76: 1–31.

611. Humphrey, P. S. & Parkes, K. C. (1963) Comments on the study of plumage succession. *Auk* 80: 496–503.

612. Hunter, J. (2005) Red-breasted Goose *Branta ruficollis.* Pp. 335–338 *in* Kear, J. (ed.) *Ducks, Geese and Swans.* Oxford Univ. Press.

613. Hunter, J. M. & Black, J. M. (1996) International Action Plan for the Red-breasted Goose (*Branta ruficollis*). Pp. 79–98 *in* Heredia, B., Rose, L. & Painter, M. (eds.) *Globally Threatened Birds in Europe: Action Plans.* Council of Europe, & BirdLife International, Strasbourg.

614. Hunter, J. M., Black, J. M., Rusev, I., Michev, T. & Munteanu, D. (1999) Red-breasted Goose *Branta ruficollis.* Pp. 328–340 *in* Madsen, J., Cracknell, G. & Fox, T. (eds.) *Goose Populations of the Western Palearctic: A Review of Status and Distribution.* Wetlands International/National Environmental Research Institute, Rønde.

615. Hupp, J. W., Schmutz, J. A., Ely, C. R., Syroechkovskiy, E. E., Kondratyev, A. V., Eldridge, W. D. & Lappo, E. (2007) Moult migration of Emperor Geese *Chen canagica* between Alaska and Russia. *J. Avian Biol.* 38: 462–470.

616. Hupp, J. W., Schmutz, J. A. & Ely, C. R. (2008) The annual migration cycle of Emperor Geese in western Alaska. *Arctic* 61: 23–34.

617. Imamura, T. & Sugimori, F. (1989) Sex determination of Eastern Spot-billed Ducks (*Anas poecilorhyncha zonorhyncha*) by plumage color in breeding season. *Sankai Birds Inst. Res. Rep.* 21: 247–252.

618. Iñigo, A., Barov, B., Orhun, C. & Gallo-Orsi, U. (2008) *Species Action Plan for the Marbled Teal Marmaronetta angustirostris in the European Union.* BirdLife International for the European Commission, Strasbourg.

619. International Zoo Yearbook (1959–89) Species of wild animals bred in captivity and multiple generation captive births (annual records). Zool. Soc. of London.

620. Irving, L. (1960) Birds of Anaktuvik Pass, Kobuk, and Old Crow: a study in arctic adaptation. *US Natl. Mus. Bull.* 217.

621. Isenmann, P. & Moali, A. (2000) *Oiseaux d'Algérie/Birds of Algeria.* Soc. Etudes Orn. Française, Paris.

622. Iverson, S. A., Esler, D. & Boyd, W. S. (2003) Plumage characteristics as an indicator of age class in the Surf Scoter. *Waterbirds,* 26: 56–61.

623. Iverson, S. A. & Esler, D. (2006) Site fidelity and the demographic implications of winter movements by a migratory bird, the Harlequin duck *Histrionicus histrionicus. J. Avian Biol.* 37: 219–228.

624. Jackson, M. F. (1959) A hybrid between Barrow's and Common Goldeneyes. *Auk* 76: 92–94.

625. Jacob, J. & Glaser, A. (1975) Chemotaxonomy of Anseriformes. *Biochem. Syst. Ecol.* 2: 215–220.

626. James, J. D. & Thompson, J. E. (2001) Black-bellied Whistling-duck (*Dendrocygna autumnalis*). *In* Poole, A. (ed.) The Birds of North America Online. Cornell Lab of Ornithology, Ithaca, NY. http://bna.birds.cornell.edu/bna/species/578

627. Jansen, J. & Ebels, E. B. (2004) Gemengd paar Rotgans × Witbuikrotgans met drie hybride jongen op Texel in december 2003–januari 2004. *Dutch Birding* 26: 114–116.

628. Jaramillo, A. (2003) *Birds of Chile.* Princeton Univ. Press.

629. Jarrett, N. (2005) Fulvous Whistling-duck *Dendrocygna bicolor.* Pp. 199–202 *in* Kear, J. (ed.) *Ducks, Geese and Swans.* Oxford Univ. Press.

630. Jarrett, N. (2005) American Black Duck *Anas rubripes.* Pp. 509–513 *in* Kear, J. (ed.) *Ducks, Geese and Swans.* Oxford Univ. Press.

631. Jefferies, R. L. & Rockwell, R. F. (2002) Foraging geese, vegetation loss and soil degradation in an Arctic salt marsh. *Appl. Veg. Sci.* 5: 7–16.

632. Jehl, J. R. & Johnson, E. (2004) Wing and tail molts of the Ruddy Duck. *Waterbirds* 27: 54–59.

633. van der Jeugd, H. P., Voslamber B., van Turnhout C., Sierdsema H., Feige N., Nienhuis J. & Koffijberg K. (2006) *Overzomerende ganzen in Nederland: grenzen aan de groei?* SOVON Vogelonderzoek Nederland, Beek-Ubbergen. (In Dutch with English summary)

634. Jiguet, F. (1999) Photo forum: hybrid American Wigeons. *Birding World* 12: 247–252.

635. Jiguet, F. (2007) Siberian White-winged Scoter, new to France. *Ornithos* 14: 38–42.

636. Johansen, H. (1945) [About races of the Bean goose.] *Dansk Orn. Foren. Tidsskr.* 39: 106–127. (In Danish with English summary)

637. Johansen, H. (1959) Birds of West-Siberia. III Non-Passerines. *J. Orn.* 100: 60–78.

638. Johnsen, A., Rindal, E., Ericson P. G. P., Zuccon, D., Kerr, K. C., Stoeckle, M. Y. & Lifjeld, J. T. (2010) DNA barcoding of Scandinavian birds reveals divergent lineages in trans-Atlantic species. *J. Orn.* 151: 565–578.

639. Johnsgard, P. A. (1960) Hybridization in the Anatidae and its taxonomic implications. *Condor* 62: 25–33.

640. Johnsgard, P. A. (1961) The taxonomy of the *Anatidae*—a behavioral analysis. *Ibis* 103A: 71–85.

641. Johnsgard, P. A. (1961) Evolutionary relationships among the North American Mallards. *Auk* 78: 3–43.

642. Johnsgard, P. A. (1965) *Handbook of Waterfowl Behavior.* Cornell Univ. Press, Ithaca, NY.

643. Johnsgard, P. A. (1968) Some putative Mandarin Duck hybrids. *Bull. Brit. Orn. Club* 88: 140–148.

644. Johnsgard, P. A. (1974) The taxonomy and relationships of the northern swans. *Wildfowl* 25: 155–161.

645. Johnsgard, P. A. (1975) *Waterfowl of North America.* Indiana Univ. Press, Bloomington.

646. Johnsgard, P. A. (1978) Ducks, geese and swans of the World. University of Nebraska Press, Lincoln and London.

647. Johnsgard, P. A. (1979) Order Anseriformes. Pp. 425–506 *in* Mayr, E. & Cottrell, G. W. (eds.) *Check-list of Birds of the World.* Vol. 1. Second edn. Mus. Comp. Zool. Cambridge, MA.

648. Johnsgard, P. A. (2010) *North America's Ducks, Geese and Swans in the 21st Century. A 2010 Supplement to Waterfowl of North America.* Rev. Edition. Univ. of Nebraska. http://digitalcommons.unl.edu/biosciwaterfowlna/

649. Johnsgard, P. A. & Carbonell, M. (1996) *Ruddy Ducks and other Stifftails.* Univ. of Oklahoma Press, Norman.

650. Johnsgard, P. A. & Hagemeyer, D. (1969) The Masked Duck in the United States. *Auk* 84: 691–695.

651. Johnson, D. H., Timm, D. E. & Springer, P. F. (1979) Morphological characteristics of Canada Geese in the Pacific Flyway. Pp. 56–80 *in* Jarvis, R. L. & Bartonek, J. C. (eds.) *Management and Biology of Pacific Flyway Geese.* Oreg. State Univ. Bookstore, Corvallis.

652. Johnson, F. A. (2009) *Variation in Population Growth Rates of Mottled Ducks in Texas and Louisiana.* US Geological Survey Administrative Report. http://www.fws.gov/migratorybirds/NewReportsPublications/SpecialTopics/BySpecies/Johnson.Mottled%20Ducks%20Admin%20Report.Final.pdf

653. Johnson, K. (1995) Green-winged Teal (*Anas carolinensis*). *In* Poole, A. (ed.) The Birds of North America Online. Cornell Lab of Ornithology, Ithaca, NY. http://bna.birds.cornell.edu/bna/species/193

654. Johnson, K. P. & Sorenson, M. D. (1999) Phylogeny and biogeography of dabbling ducks (genus: *Anas*): a comparison of molecular and morphological evidence. *Auk* 116: 792–805.

655. Johnson, O. W. (1961) Reproductive cycle of the mallard duck. *Condor* 63: 351–364.

657. Johnson, S. A. & Hawk, M. (2012) Florida's introduced birds: Muscovy Duck (*Cairina moschata*). *Univ. Florida, WEC* 254: 1–3.

658. Johnson, S. R. (1985) Adaptations of the Long-tailed Duck (*Clangula hyemalis* L.) during the period of molt in arctic Alaska. *Acta XVIII Congr. Intern. Orn.* 18: 530–540.

659. Johnson, S. R. & Troy, D. M. (1987) Nesting of Ross's Goose and blue-phase Snow Goose in the Sagavanirktok River Delta, Alaska. *Condor* 89: 665–667.

660. Johnstone, S. T. (1955) Notes on the Wildfowl Trust's collection at Slimbridge. *Avicult. Mag.* 61: 28–32.

661. Jones, R. D. (1965) Returns from Steller's Eiders banded in Izembek Bay, AK. *Wildfowl* 16: 83–85.

662. Jones, T., Martin, K., Barov, B. & Nagy, S. (eds.) (2008) *International Single Species Action Plan for the Conservation of the Western Palearctic Popuation of the Lesser White-fronted Goose Anser erythropus.* African-Eurasian Migratory Waterbird Agreement, Bonn.

663. Jónsson, J. E. & Afton, A. D. (2008) Lesser Snow Geese and Ross's Geese form mixed flocks during winter but differ in family maintenance and social status. *Wilson J. Orn.* 120: 725–731.

664. Jónsson, J. E., Ryder, J. P. & Alisauskas, R. T. (2013) Ross's Goose (*Anser rossii*). *In* Poole, A. (ed.) The Birds of North America Online. Cornell Lab of Ornithology, Ithaca, NY. http://bna.birds.cornell.edu/bna/species/162

665. Kaiser, M. J., Galanidi, M., Showler, D. A., Elliott, A. J., Caldow, R. W. G., Rees, E. I. S., Stillman, R. A. & Sutherland, W. J. (2006) Distribution and behaviour of Common Scoter (*Melanitta nigra*) relative to prey resources and environmental parameters. *Ibis* 148: 110–128.

666. Kalyakin, V. N. (2001) New data on bird fauna of Novaya Zemlya archipelago and Franz-Josef Land. *Ornithologia* 29: 8–28.

667. Kampe-Persson, H. (2010) Naturalised geese in Europe. *Ornis Svecica* 20: 155–173.

668. Kampe-Persson, H. & Lerner, H. (2007) Occurrence of hybrid geese in Sweden – a conservation problem? *Ornis Svecica* 17: 154–186.

669. Kaufman, K. (1994) Greenland White-fronted Geese: over-reported? *Birding* 26: 380.

670. Kaufman, K. (2011) *Field Guide to Advanced Birding.* Houghton Mifflin, New York.

671. Kaufman, K., Witzeman, J. & Cook, E. (1979) Pinning down the blue Ross' Goose. *Continental Birdlife* 1: 112–115.

672. Kear, J. (2005) American Wood Duck *Aix sponsa.* Pp. 461–465 *in* Kear, J. (ed.) *Ducks, Geese and Swans.* Oxford Univ. Press.

673. Kear, J. (2005) Mandarin Duck *Aix galericulata.* Pp. 465–468 *in* Kear, J. (ed.) *Ducks, Geese and Swans.* Oxford Univ. Press.

674. Kear, J. (ed.) (2005) *Ducks, Geese and Swans.* Oxford Univ. Press.

675. Kejia, Z. & Qiang, M. (2007) Large flock of Baikal Teal found in Chongming Dongtan wetland, Shanghai, China. *BirdingASIA* 8: 78–79.

676. Keller, V. (2006) Population size and trend of the Red-crested Pochard *Netta rufina* in southwest/central Europe: an update. Pp. 503–504 *in* Boere, G. C., Galbraith, C. & Stroud, D. (ed.) *Waterbirds Around the World.* The Stationary Office, Edinburgh.

677. Kellett, D. K. & Alisauskas, R. T. (2000) Body-mass dynamics of King Eiders during incubation. *Auk* 117: 812–817.

678. Kemp, J. (1991) Hybrid Pochards resembling Redheads. *Birding World* 4: 353.

679. Kennard, F. H. (1919) Notes on a new subspecies of Blue-winged Teal. *Auk* 36: 455–460.

680. Kerbes, R. H. (1994) Colonies and numbers of Ross' Geese and Lesser Snow Geese in the Queen Maud Gulf Migratory Bird Sanctuary. *Canadian Wildl. Serv. Occas. Pap.* 81: 1–47.

681. Kerr, K. C., Stoeckle, M. Y., Dove, C. J., Weigt, L. A., Francis, C. M. & Hebert, P. D. (2007) Comprehensive DNA barcode coverage of North American birds. *Mol. Ecol. Notes* 7: 535–543.

682. Kershaw, M. & Cranswick, P. A. (2003) Numbers of wintering waterbirds in Great Britain 1994/95–1998/99: I. Wildfowl and selected waterbirds. *Biol. Conserv.* 111: 91–104.

683. Kertell, K. (1991) Disappearance of the Steller's Eider from the Yukon-Kuskokwim Delta, Alaska. *Arctic* 44: 177–187.

684. Kessel, B., Rocque, D. A. & Barclay, J. S. (2002) Greater Scaup (*Aythya marila*). *In* Poole, A. (ed.) The Birds of North

America Online. Cornell Lab of Ornithology, Ithaca, NY. http://bna.birds.cornell.edu/bna/species/650

685. Kessler, L. G. & Avise, J. C. (1984) Systematic relationships among waterfowl (*Anatidae*) inferred from restriction endonuclease analysis of mitochondrial DNA. *Syst. Zool.* 33: 370–380.

686. Kestenholz, M. (1994) Body mass dynamics of wintering Tufted Duck *Aythya fuligula* and Pochard *A. ferina* in Switzerland. *Wildfowl* 45: 147–158.

687. Kilpi, M., Öst, M., Lindström, K. & Rita, H. (2001) Female characteristics and parental care mode in the crèching system of Eiders, *Somateria mollissima*. *Anim. Behav.* 62: 527–534.

688. King, B. F. (1997) *Checklist of the Birds of Eurasia*. Ibis Publishing, Vista, CA.

689. King, J. (1999) OrnithoNews: Ruddy Duck hybrid in Turkey. *Birding World* 12: 260.

690. King, J. G. (1965) Waterfowl migration spring 1964. Izembek National Wildlife Refuge. US Bureau Sport Fisheries & Wildlife Files, Anchorage, AK.

691. King, R. J. & Dau, C. P. (1992) Spring population survey of Emperor Geese (*Chen canagica*) in southwestern Alaska 2–7 May, 1991. Unpubl. US Fish & Wildlife Service, Fairbanks, AK.

692. Kirby, R. E. & Fredrickson, L. H. (1990) Molts and plumages of the Wood Duck. Pp. 29–33 *in* Frederickson, L. H., Burger, G. V., Havera, S. P., Graber, D. A., Kirby, R. E. & Taylor, T. S. (eds.) *Proc. 1988 North Amer. Wood Duck Symp.*

693. Kirby, R. E., Reed, A., Dupuis, P., Obrecht, H. H. & Quist, W. J. (2000) *Description and identification of American Black Duck, Mallard, and Hybrid Wing Plumage*. US Geological Survey, Biological Resources Division, Washington DC.

694. Kirby, R. E., Sargeant, G. A. & Shutler, D. (2004) Haldane's Rule and American Black Duck × Mallard hybridization. *Canadian J. Zool.* 82: 1827–1831.

695. Kistchinski, A. A. (1971) Biological notes on the Emperor Goose in north-east Siberia. *Ann. Rep. Wildfowl Trust* 22: 29–34.

696. Knapton, R. W. (2000) Identification of Bewick's Swan. *Birders J.* 9: 130–133.

697. Kolbe, H. (1979) *Ornamental Waterfowl*. Gresham Books, Old Woking.

698. Kolbeinsson, Y., Prainsson, G. & Petursson, G. (2001) [Rare birds in Iceland in 1998]. *Bliki* 22: 21–46. (In Icelandic)

699. Kolomiitsev, N. P. (1992) *Mergus squamatus* biology in the Kiyevka Basin (S. Primorye). Pp. 68–73 *in* Sokolov, Y. (ed.) *Ornithological Research in State Reserves*. Nauka, Moscow.

700. Kolomiitsev, N. P. (1995) New data for moult in the Chinese Merganser *Mergus squamatus*. *Russ Orn. J.* 4: 19–23.

701. Kondratiev, A. Y. (1991) The distribution and status of Bewick's Swans *Cygnus bewickii*, Tundra Swans *C. columbianus* and Whooper Swans *C. cygnus* in the "extreme northeast" of the USSR. *Wildfowl* Spec. Suppl.: 56–61.

702. Kondratiev, A. V. & Zöckler, C. (2009) Mixed pair of Ross's Goose and Barnacle Goose breeding on Kolguev, Russia, in 2006–07. *Dutch Birding* 31: 299–301.

703. Korbut, V. V. (2001) Unusual mallards (*Anas platyrhynchus* [*platyrhynchos*]) in Moscow. *Ornitologia* 29: 329–331.

704. Kortright, F. H. (1942) *The Ducks, Geese, and Swans of North America*. Stackpole, Harrisburg, PA.

705. Kostin, I. O. & Mooij, J. H. (1995) Influence of weather conditions and other factors on the reproductive cycle of Red-breasted Geese (*Branta ruficollis*) at the Taymyr Peninsula. *Wildfowl* 46: 45–54.

706. Kraege, D. (2005) *Washington State Status Report for the Aleutian Canada Goose*. Dept. of Fish & Wildlife, Olympia, WA.

707. Kraft, R. H. (1991) Status report of the Lacreek Trumpeter Swan flock. Pp. 88–90 *in* Voigt-Englund, J. (ed.) *Proc. and Papers 12th Trumpeter Swan Society Conf.* The Trumpeter Swan Society, Maple Plain, MN.

708. Krechmar, A. V. (1996) White-fronted Goose *Anser albifrons* in the Kava River region, near the northern shores of the Okhotsk Sea. *Casarca* 2: 52–65.

709. Krechmar, A. V. & Kondratiev, A. Y. (1982) Ecology of nesting of *Plilacte canagicus* on the north part of Chokotka Peninsula. *J. Zoology* 61:254–264.

710. Kreutzkamp, I. (2003) [The development of breeding populations in Greylag Goose (*Anser anser*), Canada Goose (*Branta canadensis*), and Egyptian Goose (*Alopochen aegyptiacus*) in the Hamburg report area from 1990 to 2002]. *Hamburger Avifaunistische Beiträge* 32: 153–186. (German with English summary)

711. Kristiansen, J. N. (1998) Nest site preference by Greylag Geese *Anser anser* in reedbeds of different harvest age. *Bird Study* 45: 337–343.

712. Kristiansen, J. N., Fox, A. D. & Jarrett, N. S. (1999) Resightings and recoveries of Canada Geese *Branta canadensis* ringed in West Greenland. *Wildfowl* 50: 199–203.

713. Krueger, H. (2004) Detailed guide to "White-cheeked Goose" subspecies. www.idahobirds.net/identification/white-cheeked/subspecies.html

714. Kuchel, C. R. (1977) Some aspects of the behavior and ecology of Harlequin Ducks breeding in Glacier National Park, Montana. M.Sc. thesis. Univ. of Montana, Missoula.

715. Kulikova, I. V., Zhuravlev, Y. N. & McCracken, K. G. (2004) Asymmetric hybridization and sex-biased gene flow between Eastern Spot-billed Ducks (*Anas zonorhyncha*) and Mallards (*A. platyrhynchos*) in the Russian Far East. *Auk* 121: 930–949.

716. Kulikova, I. V., Drovetski, S. V., Gibson, D. D., Harrigan, R. J., Rohwer, S., Sorenson, M. D., Winker, K., Zhuravlev, Y. N., & McCracken, K. G. (2005) Phylogeography of the mallard (*Anas platyrhynchos*): hybridization, dispersal, and lineage sorting contribute to complex geographic structure. *Auk* 122: 949–965.

717. Kuroda, N. (1924) On the Japanese geese. *Tori* 3: 194–205.

718. Kuroda, N. (1939) *Geese and Ducks of the World*. Shukyosha Shoin, Tokyo.

719. Kuroda, N. (1960) An assumed hybrid between Mallard and Wigeon. *Ann. Zool. Jap.* 33: 202–203.

720. Kutnezsov, S. B., Baranyuk, V. V. & Takekawa, J. Y. (1998) Genetic differentiation between wintering populations of Lesser Snow Geese nesting on Wrangel Island. *Auk* 115: 1053–1057.

721. Labzyuk, V. I. & Nazarov, Y. N. (1967) Rare and new birds of Southern Primorye. *Ornithologia* 8: 363–364.

722. Lack, D. (1974) *Evolution Illustrated by Waterfowl*. Blackwell Scientific Publications, Oxford.

723. Lagerquist, B. A. & Ankney, C. D. (1988) Interspecific differences in bill and tongue morphology among diving ducks (*Aythya* spp., *Oxyura jamaicensis*) *Canadian J. Zool.* 67: 2694–2699.

724. Lambillk, R. H. D. (1981) De huidige status van de

Spitsbergenf/Frans Jozef Land- populatie van de Witbuikrotgans *Branta bemicla hrota*. *Limosa* 54: 52–56.

725. Lanctot, R., Goatcher, B., Scribner, K., Talbot, S., Pierson, B., Esler, D. & Zwiefelhofer, D. (1999) Harlequin Ducks recovery from the Exxon Valdez oil spill: a population genetics perspective. *Auk* 116: 781–791.

726. Larkin, P. (2000) Eyelid colour of American Wigeon. *Brit. Birds* 93: 39–40.

727. Larned, W. W. (2012) *Steller's Eider Spring Migration Surveys, Southwest Alaska, 2011.* United States Fish & Wildlife Service, Anchorage, AK.

728. Larned, W. W., Stehn, R. & Platte, R. (2011) Waterfowl breeding population survey, Arctic Coastal Plain, Alaska, 2010. Unpubl. US Fish & Wildlife Service, Anchorage, AK.

729. Larrson, K. (1993) Inheritance of body size in the Barnacle Goose under different environmental conditions. *J. Evol. Biol.* 6: 195–208.

730. Larrson, K. & Forslund, P. (1991) Environmentally induced morphological variation in the Barnacle Goose, *Branta leucopsis. J. Evol. Biol.* 4: 319–636.

731. Larsen, J. K. & Clausen, P. (2002) Potential wind park impacts on Whooper Swans in winter: the risk of collision. Pp. 327–330 *in* Rees, E. C., Earnst, S. L. & Coulson, J. (ed.) *Proc. 4th Intern. Swan Symp.* Waterbird Society.

732. Larson, J. S. & Taber, R. D. (1980) *Criteria of Sex and Age. Wildlife Management Techniques Manual.* Wildlife Society, Washington DC.

733. Laubhan, M. K. & Metzner, K. A. (1999) Distribution and diurnal behavior of Steller's eiders wintering on the Alaska Peninsula. *Condor* 101: 694–698.

734. Laurie-Ahlberg, C. C. & McKinney, F. (1979) The nod-swim display of male Green-winged Teal (*Anas crecca*). *Anim. Behav.* 27: 165–172.

735. Laursen, K., Pihl, S., & Komdeur, J. (1992) New figures of seaduck winter populations in the Western Palearctic. *IWRB Seaduck Bull.* 1: 6–8

736. Leader, P. J. (2006) Sympatric breeding of two Spot-billed Duck *Anas poecilorhyncha* taxa in southern China. *Bull. Brit. Orn. Club* 126: 248–252.

737. Leafloor, J. O., Thompson, J. E. & Ankney, C. D. (1996) Body mass and carcass composition of fall migrant Oldsquaws. *Wilson Bull.* 108: 567–572.

738. Leafloor, J. O., Ankney, C. D. & Rusch, D. H. (1998) Environmental effects on body size of Canada Geese. *Auk* 115: 26–33.

739. Lebeda, C. S. & Ratti, J. T. (1983) Reproductive biology of Vancouver Canada Geese on Admiralty Island, Alaska. *J. Wildl. Manag.* 47: 297–306.

740. Leck, C. F. (1967) A possible hybrid between the Canada Goose and the Pink-footed Goose. *Cassinia* 50: 9–11.

741. Lee, S. Y., Scott, G. R. & Milsom, W. K. (2008) Have wing morphology or flight kinematics evolved for extreme high altitude migration in the Bar-headed Goose? *Comp. Biochem. Physiol. C. Pharmacol. Toxicol.* 148: 324–331.

742. Lehikoinen, A., Jaatinen, K. & Öst, M. (2010) Do female ornaments indicate quality in eider ducks? *Biol. Lett.* 6: 225–228.

743. Leopold, A. S. (1959) *Wildlife of Mexico: The Game Birds and Mammals.* Univ. of California Press, Berkeley.

744. Lepage, D., Gauthier, G. & Reed, A. (1998) Seasonal variation in growth of Greater Snow Goose goslings: the role of food supply. *Oecologia* 114: 226–235.

745. Lepage, M. & Doyon, M. R. (1996) Ring-necked Duck. Pp. 304–307 *in* Gauthier, J. & Aubry, Y (eds.) *The Breeding Birds of Quebec: Atlas of the Breeding Birds of Southern Quebec.* Assoc. Quebecquoise des groupes d'ornithologues, Province of Quebec Society for the Protection of Birds, Canadian Wildlife Service & Environnement Canada, Montréal.

746. Lerner, H. (2005) Fynd av några hybridgäss 2004. *Vår Fågelvärld* Suppl. 44, 49–51.

747. Leschack, C. R., McKnight, S. K. & Hepp, G. R. (1997) Gadwall (*Anas strepera*). *In* Poole, A. (ed.) The Birds of North America Online. Cornell Lab of Ornithology, Ithaca, NY. http://bna.birds.cornell.edu/bna/species/283

748. Leukering, T. (2011) Greater and Lesser Scaup: beyond crown shape. *Colorado Birds* 45: 71–75.

749. Leukering, T. & Mlodinow, S. G. (2012) The Mexican Duck in Colorado: identification and occurrence. *Colorado Birds* 46: 296–308.

750. Leuzinger, H. & Schuster, S. (2005) When and where do Ferruginous Ducks *Aythya nyroca* molt their wing feathers. *Orn. Beob.* 102: 37–39.

751. Lever, C. (1987) *Naturalized Birds of the World.* Longman Scientific & Technical, Harlow.

752. Leverkühn, P. (1890) Über Farbenvarietäten bei Vögeln. *J. Orn.* 38: 168–232.

753. Lewis, T. L., Ward, D. H., Sedinger, J. S., Reed, A. & Derksen, D. V. (2013) Brant (*Branta bernicla*). *In* Poole, A. (ed.) The Birds of North America Online. Cornell Lab of Ornithology, Ithaca, NY. http://bna.birds.cornell.edu/bna/species/337

754. Li, Z. W. D. & Mundkur, T. (2003) *Status Overview and Recommendations for Conservation of the White-headed Duck Oxyura leucocephala in Central Asia.* Wetlands International, Wageningen.

755. Li, Z. W. D. & Mundkur, T. (2004) *Numbers and Distribution of Waterbirds and Wetlands in the Asia-Pacific Region. Results of the Asian Waterbird Census 1997–2001.* Wetlands International, Kuala Lumpur.

756. Li, Z. W. D. & Mundkur, T. (2007) *Numbers and Distribution of Waterbirds and Wetlands in the Asia-Pacific Region: Results of the Asian Waterbird Census, 2002–2004.* Wetlands International, Kuala Lumpur.

757. Li, Z. W. D., Bloem, A., Delany, S., Martakis, G. & Quintero, J. O. (2009) *Status of Waterbirds in Asia – Results of the Asian Waterbird Census: 1987–2007.* Wetlands International, Kuala Lumpur.

758. Li Laixing (2001) Survey results and new records of waterfowl at Quinghai Lake. *China Crane News* 5(1): 36–37.

759. Liebherr, H. & Rutschke, E. (1993) Ergebnisse morphometrischer Untersuchungen an Saatgänsen – *Anser fabalis*. *Orn. Mitt.* 45: 299–304.

760. Limpert, R. J. & Earnst, S. L. (1994) Tundra Swan (*Cygnus columbianus*). *In* Poole, A. (ed.) The Birds of North America Online. Cornell Lab of Ornithology, Ithaca, NY. http://bna. birds.cornell.edu/bna/species/089

761. Limpert, R. J., Allen, H. A. & Sladen, W. J. L. (1987) Weights and measurements of wintering Tundra Swans. *Wildfowl* 38: 108–113.

762. Lin, Q. X., Chen, X. L. & Fang, W. Z. (2008) Discovery of Scaly-sided Merganser (*Mergus squamatus*) and *Gorsachius magnificus* in Ji'an, Jiangxi Province. *Chinese J. Zool.* 43: 13–13.

763. Lind, H. & Poulsen, H. (1963) On the morphology and behavior of a hybrid between Goosander and Shelduck

(*Mergus merganser* L. × *Tadorna tadorna* L.). *Zeitschrift f. Tierpsychologie* 20: 558–570.

764. Liu, P., Li, F., Song, H., Wang, Q., Song, Y., Liu, Y. & Piao, Z. (2010) A survey to the distribution of the Scaly-sided Merganser (*Mergus squamatus*) in Changbai Mountain range (China side). *Chinese Birds* 1: 148–155.

765. Livezey, B. C. (1986) A phylogenetic analysis of recent anseriform genera using morphological characters. *Auk* 103: 737–754.

766. Livezey, B. C. (1989) Phylogenetic relationships and incipient flightlessness of the extinct Auckland Islands Merganser. *Wilson Bull.* 101: 410–435.

767. Livezey, B. C. (1991) A phylogenetic analysis and classification of recent dabbling ducks (Tribe Anatini) based on comparative morphology. *Auk* 108: 471–507.

768. Livezey, B. C. (1993) Comparative morphometrics of *Anas* ducks, with particular reference to the Hawaiian Duck *Anas wyvilliana*, Laysan Duck *A. laysanensis*, and Eaton's Pintail *A. eatoni*. *Wildfowl* 44: 75–100.

769. Livezey, B. C. (1995) A phylogenetic analysis of the whistling and white-backed ducks (Anatidae, Dendrocygninae) using morphological characters. *Ann. Carnegie Mus.* 64: 65–97.

770. Livezey, B. C. (1995) Phylogeny and comparative ecology of stiff-tailed ducks (Anatidae: Oxyurini). *Wilson Bull.* 107: 214–234.

771. Livezey, B. C. (1995) Phylogeny and evolutionary ecology of modern seaducks (Anatidae: Mergini). *Condor* 97: 233–255.

772. Livezey, B. C. (1996) A phylogenetic analysis of geese and swans (Anseriformes: Anserinae), including selected fossil species. *Syst. Biol.* 45: 415–450.

773. Livezey, B. C. (1996) A phylogenetic analysis of modern pochards (Anatidae: Aythyini). *Auk* 113: 74–93.

774. Livezey, B. C. (1996) A phylogenetic reassessment of the tadornine-anatine divergence (Aves: Anseriformes, Anatidae). *Ann. Carnegie Mus.* 65: 27–88.

775. Livezey, B. C. (1997) A phylogenetic analysis of basal Anseriformes, the fossil *Presbyornis*, and the interordinal relationships of waterfowl. *Zool. J. Linn. Soc.* 121: 361–428.

776. Livezey, B. C. (1997) A phylogenetic analysis of modern shelducks and sheldgeese (Anatidae, Tadornini). *Ibis* 139: 51–66.

777. Livezey, B. C. (1997) An annotated phylogenetic classification of waterfowl (*Aves: Anseriformes*), including selected fossil species. *Ann. Carnegie Mus.* 67: 457–496.

778. Livezey, B. C. (1998) Erratum. *Zool. J. Linn. Soc.* 124: 397–398.

779. Livezey, B. C. & Martin, L. D. (1988) The systematic position of the Miocene anatid *Anas* [?] *blanchardi* Milne-Edwards. *J. Vert. Paleontology* 8: 196–211.

780. Lock, A. R. (1986) A census of Common Eiders breeding in Labrador and the Maritime Provinces. Pp. 30–38 *in* Reed, A. (ed.) *Eider Ducks in Canada*. Canadian Wildlife Service, Ottawa.

781. Lockwood, M. W. (1997) A closer look: Masked Duck. *Birding* 5: 386–390.

782. Lockwood, M. W. & Cooper T. W. (1999) A Texas hybrid: Cinnamon × Green-winged Teal. *Texas Birds* 1: 38–40.

783. Longcore, J. R., McAuley, D. G., Hepp, G. R. & Rhymer, J. M. (2000) American Black Duck (*Anas rubripes*). *In* Poole, A. (ed.) The Birds of North America Online. Cornell Lab of Ornithology, Ithaca, NY. http://bna.birds.cornell.edu/bna/species/481

784. Loos, E. R. (1999) Incubation in Blue-winged Teal (*Anas discors*): testing hypotheses of incubation constancy, recess frequency, weight loss, and nest success. M.Sc. thesis. Louisiana State Univ., Baton Rouge.

785. Lovvorn, J. R. & Barzen, J. A. (1988) Molt in the annual cycle of Canvasbacks. *Auk* 105: 543–552.

786. Lovvorn, J. R., Grebmeier, J. M., Cooper, L. W., Bump, J. K. & Richman, S. E. (2009) Modelling marine protected areas for threatened eiders in a climatically changing Bering Sea. *Ecol. Appl.* 19: 1596–1613.

787. Luther, D. (1996) Coues' Schnatterente. Pp. 27–28 *in Die ausgestorbenen Vögel der Welt*. Fourth edn. Westarp-Wissenschaften, Magdeburg & Spektrum, Heidelberg.

788. Ma, M. (2007) Distribution and breeding of White-headed Ducks in Xinjiang. *China Crane News* 11(2): 13–14.

789. Ma, M. & Cai, D. (2002) Breeding ecology of Bar-headed Goose in Tianshan, Xinjiang. *Casarca* 5: 177–181.

790. Ma, M. & Cai, D. (2002) Threats to Whooper Swans in Xinjiang, China. Pp. 331–333 *in* Rees, E. C., Earnst, S. L. & Coulson, J. (eds.) *Proc. 4th Intern. Swan Symp.* Waterbird Society.

791. MacInnes, C. D. (1966) Population behavior of eastern arctic Canada Geese. *J. Wildl. Manag.* 30: 536–553.

792. Mackenzie, M. J. S. (1990) White-winged Wood Duck – *Cairina scutulata* [*sic*] – the question of Indonesian albinism. *Wildfowl* 41: 163–166.

793. Maclean, G. L. (1993) *Roberts' Birds of Southern Africa*. Sixth edn. John Voelcker Book Fund, Cape Town.

794. Madge, S. & Burn, H. (1988) *Wildfowl. An Identification Guide to the Ducks, Geese and Swans of the World*. Houghton Mifflin, Boston.

795. Madsen, J. (1996) International Action Plan for the Lesser White-fronted Goose *Anser erythropus*. Pp. 67–78 *in* Heredia, B., Rose, L. & Painter, M. (eds.) *Globally Threatened Birds in Europe: Action Plans*. Council of Europe & BirdLife International, Strasbourg.

796. Madsen, J., Bregnballe, T. & Mehlum, F. (1989) Study of the breeding ecology and behaviour of the Svalbard population of Light-bellied Brent Goose *Branta bernicla hrota*. *Polar Res.* 7: 1–21.

797. Madsen, J., Fox, T. & Cracknell, J. (eds.) (1999) *Goose Populations of the Western Palearctic. A Review of Status and Distribution*. Wetlands International, Wageningen & National Environmental Research Institute, Rønde.

798. Mallory, M. & Metz, K. (1999) Common Merganser (*Mergus merganser*). *In* Poole, A. (ed.) The Birds of North America Online. Cornell Lab of Ornithology, Ithaca, NY. http://bna.birds.cornell.edu/bna/species/442

799. Manfred, B. & Ebels, E. B. (2006) Leucism in Dark-bellied Brent Goose Goose. *Dutch Birding* 28: 96–98.

800. Mank, J. E., Carlson, J. E. & Brittingham, M. C. (2004) A century of hybridization: decreasing genetic distance between American black ducks and mallards. *Conserv. Genetics* 5: 395–403.

801. Manning, T. H., Hohn, E. O. & Macpherson, A. H. (1956) The birds of Banks Island. *Natl. Mus. Canada Bull.* 143, Biol. Ser. 48. Ottawa.

802. Marchant, S. & Higgins, P. J. (eds.) (1990) *Handbook of Australian, New Zealand, & Antarctic Birds*. Vol. 1. Oxford Univ. Press, Melbourne.

803. Marchant, J. H. & Musgrove, A. J. (2011) Review of European

flyways of the Lesser White-fronted Goose *Anser erythropus*. *BTO Res. Rep.* 595.

804. Marcisz, W. J. (1981) A presumed Bufflehead × Hooded Merganser hybrid in Illinois. *Amer. Birds* 35: 340–341.

805. Marquardt, R. E (1961) Albinism in the small white-cheeked geese. *Auk* 78: 99–100.

806. Martin, J. L., LeDonne, J. R., Lee, F. B., Lebenhauer, P. A., Springer, P. F. & Timm, D. E. (1982) *Aleutian Canada Goose Recovery Plan.* US Fish & Wildlife Service, Washington DC.

807. Martin, J. P. (2002) From the Rarities Committee's files. Unusual Brent Geese in Norfolk and Hampshire. *Brit. Birds* 95: 129–136.

808. Martin, J. P. & Garner, M. (2012) From the Rarities Committee's files. Moult and ageing of male Falcated Ducks in autumn. *Brit. Birds* 105: 11-21.

809. Martin, K. (2005) *The International Single Species Action Plan for the Conservation of the Western Palearctic Population of the Lesser White-fronted Goose.* Final report of the EU LIFE-Nature project, 2009.

811. Martin, P. R. & Di Labio, B. M. (1994) Identification of Common × Barrow's Goldeneye hybrids in the field. *Birding* 26: 104–105.

812. Martin, P. R. & Di Labio, B. M. (1994) Natural hybrids between the Common Goldeneye, *Bucephala clangula*, and the Barrow's Goldeneye, *B. islandica*. *Canadian Field-Natur.* 108: 195–198.

813. Matthews, G. V. T. & Campbell, C. R. G. (1969) Weights and measurements of Greylag Geese in Scotland. *Wildfowl* 20: 86–93.

814. Mayr, E. (1942) *Systematics and the Origin of Species.* Harvard Univ. Press, Cambridge, MA.

815. Mazourek, J. C. & Gray, P. N. (1994) The Florida duck or the mallard. *Florida Wildlife* 48 (3): 29–31.

816. McCallum, J. (2014) Black Brant and hybrids. http://birdingfrontiers.com/2014/03/22/black-brant-and-hybrids/

817. McCarthy, E. (2006) *Handbook of the Avian Hybrids of the World.* Oxford Univ. Press.

818. McCracken, K. G. & Sorenson, M. D. (2005) Is homoplasy or lineage sorting the source of incongruent mtDNA and nuclear gene trees in stiff-tailed ducks (*Nomonyx-Oxyura*)? *Syst. Biol.* 54: 35–55.

819. McCracken, K. G., Afton, A. D. & Alisauskas, R. T. (1997) Nest morphology and body size of Ross's Geese and Lesser Snow Geese. *Auk* 114: 610–618.

820. McCracken, K. G., Harshman, J., McClellan, D. A. & Afton, A. D. (1999) Data set incongruence and correlated character evolution: an example of functional convergence in the hind-limb of stifftail diving ducks. *Syst. Biol.* 48: 683–714.

821. McCracken, K. G., Harshman, J., Sorenson, M. D. & Johnson, K. P. (2000) Are Ruddy Ducks and White-headed Ducks the same species? *Brit. Birds* 93: 394–398.

822. McCracken, K. G., Johnson, K. P. & Sheldon, F. H. (2001) Molecular population genetics, phylogeography, and conservation biology of the Mottled Duck (*Anas fulvigula*). *Conserv. Genetics* 2: 87–102.

823. McCracken, K. G., Sonsthagen, S. A., Talbot, S. L., Lanctot, R. B. & Scribner, K. T. (2006) *Population Genetic Structure of Common Eiders (Somateria mollissima) Nesting on Coastal Barrier Islands Adjacent to Oil Facilities in the Beaufort Sea, Alaska.* Univ. of Fairbanks, Alaska.

824. McEneaney, T. (2005) Rare color variants of the Trumpeter Swan. *Birding* 37: 148–154.

825. McGill, M. (2005) Ross's Goose *Anser rossii.* Pp. 303–305 *in* Kear, J. (ed.) *Ducks, Geese and Swans.* Oxford Univ. Press.

826. McGowan, K. (2001) Swan identification in upstate New York. http://www.birds.cornell.edu/crows/SwanID.htm

827. McHenry, M. G. (1971) Breeding and post-breeding movements of Blue-winged Teal (*Anas discors*) in southwestern Manitoba. Ph.D. thesis. Univ. of Oklahoma, Norman.

828. McIlhenny, E. A. (1937) Results of 1936 bird banding operations at Avery Island, Louisiana with special reference to sex ratios and hybrids. *Bird-Banding* 8: 117–121.

829. McLandress, M. R. (1983) Winning with warts? A threat posture suggests a function for caruncles in Ross's Geese. *Wildfowl* 34: 5–9.

830. McLandress, M. R. & McLandress, I. (1979) Blue-phase Ross's Geese and other blue-phase geese in western North America. *Auk* 96: 544–550.

831. McLeish, I. (1993) History of the Comb Duck in Oman. *Oman Bird News* 13: 4.

832. Mehlum, F. (1999) Pink-footed Goose *Anser brachyrhynchus*: Svalbard. Pp. 82–93 *in* Madsen, J., Fox, T. & Cracknell, J. (eds.) *Goose Populations of the Western Palearctic. A Review of Status and Distribution.* Wetlands International, Wageningen & National Environmental Research Institute, Rønde.

833. Meijuan Zhao, Peihao Cong, Barter, M., Fox, A. D. & Cao, L. (2012) The changing abundance and distribution of Greater White-fronted Geese *Anser albifrons* in the Yangtze River floodplain: impacts of recent hydrological changes. *Bird Conserv. Intern.* 22: 135-143.

834. Meininger, P. L. (2004) Breeding attempt of Ross's Goose at Haringvliet in 2003. *Dutch Birding* 26: 111–113.

835. Melnikov, Y. I (2001) [The numbers, distribution and migration of the Bean Goose in southern part of East Siberia]. Pp. 82–99 *in* Melnikov, Y. I. & Shaburova, N. I. (eds.) *Trans. Baykal–Lena State Nature Zapovednik* 2. Irkutsk (In Russian)

836. Mendall, H. L. (1958) *Ring-necked Duck in the Northeast.* Univ of Maine, Orono.

837. Mendall, H. L. (1980) Intergradation of eastern American Common Eiders. *Canadian Field-Natur.* 94: 286–292.

838. Mendall, H. L. (1986) Identification of eastern races of the Eider. *Canadian Wildl. Serv. Rep. Ser.* 47: 82–88.

839. Merkel, F. R. (2004) Impact of hunting and gillnet fishery on wintering eiders in Nuuk, southwest Greenland. *Waterbirds* 27: 469–479.

840. Merkel, F. R. (2004) Evidence of population decline in Common Eiders breeding in western Greenland. *Arctic* 57: 27–36.

841. Merne, O. J. & Walsh, A. (1991) An orange-legged Bewick's Swan in Co. Wexford. *Irish Birds* 4: 421–422.

842. Merrifield, K. (1998) Two presumed Mallard × Gadwall hybrids (*A. platyrhynchos* × *A. strepera*) in Lincoln County, Oregon. *Northwestern Natur.* 79: 54–58.

843. Michot, T. C. & Woodin, M. C. (2005) Redhead *Aythya americana.* Pp. 644–651 *in* Kear, J. (ed.) *Ducks, Geese and Swans.* Oxford Univ. Press.

844. Mikami, S. (1989) First Japanese records of crosses between Whistling *Cygnus columbianus columbianus* and Bewick's *Swans C. c. bewickii. Wildfowl* 40: 131–133.

845. Millard, S. (1994) Hybrid duck in Otter Tail County. *Loon* 66: 103–104.

846. Miller, M. R. (1986) Molt chronology of Northern Pintails in California. *J. Wildl. Manag.* 50: 57–64.

847. Millington, R. (1997) Separation of Black Brant, Dark-bellied Brent Goose and Pale-bellied Brent Goose. *Birding World* 10: 11–15.

848. Millington, R. (1998) The Green-winged Teal. *Birding World* 11: 430–434.

849. Millington, R. (2007) Photopage: an eclipse Green-winged Teal. *Birding World* 20: 378.

850. Millington, R. & Gantlett, S. (1999) On Canada Goose forms. *Birding World* 12: 83.

851. Milstein, P. le S. (1993) A study of the Egyptian Goose *Alopochen aegyptiacus*. Ph.D. thesis. Univ. of Pretoria.

852. Mitchell, C. (2005) Eurasian Wigeon *Anas penelope*. Pp. 499–502 *in* Kear, J. (ed.) *Ducks, Geese and Swans*. Oxford Univ. Press.

853. Mitchell, C. (2005) Northern Shoveler *Anas clypeata*. Pp. 560–564 *in* Kear, J. (ed.) *Ducks, Geese and Swans*. Oxford Univ. Press.

854. Mitchell, C., Patterson, D., Boyer, P., Cunningham, P., McDonald, R. & Meek, E. (2000) The summer status and distribution of Greylag Geese in north and west Scotland. *Scott. Birds* 21: 69–77.

855. Mitchell, C. & Pihl, S. (2005) Steller's Eider *Polysticta stelleri*. Pp. 689–692 *in* Kear, J. (ed.) *Ducks, Geese and Swans*. Oxford Univ. Press.

856. Mitchell, C. D. (1994) Trumpeter Swan (*Cygnus buccinator*), no. 105. *In* Poole, A. & Gill, F. (eds.) Birds of North America. The Birds of North America Inc., Philadelphia, PA.

857. Mitchell, C. D. & Eichholz, M. W. (2010) Trumpeter Swan (*Cygnus buccinator*). *In* Poole, A. (ed.) The Birds of North America Online. Cornell Lab of Ornithology, Ithaca, NY. http://bna.birds.cornell.edu/bna/species/105

858. Miyabayashi, Y. & Mundkur, T. (1999) *Atlas of Key Sites for Anatidae in the East Asian Flyway*. Wetlands International, Tokyo & Kuala Lumpur.

859. Miyabayashi, Y., Sugawa, H. & Kurechi, M. (1994) Inventory of goose habitat in Japan: compilation of the inventory and conservation issues identified. Pp. 35–65 *in* Miyabashi, Y. (ed.) *Inventory of Goose Habitat in Japan*. Japanese Association of Wild Geese Protection, Wakayanagi.

860. Mlodinow, S. G., Springer, P. F., Deuel, B., Semo, L. S., Leukering, T., Schonewald, T. D., Tweit, W. & Barry, J. H. (2008) Distribution and identification of Cackling Goose (*Branta hutchinsii*) subspecies. *North Amer. Birds* 62: 344–360.

861. Moffitt, J. (1926) Notes on White-fronted and Tule Geese in central California. *Condor* 28: 241–243.

862. Moison, G., Smith, R. I. & Martinson, R. K. (1967) The Green-winged Teal: its distribution, migration, and population dynamics. US Fish Wildl. Serv. Spec. Sci. Rep. Wildl. 100.

863. Mondain-Monval, J.-Y., Desnouhes, L. & Taris, J.-P. (2002) Lead shot ingestion in waterbirds in the Camargue (France). *Game & Wildl. Sci.* 19: 237–246.

864. Monval, J.-Y. & Pirot, J.-Y. (1989) *Results of the IWRB International Waterfowl Census 1967–1986: Population Estimates, Trends and Distribution in Selected Species of Ducks, Swans, and Coot Fulica atra Wintering in the Western Palearctic and West Africa*. International Wetlands Research Bureau, Slimbridge.

865. Moody, A. F. (1932) Notes on the birds at Lilford, 1930 and 1931. *Avicult. Mag.* (5)5: 31.

866. Mooij, J. H. (2000) Population dynamics and migration of white-fronted geese (*Anser albifrons*) in Eurasia. Pp. 372–393 *in* Ebbing, B. S., Mazourov, Yu.L. & Tomkovich, P.S. (eds.) *Proc. Intern. Scientific Mem. Arctic Conserv. Symp.* Ecpros Publishers. Moscow.

867. Mooij, J. H. (2010) Review of the historical distribution of the Lesser White-fronted Goose *Anser erythropus* in Europe. *Ornis Svecica* 20: 190–201.

868. Mooij, J. H. & Zöckler, C. (1999) Reflections on the systematics, distribution and status of *Anser fabalis* (Latham, 1787). *Casarca* 5: 103–120.

869. Mooij, J. H. & Zöckler, C. (2000) Reflections on the systematics, distribution and status of *Anser albifrons*. *Casarca* 6: 92–107.

871. Moores N. (2005) Baikal Teal *Anas formosa*. Pp. 605–608 *in* Kear, J. (ed.) *Ducks, Geese and Swans*. Oxford Univ. Press.

872. Moores, N. & Moores, C. (2003) A few hybrid ducks: cautionary tales of the unexpected. www.birdskorea.or.kr/ Birds/Identification/ID_Notes/BK-ID-Hybrid-Ducks.shtml

873. Moores, N. & Moores, C. (2003) Separation of female-type Barrow's Goldeneye *Bucephala islandica* and Common Goldeneye *Bucephala clangula* – more than just bill colour. http://www.birdskorea.or.kr

874. Moores, N., Kim, A., Park, M. N. & Kim, S. A. (2010) *The Anticipated Impacts of the Four Rivers Project (Republic of Korea) on Waterbirds. Preliminary Report*. Birds Korea, Busan.

875. Moreno-Arroyo, B. & Torres Esquivias, J. A. (2000) La recuperación de la malvasía cabilliblanca (*Oxyura leucocephala*) en España durante el último decenio del siglo XX. *Oxyura* 10: 5–52.

876. Morgan, A. (2001) Alaskan goose to be removed from danger list. *The Sunday Telegraph*, 5 August 2001.

877. Morlan, J. (2005) Featured photo: an apparent hybrid between Hooded Merganser and Barrow's Goldeneye at Lake Merritt, Oakland, California. *Western Birds* 36: 279–282.

878. Morozov, V. V. (2006) The Lesser White-fronted Goose *Anser erythropus* at the verge of the millennium. Pp. 380–381 *in* Boere, G. C., Galbraith, C. & Stroud, D. (eds.) *Waterbirds Around the World*. The Stationary Office, Edinburgh.

879. Morrier, A., Lesage, L., Reed, A. & Savard, J.-P. L. (1997) Étude sur l'écologie de la Macreuse à front blanc au lac Malbaie, Réserve des Laurentides, *1994–1995*. Canadian Wildlife Service, Montreal.

880. Morse, S. (2009) A challenging future for the Steller's Eider. *Endangered Species Bull.* 34(3): 22–23.

881. Moser, T. J. (2006) *The 2005 North American Trumpeter Swan Survey*. US Fish & Wildlife Service, Denver, CO.

882. Moser, T. J. & Rolley, R. E. (1990) Discrimination of giant and interior Canada Geese of the Mississippi Flyway. *Wildl. Soc. Bull.* 18: 381–388.

883. Moulton, D. W. & Marshall, A. P. (1996) Laysan Duck (*Anas laysanensis*). *In* Poole, A. (ed.) The Birds of North America Online. Cornell Lab of Ornithology, Ithaca, NY. http://bna.birds.cornell.edu/bna/species/242

884. Mowbray, T. (1999) American Wigeon (*Anas americana*). *In* Poole, A. (ed.) The Birds of North America Online. Cornell Lab of Ornithology, Ithaca, NY. http://bna.birds.cornell.edu/bna/species/401

885. Mowbray, T. B. (2002) Canvasback (*Aythya valisineria*). *In* Poole, A. (ed.) The Birds of North America Online. Cornell Lab of Ornithology, Ithaca, NY. http://bna.birds.cornell.edu/bna/species/659

886. Mowbray, T. B., Cooke, F. & Ganter, B. (2000) Snow Goose (*Anser caerulescens*). *In* Poole, A. (ed.) The Birds of North America Online. Cornell Lab of Ornithology, Ithaca, NY. http://bna.birds.cornell.edu/bna/species/514

887. Mowbray, T. B., Ely, C. R., Sedinger, J. S. & Trost, R. E. (2002) Canada Goose (*Branta canadensis*). *In* Poole, A. (ed.) The Birds of North America Online. Cornell Lab of Ornithology, Ithaca, NY. http://bna.birds.cornell.edu/bna/species/682

888. Muñoz-Fuentes, V. (2001) Genetic introgression of Ruddy Ducks in wild populations of White-headed Ducks. *Threatened Waterfowl Specialist Group News* 13: 28–30.

889. Munõz-Fuentes, V., Green, A. J., Negro, J. J. & Sorenson, M. D. (2005) Population structure and loss of genetic diversity in the endangered White-headed Duck, *Oxyura leucocephala*. *Conserv. Genetics* 6: 999–1015.

890. Muñoz-Fuentes, V., Gyllenstrand, N., Negro, J. J., Green, A. J. & Vilà, C. (2005) Microsatellite markers for two stifftail ducks: the White-headed Duck, *Oxyura leucocephala*, and the Ruddy Duck, *O. jamaicensis*. *Mol. Ecol. Notes* 5: 263–265.

891. Muñoz-Fuentes, V., Green, A. J., Sorenson, M. D., Negro, J. J. & Vilà, C. (2006) The Ruddy Duck *Oxyura jamaicensis* in Europe: natural colonization or human introduction? *Mol. Ecol.* 15: 1441–1453.

892. Muñoz-Fuentes, V., Vilà, C., Green, A. J., Negro, J. J. & Sorenson, M. D. (2007) Hybridization between White headed Ducks and introduced Ruddy Ducks in Spain. *Mol. Ecol.* 16: 629–638.

893. Muñoz-Fuentes, V., Green, A. J. & Sorenson, M. D. (2008) Comparing the genetics of wild and captive populations of White-headed Ducks *Oxyura leucocephala*: consequences for recovery programmes. *Ibis* 150: 807–815.

894. Muñoz-Fuentes, V., Green, A. J. & Negro, J. (2012) Genetic studies facilitated management decisions on the invasion of the Ruddy Duck in Europe. *Biol. Invasions* 15(4): 1–6.

895. Murase, Y. (1992) [Wintering records of a mated pair of Bewick's and Whistling Swans, *Cygnus columbianus bewickii* and *C. c. columbianus* in Kitakami, Iwate. Part 3] (in Japanese). *Strix* 11: 245–251.

896. Murase, Y. (1994) [On the bill pattern of the hybrid between Whistling and Bewick's Swans] (in Japanese). *Strix* 13: 238–242.

897. Murie, O. J. (1959) Fauna of the Aleutian Islands and Alaskan Peninsula. North Amer. Fauna no. 61.

898. Myong Sok, O. (1984) Wiederendeckung der Schopfkasarka, *Tadorna cristata*, in der Koreanischen Demokratischen Volksrepublik. *J. Orn.* 125: 102–103.

899. Nagy, E. (1950) Über Gänsebastarde. Pp. 256–266 *in* von Jordans, A. & Peus, F. (eds.) *Syllegomena Biologica*. Geest & Protig, Leipzig.

900. Ndlovu, M., Cumming, G. S. & Hockey, P. A. (2013) Influence of moult and location on patterns of daily movement by Egyptian Geese in South Africa. *Emu* 114(1): 23-29.

901. Ndlovu, M., Cumming, G. S., Hockey, P. A. & Bruinzeel, L. W. (2010) Phenotypic flexibility of a southern African duck *Alopochen aegyptiaca* during moult: do northern hemisphere paradigms apply? *J. Avian Biol.* 41: 558–564.

902. Nechaev, V. A. (1992) Status of the Swan Goose and the Mandarin Duck on Sakhalin Island, Russian Far East. *IWRB Threatened Waterfowl Res. Group Newsl.* 2: 12–14.

903. Nechaev, V. A. & Gluschenko, Y. N. (1993) Baer's Pochard *Aythya baeri* in the Far East of Russia. *IWRB Threatened Waterfowl Res. Group Newsl.* 3: 5–7.

904. Nelson, C. H. (1983) Eye-color changes in Barrow's Goldeneye and Common Goldeneye ducklings. *Wilson Bull.* 95: 482–488.

905. Nelson, C. H. (1993) The identification of Barrow's Goldeneye *Bucephala islandica* and Common Goldeneye *B. clangula americana* ducklings. *Wildfowl* 44: 178–183.

906. Nelson, C. H. (1993) *The Downy Waterfowl of North America*. Delta Station Press, Deerfield, IL.

907. Nelson, C. H. (1996) Identification of Greater Scaup, *Aythya marila*, and Lesser Scaup, *A. affinis*, ducklings. *Canadian Field-Natur.* 110: 288–293.

908. New Jersey Audubon Society (2013) Avalon seawatch. www.njaudubon.org/Portals/10/Research/PDF/Avalon%20Sea%20Watch%201993%20to%202011.pdf

909. Newth, J., Colhoun, K., Einarsson, O., McElwaine, G., Thorstensen, S., Hesketh, R., McElwaines, G., Thorstensen, S., Petersen, A., Wells, J. & Rees, E. (2013) Winter distribution of Whooper Swans *Cygnus cygnus* ringed in four geographically discrete regions in Iceland between 1988 and 2006: an update. *Wildfowl* 57: 98–119.

910. Nichols, J. D. & Johnson, F. A. (1990) Wood Duck population dynamics: a review. Pp. 83–105 in Frederickson, L. H., Burger, G. V., Havera, S. P., Graber, D. A., Kirby, R. E. & Taylor, T. S. (eds.) *Proc. 1988 North Amer. Wood Duck Symp.*

911. Nijman, V., Aliabadian, M. & Roselaar, C. S. (2010) Wild hybrids of Lesser White-fronted Goose (*Anser erythropus*) × Greater White-fronted Goose (*A. albifrons*) (*Aves: Anseriformes*) from the European migratory flyway. *Zool. Anz.* 248: 265–271.

912. Nikolaeva, N. G., Spiridonov, V. A. & Krasnov, Y. V. (2006) Existing and proposed marine protected areas and their relevance for seabird conservation: a case study in the Barents Sea region. Pp. 743–749 *in* Boere, G. C., Galbraith, C. & Stroud, D. (eds.) *Waterbirds Around the World*. The Stationary Office, Edinburgh.

913. Norderhaug, A. & Norderhaug, M. (1984) Status of the lesser white-fronted goose, *Anser erythropus*. *Swedish Wildl. Res.* 13: 171–185.

914. Norman, F. I. (1990) Macquarie Island ducks – habitats and hybrids. *Notornis* 37: 53–58.

915. Norment, C. J., Hall, A. & Hendricks, P. (1999) Important bird and mammal records in the Thelon River valley, Northwest Territories: range expansions and possible causes. *Canadian Field-Natur.* 113: 375–385.

916. Norton, A. H. (1897) A noteworthy plumage observed in the American Eider Drake (*Somateria dresseri*). *Auk* 14: 303–304.

917. Novak, J. M., Smith, L. M. & Vangilder, L. D. (1989) Genetic variability within and among wintering populations of Brant. *J. Heredity* 80: 160–163.

918. Nowak, E. (1970) The waterfowl of Mongolia. *Wildfowl* 21: 61–68.

919. Nowak, E. (1983) [The Crested Shelduck *Tadorna cristata* Kuroda, 1917 – a species threatened with extinction (summary of information and a proposal for its conservation)]. *Bonn. Zool. Beiträge* 34: 235–271. (In German)

920. Nowak, E. (1984) [On the presumed breeding and wintering range of the Crested Shelduck *Tadorna cristata*]. *J. Orn.* 125: 103–105.

921. Nudds, T. D. & Cole, R. W. (1991) Changes in populations and breeding success of boreal forest ducks. *J. Wildl. Manag.* 55: 569–573.

922. Nyeland, J. (2005) Greylag Goose *Anser anser*. Pp. 276–280 in Kear, J. (ed.) *Ducks, Geese and Swans*. Oxford Univ. Press.

923. Nygård, T., Frantzen, B., & Švažas, S. (1995) Steller's Eiders *Polysticta stelleri* wintering in Europe: numbers, distribution and origin. *Wildfowl* 46: 140–156.

924. Oberholser, H. C. (1974) *The Bird Life of Texas*. Vol. 1. Univ. of Texas Press, Austin.

925. Ogilvie, M. A. (1978) *Wild Geese*. Buteo Books, Vermillion, SD.

926. Ogilvie, M. (2005) Common Eider *Somatera mollissima*. Pp. 701–705 in Kear, J. (ed.) *Ducks, Geese and Swans*. Oxford Univ. Press.

927. Ogilvie, M. (2005) King Eider *Somateria spectabilis*. Pp. 698–701 in Kear, J. (ed.) *Ducks, Geese and Swans*. Oxford Univ. Press.

928. Ogilvie, M. & Young, S. (1998) *Photographic Handbook of the Wildfowl of the World*. New Holland, London.

929. Ohtonen, A. (1988) Bill patterns of the Whooper Swan in Finland during autumn migration. *Wildfowl* 39: 153–154.

930. Olney, P. (2005) Smew *Mergellus albellus*. Pp. 739–743 in Kear, J. (ed.) *Ducks, Geese and Swans*. Oxford Univ. Press.

931. Oreshnikova, V. S. (1985) [A hybrid of the Bean Goose (*Anser fabalis serrirostris*) and the Canada Goose (*Branta canadensis minima*)]. *Ornithologiia* 20: 191–192. (In Russian)

932. Oring, L. W. (1964) Behavior and ecology of certain ducks during the postbreeding period. *J. Wildl. Manag.* 28: 223–233.

933. Oring, L. W. (1968) Growth, molts, and plumages of the Gadwall. *Auk* 85: 355–380.

935. Orthmeyer, D. L., Takekawa, J. Y., Ely, C. R., Wege, M. L. & Newton, W. E. (1995) Morphological differences in Pacific Coast populations of Greater White-fronted Geese. *Condor* 97: 123–132.

936. Osborne, K. C. (1972) The need for caution when identifying Scaup, Ferruginous Duck and other species in the *Aythya* genus. *London Bird Rep.* 36: 86–91.

937. Ottvall, R. (2008) Feasibility study of catching and genetic screening of Swedish Lesser White-fronted Geese *Anser erythropus*. Unpubl. Dept. of Ecology, Lund Univ.

938. Owen, M. (1980) *Wild Geese of the World*. Batsford, London.

939. Owen, M. & Black, J. (2005) Barnacle Goose *Branta leucopsis*. Pp. 329–334 in Kear, J. (ed.) *Ducks, Geese and Swans*. Oxford Univ. Press.

940. Owen, M. & Montgomery, S. (1978) Body measurements of Mallard caught in Britain. *Wildfowl* 29: 123-134.

941. Owen, M. & Ogilvie, M. A. (1979) Wing molt and weights of Barnacle Geese in Spitsbergen. *Condor* 81: 42–52.

942. Owen, M., Black, J. & Liber, H. (1988) Pair bond duration and timing of its formation in Barnacle Geese. Pp. 23–38 in Weller, M. (ed.) *Waterfowl in Winter*. Univ. of Minnesota Press, Minneapolis.

943. Owens, I. P. F. & Short, R. V. (1995) Hormonal basis of sexual dimorphism in birds: implications for new theories of sexual selection. *Trends Ecol. & Evol.* 10: 44–47.

944. Oyler-McCance, S. J., Ransler, F. A., Berkman, L. K. & Quinn, T. W. (2007) A rangewide population genetic study of trumpeter swans. *Conserv. Genetics* 8: 1339–1353.

945. Palmer, R. S. (ed.) (1976) *Handbook of North American Birds*. Vols. 2–3. Yale Univ. Press, New Haven, CT.

946. Palmer, R. S. (1977) King Eider studies. *Brit. Birds* 70: 107–113.

947. Panov, E. N. (1989) [*Natural Hybridisation and Ethological Isolation in Birds*]. Nauka, Moscow. (In Russian)

948. Patrick, L. (1932) Whittier Ornithological Academy. *Avicult. Mag.* (4)10: 154–158.

949. Patten, M. A. & Heindel, M. T. (1994) Identifying Trumpeter and Tundra Swans. *Birding* 26: 306–318.

950. Patton, J. C. & Avise, J. C. (1986) Evolutionary genetics of birds, IV. Rates of protein divergence in waterfowl (Anatidae). *Genetica* 68: 129–143.

951. Paul, J.-P. & Crouzier, P. (2009) Nidification de Eider à duvet *Somateria mollissima* en Franche-Comté. *Ornithos* 16: 74–76.

952. Paulus, S. L. (1984) Molts and plumages of Gadwall in winter. *Auk* 101: 887–889.

953. Paxinos, E. E., James, H. F., Olson, S. L., Sorenson, M. D., Jackson, J. & Fleischer, R. C. (2002) mtDNA from fossils reveals a radiation of Hawaiian geese recently derived from the Canada goose (*Branta canadensis*). *Proc. Natl. Acad. Sci. USA* 99: 1399–1404.

954. Payn, W. H. (1941) The plumage changes of adolescent Shovelers. *Ibis* 83: 456–459.

955. Pearce, J. M. & Petersen, M. R. (2009) Post-fledging movements of juvenile Common Mergansers (*Mergus merganser*) in Alaska as inferred by satellite telemetry. *Waterbirds* 32: 133–137.

956. Pearce, J. M., Pierson, B. J., Talbot, S. L., Derksen, D. V., Kraege, D. K. & Scribner, K. T. (2000) A genetic evaluation of morphology used to identify harvested Canada Geese. *J. Wildl. Manag.* 64: 863–874.

957. Pearce, J. M., Talbot, S. L., Petersen, M. R. & Rearick, J. R. (2005) Limited genetic differentiation among breeding, molting, and wintering groups of the threatened Steller's eider: the role of historic and contemporary factors. *Conserv. Genetics* 6: 743–757.

958. Pearce, J., Talbot, S., Ely, C. & Derksen, D. (2006) Improving breeding population indices of Lesser and Taverner's Canada Geese through genetic analysis, progress report, March 2006. Unpubl. US Geological Survey, Anchorage, AK.

959. Pearce, J. M., Blums, P. & Lindberg, M. S. (2008) Site fidelity is an inconsistent determinant of population structure in the Hooded Merganser (*Lophodytes cucullatus*): evidence from genetic, mark-recapture, and comparative data. *Auk* 125: 711–722.

960. Pease, M. L., Rose, R. K. & Butler, M. J. (2005) Effects of human disturbances on the behavior of wintering ducks. *Wildl. Soc. Bull.* 33: 103–112.

961. Peberdy, K. (1991) The use of grazed saltmarsh by *Branta leucopsis* (Barnacle Goose) in relation to refuge establishment and management. Pp. 95–107 in Finlayson, C. M. & Larsson, T. (eds.) *Wetland Management and Restoration*. Swedish Environmental Protection Agency, Solna.

962. Pedall, I., Gonzalez, J., Sauer-Gürth, H. & Wink, M. (2007) Genetic analysis of captive Lesser White-fronted Geese (*Anser erythropus*) in Germany. *Vogelwelt* 128: 304–309.

963. Peet, N. (1998) Ruddy Duck *Oxyura jamaicensis*/White-headed Duck hybrid recorded in Turkey. *Bird Conserv. Intern.* 8: 310.

964. Perennou, C. (1992) *African Waterfowl census 1992 – Les dénombrements internationaux d'oiseaux d'eau en Afrique 1992*. International Wetlands Research Bureau, Slimbridge.

965. Perennou, C. P., Mundkur, T. & Scott, D. A. (1994) *The Asian Waterfowl Census 1987–1991: Distribution and Status of*

Asian Waterfowl. International Wetlands Research Bureau, Slimbridge & Kuala Lumpur.

966. Pérez-Arteaga, A., Gaston, K. J. & Kershaw, M. (2002) Population trends and priority conservation sites for Mexican Duck *Anas diazi. Bird Conserv. Intern.* 12: 35–52.

967. Perry, P. (1982) The use of gull nests by Eiders. *Brit. Birds* 75: 360–365.

968. Peters, J. L. (1931) *Check-list of Birds of the World.* Vol. 1. Harvard Univ. Press, Cambridge, MA.

969. Peters, J. L. & Omland, K. E. (2007) Population structure and mitochondrial polyphyly in North American Gadwalls (*Anas strepera*). *Auk* 124: 444–462.

970. Peters, J. L., Zhuravlev, Y. N., Fefelov, I., Logie, A. & Omland, K. E. (2007) Nuclear loci and coalescent methods support ancient hybridization as cause of mitochondrial paraphyly between Gadwall and Falcated duck (*Anas* spp.). *Evolution* 61: 1992–2006.

971. Peters, J. L., Zhuravlev, Y. N. & Fefelov, I. (2008) Multilocus phylogeography of a Holarctic duck: colonization of North America from Eurasia by gadwall (*Anas strepera*). *Evolution* 62: 1469–1483.

972. Peters, J. L., Bolender, K. A. & Pearce, J. M. (2012) Behavioural vs. molecular sources of conflict between nuclear and mitochondrial DNA: the role of male-biased dispersal in a Holarctic sea duck. *Mol. Ecol.* 21: 3562–3575.

973. Peters, J. L., McCracken, K. G., Pruett, C. L., Rohwer, S., Drovetski, S. V., Zhuravlev, Y. N., Kulikova, I. A., Gibson, D. D. & Winker, K. (2012) A parapatric propensity for breeding precludes the completion of speciation in common teal (*Anas crecca, sensu lato*). *Mol. Ecol.* 21: 4563–4577.

974. Peters, J. L., Sonsthagen, S. A., Lavretsky, P., Rezsutek, M., Johnson, K. P. & McCracken, K. G. (2014) Interspecific hybridization contributes to high genetic diversity and apparent effective population size in an endemic population of Mottled Ducks (*Anas fulvigula maculosa*) *Conserv. Genetics* 15: 509–520.

975. Petersen, M. R. (1981) Populations, feeding ecology and molt of Steller's Eiders. *Condor* 83: 256–262.

976. Petersen, M. R. (1990) Nest-site selection by Emperor Geese and Cackling Canada Geese. *Wilson Bull.* 102: 413–426.

977. Petersen, M. R. (1992) Reproductive ecology of Emperor Geese: annual and individual variation in nesting. *Condor* 94: 383–397.

978. Petersen, M. R. (1996) Satellite telemetry solves eider mystery. *Endangered Species Bull.* 21(5): 7.

979. Petersen, M. R. & Douglas, D. C. (2004) Winter ecology of Spectacled Eiders: environmental characteristics and population change. *Condor* 106: 79–94.

980. Petersen, M. R. & Flint, P. (2002) Population structure of Pacific Common Eiders breeding in Alaska. *Condor* 104: 780–787.

981. Petersen, M. R. & Gill, R. E. (1982) Population status of Emperor Geese along the north side of the Alaska Peninsula. *Wildfowl* 33: 31–38.

982. Petersen, M. R., Bustnes, J. O. & Systa, G. H. (2006) Breeding and moulting locations and migration patterns of the Atlantic population of Steller's eiders *Polysticta stelleri* as determined from satellite telemetry. *J. Avian Biol.* 37: 58–68.

983. Petersen, M. R., Larned, W. W. & Douglas, D. C. (1999) At-sea distribution of Spectacled Eiders: a 120-year-old mystery resolved. *Auk* 116: 1009–1020.

984. Peterson, S. R. & Ellarson, R. S. (1978) Bursae, reproductive structures and scapular color in wintering female Oldsquaws. *Auk* 95: 115–121.

985. Petkov, N., Hughes, B. & Gallo-Orsi, U. (2003) *Ferruginous Duck: From Research to Conservation.* Bird Life International, Cambrige, UK.

986. Petkov, N., Popgeorgiev, G. & Gigov, S. (2012) Evidence of landscape scale impact of windfarm development in coastal Dobrudga on the distribution of foraging flocks of Red-breasted Goose (*Branta ruficollis*) and the Ponto-Anatolian flyway population of Greater White-fronted Goose (*Anser albifrons*). Abstract/poster presented at 4th WI/IUCN GSG Meeting, Stakjiar.

987. Pettingill, O. S. (1959) King Eiders mated with Common Eiders in Iceland. *Wilson Bull.* 71: 205–207.

988. Phillips, J. C. (1922–26) *A Natural History of the Ducks.* Houghton Mifflin, Boston.

989. Pierson, B. J., Pearce, J. M., Talbot, S. L., Shields, G. F. & Scribner, K. T. (2000) Molecular genetic analysis of Aleutian Canada Geese from Buldir and the Semidi Islands, Alaska. *Condor* 102: 172–180.

990. Pihl, S. (2001) *European Species Action Plan for Steller's Eider (Polysticta stelleri).* European Union, Strasbourg.

991. Pihl, S. & Laursen, K. (1996) A reestimation of Western Palearctic wintering seaduck numbers from the Baltic Sea 1993 survey. *Gibier Faune Sauvage* 13: 191–199.

992. Pihl, S. & Fox, T. (2005) Velvet Scoter *Melanitta fusca.* Pp. 715–719 *in* Kear, J. (ed.) *Ducks, Geese and Swans.* Oxford Univ. Press.

993. Pirkola, M. & Kalinainen, P. (1984) The status, habitats and productivity of breeding Bean Goose *Anser fabalis fabalis* in Finland. *Swedish Wildl. Res.* 13: 9–48.

994. Pitman, C. C. (1965) The nesting and some other habits of *Alopochen, Nettapus, Plectropterus* and *Sarkidiornis. Wildfowl* 16: 7.

995. Pitt, F. (1944) A note on a mating of *Anser fabalis* × *Anser brachyrhynchus* and the resulting hybrids. *Bull. Brit. Orn. Club* 64: 33–35.

996. Pitt, W. S. (1944) An unusual cross. *The Field (London)* 184: 354.

997. Pittaway, R. (1992) Recognizable forms: subspecies and morphs of the Snow Goose. *Ontario Birds* 10: 72–76.

998. Ploeger, P. L. (1968) Geographical differentiation in Arctic Anatidae as a result of isolation during the last glacial. *Ardea* 56: 1–159.

999. Poole, A. F., Wood, C., Iliff, M., Silk, M. & Garner, M. (2014) Recognised and fully named. http://birdingfrontiers. com/2014/01/09/grey-bellied-brant/

1000. Popovkina, A. B. (2006) Conflicting trends in Ruddy Shelduck *Tadorna ferruginea* populations: a myth or reality? Pp. 480–481 *in* Boere, G. C., Galbraith, C. & Stroud, D. (ed.) *Waterbirds Around the World.* The Stationary Office, Edinburgh.

1001. Portenko, L. A. (1952) Age and seasonal changes in the plumage of ducks belonging to the genus *Somateria. Trudy Inst. Zool. Acad. Sci. Moscow-Leningrad, USSR* 9: 1100–1132.

1002. Poyarkov, N. D. (1984) Status of the *Anser cygnoides* population in the Amur region. *In* Present status of waterfowl resources, All-Union Seminar, 20–23 October 1984. Moscow.

1003. Poyarkov, N. D. (2006) Falcated Duck in Russia. *Threatened Wildlife Specialist Group News* 15: 21–22.

1004. Poyarkov, N. D. (2006) The Swan Goose *Anser cygnoides* research and conservation programme in Russia. Pp. 482–483 *in* Boere, G. C., Galbraith, C. & Stroud, D. (ed.) *Waterbirds Around the World*. The Stationary Office, Edinburgh.

1005. Pöysä, H. & Poysa, S. (2002) Nest-site limitation and density dependence of reproductive output in the common goldeneye *Bucephala clangula*: implications for the management of cavity-nesting birds. *J. Appl. Ecol.* 39: 502–510.

1006. Pöysä, H. & Väänänen, V.-M. (2014) Drivers of breeding numbers in a long-distance migrant, the Garganey (*Anas querquedula*): effects of climate and hunting pressure. *J. Orn.* 155: 679–687.

1007. Pranty, B., Dunn, J. L., Heinl, S. C., Kratter, A. W., Lehman, P. E., Lockwood, M. L., Mactavish, B. & Zimmer, K. J. (2008) Annual report of the ABA Checklist Committee. *Birding* 40: 32–38.

1008. Prestwich, A. A. (1960) On Mandarin Duck hybrids. *Avicult. Mag.* 66: 5–8.

1009. Prevett, J. P. & Johnson, F. C. (1977) Continued eastern expansion of breeding range of Ross's Goose. *Condor*: 121–123.

1010. Price, T. (2008) *Speciation in Birds*. Roberts & Co., Greenwood Village, CO.

1011. Prop, J. & Quinn, J. L. (2003) Colony choice in a patchy arctic environment: density-dependent reproductive sucess in red-breasted geese *Branta ruficollis*. *Oikos* 102: 571–580.

1012. Pyle, P. (2005) Molts and plumages of ducks. *Waterbirds* 28: 208–219.

1013. Pyle, P. (2007) Revision of molt and plumage terminology in Ptarmigan (*Phasianidae*: *Lagopus* spp.) based on evolutionary considerations. *Auk* 124: 508–514.

1014. Pyle, P. (2008) *Identification Guide to North American Birds*. Pt. 2. Slate Creek Press, Bolinas, CA.

1015. Pyle, P. (2013) Molt Homologies in ducks and other birds: a response to Hawkins (2011) and further thoughts on molt terminology in ducks. *Waterbirds* 36: 77–81.

1016. Pyle, R. L. & Pyle, P. (2009) *The Birds of the Hawaiian Islands: Occurrence, History, Distribution, and Status*. B. P. Bishop Museum, Honolulu, HI.

1017. Quakenbush, L. T. & Suydam, R. (1999) Periodic nonbreeding of Steller's Eiders near Barrow, Alaska, on possible causes. Pp. 34–40 *in* Goudie, R. I., Petersen, M. R. & Robertson, G. J. (eds.) *Behavior and Ecology of Sea Ducks*. Canadian Wildl. Serv. Occ. Pap. 100.

1018. Quakenbush, L. T., Day, R. H., Anderson, B. A., Pitelka, F. A. & McCaffery, B. J. (2002) Historical and present breeding season distribution of Steller's Eiders in Alaska. *Western Birds* 33: 99–120.

1019. Quakenbush, L. T., Suydam, R. S., Acker, R., Knoche, M. & Citta, J. (2009) *Migration of King and Common Eiders Past Point Barrow, Alaska, during Summer/Fall 2002 through Spring 2004: Population Trends and Effects of Wind*. Coastal Marine Institute, Fairbanks, AK.

1020. Quan, R. C., Wen, X., Tang, X., Peng, G. H. & Huang, T. F. (2001) Habitat use by wintering Ruddy Shelduck at Lashihai Lake, Lijiang, China. *Waterbirds* 24: 402–406.

1021. Quicke, D. L. (1993) *Principles and Techniques of Contemporary Taxonomy*. Blackie Academic & Professional, London.

1022. Quinn, J. L. (2005) Greater Scaup *Aythya marila*. Pp. 675–679 *in* Kear, J. (ed.) *Ducks, Geese and Swans*. Oxford Univ. Press.

1023. Quinn, J. L., Prop, J. & Kokorev, Y. (1996) The ecology of Red-breasted Geese in summer: report on a preliminary expedition to the Taimyr Peninsula in 1995. Unpubl. Wildfowl & Wetlands Trust, Slimbridge.

1024. Quinn, T. W. (1992) The genetic legacy of mother goose—phylogeographic patterns of Lesser Snow Goose *Chen caerulescens* caerulescens maternal lineages. *Mol. Ecol.* 1: 105–117.

1025. Quinn, T. W., Quinn, J. S., Cooke, F. & White, B. N. (1987) DNA marker analysis detects multiple maternity and paternity in single broods of the Lesser Snow Goose. *Nature* 326: 392–394.

1026. Quinn, T. W., Shields, G. F. & Wilson, A. C. (1991) Affinities of the Hawaiian Goose based on two types of mitochondrial DNA data. *Auk* 108: 585–593.

1027. Raffaele, H., Wiley, J., Garrido, O., Keith, A. & Raffaele, J. (1998) *A Guide to the Birds of the West Indies*. Princeton Univ. Press.

1028. Raftovich, R. V. & Wilkins, K. A. (2013) *Migratory Bird Hunting Activity and Harvest During the 2011–12 and 2012–13 Hunting Seasons*. US Fish & Wildlife Service, Laurel, MD.

1029. Rahmani, A. R. & Islam, M. Z. U. (2008) *Ducks, Geese and Swans of India: Their Status and Distribution*. Oxford Univ. Press.

1030. Raikow, R. J. (1970) Evolution of diving adaptations in the stifftail ducks. *Univ. Calif. Publ. Zool.* 94: 1–52.

1031. Randler, C. (2000) Die Bestimmung von Tauchentenhybriden des Gattung *Aythya*. *Limicola* 14: 1–35.

1032. Randler, C. (2000) Zusammenfassende Ubersicht zum Auftreten von Tafel- × Moorentenhybriden (*Aythya ferina × A. nyroca*) im westlichen Mitteleuropa. *Vogelwarte* 40: 206–211.

1033. Randler, C. (2001) Field identification of hybrid wildfowl – geese. *Alula* 7: 42–48.

1034. Randler, C. (2001) Field identification of hybrid wildfowl – *Aythya*. *Alula* 7: 148–156.

1035. Randler, C. (2002) Avian hybridization, mixed pairing and female choice. *Anim. Behav.* 63: 103–119.

1036. Randler, C. (2003) Vigilance in urban Swan Geese and their hybrids. *Waterbirds* 26: 257–260.

1037. Randler, C. (2004) Aggressive interactions in Swan Geese *Anser cygnoides* and their hybrids. *Acta Orn.* 39: 147–153.

1038. Randler, C. (2004) Frequency of bird hybrids: does detectability make all the difference? *J. Orn.* 145: 123–128.

1039. Randler, C. (2006) Behavioural and ecological correlates of natural hybridization in birds. *Ibis* 148: 459–467.

1040. Randler, C. (2008) Hybrid wildfowl in Central Europe—an overview. *Waterbirds* 31: 143–146.

1041. Randler, C. (2008) Mating patterns in avian hybrid zones—a meta-analysis and review. *Ardea* 96: 73–80.

1042. Rank, M. (1991) "Extinct" Shelduck rediscovered in China? *Bull. Oriental Bird Club* 14: 14–15.

1043. Rank, M. (1992) Crested Shelduck update. *Bull. Oriental Bird Club* 15: 10.

1044. Rasmussen, P. C. & Anderton, J. C. (2005) *Birds of South Asia. The Ripley Guide*. Smithsonian Institution, Washington DC & Lynx Edicions, Barcelona.

1045. Rassi, P., Hyvärinen, E., Juslén, A. & Mannerkoski, I. (eds.) (2010) *The 2010 Red List of Finnish Species*. Ministry of the Environment Finnish Environment Institute, Helsinki.

1046. Ratti, J. T. & Timm, D. E. (1979) Migratory behavior of Vancouver Canada Geese: recovery rate bias. Pp. 208–212 *in* Jarvis, R. L. & Bartonek, J. C. (eds.) *Management and Biology of*

Pacific Flyway Geese. Oregon State Univ. Bookstores, Corvallis.

1047. Ratti, J. T., Timm, D. E. & Robards, F. C. (1977) Weights and measurements of Vancouver Canada Geese. *Bird-Banding* 48: 354–357.

1048. Rattray, B. & Cooke, F. (1984) Genetic modelling: an analysis of a colour polymorphism in the Snow Goose (*Anser caerulescens*) *Zool. J. Linn. Soc.* 80: 437–445.

1049. Raven, G. H. & Dickson, D. L. (2009) *Surveys of Pacific Common Eiders (Somateria mollissima v-nigra) in the Bathurst Inlet area of Nunavut, 2006–2008.* Canadian Wildlife Service, Edmonton.

1050. Reeber, S. (2001) Problèmes d'identification posés par les hybrides de fuligules *Aythya sp. en Europe de l'Ouest. Ornithos* 9: 177–209.

1051. Reed, A. (2005) Surf Scoter *Melanitta perspicillata.* Pp. 712–714 *in* Kear, J. (ed.) *Ducks, Geese and Swans.* Oxford Univ. Press.

1052. Reed, A., Stehn, R. & Ward, D. (1989) Autumn use of Izembek Lagoon, Alaska, by Brant from different breeding areas. *J. Wildl. Manag.* 53: 720-725.

1053. Reed, A. & Plante, N. (1997) Decline in body mass, size and condition of Greater Snow Geese, 1975–1994. *J. Wildl. Manag.* 61: 413–419.

1054. Reed, A., Giroux, J. F. & Gauthier, G. (1998) Population size, productivity, harvest and distribution. Pp. 5–31 in Batt, B. D. J. (ed.) *The Greater Snow Goose: Report of the Arctic Goose Habitat Working Group.* US Fish & Wildlife Service, Washington DC & Canadian Wildlife Service Ottawa.

1055. Reed, A., Ward, D. H., Derksen, D. V. & Sedinger, J. S. (1998) Brant (*Branta bernicla*). *The Birds of North America Online (A. Poole, Ed.).* Ithaca: Cornell Lab of Ornithology; Retrieved from the Birds of North America Online: http://bna.birds. cornell.edu/bna/species/337

1056. Rees, E. (2005) Trumpeter Swan *Cygnus buccinator.* Pp. 234–238 in Kear, J. (ed.) *Ducks, Geese and Swans.* Oxford Univ. Press.

1057. Rees, E. (2005) Whooper Swan *Cygnus cygnus.* Pp. 249–256 *in* Kear, J. (ed.) *Ducks, Geese and Swans.* Oxford Univ. Press.

1058. Rees, E. (2010) *Bewick's Swan.* T. & A. D. Poyser, London.

1059. Rees, E., Einarsson, O. & Laubek, B. (1997) *Cygnus cygnus* Whooper swan. *BWP Update* 1(1): 27–35.

1060. Regehr, H. M. (2011) Movement rates and distances of wintering Harlequin Ducks: implications for population structure. *Waterbirds* 34: 19–31.

1061. Regehr, H. M., Smith, C. M., Arquilla, B. & Cooke, F. (2001) Post-fledging broods of migratory Harlequin Ducks accompany females to wintering areas. *Condor* 103: 408–412.

1062. Rehfisch, M. M., Blair, M. J., McKay, H. & Musgrove, A. J. (2006) The impact and status of introduced waterbirds in Africa, Asia Minor, Europe and the Middle East. *Acta Zool. Sinica* 52 (Suppl.): 572–575.

1063. Remsen, J. V., Cadena, C. D., Jaramillo, A., Nores, M., Pacheco, J. F., Pérez-Emán, J., Robbins, M. B., Stiles, F. G., Stotz, D. F. & Zimmer, K. J. (2014) A classification of the bird species of South America. Version 17/03/2014. http://www. museum.lsu.edu/~Remsen/SACCBaseline.htm

1064. René de Roland, L., Sam, T. S., Rakotondratsima, M. P. H. & Thorstrom, R. (2007) Rediscovery of the Madagascar Pochard (*Aythya innotata*) in northern Madagascar. *Bull. African Bird Club* 14: 171–174.

1065. Reynolds, C. M. (1972) Mute Swan weights in relation to breeding performance. *Wildfowl* 23: 111–118.

1066. Rheindt, F. E. & Edwards, S. V. (2011) Genetic introgression: an integral but neglected component of speciation in birds. *Auk* 128: 620–632.

1067. Rhymer, J. M. (2001) Evolutionary relationships and conservation of the Hawaiian anatids. *Stud. Avian Biol.* 22: 61–67.

1068. Rhymer, J. M. & Simberloff, D. (1996) Extinction by hybridization and introgression. *Ann. Rev. Ecol. & Syst.* 27: 83–109.

1069. Richards, B. (1999) Letter: Canada Goose forms. *Birding World* 12: 82.

1070. Ridgely, R. S. & Greenfield, P. J. (2001) *The Birds of Ecuador.* Vol. 2. Cornell Univ. Press, Ithaca, NY.

1071. Rigbäck, L. (1986) Observation av en *Aythya* hybrid. *Calidris* 15: 71–72.

1072. Robb, J. R. (1997) Physioecology of staging American Black Ducks and Mallards in autumn. Ph.D. thesis. Ohio State Univ., Columbus.

1073. Robbins, M. B., Dunn, J. L., Dittmann, D. L., Garrett, K. L., Heinl, S., Kratter, A. W., Lasley, G. & Mactavish, B. (2004) ABA Checklist Committee 2003 annual report. *Birding* 36: 38–41.

1074. Roberson, D. (1980) *Rare Birds of the West Coast of North America.* Woodcock Publications, Pacific Grove, CA.

1075. Robert, M. & Savard, J.-P. L. (2006) The St. Lawrence River Estuary and Gulf: a stronghold for Barrow's Goldeneyes wintering in eastern North America. *Waterbirds* 29: 437–450.

1076. Robert, M., Savard, J.-P. L., Fitzgerald, G. & Laporte, P. (1999) Satellite tracking of Barrow's Goldeneyes in eastern North America: location of breeding areas and molting sites. *Proc. 15th Intern. Symp. Biolotelemetry, Juneau, AK.*

1077. Robert, M., Bordage, D., Savard, J.-P. L., Fitzgerald, G. & Morneau, F. (2000) The breeding range of the Barrow's Goldeneye in eastern North America. *Wilson Bull.* 112: 1–7.

1078. Robert, M., Mittelhauser, G. H., Jobin, B., Fitzgerald, G. & Lamothe, P. (2008) New insights on Harlequin Duck population structure in eastern North America as revealed by satellite telemetry. *Waterbirds* 31 (Spec. Publ. 2): 159–172.

1079. Robertson, B. C. & Goldstien, S. J. (2012) Phylogenetic affinities of the New Zealand blue duck (*Hymenolaimus malacorhynchos*) *Notornis* 59: 49–59.

1080. Robertson, G. J. & Goudie, R. I. (1999) Harlequin Duck (*Histrionicus histrionicus*). *In* Poole, A. (ed.) The Birds of North America Online. Cornell Lab of Ornithology, Ithaca, NY. http://bna.birds.cornell.edu/bna/species/466

1081. Robertson, G. J. & Savard, J.-P. L. (2002) Long-tailed Duck (*Clangula hyemalis*). *In* Poole, A. (ed.) The Birds of North America Online. Cornell Lab of Ornithology, Ithaca, NY. http://bna.birds.cornell.edu/bna/species/651

1082. Robertson, G. J., Reed, A. & Gilchrist, H. G. (2001) Clutch, egg and body size variation among Common Eiders breeding in Hudson Bay, Canada. *Polar Res.* 20: 85–94.

1083. Robertson, G. J., Cooke, F., Goudie, R. I. & Boyd, W. S. (1997) The timing of arrival and moult chronology of Harlequin Ducks *Histrionicus histrionicus.* *Wildfowl* 48: 147–155.

1084. Robertson, G. J., Cooke, F., Goudie, R. I. & Boyd, W. S. (1998) Moult speed predicts pairing success in male Harlequin Ducks. *Anim. Behav.* 55: 1677–1684.

1085. Robertson, G. J., Mittelhauser, G. H., Chubbs, T., Trimper, P., Goudie, R. I., Thomas, P. W., Brodeur, S., Robert, M., Gilliland, S. G. & Savard, J.-P. L. (2008) Morphological variation among harlequin ducks in the Northwest Atlantic. *Waterbirds* 31 (Spec. Publ. 2): 194–203.

1086. Robinson, J. A. (2005) Tufted Duck *Aythya fuligula*. Pp. 671–675 *in* Kear, J. (ed.) *Ducks, Geese and Swans*. Oxford Univ. Press.

1087. Robinson, J. A. & Hughes, B. (2006) *International Single Species Action Plan for the Conservation of the Ferruginous Duck Aythya nyroca*. African-Eurasian Migratory Waterbird Agreement, Bonn.

1088. Robson, C. (2005) *Birds of Southeast Asia*. New Holland, London.

1089. Rockwell, R. F., Petersen, M. R. & Schmutz, J. A. (1996) The Emperor Goose: an annotated bibliography. *Biol. Papers Univ. Alaska* 25. Univ. of Alaska, Fairbanks.

1090. Rodebrand, S. (2011) Checklist of the birds of the Azores including 2011. www.birdingazores.com.

1091. Rogacheva, H. (1992) *The Birds of Central Siberia*. Druck- und Verlagsgesellschaft, Husum.

1092. Rogers, J. P. 1967. Flightless Green-winged Teal in southeast Missouri. *Wilson Bull.* 79: 339.

1093. Rohwer, F. C. (1986) The adaptive significance of clutch size in waterfowl. Ph.D. thesis. Univ. of Pennsylvania, PA.

1094. Rohwer, F. C., Johnson, W. P. & Loos, E. R. (2002) Blue-winged Teal (*Anas discors*). *In* Poole, A. (ed.) The Birds of North America Online. Cornell Lab of Ornithology, Ithaca, NY. http://bna.birds.cornell.edu/bna/species/625

1095. Rose, P. M. & Scott, D. A. (1997) *Waterfowl Population Estimates*. Second edn, Wetlands International, Wageningen.

1096. Roselaar, C. S. & Sluys, R. (1999) Dutch avifaunal list: species concepts, taxonomic instability, and taxonomic changes in 1977–1998. *Ardea* 87: 139–165.

1097. Rothschild, Lord (1921) An exhibition of hybrid ducks. *Bull. Brit. Orn. Club* 49: 93–97.

1098. Roy C. L., Herwig C. M., Hohman W. L. & Eberhardt R. T. (2012) Ring-necked Duck (*Aythya collaris*). *In* Poole, A. (ed.) The Birds of North America Online. Cornell Lab of Ornithology, Ithaca, NY. http://bna.birds.cornell.edu/bna/species/329

1099. Roy, H. (1995) Enten-Mischehen auf unseren Züchterteichen. *Geflügel-Börse* 16: 12–13.

1100. Rozenfeld, S. (2011) The number of Red-Breasted Goose (*Branta ruficollis*) and Lesser White-fronted Goose (*Anser erythropus*) on the migration routes in 2010. *Goose Bull.* 12: 8-14.

1101. Ruokonen, M. (2001) *Phylogeography and Conservation Genetics of the Lesser White-fronted Goose (Anser erythropus)*. Oulu Univ. Press.

1102. Ruokonen, M. & Aarvak, T. (2011) Typology revisited: historical taxa of the Bean Goose – Pink-footed Goose complex. *Ardea* 99: 103–112.

1103. Ruokonen, M., Kvist, L. & Lumme, J. (2000) Close relatedness between mitochondrial DNA from seven Anser goose species. *J. Evol. Biol.* 13: 532–540.

1104. Ruokonen, M., Kvist, L., Tegelström, H. & Lumme, J. (2000) Hybrids, captive breeding and restocking of the Fennoscandian lesser white-fronted goose (*Anser erythropus*) *Conserv. Genetics* 1: 277–283.

1105. Ruokonen, M., Kvist, L., Aarvak, T., Markkola, J., Morozov, V. V., Øien, I. J., Syroechkovsky Jr., E. E., Tolvanen, P. & Lumme, J. (2004) Population Genetic structure and conservation of the Lesser White-fronted Goose *Anser erythropus*. *Conserv. Genetics* 5: 501–512.

1106. Ruokonen, M., Aarvak, T. & Madsen, J. (2005) Colonisation history of the high-arctic Pink-footed Goose *Anser brachyrhynchus*. *Mol. Ecol.* 14: 171–178.

1107. Ruokonen, M., Andersson, A.-C. & Tegelström, H. (2007) Using historical captive stocks in conservation. The case of the Lesser White-fronted Goose. *Conserv. Genetics* 8: 197–207.

1108. Ruokonen, M., Litvin, K. & Aarvak, T. (2008) Taxonomy of the Bean Goose-Pink-footed Goose. *Mol. Phyl. & Evol.* 48: 554–562.

1109. Ruokonen, M., Aarvak, T., Chesser, R. K., Lundqvist, A. C. & Merilä, J. (2010) Temporal increase in mtDNA diversity in a declining population. *Mol. Ecol.* 19: 2408–2417.

1110. Rusev, I. T., Andriuschenko, Y. A., Belinskiy, A. V., Grinchenko, A. B., Zhmud, M. E., Kinda, V. V., Korziukov, A. I., Moskalenko, Y. A., Petrovich, Z. I., Popenko, V. M. & Yaremchenko, O. A. (2008) Current status of Red-breasted Goose in Azov-Black Sea region of Ukraine. *Casarca* 11: 49–60.

1111. Rush, D. H., Humburg, D. D., Samuel, M. D. & Sullivan, B. D. (eds.) (1994) Biology and management of Canada Geese. *Proc. 1991 Intern. Canada Goose Symp.*

1112. Rutt, C. (2006) Occurrence and identification of Greater White-fronted Goose in Pennsylvania. *Pennsylvania Birds* 20: 164–169.

1113. Ryan, R. A. (1972) Body weight and weight changes of wintering diving ducks. *J. Wildl. Manag.* 36: 759–765.

1114. Ryder, J. P. (1969) Timing and spacing of nests and breeding biology of Ross's Goose. Ph.D. thesis. Univ. of Saskatchewan, Saskatoon.

1115. Ryder, J. P. (1972) Biology of nesting Ross's Geese. *Ardea* 60: 185–215.

1116. Safine, D. E. (2011) *Breeding Ecology of Steller's and Spectacled Eiders Nesting near Barrow, Alaska, 2008–2010*. US Fish & Wildlife Service, Fairbanks, AK.

1117. Sage, B. L. (1960) Notes on some Pintail × Teal hybrids. *Bull. Brit. Orn. Club* 80: 80.

1118. Sage, B. L. (1962) A hybrid Red-crested Pochard × Ferruginous White-eye. Bull. *Brit. Orn. Club* 82: 138–140.

1119. Sage, B. L. (1962) Notes on some Ferruginous White-eye × Tufted Duck hybrids. *Bull. Brit. Orn. Club* 82: 55–60.

1120. Sage, B. L. (1963) Some Pochard × Lesser Scaup hybrids. *Bull. Brit. Orn. Club* 83: 75–77.

1121. Salim, M. A. (2010) Current status of Marbled Teal/Duck *Marmaronetta angustirostris* in Iraq, conservation approach. Internal report. Nature Iraq, Baghdad.

1122. Salminen, A. (1983) *Suomen sorsalinnut*. Lintutieto, Helsinki.

1123. Salomonsen, F. (1941) Mauser und Gefiederfolge der Eisent (*Clangula hyemalis* (L.)). *J. Orn.* 89: 282–337.

1124. Salomonsen, F. (1949) Some notes on the molt of the long-tailed duck (*Clangula hyemalis*). *Avicult. Mag.* 55: 59–62.

1125. Salomonsen, F. (1950) *The Birds of Greenland*. Ejnar Munksgaard, Copenhagen.

1126. Salomonsen, F. (1968) The moult migration. *Wildfowl* 19: 5–24.

1127. Sandilands, A. P. (2005) *Birds of Ontario. Habitat Requirements, Limiting Factors and Status*. UBC Press, Vancouver.

1128. Sanger, G. A. & Jones, R. D. (1984) Winter feeding ecology and trophic relationships of Oldsquaws and White-winged Scoters on Kachemak Bay, Alaska. Pp. 20–28 *in* Nettleship, D. N., Sanger, G. A. & Springer, P. F. (eds.) *Marine Birds: Their Feeding Ecology and Commercial Fisheries Relationships*. Proc. of Pacific Seabird Group Symp., Seattle, Washington, 6–8 Jan, 1982. Canadian Wildlife Service, Ottawa.

1129. Sangster, G. (2009) Acoustic differences between the scoters *Melanitta nigra nigra* and *M. n. americana. Wilson J. Orn.* 121: 696–702.

1130. Sangster, G. & Oreel, G. J. (1996) Progress in taxonomy of Taiga and Tundra Bean Geese. *Dutch Birding* 18: 310–316.

1131. Sangster, G., Hazevoet, C. J., van den Berg, A. B. & Roselaar, C. S. (1997) Dutch avifaunal list: taxonomic changes in 1977–1997. *Dutch Birding* 19: 21–28.

1132. Sangster, G., Collinson, M., Helbig, A. J., Knox, A. G., Parkin, D. T. & Prater, T. (2001) The taxonomic status of Green-winged Teal *Anas carolinensis. Brit. Birds* 94: 218–226.

1133. Sangster, G., Knox, A. G., Helbig, A. J. & Parkin, D. T. (2002) Taxonomic recommendations for European birds. *Ibis* 144: 153–159.

1134. Sangster, G., Collinson, J. M., Helbig, A. J., Knox, A. G. & Parkin, D. T. (2004) Taxonomic recommendations for British birds: second report. *Ibis* 146: 153–157.

1135. Sangster, G., Collinson, J. M., Helbig, A. J., Knox, A. G. & Parkin, D. T. (2005) Taxonomic recommendations for British birds: third report. *Ibis* 147: 821–826.

1136. Sauma, L., Carmona, R. & Brabata, G. (2005) First nesting record of the Black-bellied Whistling-duck on the Baja California Peninsula, Mexico. *Western Birds*: 36: 317–321.

1137. Savard, J.-P. L. (1996) Barrow's Goldeneye. Pp. 332–335 *in* Gauthier, J. & Aubry, Y (eds.) *The Breeding Birds of Quebec: Atlas of the Breeding Birds of Southern Quebec.* Assoc. Quebecquoise des groupes d'ornithologues, Province of Quebec Society for the Protection of Birds, Canadian Wildlife Service & Environnement Canada, Montréal.

1138. Savard, J.-P. L., Bordage, D. & Reed, A. (1998) Surf Scoter (*Melanitta perspicillata*). *In* Poole, A. (ed.) The Birds of North America Online. Cornell Lab of Ornithology, Ithaca, NY. http://bna.birds.cornell.edu/bna/species/363

1139. Savard, J.-P. L., Reed, A. & Lesage, L. (2007) Chronology of breeding and molt migration in Surf Scoters (*Melanitta perspicillata*) *Waterbirds* 30: 223–229.

1140. Savard, J.-P. L. & Robert, M. (2013) Relationships among breeding, molting and wintering areas of adult female Barrow's Goldeneyes (*Bucephala islandica*) in eastern North America. *Waterbirds* 36: 34–42.

1141. Schamber, J. L., Sedinger, J. S., Ward, D. H. & Hagmeier, K. R. (2007) Latitudinal variation in population structure of wintering Pacific Black Brant. *J. Field Orn.* 78: 74–82.

1142. Scherrer, S. & Hilsberg, T. (1982) Hybridisierung und verwandtschaftsgrade innerhalb der Anatidae – eine systematische und evolutionstheoretische Betrachtung. *J. Orn.* 123: 357–380.

1143. Schielzeth, H., Lachmann, L., Eichhorn, G. & Heinicke, T. (2003) The White-headed Duck *Oxyura leucocephala* in the Tengiz-Korgalzhyn region, central Kazakhstan. *Wildfowl* 54: 115–129.

1144. Schiøler, E. L. (1925) *Danmarks Fugle.* Bd. 1. Nordisk Forlag, Oslo.

1145. Schlüter, W. (1891) Mischling von Stockente und Gänsesäger. *Gefiederte Welt* 40: 183.

1146. Schmidt, O. (1989) Commonwealth Park mystery duck was a Redhead × Canvasback hybrid. *Oregon Birds* 15: 140–142.

1147. Schmidt, P. R. (2006) Flyway conservation in North America. Workshop introduction. Pp. 197–198 *in* Boere, G. C., Galbraith, C. & Stroud, D. (ed.) *Waterbirds Around the World.* The Stationary Office, Edinburgh.

1148. Schmitz, K. (1987) Zufallkreuzung Kolbenente × Brandgans *Netta rufina × Tadorna tadorna. Gefiederte Welt* 111: 296.

1149. Schmutz, J. (2001) Selection of habitats by Emperor Geese during brood rearing. *Waterbirds* 24: 394–401.

1150. Schmutz, J. (2005) Emperor Goose *Anser canagicus.* Pp. 293–297 *in* Kear, J. (ed.) *Ducks, Geese and Swans.* Oxford Univ. Press.

1151. Schmutz, J., Petersen, M. R., Schmutz, J. A. & Rockwell, R. F. (2011) Emperor Goose (*Anser canagicus*). *In* Poole, A. (ed.) The Birds of North America Online. Cornell Lab of Ornithology, Ithaca, NY. http://bna.birds.cornell.edu/bna/species/097

1152. Schricke, V. (2002) Elements for a Garganey (*Anas querquedula*) management plan. *Game & Wildl. Sci.* 18: 9–41.

1153. Sclater, P. L. (1890) Exhibition of, and remarks upon, a hybrid duck. *Proc. Zool. Soc. Lond.* 1890: 1–2.

1154. Scott, D. A. & Rose, P. M. (1996) *Atlas of Anatidae Populations in Africa and Western Eurasia.* Wetlands International, Wageningen.

1155. Scott, D. K. (1981) Geographical variation in the bill patterns of Bewick's Swans. *Wildfowl* 32: 123–128.

1156. Scott, M. (1999) Letters: Identification of female Green-winged Teal. *Birding World* 12: 81.

1157. Scott, N. J. & Reynolds, R. P. (1984) Phenotypic variation of the Mexican Duck (*Anas platyrhynchos diazi*) in Mexico. *Condor* 86: 266–274.

1158. Scott, P. (1947) The waterfowl registry. *Avicult. Mag.* 52: 30–34.

1159. Scott, P. (1957) *A Coloured Key to the Waterfowl of the World.* Wildfowl Trust, Slimbridge.

1160. Scott, P. (1966) The Bewick's Swans at Slimbridge. *Wildfowl Trust Ann. Rep.* 17: 20–26.

1161. Scott, P. & The Wildfowl Trust (1972) *The Swans.* Michael Joseph. London.

1162. Scribner, K. T., Talbot, S. L., Pearce, J. M., Pierson, B. J., Bollinger, K. S. & Derksen, D. V. (2003) Phylogeography of Canada Geese (*Branta canadensis*) in western North America. *Auk* 120: 889–907.

1163. Scribner, K. T., Malecki, R. A., Batt, B. D., Inman, R. L., Libants, S. & Prince, H. H. (2003) Identification of source population for Greenland Canada Geese: genetic assessment of a recent colonization. *Condor* 105: 771–782.

1164. Sea Ducks Joint Venture (2003) Sea Duck Information Series: Black Scoter. http://seaduckjv.org/wp-content/uploads/2015/01/blsc_sppfactsheet.pdf

1165. Sea Duck Joint Venture (2004) Sea Duck Information Series: Common Eider (*Somateria mollissima*). http://seaduckjv.org/infoseries/coei_sppfactsheet.pdf

1166. Sea Duck Joint Venture (2004) Sea Duck Information Series: King Eider (*Somateria spectabilis*) Info sheet #9 of 15. Downloaded from: nhttp://seaduckjv.org/infoseries/kiei_sppfactsheet.pdf

1167. Sea Duck Joint Venture (2004) Sea Duck Information Series: Spectacled Eider (*Somateria fischeri*). http:// http:// seaduckjv.org/infoseries/spei_sppfactsheet.pdf

1168. Sea Duck Joint Venture (2012) Pacific Black Scoter Breeding Survey. http://seaduckjv.org/studies/pro3/pr96.pdf

1169. Sebastián-González, E., Fuentes, C., Ferrandez, M., Echevarrias, J. L. & Green, A. J. (2013) Habitat selection of Marbled Teal and White-headed Duck during the breeding and wintering seasons in south-eastern Spain. *Bird Conserv. Intern.* 23: 344–359.

1170. Sedinger, J. S., Lensink, C. J., Ward, D. H., Anthony, R. M., Wege, M. L. & Byrd, G. V. (1993) Current status and recent dynamics of the Black Brant *Branta bernicla* breeding population. *Wildfowl* 44: 49–59.

1171. Sedinger, J. S., Flint, P. L. & Lindberg, M. S. (1995) Environmental influence on life-history traits: growth, survival and fecundity in Black Brant (*Branta bernicla*). *Ecology* 76: 2404–2414.

1172. Sedinger, J. S., Lindberg, M. S., Person, B. T., Eicholz, M. W. & Flint, P. L. (1998) Density-dependent effects on growth, body size and clutch size in Black Brant. *Auk* 115: 613–620.

1173. Serie, J. R., Trauger, D. L., Doty, H. A. & Sharp, D. E. (1982) Age-class determination of Canvasbacks. *J. Wildl. Manag.* 46: 894–904.

1174. Serie, J. R. & Sharp, D. E. (1989) Body weight and composition dynamics of fall migrating Canvasbacks. *J. Wildl. Manag.* 53:431–441.

1175. Seth-Smith, D. (1911) Exhibition of a living hybrid duck between the White-eyed Pochard (*Aythya nyroca*) and the Marbled Duck (*Marmaronetta angustirostris*). *Proc. Zool. Soc. Lond.* 1911: 558.

1176. Severin, H. J. (1981) Interessanter Entenbastard zur 4 Umschlagseite. *Falke* 28: 355, 360.

1177. Shackelton, K. (1956) Apparent hybrid Lesser White-fronted Goose × White-fronted Goose in Hampshire and Sussex. *Brit. Birds* 49: 229–230.

1178. Sheaffer, S. E., Malecki, R. A., Swift, B. L., Dunn, J. & Scribner, K. (2007) Management implications of molt migration by the Atlantic Flyway resident population of Canada Geese, *Branta canadensis. Canadian Field-Natur.* 121: 313–320.

1179. Sherony, D. F. (2008) Greenland Geese in North America. *Birding* 40(3): 46–56.

1180. Shields, G. F. (1990) Analysis of mitochondrial DNA of Pacific Black Brant (*Branta bernicla nigricans*). *Auk* 107: 620–623.

1181. Shields, G. F. & Cotter, J. P. (1998) Phylogenies of North American geese: the mitochondrial DNA record. Pp. 405–411 *in* Rusch, D. H., Samuel, M. D., Humburg, D. D. & Sullivan, B. D. (eds.) *Biology and Management of Canada Geese.* Proc. Intern. Canada Goose Symp., Milwaukee, Wisconsin.

1182. Shields, G. F. & Wilson, A. C. (1987) Subspecies of the Canada Goose (*Branta canadensis*) have distinct mitochondrial DNAs. *Evolution* 41(3): 662–666.

1183. Shields, G. F. & Wilson, A. C. (1987) Calibration of mitochondrial DNA evolution in geese. *J. Mol. Evol.* 24: 212–217.

1184. Shoffner, R. N., Wang, N., Lee, F., King, R. & Otis, J. S. (1979) Chromosome homology between the Ross's and the Emperor goose. *J. Heredity* 70: 395–400.

1185. Shokhrin, V. & Solovieva, D. (2003) Scaly-sided Merganser breeding population increase in Far East Russia. *Threatened Wildfowl Specialist Group News* 14: 43–51.

1186. Shortt, T. M. (1943) Correlation of bill and foot coloring with age and season in the Black Duck. *Wilson Bull.* 55: 3–7.

1187. Shuford, W. D. & Gardali, T. (eds.) (2008) California bird species of special concern: a ranked assessment of species, subspecies, and distinct populations of birds of immediate conservation concern in California. *Stud. Western Birds* 1. Western Field Ornithologists, Camarillo, CA & California Department of Fish & Game, Sacramento.

1188. Shurtleff, L. L. (1996) *The Wood Duck and the Mandarin: the Northern Wood Ducks.* Univ of California Press, Berkeley, California (USA).

1189. Sibley, C. G., & Ahlquist, J. E. (1990). Phylogeny and classification of birds: a study in molecular evolution. Yale Univ. Press, New Haven, Connecticut (USA).

1190. Sibley, C. G. (1938) Hybrids of and with North American Anatidae. Proc. 9th Intern. Ornithol. Congr. (Rouen, France) pp. 327–335.

1191. Sibley, C. G. (1957) The evolutionary and taxonomic significance of sexual dimorphism and hybridization in birds. *Condor* 59: 166–191.

1192. Sibley, C. G. & Monroe, B. L. (1990) *Distribution and Taxonomy of Birds of the World.* Yale Univ. Press, New Haven, CT.

1193. Sibley C. G. & Monroe, B. L. (1993) *A World Checklist of Birds.* Edwards Brothers Inc., Ann Arbor, MI.

1194. Sibley, D. (1994) A guide to finding and identifying hybrids birds. *Birding* 26: 163–177.

1195. Sibley, D. (2000) *The Sibley Guide to Birds.* Alfred A. Knopf, New York.

1196. Sibley, D. (2006) Distinguishing Trumpeter and Tundra Swans. www.sibleyguides.com/2006/02/distinguishing-trumpeter-and-tundra-swans/

1197. Sibley, D. (2010) Distinguishing Cackling and Canada Goose. www.sibleyguides.com/2007/07/identification-of-cackling-and-canada-goose/

1198. Sibley, D. (2010) Distinguishing female Barrow's and Common Goldeneyes. www.sibleyguides.com/2010/01/distinguishing-female-barrows-and-common-goldeneyes/

1199. Sibley D. (2010) Identification of (hybrid?) female goldeneyes. www.sibleyguides.com/2010/01/identification-of-hybrid-female-goldeneyes/

1200. Sibley, D. (2011) Distinguishing Eurasian and American Common Merganser. www.sibleyguides.com/2011/07/distinguishing-eurasian-and-american-common-merganser/

1201. Sibley, D. (2011) Three interesting Brants from Massachusetts. www.sibleyguides.com/2011/04/three-interesting-brant-from-massachusetts/

1202. Sibley, D. (2011) Distribution of Greater White-fronted Goose subspecies. www.sibleyguides.com/2011/03/distribution-of-greater-white-fronted-goose-subspecies/

1203. Sibley, D. (2012) Identifying sleeping female goldeneyes. www.sibleyguides.com/2012/01/identifying-sleeping-female-goldeneyes/

1204. Sibley, D. (2013) Distinguishing Green-winged and Common Teal. www.sibleyguides.com/2011/03/distinguishing-green-winged-and-common-teal/

1205. Siegfried, W. R. (1976) Social organization in Ruddy and Maccoa ducks. *Auk* 93: 560–570.

1206. Skov, H., Heinänen, S., Žydelis, R, Bellebaum, J., Bzoma, S., Dagys, M., Durinck, J., Garthe, S., Grishanov, G., Hario, M., Kieckbusch, J. K., Kube, J., Kuresoo, A., Larsson, K., Luigujoe, L., Meissner, W., Nehls, H. W., Nilsson, L., Petersen, I. K., Roos, M. M., Pihl, S., Sonntag, N., Stock, A. & Stipniece, A. (2011) *Waterbird Populations and Pressures in the Baltic Sea.* Nordic Council of Ministers, Copenhagen.

1207. Smalley, F. (1907) The supposed occurence of the Pacific Eider (*Somateria v-nigrum*) in British waters. *Brit. Birds* 1: 69–75.

1208. Smallshire, D. (1986) The frequency of hybrid ducks in the Midlands. *Brit. Birds* 79: 87–89.

1209. Smith, C. M., Cooke, F. & Goudie, R. I. (1998) Ageing Harlequin Duck *Histrionicus histrionicus* drakes using plumage characteristics. *Wildfowl* 49: 245–248.

1210. Smith, C. M., Cooke, F., Robertson, G. J., Goudie, R. I. & Boyd, W. S. (2000) Long-term pair bonds in Harlequin Ducks. *Condor* 102: 201–205.

1211. Smith, G. C., Henderson, I. S. & Robertson, P. A. (2005) A model of ruddy duck *Oxyura jamaicensis* eradication for the United Kingdom. *J. Appl. Ecol.* 42: 546–555.

1212. Smith, L. M. & Sheeley, D. G. (1993) Molt patterns of wintering Northern Pintails in the Southern High Plains. *J. Wildl. Manag.* 57: 229–238.

1213. Snow, D. W. & Perrins, C. M. (1998) *The Birds of the Western Palearctic.* Vol. 1. Compact edn. Oxford Univ. Press.

1214. Snowden, J. H. (1987) Does it whistle or does it trumpet? Trumpeter/Whistling Swans comparisons. *Central Valley Bird Club Bull.* 10(3): 60–67.

1215. Snyder, L. L. (1953) An apparently hybrid Goldeneye. *Wilson Bull.* 65: 199.

1216. Soloviewa, D. (1997) Steller's Eider: national report from Russia. Proceedings from Steller's Eider workshop. *Wetlands Intern. Seaduck Specialist Group Bull.* 7: 7–12.

1217. Soloviewa, D. V., Pihl, S., Fox, A. D. & Bustnes, J. O. (1998) *Polysticta stelleri* Steller's eider. *BWP Update* 2(3): 145–158.

1218. Soloviewa, D. V. & Shokhrin, V. (2008) Egg size, weight and fresh egg density of the Scaly-sided Merganser *Mergus squamatus* in South Primorye, Russia. *Wildfowl* 58: 106–111.

1219. Soloviewa, D. V. & Pearce, J. M. (2011) Comparative mitochondrial genetics of North American and Eurasian mergansers with an emphasis on the endangered scaly-sided merganser (*Mergus squamatus*). *Conserv. Genetics* 12: 839–844.

1220. Soloviewa, D. V. & Vartanyan, S. (2013) Lesser White-Fronted Goose *Anser erythropus*: good news about the breeding population in west Chukotka, Russia. *Wildfowl* 61: 110–120.

1221. Soloviewa, D. V., Liu, P., Antonov, A. I., Averin, A. A., Pronkevich, V. V., Shokhrin, V. P. & Cranswick, P. A. (2014) The population size and breeding range of the Scaly-sided Merganser *Mergus squamatus*. *Bird Conserv. Intern.* 24: 1–13.

1222. Soloviewa, D. V., Afanasiev, V., Fox, J. W., Shokhrin, V. & Fox, A. D. (2012) Use of geolocators reveals previously unknown Chinese and Korean Scaly-sided Merganser wintering sites. *Endangered Species Res.* 17: 217–225.

1223. Sonobe, K. & Usui, S. (1993) *A Field Guide to the Waterbirds of Asia.* Wild bird Society of Japan, Tokyo.

1224. Sonsthagen, S. A. (2006) Population genetic structure and phylogeography of common eiders (*Somateria mollissima*). Ph.D. thesis. Univ. of Alaska, Fairbanks.

1225. Sonsthagen, S. A., Talbot, S.L. & McCracken, K.G. (2007) Genetic characterization of common eiders (*Somateria mollissima*) breeding on the Yukon–Kuskokwim Delta, Alaska. *Condor* 109: 879–894.

1226. Sonsthagen, S. A., Talbot, S. L., Scribner, K. T. & McCracken, K. G. (2011) Multilocus phylogeography and population structure of common eiders breeding in North America and Scandinavia. *J. Biogeogr.* 38: 1368–1380.

1227. Sorenson, M. D., Cooper, A., Paxinos, E. E., Quinn, T. W., James, H. F., Olson, S. L. & Fleischer, R. C. (1999) Relationships of the extinct moa-nalos, flightless Hawaiian waterfowl, based on ancient DNA. *Proc. Roy. Soc. Lond.* 266: 2187–2193.

1228. Sraml, M., Christidis, L., Easteal, S., Horn, P. & Collet, C. (1996) Molecular relationships within Australasian waterfowl (Anseriformes). *Australian J. Zool.* 44: 47–58.

1229. Stehn, R. A., Dau, C. P., Conant, B. & Butler, W. I. (1993) Decline of Spectacled Eiders nesting in western Alaska. *Arctic* 46: 264–277.

1230. Steinbacher, G. (1960) Zur Balz der Tauchenten. *Vogelwelt* 81: 1–16.

1231. Steklenev, E. P. (1993) Distant hybridization of some species from the family Anatidae. *Cytology & Genetics* 27(6): 54–61.

1232. Stepanyan, L. S. (1990) [*Conspectus of the Ornithological Fauna of the USSR*]. Nauka, Moscow. (In Russian)

1233. Stepanyan, L. S. (2003) [*Conspectus of the Ornithological Fauna of Russia and Adjacent Territories (within the borders of the USSR as a historic region)*]. Nauka, Moscow. (In Russian)

1234. Stevenson, H. M. & Anderson, B. H. (1994) *Birdlife of Florida.* Univ. Press of Florida, Gainesville.

1235. Stewart, R. E. & Aldrich, J. W. (1956) Distinction of maritime and prairie populations of Blue-winged Teal. *Proc. Biol. Soc. Wash.* 69: 29–34.

1236. Stott, R. S. & Olson, D. P. (1972) An evaluation of waterfowl surveys on the New Hampshire coastline. *J. Wildl. Manag.* 36: 468–477.

1237. Stotz, D. F., Fitzpatrick, J. W., Parker, T. A. & Moskovits, D. K. (eds.) (1996) *Neotropical birds: Ecology and Conservation.* Univ. of Chicago Press.

1238. Stroud, D. A. (1982) Observations on the incubation and post-hatching behavior of the Greeland White-fronted Goose. *Wildfowl* 33: 63–72.

1239. Stutzenbaker, C. D. (1988) *The Mottled Duck, its Life History, Ecology and Management.* Texas Parks & Wildlife Dept., Austin.

1240. **Suchetet, A. (**1894**)** *Histoire du Bimaculated Duck de Pennant confondu longtemps avec l'Anas Glocitans de Pallas. Lille.*

1241. Suchetet, A. (1897) *Des Hybrides à l'état sauvage: Règne animal.* Vol. 1. J.-B. Baillère et fils, Paris.

1242. Suddaby, D., Shaw, K. D., Ellis, P. M. & Brock, K. (1994) King Eiders in Britain and Ireland in 1958–90: occurrences and ageing. *Brit. Birds* 87: 418–430.

1243. Summers, R. W., Underhill, L. G., Syroechkovski, E. E., Lappo, H. G., Prs-Jones, R. P. & Karpov, V. (1994) The breeding biology of Dark-bellied Brent Geese *Branta b. bernicla* and King Eiders *Somateria spectabilis* on the northeastern Taimyr Peninsula, especially in relation to Snowy Owl *Nyctea scandiaca* nests. *Wildfowl* 45: 110–118.

1244. Suter, H. (1953) Ein Entenbastard bei Aarau. *Orn. Beob.* 50: 9–12.

1245. Suydam, R. S., Dickson, D. L., Fadely, J. B. & Quakenbush, L. T. (2000) Population declines of King and Common Eiders of the Beaufort Sea. *Condor* 102: 219–222.

1246. Swarth, H. S. & Bryant, H. C. (1917) A study of the races of the White-fronted Goose (*Anser albifrons*) occuring in California. *Univ. Calif. Publ. Zool.* 17: 209–222.

1247. Swennen, C., Duiven, P. & Wintermans, G. J. M. (1989) Abnormal plumage in possibly senile female Eiders *Somateria mollissima*. *Wildfowl* 40: 127–130.

1248. Syroechkovsky, E. E. (1996) [Present status of the Lesser White-fronted Goose (*Anser erythropus*) populations in Taimyr and some peculiarities of the system of species migrations in the Western Palearctic]. *Casarca* 2: 71–112 (In Russian with English summary)

1249. Syroechkovski, E. E. (2000) The hypothesis about the origin of the Emperor Goose. *Casarca* 6: 45–57.

1250. Syroechkovksi, E. E. (2002) Distribution and population estimates for swans in the Siberian Arctic in the 1990s. *Waterbirds* 25 (Spec. Publ. 1): 100–113.

1251. Syroechkovski, E. E. (2006) Long-term declines in Arctic goose populations in eastern Asia. Pp. 649–662 *in* Boere, G. C., Galbraith, C. & Stroud, D. (ed.) *Waterbirds Around the World.* The Stationary Office, Edinburgh.

1252. Syroechkovski, E. E. & Litvin, K. E. (1998) Migrations of Brent Geese (*Branta bernicla bernicla*) in Russia. *Casarca* 4: 71–95.

1253. Syroechkovski, E. E. & Koblik E. A. (2011) [Field Guide to the waterfowl of Russia] (in Russian). Geese, Swans and Duck Study Group of the Northern Eurasia, Moscow, Russia, 223 pp.

1254. Takekawa, J. Y., Heath, S. R., Douglas, D. C., Perry, W. M., Javed, S., Newman, S. H., Suwal, R. N., Rahmani, A. R. & Houdhury, B. C (2009) Geographic variation in Bar-headed Geese *Anser indicus*: connectivity of wintering areas and breeding grounds across a broad front. *Wildfowl* 59: 100–123.

1255. Talbot, S. L., Pearce, J. M., Pierson, B. J., Derksen, D. V. & Scribner, K. T. (2003) Molecular status of the dusky Canada goose (*Branta canadensis occidentalis*): a genetic assessment of a translocation effort. *Conserv. Genetics* 4: 367–381.

1256. Talbot, S., Sage, K. G., Gust, J., Rearick, J., Ward, D. & Derksen, D. (2013) Multilocus phylogeography and population structure of High Arctic North American Brant Geese. Goose Specialist Group Meeting, Arcachon, January 2013. Unpubl.

1257. Tegelström, H. & Sjöberg, G. (1995) Introduced Swedish Canada geese (*Branta canadensis*) have low levels of genetic variation as revealed by DNA fingerprinting. *J. Evol. Biol.* 8: 195–207.

1258. Tegelström, H., Ruokonen, M. & Löfgren, S. (2001) The genetic status of the captive Lesser White-fronted Geese used for breeding and reintroduction in Sweden and Finland. Pp. 37–39 *in* Tolvanen, P., Øien, I. J. & Ruokolainen, K. (eds.) Fennoscandian Lesser White-fronted Goose conservation project. Annual report 2000. WWF Finland Report 13 & Norwegian Ornithological Society, NOF Rapportserie Report no. 1-2001.

1259. Tenovuo, O. & Tenovuo, R. (1983) A hybrid of an Eider *Somateria mollissima* and a merganser species (*Mergus* sp.) found in Finland *Ornis Fennica* 60: 63–64.

1260. The Trumpeter Swan Society (2014) www.trumpeterswansociety.org/index.html

1261. Thomas, P. W., Mittelhauser, G. H., Chubbs, T. E., Trimper, P. G., Goudie, R. I., Robertson, G. J., Brodeur, S., Robert, M., Gilliland, S. G. & Savard, J.-P. L. (2008) Movements of Harlequin Ducks in eastern North America. *Waterbirds* 31(Spec. Publ. 2): 188–193.

1262. Thompson, J. D. & Baldassarre, G. A. (1990) Carcass composition of nonbreeding Blue-winged Teal and Northern Pintails in Yucatan, Mexico. *Condor* 92: 1057–1065.

1263. Thompson, J. E. & Drobney, R. D. (1995) Intensity and chronology of postreproductive molts in male Canvasbacks. *Wilson Bull.* 107: 338–358.

1264. Tiedemann, R. & Noer, H. (1998) Geographic partitioning of mitochondrial DNA patterns in European Eider *Somateria mollissima. Hereditas* 128: 159–166.

1265. Timm, D. & Sellers, D. (1981) *Investigation of Tule White-fronted Geese in Alaska: 1980.* Alaska Dept. Fish & Game, Anchorage.

1266. Tipling, D. (1989) Gadwall × Chiloe Wigeon hybrid resembling American Wigeon. *Birding World* 2: 10.

1267. Titman, R. (1999) Red-breasted Merganser. *In* Poole, A. (ed.) The Birds of North America Online. Cornell Lab of Ornithology, Ithaca, NY. http://bna.birds.cornell.edu/bna/species/443

1268. Titman R. (2005) Hooded Merganser *Lophodytes cucullatus.* Pp. 744–746 *in* Kear, J. (ed.) *Ducks, Geese and Swans.* Oxford Univ. Press.

1269. Titman, R. (2005) Common Merganser *Mergus merganser.* Pp. 752–755 *in* Kear, J. (ed.) *Ducks, Geese and Swans.* Oxford Univ. Press.

1270. Titman, R. (2005) Red-breasted Merganser *Mergus serrator.* Pp. 755–758 *in* Kear, J. (ed.) *Ducks, Geese and Swans.* Oxford Univ. Press.

1271. Tkachenko, E. E. (1995) The Swan Goose in south-east Transbaikalia. *Threatened Waterfowl Res. Group Newsl.* 8: 10–11.

1272. Tobish, T. (1986) Separation of Barrow's and Common goldeneyes in all plumages. *Birding* 18: 17–30.

1273. Todd, F. S. (1979) *Waterfowl: Ducks, Geese and Swans of the World.* Seaworld Press, San Diego, CA.

1274. Todd, F. S. (1996) *Natural History of the Waterfowl.* Ibis Publishing Company, Vista, CA.

1275. Todd, W. C. (1950) Nomenclature of the White-fronted Goose. *Condor* 52: 63–68.

1276. Torres Esquivias, J. A. (2009) La malvasía cabilliblanca (*Oxyura leucocephala*) durante los primeros años del siglo XXI. *Oxyura* 12: 87–116.

1277. Torres Esquivias, J. A. & Ayala Moreno, J. M. (1986) Variation du dessin céphalique des mâles de l'Erismature à tête blanche (*Oxyura leucocephala*). *Alauda* 54: 197–206.

1278. Townshend, T. (2013) Baer's on the brink from: http://birdingfrontiers.com/2013/08/02/baers-on-the-brink/

1279. Townshend, T. (2014) Possible hybrid Baer's Pochard × Ferruginous Duck http://birdingbeijing.com/2014/05/07/possible-hybrid-baers-pochard-x-ferruginous-duck/

1280. Trapp, J. L. & Macintosh, R. A. (1978) First North American specimen of the Spotbill Duck. *Western Birds* 9: 127–128.

1281. Trauger, D. L. (1974) Eye color of female Lesser Scaup in relation to age. *Auk* 91: 243–254.

1282. Trauger, D. L., Dzubin, A. & Ryder, J. P. (1971) White geese intermediate between Ross's Geese and Lesser Snow Geese. *Auk* 88: 856–875.

1283. Trefry, S. A., Dickson, D. L. & Hoover, A. K. (2007) A Common Eider × King Eider hybrid captured on the Kent Peninsula, Nunavut. *Arctic* 60: 251–254.

1284. Trolliet, B., Girard, O. & Fouquet, M. (2003) Evaluation des populations d'oiseaux deau en Afrique de l'Ouest. *ONCFS Rapport Scientifique* 2002: 51–55.

1285. Trost, R. E. & Drut, M. S. (2001) *Waterfowl Harvest and Status, Hunter Participation and Success, and Certain Hunting Regulations in the Pacific Flyway and United States.* US Fish & Wildlife Service, Portland, OR.

1286. Tubaro, P. L. & Lijtmaer, D. A. (2002) Hybridization patterns and the evolution of reproductive isolation in ducks. *Biol. J. Linn. Soc.* 77: 193–200.

1287. Underhill, L. G., Kemper, J., Whittington, P. A. & Wolfaardt, A. C. (2000) Egyptian Geese *Alopochen aegyptiacus* moulting on Dassen Island, South Africa. *Marine Orn.* 28: 121–122.

1288. UNEP (2008) Crested Shelduck *Tadorna cristata*. World Conservation Monitoring Centre Species Information. Archived on July 20, 2008. http://apps.unep.org/publications/pmtdocuments/checklistofmammalswcmc.pdf

1289. US Fish & Wildlife Service (2002) *Steller's Eider Recovery Plan*. US Fish & Wildlife Service, Fairbanks, AK.

1290. US Fish & Wildlife Service (2005) *Waterfowl Population Status, 2005*. US Dept. Interior, Washington DC. http://www.fws.gov/migratorybirds/reports/status05/final_status_05.pdf

1291. US Fish & Wildlife Service (2009) *Waterfowl Population Status*. US Dept. Interior, Washington DC.

1292. US Fish & Wildlife Service (2011) *Waterfowl Population Status*. US Dept. Interior, Washington DC.

1293. US Fish & Wildlife Service (2012) *Waterfowl Population Status*. US Dept. Interior, Washington DC.

1294. US Fish & Wildlife Service (2013) *Waterfowl Population Status*. US Dept. Interior, Washington DC.

1295. US Geological Survey (2001) Giant Canada Goose flocks in the United States: Atlantic Flyway. www.npwrc.usgs.gov/resource/1999/gcanada/atlantic.htm

1296. Upadhyaya, S. & Saikia, P. K. (2010) Population dynamics of Cotton Pygmy-goose, *Nettapus coromandelianus coromandelianus* Gmelin in Assam (India). *NeBIO* 1(4): 22–29.

1297. Upadhyaya, S. & Saikia, P. K. (2011) Study of morphomatric biology of Cotton Pygmy-Goose *Nettapus coromandelianus coromandelianus* Gmelin. *J. Res. Biol.* 3: 191–201.

1298. Urban, E. K. (1993) Status of wildfowl in northeast and east Africa. *Wildfowl* 44: 133–148.

1299. Urdiales, C. & Pereira, P. (1993) *Identification Key of O. jamaicensis, O. leucocephala and their hybrids*. ICONA. http://www.ebd.csic.es/andy/HybridKey.pdf

1300. Uspenski, S. M. (1965) *Die Wildganse Nordeurasiens*. Franckh, Stuttgart.

1301. Uspenski, S. M. (1972) *Die Eiderenten*. A. Ziemsen Verlag, Wittenberg-Lutherstadt.

1302. Vahatalo, A. V., Rainio, K., Lehikoinen, A. & Lehikoinen, E. (2004) Spring arrival of birds depends on the North Atlantic Oscillation. *J. Avian Biol.* 35: 210–216.

1303. Vale, W. H. (1900) *Hybrid Birds, Commonly Called Mules: Their Breeding, Keeping, and Exhibition*. Feathered World, London.

1304. van De Wetering D. (1997) *Moult Characteristics and Habitat Selection of Post-Breeding male Barrow's Goldeneye (Bucephala islandica) in Northern Yukon*. Canadian Wildlife Service, Ottawa.

1305. van den Berg, A. B. (2002) Female mystery eider at IJmuiden in January 1987. *Dutch Birding* 24: 92–93.

1306. van den Berg, A. B. (2004) Population growth and vagrancy potential of Ross's Goose. *Dutch Birding* 26 (2): 107-111

1307. van den Bergh, L. M. J. (1985) Het doorwomen van de Taigarietgans *Anser fabalis fabalis* in Nederland. *Limosa* 58: 17–22. (In Dutch)

1308. van den Bergh, L. (2003) [West-Siberian Taiga Bean Goose Johansen's Goose *Anser fabalis johanseni*]. *Vogeljaar* 51: 58–64. (In Dutch with English summary)

1309. Van Impe, J. (1980) [Ecology and ethology of the Bean geese *Anser fabalis fabalis* and *Anser fabalis rossicus*]. *Gerfaut* 70: 499–588 (In French)

1310. Van Impe, J. (1982) The Lesser White-fronted Goose in the south of the province of Zeeland (Netherlands). *Veldornithologisch Tijdschrift 5: 130–140*.

1311. Van Impe, J. (2008) Changements importants dans la distribution des oies sauvages (*Anser sp. et Branta sp.*) dans le nord de la Russie européenne. *Alauda* 76: 11–22.

1312. Van Wagner, C. E. & Baker, A. J. (1986) Genetic differentiation in populations of Canada Geese (*Branta canadensis*). *Canadian J. Zool.* 64: 940–947.

1313. Van Wagner, C. E. & Baker, A. J. (1990) Association between mitochondrial DNA and morphological evolution in Canada Geese. *J. Mol. Evol.* 31: 373–382.

1314. Vangilder, L. D. & Smith, L. M. (1985) Differential distribution of wintering brant by necklace type. *Auk* 102: 645–647.

1315. Varner, D. M., Bielefeld, R. R. & Hepp, G. R. (2013) Nesting ecology of Florida Mottled Ducks using altered habitats. *J. Wildl. Manag.* 77: 1002–1009.

1316. Vaurie, C. (1965) *Birds of the Palearctic Fauna: Non-Passeriformes*. H. F. & G. Witherby, London.

1317. Vesterinen, J. (1998) Presumed *Anser indicus × Branta bernicla* hybrids recorded in Norway. *Linnut* 33: 7.

1318. Vickery, J. & Gill, J. (1999) Managing grassland for wild geese in Britain: a review. *Biol. Conserv.* 89: 93–106.

1319. Vinicombe, K. (1994) Common Teals showing mixed characters of Eurasian and North American races. *Brit. Birds* 87: 88–89.

1320. Vinicombe, K. (1998) Strange *Aythya* ducks: can Canvasbacks show white on the bill? *Birding* 30: 60–61.

1321. Vinicombe, K. (2000) Identification of Ferruginous Duck and its status in Britain and Ireland. *Brit. Birds* 93: 4–21.

1322. Vinicombe, K. (2003) The identification of a hybrid Canvasback × Common Pochard. *Brit. Birds* 96: 112–118.

1323. Voitkevich, A. A. (1966) *The Feathers and Plumage of Birds*. October House, New York.

1324. Voous, K. H. (1960) *Atlas of European Birds*. Nelson, London.

1325. Voous, K. H. (1972) Intermediate scoter. *Ardea* 60: 128–129.

1326. Voous, K. H. & Wattel, J. (1967) Waarschijnlijke bastaard Kolgans × Dwerggans uit de natuur. *Limosa* 40: 9–11.

1327. Voronov, B. A. & Pronkevich, V. V. (1991): On some ornithological findings in the Khabarovsk Krai. *Bull. Moscow Soc. Nature Res. Sec. Biol.* 96(5): 23–27.

1328. Voslamber, B. (2002) Kolgans *Anser albifrons*. Pp. 96–97 *in* SOVON Vogelonderzoek Nederland (ed.) *Atlas van de Nederlandse Broedvogels Broedvogels 1998–2000*. Nationaal Natuurhistorische Museum Naturalis, Koninklijke Nederlandse Natuurhistorische Vereniging & European Invertebrate Survey-Nederland, Leiden.

1329. Voslamber B., van der Jeugd, H. P. & Koffijberg, K. (2010) Broedende ganzen in Nederland. *De Levende Natuur 111(1): 40*.

1330. Votier, S. C., Harrop, A. H. J. & Denny, M. (2003) A review of status and identification of American Wigeon in Britain and Ireland. *Brit. Birds* 96: 2–22.

1331. Walton, K., Gotthardt, T. & Fields, T. (2012) *Alaska Species Ranking System Summary Report – Common Eider*. Pacific. Univ. of Alaska, Anchorage.

1332. Wang, X., Barter, M., Cao, L., Lei, J. & Fox, A. D. (2012) Serious contractions in wintering distribution and decline in abundance of Baer's Pochard *Aythya baeri*. *Bird Conserv. Intern.* 22: 121–127.

1333. Wang, X., Fox, A. D., Cong, P. & Cao, L. (2013) Food constraints explain distribution of wintering Lesser White-fronted Geese *Anser erythropus* in China. *Ibis* 155: 576–592.

1334. Wang, X., Fox, A. D., Zhuang, X., Cao, L., Meng, F. & Cong,

P. (2014) Shifting to an energy-poor diet for nitrogen? Not the case for wintering herbivorous Lesser White-fronted Geese in China. *J. Orn.* 155 (3): 707-712.

1335. Wang, Z. R., Shan, J. H., Li, Y. K., Tu, X. B., Jia, D. J., Hao, Y. & Zhao, J. (2010) Winter population status and endangered factors of Scaly-sided Merganser (*Mergus squamatus*) in Jiangxi Province. *Sichuan J. Zool.* 29: 597–600.

1336. Ward, J. G. & Middleton, A. L. A. (1971) Weight and histological studies of growth and regression in the Bursa of Fabricius in the Mallard, *Anas platyrhynchos. Canadian J. Zool.* 49: 11–14.

1337. Waring, D. (1993) Identification forum: female Black Scoter. *Birding World* 6: 78–79.

1338. Warren, S. M., Fox, A. D., Walsh, A. & O'Sullivan, P. (1993) Extended parent-offspring relationships in Greenland White-fronted Geese (*Anser albifrons flavirostris*). *Auk* 110: 145–148.

1339. Watkins, V. S. (2006) Intraspecific nest parasitism in Emperor Geese (*Chen canagica*): a population genetic analysis. M.Sc. thesis. Alaska Pacific Univ., Anchorage.

1340. Webster, R. E. (2006) The status of Mottled Duck (*Anas fulvigula*) in Arizona. http://azfo.org/journal/mottled_duck.html

1341. Weckstein, J. D., Afton, A. D., Zink, R. M. & Alisauskas, R. T. (2002) Hybridization and population subdivision within and between Ross's Geese and Lesser Snow Geese: a molecular perspective. *Condor* 104: 432–436.

1342. Weller, M. W. (1957) Growth, weights and plumages of the Redhead *Aythya americana. Wilson Bull.* 69: 5–38.

1343. Weller, M. W. (1959) Parasitic egg laying in the Redhead (*Aythya americana*) and other North American Anatidae. *Ecol. Monogr.* 29: 333–365.

1344. Weller, M. W. (1970) Additional notes on the plumages of the Redhead (*Aythya americana*) *Wilson Bull.* 82: 320–323.

1345. Weng, G. J. (2006) Ecology and population genetics of mottled ducks within the South Atlantic Coastal Zone. Ph.D. thesis. Univ. of Georgia, Athens.

1346. Wetlands International (2006) *Waterbird Population Estimates.* Fourth edn. Wetlands International, Wageningen.

1347. Wetlands International (2012) Results of trend analysis undertaken for CSR5 2012, presented in Annex 4. www.unep-aewa.org/meetings/en/mop/mop5_docs/pdf/mop5_14_csr5.pdf

1348. Wetlands International (2014) Waterbird population estimates. Retrieved from wpe.wetlands.org

1349. Wetmore, A. (1925) The Coues Gadwall extinct. *Condor* 27: 36.

1350. Whistler, H. (1949) *Popular Handbook of Indian Birds.* Gurney & Jackson, London.

1351. White, D. H., King, K. A., Mitchell, C. A. & Krynitsky, A. J. (1981) Body lipids and pesticide burdens of migrant Blue-winged Teal. *J. Field Orn.* 52: 23–28.

1352. Whitford, P. C. (1987) Vocal and visual communication and other social behavior in Canada Geese. Ph.D. thesis. Univ. of Wisconsin, Milwaukee.

1353. Whitford, P. C. (1998) Vocal and visual communication of Giant Canada Geese. Pp. 375–386 *in* Rusch, D. H., Samuel, M. D., Humburg, D. D. & Sullivan, B. D. (eds.) *Biology and Management of Canada Geese.* Proc. Intern. Canada Goose Symp., Milwaukee, WI.

1354. Wilkins, K. & Otto, M. (2003) Trends in duck breeding populations, 1955–2003. Unpubl. US Fish & Wildlife Service, Washington.

1355. Williams, C. L., Brust, R. C. & Rhodes, O. E. (2002) Microsatellite polymorphism and genetic structure of Florida Mottled Duck populations. *Condor* 104: 424–431.

1356. Williams, C. L., Brust, R. C., Fendley, T. T., Tiller, G. R. & Rhodes, O. E. (2005) A comparison of hybridization between mottled ducks (*Anas fulvigula*) and mallards (*A. platyrhynchos*) in Florida and South Carolina using microsatellite DNA analysis. *Conserv. Genetics* 6: 445–453.

1357. Williams, C. L., Fedynich, A. M., Pence, D. B. & Rhodes, O. E. (2005) Evaluation of allozyme and microsatellite variation in Texas and Florida Mottled Ducks. *Condor* 107: 155–161.

1358. Williams, S. O. (1980) The Mexican Duck in Mexico: natural history, distribution, and population status. Ph.D. thesis. Colorado State Univ., Fort Collins.

1359. Williamson, M. H. (1957) Polymorphism in Ross's Goose *Anser rossii*, and the detection of genetic dominance from field data. *Ibis* 99: 516–518.

1360. Wilmore, S. B. (1974) *Swans of the World.* Taplinger Publising, New York.

1362. Wilson, A. (2005) Identification and range of subspecies within the (Greater) Canada and (Lesser Canada) Cackling Goose complex (*Branta canadensis* & *B. hutchinsii*). http://www.oceanwanderers.com/CAGO.Subspecies.html

1363. Wilson, A. & Guthrie, A. (1999) Black Brant in New York State. *Kingbird* 49: 98–106.

1364. Wilson, H. M., Flint, P. L., Moran, T. L. & Powell, A. N. (2007) Survival of breeding Pacific common eiders on the Yukon-Kuskokwim Delta, Alaska. *J. Wildl. Manag.* 41: 403–410.

1365. Wilson, R. E. & McCracken, K. G. (2008) Specimen shrinkage in Cinnamon Teal. *Wilson J. Orn.* 120: 390–392.

1366. Wilson, R. E., Eaton, M. D. & McCracken, K. G. (2008) Color divergence among Cinnamon Teal (*Anas cyanoptera*) subspecies from North America and South America. *Orn. Neotrop.* 19: 307–314.

1367. Wilson, R. E., Eaton, M. D., Sonsthagen, S. A., Peters, J. L., Johnson, K. P., Simarra, B. & McCracken, K. G. (2011) Speciation, subspecies divergence, and paraphyly in the Cinnamon Teal and Blue-winged Teal. *Condor* 113: 747–761.

1368. Wilson, R. E., Eaton, M. B. & McCracken, K. G. (2012) Plumage and body size differentiation in Blue-winged teal and Cinnamon teal. *Avian Biol. Res.* 5: 107–116.

1369. Wilson, S. F. & Ankney, C. D. (1988) Variation in structural size and wing stripe of Lesser and Greater Scaup. *Rev. Canadienne Zool.* 66: 2045–2048.

1370. Winker, K., McCracken, K. G., Gibson, D. D. & Peters, J. L. (2013) Heteropatric speciation in a duck, *Anas crecca. Mol. Ecol.* 22: 5922–5935.

1371. Winter, J. (1977) Photograph of Greater Scaup × Ring-necked Duck. *Amer. Birds* 31: 397.

1372. Wishart, R. A. (1985) Moult chronology of the American Wigeon, *Anas americana*, in relation to reproduction. *Canadian Field-Natur.* 99: 172–178.

1373. Witherby, H. F., Jourdain, F. C. R., Ticehurst, N. F. & Tucker, B. W. (1944) *The Handbook of British Birds.* Vol. 3. H. F. & G. Witherby, London.

1374. Woodin, M. C. & Michot, T. C. (2002) Redhead (*Aythya americana*). *In* Poole, A. (ed.) The Birds of North America Online. Cornell Lab of Ornithology, Ithaca, NY. http://bna.birds.cornell.edu/bna/species/695

1375. Wright, K. G. & Clarkson, P. V. (1998) Harlequin Duck moulting ecology and banding synopsis in the Strait of Georgia, British Columbia: 1997 progress report. Unpubl. Harlequin Conserv. Soc., West Vancouver, BC.

1376. Würdinger, I. (2005) Bar-headed Goose *Anser indicus*. Pp. 289–293 *in* Kear, J. (ed.) *Ducks, Geese and Swans*. Oxford Univ. Press.

1377. Wynn, R. (2002) Brants: the hybrid problem. *Birdwatch* 118: 16–18.

1378. Yamashina, Y. (1953) Hybridization between a domestic drake and a Chinese Goose. Journal of the Yamashina Institute for Ornithology 1(2): 39–44.

1379. Yésou, P. & Lappo, H. G. (1992) Nidification de l'Eider de Steller *Polysticta stelleri du Taïmyr à la Péninsule de Yamal, Sibérie*. *Alauda* 60: 193–198.

1380. Yokota, Y., Kurechi, M. & Otsu, M. (1982) Distribution, numbers and status of Geese in Japan. *Aquila* 14: 209–227.

1381. Young, G. (2005) African Comb Duck *Sarkidiornis melanotos*. Pp. 391–393 *in* Kear, J. (ed.) *Ducks, Geese and Swans*. Oxford Univ. Press.

1382. Young, G. (2005) Northern Mallard *Anas platyrhynchos*. Pp. 513–517 *in* Kear, J. (ed.) *Ducks, Geese and Swans*. Oxford Univ. Press.

1383. Young, G. & Kear, J. (2005) Long-tailed Duck *Clangula hyemalis*. Pp. 723–726 *in* Kear, J. (ed.) *Ducks, Geese and Swans*. Oxford Univ. Press.

1384. Zhang, G. G., Liu, D. P., Hou, Y. Q., Jiang, H. X., Dai, M., Qian, F.-W., Lu, J., Xing, Z. & Li, F. S. (2011) Migration routes and stop-over sites determined with satellite tracking of Bar-headed Geese *Anser indicus* breeding at Qinghai Lake, China. *Waterbirds* 34: 112–116.

1385. Zhang, Y., Cao, L., Barter, M., Fox, A. D., Zhao, M., Meng, F. & Zhu, W. (2011) Changing distribution and abundance of Swan Goose *Anser cygnoides* in the Yangtze River floodplain: the likely loss of a very important wintering site. *Bird Conserv. Intern.* 21: 36-48.

1386. Zhao, Z. J. (1993) Is the Crested Shelduck extinct? *Threatened Waterfowl Res. Group Newsl.* 3: 5.

1388. Zhao, Z. J. & Pao, Z. J. (1998) The foraging behaviour of the Scaly-sided Merganser *Mergus squamatus* in the Changbai Mountains and Xiao Xingangling Mountains of China. *Forktail* 14: 76–77.

1389. Zhuravlev, Y. N., Nechaev V. A. & Kulikova I. V. (2002). Ein hybrider Erpel von Stock- und Fleckschnabelente *Anas platyrhynchos* x *A. poecilorhyncha* in Ruslands Maritim-Provinz (Primorje). Ornithologische Mitteilungen 54: 378–379.

1390. Zicus, M. C. (2005) Common Goldeneye *Bucephala clangula*. Pp. 730–735 *in* Kear, J. (ed.) *Ducks, Geese and Swans*. Oxford Univ. Press.

1391. Zimpfer, N. L., Rhodes, W. E., Silverman, E. D., Zimmerman, G. S. & Richkus, K. D. (2011) *Trends in Duck Breeding Populations, 1955–2011*. US Fish & Wildlife Service, Washington DC.

1392. Zink, R. M. (1996) Species concepts, speciation, and sexual selection. *J. Avian Biol.* 27(1): 1–6.

1393. Zink, R. M. & McKitrick, M. C. (1995) The debate over species concepts and its implications for ornithology. *Auk* 112: 701–719.

1394. Zink, R. M., Rohwer, S., Andreev, A. V. & Dittmann, D. L. (1995) Trans-Beringia comparisons of mitochondrial DNA differentiation in birds. *Condor* 97: 639–649.

1395. Zubko, V., Havrilenko, V. & Semenov, N. (2001) Restoration of the Ruddy Shelduck *Tadorna ferruginea* population in "Ascania Nova" nature reserve (southern Ukraine). *Acta Orn. (Warsaw)* 36: 97–100.

1396. Zydelis, R., Lorentsen, S.-H., Fox, A. D., Kuresoo, A., Krasnov, Y., Goryaev, Y., Bustnes, J. O., Hario, M., Nilsson, L. & Stipniece, A. (2006) Recent changes in the status of Steller's Eider *Polysticta stelleri* wintering in Europe: a decline or redistribution? *Bird Conserv. Intern.* 16: 217–236.

HYBRIDS INDEX

Numbers in **bold** refer to plate numbers where the hybrids are illustrated, other numbers refer to the caption text in the colour plate section. Page numbers in *italic* refer to the first page of the descriptions in the species accounts. Page numbers underlined refer to page(s) with relevant photographs.

SPECIES INDEX

Numbers in **bold** refer to plate numbers, other numbers refer to the caption text in the colour plate section. Page numbers in *italic* refer to the first page of the entry in the species accounts.